B&T
7/8/97
$14.97

P9-EAO-798

STANDARD
INDUSTRIAL
CLASSIFICATION
MANUAL

EXECUTIVE OFFICE OF THE PRESIDENT
OFFICE OF MANAGEMENT AND BUDGET

This book is a complete reprint of the *Standard Industrial Classification Manual* as produced by the Office of Management and Budget. It includes all the content of the original book and is published by JIST Works, Inc., Indianapolis, IN 46202.

```
┌─────────────────────────────┐
│     Margin Index appears    │
│     on last page of book    │
└─────────────────────────────┘
```

This edition distributed by JIST Works, Inc. is an unabridged reprint of the *Standard Industrial Classification Manual,* compiled by the United States Office of Management and Budget. This book was originally published in 1987.

Manufactured in the United States of America.

Contact your distributor or the publisher for quantity discounts.

See a list of other JIST titles on an order form at the end of this book.

JIST Works, Inc.
720 North Park Avenue
Indianapolis, IN 46202-3431
Phone: **1-800-648-JIST** (most areas) or **1-317-264-3720**
Fax: **1-800-JIST-FAX** or **1-317-264-3709**

ISBN: 1-56370-064-6

Preface

The Standard Industrial Classification (SIC) is the statistical classification standard underlying all establishment-based Federal economic statistics classified by industry. The SIC is used to promote the comparability of establishment data describing various facets of the U.S. economy. The classification covers the entire field of economic activities and defines industries in accordance with the composition and structure of the economy. It is revised periodically to reflect the economy's changing industrial organization. This manual incorporates the first major revision since 1972.

On February 22, 1984, the Office of Management and Budget (OMB) published a *Federal Register* notice of intent to revise the Standard Industrial Classification for 1987. In response, businesses, trade associations, individuals, and Federal, State, and local government agencies submitted proposals for over 1100 individual changes.

To provide technical advice for the 1987 SIC revision and to make recommendations on the individual proposals, OMB established a multiagency Technical Committee on Industrial Classification (TCIC). The TCIC (listed below) is chaired by OMB and consists of senior economists, statisticians, and classification specialists representing Federal agencies that use the SIC. To aid in its review, the TCIC established subcommittees for Construction; Manufacturing; Trade (Wholesale and Retail); Communications; Transportation and Public Utilities; Finance, Insurance, and Real Estate; Services; and Computers. The TCIC evaluated each of the proposed changes and recommended approximately 40 percent for acceptance and inclusion in the revised SIC.

The 1987 SIC revision has taken into account technological changes; institutional changes such as deregulation in the banking, communications, and transportation industries; and the tremendous expansion in the service sector. In addition, changes have been made to improve industry detail, coverage, and definitions, and to clarify classification concepts and the classification of individual activities.

The revision has resulted in a net increase of 19 industries for Services (Division I), 8 for Wholesale Trade, and 7 for Manufacturing, with a net decrease of 34 for the other SIC Divisions. Deleted industries are merged into other industries and new industries are created by subdividing or restructuring existing industries. Various industries have also been changed by transfers of individual activities, primarily to increase the accuracy, consistency, and usefulness of the classifications. A few industries are renumbered without any change in content as a consequence of restructuring the classification at the three-digit level.

Revision of the SIC is a large task that requires the time, energy, and cooperation of numerous individuals and organizations both inside and outside the Government. The publication of this manual is a testament to the willingness of many people to contribute to that task. In addition to the individuals and organizations who developed and submitted proposals for changing the SIC, the revision could not have been accomplished without the individual and collective contributions of the members of the TCIC and its subcommittees. In particular, the members of the Subcommittee on Coding and Interpretation (listed below), who spent many long and sometimes frustrating hours implementing the TCIC's recommendations and OMB's final decisions, are to be congratulated for their work in preparing the text of this manual. Thanks are also extended to members of the staff of the Industry and Commodity Classification Branch, Economic Surveys Division, Bureau of the Census, who provided valuable assistance in producing the manual, especially in preparing manuscripts, integrating comments, and overseeing the proofreading. Notwithstanding all this assistance and advice, the Office of Management and Budget remains responsible for final decisions on the content of the revision.

JAMES C. MILLER III
Director
Office of Management and Budget

Technical Committee on Industrial Classification

Paul Bugg, Office of Management and Budget, Chairperson
Alice K. Cullen (retired), Small Business Administration (David Hirschberg, alternate)
Linda M. Dill, Social Security Administration
Brenda Erickson, Federal Emergency Management Agency
Ron Heller, United States International Trade Commission
Thomas J. Hogan, National Science Foundation (Margaret R. Grucza, alternate)
Albert P. Keck (retired), Energy Information Administration
Zoltan Kenessey, Board of Governors of the Federal Reserve System (Charles Gilbert and Kenneth Armitage, alternates)
William F. Long, Federal Trade Commission (Susan Foster, alternate)
Brian MacDonald, Bureau of Labor Statistics (Linda P. Hardy, Wanda L. Bland, and Donald W. Rundquist (deceased), alternates)
Walter E. Neece, Bureau of the Census (C. Harvey Monk, alternate)
William G. Norris, Interstate Commerce Commission
Edward I. Reinsel, Department of Agriculture
Michael Rossetti, Department of Transportation (Rolf R. Schmitt, alternate)
Sheldon Starr, National Center for Health Statistics
William B. Sullivan, International Trade Administration
Terry J. Sutton, Bureau of Mines (Valeria W. Gross and Jeffrey Osmint, alternates)
Robert A. Wilson, Internal Revenue Service (Kenneth B. Rice, alternate)
Paula C. Young, Bureau of Economic Analysis (Mark A. Planting, alternate)

Subcommittee on Coding and Interpretation

C. Harvey Monk, Bureau of the Census, Chairperson
Wanda L. Bland, Bureau of Labor Statistics
Linda M. Dill, Social Security Administration

Contents

Introduction

The Standard Industrial Classification of Establishments

Purpose and Scope of the Classification

The Standard Industrial Classification (SIC) was developed for use in the classification of establishments by type of activity in which they are engaged; for purposes of facilitating the collection, tabulation, presentation, and analysis of data relating to establishments; and for promoting uniformity and comparability in the presentation of statistical data collected by various agencies of the United States Government, State agencies, trade associations, and private research organizations. The Standard Industrial Classification for *establishments* differs from a classification for *enterprises* (companies) or products. An enterprise consists of all establishments having more than 50 percent common direct or indirect ownership. Other classifications have been developed for use in the classification of commodities or products and also for occupations.

The Standard Industrial Classification is intended to cover the entire field of economic activities: agriculture, forestry, fishing, hunting, and trapping; mining; construction; manufacturing; transportation, communications, electric, gas, and sanitary services; wholesale trade; retail trade; finance, insurance, and real estate; personal, business, professional, repair, recreation, and other services; and public administration.

This edition of the Manual supersedes the 1972/77 edition. Appendix A presents conversion tables between the 1972/77 edition and the 1987 edition.

Principles of the Classification

In reviewing the Classification, the Technical Committee on Industrial Classification was guided by the following general principles:

(1) The Classification should conform to the existing structure of American industry.

(2) Each establishment is to be classified according to its primary activity.

(3) To be recognized as an industry, the group of establishments constituting the proposed classification must be statistically significant in the number of persons employed, the volume of business conducted, and other measures of economic activity.

11

Appendix B describes in more detail the principles and procedures used for this revision.

Structure of the Classification

The structure of the classification makes it possible to tabulate, analyze, and publish establishment data on a division, a two-digit major group, a three-digit industry group, or a four-digit industry code basis, according to the level of industrial detail considered most appropriate. An agency may use additional subdivisions within specific four-digit industries in adopting this classification for its own use, while still retaining comparability with the classifications used by other agencies.

It should be noted that the digit "9" appearing in the third- or fourth-digit position of the classification code usually designates miscellaneous three-digit industry groups or four-digit industries covering establishments not elsewhere classified. These residual classifications do not usually constitute homogeneous primary activity groups; for purposes of this classification system they are grouped together and treated as a separate industry to retain the homogeneity of the other industries in the group.

Definition of an Establishment

For purposes of this classification, an establishment is an economic unit, generally at a single physical location, where business is conducted or where services or industrial operations are performed. (For example: a factory, mill, store, hotel, movie theater, mine, farm, ranch, bank, railroad depot, airline terminal, sales office, warehouse, or central administrative office.)

Where distinct and separate economic activities are performed at a single physical location (such as construction activities operated out of the same physical location as a lumber yard), each activity should be treated as a separate establishment where: (1) no one industry description in the classification includes such combined activities; (2) the employment in each such economic activity is significant; and (3) separate reports can be prepared on the number of employees, their wages and salaries, sales or receipts, and other types of establishment data.

For activities such as construction, transportation, communications, electric, gas, and sanitary services, and similar physically dispersed operations, establishments are represented by those relatively permanent main or branch offices, terminals, stations, etc., that are either (1) directly responsible for supervising such activities, or (2) the base from which personnel operate to carry out these activities. Hence, the individual sites, projects, fields, networks, lines, or systems of such dispersed activities are not ordinarily considered to be establishments.

An establishment is not necessarily identical with the enterprise (company) which may consist of one or more establishments. Also, it is to be distinguished from subunits of the establishment such as departments. Supplemental interpretations of the definition of an establishment are included in the division, major group, industry group, and industry descriptions of the Standard Industrial Classification where appropriate. Auxiliary units, as described below, are recognized as special types of establishments.

Auxiliary Establishments

Activities

Auxiliaries are establishments primarily engaged in performing management or support services for other establishments of the same enterprise. An enterprise consists of all establishments having more than 50 percent common direct or indirect ownership. Auxiliary establishments are distinguished from operating establishments that primarily produce goods and from those that primarily provide services for personal or household use or for other enterprises. Some examples of activities commonly performed by auxiliaries are management and other general administrative functions, such as accounting, data processing, and legal services; research, development, and testing; and warehousing.

Establishment Unit

A unit that performs auxiliary functions and is located physically separate from the establishment or establishments served is treated as a separate establishment. A unit that performs auxiliary activities at the same physical location as an establishment that performs operating activities is considered a separate establishment if all of the following conditions are met:

(1) Separate reports can be prepared on the number of employees, their wages and salaries, sales or receipts, and other types of establishment data; and

(2) the unit serves other establishments of the same enterprise; and

(3) employment is significant for both the auxiliary and operating activities.

Exceptions and Borderlines

Some establishments that meet the general definition of auxiliaries are nevertheless treated as operating establishments. They are listed below:

(1) Establishments primarily engaged in producing goods or providing services for other establishments of the same enterprise when such goods or services are covered by industries in Agriculture (Major Groups 01-07 of Division A); Mining (Division B); Construction (Division C); and Manufacturing (Division D) are classified as operating establishments in such Divisions on the basis of their primary activity.

(2) Establishments, including sales branches, sales offices, and sales representatives, primarily engaged in selling tangible products for other than personal or household consumption are classified as operating establishments in Wholesale Trade, with the exception of motion pictures and prerecorded video tapes and disks of the type produced by establishments covered in Major Group 78. Establishments primarily engaged in the wholesale distribution of motion pictures and prerecorded video tapes and disks of the type produced by establishments covered in

Major Group 78 are classified in Services, Industry 7822.

(3) Establishments primarily engaged in research, development, and testing of aircraft, guided missiles, and space vehicle units and parts, covered by Industry Groups 372 or 376, are classified as operating establishments in these manufacturing industries if they are part of an enterprise that usually manufactures such products. These establishments are often funded by government contracts rather than by funds of the enterprise. Establishments of these enterprises primarily engaged in research, development, and testing of products not covered by Industry Group 372 or 376 are classified as auxiliary establishments. Establishments primarily engaged in research, development, and testing of products for other enterprises on a contract or fee basis are classified as operating establishments in Services, Industry Group 873.

(4) Research farms are classified as operating establishments in Agriculture, Forestry, and Fishing, Division A.

(5) Establishments primarily engaged in long-distance trucking, stevedoring, water transportation, or pipeline transportation for other establishments of the same enterprise are classified as operating establishments in Transportation, Division E.

(6) Establishments primarily engaged in new or replacement construction for establishments of the same enterprise covered by industries in Division E are classified as operating establishments in Construction, Division C. Establishments primarily engaged in repair and maintenance for establishments of the same enterprise covered by industries in Division E are classified as operating establishments in Division E. However, all establishments of the U.S. Postal Service are classified in Industry 4311.

(7) In Public Administration, Division J, establishments primarily engaged in performing central administrative and managerial activities are classified as operating establishments. Establishments primarily engaged in performing other auxiliary activities for establishments in Public Administration, Division J, such as warehouses, automotive maintenance shops, and recreation facilities, are classified as auxiliary establishments.

(8) Establishments primarily engaged in performing auxiliary activities for enterprises that do not have operating establishments in the United States are classified as operating establishments on the basis of the establishment's primary activity in the United States.

Specific Examples of Auxiliary Establishments

The following are examples of auxiliary establishments primarily engaged in performing management or support services for other establishments of the same enterprise:

(1) Central administrative offices primarily engaged in performing management and general administrative functions, except establishments of Public Administration, Division J. Central administrative offices may

perform such activities as general management; accounting; computing, tabulating, or data processing; purchasing; engineering and systems planning; advertising; public relations or lobbying; and legal, financial, or related managerial functions.

(2) Establishments primarily engaged in research, development, and testing for other establishments of the same enterprise, except establishments of aircraft, guided missile, and spacecraft manufacturers as defined in Exceptions and Borderlines.

(3) Warehouses and storage facilities primarily serving other establishments of the same enterprise.

(4) Maintenance and repair shops primarily serving other establishments of the same enterprise for the maintenance and repair of its own machinery and equipment.

(5) Automotive repair shops or storage garages operated by an enterprise primarily for repair or storage of its own vehicles.

(6) Establishments primarily engaged in news collection, editorial work, or advertising sales related to publishing activities for other establishments of the same enterprise.

(7) Establishments primarily providing equipment to construction establishments of the same enterprise.

(8) Establishments primarily engaged in providing field engineering support services for other establishments of the same enterprise at locations other than the parent facility, e.g., at the customer's site.

(9) Showrooms in which sales do not take place.

(10) Recreation facilities, such as gymnasiums, golf courses, and swimming pools, maintained by an enterprise for the benefit of its employees.

(11) Milk receiving stations for dairies.

Basis of Code Assignment in the SIC

Operating Establishments

Each operating establishment is assigned an industry code on the basis of its primary activity, which is determined by its principal product or group of products produced or distributed, or services rendered. Ideally, the principal product or service should be determined by its relative share of value added at the establishment. In practice, however, it is rarely possible to obtain this measure for individual products or services; typically, it is necessary to adopt some other criterion which may be expected to give approximately the same results in determining the primary activity of an establishment. It is recommended, therefore, that, when available, the following data measures be used for each of the major economic sectors in assigning industry codes:

Division	Data measure
Agriculture, forestry, and fishing (except agricultural services).	Value of production.
Mining	Value of production.

Division	*Data measure*
Construction..	Value of production.
Manufacturing...	Value of production.
Transportation, communications, electric, gas, and sanitary services.	Value of receipts or revenues.
Wholesale trade..	Value of sales.
Retail trade..	Value of sales.
Finance, insurance, and real estate...........	Value of receipts.
Services (including agricultural services).	Value of receipts or revenues.
Public administration..................................	Employment or payroll.

Occasionally, in establishments with multiple activities, the appropriate measure cannot be determined or estimated for each product or service. In some instances, an industry classification based upon the recommended output measure will not represent adequately the relative economic importance of each of the varied activities carried on at such establishments. In such cases, employment or payroll information should be used to determine the primary activity of the establishments.

Even though a data collecting organization may have no immediate need to analyze or publish establishment data at the four-digit industry level of classification, it may be useful to assign four-digit codes to each establishment report where the information is available and the incremental cost of such classification is not excessive. The four-digit code assignment should be made directly on the basis of the primary products, services, or activities reported by each establishment at the four-digit industry level of detail.[1]

Four-digit code assignment is also helpful in determining comparability with codes previously assigned from earlier editions of the manual. In this revision, for example, Industry Group 504, Professional and Commercial Equipment and Supplies, was changed by shifting some four-digit industries into this industry group and others out of it. Therefore, if four-digit industry codes were assigned previously, reclassification would not be necessary to provide comparable historical data for that industry group on the revised basis. Before an agency limits classification to less than the four-digit industry detail, consideration should also be given to possible expansion of the requirements for industry data, as well as for editing and special analyses of certain data series for which more detail would be helpful.

Auxiliary Establishments

Auxiliary establishments are assigned four-digit industry codes on the basis of the primary activity of the operating establishments they serve. In addition, they are subclassified further through the assignment of a one-digit auxiliary code, out-

---

[1] It is possible for the classification of an establishment, based on its primary activity at the two-digit major group or three-digit industry group level, to differ from that assigned on the basis of its primary activity at the four-digit industry level. This can occur where the primary activity of an establishment is classified in the four-digit industry of one industry group that is not as large as the combined activity of two or more four-digit industries within another industry group. (Note, however, that if subindustries are used, the code assignment should be made on the basis of the primary activity within the assigned four-digit industry.)

lined below, based on the primary activity performed by the auxiliary establishment.

Agencies should provide for the separate presentation of statistics on an industry basis for operating and auxiliary establishments when data for both types of establishments are presented.

Industrial Subclassification of Auxiliary Establishments

Auxiliary
Code Number   **Titles and Descriptions of Auxiliaries**

1   **Central Administrative Offices**

Auxiliary establishments primarily engaged in performing management and other general administrative functions centrally for other establishments of the same enterprise.

Accounting offices	Financial offices
Advertising offices	Head offices
Buying offices	Legal offices
Central offices	Lobbying offices
Computer operations facilities	Marketing research offices
Corporate offices	Public relations offices
Data processing facilities	Purchasing offices
District administrative offices	Recordkeeping offices
Executive offices	Regional administrative offices

2   **Research, Development, and Testing Laboratories**

Auxiliary establishments primarily engaged in performing laboratory or other physical or biological research, development, and testing for other establishments of the same enterprise.

Biological research facilities	Industrial laboratories
Chemical laboratories	Laboratories, testing of products
Engineering laboratories	Research laboratories
Food research/testing facilities	Testing facilities

3   **Warehouses**

Auxiliary establishments primarily engaged in storing raw materials, finished goods, and other products to be used or sold by other establishments of the same enterprise.

Storage yards	Warehouses

9   **Auxiliaries, Not Elsewhere Classified**

Auxiliary establishments primarily engaged in providing support services, not elsewhere classified, for other establishments of the same enterprise.

Advertising sales offices	Repair shops
Computer maintenance facilities	Security offices
Garages: maintenance, repair, motor pools	Showrooms, without sales
	Stamp redemption centers
Milk receiving stations	Trading stamp stores
Recreation centers	Trucking terminals

Treatment of Ownership Characteristics

All establishments primarily engaged in the same kind of economic activity are classified in the same four-digit industry, regardless of their types of ownership; hence, their owners may include such diverse legal organizations as corporations, partnerships, sole proprietorships, government agencies, etc.

Government establishments, therefore, are classified by their primary economic activity, rather than by type of owner.

Where applicable, agencies should publish at least summary data separately for the private and government establishments constituting an industry or industry group.

If available, these two major ownership sectors may be further subdivided by the following classification system:

Sector I. Private
- Corporation
  - Profit
  - Nonprofit (except cooperatives)
- Cooperative or mutual association (incorporated or not)
  - Profit
  - Nonprofit
- Partnership
- Sole proprietorship
- Other—estate, receivership, joint venture, personal trust, fiduciary trust, etc.

Sector II. Government
- Federal
  - Regular government
  - Quasi-government*
- State
  - Regular government
  - Quasi-government*
- Local
  - Regular government
    - County
    - City, town, village, or township
    - School districts
    - Special districts
  - Quasi-government*
- International government or foreign government
- Other—regional commissions, inter-State organizations, etc.

---

*Quasi-government includes those establishments which are controlled by the government and private sectors through joint ownership of stock or joint membership on boards of directors or other controlling bodies.

Part I

Titles and Descriptions
of Industries

DIVISION A

Agriculture, Forestry, and Fishing

The Division as a Whole

This division includes establishments primarily engaged in agricultural production, forestry, commercial fishing, hunting and trapping, and related services.

The classification of agricultural production covers establishments (e.g., farms, ranches, dairies, greenhouses, nurseries, orchards, hatcheries) primarily engaged in the production of crops, plants, vines, or trees (excluding forestry operations); and the keeping, grazing, or feeding of livestock for the sale of livestock or livestock products (including serums), for livestock increase, or for value increase. Livestock as used here includes cattle, sheep, goats, hogs, and poultry. Also included are animal specialties, such as horses, rabbits, bees, pets, fur-bearing animals in captivity, and fish in captivity. Agricultural production also includes establishments primarily engaged in the operation of sod farms, cranberry bogs, and poultry hatcheries; in the production of mushrooms, bulbs, flower seeds, and vegetable seeds; and in the growing of hydroponic crops.

Farms are the establishment units generally utilized for the purpose of industrial classification of agricultural production. A farm may consist of a single tract of land or a number of separate tracts which may be held under different tenures. For example, one tract may be owned by the farm operator and another rented. It may be operated by the operator alone or with the assistance of members of the household or hired employees, or it may be operated by a partnership, corporation, or other type of organization. When a landowner has one or more tenants, renters, croppers, or managers, the land operated by each is considered a farm.

The classification of agricultural services includes establishments primarily engaged in supplying soil preparation services, crop services, landscape and horticultural services, veterinary and other animal services, and farm labor and management services.

The classification of forestry covers establishments primarily engaged in the operation of timber tracts, tree farms, or forest nurseries; in the gathering of forest products; or in performing forestry services. Logging establishments are classified in Manufacturing, Industry 2411.

The classification of fishing and hunting and trapping covers establishments primarily engaged in commercial fishing (including shellfish and marine products); in operating fish hatcheries and fish and game preserves; and in commercial hunting and trapping.

21

Establishments which produce agricultural commodities and sell them directly to the general public for personal or household consumption are classified in Major Groups 01 and 02.

Major Group 01.—AGRICULTURAL PRODUCTION—CROPS

The Major Group as a Whole

This major group includes establishments (e.g., farms, orchards, greenhouses, nurseries) primarily engaged in the production of crops, plants, vines, and trees (excluding forestry operations). This major group also includes establishments primarily engaged in the operation of sod farms, and cranberry bogs; in the production of mushrooms, bulbs, flower seeds, and vegetable seeds; and in the growing of hydroponic crops. Seeds of field crops are classified in the same industry as crops grown for other purposes.

An establishment primarily engaged in crop production (Major Group 01) is classified in the industry (four-digit) and industry group (three-digit) which accounts for 50 percent or more of the total value of sales for its agricultural production. If the total value of sales for agricultural products of an establishment is less than 50 percent from a single four-digit industry, but 50 percent or more of the value of sales for its agricultural products derives from the products of two or more four-digit industries within the same three-digit industry group, the establishment is classified in the miscellaneous industry of that industry group; otherwise, it is classified as a general crop farm in Industry 0191. Establishments that derive 50 percent or more of the value of sales from horticultural specialties of Industry Group 018 are classified in Industry 0181 or 0182 according to their primary activity.

Industry Group No. Industry No.

011   **CASH GRAINS**

0111 Wheat

Establishments primarily engaged in the production of wheat.

Wheat farms

0112 Rice

Establishments primarily engaged in the production of rice.

Rice farms

0115 Corn

Establishments primarily engaged in the production of field corn for grain or seed. Establishments primarily engaged in the production of sweet corn are classified in Industry 0161, and those producing popcorn are classified in Industry 0119.

Corn farms, except sweet corn or popcorn

0116 Soybeans

Establishments primarily engaged in the production of soybeans.

Soybean farms

0119 Cash Grains, Not Elsewhere Classified

Establishments primarily engaged in the production of cash grains, not elsewhere classified. Included in this industry are establishments primarily engaged in the production of dry field and seed peas and beans, safflowers, sunflowers, or popcorn. This industry also includes establishments deriving 50

Industry Group No. Industry No.

011 **CASH GRAINS—Con.**

0119 Cash Grains, Not Elsewhere Classified—Con.

percent or more of their total value of sales of agricultural products from cash grains (Industry Group 011), but less than 50 percent from products of any single industry.

Barley farms	Mustard seed farms
Bean farms, dry field and seed	Oat farms
Buckwheat farms	Pea farms, dry field and seed
Cowpea farms	Popcorn farms
Flaxseed farms	Rye farms
Grain farms: except wheat, rice, corn, and soybeans	Safflower farms
	Sorghum farms, except for syrup
Lentil farms	Sunflower farms
Milo farms	

013 **FIELD CROPS, EXCEPT CASH GRAINS**

0131 Cotton

Establishments primarily engaged in the production of cotton and cottonseed.

Cotton farms	Cottonseed farms

0132 Tobacco

Establishments primarily engaged in the production of tobacco.

Tobacco farms

0133 Sugarcane and Sugar Beets

Establishments primarily engaged in the production of sugarcane and sugar beets.

Beet farms, sugar	Sugar beet farms
Cane farms, sugar	Sugarcane farms

0134 Irish Potatoes

Establishments primarily engaged in the production of potatoes, except sweet potatoes. Establishments primarily engaged in the production of sweet potatoes and yams are classified in Industry 0139.

Potato farms, Irish
Potato farms, except sweet potato and yam

0139 Field Crops, Except Cash Grains, Not Elsewhere Classified

Establishments primarily engaged in the production of field crops, except cash grains, not elsewhere classified. This industry also includes establishments deriving 50 percent or more of their total value of sales of agricultural products from field crops, except cash grains (Industry Group 013), but less than 50 percent from products of any single industry.

Alfalfa farms	Mint farms
Broomcorn farms	Peanut farms
Clover farms	Potato farms, sweet
Grass seed farms	Sweet potato farms
Hay farms	Timothy farms
Hop farms	Yam farms

016   VEGETABLES AND MELONS

0161   Vegetables and Melons

Establishments primarily engaged in the production of vegetables and melons in the open. Establishments primarily engaged in growing vegetables under glass or other protection are classified in Industry 0182; those producing dry field and seed beans and peas are classified in Industry 0119; those producing Irish potatoes are classified in Industry 0134, and those producing sweet potatoes and yams are classified in Industry 0139.

Asparagus farms	Lettuce farms
Bean farms, except dry beans	Market gardens
Beet farms, except sugar beet	Melon farms
Bok choy farms	Onion farms
Broccoli farms	Pea farms, except dry peas
Cabbage farms	Pepper farms, sweet and hot (vegetables)
Cantaloup farms	
Cauliflower farms	Romaine farms
Celery farms	Snap bean farms (bush and pole)
Corn farms, sweet	Squash farms
Cucumber farms	Tomato farms
English pea farms	Truck farms
Green lima bean farms	Vegetable farms
Green pea farms	Watermelon farms

017   FRUITS AND TREE NUTS

0171   Berry Crops

Establishments primarily engaged in the production of cranberries, bush berries, and strawberries.

Berry farms	Dewberry farms
Blackberry farms	Loganberry farms
Blueberry farms	Raspberry farms
Cranberry bogs	Strawberry farms
Currant farms	

0172   Grapes

Establishments primarily engaged in the production of grapes.

Grape farms	Vineyards

0173   Tree Nuts

Establishments primarily engaged in the production of tree nuts.

Almond groves and farms	Pecan groves and farms
Filbert groves and farms	Pistachio groves and farms
Macadamia groves and farms	Walnut groves and farms

0174   Citrus Fruits

Establishments primarily engaged in the production of citrus fruits.

Citrus groves and farms	Lime groves and farms
Grapefruit groves and farms	Orange groves and farms
Lemon groves and farms	Tangerine groves and farms

0175   Deciduous Tree Fruits

Establishments primarily engaged in the production of deciduous tree fruits. Establishments primarily growing citrus fruits are classified in Industry 0174, and those growing tropical fruits are classified in Industry 0179.

Apple orchards and farms	Persimmon orchards and farms
Apricot orchards and farms	Plum orchards and farms
Cherry orchards and farms	Pomegranate orchards and farms
Nectarine orchards and farms	Prune orchards and farms
Peach orchards and farms	Quince orchards and farms
Pear orchards and farms	

Industry Group No.	Industry No.	

017 **FRUITS AND TREE NUTS—Con.**

0179 **Fruits and Tree Nuts, Not Elsewhere Classified**

Establishments primarily engaged in the production of fruits and nuts, not elsewhere classified. This industry also includes establishments deriving 50 percent or more of their total value of sales of agricultural products from fruit and tree nuts (Industry Group 017), but less than 50 percent from products of any single industry.

Avocado orchards and farms	Kiwi fruit farms
Banana farms	Olive groves and farms
Coffee farms	Pineapple farms
Date orchards and farms	Plantain farms
Fig orchards and farms	Tropical fruit farms

018 **HORTICULTURAL SPECIALTIES**

0181 **Ornamental Floriculture and Nursery Products**

Establishments primarily engaged in the production of ornamental plants and other nursery products, such as bulbs, florists' greens, flowers, shrubbery, flower and vegetable seeds and plants, and sod. These products may be grown under cover (greenhouse, frame, cloth house, lath house) or outdoors.

Bedding plants, growing of	Nursery stock, growing of
Bulbs, growing of	Plants, ornamental: growing of
Field nurseries: growing of flowers and shrubbery, except forest shrubbery	Plants, potted: growing of
Florists' greens, cultivated: growing of	Rose growers
Flowers, growing of	Seeds, flower and vegetable: growing of
Foliage, growing of	Shrubberies, except forest shrubbery: growing of
Fruit stocks, growing of	Sod farms
Greenhouses for floral products	Vegetable bedding plants, growing of
Mats, preseeded: soil erosion—growing of	

0182 **Food Crops Grown Under Cover**

Establishments primarily engaged in the production of mushrooms or of fruits and vegetables grown under cover.

Bean sprouts grown under cover	Rhubarb grown under cover
Fruits grown under cover	Seaweed grown under cover
Greenhouses for food crops	Tomatoes grown under cover
Hydroponic crops, grown under cover	Truffles grown under cover
Mushroom spawn, production of	Vegetables grown under cover
Mushrooms , growing of	

019 **GENERAL FARMS, PRIMARILY CROP**

0191 **General Farms, Primarily Crop**

Establishments deriving 50 percent or more of their total value of sales of agricultural products from crops, including horticultural specialties, but less than 50 percent from products of any single three-digit industry group.

Crop farms, general

Major Group 02.—AGRICULTURAL PRODUCTION—LIVESTOCK AND ANIMAL SPECIALTIES

The Major Group as a Whole

This major group includes establishments (e.g., farms, ranches, dairies, feedlots, egg production facilities, broiler facilities, poultry hatcheries, apiaries) primarily engaged in the keeping, grazing, or feeding of livestock for the sale of livestock or livestock products (including serums), for livestock increase, or for value increase. Livestock, as used here, includes cattle, hogs, sheep, goats, and poultry of all kinds; also included in this major group are animal specialties, such as horses, rabbits, bees, pets, fish in captivity, and fur-bearing animals in captivity.

An establishment primarily engaged in the production of livestock or livestock products (Major Group 02) is classified in the industry (four-digit) or industry group (three-digit) which accounts for 50 percent or more of the total value of sales for its agricultural production. If the total value of sales for agricultural products of an establishment is less than 50 percent from a single four-digit industry, but 50 percent or more of the value of sales for its agricultural products derives from the products of two or more four-digit industries within the same three-digit industry group, the establishment is classified in the miscellaneous industry of that industry group; otherwise, it is classified as a general livestock farm in Industry 0291.

Industry Group No.	Industry No.	

021   **LIVESTOCK, EXCEPT DAIRY AND POULTRY**

0211   **Beef Cattle Feedlots**

Establishments primarily engaged in the fattening of beef cattle in a confined area for a period of at least 30 days, on their own account or on a contract or fee basis. Feedlot operations that are an integral part of the breeding, raising, or grazing of beef cattle are classified in Industry 0212. Establishments which feed beef cattle for periods of less than 30 days, generally in connection with their transport, are classified in Transportation, Industry 4789.

Cattle feeding farms
Cattle feedlot operations
Feedlots, cattle

Stockyards, exclusively for fattening cattle

0212   **Beef Cattle, Except Feedlots**

Establishments primarily engaged in the production or feeding of beef cattle, except feedlots. Establishments primarily raising dairy cattle are classified in Industry 0241.

Beef cattle farms, except feedlots
Cattle raising farms

Cattle ranches

0213   **Hogs**

Establishments primarily engaged in the production or feeding of hogs on their own account or on a contract or fee basis.

Feedlots, hog

Hog farms

Industry Group No.	Industry No.	
021		**LIVESTOCK, EXCEPT DAIRY AND POULTRY—Con.**

0214 Sheep and Goats

Establishments primarily engaged in the production of sheep, lambs, goats, goats' milk, wool, and mohair, including the operation of lamb feedlots, on their own account or on a contract or fee basis.

Feedlots, lamb	Sheep feeding farms and ranches
Goat farms	Sheep raising farms and ranches
Goats' milk production	Wool production
Mohair production	

0219 General Livestock, Except Dairy and Poultry

Establishments deriving 50 percent or more of their total value of sales of agricultural products from livestock and livestock products classified in Industry Group 021, but less than 50 percent from products of any single industry.

024   DAIRY FARMS

0241 Dairy Farms

Establishments primarily engaged in the production of cows' milk and other dairy products and in raising dairy heifer replacements. Such farms may process and bottle milk on the farm and sell at wholesale or retail. However, the processing and/or distribution of milk from a separate establishment not on the farm is classified in manufacturing or trade. Establishments primarily producing goats' milk are classified in Industry 0214.

Dairy farms	Milk production, dairy cattle farm
Dairy heifer replacement farms	

025   POULTRY AND EGGS

0251 Broiler, Fryer, and Roaster Chickens

Establishments primarily engaged in the production of chickens for slaughter, including those grown under contract.

Broiler chickens, raising of	Cornish hen farms
Chicken farms or ranches, raising for	Frying chickens, raising of
slaughter	Roasting chickens, raising of

0252 Chicken Eggs

Establishments primarily engaged in the production of chicken eggs, including table eggs and hatching eggs, and in the sale of cull hens.

Chicken egg farms	Started pullet farms

0253 Turkeys and Turkey Eggs

Establishments primarily engaged in the production of turkeys and turkey eggs.

Turkey egg farms and ranches	Turkey farms and ranches

0254 Poultry Hatcheries

Establishments primarily engaged in operating poultry hatcheries on their own account or on a contract or fee basis.

Chicken hatcheries	Poultry hatcheries
Egg hatcheries, poultry	

025   POULTRY AND EGGS—Con.

0259   Poultry and Eggs, Not Elsewhere Classified

Establishments primarily engaged in the production of poultry and eggs, not elsewhere classified. This industry also includes establishments deriving 50 percent or more of their total value of sales of agricultural products from poultry and eggs (Industry Group 025), but less than 50 percent from products of any single industry.

Duck farms
Egg farms, poultry: except chicken and turkey
Geese farms

Pheasant farms
Pigeon farms
Quail farms
Squab farms

027   ANIMAL SPECIALTIES

0271   Fur-Bearing Animals and Rabbits

Establishments primarily engaged in the production of fur and fur-bearing animals and rabbits.

Chinchilla farms
Fox farms
Fur farms

Game farms (fur-bearing animals)
Mink farms
Rabbit farms

0272   Horses and Other Equines

Establishments primarily engaged in the production of horses and other equines.

Burro farms
Donkey farms
Horse farms

Mule farms
Pony farms

0273   Animal Aquaculture

Establishments primarily engaged in the production of finfish and shellfish, such as crustaceans and mollusks, within a confined space and under controlled feeding, sanitation, and harvesting procedures. Establishments primarily engaged in hatching fish and in operating fishing preserves are classified in Industry 0921.

Catfish farms
Crustacean farms
Finfish farms
Fish farms, except hatcheries
Goldfish farms

Minnow farms
Mollusk farms
Tropical aquarium fish farms
Trout farms

0279   Animal Specialties, Not Elsewhere Classified

Establishments primarily engaged in the production of animal specialties, not elsewhere classified, such as pets, bees, worms, and laboratory animals. This industry also includes establishments deriving 50 percent or more of their total value of sales of agricultural products from animal specialties (Industry Group 027), but less than 50 percent from products of any single industry.

Alligator farms
Apiaries
Aviaries (e.g., parakeet, canary, love birds)
Bee farms
Cat farms
Dog farms
Earthworm hatcheries
Frog farms

Honey production
Kennels, breeding and raising own stock
Laboratory animal farms (e.g., rats, mice, guinea pigs)
Rattlesnake farms
Silk (raw) production and silkworm farms
Worm farms

Industry Group No.	Industry No.
029	

GENERAL FARMS, PRIMARILY LIVESTOCK AND ANIMAL SPECIALTIES

0291 General Farms, Primarily Livestock and Animal Specialties

Establishments deriving 50 percent or more of their total value of sales of agricultural products from livestock and animal specialties and their products, but less than 50 percent from products of any single three-digit industry group.

Animal specialty and livestock farms, general

Livestock and animal specialty farms, general

Major Group 07.—AGRICULTURAL SERVICES

The Major Group as a Whole

This major group includes establishments primarily engaged in performing soil preparation services, crop services, veterinary services, other animal services, farm labor and management services, and landscape and horticultural services, for others on a contract or fee basis. However, feedlots and poultry hatcheries operated on a contract or fee basis are included in Major Group 02.

Industry Group No.	Industry No.	
071		**SOIL PREPARATION SERVICES**
	0711	**Soil Preparation Services**

Establishments primarily engaged in land breaking, plowing, application of fertilizer, seed bed preparation, and other services for improving the soil for crop planting. Establishments primarily engaged in land clearing and earth moving for terracing and pond and irrigation construction are classified in Construction, Industry 1629.

Chemical treatment of soil for crops	Plowing
Fertilizer application for crops	Seed bed preparation
Lime spreading for crops	Weed control, crop: before planting

072   **CROP SERVICES**

0721   **Crop Planting, Cultivating, and Protecting**

Establishments primarily engaged in performing crop planting, cultivating, and protecting services . Establishments primarily engaged in complete maintenance of citrus groves, orchards, and vineyards are classified in Industry 0762. Establishments providing water for irrigation, or providing both water and irrigation services, are classified in Transportation and Public Utilities, Industry 4971.

Aerial dusting and spraying	Planting crops, with or without fertilizing
Bracing of orchard trees and vines	Pollinating
Citrus grove cultivation services	Pruning of orchard trees and vines
Cultivation services, mechanical and flame	Seeding crops, with or without fertilizing
Detasseling of corn	Seeding of sprouts and twigs
Disease control for crops, with or without fertilizing	Spraying crops, with or without fertilizing
Dusting crops, with or without fertilizing	Surgery on orchard trees and vines
Entomological service, agricultural	Thinning of crops, mechanical and chemical
Hoeing	Trees, orchard: cultivation of
Insect control for crops, with or without fertilizing	Trees, orchard: planting, pruning, bracing, spraying, removal, and surgery
Irrigation system operation services (not providing water)	Vineyard cultivation services
Orchard cultivation services	Weed control, crop: after planting

0722   **Crop Harvesting, Primarily by Machine**

Establishments primarily engaged in mechanical harvesting, picking, and combining of crops, and related activities, using machinery provided by the service firm. Farm labor contractors providing personnel for manual harvesting are classified in Industry 0761.

Industry
Group   Industry
No.   No.

072   **CROP SERVICES—Con.**

0722   **Crop Harvesting, Primarily by Machine—Con.**

Berries, machine harvesting of
Chopping and silo filling
Combining, agricultural
Cotton, machine harvesting of
Fruits, machine harvesting of
Grain, machine harvesting of
Hay mowing, raking, baling, and chopping

Nuts, machine harvesting of
Peanuts, machine harvesting of
Sugar beets, machine harvesting of
Sugarcane, machine harvesting of
Threshing service
Vegetables, machine harvesting of

0723   **Crop Preparation Services for Market, Except Cotton Ginning**

Establishments primarily engaged in performing services on crops, subsequent to their harvest, with the intent of preparing them for market or further processing. Establishments primarily engaged in buying farm products for resale to other than the general public for household consumption and which also prepare them for market or further processing are classified in Wholesale Trade. Establishments primarily engaged in stemming and redrying tobacco are classified in Manufacturing, Industry 2141.

Bean cleaning
Corn shelling
Cotton seed delinting
Drying of corn, rice, hay, fruits, and vegetables
Flax decorticating and retting
Fruit precooling, not in connection with transportation
Fruit vacuum cooling
Grain cleaning
Grain fumigation
Grain grinding, custom
Moss ginning

Nut hulling and shelling
Packaging fresh or farm-dried fruits and vegetables
Peanut shelling, custom
Potato curing
Seed cleaning
Sorting, grading, and packing of fruits and vegetables
Sweet potato curing
Tobacco grading
Vegetable precooling, not in connection with transportation
Vegetable vacuum cooling

0724   **Cotton Ginning**

Establishments primarily engaged in ginning cotton.

Cotton ginning
Cotton pickery

Gins, cotton: operation of

074   **VETERINARY SERVICES**

0741   **Veterinary Services for Livestock**

Establishments of licensed practitioners primarily engaged in the practice of veterinary medicine, dentistry, or surgery, for cattle, hogs, sheep, goats, and poultry. Establishments of licensed practitioners primarily engaged in treating all other animals are classified in Industry 0742.

Animal hospitals for livestock
Veterinarians for livestock

Veterinary services for livestock

0742   **Veterinary Services for Animal Specialties**

Establishments of licensed practitioners primarily engaged in the practice of veterinary medicine, dentistry, or surgery, for animal specialties. Animal specialties include horses, bees, fish, fur-bearing animals, rabbits, dogs, cats, and other pets and birds, except poultry. Establishments of licensed practitioners primarily engaged in veterinary medicine for cattle, hogs, sheep, goats, and poultry are classified in Industry 0741.

Animal hospitals for pets and other animal specialties
Pet hospitals
Veterinarians for pets and other animal specialties

Veterinary services for pets and other animal specialties

075   **ANIMAL SERVICES, EXCEPT VETERINARY**

    0751   **Livestock Services, Except Veterinary**

Establishments primarily engaged in performing services, except veterinary, for cattle, hogs, sheep, goats, and poultry. Dairy herd improvement associations are also included in this industry. Establishments primarily engaged in the fattening of cattle are classified in Industry 0211. Establishments engaged in incidental feeding of livestock as a part of holding them in stockyards for periods of less than 30 days (generally in the course of transportation) are classified in Transportation and Public Utilities, Industry 4789. Establishments primarily engaged in performing services, except veterinary, for animals, except cattle, hogs, sheep, goats, and poultry are classified in Industry 0752.

Artificial insemination services: livestock	Pedigree record services for cattle, hogs, sheep, goats, and poultry
Breeding of livestock	Sheep dipping and shearing
Cattle spraying	Showing of cattle, hogs, sheep, goats, and poultry
Cleaning poultry coops	
Dairy herd improvement associations	Slaughtering, custom: for individuals
Livestock breeding services	Vaccinating livestock, except by veterinarians
Milk testing for butterfat	

    0752   **Animal Specialty Services, Except Veterinary**

Establishments primarily engaged in performing services, except veterinary, for pets, equines, and other animal specialties. Establishments primarily engaged in performing services other than veterinary for cattle, hogs, sheep, goats, and poultry are classified in Industry 0751. Establishments primarily engaged in training racehorses are classified in Services, Industry 7948.

Animal shelters	Pedigree record services for pets and other animal specialties
Artificial insemination services: animal specialties	Showing of pets and other animal specialties
Boarding horses	
Boarding kennels	Training horses, except racing
Breeding of animals, other than cattle, hogs, sheep, goats, and poultry	Training of pets and other animal specialties
Dog grooming	Vaccinating pets and other animal specialties, except by veterinarians
Dog pounds	
Honey straining on the farm	

076   **FARM LABOR AND MANAGEMENT SERVICES**

    0761   **Farm Labor Contractors and Crew Leaders**

Establishments primarily engaged in supplying labor for agricultural production or harvesting. Establishments primarily engaged in machine harvesting are classified in Industry 0722.

Crew leaders, farm labor: contract	Farm labor contractors

    0762   **Farm Management Services**

Establishments primarily engaged in providing farm management services, including management or complete maintenance of citrus groves, orchards, and vineyards. Such activities may include cultivating, harvesting, or other specialized activities, but establishments primarily engaged in performing such services without farm management services are classified in the appropriate specific industry within Industry Group 072.

Citrus grove management and maintenance, with or without crop services	Vineyard management and maintenance, with or without crop services
Farm management services	
Orchard management and maintenance, with or without crop services	

078   LANDSCAPE AND HORTICULTURAL SERVICES

0781 Landscape Counseling and Planning

Establishments primarily engaged in landscape planning and in performing landscape architectural and counseling services.

Garden planning	Landscape architects
Horticultural advisory or counseling services	Landscape counseling
	Landscape planning

0782 Lawn and Garden Services

Establishments primarily engaged in performing a variety of lawn and garden services. Establishments primarily engaged in the installation of artificial turf are classified in Construction, Industry 1799.

Bermuda sprigging services	Lawn seeding services
Cemetery upkeep, independent	Lawn spraying services
Garden maintenance	Lawn sprigging services
Garden planting	Mowing highway center strips and edges
Lawn care	
Lawn fertilizing services	Seeding highway strips
Lawn mowing services	Sod laying
Lawn mulching services	Turf installation, except artificial

0783 Ornamental Shrub and Tree Services

Establishments primarily engaged in performing a variety of ornamental shrub and tree services. Establishments primarily engaged in forestry services are classified in Major Group 08. Establishments primarily engaged in general lawn and garden planting and maintenance are classified in Industry 0782, and those primarily engaged in performing shrub and tree services for farm crops are classified in Industry 0721.

Arborist services	Tree trimming for public utility lines
Ornamental bush planting, pruning, bracing, spraying, removal, and surgery	Trees, ornamental: planting, pruning, bracing, spraying, removal, and surgery
Ornamental tree planting, pruning, bracing, spraying, removal, and surgery	Utility line tree trimming services

Major Group 08. —FORESTRY

The Major Group as a Whole

This major group includes establishments primarily engaged in the operation of timber tracts, tree farms, forest nurseries, and related activities such as reforestation services and the gathering of gums, barks, balsam needles, maple sap, Spanish moss, and other forest products.

Industry Group No.	Industry No.	

081   **TIMBER TRACTS**

     0811   **Timber Tracts**

Establishments primarily engaged in the operation of timber tracts or tree farms for the purpose of selling standing timber. Establishments holding timber tracts as real property (not for sale of timber) are classified in Real Estate, Industry 6519; and logging establishments are classified in Manufacturing, Industry 2411.

Christmas tree growing   Tree farms
Timber tracts

083   **FOREST NURSERIES AND GATHERING OF FOREST PRODUCTS**

     0831   **Forest Nurseries and Gathering of Forest Products**

Establishments primarily engaged in growing trees for purposes of reforestation or in gathering forest products. The concentration or distillation of these products, when carried on in the forest, is included in this industry.

Balsam needles, gathering of   Lac production
Distillation of gums if carried on at the   Maple sap, gathering of
    gum farm   Moss, gathering of
Distillation of turpentine and rosin if   Pine gum, extraction of
    carried on at the gum farm   Rubber plantations
Forest nurseries   Spanish moss, gathering of
Gathering of forest products: (e.g.,   Sphagnum moss, gathering of
    gums, barks, seeds)   Teaberries, gathering of
Ginseng, gathering of   Tree seed gathering, extracting, and
Huckleberry greens, gathering of   selling

085   **FORESTRY SERVICES**

     0851   **Forestry Services**

Establishments primarily engaged in performing, on a contract or fee basis, services related to timber production, wood technology, forestry economics and marketing, and other forestry services, not elsewhere classified, such as cruising timber, firefighting, and reforestation.

Cruising timber   Forestry services
Estimating timber   Pest control, forest
Fire prevention, forest   Reforestation
Firefighting, forest   Timber valuation
Forest management plans, preparation
    of

Major Group 09.—FISHING, HUNTING, AND TRAPPING

The Major Group as a Whole

This major group includes establishments primarily engaged in commercial fishing (including crabbing, lobstering, clamming, oystering, and the gathering of sponges and seaweed), and the operation of fish hatcheries and fish and game preserves, in commercial hunting and trapping, and in game propagation.

Industry Group No.	Industry No.	

091 **COMMERCIAL FISHING**

0912 **Finfish**

Establishments primarily engaged in the catching or taking of finfish.

Bluefish, catching of	Pilchard, catching of
Cod, catching of	Pollack, catching of
Eels, catching of	Rays, catching of
Finfish, catching of	Salmon, catching of
Fisheries, finfish	Sea herring, catching of
Haddock, catching of	Sharks, catching of
Mackerel, catching of	Tuna, catching of
Menhaden, catching of	Whiting, catching of

0913 **Shellfish**

Establishments primarily engaged in the catching or taking of shellfish.

Clams, digging of	Oyster beds
Crabs, catching of	Oysters, dredging or tonging of
Crayfish, catching of	Shellfish, catching of
Fisheries, shellfish	Shrimp, catching of
Lobsters, catching of	Squid, catching of
Mussels, taking of	

0919 **Miscellaneous Marine Products**

Establishments primarily engaged in miscellaneous fishing activities, such as catching or taking of sea urchins, terrapins, turtles, and frogs. The gathering of seaweed and sponges is also included in this industry.

Cultured pearl production	Sponges, gathering of
Frogs, catching of	Terrapins, catching of
Sea urchins, catching of	Turtles, catching of
Seaweed, gathering of	

092 **FISH HATCHERIES AND PRESERVES**

0921 **Fish Hatcheries and Preserves**

Establishments primarily engaged in operating fish hatcheries or preserves. Establishments primarily engaged in the production of fish or frogs under controlled feeding, sanitation, and harvesting procedures are classified in Industry Group 027.

Fish hatcheries	Fishing preserves

097 **HUNTING AND TRAPPING, AND GAME PROPAGATION**

0971 **Hunting and Trapping, and Game Propagation**

Establishments primarily engaged in commercial hunting and trapping, or in the operation of game preserves.

Industry Group No.	Industry No.

097   **HUNTING AND TRAPPING, AND GAME PROPAGATION—Con.**

     0971   **Hunting and Trapping, and Game Propagation—Con.**

Animal trapping, commercial
Game management
Game preserves
Game propagation
Game retreats, operation of
Hunting carried on as a business enterprise

Hunting preserves, operation of
Trapping carried on as a business enterprise
Wildlife management

DIVISION B

Mining

The Division as a Whole

This division includes all establishments primarily engaged in mining. The term mining is used in the broad sense to include the extraction of minerals occurring naturally: solids, such as coal and ores; liquids, such as crude petroleum; and gases such as natural gas. The term mining is also used in the broad sense to include quarrying, well operations, milling (e.g., crushing, screening, washing, flotation), and other preparation customarily done at the mine site, or as a part of mining activity.

Exploration and development of mineral properties are included. Services performed on a contract or fee basis in the development or operation of mineral properties are classified separately but within this division. Establishments which have complete responsibility for operating mines, quarries, or oil and gas wells for others on a contract or fee basis are classified according to the product mined rather than as mineral services.

Mining operations are classified, by industry, on the basis of the principal mineral produced, or, if there is no production, on the basis of the principal mineral for which exploration or development work is in process. The mining of culm banks, ore dumps, and tailing piles is classified as mining according to the principal mineral product derived.

The purification and distribution of water is classified in Transportation and Public Utilities, Industry 4941, and the bottling and distribution of natural spring and mineral waters is classified in Wholesale Trade, Industry 5149.

Crushing, grinding, or otherwise preparing clay, ceramic, and refractory minerals; barite; and miscellaneous nonmetallic minerals, except fuels, not in conjunction with mining or quarrying operations, are classified in Manufacturing, Industry 3295. Dressing of stone or slabs is classified in Manufacturing, Industry 3281, whether or not mining is done at the same establishment.

Major Group 10.—METAL MINING

The Major Group as a Whole

This major group includes establishments primarily engaged in mining, developing mines, or exploring for metallic minerals (ores). These ores are valued chiefly for the metals contained, to be recovered for use as such or as constituents of alloys, chemicals, pigments or other products. This major group also includes all ore dressing and beneficiating operations, whether performed at mills operated in conjunction with the mines served or at mills, such as custom mills, operated separately. These include mills which crush, grind, wash, dry, sinter, calcine, or leach ore, or perform gravity separation or flotation operations. Magnesite and brucite operations are classified in Industry 1459, and crushed dolomite operations are classified in Industry 1422. Smelters and refineries are classified in Manufacturing, Major Group 33, and establishments engaged in producing primary magnesium metal are classified in Manufacturing, Industry 3339. The operation of brine wells or sea water plants for the production of magnesium is classified in Manufacturing, Major Group 28.

When performed by operators of the properties, exploration under preliminary phases of operation should be classified according to the type of ore expected to be found. Exploration performed on a contract or fee basis is classified in Industry 1081.

Industry Group No.	Industry No.	
101		**IRON ORES**
	1011	**Iron Ores**

Establishments primarily engaged in mining, beneficiating, or otherwise preparing iron ores and manganiferous ores valued chiefly for their iron content. This industry includes production of sinter and other agglomerates except those associated with blast furnace operations. Blast furnaces primarily engaged in producing pig iron from iron ore are classified in Manufacturing, Industry 3312.

Brown ore mining	Magnetite mining
Hematite mining	Manganiferous ore mining, valued chiefly for iron content
Iron agglomerate and pellet production	
Iron ore dressing (beneficiation) plants	Siderite mining
Iron ore mining	Sintering of iron ore at the mine
Iron ore, blocked: mining	Taconite mining
Limonite mining	

102		**COPPER ORES**
	1021	**Copper Ores**

Establishments primarily engaged in mining, milling, or otherwise preparing copper ores. This industry also includes establishments primarily engaged in the recovery of copper concentrates by precipitation and leaching of copper ore. Establishments primarily engaged in the recovery of refined copper by leaching copper concentrates are classified in Manufacturing, Major Group 33.

Chalcocite mining	Copper ore mining
Chalcopyrite mining	Cuprite mining

<table>
<tr><td>Industry
Group
No.</td><td>Industry
No.</td></tr>
</table>

103 LEAD AND ZINC ORES

1031 Lead and Zinc Ores

Establishments primarily engaged in mining, milling, or otherwise preparing lead ores, zinc ores, or lead-zinc ores.

Blende (zinc) mining	Smithsonite mining
Calamine mining	Sphalerite mining
Cerrusite mining	Willemite mining
Galena mining	Zinc ore mining
Lead ore mining	Zinc-blende (sphalerite) mining
Lead-zinc ore mining	Zincite mining

104 GOLD AND SILVER ORES

1041 Gold Ores

Establishments primarily engaged in mining gold ores from lode deposits or in the recovery of gold from placer deposits by any method. In addition to ore dressing methods such as crushing, grinding, gravity concentration, and froth flotation, this industry includes amalgamation, cyanidation, and the production of bullion at the mine, mill, or dredge site.

Bullion, gold: produced at mine, mill, or dredge site	Placer gold mining
Calaverite mining	Sylvanite mining
Lode gold mining	Telluride (gold) mining

1044 Silver Ores

Establishments primarily engaged in mining, milling, or otherwise preparing silver ores. The production of bullion at the mine or mill site is included.

Bullion, silver: produced at mine or mill site	Silver ore mining

106 FERROALLOY ORES, EXCEPT VANADIUM

1061 Ferroalloy Ores, Except Vanadium

Establishments primarily engaged in mining, milling, or otherwise preparing ferroalloy ores, except vanadium. The mining of manganiferous ores valued chiefly for their iron content is classified in Industry 1011. Establishments primarily engaged in mining vanadium ore are classified in Industry 1094, and those mining titanium ore are classified in Industry 1099.

Chromite mining	Nickel ore mining
Chromium ore mining	Psilomelane mining
Cobalt ore mining	Pyrolusite mining
Columbite mining	Rhodochrosite mining
Ferberite mining	Scheelite mining
Huebnerite mining	Tantalite mining
Manganese ore mining	Tantalum ore mining
Manganite mining	Tungsten ore mining
Molybdenite mining	Wolframite mining
Molybdenum ore mining	Wulfenite mining
Molybdite mining	

108 METAL MINING SERVICES

1081 Metal Mining Services

Establishments primarily engaged in performing metal mining services for others on a contract or fee basis, such as the removal of overburden, strip mining for metallic ores, prospect and test drilling, and mine exploration and development. Establishments which have complete responsibility for operating

Industry Group No.	Industry No.	

108   METAL MINING SERVICES—Con.

1081   Metal Mining Services—Con.

mines for others on a contract or fee basis are classified according to the product mined rather than as metal mining services. Establishments primarily performing hauling services are classified in Division E, Transportation.

Boring test holes for metal mining: on a contract basis
Draining or pumping of metal mines: on a contract basis
Drilling for metal mining: on a contract basis
Exploration for metal mining: on a contract basis
Geophysical exploration services, for metal mining: on a contract basis
Mine development for metal mining: on a contract basis

Overburden removal for metal mining: on a contract basis
Prospect drilling for metal mining: on a contract basis
Sinking shafts for metal mining: on a contract basis
Strip mining, metal: on a contract basis
Test drilling for metal mining: on a contract basis

109   MISCELLANEOUS METAL ORES

1094   Uranium-Radium-Vanadium Ores

Establishments primarily engaged in mining, milling, or otherwise preparing uranium-radium-vanadium ores.

Carnotite mining
Leaching of uranium, radium or vanadium ores at mine site
Pitchblende mining
Radium ore mining
Roscoelite (vanadium hydromica) mining

Tyuyamunite mining
Uraninite (pitchblende) mining
Uranium ore mining
Vanadium ore mining

1099   Miscellaneous Metal Ores, Not Elsewhere Classified

Establishments primarily engaged in mining, milling, or otherwise preparing miscellaneous metal ores, not elsewhere classified. Production of metallic mercury by furnacing or retorting at the mine site is also included.

Aluminum ore mining
Antimony ore mining
Bastnasite ore mining
Bauxite mining
Beryl mining
Beryllium ore mining
Cerium ore mining
Cinnabar mining
Ilmenite mining
Iridium ore mining
Mercury ore mining
Microlite mining
Monazite mining
Osmium ore mining

Palladium ore mining
Platinum group ore mining
Quicksilver (mercury) ore mining
Rare-earths ore mining
Rhodium ore mining
Ruthenium ore mining
Rutile mining
Thorium ore mining
Tin ore mining
Titaniferous-magnetite mining, valued chiefly for titanium content
Titanium ore mining
Zirconium ore mining

Major Group 12.—COAL MINING

The Major Group as a Whole

This major group includes establishments primarily engaged in producing bituminous coal, anthracite, and lignite. Included are mining operations and preparation plants (also known as cleaning plants and washeries), whether or not such plants are operated in conjunction with mine sites. The production of coal fuel briquettes and packaged fuel is classified in Manufacturing, Industry 2999. Establishments primarily engaged in the production of gas and hydrocarbon liquids from coal at the mine site are classified in Major Group 13.

Industry Group No.	Industry No.

122   BITUMINOUS COAL AND LIGNITE MINING

1221   Bituminous Coal and Lignite Surface Mining

Establishments primarily engaged in producing bituminous coal or lignite at surface mines or in developing bituminous coal or lignite surface mines. This industry includes auger mining, strip mining, culm bank mining, and other surface mining, by owners or lessees or by establishments which have complete responsibility for operating bituminous coal and lignite surface mines for others on a contract or fee basis. Bituminous coal and lignite preparation plants performing such activities as cleaning, crushing, screening or sizing are included if operated in conjunction with a mine site, or if operated independently of any type of mine.

Brown coal mining
Cleaning plants, bituminous coal
Coal mining, bituminous: surface
Coal preparation plants, bituminous or lignite
Crushing plants, bituminous coal
Culm bank recovery, bituminous coal or lignite: except on a contract basis
Hard coal surface mining, except Pennsylvania anthracite
Lignite mining
Preparation plants, bituminous coal or lignite
Screening plants, bituminous coal
Semianthracite surface mining
Semibituminous coal surface mining
Strip mining, bituminous coal: except on a contract basis
Strip mining, lignite: except on a contract basis
Subbituminous coal surface mining
Washeries, bituminous coal or lignite

1222   Bituminous Coal Underground Mining

Establishments primarily engaged in producing bituminous coal in underground mines or in developing bituminous coal underground mines. This industry includes underground mining by owners or lessees or by establishments which have complete responsibility for operating bituminous coal underground mines for others on a contract or fee basis. Bituminous coal preparation plants performing such activities as cleaning, crushing, screening or sizing are included if operated in conjunction with a mine. Independent bituminous coal preparation plants are classified in Industry 1221.

Coal mining, bituminous—underground
Hard coal underground mining, except Pennsylvania anthracite
Semianthracite mining—underground
Semibituminous coal underground mining
Subbituminous coal underground mining

Industry Group No.	Industry No.	
123		**ANTHRACITE MINING**
	1231	**Anthracite Mining**

Establishments primarily engaged in producing anthracite or in developing anthracite mines. All establishments in the United States that are classified in this industry are located in Pennsylvania. This industry includes mining by owners or lessees or by establishments which have complete responsibility for operating anthracite mines for others on a contract or fee basis. Also included are anthracite preparation plants, whether or not operated in conjunction with a mine.

Anthracite mining
Breakers, anthracite
Coal mining, anthracite
Culm bank recovery, anthracite: except on a contract basis
Dredging, anthracite

Preparation plants, anthracite
Screening plants, anthracite
Strip mining, anthracite: except on a contract basis
Washeries, anthracite

124		**COAL MINING SERVICES**
	1241	**Coal Mining Services**

Establishments primarily engaged in performing coal mining services for others on a contract or fee basis. Establishments which have complete responsibility for operating mines for others on a contract or fee basis are classified according to the product mined, rather than as mining services.

Anthracite mining services on a contract basis
Auger mining services: bituminous coal, anthracite, and lignite on a contract basis
Bituminous coal mining services on a contract basis
Culm bank recovery: bituminous coal, anthracite, and lignite on a contract basis
Draining or pumping of bituminous coal, anthracite, or lignite mines on a contract basis
Drilling for bituminous coal, anthracite, and lignite on a contract basis

Lignite mining services on a contract basis
Overburden removal for bituminous coal, anthracite, and lignite on a contract basis
Sinking shafts for bituminous coal, anthracite, and lignite on a contract basis
Stripping services: bituminous coal, anthracite, and lignite on a contract basis
Tunneling: bituminous coal, anthracite, and lignite on a contract basis

Major Group 13.—OIL AND GAS EXTRACTION

The Major Group as a Whole

This major group includes establishments primarily engaged in: (1) producing crude petroleum and natural gas; (2) extracting oil from oil sands and oil shale; (3) producing natural gasoline and cycle condensate; and (4) producing gas and hydrocarbon liquids from coal at the mine site. Types of activities included are exploration, drilling, oil and gas well operation and maintenance, the operation of natural gasoline and cycle plants, and the gasification, liquefaction, and pyrolysis of coal at the mine site. This major group also includes such basic activities as emulsion breaking and desilting of crude petroleum in the preparation of oil and gas customarily done at the field site. Pipeline transportation of petroleum, gasoline, and other petroleum products (except crude petroleum field gathering lines) is classified in Transportation and Public Utilities, Major Group 46, and of natural gas in Major Group 49. Establishments primarily engaged in petroleum refining and in the production of lubricating oils and greases are classified in Manufacturing, Major Group 29.

Industry Group No.	Industry No.	

131 **CRUDE PETROLEUM AND NATURAL GAS**

1311 **Crude Petroleum and Natural Gas**

Establishments primarily engaged in operating oil and gas field properties. Such activities may include exploration for crude petroleum and natural gas; drilling, completing, and equipping wells; operation of separators, emulsion breakers, desilting equipment, and field gathering lines for crude petroleum; and all other activities in the preparation of oil and gas up to the point of shipment from the producing property. This industry includes the production of oil through the mining and extraction of oil from oil shale and oil sands and the production of gas and hydrocarbon liquids through gasification, liquefaction, and pyrolysis of coal at the mine site. Also included are establishments which have complete responsibility for operating oil and gas wells for others on a contract or fee basis. Establishments primarily engaged in performing oil field services for operators on a contract or fee basis are classified in Industry Group 138.

Coal gasification at the mine site
Coal liquefaction at the mine site
Coal pyrolysis at the mine site
Crude oil production
Crude petroleum production

Kerogen processing
Natural gas production
Oil sand mining
Oil shale mining
Tar sands mining

132 **NATURAL GAS LIQUIDS**

1321 **Natural Gas Liquids**

Establishments primarily engaged in producing liquid hydrocarbons from oil and gas field gases. Establishments recovering liquefied petroleum gases incidental to petroleum refining or to the manufacturing of chemicals are classified in Manufacturing, Major Group 28 or 29. Establishments recovering helium from natural gas are classified in Manufacturing, Major Group 28.

Butane (natural) production
Casing-head butane and propane production

Cycle condensate production (natural gas)
Ethane (natural) production

Industry Group No.	Industry No.	

132   NATURAL GAS LIQUIDS—Con.

1321 Natural Gas Liquids—Con.

Fractionating natural gas liquids
Isobutane (natural) production
Liquefied petroleum gases (natural) production

Natural gas liquids production
Natural gasoline production
Propane (natural) production

138   OIL AND GAS FIELD SERVICES

1381 Drilling Oil and Gas Wells

Establishments primarily engaged in drilling wells for oil or gas field operations for others on a contract or fee basis. This industry includes contractors that specialize in spudding in, drilling in, redrilling, and directional drilling.

Directional drilling of oil and gas wells on a contract basis
Redrilling oil and gas wells on a contract basis
Reworking oil and gas wells on a contract basis

Spudding in oil and gas wells on a contract basis
Well drilling: gas, oil, and water intake—on a contract basis

1382 Oil and Gas Field Exploration Services

Establishments primarily engaged in performing geophysical, geological, and other exploration services for oil and gas on a contract or fee basis.

Aerial geophysical exploration, oil and gas field: on a contract basis
Exploration, oil and gas field: on a contract basis
Geological exploration, oil and gas field: on a contract basis

Geophysical exploration, oil and gas field: on a contract basis
Seismograph surveys, oil and gas field: on a contract basis

1389 Oil and Gas Field Services, Not Elsewhere Classified

Establishments primarily engaged in performing oil and gas field services, not elsewhere classified, for others on a contract or fee basis. Services included are excavating slush pits and cellars; grading, and building of foundations at well locations; well surveying; running, cutting, and pulling casings, tubes, and rods; cementing wells; shooting wells; perforating well casings; acidizing and chemically treating wells; and cleaning out, bailing, and swabbing wells. Establishments which have complete responsibility for operating oil and gas wells for others on a contract or fee basis are classified according to the product extracted rather than as oil and gas field services. Establishments primarily engaged in hauling oil and gas field supplies and equipment are classified in Division E, Transportation and Public Utilities. Establishments primarily engaged in oil and gas field machine shop work are classified in Manufacturing, Industry 3599.

Acidizing wells on a contract basis
Bailing wells on a contract basis
Building oil and gas well foundations on a contract basis
Cementing oil and gas well casings on a contract basis
Chemically treating wells on a contract basis
Cleaning lease tanks, oil and gas field: on a contract basis
Cleaning wells on a contract basis
Derrick building, repairing, and dismantling: oil and gas—on a contract basis
Dismantling of oil well rigs (oil field service) on a contract basis

Erecting lease tanks, oil and gas field: on a contract basis
Excavating slush pits and cellars on a contract basis
Fishing for tools, oil and gas field: on a contract basis
Gas compressing, natural gas at the field on a contract basis
Gas well rig building, repairing, and dismantling on a contract basis
Grading oil and gas well foundations on a contract basis
Hard banding service: on a contract basis
Hot oil treating of oil field tanks: on a contract basis

Industry Group No.	Industry No.
138	**OIL AND GAS FIELD SERVICES—Con.**
	1389 Oil and Gas Field Services, Not Elsewhere Classified—Con.

Hot shot service: on a contract basis

Hydraulic fracturing wells on a contract basis

Impounding and storing salt water in connection with petroleum production

Lease tanks, oil and gas field: erecting, cleaning, and repairing—on a contract basis

Logging wells on a contract basis

Mud service, oil field drilling: on a contract basis

Oil sampling service for oil companies on a contract basis

Oil well logging on a contract basis

Perforating well casings on a contract basis

Pipe testing service, oil and gas field: on a contract basis

Plugging and abandoning wells on a contract basis

Pumping of oil and gas wells on a contract basis

Removal of condensate gasoline from field gathering lines: on a contract basis

Roustabout service: on a contract basis

Running, cutting, and pulling casings, tubes, and rods: oil and gas field

Servicing oil and gas wells on a contract basis

Shooting wells on a contract basis

Shot-hole drilling service, oil and gas field: on a contract basis

Surveying wells on a contract basis, except seismographic

Swabbing wells: on a contract basis

Major Group 14.—MINING AND QUARRYING OF NONMETALLIC MINERALS, EXCEPT FUELS

The Major Group as a Whole

This major group includes establishments primarily engaged in mining or quarrying, developing mines, or exploring for nonmetallic minerals, except fuels. Also included are certain well and brine operations, and primary preparation plants, such as those engaged in crushing, grinding, washing, or other concentration.

Establishments primarily engaged in manufacturing cement are classified in Industry 3241; those engaged in manufacturing lime are classified in Industry 3274; those engaged in cutting and finishing stone and stone products are classified in Industry 3281; and those engaged in manufacturing brick and other structural clay products are classified in Industry Group 325.

Establishments primarily engaged in crushing, pulverizing, or otherwise treating earths, rocks, and minerals mined in Industry Group 145 or 149; or barite mined in Industry 1479, not in conjunction with mining or quarrying operations, are classified in Manufacturing, Industry 3295; establishments primarily engaged in these activities in conjunction with mines or quarries are classified in Mining. Establishments primarily engaged in crushing, pulverizing, or otherwise treating other nonmetallic minerals are classified in Mining, whether or not they are operated in conjunction with mines.

Establishments primarily engaged in manufacturing other stone, clay, glass, and concrete products from minerals mined at the same establishment are classified in Manufacturing, Major Group 32, when separate reports are not available for the mining and manufacturing activities.

Industry Group No.	Industry No.	
141		DIMENSION STONE
	1411	Dimension Stone

Establishments primarily engaged in mining or quarrying dimension stone. Also included are establishments engaged in producing rough blocks and slabs. Establishments primarily engaged in mining dimension soapstone or in mining or quarrying and shaping grindstones, pulpstones, millstones, burrstones, and sharpening stones are classified in Industry 1499. Establishments primarily engaged in dressing (shaping, polishing, or otherwise finishing) blocks and slabs are classified in Manufacturing, Industry 3281. Nepheline syenite mining operations are classified in Industry 1459.

Argillite, dimension—quarrying
Basalt, dimension—quarrying
Bluestone, dimension—quarrying
Calcareous tufa, dimension—quarrying
Diabase, dimension—quarrying
Diorite, dimension—quarrying
Dolomite, dimension—quarrying
Dolomitic marble, dimension—quarrying
Flagstone mining
Gabbro, dimension—quarrying
Gneiss, dimension—quarrying
Granite, dimension—quarrying
Greenstone, dimension—quarrying
Limestone, dimension—quarrying

Marble, dimension—quarrying
Mica schist, dimension—quarrying
Onyx marble, dimension—quarrying
Quartzite, dimension—quarrying
Rubble mining
Sandstone, dimension—quarrying
Serpentine, dimension—quarrying
Slate, dimension—quarrying
Syenite (except nepheline), dimension—quarrying
Trap rock, dimension—quarrying
Travertine, dimension—quarrying
Verde' antique, dimension—quarrying
Volcanic rock, dimension—quarrying

Industry Group No.	Industry No.
142	

142 CRUSHED AND BROKEN STONE, INCLUDING RIPRAP

1422 Crushed and Broken Limestone

Establishments primarily engaged in mining or quarrying crushed and broken limestone, including related rocks, such as dolomite, cement rock, marl, travertine, and calcareous tufa. Also included are establishments primarily engaged in the grinding or pulverizing of limestone, but establishments primarily engaged in producing lime are classified in Manufacturing, Industry 3274.

Calcareous tufa, crushed and broken—quarrying
Cement rock, crushed and broken—quarrying
Chalk mining, crushed and broken—quarrying
Dolomite, crushed and broken—quarrying

Lime rock, ground
Limestone, except bituminous: crushed and broken—quarrying
Marl, crushed and broken—quarrying
Travertine, crushed and broken—quarrying
Whiting mining, crushed and broken—quarrying

1423 Crushed and Broken Granite

Establishments primarily engaged in mining or quarrying crushed and broken granite, including related rocks, such as gneiss, syenite, and diorite.

Diorite, crushed and broken—quarrying
Gneiss, crushed and broken—quarrying
Granite, crushed and broken—quarrying

Syenite, except nepheline: crushed and broken—quarrying

1429 Crushed and Broken Stone, Not Elsewhere Classified

Establishments primarily engaged in mining or quarrying crushed and broken stone, not elsewhere classified.

Basalt, crushed and broken—quarrying
Boulder, crushed and broken—quarrying
Diabase, crushed and broken—quarrying
Dolomitic marble, crushed and broken—quarrying
Gabbro, crushed and broken—quarrying
Ganister, crushed and broken—quarrying
Grits mining (crushed stone)
Marble, crushed and broken—quarrying
Mica schist, crushed and broken—quarrying
Onyx marble, crushed and broken—quarrying

Quartzite, crushed and broken—quarrying
Riprap quarrying, except limestone or granite
Sandstone, except bituminous: crushed and broken—quarrying
Serpentine, crushed and broken—quarrying
Slate, crushed and broken—quarrying
Trap rock, crushed and broken—quarrying
Verde' antique, crushed and broken—quarrying
Volcanic rock, crushed and broken—quarrying

144 SAND AND GRAVEL

1442 Construction Sand and Gravel

Establishments primarily engaged in operating sand and gravel pits and dredges, and in washing, screening, or otherwise preparing sand and gravel for construction uses.

Common sand mining
Construction sand mining

Gravel mining
Pebble mining

Industry Group No.	Industry No.	

144   **SAND AND GRAVEL—Con.**

1446 Industrial Sand

Establishments primarily engaged in operating sand pits and dredges, and in washing, screening, and otherwise preparing sand for uses other than construction, such as glassmaking, molding, and abrasives.

Abrasive sand mining	Grinding sand mining
Blast sand mining	Industrial sand mining
Enamel sand mining	Molding sand mining
Filtration sand mining	Silica mining
Foundry sand mining	Silica sand mining
Glass sand mining	

145   **CLAY, CERAMIC, AND REFRACTORY MINERALS**

Establishments primarily engaged in mining, milling, or otherwise preparing clays and refractory minerals. Mines operated in conjunction with plants manufacturing cement, brick or other structural clay products, or pottery and related products, are included in this industry when separate reports are available. Establishments primarily engaged in grinding, pulverizing, or otherwise treating clay, ceramic, and refractory minerals not in conjunction with mining or quarrying operations are classified in Manufacturing, Industry 3295.

1455 Kaolin and Ball Clay

Establishments primarily engaged in mining, milling, or otherwise preparing kaolin or ball clay, including china clay, paper clay, and slip clay.

Ball clay mining	Paper clay mining
China clay mining	Rubber clay mining
Kaolin mining	Slip clay mining

1459 Clay, Ceramic, and Refractory Minerals, Not Elsewhere Classified

Establishments primarily engaged in mining, milling, or otherwise preparing clay, ceramic, or refractory minerals, not elsewhere classified. Establishments producing clay in conjunction with the manufacture of refractory or structural clay and pottery products are classified in Manufacturing, Major Group 32.

Andalusite mining	Fuller's earth mining
Aplite mining	Kyanite mining
Bentonite mining	Magnesite mining
Brucite mining	Nepheline syenite quarrying
Burley mining	Olivine (nongem) mining
Clays (common) quarrying—not in conjunction with manufacturing	Pegmatite (feldspar) mining
	Pinite mining
Cornwall stone mining	Plastic fire clay mining
Cyanite mining	Shale (common) quarrying-not in conjunction with manufacturing
Diaspore mining	
Dumortierite mining	Sillimanite mining
Feldspar mining	Stoneware clay mining
Fire clay mining	Syenite, nepheline—quarrying
Flint clay mining	Topaz (nongem) mining

147   **CHEMICAL AND FERTILIZER MINERAL MINING**

1474 Potash, Soda, and Borate Minerals

Establishments primarily engaged in mining, milling, or otherwise preparing natural potassium, sodium, or boron compounds. Establishments primarily engaged in mining common salt are classified in Industry 1479.

147 CHEMICAL AND FERTILIZER MINERAL MINING—Con.

1474 Potash, Soda, and Borate Minerals—Con.

Alum mining
Borate compounds mining
Borax mining
Borax, crude: ground and pulverized
Boron mineral mining
Colemanite mining
Glauber's salt mining
Kernite mining
Potash mining

Potassium compounds mining
Probertite mining
Salines mining, except common salt
Soda ash mining
Sodium compounds mining, except common salt
Trona mining
Ulexite mining

1475 Phosphate Rock

Establishments primarily engaged in mining, milling, drying, calcining, sintering, or otherwise preparing phosphate rock, including apatite. Establishments primarily engaged in the production of phosphoric acid, superphosphates, or other manufactured phosphate compounds or chemicals are classified in Manufacturing, Major Group 28.

Apatite mining

Phosphate rock mining

1479 Chemical and Fertilizer Mineral Mining, Not Elsewhere Classified

Establishments primarily engaged in mining, milling, or otherwise preparing chemical or fertilizer mineral raw materials, not elsewhere classified. Establishments primarily engaged in milling, grinding, or otherwise preparing barite not in conjunction with mining or quarry operations are classified in Manufacturing, Industry 3295; similar establishments preparing other minerals of this industry are included here. Establishments primarily engaged in producing salt by evaporation of sea water or brine are classified in Manufacturing, Industry 2899.

Alunite mining
Amblygonite mining
Arsenic mineral mining
Barite mining
Barium ore mining
Brimstone mining
Celestite mining
Fluorite mining
Fluorspar mining
Fluorspar, ground or otherwise treated
Guano mining
Lepidolite mining
Lithium mineral mining

Marcasite mining
Mineral pigment mining
Ocher mining
Pyrites mining
Pyrrhotite mining
Rock salt mining
Salt mining, common
Sienna mining
Spodumene mining
Strontianite mining
Strontium mineral mining
Sulfur mining, native
Umber mining

148 NONMETALLIC MINERALS SERVICES, EXCEPT FUELS

1481 Nonmetallic Minerals Services, Except Fuels

Establishments primarily engaged in the removal of overburden, strip mining, and other services for nonmetallic minerals, except fuels, for others on a contract or fee basis. Establishments primarily engaged in performing hauling services are classified in Division E, Transportation and Public Utilities.

Boring test holes for nonmetallic minerals, except fuels: on a contract basis
Draining or pumping of nonmetallic minerals mines, except fuels: on a contract basis
Drilling for nonmetallic minerals, except fuels: on a contract basis

Exploration for nonmetallic minerals, except fuels: on a contract basis
Geophysical exploration services, for nonmetallic minerals, except fuels: on a contract basis
Mine development for nonmetallic minerals, except fuels: on a contract basis

Industry
Group
No.
148

Industry
No.

NONMETALLIC MINERALS SERVICES, EXCEPT FUELS—Con.

1481 Nonmetallic Minerals Services, Except Fuels—Con.

Overburden removal for nonmetallic minerals, except fuels: on a contract basis

Shaft sinking for nonmetallic minerals, except fuels: on a contract basis

Strip mining for nonmetallic minerals, except fuels: on a contract basis

149   MISCELLANEOUS NONMETALLIC MINERALS, EXCEPT FUELS

1499 Miscellaneous Nonmetallic Minerals, Except Fuels

Establishments primarily engaged in mining, quarrying, milling, or otherwise preparing nonmetallic minerals, except fuels. This industry includes the shaping of natural abrasive stones at the quarry. Establishments primarily engaged in the production of blast, grinding, or polishing sand are classified in Industry 1446, and those calcining gypsum are classified in Manufacturing, Industry 3275.

Agate mining
Alabaster mining
Amethyst mining
Asbestos mining
Asphalt (native) mining
Asphalt rock mining
Bitumens (native) mining
Bituminous limestone quarrying
Bituminous sandstone quarrying
Burrstone quarrying
Calcite mining
Catlinite mining
Corundum mining
Cryolite mining
Diamond mining, industrial
Diatomaceous earth mining
Diatomite mining
Emery mining
Fill dirt pits
Garnet mining
Gem stone mining
Gilsonite mining
Grahamite mining
Graphite mining
Greensand mining
Grinding peat
Grindstone quarrying
Gypsite mining
Gypsum mining
Iceland spar mining (optical grade calcite)
Jade mining
Meerschaum mining or quarrying
Mica mining
Millstone quarrying
Muscovite mining
Natural abrasives mining (except sand)

Oilstone quarrying
Ozokerite mining
Peat humus mining
Peat mining
Perlite mining
Phlogopite mining
Pipestone mining
Pozzolana mining
Precious stones mining
Pulpstone quarrying
Pumice mining
Pumicite mining
Pyrophyllite mining
Quartz crystal mining (pure)
Reed peat mining
Rubbing stone quarrying
Ruby mining
Sapphire mining
Scoria mining
Screening peat
Scythestone quarrying
Sedge peat mining
Selenite mining
Semiprecious stones mining
Sharpening stone quarrying
Shell mining
Shredding peat
Soapstone quarrying
Steatite mining
Talc mining
Tripoli mining
Turquoise mining
Vermiculite mining
Volcanic ash mining
Whetstone quarrying
Wurtzilite mining

DIVISION C

Construction

The Division as a Whole

This division includes establishments primarily engaged in construction. The term construction includes new work, additions, alterations, reconstruction, installations, and repairs. Construction activities are generally administered or managed from a relatively fixed place of business, but the actual construction work is performed at one or more different sites. If a company has more than one relatively fixed place of business from which it undertakes or manages construction activities and for which separate data on the number of employees, payroll, receipts, and other establishment-type records are maintained, each such place of business is considered a separate construction establishment.

Three broad types of construction activity are covered: (1) building construction by general contractors or by operative builders; (2) heavy construction other than building by general contractors and special trade contractors; and (3) construction activity by other special trade contractors. Special trade contractors are primarily engaged in specialized construction activities, such as plumbing, painting, and electrical work, and work for general contractors under subcontract or directly for property owners. General contractors usually assume responsibility for an entire construction project, but may subcontract to others all of the actual construction work or those portions of the project that require special skills or equipment. General contractors thus may or may not have construction workers on their payroll.

Building construction general contractors are primarily engaged in the construction of dwellings, office buildings, stores, farm buildings, and other building construction projects. Operative builders who build on their own account for resale are also included in this division. However, investment builders who build structures on their own account for rental are classified in Real Estate, Major Group 65, but separate establishments primarily engaged in construction for the investment builder are classified in this division.

General contractors and special trade contractors for heavy construction other than building are primarily engaged in the construction of highways; pipelines, communications and power lines, and sewer and water mains; and other heavy construction projects. Special trade contractors are classified in heavy construction other than building if they are primarily engaged in activities such as grading for highway and airport runways; guardrail construction; installation of highway signs; asphalt and concrete construction of roads, highways, streets and public sidewalks; trenching; cable laying; conduit construction; underwater rock removal; pipeline wrapping; or land clearing and leveling.

53

Other special trade contractors undertake activities of a type that are either specialized to building construction or may be undertaken for building or nonbuilding projects. These activities include painting (including bridge painting and traffic lane painting) and electrical work (including work on bridges, power lines and power plants).

Establishments primarily engaged in managing construction projects for others on a contract or fee basis, but assuming no responsibility for completion of the construction project, are classified in Services, Industry 8741. Establishments primarily engaged in renting construction equipment, with or without an operator, are classified in Services, Industry Group 735.

Force account construction is construction work performed by an establishment primarily engaged in some business other than construction, for its own account and use, and by employees of the establishment. This activity is not included in this division, but is classified according to the primary activity which is or will be performed in the establishment. However, construction work performed as the primary activity of a separate establishment of an enterprise for the enterprise's own account is included in this division.

The installation of prefabricated building equipment and materials by general and special trade contractors is classified in this division. Similar installation work performed as a service incidental to sale by employees of an establishment manufacturing or selling prefabricated equipment and materials is classified according to the primary activity in the Manufacturing or Trade Divisions.

Establishments primarily engaged in the distribution and construction or installation of equipment often present classification problems. Since value added is not available for distinguishing the relative importance of sales versus installation or construction activities, payroll or employment may be used as measures yielding approximately the same results.

On this basis, separate establishments primarily engaged in the sale and installation of the following illustrative types of structures or integral parts of structures, generally site assembled, are classified in construction rather than in trade:

a. Steel work on bridges or buildings;

b. Elevators and escalators;

c. Sprinkler systems;

d. Central air-conditioning and heating equipment;

e. Communications equipment; and

f. Insulation materials.

On the other hand, establishments primarily engaged in the sale and installation of the following illustrative types of preassembled equipment are classified in trade rather than in construction:

a. Major household appliances, such as refrigerators, dishwashers, clothes washers and dryers, stoves and ranges; and

b. Partitions for banks, stores, and restaurants.

Major Group 15.—BUILDING CONSTRUCTION—GENERAL CONTRACTORS AND OPERATIVE BUILDERS

The Major Group as a Whole

This major group includes general contractors and operative builders primarily engaged in the construction of residential, farm, industrial, commercial, or other buildings. General building contractors who combine a special trade with the contracting are included in this major group.

Industry
Group
No.

Industry
No.

152　　GENERAL BUILDING CONTRACTORS—RESIDENTIAL BUILDINGS

1521　General Contractors—Single-Family Houses

General contractors primarily engaged in construction (including new work, additions, alterations, remodeling, and repair) of single-family houses.

Building alterations, single-family—general contractors
Building construction, single-family—general contractors
Custom builders, single-family houses—general contractors
Designing and erecting combined: single-family houses—general contractors
Home improvements, single-family—general contractors
House construction, single-family—general contractors
House: shell erection, single-family—general contractors
Mobile home repair, on site—general contractors
Modular housing, single-family (assembled on site)—general contractors
One-family house construction—general contractors
Prefabricated single-family houses erection—general contractors
Premanufactured housing, single-family (assembled on site)—general contractors
Remodeling buildings, single-family—general contractors
Renovating buildings, single-family—general contractors
Repairing buildings, single-family—general contractors
Residential construction, single-family—general contractors
Rowhouse (single-family) construction—general contractors
Townhouse construction—general contractors

1522　General Contractors—Residential Buildings, Other Than Single-Family

General contractors primarily engaged in construction (including new work, additions, alterations, remodeling, and repair) of residential buildings other than single-family houses.

Apartment building construction—general contractors
Building alterations, residential: except single-family—general contractors
Building construction, residential: except single-family—general contractors
Custom builders, residential: except single-family—general contractors
Designing and erecting, combined: residential, except single-family—general contractors
Dormitory construction—general contractors
Home improvements, residential: except single-family—general contractors
Hotel construction—general contractors
Motel construction—general contractors
Prefabricated building erection, residential: except single-family—general contractors
Remodeling buildings, residential: except single-family—general contractors
Renovating buildings, residential: except single-family—general contractors
Repairing buildings, residential: except single-family—general contractors
Residential construction, except single-family—general contractors

Industry Group No.	Industry No.	
153		**OPERATIVE BUILDERS**

1531 Operative Builders

Builders primarily engaged in the construction of single-family houses and other buildings for sale on their own account rather than as contractors. Establishments primarily engaged in the construction (including renovation) of buildings for lease or rental on their own account are classified in Real Estate, Industry Group 651.

Condominium developers on own account	Operative builders on own account
Cooperative apartment developers on own account	Speculative builders

154 GENERAL BUILDING CONTRACTORS—NONRESIDENTIAL BUILDINGS

1541 General Contractors—Industrial Buildings and Warehouses

General contractors primarily engaged in the construction (including new work, additions, alterations, remodeling, and repair) of industrial buildings and warehouses, such as aluminum plants, automobile assembly plants, pharmaceutical manufacturing plants, and commercial warehouses.

Aluminum plant construction—general contractors	Grain elevator construction—general contractors
Building alterations, industrial and warehouse—general contractors	Industrial building construction—general contractors
Building components manufacturing plant construction—general contractors	Industrial plant construction—general contractors
Building construction, industrial and warehouse—general contractors	Paper pulp mill construction—general contractors
Clean room construction—general contractors	Pharmaceutical manufacturing plant construction—general contractors
Cold storage plant construction—general contractors	Prefabricated building erection, industrial—general contractors
Commercial warehouse construction—general contractors	Remodeling buildings, industrial and warehouse—general contractors
Custom builders, industrial and warehouse—general contractors	Renovating buildings, industrial and warehouse—general contractors
Designing and erecting, combined: industrial—general contractors	Repairing buildings, industrial and warehouse—general contractors
Drycleaning plant construction—general contractors	Truck and automobile assembly plant construction—general contractors
Factory construction—general contractors	Warehouse construction—general contractors
Food products manufacturing or packing plant construction—general contractors	

1542 General Contractors—Nonresidential Buildings, Other Than Industrial Buildings and Warehouses

General contractors primarily engaged in the construction (including new work, additions, alterations, remodeling, and repair) of nonresidential buildings, other than industrial buildings and warehouses. Included are nonresidential buildings, such as commercial, institutional, religious, and amusement and recreational buildings. General contractors primarily engaged in the construction of industrial buildings and warehouses are classified in Industry 1541.

Administration building construction—general contractors	Building alterations, nonresidential: except industrial and warehouses—general contractors
Auditorium construction—general contractors	Building construction, nonresidential: except industrial and warehouses—general contractors
Bank building construction—general contractors	

Industry
Group
No.
154

Industry
No.

GENERAL BUILDING CONTRACTORS—NONRESIDENTIAL BUILDINGS—Con.

1542 General Contractors—Nonresidential Buildings, Other Than Industrial Buildings and Warehouses—Con.

Church, synagogue, and related building construction—general contractors

Civic center construction—general contractors

Commercial building construction—general contractors

Custom builders, nonresidential: except industrial and warehouses—general contractors

Designing and erecting, combined: commercial—general contractors

Dome construction—general contractors

Farm building construction, except residential—general contractors

Fire station construction—general contractors

Garage construction general contractors

Hospital construction—general contractors

Institutional building construction, nonresidential—general contractors

Mausoleum construction—general contractors

Museum construction—general contractors

Office building construction—general contractors

Passenger and freight terminal building construction—general contractors

Post office construction—general contractors

Prefabricated building erection, nonresidential: except industrial and warehouses—general contractors

Remodeling buildings, nonresidential: except industrial and warehouses—general contractors

Renovating buildings, nonresidential: except industrial and warehouses—general contractors

Repairing buildings, nonresidential: except industrial and warehouses—general contractors

Restaurant construction—general contractors

School building construction—general contractors

Service station construction—general contractors

Shopping center construction—general contractors

Silo construction, agricultural—general contractors

Stadium construction—general contractors

Store construction—general contractors

Major Group 16.—HEAVY CONSTRUCTION OTHER THAN BUILDING CONSTRUCTION—CONTRACTORS

The Major Group as a Whole

This major group includes general contractors primarily engaged in heavy construction other than building, such as highways and streets, bridges, sewers, railroads, irrigation projects, flood control projects and marine construction, and special trade contractors primarily engaged in activities of a type that are clearly specialized to such heavy construction and are not normally performed on buildings or building-related projects. Specialized activities that are covered here include grading for highways and airport runways; guardrail construction; installation of highway signs; trenching; underwater rock removal; and asphalt and concrete construction of roads, highways, streets and public sidewalks. Establishments primarily engaged in specialized activities that may be performed on buildings or on other heavy construction projects are classified in Major Group 17. These include contractors primarily engaged in painting (including bridge painting and traffic lane painting), electrical work (including work on bridges, power lines, and power plants), and carpentry work.

Industry Group No.	Industry No.	

161   **HIGHWAY AND STREET CONSTRUCTION, EXCEPT ELEVATED HIGHWAYS**

     1611   **Highway and Street Construction, Except Elevated Highways**

General and special trade contractors primarily engaged in the construction of roads, streets, alleys, public sidewalks, guardrails, parkways, and airports. Special trade contractors primarily engaged in the construction of private driveways and sidewalks are classified in Industry 1771.

Airport runway construction—general contractors
Alley construction—general contractors
Asphalt paving: roads, public sidewalks, and streets—contractors
Concrete construction: roads, highways, public sidewalks, and streets—contractors
Grading for highways, streets, and airport runways—contractors
Guardrail construction on highways—contractors
Highway construction, except elevated—general contractors

Highway signs, installation of—contractors
Parkway construction—general contractors
Paving construction—contractors
Resurfacing streets and highways—contractors
Road construction, except elevated—general contractors
Sidewalk construction, public—contractors
Street maintenance or repair—contractors
Street paving—contractors

162   **HEAVY CONSTRUCTION, EXCEPT HIGHWAY AND STREET CONSTRUCTION**

     1622   **Bridge, Tunnel, and Elevated Highway Construction**

General contractors primarily engaged in the construction of bridges; viaducts; elevated highways; and highway, pedestrian, and railway tunnels. General contractors engaged in subway construction are classified in Industry 1629. Special trade contractors primarily engaged in guardrail construction or installation of highway signs is classified in Industry 1611.

Abutment construction—general contractors
Bridge construction—general contractors

Causeway construction on structural supports—general contractors
Highway construction, elevated—general contractors

Industry
Group   Industry
No.   No.

162   HEAVY CONSTRUCTION, EXCEPT HIGHWAY AND STREET CONSTRUCTION—Con.

1622 Bridge, Tunnel, and Elevated Highway Construction—Con.

Overpass construction—general contractors

Trestle construction—general contractors

Tunnel construction—general contractors

Underpass construction—general contractors

Viaduct construction—general contractors

1623 Water, Sewer, Pipeline, and Communications and Power Line Construction

General and special trade contractors primarily engaged in the construction of water and sewer mains, pipelines, and communications and power lines.

Aqueduct construction—general contractors

Cable laying construction—contractors

Cable television line construction—contractors

Conduit construction—contractors

Distribution lines construction, oil and gas field—general contractors

Gas main construction—general contractors

Manhole construction—contractors

Natural gas compressing station construction—general contractors

Pipelaying—general contractors

Pipeline construction—general contractors

Pipeline wrapping—contractors

Pole line construction—general contractors

Power line construction—general contractors

Pumping station construction—general contractors

Radio transmitting tower construction—general contractors

Sewage collection and disposal line construction—general contractors

Sewer construction—general contractors

Telegraph line construction—general contractors

Telephone line construction—general contractors

Television transmitting tower construction—general contractors

Transmission line construction—general contractors

Water main line construction—general contractors

1629 Heavy Construction, Not Elsewhere Classified

General and special trade contractors primarily engaged in the construction of heavy projects, not elsewhere classified.

Athletic field construction—general contractors

Blasting, except building demolition—contractors

Breakwater construction—general contractors

Bridle path construction—general contractors

Brush clearing or cutting—contractors

Caisson drilling—contractors

Canal construction—general contractors

Central station construction—general contractors

Channel construction—general contractors

Channel cutoff construction—general contractors

Chemical complex or facilities construction—general contractors

Clearing of land—general contractors

Cofferdam construction—general contractors

Coke oven construction—general contractors

Cutting right-of-way—general contractors

Dam construction—general contractors

Dike construction—general contractors

Discharging station construction, mine—general contractors

Dock construction—general contractors

Drainage project construction—general contractors

Dredging—general contractors

Earth moving, not connected with building construction—general contractors

Flood control project construction—general contractors

Furnace construction for industrial plants—general contractors

Golf course construction—general contractors

Harbor construction—general contractors

Hydroelectric plant construction—general contractors

Industrial incinerator construction—general contractors

Industrial plant appurtenance construction—general contractors

Irrigation projects construction—general contractors

Jetty construction—general contractors

Kiln construction—general contractors

Land clearing—contractors

Land drainage—contractors

Land leveling (irrigation)—contractors

Land reclamation—contractors

Levee construction—general contractors

HEAVY CONSTRUCTION, EXCEPT HIGHWAY AND STREET CONSTRUCTION—Con.

1629   Heavy Construction, Not Elsewhere Classified—Con.

Light and power plant construction—general contractors

Loading station construction, mine—general contractors

Lock and waterway construction—general contractors

Marine construction—general contractors

Mine loading and discharging station construction—general contractors

Mining appurtenance construction—general contractors

Missile facilities construction—general contractors

Nuclear reactor containment structure construction—general contractors

Oil refinery construction—general contractors

Oven construction for industrial plants—general contractors

Oven construction, bakers'—general contractors

Petrochemical plant construction—general contractors

Petroleum refinery construction—general contractors

Pier construction—general contractors

Pile driving—contractors

Pond construction—general contractors

Power plant construction—general contractors

Railroad construction—general contractors

Railway roadbed construction—general contractors

Reclamation projects construction—general contractors

Reservoir construction—general contractors

Revetment construction—general contractors

Rock removal, underwater—contractors

Sewage treatment plant construction—general contractors

Ski tow erection—general contractors

Soil compacting service—contractors

Submarine rock removal—general contractors

Subway construction—general contractors

Tennis court construction, outdoor—general contractors

Timber removal, underwater—contractors

Tipple construction—general contractors

Trail building—general contractors

Trailer camp construction—general contractors

Trenching—contractors

Washeries construction, mining—general contractors

Waste disposal plant construction—general contractors

Water power project construction—general contractors

Water treatment plant construction—general contractors

Waterway construction—general contractors

Wharf construction—general contractors

Major Group 17.—CONSTRUCTION—SPECIAL TRADE CONTRACTORS

The Major Group as a Whole

This major group includes special trade contractors who undertake activities of a type that are specialized either to building construction, including work on mobile homes, or to both building and nonbuilding projects. These activities include painting (including bridge painting and traffic lane painting), electrical work (including work on bridges, power lines, and power plants), carpentry work, plumbing, heating, air-conditioning, roofing, and sheet metal work. Special trade contractors primarily engaged in activities that are clearly of a type specialized to heavy construction, such as grading for highways and airport runways; guardrail construction; installation of highway signs; underwater rock removal; and asphalt and concrete construction of roads, highways, streets, and public sidewalks are classified in Major Group 16.

Special trade contractors may work on subcontract from the general contractor, performing only part of the work covered by the general contract, or they may work directly for the owner. Special trade contractors for the most part perform their work at the site of construction, although they also may have shops where they perform work incidental to the job site.

Industry Group No.	Industry No.	

171 PLUMBING, HEATING AND AIR-CONDITIONING

1711 Plumbing, Heating and Air-Conditioning

Special trade contractors primarily engaged in plumbing, heating, air-conditioning, and similar work. Sheet metal work performed by plumbing, heating, and air-conditioning contractors in conjunction with the installation of plumbing, heating, and air-conditioning equipment is included here, but roofing and sheet metal work contractors are classified in Industry 1761. Special trade contractors primarily engaged in electrical work are classified in Industry 1731.

Air system balancing and testing—contractors
Air-conditioning, with or without sheet metal work—contractors
Boiler erection and installation—contractors
Drainage system installation, cesspool and septic tank—contractors
Dry well construction, cesspool—contractors
Fuel oil burner installation and servicing—contractors
Furnace repair—contractors
Gasline hookup—contractors
Heating equipment installation—contractors
Heating, with or without sheet metal work—contractors
Lawn sprinkler system installation—contractors
Mechanical contractors
Piping, plumbing—contractors

Plumbing and heating—contractors
Plumbing repair—contractors
Plumbing, with or without sheet metal work—contractors
Refrigeration and freezer work—contractors
Sewer hookups and connections for buildings—contractors
Sheet metal work combined with heating or air-conditioning—contractors
Solar heating apparatus—contractors
Sprinkler system installation—contractors
Steam fitting—contractors
Sump pump installation and servicing—contractors
Ventilating work, with or without sheet metal work—contractors
Water pump installation and servicing—contractors
Water system balancing and testing—contractors

Industry Group No.	Industry No.	

172   **PAINTING AND PAPER HANGING**

1721   **Painting and Paper Hanging**

Special trade contractors primarily engaged in painting and paper hanging. Special trade contractors primarily engaged in roof painting are classified in Industry 1761.

Bridge painting—contractors
Electrostatic painting on site (including of lockers and fixtures)—contractors
House painting—contractors
Painting of buildings and other structures, except roofs—contractors

Paper hanging—contractors
Ship painting—contractors
Traffic lane painting—contractors
Whitewashing—contractors

173   **ELECTRICAL WORK**

1731   **Electrical Work**

Special trade contractors primarily engaged in electrical work at the site. The construction of transmission lines is classified in Industry 1623, and electrical work carried on in repair shops is classified in Services, Industry Group 762. Establishments primarily engaged in monitoring of burglar and fire alarms with incidental installation are classified in Services, Industry 7382.

Burglar alarm installation—contractors
Cable splicing, electrical—contractors
Cable television hookup—contractors
Communications equipment installation—contractors
Electrical repair at site of construction—contractors
Electrical work—contractors
Electronic control system installation—contractors
Fire alarm installation—contractors

Highway lighting and electrical signal construction—contractors
Intercommunications equipment installation—contractors
Sound equipment installation—contractors
Telecommunications equipment installation—contractors
Telephone and telephone equipment installation—contractors

174   **MASONRY, STONEWORK, TILE SETTING, AND PLASTERING**

1741   **Masonry, Stone Setting, and Other Stone Work**

Special trade contractors primarily engaged in masonry work, stone setting, and other stone work. Special trade contractors primarily engaged in concrete work are classified in Industry 1771; those engaged in digging foundations are classified in Industry 1794; and those engaged in the construction of streets, highways, and alleys are classified in Industry 1611.

Bricklaying—contractors
Chimney construction and maintenance—contractors
Concrete block laying—contractors
Foundations, building of: block, stone, or brick—contractors
Marble work, exterior construction—contractors

Masonry—contractors
Refactory brick construction—contractors
Retaining wall construction: block, stone, or brick—contractors
Stone setting—contractors
Stonework erection—contractors
Tuck pointing—contractors

1742   **Plastering, Drywall, Acoustical, and Insulation Work**

Special trade contractors primarily engaged in applying plain or ornamental plaster, including the installation of lathing and other appurtenances to receive plaster, or in drywall, acoustical, and building insulation work.

Acoustical work—contractors
Ceilings, acoustical installation—contractors
Drywall construction—contractors
Insulation installation, buildings—contractors
Lathing—contractors

Plastering, plain or ornamental—contractors
Solar reflecting insulation film—contractors
Taping and finishing drywall—contractors

<table>
<tr><td>Industry Group No.</td><td>Industry No.</td></tr>
<tr><td>174</td><td></td></tr>
</table>

MASONRY, STONEWORK, TILE SETTING, AND PLASTERING—Con.

1743 Terrazzo, Tile, Marble, and Mosaic Work

Special trade contractors primarily engaged in setting and installing ceramic tile, marble, and mosaic, and in mixing marble particles and cement to make terrazzo at the site of construction. Establishments primarily engaged in manufacturing precast terrazzo steps, benches, and other terrazzo articles are classified in Manufacturing, Industry 3272.

Fresco work—contractors
Mantel work—contractors
Marble installation, interior: including finishing—contractors

Mosaic work—contractors
Terrazzo work—contractors
Tile installation, ceramic—contractors
Tile setting, ceramic—contractors

175 CARPENTRY AND FLOOR WORK

1751 Carpentry Work

Special trade contractors primarily engaged in carpentry work. Establishments primarily engaged in building and installing cabinets at the job site are classified in this industry. Establishments primarily engaged in building custom cabinets for individuals in a shop are classified in Retail Trade, Industry 5712. Carpentry work performed by general contractors engaged in building construction is classified in Major Group 15.

Cabinet work performed at the construction site
Carpentry work—contractors
Folding door installation—contractors
Framing—contractors
Garage door installation—contractors

Joinery, ship—contractors
Ship joinery—contractors
Store fixture installation—contractors
Trim and finish—contractors
Window and door (prefabricated) installation—contractors

1752 Floor Laying and Other Floor Work, Not Elsewhere Classified

Special trade contractors primarily engaged in the installation of asphalt tile, carpeting, linoleum, and resilient flooring. This industry also includes special trade contractors engaged in laying, scraping, and finishing parquet and other hardwood flooring. Establishments primarily engaged in installing stone and ceramic floor tile are classified in Industry Group 174; those installing or finishing concrete floors are classified in Industry 1771; and those installing artificial turf are classified in Industry 1799.

Asphalt tile installation—contractors
Carpet laying or removal service—contractors
Fireproof flooring construction—contractors
Floor laying, scraping, finishing, and refinishing—contractors

Flooring, wood—contractors
Hardwood flooring—contractors
Linoleum installation—contractors
Parquet flooring—contractors
Resilient floor laying—contractors
Vinyl floor tile and sheet installation—contractors

176 ROOFING, SIDING, AND SHEET METAL WORK

1761 Roofing, Siding, and Sheet Metal Work

Special trade contractors primarily engaged in the installation of roofing, siding, and sheet metal work. Sheet metal work performed by plumbing, heating, and air-conditioning contractors in conjunction with the installation of plumbing, heating, and air-conditioning equipment are classified in Industry 1711.

Architectural sheet metal work—contractors
Ceilings, metal: erection and repair—contractors

Coppersmithing, in connection with construction work—contractors
Downspout installation, metal—contractors

Industry Group No.	Industry No.	

176   ROOFING, SIDING, AND SHEET METAL WORK—Con.

1761   Roofing, Siding, and Sheet Metal Work—Con.

Duct work, sheet metal—contractors
Gutter installation, metal—contractors
Roof spraying, painting, or coating—contractors
Roofing work, including repairing—contractors
Sheet metal work: except plumbing, heating, or air-conditioning—contractors

Siding—contractors
Skylight installation—contractors
Tinsmithing, in connection with construction work—contractors

177   CONCRETE WORK

1771   Concrete Work

Special trade contractors primarily engaged in concrete work, including portland cement and asphalt. This industry includes the construction of private driveways and walks of all materials. Concrete work incidental to the construction of foundations and concrete work included in an excavation contract are classified in Industry 1794; and those engaged in construction or paving of streets, highways, and public sidewalks are classified in Industry 1611.

Asphalting of private driveways and private parking areas—contractors
Blacktop work: private driveways and private parking areas—contractors
Concrete finishers—contractors
Concrete work: private driveways, sidewalks, and parking areas—contractors
Culvert construction—contractors
Curb construction—contractors

Foundations, building of: poured concrete—contractors
Grouting work—contractors
Gunite work—contractors
Parking lot construction—contractors
Patio construction, concrete—contractors
Sidewalk construction, except public—contractors
Stucco construction—contractors

178   WATER WELL DRILLING

1781   Water Well Drilling

Special trade contractors primarily engaged in water well drilling. Establishments primarily engaged in drilling oil or gas field water intake wells on a contract or fee basis are classified in Mining, Industry 1381.

Drilling water wells—contractors
Geothermal drilling—contractors
Servicing water wells—contractors

Well drilling, water: except oil or gas field water intake—contractors

179   MISCELLANEOUS SPECIAL TRADE CONTRACTORS

1791   Structural Steel Erection

Special trade contractors primarily engaged in the erection of structural steel and of similar products of prestressed or precast concrete.

Building front installation, metal—contractors
Concrete products, structural precast or prestressed: placing of—contractors
Concrete reinforcement, placing of—contractors
Curtain wall installation—contractors
Elevator front installation, metal—contractors

Iron work, structural—contractors
Metal furring—contractors
Steel work, structural—contractors
Storage tanks, metal: erection—contractors
Store front installation, metal—contractors

1793 Glass and Glazing Work

Special trade contractors primarily engaged in glass and glazing work. Establishments primarily engaged in the installation of automotive glass are classified in Services, Industry 7536.

Glass installation, except automotive—contractors
Glass work, except automotive—contractors

Glazing work—contractors

1794 Excavation Work

Special trade contractors primarily engaged in excavation work and digging foundations, including digging and loading. Contractors in this industry may also perform incidental concrete work. Contractors primarily engaged in concrete work are classified in Industry 1771; and those primarily engaged in trenching or in earth moving and land clearing not related to building construction are classified in Major Group 16.

Excavation work—contractors
Foundation digging (excavation)—contractors

Grading: except for highways, streets, and airport runways—contractors

1795 Wrecking and Demolition Work

Special trade contractors primarily engaged in the wrecking and demolition of buildings and other structures, except marine. They may or may not sell material derived from demolishing operations. Establishments primarily engaged in marine wrecking are classified in Transportation, Industry 4499.

Concrete breaking for streets and highways—contractors
Demolition of buildings or other structures, except marine—contractors

Dismantling steel oil tanks, except oil field work—contractors
Wrecking of buildings or other structures, except marine—contractors

1796 Installation or Erection of Building Equipment, Not Elsewhere Classified

Special trade contractors primarily engaged in the installation or erection of building equipment, not elsewhere classified, such as elevators, pneumatic tube systems, and dust collecting equipment. This industry also includes contractors primarily engaged in the installation or dismantling of machinery or other industrial equipment. Contractors primarily engaged in the construction of industrial incinerator, furnace, and oven structures are classified in Industry 1629.

Conveyor system installation—contractors
Dismantling of machinery and other industrial equipment—contractors
Dumbwaiter installation—contractors
Dust collecting equipment installation—contractors
Elevator installation, conversion, and repair—contractors
Incinerator installation, small—contractors
Installation of machinery and other industrial equipment—contractors

Machine rigging—contractors
Millwrights
Pneumatic tube system installation—contractors
Power generating equipment installation—contractors
Revolving door installation—contractors
Vacuum cleaning systems, built-in—contractors

Industry
Group
No.   Industry
No.

179   MISCELLANEOUS SPECIAL TRADE CONTRACTORS—Con.

1799   Special Trade Contractors, Not Elsewhere Classified

Special trade contractors primarily engaged in construction work, not elsewhere classified, such as construction of swimming pools and fences, erection and installation of ornamental metal work, house moving, shoring work, waterproofing, dampproofing, fireproofing, sandblasting, and steam cleaning of building exteriors.

Antenna installation, except household type—contractors
Artificial turf installation—contractors
Awning installation—contractors
Bath tub refinishing—contractors
Boring for building construction—contractors
Bowling alley installation and service—contractors
Cable splicing service, nonelectrical—contractors
Caulking (construction)—contractors
Cleaning building exteriors—contractors
Cleaning new buildings after construction—contractors
Coating of concrete structures with plastics—contractors
Core drilling for building construction—contractors
Counter top installation—contractors
Dampproofing buildings—contractors
Dewatering—contractors
Diamond drilling for building construction—contractors
Epoxy application—contractors
Erection and dismantling of forms for poured concrete—contractors
Fence construction—contractors
Fire escape installation—contractors
Fireproofing buildings—contractors
Forms for poured concrete, erection and dismantling—contractors
Gas leakage detection—contractors
Gasoline pump installation—contractors
Glazing of concrete surfaces—contractors
Grave excavation—contractors
House moving—contractors
Insulation of pipes and boilers—contractors

Lead burning—contractors
Lightning conductor erection—contractors
Mobile home site setup and tie down—contractors
Ornamental metalwork—contractors
Paint and wallpaper stripping—contractors
Plastics wall tile installation—contractors
Posthole digging—contractors
Sandblasting of building exteriors—contractors
Scaffolding construction—contractors
Service and repair of broadcasting stations—contractors
Service station equipment installation, maintenance, and repair—contractors
Shoring and underpinning work—contractors
Spectator seating installation—contractors
Steam cleaning of building exteriors—contractors
Steeplejacks
Swimming pool construction—contractors
Television and radio stations, service and repair of—contractors
Test boring for construction—contractors
Tile installation, wall: plastics—contractors
Tinting glass—contractors
Wallpaper removal—contractors
Waterproofing—contractors
Weather stripping—contra tors
Welding contractors, operating at site of construction
Window shade installation—contractors

DIVISION D

Manufacturing

The Division as a Whole

The manufacturing division includes establishments engaged in the mechanical or chemical transformation of materials or substances into new products. These establishments are usually described as plants, factories, or mills and characteristically use power driven machines and materials handling equipment. Establishments engaged in assembling component parts of manufactured products are also considered manufacturing if the new product is neither a structure nor other fixed improvement. Also included is the blending of materials, such as lubricating oils, plastics resins, or liquors.

The materials processed by manufacturing establishments include products of agriculture, forestry, fishing, mining, and quarrying as well as products of other manufacturing establishments. The new product of a manufacturing establishment may be finished in the sense that it is ready for utilization or consumption, or it may be semifinished to become a raw material for an establishment engaged in further manufacturing. For example, the product of the copper smelter is the raw material used in electrolytic refineries; refined copper is the raw material used by copper wire mills; and copper wire is the raw material used by certain electrical equipment manufacturers.

The materials used by manufacturing establishments may be purchased directly from producers, obtained through customary trade channels, or secured without recourse to the market by transferring the product from one establishment to another which is under the same ownership. Manufacturing production is usually carried on for the wholesale market, for interplant transfer, or to order for industrial users, rather than for direct sale to the domestic consumer.

There are numerous borderline cases between manufacturing and other divisions of the classification system. Specific instances will be found in the descriptions of the individual industries. The following activities, although not always considered as manufacturing, are so classified:

Milk bottling and pasteurizing;
Fresh fish packaging (oyster shucking, fish filleting);
Apparel jobbing (assigning of materials to contract factories or shops for fabrication or other contract operations) as well as contracting on materials owned by others;

Publishing;
Ready-mixed concrete production;
Leather converting;
Logging;
Wood preserving;
Various service industries to the manufacturing trade, such as typesetting, engraving, plate printing,

67

and preparing electrotyping and stereotype plates, but not blue-printing or photocopying services;

Electroplating, plating, metal heat treating, and polishing for the trade;

Lapidary work for the trade;

Fabricating of signs and advertising displays.

There are also some manufacturing-type activities performed by establishments which are primarily engaged in activities covered by other divisions, and are, thus, not classified as manufacturing. A few of the more important examples are:

Agriculture, Forestry, and Fishing

Processing on farms is not considered manufacturing if the raw materials are grown on the farm and if the manufacturing activities are on a small scale without the extensive use of paid labor. Other exclusions are threshing and cotton ginning.

Mining

The dressing and beneficiating of ores; the breaking, washing, and grading of coal; the crushing and breaking of stone; and the crushing, grinding, or otherwise preparing of sand, gravel, and nonmetallic chemical and fertilizer minerals other than barite are classified in Mining.

Construction

Fabricating operations performed at the site of construction by contractors are not considered manufacturing, but the prefabrication of sheet metal, concrete, and terrazzo products and similar construction materials is included in the Manufacturing Division.

Wholesale and Retail Trade

Establishments engaged in the following types of operations are included in Wholesale or Retail Trade: cutting and selling purchased carcasses; preparing feed at grain elevators and farm supply stores; stemming leaf tobacco at wholesale establishments; and production of wiping rags. The breaking of bulk and redistribution in smaller lots, including packaging, repackaging, or bottling products, such as liquors or chemicals, is also classified as Wholesale or Retail Trade. Also included in Retail Trade are establishments primarily engaged in selling, to the general public, products produced on the same premises from which they are sold, such as bakeries, candy stores, ice cream parlors, and custom tailors.

Services

Tire retreading and rebuilding, sign painting and lettering shops, computer software production, and the production of motion picture films (including video tapes) are classified in Services. Most repair activities are classified as Services. However, some repair activity such as shipbuilding and boatbuilding and repair, the rebuilding of machinery and equipment on a factory basis, and machine shop repair are classified as manufacturing.

ABBREVIATIONS USED FOR INDEX ITEMS

mach.—machinery

mfpm—made from purchased materials or materials transferred from another establishment.

mitse—made in the same establishment as the basic materials.

Major Group 20.—FOOD AND KINDRED PRODUCTS

The Major Group as a Whole

This major group includes establishments manufacturing or processing foods and beverages for human consumption, and certain related products, such as manufactured ice, chewing gum, vegetable and animal fats and oils, and prepared feeds for animals and fowls. Products described as dietetic are classified in the same manner as nondietetic products (e.g., as candy, canned fruits, cookies). Chemical sweeteners are classified in Major Group 28.

Industry
Group Industry
No.   No.

201   MEAT PRODUCTS

2011   Meat Packing Plants

Establishments primarily engaged in the slaughtering, for their own account or on a contract basis for the trade, of cattle, hogs, sheep, lambs, and calves for meat to be sold or to be used on the same premises in canning, cooking, curing, and freezing, and in making sausage, lard, and other products. Also included in this industry are establishments primarily engaged in slaughtering horses for human consumption. Establishments primarily engaged in slaughtering, dressing, and packing poultry, rabbits, and other small game are classified in Industry 2015; and those primarily engaged in slaughtering and processing animals not for human consumption are classified in Industry 2048. Establishments primarily engaged in manufacturing sausages and meat specialties from purchased meats are classified in Industry 2013; and establishments primarily engaged in canning meat for baby food are classified in Industry 2032.

Bacon, slab and sliced—mitse	Lamb—mitse
Beef—mitse	Lard—mitse
Blood meal	Luncheon meat, except poultry—mitse
Boxed beef—mitse	Meat extracts—mitse
Canned meats, except baby foods and animal feeds—mitse	Meat packing plants
Corned beef—mitse	Meat—mitse
Cured meats—mitse	Mutton—mitse
Dried meats—mitse	Pork—mitse
Frankfurters, except poultry—mitse	Sausages—mitse
Hams, except poultry—mitse	Slaughtering plants: except animals not for human consumption
Hides and skins, cured or uncured	Variety meats edible organs—mitse
Horsemeat for human consumption—mitse	Veal—mitse

2013   Sausages and Other Prepared Meat Products

Establishments primarily engaged in manufacturing sausages, cured meats, smoked meats, canned meats, frozen meats, and other prepared meats and meat specialties, from purchased carcasses and other materials. Prepared meat plants operated by packing houses as separate establishments are also included in this industry. Establishments primarily engaged in canning or otherwise processing poultry, rabbits, and other small game are classified in Industry 2015. Establishments primarily engaged in canning meat for baby food are classified in Industry 2032. Establishments primarily engaged in the cutting up and resale of purchased fresh carcasses, for the trade, (including boxed beef) are classified in Wholesale Trade, Industry 5147.

Industry Group No.	Industry No.	
201		**MEAT PRODUCTS—Con.**
	2013	**Sausages and Other Prepared Meat Products—Con.**

Bacon, slab and sliced—mfpm
Beef—mfpm
Bologna—mfpm
Calf's-foot jelly
Canned meats, except baby foods and animal feeds—mfpm
Corned beef—mfpm
Corned meats—mfpm
Cured meats: brined, dried, and salted—mfpm
Dried meats—mfpm
Frankfurters, except poultry—mfpm
Hams, except poultry—mfpm
Headcheese—mfpm
Lard—mfpm
Luncheon meat, except poultry—mfpm
Meat extracts—mfpm

Meat products: cooked, cured, frozen, smoked, and spiced—mfpm
Pastrami—mfpm
Pigs' feet, cooked and pickled—mfpm
Pork: pickled, cured, salted, or smoked—mfpm
Potted meats—mfpm
Puddings, meat—mfpm
Sandwich spreads, meat—mfpm
Sausage casings, collagen
Sausages—mfpm
Scrapple—mfpm
Smoked meats—mfpm
Spreads, sandwich: meat—mfpm
Stew, beef and lamb—mfpm
Tripe—mfpm
Vienna sausage—mfpm

2015 Poultry Slaughtering and Processing

Establishments primarily engaged in slaughtering, dressing, packing, freezing, and canning poultry, rabbits, and other small game, or in manufacturing products from such meats, for their own account or on a contract basis for the trade. This industry also includes the drying, freezing, and breaking of eggs. Establishments primarily engaged in cleaning, oil treating, packing, and grading of eggs are classified in Wholesale Trade, Industry 5144; and those engaged in the cutting up and resale of purchased fresh carcasses are classified in Wholesale and Retail Trade.

Chickens, processed: fresh, frozen, canned, or cooked
Chickens: slaughtering and dressing
Ducks, processed: fresh, frozen, canned, or cooked
Ducks: slaughtering and dressing
Egg albumen
Egg substitutes made from eggs
Eggs: canned, dehydrated, desiccated, frozen, and processed
Eggs: drying, freezing, and breaking
Frankfurters, poultry
Game, small: fresh, frozen, canned, or cooked
Game, small: slaughtering and dressing

Geese, processed: fresh, frozen, canned, or cooked
Geese: slaughtering and dressing
Ham, poultry
Luncheon meat, poultry
Poultry, processed: fresh, frozen, canned, or cooked
Poultry: slaughtering and dressing
Rabbits, processed: fresh, frozen, canned, or cooked
Rabbits, slaughtering and dressing
Turkeys, processed: fresh, frozen, canned, or cooked
Turkeys: slaughtering and dressing

202   DAIRY PRODUCTS

This industry group includes establishments primarily engaged in: (1) manufacturing creamery butter; natural, processed, and imitation cheese; dry, condensed, and evaporated milk; ice cream and frozen dairy desserts; and special dairy products, such as yogurt and malted milk; and (2) processing (pasteurizing, homogenizing, vitaminizing, bottling) fluid milk and cream for wholesale or retail distribution. Independently operated milk receiving stations primarily engaged in the assembly and reshipment of bulk milk for use in manufacturing or processing plants are classified in Industry 5143.

2021 Creamery Butter

Establishments primarily engaged in manufacturing creamery butter.

Anhydrous butterfat
Butter oil
Butter powder

Butter, creamery and whey
Butterfat, anhydrous

Industry
Group   Industry
No.   No.
202   **DAIRY PRODUCTS—Con.**

2022   Natural, Processed, and Imitation Cheese

Establishments primarily engaged in manufacturing natural cheese (except cottage cheese), processed cheese, cheese foods, cheese spreads, and cheese analogs (imitations and substitutes). These establishments also produce byproducts, such as raw liquid whey. Establishments primarily engaged in manufacturing cottage cheese are classified in Industry 2026, and those manufacturing cheese-based salad dressings are classified in Industry 2035.

Cheese analogs	Cheese, imitation or substitutes
Cheese products, imitation or substitutes	Cheese, processed
Cheese spreads, pastes, and cheese-like preparations	Dips, cheese-based
	Processed cheese
Cheese, except cottage cheese	Sandwich spreads, cheese
	Whey, raw: liquid

2023   Dry, Condensed, and Evaporated Dairy Products

Establishments primarily engaged in manufacturing dry, condensed, and evaporated dairy products. Included in this industry are establishments primarily engaged in manufacturing mixes for the preparation of frozen ice cream and ice milk and dairy and nondairy base cream substitutes and dietary supplements.

Baby formula: fresh, processed, and bottled	Lactose, edible
Buttermilk: concentrated, condensed, dried, evaporated, and powdered	Malted milk
	Milk, whole: canned
Casein, dry and wet	Milk: concentrated, condensed, dried, evaporated, and powdered
Cream substitutes	Milkshake mix
Cream: dried, powdered, and canned	Skim milk: concentrated, dried, and powdered
Dietary supplements, dairy and nondairy base	Sugar of milk
Dry milk products: whole milk, nonfat milk, buttermilk, whey, and cream	Whey: concentrated, condensed, dried, evaporated, and powdered
Eggnog, canned: nonalcoholic	Whipped topping, dry mix
Ice cream mix, unfrozen: liquid or dry	Yogurt mix
Ice milk mix, unfrozen: liquid or dry	

2024   Ice Cream and Frozen Desserts

Establishments primarily engaged in manufacturing ice cream and other frozen desserts. Establishments primarily engaged in manufacturing frozen bakery products, such as cakes and pies, are classified in Industry 2053.

Custard, frozen	Mellorine
Desserts, frozen: except bakery	Parfait
Fruit pops, frozen	Pops, dessert: frozen-flavored ice, fruit, pudding and gelatin
Ice cream: e.g., bulk, packaged, molded, on sticks	Pudding pops, frozen
Ice milk: e.g., bulk, packaged, molded, on sticks	Sherbets and ices
	Spumoni
Ices and sherbets	Tofu frozen desserts
Juice pops, frozen	Yogurt, frozen

2026   Fluid Milk

Establishments primarily engaged in processing (e.g., pasteurizing, homogenizing, vitaminizing, bottling) fluid milk and cream, and related products, including cottage cheese, yogurt (except frozen), and other fermented milk. Establishments primarily engaged in manufacturing dry mix whipped toppings are classified in Industry 2023; those producing frozen whipped toppings are

Industry
Group   Industry
No.   No.

202   **DAIRY PRODUCTS—Con.**

2026   **Fluid Milk—Con.**

classified in Industry 2038; and those producing frozen yogurt are classified in Industry 2024.

Buttermilk, cultured	Milk production, except farm
Chocolate milk	Milk, acidophilus
Cottage cheese, including pot, bakers', and farmers' cheese	Milk, bottled
	Milk, flavored
Cream, aerated	Milk, reconstituted
Cream, bottled	Milk, ultra-high temperature
Cream, sour	Sour cream
Dips, sour cream based	Whipped cream
Eggnog, fresh: nonalcoholic	Whipped topping, except frozen or dry mix
Flavored milk drinks	
Half and half	Yogurt, except frozen
Milk processing (pasteurizing, homogenizing, vitaminizing, bottling)	

203   **CANNED, FROZEN, AND PRESERVED FRUITS, VEGETABLES, AND FOOD SPECIALTIES**

The canned products of this industry group are distinguished by their processing rather than by the container. The products may be shipped in bulk or in individual cans, bottles, retort pouch packages, or other containers.

2032   **Canned Specialties**

Establishments primarily engaged in canning specialty products, such as baby foods, nationality speciality foods, and soups, except seafood. Establishments primarily engaged in canning seafoods are classified in Industry 2091.

Baby foods (including meats), canned	Macaroni, canned
Bean sprouts, canned	Mexican foods, canned
Beans, baked: with or without meat—canned	Mincemeat, canned
	Nationality specialty foods, canned
Broth, except seafood: canned	Native foods, canned
Chicken broth and soup, canned	Pasta, canned
Chili con carne, canned	Puddings, except meat: canned
Chinese foods, canned	Ravioli, canned
Chop suey, canned	Soups, except seafood: canned
Chow mein, canned	Spaghetti, canned
Enchiladas, canned	Spanish foods, canned
Food specialties, canned	Tamales, canned
Italian foods, canned	Tortillas, canned

2033   **Canned Fruits, Vegetables, Preserves, Jams, and Jellies**

Establishments primarily engaged in canning fruits, vegetables, and fruit and vegetable juices; and in manufacturing catsup and similar tomato sauces, or natural and imitation preserves, jams, and jellies. Establishments primarily engaged in canning seafoods are classified in Industry 2091; and those manufacturing canned specialties, such as baby foods and soups, except seafood, are classified in Industry 2032.

Artichokes in olive oil, canned	Juices, fresh: fruit or vegetable
Barbecue sauce	Juices, fruit and vegetable: canned or fresh
Catsup	
Cherries, maraschino	Ketchup
Chili sauce, tomato	Marmalade
Fruit butters	Mushrooms, canned
Fruit pie mixes	Nectars, fruit
Fruits, canned	Olives, including stuffed: canned
Hominy, canned	Pastes, fruit and vegetable
Jams, including imitation	Preserves, including imitation
Jellies, edible: including imitation	Purees, fruit and vegetable
Juice, fruit: concentrated-hot pack	Sauces, tomato-based

203   **CANNED, FROZEN, AND PRESERVED FRUITS, VEGETABLES, AND FOOD SPECIALTIES—Con.**

2033   **Canned Fruits, Vegetables, Preserves, Jams, and Jellies—Con.**

Sauerkraut, canned	Tomato paste
Seasonings (prepared sauces), tomato	Tomato sauce
Spaghetti sauce	Vegetable pie mixes
Tomato juice and cocktails, canned	Vegetables, canned

2034   **Dried and Dehydrated Fruits, Vegetables, and Soup Mixes**

Establishments primarily engaged in sun drying or artificially dehydrating fruits and vegetables, or in manufacturing packaged soup mixes from dehydrated ingredients. Establishments primarily engaged in the grading and marketing of farm dried fruits, such as prunes and raisins, are classified in Wholesale Trade, Industry 5149.

Dates, dried	Prunes, dried
Dehydrated fruits, vegetables, and soups	Raisins
	Soup mixes
Fruit flour, meal, and powders	Soup powders
Fruits, sulphured	Vegetable flour, meal, and powders
Olives, dried	Vegetables, sulphured
Potato flakes, granules, and other dehydrated potato products	

2035   **Pickled Fruits and Vegetables, Vegetable Sauces and Seasonings, and Salad Dressings**

Establishments primarily engaged in pickling and brining fruits and vegetables, and in manufacturing salad dressings, vegetable relishes, sauces, and seasonings. Establishments primarily engaged in manufacturing catsup and similar tomato sauces are classified in Industry 2033, and those packing purchased pickles and olives are classified in Wholesale or Retail Trade. Establishments primarily engaged in manufacturing dry salad dressing and dry sauce mixes are classified in Industry 2099.

Blue cheese dressing	Sandwich spreads, salad dressing base
Brining of fruits and vegetables	Sauces, meat (seasoning): except tomato and dry
Cherries, brined	
French dressing	Sauces, seafood: except tomato and dry
Fruits, pickled and brined	Sauerkraut, bulk
Horseradish, prepared	Seasonings (prepared sauces), vegetable: except tomato and dry
Mayonnaise	
Mustard, prepared (wet)	Soy sauce
Olives, brined: bulk	Thousand Island dressing
Onions, pickled	Vegetable sauces, except tomato
Pickles and pickle salting	Vegetables, pickled and brined
Relishes, fruit and vegetable	Vinegar pickles and relishes
Russian dressing	Worcestershire sauce
Salad dressings, except dry mixes	

2037   **Frozen Fruits, Fruit Juices, and Vegetables**

Establishments primarily engaged in freezing fruits, fruit juices, and vegetables. These establishments also produce important byproducts such as fresh or dried citrus pulp.

Concentrates, frozen fruit juice	Fruits, quick frozen and coldpack (frozen)
Dried citrus pulp	
Frozen fruits, fruit juices, and vegetables	Vegetables, quick frozen and coldpack (frozen)
Fruit juices, frozen	

Industry Group No. 203   Industry No.

CANNED, FROZEN, AND PRESERVED FRUITS, VEGETABLES, AND FOOD SPECIALTIES—Con.

2038 Frozen Specialties, Not Elsewhere Classified

Establishments primarily engaged in manufacturing frozen food specialties, not elsewhere classified, such as frozen dinners and frozen pizza. The manufacture of some important frozen foods and specialties is classified elsewhere. For example, establishments primarily engaged in manufacturing frozen dairy specialties are classified in Industry Group 202, those manufacturing frozen bakery products are classified in Industry Group 205, those manufacturing frozen fruits and vegetables are classified in Industry 2037, and those manufacturing frozen fish and seafood specialties are classified in Industry 2092.

Dinners, frozen: packaged
French toast, frozen
Frozen dinners, packaged
Meals, frozen
Native foods, frozen
Pizza, frozen
Soups, frozen: except seafood
Spaghetti and meatballs, frozen
Waffles, frozen
Whipped topping, frozen

204 GRAIN MILL PRODUCTS

2041 Flour and Other Grain Mill Products

Establishments primarily engaged in milling flour or meal from grain, except rice. The products of flour mills may be sold plain or in the form of prepared mixes or doughs for specific purposes. Establishments primarily engaged in manufacturing prepared flour mixes or doughs from purchased ingredients are classified in Industry 2045, and those milling rice are classified in Industry 2044.

Bran and middlings, except rice
Bread and bread-type roll mixes—mitse
Buckwheat flour
Cake flour—mitse
Cereals, cracked grain—mitse
Corn grits and flakes for brewers' use
Dough, biscuit—mitse
Doughs, refrigerated or frozen—mitse
Durum flour
Farina, except breakfast food—mitse
Flour mills, cereals: except rice
Flour mixes—mitse
Flour: blended, prepared, or self-rising—mitse
Flour: buckwheat, corn, graham, rye, and wheat
Frozen doughs—mitse
Graham flour
Granular wheat flour
Grits and flakes, corn: for brewers' use
Hominy grits, except breakfast food
Meal, corn
Milling of grains, dry, except rice
Mixes, flour: e.g., pancake, cake, biscuit, doughnut—mitse
Pancake batter, refrigerated or frozen—mitse
Pizza mixes and prepared dough—mitse
Semolina (flour)
Sorghum grain flour
Wheat germ
Wheat mill feed

2043 Cereal Breakfast Foods

Establishments primarily engaged in manufacturing cereal breakfast foods and related preparations, except breakfast bars. Establishments primarily engaged in manufacturing granola bars and other types of breakfast bars are classified in Industry 2064.

Breakfast foods, cereal
Coffee substitutes made from grain
Corn flakes
Corn, hulled (cereal breakfast food)
Farina, cereal breakfast food
Granola, except bars and clusters
Hominy grits prepared as cereal breakfast food
Infants' foods, cereal type
Oatmeal (cereal breakfast food)
Oats, rolled (cereal breakfast food)
Rice breakfast foods
Wheat flakes

Industry
Group   Industry
No.   No.
204

GRAIN MILL PRODUCTS—Con.

2044 Rice Milling

Establishments primarily engaged in cleaning and polishing rice, and in manufacturing rice flour or meal. Other important products of this industry include brown rice, milled rice (including polished rice), rice polish, and rice bran.

Flour, rice	Rice polish
Milling of rice	Rice, brewers'
Polishing of rice	Rice, brown
Rice bran, flour, and meal	Rice, vitamin and mineral enriched
Rice cleaning and polishing	

2045 Prepared Flour Mixes and Doughs

Establishments primarily engaged in preparing flour mixes or doughs from purchased flour. Establishments primarily engaged in milling flour from grain and producing mixes or doughs are classified in Industry 2041.

Biscuit mixes and doughs—mfpm	Frozen doughs—mfpm
Bread and bread-type roll mixes—mfpm	Gingerbread mixes—mfpm
Cake flour—mfpm	Mixes, flour: e.g., pancake, cake, biscuit, doughnut—mfpm
Cake mixes—mfpm	Pancake batter, refrigerated or frozen—mfpm
Dough, biscuit—mfpm	Pancake mixes—mfpm
Doughnut mixes—mfpm	Pizza mixes and doughs—mfpm
Doughs, refrigerated or frozen—mfpm	
Flour: blended or self-rising—mfpm	

2046 Wet Corn Milling

Establishments primarily engaged in milling corn or sorghum grain (milo) by the wet process, and producing starch, syrup, oil, sugar, and byproducts, such as gluten feed and meal. Also included in this industry are establishments primarily engaged in manufacturing starch from other vegetable sources (e.g., potatoes, wheat). Establishments primarily engaged in manufacturing table syrups from corn syrup and other ingredients, and those manufacturing starch base dessert powders, are classified in Industry 2099.

Corn oil cake and meal	Oil, corn: crude and refined
Corn starch	Potato starch
Corn syrup (including dried), unmixed	Rice starch
Dextrine	Starch, instant
Dextrose	Starch, liquid
Feed, gluten	Starches, edible and industrial
Fructose	Steepwater concentrate
Glucose	Sugar, corn
High fructose syrup	Tapioca
Hydrol	Wheat gluten
Meal, gluten	Wheat starch

2047 Dog and Cat Food

Establishments primarily engaged in manufacturing dog and cat food from cereal, meat, and other ingredients. These preparations may be canned, frozen, or dry. Establishments primarily engaged in manufacturing feed for animals other than dogs and cats are classified in Industry 2048.

Cat food	Dog food

Industry Group No.	Industry No.	
204		GRAIN MILL PRODUCTS—Con.

2048 Prepared Feeds and Feed Ingredients for Animals and Fowls, Except Dogs and Cats

Establishments primarily engaged in manufacturing prepared feeds and feed ingredients and adjuncts for animals and fowls, except dogs and cats. Included in this industry are poultry and livestock feed and feed ingredients, such as alfalfa meal, feed supplements, and feed concentrates and feed premixes. Also included are establishments primarily engaged in slaughtering animals for animal feed. Establishments primarily engaged in slaughtering animals for human consumption are classified in Industry Group 201. Establishments primarily engaged in manufacturing dog and cat foods are classified in Industry 2047.

Alfalfa, cubed
Alfalfa, prepared as feed for animals
Animal feeds, prepared: except dog and cat
Bird food, prepared
Buttermilk emulsion for animal food
Chicken feeds, prepared
Citrus seed meal
Earthworm food and bedding
Feed concentrates
Feed premixes
Feed supplements
Feeds, prepared (including mineral): for animals and fowls—except dogs and cats
Feeds, specialty: mice, guinea pigs, minks, etc.
Fish food
Hay, cubed
Horsemeat, except for human consumption

Kelp meal and pellets
Livestock feeds, supplements, and concentrates
Meal, bone: prepared as feed for animals and fowls
Mineral feed supplements
Oats: crimped, pulverized, and rolled: except breakfast food
Oyster shells, ground: used as feed for animals and fowls
Pet food, except dog and cat: canned, frozen, and dry
Poultry feeds, supplements, and concentrates
Shell crushing for feed
Slaughtering of animals, except for human consumption
Stock feeds, dry

| 205 | | BAKERY PRODUCTS |

2051 Bread and Other Bakery Products, Except Cookies and Crackers

Establishments primarily engaged in manufacturing fresh or frozen bread and bread-type rolls and fresh cakes, pies, pastries and other similar "perishable" bakery products. Establishments primarily engaged in producing "dry" bakery products, such as biscuits, crackers, and cookies, are classified in Industry 2052. Establishments primarily engaged in manufacturing frozen bakery products, except bread and bread-type rolls, are classified in Industry 2053. Establishments producing bakery products primarily for direct sale on the premises to household consumers are classified in Retail Trade, Industry 5461.

Bagels
Bakery products, fresh: bread, cakes, doughnuts, and pastries
Bakery products, partially cooked: except frozen
Biscuits, baked: baking powder and raised
Bread, brown: Boston and other—canned
Bread, including frozen
Buns, bread-type (e.g., hamburger, hot dog), including frozen
Buns, sweet, except frozen
Cakes, bakery, except frozen

Charlotte Russe (bakery product), except frozen
Croissants, except frozen
Crullers, except frozen
Doughnuts, except frozen
Frozen bread and bread-type rolls
Knishes, except frozen
Pastries, except frozen: e.g., Danish, French
Pies, bakery, except frozen
Rolls, bread-type, including frozen
Rolls, sweet, except frozen
Sponge goods, bakery, except frozen
Sweet yeast goods, except frozen

Industry Group No.	Industry No.	
205		**BAKERY PRODUCTS—Con.**
	2052	**Cookies and Crackers**

Establishments primarily engaged in manufacturing fresh cookies, crackers, pretzels, and similar "dry" bakery products. Establishments primarily engaged in producing other fresh bakery products are classified in Industry 2051.

Bakery products, dry: e.g., biscuits, crackers, pretzels	Cracker meal and crumbs
Biscuits, baked: dry, except baking powder and raised	Crackers: e.g., graham, soda
Communion wafers	Matzoths
Cones, ice cream	Pretzels
Cookies	Rusk
	Saltines
	Zwieback

2053 Frozen Bakery Products, Except Bread

Establishments primarily engaged in manufacturing frozen bakery products, except bread and bread-type rolls. Establishments primarily engaged in manufacturing frozen bread and bread-type rolls are classified in Industry 2051.

Bakery products, frozen: except bread and bread-type rolls	Doughnuts, frozen
Cakes, frozen: pound, layer, and cheese	Pies, bakery, frozen
Croissants, frozen	Sweet yeast goods, frozen

206 **SUGAR AND CONFECTIONERY PRODUCTS**

2061 Cane Sugar, Except Refining

Establishments primarily engaged in manufacturing raw sugar, syrup, or finished (granulated or clarified) cane sugar from sugarcane. Establishments primarily engaged in refining sugar from purchased raw cane sugar or sugar syrup are classified in Industry 2062.

Cane sugar, made from sugarcane	Sugar, invert: made from sugarcane
Molasses, blackstrap: made from sugarcane	Sugar, powdered: made from sugarcane
Molasses, made from sugarcane	Sugar, raw: made from sugarcane
Sugar, granulated: made from sugarcane	Syrup, cane: made from sugarcane

2062 Cane Sugar Refining

Establishments primarily engaged in refining purchased raw cane sugar and sugar syrup.

Molasses, blackstrap: made from purchased raw cane sugar or sugar syrup	Sugar, powdered: made from purchased raw cane sugar or sugar syrup
Refineries, cane sugar	Sugar, refined: made from purchased raw cane sugar or sugar syrup
Sugar, granulated: made from purchased raw cane sugar or sugar syrup	Syrup, made from purchased raw cane sugar or sugar syrup
Sugar, invert: made from purchased raw cane sugar or sugar syrup	

2063 Beet Sugar

Establishments primarily engaged in manufacturing sugar from sugar beets.

Beet pulp, dried	Sugar, invert: made from sugar beets
Beet sugar, made from sugar beets	Sugar, liquid: made from sugar beets
Molasses beet pulp	Sugar, powdered: made from sugar beets
Molasses, made from sugar beets	Syrup, made from sugar beets
Sugar, granulated: made from sugar beets	

Industry Group No.	Industry No.	
206		SUGAR AND CONFECTIONERY PRODUCTS—Con.

2064 Candy and Other Confectionery Products

Establishments primarily engaged in manufacturing candy, including chocolate candy, other confections, and related products. Establishments primarily engaged in manufacturing solid chocolate bars from cacao beans are classified in Industry 2066, those manufacturing chewing gum are classified in Industry 2067, and those primarily engaged in roasting and salting nuts are classified in Industry 2068. Establishments primarily engaged in manufacturing confectionery for direct sale on the premises to household consumers are classified in Retail Trade, Industry 5441.

Bars, candy: including chocolate covered bars
Breakfast bars
Cake ornaments, confectionery
Candy, except solid chocolate
Chewing candy, except chewing gum
Chocolate bars, from purchased cocoa or chocolate
Chocolate candy, except solid chocolate
Confectionery
Cough drops, except pharmaceutical preparations
Dates: chocolate covered, sugared, and stuffed
Fruit peel products: candied, glazed, glace, and crystallized
Fruits: candied, glazed, and crystallized
Fudge (candy)
Granola bars and clusters
Halvah (candy)
Licorice candy
Lozenges, candy: nonmedicated
Marshmallows
Marzipan (candy)
Nuts, candy covered
Nuts, glace
Popcorn balls and candy covered popcorn products

2066 Chocolate and Cocoa Products

Establishments primarily engaged in shelling, roasting, and grinding cacao beans for the purpose of making chocolate liquor, from which cocoa powder and cocoa butter are derived, and in the further manufacture of solid chocolate bars, chocolate coatings, and other chocolate and cocoa products. Also included is the manufacture of similar products, except candy, from purchased chocolate or cocoa. Establishments primarily engaged in manufacturing candy from purchased cocoa products are classified in Industry 2064.

Baking chocolate
Bars, candy: solid chocolate
Cacao bean products: chocolate, cocoa butter, and cocoa
Cacao beans: shelling, roasting, and grinding for making chocolate liquor
Candy, solid chocolate
Chocolate bars, solid: from cacao beans
Chocolate coatings and syrups
Chocolate liquor
Chocolate syrup
Chocolate, instant
Chocolate, sweetened or unsweetened
Cocoa butter
Cocoa mix, instant
Cocoa, powdered: mixed with other substances

2067 Chewing Gum

Establishments primarily engaged in manufacturing chewing gum or chewing gum base.

Chewing gum
Chewing gum base

2068 Salted and Roasted Nuts and Seeds

Establishments primarily engaged in manufacturing salted, roasted, dried, cooked, or canned nuts or in processing grains or seeds in a similar manner for snack purposes. Establishments primarily engaged in manufacturing confectionery-coated nuts are classified in Industry 2064, and those manufacturing peanut butter are classified in Industry 2099.

Nuts, dehydrated or dried
Nuts: salted, roasted, cooked, or canned
Seeds: salted, roasted, cooked, or canned

Industry Group No.	Industry No.	
207		FATS AND OILS

2074 Cottonseed Oil Mills

Establishments primarily engaged in manufacturing cottonseed oil, cake, meal, and linters, or in processing purchased cottonseed oil other than into edible cooking oils. Establishments primarily engaged in refining cottonseed oil into edible cooking oils are classified in Industry 2079.

Cottonseed oil, cake, and meal: made in cottonseed oil mills	Cottonseed oil, deodorized Lecithin, cottonseed

2075 Soybean Oil Mills

Establishments primarily engaged in manufacturing soybean oil, cake, and meal, and soybean protein isolates and concentrates, or in processing purchased soybean oil other than into edible cooking oils. Establishments primarily engaged in refining soybean oil into edible cooking oils are classified in Industry 2079.

Lecithin, soybean Soybean flour and grits Soybean oil, cake, and meal	Soybean oil, deodorized Soybean protein concentrates Soybean protein isolates

2076 Vegetable Oil Mills, Except Corn, Cottonseed, and Soybean

Establishments primarily engaged in manufacturing vegetable oils, cake and meal, except corn, cottonseed, and soybean, or in processing similar purchased oils other than into edible cooking oils. Establishments primarily engaged in manufacturing corn oil and its byproducts are classified in Industry 2046, those which are refining vegetable oils into edible cooking oils are classified in Industry 2079, and those refining these oils for medicinal purposes are classified in Industry 2833.

Castor oil and pomace Coconut oil Linseed oil, cake, and meal Oils, vegetable: except corn, cottonseed, and soybean Oiticica oil Palm kernel oil	Peanut oil, cake, and meal Safflower oil Sunflower seed oil Tallow, vegetable Tung oil Walnut oil

2077 Animal and Marine Fats and Oils

Establishments primarily engaged in manufacturing animal oils, including fish oil and other marine animal oils, and fish and animal meal; and those rendering inedible stearin, grease, and tallow from animal fat, bones, and meat scraps. Establishments primarily engaged in manufacturing lard and edible tallow and stearin are classified in Industry Group 201; those refining marine animal oils for medicinal purposes are classified in Industry 2833; and those manufacturing fatty acids are classified in Industry 2899.

Feather meal Fish liver oils, crude Fish meal Fish oil and fish oil meal Grease rendering, inedible Meal, meat and bone: not prepared as feed Meat and bone meal and tankage	Oils, animal Oils, fish and marine animal: e.g., herring, menhaden, whale (refined), sardine Rendering plants, inedible grease and tallow Stearin, animal: inedible Tallow rendering, inedible

Industry
Group
No.

Industry
No.

207   FATS AND OILS—Con.

2079 Shortening, Table Oils, Margarine, and Other Edible Fats and Oils, Not Elsewhere Classified

Establishments primarily engaged in manufacturing shortening, table oils, margarine, and other edible fats and oils, not elsewhere classified. Establishments primarily engaged in producing corn oil are classified in Industry 2046.

Baking and frying fats (shortening)	Oil, vegetable winter stearin
Cottonseed cooking and salad oil	Olive oil
Margarine oil, except corn	Peanut cooking and salad oil
Margarine, including imitation	Shortenings, compound and vegetable
Margarine-butter blend	Soybean cooking and salad oil
Nut margarine	Vegetable cooking and salad oils,
Oil, hydrogenated: edible	except corn oil: refined
Oil, partially hydrogenated: edible	

208   BEVERAGES

2082 Malt Beverages

Establishments primarily engaged in manufacturing malt beverages. Establishments primarily engaged in bottling purchased malt beverages are classified in Industry 5181.

Ale	Malt extract, liquors, and syrups
Beer (alcoholic beverage)	Near beer
Breweries	Porter (alcoholic beverage)
Brewers' grain	Stout (alcoholic beverage)
Liquors, malt	

2083 Malt

Establishments primarily engaged in manufacturing malt or malt byproducts from barley or other grains.

Malt byproducts	Malthouses
Malt: barley, rye, wheat, and corn	Sprouts, made in malthouses

2084 Wines, Brandy, and Brandy Spirits

Establishments primarily engaged in manufacturing wines, brandy, and brandy spirits. This industry also includes bonded wine cellars which are engaged in blending wines. Establishments primarily bottling purchased wines, brandy, and brandy spirits, but which do not manufacture wines and brandy, are classified in Wholesale Trade, Industry 5182.

Brandy	Wine coolers (beverages)
Brandy spirits	Wines
Wine cellars, bonded: engaged in blend-	
ing wines	

2085 Distilled and Blended Liquors

Establishments primarily engaged in manufacturing alcoholic liquors by distillation, and in manufacturing cordials and alcoholic cocktails by blending processes or by mixing liquors and other ingredients. Establishments primarily engaged in manufacturing industrial alcohol are classified in Industry 2869, and those only bottling purchased liquors are classified in Wholesale Trade, Industry 5182.

Applejack	Ethyl alcohol for medicinal and bever-
Cocktails, alcoholic	age purposes
Cordials, alcoholic	Gin (alcoholic beverage)
Distillers' dried grains and solubles	Grain alcohol for medicinal and bever-
Eggnog, alcoholic	age purposes

Industry Group No.	Industry No.	
208		**BEVERAGES—Con.**

2085 Distilled and Blended Liquors—Con.

Liquors: distilled and blended—except brandy
Rum
Spirits, neutral, except fruit—for beverage purposes
Vodka
Whiskey: bourbon, rye, scotch type, and corn

2086 Bottled and Canned Soft Drinks and Carbonated Waters

Establishments primarily engaged in manufacturing soft drinks and carbonated waters. Establishments primarily engaged in manufacturing fruit and vegetable juices are classified in Industry Group 203; those manufacturing fruit syrups for flavoring are classified in Industry 2087; and those manufacturing nonalcoholic cider are classified in Industry 2099. Establishments primarily engaged in bottling natural spring waters are classified in Wholesale Trade, Industry 5149.

Beer, birch and root: bottled or canned
Carbonated beverages, nonalcoholic: bottled or canned
Drinks, fruit: bottled, canned, or fresh
Ginger ale, bottled or canned
Iced tea, bottled or canned
Lemonade: bottled, canned, or fresh
Mineral water, carbonated: bottled or canned
Soft drinks, bottled or canned
Tea, iced: bottled or canned
Water, pasteurized: bottled or canned

2087 Flavoring Extracts and Flavoring Syrups, Not Elsewhere Classified

Establishments primarily engaged in manufacturing flavoring extracts, syrups, powders, and related products, not elsewhere classified, for soda fountain use or for the manufacture of soft drinks, and colors for bakers' and confectioners' use. Establishments primarily engaged in manufacturing chocolate syrup are classified in Industry 2066.

Beverage bases
Bitters (flavoring concentrates)
Burnt sugar (food color)
Cocktail mixes, nonalcoholic
Coffee flavorings and syrups
Colors for bakers' and confectioners' use, except synthetic
Cordials, nonalcoholic
Drink powders and concentrates
Flavoring concentrates
Flavoring extracts, pastes, powders, and syrups
Food colorings, except synthetic
Food glace, for glazing foods
Fruit juices, concentrated: for fountain use
Fruits, crushed: for soda fountain use

| 209 | | **MISCELLANEOUS FOOD PREPARATIONS AND KINDRED PRODUCTS** |

2091 Canned and Cured Fish and Seafoods

Establishments primarily engaged in cooking and canning fish, shrimp, oysters, clams, crabs, and other seafoods, including soups; and those engaged in smoking, salting, drying, or otherwise curing fish and other seafoods for the trade. Establishments primarily engaged in shucking and packing fresh oysters in nonsealed containers, or in freezing or preparing fresh fish, are classified in Industry 2092.

Canned fish, crustacea, and mollusks
Caviar, canned
Chowders, fish and seafood: canned
Clam bouillon, broth, chowder, juice: bottled or canned
Codfish: smoked, salted, dried, and pickled
Crab meat, canned and cured
Finnan haddie (smoked haddock)
Fish and seafood cakes: canned
Fish egg bait, canned
Fish, canned and cured
Fish: cured, dried, pickled, salted, and smoked
Herring: smoked, salted, dried, and pickled
Mackerel: smoked, salted, dried, and pickled
Oysters, canned and cured
Salmon: smoked, salted, dried, canned, and pickled
Sardines, canned

Industry Group No.	Industry No.	
209		**MISCELLANEOUS FOOD PREPARATIONS AND KINDRED PRODUCTS—Con.**

2091 Canned and Cured Fish and Seafoods—Con.

Seafood products, canned and cured
Shellfish, canned and cured
Shrimp, canned and cured

Soups, fish and seafood: canned
Stews, fish and seafood: canned
Tuna fish, canned

2092 Prepared Fresh or Frozen Fish and Seafoods

Establishments primarily engaged in preparing fresh and raw or cooked frozen fish and other seafoods and seafood preparations, such as soups, stews, chowders, fishcakes, crabcakes, and shrimpcakes. Prepared fresh fish are eviscerated or processed by removal of heads, fins, or scales. This industry also includes establishments primarily engaged in the shucking and packing of fresh oysters in nonsealed containers.

Chowders, fish and seafood: frozen
Crabcakes, frozen
Crabmeat picking
Crabmeat, fresh: packed in nonsealed containers
Fish and seafood cakes, frozen
Fish fillets
Fish sticks
Fish: fresh and frozen, prepared

Oysters, fresh: shucking and packing in nonsealed containers
Seafoods, fresh and frozen
Shellfish, fresh and frozen
Shellfish, fresh: shucked, picked, or packed
Shrimp, fresh and frozen
Soups, fish and seafood: frozen
Stews, fish and seafood: frozen

2095 Roasted Coffee

Establishments primarily engaged in roasting coffee, and in manufacturing coffee concentrates and extracts in powdered, liquid, or frozen form, including freeze-dried. Coffee roasting by wholesale grocers is classified in Wholesale Trade, Industry 5149.

Coffee extracts
Coffee roasting, except by wholesale grocers

Coffee, ground: mixed with grain or chicory
Coffee, instant and freeze-dried

2096 Potato Chips, Corn Chips, and Similar Snacks

Establishments primarily engaged in manufacturing potato chips, corn chips, and similar snacks. Establishments primarily engaged in manufacturing pretzels and crackers are classified in Industry 2052; those manufacturing candy covered popcorn are classified in Industry 2064; those manufacturing salted, roasted, cooked or canned nuts and seeds are classified in Industry 2068; and those manufacturing packaged unpopped popcorn are classified in Industry 2099.

Cheese curls and puffs
Corn chips and related corn snacks
Popcorn, popped: except candy covered

Pork rinds
Potato chips and related corn snacks
Potato sticks

2097 Manufactured Ice

Establishments primarily engaged in manufacturing ice for sale. Establishments primarily engaged in manufacturing dry ice are classified in Industry 2813.

Block ice
Ice cubes
Ice plants, operated by public utilities

Ice, manufactured or artificial: except dry ice

209 MISCELLANEOUS FOOD PREPARATIONS AND KINDRED PRODUCTS— Con.

2098 Macaroni, Spaghetti, Vermicelli, and Noodles

Establishments primarily engaged in manufacturing dry macaroni, spaghetti, vermicelli, and noodles. Establishments primarily engaged in manufacturing canned macaroni and spaghetti are classified in Industry 2032, and those manufacturing fried noodles, such as Chinese noodles, are classified in Industry 2099.

Macaroni and products, dry: e.g., alphabets, rings, seashells
Noodles: egg, plain, and water

Spaghetti, dry
Vermicelli

2099 Food Preparations, Not Elsewhere Classified

Establishments primarily engaged in manufacturing prepared foods and miscellaneous food specialties, not elsewhere classified, such as baking powder, yeast, and other leavening compounds; peanut butter; packaged tea, including instant; ground spices; and vinegar and cider. Also included in this industry are establishments primarily engaged in manufacturing dry preparations, except flour mixes, consisting of pasta, rice, potatoes, textured vegetable protein, and similar products which are packaged with other ingredients to be prepared and cooked by the consumer. Establishments primarily engaged in manufacturing flour mixes are classified in Industry Group 204.

Almond pastes
Baking powder
Bouillon cubes
Box lunches for sale off premises
Bread crumbs, not made in bakeries
Butter, renovated and processed
Cake frosting mixes, dry
Chicory root, dried
Chili pepper or powder
Chinese noodles
Cider, nonalcoholic
Coconut, desiccated and shredded
Cole slaw in bulk
Cracker sandwiches made from purchased crackers
Desserts, ready-to-mix
Dips, except cheese and sour cream based
Emulsifiers, food
Fillings, cake or pie: except fruits, vegetables, and meat
Frosting, prepared
Gelatin dessert preparations
Gravy mixes, dry
Honey, strained and bottled
Jelly, corncob (gelatin)
Leavening compounds, prepared
Marshmallow creme
Meat seasonings, except sauces
Molasses, mixed or blended—mfpm
Noodles, fried (e.g., Chinese)
Noodles, uncooked: packaged with other ingredients

Pancake syrup, blended and mixed
Pasta, uncooked: packaged with other ingredients
Peanut butter
Pectin
Pepper
Pizza, refrigerated: not frozen
Popcorn, packaged: except popped
Potatoes, dried: packaged with other ingredients
Potatoes, peeled for the trade
Rice, uncooked: packaged with other ingredients
Salad dressing mixes, dry
Salads, fresh or refrigerated
Sandwiches, assembled and packaged: for wholesale market
Sauce mixes, dry
Sorghum, including custom refining
Spices, including grinding
Sugar grinding
Sugar, industrial maple: made in plants producing maple syrup
Sugar, powdered—mfpm
Syrups, sweetening: honey, maple syrup, sorghum
Tea blending
Tofu, except frozen desserts
Tortillas, fresh or refrigerated
Vegetables peeled for the trade
Vinegar
Yeast

Major Group 21.—TOBACCO PRODUCTS

The Major Group as a Whole

This major group includes establishments engaged in manufacturing cigarettes, cigars, smoking and chewing tobacco, snuff, and reconstituted tobacco and in stemming and redrying tobacco. Also included in this major group is the manufacture of nontobacco cigarettes. The manufacture of insecticides from tobacco byproducts is included in Major Group 28.

Industry Group No.	Industry No.	

211   CIGARETTES

    2111 Cigarettes

        Establishments primarily engaged in manufacturing cigarettes from tobacco or other materials.

           Cigarettes

212   CIGARS

    2121 Cigars

        Establishments primarily engaged in manufacturing cigars.

Cigarillos	Stogies
Cigars	

213   CHEWING AND SMOKING TOBACCO AND SNUFF

    2131 Chewing and Smoking Tobacco and Snuff

        Establishments primarily engaged in manufacturing chewing and smoking tobacco and snuff.

Snuff	Tobacco: chewing, smoking, and snuff

214   TOBACCO STEMMING AND REDRYING

    2141 Tobacco Stemming and Redrying

        Establishments primarily engaged in the stemming and redrying of tobacco or in manufacturing reconstituted tobacco. Establishments which sell leaf tobacco as merchant wholesalers, agents, or brokers, and which also may be engaged in stemming tobacco, are classified in Wholesale Trade, Industry 5159. Leaf tobacco warehouses which also may be engaged in stemming tobacco are classified in Transportation and Public Utilities, Industry 4221.

Tobacco thrashing (mechanical stemming)	Tobacco, stemming and redrying of

Major Group 22.—TEXTILE MILL PRODUCTS

The Major Group as a Whole

This major group includes establishments engaged in performing any of the following operations: (1) preparation of fiber and subsequent manufacturing of yarn, thread, braids, twine, and cordage; (2) manufacturing broadwoven fabrics, narrow woven fabrics, knit fabrics, and carpets and rugs from yarn; (3) dyeing and finishing fiber, yarn, fabrics, and knit apparel; (4) coating, waterproofing, or otherwise treating fabrics; (5) the integrated manufacture of knit apparel and other finished articles from yarn; and (6) the manufacture of felt goods, lace goods, nonwoven fabrics, and miscellaneous textiles.

This classification makes no distinction between the two types of organizations which operate in the textile industry: (1) the integrated mill which purchases materials, produces textiles and related articles within the establishment, and sells the finished products; and (2) the contract or commission mill which processes materials owned by others. Converters or other nonmanufacturing establishments which assign materials to contract mills for processing, other than knitting, are classified in nonmanufacturing industries; establishments which assign yarns to outside contractors or commission knitters for the production of knit products are classified in Industry Group 225.

Industry Group No.	Industry No.	

221 **BROADWOVEN FABRIC MILLS, COTTON**

2211 **Broadwoven Fabric Mills, Cotton**

Establishments primarily engaged in weaving fabrics more than 12 inches (30.48 centimeters) in width, wholly or chiefly by weight of cotton. Establishments primarily engaged in weaving or tufting carpet and rugs are classified in Industry 2273; those making tire cord and fabrics are classified in Industry 2296; and those engaged in finishing cotton broadwoven fabrics are classified in Industry 2261.

Airplane cloth, cotton
Alpacas, cotton
Automotive fabrics, cotton
Awning stripes, cotton—mitse
Balloon cloth, cotton
Bandage cloths, cotton
Bark cloth, cotton
Basket weave fabrics, cotton
Bathmats, cotton: made in weaving mills
Batiste, cotton
Bedspreads, cotton: made in weaving mills
Bird's-eye diaper cloth, cotton
Blankets and blanketings, cotton—mitse
Bombazine, cotton
Book cloth—mitse
Broadcloth, cotton
Brocade, cotton
Brocatelle, cotton
Buckram—mitse
Bunting—mitse
Butter cloths
Cambric, cotton
Camouflage nets—mitse
Canton flannels, cotton
Canvas—mitse

Casement cloth, cotton
Chambrays
Cheesecloth
Chenilles, tufted textile—mitse
Cheviots, cotton
Chintz, cotton
Corduroys, cotton
Cotton broadwoven goods
Cottonades
Coutil, cotton
Coverts, cotton
Crash toweling, cotton
Crepes, cotton
Cretonne, cotton
Crinoline
Damasks, cotton
Denims
Diaper fabrics
Dimities
Dishcloths, woven: made in weaving mills
Draperies and drapery fabrics, cotton—mitse
Dress fabrics, cotton
Drills, cotton
Duck, cotton
Duvetyn, cotton
Elastic fabrics, cotton: more than 12

221   BROADWOVEN FABRIC MILLS, COTTON—Con.

2211   Broadwoven Fabric Mills, Cotton—Con.

inches in width
Express stripes, cotton
Filter cloth, cotton
Flannelette
Flannels, cotton
Furniture denim
Gabardine, cotton
Galatea, cotton
Gauze—mitse
Ginghams
Glass toweling, cotton
Glove fabrics, cotton—mitse
Grosgrain, cotton
Handkerchief fabrics, cotton
Hickory stripes, cotton
Huck toweling
Interlining material, cotton
Jacquard woven fabrics, cotton
Jean fabrics, cotton
Laundry fabrics, cotton
Laundry nets—mitse
Lawns, cotton
Leno fabrics, cotton
Long cloth, cotton
Luggage fabrics, cotton
Marquisettes, cotton
Matelasse, cotton
Mitten flannel, cotton
Moleskins—mitse
Momie crepe, cotton
Mosquito netting—mitse
Muslin, cotton
Nainsook, cotton
Nets and nettings—mitse
Opaline, cotton
Organdy, cotton
Osnaburgs
Outing flannel, cotton
Oxfords (cotton fabrics)
Pajama checks, textile
Percale
Percaline, cotton
Pile fabrics, cotton
Pillow tubing—mitse
Pillowcases—mitse
Pin checks, cotton
Pin stripes, cotton
Piques, cotton
Plaids, cotton
Plisse crepe, cotton
Plushes, cotton

Pocketing twill, cotton
Pongee, cotton
Poplin, cotton
Press cloth
Print cloths, cotton
Ratine, cotton
Rep, cotton
Sailcloth—mitse
Sateens, cotton
Scrim, cotton
Scrub cloths—mitse
Seat cover cloth, automobile: cotton
Seersuckers, cotton
Sheets and sheetings, cotton—mitse
Shirting fabrics, cotton
Shoe fabrics—mitse
Silesia, cotton
Slipcover fabrics, cotton
Stretch fabrics, cotton
Suiting fabrics, cotton
Surgical fabrics, cotton
Table cover fabrics, cotton
Table damask, cotton
Tapestry fabrics, cotton
Tarlatan, cotton
Tentage—mitse
Terry woven fabrics, cotton
Tickings—mitse
Tobacco cloths—mitse
Towels and toweling, cotton: made in
   weaving mills
Tracing cloth, cotton
Trouserings, cotton
Tubing, seamless: cotton
Twills, cotton
Typewriter ribbon cloth, cotton
Umbrella cloth, cotton
Underwear fabrics, woven: cotton
Upholstery fabrics, cotton
Velours
Velveteens
Voiles, cotton
Waffle cloth, cotton
Washcloths, woven: made in weaving
   mills
Weaving mills, cotton broadwoven fab-
   rics
Wignan, cotton
Window shade cloth, cotton
Yarn-dyed fabrics, cotton

222   BROADWOVEN FABRIC MILLS, MANMADE FIBER AND SILK

2221   Broadwoven Fabric Mills, Manmade Fiber and Silk

Establishments primarily engaged in weaving fabrics more than 12 inches
(30.48 centimeters) in width, wholly or chiefly by weight of silk and manmade
fibers including glass. Establishments primarily engaged in weaving or tufting
carpets and rugs from these fibers are classified in Industry 2273; those manufacturing tire cord and fabrics are classified in Industry 2296; and those engaged in finishing manmade fiber and silk broadwoven goods are classified in
Industry 2262.

Acetate broadwoven fabrics
Acrylic broadwoven fabrics
Automotive fabrics, manmade fiber
Bedspreads, silk and manmade fiber—
   mitse

Blanketings, manmade fiber
Canton crepes
Comforters, manmade fiber—mitse
Crepe satins
Draperies and drapery fabrics, man-

222   **BROADWOVEN FABRIC MILLS, MANMADE FIBER AND SILK—Con.**

2221   Broadwoven Fabric Mills, Manmade Fiber and Silk—Con.

made fiber and silk—mitse
Dress fabrics, manmade fiber and silk
Duvetyn, manmade fiber and silk
Elastic fabrics, manmade fiber and silk:
  more than 12 inches in width
Failles
Fiberglass fabrics
Flat crepes
French crepes
Fur-type fabrics, manmade fiber
Georgettes
Glass broadwoven fabrics
Jacquard woven fabrics, manmade fiber
  and silk
Leno fabrics, manmade fiber and silk
Lining fabrics, manmade fiber and silk:
  except glove lining fabrics
Linings, rayon or silk—mitse
Marquisettes, manmade fiber
Modacrylic broadwoven fabrics
Necktie fabrics, manmade fiber and
  silk: broadwoven
Nylon broadwoven fabrics
Nytril broadwoven fabrics
Paper broadwoven fabrics
Parachute fabrics
Pile fabrics, manmade fiber and silk
Plushes, manmade fiber and silk
Polyester broadwoven fabrics
Polyethylene broadwoven fabrics
Polypropylene broadwoven fabrics
Pongee, manmade fiber and silk

Poplin, manmade fiber
Quilts, manmade fiber and silk—mitse
Rayon broadwoven fabrics
Saran broadwoven fabrics
Satins
Serges, manmade fiber
Shantungs, manmade fiber and silk
Shirting fabrics, manmade fiber and
  silk
Silk broadwoven fabrics
Slipcover fabrics, manmade fiber and
  silk
Spandex broadwoven fabrics
Suiting fabrics, manmade fiber and silk
Taffetas
Tapestry fabrics, manmade fiber and
  silk
Textile mills, broadwoven: silk, and
  manmade fiber including glass
Textile warping, on a contract basis
Twills, manmade fiber
Typewriter ribbon cloth, manmade
  fiber
Underwear fabrics, except knit: man-
  made fiber and silk
Upholstery fabrics, manmade fiber and
  silk
Velvets, manmade fiber and silk
Vinal broadwoven fabrics
Vinyon broadwoven fabrics
Voiles, manmade fiber and silk

223   **BROADWOVEN FABRIC MILLS, WOOL (INCLUDING DYEING AND
                   FINISHING)**

2231   Broadwoven Fabric Mills, Wool (Including Dyeing and Finishing)

Establishments primarily engaged in weaving fabrics more than 12 inches
(30.48 centimeters) in width, wholly or chiefly by weight of wool, mohair, or
similar animal fibers; dyeing and finishing all woven wool fabrics or dyeing
wool, tops, or yarn; and those shrinking and sponging wool goods for the trade.
Establishments primarily engaged in weaving or tufting wool carpets and rugs
are classified in Industry 2273.

Alpacas, mohair: woven
Billiard cloths—mitse
Blankets and blanketings, wool and
  similar animal fibers—mitse
Bleaching yarn and fabrics, wool and
  similar animal fibers: except knit
Burling and mending wool cloth for the
  trade
Calendering of wool, mohair, and simi-
  lar animal fiber fabrics: except knit
Cloth, wool: mending for the trade
Dyeing and finishing of wool and simi-
  lar animal fibers: except knit
Fabric finishing of wool, mohair, and
  similar animal fibers: except knit
Fabrics, animal fiber: broadwoven wool,
  mohair, and similar animal fibers
Fabrics, broadwoven: wool, mohair, and
  similar animal fibers
Felts: wool, mohair, and similar animal
  fibers: woven
Finishing of wool, mohair, and similar
  animal fiber fabrics: except knit

Flannels: wool, mohair, and similar
  animal fibers
Haircloth: wool, mohair, and similar
  animal fibers
Mill menders, contract: wool, mohair,
  and similar animal fibers
Napping of wool, mohair, and similar
  animal fiber fabrics
Narrow fabrics, dyeing and finishing:
  wool, mohair, and similar animal
  fibers
Overcoatings: wool, mohair, and similar
  animal fibers
Pantings: wool, mohair, and similar
  animal fibers
Papermakers' felts, woven: wool,
  mohair, and similar animal fibers
Raw stock dyeing and finishing: wool,
  mohair, and similar animal fibers
Refinishing and sponging cloths: wool,
  mohair, and similar animal fibers,
  for the trade
Serges of wool, mohair, and similar

223   BROADWOVEN FABRIC MILLS, WOOL (INCLUDING DYEING AND FINISHING)—Con.

2231   Broadwoven Fabric Mills, Wool (Including Dyeing and Finishing)—Con.

animal fibers
Shrinking cloth of wool, mohair, and similar animal fibers: for the trade
Skirtings
Sponging and refinishing cloth: wool and similar animal fiber for the trade
Suitings: wool, mohair, and similar animal fibers
Trouserings: wool, mohair, and similar animal fibers

Upholstery fabrics, wool
Weaving mills, broadwoven fabrics: wool, mohair, and similar animal fibers
Wool felts, woven
Worsted fabrics, broadwoven
Yarn bleaching, dyeing, and finishing: wool, mohair, and similar animal fibers

224   NARROW FABRIC AND OTHER SMALLWARES MILLS: COTTON, WOOL, SILK, AND MANMADE FIBER

2241   Narrow Fabric and Other Smallwares Mills: Cotton, Wool, Silk, and Manmade Fiber

Establishments primarily engaged in weaving or braiding narrow fabrics of cotton, wool, silk, and manmade fibers, including glass fibers. These fabrics are generally 12 inches or less in width in their final form but may be made initially in wider widths that are specially constructed for cutting to narrower widths. Also included in this industry are establishments primarily engaged in producing fabric-covered elastic yarn or thread.

Apparel webbing
Banding, spindle
Beltings, woven or braided
Bindings, textile—mitse
Braids, textile
Braids, tubular nylon and plastics
Cords, fabric
Elastic narrow fabrics, woven or braided
Elastic webbing
Electric insulating tapes and braids, except plastic
Fabrics, animal fiber: narrow woven
Fringes, weaving
Gimps—mitse
Glass narrow fabrics
Glove lining fabrics
Hat band fabrics
Hose fabrics, tubular
Insulating tapes and braids, electric, except plastics
Labels, woven
Lace, auto wind
Laces, corset and shoe: textile
Lacings—mitse

Narrow woven fabrics: cotton, rayon, wool, silk, glass, and manmade fiber
Ribbons—mitse
Rickrack braid
Rubber thread and yarns, fabric covered
Shoe laces, except leather
Slide fastener tapes
Strapping webs
Tapes, fabric
Textile mills, narrow woven fabric: cotton, wool, silk, and manmade fibers—including glass
Thread, elastic: fabric covered
Tie tapes, woven or braided
Trimmings, textile—mitse
Venetian blind tapes
Weaving mills, narrow fabric: cotton, wool, silk, and manmade fibers—including glass
Webbing, woven: except jute
Wicking
Yarn, elastic: fabric covered
Zipper tape

225   KNITTING MILLS

This industry group includes three types of organizations which operate in the knitting mill industry: (1) the integrated mill which purchases materials, produces textiles and related articles within the establishment, and sells the finished products; (2) the contract or commission mill which processes materials owned by others; and (3) establishments commonly known as jobbers or converters of knit goods which perform the entrepreneurial functions of a manufacturing company, such as buying the raw material, designing and pre-

Industry Group No.	Industry No.	
225		**KNITTING MILLS—Con.**

paring samples, and assigning yarns to others for knitting products on their account.

2251 Women's Full-Length and Knee-Length Hosiery, Except Socks

Establishments primarily engaged in knitting, dyeing, or finishing women's and misses' full-length and knee-length hosiery (except socks) both seamless and full-fashion, and panty hose. Establishments primarily engaged in knitting, dyeing, or finishing women's and misses' knee-length socks and anklets are classified in Industry 2252. Establishments primarily engaged in manufacturing elastic (orthopedic) hosiery are classified in Industry 3842.

Dyeing and finishing women's full-length and knee-length hosiery, except socks
Hosiery, women's full-length and knee-length, except socks
Nylons, women's full-length and knee-length

Panty hose, women's
Stockings, women's full-length and knee-length, except socks
Tights, women's

2252 Hosiery, Not Elsewhere Classified

Establishments primarily engaged in knitting, dyeing, or finishing hosiery, not elsewhere classified. Establishments primarily engaged in manufacturing women's full-length and knee-length hosiery (except socks), and panty hose are classified in Industry 2251. Establishments primarily engaged in manufacturing elastic (orthopedic) hosiery are classified in Industry 3842.

Anklets, hosiery
Boys' hosiery
Children's hosiery
Dyeing and finishing hosiery, except women's full-length and knee-length
Girls' hosiery
Hosiery, except women's and misses' full-length and knee-length
Leg warmers

Men's hosiery
Nylons, except women's full-length and knee-length
Socks
Socks, slipper—mitse
Stockings, except women's and misses' full-length and knee-length
Tights, except women's

2253 Knit Outerwear Mills

Establishments primarily engaged in knitting outerwear from yarn or in manufacturing outerwear from knit fabrics produced in the same establishment. Establishments primarily engaged in hand knitting outerwear for the trade are included in this industry. Establishments primarily engaged in knitting gloves and mittens are classified in Industry 2259, and those manufacturing outerwear from purchased knit fabrics are classified in Major Group 23.

Bathing suits—mitse
Bathrobes—mitse
Beachwear—mitse
Blouses—mitse
Body stockings—mitse
Caps—mitse
Collar and cuff sets—mitse
Dresses, hand-knit
Dresses—mitse
Dyeing and finishing knit outerwear, except hosiery, gloves, and nightwear
Hats—mitse
Headwear—mitse
Housecoats—mitse
Jackets—mitse
Jerseys and sweaters—mitse
Jogging suits—mitse
Leotards—mitse
Lounging robes—mitse
Mufflers—mitse

Neckties—mitse
Pants, outerwear—mitse
Scarfs—mitse
Shawls—mitse
Shirts, outerwear—mitse
Shoulderettes—mitse
Ski suits—mitse
Skirts—mitse
Slacks—mitse
Suits—mitse
Sweat bands—mitse
Sweat pants—mitse
Sweat shirts—mitse
Sweaters and sweater coats—mitse
T-shirts, outerwear—mitse
Tank tops—mitse
Ties—mitse
Trousers—mitse
Warmup and jogging suits—mitse
Wristlets—mitse

Industry Group No.	Industry No.	
225		**KNITTING MILLS—Con.**

2254 Knit Underwear and Nightwear Mills

Establishments primarily engaged in knitting underwear and nightwear from yarn or in manufacturing underwear and nightwear from knit fabrics produced in the same establishment. Establishments primarily engaged in manufacturing underwear and nightwear from purchased knit fabrics are classified in Major Group 23. Establishments primarily engaged in knitting robes are classified in Industry 2253.

Briefs, underwear—mitse	Panties—mitse
Drawers, apparel—mitse	Shirts, underwear—mitse
Dyeing and finishing knit underwear	Shorts, underwear—mitse
Gowns, night—mitse	Slips—mitse
Negligees—mitse	Step-ins—mitse
Nightgowns—mitse	T-shirts, underwear—mitse
Nightwear—mitse	Underwear—mitse
Pajamas—mitse	Union suits—mitse

2257 Weft Knit Fabric Mills

Establishments primarily engaged in knitting weft (circular) fabrics or in dyeing, or finishing weft (circular) knit fabrics.

Circular knit fabrics	Fabrics, weft knit
Cloth, circular knit	Jersey fabrics
Dyeing and finishing circular knit fabrics	Knit fabrics, weft (circular): knitting, dyeing, or finishing
Dyeing and finishing weft knit fabrics	Pile fabrics, circular knit
Fabrics, circular knit	Weft knit fabrics

2258 Lace and Warp Knit Fabric Mills

Establishments primarily engaged in knitting, dyeing, or finishing warp (flat) knit fabrics, or in manufacturing, dyeing, or finishing lace goods.

Bed sets, lace	Lace goods: curtains, bedspreads, table covers, flouncings, and insertions
Cloth, warp knit—mitse	Lace, knit
Covers, lace: chair, dresser, piano, and table	Laces: Barmen, bobbinet, levers, and Nottingham
Curtains and curtain fabrics, lace	Mosquito netting, warp knit—mitse
Dyeing and finishing lace goods	Netting made on a lace or net machine
Dyeing and finishing warp knit fabrics	Netting, knit—mitse
Edgings, lace	Pile fabrics, warp knit
Fabrics, warp knit—mitse	Tricot fabrics
Finishing of warp knit fabrics	Warp (flat) knit fabrics
Galloons, lace	
Knit fabrics, warp: knitting, dyeing, or finishing	

2259 Knitting Mills, Not Elsewhere Classified

Establishments primarily engaged in knitting gloves and other articles, not elsewhere classified. Establishments primarily engaged in manufacturing woven or knit fabric gloves and mittens from purchased fabrics are classified in Industry 2381.

Bags and bagging—mitse	Gloves—mitse
Bedspreads—mitse	Linings, shoe—mitse
Curtains—mitse	Meat bagging—mitse
Dishcloths—mitse	Mittens—mitse
Dyeing and finishing knit gloves and mittens	Stockinettes—mitse
Elastic girdle blanks—mitse	Towels—mitse
Girdles (elastic) and other foundation garments—mitse	Washcloths—mitse

Industry
Group
No.
226

Industry
No.

DYEING AND FINISHING TEXTILES, EXCEPT WOOL FABRICS AND KNIT GOODS

2261 Finishers of Broadwoven Fabrics of Cotton

Establishments primarily engaged in finishing purchased cotton broadwoven fabrics, or finishing such fabrics, on a commission basis. These finishing operations include bleaching, dyeing, printing (roller, screen, flock, plisse), and other mechanical finishing, such as preshrinking, calendering, and napping. Also included in this industry are establishments primarily engaged in shrinking and sponging of cotton broadwoven fabrics for the trade and chemical finishing for water repellency, fire resistance, and mildew proofing. Establishments primarily engaged in finishing wool broadwoven fabrics are classified in Industry 2231; those finishing knit goods are classified in Industry Group 225; and those coating or impregnating fabrics are classified in Industry 2295.

Bleaching cotton broadwoven fabrics
Bleaching, kier: continuous machine
Calendering of cotton broadwoven fabrics
Dyeing cotton broadwoven fabrics
Embossing cotton broadwoven fabrics
Finishing of cotton broadwoven fabrics
Fire resistance finishing of cotton broadwoven fabrics
Flocking of cotton broadwoven fabrics
Mercerizing cotton broadwoven fabrics
Mildew proofing cotton broadwoven fabrics

Napping of cotton broadwoven fabrics
Preshrinking cotton broadwoven fabrics for the trade
Printing and finishing of cotton broadwoven fabrics
Refinishing and sponging cotton broadwoven fabrics for the trade
Shrinking cotton broadwoven fabrics for the trade
Sueding cotton broadwoven goods
Teaseling cotton broadwoven goods
Water repellency finishing of cotton broadwoven fabrics

2262 Finishers of Broadwoven Fabrics of Manmade Fiber and Silk

Establishments primarily engaged in finishing purchased manmade fiber and silk broadwoven fabrics or finishing such fabrics on a commission basis. These finishing operations include bleaching, dyeing, printing (roller, screen, flock, plisse), and other mechanical finishing, such as preshrinking, calendering, and napping. Establishments primarily engaged in finishing wool broadwoven fabrics are classified in Industry 2231; those finishing knit goods are classified in Industry Group 225; and those coating or impregnating fabrics are classified in Industry 2295.

Bleaching manmade fiber and silk broadwoven fabrics
Calendering of manmade fiber and silk broadwoven fabrics
Dyeing manmade fiber and silk broadwoven fabrics
Embossing manmade fiber and silk broadwoven fabrics
Finishing of manmade fiber and silk broadwoven fabrics
Fire resistance finishing of manmade fiber and silk broadwoven fabrics
Flocking of manmade fiber and silk broadwoven fabrics
Mildew proofing manmade fiber and silk broadwoven fabrics

Napping of manmade fiber and silk broadwoven fabrics
Preshrinking manmade fiber and silk broadwoven fabrics for the trade
Printing manmade fiber and silk broadwoven fabrics
Refinishing of manmade fiber and silk broadwoven fabrics
Shrinking manmade fiber and silk broadwoven fabrics for the trade
Silk broadwoven fabric finishing
Sueding manmade fiber and silk broadwoven fabrics
Teaseling manmade fiber and silk broadwoven fabrics

2269 Finishers of Textiles, Not Elsewhere Classified

Establishments primarily engaged in dyeing and finishing textiles, not elsewhere classified, such as bleaching, dyeing, printing, and finishing of raw stock, yarn, braided goods, and narrow fabrics, except wool and knit fabrics.

226   **DYEING AND FINISHING TEXTILES, EXCEPT WOOL FABRICS AND
KNIT GOODS—Con.**

2269   **Finishers of Textiles, Not Elsewhere Classified—Con.**

These establishments perform finishing operations on purchased textiles or on a commission basis.

Bleaching raw stock, yarn, and narrow fabrics: except knit and wool	Gassing yarn
	Labels, cotton: printed
Braided goods, except wool: bleaching, dyeing, printing, and other finishing	Linen fabrics: dyeing, finishing, and printing
Cloth mending, except wool: for the trade	Mercerizing yarn, braided goods, and narrow fabrics: except knit and wool
Dyeing raw stock, yarn, and narrow fabrics: except knit and wool	Mill enders, contract: cotton, silk, and manmade fiber
Embossing linen broadwoven fabrics	Printing narrow fabrics, except knit and wool
Finishing of raw stock, yarn, and narrow fabrics: except knit and wool	

227   **CARPETS AND RUGS**

2273   **Carpets and Rugs**

Establishments primarily engaged in manufacturing woven, tufted, and other carpets and rugs, such as art squares, floor mattings, needle punch carpeting, and door mats and mattings, from textile materials or from twisted paper, grasses, reeds, coir, sisal, jute, or rags.

Aircraft floor coverings, except rubber or plastics	Dyeing and finishing of rugs and carpets
Art squares, textile fiber	Floor coverings, textile fiber
Art squares: twisted paper, grass, reed, coir, sisal, jute, and rag	Floor coverings: twisted paper, grass, reed, coir, sisal, jute, and rag
Automobile floor coverings, except rubber or plastics	Mats and matting, textile
Axminster carpets	Mats and matting: twisted paper, grass, reed, coir, sisal, jute, and rag
Bathmats and sets, textile	Rugs, except rubber or plastics
Carpets, textile fiber	Scatter rugs, except rubber or plastics
Carpets: twisted paper, grass, reed, coir, sisal, jute, and rag	Smyrna carpets and rugs, machine woven
Chenille rugs	Wilton carpets
Door mats: twisted paper, grass, reed, coir, sisal, jute, and rag	

228   **YARN AND THREAD MILLS**

2281   **Yarn Spinning Mills**

Establishments primarily engaged in spinning yarn wholly or chiefly by weight of cotton, manmade fibers, silk, wool, mohair, or similar animal fibers. Establishments primarily engaged in dyeing or finishing purchased yarns or finishing yarns on a commission basis are classified in Industry 2231 if the yarns are of wool and in Industry 2269 if they are of other fibers. Establishments primarily engaged in producing specialty yarns or producing spun yarns of other fibers are classified in Industry 2299.

Acetate yarn, made from purchased staple: spun	Embroidery yarn: cotton, silk, wool, and manmade staple
Acrylic yarn, made from purchased staple: spun	Knitting yarn: cotton, silk, wool, and manmade staple
Carded yarn, cotton	Manmade staple fiber yarn, spun
Carpet yarn, cotton	Modacrylic yarn, made from purchased staple: spun
Combed yarn, cotton	
Cordage yarn, cotton	Nylon yarn, spinning of staple
Crochet yarn: cotton, silk, wool, and manmade staple	Polyester yarn, made from purchased staple: spun
Darning yarn: cotton, silk, wool, and manmade staple	Polypropylene yarn, made from purchased staple: spun

228 YARN AND THREAD MILLS—Con.

2281 Yarn Spinning Mills—Con.

Rayon yarn, made from purchased staple: spun
Spinning yarn: cotton, silk, wool, and manmade staple
Spun yarn: cotton, silk, manmade fiber, wool, and animal fiber

Weaving yarn: cotton, silk, wool, and manmade staple
Yarn, spun: cotton, silk, manmade fiber, wool, and animal fiber
Yarn: cotton, silk, wool, and manmade staple

2282 Yarn Texturizing, Throwing, Twisting, and Winding Mills

Establishments primarily engaged in texturizing, throwing, twisting, winding, or spooling purchased yarns or manmade fiber filaments wholly or chiefly by weight of cotton, manmade fibers, silk, or wool, mohair or similar animal fibers, or in performing such activities on a commission basis. Establishments primarily engaged in dyeing or finishing purchased yarns or finishing yarns on a commission basis are classified in Industry 2231 if the yarns are of wool and in Industry 2269 if they are of other fibers. Establishments primarily engaged in producing and texturizing manmade fiber filaments and yarns in the same plant are classified in Industries 2823 or 2824.

Acetate filament yarn: throwing, twisting, winding, or spooling
Acrylic and modacrylic filament yarn: throwing, winding, or spooling
Animal fiber yarn: twisting, winding, or spooling
Beaming yarns for the trade
Mohair yarn: twisting, winding, or spooling
Nylon yarn: throwing, twisting, winding, or spooling
Polyester filament yarn: throwing, twisting, winding, or spooling
Polypropylene filament yarn: throwing, twisting, winding, or spooling

Rayon yarn, filament: throwing, twisting, winding
Spooling yarn: cotton, silk, and manmade fiber continuous filament
Textured yarns—mfpm
Throwing, winding, or spooling of yarn: silk, wool and manmade fiber continuous filament
Twisting yarn: silk, wool, and manmade fiber continuous filament
Winding yarn: cotton, silk, wool, and manmade fiber continuous filament
Wool yarn: twisting, winding, or spooling

2284 Thread Mills

Establishments primarily engaged in manufacturing thread of cotton, silk, manmade fibers, wool or similar animal fibers. Important products of this industry include sewing, crochet, darning, embroidery, tatting, hand-knitting, and other handicraft threads. Establishments primarily engaged in manufacturing thread of flax, hemp, and ramie are classified in Industry 2299.

Cotton thread
Crochet thread: cotton, silk, manmade fibers, and wool
Darning thread: cotton, silk, manmade fibers, and wool
Embroidery thread: cotton, silk, manmade fibers, and wool
Hand-knitting thread: cotton, silk, manmade fibers, and wool
Manmade fiber thread
Nylon thread

Polyester thread
Rayon thread
Sewing thread: cotton, silk, manmade fibers, and wool
Silk thread
Spinning thread: cotton, silk, manmade fibers, and wool
Tatting thread: cotton, silk, manmade fibers, and wool
Thread: except flax, hemp, and ramie

229 MISCELLANEOUS TEXTILE GOODS

2295 Coated Fabrics, Not Rubberized

Establishments primarily engaged in manufacturing coated, impregnated, or laminated textiles, and in the special finishing of textiles, such as varnishing and waxing. Establishments primarily engaged in rubberizing purchased fab-

Industry
Group   Industry
No.   No.

229   MISCELLANEOUS TEXTILE GOODS—Con.

2295   Coated Fabrics, Not Rubberized—Con.

rics are classified in Industry 3069, and those engaged in dyeing and finishing textiles are classified in Industry Group 226 or Industry 2231.

Buckram: varnished, waxed, and impregnated
Cambric: varnished, waxed, and impregnated
Cloth, varnished glass
Coating and impregnating of fabrics, except rubberizing
Fabrics, coated and impregnated: except rubberized
Laminating of fabrics
Leather, artificial or imitation
Mats, varnished glass
Metallizing of fabrics
Oilcloth
Plastics coated fabrics
Pyroxylin coated fabrics
Resin coated fabrics
Sealing or insulating tape for pipe, fiberglass coated with tar or asphalt
Sleeving, textile: saturated
Tape, varnished: plastics and other coated: except magnetic—mfpm
Tubing, textile: varnished
Waxing of cloth
Yarns, plastics coated: made from purchased yarns

2296   Tire Cord and Fabrics

Establishments primarily engaged in manufacturing cord and fabric of manmade fibers, cotton, glass, steel, or other materials for use in reinforcing rubber tires, industrial belting, fuel cells, and similar uses.

Cord for reinforcing rubber tires, industrial belting, and fuel cells
Fabrics for reinforcing rubber tires, industrial belting, and fuel cells
Glass tire cord and tire cord fabrics
Steel tire cord and tire cord fabrics

2297   Nonwoven Fabrics

Establishments primarily engaged in manufacturing nonwoven fabrics (by bonding and/or interlocking of fibers) by mechanical, chemical, thermal or solvent means, or by combinations thereof. Establishments primarily engaged in producing woven felts are classified in Industry 2231; and those producing other felts are classified in Industry 2299.

Bonded-fiber fabrics, except felt
Fabrics, bonded fiber: except felt
Fabrics, nonwoven: except felts
Ribbon, nonwoven (yarn bonded by plastics)
Spunbonded fabrics

2298   Cordage and Twine

Establishments primarily engaged in manufacturing rope, cable, cordage, twine, and related products from abaca (Manila), sisal, henequen, hemp, cotton, paper, jute, flax, manmade fibers including glass, and other fibers.

Binder and baler twine
Blasting mats, rope
Cable, fiber
Camouflage nets, not made in weaving mills
Cargo nets (cordage)
Cord, braided
Cordage: abaca (Manila), sisal, henequen, hemp, jute, and other fibers
Fish nets and seines, made in cordage or twine mills
Fishing lines, nets, seines: made in cordage or twine mills
Hard fiber cordage and twine
Insulator pads, cordage
Nets, rope
Rope, except asbestos and wire
Slings, rope
Soft fiber cordage and twine
Trawl twine
Twine
Wire rope centers

2299   Textile Goods, Not Elsewhere Classified

Establishments primarily engaged in manufacturing textile goods, not elsewhere classified, including linen goods, jute goods, felt goods, padding and upholstery filling and processed waste and recovered fibers and flock. Establishments primarily engaged in processing textile fibers to prepare them for spin-

Industry
Group
No.

Industry
No.

229   MISCELLANEOUS TEXTILE GOODS—Con.

2299   Textile Goods, Not Elsewhere Classified—Con.

ning, such as wool scouring and carbonizing and combing and converting tow to top, are also classified here. Establishments primarily engaged in manufacturing woven wool felts and wool haircloth are classified in Industry 2231, and those manufacturing needle punch carpeting are classified in Industry 2273 . Establishments primarily engaged in manufacturing embroideries are classified in Industry Group 239. Establishments primarily engaged in manufacturing lace goods are classified in Industry 2258. Establishments primarily engaged in sorting wiping rags or waste are classified in Wholesale Trade, Industry 5093.

Apparel filling: cotton mill waste, kapok, and related materials
Bagging, jute: made in jute weaving mills
Batts and batting: cotton mill waste, kapok, and related materials
Burlap, jute
Carbonized rags
Coir yarns and roving
Crash, linen
Fabrics: linen, jute, hemp, ramie
Felt goods, except woven felts and hats: wool, hair, jute, or other fiber
Felts, pressed or needle loom
Fibers, textile: recovery from textile mill waste and rags
Flax yarns and roving
Flock (recovered textile fibers)
Garnetting of textile waste and rags
Grease, wool
Hair, curled: for upholstery, pillow, and quilt filling
Handwoven fabrics
Hemp yarn, thread, roving, and textiles
Linings, carpet: felt except woven
Mats, felt: except woven
Narrow woven fabrics: linen, jute, hemp, and ramie
Noils, wool and mohair
Oakum
Packing, twisted jute
Padding and wadding, textile
Pads and padding, felt: except woven
Pads, fiber: henequen, sisal, istle
Pillow filling: curled hair (e.g., cotton waste, moss, hemp tow, kapok)
Pipe and boiler covering, felt
Polishing felts, except woven

Preparing textile fibers for spinning (scouring and combing)
Pressed felts
Processing of textile mill waste and recovering fibers
Punched felts
Quilt filling: curled hair (e.g., cotton waste, moss, hemp tow, kapok)
Ramie yarn, thread, roving, and textiles
Rayon tops, combing and converting
Recovering textile fibers from clippings and rags
Roves, flax and jute
Rugbacking, jute or other fiber
Slubs and nubs (cutting up fibers for use in tweeds)
Textile mills: linen, jute, hemp, and ramie yarn, thread, and fabrics
Thread: linen, hemp, and ramie
Tops, combing and converting
Tops, manmade fiber
Tow to top mills
Towels and towelings, linen and linen-and-cotton mixtures—mitse
Trimming felts, except woven
Upholstery filling, textile
Wads and wadding, textile
Webbing, jute
Wool felts, pressed or needle loom
Wool scouring and carbonizing
Wool shoddy
Wool tops, combing and converting
Wool waste processing
Yarn, specialty and novelty
Yarn: flax, jute, hemp, and ramie
Yarn: metallic, ceramic, or paper fibers

Major Group 23.—APPAREL AND OTHER FINISHED PRODUCTS MADE FROM FABRICS AND SIMILAR MATERIALS

The Major Group as a Whole

This major group, known as the cutting-up and needle trades, includes establishments producing clothing and fabricating products by cutting and sewing purchased woven or knit textile fabrics and related materials, such as leather, rubberized fabrics, plastics, and furs. Also included are establishments that manufacture clothing by cutting and joining (for example, by adhesives) materials such as paper and nonwoven textiles. Included in the apparel industries are three types of establishments: (1) the regular or inside factories; (2) contract factories; and (3) apparel jobbers. The regular factories perform all of the usual manufacturing functions within their own plant; the contract factories manufacture apparel from materials owned by others; and apparel jobbers perform the entrepreneurial functions of a manufacturing company, such as buying raw materials, designing and preparing samples, arranging for the manufacture of clothing from their materials, and selling of the finished apparel.

Knitting mills are classified in Industry 2253 if primarily knitting outerwear, and in Industry 2254 if primarily knitting underwear and nightwear. Custom tailors and dressmakers not operating on a factory basis are classified in Retail Trade, Industry 5699; and establishments which purchase and resell finished garments but do not perform the functions of the apparel jobbers are classified in Wholesale Trade, Industry Group 513.

Industry Group No.	Industry No.	
231		**MEN'S AND BOYS' SUITS, COATS, AND OVERCOATS**
	2311	**Men's and Boys' Suits, Coats, and Overcoats**

Establishments primarily engaged in manufacturing men's and boys' tailored suits, coats, and overcoats from purchased woven or knit fabrics. Establishments primarily engaged in manufacturing uniforms (except athletic and work uniforms) are also included in this industry. Establishments primarily engaged in manufacturing men's work uniforms and clothing are classified in Industry 2326, and those manufacturing men's and boys' athletic uniforms are classified in Industry 2329. Knitting mills primarily engaged in manufacturing suits and coats are classified in Industry 2253.

Coats, tailored: men's and boys'—mfpm
Firefighters' dress uniforms, men's
Formal jackets, men's and boys'
Jackets, tailored suit-type: men's and boys'
Military uniforms, tailored: men's and boys'
Overcoats: men's and boys'

Police uniforms, men's
Suits, tailored: men's and boys'—mfpm
Tailored dress and sport coats: men's and boys'
Topcoats: men's and boys'
Tuxedos
Uniforms, tailored: men's and boys'
Vests, tailored: men's and boys'

232		**MEN'S AND BOYS' FURNISHINGS, WORK CLOTHING, AND ALLIED GARMENTS**
	2321	**Men's and Boys' Shirts, Except Work Shirts**

Establishments primarily engaged in manufacturing men's and boys' shirts (including polo and sport shirts) from purchased woven or knit fabrics. Establishments primarily engaged in manufacturing work shirts are classified in In-

232   **MEN'S AND BOYS' FURNISHINGS, WORK CLOTHING, AND ALLIED GARMENTS—Con.**

2321 **Men's and Boys' Shirts, Except Work Shirts—Con.**

dustry 2326. Knitting mills primarily engaged in manufacturing outerwear are classified in Industry 2253.

Blouses, boys'—mfpm	Sport shirts: men's and boys'—mfpm
Collars, men's and boys'—mfpm	Sweatshirts: men's and boys'—mfpm
Flannel shirts, except work shirts: men's, youths', and boys'	T-shirts, outerwear: men's and boys'—mfpm
Polo shirts: men's and boys'—mfpm	Tank tops: men's and boys'—mfpm
Shirts, outerwear; except work shirts: men's and boys'—mfpm	Uniform shirts, except athletic or work: men's and boys'—mfpm

2322 **Men's and Boys' Underwear and Nightwear**

Establishments primarily engaged in manufacturing men's and boys' underwear and nightwear from purchased woven or knit fabrics. Knitting mills primarily engaged in manufacturing underwear and nightwear are classified in Industry 2254; and those manufacturing men's and boys' robes are classified in Industry 2384.

Briefs, underwear: men's and boys'—mfpm	Shorts, underwear: men's and boys'—mfpm
Nightshirts: men's and boys'—mfpm	T-shirts, underwear: men's and boys'—mfpm
Nightwear: men's and boys'—mfpm	Underwear: men's and boys'—mfpm
Pajamas: men's and boys'—mfpm	
Shirts, underwear: men's and boys'—mfpm	

2323 **Men's and Boys' Neckwear**

Establishments primarily engaged in manufacturing men's and boys' neckties, scarves, and mufflers from purchased woven or knit fabrics. Knitting mills primarily engaged in manufacturing neckties, scarves, and mufflers are classified in Industry 2253.

Ascots: men's and boys'—mfpm	Neckties: men's and boys'—mfpm
Bow ties: men's and boys'—mfpm	Scarves: men's and boys'—mfpm
Mufflers: men's and boys'—mfpm	Ties, handsewn—mfpm

2325 **Men's and Boys' Separate Trousers and Slacks**

Establishments primarily engaged in manufacturing men's and boys' separate trousers and slacks from purchased woven or knit fabrics, including jeans, dungarees, and jean-cut casual slacks. Establishments primarily engaged in manufacturing complete suits are classified in Industry 2311; those manufacturing workpants (excluding jeans and dungarees) are classified in Industry 2326. Knitting mills primarily engaged in manufacturing men's and boys' separate trousers and slacks are classified in Industry 2253.

Dungarees: men's and boys'—mfpm	Slacks (separate): men's and boys'—mfpm
Jean-cut casual slacks: men's and boys'—mfpm	Slacks, jean-cut casual: men's and boys'—mfpm
Jeans: men's and boys'—mfpm	Trousers (separate): men's and boys'—mfpm
Pants, dress (separate): men's and boys'—mfpm	

2326 **Men's and Boys' Work Clothing**

Establishments primarily engaged in manufacturing men's and boys' work shirts, workpants (excluding jeans and dungarees), other work clothing, and

Industry Group No.	Industry No.
232	

MEN'S AND BOYS' FURNISHINGS, WORK CLOTHING, AND ALLIED GARMENTS—Con.

2326 Men's and Boys' Work Clothing—Con.

washable service apparel. Establishments primarily engaged in manufacturing separate trousers and slacks are classified in Industry 2325.

Aprons, work, except rubberized and plastics: men's—mfpm
Coveralls, work: men's and boys'—mfpm
Industrial garments: men's and boys'—mfpm
Jackets, overall and work: men's and boys'—mfpm
Laboratory coats: men's—mfpm
Medical uniforms, men's—mfpm
Overall jackets: men's and boys'—mfpm
Overalls, work: men's and boys'—mfpm

Pants, work, except jeans and dungarees: men's and boys'—mfpm
Service apparel, washable: men's—mfpm
Shirts, work: men's and boys'—mfpm
Suits, work: men's—mfpm
Uniforms, nontailored work type: men's—mfpm
Uniforms, work: men's—mfpm
Work garments, waterproof, men's and boys'; except raincoats—mfpm
Workpants, except jeans and dungarees: men's and boys'—mfpm

2329 Men's and Boys' Clothing, Not Elsewhere Classified

Establishments primarily engaged in manufacturing men's and boys' clothing, not elsewhere classified, from purchased woven or knit fabrics. Establishments primarily engaged in manufacturing leather and sheep-lined garments are classified in Industry 2386. Knitting mills primarily engaged in manufacturing outerwear are classified in Industry 2253.

Athletic clothing: men's and boys'—mfpm
Bathing suits: men's and boys'—mfpm
Coats, except tailored or work: men's and boys'—mfpm
Coats, oiled fabric and blanket-lined: men's and boys'—mfpm
Down-filled clothing: men's and boys'—mfpm
Feather-filled clothing: men's and boys'—mfpm
Field jackets, military—mfpm
Gymnasium clothing: men's and boys'—mfpm
Hunting coats and vests, men's—mfpm
Jackets, nontailored except work: men's and boys'—mfpm
Jackets, sport, nontailored: men's and boys'—mfpm
Knickers, dress (separate): men's and boys'—mfpm
Lumberjackets: men's and boys'—mfpm
Mackinaws: men's and boys'—mfpm
Melton jackets: men's and boys'—mfpm
Pants, athletic and gymnasium: men's and boys'—mfpm

Pants, men's and boys': sweat, athletic, gymnasium, ski, and snow—mfpm
Riding clothes: men's and boys'—mfpm
Shirt and slack suits, nontailored: men's and boys'—mfpm
Shorts, outerwear: men's and boys'—mfpm
Ski suits: men's and boys'—mfpm
Sports clothing, nontailored: men's and boys'—mfpm
Suits, men's and boys': warm-up, jogging, snow, and ski—mfpm
Sweater jackets: men's and boys'—mfpm
Sweater vests: men's and boys'—mfpm
Sweaters: men's and boys'—mfpm
Swimsuits: men's and boys'—mfpm
Swimwear, men's and boys'—mfpm
Uniforms, athletic and gymnasium: men's and boys'—mfpm
Vests, nontailored including sweater—men's and boys'—mfpm
Windbreakers: men's and boys'—mfpm

233	

WOMEN'S, MISSES', AND JUNIORS' OUTERWEAR

2331 Women's, Misses', and Juniors' Blouses and Shirts

Establishments primarily engaged in manufacturing women's, misses', and juniors' blouses and shirts from purchased woven or knit fabrics. Knitting mills primarily engaged in manufacturing outerwear are classified in Industry 2253. Establishments primarily engaged in manufacturing girls', children's, and infants' blouses and shirts are classified in Industry 2361.

Blouses: women's, misses', and juniors'—mfpm
Shirts, outerwear: women's, misses', and juniors'—mfpm
Sweatshirts: women's, misses', and juniors'—mfpm

T-shirts, outerwear: women's, misses', and juniors'—mfpm
Tank tops, outerwear: women's, misses', and juniors'—mfpm

WOMEN'S, MISSES', AND JUNIORS' OUTERWEAR—Con.

2335 Women's, Misses', and Juniors' Dresses

Establishments primarily engaged in manufacturing women's, misses', and juniors' dresses (including ensemble dresses), from purchased woven or knit fabrics, including woven or knit fabrics of paper, whether sold by the piece or by the dozen. Establishments primarily engaged in manufacturing girls', children's, and infants' dresses are classified in Industry 2361. Knitting mills primarily engaged in manufacturing knit dresses are classified in Industry 2253.

Bridal dresses or gowns: women's, misses', and juniors'—mfpm
Dresses, paper, cut and sewn: women's, misses', and juniors'—mfpm
Dresses: women's, misses', and juniors'—mfpm
Ensemble dresses: women's, misses', and juniors'—mfpm

Gowns, formal: women's, misses', and juniors'—mfpm
Gowns, wedding: women's, misses', and juniors'—mfpm
Housedresses: women's, misses', and juniors'—mfpm
Wedding dresses: women's, misses', and juniors'—mfpm

2337 Women's, Misses', and Juniors' Suits, Skirts, and Coats

Establishments primarily engaged in manufacturing women's, misses', and juniors' suits, pantsuits, skirts, coats, except fur coats and raincoats, and tailored jackets and vests, from purchased woven or knit fabrics. These garments are generally tailored and usually lined. Establishments primarily engaged in manufacturing fur clothing are classified in Industry 2371; and those manufacturing raincoats are classified in Industry 2385. Knitting mills primarily engaged in manufacturing knit outerwear are classified in Industry 2253.

Capes, except fur and vulcanized rubber: women's, misses', and juniors'— mfpm
Coats, except fur and raincoats: women's, misses', and juniors'—mfpm
Jackets, tailored, except fur, sheeplined, and leather: women's, misses', and juniors'—mfpm
Jumpsuits: women's, misses', and juniors'—mfpm
Pantsuits: women's, misses', and juniors'—mfpm

Skirts, except tennis skirts: women's, misses', and juniors'—mfpm
Suits, except playsuits and athletic: women's, misses', and juniors'—mfpm
Uniforms, except athletic and service apparel: women's, misses', and juniors'—mfpm
Vests, except tailored: women's, misses', and juniors'—mfpm

2339 Women's, Misses', and Juniors' Outerwear, Not Elsewhere Classified

Establishments primarily engaged in manufacturing women's, misses', and juniors' outerwear, not elsewhere classified, from purchased woven or knit fabrics. Knitting mills primarily engaged in manufacturing outerwear are classified in Industry 2253.

Aprons, except rubberized and plastics: women's, misses', and juniors'
Athletic uniforms: women's, misses', and juniors'
Bathing suits: women's, misses', and juniors'—mfpm
Beachwear: women's, misses', and juniors'—mfpm
Coats, service apparel (e.g., medical and lab)
Collar and cuff sets: women's, misses' and juniors'— mfpm
Culottes: women's, misses', and juniors'—mfpm
Dickeys: women's, misses' and juniors'—mfpm

Down-filled coats, jackets, and vests: women's, misses', and juniors'—mfpm
Feather-filled coats, jackets, and vests: women's, misses', and juniors'—mfpm
Jackets, not tailored: women's, misses', and juniors'
Jackets, service apparel (e.g., medical and lab)
Jean-cut casual slacks: women's, misses', and juniors'—mfpm
Jeans: women's, misses', and juniors'
Jogging suits: women's, misses', and juniors'—mfpm
Knickers: women's, misses', and jun-

233   WOMEN'S, MISSES', AND JUNIORS' OUTERWEAR—Con.

2339   Women's, Misses', and Juniors' Outerwear, Not Elsewhere Classified—Con.

iors'—mfpm
Leotards: women's, misses', and juniors'—mfpm
Neckwear: women's, misses' and juniors'—mfpm
Pants outfits, except pantsuits: women's, misses', and juniors'—mfpm
Playsuits: women's, misses', and juniors'—mfpm
Riding habits: women's, misses', and juniors'—mfpm
Scarves, hoods, and headbands: women's, misses', and juniors'—mfpm
Service apparel, washable: e.g., nurses', maids', waitresses', laboratory uniforms: women's, misses', and jun
Shorts, outerwear: women's, misses', and juniors' —mfpm
Ski jackets, vests, and pants: women's, misses', and juniors'—mfpm
Ski suits: women's, misses', and juniors'—mfpm
Skirts, tennis: women's, misses', and juniors'—mfpm
Slacks: women's, misses', and juniors'—mfpm

Smocks: women's, misses', and juniors'—mfpm
Snowsuits: women's, misses', and juniors'—mfpm
Suits, women's, misses', and juniors': ski, swim, snow, play, warm-up, and jogging—mfpm
Sweat pants: women's, misses', and juniors'—mfpm
Swimsuits: women's, misses', and juniors'—mfpm
Ties: women's, misses', and juniors'—mfpm
Uniforms, athletic: women's, misses', and juniors'—mfpm
Uniforms, washable service apparel (nurses', maid, waitresses', laboratory): women's, misses', and juniors'—m
Vests, not tailored: women's, misses' and juniors—mfpm
Warmup suits: women's, misses', and juniors'—mfpm
Windbreakers: women's, misses', and juniors'—mfpm

234   WOMEN'S, MISSES', CHILDREN'S, AND INFANTS' UNDERGARMENTS

2341   Women's, Misses', Children's, and Infants' Underwear and Nightwear

Establishments primarily engaged in manufacturing women's, misses', children's, and infants' underwear and nightwear from purchased woven or knit fabrics. Knitting mills primarily engaged in manufacturing underwear and nightwear are classified in Industry 2254. Establishments primarily engaged in manufacturing women's and misses' robes and dressing gowns are classified in Industry 2384, and those manufacturing children's and infants' robes are classified in Industry 2369. Establishments primarily engaged in manufacturing brassieres, girdles, and allied garments are classified in Industry 2342.

Bedjackets: women's, misses', and juniors'—mfpm
Bra-slips: women's and misses'—mfpm
Briefs: women's, misses', children's, and infants'—mfpm
Camisoles: women's, misses', children's, and infants'—mfpm
Chemises: women's, misses', children's, and infants'—mfpm
Negligees: women's, misses', children's, and infants'—mfpm
Nightgowns: women's, misses', children's, and infants'—mfpm
Nightwear: women's, misses', children's, and infants'—mfpm

Pajamas: women's, misses', children's, and infants'—mfpm
Panties: women's, misses', children's, and infants'—mfpm
Slips: women's, misses', children's, and infants'—mfpm
T-shirts, underwear: women's, misses', children's, and infants'—mfpm
Teddies: women's, misses', children's, and infants'—mfpm
Training pants (underwear) except rubber or rubberized fabric: children's and infants'—mfpm
Underwear: women's, misses', children's, and infants'—mfpm

2342   Brassieres, Girdles, and Allied Garments

Establishments primarily engaged in manufacturing brassieres, girdles, corsets, corset accessories, and allied garments. Establishments primarily engaged in manufacturing surgical and orthopedic appliances are classified in Industry 3842.

Industry Group No.	Industry No.	
234		**WOMEN'S, MISSES', CHILDREN'S, AND INFANTS' UNDERGARMENTS—Con.**
	2342	**Brassieres, Girdles, and Allied Garments—Con.**

Brassieres—mfpm
Corset accessories: e.g., clasps and stays—mfpm
Corsets and allied garments, except surgical: women's and misses'—mfpm

Foundation garments, women's—mfpm
Girdles, women's and misses'—mfpm
Maternity bras and corsets—mfpm
Panty girdles—mfpm

| 235 | | **HATS, CAPS, AND MILLINERY** |
| | 2353 | **Hats, Caps, and Millinery** |

Establishments primarily engaged in manufacturing hats, caps, and millinery, and hat bodies. Establishments primarily engaged in manufacturing millinery trimmings are classified in Industry 2396. Establishments primarily engaged in manufacturing hats and caps of paper are classified in Industry 2679; those manufacturing caps of rubber are classified in Industry 3069; those manufacturing caps of plastics are classified in Industry 3089; and those manufacturing fur hats are classified in Industry 2371.

Baseball caps, except plastics
Caps: textiles, straw, fur-felt, and wool-felt—mfpm
Chauffeurs' hats and caps, cloth
Harvest hats, straw
Hat bodies: fur-felt, straw, and wool-felt
Hats, trimmed
Hats: textiles, straw, fur-felt, and wool-felt

Helmets, jungle-cloth: wool-lined
Millinery
Opera hats
Panama hats
Police hats and caps, except protective head gear
Uniform hats and caps, except protective head gear

| 236 | | **GIRLS', CHILDREN'S, AND INFANTS' OUTERWEAR** |
| | 2361 | **Girls', Children's, and Infants' Dresses, Blouses, and Shirts** |

Establishments primarily engaged in manufacturing girls', children's, and infants' dresses, blouses, and shirts from purchased woven or knit fabrics. Knitting mills primarily engaged in manufacturing outerwear are classified in Industry 2253.

Blouses: girls', children's, and infants'—mfpm
Dresses: girls', children's, and infants'—mfpm
Middies: girls', children's, and infants'—mfpm
Shirts, outerwear: girls', children's, and infants'—mfpm

Sweat shirts: girls', children's, and infants'—mfpm
T-shirts, outerwear: girls', children's, and infants'—mfpm
Tank tops: girls', children's, and infants'—mfpm

2369 Girls', Children's, and Infants' Outerwear, Not Elsewhere Classified

Establishments primarily engaged in manufacturing girls', children's, and infants' outerwear, not elsewhere classified, from purchased woven or knit fabrics. Knitting mills primarily engaged in manufacturing outerwear are classified in Industry 2253.

Bathing suits: girls', children's, and infants'—mfpm
Bathrobes: girls', children's, and infants'—mfpm
Beachwear: girls', children's, and infants'—mfpm
Buntings: infants'—mfpm
Coat and legging sets: girls' and children's—mfpm
Coats: girls', children's, and infants'—mfpm

Culottes: girls' and children's—mfpm
Headwear: girls', children's, and infants'—mfpm
Housecoats: girls', children's, and infants'—mfpm
Jackets: girls', children's, and infants'—mfpm
Jeans: girls', children's, and infants'—mfpm
Jogging suits: girls', children's, and infants'—mfpm

Industry Group No.	Industry No.	
236		**GIRLS', CHILDREN'S, AND INFANTS' OUTERWEAR—Con.**
	2369	**Girls', Children's, and Infants' Outerwear, Not Elsewhere Classified—Con.**

Leggings: girls', children's, and infants'—mfpm

Leotards: girls', children's, and infants'—mfpm

Lounging robes: girls', children's, and infants'—mfpm

Pantsuits: girls', children's, and infants'—mfpm

Playsuits: girls', children's, and infants'—mfpm

Robes, lounging: girls', children's, and infants'—mfpm

Rompers: infants'—mfpm

Shorts, outerwear: girls' and children's—mfpm

Ski suits: girls' and children's—mfpm

Skirts: girls', children's, and infants'—mfpm

Slacks: girls' and children's—mfpm

Snowsuits: girls' and children's—mfpm

Suits and rompers: children's and infants'—mfpm

Suits: girls' and children's—mfpm

Sunsuits: girls', children's, and infants'—mfpm

Sweat suits: girls', children's, and infants'—mfpm

Warmup suits: girls', children's, and infants'—mfpm

237   FUR GOODS

2371 Fur Goods

Establishments primarily engaged in manufacturing fur coats, and other clothing, accessories, and trimmings made of fur. Establishments primarily engaged in manufacturing sheep-lined clothing are classified in Industry 2386, and those engaged in dyeing and dressing of furs are classified in Industry 3999.

Apparel, fur

Capes, fur

Caps, fur

Clothing, fur

Coat linings, fur

Coats, fur

Fur finishers and liners for the fur goods trade: buttonhole making

Fur plates and trimmings

Glazing furs

Glove linings, fur

Hats, fur

Jackets, fur

Mounting heads on fur neckpieces

238   MISCELLANEOUS APPAREL AND ACCESSORIES

2381 Dress and Work Gloves, Except Knit and All-Leather

Establishments primarily engaged in manufacturing dress, semidress, and work gloves and mittens from purchased woven or knit fabrics, or from these materials combined with leather or plastics. Knitting mills primarily engaged in manufacturing gloves and mittens are classified in Industry 2259; establishments primarily engaged in manufacturing leather gloves are classified in Industry 3151; those manufacturing sporting and athletic gloves are classified in Industry 3949; and those manufacturing safety gloves are classified in Industry 3842.

Dyeing gloves, woven or knit: for the trade

Glove linings, except fur

Gloves and mittens, woven or knit—mfpm

2384 Robes and Dressing Gowns

Establishments primarily engaged in manufacturing men's, boys', and women's robes and dressing gowns from purchased woven or knit fabrics. Establishments primarily engaged in manufacturing girls', children's, and infants' robes from purchased fabric are classified in Industry 2369. Knitting mills primarily engaged in manufacturing knit robes and dressing gowns are classified in Industry 2253.

Bathrobes, men's, boys', and women's—mfpm

Industry Group No.	Industry No.
238	

MISCELLANEOUS APPAREL AND ACCESSORIES—Con.

2384 Robes and Dressing Gowns—Con.

Caftans—mfpm
Dressing gowns, men's and women's
Dusters (apparel)
Housecoats, except children's and infants'—mfpm

Jackets, smoking: men's—mfpm
Lounging robes and dressing gowns, men's, boys', and women's—mfpm

2385 Waterproof Outerwear

Establishments primarily engaged in manufacturing raincoats and other waterproof outerwear from purchased rubberized fabrics, plastics, and similar materials. Included in this industry are establishments primarily engaged in manufacturing waterproof or water-repellant outerwear from purchased woven or knit fabrics other than wool. Establishments primarily engaged in manufacturing men's and boys' oiled-fabric work clothing are classified in Industry 2326, and those manufacturing vulcanized rubber clothing and clothing made from rubberized fabrics produced in the same establishment are classified in Industry 3069.

Aprons, waterproof: except vulcanized rubber—mfpm
Bibs, waterproof—mfpm
Clothing, waterproof—mfpm
Diaper covers, waterproof: except vulcanized rubber
Pants, waterproof—mfpm

Plastics gowns
Raincoats, except vulcanized rubber—mfpm
Waterproof and water-repellent outerwear, except vulcanized rubber, oiled and wool—mfpm

2386 Leather and Sheep-Lined Clothing

Establishments primarily engaged in manufacturing leather and sheep-lined clothing. Establishments primarily engaged in manufacturing leather gloves and mittens are classified in Industry 3151, and those manufacturing fur clothing are classified in Industry 2371.

Caps, leather
Clothing, leather or sheep-lined
Coats, leather or sheep-lined
Garments, leather or sheep-lined
Hats, leather

Jackets, leather (except welders') or sheep-lined
Pants, leather
Vests, leather or sheep-lined

2387 Apparel Belts

Establishments primarily engaged in manufacturing apparel belts of any material.

Belts, apparel: made of any material

2389 Apparel and Accessories, Not Elsewhere Classified

Establishments primarily engaged in manufacturing suspenders, garters, handkerchiefs, and other apparel, not elsewhere classified, such as academic caps and gowns, vestments, and theatrical costumes. Also included are establishments primarily engaged in manufacturing clothing by cutting and joining (for example, by adhesives) materials such as paper and nonwoven textiles.

Arm bands, elastic—mfpm
Band uniforms—mfpm
Burial garments—mfpm
Caps and gowns, academic—mfpm
Costumes: e.g., lodge, masquerade, theatrical—mfpm
Cummerbunds—mfpm
Footlets—mfpm
Garter belts—mfpm
Garters—mfpm

Gowns, hospital: surgical and patient—mfpm
Gowns: academic, choir, clerical—mfpm
Handkerchiefs, except paper—mfpm
Prayer shawls—mfpm
Regalia—mfpm
Suspenders—mfpm
Uniforms, band—mfpm
Vestments, academic and clerical—mfpm

Industry
Group   Industry
No.   No.

239   MISCELLANEOUS FABRICATED TEXTILE PRODUCTS

2391   Curtains and Draperies

Establishments primarily engaged in manufacturing curtains and draperies from purchased materials. Establishments primarily engaged in manufacturing lace curtains on lace machines are classified in Industry 2258, and those manufacturing shower curtains are classified in Industry 2392.

Cottage sets (curtains)—mfpm
Curtains, window—mfpm

Draperies, plastics and textile—mfpm

2392   Housefurnishings, Except Curtains and Draperies

Establishments primarily engaged in manufacturing housefurnishings, such as blankets, bedspreads, sheets, tablecloths, towels, and shower curtains from purchased materials. Establishments primarily engaged in manufacturing curtains and draperies are classified in Industry 2391. Establishments producing housefurnishings primarily of fabric woven at the same establishment are classified in Industries 2211, 2221, 2231, or 2299 according to fiber.

Bags, garment storage: except paper or
  plastics film
Bags, laundry—mfpm
Bath mitts (washcloths)
Bedspreads and bed sets—mfpm
Blanket bags, plastic
Blankets—mfpm
Boat cushions
Bridge sets (cloths and napkins)
Chair covers, cloth
Chair pads, except felt
Comforters or comfortables—mfpm
Curtains, shower—mfpm
Cushions, except spring and carpet
  cushions
Dishcloths, nonwoven textile
Dust cloths
Dusters, fabric
Dusting cloths, plain
Hassocks, textile
Housefurnishings, except curtains and
  draperies
Ironing board pads—mfpm
Linings, carpet: textile, except felt
Lunch cloths—mfpm

Mattress pads
Mattress protectors, except rubber
Mops, floor and dust
Napkins, fabric and nonwoven tex-
  tiles—mfpm
Pads and padding, table: except asbes-
  tos, felt, rattan, reed, and willow
Pillowcases—mfpm
Pillows, bed—mfpm
Placemats, plastics and textiles
Polishing cloths, plain
Quilts—mfpm
Scarves: e.g., table, dresser—mfpm
Sheets, fabric—mfpm
Sheets, hospital: nonwoven textile
Shoe bags—mfpm
Slipcovers: made of fabrics, plastics,
  and other material—except paper
Table mats, plastics and textiles
Tablecloths, plastics
Tablecloths—mfpm
Towels, fabric and nonwoven textiles—
  mfpm
Wardrobe bags—mfpm
Washcloths—mfpm

2393   Textile Bags

Establishments primarily engaged in manufacturing shipping and other industrial bags from purchased fabrics. Establishments primarily engaged in manufacturing plastics bags are classified in Industry 2673; those manufacturing laundry, wardrobe, shoe, and other textile housefurnishing bags are classified in Industry 2392; and those manufacturing luggage are classified in Industry 3161.

Bags and containers, textile: except
  sleeping bags—insulated or not—
  mfpm
Bags, textile: including canvas—except
  laundry, garment, and sleeping—
  mfpm

Duffel bags, canvas
Flour bags, fabric—mfpm
Knapsacks, canvas
Tea bags, fabric—mfpm

Industry
Group
No.
239

Industry
No.

MISCELLANEOUS FABRICATED TEXTILE PRODUCTS—Con.

2394 Canvas and Related Products

Establishments primarily engaged in manufacturing awnings, tents, and related products from purchased fabrics. Establishments primarily engaged in manufacturing canvas bags are classified in Industry 2393.

Air cushions, canvas
Awnings, fabric—mfpm
Canopies, fabric—mfpm
Canvas products, except bags and knapsacks—mfpm
Cloths, drop: fabric—mfpm
Covers, fabric—mfpm
Curtains: dock and welding—mfpm
Liners and covers, fabric: pond, pit, and landfill—mfpm

Pneumatic mattresses—mfpm
Sails—mfpm
Shades, canvas
Swimming pool covers and blankets, fabric—mfpm
Tarpaulins, fabric—mfpm
Tents—mfpm

2395 Pleating, Decorative and Novelty Stitching, and Tucking for the Trade

Establishments primarily engaged in pleating, decorative and novelty stitching, and tucking for the trade. Establishments primarily engaged in performing similar services for individuals are classified in service industries. Establishments primarily engaged in manufacturing trimmings are classified in Industry 2396.

Appliqueing, for the trade
Art needlework—mfpm
Buttonhole making, except fur: for the trade
Crochet ware, machine-made
Emblems, embroidered
Embroideries: metallic, beaded, and sequined
Embroidery products, except Schiffli machine
Eyelet making, for the trade
Hemstitching, for the trade
Lace, burnt-out

Looping, for the trade
Permanent pleating and pressing, for the trade
Pleating, for the trade
Quilted fabrics or cloth
Quilting, for the trade
Ruffling, for the trade
Scalloping, for the trade
Stitching, decorative and novelty: for the trade
Swiss loom embroideries
Tucking, for the trade

2396 Automotive Trimmings, Apparel Findings, and Related Products

Establishments primarily engaged in manufacturing automotive trimmings, apparel findings, and related products. Included in this industry are establishments primarily engaged in printing and stamping on fabric articles.

Apparel findings and trimmings—mfpm
Bindings, bias—mfpm
Bindings, cap and hat—mfpm
Collar linings, for men's coats
Findings, suit and coat: e.g., coat fronts, pockets
Hat findings, men's
Hatters' fur
Linings, handbag or pocketbook
Linings, hat: men's
Linings, luggage
Linings: e.g., suit, coat, shirt, skirt, dress, necktie, millinery
Luggage linings
Millinery trimmings—mfpm
Pads, shoulder: e.g., for coats and suits
Passementeries—mfpm

Printing and embossing on fabric articles
Printing on fabric articles
Ribbons and bows, cut and sewed
Silk screening on fabric articles
Stamping fabrics for embroidering
Straps, shoulder: for women's underwear—mfpm
Sweatbands, hat and cap
Tip printing and stamping on fabric articles
Trimmings, fabric: auto, furniture, millinery, dress, coat, and suit—mfpm
Trimmings, hat: men's
Veils and veiling, hat
Visors, cap
Waistbands, trouser

2397 Schiffli Machine Embroideries

Establishments primarily engaged in manufacturing Schiffli machine embroideries.

Industry Group No.	Industry No.	
239		**MISCELLANEOUS FABRICATED TEXTILE PRODUCTS—Con.**
	2397	**Schiffli Machine Embroideries—Con.**

Embroideries, Schiffli machine

2399 Fabricated Textile Products, Not Elsewhere Classified

Establishments primarily engaged in manufacturing fabricated textile products, not elsewhere classified.

Aprons, breast (harness)
Badges, made from fabric
Bags, sleeping
Bandoleers
Banners, made from fabric
Belting, fabric—mfpm
Belts, money: made of any material
Blankets, horse—mfpm
Cheese bandages—mfpm
Covers, automobile tire and seat— mfpm
Diapers, except disposable—mfpm
Emblems, made from fabrics
Fishing nets—mfpm
Flags, fabric

Glove mending on factory basis
Hammocks, fabric—mfpm
Insignia, military: textile
Nets, launderers' and dyers'
Parachutes
Pennants
Powder puffs and mitts
Saddle cloths
Safety strap assemblies, automobile: except leather
Seat belts, automobile and aircraft: except leather
Strap assemblies, tie down: aircraft— except leather
Welts—mfpm

Major Group 24.—LUMBER AND WOOD PRODUCTS, EXCEPT FURNITURE

The Major Group as a Whole

This major group includes establishments engaged in cutting timber and pulpwood; merchant sawmills, lath mills, shingle mills, cooperage stock mills, planing mills, and plywood mills and veneer mills engaged in producing lumber and wood basic materials; and establishments engaged in manufacturing finished articles made entirely or mainly of wood or related materials. Certain types of establishments producing wood products are classified elsewhere. For example, furniture and office and store fixtures are classified in Major Group 25; musical instruments, toys and playground equipment, and caskets are classified in Major Group 39. Woodworking in connection with construction, in the nature of reconditioning and repair, or performed to individual order, is classified in nonmanufacturing industries. Establishments engaged in integrated operations of logging combined with sawmills, pulp mills, or other converting activity, with the logging not separately reported, are classified according to the primary product shipped.

Industry Group No.	Industry No.	
241		**LOGGING**
	2411	**Logging**

Establishments primarily engaged in cutting timber and in producing rough, round, hewn, or riven primary forest or wood raw materials, or in producing wood chips in the field. Independent contractors engaged in estimating or trucking timber, but who perform no cutting operations, are classified in nonmanufacturing industries. Establishments primarily engaged in the collection of bark, sap, gum, and other forest products are classified in Forestry, Major Group 08.

Bolts, wood: e.g., handle, heading, shingle, stave
Burls, wood
Driving timber
Fuel wood harvesting
Last blocks, wood: hewn or riven
Logging contractors
Logs
Mine timbers, hewn
Peeler logs
Pickets and paling: round or split
Piling, wood: untreated
Pole cutting contractors
Poles, wood: untreated
Posts, wood: hewn, round, or split
Pulpwood camps
Pulpwood contractors engaged in cutting
Rails, fence: round or split
Saw logs
Skidding logs
Stumping for turpentine or powder manufacturing
Stumps
Timber (product of logging camps)
Veneer logs
Wood chips, produced in the field

242		**SAWMILLS AND PLANING MILLS**
	2421	**Sawmills and Planing Mills, General**

Establishments primarily engaged in sawing rough lumber and timber from logs and bolts, or resawing cants and flitches into lumber, including box lumber and softwood cut stock; planing mills combined with sawmills; and separately operated planing mills which are engaged primarily in producing surfaced lumber and standard workings or patterns of lumber. This industry includes establishments primarily engaged in sawing lath and railroad ties

Industry
Group   Industry
No.   No.

242   SAWMILLS AND PLANING MILLS—Con.

2421   Sawmills and Planing Mills, General—Con.

and in producing tobacco hogshead stock, wood chips, and snow fence lath. Establishments primarily engaged in manufacturing box shook or boxes are classified in Industry Group 244; those manufacturing sash, doors, wood molding, window and door frames, and other fabricated millwork are classified in Industry Group 243; and those manufacturing hardwood dimension and flooring are classified in Industry 2426.

Cants, resawed (lumber)
Ceiling lumber, dressed
Chipper mills
Custom sawmills
Cut stock, softwood
Flitches (veneer stock), made in sawmills
Flooring (dressed lumber), softwood
Fuelwood, from mill waste
Furniture dimension stock, softwood
Kiln drying of lumber
Lath, made in sawmills and lathmills
Lumber stacking or sticking
Lumber: rough, sawed, or planed

Planing mills, independent: except millwork
Resawing lumber into smaller dimensions
Sawdust and shavings
Sawmills, except special product mills
Siding, dressed lumber
Silo stock, wood: sawed
Snow fence lath
Stud mills
Ties, railroad: sawed
Tobacco hogshead stock
Wood chips produced at mill

2426   Hardwood Dimension and Flooring Mills

Establishments primarily engaged in manufacturing hardwood dimension lumber and workings therefrom; and other hardwood dimension, semifabricated or ready for assembly; hardwood flooring; and wood frames for household furniture. Establishments primarily engaged in manufacturing stairwork, molding, and trim are classified in Industry 2431; and those manufacturing textile machinery bobbins, picker sticks, and shuttles are classified in Industry 3552.

Blanks, wood: for bowling pins, handles, and textile machinery accessories
Blocks, wood: for bowling pins, handles, and textile machinery accessories
Bobbin blocks and blanks, wood
Brush blocks, wood: turned and shaped
Carvings, furniture: wood
Chair frames for upholstered furniture, wood
Chair seats, hardwood
Dimension, hardwood
Flooring, hardwood
Frames for upholstered furniture, wood
Furniture dimension stock, hardwood
Furniture squares, hardwood

Furniture turnings and carvings, wood
Gun stocks, wood
Handle blanks, wood
Handle stock, sawed or planed
Lumber, hardwood dimension
Parquet flooring, hardwood
Picker stick blanks
Rounds or rungs, ladder and furniture: hardwood
Shuttle blocks: hardwood
Spool blocks and blanks, wood
Stock, chair: hardwood—turned, shaped, or carved
Table slides, for extension tables: wood
Turnings, furniture: wood
Vehicle stock, hardwood

2429   Special Product Sawmills, Not Elsewhere Classified

Mills primarily engaged in manufacturing excelsior, wood shingles, and cooperage stock; and in sawing special products, not elsewhere classified.

Barrel heading and staves, sawed or split
Cooperage stock mills
Cooperage stock: staves, heading, and hoops—sawed or split
Excelsior, including pads and wrappers: wood
Hoops, wood: for tight or slack cooperage—sawed or split

Sawmills, special product: except lumber and veneer mills
Shakes (hand split shingles)
Shingle mills, wood
Shingles, wood: sawed or hand split
Wood wool (excelsior)
Wrappers, excelsior

**243   MILLWORK, VENEER, PLYWOOD, AND STRUCTURAL WOOD
              MEMBERS**

2431 Millwork

Establishments primarily engaged in manufacturing fabricated wood millwork, including wood millwork covered with materials such as metal and plastics. Planing mills primarily engaged in producing millwork are included in
this industry, but planing mills primarily producing standard workings or patterns of lumber are classified in Industry 2421. Establishments primarily manufacturing wood kitchen cabinets and bathroom vanities for permanent installation are classified in Industry 2434.

Awnings, wood	Porch work, wood
Blinds (shutters), wood	Railings, stair: wood
Brackets, wood	Sash, door and window: wood and cov-
Door jambs, wood	ered wood
Door trim, wood	Screens, door and window: wood
Door units, prehung: wood and covered	Shutters, door and window: wood and
wood	covered wood
Doors, combination screen-storm: wood	Silo staves, wood
Doors, wood and covered wood	Staircases and stairs, wood
Floor baseboards, wood	Trellises, wood
Garage doors, overhead: wood	Trim, wood and covered wood
Jalousies, glass: wood frame	Venetian blind slats, wood
Louver windows and doors, glass with	Wainscots, wood
wood frame	Weather strip, wood
Millwork products	Window frames and sash, wood and
Moldings, wood and covered wood: un-	covered wood
finished and prefinished	Window screens, wood
Newel posts, wood	Window trim, wood and covered wood
Ornamental woodwork: e.g., cornices	Window units, wood and covered wood
and mantels	Woodwork, interior and ornamental:
Panel work, wood	e.g., windows, doors, sash, and man-
Planing mills, millwork	tels

2434 Wood Kitchen Cabinets

Establishments primarily engaged in manufacturing wood kitchen cabinets
and wood bathroom vanities, generally for permanent installation. Establishments primarily engaged in manufacturing free-standing cabinets and vanities
are classified in Major Group 25. Establishments primarily engaged in building custom cabinets for individuals are classified in Retail Trade, Industry
5712.

Cabinets, wood: to be installed	Vanities, bathroom, wood: to be in-
Kitchen cabinets, wood: to be installed	stalled

2435 Hardwood Veneer and Plywood

Establishments primarily engaged in producing commercial hardwood
veneer and those primarily engaged in manufacturing commercial plywood or
prefinished hardwood plywood. This includes nonwood backed or faced veneer
and nonwood faced plywood, from veneer produced in the same establishment
or from purchased veneer. Establishments primarily engaged in the production of veneer which is used in the same establishment for the manufacture of
wood containers, such as fruit and vegetable baskets and wood boxes are classified in Industry Group 244.

Hardwood plywood composites	Plywood, hardwood or hardwood faced
Hardwood veneer or plywood	Prefinished hardwood plywood
Panels, hardwood plywood	Veneer mills, hardwood

243   **MILLWORK, VENEER, PLYWOOD, AND STRUCTURAL WOOD
             MEMBERS—Con.**

2436   **Softwood Veneer and Plywood**

Establishments primarily engaged in producing commercial softwood veneer and plywood, from veneer produced in the same establishment or from purchased veneer. Establishments primarily engaged in producing commercial hardwood veneer and plywood are classified in Industry 2435. Establishments primarily engaged in the production of veneer which is used in the same establishment for the manufacture of wood containers such as fruit and vegetable baskets and wood boxes are classified in Industry Group 244.

Panels, softwood plywood	Softwood veneer or plywood
Plywood, softwood	Veneer mills, softwood
Softwood plywood composites	

2439   **Structural Wood Members, Not Elsewhere Classified**

Establishments primarily engaged in producing laminated or fabricated trusses, arches, and other structural members of lumber. Establishments primarily engaged in fabrication on the site of construction are classified in Division C, Construction. Establishments primarily engaged in producing prefabricated wood buildings, sections, and panels are classified in Industry 2452.

Structural members, laminated wood:	Trusses, wood
arches, trusses, timbers, and parallel	
chord ceilings	

244   **WOOD CONTAINERS**

2441   **Nailed and Lock Corner Wood Boxes and Shook**

Establishments primarily engaged in manufacturing nailed and lock corner wood boxes (lumber or plywood), and shook for nailed and lock corner boxes.

Ammunition boxes, wood	Flats, wood: greenhouse
Box cleats, wood	Packing cases, wood: nailed or lock corner
Boxes, wood: plain or fabric covered, nailed or lock corner	Shipping cases, wood: nailed or lock corner
Carrier trays, wood	Shook, box
Chests for tools, wood	Trunk slats, wood
Cigar boxes, wood and part wood	
Egg cases, wood	

2448   **Wood Pallets and Skids**

Establishments primarily engaged in manufacturing wood or wood and metal combination pallets and skids.

Pallet containers, wood or wood and metal combination	Pallets, wood or wood and metal combination

2449   **Wood Containers, Not Elsewhere Classified**

Establishments primarily engaged in manufacturing wood containers, not elsewhere classified, such as cooperage, wirebound boxes and crates, and other veneer and plywood containers. Establishments primarily engaged in manufacturing tobacco hogshead stock are classified in Industry 2421, and those manufacturing cooperage stock are classified in Industry 2429.

Barrels, wood: coopered	Buckets, wood: coopered
Baskets, fruit and vegetable: e.g., till, berry, climax, round stave	Casks, wood: coopered
Berry cups, veneer and splint	Chicken coops (crates), wood: wirebound for shipping poultry
Boxes, wood: wirebound	Climax baskets

Industry Group No.	Industry No.	
244		**WOOD CONTAINERS—Con.**
	2449	**Wood Containers, Not Elsewhere Classified—Con.**

Containers made of staves	Kegs, wood: coopered
Containers, veneer and plywood: except nailed and lock corner boxes	Kits, wood: coopered
	Market baskets, fruit and vegetable: veneer and splint
Cooperage	Pails, plywood
Coopered tubs	Pails, wood: coopered
Crates: berry, butter, fruit, and vegetable—wood, wirebound	Splint baskets, for fruits and vegetables
Drums, plywood	Tanks, wood: coopered
Drums, shipping: wood—wirebound	Tierces (cooperage)
Firkins and kits, wood: coopered	Till baskets, veneer and splint
Fruit baskets, veneer and splint	Tobacco hogsheads
Hampers, fruit and vegetable: veneer and splint	Tubs, wood: coopered
	Vats, wood: coopered
Hogsheads, wood: coopered	Vegetable baskets, veneer and splint
Hot tubs, coopered	

245   WOOD BUILDINGS AND MOBILE HOMES

2451   Mobile Homes

Establishments primarily engaged in manufacturing mobile homes and non-residential mobile buildings. These units are generally more than 35 feet long, at least 8 feet wide, do not have facilities for storage of water or waste, and are equipped with wheels. Trailers that are generally 35 feet long or less, 8 feet wide or less, and with self-contained facilities are classified in Industry 3792. Portable wood buildings not equipped with wheels are classified in Industry 2452.

Buildings, mobile: commercial use	Mobile classrooms
Mobile buildings for commercial use (e.g., offices, banks)	Mobile dwellings
	Mobile homes, except recreational

2452   Prefabricated Wood Buildings and Components

Establishments primarily engaged in manufacturing prefabricated wood buildings, sections, and panels. Establishments primarily engaged in fabricating buildings on the site of construction are classified in Division C, Construction.

Buildings, prefabricated and portable: wood	Houses, portable: prefabricated wood—except mobile homes
Chicken coops, prefabricated: wood	Log cabins, prefabricated: wood
Corn cribs, prefabricated: wood	Marinas, prefabricated: wood
Farm buildings, prefabricated or portable: wood	Panels for prefabricated wood buildings
	Sauna rooms, prefabricated: wood
Floors, prefabricated: wood	Sections for prefabricated wood buildings
Geodesic domes, prefabricated: wood	

249   MISCELLANEOUS WOOD PRODUCTS

2491   Wood Preserving

Establishments primarily engaged in treating wood, sawed or planed in other establishments, with creosote or other preservatives to prevent decay and to protect against fire and insects. This industry also includes the cutting, treating, and selling of poles, posts, and piling, but establishments primarily engaged in manufacturing other wood products, which they may also treat with preservatives, are not included.

Bridges and trestles, wood: treated	Millwork, treated
Creosoting of wood	Mine props, treated
Crossties, treated	Mine ties, wood: treated
Flooring, wood block: treated	Piles, foundation and marine construc-

Industry Group No.	Industry No.	

249

MISCELLANEOUS WOOD PRODUCTS—Con.

2491 Wood Preserving—Con.

tion: treated
Piling, wood: treated
Poles and pole crossarms, treated
Poles, cutting and preserving
Posts, wood: treated
Preserving of wood (creosoting)
Railroad cross bridge and switch ties, treated

Railway crossties, wood: treated
Structural lumber and timber, treated
Vehicle lumber, treated
Wood fence: pickets, poling, rails—treated
Wood products, creosoted

2493 Reconstituted Wood Products

Establishments primarily engaged in manufacturing reconstituted wood products. Important products of this industry are hardboard, particleboard, insulation board, medium density fiberboard, waferboard, and oriented strandboard.

Board, bagasse
Flakeboard
Hardboard
Insulating siding, board—mitse
Insulation board, cellular fiber or hard pressed (without gypsum)—mitse
Lath, fiber
MDF (medium density fiberboard)

Medium density fiberboard (MDF)
Particleboard
Reconstituted wood panels
Strandboard, oriented
Waferboard
Wall tile, fiberboard
Wallboard, wood fiber: cellular fiber or hard pressed—mitse

2499 Wood Products, Not Elsewhere Classified

Establishments primarily engaged in manufacturing miscellaneous wood products, not elsewhere classified, and products from rattan, reed, splint, straw, veneer, veneer strips, wicker, and willow.

Applicators, wood
Bakers' equipment, wood
Baskets, except fruit, vegetable, fish, and bait: (e.g., rattan, reed, straw)
Battery separators, wood
Bearings, wood
Beekeeping supplies, wood
Bentwood (steam bent) products, except furniture
Blocks, tackle: wood
Blocks, tailors' pressing: wood
Boards, bulletin: wood and cork
Boards: clip, ironing, meat, and pastry—wood
Boot and shoe lasts, regardless of material
Bowls, wood: turned and shaped
Briquettes, sawdust or bagasse: nonpetroleum binder
Bungs, wood
Buoys, cork
Bushings, wood
Cane, chair: woven of reed or rattan
Carpets, cork
Cloth winding reels, wood
Clothes dryers (clothes horses), wood
Clothes drying frames, wood
Clothespins, wood
Clubs, police: wood
Cooling towers, wood or wood and sheet metal combination
Cork products
Corks, bottle
Covers, bottle and demijohn: willow, rattan, and reed
Curtain stretchers, wood
Dishes, wood
Display forms for boots and shoes, regardless of material

Dowels, wood
Extension planks, wood
Faucets, wood
Fellies, wood
Fencing, wood: except rough pickets, poles, and rails
Firewood and fuel wood containing fuel binder
Flour, wood
Frames: medallion, mirror, photograph, and picture—wood or metal
Furniture inlays (veneers)
Garment hangers, wood
Gavels, wood
Grain measures, wood: turned and shaped
Hammers, meat: wood
Hampers, laundry: rattan, reed, splint, veneer, and willow
Handles, wood: turned and shaped
Hubs, wood
Insulating materials, cork
Jacks, ladder: wood
Knobs, wood
Ladders, wood
Last sole patterns, regardless of material
Letters, wood
Life preservers, cork
Mallets, wood
Market baskets, except fruit and vegetable: veneer and splint
Marquetry, wood
Mashers, potato: wood
Masts, wood
Mauls, wood
Moldings, picture frame: finished
Novelties, wood fiber
Oars, wood

Industry Group No.	Industry No.	
249		**MISCELLANEOUS WOOD PRODUCTS—Con.**
	2499	**Wood Products, Not Elsewhere Classified—Con.**

Pads, table: rattan, reed, and willow
Paint sticks, wood
Pencil slats
Plugs, wood
Poles, wood: e.g., clothesline, tent, flag
Pressed logs of sawdust and other wood particles, nonpetroleum binder
Pulleys, wood
Racks, for drying clothes: wood
Rattan ware, except furniture
Reed ware, except furniture
Reels, cloth winding: wood
Reels, for drying clothes: wood
Reels, plywood
Rollers, wood
Rolling pins, wood
Rules and rulers: wood, except slide
Saddle trees, wood
Sawdust, reground
Scaffolds, wood
Scoops, wood
Seat covers, rattan
Seats, toilet: wood
Shoe stretchers, regardless of material
Shoe trees, regardless of material

Signboards, wood
Skewers, wood
Snow fence
Spars, wood
Spigots, wood
Spokes, wood
Spools, except for textile machinery: wood
Stakes, surveyors': wood
Stepladders, wood
Stoppers, cork
Tile, cork
Tool handles, wood: turned and shaped
Toothpicks, wood
Trays: wood, wicker, and bagasse
Trophy bases, wood
Vats, wood: except coopered
Washboards, wood and part wood
Webbing: cane, reed, and rattan
Willow ware, except furniture
Wood, except furniture: turned and carved
Woodenware, kitchen and household
Yardsticks, wood

Major Group 25.—FURNITURE AND FIXTURES

The Major Group as a Whole

This major group includes establishments engaged in manufacturing household, office, public building, and restaurant furniture; and office and store fixtures. Establishments primarily engaged in the production of millwork are classified in Industry 2431; those manufacturing wood kitchen cabinets are classified in Industry 2434; those manufacturing cut stone and concrete furniture are classified in Major Group 32; those manufacturing laboratory and hospital furniture, except hospital beds, are classified in Major Group 38; those manufacturing beauty and barber shop furniture are classified in Major Group 39; and those engaged in woodworking to individual order or in the nature of reconditioning and repair are classified in nonmanufacturing industries.

Industry Group No.	Industry No.	

251   HOUSEHOLD FURNITURE

2511   Wood Household Furniture, Except Upholstered

Establishments primarily engaged in manufacturing wood household furniture commonly used in dwellings. This industry also includes establishments manufacturing camp furniture. Establishments engaged in manufacturing upholstered furniture are classified in Industry 2512; those manufacturing reed, rattan, and similar furniture are classified in Industry 2519; those manufacturing television, radio, phonograph, and sewing machine cabinets are classified in Industry 2517; and those manufacturing kitchen cabinets and bathroom vanities are classified in Industry 2434.

Beds, including folding and cabinet beds: household—wood
Bookcases, household: wood
Breakfast sets (furniture), wood
Bridge sets (furniture), wood
Buffets (furniture)
Cedar chests
Chairs, bentwood
Chairs, household: except upholstered—wood
Chests, silverware: wood (floor standing)
Chiffoniers and chifforobes
China closets
Coffee tables, wood
Console tables, wood
Cots, household: wood
Cradles, wood
Cribs, wood
Desks, household: wood
Dining room furniture, wood
Dressers
Dressing tables
End tables, wood
Frames for box springs, bedsprings, or water beds: wood
Furniture, household, wood: porch, lawn, garden, and beach

Furniture, household, wood: unassembled or knock-down
Furniture, household, wood: unfinished
Furniture: household, clubroom, novelty—wood, except upholstered
Headboards, wood
High chairs, children's: wood
Juvenile furniture, wood: except upholstered
Magazine racks, wood
Nursery furniture, wood
Playpens, children's: wood
Rockers, wood: except upholstered
Room dividers, household: wood
Screens, privacy: wood
Secretaries, household: wood
Stands: telephone, bedside, and smoking—wood
Stools, household: wood
Storage chests, household: wood
Swings, porch: wood
Tables, household: wood
Tea wagons, wood
Vanity dressers
Wardrobes, household: wood
Whatnot shelves, wood

2512   Wood Household Furniture, Upholstered

Establishments primarily engaged in manufacturing upholstered furniture on wood frames. Shops primarily engaged in reupholstering furniture, or up-

Industry
Group   Industry
No.   No.

251   HOUSEHOLD FURNITURE—Con.

2512   Wood Household Furniture, Upholstered—Con.

holstering frames to individual order, are classified in Services, Industry 7641, or Retail Trade, Industry 5712. Establishments primarily engaged in manufacturing dual-purpose sleep furniture, such as convertible sofas and chair beds, are classified in Industry 2515, regardless of the material used in the frame. Establishments primarily engaged in manufacturing wood frames for upholstered furniture are classified in Industry 2426.

Chairs, upholstered on wood frames, except convertible beds	Living room furniture, upholstered on wood frames, except convertible beds
Couches, upholstered on wood frames, except convertible beds	Recliners, upholstered on wood frames
	Rockers, upholstered on wood frames
Furniture, household: upholstered on wood frames, except convertible beds	Sofas, upholstered on wood frames, except convertible beds
Juvenile furniture, upholstered on wood frames, except convertible beds	

2514   Metal Household Furniture

Establishments primarily engaged in manufacturing metal household furniture of a type commonly used in dwellings. Establishments primarily engaged in manufacturing dual-purpose sleep furniture, such as convertible sofas and chair beds, are classified in Industry 2515, regardless of the material used in the frame.

Backs for metal household furniture	Garden furniture, metal
Beds, including folding and cabinet beds: household—metal	Gliders (furniture), metal
Bookcases, household: metal	Hammocks, metal or fabric and metal combination
Breakfast sets (furniture), metal	Juvenile furniture, metal
Bridge sets (furniture), metal	Lawn furniture, metal
Cabinets, kitchen: metal	Novelty furniture, metal
Cabinets, medicine: metal	Nursery furniture, metal
Cabinets, radio and television: metal	Playpens, children's: metal
Camp furniture, metal	Seats for metal household furniture
Chairs, household: metal	Serving carts, household: metal
Cots, household: metal	Smoking stands, metal
Cribs, metal	Stools, household: metal
Dinette sets, metal	Swings, porch: metal
Frames for box springs or bedsprings, metal	Tables, household: metal
Furniture, clubroom: metal	Tea wagons, metal
Furniture, household: metal	Vanities, household: metal
Furniture, household: upholstered on metal frames, except dual-purpose sleep furniture	

2515   Mattresses, Foundations, and Convertible Beds

Establishments primarily engaged in manufacturing innerspring mattresses, box spring mattresses, and noninnerspring mattresses containing felt, foam rubber, urethane, hair, or any other filling material; and assembled wire springs (fabric, coil, or box) for use on beds, couches, and cots. This industry also includes establishments primarily engaged in manufacturing dual-purpose sleep furniture, such as convertible sofas and chair beds, regardless of the material used in the frame. Establishments primarily engaged in manufacturing automobile seats and backs are classified in Industry 2531; those manufacturing individual wire springs are classified in Industry 3495; and those manufacturing paddings and upholstery filling are classified in Industry 2299.

Beds, sleep-system ensembles: flotation and adjustable	Beds, sofa and chair: on frames of any material

Industry Group No.	Industry No.	
251		**HOUSEHOLD FURNITURE—Con.**

2515　Mattresses, Foundations, and Convertible Beds—Con.

Bedsprings, assembled
Box springs, assembled
Chair and couch springs, assembled
Cot springs, assembled
Cushion springs, assembled
Cushions, spring
Foundations, bed: spring, foam, and platform
Mattresses, containing felt, foam rubber, urethane, etc.
Mattresses: innerspring, box spring, and noninnerspring
Sofas, convertible
Spring cushions

2517　Wood Television, Radio, Phonograph, and Sewing Machine Cabinets

Establishments primarily engaged in manufacturing wood cabinets for radios, television sets, phonographs, and sewing machines.

Audio cabinets, wood
Cabinets, wood: radio, television, phonograph, and sewing machines
Phonograph cabinets and cases, wood
Radio cabinets and cases, wood
Sewing machine cabinets and cases, wood
Stereo cabinets, wood
Television cabinets, wood

2519　Household Furniture, Not Elsewhere Classified

Establishments primarily engaged in manufacturing reed, rattan, and other wicker furniture, plastics and fiberglass household furniture and cabinets, and household furniture, not elsewhere classified.

Bassinets, reed and rattan
Cabinets, radio and television: plastics
Camp furniture, reed and rattan
Chairs, cane
Furniture, household: glass and plastics (including fiberglass)
Furniture, household: rattan, reed, malacca, fiber, willow, and wicker
Garden furniture: except wood, metal, stone, and concrete
Household furniture: rattan, reed, malacca, fiber, willow, and wicker
Juvenile furniture, rattan and reed
Lawn furniture: except wood, metal, stone, and concrete

| 252 | | **OFFICE FURNITURE** |

2521　Wood Office Furniture

Establishments primarily engaged in manufacturing office furniture, chiefly of wood.

Benches, office: wood
Bookcases, office: wood
Cabinets, office: wood
Chairs, office: wood
Desks, office: wood
Filing boxes, cabinets, and cases: wood
Furniture, office: wood
Modular furniture systems, office, wood
Panel furniture systems, office, wood
Partitions, office: not for floor attachment—wood
Stools, office: wood
Tables, office: wood

2522　Office Furniture, Except Wood

Establishments primarily engaged in manufacturing office furniture, except furniture chiefly of wood. Establishments primarily engaged in manufacturing safes and vaults are classified in Industry 3499.

Benches, office: except wood
Bookcases, office: except wood
Cabinets, office: except wood
Chairs, office: except wood
Desks, office: except wood
File drawer frames: except wood
Filing boxes, cabinets, and cases: except wood
Furniture, office: except wood
Modular furniture systems, office: except wood
Panel furniture systems, office: except wood
Partitions, office: not for floor attachment—except wood
Stools, office: rotating—except wood
Tables, office: except wood
Wall cases, office: except wood

Industry Group No.	Industry No.	
253		**PUBLIC BUILDING AND RELATED FURNITURE**
	2531	**Public Building and Related Furniture**

Establishments primarily engaged in manufacturing furniture for schools, theaters, assembly halls, churches, and libraries. Establishments primarily engaged in manufacturing seats for public conveyances, as well as seats for automobiles and aircraft, are included in this industry. Establishments primarily engaged in manufacturing stone furniture are classified in Industry 3281, and those manufacturing concrete furniture are classified in Industry 3272.

Benches for public buildings
Blackboards, wood
Bleacher seating, portable
Chairs, portable folding
Church furniture, except stone or concrete
Furniture: church, library, school, theater, and other public buildings

Pews, church
School furniture, except stone and concrete
Seats: automobile, vans, aircraft, railroad, and other public conveyances
Stadium seating

254		**PARTITIONS, SHELVING, LOCKERS, AND OFFICE AND STORE FIXTURES**
	2541	**Wood Office and Store Fixtures, Partitions, Shelving, and Lockers**

Establishments primarily engaged in manufacturing shelving, lockers, and office and store fixtures, plastics laminated fixture tops, and related fabricated products, chiefly of wood. Prefabricated partitions are included in this industry if designed to be attached to the floor and are classified in Industry 2521 if designed to be free-standing or part of an office furniture panel system. Establishments primarily engaged in manufacturing refrigerated cabinets, showcases, and display cases are classified in Industry 3585.

Bar fixtures, wood
Butchers' store fixtures, wood
Cabinets, show, display, and storage: except refrigerated—wood
Counters and counter display cases, except refrigerated—wood
Display cases and fixtures, not refrigerated: wood
Drainboards, plastics laminated
Fixture tops, plastics laminated
Fixtures, display: office and store—wood
Garment racks, wood
Lockers, not refrigerated: wood

Lunchroom fixtures, wood
Partitions, prefabricated: wood—for floor attachment
Pedestals, statuary: wood
Racks, merchandise display: wood
Shelving, office and store: wood
Showcases, not refrigerated: wood
Sink tops, plastics laminated
Store fronts, prefabricated: wood
Table or counter tops, plastics laminated
Telephone booths, wood
Window backs, store and lunchroom: prefabricated—wood

	2542	**Office and Store Fixtures, Partitions, Shelving, and Lockers, Except Wood**

Establishments primarily engaged in manufacturing office and store fixtures, shelving, storage racks, lockers, and related fabricated products, chiefly of materials other than wood. Prefabricated partitions are included in this industry if designed to be attached to the floor and are classified in Industry 2522 if designed to be free-standing or part of an office furniture panel system. Establishments primarily engaged in manufacturing refrigerated cabinets, showcases, and display cases are classified in Industry 3585 and those manufacturing safes and vaults are classified in Industry 3499.

Bar fixtures, except wood
Butchers' store fixtures, except wood
Cabinets, show, display, and storage: not refrigerated—except wood
Carrier cases and tables, mail: except wood

Counters and counter display cases, not refrigerated: except wood
Display cases and fixtures, not refrigerated: except wood
Fixtures, display: office and store—except wood

Industry Group No.	Industry No.	

254   PARTITIONS, SHELVING, LOCKERS, AND OFFICE AND STORE FIXTURES—Con.

2542   Office and Store Fixtures, Partitions, Shelving, and Lockers, Except Wood—Con.

Garment racks, except wood
Lockers, not refrigerated: except wood
Lunchroom fixtures, except wood
Mail pouch racks, except wood
Mailing racks, postal service: except wood
Pallet racks, except wood
Partitions, prefabricated: except wood and free-standing
Postal service lock boxes, except wood
Racks, merchandise display and storage: except wood
Shelving angles and slotted bars, except wood
Shelving, office and store: except wood
Showcases, not refrigerated: except wood
Sorting racks, mail: except wood
Stands, merchandise display: except wood
Telephone booths, except wood

259   MISCELLANEOUS FURNITURE AND FIXTURES

2591   Drapery Hardware and Window Blinds and Shades

Establishments primarily engaged in manufacturing curtain and drapery rods, poles, and fixtures; and venetian blinds and other window blinds and shades, except of canvas. Establishments primarily engaged in manufacturing canvas shades and awnings are classified in Industry 2394.

Blinds, venetian
Blinds, vertical
Curtain rods, poles, and fixtures
Drapery rods, poles, and fixtures
Porch shades, wood slat
Shade pulls, window
Shades, window: except canvas
Window shade rollers and fittings

2599   Furniture and Fixtures, Not Elsewhere Classified

Establishments primarily engaged in manufacturing furniture and fixtures, not elsewhere classified, including hospital beds and furniture specially designed for use in restaurants, bars, cafeterias, bowling centers, and ships.

Bar furniture
Beds, hospital
Bowling center furniture
Cafeteria furniture
Carts, restaurant
Dish carts, restaurant
Factory furniture: stools, work benches, tool stands, and cabinets
Food trucks, restaurant
Food wagons, restaurant
Restaurant furniture
Ship furniture
Stools, metal: with casters—not household or office
Tray trucks, restaurant
Work benches, industrial

Major Group 26.—PAPER AND ALLIED PRODUCTS

The Major Group as a Whole

This major group includes establishments primarily engaged in the manufacture of pulps from wood and other cellulose fibers, and from rags; the manufacture of paper and paperboard; and the manufacture of paper and paperboard into converted products, such as paper coated off the paper machine, paper bags, paper boxes, and envelopes. Also included are establishments primarily engaged in manufacturing bags of plastics film and sheet. Certain types of converted paper products are classified elsewhere, such as abrasive paper which is in Industry 3291; carbon paper in Industry 3955; and photosensitized and blueprint paper in Industry 3861.

Industry Group No.	Industry No.
261		**PULP MILLS**

2611 Pulp Mills

Establishments primarily engaged in manufacturing pulp from wood or from other materials, such as rags, linters, wastepaper, and straw. Establishments engaged in integrated logging and pulp mill operations are classified according to the primary products shipped. Establishments engaged in integrated operations of producing pulp and manufacturing paper, paperboard, or products thereof are classified in Industry 2621 if primarily shipping paper or paper products; in Industry 2631 if primarily shipping paperboard or paperboard products; and in Industry 2611 if primarily shipping pulp. Establishments primarily engaged in cutting pulpwood are classified in Industry 2411.

Deinking of newsprint
Fiber pulp: made from wood, rags, wastepaper, linters, straw, and bagasse
Pulp mills

Pulp: soda, sulfate, sulfite, groundwood, rayon, and semichemical
Rayon pulp
Wood pulp

262 **PAPER MILLS**

2621 Paper Mills

Establishments primarily engaged in manufacturing paper from wood pulp and other fiber pulp, and which may also manufacture converted paper products. Establishments primarily engaged in integrated operations of producing pulp and manufacturing paper are included in this industry if primarily shipping paper or paper products. Establishments primarily engaged in manufacturing converted paper products from purchased paper stock are classified in Industry Group 265 or 267.

Absorbent paper—mitse
Asbestos paper and asbestos filled paper—mitse
Asphalt paper: laminated—mitse
Asphalt sheathing—mitse
Bag paper—mitse
Blotting paper—mitse
Bond paper—mitse
Book paper—mitse
Bristols, except bogus—mitse
Building paper: sheathing, insulation, saturating, and dry felts—mitse
Capacitor paper—mitse

Catalog paper—mitse
Cigarette paper—mitse
Cleansing tissue stock—mitse
Condenser paper—mitse
Construction paper—mitse
Cotton fiber paper—mitse
Cover paper—mitse
Dry felts, except textile—mitse
Facial tissue stock—mitse
Felts, building—mitse
Filter paper—mitse
Glassine wrapping paper—mitse
Greaseproof wrapping paper—mitse

Industry Group No.	Industry No.	

262　　PAPER MILLS—Con.

2621　Paper Mills—Con.

Groundwood paper—mitse
Hanging paper (wallpaper stock)—mitse
Kraft sheathing paper—mitse
Kraft wrapping paper—mitse
Lining paper—mitse
Lithograph paper—mitse
Manila wrapping paper—mitse
Matrix paper—mitse
Milk filter disks—mitse
Napkin stock, paper—mitse
News tablet paper—mitse
Newsprint—mitse
Offset paper—mitse
Paper mills—mitse
Paper, building—mitse
Paper—mitse
Parchment paper—mitse
Poster paper—mitse

Printing paper—mitse
Publication paper—mitse
Roofing felt stock—mitse
Rope and jute wrapping paper—mitse
Rotogravure paper—mitse
Saturated felts—mitse
Shipping sack paper—mitse
Tagboard, made in paper mills—mitse
Tar paper, building and roofing—mitse
Text paper—mitse
Thin paper—mitse
Tissue paper—mitse
Toilet tissue stock—mitse
Toweling paper—mitse
Wallpaper stock (hanging paper)—mitse
Wrapping paper—mitse
Writing paper—mitse

263　　PAPERBOARD MILLS

2631　Paperboard Mills

Establishments primarily engaged in manufacturing paperboard, including paperboard coated on the paperboard machine, from wood pulp and other fiber pulp; and which may also manufacture converted paperboard products. Establishments primarily engaged in integrated operations of producing pulp and manufacturing paperboard are included in this industry if primarily shipping paperboard or paperboard products. Establishments primarily engaged in manufacturing converted paperboard products from purchased paperboard are classified in Industry Group 265 or 267. Establishments primarily engaged in manufacturing insulation board and other reconstituted wood fiberboard are classified in Industry 2493.

Binders' board—mitse
Bottle cap board—mitse
Boxboard—mitse
Bristols, bogus—mitse
Cardboard—mitse
Chipboard (paperboard)—mitse
Clay coated board—mitse
Container board—mitse
Folding boxboards—mitse
Leatherboard—mitse
Liner board, kraft and jute—mitse
Manila lined board—mitse
Matrix board—mitse
Milk carton board—mitse
Newsboard—mitse

Paperboard mills, except building board mills
Paperboard, except building board—mitse
Patent coated paperboard—mitse
Pressboard—mitse
Setup boxboard—mitse
Shoe board—mitse
Special food board—mitse
Stencil board—mitse
Strawboard, except building board—mitse
Tagboard—mitse
Wet machine board—mitse

265　　PAPERBOARD CONTAINERS AND BOXES

2652　Setup Paperboard Boxes

Establishments primarily engaged in manufacturing setup paperboard boxes from purchased paperboard.

Boxes, newsboard: metal edged—mfpm
Boxes, setup paperboard—mfpm

Filing boxes, paperboard—mfpm

2653　Corrugated and Solid Fiber Boxes

Establishments primarily engaged in manufacturing corrugated and solid fiber boxes and related products from purchased paperboard of fiber stock. Im-

Industry
Group
No.
265

Industry
No.

PAPERBOARD CONTAINERS AND BOXES—Con.

2653 Corrugated and Solid Fiber Boxes—Con.

portant products of this industry include corrugated and solid fiberboard boxes, pads, partitions, display items, pallets, single face products, and corrugated sheets.

Boxes, corrugated and solid fiber—mfpm
Containers, corrugated and solid fiber-board—mfpm
Display items, corrugated and solid fiberboard—mfpm
Hampers, shipping: paperboard and solid fiber—mfpm

Pads, corrugated and solid fiberboard—mfpm
Pallets, corrugated and solid fiber-board—mfpm
Partitions, corrugated and solid fiber-board—mfpm
Sheets, corrugated and solid fiber-board—mfpm

2655 Fiber Cans, Tubes, Drums, and Similar Products

Establishments primarily engaged in manufacturing from purchased materials fiber cans, cones, drums, and similar products, with or without metal ends, and vulcanized fiber boxes.

Ammunition cans or tubes, paperboard laminated with metal foil—mfpm
Bobbins, fiber—mfpm
Bottles, paper fiber—mfpm
Boxes, vulcanized fiber—mfpm
Candelabra tubes, fiber—mfpm
Cans, composite: foil-fiber and other combinations—mfpm
Cans, fiber (metal-end or all-fiber)—mfpm
Cases, mailing: paper fiber (metal-end or all-fiber)—mfpm
Cones, fiber: for winding yarn, string, ribbons, or cloth—mfpm
Containers, laminated phenolic and vulcanized fiber—mfpm
Containers, liquid tight fiber (except sanitary food containers)—mfpm
Cores, fiber (metal-end or all-fiber)—mfpm

Drums, fiber (metal-end or all-fiber)—mfpm
Hampers, shipping: vulcanized fiber—mfpm
Mailing cases and tubes, paper fiber (metal-end or all-fiber)—mfpm
Pans and voids, fiber or cardboard—mfpm
Ribbon blocks, fiber—mfpm
Spools, fiber (metal-end or all-fiber)—mfpm
Textile reels, fiber—mfpm
Textile spinning bobbins, fiber (metal-end or all-fiber)—mfpm
Tubes, fiber or paper (with or without metal ends)—mfpm
Tubes, for chemical and electrical uses: impregnated paper or fiber—mfpm
Wastebaskets, fiber (metal-end or all-fiber)—mfpm

2656 Sanitary Food Containers, Except Folding

Establishments primarily engaged in manufacturing nonfolding food containers from special foodboard. Important products of this industry include fluid milk containers, round nested food containers, paper cups for hot or cold drinks, and stamped plates, dishes, spoons, and similar products. Establishments primarily engaged in manufacturing similar items of plastics materials are classified in Industry Group 308 and those making folding sanitary cartons are classified in Industry 2657.

Containers, food, sanitary: except folding—mfpm
Cups, paper: except those made from pressed or molded pulp—mfpm
Dishes, paper: except those made from pressed or molded pulp—mfpm
Drinking cups, paper: except those made from pressed or molded pulp—mfpm
Drinking straws, except glass or plastics—mfpm
Food containers, nonfolding paperboard, sanitary—mfpm
Food containers, sanitary: except folding—mfpm

Frozen food containers, nonfolding paperboard—mfpm
Ice cream containers, nonfolding paper-board—mfpm
Milk cartons, paperboard—mfpm
Plates, paper: except those made from pressed or molded pulp—mfpm
Soda straws, except glass or plastics—mfpm
Spoons, paper: except those made from pressed or molded pulp—mfpm
Utensils, paper: except those made from pressed or molded pulp—mfpm

Industry Group No.	Industry No.

265   PAPERBOARD CONTAINERS AND BOXES—Con.

2657   Folding Paperboard Boxes, Including Sanitary

Establishments primarily engaged in manufacturing folding paperboard boxes from purchased paperboard, including folding sanitary food boxes or cartons except milk cartons.

Boxes, folding paperboard—mfpm
Cartons, folding, except milk cartons: paperboard—mfpm
Frozen food containers, folding paperboard—mfpm
Ice cream containers, folding paperboard—mfpm

Pails, folding sanitary food: paperboard—mfpm
Paperboard backs for blister or skin packages—mfpm

267   CONVERTED PAPER AND PAPERBOARD PRODUCTS, EXCEPT CONTAINERS AND BOXES

2671   Packaging Paper and Plastics Film, Coated and Laminated

Establishments primarily engaged in manufacturing coated or laminated flexible materials made of combinations of paper, plastics film, metal foil, and similar materials (excluding textiles) for packaging purposes. These are made from purchased sheet materials or plastics resins and may be printed in the same establishment. Establishments primarily engaged in manufacturing coated or laminated paper for other purposes are classified in Industry 2672, including establishments manufacturing all gummed or pressure sensitive tape; those manufacturing unsupported plastics film are classified in Industry 3081; those manufacturing aluminum foil are classified in Industry 3497; and those manufacturing paper from pulp are classified in Industry 2621.

Bread wrappers, waxed or laminated—mfpm
Coated paper for packaging—mfpm
Metallic covered paper for packaging—mfpm
Paper, coated or laminated: for packaging—mfpm
Plastics film, coated or laminated: for packaging—mfpm

Resinous impregnated paper for packaging—mfpm
Thermoplastics coated paper for packaging—mfpm
Waxed paper for packaging—mfpm
Wrapping paper, coated or laminated—mfpm

2672   Coated and Laminated Paper, Not Elsewhere Classified

Establishments primarily engaged in manufacturing coated, laminated, or processed paper and film from purchased paper, except for packaging. Also included are establishments primarily manufacturing gummed paper products and pressure sensitive tape with backing of any material other than rubber, for any application. Establishments primarily engaged in manufacturing coated and laminated paper for packaging are classified in Industry 2671; those manufacturing carbon paper are classified in Industry 3955; and those manufacturing photographic and blueprint paper are classified in Industry 3861.

Book paper, coated—mfpm
Cellophane adhesive tape—mfpm
Cloth-lined paper—mfpm
Condenser paper—mfpm
Enameled paper—mfpm
Fancy paper, coated and glazed: except for packaging—mfpm
Flypaper—mfpm
Gummed paper—mfpm
Gummed tape, cloth and paper base—mfpm

Litmus paper—mfpm
Masking tape—mfpm
Metallic covered paper, except for packaging—mfpm
Oiled paper—mfpm
Paper, coated and laminated: except for packaging—mfpm
Pressure sensitive paper and tape, except rubber backed—mfpm
Printing paper, coated—mfpm
Resinous impregnated paper, except for

267   **CONVERTED PAPER AND PAPERBOARD PRODUCTS, EXCEPT
               CONTAINERS AND BOXES—Con.**

2672   Coated and Laminated Paper, Not Elsewhere Classified—Con.

packaging—mfpm
Tape, pressure sensitive: except rubber
  backed—mfpm
Tar paper: except building or roofing
  and packaging—mfpm

Thermoplastics coated paper, except for
  packaging—mfpm
Transfer paper, gold and silver—mfpm
Waxed paper, except for packaging—
  mfpm

2673   Plastics, Foil, and Coated Paper Bags

Establishments primarily engaged in manufacturing bags of unsupported plastics film, coated paper, metal foil, or laminated combinations of these materials, whether or not printed. Establishments primarily engaged in manufacturing uncoated paper bags and multiwall bags and sacks are classified in Industry 2674; those manufacturing textile bags are classified in Industry 2393; and those manufacturing garment storage bags, except of plastics film and paper, are classified in Industry 2392.

Frozen food bags—mfpm
Garment storage bags, coated paper or
  plastics film—mfpm
Merchandise bags, plastics—mfpm
Pliofilm bags—mfpm
Trash bags, plastics film, foil, and
  coated paper—mfpm

Wardrobe bags (closet accessories), plastics film or coated paper—mfpm
Waste bags, plastics film and laminated—mfpm

2674   Uncoated Paper and Multiwall Bags

Establishments primarily engaged in manufacturing uncoated paper bags, or manufacturing multiwall bags and sacks, whether or not coated or containing plastics film or metal foil. Establishments primarily engaged in manufacturing bags from plastics, unsupported film, foil, coated paper, or laminated or coated combinations of these materials, are classified in Industry 2673; and those manufacturing textile bags are classified in Industry 2393.

Bags, paper: uncoated—mfpm
Glassine bags, uncoated paper—mfpm
Grocers' bags and sacks, uncoated
  paper—mfpm
Merchandise bags, uncoated paper—
  mfpm

Multiwall bags, paper—mfpm
Sacks, multiwall or heavy-duty ship-
  ping sack—mfpm
Shipping sacks, paper—mfpm
Shopping bags, uncoated paper—mfpm
Variety bags, uncoated paper—mfpm

2675   Die-Cut Paper and Paperboard and Cardboard

Establishments primarily engaged in die-cutting purchased paper and paperboard; and in manufacturing cardboard by laminating, lining, or surface-coating paperboard. Establishments primarily engaged in laminating building paper from purchased paper are classified in Industry 2679.

Board, chip: pasted—mfpm
Bottle caps and tops, die-cut from pur-
  chased paper or paperboard
Card cutting—mfpm
Cardboard foundations and cutouts—
  mfpm
Cardboard panels and cutouts—mfpm
Cardboard: pasted, laminated, lined,
  and surface coated—mfpm
Cards, cut and designed: unprinted—
  mfpm
Cards, plain paper: die-cut or rotary-cut
  from purchased materials
Cards, tabulating and time recording:
  die-cut from purchased paperboard

Cutouts, paper and paperboard: die-cut
  from purchased material
Die-cut paper and paperboard—mfpm
Egg cartons, die-cut paper and paper-
  board—mfpm
Egg case fillers and flats, die-cut from
  purchased paper or paperboard
Filing folders—mfpm
Index and other cut cards—mfpm
Jacquard cards—mfpm
Jewelers' cards—mfpm
Lace, paper: die-cut from purchased
  materials
Letters, cardboard—mfpm
Library cards, paperboard—mfpm

267   **CONVERTED PAPER AND PAPERBOARD PRODUCTS, EXCEPT CONTAINERS AND BOXES—Con.**

2675 Die-Cut Paper and Paperboard and Cardboard—Con.

Liners for freight car doors: reinforced with metal strip—mfpm
Manila folders—mfpm
Milk filter disks, die-cut from purchased paper
Newsboard, pasted—mfpm
Paperboard: pasted, lined, laminated, or surface coated—mfpm
Photograph folders, mats, and mounts—mfpm
Stencil board—mfpm
Stencil cards for addressing machines—mfpm
Tabulating cards, printed or unprinted: die-cut from purchased paperboard
Time recording cards, die-cut from purchased paperboard
Waterproof cardboard—mfpm

2676 Sanitary Paper Products

Establishments primarily engaged in manufacturing sanitary paper products from purchased paper, such as facial tissues and handkerchiefs, table napkins, toilet paper, towels, disposable diapers, and sanitary napkins and tampons.

Cleansing tissues—mfpm
Diapers, disposable—mfpm
Facial tissues—mfpm
Handkerchiefs, paper—mfpm
Napkins, paper—mfpm
Napkins, sanitary—mfpm
Tampons—mfpm
Toilet paper—mfpm
Towels, paper—mfpm

2677 Envelopes

Establishments primarily engaged in manufacturing envelopes of any description from purchased paper and paperboard. Establishments primarily engaged in manufacturing stationery are classified in Industry 2678.

Envelopes, printed or unprinted: paper, glassine, cellophane, and pliofilm—mfpm

2678 Stationery, Tablets, and Related Products

Establishments primarily engaged in manufacturing stationery, tablets, looseleaf fillers, and related items from purchased paper. Establishments primarily engaged in manufacturing envelopes are classified in Industry 2677.

Correspondence-type tablets—mfpm
Desk pads, paper—mfpm
Fillers for looseleaf devices, except printed forms—mfpm
Looseleaf fillers and ream paper in filler sizes, except printed—mfpm
Memorandum books, except printed—mfpm
Newsprint tablets and pads—mfpm
Notebooks, including mechanically bound by wire, plastics, etc.—mfpm
Papeteries—mfpm
Stationery—mfpm
Tablets and pads, book and writing—mfpm
Writing paper and envelopes, boxed sets—mfpm

2679 Converted Paper and Paperboard Products, Not Elsewhere Classified

Establishments primarily engaged in manufacturing miscellaneous converted paper or paperboard products, not elsewhere classified, from purchased paper or paperboard. Also included in this industry are pressed and molded pulp goods, such as papier-mache articles, other than statuary and art goods.

Building paper, laminated—mfpm
Cigarette paper, book—mfpm
Conduits, fiber (pressed pulp)—mfpm
Confetti—mfpm
Crepe paper—mfpm
Cups, pressed and molded pulp—mfpm
Dishes, pressed and molded pulp—mfpm
Doilies, paper—mfpm
Egg cartons, molded pulp—mfpm
Egg case filler flats, molded pulp—mfpm
Excelsior, paper—mfpm
False faces, papier-mache—mfpm
Filter paper, converted—mfpm
Foil board—mfpm

267 CONVERTED PAPER AND PAPERBOARD PRODUCTS, EXCEPT
CONTAINERS AND BOXES—Con.

2679 Converted Paper and Paperboard Products, Not Elsewhere Classified—Con.

Fuel cell forms, cardboard—mfpm
Gift wrap paper—mfpm
Halloween lanterns, papier-mache—
mfpm
Hats, paper—mfpm
Honeycomb core and board—mfpm
Insulating batts, fills, and blankets:
paper—mfpm
Insulation, cellulose—mfpm
Masks, papier-mache—mfpm
Novelties, paper—mfpm
Pallet spacers, fiber—mfpm
Paper, building: laminated—mfpm
Paper, corrugated—mfpm
Paper, crepe and crepe paper prod-
ucts—mfpm
Papier-mache articles, except statuary
and art goods—mfpm
Pin tickets, paper—mfpm
Pipe and fittings, molded pulp—mfpm

Plates, pressed and molded pulp—
mfpm
Pressed products from wood pulp—
mfpm
Pulp products, pressed and molded:
except statuary—mfpm
Rolls, paper: adding machine, telegraph
tape, etc.—mfpm
Spoons, pressed and molded pulp—
mfpm
Tags, paper: unprinted—mfpm
Telegraph tape, paper—mfpm
Teletypewriter paper, rolls with
carbon—mfpm
Utensils, pressed and molded pulp—
mfpm
Wallcoverings: paper—mfpm
Wallpaper, embossed plastics: made on
textile backing—mfpm
Wallpaper—mfpm

Major Group 27.—PRINTING, PUBLISHING, AND ALLIED INDUSTRIES

The Major Group as a Whole

This major group includes establishments engaged in printing by one or more common processes, such as letterpress; lithography (including offset), gravure, or screen; and those establishments which perform services for the printing trade, such as bookbinding and plate-making. This major group also includes establishments engaged in publishing newspapers, books, and periodicals, regardless of whether or not they do their own printing. News syndicates are classified in Services, Industry 7383. Establishments primarily engaged in textile printing and finishing fabrics are classified in Major Group 22, and those engaged in printing and stamping on fabric articles are classified in Industry 2396. Establishments manufacturing products that contain incidental printing, such as advertising or instructions, are classified according to the nature of the products—for example, as cartons, bags, plastics film, or paper.

Industry Group No.	Industry No.	

271 **NEWSPAPERS: PUBLISHING, OR PUBLISHING AND PRINTING**

2711 Newspapers: Publishing, or Publishing and Printing

Establishments primarily engaged in publishing newspapers, or in publishing and printing newspapers. These establishments carry on the various operations necessary for issuing newspapers, including the gathering of news and the preparation of editorials and advertisements, but may or may not perform their own printing. Commercial printing is frequently carried on by establishments engaged in publishing and printing newspapers, but, even though the commercial printing may be of major importance, such establishments are included in this industry. Establishments not engaged in publishing newspapers, but which print newspapers for publishers, are classified in Industry Group 275. News syndicates are classified in Services, Industry 7383.

Commercial printing and newspaper publishing combined
Job printing and newspaper publishing combined
Newspaper branch offices, editorial and advertising
Newspapers: publishing and printing, or publishing only

272 **PERIODICALS: PUBLISHING, OR PUBLISHING AND PRINTING**

2721 Periodicals: Publishing, or Publishing and Printing

Establishments primarily engaged in publishing periodicals, or in publishing and printing periodicals. These establishments carry on the various operations necessary for issuing periodicals, but may or may not perform their own printing. Establishments not engaged in publishing periodicals, but which print periodicals for publishers, are classified in Industry Group 275.

Comic books: publishing and printing, or publishing only
Magazines: publishing and printing, or publishing only
Periodicals: publishing and printing, or publishing only
Statistical reports (periodicals), publishing and printing, or publishing only
Television schedules: publishing and printing, or publishing only
Trade journals, publishing and printing, or publishing only

273   BOOKS

2731   Books: Publishing, or Publishing and Printing

Establishments primarily engaged in publishing, or in publishing and printing, books and pamphlets. Establishments primarily engaged in printing or in printing and binding (but not publishing) books and pamphlets are classified in Industry 2732.

Book club publishing and printing, or publishing only
Books: publishing and printing, or publishing only
Music books: publishing and printing, or publishing only

Pamphlets: publishing and printing, or publishing only
Textbooks: publishing and printing, or publishing only

2732   Book Printing

Establishments primarily engaged in printing, or in printing and binding, books and pamphlets, but not engaged in publishing. Establishments primarily engaged in publishing, or in publishing and printing, books and pamphlets are classified in Industry 2731. Establishments engaged in both printing and binding books, but primarily binding books printed elsewhere, are classified in Industry 2789.

Books: printing or printing and binding, not publishing
Music books: printing or printing and binding, not publishing

Pamphlets: printing or printing and binding, not publishing
Textbooks: printing or printing and binding, not publishing

274   MISCELLANEOUS PUBLISHING

2741   Miscellaneous Publishing

Establishments primarily engaged in miscellaneous publishing activities, not elsewhere classified, whether or not engaged in printing. Establishments primarily engaged in offering financial, credit, or other business services, and which may publish directories as part of this service, are classified in Division I, Services.

Atlases: publishing and printing, or publishing only
Business service newsletters: publishing and printing, or publishing only
Calendars: publishing and printing, or publishing only
Catalogs: publishing and printing, or publishing only
Directories: publishing and printing, or publishing only
Globe covers (maps): publishing and printing, or publishing only
Guides: publishing and printing, or publishing only
Maps: publishing and printing, or publishing only
Micropublishing
Multimedia educational kits: publishing and printing, or publishing only

Music, sheet: publishing and printing, or publishing only
Patterns, paper, including clothing patterns: publishing and printing, or publishing only
Race track programs: publishing and printing, or publishing only
Racing forms: publishing and printing, or publishing only
Shopping news: publishing and printing, or publishing only
Technical manuals and papers: publishing and printing, or publishing only
Telephone directories: publishing and printing, or publishing only
Yearbooks: publishing and printing, or publishing only

275   COMMERCIAL PRINTING

2752   Commercial Printing, Lithographic

Establishments primarily engaged in printing by the lithographic process. The greater part of the work in this industry is performed on a job or custom basis; but in some cases lithographed calendars, maps, posters, decalcomanias,

275   COMMERCIAL PRINTING—Con.

2752 Commercial Printing, Lithographic—Con.

or other products are made for sale. Offset printing, photo-offset printing, and photolithographing are also included in this industry. Establishments primarily engaged in lithographing books and pamphlets, without publishing, are classified in Industry 2732. Establishments primarily engaged in publishing or printing greeting cards are classified in Industry 2771. Establishments primarily engaged in preparing lithographic or offset plates and in related services are classified in Industry 2796. Establishments primarily engaged in providing photocopying services are classified in Services, Industry 7334.

Advertising posters, lithographed
Atlases, lithographed
Billheads, lithographed
Bread wrappers, lithographed
Business forms, except manifold: lithographed
Calendars, lithographed: not published
Cards, lithographed
Circulars, lithographed
Color cards, paint: offset printing
Color lithography
Coupons, lithographed
Decalcomanias (dry transfers), lithographed
Fashion plates, lithographed
Instant printing, except photocopy service
Labels, lithographed
Letters, circular and form: lithographed
Lithographing on metal or paper
Maps, lithographed
Menus, lithographed
Newspapers, lithographed: not published
Offset printing

Periodicals, lithographed: not published
Photo-offset printing
Photolithographing
Planographing
Playing cards, lithographed
Postcards, picture: lithographed
Posters, lithographed
Printing from lithographic or offset plates
Printing, commercial or job: lithographic and offset
Printing, lithographic
Quick printing, except photocopy service
Schedules, transportation: lithographed
Seals, lithographed
Souvenir cards, lithographed
Tags, lithographed
Tickets, lithographed
Trading stamps, lithographed
Transferring designs (lithographing)
Transfers, decalcomania and dry: lithographed
Visiting cards, lithographed
Wrappers, lithographed

2754 Commercial Printing, Gravure

Establishments primarily engaged in gravure printing. Establishments primarily engaged in making and preparing plates for printing are classified in Industry 2796.

Bread wrappers: gravure printing
Business forms, except manifold: gravure printing
Calendars, gravure printing: not publishing
Cards, except greeting: gravure printing
Catalogs: gravure printing (not publishing)
Circulars: gravure printing
Color printing: gravure
Coupons: gravure printing
Directories: gravure printing (not publishing)
Envelopes: gravure printing
Facsimile letters: gravure printing
Fashion plates: gravure printing
Gravure printing
Imprinting: gravure
Intaglio printing
Labels: gravure printing
Letters, circular and form: gravure printing
Magazines: gravure printing (not publishing)
Maps: gravure printing (not publishing)
Menus: gravure printing

Music, sheet: gravure printing (not publishing)
Newspapers: gravure printing (not publishing)
Periodicals: gravure printing (not publishing)
Photogravure printing
Playing cards: gravure printing
Postcards, picture: gravure printing
Posters: gravure printing
Printing, commercial or job: gravure
Printing: gravure, photogravure, rotary photogravure, and rotogravure
Rotary photogravure printing
Rotogravure printing
Schedules, transportation: gravure printing
Seals: gravure printing
Souvenir cards: gravure printing
Stationery: gravure printing
Telephone directories, gravure printing: not publishing
Tickets: gravure printing
Trading stamps: gravure printing
Visiting cards: gravure printing
Wrappers: gravure printing

275   COMMERCIAL PRINTING—Con.

2759   **Commercial Printing, Not Elsewhere Classified**

Establishments primarily engaged in commercial or job printing, not elsewhere classified. This industry includes general printing shops, not elsewhere
classified, as well as shops specializing in printing newspapers and periodicals
for others.

Announcements, engraved
Bags, plastics: printed only, except lith-
ographed or gravure (bags not made
in printing plants)
Banknotes, engraved
Bread wrappers, printed: except litho-
graphed or gravure
Business forms, except manifold, litho-
graphed or gravure printed
Calendars, printed: except lithographed
or gravure
Cards, except greeting cards: engraving
of
Cards, printed: except greeting, litho-
graphed or gravure
Catalogs, printed: except lithographed
or gravure (not publishing)
Circulars, printed: except lithographed
or gravure
Color printing: except lithographed or
gravure
Coupons, printed: except lithographed
or gravure
Currency, engraving of
Decalcomanias, printed: except litho-
graphed or gravure
Directories, printed: except litho-
graphed or gravure (not publishing)
Embossing on paper
Envelopes, printed: except lithographed
or gravure
Fashion plates, printed: except litho-
graphed or gravure
Flexographic printing
Gummed labels and seals, printed:
except lithographed or gravure
Halftones, engraved
Imprinting, except lithographed or gra-
vure
Invitations, engraved
Labels, printed: except lithographed or
gravure
Letterpress printing
Letters, circular and form: except litho-
graphed or gravure printed
Magazines, printed: except litho-
graphed or gravure (not publishing)
Maps, engraved
Maps, printed: except lithographed or
gravure (not publishing)
Menus, except lithographed or gravure
printed

Music, sheet: except lithographed or
gravure (not publishing)
Newspapers, printed: except litho-
graphed or gravure (not publishing)
Periodicals, printed: except litho-
graphed or gravure (not publishing)
Plateless engraving
Playing cards, printed: except litho-
graphed or gravure
Postcards, picture: except lithographed
or gravure printed
Posters, including billboard: except lith-
ographed or gravure
Printing from engraved and etched
plates
Printing, commercial or job: engraved
plate
Printing, commercial or job: except lith-
ographic or gravure
Printing, flexographic
Printing, letterpress
Printing, screen: except on textiles or
finished fabric articles
Schedules, transportation: except litho-
graphed or gravure
Screen printing on glass, plastics,
paper, and metal, including highway
signs
Seals: printing except lithographic or
gravure
Security certificates, engraved
Souvenir cards: except lithographed or
gravure
Stationery: except lithographed or gra-
vure
Stock certificates, engraved
Tags, printed: except lithographed or
gravure
Telephone directories, except litho-
graphed or gravure (not publishing)
Thermography, except lithographed or
gravure
Tickets, printed: except lithographed or
gravure
Trading stamps, printed: except lithographed or gravure
Visiting cards, printed: except litho-
graphed or gravure
Wrappers, printed: except lithographed
or gravure

276   **MANIFOLD BUSINESS FORMS**

2761   **Manifold Business Forms**

Establishments primarily engaged in designing and printing, by any process,
special forms for use in the operation of a business, in single and multiple
sets, including carbonized or interleaved with carbon or otherwise processed
for multiple reproduction.

Industry
Group   Industry
No.   No.

276   MANIFOLD BUSINESS FORMS—Con.

2761 Manifold Business Forms—Con.

Autographic register forms, printed   Fanfold forms
Business forms, manifold   Sales books
Computer forms, manifold or continu-   Strip forms (manifold business forms)
ous (excludes paper simply lined)   Tabulating card set forms (business
Continuous forms, office and business: forms)
carbonized or multiple reproduction   Unit sets (manifold business forms)

277   GREETING CARDS

2771 Greeting Cards

Establishments primarily engaged in publishing, printing by any process, or
both, of greeting cards for all occasions. Establishments primarily engaged in
producing hand painted greeting cards are classified in Services, Industry
8999.

Birthday cards, except hand painted   Greeting cards, except hand painted
Christmas cards, except hand painted   Valentine cards, except hand painted
Easter cards, except hand painted

**278   BLANKBOOKS, LOOSELEAF BINDERS, AND BOOKBINDING AND
RELATED WORK**

2782 Blankbooks, Looseleaf Binders and Devices

Establishments primarily engaged in manufacturing blankbooks, looseleaf
devices, and library binders; and in ruling paper.

Account books   Looseleaf devices and binders
Albums   Looseleaf forms and fillers, pen ruled
Binders, looseleaf   or printed only
Blankbook making   Memorandum books, printed
Chart and graph paper, ruled   Paper ruling
Checkbooks   Passbooks
Diaries   Receipt books
Inventory blankbooks   Record albums
Ledgers and ledger sheets   Sample books
Library binders, looseleaf   Scrapbooks

2789 Bookbinding and Related Work

Establishments primarily engaged in edition, trade, job, and library bookbinding. Also included in this industry are establishments primarily engaged
in book or paper bronzing, gilding, and edging; in map and sample mounting;
and in other services related to bookbinding. Establishments primarily binding books printed elsewhere are classified in this industry, but those primarily
binding books printed in the same establishment are classified in Industry
Group 273.

Beveling of cards   Pamphlets, binding only
Binding only: books, pamphlets, maga-   Paper bronzing, gilding, edging, and
zines, etc.   deckling
Book gilding, bronzing, edging, deck-   Paper cutting, except die-cutting
ling, embossing, and gold stamping   Rebinding books, magazines, or pam-
Bookbinding: edition, job, library, and   phlets
trade   Repairing books (bookbinding)
Bronzing books, cards, or paper   Swatches and samples, mounting for
Display mounting   the trade
Edging books, cards, or paper   Trade binding services
Magazines, binding only
Mounting of maps and samples, for the
trade

279   **SERVICE INDUSTRIES FOR THE PRINTING TRADE**

2791   **Typesetting**

Establishments primarily engaged in typesetting for the trade, including advertisement typesetting.

Advertisement typesetting	Photocomposition
Composition, hand: for the printing trade	Phototypesetting
	Typesetting for the printing trade
Composition, machine: e.g., linotype, monotype—for the printing trade	Typesetting, computer controlled
	Typographic composition

2796   **Platemaking and Related Services**

Establishments primarily engaged in making plates for printing purposes and in related services. Also included are establishments primarily engaged in making positives or negatives from which offset lithographic plates are made. These establishments do not print from the plates which they make, but prepare them for use by others. Engraving for purposes other than printing is classified in Industry 3479.

Color separations for printing	Letterpress plates, preparation of
Electrotype plates	Linecuts
Electrotyping for the trade	Lithographic plates, positives or negatives: preparation of
Embossing plates for printing	
Engraving on copper, steel, wood, or rubber plates for printing purposes	Offset plates, positives or negatives: preparation of
Engraving on textile printing plates and cylinders	Photoengraving for the trade
	Plates and cylinders, rotogravure printing: preparation of
Engraving, steel line: for printing purposes	Plates, printing: preparation of
Etching on copper, steel, wood, or rubber plates for printing purposes	Stereotype plates
Flexographic plates, preparation of	Stereotyping for the trade
Gravure plates and cylinders, preparation of	

Major Group 28.—CHEMICALS AND ALLIED PRODUCTS

The Major Group as a Whole

This major group includes establishments producing basic chemicals, and establishments manufacturing products by predominantly chemical processes. Establishments classified in this major group manufacture three general classes of products: (1) basic chemicals, such as acids, alkalies, salts, and organic chemicals; (2) chemical products to be used in further manufacture, such as synthetic fibers, plastics materials, dry colors, and pigments; and (3) finished chemical products to be used for ultimate consumption, such as drugs, cosmetics, and soaps; or to be used as materials or supplies in other industries, such as paints, fertilizers, and explosives. The mining of natural alkalies and other natural potassium, sodium, and boron compounds, of natural rock salt, and of other natural chemicals and fertilizers are classified in Mining, Industry Group 147. Establishments primarily engaged in manufacturing nonferrous metals and high-percentage ferroalloys are classified in Major Group 33; those manufacturing silicon carbide are classified in Major Group 32; those manufacturing baking powder, other leavening compounds, and starches are classified in Major Group 20; and those manufacturing artists' colors are classified in Major Group 39. Establishments primarily engaged in packaging, repackaging, and bottling of purchased chemical products, but not engaged in manufacturing chemicals and allied products, are classified in Wholesale or Retail Trade industries.

Industry Group No.	Industry No.	

281   **INDUSTRIAL INORGANIC CHEMICALS**

This industry group includes establishments primarily engaged in manufacturing basic industrial inorganic chemicals. Establishments primarily engaged in manufacturing formulated agricultural pesticides are classified in Industry 2879; those manufacturing medicinal chemicals, drugs, and medicines are classified in Industry Group 283; and those manufacturing soap and cosmetics are classified in Industry Group 284.

2812 Alkalies and Chlorine

Establishments primarily engaged in manufacturing alkalies and chlorine. Establishments primarily engaged in mining natural alkalies are classified in Mining, Industry 1474.

Alkalies, not produced at mines
Caustic potash
Caustic soda
Chlorine, compressed or liquefied
Potassium carbonate
Potassium hydroxide
Sal soda (washing soda)

Soda ash, not produced at mines
Sodium bicarbonate, not produced at mines
Sodium carbonate (soda ash), not produced at mines
Sodium hydroxide (caustic soda)
Washing soda (sal soda)

2813 Industrial Gases

Establishments primarily engaged in manufacturing industrial gases (including organic) for sale in compressed, liquid, and solid forms. Establishments primarily engaged in manufacturing fluorine and sulfur dioxide are classified in Industry 2819; those manufacturing household ammonia are classified in Industry 2842; those manufacturing other ammonia are classified in Industry 2873; those manufacturing chlorine are classified in Industry 2812; and those

281   INDUSTRIAL INORGANIC CHEMICALS—Con.

2813   **Industrial Gases—Con.**

manufacturing fluorocarbon gases are classified in Industry 2869. Distributors of industrial gases and establishments primarily engaged in shipping liquid oxygen are classified in Wholesale Trade, Industry 5169.

Acetylene	Helium
Argon	Hydrogen
Carbon dioxide	Neon
Dry ice (solid carbon dioxide)	Nitrogen
Gases, industrial: compressed, liquefied,	Nitrous oxide
or solid	Oxygen, compressed and liquefied

2816   **Inorganic Pigments**

Establishments primarily engaged in manufacturing inorganic pigments. Important products of this industry include black pigments, except carbon black, white pigments, and color pigments. Organic color pigments, except animal black and bone black, are classified in Industry 2865, and those manufacturing carbon black are classified in Industry 2895.

Animal black	Metallic pigments, inorganic
Barium sulfate, precipitated (blanc fixe)	Mineral colors and pigments
Barytes pigments	Minium (pigments)
Black pigments, except carbon black	Ochers
Blanc fixe (barium sulfate, precipitated)	Paint pigments, inorganic
Bone black	Pearl essence
Chrome pigments: chrome green, chrome yellow, chrome orange, and zinc yellow	Pigments, inorganic
	Prussian blue pigments
	Red lead pigments
Color pigments, inorganic	Satin white pigments
Ferric oxide pigments	Siennas
Iron blue pigments	Titanium pigments
Iron colors	Ultramarine pigments
Iron oxide, black	Umbers
Iron oxide, magnetic	Vermilion pigments
Iron oxide, yellow	White lead pigments
Lamp black	Whiting
Lead oxide pigments	Zinc oxide pigments
Lead pigments	Zinc pigments: zinc yellow and zinc sulfide
Litharge	
Lithopone	

2819   **Industrial Inorganic Chemicals, Not Elsewhere Classified**

Establishments primarily engaged in manufacturing industrial inorganic chemicals, not elsewhere classified. Establishments primarily engaged in mining, milling, or otherwise preparing natural potassium, sodium, or boron compounds (other than common salt) are classified in Industry 1474. Establishments primarily engaged in manufacturing household bleaches are classified in Industry 2842; those manufacturing phosphoric acid are classified in Industry 2874; and those manufacturing nitric acid, anhydrous ammonia, and other nitrogenous fertilizer materials are classified in Industry 2873.

Activated carbon and charcoal	Ammonium compounds, except for fertilizer
Alkali metals	
Alumina	Ammonium perchlorate
Aluminum chloride	Ammonium thiosulfate
Aluminum compounds	Barium compounds
Aluminum hydroxide (alumina trihydrate)	Bauxite, refined
	Beryllium oxide
Aluminum oxide	Bleach (calcium hypochlorite), industrial
Aluminum sulfate	
Alums	Bleach (sodium hypochlorite), industrial
Ammonia alum	Bleaches, industrial
Ammonium chloride, hydroxide, and molybdate	Bleaching powder, industrial
	Borax (sodium tetraborate)

281 INDUSTRIAL INORGANIC CHEMICALS—Con.

2819 Industrial Inorganic Chemicals, Not Elsewhere Classified—Con.

Boric acid
Boron compounds, not produced at mines
Borosilicate
Brine
Bromine, elemental
Calcium carbide, chloride, and hypochlorite
Calcium compounds, inorganic
Calcium metal
Carbide
Catalysts, chemical
Cerium salts
Cesium metal
Charcoal, activated
Chlorosulfonic acid
Chromates and bichromates
Chromic acid
Chromium compounds, inorganic
Chromium salts
Cobalt 60 (radioactive)
Cobalt chloride
Cobalt sulfate
Copper chloride
Copper iodide and oxide
Copper sulfate
Cyanides
Desiccants, activated: silica gel
Dichromates
Ferric chloride
Ferric oxides, except pigments
Ferrocyanides
Fissionable material production
Fluorine, elemental
Fuel propellants, solid: inorganic
Fuels, high energy: inorganic
Glauber's salt
Heavy water
High purity grade chemicals, inorganic: refined from technical grades
Hydrated alumina silicate powder
Hydrazine
Hydrochloric acid
Hydrocyanic acid
Hydrofluoric acid
Hydrogen peroxide
Hydrogen sulfide
Hydrosulfites
Hypophosphites
Indium chloride
Inorganic acids, except nitric or phosphoric
Iodides
Iodine, elemental
Iodine, resublimed
Iron sulphate
Isotopes, radioactive
Laboratory chemicals, inorganic
Lead oxides, other than pigments
Lead silicate
Lime bleaching compounds
Lithium compounds
Lithium metal
Luminous compounds, radium
Magnesium carbonate
Magnesium chloride
Magnesium compounds, inorganic
Manganese dioxide powder, synthetic
Mercury chlorides (calomel, corrosive sublimate), except U.S.P.
Mercury compounds, inorganic
Mercury oxides

Mercury, redistilled
Metals, liquid
Mixed acid
Muriate of potash, not produced at mines
Nickel ammonium sulfate
Nickel carbonate
Nickel compounds, inorganic
Nickel sulfate
Nuclear cores, inorganic
Nuclear fuel reactor cores, inorganic
Nuclear fuel scrap reprocessing
Oleum (fuming sulfuric acid)
Oxidation catalyst made from porcelain
Perchloric acid
Peroxides, inorganic
Phosphates, except defluorinated and ammoniated
Phosphorus and phosphorus oxychloride
Potash alum
Potassium aluminum sulfate
Potassium bichromate and chromate
Potassium bromide
Potassium chlorate
Potassium chloride
Potassium compounds, inorganic: except potassium hydroxide and carbonate
Potassium cyanide
Potassium hypochlorate
Potassium iodide
Potassium metal
Potassium nitrate and sulfate
Potassium permanganate
Propellants for missiles, solid: inorganic
Radium chloride
Radium luminous compounds
Rare earth metal salts
Reagent grade chemicals, inorganic: refined from technical grades
Rubidium metal
Salt cake (sodium sulfate)
Salts of rare earth metals
Scandium
Silica gel
Silica, amorphous
Silicofluorides
Silver bromide, chloride, and nitrate
Silver compounds, inorganic
Soda alum
Sodium aluminate
Sodium aluminum sulfate
Sodium antimoniate
Sodium arsenite, technical
Sodium bichromate and chromate
Sodium borates
Sodium borohydride
Sodium bromide, not produced at mines
Sodium chlorate
Sodium compounds, inorganic
Sodium cyanide
Sodium hydrosulfite
Sodium molybdate
Sodium perborate
Sodium peroxide
Sodium phosphate
Sodium polyphosphate
Sodium silicate
Sodium silicofluoride
Sodium stannate
Sodium sulfate-bulk or tablets

281   INDUSTRIAL INORGANIC CHEMICALS—Con.

2819 Industrial Inorganic Chemicals, Not Elsewhere Classified—Con.

Sodium tetraborate, not produced at
   mines
Sodium thiosulfate
Sodium tungstate
Sodium uranate
Sodium, metallic
Stannic and stannous chloride
Strontium carbonate, precipitated, and
   oxide
Strontium nitrate
Sublimate, corrosive
Sulfate of potash and potash magnesia,
   not produced at mines
Sulfides and sulfites
Sulfocyanides
Sulfur chloride

Sulfur dioxide
Sulfur hexafluoride gas
Sulfur, recovered or refined, including
   from sour natural gas
Sulfuric acid
Tanning agents, synthetic inorganic
Thiocyanates, inorganic
Tin chloride
Tin compounds, inorganic
Tin oxide
Tin salts
Tungsten carbide powder, except abra-
   sives or by metallurgical process
Uranium slug, radioactive
Water glass
Zinc chloride

282   PLASTICS MATERIALS AND SYNTHETIC RESINS, SYNTHETIC
RUBBER, CELLULOSIC AND OTHER MANMADE FIBERS, EXCEPT
GLASS

This group includes chemical establishments primarily engaged in manufacturing plastics materials and synthetic resins, synthetic rubbers, and cellulosic and other manmade fibers. Establishments primarily engaged in the manufacture of rubber products, and those primarily engaged in the compounding of purchased resins or the fabrication of plastics sheets, rods, and miscellaneous plastics products, are classified in Major Group 30; and textile mills primarily engaged in throwing, spinning, weaving, or knitting textile products from manufactured fibers are classified in Major Group 22.

2821 Plastics Materials, Synthetic Resins, and Nonvulcanizable Elastomers

Establishments primarily engaged in manufacturing synthetic resins, plastics materials, and nonvulcanizable elastomers. Important products of this industry include: cellulose plastics materials; phenolic and other tar acid resins; urea and melamine resins; vinyl resins; styrene resins; alkyd resins; acrylic resins; polyethylene resins; polypropylene resins; rosin modified resins; coumarone-indene and petroleum polymer resins; miscellaneous resins, including polyamide resins, silicones, polyisobutylenes, polyesters, polycarbonate resins, acetal resins, and fluorohydrocarbon resins; and casein plastics. Establishments primarily engaged in manufacturing fabricated plastics products or plastics film, sheet, rod, nontextile monofilaments and regenerated cellulose products, and vulcanized fiber are classified in Industry Group 308, whether from purchased resins or from resins produced in the same plant. Establishments primarily engaged in compounding purchased resins are classified in Industry 3087. Establishments primarily manufacturing adhesives are classified in Industry 2891.

Acetal resins
Acetate, cellulose (plastics)
Acrylic resins
Acrylonitrile-butadiene-styrene resins
Alcohol resins, polyvinyl
Alkyd resins
Allyl resins
Butadiene copolymers, containing less
   than 50 percent butadiene
Carbohydrate plastics

Casein plastics
Cellulose nitrate resins
Cellulose propionate (plastics)
Coal tar resins
Condensation plastics
Coumarone-indene resins
Cresol resins
Cresol-furfural resins
Dicyandiamine resins
Diisocyanate resins

282   PLASTICS MATERIALS AND SYNTHETIC RESINS, SYNTHETIC
      RUBBER, CELLULOSIC AND OTHER MANMADE FIBERS, EXCEPT
      GLASS—Con.

2821   Plastics Materials, Synthetic Resins, and Nonvulcanizable Elastomers—Con.

Elastomers, nonvulcanizable (plastics)
Epichlorohydrin bisphenol
Epichlorohydrin diphenol
Epoxy resins
Ester gum
Ethyl cellulose plastics
Ethylene-vinyl acetate resins
Fluorohydrocarbon resins
Ion exchange resins
Ionomer resins
Isobutylene polymers
Lignin plastics
Melamine resins
Methyl acrylate resins
Methyl cellulose plastics
Methyl methacrylate resins
Molding compounds, plastics
Nitrocellulose plastics (pyroxylin)
Nylon resins
Petroleum polymer resins
Phenol-furfural resins
Phenolic resins
Phenoxy resins
Phthalic alkyd resins
Phthalic anhydride resins
Polyacrylonitrile resins
Polyamide resins

Polycarbonate resins
Polyesters
Polyethylene resins
Polyhexamethylenediamine adipamide
  resins
Polyisobutylenes
Polymerization plastics, except fibers
Polypropylene resins
Polystyrene resins
Polyurethane resins
Polyvinyl chloride resins
Polyvinyl halide resins
Polyvinyl resins
Protein plastics
Pyroxylin
Resins, synthetic
Rosin modified resins
Silicone fluid solution (fluid for sonar
  transducers)
Silicone resins
Soybean plastics
Styrene resins
Styrene-acrylonitrile resins
Tar acid resins
Urea resins
Vinyl resins

2822   Synthetic Rubber (Vulcanizable Elastomers)

Establishments primarily engaged in manufacturing synthetic rubber by polymerization or copolymerization. An elastomer for the purpose of this classification is a rubber-like material capable of vulcanization, such as copolymers of butadiene and styrene, or butadiene and acrylonitrile, polybutadienes, chloroprene rubbers, and isobutylene-isoprene copolymers. Butadiene copolymers containing less than 50 percent butadiene are classified in Industry 2821. Natural chlorinated rubbers and cyclized rubbers are considered as semifinished products and are classified in Industry 3069.

Acrylate type rubbers
Acrylate-butadiene rubbers
Acrylic rubbers
Butadiene rubbers
Butadiene-acrylonitrile   copolymers
  (more than 50 percent butadiene)
Butadiene-styrene copolymers (more
  than 50 percent butadiene)
Butyl rubber
Chlorinated rubbers, synthetic
Chloroprene type rubbers
Chlorosulfonated polyethylenes
Cyclo rubbers, synthetic
EPDM polymers
Elastomers, vulcanizable (synthetic
  rubber)
Epichlorohydrin elastomers
Estane
Ethylene-propylene rubbers
Fluoro rubbers
Fluorocarbon derivative rubbers
Isobutylene-isoprene rubbers
Isocyanate type rubber
Isoprene rubbers, synthetic

N-type rubber
Neoprene
Nitrile type rubber
Nitrile-butadiene rubbers
Nitrile-chloroprene rubbers
Polybutadienes
Polyethylenes, chlorosulfonated
Polyisobutylene (synthetic rubber)
Polyisobutylene-isoprene elastomers
Polymethylene rubbers
Polysulfides
Pyridine-butadiene copolymers
Pyridine-butadiene rubbers
Rubber, synthetic
S-type rubber
Silicone rubbers
Stereo regular elastomers
Styrene-butadiene rubbers (50 percent
  or less styrene content)
Styrene-chloroprene rubbers
Styrene-isoprene rubbers
Thiol rubbers
Urethane rubbers
Vulcanized oils

Industry Group No.	Industry No.	
282		**PLASTICS MATERIALS AND SYNTHETIC RESINS, SYNTHETIC RUBBER, CELLULOSIC AND OTHER MANMADE FIBERS, EXCEPT GLASS—Con.**

2823 Cellulosic Manmade Fibers

Establishments primarily engaged in manufacturing cellulosic fibers (including cellulose acetate and regenerated cellulose such as rayon by the viscose or cuprammonium process) in the form of monofilament, yarn, staple, or tow suitable for further manufacturing on spindles, looms, knitting machines, or other textile processing equipment.

Acetate fibers
Cellulose acetate monofilament, yarn, staple, or tow
Cellulose fibers, manmade
Cigarette tow, cellulosic fiber
Cuprammonium fibers
Fibers, rayon
Horsehair, artificial: rayon
Nitrocellulose fibers
Rayon primary products: fibers, straw, strips, and yarn

Rayon yarn, made in chemical plants
Regenerated cellulose fibers
Textured yarns and fibers, cellulosic: made in chemical plants
Triacetate fibers
Viscose fibers, bands, strips, and yarn
Yarn, cellulosic: made in chemical plants

2824 Manmade Organic Fibers, Except Cellulosic

Establishments primarily engaged in manufacturing manmade organic fibers, except cellulosic (including those of regenerated proteins, and of polymers or copolymers of such components as vinyl chloride, vinylidene chloride, linear esters, vinyl alcohols, acrylonitrile, ethylenes, amides, and related polymeric materials), in the form of monofilament, yarn, staple, or tow suitable for further manufacturing on spindles, looms, knitting machines, or other textile processing equipment. Establishments primarily engaged in manufacturing textile glass fibers are classified in Industry 3229.

Acrylic fibers
Acrylonitrile fibers
Anidex fibers
Casein fibers
Elastomeric fibers
Fibers, manmade: except cellulosic
Fluorocarbon fibers
Horsehair, artificial: nylon
Linear esters fibers
Modacrylic fibers
Nylon fibers and bristles
Olefin fibers
Organic fibers, synthetic: except cellulosic

Polyester fibers
Polyvinyl ester fibers
Polyvinylidene chloride fibers
Protein fibers
Saran fibers
Soybean fibers (manmade textile materials)
Textured fibers and yarns, noncellulosic: made in chemical plants
Vinyl fibers
Vinylidene chloride fibers
Zein fibers

283		**DRUGS**

This group includes establishments primarily engaged in manufacturing, fabricating, or processing medicinal chemicals and pharmaceutical products. Also included in this group are establishments primarily engaged in the grading, grinding, and milling of botanicals.

2833 Medicinal Chemicals and Botanical Products

Establishments primarily engaged in: (1) manufacturing bulk organic and inorganic medicinal chemicals and their derivatives and (2) processing (grading, grinding, and milling) bulk botanical drugs and herbs. Included in this industry are establishments primarily engaged in manufacturing agar-agar and

Industry Group No.
283

Industry No.

DRUGS—Con.

2833 Medicinal Chemicals and Botanical Products—Con.

similar products of natural origin, endocrine products, manufacturing or isolating basic vitamins, and isolating active medicinal principals such as alkaloids from botanical drugs and herbs.

Adrenal derivatives: bulk, uncompounded
Agar-agar (ground)
Alkaloids and salts
Anesthetics, in bulk form
Antibiotics: bulk uncompounded
Atropine and derivatives
Barbituric acid and derivatives: bulk, uncompounded
Botanical products, medicinal: ground, graded, and milled
Brucine and derivatives
Caffeine and derivatives
Chemicals, medicinal: organic and inorganic—bulk, uncompounded
Cinchona and derivatives
Cocaine and derivatives
Codeine and derivatives
Digitoxin
Drug grading, grinding, and milling
Endocrine products
Ephedrine and derivatives
Ergot alkaloids
Fish liver oils, refined and concentrated for medicinal use
Gland derivatives: bulk, uncompounded
Glycosides
Herb grinding, grading, and milling
Hormones and derivatives
Insulin: bulk, uncompounded
Kelp plants
Mercury chlorides, U.S.P.
Mercury compounds, medicinal: organic and inorganic
Morphine and derivatives
N-methylpiperazine
Oils, vegetable and animal: medicinal grade—refined and concentrated
Opium derivatives
Ox bile salts and derivatives: bulk, uncompounded
Penicillin: bulk, uncompounded
Physostigmine and derivatives
Pituitary gland derivatives: bulk, uncompounded
Procaine and derivatives: bulk, uncompounded
Quinine and derivatives
Reserpines
Salicylic acid derivatives, medicinal grade
Strychnine and derivatives
Sulfa drugs: bulk, uncompounded
Sulfonamides
Theobromine
Vegetable gelatin (agar-agar)
Vitamins, natural and synthetic: bulk, uncompounded

2834 Pharmaceutical Preparations

Establishments primarily engaged in manufacturing, fabricating, or processing drugs in pharmaceutical preparations for human or veterinary use. The greater part of the products of these establishments are finished in the form intended for final consumption, such as ampoules, tablets, capsules, vials, ointments, medicinal powders, solutions, and suspensions. Products of this industry consist of two important lines, namely: (1) pharmaceutical preparations promoted primarily to the dental, medical, or veterinary professions, and (2) pharmaceutical preparations promoted primarily to the public.

Adrenal pharmaceutical preparations
Analgesics
Anesthetics, packaged
Antacids
Anthelmintics
Antibiotics, packaged
Antihistamine preparations
Antipyretics
Antiseptics, medicinal
Astringents, medicinal
Barbituric acid pharmaceutical preparations
Belladonna pharmaceutical preparations
Botanical extracts: powdered, pilular, solid, and fluid, except diagnostics
Chlorination tablets and kits (water purification)
Cold remedies
Cough medicines
Cyclopropane for anesthetic use (U.S.P. par N.F.), packaged
Dermatological preparations
Dextrose and sodium chloride injection, mixed
Dextrose injection
Digitalis pharmaceutical preparations
Diuretics
Effervescent salts
Emulsifiers, fluorescent inspection
Emulsions, pharmaceutical
Fever remedies
Galenical preparations
Hormone preparations, except diagnostics
Insulin preparations
Intravenous solutions
Iodine, tincture of
Laxatives
Liniments
Lip balms
Lozenges, pharmaceutical
Medicines, capsuled or ampuled
Nitrofuran preparations

283   DRUGS—Con.

2834   Pharmaceutical Preparations—Con.

Ointments	Spirits, pharmaceutical
Parenteral solutions	Suppositories
Penicillin preparations	Syrups, pharmaceutical
Pharmaceuticals	Tablets, pharmaceutical
Pills, pharmaceutical	Thyroid preparations
Pituitary gland pharmaceutical preparations	Tinctures, pharmaceutical
Poultry and animal remedies	Tranquilizers and mental drug preparations
Powders, pharmaceutical	Vermifuges
Procaine pharmaceutical preparations	Veterinary pharmaceutical preparations
Proprietary drug products	Vitamin preparations
Remedies, human and animal	Water decontamination or purification tablets
Sodium chloride solution for injection, U.S.P.	Water, sterile: for injections
Sodium salicylate tablets	Zinc ointment
Solutions, pharmaceutical	

2835   In Vitro and In Vivo Diagnostic Substances

Establishments primarily engaged in manufacturing in vitro and in vivo diagnostic substances, whether or not packaged for retail sale. These materials are chemical, biological, or radioactive substances used in diagnosing or monitoring the state of human or veterinary health by identifying and measuring normal or abnormal constituents of body fluids or tissues.

Angiourographic diagnostic agents	Enzyme and isoenzyme diagnostic reagents
Barium diagnostic agents	
Blood derivative diagnostic reagents	Hematology diagnostic reagents
Clinical chemistry reagents (including toxicology)	In vitro diagnostics
	In vivo diagnostics
Clinical chemistry standards and controls (including toxicology)	In vivo radioactive reagents
	Iodinated diagnostic agents
Coagulation diagnostic reagents	Metabolite diagnostic reagents
Cold kits for labeling with technetium	Microbiology, virology, and serology diagnostic products
Contrast media diagnostic products (e.g., iodine and barium)	Pregnancy test kits
Cytology and histology diagnostic products	Radioactive diagnostic substances
	Technetium products
Diagnostic agents, biological	Viral test diagnostic reagents
Electrolyte diagnostic reagents	

2836   Biological Products, Except Diagnostic Substances

Establishments primarily engaged in the production of bacterial and virus vaccines, toxoids, and analogous products (such as allergenic extracts), serums, plasmas, and other blood derivatives for human or veterinary use, other than in vitro and in vivo diagnostic substances. Included in this industry are establishments primarily engaged in the production of microbiological products for other uses. Establishments primarily engaged in manufacturing in vitro and in vivo diagnostic substances are classified in Industry 2835.

Agar culture media, except in vitro and in vivo	Biological and allied products: antitoxins, bacterins, vaccines, viruses, except in vitro and in vivo
Aggressins, except in vitro and in vivo	
Allergenic extracts, except in vitro and in vivo	Blood derivatives, for human or veterinary use, except in vitro and in vivo
Allergens	Coagulation products
Anti-hog-cholera serums	Culture media or concentrates, except in vitro and in vivo
Antigens	
Antiserums	Diphtheria toxin
Antitoxins	Hematology products, except in vitro and in vivo reagents
Antivenin	
Bacterial vaccines	Plasmas
Bacterins, except in vitro and in vivo	Pollen extracts, except in vitro and in vivo
Bacteriological media, except in vitro and in vivo	
	Serobacterins

Industry Group No.	Industry No.	
283		**DRUGS—Con.**

2836 Biological Products, Except Diagnostic Substances—Con.

Serums, except in vitro and in vivo	Vaccines
Toxins	Venoms
Toxoids, except in vitro and in vivo	Viruses
Tuberculins	

284 SOAP, DETERGENTS, AND CLEANING PREPARATIONS; PERFUMES, COSMETICS, AND OTHER TOILET PREPARATIONS

This industry group includes establishments primarily engaged in manufacturing soap and other detergents and in producing glycerin from vegetable and animal fats and oils; specialty cleaning, polishing, and sanitation preparations; and surface active preparations used as emulsifiers, wetting agents, and finishing agents, including sulfonated oils; and perfumes, cosmetics, and other toilet preparations.

2841 Soap and Other Detergents, Except Specialty Cleaners

Establishments primarily engaged in manufacturing soap, synthetic organic detergents, inorganic alkaline detergents, or any combination thereof, and establishments producing crude and refined glycerin from vegetable and animal fats and oils. Establishments primarily engaged in manufacturing shampoos or shaving products, whether from soap or synthetic detergents, are classified in Industry 2844; and those manufacturing synthetic glycerin are classified in Industry 2869.

Detergents, synthetic organic and inorganic alkaline	Presoaks
Dishwashing compounds	Scouring compounds
Dye removing cream, soap base	Soap: granulated, liquid, cake, flaked, and chip
Glycerin, crude and refined: from fats—except synthetic	Textile soap
Mechanics' paste	Washing compounds

2842 Specialty Cleaning, Polishing, and Sanitation Preparations

Establishments primarily engaged in manufacturing furniture, metal, and other polishes; waxes and dressings for fabricated leather and other materials; household, institutional, and industrial plant disinfectants; nonpersonal deodorants; drycleaning preparations; household bleaches; and other sanitation preparations. Establishments primarily engaged in manufacturing industrial bleaches are classified in Industry 2819, and those manufacturing household pesticidal preparations are classified in Industry 2879.

Ammonia, household	Drycleaning preparations
Aqua ammonia, household	Dust mats, gelatin
Beeswax, processing of	Dusting cloths, chemically treated
Belt dressing	Dye removing cream, petroleum base
Blackings	Fabric softeners
Burnishing ink	Floor wax emulsion
Chlorine bleaching compounds, household: liquid or dry	Floor waxes
Cleaning and polishing preparations	Furniture polish and wax
Cloths, dusting and polishing: chemically treated	Glass window cleaning preparations
Degreasing solvent	Harness dressing
Deodorants, nonpersonal	Household bleaches, dry or liquid
Disinfectants, household and industrial plant	Industrial plant disinfectants and deodorants
Drain pipe solvents and cleaners	Ink eradicators
Dressings for fabricated leather and other materials	Ink, burnishing
	Leather dressings and finishes
	Lye, household
	Paint and wallpaper cleaners

284   SOAP, DETERGENTS, AND CLEANING PREPARATIONS; PERFUMES,
             COSMETICS, AND OTHER TOILET PREPARATIONS—Con.

2842   **Specialty Cleaning, Polishing, and Sanitation Preparations—Con.**

Polishes: furniture, automobile, metal,
  shoe, and stove
Re-refining drycleaning fluid
Rug, upholstery, and drycleaning deter-
  gents and spotters
Rust removers
Saddle soap
Sanitation preparations
Shoe cleaners and polishes
Sodium hypochlorite (household bleach)

Stain removers
Starch preparations, laundry
Starches, plastics
Sweeping compounds, oil and water ab-
  sorbent, clay or sawdust
Wallpaper cleaners
Wax removers
Waxes for wood, fabricated leather, and
  other materials
Window cleaning preparations

2843   **Surface Active Agents, Finishing Agents, Sulfonated Oils, and Assistants**

Establishments primarily engaged in producing surface active preparations
for use as wetting agents, emulsifiers, and penetrants. Establishments engaged
in producing sulfonated oils and fats and related products are also included.

Assistants, textile and leather process-
  ing
Calcium salts of sulfonated oils, fats, or
  greases
Cod oil, sulfonated
Emulsifiers, except food and pharma-
  ceutical
Finishing agents, textile and leather
Mordants
Oil, turkey red
Oils, soluble (textile assistants)

Penetrants
Sodium salts of sulfonated oils, fats, or
  greases
Softeners (textile assistants)
Soluble oils and greases
Sulfonated oils, fats, and greases
Surface active agents
Textile processing assistants
Textile scouring compounds and wet-
  ting agents
Thin water (admixture)

2844   **Perfumes, Cosmetics, and Other Toilet Preparations**

Establishments primarily engaged in manufacturing perfumes (natural and
synthetic), cosmetics, and other toilet preparations. This industry also includes
establishments primarily engaged in blending and compounding perfume
bases; and those manufacturing shampoos and shaving products, whether
from soap or synthetic detergents. Establishments primarily engaged in manufacturing synthetic perfume and flavoring materials are classified in Industry
2869, and those manufacturing essential oils are classified in Industry 2899.

Bath salts
Bay rum
Body powder
Colognes
Concentrates, perfume
Cosmetic creams
Cosmetic lotions and oils
Cosmetics
Dentifrices
Denture cleaners
Deodorants, personal
Depilatories, cosmetic
Dressings, cosmetic
Face creams and lotions
Face powders
Hair coloring preparations
Hair preparations: dressings, rinses,
  tonics, and scalp conditioners
Home permanent kits
Lipsticks

Manicure preparations
Mouthwashes
Perfume bases, blending and com-
  pounding
Perfumes, natural and synthetic
Rouge, cosmetic
Sachet
Shampoos, hair
Shaving preparations: e.g., cakes,
  creams, lotions, powders, tablets
Soap impregnated papers and paper
  washcloths
Suntan lotions and oils
Talcum powders
Toilet creams, powders, and waters
Toilet preparations
Toothpastes and powders
Towelettes, premoistened
Washes, cosmetic

285   PAINTS, VARNISHES, LACQUERS, ENAMELS, AND ALLIED PRODUCTS

2851 Paints, Varnishes, Lacquers, Enamels, and Allied Products

Establishments primarily engaged in manufacturing paints (in paste and ready-mixed form); varnishes; lacquers; enamels and shellac; putties, wood fillers, and sealers; paint and varnish removers; paint brush cleaners; and allied paint products. Establishments primarily engaged in manufacturing carbon black are classified in Industry 2895; those manufacturing bone black, lamp black, and inorganic color pigments are classified in Industry 2816; those manufacturing organic color pigments are classified in Industry 2865; those manufacturing plastics materials are classified in Industry 2821; those manufacturing printing ink are classified in Industry 2893; those manufacturing caulking compounds and sealants are classified in Industry 2891; those manufacturing artists' paints are classified in Industry 3952; and those manufacturing turpentine are classified in Industry 2861.

Calcimines, dry and paste
Coating, air curing
Colors in oil, except artists'
Dispersions, thermoplastics and colloidal: paint
Dopes, paint
Driers, paint
Enamels, except dental and china painting
Epoxy coatings, made from purchased resin
Intaglio ink vehicle
Japans, baking and drying
Kalsomines, dry or paste
Lacquer bases and dopes
Lacquer thinner
Lacquer, clear and pigmented
Lacquers, plastics
Lead-in-oil paints
Linoleates, paint driers
Lithographic varnishes
Marine paints
Naphthanate driers
Oleate driers
Paint driers
Paint removers
Paintbrush cleaners

Paints, asphalt and bituminous
Paints, plastics texture: paste and dry
Paints, waterproof
Paints: oil and alkyd vehicle, and water thinned
Phenol formaldehyde coatings, baking and air curing
Plastics base paints and varnishes
Plastisol coating compound
Polyurethane coatings
Primers, paint
Putty
Resinate driers
Shellac, protective coating
Soyate driers
Stains: varnish, oil, and wax
Tallate driers
Thinners, paint: prepared
Undercoatings, paint
Varnish removers
Varnishes
Vinyl coatings, strippable
Vinyl plastisol
Water paints
Wood fillers and sealers
Wood stains
Zinc oxide in oil, paint

286   INDUSTRIAL ORGANIC CHEMICALS

Establishments primarily engaged in manufacturing industrial organic chemicals. Important products of this group include: (1) noncyclic organic chemicals, such as acetic, chloroacetic, adipic, formic, oxalic and tartaric acids, and their metallic salts; chloral, formaldehyde, and methylamine; (2) solvents such as amyl, butyl, and ethyl alcohols; methanol; amyl, butyl and ethyl acetates; ethyl ether, ethylene glycol ether, and diethylene glycol ether; acetone, carbon disulfide, and chlorinated solvents, such as carbon tetrachloride, perchloroethylene, and trichloroethylene; (3) polyhydric alcohols, such as ethylene glycol, sorbitol, pentaerythritol, synthetic glycerin; (4) synthetic perfume and flavoring materials, such as coumarin, methyl salicylate, saccharin, citral, citronellal, synthetic geraniol, ionone, terpineol, and synthetic vanillin; (5) rubber processing chemicals, such as accelerators and antioxidants, both cyclic and acyclic; (6) plasticizers, both cyclic and acyclic, such as esters of phosphoric acid, phthalic anhydride, adipic acid, lauric acid, oleic acid, sebacic acid, and

Industry
Group   Industry
No.   No.

286   **INDUSTRIAL ORGANIC CHEMICALS—Con.**

stearic acid; (7) synthetic tanning agents, such as naphthalene sulfonic acid condensates; (8) chemical warfare gases; (9) esters, amines, etc., of polyhydric alcohols and fatty and other acids; (10) cyclic crudes and intermediates; (11) cyclic dyes and organic pigments; and (12) natural gum and wood chemicals. Establishments primarily engaged in manufacturing plastics materials and nonvulcanizable elastomers are classified in Industry 2821; those manufacturing synthetic rubber are classified in Industry 2822; those manufacturing essential oils are classified in Industry 2899; those manufacturing rayon and other manmade fibers are classified in Industries 2823 and 2824; those manufacturing specialty cleaning, polishing, and sanitation preparations are classified in Industry 2842; those manufacturing paints are classified in Industry 2851; and those manufacturing inorganic pigments are classified in Industry 2816. Distillers engaged in the manufacture of grain alcohol for beverage purposes are classified in Industry 2085.

2861   Gum and Wood Chemicals

Establishments primarily engaged in manufacturing hardwood and softwood distillation products, wood and gum naval stores, charcoal, natural dyestuffs, and natural tanning materials. Establishments primarily engaged in manufacturing synthetic organic tanning materials are classified in Industry 2869, and those manufacturing synthetic organic dyes are classified in Industry 2865.

Acetate of lime, natural
Acetone, natural
Annato extract
Brazilwood extract
Brewers' pitch, product of softwood distillation
Calcium acetate, product of hardwood distillation
Charcoal, except activated
Chestnut extract
Dragon's blood
Dyeing and extract materials, natural
Dyestuffs, natural
Ethyl acetate, natural
Fustic wood extract
Gambier extract
Gum naval stores, processing but not gathering or warehousing
Hardwood distillates
Hemlock extract
Logwood extract
Mangrove extract
Methanol, natural (wood alcohol)
Methyl acetone
Methyl alcohol, natural (wood alcohol)
Myrobalans extract
Naval stores, wood

Oak extract
Oils, wood: product of hardwood distillation
Pine oil, produced by distillation of pine gum or pine wood
Pit charcoal
Pitch, wood
Pyroligneous acid
Quebracho extract
Quercitron extract
Rosin, produced by distillation of pine gum or pine wood
Softwood distillates
Sumac extract
Tall oil, except skimmings
Tanning extracts and materials, natural
Tar and tar oils, products of wood distillation
Turpentine, produced by distillation of pine gum or pine wood
Valonia extract
Wattle extract
Wood alcohol, natural
Wood creosote
Wood distillates

2865   Cyclic Organic Crudes and Intermediates, and Organic Dyes and Pigments

Establishments primarily engaged in manufacturing cyclic organic crudes and intermediates, and organic dyes and pigments. Important products of this industry include: (1) aromatic chemicals, such as benzene, toluene, mixed xylenes naphthalene; (2) synthetic organic dyes; and (3) synthetic organic pigments. Establishments primarily engaged in manufacturing coal tar crudes in chemical recovery ovens are classified in Industry 3312, and petroleum refin-

INDUSTRIAL ORGANIC CHEMICALS—Con.

2865 Cyclic Organic Crudes and Intermediates, and Organic Dyes and Pigments—Con.

eries which produce such products as byproducts of petroleum refining are classified in Industry 2911.

Acid dyes, synthetic
Acids, coal tar: derived from coal tar distillation
Alkylated diphenylamines, mixed
Alkylated phenol, mixed
Aminoanthraquinone
Aminoazobenzene
Aminoazotoluene
Aminophenol
Aniline
Aniline oil
Anthracene
Anthraquinone dyes
Azine dyes
Azo dyes
Azobenzene
Azoic dyes
Benzaldehyde
Benzene hexachloride (BHC)
Benzene, made in chemical plants
Benzoic acid
Biological stains
Chemical indicators
Chlorobenzene
Chloronaphthalene
Chlorophenol
Chlorotoluene
Coal tar crudes, derived from coal tar distillation
Coal tar distillates
Coal tar intermediates
Color lakes and toners
Color pigments, organic: except animal black and bone black
Colors, dry: lakes, toners, or full strength organic colors
Colors, extended (color lakes)
Cosmetic dyes, synthetic
Creosote oil, made in chemical plants
Cresols, made in chemical plants
Cresylic acid, made in chemical plants
Cyclic crudes, coal tar: product of coal tar distillation
Cyclic intermediates, made in chemical plants
Cyclohexane
Diphenylamine
Drug dyes, synthetic
Dye (cyclic) intermediates

Dyes, food: synthetic
Dyes, synthetic organic
Eosine toners
Ethylbenzene
Hydroquinone
Isocyanates
Lake red C toners
Leather dyes and stains, synthetic
Lithol rubine lakes and toners
Maleic anhydride
Methyl violet toners
Naphtha, solvent: made in chemical plants
Naphthalene chips and flakes
Naphthalene, made in chemical plants
Naphthol, alpha and beta
Nitro dyes
Nitroaniline
Nitrobenzene
Nitrophenol
Nitroso dyes
Oils: light, medium, and heavy: made in chemical plants
Organic pigments (lakes and toners)
Orthodichlorobenzene
Paint pigments, organic
Peacock blue lake
Pentachlorophenol
Persian orange lake
Phenol
Phloxine toners
Phosphomolybdic acid lakes and toners
Phosphotungstic acid lakes and toners
Phthalic anhydride
Phthalocyanine toners
Pigment scarlet lake
Pitch, product of coal tar distillation
Pulp colors, organic
Quinoline dyes
Resorcinol
Scarlet 2 R lake
Stilbene dyes
Styrene
Styrene monomer
Tar, product of coal tar distillation
Toluene, made in chemical plants
Toluidines
Vat dyes, synthetic
Xylene, made in chemical plants

2869 Industrial Organic Chemicals, Not Elsewhere Classified

Establishments primarily engaged in manufacturing industrial organic chemicals, not elsewhere classified. Important products of this industry include: (1) aliphatic and other acyclic organic chemicals, such as ethylene, butylene, and butadiene; acetic, chloroacetic, adipic, formic, oxalic, and tartaric acids and their metallic salts; chloral, formaldehyde, and methylamine; (2) solvents, such as amyl, butyl, and ethyl alcohols; methanol; amyl, butyl, and ethyl acetates; ethyl ether, ethylene glycol ether, and diethylene glycol ether; acetone, carbon disulfide and chlorinated solvents, such as carbon tetrachloride, perchloroethylene, and trichloroethylene; (3) polyhydric alcohols, such as

Industry
Group   Industry
No.   No.

286   **INDUSTRIAL ORGANIC CHEMICALS—Con.**

2869 **Industrial Organic Chemicals, Not Elsewhere Classified—Con.**

ethylene glycol, sorbitol, pentaerythritol, synthetic glycerin; (4) synthetic perfume and flavoring materials, such as coumarin, methyl salicylate, saccharin, citral, citronellal, synthetic geraniol, ionone, terpineol, and synthetic vanillin; (5) rubber processing chemicals, such as accelerators and antioxidants, both cyclic and acyclic; (6) plasticizers, both cyclic and acyclic, such as esters of phosphoric acid, phthalic anhydride, adipic acid, lauric acid, oleic acid, sebacic acid, and stearic acid; (7) synthetic tanning agents, such as naphthalene sulfonic acid condensates; (8) chemical warfare gases; and (9) esters, amines, etc., of polyhydric alcohols and fatty and other acids. Establishments primarily engaged in manufacturing plastics materials and nonvulcanizable elastomers are classified in Industry 2821; those manufacturing synthetic rubber are classified in Industry 2822; those manufacturing essential oils are classified in Industry 2899; those manufacturing wood distillation products, naval stores and natural dyeing and tanning materials are classified in Industry 2861; those manufacturing manmade textile fibers are classified in Industries 2823 and 2824; those manufacturing specialty cleaning, polishing, and sanitation preparations are classified in Industry 2842; those manufacturing paints are classified in Industry 2851; those manufacturing urea are classified in Industry 2873; those manufacturing organic pigments are classified in Industry 2865; those manufacturing inorganic pigments are classified in Industry 2816 and those manufacturing aliphatics and aromatics as byproducts of petroleum refining are classified in Industry 2911. Distilleries engaged in the manufacture of grain alcohol for beverage purposes are classified in Industry 2085.

Acetaldehyde
Acetates, except natural acetate of lime
Acetic acid, synthetic
Acetic anhydride
Acetin
Acetone, synthetic
Acid esters and amines
Acids, organic
Acrolein
Acrylonitrile
Adipic acid
Adipic acid esters
Adiponitrile
Alcohol, aromatic
Alcohol, fatty: powdered
Alcohol, methyl: synthetic (methanol)
Alcohols, industrial: denatured (nonbeverage)
Algin products
Amyl acetate and alcohol
Aspartome
Bromochloromethane
Butadiene, made in chemical plants
Butyl acetate, alcohol, and propionate
Butyl ester solution of 2, 4-D
Butylene, made in chemical plants
Calcium oxalate
Camphor, synthetic
Caprolactam
Carbon bisulfide (disulfide)
Carbon tetrachloride
Casing fluids for curing fruits, spices, and tobacco
Cellulose acetate, unplasticized
Chemical warfare gases

Chloral
Chlorinated solvents
Chloroacetic acid and metallic salts
Chloroform
Chloropicrin
Citral
Citrates
Citric acid
Citronellal
Coumarin
Cream of tartar
Cyclopropane
DDT, technical
Decahydronaphthalene
Dichlorodifluoromethane
Diethylcyclohexane (mixed isomers)
Diethylene glycol ether
Dimethyl divinyl acetylene (di-isopropenyl acetylene)
Dimethylhydrazine, unsymmetrical
Enzymes, except diagnostic substances
Esters of phosphoric, adipic, lauric, oleic, sebacic, and stearic acids
Esters of phthalic anhydride
Ethanol, industrial
Ether
Ethyl acetate, synthetic
Ethyl alcohol, industrial (nonbeverage)
Ethyl butyrate
Ethyl cellulose, unplasticized
Ethyl chloride
Ethyl ether
Ethyl formate
Ethyl nitrite
Ethyl perhydrophenanthrene

Industry
Group
No.
286

Industry
No.

INDUSTRIAL ORGANIC CHEMICALS—Con.

2869 Industrial Organic Chemicals, Not Elsewhere Classified—Con.

Ethylene glycol
Ethylene glycol ether
Ethylene glycol, inhibited
Ethylene oxide
Ethylene, made in chemical plants
Fatty acid esters and amines
Ferric ammonium oxalate
Flavors and flavoring materials, synthetic
Fluorinated hydrocarbon gases
Formaldehyde (formalin)
Formic acid and metallic salts
Fuel propellants, solid: organic
Fuels, high energy: organic
Geraniol, synthetic
Glycerin, except from fats (synthetic)
Grain alcohol, industrial (nonbeverage)
Hexamethylenediamine
Hexamethylenetetramine
High purity grade chemicals, organic: refined from technical grades
Hydraulic fluids, synthetic base
Industrial organic cyclic compounds
Ionone
Isopropyl alcohol
Ketone, methyl ethyl
Ketone, methyl isobutyl
Laboratory chemicals, organic
Lauric acid esters
Lime citrate
Malononitrile, technical grade
Metallic salts of acyclic organic chemicals
Metallic stearate
Methanol, synthetic (methyl alcohol)
Methyl chloride
Methyl perhydrofluorine
Methyl salicylate
Methylamine
Methylene chloride
Monochlorodifluoromethane
Monomethylparaminophenol sulfate
Monosodium glutamate
Mustard gas
Naphthalene sulfonic acid condensates
Naphthenic acid soaps
Normal hexyl decalin
Nuclear fuels, organic
Oleic acid esters
Organic acid esters
Organic chemicals, acyclic
Oxalates
Oxalic acid and metallic salts
Pentaerythritol
Perchloroethylene

Perfume materials, synthetic
Phosgene
Phthalates
Plasticizers, organic: cyclic and acyclic
Polyhydric alcohol esters and amines
Polyhydric alcohols
Potassium bitartrate
Propellants for missiles, solid: organic
Propylene glycol
Propylene, made in chemical plants
Quinuclidinol ester of benzylic acid
Reagent grade chemicals, organic: refined from technical grades, except diagnostic and substances
Rocket engine fuel, organic
Rubber processing chemicals, organic: accelerators and antioxidants
Saccharin
Sebacic acid
Silicones
Sodium acetate
Sodium alginate
Sodium benzoate
Sodium glutamate
Sodium pentachlorophenate
Sodium sulfoxalate formaldehyde
Solvents, organic
Sorbitol
Stearic acid salts
Sulfonated naphthalene
Sweetners, synthetic
Tackifiers, organic
Tannic acid
Tanning agents, synthetic organic
Tartaric acid and metallic salts
Tartrates
Tear gas
Terpineol
Tert-butylated bis (p-phenoxyphenyl) ether fluid
Tetrachloroethylene
Tetraethyl lead
Thioglycolic acid, for permanent wave lotions
Trichloroethylene
Trichlorophenoxyacetic acid
Trichlorotrifluoroethane tetrachlorodifluoroethane isopropyl alcohol
Tricresyl phosphate
Tridecyl alcohol
Trimethyltrithiophosphite (rocket propellants)
Triphenyl phosphate
Vanillin, synthetic
Vinyl acetate

287   AGRICULTURAL CHEMICALS

This group includes establishments primarily engaged in manufacturing nitrogenous and phosphatic basic fertilizers, mixed fertilizers, pesticides, and other agricultural chemicals. Establishments primarily engaged in manufacturing basic chemicals, which require further processsing or formulation before use as agricultural pest control agents, are classified in Industry Groups 281 or 286.

Industry
Group   Industry
No.   No.
287   AGRICULTURAL CHEMICALS—Con.

2873 Nitrogenous Fertilizers

Establishments primarily engaged in manufacturing nitrogenous fertilizer materials or mixed fertilizers from nitrogenous materials produced in the same establishment. Included are ammonia fertilizer compounds and anhydrous ammonia, nitric acid, ammonium nitrate, ammonium sulfate and nitrogen solutions, urea, and natural organic fertilizers (except compost) and mixtures.

Ammonia liquor
Ammonium nitrate and sulfate
Anhydrous ammonia
Aqua ammonia, made in ammonia plants
Fertilizers, mixed: made in plants producing nitrogenous fertilizer materials

Fertilizers: natural (organic), except compost
Nitric acid
Nitrogen solutions (fertilizer)
Plant foods, mixed: made in plants producing nitrogenous fertilizer materials
Urea

2874 Phosphatic Fertilizers

Establishments primarily engaged in manufacturing phosphatic fertilizer materials, or mixed fertilizers from phosphatic materials produced in the same establishment. Included are phosphoric acid; normal, enriched, and concentrated superphosphates; ammonium phosphates; nitro-phosphates; and calcium meta-phosphates.

Ammonium phosphates
Calcium meta-phosphates
Defluorinated phosphates
Diammonium phosphates
Fertilizers, mixed: made in plants producing phosphatic fertilizer materials

Phosphoric acid
Plant foods, mixed: made in plants producing phosphatic fertilizer materials
Superphosphates, ammoniated and not ammoniated

2875 Fertilizers, Mixing Only

Establishments primarily engaged in mixing fertilizers from purchased fertilizer materials.

Compost
Fertilizers, mixed: made in plants not manufacturing fertilizer materials

Potting soil, mixed

2879 Pesticides and Agricultural Chemicals, Not Elsewhere Classified

Establishments primarily engaged in the formulation and preparation of ready-to-use agricultural and household pest control chemicals, including insecticides, fungicides, and herbicides, from technical chemicals or concentrates; and the production of concentrates which require further processing before use as agricultural pesticides. This industry also includes establishments primarily engaged in manufacturing or formulating agricultural chemicals, not elsewhere classified, such as minor or trace elements and soil conditioners. Establishments primarily engaged in manufacturing basic or technical agricultural pest control chemicals are classified in Industry Group 281 if the chemicals are inorganic and in Industry Group 286 if they are organic. Establishments primarily engaged in manufacturing agricultural lime products are classified in Major Group 32.

Agricultural disinfectants
Agricultural pesticides
Arsenates: calcium, copper, and lead-formulated

Arsenites, formulated
Bordeaux mixture
Calcium arsenate and arsenite, formulated

287 AGRICULTURAL CHEMICALS—Con.

2879 Pesticides and Agricultural Chemicals, Not Elsewhere Classified—Con.

Cattle dips
Copper arsenate, formulated
DDT (insecticide), formulated
Defoliants
Elements, minor or trace (agricultural chemicals)
Exterminating products, for household and industrial use
Fly sprays
Fungicides
Growth regulants, agricultural
Herbicides
Household insecticides
Insect powder, household
Insecticides, agricultural
Lead arsenate, formulated
Lime-sulfur, dry and solution
Lindane, formulated
Moth repellants
Nicotine and salts

Nicotine bearing insecticides
Paris green (insecticide)
Pesticides, household
Phytoactin
Plant hormones
Poison: ant, rat, roach, and rodent—household
Pyrethrin bearing preparations
Pyrethrin concentrates
Rodenticides
Rotenone bearing preparations
Rotenone concentrates
Sheep dips, chemical
Sodium arsenite (formulated)
Soil conditioners
Sulfur dust (insecticide)
Thiocyanates, organic (formulated)
Trace elements (agricultural chemicals)
Xanthone (formulated)

289 MISCELLANEOUS CHEMICAL PRODUCTS

2891 Adhesives and Sealants

Establishments primarily engaged in manufacturing industrial and household adhesives, glues, caulking compounds, sealants, and linoleum, tile, and rubber cements from vegetable, animal, or synthetic plastics materials, purchased or produced in the same establishment. Establishments primarily engaged in manufacturing gelatin and sizes are classified in Industry 2899, and those manufacturing vegetable gelatin or agar-agar are classified in Industry 2833.

Adhesives
Adhesives, plastics
Caulking compounds
Cement (cellulose nitrate base)
Cement, linoleum
Cement, mending
Epoxy adhesives
Glue, except dental: animal, vegetable, fish, casein, and synthetic resin
Iron cement, household
Joint compounds

Laminating compounds
Mucilage
Paste, adhesive
Porcelain cement, household
Rubber cement
Sealing compounds for pipe threads and joints
Sealing compounds, synthetic rubber and plastics
Wax, sealing

2892 Explosives

Establishments primarily engaged in manufacturing explosives. Establishments primarily engaged in manufacturing ammunition for small arms are classified in Industry 3482, and those manufacturing fireworks are classified in Industry 2899.

Amatol (explosives)
Azides (explosives)
Blasting powder and blasting caps
Carbohydrates, nitrated (explosives)
Cordeau detonant (explosives)
Cordite (explosives)
Detonating caps for safety fuses
Detonators (explosive compounds)
Dynamite
Explosive cartridges for concussion forming of metal
Explosive compounds
Explosives
Fulminate of mercury (explosive compounds)

Fuse powder
Fuses, safety
Gunpowder
High explosives
Lead azide (explosives)
Mercury azide (explosives)
Nitrocellulose powder (explosives)
Nitroglycerin (explosives)
Nitromannitol (explosives)
Nitrostarch (explosives)
Nitrosugars (explosives)
Pentolite (explosives)
Permissible explosives
Picric acid (explosives)
Powder, explosive: pellet, smokeless,

Industry Group No.	Industry No.	
289		MISCELLANEOUS CHEMICAL PRODUCTS—Con.

2892 Explosives—Con.

and sporting	TNT (trinitrotoluene)
RDX (explosives)	Tetryl (explosives)
Squibbs, electric	Well shooting torpedoes (explosives)
Styphnic acid	

2893 Printing Ink

Establishments primarily engaged in manufacturing printing ink, including gravure ink, screen process ink, and lithographic ink. Establishments primarily engaged in manufacturing writing ink and fluids are classified in Industry 2899, and those manufacturing drawing ink are classified in Industry 3952.

Bronze ink	Letterpress ink
Flexographic ink	Lithographic ink
Gold ink	Offset ink
Gravure ink	Printing ink: base or finished
Ink, duplicating	Screen process ink

2895 Carbon Black

Establishments primarily engaged in manufacturing carbon black (channel and furnace black). Establishments primarily engaged in manufacturing bone and lamp black are classified in Industry 2816.

Carbon black	Furnace black
Channel black	

2899 Chemicals and Chemical Preparations, Not Elsewhere Classified

Establishments primarily engaged in manufacturing miscellaneous chemical preparations, not elsewhere classified, such as fatty acids, essential oils, gelatin (except vegetable), sizes, bluing, laundry sours, writing and stamp pad ink, industrial compounds, such as boiler and heat insulating compounds, metal, oil, and water treating compounds, waterproofing compounds, and chemical supplies for foundries. Establishments primarily engaged in manufacturing vegetable gelatin (agar-agar) are classified in Industry 2833; those manufacturing dessert preparations based on gelatin are classified in Industry 2099; those manufacturing printing ink are classified in Industry 2893; and those manufacturing drawing ink are classified in Industry 3952.

Acid resist for etching	Deicing fluid
Acid, battery	Desalter kits, sea water
Anise oil	Dextrine sizes
Antifreeze compounds, except industrial alcohol	Drilling mud
	Dyes, household
Bay oil	Essential oils
Binders (chemical foundry supplies)	Ethylene glycol antifreeze preparations
Bluing	Eucalyptus oil
Boiler compounds, antiscaling	Exothermics for metal industries
Bombs, flashlight	Facings (chemical foundry supplies)
Caps, for toy pistols	Fatty acids: margaric, oleic, and stearic
Carbon removing solvent	Fire extinguisher charges
Chemical cotton (processed cotton linters)	Fire retardant chemical preparations
	Fireworks
Chemical supplies for foundries	Flares
Citronella oil	Fluidifier (retarder) for concrete
Concrete curing compounds (blends of pigments, waxes, and resins)	Fluorescent inspection oil
	Fluxes: brazing, soldering, galvanizing, and welding
Concrete hardening compounds	Foam charge mixtures
Core oil and binders	Food contamination testing and screening kits
Core wash	
Core wax	Foundry supplies, chemical preparations
Correction fluid	
Corrosion preventive lubricant, synthetic base: for jet engines	Frit

Industry
Group
No.

Industry
No.

289   **MISCELLANEOUS CHEMICAL PRODUCTS—Con.**

     2899   **Chemicals and Chemical Preparations, Not Elsewhere Classified—Con.**

Fuel tank and engine cleaning chemicals, automotive and aircraft
Fusees: highway, marine, and railroad
Gelatin capsules, empty
Gelatin: edible, technical, photographic, and pharmaceutical
Glue size
Grapefruit oil
Grouting material (concrete mending compound)
Gum sizes
Gun slushing compounds
Heat insulating compounds
Heat treating salts
Hydrofluoric acid compound, for etching and polishing glass
Igniter grains, boron potassium nitrate
Incense
Industrial sizes
Insulating compounds
Jet fuel igniters
Laundry sours
Lemon oil
Lighter fluid
Magnetic inspection oil and powder
Margaric acid
Metal drawing compound lubricants
Metal treating compounds
Military pyrotechnics
Napalm
Oil treating compounds
Oleic acid (red oil)
Orange oil
Orris oil
Ossein

Oxidizers, inorganic
Packers' salt
Parting compounds (chemical foundry supplies)
Patching plaster, household
Penetrants, inspection
Peppermint oil
Plating compounds
Pyrotechnic ammunition: flares, signals, flashlight bombs, and rockets
Railroad torpedoes
Red oil (oleic acid)
Rifle bore cleaning compounds
Rosin sizes
Rubber processing preparations
Rust resisting compounds
Salt
Signal flares, marine
Sizes: animal, vegetable, and synthetic plastics materials
Sodium chloride, refined
Soil testing kits
Spearmint oil
Spirit duplicating fluid
Stearic acid
Stencil correction compounds
Tints and dyes, household
Torches (fireworks)
Vegetable oils, vulcanized or sulfurized
Water treating compounds
Water, distilled
Waterproofing compounds
Wintergreen oil
Wood, plastic
Writing ink and fluids

Major Group 29.—PETROLEUM REFINING AND RELATED INDUSTRIES

The Major Group as a Whole

This major group includes establishments primarily engaged in petroleum refining, manufacturing paving and roofing materials, and compounding lubricating oils and greases from purchased materials. Establishments manufacturing and distributing gas to consumers are classified in public utilities industries, and those primarily engaged in producing coke and byproducts are classified in Major Group 33.

Industry
Group
No.

Industry
No.

291   PETROLEUM REFINING

2911 Petroleum Refining

Establishments primarily engaged in producing gasoline, kerosene, distillate fuel oils, residual fuel oils, and lubricants, through fractionation or straight distillation of crude oil, redistillation of unfinished petroleum derivatives, cracking or other processes. Establishments of this industry also produce aliphatic and aromatic chemicals as byproducts. Establishments primarily engaged in producing natural gasoline from natural gas are classified in mining industries. Those manufacturing lubricating oils and greases by blending and compounding purchased materials are included in Industry 2992. Establishments primarily re-refining used lubricating oils are classified in Industry 2992. Establishments primarily engaged in manufacturing cyclic and acyclic organic chemicals are classified in Major Group 28.

Acid oil, produced in petroleum refineries

Alkylates, produced in petroleum refineries

Aromatic chemicals, made in petroleum refineries

Asphalt and asphaltic materials: liquid and solid—produced in petroleum refineries

Benzene, produced in petroleum refineries

Butadiene, produced in petroleum refineries

Butylene, produced in petroleum refineries

Coke, petroleum: produced in petroleum refineries

Ethylene, produced in petroleum refineries

Fraction products of crude petroleum, produced in petroleum refineries

Gas, refinery or still oil: produced in petroleum refineries

Gases, liquefied petroleum: produced in petroleum refineries

Gasoline blending plants

Gasoline, except natural gasoline

Greases, lubricating: produced in petroleum refineries

Hydrocarbon fluid, produced in petroleum refineries

Jet fuels

Kerosene

Mineral jelly, produced in petroleum refineries

Mineral oils, natural: produced in petroleum refineries

Mineral waxes, natural: produced in petroleum refineries

Naphtha, produced in petroleum refineries

Naphthenic acids, produced in petroleum refineries

Oils, partly refined: sold for rerunning—produced in petroleum refineries

Oils: fuel, lubricating, and illuminating—produced in petroleum refineries

Paraffin wax, produced in petroleum refineries

Petrolatums, produced in petroleum refineries

Petroleum refining

Propylene, produced in petroleum refineries

Road materials, bituminous: produced in petroleum refineries

Road oils, produced in petroleum refineries

Solvents, produced in petroleum refineries

Tar or residuum, produced in petroleum refineries

Industry Group No.	Industry No.	
295		**ASPHALT PAVING AND ROOFING MATERIALS**

2951 Asphalt Paving Mixtures and Blocks

Establishments primarily engaged in manufacturing asphalt and tar paving mixtures; and paving blocks made of asphalt and various compositions of asphalt or tar with other materials. Establishments primarily engaged in manufacturing brick, concrete, granite, and stone paving blocks are classified in Major Group 32.

Asphalt and asphaltic mixtures for paving, not made in refineries
Asphalt paving blocks, not made in petroleum refineries
Asphaltic concrete, not made in petroleum refineries
Coal tar paving materials, not made in petroleum refineries

Composition blocks for paving
Concrete, bituminous
Mastic floor composition, hot and cold
Road materials, bituminous: not made in petroleum refineries
Tar and asphalt mixtures for paving, not made in petroleum refineries

2952 Asphalt Felts and Coatings

Establishments primarily engaged in manufacturing, from purchased materials, asphalt and other saturated felts in roll or shingle form, either smooth or faced with grit, and in manufacturing roofing cements and coatings. Establishments primarily engaged in manufacturing paint are classified in Industry 2851, and those manufacturing linoleum and tile cement are classified in Industry 2891.

Asphalt roof cement—mfpm
Asphalt saturated board—mfpm
Brick siding, asphalt—mfpm
Coating compounds, tar—mfpm
Fabrics, roofing: asphalt or tar saturated—mfpm
Insulating siding, impregnated—mfpm
Mastic roofing composition—mfpm
Pitch, roofing—mfpm
Roof cement: asphalt, fibrous, and plastics—mfpm

Roof coatings and cements: liquid and plastics—mfpm
Roofing felts, cements, and coatings: asphalt, tar, and composition—mfpm
Roofing, asphalt or tar saturated felt: built-up, roll, and shingle—mfpm
Sheathing, asphalt saturated—mfpm
Shingles, asphalt or tar saturated felt: strip and individual—mfpm
Siding, insulating: impregnated—mfpm
Tar paper, roofing—mfpm

299		**MISCELLANEOUS PRODUCTS OF PETROLEUM AND COAL**

2992 Lubricating Oils and Greases

Establishments primarily engaged in blending, compounding, and re-refining lubricating oils and greases from purchased mineral, animal, and vegetable materials. Petroleum refineries engaged in the production of lubricating oils and greases are classified in Industry 2911.

Brake fluid, hydraulic—mfpm
Cutting oils, blending and compounding from purchased material
Greases, lubricating—mfpm
Hydraulic fluids—mfpm
Lubricating greases and oils—mfpm

Re-refining lubricating oils and greases—mfpm
Rust arresting compounds, animal and vegetable oil base—mfpm
Transmission fluid—mfpm

2999 Products of Petroleum and Coal, Not Elsewhere Classified

Establishments primarily engaged in manufacturing packaged fuel, powdered fuel, and other products of petroleum and coal, not elsewhere classified.

Calcined petroleum coke—mfpm
Coke, petroleum: not produced in petroleum refineries
Fireplace logs, made from coal

Fuel briquettes or boulets, made with petroleum binder
Waxes, petroleum: not produced in petroleum refineries

Major Group 30.—RUBBER AND MISCELLANEOUS PLASTICS PRODUCTS

The Major Group as a Whole

This major group includes establishments manufacturing products, not elsewhere classified, from plastics resins and from natural, synthetic, or reclaimed rubber, gutta percha, balata, or gutta siak. Numerous products made from these materials are included in other major groups, such as boats in Major Group 37, and toys, buckles, and buttons in Major Group 39. This group includes establishments primarily manufacturing tires, but establishments primarily recapping and retreading automobile tires are classified in Services, Industry 7534. Establishments primarily engaged in manufacturing synthetic rubber and synthetic plastics resins are classified in Industry Group 282.

Industry Group No.	Industry No.	
301		**TIRES AND INNER TUBES**
	3011	**Tires and Inner Tubes**

Establishments primarily engaged in manufacturing pneumatic casings, inner tubes, and solid and cushion tires for all types of vehicles, airplanes, farm equipment, and children's vehicles; tiring; camelback; and tire repair and retreading materials. Establishments primarily engaged in retreading tires are classified in Services, Industry 7534.

Camelback for tire retreading
Inner tubes: airplane, automobile, bicycle, motorcycle, and tractor
Pneumatic casings (rubber tires)
Tire sundries and tire repair materials, rubber
Tires, cushion or solid rubber
Tiring, continuous lengths: rubber, with or without metal core

302		**RUBBER AND PLASTICS FOOTWEAR**
	3021	**Rubber and Plastics Footwear**

Establishments primarily engaged in manufacturing fabric upper footwear having rubber or plastics soles vulcanized, injection molded, or cemented to the uppers, and rubber and plastics protective footwear. Establishments primarily engaged in manufacturing rubber, composition, and fiber heels, soles, soling strips, and related shoe making and repairing materials are classified in Industry 3069; those manufacturing plastics soles and soling strips are classified in Industry 3089; and those manufacturing other footwear of rubber or plastics are classified in Industry Group 314.

Arctics, rubber or rubber soled fabric
Boots, plastics
Boots, rubber or rubber soled fabric
Canvas shoes, rubber soled
Footholds, rubber
Footwear, rubber or rubber soled fabric
Gaiters, rubber or rubber soled fabric
Galoshes, plastics
Galoshes, rubber or rubber soled fabric
Overshoes, plastics
Overshoes, rubber or rubber soled fabric
Pacs, rubber or rubber soled fabric
Sandals, rubber
Shoes, plastics soles molded to fabric uppers
Shoes, rubber or rubber soled fabric uppers
Shower sandals or slippers, rubber

305 GASKETS, PACKING, AND SEALING DEVICES AND RUBBER AND PLASTICS HOSE AND BELTING

3052 Rubber and Plastics Hose and Belting

Establishments primarily engaged in manufacturing rubber and plastics hose and belting, including garden hose. Establishments primarily engaged in manufacturing rubber tubing are classified in Industry Group 306; those manufacturing plastics tubing are classified in Industry 3082; and those manufacturing flexible metallic hose are classified in Industry 3599.

Air brake and air line hose, rubber or rubberized fabric
Automobile hose, plastics or rubber
Belting, rubber: e.g., conveyor, elevator, transmission
Firehose, rubber
Garden hose, plastics or rubber
Heater hose, plastics or rubber

Hose, plastics or rubber
Hose: cotton fabric, rubber lined
Pneumatic hose, rubber or rubberized fabric: e.g., air brake and air line
V-belts, rubber or plastics
Vacuum cleaner hose, plastics or rubber

3053 Gaskets, Packing, and Sealing Devices

Establishments primarily engaged in manufacturing gaskets, gasketing materials, compression packings, mold packings, oil seals, and mechanical seals. Included are gaskets, packing, and sealing devices made of leather, rubber, metal, asbestos, and plastics.

Gaskets, regardless of material
Grease retainers, leather
Grease seals, asbestos
Oil seals, asbestos
Oil seals, leather
Oil seals, rubber
Packing for steam engines, pipe joints, air compressors, etc.

Packing, metallic
Packing, rubber
Packing: cup, U-valve, etc.—leather
Steam and other packing
Washers, leather

306 FABRICATED RUBBER PRODUCTS, NOT ELSEWHERE CLASSIFIED

3061 Molded, Extruded, and Lathe-Cut Mechanical Rubber Goods

Establishments primarily engaged in manufacturing molded, extruded, and lathe-cut mechanical rubber goods. The products are generally parts for machinery and equipment. Establishments primarily engaged in manufacturing other industrial rubber goods, rubberized fabric, and miscellaneous rubber specialties and sundries are classified in Industry 3069.

Appliance mechanical rubber goods: molded, extruded, and lathe-cut
Automotive mechanical rubber goods: molded, extruded, and lathe-cut
Mechanical rubber goods: molded, extruded, and lathe-cut
Off-highway machinery and equipment mechanical rubber goods: molded, extruded, and lathe-cut

Oil and gas field machinery and equipment mechanical rubber goods: molded, extruded, and lathe-cut
Rubber goods, mechanical: molded, extruded, and lathe-cut
Surgical and medical tubing: extruded and lathe-cut

3069 Fabricated Rubber Products, Not Elsewhere Classified

Establishments primarily engaged in manufacturing industrial rubber goods, rubberized fabrics, and vulcanized rubber clothing, and miscellaneous rubber specialties and sundries, not elsewhere classified. Included in this industry are establishments primarily engaged in reclaiming rubber and rubber articles. Establishments primarily engaged in the wholesale distribution of scrap rubber are classified in Wholesale Trade, Industry 5093. Establishments primarily engaged in rebuilding and retreading tires are classified in Services,

Industry
Group   Industry
No.   No.

306   **FABRICATED RUBBER PRODUCTS, NOT ELSEWHERE CLASSIFIED—Con.**

    3069   **Fabricated Rubber Products, Not Elsewhere Classified—Con.**

Industry 7534; those manufacturing rubberized clothing from purchased materials are classified in Industry 2385; and those manufacturing gaskets and packing are classified in Industry 3053.

Acid bottles, rubber
Air supported rubber structures
Aprons, vulcanized rubber and rubberized fabric—mitse
Bags, rubber or rubberized fabric
Balloons, advertising and toy: rubber
Balloons, metal foil laminated with rubber
Balls, rubber: except athletic equipment
Bath sprays, rubber
Bathing caps and suits, rubber—mitse
Battery boxes, jars, and parts: hard rubber
Bibs, vulcanized rubber and rubberized fabric—mitse
Bottles, rubber
Boxes, hard rubber
Brake lining, rubber
Brushes, rubber
Bulbs for medicine droppers, syringes, atomizers, and sprays: rubber
Bushings, rubber
Capes, vulcanized rubber and rubberized fabric—mitse
Caps, rubber—mitse
Castings, rubber
Chlorinated rubbers, natural
Cloaks, vulcanized rubber and rubberized fabric—mitse
Clothing, vulcanized rubber and rubberized fabric—mitse
Combs, hard rubber
Culture cups, rubber
Custom compounding of rubber materials
Cyclo rubbers, natural
Diaphragms, rubber: separate and in kits
Dress shields, vulcanized rubber and rubberized fabric—mitse
Druggists' sundries, rubber
Erasers: rubber, or rubber and abrasive combined
Fabrics, rubberized
Film, rubber
Finger cots, rubber
Flooring, rubber: tile or sheet
Foam rubber
Fountain syringes, rubber
Friction tape, rubber
Fuel cells, rubber
Fuel tanks, collapsible: rubberized fabric
Funnels, rubber
Gloves: e.g., surgeons', electricians', household—rubber
Grips and handles, rubber
Grommets, rubber
Gutta percha compounds
Hair curlers, rubber
Hairpins, rubber
Handles, rubber
Hard rubber products
Hard surface floor coverings: rubber

Heels, boot and shoe: rubber, composition, and fiber
Jar rings, rubber
Laboratory sundries: e.g., cases, covers, funnels, cups, bottles—rubber
Latex, foamed
Lifejackets: inflatable rubberized fabric
Liferafts, rubber
Liner strips, rubber
Linings, vulcanizable elastomeric: rubber
Mallets, rubber
Mats and matting: e.g., bath, door—rubber
Mattress protectors, rubber
Mattresses, pneumatic: fabric coated with rubber
Medical sundries, rubber
Mittens, rubber
Mouthpieces for pipes and cigarette holders, rubber
Nipples, rubber
Orthopedic sundries, molded rubber
Pacifiers, rubber
Pads, kneeling: rubber
Pants, baby: vulcanized rubber and rubberized fabric—mitse
Pillows, sponge rubber
Pipe stems and bits, tobacco: hard rubber
Platens, except printers': solid or covered rubber
Plumbers' rubber goods
Pontoons, rubber
Printers' blankets, rubber
Printers' rolls, rubber
Prophylactics, rubber
Pump sleeves, rubber
Reclaimed rubber (reworked by manufacturing processes)
Rods, hard rubber
Roll coverings: rubber for papermill; industrial, steelmills, printers'
Roller covers, printers': rubber
Rolls, solid or covered rubber
Roofing, single ply membrane: rubber
Rubber heels, soles, and soling strips
Rubber-covered motor mounting rings (rubber bonded)
Rubberbands
Rug backing compounds, latex
Separators, battery: rubber
Sheeting, rubber or rubberized fabric
Sheets, hard rubber
Sleeves, pump: rubber
Soles, boot and shoe: rubber, composition, and fiber
Soling strips, boot and shoe: rubber, composition, and fiber
Spatulas, rubber
Sponge rubber and sponge rubber products
Stair treads, rubber
Stationers' sundries, rubber
Stoppers, rubber

Industry
Group   Industry
No.   No.

306   FABRICATED RUBBER PRODUCTS, NOT ELSEWHERE CLASSIFIED— Con.

3069   Fabricated Rubber Products, Not Elsewhere Classified—Con.

Tape, pressure sensitive (including friction), rubber
Teething rings, rubber
Thermometer cases, rubber
Thread, rubber: except fabric covered
Tile, rubber
Top lift sheets, rubber
Top roll covering, for textile mill machinery: rubber
Toys, rubber: except dolls
Trays, rubber
Tubing, rubber: except extruded and lathe-cut

Type, rubber
Urinals, rubber
Valves, hard rubber
Wainscoting, rubber
Wallcoverings, rubber
Water bottles, rubber
Weather strip, sponge rubber
Wet suits, rubber

308   MISCELLANEOUS PLASTICS PRODUCTS

3081   Unsupported Plastics Film and Sheet

Establishments primarily engaged in manufacturing unsupported plastics film and sheet, from purchased resins or from resins produced in the same plant. Establishments primarily engaged in manufacturing plastics film and sheet for blister and bubble formed packaging are classified in Industry 3089.

Cellulosic plastics film and sheet, unsupported
Film, plastics: unsupported
Photographic, micrographic, and X-ray plastics, sheet, and film: unsupported
Polyester film and sheet, unsupported
Polyethylene film and sheet, unsupported

Polypropylene film and sheet, unsupported
Polyvinyl film and sheet, unsupported
Sheet, plastics: unsupported
Vinyl and vinyl copolymer film and sheet, unsupported

3082   Unsupported Plastics Profile Shapes

Establishments primarily engaged in manufacturing unsupported plastics profiles, rods, tubes, and other shapes. Establishments primarily engaged in manufacturing plastics hose are classified in Industry 3052.

Profiles, unsupported plastics
Rods, unsupported plastics

Tubes, unsupported plastics

3083   Laminated Plastics Plate, Sheet, and Profile Shapes

Establishments primarily engaged in manufacturing laminated plastics plate, sheet, profiles, rods, and tubes. Establishments primarily engaged in manufacturing laminated flexible packaging are classified in Industry Group 267.

Plastics, laminated: plate, rods, tubes, profiles and sheet, except flexible packaging
Thermoplastics laminates: rods, tubes, plates, and sheet, except flexible packaging

Thermosetting laminates: rods, tubes, plates, and sheet, except flexible packaging

3084   Plastics Pipe

Establishments primarily engaged in manufacturing plastics pipe. Establishments primarily engaged in manufacturing plastics pipe fittings are classified in Industry 3089.

Pipe, plastics

Industry Group No.
308

Industry No.

MISCELLANEOUS PLASTICS PRODUCTS—Con.

3085 Plastics Bottles

Establishments primarily engaged in manufacturing plastics bottles.

Bottles, plastics

3086 Plastics Foam Products

Establishments primarily engaged in manufacturing plastics foam products.

Cups, foamed plastics
Cushions, carpet and rug: plastics foam
Foamed plastics products
Ice chests or coolers, portable: foamed plastics

Insulation and cushioning: foamed plastics
Packaging foamed plastics
Plates, foamed plastics
Shipping pads, plastics foam

3087 Custom Compounding of Purchased Plastics Resins

Establishments primarily engaged in custom compounding of purchased plastics resins.

Custom compounding of purchased resins

3088 Plastics Plumbing Fixtures

Establishments primarily engaged in manufacturing plastics plumbing fixtures. Establishments primarily engaged in assembling plastics plumbing fixture fittings are classified in Industry 3432. Establishments primarily engaged in manufacturing plastics plumbing fixture components are classified in Industry 3089.

Bathroom fixtures, plastics
Drinking fountains, except mechanically refrigerated: plastics
Flush tanks, plastics
Hot tubs, plastics or fiberglass
Laundry tubs, plastics
Lavatories, plastics
Plumbing fixtures, plastics

Portable chemical toilets, plastics
Shower stalls, plastics
Sinks, plastics
Toilet fixtures, plastics
Tubs, plastics: bath, shower, and laundry
Urinals, plastics
Water closets, plastics

3089 Plastics Products, Not Elsewhere Classified

Establishments primarily engaged in manufacturing plastics products, not elsewhere classified. Establishments primarily engaged in manufacturing artificial leather are classified in Industry 2295.

Air mattresses, plastics
Aquarium accessories, plastics
Awnings, fiberglass and plastics combination
Bands, plastics
Bathware, plastics: except plumbing fixtures
Battery cases, plastics
Bearings, plastics
Billfold inserts, plastics
Blister packaging, plastics
Boats, nonrigid: plastics
Bolts, plastics
Bowl covers, plastics
Boxes, plastics
Brush handles, plastics
Bubble formed packaging, plastics
Buckets, plastics
Buoys and floats, plastics
Caps, plastics
Carafes, plastics
Casein products, molded for the trade

Cases, plastics
Casting of plastics for the trade, except foam plastics
Ceiling tile, unsupported plastics
Celluloid products, molded for the trade
Closures, plastics
Clothes hangers, plastics
Clothespins, plastics
Combs, plastics
Composition stone, plastics
Containers, plastics: except foam, bottles, and bags
Corrugated panels, plastics
Cotter pins, plastics
Counter coverings, plastics
Cups, plastics: except foam
Dinnerware, plastics: except foam
Dishes, plastics: except foam
Doors, folding: plastics or plastics coated fabric
Downspouts, plastics
Drums, plastics (containers)

Industry
Group
No.
Industry
No.

308   MISCELLANEOUS PLASTICS PRODUCTS—Con.

3089   Plastics Products, Not Elsewhere Classified—Con.

Engraving of plastics
Fascia, plastics (siding)
Fittings for pipe, plastics
Fittings, plastics
Flat panels, plastics
Floor coverings, plastics
Flower pots, plastics
Food casings, plastics
Garbage containers, plastics
Gate hooks, plastics
Glazing panels, plastics
Gloves and mittens, plastics
Grower pots, plastics
Gutters, plastics: glass fiber reinforced
Hardware, plastics
Heels, boot and shoe: plastics
Holders, plastics: papertowel, grocery bag, dust mop and broom
Hospitalware, plastics: except foam
Ice buckets, plastics: except foam
Ice chests or coolers, portable, plastics: except insulated or foam plastics
Jars, plastics
Kitchenware, plastics: except foam
Laboratoryware, plastics
Ladders, plastics
Lamp bases, plastics
Lamp shades, plastics
Lenses, plastics: except ophthalmic or optical
Lifejackets, plastics
Liferafts, nonrigid: plastics
Lock washers, plastics
Machine nuts, plastics
Microwaveware, plastics
Molding of plastics for the trade, except foam
Monofilaments, plastics: not suited for textile use
Netting, plastics
Nuts, plastics
Organizers for closets, drawers, and shelves: plastics
Ovenware, plastics
Pails, plastics
Picnic jugs, plastics
Planters, plastics

Pontoons, nonrigid: plastics
Printer acoustic covers, plastics
Rivets, plastics
Saucers, plastics: except foam
Screw eyes, plastics
Scrubbing pads, plastics
Septic tanks, plastics
Shutters, plastics
Siding, plastics
Sinkware, plastics
Skirts, plastics (siding)
Soffit, plastics (siding)
Soles, boot and shoe: plastics
Soling strips, boot and shoe: plastics
Sponges, plastics
Spouting, plastics: glass fiber reinforced
Spring pins, plastics
Spring washers, plastics
Suitcase shells, plastics
Swimming pool covers and blankets: plastics
Tableware, plastics: except foam
Tires, plastics
Tissue dispensers, plastics
Toggle bolts, plastics
Tool handles, plastics
Tops, plastics (e.g., dispenser, shaker)
Trash containers, plastics
Trays, plastics: except foam
Tubs, plastics (containers)
Tumblers, plastics: except foam
Unions, plastics
Utility containers, plastics
Vials, plastics
Vulcanized fiber plate, sheet, rods and tubes
Wall coverings, plastics
Warmers, bottle: plastics, except foam
Washers, plastics
Watering pots, plastics
Window frames and sash, plastics
Window screening, plastics
Windows, louver: plastics
Windows, storm: plastics
Windshields, plastics
Work gloves, plastics

Major Group 31.—LEATHER AND LEATHER PRODUCTS

The Major Group as a Whole

This major group includes establishments engaged in tanning, currying, and finishing hides and skins, leather converters, and establishments manufacturing finished leather and artificial leather products and some similar products made of other materials.

Industry Group No.	Industry No.	

311   LEATHER TANNING AND FINISHING

3111   Leather Tanning and Finishing

Establishments primarily engaged in tanning, currying, and finishing hides and skins into leather. This industry also includes leather converters, who buy hides and skins and have them processed into leather on a contract basis by others.

Bag leather
Belting butts, curried or rough
Belting leather
Bookbinders' leather
Bridle leather
Buffings, russet
Case leather
Chamois leather
Collar leather
Coloring of leather
Cutting of leather
Die-cutting of leather
Embossing of leather
Exotic leathers
Fancy leathers
Fleshers, leather (flesh side of split leather)
Garment leather
Glove leather
Handbag leather
Harness leather
Japanning of leather
Lace leather
Latigo leather
Leather coloring, cutting, embossing, japanning, and welting

Leather converters
Leather: tanning, currying, and finishing
Lining leather
Mechanical leather
Parchment leather
Patent leather
Rawhide
Roller leather
Saddlery leather
Shearling (prepared sheepskin)
Skirting leather
Skivers, leather
Sole leather
Specialty leathers
Splits, leather
Strap leather
Sweatband leather
Tanneries, leather
Upholstery leather
Upper leather
Vellum leather
Welting leather
Wet blues

313   BOOT AND SHOE CUT STOCK AND FINDINGS

3131   Boot and Shoe Cut Stock and Findings

Establishments primarily engaged in manufacturing leather soles, inner soles, and other boot and shoe cut stock and findings. This industry also includes finished wood heels. Establishments primarily engaged in manufacturing heels, soling strips, and soles made of rubber, composition, plastics, and fiber are classified in Major Group 30.

Bows, shoe
Box toes, leather (shoe cut stock)
Buckles, shoe
Caps, heel and toe: leather or metal
Clasps, shoe
Counters (shoe cut stock)
Cut stock for boots and shoes
Findings, boot and shoe
Heel caps, leather or metal
Heel lifts, leather
Heels, boot and shoe: finished wood or leather

Inner soles, leather
Laces, boot and shoe: leather
Leather welting
Linings, boot and shoe: leather
Ornaments, shoe
Pegs, shoe
Quarters (shoe cut stock)
Rands (shoe cut stock)
Shanks, shoe
Shoe cut stock
Shoe soles: except rubber, composition, plastics, and fiber

313   BOOT AND SHOE CUT STOCK AND FINDINGS—Con.

3131   Boot and Shoe Cut Stock and Findings—Con.

Soles, boot and shoe: except rubber,
  composition, plastics, and fiber
Stays, shoe
Taps, shoe: regardless of material
Tips, shoe: regardless of material
Toe caps, leather or metal
Tongues, boot and shoe: leather

Top lifts, boot and shoe
Trimmings, shoe: leather
Uppers (shoe cut stock)
Vamps, leather
Wood heel blocks, for sale as such
Wood heels, finished (shoe findings)

314   FOOTWEAR, EXCEPT RUBBER

3142   House Slippers

Establishments primarily engaged in manufacturing house slippers of leather or other materials.

House slippers
Slipper socks, made from purchased
  socks

3143   Men's Footwear, Except Athletic

Establishments primarily engaged in the production of men's footwear designed primarily for dress, street, and work. Establishments primarily engaged in the production of such protective footwear as rubbers, rubber boots, storm shoes, galoshes, and other footwear with rubber soles vulcanized to the uppers are classified in Industry 3021. Establishments primarily engaged in the production of athletic shoes and youths' and boys' shoes are classified in Industry 3149, and those manufacturing orthopedic extension shoes are classified in Industry 3842.

Boots, dress and casual: men's
Casual shoes, men's: except athletic
  and rubber footwear
Dress shoes, men's
Footwear, men's: except house slippers,
  athletic, and vulcanized rubber footwear

Footwear, men's: leather or vinyl with
  molded or vulcanized soles
Orthopedic shoes, men's: except extension shoes
Shoes, men's: except house slippers,
  athletic, rubber, and extension shoes
Work shoes, men's

3144   Women's Footwear, Except Athletic

Establishments primarily engaged in the production of women's footwear designed primarily for dress, street, and work. Establishments primarily engaged in the production of athletic shoes and misses', children's, infants', and babies' footwear are classified in Industry 3149. Establishments primarily engaged in the production of rubber or plastics footwear are classified in Industry 3021, and those manufacturing orthopedic extension shoes are classified in Industry 3842.

Boots: women's canvas and leather—
  except athletic
Footwear, women's: except house slippers, athletic, and vulcanized rubber
  footwear
Footwear, women's: leather or vinyl
  with molded or vulcanized soles

Orthopedic shoes, women's: except extension shoes
Shoes, women's: except house slippers,
  athletic, and rubber footwear

3149   Footwear, Except Rubber, Not Elsewhere Classified

Establishments primarily engaged in the production of shoes, not elsewhere classified, such as misses', youths', boys', children's, and infants' footwear and athletic footwear. Establishments primarily engaged in the production of

Industry Group No.	Industry No.	
314		**FOOTWEAR, EXCEPT RUBBER—Con.**

3149 Footwear, Except Rubber, Not Elsewhere Classified—Con.

rubber or plastics footwear are classified in Industry 3021, and those manufacturing orthopedic extension shoes are classified in Industry 3842.

Athletic shoes, except rubber
Ballet slippers
Footwear, children's: house slippers and vulcanized rubber footwear
Footwear, children's: leather or vinyl with molded or vulcanized shoes

Moccasins
Orthopedic shoes, children's: except extension shoes
Sandals, children's: except rubber
Shoe dyeing for the trade

315   LEATHER GLOVES AND MITTENS

3151 Leather Gloves and Mittens

Establishments primarily engaged in manufacturing dress, semidress, and work gloves exclusively of leather or leather with lining of other material. Establishments primarily engaged in manufacturing sporting and athletic gloves are classified in Industry 3949; those manufacturing dress, semidress, and work gloves and mittens of cloth or cloth and leather combined are classified in Industry 2381; and those manufacturing safety gloves are classified in Industry 3842.

Dress and semidress gloves, leather
Gloves, leather
Mittens, leather

Welders' gloves
Work gloves, leather

316   LUGGAGE

3161 Luggage

Establishments primarily engaged in manufacturing luggage of leather or other materials.

Attache cases, regardless of material
Bags (luggage), regardless of material
Binocular cases
Boxes, hat: except paper or paperboard
Briefcases, regardless of material
Camera carrying bags, regardless of material
Cases, luggage
Luggage, regardless of material

Musical instrument cases
Sample cases, regardless of material
Satchels, regardless of material
Shoe kits, regardless of material
Suitcases, regardless of material
Traveling bags, regardless of material
Trunks, regardless of material
Valises, regardless of material
Wardrobe bags (luggage)

317   HANDBAGS AND OTHER PERSONAL LEATHER GOODS

3171 Women's Handbags and Purses

Establishments primarily engaged in manufacturing women's handbags and purses of leather or other materials, except precious metal. Establishments primarily engaged in manufacturing precious metal handbags and purses are classified in Industry 3911.

Handbags, women's: of all materials, except precious metal
Pocketbooks, women's: of all materials, except precious metal

Purses, women's: of all materials, except precious metal

3172 Personal Leather Goods, Except Women's Handbags and Purses

Establishments primarily engaged in manufacturing small articles normally carried on the person or in a handbag, such as billfolds, key cases, and coin purses of leather or other materials, except precious metal. Establishments

Industry Group No. 317

Industry No.

HANDBAGS AND OTHER PERSONAL LEATHER GOODS—Con.

3172 Personal Leather Goods, Except Women's Handbags and Purses—Con.

primarily engaged in manufacturing similar personal goods of precious metals are classified in Industry 3911.

Billfolds, regardless of material
Card cases, except precious metal
Cases, jewelry: regardless of material
Checkbook covers, regardless of material
Cigar cases, except precious metal
Cigarette cases, except precious metal
Coin purses, regardless of material
Comb cases, except precious metal
Compacts, solid leather
Cosmetic bags, regardless of material
Eyeglass cases, regardless of material
Handbags, men's: regardless of material

Key cases, regardless of material
Leather goods, small: personal
Pocketbooks, men's: regardless of material
Purses, men's: regardless of material
Sewing cases, regardless of material
Tobacco pouches, regardless of material
Toilet kits and cases, regardless of material
Vanity cases, leather
Wallets, regardless of material
Watch straps, except metal

319 LEATHER GOODS, NOT ELSEWHERE CLASSIFIED

3199 Leather Goods, Not Elsewhere Classified

Establishments primarily engaged in manufacturing leather goods, not elsewhere classified, such as saddlery, harnesses, whips, embossed leather goods, leather desk sets, razor strops, and leather belting. Establishments primarily engaged in manufacturing gaskets and packing are classified in Industry 3053. Establishments primarily engaged in manufacturing leather and sheep-lined clothing are classified in Industry 2386.

Aprons, leather: e.g., blacksmiths', welders'
Aprons, textile machinery: leather
Bags, feed: for horses
Belt laces, leather
Belts, safety: leather
Boots, horse
Boxes, leather
Burnt leather goods for the trade
Collars and collar pads (harness)
Corners, luggage: leather
Crops, riding
Desk sets, leather
Dog furnishings, leather: e.g., collars, leashes, harnesses, muzzles
Embossed leather goods for the trade
Fly nets (harness)
Halters (harness)
Handles, whip and luggage: leather
Harnesses and harness parts

Helmets, except athletic: leather
Holsters, leather
Jackets, welders': leather
Lashes (whips)
Leather belting for machinery: flat, solid, twisted, and built-up
Leggings, welders': leather
Mill strapping for textile mills, leather
Novelties, leather
Puttees, canvas and leather
Razor strops
Saddles and parts
Seatbelts, leather
Sleeves, welders': leather
Spats
Stirrups, wood and metal
Straps, except watch straps: leather
Whips, horse
Whipstocks

Major Group 32.—STONE, CLAY, GLASS, AND CONCRETE PRODUCTS

The Major Group as a Whole

This major group includes establishments engaged in manufacturing flat glass and other glass products, cement, structural clay products, pottery, concrete and gypsum products, cut stone, abrasive and asbestos products, and other products from materials taken principally from the earth in the form of stone, clay, and sand. When separate reports are available for mines and quarries operated by manufacturing establishments classified in this major group, the mining and quarrying activities are classified in Division B, Mining. When separate reports are not available, the mining and quarrying activities, other than those of Industry 3295, are classified herein with the manufacturing operations.

If separate reports are not available for crushing, grinding, and other preparation activities of Industry 3295, these establishments are classified in Division B, Mining.

Industry Group No.	Industry No.	
321		**FLAT GLASS**
	3211	**Flat Glass**

Establishments primarily engaged in manufacturing flat glass. This industry also produces laminated glass, but establishments primarily engaged in manufacturing laminated glass from purchased flat glass are classified in Industry 3231.

Building glass, flat	Picture glass
Cathedral glass	Plate glass blanks for optical or ophthalmic uses
Float glass	
Glass, colored: cathedral and antique	Plate glass, polished and rough
Glass, flat	Sheet glass
Insulating glass, sealed units—mitse	Sheet glass blanks for optical or ophthalmic uses
Laminated glass, made from glass produced in the same establishment	Skylight glass
Multiple-glazed insulating units—mitse	Spectacle glass
Opalescent flat glass	Structural glass, flat
Ophthalmic glass, flat	Tempered glass—mitse
Optical glass, flat	Window glass, clear and colored

322   **GLASS AND GLASSWARE, PRESSED OR BLOWN**

This group includes establishments primarily engaged in manufacturing glass and glassware, pressed, blown, or shaped from glass produced in the same establishment. Establishments primarily engaged in manufacturing glass products made from purchased glass are classified in Industry 3231.

3221   **Glass Containers**

Establishments primarily engaged in manufacturing glass containers for commercial packing and bottling, and for home canning.

Ampoules, glass	Jugs for packing, bottling, and canning: glass
Bottles for packing, bottling, and canning: glass	Medicine bottles, glass
Carboys, glass	Milk bottles, glass
Containers for packing, bottling, and canning: glass	Packers' ware (containers), glass
Cosmetic jars, glass	Vials, glass: made in glassmaking establishments
Fruit jars, glass	Water bottles, glass
Jars for packing, bottling, and canning: glass	

322   GLASS AND GLASSWARE, PRESSED OR BLOWN—Con.

3229   Pressed and Blown Glass and Glassware, Not Elsewhere Classified

Establishments primarily engaged in manufacturing glass and glassware, not elsewhere classified, pressed, blown, or shaped from glass produced in the same establishment. Establishments primarily engaged in manufacturing textile glass fibers are also included in this industry, but establishments primarily engaged in manufacturing glass wool insulation products are classified in Industry 3296. Establishments primarily engaged in manufacturing fiber optic cables are classified in Industry 3357, and those manufacturing fiber optic medical devices are classified in Industry Group 384. Establishments primarily engaged in the production of pressed lenses for vehicular lighting, beacons, and lanterns are also included in this industry, but establishments primarily engaged in the production of optical lenses are classified in Industry 3827. Establishments primarily engaged in manufacturing glass containers are classified in Industry 3221, and those manufacturing complete electric light bulbs are classified in Industry 3641.

Art glassware, made in glassmaking plants
Ashtrays, glass
Barware, glass
Battery jars, glass
Blocks, glass
Bowls, glass
Bulbs for electric lights, without filaments or sockets—mitse
Candlesticks, glass
Centerpieces, glass
Chimneys, lamp: glass—pressed or blown
Christmas tree ornaments, from glass—mitse
Clip cups, glass
Cooking utensils, glass and glass ceramic
Drinking straws, glass
Fiber optics strands
Fibers, glass, textile
Flameware, glass and glass ceramic
Frying pans, glass and glass ceramic
Glass blanks for electric light bulbs
Glass brick
Glassware, except glass containers for packing, bottling, and canning
Glassware: art, decorative, and novelty
Goblets, glass
Illuminating glass: light shades, reflectors, lamp chimneys, and globes
Industrial glassware and glass products, pressed or blown
Inkwells, glass

Insulators, electrical: glass
Lamp parts, glass
Lamp shades, glass
Lantern globes, glass: pressed or blown
Lens blanks, optical and ophthalmic
Lenses, glass: for lanterns, flashlights, headlights, and searchlights
Level vials for instruments, glass
Light shades, glass: pressed or blown
Lighting glassware, pressed or blown
Novelty glassware: made in glassmaking plants
Ophthalmic glass, except flat
Optical glass blanks
Photomask blanks, glass
Reflectors for lighting equipment, glass: pressed or blown
Refrigerator dishes and jars, glass
Scientific glassware, pressed or blown: made in glassmaking plants
Stemware, glass
Tableware, glass and glass ceramic
Tea kettles, glass and glass ceramic
Technical glassware and glass products, pressed or blown
Television tube blanks, glass
Textile glass fibers
Tobacco jars, glass
Trays, glass
Tubing, glass
Tumblers, glass
Vases, glass
Yarn, fiberglass: made in glass plants

323   GLASS PRODUCTS, MADE OF PURCHASED GLASS

3231   Glass Products, Made of Purchased Glass

Establishments primarily engaged in manufacturing glass products from purchased glass. Establishments primarily engaged in manufacturing optical lenses, except ophthalmic, are classified in Industry 3827, and those manufacturing ophthalmic lenses are classified in Industry 3851.

Aquariums and reflectors, made from purchased glass
Art glass, made from purchased glass

Christmas tree ornaments, made from purchased glass
Cut and engraved glassware, made

323 GLASS PRODUCTS, MADE OF PURCHASED GLASS—Con.

3231 Glass Products, Made of Purchased Glass—Con.

from purchased glass

Decorated glassware: e.g., chipped, engraved, etched, sandblasted—made from purchased glass

Doors, made from purchased glass

Enameled glass, made from purchased glass

Encrusting gold, silver, or other metals on glass products: made from purchased glass

Flowers, foliage, fruits and vines: artificial glass—made from purchased glass

Fruit, artificial: made from purchased glass

Furniture tops, glass: cut, beveled, and polished

Glass, scientific apparatus: for druggists', hospitals, laboratories—made from purchased glass

Glass, sheet: bent—made from purchased glass

Grasses, artificial: made from purchased glass

Ground glass, made from purchased glass

Industrial glassware, made from purchased glass

Laboratory glassware, made from purchased glass

Laminated glass, made from purchased glass

Leaded glass, made from purchased glass

Medicine droppers, made from purchased glass

Mirrors, framed or unframed: made from purchased glass

Mirrors, transportation equipment: made from purchased glass

Multiple-glazed insulating units, made from purchased glass

Novelties, glass: e.g., fruit, foliage, flowers, animals, made from purchased glass

Ornamented glass, made from purchased glass

Plants and foliage, artificial: made from purchased glass

Reflector glass beads, for highway signs and other reflectors: made from purchased glass

Safety glass, made from purchased glass

Silvered glass, made from purchased glass

Stained glass, made from purchased glass

Table tops, made from purchased glass

Technical glassware, made from purchased glass

Tempered glass, made from purchased glass

Test tubes, made from purchased glass

Vials, made from purchased glass

Watch crystals, made from purchased glass

Windows, stained glass: made from purchased glass

Windshields, made from purchased glass

324 CEMENT, HYDRAULIC

3241 Cement, Hydraulic

Establishments primarily engaged in manufacturing hydraulic cement, including portland, natural, masonry, and pozzolana cements.

Cement, hydraulic: portland, natural, masonry, and pozzolana

325 STRUCTURAL CLAY PRODUCTS

3251 Brick and Structural Clay Tile

Establishments primarily engaged in manufacturing brick and structural clay tile. Establishments primarily engaged in manufacturing clay firebrick are classified in Industry 3255; those manufacturing nonclay firebrick are classified in Industry 3297; those manufacturing sand lime brick are classified in Industry 3299; and those manufacturing glass brick are classified in Industry 3229.

Book tile, clay

Brick: common, face, glazed, vitrified, and hollow—clay

Building tile, clay

Ceramic glazed brick, clay

Chimney blocks, radial—clay

Corncrib tile

Facing tile, clay

Fireproofing tile, clay

Floor arch tile, clay

Flooring brick, clay

Furring tile, clay

Partition tile, clay

Paving brick, clay

Silo tile

Slumped brick

Structural tile, clay

Industry Group No.	Industry No.	
325		**STRUCTURAL CLAY PRODUCTS—Con.**

3253   Ceramic Wall and Floor Tile

Establishments primarily engaged in manufacturing ceramic wall and floor tile. Establishments primarily engaged in manufacturing structural clay tile are classified in Industry 3251, and those manufacturing drain tile are classified in Industry 3259.

Ceramic tile, floor and wall	Mosaic tile, ceramic
Enamel tile, floor and wall: clay	Promenade tile, clay
Faience tile	Quarry tile, clay

3255   Clay Refractories

Establishments primarily engaged in manufacturing clay firebrick and other heat resisting clay products. Establishments primarily engaged in manufacturing nonclay refractories and all graphite refractories, whether of carbon bond or ceramic bond, are classified in Industry 3297.

Brick, clay refractory: fire clay and high alumina	Hot top refractories, clay
Castable refractories, clay	Insulating firebrick and shapes, clay
Cement, clay refractory	Kiln furniture, clay
Clay refractories	Ladle brick, clay
Crucibles, fire clay	Melting pots, glasshouse: clay
Fire clay blocks, bricks, tile, and special shapes	Mortars, clay refractory
Firebrick, clay	Plastics fire clay bricks
Floaters, glasshouse: clay	Plastics refractories, clay
Foundry refractories, clay	Rings, glasshouse: clay
Glasshouse refractories	Saggers
Heater radiants, clay	Stoppers, glasshouse: clay
	Tank blocks, glasshouse: clay
	Tile, clay refractory

3259   Structural Clay Products, Not Elsewhere Classified

Establishments primarily engaged in manufacturing clay sewer pipe and structural clay products, not elsewhere classified.

Adobe brick	Lining, stove and flue: clay
Architectural terra cotta	Roofing tile, clay
Blocks, segment: clay	Sewer pipe and fittings, clay
Chimney pipe and tops, clay	Thimbles, chimney: clay
Conduit, vitrified clay	Tile, filter underdrain: clay
Coping, wall: clay	Tile, sewer: clay
Drain tile, clay	
Liner brick and plates, for lining sewers, tanks, etc.: vitrified clay	

Industry Group No.		
326		**POTTERY AND RELATED PRODUCTS**

3261   Vitreous China Plumbing Fixtures and China and Earthenware Fittings and Bathroom Accessories

Establishments primarily engaged in manufacturing vitreous china plumbing fixtures and china and earthenware fittings and bathroom accessories.

Bathroom accessories, vitreous china and earthenware	Laundry trays, vitreous china
Bidets, vitreous china	Lavatories, vitreous china
Bolt caps, vitreous china and earthenware	Plumbing fixtures, vitreous china
Closet bowls, vitreous china	Sinks, vitreous china
Drinking fountains, vitreous china	Soap dishes, vitreous china and earthenware
Faucet handles, vitreous china and earthenware	Toilet fixtures, vitreous china
Flush tanks, vitreous china	Towel bar holders, vitreous china and earthenware
	Urinals, vitreous china

POTTERY AND RELATED PRODUCTS—Con.

3262 Vitreous China Table and Kitchen Articles

Establishments primarily engaged in manufacturing vitreous china table and kitchen articles for use in households and in hotels, restaurants, and other commercial institutions for preparing, serving, or storing food or drink. Establishments primarily engaged in manufacturing fine (semivitreous) earthenware (whiteware) table and kitchen articles are classified in Industry 3263.

Bone china
Commercial and household tableware
 and kitchenware: vitreous china
Cooking ware, china

Dishes: commercial and household—vitreous china
Table articles, vitreous china

3263 Fine Earthenware (Whiteware) Table and Kitchen Articles

Establishments primarily engaged in manufacturing fine (semivitreous) earthenware table and kitchen articles for preparing, serving, or storing food or drink. Establishments primarily engaged in manufacturing vitreous china table and kitchen articles are classified in Industry 3262.

Cooking ware, fine earthenware
Earthenware: commercial and household—semivitreous
Kitchenware, semivitreous earthenware

Tableware: commercial and household—semivitreous
Whiteware, fine type semivitreous tableware and kitchenware

3264 Porcelain Electrical Supplies

Establishments primarily engaged in manufacturing porcelain electronic and other electrical insulators, molded porcelain parts for electrical devices, spark plug and steatitic porcelain, and electronic and electrical supplies from clay and other ceramic materials.

Alumina porcelain insulators
Beryllia porcelain insulators
Cleats, porcelain
Ferrite
Insulators, porcelain
Knobs, porcelain

Magnets, permanent: ceramic or ferrite
Porcelain parts, molded: for electrical and electronic devices
Spark plugs, porcelain
Titania porcelain insulators
Tubes, porcelain

3269 Pottery Products, Not Elsewhere Classified

Establishments primarily engaged in firing and decorating white china and earthenware for the trade and manufacturing art and ornamental pottery, industrial and laboratory pottery, stoneware and coarse earthenware table and kitchen articles, unglazed red earthenware florists' articles, and other pottery products, not elsewhere classified.

Art and ornamental ware, pottery
Ashtrays, pottery
Ceramic articles for craft shops
Chemical porcelain
Chemical stoneware (pottery products)
China firing and decorating, for the trade
Cones, pyrometric: earthenware
Cooking ware: stoneware, coarse earthenware, and pottery
Crockery
Decalcomania work on china and glass, for the trade
Earthenware table and kitchen articles, coarse
Encrusting gold, silver, or other metal on china, for the trade
Figures, pottery: china, earthenware, and stoneware

Filtering media, pottery
Florists' articles, red earthenware
Flower pots, red earthenware
Forms for dipped rubber products, pottery
Grinding media, pottery
Heater parts, pottery
Kitchen articles, coarse earthenware
Lamp bases, pottery
Pottery: art, garden, decorative, industrial, and laboratory
Pyrometer tubes
Rockingham earthenware
Smokers' articles, pottery
Stationery articles, pottery
Textile guides, porcelain
Vases, pottery (china, earthenware, and stoneware)

Industry
Group
No.

Industry
No.

327   CONCRETE, GYPSUM, AND PLASTER PRODUCTS

3271   Concrete Block and Brick

Establishments primarily engaged in manufacturing concrete building block and brick from a combination of cement and aggregate. Contractors engaged in concrete construction work are classified in Division C, Construction, and establishments primarily engaged in mixing and delivering ready-mixed concrete are classified in Industry 3273.

Architectural block, concrete: e.g., fluted, screen, split, slump, ground face
Blocks, concrete and cinder
Brick, concrete
Paving blocks, concrete
Plinth blocks, precast terrazzo

3272   Concrete Products, Except Block and Brick

Establishments primarily engaged in manufacturing concrete products, except block and brick, from a combination of cement and aggregate. Contractors engaged in concrete construction work are classified in Division C, Construction, and establishments primarily engaged in mixing and delivering ready-mixed concrete are classified in Industry 3273.

Areaways, basement window: concrete
Art marble, concrete
Ashlar, cast stone
Bathtubs, concrete
Battery wells and boxes, concrete
Building materials, concrete: except block and brick
Building stone, artificial: concrete
Burial vaults, concrete and precast terrazzo
Cast stone, concrete
Catch basin covers, concrete
Ceiling squares, concrete
Chimney caps, concrete
Church furniture, concrete
Columns, concrete
Concrete products, precast: except block and brick
Concrete, dry mixture
Conduits, concrete
Copings, concrete
Cribbing, concrete
Crossing slabs, concrete
Culvert pipe, concrete
Cylinder pipe, prestressed concrete
Cylinder pipe, pretensioned concrete
Door frames, concrete
Drain tile, concrete
Fireplaces, concrete
Floor filler tiles, concrete
Floor slabs, precast concrete
Floor tile, precast terrazzo
Fountains, concrete
Fountains, wash: precast terrazzo
Garbage boxes, concrete
Grave markers, concrete
Grave vaults, concrete
Grease traps, concrete
Housing components, prefabricated: concrete
Incinerators, concrete
Irrigation pipe, concrete
Joists, concrete
Laundry trays, concrete
Lintels, concrete

Manhole covers and frames, concrete
Mantels, concrete
Mattresses for river revetment, concrete articulated
Meter boxes, concrete
Monuments, concrete
Panels and sections, prefabricated: concrete
Paving materials, prefabricated concrete, except blocks
Pier footings, prefabricated concrete
Piling, prefabricated concrete
Pipe, concrete
Pipe, lined with concrete
Poles, concrete
Posts, concrete
Pressure pipe, reinforced concrete
Prestressed concrete products
Roofing tile and slabs, concrete
Septic tanks, concrete
Sewer pipe, concrete
Shower receptors, concrete
Siding, precast stone
Sills, concrete
Silo staves, cast stone
Silos, prefabricated concrete
Slabs, crossing: concrete
Spanish floor tile, concrete
Squares for walls and ceilings, concrete
Steps, prefabricated concrete
Stone, cast concrete
Stools, precast terrazzo
Storage tanks, concrete
Tanks, concrete
Terrazzo products, precast
Thresholds, precast terrazzo
Ties, railroad: concrete
Tile, precast terrazzo or concrete
Tombstones, precast terrazzo or concrete
Wall base, precast terrazzo
Wall squares, concrete
Wash foundations, precast terrazzo
Well curbing, concrete
Window sills, cast stone

327   **CONCRETE, GYPSUM, AND PLASTER PRODUCTS—Con.**

3273 Ready-Mixed Concrete

Establishments primarily engaged in manufacturing portland cement concrete manufactured and delivered to a purchaser in a plastic and unhardened state. This industry includes production and sale of central-mixed concrete, shrink-mixed concrete, and truck-mixed concrete.

Central-mixed concrete	Shrink-mixed concrete
Ready-mixed concrete, production and distribution	Truck-mixed concrete

3274 Lime

Establishments primarily engaged in manufacturing quicklime, hydrated lime, and "dead-burned" dolomite from limestone, dolomite shells, or other substances.

Agricultural lime	Hydrated lime
Building lime	Lime plaster
Dolomite, dead-burned	Masons' lime
Dolomitic lime	Quicklime

3275 Gypsum Products

Establishments primarily engaged in manufacturing plaster, plasterboard, and other products composed wholly or chiefly of gypsum, except articles of plaster of paris and papier-mache.

Acoustical plaster, gypsum	Insulating plaster, gypsum
Agricultural gypsum	Orthopedic plaster, gypsum
Board, gypsum	Panels, plaster: gypsum
Building board, gypsum	Plaster and plasterboard, gypsum
Cement, Keene's	Plaster of paris
Gypsum products: e.g., block, board, plaster, lath, rock, tile	Wallboard, gypsum

328   **CUT STONE AND STONE PRODUCTS**

3281 Cut Stone and Stone Products

Establishments primarily engaged in cutting, shaping, and finishing granite, marble, limestone, slate, and other stone for building and miscellaneous uses. Establishments primarily engaged in buying or selling partly finished monuments and tombstones, but performing no work on the stones other than lettering, finishing, or shaping to custom order, are classified in Division F, Wholesale Trade or Division G, Retail Trade. The cutting of grindstones, pulpstones, and whetstones at the quarry is classified in Division B, Mining.

Altars, cut stone	Paving blocks, cut stone
Baptismal fonts, cut stone	Pedestals, marble
Benches, cut stone	Pulpits, cut stone
Blackboards, slate	Roofing, slate
Burial vaults, stone	Slate and slate products
Church furniture, cut stone	Statuary, marble
Curbing, granite and stone	Stone, cut and shaped
Cut stone products	Stone, quarrying and processing of own stone products
Desk set bases, onyx	
Dimension stone for buildings	Switchboard panels, slate
Flagstones	Table tops, marble
Furniture, cut stone	Tombstones, cut stone: not including only finishing or lettering to order
Granite, cut and shaped	
Lamp bases, onyx	Urns, cut stone
Limestone, cut and shaped	Vases, cut stone
Marble, building: cut and shaped	
Monuments, cut stone: not including only finishing or lettering to order	

329 ABRASIVE, ASBESTOS, AND MISCELLANEOUS NONMETALLIC MINERAL PRODUCTS

3291 Abrasive Products

Establishments primarily engaged in manufacturing abrasive grinding wheels of natural or synthetic materials, abrasive-coated products, and other abrasive products. The cutting of grindstones, pulpstones, and whetstones at the quarry is classified in Division B, Mining .

Abrasive buffs, bricks, cloth, paper, sticks, stones, wheels, etc.
Abrasive grains, natural and artificial
Abrasive-coated products
Abrasives, aluminous
Aluminum oxide (fused) abrasives
Boron carbide abrasives
Bort, crushing
Buffing and polishing wheels, abrasive and nonabrasive
Cloth: garnet, emery, aluminum oxide, and silicon carbide coated
Corundum abrasives
Diamond dressing wheels
Diamond powder
Emery abrasives
Garnet abrasives
Grinding balls, ceramic
Grindstones, artificial
Grit, steel
Hones
Metallic abrasives

Oilstones, artificial
Pads, scouring: soap impregnated
Paper: garnet, emery, aluminum oxide, and silicon carbide coated
Polishing rouge (abrasive)
Polishing wheels
Pumice and pumicite abrasives
Rouge, polishing
Rubbing stones, artificial
Sandpaper
Scythestones, artificial
Silicon carbide abrasives
Sponges, scouring: metallic
Steel shot abrasives
Steel wool
Tripoli
Tungsten carbide abrasives
Wheels, abrasive: except dental
Wheels, diamond abrasive
Wheels, grinding: artificial
Whetstones, artificial

3292 Asbestos Products

Establishments primarily engaged in manufacturing asbestos textiles, asbestos building materials, except asbestos paper, insulating materials for covering boilers and pipes, and other products composed wholly or chiefly of asbestos. Establishments primarily engaged in manufacturing asbestos paper are classified in Industry 2621, and those manufacturing gaskets and packing are classified in Industry 3053.

Asbestos cement products: e.g., siding, pressure pipe, conduits, ducts
Asbestos products: except packing and gaskets
Blankets, insulating for aircraft: asbestos
Boiler covering (heat insulating material), except felt
Brake lining, asbestos
Brake pads, asbestos
Building materials, asbestos: except asbestos paper
Carded fiber, asbestos
Cloth, asbestos
Clutch facings, asbestos
Cord, asbestos
Felt, woven amosite: asbestos
Floor tile, asphalt
Friction materials, asbestos: woven
Insulation, molded asbestos

Mattresses, asbestos
Millboard, asbestos
Pipe and boiler covering, except felt
Pipe covering (insulation), laminated asbestos paper
Pipe, pressure: asbestos cement
Roofing, asbestos felt roll
Rope, asbestos
Sheet, asbestos cement: flat or corrugated
Shingles, asbestos cement
Siding, asbestos cement
Table pads and padding, asbestos
Tape, asbestos
Textiles, asbestos: except packing
Thread, asbestos
Tile, vinyl asbestos
Tubing, asbestos
Wick, asbestos
Yarn, asbestos

3295 Minerals and Earths, Ground or Otherwise Treated

Establishments operating without a mine or quarry and primarily engaged in crushing, grinding, pulverizing, or otherwise preparing clay, ceramic, and refractory minerals; barite; and miscellaneous nonmetallic minerals, except

329   ABRASIVE, ASBESTOS, AND MISCELLANEOUS NONMETALLIC
MINERAL PRODUCTS—Con.

3295 Minerals and Earths, Ground or Otherwise Treated—Con.

fuels. These minerals are the crude products mined by establishments of Industry Groups 145 and 149, and by those of Industry 1479 mining barite. Also included are establishments primarily crushing slag and preparing roofing granules. The beneficiation or preparation of other minerals and metallic ores, and the cleaning and grading of coal, are classified in Division B, Mining, whether or not the operation is associated with a mine.

Barite, ground or otherwise treated
Barium, ground or otherwise treated
Blast furnace slag
Clay for petroleum refining, chemically processed
Clay, ground or otherwise treated
Desiccants, activated: clay
Diatomaceous earth, ground or otherwise treated
Feldspar, ground or otherwise treated
Filtering clays, treated purchased materials
Flint, ground or otherwise treated
Foundry facings, ground or otherwise treated
Fuller's earth, ground or otherwise treated
Graphite, natural: ground, pulverized, refined, or blended
Kaolin, ground or otherwise treated
Lead, black (natural graphite): ground, refined, or blended

Magnesite, crude: ground, calcined, or dead-burned
Mica, ground or otherwise treated
Perlite aggregate
Perlite, expanded
Plumbago: ground, refined, or blended
Pulverized earth
Pumice, ground or otherwise treated
Pyrophyllite, ground or otherwise treated
Roofing granules
Shale, expanded
Silicon, ultra high purity: treated purchased materials
Slag, crushed or ground
Spar, ground or otherwise treated
Steatite, ground or otherwise treated
Talc, ground or otherwise treated
Vermiculite, exfoliated

3296 Mineral Wool

Establishments primarily engaged in manufacturing mineral wool and mineral wool insulation products made of such siliceous materials as rock, slag, and glass, or combinations thereof. Establishments primarily engaged in manufacturing asbestos insulation products are classified in Industry 3292, and those manufacturing textile glass fibers are classified in Industry 3229.

Acoustical board and tile, mineral wool
Fiberglass insulation
Glass wool

Insulation: rock wool, fiberglass, slag, and silica minerals
Mineral wool roofing mats

3297 Nonclay Refractories

Establishments primarily engaged in manufacturing refractories and crucibles made of materials other than clay. This industry includes establishments primarily engaged in manufacturing all graphite refractories, whether of carbon bond or ceramic bond. Establishments primarily engaged in manufacturing clay refractories are classified in Industry 3255.

Alumina fused refractories
Brick, bauxite
Brick, carbon
Brick, refractory: chrome, magnesite, silica, and other nonclay
Brick, silicon carbide
Castable refractories, nonclay
Cement, magnesia
Cement: high temperature, refractory (nonclay)
Crucibles: graphite, magnesite, chrome, silica, or other nonclay materials
Dolomite and dolomite-magnesite brick and shapes

Gunning mixes, nonclay
High temperature mortar, nonclay
Hot top refractories, nonclay
Nonclay refractories
Plastics refractories, nonclay
Pyrolytic graphite
Ramming mixes, nonclay
Refractories, castable: nonclay
Refractories, graphite: carbon bond or ceramic bond
Refractory cement, nonclay
Retorts, graphite

Industry Group No.	Industry No.	
329		**ABRASIVE, ASBESTOS, AND MISCELLANEOUS NONMETALLIC MINERAL PRODUCTS—Con.**

3299 Nonmetallic Mineral Products, Not Elsewhere Classified

Establishments primarily engaged in the factory production of goods made of plaster of paris and papier-mache, and in manufacturing sand lime products and other nonmetallic mineral products, not elsewhere classified.

Architectural sculptures, plaster of paris: factory production only
Art goods: plaster of paris, papier-mache, and scagliola
Blocks, sand lime
Brackets, architectural: plaster—factory production only
Built-up mica
Ceramic fiber
Columns, papier-mache or plaster of paris
Ecclesiastical statuary: gypsum, clay, or papier-mache—factory production only
Floor composition, magnesite
Flower boxes, plaster of paris: factory production only
Fountains, plaster of paris: factory production only
Gravel painting
Images, small: gypsum, clay, or papier-mache—factory production only
Insulsleeves (foundry materials)
Mica products, built-up and sheet, except radio parts
Mica splitting

Mica, laminated
Moldings, architectural: plaster of paris—factory production only
Ornamental and architectural plaster work: e.g., mantels and columns
Panels, papier-mache or plaster of paris
Pedestals, statuary: plaster of paris or papier-mache—factory production only
Plaques: clay, plaster, or papier-mache—factory production only
Sculptures, architectural: gypsum, clay, or papier-mache—factory production only
Statuary: gypsum, clay, papier-mache, scagliola, and metal—factory production only
Stucco
Synthetic stones, for gem stones and industrial use
Tile, sand lime
Tubing for electrical purposes, quartz
Urns, gypsum or papier-mache: factory production only
Vases, gypsum or papier-mache: factory production only

Major Group 33.—PRIMARY METAL INDUSTRIES

The Major Group as a Whole

This major group includes establishments engaged in smelting and refining ferrous and nonferrous metals from ore, pig, or scrap; in rolling, drawing, and alloying metals; in manufacturing castings and other basic metal products; and in manufacturing nails, spikes, and insulated wire and cable. This major group includes the production of coke. Establishments primarily engaged in manufacturing metal forgings or stampings are classified in Industry Group 346.

Industry Group No.

Industry No.

331 **STEEL WORKS, BLAST FURNACES, AND ROLLING AND FINISHING MILLS**

3312 Steel Works, Blast Furnaces (Including Coke Ovens), and Rolling Mills

Establishments primarily engaged in manufacturing hot metal, pig iron, and silvery pig iron from iron ore and iron and steel scrap; converting pig iron, scrap iron, and scrap steel into steel; and in hot-rolling iron and steel into basic shapes, such as plates, sheets, strips, rods, bars, and tubing. Merchant blast furnaces and byproduct or beehive coke ovens are also included in this industry. Establishments primarily engaged in manufacturing ferro and nonferrous additive alloys by electrometallurgical processes are classified in Industry 3313.

Armor plate, made in steel works or rolling mills
Axles, rolled or forged: made in steel works or rolling mills
Bars, iron: made in steel works or rolling mills
Bars, steel: made in steel works or hot-rolling mills
Beehive coke oven products
Billets, steel
Blackplate
Blast furnace products
Blooms
Car wheels, rolled
Chemical recovery coke oven products
Coal gas, derived from chemical recovery coke ovens
Coal tar crudes, derived from chemical recovery coke ovens
Coke, produced in beehive ovens
Coke, produced in chemical recovery coke ovens
Distillates, derived from chemical recovery coke ovens
Fence posts, iron and steel: made in steel works or rolling mills
Flats, iron and steel: made in steel works or hot-rolling mills
Forgings, iron and steel: made in steel works or rolling mills
Frogs, iron and steel: made in steel works or rolling mills
Galvanized hoops, pipes, plates, sheets, and strips: iron and steel
Gun forgings, iron and steel: made in steel works or rolling mills
Hoops, galvanized iron and steel
Hoops, iron and steel: made in steel works or hot-rolling mills
Hot-rolled iron and steel products
Ingots, steel
Iron sinter, made in steel mills
Iron, pig
Nut rods, iron and steel: made in steel works or rolling mills
Pipe, iron and steel: made in steel works or rolling mills
Plates, made in steel works or rolling mills
Rail joints and fastenings, made in steel works or rolling mills
Railroad crossings, iron and steel: made in steel works or rolling mills
Rails, iron and steel
Rails, rerolled or renewed
Rods, iron and steel: made in steel works or rolling mills
Sheet pilings, plain: iron and steel—made in steel works or rolling mills
Sheets, steel: made in steel works or hot-rolling mills
Shell slugs, steel: made in steel works or rolling mills
Skelp, iron and steel
Slabs, steel
Spike rods, made in steel works or rolling mills
Sponge iron
Stainless steel
Steel works producing bars, rods, plates, sheets, structural shapes, etc.
Strips, galvanized iron and steel: made in steel works or rolling mills
Strips, iron and steel: made in steel works or hot-rolling mills
Structural shapes, iron and steel
Tar, derived from chemical recovery coke ovens

Industry Group No.	Industry No.	
331		**STEEL WORKS, BLAST FURNACES, AND ROLLING AND FINISHING MILLS—Con.**

3312 Steel Works, Blast Furnaces (Including Coke Ovens), and Rolling Mills—Con.

Terneplate
Ternes, iron and steel: long or short
Tie plates, iron and steel
Tin-free steel
Tinplate
Tool steel
Tube rounds
Tubes, iron and steel: made in steel works or rolling mills

Tubing, seamless: steel
Well casings, iron and steel: made in steel works or rolling mills
Wheels, car and locomotive: iron and steel—mitse
Wire products, iron and steel: made in steel works or rolling mills
Wrought pipe and tubing, made in steel works or rolling mills

3313 Electrometallurgical Products, Except Steel

Establishments primarily engaged in manufacturing ferro and nonferrous metal additive alloys by electrometallurgical or metallothermic processes, including high percentage ferroalloys and high percentage nonferrous additive alloys. Establishments primarily engaged in manufacturing electrometallurgical steel are classified in Industry 3312.

Additive alloys, except copper
Ferroalloys (including high percentage)
Ferrochromium
Ferromanganese
Ferromolybdenum
Ferrophosphorus
Ferrosilicon
Ferrotitanium
Ferrotungsten

Ferrovanadium
High percentage ferroalloys
Manganese metal
Molybdenum silicon
Nonferrous additive alloys, high percentage: except copper
Spiegeleisen
Tungsten carbide powder by metallurgical process

3315 Steel Wiredrawing and Steel Nails and Spikes

Establishments primarily engaged in drawing wire from purchased iron or steel rods, bars, or wire and which may be engaged in the further manufacture of products made from wire; establishments primarily engaged in manufacturing steel nails and spikes from purchased materials are also included in this industry. Rolling mills engaged in the production of ferrous wire from wire rods or hot-rolled bars produced in the same establishment are classified in Industry 3312. Establishments primarily engaged in drawing nonferrous wire are classified in Industry Group 335.

Barbed and twisted wire: made in wiredrawing plants
Baskets, steel: made in wiredrawing plants
Brads, steel: wire or cut
Cable, steel: insulated or armored
Chain link fencing, steel: made in wiredrawing plants
Fence gates, posts, and fittings: steel—made in wiredrawing plants
Form ties, made in wiredrawing plants
Horseshoe nails
Nails, steel: wire or cut
Paper clips, steel: made in wiredrawing plants
Spikes, steel: wire or cut
Staples, steel: wire or cut
Steel wire cages, made in wiredrawing plants

Tacks, steel: wire or cut
Tie wires, made in wiredrawing plants
Welded steel wire fabric, made in wiredrawing plants
Wire carts: household, grocery, and industrial—made in wiredrawing plants
Wire cloth, steel: made in wiredrawing plants
Wire garment hangers, steel: made in wiredrawing plants
Wire products, ferrous: made in wiredrawing plants
Wire, ferrous: made in wiredrawing plants
Wire, steel: insulated or armored

Industry
Group   Industry
No.   No.

331   **STEEL WORKS, BLAST FURNACES, AND ROLLING AND FINISHING MILLS—Con.**

3316   **Cold-Rolled Steel Sheet, Strip, and Bars**

Establishments primarily engaged in: (1) cold-rolling steel sheets and strip from purchased hot-rolled sheets; (2) cold-drawing steel bars and steel shapes from purchased hot-rolled steel bars; and (3) producing other cold finished steel. Establishments primarily engaged in the production of steel, including hot-rolled steel sheets, and further cold-rolling such sheets are classified in Industry 3312.

Cold-finished steel bars: not made in hot-rolling mills
Cold-rolled steel strip, sheet, and bars: not made in hot-rolling mills
Corrugating iron and steel, cold-rolled: not made in hot-rolling mills
Flat bright steel strip, cold-rolled: not made in hot-rolling mills

Razor blade strip steel, cold-rolled: not made in hot-rolling mills
Sheet steel, cold-rolled: not made in hot-rolling mills
Wire, flat: cold-rolled strip—not made in hot-rolling mills

3317   **Steel Pipe and Tubes**

Establishments primarily engaged in the production of welded or seamless steel pipe and tubes and heavy riveted steel pipe from purchased materials. Establishments primarily engaged in the production of steel, including steel skelp or steel blanks, tube rounds, or pierced billets, are classified in Industry 3312.

Boiler tubes, wrought—mfpm
Conduit: welded, lock joint, and heavy riveted—mfpm
Pipe, seamless steel—mfpm
Pipe, wrought: welded, lock joint, and heavy riveted—mfpm
Tubes, seamless steel—mfpm

Tubing, mechanical and hypodermic sizes: cold-drawn stainless steel—mfpm
Well casing, wrought: welded, lock joint, and heavy riveted—mfpm
Wrought pipe and tubes: welded, lock joint, and heavy riveted—mfpm

332   **IRON AND STEEL FOUNDRIES**

This industry group includes establishments primarily engaged in manufacturing iron and steel castings. These establishments generally operate on a job or order basis, manufacturing castings for sale to others or for interplant transfer. Establishments which produce iron and steel castings and which are also engaged in fabricating operations, such as machining and assembling, in manufacturing a specified product are classified in the industry of the specified product. Iron and steel castings are made, to a considerable extent, by establishments that are classified in other industries and that operate foundry departments for the production of castings for incorporation, in the same establishment, into such products as stoves, furnaces, plumbing fixtures, and motor vehicles. Establishments primarily engaged in the manufacture and rolling of steel and also making steel castings are classified in Industry 3312. Establishments primarily engaged in manufacturing nonferrous castings are classified in Industry Group 336.

3321   **Gray and Ductile Iron Foundries**

Establishments primarily engaged in manufacturing gray and ductile iron castings, including cast iron pressure and soil pipes and fittings.

Brake shoes, railroad: cast iron
Car wheels, railroad: chilled cast iron

Castings, compacted graphite iron
Castings, gray iron and semisteel

Industry Group No.	Industry No.	

332   **IRON AND STEEL FOUNDRIES—Con.**

3321   **Gray and Ductile Iron Foundries—Con.**

Cooking utensils, cast iron
Couplings, pipe: pressure and soil pipe—cast iron
Ductile iron castings
Elbows, pipe: pressure and soil pipe—cast iron
Fittings, soil and pressure pipe: cast iron
Foundries, gray iron and semisteel
Gas pipe, cast iron
Gray iron foundries
Ingot molds and stools

Manhole covers, metal
Nipples, pipe: pressure and soil pipe—cast iron
Nodular iron castings
Pipe and fittings, soil and pressure: cast iron
Railroad car wheels, chilled cast iron
Rolling mill rolls, iron: not machined
Sash balances, cast iron
Sewer pipe, cast iron
Water pipe, cast iron

3322   **Malleable Iron Foundries**

Establishments primarily engaged in manufacturing malleable iron castings.

Castings, malleable iron
Foundries, malleable iron

Pearlitic castings, malleable iron

3324   **Steel Investment Foundries**

Establishments primarily engaged in manufacturing steel investment castings.

Investment castings, steel

3325   **Steel Foundries, Not Elsewhere Classified**

Establishments primarily engaged in manufacturing steel castings, not elsewhere classified.

Alloy steel castings, except investment
Bushings, cast steel: except investment
Cast steel railroad car wheels
Castings, steel: except investment

Foundries, steel: except investment
Rolling mill rolls, steel: not machined
Steel foundries, except investment

333   **PRIMARY SMELTING AND REFINING OF NONFERROUS METALS**

3331   **Primary Smelting and Refining of Copper**

Establishments primarily engaged in smelting copper from the ore, and in refining copper by electrolytic or other processes. Establishments primarily engaged in rolling, drawing, or extruding copper are classified in Industry 3351.

Bars, refinery: primary copper
Blister copper
Blocks, copper
Copper ingots and refinery bars, primary

Copper smelting and refining, primary
Pigs, copper
Primary smelting and refining of copper
Slabs, copper: primary

3334   **Primary Production of Aluminum**

Establishments primarily engaged in producing aluminum from alumina and in refining aluminum by any process. Establishments primarily engaged in rolling, drawing, or extruding aluminum are classified in Industry Group 335.

Aluminum ingots and primary production shapes, from bauxite or alumina
Extrusion ingot, aluminum: primary

Pigs, aluminum
Slabs, aluminum: primary

Industry
Group
No.

Industry
No.

333 **PRIMARY SMELTING AND REFINING OF NONFERROUS METALS—
Con.**

**3339 Primary Smelting and Refining of Nonferrous Metals, Except Copper and
Aluminum**

Establishments primarily engaged in smelting and refining nonferrous
metals, except copper and aluminum. Establishments primarily engaged in
rolling, drawing, and extruding these nonferrous primary metals are classified
in Industry 3356, and the production of bullion at the site of the mine is classified in Division B, Mining.

Antifriction bearing metals, lead-base:
primary
Antimony refining, primary
Babbitt metal, primary
Beryllium metal
Bismuth refining, primary
Blocks, zinc, primary
Cadmium refining, primary
Chromium refining, primary
Cobalt refining, primary
Columbium refining, primary
Germanium refining, primary
Gold refining, primary
Ingots, primary: nonferrous metals,
except copper and aluminum
Iridium refining, primary
Lead pigs, blocks, ingots, and refinery
shapes: primary
Lead smelting and refining, primary
Magnesium refining, primary
Nickel refining, primary
Nonferrous refining, primary: except
copper and aluminum
Nonferrous smelting, primary: except
copper and aluminum
Pigs, primary: nonferrous metals,
except copper and aluminum
Platinum-group metals refining, pri-
mary

Precious metal refining, primary
Primary refining of nonferrous metal:
except copper and aluminum
Primary smelting of nonferrous metal:
except copper and aluminum
Refining of nonferrous metal, primary:
except copper and aluminum
Rhenium refining, primary
Selenium refining, primary
Silicon refining, primary (over 99 per-
cent pure)
Silicon, epitaxial (silicon alloy)
Silicon, pure
Silver refining, primary
Slabs, primary: nonferrous metals,
except copper and aluminum
Smelting of nonferrous metal, primary:
except copper and aluminum
Spelter (zinc), primary
Tantalum refining
Tellurium refining, primary
Tin base alloys, primary
Tin refining, primary
Titanium metal sponge and granules
Zinc dust, primary
Zirconium metal sponge and granules

334 **SECONDARY SMELTING AND REFINING OF NONFERROUS METALS**

3341 Secondary Smelting and Refining of Nonferrous Metals

Establishments primarily engaged in recovering nonferrous metals and
alloys from new and used scrap and dross or in producing alloys from purchased refined metals. This industry includes establishments engaged in both
the recovery and alloying of precious metals. Plants engaged in the recovery
of tin through secondary smelting and refining, as well as by chemical processes, are included in this industry. Establishments primarily engaged in assembling, sorting, and breaking up scrap metal, without smelting and refining, are classified in Wholesale Trade, Industry 5093.

Aluminum extrusion ingot, secondary
Aluminum smelting and refining, sec-
ondary
Antimonial lead refining, secondary
Babbitt metal smelting and refining,
secondary
Brass smelting and refining, secondary
Bronze smelting and refining, second-
ary
Copper smelting and refining, second-
ary
Detinning of cans
Detinning of scrap

Germanium refining, secondary
Gold smelting and refining, secondary
Ingots, nonferrous: smelting and refin-
ing—secondary
Iridium smelting and refining, second-
ary
Lead smelting and refining, secondary
Magnesium smelting and refining, sec-
ondary
Nickel smelting and refining, secondary
Nonferrous metal smelting and refin-
ing, secondary
Platinum-group metals smelting and

Industry Group No.	Industry No.	

334   SECONDARY SMELTING AND REFINING OF NONFERROUS METALS— Con.

3341   Secondary Smelting and Refining of Nonferrous Metals—Con.

refining, secondary
Precious metal smelting and refining, secondary
Recovering and refining of nonferrous metals
Recovery of silver from used photographic film
Secondary refining and smelting of nonferrous metals

Selenium refining, secondary
Silver smelting and refining, secondary
Solder (base metal), pig and ingot: secondary
Tin smelting and refining, secondary
Zinc dust, reclaimed
Zinc smelting and refining, secondary

335   ROLLING, DRAWING, AND EXTRUDING OF NONFERROUS METALS

3351   Rolling, Drawing, and Extruding of Copper

Establishments primarily engaged in rolling, drawing, and extruding copper, brass, bronze, and other copper base alloy basic shapes, such as plate, sheet, strip, bar, and tubing. Establishments primarily engaged in recovering copper and its alloys from scrap or dross are classified in Industry 3341.

Bands, shell: copper and copper alloy— made in copper rolling mills
Bars, copper and copper alloy
Brass rolling and drawing
Bronze rolling and drawing
Cartridge cups, discs, and sheets: copper and copper alloy
Cups, primer and cartridge: copper and copper alloy
Extruded shapes, copper and copper alloy
Pipe, extruded and drawn: brass, bronze, and copper
Plates, copper and copper alloy
Primer cups, copper and copper alloy

Rails, rolled and drawn: brass, bronze, and copper
Rods, copper and copper alloy
Rolling, drawing, and extruding of copper and copper alloys
Rotating bands, copper and copper alloy
Sheets, copper and copper alloy
Shell discs, copper and copper alloy
Slugs, copper and copper alloy
Strip, copper and copper alloy
Tubing, copper and copper alloy
Wire, copper and copper alloy: made in brass mills

3353   Aluminum Sheet, Plate, and Foil

Establishments primarily engaged in flat rolling aluminum and aluminum-base alloy basic shapes, such as sheet, plate, and foil, including establishments producing welded tube. Also included are establishments primarily producing similar products by continuous casting.

Coils, sheet: aluminum
Foil, plain aluminum
Plates, aluminum

Sheets, aluminum
Tubes, welded: aluminum

3354   Aluminum Extruded Products

Establishments primarily engaged in extruding aluminum and aluminum-base alloy basic shapes, such as rod and bar, pipe and tube, and tube blooms, including establishments producing tube by drawing.

Bars, aluminum: extruded
Coils, rod: aluminum—extruded
Extruded shapes, aluminum
Pipe, aluminum: extruded

Rods, aluminum: extruded
Tube blooms, aluminum: extruded
Tube, aluminum: extruded or drawn

3355   Aluminum Rolling and Drawing, Not Elsewhere Classified

Establishments primarily engaged in rolling, drawing, and other operations resulting in the production of aluminum ingot, including extrusion ingot, and aluminum and aluminum-base alloy basic shapes, not elsewhere classified, such as rolled and continuous cast rod and bar. Establishments primarily en-

**335   ROLLING, DRAWING, AND EXTRUDING OF NONFERROUS METALS—
        Con.**

3355   Aluminum Rolling and Drawing, Not Elsewhere Classified—Con.

gaged in producing aluminum powder, flake, and paste are classified in Industry 3399, and those producing aluminum wire and cable from purchased wire bars, rods, or wire are classified in Industry 3357.

Bars, aluminum: rolled	Ingot, aluminum: made in rolling mills
Cable, aluminum: made in rolling mills	Rails, aluminum: rolled and drawn
Coils, wire: aluminum—made in rolling mills	Rods, aluminum: rolled
mills	Slugs, aluminum
Extrusion ingot, aluminum: made in	Structural shapes, rolled aluminum
rolling mills	Wire, aluminum: made in rolling mills

**3356   Rolling, Drawing, and Extruding of Nonferrous Metals, Except Copper and
        Aluminum**

Establishments primarily engaged in rolling, drawing, and extruding nonferrous metals other than copper and aluminum. The products of this industry are in the form of basic shapes, such as plate, sheet, strip, bar, and tubing. Establishments primarily engaged in recovering nonferrous metals and alloys from scrap or dross are classified in Industry 3341; those manufacturing gold, silver, tin, and other foils, except aluminum, are classified in Industry 3497; and those manufacturing aluminum foil are classified in Industry 3353.

Battery metal	Silver and silver alloy bars, rods,
Britannia metal, rolling and drawing	sheets, strip, and tubing
Extruded shapes, nonferrous metals	Silver rolling and drawing
and alloys, except copper and alumi-	Solder wire, bar: acid core and rosin
num	core
Gold and gold alloy bars, sheets, strip,	Tin and tin alloy bars, pipe, rods,
and tubing	sheets, strip, and tubing
Gold rolling and drawing	Tin rolling and drawing
Lead and lead alloy bars, pipe, plates,	Titanium and titanium alloy bars, rods,
rods, sheets, strip, and tubing	billets, sheets, strip, and tubing
Lead rolling, drawing, and extruding	Titanium from sponge
Magnesium and magnesium alloy bars,	Tungsten basic shapes
rods, shapes, sheets, strip, and tubing	Welding rods
Magnesium rolling, drawing, and ex-	Wire, nonferrous except copper and
truding	aluminum: made in rolling mills
Nickel and nickel alloy pipe, plates,	Zinc and zinc alloy bars, plates, pipe,
sheets, strips, and tubing	rods, sheets, tubing, and wire
Nonferrous rolling, drawing, and ex-	Zinc rolling, drawing, and extruding
truding: except copper and aluminum	Zirconium and zirconium alloy bars,
Platinum and platinum alloy sheets	rods, billets, sheets, strip, and tubing
and tubing	
Platinum-group metals rolling, draw-	
ing, and extruding	

3357   Drawing and Insulating of Nonferrous Wire

Establishments primarily engaged in drawing, drawing and insulating, and insulating wire and cable of nonferrous metals from purchased wire bars, rods, or wire. Also included are establishments primarily engaged in manufacturing insulated fiber optic cable. Establishments primarily engaged in manufacturing glass fiber optic materials are classified in Industry 3229, and those manufacturing fabricated wire products from purchased wire are classified in Industry 3496.

Apparatus wire and cord: made in wire-	Coaxial cable, nonferrous
drawing plants	Communications wire and cable, non-
Automotive and aircraft wire and	ferrous
cable, nonferrous	Cord sets, flexible: made in wiredraw-
Cable, nonferrous: bare, insulated, or	ing plants
armored—mfpm	Fiber optic cable

Industry
Group   Industry
No.   No.

335   ROLLING, DRAWING, AND EXTRUDING OF NONFERROUS METALS—Con.

3357   Drawing and Insulating of Nonferrous Wire—Con.

Magnet wire, insulated
Shipboard cable, nonferrous
Signal and control cable, nonferrous
Weatherproof wire and cable, nonferrous
Wire cloth, nonferrous: made in wire-drawing plants

Wire screening, nonferrous: made in wiredrawing plants
Wire, nonferrous: bare, insulated, or armored—mfpm

336   NONFERROUS FOUNDRIES (CASTINGS)

This industry group includes establishments primarily engaged in manufacturing castings and die-castings of aluminum, brass, bronze, and other nonferrous metals and alloys. These establishments generally operate on a job or order basis, manufacturing castings for sale to others or for interplant transfer. Establishments which produce nonferrous castings and which are also engaged in fabricating operations, such as machining and assembling, in manufacturing a specified product are classified in the industry of the specified product. Nonferrous castings are made to a considerable extent by establishments classified in other industries that operate foundry departments for the production of castings for incorporation, in the same establishment, into such products as machinery and motor vehicles. Establishments primarily engaged in manufacturing iron and steel castings are classified in Industry Group 332.

3363   Aluminum Die-Castings

Establishments primarily engaged in manufacturing die-castings of aluminum (including alloys).

Aluminum die-casting, including alloys

3364   Nonferrous Die-Castings, Except Aluminum

Establishments primarily engaged in manufacturing nonferrous metal die-castings, except aluminum.

Beryllium die-castings
Copper die-castings
Die-casting nonferrous metals, except aluminum

Lead die-castings
Magnesium die-castings
Titanium die-castings
Zinc die-castings

3365   Aluminum Foundries

Establishments primarily engaged in manufacturing aluminum (including alloys) castings, except die-castings.

Aluminum and aluminum-base alloy castings, except die-castings
Castings, aluminum: except die-castings
Cooking utensils, cast aluminum: except die-castings
Foundries, aluminum: except die-castings
Hospital utensils, cast aluminum: except die-castings

Household utensils, cast aluminum: except die-castings
Kitchen utensils, cast aluminum: except die-castings
Machinery castings, aluminum: except die-castings
Pressure cookers, domestic: cast aluminum, except die-castings

3366   Copper Foundries

Establishments primarily engaged in manufacturing copper (including alloys) castings, except die-castings.

Bushings and bearings, except die-castings: brass, bronze, and copper

Industry Group No.	Industry No.	
336		**NONFERROUS FOUNDRIES (CASTINGS)—Con.**

3366 Copper Foundries—Con.

Castings, except die-castings: brass, bronze, copper, and copper-base alloy
Copper and copper-base alloy castings, except die-castings
Copper foundries, except die-castings
Foundries: brass, bronze, copper, and copper-base alloy—except die-castings

Machinery castings: brass, copper, and copper-base alloy—except die-castings
Propellers, ship and screw: cast brass, bronze, copper, and copper-base—except die-castings

3369 Nonferrous Foundries, Except Aluminum and Copper

Establishments primarily engaged in manufacturing nonferrous metal castings (including alloys), except all die-castings and other castings of aluminum or copper.

Beryllium castings, except die-castings
Castings, except die-castings and castings of aluminum and copper
Castings, precision, except die-castings: industrial and aircraft use—cobalt-chromium
Machinery castings, nonferrous: except aluminum, copper, copper alloys, and die-castings
Magnesium castings, except die-castings

Nonferrous metal foundries, except aluminum, copper, and die-castings
Nonferrous metal machinery castings: except aluminum, copper, and die-castings
Titanium castings, except die-castings
White metal castings, except die-castings: lead, antimony, and tin
Zinc castings, except die-castings

| 339 | | **MISCELLANEOUS PRIMARY METAL PRODUCTS** |

3398 Metal Heat Treating

Establishments primarily engaged in heat treating of metal for the trade.

Annealing of metal for the trade
Brazing (hardening) metal for the trade
Burning metal for the trade
Hardening of metal for the trade
Heat treating of metal for the trade

Shot peening-treating steel to reduce fatigue
Stainless steel, brazing (hardening) for the trade
Tempering of metal for the trade

3399 Primary Metal Products, Not Elsewhere Classified

Establishments primarily engaged in manufacturing primary metal products, not elsewhere classified, such as nonferrous nails, brads, and spikes, and metal powder, flakes, and paste.

Aluminum atomized powder
Balls, steel
Brads, nonferrous metal (including wire)
Flakes, metal
Iron, powdered
Laminating steel for the trade
Nails, nonferrous metal (including wire)
Paste, metal
Powder, metal: except artists' materials

Reclaiming ferrous metals from clay
Recovery of iron ore from open hearth slag
Silver powder, except artists' materials
Spikes, nonferrous metal (including wire)
Staples, nonferrous metal (including wire)
Tacks, nonferrous metal (including wire)

Major Group 34.—FABRICATED METAL PRODUCTS, EXCEPT MACHINERY AND TRANSPORTATION EQUIPMENT

The Major Group as a Whole

This major group includes establishments engaged in fabricating ferrous and nonferrous metal products, such as metal cans, tinware, handtools, cutlery, general hardware, nonelectric heating apparatus, fabricated structural metal products, metal forgings, metal stampings, ordnance (except vehicles and guided missiles), and a variety of metal and wire products, not elsewhere classified. Certain important segments of the metal fabricating industries are classified in other major groups, such as machinery in Major Groups 35 and 36; transportation equipment, including tanks, in Major Group 37; professional scientific and controlling instruments, watches, and clocks in Major Group 38; and jewelry and silverware in Major Group 39. Establishments primarily engaged in producing ferrous and nonferrous metals and their alloys are classified in Major Group 33.

Industry Group No.	Industry No.	
341		**METAL CANS AND SHIPPING CONTAINERS**

3411 Metal Cans

Establishments primarily engaged in manufacturing metal cans from purchased materials. Establishments primarily engaged in manufacturing foil containers are classified in Industry 3497.

Beer cans, metal
Can lids and ends, metal
Cans, aluminum
Cans, metal
Food containers, metal
General line cans, metal
Ice cream cans, metal

Milk cans, metal
Oil cans, metal
Packers' cans, metal
Pails, except shipping and stamped: metal
Pans, tinned
Tin cans

3412 Metal Shipping Barrels, Drums, Kegs, and Pails

Establishments primarily engaged in manufacturing metal shipping barrels, drums, kegs, and pails.

Containers, shipping: barrels, kegs, drums, packages—liquid tight (metal)
Drums, shipping: metal

Milk (fluid) shipping containers, metal
Pails, shipping: metal—except tinned

342 **CUTLERY, HANDTOOLS, AND GENERAL HARDWARE**

3421 Cutlery

Establishments primarily engaged in manufacturing safety razors, razor blades, scissors, shears, and other cutlery of metal, except precious metal and table cutlery with handles of metal. Establishments primarily engaged in manufacturing precious metal cutlery and table cutlery with handles of metal are classified in Industry 3914; those manufacturing electric razors, knives, or scissors are classified in Industry 3634; those manufacturing hair clippers for human use are classified in Industry 3999 and for animal use in Industry 3523; and those manufacturing power hedge shears and trimmers are classified in Industry 3524.

Barbers' scissors
Butchers' knives

Carving sets: except all metal
Cleavers

342   CUTLERY, HANDTOOLS, AND GENERAL HARDWARE—Con.

3421   Cutlery—Con.

Clippers, fingernail and toenail
Cutlery, except table cutlery with handles of metal
Forks, table: except all metal
Hedge shears and trimmers, except power
Kitchen cutlery
Knife blades
Knife blanks
Knives, table: metal, except all metal
Knives: butchers', hunting, pocket, table—except all metal table and electric

Potato peelers, hand
Razor blades
Razors: safety and straight
Safety razor blades
Scissors, hand
Shears, hand
Shears, metal cutting: hand
Snips, tinners'
Swords
Table cutlery, except table cutlery with handles of metal
Tailors' scissors

3423   Hand and Edge Tools, Except Machine Tools and Handsaws

Establishments primarily engaged in manufacturing files and other hand and edge tools for metalworking, woodworking, and general maintenance. Establishments primarily engaged in manufacturing handsaws and saw blades are classified in Industry 3425; and those manufacturing metal cutting dies, power driven handtools, and attachments and accessories for machine tools are classified in Major Group 35.

Adzes
Awls
Axes
Bits (edge tools for woodworking)
Blow torches
C-clamps
Can openers, except electric
Cane knives
Cant hooks (handtools)
Carpenters' handtools, except saws
Caulking guns
Caulking tools, hand
Chisels
Clamps, hand
Corn knives
Counterbores and countersinking bits, woodworking
Countersinks
Cutters, glass
Cutting dies: except metal cutting
Drawknives
Drill bits, woodworking
Drills, hand: except power
Edge tools for woodworking: augers, bits, gimlets, countersinks, etc.
Engravers' tools, hand
Fence stretchers (handtools)
Files, including recutting and resharpening
Forks: garden, hay and manure, stone and ballast
Garden handtools
Gouges, woodworking
Guns, caulking
Hammers (handtools)
Hatchets
Hay knives
Hoes, garden and masons'
Hooks: bush, grass, baling, and husking
Ironworkers' handtools
Jacks: lifting, screw, and ratchet (handtools)
Jewelers' handtools
Knives, agricultural and industrial
Leaf skimmers and swimming pool rakes

Levels, carpenters'
Machetes
Machine knives, except metal cutting
Mallets, printers'
Masons' handtools
Mattocks (handtools)
Mauls, metal (handtools)
Mechanics' handtools
Mitre boxes, metal
Peavies (handtools)
Picks (handtools)
Planes, woodworking: hand
Pliers (handtools)
Plumbers' handtools
Post hole diggers, hand
Prying bars (handtools)
Pullers: wheel, gear, and bearing (handtools)
Punches (handtools)
Putty knives
Rakes, handtools
Rasps, including recutting and resharpening
Rules and rulers: metal, except slide
Scoops, hand: metal
Scrapers, woodworking: hand
Screw drivers
Scythes
Shovels, hand
Sickles, hand
Sledges (handtools)
Soldering guns and tools, hand: electric
Soldering iron tips and tiplets
Soldering irons and coppers
Spades, hand
Squares, carpenter
Stone forks (handtools)
Stonecutters' handtools
Strapping tools, steel
Test plugs: plumbers' handtools
Tinners' handtools, except snips
Tongs, oyster
Tools and equipment for use with sporting arms
Tools, hand: except power driven tools

Industry
Group   Industry
No.   No.

342   **CUTLERY, HANDTOOLS, AND GENERAL HARDWARE—Con.**

3423   **Hand and Edge Tools, Except Machine Tools and Handsaws—Con.**

and saws	Vises, except machine
Trowels	Wrenches (handtools)
Vises, carpenters'	Yardsticks, metal

3425   **Saw Blades and Handsaws**

Establishments primarily engaged in manufacturing handsaws and saw blades for hand and power driven saws. Establishments primarily engaged in manufacturing power driven sawing machines are classified in Major Group 35.

Chain type saw blades	Saws, hand: metalworking or wood-
Saw blades, for hand or power saws	working

3429   **Hardware, Not Elsewhere Classified**

Establishments primarily engaged in manufacturing miscellaneous metal products usually termed hardware, not elsewhere classified. Establishments primarily engaged in manufacturing bolts and nuts are classified in Industry 3452; those manufacturing nails and spikes are classified in Major Group 33; those manufacturing cutlery are classified in Industry 3421; those manufacturing handtools are classified in Industry 3423; and those manufacturing pole line and transmission hardware are classified in Industry Group 364.

Andirons	Key blanks
Angle irons, hardware	Keys
Animal traps, iron and steel: except wire	Ladder jacks, metal
Bellows, hand	Locks and lock sets: except safe, vault, and coin-operated
Brackets, iron and steel	Locks, trigger, for guns
Builders' hardware, including locks and lock sets	Luggage hardware
Cabinet hardware, including locks and lock sets	Luggage racks, car top
Car seals, metal	Marine hardware
Casket hardware	Metal fasteners, spring and cold-rolled steel, not made in rolling mills
Casters, industrial	Motor vehicle hardware
Chain fittings	Nozzles, fire fighting
Chair glides	Nut crackers and pickers, metal
Clamps, hose	Organ hardware
Clamps, metal	Padlocks
Couplings, hose	Parachute hardware
Crab traps, steel: except wire	Piano hardware
Cuffs, leg: iron	Pulleys, metal: except power transmis- sion equipment
Door bolts and checks	Rope fittings
Door locks and lock sets	Saddlery hardware
Door opening and closing devices, except electrical	Sleeper mechanisms, for convertible beds
Dzus fasteners	Suitcase hardware, including locks
Fireplace equipment (hardware)	Tackle blocks, metal
Furniture hardware, including casters	Thimbles, wire rope
Gun trigger locks	Time locks
Handcuffs	Trimmings, trunk: metal
Harness hardware	Trunk hardware, including locks
Hinge tubes	Turnbuckles
Hinges	Utility carriers, car top
Horse bits	Vacuum bottles and jugs
Ice chests or coolers, portable, except insulated foam plastics	Vehicle hardware: aircraft, automobile, railroad, etc.

343   **HEATING EQUIPMENT, EXCEPT ELECTRIC AND WARM AIR; AND PLUMBING FIXTURES**

3431 Enameled Iron and Metal Sanitary Ware

Establishments primarily engaged in manufacturing enameled iron, cast iron, or pressed metal sanitary ware. Establishments primarily engaged in manufacturing plastics plumbing fixtures are classified in Industry 3088; those manufacturing vitreous and semivitreous pottery sanitary ware are classified in Industry 3261; and those manufacturing porcelain enameled kitchen, household, and hospital ware are classified in Industry 3469.

Bathroom fixtures: enameled iron, cast iron, and pressed metal	Portable chemical toilets (metal)
Bathtubs: enameled iron, cast iron, and pressed metal	Shower receptors, metal
Drinking fountains, except mechanically refrigerated: metal	Shower stalls, metal
Flush tanks, metal	Sinks: enameled iron, cast iron, and pressed metal
Laundry tubs, enameled iron and other metal	Toilet fixtures: enameled iron, cast iron, and pressed metal
Lavatories, enameled iron and other metal	Urinals: enameled iron, cast iron, and pressed metal
Plumbing fixtures: enameled iron, cast iron, and pressed metal	Water closets: enameled iron, cast iron, and pressed metal

3432 Plumbing Fixture Fittings and Trim

Establishments primarily engaged in manufacturing metal plumbing fixture fittings and trim. Also included in this industry are establishments engaged in the assembly of plastics components into plumbing fixture fittings. Establishments primarily engaged in the manufacture of steam or water line valves are classified in Industry Group 349. Establishments primarily engaged in manufacturing china and earthenware plumbing fixture fittings are classified in Industry 3261, and those manufacturing plastics plumbing fixture components are classified in Industry 3089.

Backflow preventors	Nozzles, plumbers'
Brass goods, plumbers'	Plumbers' brass goods
Breakers, vacuum: plumbing	Plumbing fixture fittings and trim
Bubblers, drinking fountain	Sanitary pipe fittings
Cocks, drain (including basin)	Shower rods
Drains, plumbers'	Spigots, metal and plastics
Faucets, metal and plastics	Sprinklers, lawn
Flush valves	Stopcocks (plumbers' supplies)
Interceptors, plumbers'	Water traps
Nozzles, lawn hose	

3433 Heating Equipment, Except Electric and Warm Air Furnaces

Establishments primarily engaged in manufacturing heating equipment, except electric and warm air furnaces, including gas, oil, and stoker coal fired equipment for the automatic utilization of gaseous, liquid, and solid fuels. Establishments primarily engaged in manufacturing warm air furnaces are classified in Industry 3585; cooking stoves and ranges are classified in Industry 3631; boiler shops primarily engaged in the production of industrial, power, and marine boilers are classified in Industry 3443; and those manufacturing industrial process furnaces and ovens are classified in Industry 3567.

Boilers, low-pressure heating: steam or hot water	Gas heaters, room
Fireplace inserts	Gas infrared heating units
Furnaces, domestic: steam or hot water	Gas-oil burners, combination
Gas burners, domestic	Heaters, swimming pool: oil or gas
	Heating apparatus, except electric or

Industry Group No.	Industry No.
343	

HEATING EQUIPMENT, EXCEPT ELECTRIC AND WARM AIR; AND PLUMBING FIXTURES—Con.

3433　Heating Equipment, Except Electric and Warm Air Furnaces—Con.

warm air
Kerosene space heaters
Logs, fireplace: gas
Oil burners, domestic and industrial
Radiators, except electric
Range boilers, galvanized iron and nonferrous metal
Room heaters, except electric
Salamanders, coke and gas burning
Solar energy collectors, liquid or gas

Solar heaters
Space heaters, except electric
Stokers, mechanical: domestic and industrial
Stoves, household: heating—except electric
Stoves, wood and coal burning
Unit heaters, domestic: except electric
Wall heaters, except electric

344　FABRICATED STRUCTURAL METAL PRODUCTS

3441　Fabricated Structural Metal

Establishments primarily engaged in fabricating iron and steel or other metal for structural purposes, such as bridges, buildings, and sections for ships, boats, and barges. Establishments primarily engaged in manufacturing metal doors, sash, frames, molding, and trim are classified in Industry 3442; and establishments doing fabrication work at the site of construction are classified in Division C, Construction.

Barge sections, prefabricated metal
Boat sections, prefabricated metal
Expansion joints (structural shapes): iron and steel
Floor jacks, metal
Floor posts, adjustable: metal
Gates, dam: metal plate
Highway bridge sections, prefabricated metal
Joists, open web steel: long-span series
Radio and television tower sections, prefabricated metal

Railway bridge sections, prefabricated metal
Ship sections, prefabricated metal
Steel joists, open web: long-span series
Steel railroad car racks (for transporting motor vehicles fabricated)
Structural steel, fabricated
Tower sections, transmission: prefabricated metal

3442　Metal Doors, Sash, Frames, Molding, and Trim

Establishments primarily engaged in manufacturing ferrous and nonferrous metal doors, sash, window and door frames and screens, molding, and trim. Establishments primarily engaged in manufacturing metal covered wood doors, windows, sash, door frames, molding, and trim are classified in Industry 2431.

Baseboards, metal
Casements, aluminum
Door and jamb assemblies, prefabricated: metal
Door frames and sash, metal
Doors, louver: all metal or metal frame
Doors, metal
Fire doors, metal
Garage doors, overhead: metal
Hangar doors, sheet metal
Jalousies, all metal or metal frame
Louver windows, all metal or metal frame
Moldings and trim, metal: except automobile

Rolling doors for industrial buildings and warehouses, metal
Screen doors, metal
Screens, door and window: metal frame
Shutters, door and window: metal
Store fronts, prefabricated: metal, except porcelain enameled
Storm doors and windows, metal
Trim and molding, except automobile: metal
Weather strip, metal
Window frames and sash, metal

3443　Fabricated Plate Work (Boiler Shops)

Establishments primarily engaged in manufacturing power and marine boilers, pressure and nonpressure tanks, processing and storage vessels, heat ex-

Industry
Group   Industry
No.   No.

344   FABRICATED STRUCTURAL METAL PRODUCTS—Con.

3443   Fabricated Plate Work (Boiler Shops)—Con.

changers, weldments and similar products, by the process of cutting, forming and joining metal plates, shapes, bars, sheet, pipe mill products and tubing to custom or standard design, for factory or field assembly. Establishments primarily engaged in manufacturing warm air heating furnaces are classified in Industry 3585; those manufacturing other nonelectric heating apparatus, except power boilers, are classified in Industry 3433; those manufacturing household cooking apparatus are classified in Industry 3631; and those manufacturing industrial process furnaces and ovens are classified in Industry 3567.

Absorbers, gas
Accumulators (industrial pressure vessels)
Acetylene cylinders
Aftercooler shells
Air preheaters, nonrotating: plate type
Air receiver tanks, metal plate
Airlocks
Annealing boxes, pots, and covers
Atomic waste casks
Autoclaves, industrial
Baffles
Bails, ladle
Bins, prefabricated metal plate
Boiler shop products: industrial boilers, smokestacks, and steel tanks
Boilers: industrial, power, and marine
Boxes, condenser: metal plate
Breechings, metal plate
Buoys, metal
Cable trays, metal plate
Caissons, metal plate
Cars for hot metal
Casing, boiler: metal plate
Casings, scroll
Chutes, metal plate
Condensers, barometric
Condensers, steam
Containers, shipping: metal plate (bombs, etc.)—except missile casings
Cooling towers, metal plate
Cryogenic tanks, for liquids and gases: metal plate
Culverts, metal plate
Cupolas, metal plate
Cyclones, industrial: metal plate
Cylinders, pressure: metal plate
Digesters, process: metal plate
Ducting, metal plate
Economizers (boilers)
Evaporators (process vessels), metal plate
Exchangers, heat: industrial, scientific, and nuclear
Farm storage tanks, metal plate
Fermenters (process vessels), metal plate
Floating covers, metal plate
Flumes, metal plate
Forms, collapsible: for tunnels
Fractionating columns, metal plate
Fuel tanks, metal plate
Fumigating chambers, metal plate
Gas holders, metal plate
Gas tanks, metal plate
Heat transfer drives (finned tubing)
High vacuum coaters, metal plate
Hoods, industrial: metal plate

Hooks, crane: laminated plate
Hoppers, metal plate
Housing cabinets for radium, metal plate
Housings, pressure
Hydropneumatic tanks, metal plate
Intercooler shells
Jackets, industrial: metal plate
Kettles (process vessels), metal plate
Knockouts, free water: metal plate
Ladles, metal plate
Liners, industrial: metal plate
Liquid oxygen tanks, metal plate
Melting pots, for metal
Missile silos and components, metal plate
Mixers for hot metal
Nuclear core structurals, metal plate
Nuclear shielding, metal plate
Oil storage tanks, metal plate
Penstocks, metal plate
Perforating on heavy metal
Pile shells, metal plate
Pipe, large diameter: metal plate—made by plate fabricators
Plate work, fabricated: cutting, punching, bending, and shaping
Precipitators (process vessels), metal plate
Pressure vessels, industrial: metal plate—made in boiler shops
Pressurizers and auxiliary equipment, nuclear: metal plate
Reactor containment vessels, metal plate
Reactors, nuclear: military and industrial
Retorts, industrial
Rocket transportation casings
Separators, industrial process: metal plate
Septic tanks, metal plate
Skid tanks, metal plate
Smelting pots and retorts
Smokestacks, boiler plate
Space simulation chambers, metal plate
Spheres, for liquids or gas: metal plate
Standpipes
Steam jet aftercoolers
Steam jet inter condensers
Sterilizing chambers, metal plate
Stills, pressure: metal plate
Storage tanks, metal plate
Surge tanks, metal plate
Tanks for tank trucks, metal plate
Tanks, metal plate: lined
Tanks, standard and custom fabricated: metal plate—made in boiler shops

Industry
Group   Industry
No.   No.

344   **FABRICATED STRUCTURAL METAL PRODUCTS—Con.**

3443   **Fabricated Plate Work (Boiler Shops)—Con.**

Towers, tank: metal plate
Towers: bubble, cooling, fractionating—
  metal plate
Trash racks, metal plate
Troughs, industrial: metal plate
Truss plates, metal
Tunnel lining, metal plate
Tunnels, vacuum: metal plate

Tunnels, wind
Vacuum tanks, metal plate
Vats, metal plate
Vessels, process and storage: metal
  plate (made in boiler shops)
Water tanks, metal plate
Weldments

3444   **Sheet Metal Work**

Establishments primarily engaged in manufacturing sheet metal work for
buildings (not including fabrication work done by construction contractors at
the place of construction), and manufacturing stovepipes, light tanks, and
other products of sheet metal.

Air cowls, scoops, or airports (ship ven-
  tilators), sheet metal
Awnings, sheet metal
Bins, prefabricated: sheet metal
Booths, spray: prefabricated sheet
  metal
Canopies, sheet metal
Casings, sheet metal
Coal chutes, prefabricated sheet metal
Cooling towers, sheet metal
Cornices, sheet metal
Culverts, sheet metal
Dampers, sheet metal
Door hoods, aluminum
Downspouts, sheet metal
Ducts, sheet metal
Eaves, sheet metal
Elbows for conductor pipe, hot air
  ducts, and stovepipe: sheet metal
Flooring, cellular steel
Flues, stove and furnace: sheet metal
Flumes, sheet metal
Forming machine work for the trade,
  except stampings: sheet metal
Forms for concrete, sheet metal
Furnace casings, sheet metal
Guardrails, highway: sheet metal
Gutters, sheet metal
Hoods, range: sheet metal

Hoppers, sheet metal
Housings for business machines, sheet
  metal: except stamped
Irrigation pipe, sheet metal
Joists, sheet metal
Laundry hampers, sheet metal
Louvers, sheet metal
Machine guards, sheet metal
Mail chutes, sheet metal
Mail collection or storage boxes, sheet
  metal
Pile shells, sheet metal
Pipe, sheet metal
Post office collection boxes
Radiator shields and enclosures, sheet
  metal
Restaurant sheet metal work
Roof deck, sheet metal
Sheet metal specialties, not stamped
Siding, sheet metal
Skylights, sheet metal
Spouts, sheet metal
Stove boards, sheet metal
Stove pipe and flues, sheet metal
Studs, sheet metal
Troughs, elevator: sheet metal
Vats, sheet metal
Ventilators, sheet metal
Wells, light: sheet metal

3446   **Architectural and Ornamental Metal Work**

Establishments primarily engaged in manufacturing architectural and ornamental metal work, such as stairs and staircases, open steel flooring (grating),
fire escapes, grilles, railings, and fences and gates, except those made from
wire. Establishments primarily engaged in manufacturing fences and gates
from purchased wire are classified in Industry 3496; those manufacturing prefabricated metal buildings and parts are classified in Industry 3448; and those
manufacturing miscellaneous metal work are classified in Industry 3449.

Acoustical suspension systems, metal
Balconies, metal
Bank fixtures, ornamental metal
Bannisters, railings, guards, etc.: made
  from metal pipe
Brasswork, ornamental: structural
Channels, furring
Elevator guide rails, metal
Fences and posts, ornamental iron and
  steel

Fire escapes, metal
Flagpoles, metal
Flooring, open steel (grating)
Gates, ornamental metal
Gratings (open steel flooring)
Gratings, tread: fabricated metal
Ladders, chain: metal
Ladders, for permanent installation:
  metal
Lamp posts, metal

344   **FABRICATED STRUCTURAL METAL PRODUCTS—Con.**

3446 Architectural and Ornamental Metal Work—Con.

Lintels, light gauge steel
Ornamental and architectural metal
work
Partitions and grillework, ornamental
metal
Pipe bannisters, railings, and guards
Purlins, light gauge steel

Railings, prefabricated metal
Registers, air: metal
Scaffolds, metal (mobile or stationary)
Stair railings, metal
Staircases, prefabricated metal
Stairs, prefabricated metal
Treads, stair: fabricated metal

3448 Prefabricated Metal Buildings and Components

Establishments primarily engaged in manufacturing portable and other prefabricated metal buildings and parts and prefabricated exterior metal panels.

Buildings, prefabricated: metal
Carports, prefabricated: metal
Docks, building, prefabricated: metal
Dwellings, prefabricated: metal
Farm buildings, prefabricated: metal
Garages, prefabricated: metal
Greenhouses, prefabricated: metal
Houses, prefabricated: metal
Panels for prefabricated metal buildings

Portable buildings, prefabricated metal
Prefabricated buildings, metal
Ramps, prefabricated: metal
Sections for prefabricated metal buildings
Silos, metal
Utility buildings, prefabricated: metal

3449 Miscellaneous Structural Metal Work

Establishments primarily engaged in manufacturing miscellaneous structural metal work, such as metal plaster bases, fabricated bar joists, and concrete reinforcing bars. Also included in this industry are establishments primarily engaged in custom roll forming of metal.

Bars, concrete reinforcing: fabricated
steel
Curtain wall, metal
Custom roll formed products, metal

Joists, fabricated bar
Landing mats, aircraft: metal
Lath, expanded metal
Plastering accessories, metal

345   **SCREW MACHINE PRODUCTS, AND BOLTS, NUTS, SCREWS, RIVETS,
AND WASHERS**

3451 Screw Machine Products

Establishments primarily engaged in manufacturing automatic or hand screw machine products from rod, bar, or tube stock of metal, fiber, plastics or other material. The products of this industry consist of a wide variety of unassembled parts and are usually manufactured on a job or order basis. Establishments included in this industry may perform assembly of some parts manufactured in the same establishment, but establishments primarily engaged in producing assembled components are classified according to the nature of the components. Establishments primarily engaged in manufacturing standard bolts, nuts, rivets, screws, and other industrial fasteners on headers, threaders, and nut forming machines are classified in Industry 3452.

Screw machine products: produced on a
job or order basis

3452 Bolts, Nuts, Screws, Rivets, and Washers

Establishments primarily engaged in manufacturing metal bolts, nuts, screws, rivets, washers, formed and threaded wire goods, and special industrial fasteners. Rolling mills engaged in manufacturing similar products are classified in Major Group 33; establishments primarily engaged in manufacturing

Industry
Group   Industry
No.   No.

345   SCREW MACHINE PRODUCTS, AND BOLTS, NUTS, SCREWS, RIVETS, AND WASHERS—Con.

3452   Bolts, Nuts, Screws, Rivets, and Washers—Con.

screw machine products are classified in Industry 3451; and those manufacturing plastics fasteners are classified in Industry 3089.

Bolts, metal	Screw eyes, metal
Cotter pins, metal	Screw hooks
Dowel pins, metal	Screws, metal
Gate hooks	Spring pins, metal
Lock washers	Spring washers, metal
Machine keys	Toggle bolts, metal
Nuts, metal	Washers, metal
Rivets, metal	Wood screws, metal

346   METAL FORGINGS AND STAMPINGS

This industry group includes establishments primarily engaged in manufacturing metal forgings or metal stampings. These establishments generally operate on a job or order basis, manufacturing metal stampings or forgings for sale to others or for interplant transfer. Establishments which produce metal stampings or forgings for incorporation in end products produced in the same establishment are classified on the basis of the end product. Establishments further processing forgings or stampings are classified according to the particular product or process.

3462   Iron and Steel Forgings

Establishments primarily engaged in manufacturing iron and steel forgings, with or without the use of dies.

Aircraft forgings, ferrous: not made in rolling mills	Hammer forgings, not made in rolling mills
Anchors, forged: not made in rolling mills	Horseshoes, not made in rolling mills
Anvils, forged: not made in rolling mills	Internal combustion engine (stationary and mobile) forgings, ferrous: not made in rolling mills
Armor plate, forged iron and steel: not made in rolling mills	Machinery forgings, ferrous: not made in rolling mills
Automotive forgings, ferrous: not made in rolling mills	Mechanical power transmission forgings, ferrous: not made in rolling mills
Axles, railroad: forged—not made in rolling mills	Missile forgings, ferrous: not made in rolling mills
Bumping posts, railroad: forged—not made in rolling mills	Nuclear power plant forgings, ferrous: not made in rolling mills
Bus, truck and trailer forgings, ferrous: not made in rolling mills	Ordnance forgings, ferrous: not made in rolling mills
Calks, horseshoe: forged—not made in rolling mills	Pole line hardware forgings, ferrous: not made in rolling mills
Chains, forged steel: not made in rolling mills	Press forgings, iron and steel: not made in rolling mills
Construction and mining equipment forgings, ferrous: not made in rolling mills	Pump and compressor forgings, ferrous: not made in rolling mills
Crankshafts, forged steel: not made in rolling mills	Railroad wheels, axles, frogs, and related equipment: forged—mfpm
Engine forgings, ferrous: not made in rolling mills	Switches, railroad: forged—not made in rolling mills
Flange, valve, and pipe fitting forgings, ferrous: not made in rolling mills	Turbine engine forgings, ferrous: not made in rolling mills
Forgings, iron and steel: not made in rolling mills	Upset forgings, iron and steel: not made in rolling mills
Gears, forged steel: not made in rolling mills	Wheels, car and locomotive: forged—not made in rolling mills

Industry Group No.

346

Industry No.

METAL FORGINGS AND STAMPINGS—Con.

3463 Nonferrous Forgings

Establishments primarily engaged in manufacturing nonferrous forgings, with or without the use of dies.

Aircraft forgings, nonferrous: not made in hot-rolling mills
Aluminum forgings, not made in hot-rolling mills
Automotive forgings, nonferrous: not made in hot-rolling mills
Bearing and bearing race forgings, nonferrous: not made in hot-rolling mills
Engine and turbine forgings, nonferrous: not made in hot-rolling mills
Flange, valve and pipe fitting forgings, nonferrous: not made in hot-rolling mills
Machinery forgings, nonferrous: not made in hot-rolling mills
Mechanical power transmission forgings, nonferrous: not made in hot-rolling mills

Missile forgings, nonferrous: not made in hot-rolling mills
Nonferrous forgings, not made in hot-rolling mills
Ordnance forgings, nonferrous: not made in hot-rolling mills
Plumbing fixture forgings, nonferrous: not made in hot-rolling mills
Pole line hardware forgings, nonferrous: not made in hot-rolling mills
Pump and compressor forgings, nonferrous: not made in hot-rolling mills
Titanium forgings, not made in hot-rolling mills

3465 Automotive Stampings

Establishments primarily engaged in manufacturing automotive stampings, such as body parts, hubs, and trim.

Automotive stampings: e.g., fenders, tops, hub caps, body parts, trim
Body parts, automotive: stamped

Moldings and trim, automotive: stamped

3466 Crowns and Closures

Establishments primarily engaged in manufacturing metal crowns and closures.

Bottle caps and tops, stamped metal
Closures, stamped metal
Crowns, jar: stamped metal

Jar crowns and tops, stamped metal
Tops, jar: stamped metal

3469 Metal Stampings, Not Elsewhere Classified

Establishments primarily engaged in manufacturing metal stampings and spun products, not elsewhere classified, including porcelain enameled products. Products of this industry include household appliance housings and parts; cooking and kitchen utensils; and other nonautomotive job stampings.

Appliance parts, porcelain enameled
Ashcans, stamped and pressed metal
Ashtrays, stamped metal
Automobile license tags, stamped metal
Bottle openers, stamped metal
Capacitor and condenser cans and cases: stamped metal
Cash and stamp boxes, stamped metal
Chassis, radio and television: stamped metal
Cookers, pressure: stamped or drawn
Cooking ware, porcelain enameled
Electronic enclosures: stamped or pressed
Fins, tube: stamped metal
Floor tile, stamped metal
Furniture components, porcelain enameled
Garbage cans, stamped and pressed metal
Helmets, steel

Honeycombed metal
Household utensils, stamped and pressed metal
Housings for business machines, stamped metal
Ice cream dippers
Ironer parts, porcelain enameled
Kitchen utensils, porcelain enameled
Kitchen utensils, stamped and pressed metal
Lunch boxes, stamped metal
Machine parts, stamped and pressed metal
Mail boxes, except collection boxes
Pails, stamped and pressed metal: except tinned and shipping type
Pans, stamped and pressed metal: except tinned
Patterns on metal
Perforated metal, stamped
Perforating on light metal

Industry Group No.	Industry No.	
346		**METAL FORGINGS AND STAMPINGS—Con.**

3469 Metal Stampings, Not Elsewhere Classified—Con.

Rigidizing metal
Spinning metal, for the trade
Stamping metal, for the trade
Store fronts, porcelain enameled
Stove parts, porcelain enameled
Table tops, porcelain enameled
Teakettles, except electric: stamped metal
Tool boxes, stamped metal
Utensils, metal, except cast: household, commercial, and hospital
Utensils, porcelain enameled: household, commercial, and hospital
Washing machine parts, porcelain enameled
Wastebaskets, stamped metal

347   COATING, ENGRAVING, AND ALLIED SERVICES

3471 Electroplating, Plating, Polishing, Anodizing, and Coloring

Establishments primarily engaged in all types of electroplating, plating, anodizing, coloring, and finishing of metals and formed products for the trade. Also included in this industry are establishments which perform these types of activities, on their own account, on purchased metals or formed products. Establishments that both manufacture and finish products are classified according to the products.

Anodizing of metals and formed products, for the trade
Buffing, for the trade
Chromium plating of metals and formed products, for the trade
Cleaning and descaling metal products, for the trade
Coloring and finishing of aluminum and formed products, for the trade
Decontaminating and cleaning of missile and satellite parts, for the trade
Decorative plating and finishing of formed products, for the trade
Depolishing metal, for the trade
Electrolizing steel, for the trade
Electroplating of metals and formed products, for the trade
Finishing metal products and formed products, for the trade
Gold plating, for the trade
Plating of metals and formed products, for the trade
Polishing of metals and formed products, for the trade
Rechroming auto bumpers, for the trade
Sandblasting of metal parts, for the trade
Tumbling (cleaning and polishing) of machine parts, for the trade

3479 Coating, Engraving, and Allied Services, Not Elsewhere Classified

Establishments primarily engaged in performing the following types of services on metals, for the trade: (1) enameling, lacquering, and varnishing metal products; (2) hot dip galvanizing of mill sheets, plates and bars, castings, and formed products fabricated of iron and steel; hot dip coating such items with aluminum, lead, or zinc; retinning cans and utensils; (3) engraving, chasing and etching jewelry, silverware, notarial and other seals, and other metal products for purposes other than printing; and (4) other metal services, not elsewhere classified. Also included in this industry are establishments which perform these types of activities on their own account on purchased metals or formed products. Establishments that both manufacture and finish products are classified according to the products.

Bonderizing of metal and metal products, for the trade
Chasing on metals for the trade, for purposes other than printing
Coating (hot dipping) of metals and formed products, for the trade
Coating and wrapping steel pipe
Coating of metals with plastics and resins, for the trade
Coating of metals with silicon, for the trade
Coating, rust preventive
Dipping metal in plastics solution as a preservative, for the trade
Enameling (including porcelain) of metal products, for the trade
Engraving jewelry, silverware, and metal for the trade: except printing
Etching on metals for purposes other than printing
Etching: photochemical, for the trade
Galvanizing of iron and steel and end formed products, for the trade
Japanning of metal
Jewelry enameling, for the trade
Lacquering of metal products, for the trade
Name plates: engraved and etched

Industry
Group   Industry
No.   No.

347   COATING, ENGRAVING, AND ALLIED SERVICES—Con.

3479   Coating, Engraving, and Allied Services, Not Elsewhere Classified—Con.

Painting (enameling and varnishing) of metal products, for the trade
Pan glazing, for the trade
Parkerizing, for the trade
Phosphate coating of metal and metal products, for the trade
Retinning of cans and utensils, not done in rolling mills

Rust proofing (hot dipping) of metals and formed products, for the trade
Sherardizing of metals and metal products, for the trade
Varnishing of metal products, for the trade

348   ORDNANCE AND ACCESSORIES, EXCEPT VEHICLES AND GUIDED MISSILES

3482   Small Arms Ammunition

Establishments primarily engaged in manufacturing ammunition for small arms having a bore of 30 mm. (or 1.18 inch) or less. Establishments primarily engaged in manufacturing ammunition, except for small arms, are classified in Industry 3483; those manufacturing blasting and detonating caps and safety fuses are classified in Industry 2892; and those manufacturing fireworks are classified in Industry 2899.

Ammunition and component parts, small arms: 30 mm. (or 1.18 inch) or less
Bullet jackets and cores, 30 mm. (or 1.18 inch) or less
Cartridge cases for ammunition, 30 mm. (or 1.18 inch) or less
Cartridges, 30 mm. (or 1.18 inch) or less
Cores, bullet: 30 mm. (or 1.18 inch) or less
Paper shells, 30 mm. (or 1.18 inch) or less

Pellets, ammunition: pistol and air rifle
Percussion caps, for ammunition of 30 mm. (or 1.18 inch) or less
Shells, small arms: 30 mm. (or 1.18 inch) or less
Shot, BB
Shot, lead
Shot, pellet
Shot, steel ammunition
Shotgun ammunition
Wads, ammunition: 30 mm. (or 1.18 inch) or less

3483   Ammunition, Except for Small Arms

Establishments primarily engaged in manufacturing ammunition, not elsewhere classified, or in loading and assembling ammunition more than 30 mm. (or more than 1.18 inch), including component parts. This industry also includes establishments primarily engaged in manufacturing bombs, mines, torpedoes, grenades, depth charges, chemical warfare projectiles, and their component parts. Establishments primarily engaged in manufacturing small arms ammunition are classified in Industry 3482; those manufacturing explosives are classified in Industry 2892; and those manufacturing military pyrotechnics are classified in Industry 2899.

Ammunition and component parts, more than 30 mm. (or more than 1.18 inch)
Ammunition loading and assembling plants
Arming and fusing devices for missiles
Bag loading plants, ammunition
Bomb loading and assembling plants
Bombcluster adapters
Bombs and parts
Boosters and bursters
Canisters, ammunition
Caps, bomb
Chemical warfare projectiles and components
Depth charges and parts (ordnance)
Detonators for ammunition more than 30 mm. (or more than 1.18 inch)

Detonators: mine, bomb, depth charge, and chemical warfare projectile
Fin assemblies, mortar: more than 30 mm. (or more than 1.18 inch)
Fin assemblies, torpedo and bomb
Fuses for ammunition more than 30 mm. (or more than 1.18 inch)
Fuses: mine, torpedo, bomb, depth charge, and chemical warfare projectile
Grenades and parts
Jet propulsion projectiles, complete
Loading and assembling bombs, powder bags, and shells: more than 30 mm. (or more than 1.18 inch)
Mines and parts (ordnance)
Missile warheads
Mortar shells, more than 30 mm. (or

348   ORDNANCE AND ACCESSORIES, EXCEPT VEHICLES AND GUIDED MISSILES—Con.

3483   Ammunition, Except for Small Arms—Con.

more than 1.18 inch)
Primers for ammunition, more than 30
mm. (or more than 1.18 inch)
Projectile forgings, machined: for ammunition more than 30 mm. (or more
than 1.18 inch)

Rockets (ammunition)
Shells, artillery: more than 30 mm. (or
more than 1.18 inch)
Torpedoes and parts (ordnance)
Tracer igniters for ammunition more
than 30 mm. (or more than 1.18 inch)

3484   Small Arms

Establishments primarily engaged in manufacturing small firearms having a bore 30 mm. (or 1.18 inch) or less, and parts for small firearms. Also includ-ed in this industry are establishments primarily engaged in manufacturing certain weapons more than 30 mm. which are carried and employed by the individual, such as grenade launchers and heavy field machine guns. Estab-lishments primarily engaged in manufacturing artillery and mortars having a bore more than 30 mm. (or more than 1.18 inch), and component parts, are classified in Industry 3489.

Barrels, gun: 30 mm. (or 1.18 inch) or
less
Carbines, 30 mm. (or 1.18 inch) or less
Carts, machine gun and machine gun
ammunition
Clips, gun: 30 mm. (or 1.18 inch) or less
Cylinders and clips, gun: 30 mm. (or
1.18 inch) or less
Firearms, 30 mm. (or 1.18 inch) or less
Grenade launchers
Gun sights, except optical: 30 mm. (or
1.18 inch) or less
Guns, 30 mm. (or 1.18 inch) or less
Guns, dart: except toy
Guns: BB and pellet
Links, for ammunition 30 mm. (or 1.18
inch) or less
Machine gun belts, metallic: 30 mm. (or
1.18 inch) or less
Machine guns and parts, 30 mm. (or
1.18 inch) or less

Magazines, gun: 30 mm. (or 1.18 inch)
or less
Mounts for guns, 30 mm. (or 1.18 inch)
or less
Pistols and parts, except toy
Pyrotechnic pistols and projectors
Recoil mechanisms for guns, 30 mm. (or
1.18 inch) or less
Revolvers and parts
Rifles and parts, 30 mm. (or 1.18 inch)
or less
Rifles, high compression pneumatic: 30
mm. (or 1.18 inch) or less
Rifles: BB and pellet
Rifles: pneumatic, spring loaded, and
compressed air—except toy
Shotguns and parts
Submachine guns and parts

3489   Ordnance and Accessories, Not Elsewhere Classified

Establishments primarily engaged in manufacturing ordnance and accesso-ries, not elsewhere classified, such as naval, aircraft, antiaircraft, tank, coast, and field artillery having a bore more than 30 mm. (or more than 1.18 inch), and components. Establishments primarily engaged in manufacturing small arms and parts 30 mm. (or 1.18 inch) or less are classified in Industry 3484; those manufacturing tanks are classified in Industry 3795; and those manufac-turing guided missiles are classified in Industry Group 376.

Antisubmarine projectors (ordnance)
Antitank rocket launchers
Artillery parts for artillery more than
30 mm. (or more than 1.18 inch)
Artillery, more than 30 mm. (or more
than 1.18 inch): aircraft, antiaircraft,
field, naval, and tank
Barrels, gun: more than 30 mm. (or
more than 1.18 inch)
Bofors guns
Cannons, more than 30 mm. (or more
than 1.18 inch)
Carriages, gun: for artillery more than
30 mm. (or more than 1.18 inch)

Catapult guns
Depth charge release pistols and projec-
tors
Flame throwers (ordnance)
Gun turrets and parts for artillery
more than 30 mm. (or more than 1.18
inch)
Guns, more than 30 mm. (or more than
1.18 inch)
Howitzers, more than 30 mm. (or more
than 1.18 inch)
Limbers, gun and caisson
Links for ammunition more than 30
mm. (or more than 1.18 inch)

Industry Group No.	Industry No.	
348		**ORDNANCE AND ACCESSORIES, EXCEPT VEHICLES AND GUIDED MISSILES—Con.**
	3489	**Ordnance and Accessories, Not Elsewhere Classified—Con.**

Livens projectors (ordnance)
Machine guns, more than 30 mm. (or more than 1.18 inch)
Mortars, more than 30 mm. (or more than 1.18 inch)
Oerlikon guns
Projectors: antisub, depth charge release, grenade, livens, and rocket

Recoil mechanisms for guns more than 30 mm. (or more than 1.18 inch)
Rifles, recoilless
Rocket launchers, hand-held
Smoke generators (ordnance)
Tampions for guns more than 30 mm. (or more than 1.18 inch)
Torpedo tubes (ordnance)

349   MISCELLANEOUS FABRICATED METAL PRODUCTS

3491   Industrial Valves

Establishments primarily engaged in manufacturing industrial valves. Establishments primarily engaged in manufacturing fluid power valves are classified in Industry 3492; those manufacturing plumbing fixture fittings and trim are classified in Industry 3432; and those manufacturing plumbing and heating valves are classified in Industry 3494.

Boiler gauge cocks
Compressed gas cylinder valves
Fire hydrant valves
Gas valves and parts, industrial
Pop safety valves, over 15 lbs. w.s.p.
Pressure valves, industrial: except power transfer
Steam traps, over 15 lbs. w.s.p.

Valves, automatic control: industrial, except fluid power
Valves, industrial: gate, globe, check, pop safety, and relief
Valves, nuclear
Valves, relief: over 15 lbs. w.s.p.
Valves, solenoid: except fluid power
Water works valves

3492   Fluid Power Valves and Hose Fittings

Establishments primarily engaged in manufacturing hydraulic and pneumatic valves, hose and tube fittings, and hose assemblies for fluid power systems. Establishments primarily engaged in manufacturing fluid power cylinders are classified in Industry 3593; those manufacturing fluid power pumps are classified in Industry 3594; and those manufacturing hydraulic intake and exhaust motor vehicle valves are classified in Industry 3592.

Control valves, fluid power: metal
Electrohydraulic servo valves, fluid power: metal
Hose fittings and assemblies, fluid power: metal
Hydraulic valves, including aircraft: fluid power—metal
Pneumatic valves, including aircraft: fluid power—metal

Pressure control valves, fluid power: metal
Solenoid valves, fluid power: metal
Tube fittings and assemblies, fluid power: metal
Valves, automatic control: fluid power—metal
Valves, hydraulic and pneumatic control: fluid power—metal

3493   Steel Springs, Except Wire

Establishments primarily engaged in manufacturing leaf springs, hot wound springs, and coiled flat springs. Establishments primarily engaged in manufacturing wire springs are classified in Industry 3495.

Automobile springs
Coiled flat springs
Flat springs, sheet or strip stock
Helical springs, hot wound: for railroad equipment and vehicles
Hot wound springs, except wire springs

Leaf springs: automobile, locomotive, and other vehicle
Railroad equipment springs
Steel springs, except wire
Torsion bar springs

349　　　　MISCELLANEOUS FABRICATED METAL PRODUCTS—Con.

3494　Valves and Pipe Fittings, Not Elsewhere Classified

Establishments primarily engaged in manufacturing metal valves and pipe fittings, not elsewhere classified, such as plumbing and heating valves, and pipe fittings, flanges, and unions, except from purchased pipes. Establishments primarily engaged in manufacturing plastics pipe fittings are classified in Industry 3089; those manufacturing plumbing fixture fittings and trim are classified in Industry 3432; and those manufacturing fittings and couplings for garden hose are classified in Industry 3429. Establishments primarily engaged in manufacturing fluid power valves are classified in Industry 3492, and those manufacturing other industrial valves are classified in Industry 3491. Establishments primarily engaged in fabricating pipe fittings from purchased metal pipe by processes such as cutting, threading, and bending are classified in Industry 3498.

Boiler couplings and drains, metal
Couplings, pipe: except pressure and soil pipe—metal
Elbows, pipe: except pressure and soil pipe—metal
Flanges and flange unions, pipe: metal
Line strainers, for use in piping systems—metal
Pipe fittings, except plumbers' brass goods: metal

Pipe hangers, metal
Plumbing and heating valves, metal
Reducer returns, pipe: metal
Steam fittings and specialties, except plumbers' brass goods and fittings, metal
Stop cocks, except drain: metal
Unions, pipe: metal
Well adapters, tipless: metal
Y bends and branches, pipe: metal

3495　Wire Springs

Establishments primarily engaged in manufacturing wire springs from purchased wire. Establishments primarily engaged in assembling wire bedsprings or seats are classified in Major Group 25.

Clock springs, precision: made from purchased wire
Furniture springs, unassembled: made from purchased wire
Gun springs, precision: made from purchased wire
Hairsprings, made from purchased wire
Instrument springs, precision: made from purchased wire

Mechanical springs, precision: made from purchased wire
Sash balances, spring
Spring units for seats, made from purchased wire
Springs, except complete bedsprings: made from purchased wire
Upholstery springs, unassembled: made from purchased wire

3496　Miscellaneous Fabricated Wire Products

Establishments primarily engaged in manufacturing miscellaneous fabricated wire products from purchased wire, such as noninsulated wire rope and cable; fencing; screening, netting, paper machine wire cloth; hangers, paper clips, kitchenware, and wire carts. Rolling mills engaged in manufacturing wire products are classified in Major Group 33. Establishments primarily engaged in manufacturing steel nails and spikes from purchased wire or rod are classified in Industry 3315; those manufacturing nonferrous wire nails and spikes from purchased wire or rod are classified in Industry 3399; those drawing and insulating nonferrous wire are classified in Industry 3357; and those manufacturing wire springs are classified in Industry 3495.

Antisubmarine and torpedo nets, made from purchased wire
Barbed wire, made from purchased wire
Baskets, made from purchased wire
Belts, conveyor: made from purchased wire

Belts, drying: made from purchased wire
Bird cages, made from purchased wire
Bottle openers, made from purchased wire
Cable, uninsulated wire: made from purchased wire

349 MISCELLANEOUS FABRICATED METAL PRODUCTS—Con.

3496 Miscellaneous Fabricated Wire Products—Con.

Cages, wire: made from purchased wire
Carts, grocery: made from purchased wire
Chain, welded: made from purchased wire
Chain, wire: made from purchased wire
Clips and fasteners, made from purchased wire
Cloth, woven wire: made from purchased wire
Concrete reinforcing mesh, made from purchased wire
Cylinder wire cloth, made from purchased wire
Delivery cases, made from purchased wire
Diamond cloth, made from purchased wire
Door mats, made from purchased wire
Fabrics, woven wire: made from purchased wire
Fencing, made from purchased wire
Florists' designs, made from purchased wire
Fourdrinier wire cloth, made from purchased wire
Gates, fence: made from purchased wire
Grilles and grillework, woven wire: made from purchased wire
Guards, made from purchased wire
Hangers, garment: made from purchased wire
Hardware cloth, woven wire: made from purchased wire
Hog rings, made from purchased wire
Insect screening, woven wire: made from purchased wire
Key rings, made from purchased wire
Keys, can: made from purchased wire
Kitchen wire goods, made from purchased wire
Lamp frames, wire: made from purchased wire
Lath, woven wire: made from purchased wire
Mats and matting, made from purchased wire

Mesh, made from purchased wire
Netting, woven wire: made from purchased wire
Paper clips and fasteners, made from purchased wire
Paper machine wire cloth, made from purchased wire
Partitions and grillework, made from purchased wire
Postal screen wire equipment—mfpm
Potato mashers, made from purchased wire
Poultry netting, made from purchased wire
Racks without rigid framework, made from purchased wire
Rods, gas welding: made from purchased wire
Rope, uninsulated wire: made from purchased wire
Screening, woven wire: made from purchased wire
Shelving without rigid framework, made from purchased wire
Sieves, made from purchased wire
Skid chains, made from purchased wire
Slings, lifting: made from purchased wire
Spiral cloth, made from purchased wire
Staples, wire: made from purchased wire
Strand, uninsulated wire: made from purchased wire
Ties, bale: made from purchased wire
Tire chains, made from purchased wire
Traps, animal and fish: made from purchased wire
Trays, made from purchased wire
Wire and wire products mfpm: except insulated wire, and nails and spikes
Wire winding of purchased wire
Wire, concrete reinforcing: made from purchased wire
Woven wire products, made from purchased wire

3497 Metal Foil and Leaf

Establishments primarily engaged in manufacturing gold, silver, tin, and other metal foil (including converted metal foil) and leaf. Also included are establishments primarily engaged in converting metal foil (including aluminum) into wrappers, cookware, dinnerware, and containers, except bags and liners. Establishments primarily engaged in manufacturing plain aluminum foil are classified in Industry 3353.

Copper foil, not made in rolling mills
Foil containers for bakery goods and frozen foods, except bags and liners
Foil, except aluminum: not made in rolling mills
Foil, laminated to paper or other materials
Gold beating (manufacturing of gold leaf and foil)
Gold foil and leaf, not made in rolling mills

Lead foil, not made in rolling mills
Leaf, metal
Magnesium and magnesium base alloy foil, not made in rolling mills
Nickel foil, not made in rolling mills
Platinum and platinum base alloy foil
Silver foil and leaf
Tin foil, not made in rolling mills
Zinc foil, not made in rolling mills

Industry
Group
No.
349

Industry
No.

MISCELLANEOUS FABRICATED METAL PRODUCTS—Con.

3498 Fabricated Pipe and Pipe Fittings

Establishments primarily engaged in fabricating pipe and pipe fittings from purchased metal pipe, by processes such as cutting, threading, and bending. Establishments primarily engaged in manufacturing cast iron pipe and fittings, including cast and forged pipe fittings which have been machined and threaded, are classified in Industry 3321; those manufacturing welded and heavy riveted pipe and seamless steel pipe are classified in Industry 3317; and those manufacturing products such as banisters, railings, and guards from pipe are classified in Industry 3446.

Bends, pipe: fabricated from purchased metal pipe
Coils, pipe: fabricated from purchased metal pipe
Couplings, pipe: fabricated from purchased metal pipe
Manifolds, pipe: fabricated from purchased metal pipe
Nipples, metal pipe: except pressure and soil pipe
Pipe and fittings, fabricated from purchased metal pipe

Pipe headers, welded: fabricated from purchased metal pipe
Pipe, fabricated from purchased metal pipe
Piping systems, metal: for pulp, paper, and chemical industries
Sections, pipe: fabricated from purchased metal pipe
Tube fabricating (contract bending and shaping); metal

3499 Fabricated Metal Products, Not Elsewhere Classified

Establishments primarily engaged in manufacturing fabricated metal products, not elsewhere classified, such as fire or burglary resistive steel safes and vaults and similar fire or burglary resistive products; and collapsible tubes of thin flexible metal. Also included are establishments primarily engaged in manufacturing metal boxes, metal ladders, and metal household articles, such as ice cream freezers and ironing boards. Establishments primarily engaged in manufacturing concrete burial vaults are classified in Industry 3272, and metal burial vaults are classified in Industry 3995. Establishments primarily engaged in manufacturing advertising novelties are classified in Industry 3993.

Aerosol valves, metal
Ammunition boxes, metal
Aquarium accessories, metal
Automobile seat frames, metal
Bank chests, metal
Barricades, metal
Book ends, metal
Boxes for packing and shipping, metal
Chair frames, metal
Chests, fire or burglary resistive: metal
Collapsible tubes for viscous products, metal
Doors, safe and vault: metal
Drain plugs, magnetic: metal
Drill stands, metal
Ferrules, metal
Fountains, metal (except drinking)
Friction material, made from powdered metal
Furniture parts, metal
Hoops, metal: other than wire
Ice cream freezers, household, nonelectric: metal
Ironing boards, metal
Ladder assemblies, combination workstand: metal
Ladders, metal: portable

Linings, safe and vault: metal
Locks, safe and vault: metal
Machine bases, metal
Magnets, permanent: metallic
Marine horns, compressed air or steam: metal
Money chests, metal
Novelties and specialties, metal: except advertising novelties
Powder metal products, custom molding
Reels, cable: metal
Safe deposit boxes and chests, metal
Safes, metal
Shims, metal
Spray nozzles, aerosol
Stabilizing bars (cargo), metal
Strapping, metal
Tablets, metal
Target drones for use by ships, metal
Toilet ware, metal: except silver, nickel silver, pewter, and plated
Trophies, metal: except silver, nickel silver, pewter, and plated
Vaults, except burial vaults: metal
Wheels, stamped metal, disc type: wheelbarrow, stroller, lawnmower

Major Group 35.—INDUSTRIAL AND COMMERCIAL MACHINERY AND COMPUTER EQUIPMENT

The Major Group as a Whole

This major group includes establishments engaged in manufacturing industrial and commercial machinery and equipment and computers. Included are the manufacture of engines and turbines; farm and garden machinery; construction, mining, and oil field machinery; elevators and conveying equipment; hoists, cranes, monorails, and industrial trucks and tractors; metalworking machinery; special industry machinery; general industrial machinery; computer and peripheral equipment and office machinery; and refrigeration and service industry machinery. Machines powered by built-in or detachable motors ordinarily are included in this major group, with the exception of electrical household appliances. Power-driven handtools are included in this major group, whether electric or otherwise driven. Establishments primarily engaged in manufacturing electrical equipment are classified in Major Group 36, and those manufacturing handtools, except powered, are classified in Major Group 34.

Industry
Group   Industry
No.   No.

351   ENGINES AND TURBINES

3511 Steam, Gas, and Hydraulic Turbines, and Turbine Generator Set Units

Establishments primarily engaged in manufacturing steam turbines; hydraulic turbines; gas turbines, except aircraft; and complete steam, gas, and hydraulic turbine generator set units. Also included in this industry are the manufacture of wind and solar powered turbine generators and windmills for generating electric power. Establishments primarily engaged in manufacturing nonautomotive type generators are classified in Industry 3621; those manufacturing aircraft turbines are classified in Industry 3724; and those manufacturing windmill heads and towers for pumping water for agricultural use are classified in Industry 3523.

Gas turbines, mechanical drive
Governors, steam
Hydraulic turbines
Solar powered turbine-generator sets
Steam engines, except locomotives
Steam turbines
Tank turbines
Turbine generator set units, complete: steam, gas, and hydraulic

Turbines: steam, hydraulic, and gas— except aircraft type
Turbogenerators
Water turbines
Wind powered turbine-generator sets
Windmills for generating power

3519 Internal Combustion Engines, Not Elsewhere Classified

Establishments primarily engaged in manufacturing diesel, semidiesel, or other internal combustion engines, not elsewhere classified, for stationary, marine, traction, and other uses. Establishments primarily engaged in manufacturing aircraft engines are classified in Industry 3724, and those manufacturing automotive engines, except diesel, are classified in Industry 3714.

Diesel and semidiesel engines: for stationary, marine, traction, etc.
Diesel engine parts
Engines and engine parts, internal combustion— military tank
Engines, internal combustion: except aircraft and nondiesel automotive

Engines: diesel and semidiesel and dual fuel—except aircraft
Gas and diesel engine rebuilding, on a factory basis
Governors, diesel engine
Internal combustion engines, except aircraft and nondiesel automotive

Industry Group No.	Industry No.	
351		**ENGINES AND TURBINES—Con.**
	3519	**Internal Combustion Engines, Not Elsewhere Classified—Con.**

Marine engines: diesel, semidiesel, and other internal combustion
Outboard motors, except electric
Semidiesel engines for stationary, marine, traction, or other uses

Tank engines and engine parts, internal combustion: military

352 FARM AND GARDEN MACHINERY AND EQUIPMENT

3523 Farm Machinery and Equipment

Establishments primarily engaged in manufacturing farm machinery and equipment, including wheel tractors, for use in the preparation and maintenance of the soil; planting and harvesting of the crop; preparing crops for market on the farm; or for use in performing other farm operations and processes. Included in this industry are establishments primarily engaged in manufacturing commercial mowing and other turf and grounds care equipment. Establishments primarily engaged in manufacturing farm handtools are classified in Industry Group 342, and those manufacturing garden tractors, lawnmowers and other lawn and garden equipment are classified in Industry 3524.

Agricultural implements and machinery
Ammonia applicators and attachments (agricultural machinery)
Bale throwers
Balers, farm: e.g., hay, straw, cotton
Barn cleaners
Barn stanchions and standards
Blowers and cutters, ensilage
Blowers, forage
Brooders
Cabs, agricultural machinery
Calf savers (farm equipment)
Cattle feeding, handling, and watering equipment
Cattle oilers (farm equipment)
Chicken brooders
Cleaning machines for fruits, grains, and vegetables: farm
Combines (harvester-threshers)
Conveyors, farm (agricultural machinery)
Corn pickers and shellers, farm
Corrals, portable
Cotton picker and stripper harvesting machinery
Cream separators, farm
Crop driers, farm
Crushers, feed (agricultural machinery)
Cultivators, agricultural field and row crop
Cutters, ensilage
Dairy equipment, farm
Drags (agricultural equipment)
Driers: grain, hay, and seed (agricultural implements)
Dusters, mechanical: agricultural
Elevators, farm
Farm machinery and equipment
Feed grinders, crushers, and mixers (agricultural machinery)
Feeders, chicken
Fertilizing machinery, farm
Field type rotary tillers (agricultural machinery)
Fruit, vegetable, berry, and grape harvesting machines

Gates, holding (farm equipment)
Grading, cleaning, and sorting machines: fruit, grain, and vegetable
Grain drills, including legume planters (agricultural machinery)
Grain stackers
Greens mowing equipment
Grounds mowing equipment
Hair clippers for animal use, hand and electric
Hammer and roughage mills (agricultural machinery)
Harrows: disc, spring, and tine
Harvesting machines
Haying machines: mowers, rakes, loaders, stackers, balers, presses, etc.
Hog feeding, handling, and watering equipment
Hulling machinery, agricultural
Incubators, except laboratory and infant
Irrigation equipment, self-propelled
Land rollers and levelers (agricultural machinery)
Listers
Loaders, farm type (general utility)
Milking machines
Mowers and mower-conditioners, hay
Peanut combines, diggers, packers, and threshers (agricultural equipment)
Planting machines, agricultural
Plows, agricultural: disc, moldboard, chisel, etc.
Potato diggers, harvesters, and planters (agricultural machinery)
Poultry brooders, feeders, and waterers
Poultry vision control devices
Presses and balers, farm: hay, cotton, etc.
Rakes, hay (agricultural machinery)
Rotary hoes (agricultural machinery)
Roughage mills (agricultural machinery)
Seeders (agricultural machinery)
Separators, grain and berry: farm
Shears, sheep: power
Shellers, nut (agricultural machinery)

352   FARM AND GARDEN MACHINERY AND EQUIPMENT—Con.

3523 Farm Machinery and Equipment—Con.

Shredders (agricultural machinery)
Silo fillers (agricultural machinery)
Soil pulverizers and packers (agricultural machinery)
Sorting machines for agricultural products
Sprayers, hand: agricultural
Spraying machines (agricultural machinery)
Spreaders, fertilizer
Tobacco curers

Tractors, wheel: farm type
Trailers and wagons, farm
Transplanters
Turf equipment, commercial
Vine pullers
Volume guns (irrigation equipment)
Water troughs
Weeding machines, farm
Windmills for pumping water (agricultural machinery)
Windrowers (agricultural machinery)

3524 Lawn and Garden Tractors and Home Lawn and Garden Equipment

Establishments primarily engaged in manufacturing lawnmowers, lawn and garden tractors, and other lawn and garden equipment used for home lawn and garden care. Also included are establishments primarily engaged in manufacturing snowblowers and throwers for residential use. Establishments primarily engaged in manufacturing farm machinery and equipment (including commercial mowing and other turf and grounds care equipment) are classified in Industry 3523; those manufacturing hand lawn and garden shears and pruners are classified in Industry 3421; and those manufacturing other garden handtools are classified in Industry 3423.

Blowers, residential lawn
Carts for lawn and garden use
Cultivators (garden tractor equipment)
Grass catchers, lawnmower
Hedge trimmers, power
Lawn edgers, power
Lawn rollers, residential
Lawnmowers, hand and power: residential
Loaders (garden tractor equipment)

Mulchers, residential lawn and garden
Plows (garden tractor equipment)
Rototillers (garden machinery)
Seeders, residential lawn and garden
Snowblowers and throwers, residential
Tractors, lawn and garden
Vacuums, residential lawn
Wagons for residential lawn and garden use

353   CONSTRUCTION, MINING, AND MATERIALS HANDLING MACHINERY AND EQUIPMENT

3531 Construction Machinery and Equipment

Establishments primarily engaged in manufacturing heavy machinery and equipment of a type used primarily by the construction industries, such as bulldozers; concrete mixers; cranes, except industrial plant overhead and truck-type cranes; dredging machinery; pavers; and power shovels. Also included in this industry are establishments primarily engaged in manufacturing forestry equipment and certain specialized equipment, not elsewhere classified, similar to that used by the construction industries, such as elevating platforms, ship cranes and capstans, aerial work platforms, and automobile wrecker hoists. Establishments primarily engaged in manufacturing mining equipment are classified in Industry 3532; those manufacturing well-drilling machinery are classified in Industry 3533; those manufacturing industrial plant overhead traveling cranes are classified in Industry 3536; and those manufacturing industrial truck-type cranes are classified in Industry 3537.

Aerial work platforms, hydraulic or electric truck or carrier mounted
Aggregate spreaders
Asphalt plants, including travel—mix type

Automobile wrecker hoists
Backfillers, self-propelled
Backhoes
Ballast distributors (railway track equipment)

Industry Group No.	Industry No.	
353		**CONSTRUCTION, MINING, AND MATERIALS HANDLING MACHINERY AND EQUIPMENT**—Con.
	3531	**Construction Machinery and Equipment**—Con.

Batching plants, bituminous
Batching plants, for aggregate concrete and bulk cement
Blades for graders, scrapers, dozers, and snowplows
Breakers, paving
Buckets, excavating: e.g., clamshell, concrete, dragline, drag scraper, shovel
Bulldozers, construction
Cabs, construction machinery
Capstans, ship
Carriers, crane
Chip spreaders, self-propelled
Chippers, commercial: brush, limb, and log
Concrete buggies, powered
Concrete grouting equipment
Concrete gunning equipment
Concrete plants
Construction machinery, except mining
Cranes, construction
Cranes, except industrial plant
Crushers, mineral: portable
Derricks, except oil and gas field
Distributors (construction machinery)
Ditchers, ladder: vertical boom or wheel
Dozers, tractor mounted: material moving
Draglines, powered
Drags, road (construction and road maintenance equipment)
Dredging machinery
Excavators: e.g., cable, clamshell, crane, derrick, dragline, power shovel
Extractors, piling
Finishers and spreaders, construction
Finishers, concrete and bituminous: powered
Grader attachments, elevating
Graders, road (construction machinery)
Grapples: rock, wood, etc.
Grinders, stone: portable
Hammer mills (rock and ore crushing machines), portable
Hammers, pile driving
Line markers, self-propelled
Locomotive cranes
Log splitters
Logging equipment

Mixers: e.g., concrete, ore, sand, slag, plaster, mortar, bituminous
Mortar mixers
Mud jacks
Pavers
Pile-driving equipment
Planers, bituminous
Plaster mixers
Plows, construction: excavating and grading
Post hole diggers, powered
Power cranes, draglines, and shovels
Pulverizers, stone: portable
Railway track equipment: e.g., rail layers, ballast distributors
Rakes, land clearing: mechanical
Road construction and maintenance machinery
Rock crushing machinery, portable
Rollers, road
Rollers, sheepsfoot and vibratory
Sand mixers
Scarifiers, road
Scrapers, construction
Screeds and screeding machines
Screeners, portable
Ship cranes and derricks
Ship winches
Shovel loaders
Shovels, power
Silos, cement (batch plant)
Slag mixers
Snowplow attachments
Soil compactors: vibratory
Spreaders and finishers, construction
Subgraders, construction equipment
Subsoiler attachments, tractor-mounted
Surfacers, concrete grinding
Tampers, powered
Tamping equipment, rail
Teeth, bucket and scarifier
Tractors, construction
Tractors, crawler
Tractors, tracklaying
Trenching machines
Trucks, off-highway
Vibrators for concrete construction
Wellpoint systems
Winches, all types
Work platforms, elevated

3532   Mining Machinery and Equipment, Except Oil and Gas Field Machinery and Equipment

Establishments primarily engaged in manufacturing heavy machinery and equipment used by the mining industries, such as coal breakers, mine cars, mineral cleaning machinery, concentration machinery, core drills, coal cutters, portable rock drills, and rock crushing machinery. Establishments primarily engaged in manufacturing construction machinery are classified in Industry 3531; those manufacturing welldrilling machinery are classified in Industry 3533; and those manufacturing coal and ore conveyors are classified in Industry 3535.

Amalgamators (metallurgical and mining machinery)

Auger mining equipment
Bits, rock: except oil and gas field tools

**353   CONSTRUCTION, MINING, AND MATERIALS HANDLING MACHINERY
AND EQUIPMENT—Con.**

**3532   Mining Machinery and Equipment, Except Oil and Gas Field Machinery and
Equipment—Con.**

Cages, mine shaft
Car dumpers, mining
Clarifying machinery, mineral
Classifiers, metallurgical and mining
Cleaning machinery, mineral
Coal breakers, cutters, and pulverizers
Concentration machinery (metallurgical and mining)
Crushers, mineral: stationary
Drills and drilling equipment, mining: except oil and gas field
Drills, core
Drills, rock: portable
Feeders, ore and aggregate
Flotation machinery (mining machinery)
Grinders, stone: stationary
Hammer mills (rock and ore crushing machines), stationary
Loading machines, underground: mobile

Mining cars and trucks (dollies)
Mining equipment, except oil and gas field: rebuilding on a factory basis
Mining machinery and equipment, except oil and gas field
Ore crushing, washing, screening, and loading machinery
Pellet mills (mining machinery)
Plows, coal
Pulverizers, stone: stationary
Scraper loaders, underground
Screeners, stationary
Sedimentation machinery, mineral
Separating machinery, mineral
Shuttle cars, underground
Stamping mill mining machinery
Washers, aggregate and sand: stationary type

3533   Oil and Gas Field Machinery and Equipment

Establishments primarily engaged in manufacturing machinery and equipment for use in oil and gas fields or for drilling water wells, including portable drilling rigs. Establishments primarily engaged in manufacturing offshore oil and gas well drilling and production platforms are classified in Industry 3731.

Bits, rock: oil and gas field tools
Derricks, oil and gas field
Drill rigs, all types
Drilling tools for gas, oil, or water wells
Gas well machinery and equipment

Oil and gas field machinery and equipment
Water well drilling machinery
Well logging equipment
Well surveying machinery

3534   Elevators and Moving Stairways

Establishments primarily engaged in manufacturing passenger or freight elevators, automobile lifts, dumbwaiters, and moving stairways. Establishments primarily engaged in manufacturing commercial conveyor systems and equipment are classified in Industry 3535, and those manufacturing farm elevators are classified in Industry 3523.

Automobile lifts (elevators)
Dumbwaiters
Elevator fronts
Elevators and elevator equipment, passenger and freight
Elevators, powered: nonfarm

Escalators, passenger and freight
Lifts (elevators), passenger and freight
Stair elevators: motor powered
Stairways, moving
Walkways, moving

3535   Conveyors and Conveying Equipment

Establishments primarily engaged in manufacturing conveyors and conveying equipment for installation in factories, warehouses, mines, and other industrial and commercial establishments. Establishments primarily engaged in manufacturing farm elevators and conveyors are classified in Industry 3523; those manufacturing passenger or freight elevators, dumbwaiters, and moving stairways are classified in Industry 3534; and those manufacturing overhead traveling cranes and monorail systems are classified in Industry 3536.

Belt conveyor systems for general industrial use

Industry
Group
No.

Industry
No.

353   **CONSTRUCTION, MINING, AND MATERIALS HANDLING MACHINERY AND EQUIPMENT—Con.**

3535   **Conveyors and Conveying Equipment—Con.**

Bucket type conveyor systems for general industrial use
Buckets, elevator or conveyor for general industrial use
Conveyor systems for general industrial use
Mine conveyors
Overhead conveyor systems for general industrial use
Passenger baggage belt loaders
Pneumatic tube conveyor systems for general industrial use
Robotic conveyors for general industrial use

3536   **Overhead Traveling Cranes, Hoists, and Monorail Systems**

Establishments primarily engaged in manufacturing overhead traveling cranes, hoists, and monorail systems for installation in factories, warehouses, marinas, and other industrial and commercial establishments. Establishments primarily engaged in manufacturing cranes except industrial types, automobile wrecker hoists, and aerial work platforms are classified in Industry 3531, and those manufacturing aircraft loading hoists are classified in Industry 3537.

Boat lifts
Cranes, overhead traveling
Davits
Hoists, except aircraft loading and automobile wrecker hoists
Hoists, hand
Hoists, overhead
Monorail systems

3537   **Industrial Trucks, Tractors, Trailers, and Stackers**

Establishments primarily engaged in manufacturing industrial trucks, tractors, trailers, stackers (truck type), and related equipment, used for handling materials on floors and paved surfaces in and around industrial and commercial plants, depots, docks, airports, and terminals. Establishments primarily engaged in manufacturing motor vehicles and motor vehicle type trailers are classified in Industry Group 371; those manufacturing farm type wheel tractors are classified in Industry 3523; those manufacturing tractor shovel loaders and tracklaying tractors are classified in Industry 3531; and those manufacturing wood pallets and skids are classified in Industry 2448.

Adapters for multiweapon rack loading on aircraft
Aircraft engine cradles
Aircraft loading hoists
Boat cradles
Bomb lifts
Bomb trucks
Cabs for industrial trucks and tractors
Cars, industrial: except automotive cars and trucks and mining cars
Containers, air cargo: metal
Cranes, mobile industrial truck
Die and strip handlers
Docks, loading: portable, adjustable, and hydraulic
Dollies (hand or power trucks), industrial: except mining
Drum cradles
Engine stands and racks, metal
Forklift trucks
Hoists, aircraft loading
Hoppers, end dump
Hospital dollies
Industrial truck cranes
Industrial trucks and tractors
Laundry containers on wheels
Lift trucks, industrial: fork, platform, straddle, etc.
Mobile straddle carriers
Pallet assemblies for landing mats
Pallet loaders and unloaders
Palletizers and depalletizers
Pallets, metal
Platforms, cargo: metal
Ramps, aircraft—loading
Ramps, loading: portable, adjustable, and hydraulic
Skid boxes, metal
Skids, metal
Stackers, power (industrial truck stackers)
Stacking carts
Stacking machines, automatic
Stands, ground servicing aircraft
Straddle carriers, mobile
Tables, lift: hydraulic
Tractors, industrial: for use in plants, depots, docks, and terminals
Truck trailers for use in plants, depots, docks, and terminals
Trucks, industrial (except mining): for freight, baggage, etc.
Tunnel kiln cars

354   METALWORKING MACHINERY AND EQUIPMENT

3541   Machine Tools, Metal Cutting Types

Establishments primarily engaged in manufacturing metal cutting type machine tools, not supported in the hands of an operator when in use, that shape metal by cutting or use of electrical techniques; the rebuilding of such machine tools, and the manufacture of replacement parts for them. Also included in this industry are metalworking machine tools designed primarily for home workshops. Establishments primarily engaged in the manufacture of electric and gas welding and soldering equipment are classified in Industry 3548, and those manufacturing portable power-driven handtools are classified in Industry 3546.

Automatic chucking machines
Boring machine tools, metalworking
Boring mills
Boring, drilling, and milling machine combinations
Broaching machines
Brushing machines (metalworking machinery)
Buffing and polishing machines (machine tools)
Burnishing machines (machine tools)
Centering machines
Chemical milling machines
Countersinking machines
Cutoff machines (metalworking machinery)
Cutting machines, pipe (machine tools)
Cylinder reboring machines
Deburring machines
Diesinking machines
Drill presses (machine tools)
Drilling machine tools (metal cutting)
Duplicator, machine tools
Electrical discharge erosion machines
Electrical discharge grinding machines
Electrochemical milling machines
Electrolytic metal cutting machine tools
Electron-discharge metal cutting machine tools
Facing machines
Filing machines, metal (machine tools)
Flange facing machines
Gear chamfering machines (machine tools)
Gear cutting and finishing machines
Gear tooth grinding machines (machine tools)
Grinding machines, metalworking
Grooving machines (machine tools)
Home workshop machine tools, metalworking
Honing and lapping machines
Jig boring machines
Jig grinding machines

Keyseating machines (machine tools)
Lapping machines
Lathes, metal cutting
Machine tool replacement and repair parts, metal cutting types
Machine tools, metal cutting: e.g., exotic, chemical, explosive
Metal polishing lathes
Milling machines (machine tools)
Pipe cutting and threading machines (machine tools)
Planers, metal cutting
Plasma process metal cutting machines, except welding machines
Pointing, chamfering, and burring machines
Polishing machines (machine tools)
Reaming machines
Rebuilt machine tools, metal cutting types
Regrinding machines, crankshaft
Rifle working machines (machine tools)
Robots for drilling and cutting—machine type, metalworking
Robots for grinding, polishing, and deburring—metalworking
Sawing and cutoff machines (metalworking machinery)
Saws, power: metal cutting
Screw and nut slotting machines
Screw machines, automatic
Shapers and slotters, metal cutting
Shaving machines (metalworking)
Slotting machines (machine tools)
Tapping machines
Threading machines (machine tools)
Turning machines (lathes)
Turret lathes, metal cutting
Ultrasonic assisted grinding machines (metalworking)
Ultrasonic metal cutting machine tools
Valve grinding machines
Vertical turning and boring machines (metalworking)

3542   Machine Tools, Metal Forming Types

Establishments primarily engaged in manufacturing metal forming machine tools, not supported in the hands of an operator while in use, for pressing, hammering, extruding, shearing, die-casting, or otherwise forming metal into shape. This industry also includes the rebuilding of such machine tools and the manufacture of repair parts for them. Establishments primarily engaged in the manufacture of electric and gas welding equipment and soldering equip-

Industry
Group
No.
354

Industry
No.

METALWORKING MACHINERY AND EQUIPMENT—Con.

3542 Machine Tools, Metal Forming Types—Con.

ment are classified in Industry 3548; those manufacturing portable power-driven handtools are classified in Industry 3546; and those manufacturing rolling mill machinery and equipment are classified in Industry 3547.

Arbor presses
Beaders, metal (machines)
Bending and forming machines
Brakes, metal forming
Bulldozers, metalworking
Can making machines
Chemical explosives metal forming machines
Die-casting machines
Drop hammers, for forging and shaping metal
Elastic membrane metal forming machines
Electroforming machines
Extruding machines (machine tools), metal
Forging machinery and hammers
Hammers, power (forging machinery)
Headers
High energy rate metal forming machines
Knurling machines
Machine tools, metal forming types: including rebuilding
Magnetic forming machines
Mechanical-pneumatic or hydraulic metal forming machines

Metal deposit forming machines
Nail heading machines
Plasma jet spray metal forming machines
Presses: forming, stamping, punching, and shearing (machine tools)
Presses: hydraulic and pneumatic, mechanical and manual
Punching and shearing machines
Rebuilt machine tools, metal forming types
Riveting machines
Robots for metal forming: e.g., pressing, hammering, extruding
Shearing machines, power
Sheet metalworking machines
Shock wave metal forming machines
Spinning lathes
Spinning machines, metal
Spline rolling machines
Spring winding and forming machines
Stretching machines
Swaging machines
Thread rolling machines
Ultrasonically assisted metal forming machines
Upsetters (forging machines)

3543 Industrial Patterns

Establishments primarily engaged in manufacturing industrial patterns.

Cores, sand (foundry)
Foundry cores

Foundry patternmaking
Patterns, industrial

3544 Special Dies and Tools, Die Sets, Jigs and Fixtures, and Industrial Molds

Establishments commonly known as contract tool and die shops and primarily engaged in manufacturing, on a job or order basis, special tools and fixtures for use with machine tools, hammers, die-casting machines, and presses. The products of establishments classified in this industry include a wide variety of special toolings, such as dies; punches; diesets and components, and subpresses; jigs and fixtures; and special checking devices. Establishments primarily engaged in manufacturing molds for die-casting and foundry casting; metal molds for plaster working, rubber working, plastics working, glass working and similar machinery are also included. Establishments primarily engaged in manufacturing molds for heavy steel ingots are classified in Industry 3321, and those manufacturing cutting dies, except metal cutting, are classified in Industry 3423.

Diamond dies, metalworking
Dies and die holders for metal die-casting and metal cutting and forming, except threading
Dies, metalworking, except threading
Dies, plastics forming
Dies, steel rule
Diesets for metal stamping (presses)
Extrusion dies
Forms, metal (molds): for foundry and plastics working machinery

Industrial molds
Jigs and fixtures (metalworking machinery accessories)
Jigs: inspection, gauging, and checking
Punches, forming and stamping
Subpresses, metalworking
Welding positioners (jigs)
Wiredrawing and straightening dies

Industry
Group
No.
354

Industry
No.

METALWORKING MACHINERY AND EQUIPMENT—Con.

3545 Cutting Tools, Machine Tool Accessories, and Machinists' Precision Measuring Devices

Establishments primarily engaged in manufacturing cutting tools, machinists' precision measuring tools, and attachments and accessories for machine tools and for other metalworking machinery, not elsewhere classified. Establishments primarily engaged in manufacturing handtools, except power-driven types, are classified in Industry Group 342.

Angle rings
Arbors (machine tool accessories)
Bits for use on lathes, planers, shapers, etc.
Blanks, cutting tool
Boring machine attachments (machine tool accessories)
Broaches (machine tool accessories)
Calipers and dividers
Cams (machine tool accessories)
Chasers (machine tool accessories)
Chucks: drill, lathe, and magnetic (machine tool accessories)
Clamps, machine tool
Collars (machine tool accessories)
Collets (machine tool accessories)
Comparators (machinists' precision tools)
Counterbores, metalworking
Countersinks and countersink drill combinations (machine tool accessories)
Cutters, milling
Cutting tools and bits for use on lathes, planers, shapers, etc.
Diamond cutting tools for turning, boring, burnishing, etc.
Diamond dressing and wheel crushing attachments
Dies, thread cutting
Dressers, abrasive wheel: diamond point and other
Drill bits, metalworking
Drill bushings (drilling jig)
Drilling machine attachments and accessories (machine tool accessories)
Drills (machine tool accessories)
Files, machine tool
Gauge blocks
Gauges, except optical (machine tool accessories)

Hobs
Honing heads
Hopper feed devices
Inserts, cutting tool
Knives, shear
Lathe attachments and cutting tools (machine tool accessories)
Letter pins (gauging and measuring)
Machine knives, metalworking
Machine tool attachments and accessories
Mandrels
Measuring tools and machines, machinists' metalworking type
Micrometers
Milling machine attachments (machine tool accessories)
Precision tools, machinists'
Pushers
Reamers, machine tool
Scales, measuring (machinists' precision tools)
Shaping tools (machine tool accessories)
Shear knives
Sockets (machine tool accessories)
Tables, rotary: indexing
Taps, machine tool
Threading toolholders
Threading tools (machine tool accessories)
Tips, cutting tool
Toolholders
Tools and accessories for machine tools
Verniers (machinists' precision tools)
Vises, machine (machine tool accessories)
Wheel turning equipment, diamond point and other (machine tool accessories)

3546 Power-Driven Handtools

Establishments primarily engaged in manufacturing power-driven handtools, such as drills and drilling tools, pneumatic and snagging grinders, and electric hammers. Establishments primarily engaged in manufacturing metal cutting type and metal forming type machines (including home workshop tools) which are not supported in the hands of an operator are classified in Industries 3541 and 3542; and those primarily manufacturing power-driven heavy construction or mining handtools are classified in Industry Group 353.

Attachments for portable drills
Buffing machines, hand: electric
Cartridge-activated hand power tools
Caulking hammers
Chain saws, portable
Chipping hammers, electric

Drills (except rock drilling and coring), portable: electric and pneumatic
Drills, hand: electric
Flexible shaft metalworking machines, portable
Grinders, pneumatic and electric: port-

Industry Group No.	Industry No.	
354		**METALWORKING MACHINERY AND EQUIPMENT—Con.**

3546 Power-Driven Handtools—Con.

able (metalworking machinery)
Grinders, snagging
Guns, pneumatic: chip removal
Hammers: portable electric and pneumatic: e.g., chipping, riveting, caulking
Handtools, power-driven: woodworking or metalworking

Masonry and concrete drilling tools, power: portable
Powder-actuated hand tools
Riveting hammers
Sanders, hand: electric
Saws, portable hand held: power-driven—woodworking or metalworking

3547 Rolling Mill Machinery and Equipment

Establishments primarily engaged in manufacturing rolling mill machinery and processing equipment for metal production, such as cold forming mills, structural mills, and finishing equipment.

Bar mills
Billet mills
Blooming and slabbing mills
Cleaning lines, electrolytic (rolling mill equipment)
Cold forming type mills (rolling mill machinery)
Ferrous and nonferrous mill equipment, auxiliary
Finishing equipment, rolling mill
Galvanizing lines (rolling mill equipment)
Hot strip mill machinery
Mill tables (rolling mill equipment)
Picklers and pickling lines, sheet and strip (rolling mill equipment)

Pipe and tube mills
Plate rolling mill machinery
Rod mills (rolling mill equipment)
Roller levelers (rolling mill machinery)
Rolling mill machinery and equipment
Rolls for rolling mill machinery, machined
Steel rolling machinery
Straightening machinery (rolling mill equipment)
Structural mills (rolling mill machinery)
Tube mill machinery

3548 Electric and Gas Welding and Soldering Equipment

Establishments primarily engaged in manufacturing electric and gas welding and soldering equipment and accessories. Also included are establishments primarily engaged in coating welding wire from purchased wire or from wire drawn in the same establishment. Establishments primarily engaged in manufacturing handheld soldering irons are classified in Industry 3423, and those manufacturing electron beam, ultrasonic, and laser welding equipment are classified in Industry 3699.

Arc-welder transformers (separate)
Arc-welders, transformer-rectifier
Arc-welding generators, a.c. and d.c.
Electrode holders for electric welding apparatus
Electrodes, electric welding
Gas welding equipment
Generators (separate) for arc-welders
Resistance welders, electric
Robots for welding, soldering, or brazing

Seam welding apparatus, gas and electric
Soldering equipment, except soldering irons
Spot welding apparatus, gas and electric
Transformers (separate) for arc-welders
Welding accessories, electric and gas
Welding and cutting apparatus, gas or electric
Welding wire, bare and coated

3549 Metalworking Machinery, Not Elsewhere Classified

Establishments primarily engaged in manufacturing metalworking machinery, not elsewhere classified. Establishments primarily engaged in manufacturing automotive maintenance equipment are classified in Industry 3559.

Assembly machines, e.g., rotary transfer, in-line transfer, special purpose: including robotic
Coil winding machines for springs
Coilers (metalworking machines)
Cradle assemblies (wire making equipment)

Cutting up lines
Draw benches
Drawing machinery and equipment, except wiredrawing dies
Marking machines, metalworking
Pail mills
Propeller straightening presses

Industry Group No.	Industry No.
354	

METALWORKING MACHINERY AND EQUIPMENT—Con.

3549 Metalworking Machinery, Not Elsewhere Classified—Con.

Rotary slitters (metalworking machines)
Screwdowns and boxes

Screwdriving machines
Wiredrawing and fabricating machinery and equipment, except dies

355 SPECIAL INDUSTRY MACHINERY, EXCEPT METALWORKING MACHINERY

3552 Textile Machinery

Establishments primarily engaged in manufacturing machinery for the textile industries, including parts, attachments, and accessories. Establishments primarily engaged in manufacturing industrial sewing machines are classified in Industry 3559, and those manufacturing household sewing machines are classified in Industry 3639.

Beaming machines, textile
Bleaching machinery, textile
Bobbins for textile machinery
Braiding machines, textile
Carbonizing equipment (wool processing machinery)
Card clothing for textile machines
Carding machines, textile
Cloth spreading machines
Cloth stripping machines
Combing machines, textile
Creels, textile machinery
Drawing frames, textile
Drying machines, textile: for stock, yarn, and cloth
Dyeing machinery, textile
Embroidery machines
Finishing machinery, textile
Frames, doubling and twisting (textile machinery)
Garnetting machines, textile
Heddles for loom harnesses, wire
Hosiery machines
Jacquard card cutting machines
Jacquard loom parts and attachments
Knitting machines
Knot tying machines (textile machinery)
Lace and net machines
Lace machine bobbins, wood or metal
Loom bobbins, wood or metal

Looms (textile machinery)
Loopers (textile machinery)
Mercerizing machinery
Napping machines (textile machinery)
Picker machines (textile machinery)
Picker sticks for looms
Printing machinery, textile
Reeds, loom
Rope and cordage machines
Roving machines (textile machinery)
Shuttles for textile weaving
Silk screens for the textile industry
Slashing machines (textile machinery)
Spindles, textile
Spinning machines, textile
Spools, textile machinery: wood
Textile finishing machinery: bleaching, dyeing, mercerizing, and printing
Textile machinery parts
Textile machinery, except sewing machines
Textile turnings and shapes, wood
Thread making machines (spinning machinery), textile
Tufting machines
Warp and knot tying machines (textile machinery)
Warping machines (textile machinery)
Winders (textile machinery)
Wool and worsted finishing machines
Yarn texturizing machines

3553 Woodworking Machinery

Establishments primarily engaged in manufacturing machinery for sawmills, for making particleboard and similar products, and for otherwise working or producing wood products. Establishments primarily engaged in manufacturing handtools such as planes, axes, drawknives, and handsaws are classified in Industry Group 342, and those manufacturing portable power-driven handtools in Industry 3546.

Bandsaws, woodworking
Box making machines for wooden boxes
Cabinet makers' machinery
Furniture makers' machinery (woodworking)
Jointers (woodworking machines)
Lathes, wood turning: including accessories
Mortisers (woodworking machines)
Pattern makers' machinery (woodworking)

Planers, woodworking
Planing mill machinery
Presses, woodworking: particleboard, hardboard, medium density fiberboard (MDF), and plywood
Sanding machines, except portable floor sanders (woodworking machinery)
Sawmill machines
Saws, power: bench and table (woodworking machinery)—except portable

Industry
Group   Industry
No.   No.

**355   SPECIAL INDUSTRY MACHINERY, EXCEPT METALWORKING
         MACHINERY—Con.**

3553   Woodworking Machinery—Con.

Scarfing machines (woodworking machinery)
Shapers, woodworking machinery
Surfacers (woodworking machines)
Tenoners (woodworking machines)

Veneer mill machines
Venetian blind machines (woodworking machinery)
Woodworking machines

3554   Paper Industries Machinery

Establishments primarily engaged in manufacturing machinery for the pulp, paper, and paper product industries. Establishments primarily engaged in manufacturing printing trades machinery are classified in Industry 3555.

Bag and envelope making machinery (paper machinery)
Box making machines for paper boxes
Coating and finishing machinery, paper
Corrugating machines for paper
Cutting and folding machines, paper
Die-cutting and stamping machinery (paper converting machinery)
Folding machines, paper: except office machines

Fourdrinier machines (paper manufacturing machinery)
Paper mill machinery: e.g., plating, slitting, waxing
Paper product machines, except printing machines
Pulp mill machinery
Sandpaper manufacturing machines

3555   Printing Trades Machinery and Equipment

Establishments primarily engaged in manufacturing machinery and equipment used by the printing and bookbinding trades. Establishments primarily engaged in manufacturing textile printing machinery are classified in Industry 3552.

Advertising and newspaper mats
Blocks, engravers': wood
Bookbinders' machines
Bronzing and dusting machines for the printing trade
Chases and galleys, printers'
Collating machines for printing and bookbinding trade use
Copy holders, printers'
Electrotyping machines
Engraving machinery and equipment (printing trades machinery)
Envelope printing presses
Etching machines (printing trades machinery)
Foundry type for printing
Gelatin rolls used in printing
Gravure presses
Intertype machines
Leads, printers'
Linotype machines

Lithographic stones
Monotype machines
Paper ruling and sewing machines (bookbinders' machinery)
Photoengraving machines
Planes, printers'
Plates, metal: engravers'
Presses, printing
Printers' machines and equipment
Rules, printers'
Slugs, printers'
Stereotyping machines
Sticks, printers'
Type: lead, steel, brass, copper faced, etc.
Typecases, printers'
Typecasting, founding, and melting machines
Typesetting machines: intertypes, linotypes, monotypes, etc.
Typographic numbering machines

3556   Food Products Machinery

Establishments primarily engaged in manufacturing machinery for use by the food products and beverage manufacturing industries and similar machinery for use in manufacturing animal foods. Establishments primarily engaged in manufacturing food packaging machinery are classified in Industry 3565, and those manufacturing industrial refrigeration machinery are classified in Industry Group 358.

Bakery machinery
Biscuit cutters (machines)
Bread slicing machines

Brewers' and maltsers' machinery
Butter making and butter working machinery

Industry Group No. 355

Industry No.

SPECIAL INDUSTRY MACHINERY, EXCEPT METALWORKING MACHINERY—Con.

3556 Food Products Machinery—Con.

Cheese making machinery
Chewing gum machinery
Chocolate processing machinery
Choppers, food: commercial types
Cider presses
Coffee roasting and grinding machines
Condensed and evaporated milk machinery
Confectionery machinery
Corn popping machines, industrial type
Cracker making machines
Cream separators, industrial
Cutters, biscuit (machines)
Dairy products machinery and equipment
Dehydrating equipment, food processing
Dies, biscuit cutting
Distillery machinery
Dough mixing machinery
Dry milk processing machinery
Fish and shellfish processing machinery
Flour mill machinery
Food choppers, grinders, mixers, and slicers: commercial type
Grain mill machinery
Grinders, food: commercial types
Homogenizing machinery: dairy, fruit, vegetable, and other foods
Ice cream manufacturing machinery

Juice extractors, fruit and vegetable: commercial type
Macaroni machinery: for making macaroni, spaghetti, and noodles
Malt mills
Meat and poultry processing machinery
Meat grinders
Milk processing machinery
Mills and presses: beet, cider, and sugarcane
Mixers and whippers, electric: for food manufacturing industries
Mixers, feed: except agricultural machinery
Mixers, food: commercial types
Oilseed crushing and extracting machinery
Ovens, bakery
Pasteurizing equipment, dairy and other food
Peanut roasting machines
Potato peelers, electric
Presses: cheese, beet, cider, and sugarcane
Sifting machines, food
Slicing machines, fruit and vegetable: commercial types
Stuffers, sausage
Sugar plant machinery
Vegetable oil processing machinery

3559 Special Industry Machinery, Not Elsewhere Classified

Establishments primarily engaged in manufacturing special industry machinery, not elsewhere classified, such as smelting and refining equipment, cement making, clayworking, cotton ginning, glass making, hat making, incandescent lamp making, leather working, paint making, rubber working, cigar and cigarette making, tobacco working, shoe making, and stone working machinery, and industrial sewing machines, and automotive maintenance machinery and equipment.

Ammunition and explosives loading machinery
Anodizing equipment (except rolling mill lines)
Bag sewing and closing machines (industrial sewing machines)
Balancing equipment, automotive wheel
Boot making and repairing machinery
Brick making machines
Broom making machinery
Buttonhole and eyelet machines and attachments, industrial
Cement making machinery
Chemical kilns
Chemical machinery and equipment
Cigarette and cigar making machines
Clayworking and tempering machines
Concrete products machinery
Control rod drive mechanisms for use on nuclear reactors
Cork working machinery
Degreasing machines, automotive (garage equipment)
Degreasing machines, industrial

Desalination equipment
Die and hub cutting equipment (jewelry manufacturing)
Drying kilns, lumber
Electric screening equipment
Electron tube making machinery
Electroplating machinery and equipment, except rolling mill lines
Foundry machinery and equipment
Frame straighteners, automotive (garage equipment)
Fur sewing machines
Ginning machines, cotton
Glass making machinery: blowing, molding, forming, grinding, etc.
Hat making and hat renovating machinery
Jewelers' machines
Kilns: cement, wood, and chemical
Lamp making machinery, incandescent
Leather working machinery
Metal finishing equipment for plating, except rolling mill lines
Metal pickling equipment, except rolling mill lines

355   **SPECIAL INDUSTRY MACHINERY, EXCEPT METALWORKING MACHINERY—Con.**

3559   **Special Industry Machinery, Not Elsewhere Classified—Con.**

Metal smelting and refining machinery, except furnaces and ovens
Nuclear reactor control rod drive mechanisms
Optical lens machinery
Ozone machines
Packup assemblies (wheel overhaul)
Paint making machinery
Petroleum refinery equipment
Pharmaceutical machinery
Plastics working machinery
Pottery making machinery
Robots, plastics: for molding and forming
Rubber products machinery
Rubber working machinery
Scouring machines, tannery
Semiconductor manufacturing machinery

Sewing machines and attachments, industrial
Shoe making and repairing machinery
Silver recovery equipment, electrolytic
Stone tumblers
Stone working machinery
Synthetic filament extruding machines
Tannery machines
Tile making machines
Tire grooving machines
Tire retreading machinery and equipment
Tire shredding machinery
Tobacco products machinery
Wheel mounting and balancing equipment, automotive
Wood drying kilns
Zipper making machinery

356   **GENERAL INDUSTRIAL MACHINERY AND EQUIPMENT**

3561   **Pumps and Pumping Equipment**

Establishments primarily engaged in manufacturing pumps and pumping equipment for general industrial, commercial, or household use, except fluid power pumps and motors. Included are establishments primarily engaged in manufacturing domestic water and sump pumps. Establishments primarily engaged in manufacturing fluid power pumps and motors are classified in Industry 3594; those manufacturing measuring and dispensing pumps for gasoline service station use are classified in Industry 3586; those manufacturing vacuum pumps, except laboratory, are classified in Industry 3563; those manufacturing laboratory vacuum pumps are classified in Industry 3821; and those manufacturing pumps for motor vehicles are classified in Industry 3714.

Cylinders, pump
Domestic water pumps
Hydrojet marine engine units
Pump jacks

Pumps, domestic: water or sump
Pumps, general industrial type
Pumps, oil well and oil field

3562   **Ball and Roller Bearings**

Establishments primarily engaged in manufacturing ball and roller bearings (including ball or roller bearing pillow block, flange, takeup cartridge and hangar units) and parts. Establishments primarily engaged in manufacturing plain bearings are classified in Industry 3568.

Bearings, ball and roller
Flange units for ball or roller bearings
Pillow block units for ball or roller bearings

Pillow blocks, with ball or roller bearings
Races, ball and roller bearing

3563   **Air and Gas Compressors**

Establishments primarily engaged in manufacturing air and gas compressors for general industrial use, and in manufacturing nonagricultural spraying and dusting equipment. Establishments primarily engaged in manufacturing refrigeration and air-conditioning compressors and compressing units are classified in Industry 3585; those manufacturing pneumatic pumps and motors for fluid power transmission are classified in Industry 3594; those manufactur-

Industry
Group   Industry
No.   No.

356   GENERAL INDUSTRIAL MACHINERY AND EQUIPMENT—Con.

3563   Air and Gas Compressors—Con.

ing agricultural spraying and dusting equipment are classified in Industry 3523; and those manufacturing laboratory vacuum pumps are classified in Industry 3821.

Compressors, air and gas: for general industrial use	Sprayers, hand: except agricultural
Dusting outfits for metal, paints, and chemicals (portable or vehicular)	Spraying outfits for metals, paints, and chemicals (compressor units)
Paint sprayers	Tire inflators, hand or compressor operated
Robots for spraying, painting—industrial	Vacuum pumps, except laboratory

3564   Industrial and Commercial Fans and Blowers and Air Purification Equipment

Establishments primarily engaged in manufacturing industrial and commercial blowers, industrial and commercial exhaust and ventilating fans, and attic fans, or in manufacturing dust collection and other air purification equipment for heating, ventilating and air-conditioning systems or for industrial gas cleaning systems. Establishments primarily engaged in manufacturing air-conditioning units are classified in Industry 3585; those manufacturing free air-circulating fans for use on desks, pedestals, or wall brackets as well as household window-type fans and roll-abouts, and kitchen and household ventilating and exhaust electric fans, except attic, are classified in Industry 3634.

Air cleaning systems	Fans, except household
Air purification and dust collection equipment	Filters, air: for furnaces and air-conditioning equipment
Aircurtains (blower)	Furnace blowers (blower filter units)
Attic fans	Precipitators, electrostatic
Blowers, commercial and industrial	Turboblowers, industrial
Dust and fume collecting equipment, industrial	Ventilating, blowing, and exhaust fans: except household and kitchen
Exhaust fans, except household and kitchen	

3565   Packaging Machinery

Establishments primarily engaged in manufacturing packaging machinery, including wrapping and bottling machinery.

Aerating machines, for beverages	Carton packing machines
Bag opening, filling and closing machines	Label moisteners, industrial type
Bottling machinery: washing, sterilizing, filling, capping, and labeling	Labeling machinery, industrial type
Bread wrapping machines	Packaging machinery
	Wrapping machines

3566   Speed Changers, Industrial High-Speed Drives, and Gears

Establishments primarily engaged in manufacturing speed changers, industrial high-speed drives, except hydrostatic drives, and gears. Establishments primarily engaged in manufacturing automotive power transmission equipment are classified in Industry 3714; those manufacturing aircraft power transmission equipment are classified in Industry 3728; and those manufacturing industrial hydrostatic drives (transmissions) are classified in Industry 3594.

Drives, high-speed industrial: except hydrostatic	Gears, power transmission: except motor vehicle and aircraft
Gearmotors (power transmission equipment)	Reducers, speed
	Reduction gears and gear units for tur-

Industry Group No.
356

Industry No.

GENERAL INDUSTRIAL MACHINERY AND EQUIPMENT—Con.

3566 Speed Changers, Industrial High-Speed Drives, and Gears—Con.

bines, except automotive and aircraft
Speed changers (power transmission equipment)
Speed reducers (power transmission equipment)

Torque converters, except motor vehicle

3567 Industrial Process Furnaces and Ovens

Establishments primarily engaged in manufacturing industrial process furnaces, ovens, induction and dielectric heating equipment, and related devices. Establishments primarily engaged in manufacturing bakery ovens are classified in Industry 3556; those manufacturing cement, wood, and chemical kilns are classified in Industry 3559; those manufacturing cremating ovens are classified in Industry 3569; and those manufacturing laboratory furnaces and ovens are classified in Industry 3821.

Calcining kilns (industrial furnaces)
Ceramic kilns and furnaces
Core baking and mold drying ovens
Dielectric heating equipment
Distillation ovens, charcoal and coke
Driers and redriers, industrial process
Enameling ovens
Furnaces, industrial process
Heat treating ovens
Heating equipment, induction
Heating units and devices, industrial: electric
Incinerators, metal: domestic and commercial
Induction heating equipment

Infrared ovens, industrial
Japanning ovens
Kilns: except cement, chemical, and wood
Lacquering ovens
Metal melting furnaces, industrial
Ovens, industrial process: except bakery
Paint baking and drying ovens
Radiant heating systems, industrial process: e.g., dryers, cookers'
Rubber curing ovens
Sherardizing ovens
Smelting ovens
Vacuum furnaces and ovens

3568 Mechanical Power Transmission Equipment, Not Elsewhere Classified

Establishments primarily engaged in manufacturing mechanical power transmission equipment and parts, for industrial machinery. Establishments primarily engaged in manufacturing motor vehicle power transmission equipment are classified in Industry 3714; those manufacturing aircraft power transmission equipment are classified in Industry 3728; those manufacturing ball and roller bearings are classified in Industry 3562; and those manufacturing speed changers, industrial high-speed drives, and gears are classified in Industry 3566.

Ball joints, except motor vehicle and aircraft
Bearings, plain
Belting, chain
Chain, power transmission
Clutches, except motor vehicle
Collars, shaft (power transmission equipment)
Couplings, shaft: rigid, flexible, universal joint, etc.
Drive chains, bicycle and motorcycle

Joints, swivel: except motor vehicle and aircraft
Joints, universal: except motor vehicle
Pillow blocks, with plain bearings
Pivots, power transmission
Pulleys, power transmission
Railroad car journal bearings, plain
Shafts, flexible
Sprockets (power transmission equipment)

3569 General Industrial Machinery and Equipment, Not Elsewhere Classified

Establishments primarily engaged in manufacturing machinery, equipment, and components for general industrial use, and for which no special classification is provided. Machine shops primarily engaged in producing machine and equipment parts, usually on a job or order basis, are classified in Industry 3599.

356   **GENERAL INDUSTRIAL MACHINERY AND EQUIPMENT—Con.**

3569   **General Industrial Machinery and Equipment, Not Elsewhere Classified— Con.**

Altitude testing chambers
Baling machines for scrap metal, paper, and similar materials
Blast cleaning equipment, dustless: except metalworking
Brake burnishing and washing machines
Bridge and gate machinery, hydraulic
Burnishing and washing machines, brake
Centrifuges, industrial
Cremating ovens
Driers and reel, firehose
Filter elements, fluid: hydraulic line
Filters, fluid, general line industrial: except internal combustion engine
Filters, pipeline
Firefighting apparatus, except automotive and chemical
Firehose, except rubber
Gas producers (machinery)
Gas separators (machinery)
Generators, gas
Generators: steam, liquid oxygen, and nitrogen
Heaters, swimming pool: electric
Hose, fire: except rubber
Ice crushers, except household

Jacks, hydraulic: for general industrial use
Lubricating systems, centralized
Lubrication equipment, industrial
Lubrication machinery, automatic
Ordnance testing chambers
Ovens, surveillance: for aging and testing powder
Powder testing chambers
Presses, metal baling
Purifiers, centrifugal
Reels and racks, firehose
Robots for general industrial use
Screening and sifting machines for general industrial use
Screws, jack
Separators for steam, gas, vapor, and air (machinery)
Sifting and screening machines for general industrial use
Sprinkler systems, fire: automatic
Steam separators (machinery)
Strainers, pipeline
Temperature testing chambers
Testing chambers for altitude, temperature, ordnance, and power
Vapor separators (machinery)

357   **COMPUTER AND OFFICE EQUIPMENT**

3571   **Electronic Computers**

Establishments primarily engaged in manufacturing electronic computers. Electronic computers are machines which: (1) store the processing program or programs and the data immediately necessary for execution of the program; (2) can be freely programmed in accordance with the requirements of the user; (3) perform arithmetical computations specified by the user; and (4) execute, without human intervention, a processing program which requires them to modify their execution by logical decision during the processing run. Included in this industry are digital computers, analog computers, and hybrid digital/ analog computers. Establishments primarily engaged in manufacturing machinery or equipment which incorporate computers or a central processing unit for the purpose of performing functions such as measuring, displaying, or controlling process variables are classified based on the manufactured end product.

Computers: digital, analog, and hybrid
Mainframe computers
Microcomputers

Minicomputers
Personal computers

3572   **Computer Storage Devices**

Establishments primarily engaged in manufacturing computer storage devices.

Auxiliary computer storage units
Computer storage units
Disk drives, computer
Drum drives, computer

Magnetic storage devices for computers
Optical storage devices for computers
Recorders, tape: for computers
Tape storage units, computer

Industry Group No.	Industry No.	

357   **COMPUTER AND OFFICE EQUIPMENT—Con.**

3575   **Computer Terminals**

Establishments primarily engaged in manufacturing computer terminals. Establishments primarily engaged in manufacturing point-of-sale, funds transfer, and automatic teller machines are classified in Industry 3578.

Cathode ray tube (CRT) teleprinter, multistation	Multistation CRT/teleprinters
Computer terminals	Teleprinters (computer terminals)

3577   **Computer Peripheral Equipment, Not Elsewhere Classified**

Establishments primarily engaged in manufacturing computer peripheral equipment, not elsewhere classified, including printers, plotters, and graphic displays. Establishments primarily engaged in manufacturing modems and other communications interface equipment are classified in Industry 3661.

Card punching and sorting machines	Keypunch/verify cards, computer peripheral equipment
Card-type conversion equipment, computer peripheral equipment	Magnetic ink recognition devices, computer peripheral equipment
Computer output to microfilm units, computer peripheral equipment	Media-to-media data conversion equipment, computer peripheral equipment
Computer paper tape punchers and devices, computer peripheral equipment	Optical scanning devices, computer peripheral equipment
Decoders, computer peripheral equipment	Plotter controllers, computer peripheral equipment
Disk pack inspectors, computer peripheral equipment	Plotters, computer
Document entry conversion devices, computer peripheral equipment	Printers, computer
Graphic displays, except graphic terminals: computer peripheral equipment	Punch card equipment: card readers, tabulators, collators, sorters, and interpreters
Input/output equipment, computer: except terminals	Tape cleaners, magnetic: computer peripheral equipment
Key-disk or diskette equipment, computer peripheral equipment	Tape print units, computer peripheral equipment
Key-tape equipment: reel, cassette, or cartridge	
Keying equipment, computer peripheral equipment	

3578   **Calculating and Accounting Machines, Except Electronic Computers**

Establishments primarily engaged in manufacturing point-of-sale devices, funds transfer devices, and other calculating and accounting machines, except electronic computers. Included are electronic calculating and accounting machines which must be paced by operator intervention, even when augmented by attachments. These machines may include program control or have input/output capabilities.

Accounting machines, operator paced	Change making machines
Adding machines	Coin counters
Automatic teller machines (ATM)	Funds transfer devices
Billing machines	Point-of-sale devices
Bookkeeping machines	Registers, credit account
Calculating machines, operator paced	
Cash registers, including adding machines with cash drawers	

3579   **Office Machines, Not Elsewhere Classified**

Establishments primarily engaged in manufacturing office machines and devices, not elsewhere classified, including typewriters and word processing equipment. Establishments primarily engaged in manufacturing photocopy and microfilm equipment are classified in Industry 3861.

357   COMPUTER AND OFFICE EQUIPMENT—Con.

3579 Office Machines, Not Elsewhere Classified—Con.

Address labeling machines
Addressing machines, plates and plate embossers
Binding machines, plastics and adhesive: for store or office use
Canceling machinery, post office
Check writing, endorsing, signing, numbering, and protecting machines
Coin wrapping machines
Collating machines for store or office use
Dating devices and machines, except rubber stamps
Dictating machines, office types
Duplicating machines
Embossing machines for store and office use
Envelope stuffing, sealing, and addressing machines
Forms handling equipment for store and office use
Gummed tape moisteners for store and office use
Letter folding, stuffing, and sealing machines
List finders, automatic
Mail tying (bundling) machines
Mailing machines
Numbering machines, office and store: mechanical
Paper cutters and trimmers (hand office equipment)
Pencil sharpeners
Perforators (office machines)
Postage meters
Punches, paper: hand
Registers, autographic
Scalers for gummed tape: hand
Shorthand machines
Slipsheeting machines
Sorters, filing: office
Staple removers
Stapling machines, office
Ticket counting machines
Time-stamps containing clock mechanisms
Timeclocks and time recording devices
Typewriters
Voting machines
Word processing equipment

358   REFRIGERATION AND SERVICE INDUSTRY MACHINERY

3581 Automatic Vending Machines

Establishments primarily engaged in manufacturing automatic vending machines and coin-operated mechanisms for such machines.

Locks, coin-operated
Mechanisms for coin-operated machines
Merchandising machines, automatic
Vending machines for merchandise: coin-operated

3582 Commercial Laundry, Drycleaning, and Pressing Machines

Establishments primarily engaged in manufacturing laundry and drycleaning equipment and pressing machines for commercial and industrial use. Establishments primarily engaged in manufacturing household laundry equipment, including coin-operated washers and dryers, are classified in Industry 3633.

Drycleaning equipment and machinery, commercial
Dryers, laundry: commercial, including coin-operated
Extractors and driers, commercial laundry
Feather cleaning and sterilizing machinery
Ironers, commercial laundry and drycleaning
Laundry machinery and equipment, commercial, including coin-operated
Pressing machines, commercial laundry and drycleaning
Rug cleaning, drying, and napping machines: commercial laundry
Washing machines, laundry: commercial, including coin-operated

3585 Air-Conditioning and Warm Air Heating Equipment and Commercial and Industrial Refrigeration Equipment

Establishments primarily engaged in manufacturing refrigeration equipment and systems and similar equipment for commercial and industrial use; complete air-conditioning units for domestic, commercial, and industrial use; and warm air furnaces. Establishments primarily engaged in manufacturing soda fountains and beer dispensing equipment and humidifiers and dehumidifiers, except portable, are also classified in this industry. Establishments pri-

Industry Group No.	Industry No.	
358		**REFRIGERATION AND SERVICE INDUSTRY MACHINERY—Con.**

3585 Air-Conditioning and Warm Air Heating Equipment and Commercial and Industrial Refrigeration Equipment—Con.

marily engaged in manufacturing household refrigerators and home and farm freezers are classified in Industry 3632, and those manufacturing electric air-space heaters and portable humidifiers and dehumidifiers are classified in Industry 3634.

Air-conditioners, motor vehicle
Air-conditioning and heating combination units
Air-conditioning compressors
Air-conditioning condensers and condensing units
Air-conditioning units, complete: domestic and industrial
Beer dispensing equipment
Cabinets, show and display: refrigerated
Cases, show and display: refrigerated
Cold drink dispensing equipment, except coin-operated
Compressors for refrigeration and air-conditioning
Condensers and condensing units: refrigeration and air-conditioning
Coolers, milk and water: electric
Counters and counter display cases, refrigerated
Dehumidifiers, except portable: electric

Electric warm air furnaces
Evaporative condensers (heat transfer equipment)
Fountains, drinking: mechanically refrigerated
Furnaces: gravity air flow
Heat pumps, electric
Humidifying equipment, except portable
Ice boxes, industrial
Ice making machinery
Lockers, refrigerated
Refrigeration compressors
Refrigeration machinery and equipment, industrial
Room coolers, portable
Showcases, refrigerated
Siphons, soda water
Snow making machinery
Soda fountains, parts, and accessories
Tanks, soda water

3586 Measuring and Dispensing Pumps

Establishments primarily engaged in manufacturing measuring and dispensing pumps commonly used in service stations for dispensing gasoline, oil, and grease, including grease guns. Establishments primarily engaged in manufacturing pumps and pumping equipment for general industrial use are classified in Industry Group 356.

Dispensing and measuring pumps, gasoline and oil

Grease guns (lubricators)

3589 Service Industry Machinery, Not Elsewhere Classified

Establishments primarily engaged in manufacturing machines and equipment, not elsewhere classified, for use in service industries, such as floor sanding machines, industrial vacuum cleaners, scrubbing machines, commercial cooking and food warming equipment, and commercial dishwashing machines. Establishments primarily engaged in manufacturing household electrical appliances are classified in Industry Group 363.

Cafeteria food warming equipment
Carpet sweepers, except household electric vacuum sweepers
Carwashing machinery, including coin-operated
Cookers, steam: restaurant type
Cooking equipment, commercial
Corn popping machines, commercial type
Dirt sweeping units, industrial
Dishwashing machines, commercial
Floor sanding, washing, and polishing machines: commercial type
Food warming equipment, commercial
Fryers, commercial

Garbage disposers, commercial
Janitors' carts
Mop wringers
Ovens, cafeteria food warming: portable
Ovens, microwave (cooking equipment): commercial
Pressure cookers, steam: commercial
Sanding machines, floor
Scrubbing machines
Servicing machines, coin-operated: except drycleaning and laundry
Sewage treatment equipment
Sewer cleaning equipment, power
Sludge processing equipment
Vacuum cleaners and sweepers, elec-

358   **REFRIGERATION AND SERVICE INDUSTRY MACHINERY—Con.**

3589 **Service Industry Machinery, Not Elsewhere Classified—Con.**

tric: industrial and commercial	Water purification equipment, house-
Water conditioners, for swimming pools	hold type
Water filters and softeners, household	Water treatment equipment, industrial
type	

359   **MISCELLANEOUS INDUSTRIAL AND COMMERCIAL MACHINERY AND EQUIPMENT**

3592 **Carburetors, Pistons, Piston Rings, and Valves**

Establishments primarily engaged in manufacturing carburetors, pistons, piston rings, and engine intake and exhaust valves. Establishments primarily engaged in manufacturing metallic packing are classified in Industry 3053, and those primarily engaged in manufacturing machine repair and equipment parts (except electric), on a job or order basis for others, are classified in Industry 3599.

Carburetors, all types	Valves, engine: intake and exhaust
Pistons and piston rings	

3593 **Fluid Power Cylinders and Actuators**

Establishments primarily engaged in manufacturing hydraulic and pneumatic cylinders and actuators for use in fluid power systems.

Fluid power actuators, hydraulic and	Hydraulic cylinders, fluid power
pneumatic	Pneumatic cylinders, fluid power

3594 **Fluid Power Pumps and Motors**

Establishments primarily engaged in manufacturing hydraulic and pneumatic fluid power pumps and motors, including hydrostatic transmissions. Establishments primarily engaged in manufacturing pumps for motor vehicles are classified in Industry 3714.

Fluid power pumps and motors	Motors, air or hydraulic fluid power
Hydraulic pumps, aircraft	Motors, pneumatic
Hydrostatic drives (transmissions)	Pumps, hydraulic power transfer
Hydrostatic transmissions	

3596 **Scales and Balances, Except Laboratory**

Establishments primarily engaged in manufacturing weighing and force-measuring machines and devices of all types, except those regarded as scientific apparatus for laboratory work which are classified in Industry 3821.

Baby scales	Railroad track scales
Balances, except laboratory	Scales, except laboratory
Bathroom scales	Weighing machines and apparatus,
Industrial scales	except laboratory
Motor truck scales	

3599 **Industrial and Commercial Machinery and Equipment, Not Elsewhere Classified**

Establishments primarily engaged in manufacturing machinery and equipment and parts, not elsewhere classified, such as amusement park equipment and flexible metal hose and tubing. This industry also includes establishments primarily engaged in producing or repairing machinery and equipment parts, not elsewhere classified, on a job or order basis for others. Establishments primarily engaged in manufacturing motor vehicle engine filters are classified in

359 MISCELLANEOUS INDUSTRIAL AND COMMERCIAL MACHINERY AND EQUIPMENT—Con.

3599 Industrial and Commercial Machinery and Equipment, Not Elsewhere Classified—Con.

Industry 3714, and those manufacturing coin-operated amusement machines are classified in Industry 3999.

Amusement rides for carnivals	Grinding castings for the trade
Bellows, industrial: metal	Hose, flexible metallic
Boiler tube cleaners	Leak detectors, water
Carousels (merry-go-rounds)	Machine shops, jobbing and repair
Catapults	Propellers, ship and boat: machined
Chemical milling job shops	Riddles, sand (hand sifting or screening
Cleaners, boiler tube	apparatus)
Crankshaft and camshaft machining	Sludge tables
Cups, oil and grease: metal	Swage blocks
Electrical discharge machining (EDM)	Ties, form: metal
Fan forges	Tubing, flexible metallic
Ferris wheels	Weather vanes
Filters, internal combustion engine: oil, gasoline, air intake, except motor vehicle engine	

Major Group 36.—ELECTRONIC AND OTHER ELECTRICAL EQUIPMENT AND COMPONENTS, EXCEPT COMPUTER EQUIPMENT

The Major Group as a Whole

This major group includes establishments engaged in manufacturing machinery, apparatus, and supplies for the generation, storage, transmission, transformation, and utilization of electrical energy. Included are the manufacturing of electricity distribution equipment; electrical industrial apparatus; household appliances; electrical lighting and wiring equipment; radio and television receiving equipment; communications equipment; electronic components and accessories; and other electrical equipment and supplies. The manufacture of household appliances is included in this group, but industrial machinery and equipment powered by built-in or detachable electric motors is classified in Major Group 35. Establishments primarily engaged in manufacturing instruments are classified in Major Group 38.

Industry Group No.	Industry No.	

361   **ELECTRIC TRANSMISSION AND DISTRIBUTION EQUIPMENT**

3612   **Power, Distribution, and Specialty Transformers**

Establishments primarily engaged in manufacturing power, distribution, instrument, and specialty transformers. Establishments primarily engaged in manufacturing radio frequency or voice frequency electronic transformers, coils, or chokes are classified in Industry 3677, and those manufacturing resistance welder transformers are classified in Industry 3548.

Airport lighting transformers
Autotransformers for switchboards, except telephone switchboards
Autotransformers, electric (power transformers)
Ballasts for lighting fixtures
Control transformers
Current limiting reactors, electrical
Distribution transformers, electric
Doorbell transformers, electric
Electric furnace transformers
Feeder voltage regulators and boosters (electric transformers)
Fluorescent ballasts (transformers)
Generator voltage regulators, electric induction and step type
Ignition transformers
Instrument transformers, except portable
Isolation transformers
Lighting transformers, fluorescent

Lighting transformers, street and airport
Line voltage regulators
Luminous tube transformers
Machine tool transformers
Ratio transformers
Rectifier transformers
Signaling transformers, electric
Specialty transformers
Street lighting transformers
Toy transformers
Transformers, electric power
Transformers, for electronic meters
Transformers, reactor
Tripping transformers
Vibrators, interrupter
Voltage regulating transformers, electric power
Voltage regulators, transmission and distribution

3613   **Switchgear and Switchboard Apparatus**

Establishments primarily engaged in manufacturing switchgear and switchboard apparatus. Important products of this industry include power switches, circuit breakers, power switching equipment, and similar switchgear for general industrial application; switchboards and cubicles, control and metering panels, fuses and fuse mountings, and similar switchboard apparatus and supplies. Establishments primarily engaged in manufacturing relays are classified in Industry 3625. Establishments manufacturing switches other than switch-

Industry Group No.	Industry No.	
361		**ELECTRIC TRANSMISSION AND DISTRIBUTION EQUIPMENT—Con.**
	3613	**Switchgear and Switchboard Apparatus—Con.**

gear type are classified in Industry 3625 if the switches are of the type used as industrial controls, in Industry 3679 if the switches are of the type used in electronic devices, and in Industry 3643 if the switches are of other types used in wiring circuits.

Air circuit breakers
Bus bar structures
Circuit breakers, power
Control panels, electric power distribution
Cubicles (electric switchboard equipment)
Distribution boards, electric
Distribution cutouts
Fuse clips and blocks, electric
Fuse devices, power: 600 volts and over
Fuse mountings, electric power
Fuses, electric
Generator control and metering panels

Knife switches, electric
Metering panels, electric
Panelboards and distribution boards, electric
Panels, electric control and metering
Power connectors
Power switching equipment
Regulators, power
Switchboards and parts, power
Switches, electric power: except snap, push button, tumbler, and solenoid
Switchgear and switchgear accessories
Time switches, electrical switchgear apparatus

362   ELECTRICAL INDUSTRIAL APPARATUS

3621   Motors and Generators

Establishments primarily engaged in manufacturing electric motors (except engine starting motors) and power generators; motor generator sets; railway motors and control equipment; and motors, generators, and control equipment for gasoline, electric, and oil-electric buses and trucks. Establishments primarily engaged in manufacturing turbogenerators are classified in Industry 3511; those manufacturing starting motors and battery charging generators for internal combustion engines are classified in Industry 3694; and those manufacturing generators for welding equipment are classified in Industry 3548.

Armatures, industrial
Coils for motors and generators
Collector rings for motors and generators
Commutators, electric motor
Control equipment for buses and trucks
Converters, phase and rotary: electrical equipment
Dynamos, electric: except automotive
Dynamotors
Exciter assemblies, motor and generator
Frequency converters (electric generators)
Generating apparatus and parts, electrical: except internal combustion engine and arc-welding
Generator sets: gasoline, diesel, and dual fuel
Generators and sets, electric: except internal combustion engine, welding, and turbogenerators
Generators for gas-electric and oil-electric vehicles
Generators for storage battery chargers, except internal combustion engine and aircraft

Inverters, rotating: electrical
Motor generator sets, except automotive and turbogenerators
Motor housings
Motors, electric: except engine starting motors and gear motors
Power generators
Railway motors and control equipment, electric
Resolvers
Rotary converters (electrical equipment)
Rotor retainers and housings
Rotors for motors
Servomotors
Sliprings for motors and generators
Starting equipment, for streetcars
Stators for motors
Storage battery chargers, engine generator type
Synchronous condensers and timing motors, electric
Synchros
Torque motors, electric

3624   Carbon and Graphite Products

Establishments primarily engaged in manufacturing carbon, graphite, and metal-graphite brushes and brush stock; carbon or graphite electrodes for

Industry
Group   Industry
No.   No.

362   **ELECTRICAL INDUSTRIAL APPARATUS—Con.**

3624   **Carbon and Graphite Products—Con.**

thermal and electrolytic uses; carbon and graphite fibers; and other carbon, graphite, and metal-graphite products.

Brush blocks, carbon or molded graphite
Brushes and brush stock contacts:
carbon and graphite—electric
Carbon specialties for electrical use

Carbons, electric
Electrodes for thermal and electrolytic
uses, carbon and graphite
Fibers, carbon and graphite
Lighting carbons

3625   **Relays and Industrial Controls**

Establishments primarily engaged in manufacturing relays; motor starters and controllers; and other industrial controls and control accessories. Establishments primarily engaged in manufacturing automatic temperature controls are classified in Industry 3822, and those manufacturing industrial process control instruments are classified in Industry 3823.

Armature relays
Control circuit devices: magnet and
solid-state
Control circuit relays, industrial
Controls and control accessories, indus-
trial
Controls for adjustable speed drives
Crane and hoist controls, including
metal mill
Electromagnetic brakes and clutches
Industrial controls: push button, selec-
tor switches, and pilot
Marine and navy auxiliary controls
Motor control accessories, including
overload relays

Motor control centers
Motor controls, electric
Motor starters, contactors, and control-
lers, industrial
Numerical controls
Relays
Rheostats, industrial control
Solenoid switches, industrial
Timing devices, mechanical and solid-
state, except clockwork
Truck controls, industrial battery
Vacuum relays

3629   **Electrical Industrial Apparatus, Not Elsewhere Classified**

Establishments primarily engaged in manufacturing industrial and commercial electric apparatus and equipment, not elsewhere classified, such as fixed and variable capacitors and rectifiers for industrial applications. Establishments primarily engaged in manufacturing electronic capacitors and rectifiers are classified in Industry Group 367.

Battery chargers, rectifying or nonrotating
Capacitors, a.c.: for motors and fluorescent lamp ballasts
Capacitors, except electronic: fixed and
variable
Condensers for motors and generators
Condensers, except electronic: fixed and
variable
Current collector wheels for trolley rigging

Electrochemical generators (fuel cells)
Inverters, nonrotating: electrical
Mercury arc rectifiers (electrical appa-
ratus)
Power conversion units, a.c. to d.c.:
static—electric
Rectifiers (electrical apparatus)
Series capacitors, except electronic
Thermoelectric generators

363   **HOUSEHOLD APPLIANCES**

3631   **Household Cooking Equipment**

Establishments primarily engaged in manufacturing household electric and nonelectric cooking equipment, such as stoves, ranges, and ovens, except portable electric appliances. This industry includes establishments primarily engaged in manufacturing microwave and convection ovens, including portable. Establishments primarily engaged in manufacturing other electric household cooking appliances, such as portable ovens, hot plates, grills, percolators, and

Industry Group No.	Industry No.	
363		HOUSEHOLD APPLIANCES—Con.

3631 Household Cooking Equipment—Con.

toasters, are classified in Industry 3634. Establishments primarily engaged in manufacturing commercial cooking equipment are classified in Industry 3589.

Barbecues, grills, and braziers for outdoor cooking
Convection ovens, household: including portable
Microwave ovens, household: including portable

Ovens, household: excluding portable appliances other than microwave and convection
Ranges, household cooking: electric and gas
Stoves, disk

3632 Household Refrigerators and Home and Farm Freezers

Establishments primarily engaged in manufacturing household refrigerators and home and farm freezers. Establishments primarily engaged in manufacturing commercial and industrial refrigeration equipment, packaged room coolers, and all refrigeration compressor and condenser units are classified in Industry 3585, and those manufacturing portable room dehumidifiers are classified in Industry 3634.

Freezers, home and farm
Ice boxes, household
Refrigerator cabinets, household

Refrigerators, mechanical and absorption: household

3633 Household Laundry Equipment

Establishments primarily engaged in manufacturing laundry equipment, such as washing machines, dryers, and ironers, for household use, including coin-operated. Establishments primarily engaged in manufacturing commercial laundry equipment are classified in Industry 3582, and those manufacturing portable electric irons are classified in Industry 3634.

Drycleaning and laundry machines, household: including coin-operated
Dryers, laundry: household, including coin-operated
Ironers and mangles, household, except portable irons

Laundry machinery, household, including coin-operated
Washing machines, household: including coin-operated
Wringers, domestic laundry

3634 Electric Housewares and Fans

Establishments primarily engaged in manufacturing electric housewares for heating, cooking, and other purposes; and electric household fans, except attic fans. Important products of this industry include household-type ventilation and exhaust fans; portable household cooking appliances, except convection and microwave ovens; electric space heaters; electrically heated bedcoverings, electric scissors; and portable humidifiers and dehumidifiers. Establishments primarily engaged in manufacturing attic fans and industrial and commercial exhaust and ventilation fans are classified in Industry 3564; and those manufacturing room air-conditioners and humidifying and dehumidifying equipment, except portable, are classified in Industry 3585.

Air purifiers, portable
Bedcoverings, electric
Blankets, electric
Blenders, electric
Blowers, portable: electric
Bottle warmers, household: electric
Broilers, electric
Can openers, electric
Casseroles, electric
Chafing dishes, electric

Cigar lighters, electric
Cigarette lighters, electric
Coffee makers, household: electric
Cooking appliances, household: electric, except convection and microwave ovens
Crock pots, electric
Curling irons, electric
Deep fat fryers, household: electric
Dehumidifiers, electric: portable

Industry Group No.	Industry No.	

363   HOUSEHOLD APPLIANCES—Con.

3634   Electric Housewares and Fans—Con.

Desk fans, electric
Driers: hand, face, and hair—electric
Dry shavers (electric razors)
Egg cookers, electric
Fans, household: electric, except attic fans
Floor fans, electric
Food mixers, household: electric
Fryers, household: electric
Griddles and grills, household: electric
Hair curlers, electric
Hair driers, electric: except equipment designed for beauty parlor use
Hassock fans, electric
Heaters, immersion: household—electric
Heaters, space: electric
Heaters, tape
Heating pads, electric
Heating units for electric appliances
Heating units, baseboard or wall: electric (radiant heating element)
Hotplates, electric
Humidifiers, electric: portable
Ice crushers, electric
Irons, domestic: electric
Juice extractors, electric
Knives, electric
Massage machines, electric: except designed for beauty and barber shop

Ovens, household: portable: except microwave and convection ovens
Percolators, electric
Popcorn poppers for home use: electric
Propeller fans, window-type (household)
Radiators, electric
Razors, electric
Roasters, electric
Sandwich toasters and grills, household: electric
Sauna heaters, electric
Scissors, electric
Shoe polishers, electric
Tea kettles, electric
Toasters, household: electric
Toothbrushes, electric
Trays, warming: electric
Trouser pressers, electric
Unit heaters, household: electric
Urns, electric: household
Vaporizers, electric: household
Ventilating fans, electric: household—kitchen
Waffle irons, electric
Wall heaters, household: electric
Water pulsating devices, electric
Whippers, household: electric

3635   Household Vacuum Cleaners

Establishments primarily engaged in manufacturing vacuum cleaners for household use. Establishments primarily engaged in manufacturing vacuum cleaners for industrial use are classified in Industry 3589. Establishments primarily engaged in installation of central vacuum cleaner systems are classified in Construction, Industry 1796.

Vacuum cleaners and sweepers, electric: household

3639   Household Appliances, Not Elsewhere Classified

Establishments primarily engaged in manufacturing household appliances, not elsewhere classified, such as water heaters, dishwashers, food waste disposal units, and household sewing machines.

Buttonhole and eyelet machines and attachments, household
Dishwashing machines, household
Floor waxers and polishers, household: electric
Garbage disposal units, household

Sewing machines and attachments, household
Trash compactors, household
Water heaters, household: including nonelectric

364   ELECTRIC LIGHTING AND WIRING EQUIPMENT

3641   Electric Lamp Bulbs and Tubes

Establishments primarily engaged in manufacturing electric bulbs, tubes, and related light sources. Important products of this industry include incandescent filament lamps, vapor and fluorescent lamps, photoflash and photoflood lamps, and electrotherapeutic lamp units for ultraviolet and infrared radiation. Establishments primarily engaged in manufacturing glass blanks for bulbs are classified in Industry 3229.

Industry
Group
No.

Industry
No.

364   **ELECTRIC LIGHTING AND WIRING EQUIPMENT—Con.**

3641   **Electric Lamp Bulbs and Tubes—Con.**

Electrodes, cold cathode fluorescent lamp
Electrotherapeutic lamp units for ultra-violet and infrared radiation
Filaments for electric lamps
Flashlight bulbs, photographic
Glow lamp bulbs
Infrared lamp bulbs
Lamp (bulb) parts, electric
Lamp bulbs and tubes, electric: incandescent filament, fluorescent, and vapor

Lamp bulbs and tubes, health: infrared and ultraviolet radiation
Lamps, sealed beam
Lead-in wires, electric lamp: made from purchased wire
Light bulbs, electric: complete
Photoflash and photoflood lamp bulbs and tubes
Strobotrons
Ultraviolet lamps

3643   **Current-Carrying Wiring Devices**

Establishments primarily engaged in manufacturing current-carrying wiring devices.

Bus bars (electrical conductors)
Caps and plugs, attachment: electric
Connectors and terminals for electrical devices
Contacts, electrical: except carbon and graphite
Convenience outlets, electric
Cord connectors, electric
Current taps, attachment plug and screw shell types
Cutouts, switch and fuse
Dial light sockets, radio
Fluorescent starters
Fuse cutouts
Ground clamps (electric wiring devices)
Lamp sockets and receptacles (electric wiring devices)

Lightning arrestors and coils
Lightning protection equipment
Plugs, electric
Rail bonds, electric: for propulsion and signal circuits
Snap switches, (electric wiring devices)
Sockets, electric
Solderless connectors (electric wiring devices)
Starting switches, fluorescent lamp
Switch cutouts
Switches for electric wiring: e.g., snap, tumbler, pressure, pushbutton
Trolley line material, overhead

3644   **Noncurrent-Carrying Wiring Devices**

Establishments primarily engaged in manufacturing noncurrent-carrying wiring devices. Important products of this industry include conduits and fittings; electrical insulators, except porcelain and other ceramic insulators and glass insulators; outlet, switch, and fuse boxes; and pole line hardware. Establishments primarily engaged in manufacturing ceramic insulators are classified in Industry 3264, and those manufacturing glass insulators are classified in Industry 3229.

Boxes, electric wiring: junction, outlet, switch, and fuse
Conduits and fittings, electrical
Face plates (wiring devices)
Insulators, electrical: except glass and ceramic

Pole line hardware
Raceways
Snubbers for CATV systems

3645   **Residential Electric Lighting Fixtures**

Establishments primarily engaged in manufacturing residential electric lighting fixtures and equipment, fixed or portable. Establishments primarily engaged in producing glassware for lighting fixtures are classified in Major Group 32; those manufacturing electric light bulbs, tubes, and related light sources are classified in Industry 3641; those manufacturing lamp shades, except glass and metal, are classified in Industry 3999; and those manufacturing nonelectric fixtures and portable electric flashlights, lanterns, and similar lamps are classified in Industry 3648.

Industry
Group   Industry
No.   No.

364   ELECTRIC LIGHTING AND WIRING EQUIPMENT—Con.

3645   Residential Electric Lighting Fixtures—Con.

Boudoir lamps
Chandeliers, residential
Desk lamps, residential
Floor lamps
Fluorescent lighting fixtures, residential
Lamp shades, metal
Lamps (lighting fixtures), residential: electric

Light shades, metal
Lighting fixtures, residential, electric: e.g., garden, patio, walkway, yard
Lights, yard: electric
Table lamps
Wall lamps

3646   Commercial, Industrial, and Institutional Electric Lighting Fixtures

Establishments primarily engaged in manufacturing commercial, industrial, and institutional electric lighting fixtures. Establishments primarily engaged in producing glassware for lighting fixtures are classified in Major Group 32; those manufacturing residential lighting fixtures are classified in Industry 3645; and those manufacturing vehicular lighting fixtures are classified in Industry 3647.

Chandeliers, commercial
Commercial lighting fixtures
Desk lamps, commercial
Fluorescent lighting fixtures, commercial

Lighting fixtures, commercial
Luminous panel ceilings

3647   Vehicular Lighting Equipment

Establishments primarily engaged in manufacturing vehicular lighting equipment. Establishments primarily engaged in manufacturing sealed-beam lamps are classified in Industry 3641.

Aircraft lighting fixtures
Automotive lighting fixtures
Bicycle lamps
Boat and ship lighting fixtures
Clearance lamps and reflectors, motor vehicle
Dome lights, motor vehicle
Flasher lights, automobile
Fog lights, motor vehicle
Headlights (fixtures), vehicular

Lamps, marker and clearance: motor vehicle
Lighting fixtures, vehicular
Locomotive and railroad car lights
Marker lamps, motor vehicle
Motorcycle lamps
Parking lights, automotive
Reflectors, clearance: vehicular
Spotlights, motor vehicle
Tail lights, motor vehicle

3648   Lighting Equipment, Not Elsewhere Classified

Establishments primarily engaged in manufacturing lighting fixtures and equipment, electric and nonelectric, not elsewhere classified, including flashlights and similar portable lamps, searchlights, ultraviolet lamp fixtures, and infrared lamp fixtures. Establishments primarily engaged in manufacturing electric light bulbs, tubes, and related light sources are classified in Industry 3641; those producing glassware for lighting fixtures are classified in Major Group 32; and those manufacturing traffic signals are classified in Industry 3669.

Arc lamps, except electrotherapeutic
Area and sports luminaries
Decorative area lighting fixtures, except residential
Flashlights
Floodlights
Fountain lighting fixtures
Gas lighting fixtures
Lamp fixtures, infrared
Lanterns: electric, gas, carbide, kerosene, and gasoline
Lighting fixtures, airport: runway, approach, taxi, and ramp

Lighting fixtures, residential, except electric
Miners' lamps
Reflectors for lighting equipment: metal
Searchlights
Spotlights, except vehicular
Stage lighting equipment
Street lighting fixtures, except traffic signals
Swimming pool lighting fixtures
Ultraviolet lamp fixtures
Underwater lighting fixtures

365   **HOUSEHOLD AUDIO AND VIDEO EQUIPMENT, AND AUDIO RECORDINGS**

3651   **Household Audio and Video Equipment**

Establishments primarily engaged in manufacturing electronic audio and video equipment for home entertainment (including automotive), such as television sets, radio broadcast receivers, tape players, phonographs, and video recorders and players. This industry also includes establishments primarily engaged in manufacturing public address systems and music distribution apparatus. Establishments primarily engaged in manufacturing phonograph records and prerecorded audio tapes are classified in Industry 3652; those manufacturing telephone answering machines are classified in Industry 3661; those manufacturing motion picture reproduction equipment are classified in Industry 3861; and those manufacturing phonograph needles and cartridges are classified in Industry 3679. Establishments primarily engaged in manufacturing separate cabinets for home electronic equipment are classified in Major Group 25.

Amplifiers: radio, public address, or musical instrument
Audio recorders and players: automotive and household
Clock radio and telephone combinations
Clock radios
Coin-operated phonographs
Disc players, compact
Electronic kits for home assembly: radio and television receiving sets, and phonograph equipment
FM and AM tuners
Home tape recorders: cassette, cartridge, and reel
Juke boxes
Loudspeakers, electrodynamic and magnetic
Microphones
Music distribution apparatus, except records or tape
Musical instrument amplifiers
Phonograph and radio combinations
Phonograph turntables
Phonographs, including coin-operated
Pickup heads, phonograph
Pillows, stereo
Public address systems
Radio and phonograph combinations
Radio receiving sets
Recording machines, music and speech: except dictation and telephone answering machines
Speaker systems
Tape players, household
Tape recorders, household
Television receiving sets
Turntables, for phonographs
Video camera-audio recorders, household
Video cassette recorders/players
Video triggers (remote control television devices)

3652   **Phonograph Records and Prerecorded Audio Tapes and Disks**

Establishments primarily engaged in manufacturing phonograph records and prerecorded audio tapes and disks. Establishments primarily engaged in the design, development, and production of prepackaged computer software are classified in Services, Industry Group 737; and those reproducing prerecorded video tape cassettes and disks are classified in Services, Major Group 78.

Compact disc, prerecorded: except video
Discs, laser: audio prerecorded
Magnetic tape, audio: prerecorded
Phonograph record blanks
Phonograph records (including preparation of the master)
Prerecorded audio magnetic tape

366   **COMMUNICATIONS EQUIPMENT**

3661   **Telephone and Telegraph Apparatus**

Establishments primarily engaged in manufacturing wire telephone and telegraph equipment. Included are establishments manufacturing modems and other telephone and telegraph communications interface equipment. Estab-

366 COMMUNICATIONS EQUIPMENT—Con.

3661 Telephone and Telegraph Apparatus—Con.

lishments primarily engaged in manufacturing cellular radio telephones are classified in Industry 3663.

Autotransformers for telephone switchboards
Carrier equipment, telephone and telegraph
Communications headgear, telephone
Data sets, telephone and telegraph
Facsimile equipment
Headsets, telephone
Message concentrators
Modems
Multiplex equipment, telephone and telegraph
PBX equipment, manual and automatic
Switchboards, telephone and telegraph

Switching equipment, telephone
Telegraph office switching equipment
Telephone answering machines
Telephone central office equipment, dial and manual
Telephone dialing devices, automatic
Telephone sets, except cellular radio telephone
Telephone station equipment and parts, wire
Telephones, sound powered (no battery)
Telephones, underwater
Toll switching equipment, telephone

3663 Radio and Television Broadcasting and Communications Equipment

Establishments primarily engaged in manufacturing radio and television broadcasting and communications equipment. Important products of this industry are closed-circuit and cable television equipment; studio equipment; light communications equipment; transmitters, transceivers and receivers (except household and automotive); cellular radio telephones; communication antennas; receivers; RF power amplifiers; and fixed and mobile radio systems. Establishments primarily engaged in manufacturing household audio and video equipment are classified in Industry 3651; those manufacturing intercommunications equipment are classified in Industry 3669; and those manufacturing consumer radio and television receiving antennas are classified in Industry 3679.

Airborne radio communications equipment
Amplifiers: RF power and IF
Antennas, transmitting and communications
Broadcast equipment (including studio), radio and television
Cable television equipment
Cameras, television
Carrier equipment, radio communications
Cellular radio telephones
Citizens' band (CB) radios
Closed circuit television equipment
Digital encoders
Encryption devices
Light communications equipment
Marine radio communications equipment
Microwave communications equipment
Mobile communications equipment
Multiplex equipment, radio

Pagers (one-way)
Phototransmission equipment
Radio and television switching equipment
Radio receiver networks
Radio transmitting and communications antennas and ground equipment
Receivers, radio communications
Satellites, communications
Space satellite communications equipment
Studio equipment, radio and television broadcasting
Telemetering equipment, electronic
Television monitors
Television transmitting antennas and ground equipment
Transceivers
Transmitter-receivers, radio
Transmitting apparatus, radio and television

3669 Communications Equipment, Not Elsewhere Classified

Establishments primarily engaged in manufacturing communications and related equipment, not elsewhere classified. Important products of this industry are intercommunication equipment, traffic signaling equipment, and fire and burglar alarm apparatus.

Burglar alarm apparatus, electric

Fire alarm apparatus, electric

366   COMMUNICATIONS EQUIPMENT—Con.

3669   Communications Equipment, Not Elsewhere Classified—Con.

Fire detection systems, electric
Highway signals, electric
Intercommunications equipment, electronic
Marine horns, electric
Pedestrian traffic control equipment
Railroad signaling devices, electric
Signaling apparatus, electric

Signals: railway, highway, and traffic—electric
Sirens, electric: vehicle, marine, industrial, and air raid
Smoke detectors
Traffic signals, electric

367   ELECTRONIC COMPONENTS AND ACCESSORIES

3671   Electron Tubes

Establishments primarily engaged in manufacturing electron tubes and tube parts. Establishments primarily engaged in manufacturing X-ray tubes and parts are classified in Industry 3844.

Cathode ray tubes
Electron beam (beta ray) generator tubes
Electron tube parts, except glass blanks: bases, getters, and guns
Electron tubes
Gas and vapor tubes
Geiger Mueller tubes
Klystron tubes
Light sensing and emitting tubes
Magnetron tubes

Photomultiplier tubes
Picture tube reprocessing
Planar triode tubes
Receiving type electron tubes
Television tubes
Transmitting electron tubes
Traveling wave tubes
Tubes for operating above the X-ray spectrum (with shorter wavelength)
Vacuum tubes

3672   Printed Circuit Boards

Establishments primarily engaged in manufacturing printed circuit boards.

Circuit boards, television and radio: printed
Printed circuit boards

Printed circuits
Wiring boards

3674   Semiconductors and Related Devices

Establishments primarily engaged in manufacturing semiconductors and related solid-state devices. Important products of this industry are semiconductor diodes and stacks, including rectifiers, integrated microcircuits (semiconductor networks), transistors, solar cells, and light sensing and emitting semiconductor (solid-state) devices.

Computer logic modules
Controlled rectifiers, solid-state
Diodes, solid-state (germanium, silicon, etc.)
Fuel cells, solid-state
Gunn effect devices
Hall effect devices
Hybrid integrated circuits
Infrared sensors, solid-state
Laser diodes
Light emitting diodes
Light sensitive devices, solid-state
Magnetic bubble memory device
Magnetohydrodynamic (MHD) devices
Memories, solid-state
Metal oxide silicon (MOS) devices
Microcircuits, integrated (semiconductor)
Microprocessors
Modules, solid-state
Molecular devices, solid-state
Monolithic integrated circuits (solid-state)
Optical isolators

Parametric diodes
Photoconductive cells
Photoelectric cells, solid-state (electronic eye)
Photoelectric magnetic devices
Photovoltaic devices, solid-state
Random access memories (RAMS)
Read only memories (ROMS)
Rectifiers, solid-state
Schottky diodes
Semiconductor circuit networks (solid-state integrated circuits)
Semiconductor devices
Silicon wafers, chemically doped
Solar cells
Solid-state electronic devices
Strain gages, solid-state
Stud bases or mounts for semiconductor devices
Switches, silicon control
Thermionic devices, solid-state
Thermoelectric devices, solid-state
Thin film circuits
Thyristors

367   ELECTRONIC COMPONENTS AND ACCESSORIES—Con.

3674   Semiconductors and Related Devices—Con.

Transistors	Variable capacitance diodes
Tunnel diodes	Wafers (semiconductor devices)
Ultraviolet sensors, solid-state	Zener diodes

3675   Electronic Capacitors

Establishments primarily engaged in manufacturing electronic capacitors. Establishments primarily engaged in manufacturing electrical capacitors are classified in Industry 3629.

Capacitors, electronic: fixed and variable	Condensers, electronic

3676   Electronic Resistors

Establishments primarily engaged in manufacturing electronic resistors. Establishments primarily engaged in manufacturing resistors for telephone and telegraph apparatus are classified in Industry 3661.

Resistor networks	Varistors
Resistors, electronic	
Thermistors, except temperature sensors	

3677   Electronic Coils, Transformers, and Other Inductors

Establishments primarily engaged in manufacturing electronic coils, transformers, and inductors. Establishments primarily engaged in manufacturing electrical transformers are classified in Industry 3612; those manufacturing transformers and inductors for telephone and telegraph apparatus are classified in Industry 3661, and those manufacturing semiconductors and related devices are classified in Industry 3674.

Baluns	Coupling transformers
Coil windings, electronic	Flyback transformers
Coils, chokes and other inductors, electronic	Transformers, electronic types
Constant impedance transformers	Transformers: power supply electronic type

3678   Electronic Connectors

Establishments primarily engaged in manufacturing electronic connectors. Establishments primarily engaged in manufacturing electrical connectors are classified in Industry 3643; those manufacturing electronic capacitors are classified in Industry 3675; and those manufacturing electronic coils, transformers, and other inductors are classified in Industry 3677.

Connectors, electronic: e.g., coaxial, cylindrical, rack and panel, printed circuit

3679   Electronic Components, Not Elsewhere Classified

Establishments primarily engaged in manufacturing electronic components, not elsewhere classified, such as receiving antennas, switches, and waveguides. Establishments primarily engaged in manufacturing radio and television transmitting antennas are classified in Industry 3663.

Antennas, receiving: automobile, home, and portable	Commutators, electronic
	Cores, magnetic
Antennas, satellite: home type	Cryogenic cooling devices (e.g., cryostats) for infrared detectors and
Attenuators	

Industry Group No.   Industry No.

367   ELECTRONIC COMPONENTS AND ACCESSORIES—Con.

3679   Electronic Components, Not Elsewhere Classified—Con.

masers
Crystals and crystal assemblies, radio
Delay lines
Harness assemblies for electronic use: wire and cable
Headphones, radio
Heads, recording for speech and musical equipment
Hermetic seals for electronic equipment
Impedance conversion units, high frequency
Liquid crystal displays
Loads, electronic
Microwave components
Oscillators, except laboratory type
Parametric amplifiers
Passive repeaters
Phonograph needle cartridges
Phonograph needles
Piezoelectric crystals
Power supplies, static, and variable frequency
Pulse forming networks
Quartz crystals for electronic application

Recording and playback heads, magnetic
Recording heads for speech and musical equipment
Rectifiers, electronic: except solid-state
Resonant reed devices, electronic
Rheostats, electronic
Sockets, electronic tube
Solenoids for electronic applications
Static power supply converters for electronic applications
Step positioners for transmitting equipment
Styli, phonograph record cutting
Switches, electronic
Switches, stepping
Transducers for use in measuring and testing instruments and equipments
Tube retainers, electronic
Tube spacers, mica
Tube transformer assemblies used in firing electronic tubes
Video triggers, except remote control television devices
Voice controls
Waveguides and fittings

369   MISCELLANEOUS ELECTRICAL MACHINERY, EQUIPMENT, AND SUPPLIES

3691   Storage Batteries

Establishments primarily engaged in manufacturing storage batteries.

Alkaline cell storage batteries
Batteries, rechargeable
Lead acid batteries (storage batteries)

Nickel cadmium storage batteries
Storage batteries

3692   Primary Batteries, Dry and Wet

Establishments primarily engaged in manufacturing primary batteries, dry or wet.

Batteries, primary: dry or wet
Dry cell batteries, single and multiple cell

3694   Electrical Equipment for Internal Combustion Engines

Establishments primarily engaged in manufacturing electrical equipment for internal combustion engines. Important products of this industry include armatures, starting motors, alternators, and generators for automobiles and aircraft; and ignition apparatus for internal combustion engines, including spark plugs, magnetos, coils, and distributors.

Alternators, motor vehicle
Armatures, motor vehicle
Battery cable wiring sets for internal combustion engines
Battery charging generators for internal combustion engines
Breaker point sets, internal combustion engine
Coils, ignition: internal combustion engines
Distributors, motor vehicle engine
Generators, aircraft and motor vehicle

Harness wiring sets for internal combustion engines
Ignition cable sets or wire assemblies for internal combustion engines
Ignition systems, high frequency
Motors, starting: motor vehicle and aircraft
Regulators, voltage: motor vehicle
Spark plugs for internal combustion engines
Voltage regulators, motor vehicle

Industry Group No.	Industry No.	
369		MISCELLANEOUS ELECTRICAL MACHINERY, EQUIPMENT, AND SUPPLIES—Con.

3695 Magnetic And Optical Recording Media

Establishments primarily engaged in manufacturing blank tape, disk, or cassette magnetic or optical recording media for use in recording audio, video, or other signals. Establishments primarily engaged in manufacturing blank or recorded records and prerecorded audio tapes are classified in Industry 3652; those manufacturing prepackaged computer software are classified in Services, Industry 7372; and those manufacturing prerecorded video tape cassettes and disks are classified in Services, Major Group 78.

Audio range tapes, blank
Computer software tape and disks, blank: rigid and floppy
Instrumentation type tape, blank
Magnetic recording tape, blank: reels, cassettes, and disks
Optical disks and tape, blank
Video recording tape, blank

3699 Electrical Machinery, Equipment, and Supplies, Not Elsewhere Classified

Establishments primarily engaged in manufacturing electrical machinery, equipment, and supplies, not elsewhere classified, including high energy particle acceleration systems and equipment, electronic simulators, appliance and extension cords, bells and chimes, and insect traps.

Accelerating waveguide structures
Amplifiers; magnetic, pulse, and maser
Appliance cords for e.g., electric irons, grills, waffle irons—mfpm
Atom smashers (particle accelerators)
Bells, electric
Betatrons
Chimes, electric
Christmas tree lighting sets, electric
Clothing, electrically heated
Cyclotrons
Door opening and closing devices, electrical
Dynamotrons
Electric fence chargers
Electron beam metal cutting, forming, and welding machines
Electron linear accelerators
Electrostatic particle accelerators
Extension cords, made from purchased insulated wire
Flight simulators (training aids), electronic
Flytraps, electrical
Gongs, electric
Grids, electric
Lamps, insect: electric
Laser welding, drilling and cutting equipment
Linear accelerators
Logs, fireplace: electric
Maser amplifiers
Ornaments, Christmas tree: electric
Outboard motors, electric
Particle accelerators, high voltage
Teaching machines and aids, electronic
Trouble lights—mfpm
Ultrasonic cleaning equipment, except medical and dental
Ultrasonic generators sold separately for inclusion in tools and equipment
Ultrasonic welding machines and equipment
Waveguide pressurization equipment

234

Major Group 37.—TRANSPORTATION EQUIPMENT

The Major Group as a Whole

This major group includes establishments engaged in manufacturing equipment for transportation of passengers and cargo by land, air, and water. Important products produced by establishments classified in this major group include motor vehicles, aircraft, guided missiles and space vehicles, ships, boats, railroad equipment, and miscellaneous transportation equipment, such as motorcycles, bicycles, and snowmobiles. Establishments primarily engaged in manufacturing mobile homes are classified in Industry 2451. Establishments primarily engaged in manufacturing equipment used for moving materials on farms; in mines and on construction sites; in individual plants; in airports; or on other locations off the highway are classified in Major Group 35.

Industry Group No.   Industry No.

371   MOTOR VEHICLES AND MOTOR VEHICLE EQUIPMENT

3711   Motor Vehicles and Passenger Car Bodies

Establishments primarily engaged in manufacturing or assembling complete passenger automobiles, trucks, commercial cars and buses, and special purpose motor vehicles which are for highway use. This industry also includes establishments primarily engaged in manufacturing chassis and passenger car bodies. Such establishments may also manufacture motor vehicle parts, but establishments primarily engaged in manufacturing motor vehicle parts except chassis and passenger car bodies are classified in Industry 3714. Establishments primarily engaged in manufacturing truck and bus bodies and in assembling them on purchased chassis are classified in Industry 3713; those manufacturing motor homes on purchased chassis are classified in Industry 3716; those manufacturing motorcycles are classified in Industry 3751; those manufacturing industrial tractors are classified in Industry 3537; those manufacturing other wheel tractors, except contractors off-highway types, are classified in Industry 3523; those manufacturing tracklaying and contractors' off-highway type tractors are classified in Industry 3531; those manufacturing combat tanks and self-propelled weapons are classified in Industry 3795; and those manufacturing stamped body parts for passenger cars are classified in Industry 3465.

Ambulances (motor vehicles)
Amphibian motor vehicles, except tanks
Assembling complete automobiles, trucks, commercial cars, and buses
Automobiles
Bodies, passenger automobile
Brooms, powered (motor vehicles)
Car bodies, including fiberglass
Cars, armored
Cars, electric: for highway use
Chassis, motor vehicle
Fire department vehicles (motor vehicles)
Flushers, street (motor vehicles)
Hearses (motor vehicles)

Mobile lounges (motor vehicle)
Motor buses, except trackless trolley
Motor homes, self-contained—mitse
Motor trucks, except off-highway
Motor vehicles, including amphibian
Patrol wagons (motor vehicles)
Personnel carriers, for highway use
Road oilers (motor vehicles)
Snowplows (motor vehicles)
Station wagons (motor vehicles)
Street sprinklers and sweepers (motor vehicles)
Taxicabs
Tractors, truck: for highway use
Universal carriers, military

371 MOTOR VEHICLES AND MOTOR VEHICLE EQUIPMENT—Con.

3713 Truck and Bus Bodies

Establishments primarily engaged in manufacturing truck and bus bodies and cabs for sale separately or for assembly on purchased chassis, or in assembling truck and bus bodies on purchased chassis. Establishments primarily engaged in manufacturing complete trucks and buses are classified in Industry 3711; those manufacturing stamped body parts for trucks and buses are classified in Industry 3465; those manufacturing truck trailers and demountable cargo containers are classified in Industry 3715; those manufacturing cabs for agricultural tractors are classified in Industry 3523; those manufacturing cabs for industrial trucks are classified in Industry 3537; and those manufacturing cabs for off-highway construction trucks are classified in Industry 3531.

Ambulance bodies	Truck beds
Automobile wrecker-truck body	Truck bodies, motor vehicle
Bodies, dump	Truck cabs for motor vehicles
Bus bodies, motor vehicle	Truck tops
Hearse bodies	Van-type bodies, all purpose

3714 Motor Vehicle Parts and Accessories

Establishments primarily engaged in manufacturing motor vehicle parts and accessories, but not engaged in manufacturing complete motor vehicles or passenger car bodies. Establishments primarily engaged in manufacturing or assembling complete automobiles and trucks are classified in Industry 3711; those manufacturing tires and tubes are classified in Industry 3011; those manufacturing automobile glass are classified in Major Group 32; those manufacturing automobile stampings are classified in Industry 3465; those manufacturing vehicular lighting equipment are classified in Industry 3647; those manufacturing ignition systems are classified in Industry 3694; those manufacturing storage batteries are classified in Industry 3691; and those manufacturing carburetors, pistons, piston rings, and engine intake and exhaust valves are classified in Industry 3592.

Air brakes, motor vehicle	Engines and parts, except diesel: motor vehicle
Automotive wiring harness sets, except ignition	Exhaust systems and parts, motor vehicle
Axle housings and shafts, motor vehicle	Fifth wheels
Axles, motor vehicle	Filters: oil, fuel, and air—motor vehicle
Ball joints, motor vehicle	Frames, motor vehicle
Bearings, motor vehicle: except ball and roller	Fuel pumps, motor vehicle
Brake drums	Fuel systems and parts, motor vehicle
Brakes and brake parts, motor vehicle	Gas tanks, motor vehicle
Bumpers and bumperettes, motor vehicle	Gears, motor vehicle
Camshafts, motor vehicle gasoline engine	Governors, motor vehicle
Cleaners, air: motor vehicle	Heaters, motor vehicle
Connecting rods, motor vehicle: gasoline engine	Hoods, motor vehicle
Control equipment, motor vehicle: acceleration mechanisms and governors	Horns, motor vehicle
Crankshaft assemblies, motor vehicle: gasoline engine	Hydraulic fluid power pumps for automotive steering mechanisms
Cylinder heads, motor vehicle: gasoline engines	Instrument board assemblies, motor vehicle
Defrosters, motor vehicle	Lubrication systems and parts, motor vehicle
Differentials and parts, motor vehicle	Manifolds, motor vehicle: gasoline engine
Directional signals, motor vehicle	Motor vehicle gasoline engine rebuilding on a factory basis
Drive shafts, motor vehicle	Motor vehicle parts and accessories, except motor vehicle stampings
Dump-truck lifting mechanisms	Mufflers, exhaust: motor vehicle

Industry Group No.	Industry No.
371	

MOTOR VEHICLES AND MOTOR VEHICLE EQUIPMENT—Con.

3714 Motor Vehicle Parts and Accessories—Con.

Oil filters, motor vehicle
PCV valves
Pipes, fuel: motor vehicle
Power transmission equipment, motor vehicle
Pumps, motor vehicle: oil, water, fuel, and power steering
Radiators and radiator shells and cores, motor vehicle
Rear axle housings, motor vehicle
Rebuilding motor vehicle gasoline engines and transmissions on a factory basis
Rims, wheel: motor vehicle
Sanders, motor vehicle safety
Shock absorbers, motor vehicle
Steering mechanisms, motor vehicle
Thermostats, motor vehicle

Third axle attachments or six wheel units for motor vehicles
Tie rods, motor vehicle
Tire valve cores
Tops, motor vehicle: except stamped metal
Transmission housings and parts, motor vehicle
Transmissions, motor vehicle
Universal joints, motor vehicle
Vacuum brakes, motor vehicle
Wheels, motor vehicle
Windshield frames, motor vehicle
Windshield wiper systems, all types
Winterfronts, motor vehicle
Wiring harness sets motor vehicles: except ignition

3715 Truck Trailers

Establishments primarily engaged in manufacturing truck trailers, truck trailer chassis for sale separately, detachable trailer bodies (cargo containers) for sale separately, and detachable trailer (cargo container) chassis, for sale separately.

Bus trailers, tractor type
Demountable cargo containers
Motor truck trailers
Semitrailers for missile transportation

Semitrailers for truck tractors
Trailers, fifth-wheel type: for transporting horses
Truck trailers

3716 Motor Homes

Establishments primarily engaged in manufacturing self-contained motor homes on purchased chassis. Establishments engaged in manufacturing self-contained motor homes on chassis manufactured in the same establishment are classified in Industry 3711. Establishments primarily engaged in manufacturing mobile homes are classified in Industry 2451; and those manufacturing travel trailers and pickup campers are classified in Industry 3792. Establishments primarily engaged in van conversion on a custom basis are classified in Services, Industry 7532.

Self-contained motor homes: made on purchased chassis

Vans, self-propelled: conversion on a factory basis for recreational use

372 AIRCRAFT AND PARTS

3721 Aircraft

Establishments primarily engaged in manufacturing or assembling complete aircraft. This industry also includes establishments owned by aircraft manufacturers and primarily engaged in research and development on aircraft, whether from enterprise funds or on a contract or fee basis. Also included are establishments engaged in repairing and rebuilding aircraft on a factory basis. Establishments primarily engaged in manufacturing engines and other aircraft parts and auxiliary equipment are classified in Industries 3724 and 3728; and those manufacturing guided missiles and space vehicles and parts are classified in Industry Group 376. Establishments primarily engaged in the repair of aircraft, except on a factory basis, are classified in Transportation,

372   **AIRCRAFT AND PARTS—Con.**

    3721 Aircraft—Con.

Industry 4581; and research and development on aircraft by establishments not owned by aircraft manufacturers are classified in Services, Industry 8731.

Aircraft	Dirigibles
Airplanes, fixed or rotary wing	Gliders (aircraft)
Airships	Hang gliders
Autogiros	Helicopters
Balloons (aircraft)	Research and development on aircraft
Blimps	by the manufacturer

    3724 Aircraft Engines and Engine Parts

Establishments primarily engaged in manufacturing aircraft engines and engine parts. This industry also includes establishments owned by aircraft engine manufacturers and primarily engaged in research and development on aircraft engines and engine parts whether from enterprise funds or on a contract or fee basis. Also included are establishments engaged in repairing and rebuilding aircraft engines on a factory basis. Establishments primarily engaged in manufacturing guided missile and space vehicle propulsion units and parts are classified in Industry 3764; those manufacturing aircraft intake and exhaust valves and pistons are classified in Industry 3592; and those manufacturing aircraft internal combustion engine filters are classified in Industry 3714. Establishments primarily engaged in the repair of aircraft engines, except on a factory basis, are classified in Transportation, Industry 4581; and research and development on aircraft engines on a contract or fee basis by establishments not owned by aircraft engine manufacturers are classified in Services, Industry 8731.

Air scoops, aircraft	Jet assisted takeoff devices (JATO)
Aircraft engines and engine parts, internal combustion and jet propulsion	Lubricating systems, aircraft
	Pumps, aircraft engine
Airfoils, aircraft engine	Research and development on aircraft
Cooling systems, aircraft engine	engines and engine parts by the manufacturer
Engine heaters, aircraft	
Engine mount parts, aircraft	Rocket motors, aircraft
Exhaust systems, aircraft	Starters, aircraft: nonelectric
External power units, aircraft: for	Turbines, aircraft type
hand-inertia starters	Turbo-superchargers, aircraft

    3728 Aircraft Parts and Auxiliary Equipment, Not Elsewhere Classified

Establishments primarily engaged in manufacturing aircraft parts and auxiliary equipment, not elsewhere classified. This industry also includes establishments owned by manufacturers of aircraft parts and auxiliary equipment and primarily engaged in research and development on aircraft parts, whether from enterprise funds or on a contract or fee basis. Establishments primarily engaged in manufacturing or assembling complete aircraft are classified in Industry 3721; those manufacturing aircraft engines and parts are classified in Industry 3724; those manufacturing aeronautical instruments are classified in Industry 3812; those manufacturing aircraft engine electrical (aeronautical electrical) equipment are classified in Industry 3694; and those manufacturing guided missile and space vehicle parts and auxiliary equipment are classified in Industry 3769. Establishments not owned by manufacturers of aircraft parts but primarily engaged in research and development on aircraft parts on a contract or fee basis are classified in Services, Industry 8731.

372   AIRCRAFT AND PARTS—Con.

3728   Aircraft Parts and Auxiliary Equipment, Not Elsewhere Classified—Con.

Adapter assemblies, hydromatic propeller

Ailerons, aircraft

Aircraft armament, except guns

Aircraft arresting device system

Aircraft assemblies, subassemblies, and parts, except engines

Aircraft body assemblies and parts

Aircraft power transmission equipment

Aircraft propeller parts

Airframe assemblies, except for guided missiles

Airplane brake expanders

Alighting assemblies (landing gear), aircraft

Beaching gear, aircraft

Blades, aircraft propeller: metal or wood

Bomb racks, aircraft

Brakes, aircraft

Chaffing dispensers, aircraft

Countermeasure dispensers, aircraft

Deicing equipment, aircraft

Dive brakes, aircraft

Dusting and spraying equipment, aircraft

Dynetric balancing stands, aircraft

Elevators, aircraft

Empennage (tail) assemblies and parts, aircraft

Fins, aircraft

Flaps, aircraft wing

Fuel tanks, aircraft: including self-sealing

Fuselage assemblies, aircraft

Gears, power transmission: aircraft

Governors, aircraft propeller feathering

Hubs, aircraft propeller

Instrument panel mockups: aircraft training units

Landing gear, aircraft

Landing skis and tracks, aircraft

Link trainers (aircraft training mechanisms)

Nacelles, aircraft

Oleo struts, aircraft

Oxygen systems for aircraft

Panel assemblies (hydromatic propeller test stands), aircraft

Pontoons, aircraft

Propeller alining tables

Propellers, variable and fixed pitch and parts—aircraft

Pumps, propeller feathering

Refueling equipment, airplane: for use in flight

Research and development on aircraft parts and auxiliary equipment by the manufacturer

Roto-blades for helicopters

Rudders, aircraft

Seat ejector devices, aircraft

Spinners, aircraft propeller

Stabilizers, aircraft

Target drones, aircraft

Targets, trailer type: aircraft

Tow targets, aircraft

Training aids, aircraft: except electronic

Transmissions, aircraft

Turret test fixtures, aircraft

Turrets and turret drives, aircraft

Wheels, aircraft

Wing assemblies and parts, aircraft

373   SHIP AND BOAT BUILDING AND REPAIRING

3731   Ship Building and Repairing

Establishments primarily engaged in building and repairing ships, barges, and lighters, whether self-propelled or towed by other craft. This industry also includes the conversion and alteration of ships and the manufacture of off-shore oil and gas well drilling and production platforms (whether or not self-propelled). Establishments primarily engaged in fabricating structural assemblies or components for ships, or subcontractors engaged in ship painting, joinery, carpentry work, and electrical wiring installation, are classified in other industries.

Barges, building and repairing

Cargo vessels, building and repairing

Combat ships, building and repairing

Crew boats, building and repairing

Dredges, building and repairing

Drilling and production platforms, floating, oil and gas

Drydocks, floating

Ferryboats, building and repairing

Fireboats, building and repairing

Fishing vessels, large: seiners and trawlers—building and repairing

Hydrofoil vessels

Landing ships, building and repairing

Lighters, marine: building and repairing

Lighthouse tenders, building and repairing

Marine rigging

Naval ships, building and repairing

Offshore supply boats, building and repairing

Passenger-cargo vessels, building and repairing

Patrol boats, building and repairing

Radar towers, floating

Sailing vessels, commercial: building and repairing

Scows, building and repairing

Seiners, building and repairing

Shipbuilding and repairing

Submarine tenders, building and re-

Industry Group No.	Industry No.	
373		SHIP AND BOAT BUILDING AND REPAIRING—Con.

3731 Ship Building and Repairing—Con.

pairing
Tankers (ships), building and repairing
Tenders (ships), building and repairing
Towboats, building and repairing

Transport vessels, passenger and troop: building and repairing
Trawlers, building and repairing
Tugboats, building and repairing

3732 Boat Building and Repairing

Establishments primarily engaged in building and repairing boats. Establishments primarily engaged in manufacturing rubber and nonrigid plastics boats are classified in Major Group 30. Establishments primarily engaged in operating marinas and which perform incidental boat repair are classified in Transportation, Industry 4493; membership yacht clubs are classified in Services, Industry 7997; and those performing outboard motor repair are classified in Services, Industry 7699.

Boat kits, not a model
Boats, fiberglass: building and repairing
Boats, rigid: plastics
Boats: motorboats, sailboats, rowboats, and canoes—building and repairing
Canoes, building and repairing
Dinghies, building and repairing
Dories, building and repairing
Fishing boats, small
Houseboats, building and repairing

Hydrofoil boats
Kayaks, building and repairing
Lifeboats, building and repairing
Liferafts, except inflatable (rubber and plastics)
Motorboats, inboard and outboard: building and repairing
Pontoons, except aircraft and inflatable (rubber and plastics)
Skiffs, building and repairing

374 RAILROAD EQUIPMENT

3743 Railroad Equipment

Establishments primarily engaged in building and rebuilding locomotives (including frames and parts, not elsewhere classified) of any type or gauge; and railroad, street, and rapid transit cars and car equipment for operation on rails for freight and passenger service. Establishments primarily engaged in manufacturing mining cars are classified in Industry 3532. Repair shops, owned and operated by railroads or local transit companies, repairing locomotives or cars for their own use are classified in Transportation, Major Groups 40 and 41. Establishments primarily engaged in repairing railroad cars on a contract or fee basis are classified in Transportation, Industry 4789; and those repairing locomotive engines on a contract or fee basis are classified in Services, Industry 7699.

Brakes, railway: air and vacuum
Cars and car equipment, freight or passenger
Dining cars and car equipment
Engines, steam (locomotives)
Freight cars and car equipment
Industrial locomotives and parts
Interurban cars and car equipment
Locomotives, locomotive frames, and parts
Lubrication systems, locomotive
Mining locomotives and parts

Railroad car rebuilding
Railway maintenance cars
Railway motor cars
Rapid transit cars and equipment
Sleeping cars, railroad
Streetcars and car equipment
Switching locomotives and parts, electric and nonelectric
Tank freight cars and car equipment
Tenders, locomotive
Trolley buses, trackless

375   MOTORCYCLES, BICYCLES, AND PARTS

3751   Motorcycles, Bicycles, and Parts

Establishments primarily engaged in manufacturing motorcycles, bicycles, and similar equipment, and parts. Establishments primarily engaged in manufacturing children's vehicles, except bicycles, are classified in Industry 3944. Establishments primarily engaged in manufacturing golf carts and other similar personnel carriers are classified in Industry 3799.

Bicycles and parts	Mopeds and parts
Brakes, bicycle: friction clutch and other	Motor scooters and parts
	Motorbikes and parts
Frames, motorcycle and bicycle	Motorcycles and parts
Gears, motorcycle and bicycle	Saddles, motorcycle and bicycle
Handle bars, motorcycle and bicycle	Seat posts, motorcycle and bicycle

376   GUIDED MISSILES AND SPACE VEHICLES AND PARTS

3761   Guided Missiles and Space Vehicles

Establishments primarily engaged in manufacturing complete guided missiles and space vehicles. This industry also includes establishments owned by guided missile and space vehicle manufacturers and primarily engaged in research and development on these products, whether from enterprise funds or on a contract or fee basis. Establishments primarily engaged in manufacturing guided missile and space vehicle propulsion units and propulsion unit parts are classified in Industry 3764; those manufacturing space satellites are classified in Industry 3669; those manufacturing guided missile and space vehicle airborne and ground guidance, checkout, and launch electronic systems and components are classified in Industry 3812; and those manufacturing guided missile and space vehicle airframes, nose cones, and space capsules are classified in Industry 3769. Research and development on guided missiles and space vehicles, on a contract or fee basis, by establishments not owned by guided missile or space vehicle manufacturers are classified in Services, Industry 8731.

Ballistic missiles, complete	Rockets (guided missiles), space and military: complete
Guided missiles, complete	
Research and development on guided missiles and space vehicles, by the manufacturer	Space vehicles, complete

3764   Guided Missile and Space Vehicle Propulsion Units and Propulsion Unit Parts

Establishments primarily engaged in manufacturing guided missile propulsion units and propulsion unit parts. This industry also includes establishments owned by manufacturers of guided missile and space vehicle propulsion units and parts and primarily engaged in research and development on such products, whether from enterprise funds or on a contract or fee basis. Research and development on guided missile and space propulsion units, on a contract or fee basis by establishments not owned by manufacturers of guided missile and space vehicle propulsion units and parts, are classified in Services, Industry 8731.

Engines and engine parts, guided missile	Research and development on guided missile and space vehicle engines, by the manufacturer
Propulsion units for guided missiles and space vehicles	Rocket motors, guided missile

Industry
Group   Industry
No.   No.

376   **GUIDED MISSILES AND SPACE VEHICLES AND PARTS—Con.**

3769   **Guided Missile and Space Vehicle Parts and Auxiliary Equipment, Not Elsewhere Classified**

Establishments primarily engaged in manufacturing guided missile and space vehicle parts and auxiliary equipment, not elsewhere classified. This industry also includes establishments owned by manufacturers of guided missile and space vehicle parts and auxiliary equipment, not elsewhere classified, and primarily engaged in research and development on such products, whether from enterprise funds or on a contract or fee basis. Establishments primarily engaged in manufacturing navigational and guidance systems are classified in Industry 3812. Research and development on guided missile and space vehicle parts, on a contract or fee basis by establishments not owned by manufacturers of such products, are classified in Services, Industry 8731.

Airframe assemblies, for guided missiles
Casings for missiles and missile components shipping and storage
Nose cones, guided missile

Research and development on guided missile and space vehicle components, by the manufacturer
Space capsules

379   **MISCELLANEOUS TRANSPORTATION EQUIPMENT**

3792   **Travel Trailers and Campers**

Establishments primarily engaged in manufacturing travel trailers and campers for attachment to passenger cars or other vehicles, pickup coaches (campers) and caps (covers) for mounting on pickup trucks. Travel trailers are generally 35 feet long or less, 8 feet wide or less, and have storage facilities for water and waste. Establishments primarily engaged in manufacturing mobile homes are classified in Industry 2451.

Campers, for mounting on trucks
Camping trailers and chassis
Pickup coaches (campers), for mounting on pickup trucks

Pickup covers, canopies or caps
Tent-type camping trailers
Travel trailer chassis
Truck campers (slide-in campers)

3795   **Tanks and Tank Components**

Establishments primarily engaged in manufacturing complete tanks, specialized components for tanks, and self-propelled weapons. Establishments primarily engaged in manufacturing military vehicles, except tanks and self-propelled weapons, are classified in Industry Group 371, and those manufacturing tank engines are classified in Industry Group 351.

Amphibian tanks, military
Tank components, specialized: military
Tank recovery vehicles

Tanks, military: including factory rebuilding

3799   **Transportation Equipment, Not Elsewhere Classified**

Establishments primarily engaged in manufacturing transportation equipment, not elsewhere classified. Establishments primarily engaged in manufacturing industrial trucks, tractors, trailers, and stackers are classified in Industry 3537, and those manufacturing children's vehicles except bicycles are classified in Industry 3944.

All terrain vehicles (ATV)
Automobile trailer chassis, except travel trailer
Autos, midget: power driven

Boat trailers
Caddy cars
Cars, electric: off-highway
Electrocars for transporting golfers

Industry Group No.	Industry No.	

379   **MISCELLANEOUS TRANSPORTATION EQUIPMENT—Con.**

    3799   **Transportation Equipment, Not Elsewhere Classified—Con.**

Gocarts, except children's
Golf carts, powered
Pushcarts
Snowmobiles
Towing bars and systems

Trailer hitches
Trailers for transporting horses, except fifth-wheel type
Wheelbarrows

Major Group 38.—MEASURING, ANALYZING, AND CONTROLLING INSTRUMENTS; PHOTOGRAPHIC, MEDICAL AND OPTICAL GOODS; WATCHES AND CLOCKS

The Major Group as a Whole

This major group includes establishments engaged in manufacturing instruments (including professional and scientific) for measuring, testing, analyzing, and controlling, and their associated sensors and accessories; optical instruments and lenses; surveying and drafting instruments; hydrological, hydrographic, meteorological, and geophysical equipment; search, detection, navigation, and guidance systems and equipment; surgical, medical, and dental instruments, equipment, and supplies; ophthalmic goods; photographic equipment and supplies; and watches and clocks.

Industry Group No. | Industry No.

381 SEARCH, DETECTION, NAVIGATION, GUIDANCE, AERONAUTICAL, AND NAUTICAL SYSTEMS, INSTRUMENTS, AND EQUIPMENT

3812 Search, Detection, Navigation, Guidance, Aeronautical, and Nautical Systems and Instruments

Establishments primarily engaged in manufacturing search, detection, navigation, guidance, aeronautical, and nautical systems and instruments. Important products of this industry are radar systems and equipment; sonar systems and equipment; navigation systems and equipment; countermeasures equipment; aircraft and missile control systems and equipment; flight and navigation sensors, transmitters, and displays; gyroscopes; airframe equipment instruments; and speed, pitch, and roll navigational instruments and systems. Establishments primarily engaged in manufacturing aircraft engine instruments or meteorological systems and equipment, including weather tracking equipment, are classified in Industry 3829.

Acceleration indicators and systems components, aerospace types
Air traffic control radar systems and equipment
Airborne integrated data systems/flight recorders
Aircraft flight instruments
Airframe equipment instruments
Airspeed instrumentation (aeronautical instruments)
Altimeters, aeronautical
Angle-of-attack instrumentation
Angle-of-yaw instrumentation
Artificial horizon instrumentation
Automatic pilots
Bank and turn indicators and components (aeronautical instruments)
Cabin environment indicators, transmitters, and sensors
Compasses, gyroscopic and magnetic except portable
Distance measuring equipment (DME), aeronautical
Driftmeters, aeronautical
Fathometers
Glide slope instrumentation
Gyrocompasses
Gyrogimbals

Gyropilots
Gyroscopes
Heads-up display (HUD) systems, aeronautical
Horizon situation instrumentation
Hydrophones
Inertial navigation systems, aeronautical
Infrared homing systems, aeronautical
Instrument landing system instrumentation, airborne or airport
Light reconnaissance and surveillance systems and equipment
Machmeters
Missile guidance systems and equipment
Nautical instruments
Navigational instruments
Omnibearing instrumentation
Pictorial situation instrumentation
Position indicators, airframe equipment: e.g., for landing gear, stabilizers
Radar systems and equipment
Radio magnetic instrumentation (RMI)
Rate-of-climb instrumentation
Sextants, except surveying
Sonabuoys

381   **SEARCH, DETECTION, NAVIGATION, GUIDANCE, AERONAUTICAL, AND NAUTICAL SYSTEMS, INSTRUMENTS, AND EQUIPMENT—Con.**

3812   **Search, Detection, Navigation, Guidance, Aeronautical, and Nautical Systems and Instruments—Con.**

Sonar fish finders
Sonar systems and equipment
Space vehicle guidance systems and equipment

Taffrail logs
Warfare countermeasures equipment
Wheel position indicators and transmitters, aircraft

382   **LABORATORY APPARATUS AND ANALYTICAL, OPTICAL, MEASURING, AND CONTROLLING INSTRUMENTS**

3821   **Laboratory Apparatus and Furniture**

Establishments primarily engaged in manufacturing laboratory apparatus and furniture. Important products of this industry include laboratory balances and scales, laboratory furnaces and ovens, laboratory centrifuges, and various components, parts, and accessories for laboratory apparatus. Laboratory instruments are classified elsewhere, generally in other industries of Industry Group 382.

Autoclaves, laboratory
Balances, laboratory
Bunsen burners
Calorimeters, laboratory type
Centrifuges, laboratory
Crushing and grinding apparatus, laboratory
Distilling apparatus, laboratory type
Dryers, laboratory
Evaporation apparatus, laboratory type
Freezers, laboratory
Furnaces, laboratory: except dental
Furniture, laboratory
Granulators, laboratory
Hotplates, laboratory

Incubators, laboratory
Laboratory equipment: fume hoods, distillation racks, benches, and cabinets
Melting point apparatus, laboratory
Microtomes
Ovens, laboratory
Particle size reduction apparatus, laboratory
Pipettes, hemocytometer
Sample preparation apparatus, laboratory type
Shakers and stirrers, laboratory
Sterilizers, laboratory
Worktables, laboratory

3822   **Automatic Controls for Regulating Residential and Commercial Environments and Appliances**

Establishments primarily engaged in manufacturing temperature and related controls for heating and air-conditioning installations and refrigeration applications, which are electrically, electronically, or pneumatically actuated, and which measure and control variables such as temperature and humidity; and automatic regulators used as components of household appliances. Establishments primarily engaged in manufacturing industrial process controls are classified in Industry 3823; those manufacturing motor control switches are classified in Industry 3625; those manufacturing switches for household appliances are classified in Industry 3643; and those manufacturing appliance timers are classified in Industry 3873.

Air flow controllers, air-conditioning and refrigeration: except valves
Appliance regulators, except switches
Building services monitoring controls, automatic
Clothes dryer controls, including dryness controls
Combination limit and fan controls
Combination oil and hydronic controls
Damper operators: pneumatic, thermostatic, and electric
Electric air cleaner controls, automatic
Electric heat proportioning controls, modulating controls

Electric space heater controls, automatic
Energy cutoff controls, residential and commercial types
Fan control, temperature responsive
Flame safety controls for furnaces and boilers
Float controls, residential and commercial types
Gas burner automatic controls, except valves
Gradual switches, pneumatic
Humidistats: wall, duct, and skeleton
Humidity controls, air-conditioning

Industry Group No.	Industry No.	
382		**LABORATORY APPARATUS AND ANALYTICAL, OPTICAL, MEASURING, AND CONTROLLING INSTRUMENTS—Con.**
	3822	**Automatic Controls for Regulating Residential and Commercial Environments and Appliances—Con.**

types
Hydronic circulator control, automatic
Hydronic limit control
Hydronic pressure and temperature controls
Ice bank controls
Ice maker controls
Ignition controls for gas appliances and furnaces, automatic
In-built thermostats, filled system and bimetal types
Incinerator control systems, residential and commercial types
Limit controls, residential and commercial heating types
Line or limit control for electric heat
Liquid level controls, residential and commercial heating types
Oven temperature controls, nonindustrial
Pneumatic relays, air-conditioning type
Pressure controllers, air-conditioning system type
Primary oil burner controls, including stack controls and cadmium cells

Refrigeration controls, pressure
Refrigeration thermostats
Refrigeration/air-conditioning defrost controls
Sequencing controls for electric heat
Static pressure regulators
Steam pressure controls, residential and commercial type
Surface burner controls, temperature
Switches, pneumatic positioning remote
Switches, thermostatic
Temperature controls, automatic: residential and commercial types
Temperature sensors for motor windings
Thermocouples, vacuum: glass
Thermostats: air-conditioning, refrigeration, comfort heating, appliance
Time program controls, air-conditioning systems
Vapor heating controls
Water heater controls

3823 Industrial Instruments for Measurement, Display, and Control of Process Variables; and Related Products

Establishments primarily engaged in manufacturing industrial instruments and related products for measuring, displaying (indicating and/or recording), transmitting, and controlling process variables in manufacturing, energy conversion, and public service utilities. These instruments operate mechanically, pneumatically, electronically, or electrically to measure process variables, such as temperature, humidity, pressure, vacuum, combustion, flow, level, viscosity, density, acidity, alkalinity, specific gravity, gas and liquid concentration, sequence, time interval, mechanical motion, and rotation. Establishments primarily engaged in manufacturing electrical integrating meters are classified in Industry 3825; those manufacturing residential and commercial comfort controls are classified in Industry 3822; those manufacturing all liquid-in-glass and bimetal thermometers and glass hydrometers are classified in Industry 3829; those manufacturing recorder charts are classified in Industry Group 275; and those manufacturing analytical and optical instruments are classified in Industries 3826 and 3827.

Absorption analyzers, industrial process type: e.g., infrared, X-ray
Analyzers, industrial process type
Annunciators, relay and solid-state types: industrial display
Boiler controls: industrial, power, and marine type
Buoyancy instruments, industrial process type
Chromatographs, industrial process type
Combustion control instruments, except commercial and household furnace type
Computer interface equipment for industrial process control

Controllers for process variables: electric, electronic, and pneumatic
Coulometric analyzers, industrial process type
Data loggers, industrial process type
Density and specific gravity instruments, industrial process type
Differential pressure instruments, industrial process type
Digital displays of process variables
Draft gauges, industrial process type
Electrodes used in industrial process measurement
Electrolytic conductivity instruments, industrial process type
Flow instruments, industrial process

Industry Group No.
382

Industry No.

LABORATORY APPARATUS AND ANALYTICAL, OPTICAL, MEASURING, AND CONTROLLING INSTRUMENTS—Con.

3823 Industrial Instruments for Measurement, Display, and Control of Process Variables; and Related Products—Con.

type
Fluidic devices, circuits, and systems for process control
Gas and liquid analysis instruments, industrial process type
Gas flow computers, industrial process type
Humidity instruments, industrial process type
Hydrometers, industrial process type
Industrial process control instruments
Infrared instruments, industrial process type
Level and bulk measuring instruments, industrial process type
Liquid analysis instruments, industrial process type
Liquid concentration instruments, industrial process type
Liquid level instruments, industrial process type
Magnetic flow meters, industrial process type
Manometers, industrial process type
Moisture meters, industrial process type
Nuclear reactor controls
PH instruments, industrial process type
Panelboard indicators, recorders and controllers: receiver type
Potentiometric self-balancing instruments, except X-Y plotters

Pressure gauges, dial and digital
Pressure instruments, industrial process type
Primary elements for process flow measurement: orifice plates
Programmers, process type
Pyrometers, industrial process type
Refractometers, industrial process type
Resistance thermometers and bulbs, industrial process type
Telemetering instruments, industrial process type
Temperature instruments: industrial process type, except glass and bimetal
Thermal conductivity instruments, industrial process type
Thermistors, industrial process type
Thermocouples, industrial process type
Thermometers, filled system: industrial process type
Time cycle and program controllers, industrial process type
Transmitters of process variables, standard signal conversion
Turbidity instruments, industrial process type
Turbine flow meters, industrial process type
Viscosimeters, industrial process type
Water quality monitoring and control systems

3824 Totalizing Fluid Meters and Counting Devices

Establishments primarily engaged in manufacturing totalizing (registering) meters monitoring fluid flows, such as watermeters and gasmeters; and producers of mechanical and electromechanical counters and associated metering devices. Establishments primarily engaged in manufacturing electricity integrating meters and electronic frequency counters are classified in Industry 3825, and those manufacturing industrial process instruments are classified in Industry 3823.

Controls, revolution and timing instruments
Counter type registers
Counters, revolution
Counters: mechanical, electrical, and electronic totalizing
Electromechanical counters
Electronic totalizing counters
Gasmeters: domestic, large capacity, and industrial
Gasoline dispensing meters (except pumps)
Gauges for computing pressure-temperature corrections
Impeller and counter driven flow meters
Integrating meters, nonelectric
Linear counters
Magnetic counters
Measuring wheels
Meters: gas, liquid, tallying, and mechanical measuring—except electrical
Odometers

Parking meters
Pedometers
Positive displacement meters
Predetermined counters
Production counters
Propeller type meters with registers
Registers, linear tallying
Rotary type meters, consumption registering
Speed indicators and recorders, vehicle
Speedometers
Tachometer, centrifugal
Tally counters
Tallying meters: except electrical instruments, watches, and clocks
Tank truck meters
Taximeters
Totalizing meters, consumption registering, except aircraft
Turbine meters, consumption registering
Vehicle tank meters
Watermeters, consumption registering

382   LABORATORY APPARATUS AND ANALYTICAL, OPTICAL,
             MEASURING, AND CONTROLLING INSTRUMENTS—Con.

3825   Instruments for Measuring and Testing of Electricity and Electrical Signals

Establishments primarily engaged in manufacturing instruments for measuring the characteristics of electricity and electrical signals, such as voltmeters, ammeters, wattmeters, watt-hour meters, demand meters, and equipment for testing the electrical characteristics of electrical, radio, and communication circuits and of internal combustion engines. Establishments primarily engaged in the manufacturing of electronic checkout, monitoring, evaluating, and other electronic support equipment for electronic navigational, radar, and sonar systems are classified in Industry 3812, and those manufacturing similar equipment for communications systems classified in Industry Group 366.

Alternator and generator testers
Ammeters
Ampere-hour meters
Analog-to-digital converters, electronic instrumentation type
Analyzers for testing electrical characteristics
Audiometers, except medical
Automotive ammeters and voltmeters
Battery testers, electrical
Bleed control cabinets (engine testers)
Bridges, electrical: e.g., Kelvin, Wheatstone, vacuum tube, and megohm
Current measuring equipment
Decade boxes: capacitance, inductance, and resistance
Demand meters, electric
Digital panel meters, electricity measuring
Digital test equipment, electronic and electrical circuits and equipment
Digital-to-analog converters, electronic instrumentation type
Diode and transistor testers
Distortion meters and analyzers
Elapsed time meters, electronic
Electron tube test equipment
Electronic test equipment for testing electrical characteristics
Energy measuring equipment, electrical
Field strength and intensity measuring equipment, electrical
Frequency meters: electrical, mechanical, and electronic
Frequency synthesizers
Function generators
Galvanometers, except geophysical
Ignition testing instruments
Impedance measuring equipment
Indicating instruments, electric
Instrument relays, all types
Instrument shunts
Instruments for measuring electrical quantities
Instruments, electric: for testing electrical characteristics
Integrated-circuit testers
Integrating electricity meters
Internal combustion engine analyzers, to test electrical characteristics
Laboratory standards, electric: resistance, inductance, and capacitance
Logic circuit testers
Measuring equipment for electronic and electrical circuits and equipment
Measuring instruments and meters, electric

Meters, electric: pocket, portable, panelboard, and graphic recording
Meters, power factor and phase angle
Microwave test equipment
Multimeters
Network analyzers
Ohmmeters
Oscillators, audiofrequency and radiofrequency (instrument types)
Oscillographs and oscilloscopes
Potentiometric instruments, except industrial process type
Power measuring equipment, electrical
Pulse (signal) generators
Radar testing instruments, electric
Radio apparatus analyzers for testing electrical characteristics
Radio set analyzers, electrical
Radio tube checkers, electrical
Radiofrequency measuring equipment
Recorders, oscillographic
Reflectometers, sliding shorts
Resistance measuring equipment
Semiconductor test equipment
Signal generators and averages
Spark plug testing instruments, electric
Spectrum analyzers
Standard cells
Standards and calibration equipment for electrical measuring, except laboratory
Standing wave ratio measuring equipment
Stroboscopes
Sweep generators
Sweep oscillators
Synchroscopes
Tachometer generators
Test equipment for electronic and electrical circuits and equipment
Test sets, ignition harness
Time code generators
Transformers, instrument: portable
Tube testers
Volt-ohm milliammeters
Voltmeters
Watt-hour and demand meters, combined
Watt-hour and time switch meters, combined
Watt-hour meters, electric
Wattmeters
Waveform measuring and/or analyzing equipment
X-Y recorders (plotters), except computer peripheral equipment

LABORATORY APPARATUS AND ANALYTICAL, OPTICAL, MEASURING, AND CONTROLLING INSTRUMENTS—Con.

3826 Laboratory Analytical Instruments

Establishments primarily engaged in manufacturing laboratory instruments and instrumentation systems for chemical or physical analysis of the composition or concentration of samples of solid, fluid, gaseous, or composite material. Establishments primarily engaged in manufacturing instruments for monitoring and analyzing continuous samples from medical patients are classified in Industry 3845, and from industrial process streams are classified in Industry 3823.

Amino acid analyzers, laboratory type
Automatic chemical analyzers, laboratory type
Chromatographic instruments, laboratory type
Colorimeters, laboratory type
Coulometric analyzers, laboratory type
Densitometers, analytical
Differential thermal analysis instruments
Electrolytic conductivity instruments, laboratory type
Electron paramagnetic spin type apparatus
Electrophoresis instruments
Elemental analyzers (CHNOS)
Flame photometers
Gas analyzers, laboratory type
Gas chromatographic instruments, laboratory type
Infrared type analytical instruments, laboratory type
Liquid chromatographic instruments, laboratory type
Magnetic resonance imaging type apparatus, except diagnostic
Mass spectrometers
Mass spectroscopy instrumentation
Microprobes: electron, ion, laser, X-ray
Microscopes, electron and proton
Moisture analysers, laboratory type
Monochrometers, laboratory type
Nephelometers, except meteorological

Neutron activation analysis instruments
Osmometers
PH measuring equipment
Particle size analyzers
Photometers, except photographic exposure meters
Polariscopes
Polarizers
Polarographic equipment
Protein analyzers, laboratory type
Redox (oxidation-reduction potential) instruments
Refractometers, laboratory
Specific ion measuring instruments, laboratory type
Spectrofluorometers
Spectrographs
Spectrometers: electron diffraction, mass, nmr, raman, x-ray
Spectrophotometers: atomic absorption, atomic emission, flame, fluorescence, infrared, raman, visible, ultrav
Surface area analyzers
Thermal analysis instruments, laboratory type
Thermal conductivity instruments and sensors
Thermogravimetric analyzers
Titrimeters
Turbidometers
Ultraviolet-type analytical instruments

3827 Optical Instruments and Lenses

Establishments primarily engaged in manufacturing instruments and apparatus that measure an optical property and optically project, measure, or magnify an image, such as binoculars, microscopes, prisms, and lenses. Included are establishments primarily engaged in manufacturing optical sighting and fire control equipment.

Aiming circles (fire control equipment)
Binoculars
Boards: plotting, spotting, and gun fire adjustment
Borescopes
Cinetheodolites
Coddington magnifying instruments
Contour projectors
Correctors: percentage, wind, and roll (sighting and fire control equipment)
Fuse setters (fire control equipment)
Glasses, field or opera
Gratings, diffraction
Gun sights, optical

Interferometers
Lens coating
Lens grinding, except ophthalmic
Lens mounts
Lenses, optical: photographic, magnifying, projection, and instrument
Light sources, standard
Lupes magnifying instruments, optical
Magnifying instruments, optical
Metallographs
Microprojectors
Microscopes, except electron, proton, and corneal
Mirrors, optical

Industry Group No.	Industry No.	
382		**LABORATORY APPARATUS AND ANALYTICAL, OPTICAL, MEASURING, AND CONTROLLING INSTRUMENTS—Con.**

3827 Optical Instruments and Lenses—Con.

Optical alignment and display instruments, except photographic
Optical comparators
Optical test and inspection equipment
Periscopes
Phototheodolites
Prisms, optical
Reflectors, optical

Searchlight mirrors and reflectors
Sighting and fire control equipment, optical
Spyglasses
Telescopes
Telescopic sights
Triplet magnifying instruments, optical

3829 Measuring and Controlling Devices, Not Elsewhere Classified

Establishments primarily engaged in manufacturing measuring and controlling devices, not elsewhere classified, including meteorological instruments. Important products of this industry are physical properties testing equipment, nuclear radiation detection and monitoring instrumentation, aircraft engine instruments (except flight), and liquid-in-glass and bimetal thermometers. Also included in this industry are establishments primarily engaged in manufacturing surveying and drafting instruments, such as alidades, transits, sextants, theodolites, slide rules, and T-squares.

Accelerometers, except aerospace type
Actinometers, meteorological
Alidades, surveying
Anamometers
Barographs
Barometers, mercury and aneroid types
Cable testing machines
Ceilometers
Chronometers, electronic
Clinical thermometers, including digital
Compasses, magnetic: portable type
Count rate meters, nuclear radiation
Drafting instruments and machines
Dynamometer instruments
Electrogamma ray loggers
Evaporation meters
Fare registers: e.g., for streetcars and buses
Fatigue testing machines, industrial: mechanical
Fuel densitometers, aircraft engine
Fuel mixture indicators, aircraft engine
Fuel system instruments, aircraft
Fuel totalizers, aircraft engine
Gauges except electric, motor vehicle: oil pressure and water temperature
Gauging instruments, thickness: ultrasonic
Geiger counters
Hardness testing equipment
Humidity instruments, except industrial process and air-conditioning type
Hydrometers, except industrial process type
Hygrometers, except industrial process type
Hygrothermographs
Instrumentation for reactor controls, auxiliary
Ion chambers
Kinematic test and measuring equipment
Level gauges, radiation type
Levels and tapes, surveying
Magnetometers

Map plotting instruments
Meteorogic tracking systems
Meteorological instruments
Nephoscopes
Nuclear instrument modules
Nuclear radiation detection and monitoring instruments
Personnel dosimetry devices
Photogrammetrical instruments
Photopitometers
Physical properties testing and inspection equipment
Pitometers
Pressure and vacuum indicators, aircraft engine
Pulse analyzers, nuclear monitoring
Pyrheliometers
Radiation measuring and detecting (radiac) equipment
Rain gauges
Restitution apparatus, photogrammetrical
Sample changers, nuclear radiation
Scalers, nuclear radiation
Scintillation detectors
Seismographs
Seismometers
Seismoscopes
Sextants, surveying
Solarimeters
Spectrometers, liquid scintillation and nuclear
Stereotopographs
Stress, strain, and flaw detecting and measuring equipment
Surveying instruments
Synchronizers, aircraft engine
Testers for checking hydraulic controls on aircraft
Testing equipment: abrasion, shearing strength, tensile strength, and torsion
Theodolites, surveying
Thermocouples, except industrial process, aircraft type, and glass vacuum
Thermohydrometers

Industry Group No.	Industry No.	

382   LABORATORY APPARATUS AND ANALYTICAL, OPTICAL, MEASURING, AND CONTROLLING INSTRUMENTS—Con.

3829   Measuring and Controlling Devices, Not Elsewhere Classified—Con.

Thermometers, liquid-in-glass and bi-metal types
Thrust power indicators, aircraft engine
Toll booths, automatic
Transducers, pressure
Transits, surveying
Turnstiles, equipped with counting mechanisms

Ultrasonic testing equipment
Vibration meters, analyzers, and calibrators
Viscosimeters, except industrial process type
Weather tracking equipment
Whole body counters, nuclear
Wind direction indicators

384   SURGICAL, MEDICAL, AND DENTAL INSTRUMENTS AND SUPPLIES

3841   Surgical and Medical Instruments and Apparatus

Establishments primarily engaged in manufacturing medical, surgical, ophthalmic, and veterinary instruments and apparatus. Establishments primarily engaged in manufacturing surgical and orthopedic appliances are classified in Industry 3842; those manufacturing electrotherapeutic and electromedical apparatus are classified in Industry 3845; and those manufacturing X-ray apparatus are classified in Industry 3844.

Anesthesia apparatus
Biopsy instruments and equipment
Blood pressure apparatus
Blood transfusion equipment
Bone drills
Bone plates and screws
Bone rongeurs
Bronchoscopes, except electromedical
Cannulae
Catheters
Clamps, surgical
Corneal microscopes
Cystoscopes, except electromedical
Diagnostic apparatus, physicians'
Eye examining instruments and apparatus
Fixation appliances, internal
Forceps, surgical
Gastroscopes, except electromedical
Hemodialysis apparatus
Holders, surgical needle
Hypodermic needles and syringes
IV transfusion apparatus
Inhalation therapy equipment
Inhalators, surgical and medical
Instruments and apparatus, except electromedical: medical, surgical, ophthalmic, and veterinary
Instruments, microsurgical: except electromedical
Knives, surgical
Metabolism apparatus

Muscle exercise apparatus, ophthalmic
Needle holders, surgical
Needles, suture
Operating tables
Ophthalmic instruments and apparatus
Ophthalmometers and ophthalmoscopes
Optometers
Otoscopes, except electromedical
Oxygen tents
Pelvimeters
Physiotherapy equipment, electrical
Probes, surgical
Retinoscopes, except electromedical
Retractors
Rifles for propelling hypodermics into animals
Saws, surgical
Skin grafting equipment
Slit lamps (ophthalmic goods)
Speculums
Sphygmomanometers
Stethoscopes and stethographs
Suction therapy apparatus
Surgical instruments and apparatus, except electromedical
Surgical knife blades and handles
Surgical stapling devices
Tonometers, medical
Trocars
Ultrasonic medical cleaning equipment
Veterinarians' instruments and apparatus

3842   Orthopedic, Prosthetic, and Surgical Appliances and Supplies

Establishments primarily engaged in manufacturing orthopedic, prosthetic, and surgical appliances and supplies, arch supports and other foot appliances; fracture appliances, elastic hosiery, abdominal supporters, braces, and trusses; bandages; surgical gauze and dressings; sutures; adhesive tapes and medicated plasters; and personal safety appliances and equipment. Establishments primarily engaged in manufacturing surgical and medical instruments are classified in Industry 3841. Establishments primarily engaged in manufacturing or-

Industry Group No. **384**

Industry No.

SURGICAL, MEDICAL, AND DENTAL INSTRUMENTS AND SUPPLIES—Con.

3842 Orthopedic, Prosthetic, and Surgical Appliances and Supplies—Con.

thopedic or prosthetic appliances and in the personal fitting to the individual prescription by a physician are classified in Retail Trade, Industry 5999.

Abdominal supporters, braces, and trusses
Absorbent cotton, sterilized
Adhesive tape and plasters, medicated or nonmedicated
Applicators, cotton tipped
Atomizers, medical
Autoclaves, hospital and surgical
Bandages and dressings, surgical and orthopedic
Bandages: plastics, muslin, and plaster of paris
Belts: sanitary, surgical, and corrective
Braces, elastic
Braces, orthopedic
Bulletproof vests
Canes, orthopedic
Cervical collars
Clothing, fire resistant and protective
Colostomy appliances
Corn remover and bunion pads
Corsets, surgical
Cosmetic restorations
Cotton, absorbent: sterilized
Cotton, including cotton balls
Crutches and walkers
Drapes, surgical: cotton
Dressings, surgical
Ear stoppers
Elastic hosiery, orthopedic
Extension shoes, orthopedic
First aid, snake bite, and burn kits
Foot appliances, orthopedic
Fracture appliances, surgical
Gas masks
Gauze, surgical: not made in weaving mills
Grafts, artificial: for surgery—made of braided or mesh artificial fibers
Gynecological supplies and appliances
Hearing aids
Helmets, space
Hosiery, support
Hydrotherapy equipment
Implants, surgical
Infant incubators
Intrauterine devices
Iron lungs
Life preservers, except cork and inflatable
Ligatures, medical
Limbs, artificial
Linemen's safety belts
Models, anatomical
Noise protectors, personal
Orthopedic devices and materials
Pads, incontinent and bed
Personal safety appliances and equipment
Plugs, ear and nose
Prosthetic appliances and supplies
Radiation shielding aprons, gloves, and sheeting
Respirators
Respiratory protection equipment, personal
Restraints, patient
Safety appliances and equipment, personal
Safety gloves, all materials
Socks, stump
Space suits
Splints, pneumatic and wood
Sponges, surgical
Sterilizers, hospital and surgical
Stockinette, surgical
Stretchers
Suits, firefighting: asbestos
Supports: abdominal, ankle, arch, and kneecap
Surgical appliances and supplies, except medical instruments
Suspensories
Sutures
Swabs, sanitary cotton
Tongue depressors
Traction apparatus
Trusses: orthopedic and surgical
Welders' hoods
Wheel chairs
Whirlpool baths, hydrotherapy equipment

3843 Dental Equipment and Supplies

Establishments primarily engaged in manufacturing artificial teeth, dental metals, alloys, and amalgams, and a wide variety of equipment, instruments, and supplies used by dentists, dental laboratories, and dental colleges. Dental laboratories constructing artificial dentures, bridges, inlays, and other dental restorations on specifications from dentists are classified in Services, Industry 8072.

Abrasive points, wheels, and disks: dental
Autoclaves, dental
Broaches, dental
Burs, dental
Cabinets, dental
Cement, dental
Chairs, dentists'
Compounds, dental
Cutting instruments, dental
Dental alloys for amalgams
Dental engines
Dental equipment and supplies
Dental hand instruments, including for-

Industry
Group   Industry
No.   No.

**384   SURGICAL, MEDICAL, AND DENTAL INSTRUMENTS AND SUPPLIES—
            Con.**

3843   Dental Equipment and Supplies—Con.

ceps
Dental laboratory equipment
Dental metal
Denture materials
Drills, dental
Enamels, dentists'
Forceps, dental
Furnaces, laboratory: dental
Glue, dental
Gold, dental
Hand pieces and parts, dental

Impression material, dental
Investment material, dental
Orthodontic appliances
Plaster, dental
Pliers, dental
Sterilizers, dental
Teeth, artificial: not made in dental
laboratories
Tools, dentists'
Ultrasonic dental equipment
Wax, dental

3844   X-Ray Apparatus and Tubes and Related Irradiation Apparatus

Establishments primarily engaged in manufacturing radiographic X-ray,
fluoroscopic X-ray, and therapeutic X-ray apparatus and tubes for medical, industrial, research, and control applications, or in manufacturing other irradiation equipment, including gamma and beta-ray equipment.

Beta-ray irradiation equipment
Fluoroscopes
Fluoroscopic X-ray apparatus and tubes
Gamma ray irradiation equipment
Irradiation equipment
Lamps, X-ray
Nuclear irradiation equipment
Radiographic X-ray apparatus and
tubes: medical, industrial, and re-
search

Radium equipment
Therapeutic X-ray apparatus and tubes:
medical, industrial, and research
X-ray apparatus and tubes: medical, in-
dustrial, research, and control
X-ray generators

3845   Electromedical and Electrotherapeutic Apparatus

Establishments primarily engaged in manufacturing electromedical and
electrotherapeutic apparatus. Establishments primarily engaged in manufacturing electrotherapeutic lamp units for ultraviolet and infrared radiation are
classified in Industry 3641.

Arc lamp units, electrotherapeutic:
except infrared and ultraviolet
Audiological equipment, electromedical
Automated blood and body fluid analyz-
ers, except laboratory
Bronchoscopes, electromedical
Cardiographs
Colonscopes, electromedical
Computerized axial tomography (CT/
CAT scanner) apparatus
Cystoscopes, electromedical
Defibrilators
Dialyzers, electromedical
Diathermy apparatus, electromedical
Electrocardiographs
Electroencephalographs
Electromedical apparatus
Electromyographs
Endoscopic equipment, electromedical:
e.g., bronchoscopes, cystoscopes, and
colonoscopes
Gastroscopes, electromedical

Laser systems and equipment, medical
Lithotripters
Magnetic resonance imaging device (di-
agnostic), nuclear
Otoscopes, electromedical
Pacemakers
Patient monitoring equipment: inten-
sive care/coronary care unit
Phonocardiographs
Position emission tomography (PET
scanner)
Respiratory analysis equipment, elec-
tromedical
Retinoscopes, electromedical
Surgical support systems: heart-lung
machines, except iron lungs and
blood flow systems
Transcutaneous electrical nerve stimu-
lators (TENS)
Ultrasonic medical equipment, except
cleaning
Ultrasonic scanning devices, medical

385   OPHTHALMIC GOODS

3851   Ophthalmic Goods

Establishments primarily engaged in manufacturing ophthalmic frames,
lenses, and sunglass lenses. Establishments primarily engaged in manufactur-

Industry Group No.	Industry No.	

385   **OPHTHALMIC GOODS—Con.**

3851   **Ophthalmic Goods—Con.**

ing molded glass blanks are classified in Industry 3229. Establishments primarily engaged in grinding lenses and fitting glasses to prescription are classified in Retail Trade, Industry 5995.

Contact lenses
Eyeglasses, lenses, and frames
Eyes, glass and plastics
Frames and parts, eyeglass and spectacle
Glasses, sun or glare
Goggles: sun, safety, industrial, and underwater
Intra ocular lenses
Lens coating, ophthalmic
Lens grinding, ophthalmic, except prescription

Lenses, ophthalmic
Lorgnettes
Magnifiers (readers and simple magnifiers)
Mountings, eyeglass and spectacle
Ophthalmic lens grinding, except prescription
Protectors, eye
Spectacles
Temples and fronts, ophthalmic

386   **PHOTOGRAPHIC EQUIPMENT AND SUPPLIES**

3861   **Photographic Equipment and Supplies**

Establishments primarily engaged in manufacturing: (1) photographic apparatus, equipment, parts, attachments, and accessories, such as still and motion picture camera and projection apparatus; photocopy and microfilm equipment; blueprinting and diazotype (white printing) apparatus and equipment; and other photographic equipment; and (2) sensitized film, paper, cloth, and plates, and prepared photographic chemicals for use therewith. Establishments primarily engaged in manufacturing photographic paper stock (unsensitized), and paper mats, mounts, easels, and folders for photographic use, are classified in Major Group 26; those manufacturing photographic lenses are classified in Industry 3827; those manufacturing photographic glass are classified in Major Group 32; those manufacturing chemicals for technical purposes, not specifically prepared and packaged for use in photography, are classified in Major Group 28; and those manufacturing photographic flash, flood, enlarger, and projection lamp bulbs are classified in Industry 3641.

Aerial cameras
Blueprint cloth or paper, sensitized
Blueprint reproduction machines and equipment
Brownprint paper and cloth, sensitized
Brownprint reproduction machines and equipment
Cameras, microfilm
Cameras, still and motion picture
Densitometers
Developers, prepared photographic: not made in chemical plants
Developing machines and equipment, still or motion picture
Diazo (whiteprint) paper and cloth, sensitized
Diazotype (whiteprint) reproduction machines and equipment
Driers, photographic
Editing equipment, motion picture: rewinds, viewers, titlers, and splicers
Enlargers, photographic
Exposure meters, photographic
Film, sensitized: motion picture, X-ray, still camera, and special purpose
Fixers, prepared photographic: not made in chemical plants

Flashlight apparatus for photographers, except bulbs
Graphic arts plates, sensitized
Hangers: photographic film, plate, and paper
Heat sensitized paper made from purchased paper
Holders: photographic film, plate, and paper
Lantern slide plates, sensitized
Lens shades, camera
Light meters, photographic
Metallic emulsion sensitized paper and cloth, photographic
Microfiche cameras
Microfiche readers and reader printers
Microfilm equipment: cameras, projectors, and readers
Motion picture apparatus and equipment
Motion picture film
Photocopy machines
Photoflash equipment, except lamp bulbs
Photographic chemicals, packaged
Photographic equipment and accessories

Industry Group No.	Industry No.	
386		**PHOTOGRAPHIC EQUIPMENT AND SUPPLIES—Con.**
	3861	**Photographic Equipment and Supplies—Con.**

Photographic instruments, electronic
Photographic paper and cloth, sensitized
Photographic sensitized goods
Photoreconnaissance systems
Plates, photographic: sensitized
Printing equipment, photographic
Printing frames, photographic
Processing equipment, photographic
Projectors, still and motion picture: silent and sound
Range finders, photographic
Reels, film
Screens, projection
Sensitometers, photographic

Shutters, camera
Sound recording and reproducing equipment, motion picture
Stands, camera and projector
Stereopticons
Tanks: photographic developing, fixing, and washing
Toners, prepared photographic, packaged
Trays, photographic printing and processing
Tripods, camera and projector
Washers, photographic print and film
X-ray film
X-ray plates, sensitized

387		**WATCHES, CLOCKS, CLOCKWORK OPERATED DEVICES, AND PARTS**
	3873	**Watches, Clocks, Clockwork Operated Devices, and Parts**

Establishments primarily engaged in manufacturing clocks (including electric), watches, watchcases, mechanisms for clockwork operated devices, and clock and watch parts. This industry includes establishments primarily engaged in assembling clocks and watches from purchased movements and cases. Establishments primarily engaged in manufacturing timeclocks are classified in Industry 3579; those manufacturing glass crystals are classified in Industry 3231; and those manufacturing plastics crystals are classified in Industry 3089.

Appliance timers
Chronographs, spring wound
Chronometers, spring wound
Clock materials and parts, except crystals and jewels
Clocks, assembling of
Clocks, except timeclocks
Mechanisms for clockwork operated devices

Movements, watch or clock
Timers for industrial use, clockwork mechanism only
Watchcases
Watches and parts: except crystals and jewels

Major Group 39.—MISCELLANEOUS MANUFACTURING INDUSTRIES

The Major Group as a Whole

This major group includes establishments primarily engaged in manufacturing products not classified in any other manufacturing major group. Industries in this group fall into the following categories: jewelry, silverware, and plated ware; musical instruments; dolls, toys, games, and sporting and athletic goods; pens, pencils, and artists' materials; buttons, costume novelties, miscellaneous notions; brooms and brushes; caskets; and other miscellaneous manufacturing industries.

Industry
Group
No.

Industry
No.

391 JEWELRY, SILVERWARE, AND PLATED WARE

3911 Jewelry, Precious Metal

Establishments primarily engaged in manufacturing jewelry and other articles worn on or carried about the person, made of precious metals (including base metals clad or rolled with precious metals), with or without stones. Products of this industry include cigarette cases and lighters, vanity cases and compacts; trimmings for umbrellas and canes; and jewel settings and mountings. Establishments primarily engaged in manufacturing costume jewelry from nonprecious metals and other materials are classified in Industry 3961.

Cases: cigar, cigarette, and vanity—precious metal
Cigar lighters, precious metal or based metal clad with precious metal
Cigarette lighters, precious metal
Collar buttons, precious metal and precious or semiprecious stones
Compacts, precious metal
Cuff buttons, precious metal and precious or semiprecious stones
Handbags, precious metal
Handles, umbrella and parasol: gold and silver
Jewel settings and mountings, precious metal
Jewelry, made of precious metal or precious or semiprecious stones

Jewelry, natural or cultured pearls
Medals of precious or semiprecious metals
Mountings, gold and silver: for pens, leather goods, and umbrellas
Pins, precious metal
Rings, precious metal
Rosaries and other small religious articles, precious metal
Shirt studs, precious metal and precious or semiprecious stones
Trimmings, precious metal: e.g., for canes, umbrellas
Watchbands, precious metal

3914 Silverware, Plated Ware, and Stainless Steel Ware

Establishments primarily engaged in manufacturing flatware (including knives, forks, and spoons), hollowware, ecclesiastical ware, trophies, trays, and related products made of sterling silver; of metal plated with silver, gold, or other metal; of nickel silver; of pewter; or of stainless steel. Also included are establishments primarily engaged in manufacturing table flatware with blades and handles of metal. Establishments primarily engaged in manufacturing other metal cutlery are classified in Industry 3421, and those manufacturing metal trophies, trays and toilet ware, other than silver, nickel silver, pewter, stainless steel, and plated, are classified in Industry 3499.

Carving sets, with metal handles and blades
Cutlery, with metal handles and blades
Ecclesiastical ware: silver, nickel silver, pewter, and plated

Flatware, table: with metal handles and blades
Hollowware, silver, nickel silver, pewter, stainless steel, and plated
Loving cups, silver, nickel silver,

Industry Group No.	Industry No.	
391		**JEWELRY, SILVERWARE, AND PLATED WARE—Con.**

3914 Silverware, Plated Ware, and Stainless Steel Ware—Con.

pewter, and plated
Silversmithing
Silverware: nickel silver, silver plated, solid silver, and sterling
Table and kitchen cutlery, all metal
Toilet ware: silver, nickel silver, pewter, and plated

Trays: silver, nickel silver, pewter, stainless steel, and plated
Trophies: silver, nickel silver, pewter, and plated

3915 Jewelers' Findings and Materials, and Lapidary Work

Establishments primarily engaged in manufacturing unassembled jewelry parts and stock shop products, such as sheet, wire, and tubing; and establishments of lapidaries primarily engaged in cutting, slabbing, tumbling, carving, engraving, polishing or faceting stones from natural or manmade precious or semiprecious gem raw materials, either for sale or on a contract basis for the trade; in recutting, repolishing, and setting gem stones; or in cutting, drilling, and otherwise preparing jewels for instruments, dies, watches, chronometers, and other industrial uses. This industry includes the drilling, sawing, and peeling of real or cultured pearls. Establishments primarily engaged in manufacturing synthetic stones for gem stones and industrial use are classified in Industry 3299, and those manufacturing artificial pearls are classified in Industry 3961.

Diamond cutting and polishing
Diamond points for phonograph needles
Jewel bearings, synthetic
Jewel cutting, drilling, polishing, recutting, or setting
Jewel preparing: for instruments, tools, watches, and jewelry
Jewelers' findings and materials
Jewelry parts, unassembled

Jewelry polishing for the trade
Jewelry soldering for the trade
Lapidary work, contract and other
Machine chain, platinum or karat gold
Pearls: drilling, sawing, or peeling of
Pin stems (jewelry findings)
Soldering for the jewelry trade
Stones: preparation of real and imitation gems for settings

393 MUSICAL INSTRUMENTS

3931 Musical Instruments

Establishments primarily engaged in manufacturing pianos, with or without player attachments; organs; other musical instruments; and parts and accessories for musical instruments.

Accordions and parts
Autophones (organs with perforated music rolls)
Banjos and parts
Bassoons
Bells (musical instruments)
Blowers, pipe organ
Bugles and parts (musical instruments)
Calliopes (steam organs)
Carillon bells
Cellos and parts
Chimes and parts (musical instruments)
Clarinets and parts
Concertinas and parts
Cornets and parts
Cymbals and parts
Drummers' traps
Drums, parts, and accessories (musical instruments)
Electric musical instruments
Electronic musical instruments
Flutes and parts
Fretted instruments and parts

Guitars and parts, electric and nonelectric
Harmonicas
Harps and parts
Harpsichords
Heads, banjo and drum
Mandolins and parts
Marimbas
Mouthpieces for musical instruments
Music rolls, perforated
Music stands
Musical instrument accessories: e.g., reeds, mouthpieces, stands, traps
Musical instruments, including electric and electronic
Oboes
Ocarinas
Octophones
Organ parts and materials, except organ hardware
Organs, all types: e.g., pipe, reed, hand, street, barrel, electronic, player
Percussion musical instruments

Industry Group No.	Industry No.	

393   MUSICAL INSTRUMENTS—Con.

3931   Musical Instruments—Con.

Piano parts and materials, except piano hardware
Pianos, all types: e.g., vertical, grand, spinet, player, coin-operated
Piccolos and parts
Saxophones and parts
Stringed musical instruments and parts
Strings, musical instrument
Synthesizers, music
Trombones and parts

Trumpets and parts
Ukuleles and parts
Vibraphones
Violas and parts
Violins and parts
Woodwind and brass wind musical instrument
Xylophones and parts
Zithers and parts

394   DOLLS, TOYS, GAMES AND SPORTING AND ATHLETIC GOODS

3942   Dolls and Stuffed Toys

Establishments primarily engaged in manufacturing dolls, doll parts, and doll clothing, except doll wigs. Establishments primarily engaged in manufacturing stuffed toys are also included in this industry. Doll wigs are classified in Industry 3999.

Dolls, doll parts, and doll clothing: except wigs

Dolls, miniature: collectors'
Stuffed toys (including animals)

3944   Games, Toys, and Children's Vehicles, Except Dolls and Bicycles

Establishments primarily engaged in manufacturing games and game sets for adults and children, and mechanical and nonmechanical toys. Important products of this industry include games; toy furniture; doll carriages and carts; construction sets; mechanical trains; toy guns and rifles; baby carriages and strollers; children's tricycles, coaster wagons, play cars, sleds, and other children's outdoor wheel goods and vehicles, except bicycles. Included are establishments primarily engaged in manufacturing electronic board games; electronic toys; and electronic game machines, except coin-operated. Establishments primarily engaged in manufacturing dolls and stuffed toys are classified in Industry 3942; those manufacturing bicycles are classified in Industry 3751; those manufacturing sporting and athletic goods for children and adults are classified in Industry 3949; those manufacturing coin-operated game machines are classified in Industry 3999; those manufacturing electronic video game cartridges are classified in Services, Industry 7372; and those manufacturing rubber toys, except dolls, are classified in Industry 3069.

Airplanes, toy
Automobiles and trucks, toy
Automobiles, children's pedal driven
Banks, toy
Baskets, toy
Bells, toy
Blocks, toy
Carriages, baby
Cars, play (children's vehicles)
Craft and hobby kits and sets
Cycles, sidewalk: children's
Darts and dart games
Dishes, toy
Doll carriages and carts
Drums, toy
Electronic game machines, except coin-operated
Electronic toys
Engines, miniature
Erector sets, toy
Games for children and adults: puzzles, bingo, marbles, poker chips, and chess

Gocarts, children's
Guns, toy
Hobbyhorses
Horns, toy
Kites
Magic lanterns (toys)
Models, toy and hobby: e.g., airplane, boat, ship, railroad equipment
Musical instruments, toy
Paint sets, children's
Pistols, toy
Poker chips
Rifles, toy
Rocking horses
Science kits: microscopes, chemistry sets, and natural science sets
Scooters, children's
Sleds, children's
Strollers, baby (vehicles)
Structural toy sets
Sulkies, baby (vehicles)
Tenders, baby (vehicles)
Toys: except dolls, bicycles, rubber toys,

DOLLS, TOYS, GAMES AND SPORTING AND ATHLETIC GOODS—Con.

3944 Games, Toys, and Children's Vehicles, Except Dolls and Bicycles—Con.

and stuffed toys
Trains and equipment, toy: electric and
mechanical
Tricycles, children's
Vehicles except bicycles, children's

Video game machines, except coin-operated
Wagons, children's: coaster, express,
and play
Walkers, baby (vehicles)

3949 Sporting and Athletic Goods, Not Elsewhere Classified

Establishments primarily engaged in manufacturing sporting and athletic goods, not elsewhere classified, such as fishing tackle; golf and tennis goods; baseball, football, basketball, and boxing equipment; roller skates and ice skates; gymnasium and playground equipment; billiard and pool tables; and bowling alleys and equipment. Establishments primarily engaged in manufacturing athletic apparel are classified in Major Group 23; those manufacturing athletic footwear are classified in Industries 3021 and 3149; those manufacturing small arms ammunition are classified in Industry 3482; and those manufacturing small arms are classified in Industry 3484.

Ammunition belts, sporting type: of all
materials
Archery equipment
Arrows, archery
Athletic and sporting goods: except
clothing, footwear, small arms, and
ammunition
Badminton equipment
Bait, fishing: artificial
Balls: baseball, basketball, football,
golf, tennis, pool, and bowling
Baseball equipment and supplies,
except uniforms and footwear
Bases, baseball
Basketballs and basketball equipment
and supplies, except uniforms and
footwear
Baskets, fish and bait
Bats, game: e.g., baseball, softball,
cricket
Billiard and pool balls, cues, cue tips,
and tables
Billiard chalk
Bobsleds
Boomerangs
Bowling alleys and accessories
Bowling pin machines, automatic
Bowling pins
Bows, archery
Boxing equipment
Bridges, billiard and pool
Buckets, fish and bait
Cartridge belts, sporting type
Cases, gun and rod (sporting equip-
ment)
Creels, fish
Cricket equipment
Croquet sets
Decoys, duck and other game birds
Dumbbells
Exercise cycles
Exercising machines
Fencing equipment (sporting goods)
Fishing tackle (except lines, nets, and
seines)
Flies, artificial: for fishing
Floats for fish lines
Footballs and football equipment and
supplies, except uniforms and foot-
wear

Game calls
Gloves, sport and athletic: e.g., boxing,
baseball, racketball, handball
Golf carts, hand
Golfing equipment: e.g., caddy carts
and bags, clubs, tees, balls
Guards: e.g., football, basketball, soccer,
lacrosse
Gymnasium and playground equipment
Helmets, athletic
Hockey equipment, except uniforms
and footwear
Indian clubs
Jogging machines
Lacrosse equipment
Mallets, sports: e.g., polo, croquet
Masks, sports: e.g., baseball, fencing,
hockey
Nets: e.g., badminton, basketball,
tennis—not made in weaving mills
Pads, athletic: e.g., football, basketball,
soccer, lacrosse
Pigeons, clay (targets)
Pinsetters for bowling, automatic
Playground equipment
Polo equipment, except apparel and
footwear
Pool balls, pockets, tables, and equip-
ment
Protectors, sports: e.g., baseball, basket-
ball, hockey
Rackets and frames, sports: e.g., tennis,
badminton, squash, racketball, la-
crosse
Rowing machines
Sailboards
Scoops, crab and fish
Scuba diving equipment, except cloth-
ing
Shafts, golf club
Sinkers (fishing tackle)
Skateboards
Skates and parts, ice and roller
Skin diving equipment, except clothing
Skis and skiing equipment, except ap-
parel
Snowshoes
Soccer equipment, except apparel
Spearguns
Spears, fishing

Industry Group No.	Industry No.	
394		**DOLLS, TOYS, GAMES AND SPORTING AND ATHLETIC GOODS—Con.**

3949 Sporting and Athletic Goods, Not Elsewhere Classified—Con.

Sporting goods: except clothing, footwear, small arms, and ammunition
Squash equipment, except apparel
Stand boards
Sticks, sports: e.g., hockey, lacrosse
Striking (punching) bags
Strings, tennis racket
Surfboards
Swimming pools, plastics
Tables: billiard, pool, bagatelle, and ping pong
Target shooting equipment, except small arms and ammunition
Targets, archery and rifle shooting
Targets, clay
Tennis goods: e.g., balls, frames, rackets
Toboggans
Track and field athletic equipment, except apparel and footwear
Trap racks (clay targets)
Treadmills
Wading pools, plastics coated fabric
Windsurfing boards and equipment

395 PENS, PENCILS, AND OTHER ARTISTS' MATERIALS

3951 Pens, Mechanical Pencils, and Parts

Establishments primarily engaged in manufacturing pens (including ballpoint pens), refill cartridges, mechanical pencils, fine and broad tipped markers, and parts.

Cartridges, refill: for ballpoint pens
Fountain pens and fountain pen desk sets
Markers, soft tip: e.g., felt, fabric, plastics
Meter pens
Nibs (pen points): gold, steel, or other metal
Pencils and pencil parts, mechanical
Penholders and parts
Penpoints: gold, steel, or other metal
Pens and pen parts: fountain, stylographic, and ballpoint

3952 Lead Pencils, Crayons, and Artists' Materials

Establishments primarily engaged in manufacturing lead pencils, pencil leads, and crayons; and materials and equipment for artwork, such as airbrushes, drawing tables and boards, palettes, sketch boxes, pantographs, artists' colors and waxes, pyrography goods, drawing inks, and drafting materials. Establishments primarily engaged in manufacturing mechanical pencils are classified in Industry 3951, and those manufacturing drafting instruments are classified in Industry 3829.

Artists' materials, except drafting instruments
Boards, drawing: artists'
Boxes, sketching and paint
Brushes, air: artists'
Burnishers and cushions, gilders'
Canvas board, artists'
Canvas, artists': prepared on frames
Chalk: e.g., carpenters', blackboard, marking, artists', tailors'
Colors, artists': water and oxide ceramic glass
Crayons: chalk, gypsum, charcoal, fusains, pastel, and wax
Drafting materials, except instruments
Drawing tables and boards, artists'
Easels, artists'
Enamels, china painting
Eraser guides and shields
Frames for artists' canvases
Frisket paper (artists' material)
Gold or bronze mixtures, powders, paints, and sizes: artists'
India ink
Ink, drawing: black and colored
Lettering instruments, artists'
Maulsticks, artists'
Modeling clay
Paints for burnt wood or leather work, platinum
Paints for china painting
Paints, artists'
Palettes, artists'
Pantographs for drafting
Pastels, artists'
Pencil holders
Pencil lead: black, indelible, or colored
Pencils, except mechanical
Pyrography materials
Sizes, artists': gold and bronze
Sketching boxes, artists'
Tracing cloth (drafting material)
Walnut oil, artists'
Water colors, artists'
Wax, artists'

Industry Group No.	Industry No.	
395		**PENS, PENCILS, AND OTHER ARTISTS' MATERIALS—Con.**
	3953	**Marking Devices**

Establishments primarily engaged in manufacturing rubber and metal hand-stamps, dies, and seals; steel letters and figures; and stencils for use in painting or marking. Establishments primarily engaged in manufacturing felt tip markers are classified in Industry 3951.

Dies, hand seal
Figures (marking devices), metal
Hand stamps, stencils, and brands
Irons, marking or branding
Letters (marking devices), metal
Numbering stamps, with rubber type: hand
Pads, inking and stamping
Paper stencils

Printing dies, rubber
Screens, textile printing
Seal presses, notary, hand
Seals, hand (dies)
Stamps, hand: time, date, postmark, cancelling, shoe, and textile marking
Stencils for use in painting and marking: e.g., metal, cardboard

3955   Carbon Paper and Inked Ribbons

Establishments primarily engaged in manufacturing carbon paper; spirit or gelatin process and other stencil paper; and inked or carbon ribbons for business machines.

Carbon paper
Ribbons, inked: e.g., typewriter, adding machine, cash register

Stencil paper for typewriters
Stencil paper, gelatin or spirit process

396   COSTUME JEWELRY, COSTUME NOVELTIES, BUTTONS, AND MISCELLANEOUS NOTIONS, EXCEPT PRECIOUS METAL

3961   Costume Jewelry and Costume Novelties, Except Precious Metal

Establishments primarily engaged in manufacturing costume jewelry, costume novelties, and ornaments made of all materials, except precious metal, precious or semiprecious stones, and rolled goldplate and gold-filled materials. Establishments primarily engaged in manufacturing jewelry of precious and semiprecious metal are classified in 3911; those manufacturing leather compacts and vanity cases are classified in Industry 3172; and those manufacturing synthetic stones for gem stone and industrial use are classified in Industry 3299.

Compacts, except precious metal and solid leather
Costume jewelry, except precious metal and precious or semiprecious stones
Cuff-links and studs, except precious metal and gems
Novelties, costume: except precious metal and gems
Ornaments, costume: except precious metal and gems

Pearls, artificial
Rings, finger: gold-plated wire
Rosaries and other small religious articles, except precious metal
Vanity cases, except precious metal and leather
Watchbands, base metal

3965   Fasteners, Buttons, Needles, and Pins

Establishments primarily engaged in manufacturing notions, such as slide and snap fasteners and zippers, machine and hand needles, pins, hooks and eyes, buckles, buttons, button parts, and button blanks. Establishments primarily engaged in manufacturing these products from precious metals or from precious or semiprecious stones are classified in Industry 3911.

Buckle blanks and molds
Buckles and buckle parts, except shoe buckles
Button backs and parts

Button blanks and molds
Button coloring for the trade
Buttons, except precious metal and precious or semiprecious stones

Industry Group No.	Industry No.	
396		**COSTUME JEWELRY, COSTUME NOVELTIES, BUTTONS, AND MISCELLANEOUS NOTIONS, EXCEPT PRECIOUS METAL—Con.**

3965 Fasteners, Buttons, Needles, and Pins—Con.

Collar buttons, except precious metal and precious or semiprecious stones
Cuff buttons, except precious metal and precious or semiprecious stones
Eyelets, metal: for clothing, fabrics, boots and shoes, and paper
Fasteners: glove, slide, snap, and hook-and-eye
Hair curlers, except equipment designed for beauty parlor use

Hairpins, except rubber
Hooks and eyes
Hooks, crochet
Needles, hand and machine
Pins, except jewelry: toilet, safety, hatpins, and hairpins—steel or brass
Shirt studs, except precious metal and precious or semiprecious stones
Tape, hook-and-eye and snap fastener
Zippers (slide fasteners)

399 MISCELLANEOUS MANUFACTURING INDUSTRIES

3991 Brooms and Brushes

Establishments primarily engaged in manufacturing household, industrial, and street sweeping brooms; and brushes, such as paintbrushes, toothbrushes, toilet brushes, and household and industrial brushes.

Artists' brushes, hand
Brooms, hand and machine: bamboo, wire, fiber, splint, or other material
Brushes for vacuum cleaners, carpet sweepers, and other rotary machines
Brushes, household and industrial
Hair pencils (artists' brushes)
Paint rollers
Paintbrushes

Push brooms
Shaving brushes
Street sweeping brooms, hand and machine
Toilet brushes
Toothbrushes, except electric
Varnish brushes
Whisk brooms

3993 Signs and Advertising Specialties

Establishments primarily engaged in manufacturing electrical, mechanical, cutout, or plate signs and advertising displays, including neon signs, and advertising specialties. Sign painting shops doing business on a custom basis are classified in Services, Industry 7389. Establishments primarily engaged in manufacturing electric signal equipment are classified in Industry 3669, and those manufacturing commercial lighting fixtures are classified in Industry 3646.

Advertising displays, except printed
Advertising specialties—mfpm
Cutouts and displays, window and lobby
Displays, paint process
Electrical signs and advertising displays

Letters for signs, metal
Name plates, metal: except e.g., engraved, etched, chased
Neon signs
Scoreboards, electric
Signs, not made in custom sign painting shops

3995 Burial Caskets

Establishments primarily engaged in manufacturing burial caskets and cases, including shipping cases, of wood or other material except concrete.

Burial cases, metal and wood
Burial vaults, fiberglass

Caskets, metal and wood
Grave vaults, metal

3996 Linoleum, Asphalted-Felt-Base, and Other Hard Surface Floor Coverings, Not Elsewhere Classified

Establishments primarily engaged in manufacturing linoleum, asphalted-felt-base, and other hard surface floor coverings, not elsewhere classified. Establishments primarily engaged in manufacturing rubber floor coverings are

Industry Group No.	Industry No.	
399		**MISCELLANEOUS MANUFACTURING INDUSTRIES—Con.**
	3996	**Linoleum, Asphalted-Felt-Base, and Other Hard Surface Floor Coverings, Not Elsewhere Classified—Con.**

classified in Industry 3069, and those manufacturing cork floor and wall tile are classified in Industry 2499.

Carpets, asphalted-felt-base (linoleum)
Floor coverings, asphalted-felt-base (linoleum)
Hard surfaced floor coverings, except rubber and cork

Linoleum
Tile, floor: supported plastics

3999 Manufacturing Industries, Not Elsewhere Classified

Establishments primarily engaged in manufacturing miscellaneous fabricated products, including beauty shop and barber shop equipment; hair work; tobacco pipes and cigarette holders; coin-operated amusement machines; matches; candles; lamp shades; feathers; artificial trees and flowers made from all materials, except glass; dressed and dyed furs; umbrellas, parasols, and canes; and other articles, not elsewhere classified.

Advertising curtains
Amusement machines, coin-operated: except coin-operated phonographs
Artificial and preserved flowers, foliage, fruits, and vines: except glass
Artificial flower arrangements
Atomizers, other than medical
Badges for policemen and firemen—metal
Barber shop equipment
Barbers' clippers, hand and electric
Beach umbrellas
Beaded novelties
Beads, unassembled
Beauty shop equipment
Beekeeping supplies, except wood
Bone novelties
Book matches
Boutiquing: for the trade (decorating gift items)
Bric-a-brac
Bristles, dressing of
Burnt wood articles
Buttons: Red Cross, union, and identification
Calendars, framed
Candles
Canes and cane trimmings, except precious metal
Chairs, hydraulic: barber and beauty shop
Christmas tree ornaments, except electrical and glass
Christmas trees, artificial
Cigar and cigarette holders
Cigarette filters, not made in chemical plants
Cigarette lighter flints
Cleaners, pipe and cigarette holder
Combs, except hard rubber
Curlers, hair: designed for beauty parlors
Curls, artificial (hair)
Decalcomania work, except on china or glass: for the trade
Desk pads, except paper
Doll wigs
Down (feathers)
Dressing of furs: bleaching, blending, currying, scraping, and tanning

Driers, hair: designed for beauty parlors
Dusters, feather
Embroidery kits
Feathers: curling, dyeing, and renovating—for the trade
Figures, wax: mannikins
Fingerprint equipment, except cameras and optical equipment
Fire extinguishers, portable
Flocking metal products for the trade
Fly swatters
Forms: display, dress, and show—except shoe display forms
Frames and handles, handbag and luggage: except precious metal
Fruits, artificial, except glass
Fur stripping
Furniture, beauty shop and barber shop
Furs, dressed: bleached, curried, scraped, tanned, and dyed
Games, coin-operated: pinball and other
Globes, geographical
Gold stamping for the trade, except books
Grasses, artificial and preserved: except glass
Grenades, hand (fire extinguishers)
Grinding purchased nut shells
Hair clippers for human use, hand and electric
Hair goods: braids, nets, switches, toupees, and wigs
Hair, dressing of, for the trade
Hairpin mountings
Hat blocks and display forms
Honeycomb foundations (beekeepers' supplies)
Hosiery kits, sewing and mending
Identification plates
Identification tags, except paper
Lamp shade frames
Lamp shades: except metal and glass
Lighters, cigar and cigarette: except precious metal and electric
Mannikins and display forms
Marionettes (puppets)
Massage machines, electric: designed for beauty and barber shops
Matches and match books

Industry
Group
No.
399

Industry
No.

MISCELLANEOUS MANUFACTURING INDUSTRIES—Con.

3999   Manufacturing Industries, Not Elsewhere Classified—Con.

Military insignia, except textile
Models, except toy and hobby
Mosaics: ivory, shell, horn, and bone
Mountings, comb and hairpin: except precious metal
Music boxes
Musical chests
Novelties: bone, beaded, and shell
Pads, permanent waving
Painting instrument dials, for the trade
Parasols and frames: handles, parts, and trimmings—except precious metal
Pelts: scraping, currying, tanning, bleaching, and dyeing
Permanent wave equipment and machines
Picture plaques, laminated
Pipes, pipestems, and bits: tobacco—except hard rubber
Plaques, picture: laminated
Plumes, feather
Preparation of slides and exhibits, for classroom use
Printing eyeglass frames for the trade
Puppets
Scenery for theaters, opera houses, halls, and schools
Sewing kits, novelty: other than sewing cases and cabinets
Shades, lamp and candle: except glass and metal

Shell novelties
Shoe patterns
Slot machines
Smokers, bee (beekeepers' supplies)
Soap dispensers
Sponges, bleaching and dyeing of
Stage hardware and equipment, except lighting equipment
Stereographs, photographic
Sterilizers, beauty and barber shop
Straw goods
Stringing beads for the trade
Tape measures
Tear gas devices and equipment
Tinsel
Transformations, hair
Treating clock and watch dials with luminous material
Trees, Christmas, artificial
Trimmings, feather
Umbrellas and parts, except precious metal
Umbrellas: beach, garden, and wagon
Veils made of hair
Vibrators, electric: designed for beauty and barber shops
Walnut shell flour
Wigs, including doll wigs, toupees, or wiglets, except custom made
Wind chimes
Wool pulling
Wreaths, artificial

DIVISION E

Transportation, Communications, Electric, Gas, and Sanitary Services

The Division as a Whole

This division includes establishments providing, to the general public or to other business enterprises, passenger and freight transportation, communications services, or electricity, gas, steam, water or sanitary services, and all establishments of the United States Postal Service.

For many of the industries in this division, the establishments have activities, workers, and physical facilities distributed over an extensive geographic area. For this division, the establishment is represented by a relatively permanent office, shop, station, terminal, or warehouse, etc. that is either (1) directly responsible for supervising such activities or (2) the base from which personnel operate to carry out these activities.

Many of the industries are engaged in various related activities. For example, establishments of communications, pipeline, and utility enterprises include a variety of activities, such as power generation, pumping, transmission, and distribution. Establishments primarily engaged in such activities are all classified in this division. Establishments primarily engaged in new or replacement construction for establishments of these types of enterprises are classified as operating establishments in Division C, Construction. Locations engaged in activities such as sales of electric appliances to household consumers are classified in Division G, Retail Trade.

The establishments classified in this division furnish services to the general public or to other business enterprises; establishments which furnish similar services only to other establishments of the same enterprise are classified as auxiliary to the establishments or units of the enterprise which they serve. However, separate establishments primarily engaged in long-distance trucking, stevedoring, water transportation, or pipeline transportation are classified according to their activity and not as auxiliaries, even though they serve only establishments of the same enterprise.

Major Group 40.—RAILROAD TRANSPORTATION

The Major Group as a Whole

This major group includes establishments furnishing transportation by line-haul railroad, and switching and terminal establishments. Railways serving a single municipality, contiguous municipalities, or a municipality and its suburban areas are classified in Major Group 41. Other services related to railroad transportation are classified in Major Group 47. Lessors of railroad property are classified in Real Estate, Industry 6517.

Industry Group No.	Industry No.	

401 **RAILROADS**

4011 **Railroads, Line-Haul Operating**

Establishments primarily engaged in line-haul railroad passenger and freight operations. Railways primarily engaged in furnishing passenger transportation confined principally to a single municipality, contiguous municipalities, or a municipality and its suburban areas are classified in Major Group 41.

Electric railroads, line-haul operating
Interurban railways

Railroads, line-haul operating

4013 **Railroad Switching and Terminal Establishments**

Establishments primarily engaged in the furnishing of terminal facilities for rail passenger or freight traffic for line-haul service, and in the movement of railroad cars between terminal yards, industrial sidings and other local sites. Terminal companies do not necessarily operate any vehicles themselves, but may operate the stations and terminals. Lessors of railway property are classified in Real Estate, Industry 6517.

Belt line railroads
Logging railroads
Railroad terminals

Stations operated by railway terminal companies

Major Group 41.—LOCAL AND SUBURBAN TRANSIT AND INTERURBAN HIGHWAY PASSENGER TRANSPORTATION

The Major Group as a Whole

This major group includes establishments primarily engaged in furnishing local and suburban passenger transportation, such as those providing passenger transportation within a single municipality, contiguous municipalities, or a municipality and its suburban areas, by bus, rail, or subway, either separately or in combination, and establishments engaged in furnishing transportation to local scenic features. Also included are establishments primarily engaged in furnishing highway passenger transportation and establishments furnishing highway passenger terminal or maintenance facilities. Intercity bus lines are included in this major group, but interurban railways are classified in Major Group 40.

Industry Group No.	Industry No.	
411		**LOCAL AND SUBURBAN PASSENGER TRANSPORTATION**

Establishments primarily engaged in furnishing road or rail passenger transportation confined principally to a municipality, contiguous municipalities, or a municipality and its suburban areas, other than by taxicab, school bus, or charter service. Establishments primarily engaged in furnishing local and suburban passenger transportation by water are classified in Major Group 44 and those providing local and suburban transportation by air are classified in Major Group 45.

4111 Local and Suburban Transit

Establishments primarily engaged in furnishing local and suburban mass passenger transportation over regular routes and on regular schedules, with operations confined principally to a municipality, contiguous municipalities, or a municipality and its suburban areas. Also included in this industry are establishments primarily engaged in furnishing passenger transportation by automobile, bus, or rail to, from, or between airports or rail terminals, over regular routes, and those providing bus and rail commuter services.

Airport limousine scheduled service
Airport transportation service, local: road or rail
Bus line operation, local
Cable cars, except aerial, amusement and scenic
City and suburban bus line operation
Commuter bus operation
Commuter rail passenger operation
Elevated railway operation
Local railway passenger operation
Monorails, regular route: except amusement and scenic
Passenger transportation, regular route, road or rail: between airports and terminals
Streetcar operation
Suburban and urban railway operation
Subway operation
Trolley operation, except amusement and scenic

4119 Local Passenger Transportation, Not Elsewhere Classified

Establishments primarily engaged in furnishing miscellaneous passenger transportation, where such operations are principally within a municipality, contiguous municipalities, or a municipality and its suburban areas. Establishments primarily engaged in renting passenger automobiles without drivers are classified in Services, Industry Group 751. Establishments primarily oper-

411   **LOCAL AND SUBURBAN PASSENGER TRANSPORTATION—Con.**

4119   **Local Passenger Transportation, Not Elsewhere Classified—Con.**

ating ski lifts, tows, and other recreational lifts are classified in Services, Industry 7999.

Aerial tramways, except amusement and scenic	Cog railways, except amusement and scenic
Ambulance service, road	Hearse rental with drivers
Automobile rental with drivers	Limousine rental with drivers
Cable cars, aerial: except amusement and scenic	Sightseeing buses
	Vanpool operation

412   **TAXICABS**

4121   **Taxicabs**

Establishments primarily engaged in furnishing passenger transportation by automobiles not operated on regular schedules or between fixed terminals. Taxicab fleet owners and organizations are included, regardless of whether drivers are hired or rent their cabs or are otherwise compensated. Establishments primarily engaged in furnishing passenger transportation by automobile or bus, to, from, or between airports or rail terminals, over regular routes, are classified in Industry 4111. Taxicab associations and similar organizations which do not operate taxicabs, but supply maintenance and repair services to their members, are classified in Industry 4173.

Taxicab operation

413   **INTERCITY AND RURAL BUS TRANSPORTATION**

4131   **Intercity and Rural Bus Transportation**

Establishments primarily engaged in furnishing bus transportation, over regular routes and on regular schedules, the operations of which are principally outside a single municipality, outside one group of contiguous municipalities, and outside a single municipality and its suburban areas. Charter bus transportation services are classified in Industry Group 414.

Intercity bus lines	Interurban bus lines
Interstate bus lines	

414   **BUS CHARTER SERVICE**

4141   **Local Bus Charter Service**

Establishments primarily engaged in furnishing local bus charter service where such operations are principally within a single municipality, contiguous municipalities, or a municipality and its suburban areas.

Bus charter service, local

4142   **Bus Charter Service, Except Local**

Establishments primarily engaged in furnishing bus charter service, except local, where such operations are principally outside a single municipality, outside one group of contiguous municipalities, and outside a single municipality and its suburban areas.

Bus charter service, except local

Industry
Group   Industry
No.   No.

415   SCHOOL BUSES

4151   School Buses

Establishments primarily engaged in operating buses to transport pupils to and from school. School bus establishments operated by educational institutions should be treated as auxiliaries.

School buses

417   TERMINAL AND SERVICE FACILITIES FOR MOTOR VEHICLE PASSENGER TRANSPORTATION

4173   Terminal and Service Facilities for Motor Vehicle Passenger Transportation

Establishments primarily engaged in the operation of motor vehicle passenger terminals and of maintenance and service facilities, not operated by companies that also furnish motor vehicle passenger transportation. Establishments that are owned by motor vehicle passenger transportation companies and are primarily engaged in operating terminals for use of such vehicles are classified in the same industry as the establishments providing the motor vehicle transportation. Separate maintenance and service facilities operated by companies furnishing motor vehicle passenger transportation should be treated as auxiliaries. Establishments which provide motor vehicle maintenance or service for the general public are classified in Services, Industry Group 753.

Bus terminal operation
Maintenance facilities for motor vehicle
    passenger transportation

Major Group 42.—MOTOR FREIGHT TRANSPORTATION AND WAREHOUSING

The Major Group as a Whole

This major group includes establishments furnishing local or long-distance trucking or transfer services, or those engaged in the storage of farm products, furniture and other household goods, or commercial goods of any nature. The operation of terminal facilities for handling freight, with or without maintenance facilities, is also included. Establishments primarily engaged in the storage of natural gas are classified in Industry 4922. Field warehousing is classified in Services, Industry 7389. Establishments of the United States Postal Service are classified in Major Group 43.

Industry
Group   Industry
No.   No.

421   **TRUCKING AND COURIER SERVICES, EXCEPT AIR**

     4212   **Local Trucking Without Storage**

Establishments primarily engaged in furnishing trucking or transfer services without storage for freight generally weighing more than 100 pounds, in a single municipality, contiguous municipalities, or a municipality and its suburban areas. Establishments primarily engaged in furnishing local courier services for letters, parcels, and packages generally weighing less than 100 pounds are classified in Industry 4215; those engaged in collecting and disposing of refuse by processing or destruction of materials are classified in Industry 4953; those engaged in removing overburden from mines or quarries are classified in Division B, Mining; and construction contractors hauling dirt and rock as a part of their construction activity are classified in Division C, Construction.

Baggage transfer	Hauling, by dump truck
Carting, by truck or horse drawn wagon	Local trucking, without storage
	Log trucking
Debris removal, local carting only	Mail carriers, bulk, contract: local
Draying, local: without storage	Refuse, local collecting and transporting: without disposal
Farm to market hauling	
Furniture moving, local: without storage	Rental of trucks with drivers
	Safe moving, local
Garbage, local collecting and transporting: without disposal	Star routes, local
	Truck rental for local use, with drivers
Hauling live animals, local	Trucking timber

     4213   **Trucking, Except Local**

Establishments primarily engaged in furnishing "over-the-road" trucking services or trucking services and storage services, including household goods either as common carriers or under special or individual contracts or agreements, for freight generally weighing more than 100 pounds. Such operations are principally outside a single municipality, outside one group of contiguous municipalities, or outside a single municipality and its suburban areas. Establishments primarily engaged in furnishing air courier services for individually addressed letters, parcels, and packages generally weighing less than 100 pounds are classified in Industry 4513 and other courier services for individually addressed letters, parcels, and packages generally weighing less than 100 pounds are classified in Industry 4215.

Industry Group No.	Industry No.	
421		**TRUCKING AND COURIER SERVICES, EXCEPT AIR—Con.**
	4213	**Trucking, Except Local—Con.**

Long-distance trucking
Over-the-road trucking
Trucking rental with drivers, except for
   local use

Trucking, except local

4214 Local Trucking With Storage

Establishments primarily engaged in furnishing both trucking and storage services, including household goods, within a single municipality, contiguous municipalities, or a municipality and its suburban areas. Establishments primarily engaged in furnishing warehousing and storage of household goods when not combined with trucking are classified in Industry 4226. Establishments primarily engaged in furnishing local courier services for letters, parcels, and packages weighing less than 100 pounds are classified in Industry 4215.

Furniture moving, local: combined with
   storage
Household goods moving, local: combined with storage

Trucking, local: combined with storage

4215 Courier Services, Except by Air

Establishments primarily engaged in the delivery of individually addressed letters, parcels, and packages (generally under 100 pounds), except by means of air transportation or by the United States Postal Service. Delivery is usually made by street or highway within a local area or between cities. Establishments primarily engaged in furnishing air delivery of individually addressed letters, parcels, and packages, except by the United States Postal Service, are classified in Industry 4513, and establishments of the United States Postal Service are classified in Industry 4311. Establishments primarily engaged in the delivery of advertising and other unaddressed letters, parcels, and packages are classified in Industry 7319. Establishments primarily engaged in undertaking the transportation of goods from shippers to receivers for a charge covering the entire transportation, but making use of other transportation establishments to effect the entire delivery, are classified in Industry 4731. Establishments primarily engaged in furnishing armored car services are classified in Services, Industry 7381.

Courier services, except by air
Letter delivery, private: except air
Mail delivery, private: except air

Package delivery, private: except air
Parcel delivery, private: except air

422   PUBLIC WAREHOUSING AND STORAGE

4221 Farm Product Warehousing and Storage

Establishments primarily engaged in the warehousing and storage of farm products. Establishments primarily engaged in refrigerated warehousing are classified in Industry 4222.

Bean elevators, except sales
Cotton compresses and warehouses
Farm product warehousing and storage,
   other than cold storage

Grain elevators, storage only
Potato cellars
Tobacco warehousing and storage
Wool and mohair warehousing

422   PUBLIC WAREHOUSING AND STORAGE—Con.

4222   Refrigerated Warehousing and Storage

Establishments primarily engaged in the warehousing and storage of perishable goods under refrigeration. The establishments may also rent locker space for the storage of food products for individual households and provide incidental services for processing, preparing, or packaging such food for storage. Establishments primarily selling frozen foods for home freezers (freezer and locker meat provisioners) are classified in Retail Trade, Industry 5421.

Cheese warehouses	Storage, frozen or refrigerated goods
Cold storage locker rental	Warehousing, cold storage or refrigerated
Food lockers, rental	
Frozen food locker rental	

4225   General Warehousing and Storage

Establishments primarily engaged in the warehousing and storage of a general line of goods. The warehousing of goods at foreign trade zones is classified in Industry 4226. Field warehousing is classified in Services, Industry 7389.

General warehousing and storage	Warehousing, self-storage
Miniwarehouse warehousing	

4226   Special Warehousing and Storage, Not Elsewhere Classified

Establishments primarily engaged in the warehousing and storage of special products, not elsewhere classified, such as household goods, automobiles (dead storage only), furs (for the trade), textiles, whiskey, and goods at foreign trade zones. Warehouses primarily engaged in blending wines are classified in Wholesale Trade, Industry 5182.

Automobile dead storage	Storage of goods at foreign trade zones
Fur storage for the trade	Storage, special: except farm products and cold storage
Furniture storage, without local trucking	Textile warehousing
Household goods warehousing and storage, without local trucking	Warehousing of goods at foreign trade zones
Lumber terminals, storage for hire	Warehousing, special: except farm products and cold storage
Oil and gasoline storage caverns for hire	Whiskey warehousing
Petroleum and chemical bulk stations and terminals for hire	

423   TERMINAL AND JOINT TERMINAL MAINTENANCE FACILITIES FOR MOTOR FREIGHT TRANSPORTATION

4231   Terminal and Joint Terminal Maintenance Facilities for Motor Freight Transportation

Establishments primarily engaged in the operation of terminal facilities used by highway-type property carrying vehicles. Also included are terminals which provide maintenance and service for motor vehicles. Terminals operated by motor freight transportation companies for their own use are classified in Industry Group 421. Separate maintenance and service facilities operated by motor freight transportation companies are classified as auxiliary. Establishments primarily engaged in the repair of trucks are classified in Services, Industry Group 753.

Freight trucking terminals, with or without maintenance facilities

Major Group 43.—UNITED STATES POSTAL SERVICE

The Major Group as a Whole

This major group includes all establishments of the United States Postal Service. Post Office contract stations are classified in Services, Industry 7389. Establishments primarily transporting mail on a contract basis for the Unites States Postal Service are classified in Industry Group 421 and Major Group 45. Private postal services primarily engaged in the delivery of unaddressed advertising materials are classified in Services, Industry 7319, and private establishments delivering individually addressed letters, parcels, and packages are classified in Industry Group 421 and Major Group 45.

Industry Group No.	Industry No.	
431		**UNITED STATES POSTAL SERVICE**
	4311	**United States Postal Service**

This industry includes all establishments of the U.S. Postal Service.

United States Postal Service

Major Group 44.—WATER TRANSPORTATION

The Major Group as a Whole

This major group includes establishments engaged in freight and passenger transportation on the open seas or inland waters, and establishments furnishing such incidental services as lighterage, towing, and canal operation. This major group also includes excursion boats, sightseeing boats, and water taxis. Cargo handling operations when carried on by transportation companies and separately reported are classified in Industry 4491. When separate reports for cargo handling are not available, these operations are classified with the transportation establishment. Establishments engaged in the operation of charter or party fishing boats are classified in Services, Industry 7999.

Industry Group No.	Industry No.	

441   **DEEP SEA FOREIGN TRANSPORTATION OF FREIGHT**

      4412   **Deep Sea Foreign Transportation of Freight**

Establishments primarily engaged in operating vessels for the transportation of freight on the deep seas between the United States and foreign ports. Establishments operating vessels for the transportation of freight which travel to foreign ports and also to noncontiguous territories are classified in this industry.

Deep sea foreign transportation of
   freight

442   **DEEP SEA DOMESTIC TRANSPORTATION OF FREIGHT**

      4424   **Deep Sea Domestic Transportation of Freight**

Establishments primarily engaged in operating vessels for the transportation of freight on the deep seas between ports of the United States, the Panama Canal Zone, Puerto Rico, and United States island possessions or protectorates. Also included are operations limited to the coasts of Alaska, Hawaii, or Puerto Rico. Establishments performing transportation of freight on the intracoastal waterways paralleling the Atlantic and Gulf coasts are classified in Industry 4449.

Coastwise transportation of freight	Intercoastal transportation of freight
Domestic freight transportation, deep sea	Water transportation of freight to non-contiguous territories

443   **FREIGHT TRANSPORTATION ON THE GREAT LAKES—ST. LAWRENCE SEAWAY**

      4432   **Freight Transportation on the Great Lakes—St. Lawrence Seaway**

Establishments primarily engaged in the transportation of freight on the Great Lakes and the St. Lawrence Seaway, either between United States ports or between United States and Canadian ports.

Great Lakes and St. Lawrence Seaway
   freight transportation

444   **WATER TRANSPORTATION OF FREIGHT, NOT ELSEWHERE CLASSIFIED**

   4449   Water Transportation of Freight, Not Elsewhere Classified

Establishments primarily engaged in the transportation of freight on all inland waterways, including the intracoastal waterways on the Atlantic and Gulf Coasts. Transportation of freight on the Great Lakes and the St. Lawrence Seaway is classified in Industry 4432. Establishments primarily engaged in providing lighterage and towing or tugboat services are classified in Industry Group 449.

Canal barge operations
Canal freight transportation
Intracoastal freight transportation
Lake freight transportation, except on the Great Lakes

Log rafting and towing
River freight transportation, except on the St. Lawrence Seaway
Transportation of freight on bays and sounds of the oceans

448   **WATER TRANSPORTATION OF PASSENGERS**

   4481   Deep Sea Transportation of Passengers, Except by Ferry

Establishments primarily engaged in operating vessels for the transportation of passengers on the deep seas.

Deep sea transportation of passengers

   4482   Ferries

Establishments primarily engaged in operating ferries for the transportation of passengers or vehicles. Establishments primarily engaged in providing lighterage services are classified in Industry 4499.

Car lighters (ferries)
Ferries, operation of

Railroad ferries

   4489   Water Transportation of Passengers, Not Elsewhere Classified

Establishments primarily engaged in furnishing water transportation of passengers, not elsewhere classified.

Airboats (swamp buggy rides)
Excursion boat operations
Passenger water transportation on rivers and canals

Sightseeing boats
Water taxis, operation of

449   **SERVICES INCIDENTAL TO WATER TRANSPORTATION**

   4491   Marine Cargo Handling

Establishments primarily engaged in activities directly related to marine cargo handling from the time cargo, for or from a vessel, arrives at shipside, dock, pier, terminal, staging area, or in-transit area until cargo loading or unloading operations are completed. Included in this industry are establishments primarily engaged in the transfer of cargo between ships and barges, trucks, trains, pipelines, and wharfs. Cargo handling operations carried on by transportation companies and separately reported are classified here. This industry includes the operation and maintenance of piers, docks, and associated buildings and facilities; but lessors of such facilities are classified in Real Estate, Industry 6512.

Docks, including buildings and facilities: operation and maintenance
Loading vessels
Marine cargo handling
Piers, including buildings and facilities: operation and maintenance

Ship hold cleaning
Stevedoring
Unloading vessels
Waterfront terminal operation

Industry Group No.	Industry No.	
449		SERVICES INCIDENTAL TO WATER TRANSPORTATION—Con.

4492 Towing and Tugboat Services

Establishments primarily engaged in furnishing marine towing and tugboat services in the performance of auxiliary or terminal services in harbor areas. The vessels used in performing these services do not carry cargo or passengers.

Docking of ocean vessels	Towing services, marine
Shifting of floating equipment within harbors	Tugboat service
	Undocking of ocean vessels

4493 Marinas

Establishments primarily engaged in operating marinas. These establishments rent boat slips and store boats, and generally perform a range of other services including cleaning and incidental boat repair. They frequently sell food, fuel, and fishing supplies, and may sell boats. Establishments primarily engaged in building or repairing boats and ships are classified in Manufacturing, Industry Group 373. Establishments primarily engaged in the operation of charter or party fishing boats or rental of small recreational boats are classified in Services, Industry 7999.

Boat yards, storage and incidental repair	Marine basins, operation of
Marinas	Yacht basins, operation of

4499 Water Transportation Services, Not Elsewhere Classified

Establishments primarily engaged in furnishing miscellaneous services incidental to water transportation, not elsewhere classified, such as lighterage, boat hiring, except for pleasure; chartering of vessels; canal operation; ship cleaning, except hold cleaning; and steamship leasing. Establishments primarily engaged in ship hold cleaning are classified in Industry 4491; and those primarily engaged in the operation of charter or party fishing boats or rental of small recreational boats are classified in Services, Industry 7999.

Boat cleaning	Marine salvaging
Boat hiring, except pleasure	Marine surveyors, except cargo
Boat livery, except pleasure	Marine wrecking: ships for scrap
Boat rental, commercial	Piloting vessels in and out of harbors
Canal operation	Ship cleaning, except hold cleaning
Cargo salvaging, from distressed vessels	Ship registers: survey and classification
Chartering of commercial boats	of ships and marine equipment
Dismantling ships	Steamship leasing
Lighterage	
Marine railways for drydocking, operation of	

Major Group 45.—TRANSPORTATION BY AIR

The Major Group as a Whole

This major group includes establishments engaged in furnishing domestic and foreign transportation by air and also those operating airports and flying fields and furnishing terminal services. Establishments primarily engaged in performing services which may incidentally use airplanes (e.g., crop dusting and aerial photography) are classified according to the service performed.

Industry Group No.	Industry No.	

451   **AIR TRANSPORTATION, SCHEDULED, AND AIR COURIER SERVICES**

     4512   **Air Transportation, Scheduled**

Establishments primarily engaged in furnishing air transportation over regular routes and on regular schedules. This industry includes Alaskan carriers operating over regular or irregular routes.

Air cargo carriers, scheduled

Air passenger carriers, scheduled

     4513   **Air Courier Services**

Establishments primarily engaged in furnishing air delivery of individually addressed letters, parcels, and packages (generally under 100 pounds), except by the U.S. Postal Service. While these establishments deliver letters, parcels, and packages by air, the initial pick-up and the final delivery are often made by other modes of transportation, such as by truck, bicycle, or motorcycle. Separate establishments of air courier companies engaged in providing pick-up and delivery only; "drop-off points"; or distribution centers are all classified in this industry. Establishments of the U.S. Postal Service are classified in Industry 4311; and establishments furnishing delivery of individually addressed letters, parcels, or packages (generally under 100 pounds) other than by air are classified in Industry 4215. Establishments primarily engaged in undertaking the transportation of goods from shippers to receivers for charges covering the entire transportation, but making use of other transportation establishments to effect the entire delivery, are classified in Industry 4731.

Courier services, air
Letter delivery, private: air

Package delivery, private: air
Parcel delivery, private: air

452   **AIR TRANSPORTATION, NONSCHEDULED**

     4522   **Air Transportation, Nonscheduled**

Establishments primarily engaged in furnishing nonscheduled air transportation. Also included in this industry are establishments primarily engaged in furnishing airplane sightseeing services, air taxi services and helicopter passenger transportation services to, from, or between local airports, whether or not scheduled.

Air cargo carriers, nonscheduled
Air passenger carriers, nonscheduled
Air taxi services
Ambulance services, air

Flying charter services
Helicopter carriers
Sightseeing airplane services

458   AIRPORTS, FLYING FIELDS, AND AIRPORT TERMINAL SERVICES

4581   Airports, Flying Fields, and Airport Terminal Services

Establishments primarily engaged in operating and maintaining airports and flying fields; in servicing, repairing (except on a factory basis), maintaining, and storing aircraft; and in furnishing coordinated handling services for airfreight or passengers at airports. This industry also includes private establishments primarily engaged in air traffic control operations. Government air traffic control operations are classified in Public Administration, Industry 9621. Aircraft modification centers and establishments primarily engaged in factory type overhaul of aircraft are classified in Manufacturing, Major Group 37, and flying fields maintained by aviation clubs are classified in Services, Industry 7997.

Air traffic control, except government
Aircraft cleaning and janitorial service
Aircraft servicing and repairing, except
  on a factory basis
Aircraft storage at airports
Aircraft upholstery repair
Airfreight handling at airports

Airport hangar rental
Airport leasing, if operating airport
Airport terminal services
Airports
Flying fields, except those maintained
  by aviation clubs
Hangar operation

Major Group 46.—PIPELINES, EXCEPT NATURAL GAS

The Major Group as a Whole

This major group includes establishments primarily engaged in the pipeline transportation of petroleum and other commodities, except natural gas. Pipelines operated by petroleum producing or refining companies and separately reported are included. Establishments primarily engaged in natural gas transmission are classified in Industry 4922.

Industry
Group
No.

Industry
No.

461   **PIPELINES, EXCEPT NATURAL GAS**

4612 Crude Petroleum Pipelines

Establishments primarily engaged in the pipeline transportation of crude petroleum. Field gathering lines are classified in Mining, Major Group 13.

Crude petroleum pipelines

4613 Refined Petroleum Pipelines

Establishments primarily engaged in the pipeline transportation of refined products of petroleum, such as gasoline and fuel oil.

Gasoline pipelines, common carriers   Refined petroleum pipelines

4619 Pipelines, Not Elsewhere Classified

Establishments primarily engaged in the pipeline transportation of commodities, except crude petroleum, refined products of petroleum, and natural gas. Establishments primarily engaged in the pipeline transportation of refined petroleum are classified in Industry 4613, and those engaged in natural gas transmission are classified in Industry 4922.

Coal pipeline operation   Slurry pipeline operation
Pipeline operation, except petroleum
  and natural gas pipelines

Major Group 47.—TRANSPORTATION SERVICES

The Major Group as a Whole

This major group includes establishments furnishing services incidental to transportation, such as forwarding and packing services, and the arrangement of passenger and freight transportation.

Industry Group No.   Industry No.

472   ARRANGEMENT OF PASSENGER TRANSPORTATION

4724   Travel Agencies

Establishments primarily engaged in furnishing travel information and acting as agents in arranging tours, transportation, rental of cars, and lodging for travelers. Tour operators primarily engaged in arranging and assembling tours for sale through travel agents are classified in Industry 4725.

Tourist agencies for the arrangement of transportation, lodging, and car rental

Travel agencies

4725   Tour Operators

Establishments primarily engaged in arranging and assembling tours for sale through travel agents. Tour operators primarily engaged in selling their own tours directly to travelers are also included in this industry.

Tour operation (travel)
Tours, except sightseeing buses, boats, and airplanes

Wholesale tour operator

4729   Arrangement of Passenger Transportation, Not Elsewhere Classified

Establishments primarily engaged in arranging passenger transportation, not elsewhere classified, such as ticket offices, not operated by transportation companies, for railroads, buses, ships, and airlines.

Airline ticket offices, not operated by transportation companies
Arrangement of carpools and vanpools
Bus ticket offices, not operated by transportation companies

Railroad ticket offices, not operated by transportation companies
Steamship ticket offices, not operated by transportation companies

473   ARRANGEMENT OF TRANSPORTATION OF FREIGHT AND CARGO

4731   Arrangement of Transportation of Freight and Cargo

Establishments primarily engaged in furnishing shipping information and acting as agents in arranging transportation for freight and cargo. Also included in this industry are freight forwarders which undertake the transportation of goods from the shippers to receivers for a charge covering the entire transportation, and, in turn, make use of the services of other transportation establishments as instrumentalities in effecting delivery.

Agents, shipping
Auditors, freight rate
Brokers, shipping
Brokers, transportation
Consultants, tariff
Customhouse brokers
Customs clearance of freight
Domestic forwarding
Foreign forwarding
Freight agencies, railroad: not operated by railroad companies

Freight consolidation
Freight forwarding
Freight rate auditors
Freight rate information service
Shipping documents preparation
Tariff consultant
Tariff rate information service
Transport clearinghouse
Transportation rate services

Industry Group No.	Industry No.	
474		**RENTAL OF RAILROAD CARS**

4741 Rental of Railroad Cars

Establishments primarily engaged in renting railroad cars, whether or not also performing services connected with the use thereof, or in performing services connected with the rental of railroad cars. Establishments, such as banks and insurance companies, which purchase and lease railroad cars as investments are classified based on their primary activity.

Grain leveling in railroad cars
Grain trimming service for railroad shipment
Precooling of fruits and vegetables in connection with transportation

Railroad car cleaning, icing, ventilating, and heating
Rental of railroad cars

478 MISCELLANEOUS SERVICES INCIDENTAL TO TRANSPORTATION

4783 Packing and Crating

Establishments primarily engaged in packing, crating, and otherwise preparing goods for shipping. Establishments primarily engaged in packaging and labeling merchandise for purposes other than shipping (retail packaging) are classified in Industry 7389.

Crating goods for shipping

Packing goods for shipping

4785 Fixed Facilities and Inspection and Weighing Services for Motor Vehicle Transportation

Establishments primarily engaged in the inspection and weighing of goods in connection with transportation or in the operation of fixed facilities for motor vehicle transportation, such as toll roads, highway bridges, and other fixed facilities, except terminals.

Cargo checkers and surveyors, marine
Highway bridges, operation of
Inspection services connected with transportation
Toll bridge operation

Toll roads, operation of
Tunnel operation, vehicular
Weighing services connected with transportation

4789 Transportation Services, Not Elsewhere Classified

Establishments primarily engaged in furnishing transportation or services incidental to transportation, not elsewhere classified. Included in this industry are stockyards that do not buy, sell, or auction livestock; sleeping and dining car operations not performed by railroads; and horse-drawn cabs and carriages for hire.

Cabs, horse-drawn: for hire
Car loading
Carriages, horse-drawn: for hire
Cleaning railroad ballasts
Dining car operations, not performed by line-haul railroad companies
Freight car loading and unloading, not trucking
Parlor car operations, not performed by line-haul railroad companies
Pipeline terminal facilities independently operated

Railroad car repair, on a contract or fee basis
Sleeping car and other passenger car operations, not performed by railroads
Space flight operations, except government
Stockyards, not primarily for fattening or selling livestock

282

Major Group 48.—COMMUNICATIONS

The Major Group as a Whole

This major group includes establishments furnishing point-to-point communications services, whether intended to be received aurally or visually; and radio and television broadcasting. This major group also includes establishments primarily engaged in providing paging and beeper services and those engaged in leasing telephone lines or other methods of telephone transmission, such as optical fiber lines and microwave or satellite facilities, and reselling the use of such methods to others. Establishments primarily engaged in furnishing telephone answering services are classified in Services, Industry 7389.

Industry Group No.	Industry No.	

481   TELEPHONE COMMUNICATIONS

4812   Radiotelephone Communications

Establishments primarily engaged in providing two-way radiotelephone communications services, such as cellular telephone services. This industry also includes establishments primarily engaged in providing telephone paging and beeper services and those engaged in leasing telephone lines or other methods of telephone transmission, such as optical fiber lines and microwave or satellite facilities, and and reselling the use of such methods to others. Establishments primarily engaged in furnishing telephone answering services are classified in Services, Industry 7389.

Beeper (radio pager) communications services
Cellular telephone services

Paging services: radiotelephone
Radiotelephone communications

4813   Telephone Communications, Except Radiotelephone

Establishments primarily engaged in furnishing telephone voice and data communications, except radiotelephone and telephone answering services. This industry also includes establishments primarily engaged in leasing telephone lines or other methods of telephone transmission, such as optical fiber lines and microwave or satellite facilities, and reselling the use of such methods to others. Establishments primarily engaged in furnishing radiotelephone communications are classified in Industry 4812, and those furnishing telephone answering services are classified in Services, Industry 7389.

Data telephone communications
Local telephone communications, except radio telephone
Long distance telephone communications

Voice telephone communications, except radio telephone

482   TELEGRAPH AND OTHER MESSAGE COMMUNICATIONS

4822   Telegraph and Other Message Communications

Establishments primarily engaged in furnishing telegraph and other nonvocal message communications services, such as cablegram, electronic mail, and facsimile transmission services.

Cablegram services
Electronic mail services
Facsimile transmission services
Mailgram services
Photograph transmission services
Radio telegraph services

Telegram services
Telegraph cable services
Telegraph services
Teletypewriter services
Telex services

Industry Group No.	Industry No.	
483		**RADIO AND TELEVISION BROADCASTING STATIONS**
	4832	**Radio Broadcasting Stations**

Establishments primarily engaged in broadcasting aural programs by radio to the public. Included in this industry are commercial, religious, educational, and other radio stations. Also included here are establishments primarily engaged in radio broadcasting and which produce radio program materials. Separate establishments primarily engaged in producing radio program materials are classified in Services, Industry 7922.

Radio broadcasting stations

4833 Television Broadcasting Stations

Establishments primarily engaged in broadcasting visual programs by television to the public, except cable and other pay television services. Included in this industry are commercial, religious, educational, and other television stations. Also included here are establishments primarily engaged in television broadcasting and which produce taped television program materials. Separate establishments primarily engaged in producing taped television program materials are classified in Services, Industry 7812. Establishments primarily engaged in furnishing cable and other pay television services are classified in Industry 4841.

Television broadcasting stations

484 CABLE AND OTHER PAY TELEVISION SERVICES

4841 Cable and Other Pay Television Services

Establishments primarily engaged in the dissemination of visual and textual television programs, on a subscription or fee basis. Included in this industry are establishments which are primarily engaged in cablecasting and which also produce taped program materials. Separate establishments primarily engaged in producing taped television or motion picture program materials are classified in Services, Industry 7812.

Cable television services
Closed circuit television services
Direct broadcast satellite (DBS) services
Multipoint distribution systems (MDS) services

Satellite master antenna systems (SMATV) services
Subscription television services

489 COMMUNICATIONS SERVICES, NOT ELSEWHERE CLASSIFIED

4899 Communications Services, Not Elsewhere Classified

Establishments primarily engaged in furnishing communications services, not elsewhere classified. Establishments primarily engaged in providing online information retrieval services on a contract or fee basis are classified in Services, Industry 7375.

Radar station operation
Radio broadcasting operated by cab companies
Satellite earth stations

Satellite or missile tracking stations, operated on a contract basis
Tracking missiles by telemetry and photography on a contract basis

Major Group 49.—ELECTRIC, GAS, AND SANITARY SERVICES

The Major Group as a Whole

This major group includes establishments engaged in the generation, transmission, and/or distribution of electricity or gas or steam. Such establishments may be combinations of any of the above three services and also include other types of services, such as transportation, communications, and refrigeration. Water and irrigation systems, and sanitary systems engaged in the collection and disposal of garbage, sewage, and other wastes by means of destroying or processing materials, are also included. If one service of a combination system does not constitute 95 percent or more of revenues, the establishment should be classified as a combination in Industry Group 493, with the subgroup being determined by the major service supplied.

Industry Group No.	Industry No.	

491   **ELECTRIC SERVICES**

     4911   **Electric Services**

         Establishments engaged in the generation, transmission, and/or distribution of electric energy for sale.

            Electric power generation, transmission, or distribution

492   **GAS PRODUCTION AND DISTRIBUTION**

     4922   **Natural Gas Transmission**

         Establishments engaged in the transmission and/or storage of natural gas for sale.

            Natural gas storage   Pipelines, natural gas
            Natural gas transmission

     4923   **Natural Gas Transmission and Distribution**

         Establishments engaged in both the transmission and distribution of natural gas for sale.

            Natural gas transmission and distribution

     4924   **Natural Gas Distribution**

         Establishments engaged in the distribution of natural gas for sale.

            Natural gas distribution

     4925   **Mixed, Manufactured, or Liquefied Petroleum Gas Production and/or Distribution**

         Establishments engaged in the manufacture and/or distribution of gas for sale, including mixtures of manufactured with natural gas. Establishments distributing liquefied petroleum (LP) gas in steel containers are classified in Retail Trade, Industry 5984.

            Blue gas, carbureted: production and distribution   Liquefied petroleum (LP) gas, distribution through mains
            Coke oven gas, production and distribution   Manufactured gas production and distribution
            Coke ovens, byproduct: operated for manufacture or distribution of gas   Synthetic natural gas from naphtha, production and distribution
            Gas, mixed natural and manufactured: production and distribution

Industry
Group
No.

Industry
No.

493 COMBINATION ELECTRIC AND GAS, AND OTHER UTILITY SERVICES

Establishments providing electric or gas services in combination with other services. Establishments are classified here only if one service does not constitute 95 percent or more of revenues.

4931 Electric and Other Services Combined

Establishments primarily engaged in providing electric services in combination with other services, with electric services as the major part though less than 95 percent of the total.

Electric and other services combined
(electric less than 95 percent of total)

4932 Gas and Other Services Combined

Establishments primarily engaged in providing gas services in combination with other services, with gas services as the major part though less than 95 percent of the total.

Gas and other services combined (gas
less than 95 percent of total)

4939 Combination Utilities, Not Elsewhere Classified

Establishments primarily engaged in providing combinations of electric, gas, and other services, not elsewhere classified.

Utilities, combination of

494 WATER SUPPLY

4941 Water Supply

Establishments primarily engaged in distributing water for sale for domestic, commercial, and industrial use. Systems distributing water primarily for irrigation service are classified in Industry 4971.

Water supply systems, except irrigation

495 SANITARY SERVICES

4952 Sewerage Systems

Establishments primarily engaged in the collection and disposal of wastes conducted through a sewer system, including such treatment processes as may be provided.

Sewerage systems

4953 Refuse Systems

Establishments primarily engaged in the collection and disposal of refuse by processing or destruction or in the operation of incinerators, waste treatment plants, landfills, or other sites for disposal of such materials. Establishments primarily engaged in collecting and transporting refuse without such disposal are classified in Transportation, Industry 4212.

Acid waste, collection and disposal of
Ashes, collection and disposal of
Dumps, operation of
Garbage: collecting, destroying, and
  processing
Hazardous waste material disposal sites
Incinerator operation

Landfill, sanitary: operation of
Radioactive waste materials, disposal of
Refuse systems
Rubbish collection and disposal
Sludge disposal sites
Street refuse systems
Waste materials disposal at sea

Industry Group No.	Industry No.	

495   **SANITARY SERVICES—Con.**

4959   **Sanitary Services, Not Elsewhere Classified**

Establishments primarily engaged in furnishing sanitary services, not elsewhere classified.

Beach maintenance cleaning	Snowplowing
Malaria control	Sweeping service: road, airport, parking lot, etc.
Mosquito eradication	
Oil spill cleanup	Vacuuming of airport runways

496   **STEAM AND AIR-CONDITIONING SUPPLY**

4961   **Steam and Air-Conditioning Supply**

Establishments engaged in the production and/or distribution of steam and heated or cooled air for sale.

Air-conditioning supply services	Steam heating systems (suppliers of heat)
Cooled air suppliers	
Distribution of cooled air	Steam supply systems, including geothermal
Geothermal steam production	

497   **IRRIGATION SYSTEMS**

4971   **Irrigation Systems**

Establishments primarily engaged in operating water supply systems for the purpose of irrigation. Establishments primarily engaged in operating irrigation systems for others, but which do not themselves provide water, are classified in Agricultural Services, Industry 0721.

Impounding reservoirs, irrigation	Water distribution or supply systems for irrigation
Irrigation system operation	

DIVISION F

Wholesale Trade

The Division as a Whole

This division includes establishments or places of business primarily engaged in selling merchandise to retailers; to industrial, commercial, institutional, farm, construction contractors, or professional business users; or to other wholesalers; or acting as agents or brokers in buying merchandise for or selling merchandise to such persons or companies.

The chief functions of establishments included in Wholesale Trade are selling goods to trading establishments, or to industrial, commercial, institutional, farm, construction contractors, or professional business users; and bringing buyer and seller together. In addition to selling, functions frequently performed by wholesale establishments include maintaining inventories of goods; extending credit; physically assembling, sorting, and grading goods in large lots; breaking bulk and redistribution in smaller lots; delivery; refrigeration; and various types of promotion such as advertising and label designing.

The principal types of establishments included are: (1) merchant wholesalers—wholesalers who take title to the goods they sell, such as wholesale merchants or jobbers, industrial distributors, voluntary group wholesalers, exporters, importers, cash-and-carry wholesalers, drop shippers, truck distributors, retailer cooperative warehouses, terminal elevators, cooperative buying associations, and assemblers, buyers or cooperatives engaged in the marketing of farm products; (2) sales branches and sales offices (but not retail stores) maintained by manufacturing, refining or mining enterprises apart from their plants or mines for the purpose of marketing their products; and (3) agents, merchandise or commodity brokers, and commission merchants.

Establishments primarily engaged in selling merchandise to construction contractors, institutions, industrial users, or businesses are included in Wholesale Trade with a few exceptions. These exceptions are made necessary because of sales to both the general public for personal or household consumption and to businesses, industrial users, or construction contractors. These exceptions are lumber yards; paint, glass, and wallpaper stores; typewriter stores; stationery stores; and gasoline service stations which are classified in Retail Trade, Division G.

However, establishments that sell similar products only to institutions, industrial users, and establishments that sell merchandise for use exclusively by business establishments or to other wholesalers are classified in Wholesale Trade. Establishments primarily engaged in selling such merchandise as plumbing equipment; electrical supplies; used automobile parts; and office furniture are classified in Whole-

287

sale Trade, even if a higher proportion of their sales is made to individuals for household use. Establishments primarily engaged in the wholesale distribution of used products are classified on the basis of the products sold.

Guidelines for the classification of establishments primarily engaged in the wholesale distribution and construction or installation of equipment manufactured by other establishments are outlined in the Introduction to Division C, Construction.

Major Group 50.—WHOLESALE TRADE—DURABLE GOODS

The Major Group as a Whole

This major group includes establishments primarily engaged in the wholesale distribution of durable goods.

Industry Group No.	Industry No.	

501   MOTOR VEHICLES AND MOTOR VEHICLE PARTS AND SUPPLIES

5012   Automobiles and Other Motor Vehicles

Establishments primarily engaged in the wholesale distribution of new and used passenger automobiles, trucks, trailers, and other motor vehicles, including motorcycles, motor homes, and snowmobiles. Automotive distributors primarily engaged in selling at retail to individual consumers for personal use, and also selling a limited amount of new and used passenger automobiles and trucks at wholesale, are classified in Retail Trade, Industry 5511.

Ambulances—wholesale
Automobile auction—wholesale
Automobiles—wholesale
Bodies, automotive—wholesale
Buses—wholesale
Campers (pickup coaches) for mounting on trucks—wholesale
Mopeds—wholesale
Motor homes—wholesale
Motor scooters—wholesale
Motor vehicles, commercial—wholesale
Motorcycles—wholesale
Popup campers—wholesale
Recreational vehicles—wholesale
Snowmobiles—wholesale
Taxicabs—wholesale
Trailers for passenger automobiles—wholesale
Truck tractors—wholesale
Truck trailers—wholesale
Trucks—wholesale
Vans—wholesale

5013   Motor Vehicle Supplies and New Parts

Establishments primarily engaged in the wholesale distribution of motor vehicle supplies, accessories, tools, and equipment; and new motor vehicle parts.

Automobile engine testing equipment, electrical—wholesale
Automobile glass—wholesale
Automobile service station equipment—wholesale
Automotive accessories—wholesale
Automotive engines, new—wholesale
Automotive parts, new —wholesale
Automotive stampings—wholesale
Automotive supplies—wholesale
Batteries, automotive—wholesale
Engine electrical equipment, automotive—wholesale
Garage service equipment—wholesale
Hardware, automotive—wholesale
Motorcycle parts—wholesale
Pumps, measuring and dispensing: gasoline and oil—wholesale
Seat belts, automotive—wholesale
Seat covers, automotive—wholesale
Service station equipment, automobile—wholesale
Testing equipment, electrical: automotive—wholesale
Tools and equipment, automotive—wholesale
Wheels, motor vehicle: new—wholesale

5014   Tires and Tubes

Establishments primarily engaged in the wholesale distribution of tires and tubes for passenger and commercial vehicles.

Repair materials, tire and tube—wholesale
Tires and tubes, new—wholesale
Tires, used—wholesale

5015   Motor Vehicle Parts, Used

Establishments primarily engaged in the distribution at wholesale or retail of used motor vehicle parts. This industry includes establishments primarily engaged in dismantling motor vehicles for the purpose of selling parts. Estab-

501 MOTOR VEHICLES AND MOTOR VEHICLE PARTS AND SUPPLIES— Con.

5015 Motor Vehicle Parts, Used—Con.

lishments primarily engaged in dismantling motor vehicles for scrap are classified in Industry 5093.

Automobile engines, used—wholesale or retail
Automobile parts, used—wholesale or retail

Motor vehicle parts, used—wholesale or retail

502 FURNITURE AND HOMEFURNISHINGS

5021 Furniture

Establishments primarily engaged in the wholesale distribution of furniture, including bedsprings, mattresses, and other household furniture; office furniture; and furniture for public parks and buildings. Establishments primarily engaged in the wholesale distribution of partitions, shelving, lockers, and store fixtures are classified in Industry 5046.

Bar furniture—wholesale
Bedsprings—wholesale
Cafeteria furniture—wholesale
Chairs: household, office, and public building—wholesale
Church pews—wholesale
Desks, including school—wholesale
Furniture, juvenile—wholesale

Furniture, unfinished—wholesale
Furniture: household, office, restaurant, and public building—wholesale
Lawn furniture—wholesale
Mattresses—wholesale
School desks—wholesale
Theater seats—wholesale
Waterbeds—wholesale

5023 Homefurnishings

Establishments primarily engaged in the wholesale distribution of homefurnishings and housewares, including antiques; china; glassware and earthenware; lamps (including electric); curtains and draperies; linens and towels; and carpets, linoleum, and all other types of hard and soft surface floor coverings. Establishments primarily engaged in the wholesale distribution of other electrical household goods are classified in Industry 5064, and those distributing precious metal flatware are classified in Industry 5094.

Aluminumware—wholesale
Bedspreads—wholesale
Blankets—wholesale
Carpets—wholesale
China—wholesale
Crockery—wholesale
Curtains—wholesale
Draperies—wholesale
Floor coverings—wholesale
Glassware, household—wholesale
Homefurnishings—wholesale

Kitchen tools and utensils, except precious metal flatware—wholesale
Lamps: floor, boudoir, desk—wholesale
Linens—wholesale
Linoleum—wholesale
Pillowcases—wholesale
Rugs—wholesale
Sheets, textile—wholesale
Slipcovers, furniture—wholesale
Table linens—wholesale

503 LUMBER AND OTHER CONSTRUCTION MATERIALS

5031 Lumber, Plywood, Millwork, and Wood Panels

Establishments, with or without yards, primarily engaged in the wholesale distribution of rough, dressed, and finished lumber (but not timber); plywood; reconstituted wood fiber products; doors and windows and their frames (all materials); wood fencing; and other wood or metal millwork.

Composite board products, wood-based—wholesale
Door frames, all materials—wholesale
Enameled tileboard (hardboard)—wholesale

Fencing, wood—wholesale
Hardboard—wholesale
Kitchen cabinets to be built in—wholesale
Lumber: rough, dressed, and finished—

Industry Group No.	Industry No.	

503   LUMBER AND OTHER CONSTRUCTION MATERIALS—Con.

5031   Lumber, Plywood, Millwork, and Wood Panels—Con.

wholesale
Medium density fiberboard—wholesale
Metal doors, sash and trim—wholesale
Millwork—wholesale
Molding, all materials—wholesale
Paneling, wood—wholesale
Particleboard—wholesale
Plywood—wholesale
Shingles, wood—wholesale

Structural assemblies, prefabricated: wood—wholesale
Veneer—wholesale
Wallboard—wholesale
Window frames, all materials—wholesale
Windows and doors—wholesale
Wood siding—wholesale

5032   Brick, Stone, and Related Construction Materials

Establishments primarily engaged in the wholesale distribution of stone, cement, lime, construction sand, and gravel; brick (except refractory); asphalt and concrete mixtures; and concrete, stone, and structural clay products (other than refractories). Distributors of industrial sand and of refractory materials are classified in Industry 5085. Establishments primarily engaged in producing ready-mixed concrete are classified in Manufacturing, Industry 3273.

Aggregate—wholesale
Asphalt mixtures—wholesale
Blocks, building—wholesale
Brick, except refractory—wholesale
Building stone—wholesale
Cement—wholesale
Ceramic construction materials, except refractory—wholesale
Ceramic wall and floor tile—wholesale
Cinders—wholesale
Clay construction materials, except refractory—wholesale
Concrete building products—wholesale
Concrete mixtures—wholesale
Granite building stone—wholesale
Gravel—wholesale

Lime, except agricultural—wholesale
Limestone—wholesale
Marble building stone—wholesale
Masons' materials—wholesale
Paving mixtures—wholesale
Plaster—wholesale
Sand, construction—wholesale
Sewer pipe, clay—wholesale
Stone, building—wholesale
Stone, crushed or broken—wholesale
Stucco—wholesale
Terra cotta—wholesale
Tile, clay or other ceramic: except refractory—wholesale
Tile, structural clay—wholesale

5033   Roofing, Siding, and Insulation Materials

Establishments primarily engaged in the wholesale distribution of roofing and siding (except wood) and insulation materials.

Asphalt felts and coatings—wholesale
Felts, tarred—wholesale
Fiberglass insulation materials—wholesale
Insulation, thermal—wholesale
Mineral wool insulation materials—wholesale

Roofing, asphalt and sheet metal—wholesale
Shingles, except wood—wholesale
Siding, except wood—wholesale

5039   Construction Materials, Not Elsewhere Classified

Establishments primarily engaged in the wholesale distribution of mobile homes and of construction materials, not elsewhere classified, including prefabricated buildings and glass. Establishments selling construction materials to the general public and known as retail in the trade are classified in Retail Trade, Industry 5211. Establishments primarily engaged in marketing heavy structural metal products are classified in Industry 5051.

Architectural metalwork—wholesale
Awnings—wholesale
Fencing and accessories, wire—wholesale
Glass, flat: except automotive—wholesale
Grain storage bins—wholesale
Metal buildings—wholesale

Mobile homes—wholesale
Plate glass—wholesale
Prefabricated buildings—wholesale
Septic tanks—wholesale
Structural assemblies, prefabricated: nonwood—wholesale
Window glass—wholesale

Industry
Group   Industry
No.   No.

504   PROFESSIONAL AND COMMERCIAL EQUIPMENT AND SUPPLIES

5043   Photographic Equipment and Supplies

Establishments primarily engaged in the wholesale distribution of photographic equipment and supplies. Establishments primarily engaged in the wholesale distribution of photocopy, microfilm, and similar equipment are classified in Industry 5044.

Cameras, equipment, and supplies—wholesale	Motion picture cameras, equipment, and supplies—wholesale
Darkroom apparatus—wholesale	Photographic cameras, projectors, equipment and supplies—wholesale
Developing apparatus, photographic—wholesale	Printing apparatus, photographic—wholesale
Film, photographic—wholesale	Projection apparatus, motion picture and slide: photographic—wholesale
Identity recorders for photographing checks and fingerprints—wholesale	

5044   Office Equipment

Establishments primarily engaged in the wholesale distribution of office machines and related equipment, including photocopy and microfilm equipment and safes and vaults. These establishments frequently also sell office supplies. However, establishments primarily engaged in wholesaling most office supplies are classified in Industry Group 511. Establishments primarily engaged in wholesaling office furniture are classified in Industry 5021, and those wholesaling computers and peripheral equipment are classified in Industry 5045.

Accounting machines—wholesale	Duplicating machines—wholesale
Adding machines—wholesale	Mailing machines—wholesale
Addressing machines—wholesale	Microfilming equipment—wholesale
Bank automatic teller machines—wholesale	Mimeograph equipment—wholesale
Blueprinting equipment—wholesale	Photocopy machines—wholesale
Brownprinting equipment—wholesale	Typewriters—wholesale
Calculating machines—wholesale	Vaults and safes—wholesale
Cash registers—wholesale	Whiteprinting equipment—wholesale

5045   Computers and Computer Peripheral Equipment and Software

Establishments primarily engaged in the wholesale distribution of computers, computer peripheral equipment, and computer software. These establishments frequently also may sell related supplies, but establishments primarily engaged in wholesaling supplies are classified according to the individual product (for example, computer paper in Industry 5112). Establishments primarily engaged in the wholesale distribution of modems and other electronic communications equipment are classified in Industry 5065. Establishment primarily engaged in selling computers and computer peripheral equipment and software for other than business or professional use are classified in Retail Trade, Industry 5734.

Computer terminals—wholesale	Peripheral equipment, computer—wholesale
Computers—wholesale	Printers, computer—wholesale
Disk drives—wholesale	Software, computer—wholesale
Keying equipment—wholesale	

5046   Commercial Equipment, Not Elsewhere Classified

Establishments primarily engaged in the wholesale distribution of commercial and related machines and equipment, not elsewhere classified, such as commercial cooking and food service equipment; partitions, shelving, lockers, and store fixtures; electrical signs; and balances and scales, except laboratory.

Industry
Group
No.

Industry
No.

504 **PROFESSIONAL AND COMMERCIAL EQUIPMENT AND SUPPLIES— Con.**

5046 Commercial Equipment, Not Elsewhere Classified—Con.

Balances, except laboratory—wholesale
Coffee urns, commercial—wholesale
Cooking equipment, commercial— wholesale
Fixtures, store, not refrigerated— wholesale
Food warming equipment, commercial—wholesale
Lockers, not refrigerated—wholesale
Mannequins—wholesale
Merchandising machines, automatic— wholesale

Neon signs—wholesale
Ovens, microwave: commercial—wholesale
Partitions—wholesale
Phonographs, coin-operated—wholesale
Scales, except laboratory—wholesale
Shelving—wholesale
Signs, electrical—wholesale
Soda fountain fixtures, except refrigerated—wholesale
Vending machines—wholesale

5047 Medical, Dental, and Hospital Equipment and Supplies

Establishments primarily engaged in the wholesale distribution of surgical and other medical instruments, apparatus, and equipment; dentist equipment; artificial limbs; operating room and hospital equipment; X-ray machines; and other electromedical equipment and apparatus used by physicians and in hospitals. Also included in this industry are establishments primarily engaged in the wholesale distribution of professional supplies used by medical and dental practitioners.

Baths, whirlpool—wholesale
Beds, hospital—wholesale
Dental equipment—wholesale
Dental laboratory equipment—wholesale
Dentists' professional supplies—wholesale
Diagnostic equipment, medical—wholesale
Electromedical equipment—wholesale
Hearing aids—wholesale
Hospital equipment—wholesale
Hospital furniture—wholesale
Industrial safety devices: first-aid kits, face and eye masks—wholesale

Laboratory equipment, dental and medical—wholesale
Medical equipment—wholesale
Medical glass—wholesale
Orthopedic equipment—wholesale
Patient monitoring equipment—wholesale
Physicians' equipment—wholesale
Physicians' supplies—wholesale
Surgical and medical instruments— wholesale
Surgical equipment—wholesale
Therapy equipment—wholesale
X-ray machines and parts, medical— wholesale

5048 Ophthalmic Goods

Establishments primarily engaged in the wholesale distribution of professional equipment and goods used, prescribed, or sold by ophthalmologists, optometrists, and opticians, including ophthalmic frames, lenses, and sunglass lenses.

Contact lenses—wholesale
Frames, ophthalmic—wholesale
Lenses, ophthalmic—wholesale

Ophthalmic goods—wholesale
Optometric equipment and supplies— wholesale

5049 Professional Equipment and Supplies, Not Elsewhere Classified

Establishments primarily engaged in the wholesale distribution of professional equipment and supplies, not elsewhere classified, such as drafting instruments, laboratory equipment, and scientific instruments.

Analytical instruments: photometers, spectrographs, and chromatographic instruments—wholesale
Architects' equipment and supplies— wholesale
Drafting instruments and tables— wholesale

Engineers' equipment and supplies— wholesale
Laboratory equipment, except medical or dental—wholesale
Scientific instruments—wholesale

Industry
Group
No.

Industry
No.

505   METALS AND MINERALS, EXCEPT PETROLEUM

5051   Metals Service Centers and Offices

Establishments primarily engaged in marketing semifinished metal products, except precious metals. Establishments in this industry may operate with warehouses (metals service centers) or without warehouses (metals sales offices). Establishments primarily engaged in marketing precious metals are classified in Industry 5094.

Aluminum bars, rods, ingots, sheets, pipes, plates, etc.—wholesale
Anode metal—wholesale
Bale ties, wire—wholesale
Bars, metal—wholesale
Bearing piles, iron and steel—wholesale
Black plate, iron and steel—wholesale
Castings, rough: iron and steel—wholesale
Concrete reinforcing bars—wholesale
Copper sheets, plates, bars, rods, pipes, etc.—wholesale
Ferroalloys—wholesale
Forgings, ferrous—wholesale
Forms, concrete construction: steel—wholesale
Foundry products—wholesale
Ingots—wholesale
Iron and steel flat products—wholesale
Iron and steel semifinished products—wholesale
Lead—wholesale
Mercury—wholesale
Metals, except precious—wholesale
Nails—wholesale
Nonferrous metal, except precious: e.g., sheets, bars, rods—wholesale
Pig iron—wholesale

Piling, iron and steel—wholesale
Pipe and tubing, steel—wholesale
Pipe, cast iron—wholesale
Plates, metal—wholesale
Rails and accessories—wholesale
Reinforcement mesh, wire—wholesale
Rods, metal—wholesale
Sheets, galvanized or other coated—wholesale
Sheets, metal—wholesale
Steel—wholesale
Strip, metal—wholesale
Structural shapes, iron and steel—wholesale
Terneplate—wholesale
Tin and tin base metals, shapes, forms, etc.—wholesale
Tin plate bars—wholesale
Tin plate—wholesale
Track spikes—wholesale
Tubing, metal—wholesale
Wire rods—wholesale
Wire rope or cable, not insulated—wholesale
Wire screening—wholesale
Wire, not insulated—wholesale
Zinc—wholesale

5052   Coal and Other Minerals and Ores

Establishments primarily engaged in the wholesale distribution of coal and coke; copper, iron, lead, and other metallic ores, including precious metal ores; and crude nonmetallic minerals (including concentrates), except crude petroleum. Establishments primarily engaged in the wholesale distribution of nonmetallic minerals used in construction, such as sand and gravel, are included in Industry 5032.

Coal—wholesale
Coke—wholesale
Copper ore—wholesale
Gold ore—wholesale
Iron ore—wholesale
Lead ore—wholesale

Metallic concentrates—wholesale
Metallic ores—wholesale
Nonmetallic minerals and concentrates, crude: except petroleum—wholesale
Silver ore—wholesale
Zinc ore—wholesale

506   ELECTRICAL GOODS

This industry group includes establishments primarily engaged in the wholesale distribution of electrical generating, distributing, and wiring equipment. It also includes household appliances, whether electrically, manually, or mechanically powered. This industry group does not include electrical commercial and industrial machines in which electricity does the work directly, e.g., heating, turning a shaft, or ionizing a substance, or electrically powered commercial and industrial machines, which are classified in Industry Group 504 or 508.

Industry
Group Industry
No.   No.

506 ELECTRICAL GOODS—Con.

5063 Electrical Apparatus and Equipment, Wiring Supplies, and Construction Materials

Establishments primarily engaged in the wholesale distribution of electrical power equipment for the generation, transmission, distribution, or control of electric energy; electrical construction materials for outside power transmission lines and for electrical systems; and electric light fixtures and bulbs. Construction contractors primarily engaged in installing electrical systems and equipment from their own stock are classified in Construction, Industry 1731.

Alarm signal systems—wholesale
Batteries, except automotive—wholesale
Boxes and fittings, electrical—wholesale
Bus bars and trolley ducts—wholesale
Cable conduit—wholesale
Capacitors, except electronic—wholesale
Circuit breakers—wholesale
Coaxial cable—wholesale
Conduits and raceways—wholesale
Construction materials, electrical: interior and exterior—wholesale
Distribution equipment, electrical—wholesale
Flashlights—wholesale
Fuses and accessories—wholesale
Generators, electrical—wholesale
Hanging and fastening devices, electrical—wholesale
Industrial motor controls—wholesale
Insulators, electrical—wholesale
Lamp bulbs —wholesale
Light bulbs, electric—wholesale
Lighting fixtures: residential, commercial, and industrial—wholesale
Lugs and connectors, electrical—wholesale
Motor controls, electric—wholesale

Motors, electric—wholesale
Panelboards—wholesale
Pole line hardware—wholesale
Power transmission equipment, electric—wholesale
Receptacles, electrical—wholesale
Relays—wholesale
Safety switches—wholesale
Service entrance equipment, electrical—wholesale
Signaling equipment, electrical—wholesale
Storage batteries, industrial—wholesale
Switchboards, electrical distribution—wholesale
Switches, except electronic—wholesale
Switchgear—wholesale
Time switches—wholesale
Transformers, electric: except electronic—wholesale
Transmission equipment, electrical—wholcsale
Unit substations—wholesale
Wire rope or cable, insulated—wholesale
Wire, insulated—wholesale
Wiring devices—wholesale
Wiring materials, interior—wholesale
Wiring supplies—wholesale

5064 Electrical Appliances, Television and Radio Sets

Establishments primarily engaged in the wholesale distribution of radio and television receiving sets, other household electronic sound or video equipment, self-contained air-conditioning room units, and household electrical appliances. Also included are establishments primarily engaged in the wholesale distribution of household nonelectric laundry equipment and refrigerators and freezers.

Air-conditioning room units, self-contained—wholesale
Answering machines, telephone—wholesale
Clothes dryers, household: electric and gas—wholesale
Dishwashers, household: electric—wholesale
Electric appliances, household—wholesale
Electric housewares and household fans—wholesale
Electric irons—wholesale
Electric ranges—wholesale
Electric razors—wholesale
Electric washing machines—wholesale
Freezers, household—wholesale

Garbage disposals, electric—wholesale
Humidifiers and dehumidifiers, portable—wholesale
Ironers, household: electric—wholesale
Microwave ovens, household—wholesale
Motor vehicle radios—wholesale
Percolators, electric—wholesale
Phonographs, except coin-operated—wholesale
Radios, receiving only, household and automotive—wholesale
Refrigerators, household: electric and gas—wholesale
Sewing machines, household: electric—wholesale
Stereo equipment—wholesale

506   **ELECTRICAL GOODS—Con.**

5064   **Electrical Appliances, Television and Radio Sets—Con.**

Stoves, cooking or heating, household:
electric—wholesale
Tape players and recorders, household—wholesale
Television sets—wholesale
Toothbrushes, electric—wholesale
Vacuum cleaners, household—wholesale

Video disc players—wholesale
Waffle irons, electric—wholesale
Washing machines, household: electric—wholesale
Water heaters, electric—wholesale

5065   **Electronic Parts and Equipment, Not Elsewhere Classified**

Establishments primarily engaged in the wholesale distribution of electronic parts and electronic communications equipment, not elsewhere classified, such as telephone and telegraphic equipment; radio and television broadcasting and communications equipment; and intercommunications equipment. Establishments primarily engaged in the wholesale distribution of radio and television receiving sets, phonographs, and other household sound or video equipment are classified in Industry 5064.

Amateur radio communications equipment—wholesale
Capacitors, electronic—wholesale
Cassettes, recording—wholesale
Cathode ray picture tubes—wholesale
Citizens' band radios—wholesale
Coils, electronic—wholesale
Communications equipment, except household—wholesale
Condensers, electronic—wholesale
Connectors, electronic—wholesale
Diodes—wholesale
Diskettes—wholesale
Electronic parts—wholesale
Electronic tubes: receiving, transmitting, and industrial—wholesale
Intercommunications equipment, electronic—wholesale

Magnetic recording tape—wholesale
Modems—wholesale
Public address equipment—wholesale
Radio parts and accessories—wholesale
Rectifiers, electronic—wholesale
Resistors, electronic—wholesale
Semiconductor devices—wholesale
Tapes, audio and video recording—wholesale
Telegraph equipment—wholesale
Telephone equipment—wholesale
Television receiving and transmitting tubes—wholesale
Transformers, electronic—wholesale
Transistors—wholesale
Transmitters—wholesale

507   **HARDWARE, AND PLUMBING AND HEATING EQUIPMENT AND SUPPLIES**

5072   **Hardware**

Establishments primarily engaged in the wholesale distribution of cutlery and general hardware, including handsaws; saw blades; brads, staples, and tacks; and bolts, nuts, rivets, and screws. Establishments primarily engaged in the wholesale distribution of nails, noninsulated wire, and screening are classified in Industry 5051.

Bolts, nuts, rivets, and screws—wholesale
Brads—wholesale
Builders' hardware—wholesale
Cutlery—wholesale
Fasteners, hardware—wholesale
Handsaws—wholesale
Handtools, except automotive and machinists' precision—wholesale

Hardware, heavy—wholesale
Hardware, shelf or light—wholesale
Locks and related materials—wholesale
Power handtools—wholesale
Saw blades—wholesale
Staples—wholesale
Tacks—wholesale
Washers, hardware—wholesale

5074   **Plumbing and Heating Equipment and Supplies (Hydronics)**

Establishments primarily engaged in the wholesale distribution of hydronic plumbing and heating equipment and supplies. Construction contractors pri-

507   HARDWARE, AND PLUMBING AND HEATING EQUIPMENT AND SUPPLIES—Con.

5074   Plumbing and Heating Equipment and Supplies (Hydronics)—Con.

marily engaged in installing plumbing and heating equipment from their own stock are classified in Construction, Industry 1711.

Boilers, power: industrial—wholesale
Boilers, steam and hot water heating—wholesale
Burners, fuel oil and distillate oil—wholesale
Convectors—wholesale
Fireplaces, prefabricated—wholesale
Furnaces, except electric and warm air—wholesale
Hydronic heating equipment and supplies—wholesale
Metal sanitary ware—wholesale
Oil burners—wholesale
Pipe and boiler covering—wholesale
Plumbers' brass goods, fittings, and valves—wholesale
Plumbing and heating valves—wholesale
Plumbing fixtures, equipment, and supplies—wholesale

Radiators and parts, heating: nonelectric—wholesale
Ranges, except electric—wholesale
Sanitary ware, china or enameled iron—wholesale
Sauna heaters, except electric—wholesale
Solar heating panels and equipment—wholesale
Steam fittings—wholesale
Stoves, cooking: except electric—wholesale
Stoves, wood burning—wholesale
Valves, plumbing and heating—wholesale
Water conditioning equipment—wholesale
Water heaters, except electric—wholesale
Water softeners—wholesale

5075   Warm Air Heating and Air-Conditioning Equipment and Supplies

Establishments primarily engaged in the wholesale distribution of warm air heating and air-conditioning equipment and supplies. Construction contractors primarily engaged in installing warm air heating and air-conditioning equipment are classified in Construction, Industry 1711.

Air pollution control equipment and supplies—wholesale
Air-conditioning equipment, except room units—wholesale
Automotive air-conditioners—wholesale
Compressors, air-conditioning—wholesale
Condensing units, air-conditioning—wholesale

Dust collection equipment—wholesale
Furnaces, heating: electric—wholesale
Furnaces, warm air—wholesale
Humidifiers and dehumidifiers, except portable—wholesale
Ventilating equipment and supplies—wholesale
Warm air heating and cooling equipment—wholesale

5078   Refrigeration Equipment and Supplies

Establishments primarily engaged in the wholesale distribution of refrigeration equipment and supplies. Construction contractors primarily engaged in the installation of refrigeration equipment from their own stock are classified in Construction, Industry 1711.

Beverage coolers—wholesale
Cold storage machinery—wholesale
Condensing units, refrigeration—wholesale
Display cases, refrigerated—wholesale
Drinking water coolers, mechanical—wholesale
Fixtures, refrigerated—wholesale

Ice cream cabinets—wholesale
Ice making machines—wholesale
Refrigerators, commercial: reach-in and walk-in—wholesale
Show cases, refrigerated—wholesale
Soda fountain fixtures, refrigerated—wholesale

508   MACHINERY, EQUIPMENT, AND SUPPLIES

5082   Construction and Mining (Except Petroleum) Machinery and Equipment

Establishments primarily engaged in the wholesale distribution of construction or mining cranes, excavating machinery and equipment, power shovels, road construction and maintenance machinery, tractor-mounting equipment

508 MACHINERY, EQUIPMENT, AND SUPPLIES—Con.

5082 Construction and Mining (Except Petroleum) Machinery and Equipment—Con.

and other specialized machinery and equipment used in the construction, mining, and logging industries. Establishments engaged in marketing oil well machinery and equipment are classified in Industry 5084.

Bituminous processing equipment—wholesale
Concrete processing equipment—wholesale
Construction machinery and equipment—wholesale
Cranes, construction—wholesale
Crushing, pulverizing and screening machinery for construction and mining—wholesale
Dredges and draglines, except ships—wholesale
Excavating machinery and equipment—wholesale
Forestry equipment—wholesale
Front-end loaders—wholesale
Graders, motor—wholesale
Logging equipment—wholesale
Mineral beneficiation machinery—wholesale

Mining machinery and equipment, except petroleum—wholesale
Mixers, construction and mining—wholesale
Pavers—wholesale
Quarrying machinery and equipment—wholesale
Road construction and maintenance machinery—wholesale
Scaffolding—wholesale
Shovels, power—wholesale
Tracklaying equipment—wholesale
Tractor-mounting equipment—wholesale
Tractors, construction—wholesale
Well points (drilling equipment)—wholesale

5083 Farm and Garden Machinery and Equipment

Establishments primarily engaged in the wholesale distribution of agricultural machinery and equipment for use in the preparation and maintenance of the soil, the planting and harvesting of crops, and other operations and processes pertaining to work on the farm or the lawn or garden; and dairy and other livestock equipment.

Agricultural machinery—wholesale
Cream separators, farm—wholesale
Cultivating machinery and equipment—wholesale
Dairy farm machinery and equipment—wholesale
Farm machinery and equipment—wholesale
Garden machinery and equipment—wholesale
Harvesting machinery and equipment—wholesale
Haying machinery—wholesale
Irrigation equipment—wholesale

Land preparation machinery, agricultural—wholesale
Lawn machinery and equipment—wholesale
Milking machinery and equipment—wholesale
Mowers, power—wholesale
Planting machinery and equipment—wholesale
Poultry equipment—wholesale
Tractors, agricultural—wholesale
Wind machines (frost protection equipment)—wholesale

5084 Industrial Machinery and Equipment

Establishments primarily engaged in the wholesale distribution of industrial machinery and equipment, not elsewhere classified.

Blanks, tips and inserts—wholesale
Broaches—wholesale
Cement making machinery—wholesale
Chainsaws—wholesale
Citrus processing machinery—wholesale
Compressors, except air-conditioning and refrigeration—wholesale
Controlling instruments and accessories, industrial—wholesale
Conveyor systems—wholesale
Counterbores—wholesale
Countersinks—wholesale

Cranes, industrial—wholesale
Cream separators, except farm—wholesale
Crushing machinery and equipment, industrial—wholesale
Dairy products manufacturing machinery—wholesale
Derricks—wholesale
Dies, metalworking—wholesale
Diesel engines and engine parts, industrial—wholesale
Drilling bits—wholesale
Elevators—wholesale

Industry Group No.	Industry No.
508	

MACHINERY, EQUIPMENT, AND SUPPLIES—Con.

5084 Industrial Machinery and Equipment—Con.

Fans, industrial—wholesale
Food product manufacturing machinery—wholesale
Heat exchange equipment, industrial—wholesale
Hobs—wholesale
Hoists—wholesale
Indicating instruments and accessories—wholesale
Jigs—wholesale
Ladders—wholesale
Lift trucks—wholesale
Machine tool accessories—wholesale
Machine tools—wholesale
Machinists' precision measuring tools—wholesale
Materials handling equipment—wholesale
Measuring and testing equipment, electrical, except automotive—wholesale
Metal refining machinery and equipment—wholesale
Metalworking machinery—wholesale
Metalworking tools: drills, taps, dies, grinding wheels, and files—wholesale
Milk products manufacturing machinery and equipment—wholesale
Oil refining machinery, equipment, and supplies—wholesale
Oil well machinery, equipment, and supplies—wholesale
Oil well supply houses—wholesale
Packing machinery and equipment—wholesale
Paint spray equipment, industrial—wholesale
Paper manufacturing machinery—wholesale
Power plant machinery, except electrical—wholesale

Printing trades machinery, equipment, and supplies—wholesale
Pulp (wood) manufacturing machinery—wholesale
Pulverizing machinery and equipment, industrial—wholesale
Pumps and pumping equipment, industrial—wholesale
Reamers—wholesale
Recapping machinery for tires—wholesale
Recording instruments and accessories—wholesale
Screening machinery and equipment, industrial—wholesale
Sewing machines, industrial—wholesale
Shoe manufacturing and repairing machinery—wholesale
Smelting machinery and equipment—wholesale
Stackers, industrial—wholesale
Tapping attachments—wholesale
Textile machinery and equipment—wholesale
Threading tools—wholesale
Tool holders (e.g., chucks, turrets)—wholesale
Tractors, industrial—wholesale
Trailers, industrial—wholesale
Trucks, industrial—wholesale
Twist drills—wholesale
Water pumps, industrial—wholesale
Welding machinery and equipment—wholesale
Winches—wholesale
Woodworking machinery—wholesale

5085 Industrial Supplies

Establishments primarily engaged in the wholesale distribution of industrial supplies, not elsewhere classified.

Abrasives—wholesale
Barrels, new and reconditioned—wholesale
Bearings—wholesale
Bort—wholesale
Bottlers' supplies: caps, bottles, etc.—wholesale
Bottles, glass or plastics—wholesale
Box shooks—wholesale
Boxes, crates, etc., other than paper—wholesale
Cans for fruits and vegetables—wholesale
Chain, power transmission—wholesale
Cooperage stock—wholesale
Cordage—wholesale
Cork—wholesale
Crates, except paper—wholesale
Crowns and closures, metal—wholesale
Diamonds, industrial: natural and crude—wholesale
Drums, new and reconditioned—wholesale
Gaskets—wholesale
Gears—wholesale
Glass bottles—wholesale

Grommets—wholesale
Hose, belting, and packing: industrial—wholesale
Hydraulic and pneumatic pistons and valves—wholesale
Industrial fittings—wholesale
Industrial sewing thread—wholesale
Industrial wheels—wholesale
Ink, printers'—wholesale
Lapidary equipment—wholesale
Leather belting, packing—wholesale
Mill supplies—wholesale
Pails, metal—wholesale
Pistons and valves, industrial—wholesale
Power transmission supplies, mechanical—wholesale
Refractory material—wholesale
Rope, except wire rope—wholesale
Rubber goods, mechanical—wholesale
Seals, gaskets, and packing—wholesale
Sprockets—wholesale
Textile printers' supplies—wholesale
Twine—wholesale
Valves and fittings, except plumbers'—wholesale

Industry Group No.	Industry No.	
508		MACHINERY, EQUIPMENT, AND SUPPLIES—Con.

5087 Service Establishment Equipment and Supplies

Establishments primarily engaged in the wholesale distribution of equipment and supplies for barber shops, beauty parlors, power laundries, drycleaning plants, upholsterers, undertakers, and related personal service establishments.

Barber shop equipment and supplies—
  wholesale
Beauty parlor equipment and sup-
  plies—wholesale
Boot and shoe cut stock and findings—
  wholesale
Carnival and amusement park equip-
  ment—wholesale
Carwash equipment and supplies—
  wholesale
Caskets, burial—wholesale
Chairs, hydraulic: beauty and barber
  shop—wholesale
Concrete burial vaults and boxes—
  wholesale
Drycleaning plant equipment and sup-
  plies—wholesale
Dryers, beauty shop—wholesale
Findings, shoe repair—wholesale
Firefighting equipment—wholesale

Janitors' supplies—wholesale
Laundry equipment and supplies—
  wholesale
Morticians' goods—wholesale
Shoe heels—wholesale
Shoe patterns—wholesale
Shoe repair materials—wholesale
Soles, shoe—wholesale
Sprinkler systems, except agricultur-
  al—wholesale
Tailors' supplies—wholesale
Undertakers' equipment and supplies—
  wholesale
Upholsterers' equipment and supplies,
  except fabrics—wholesale
Upholstery filling and padding—whole-
  sale
Vacuum cleaning systems—wholesale
Voting machines—wholesale

5088 Transportation Equipment and Supplies, Except Motor Vehicles

Establishments primarily engaged in the wholesale distribution of transportation equipment and supplies. Establishments primarily engaged in the wholesale distribution of motor vehicles and motor vehicle parts are classified in Industry Group 501, and those distributing pleasure boats are classified in Industry 5091.

Aeronautical equipment and supplies—
  wholesale
Aircraft and parts—wholesale
Aircraft engines and engine parts—
  wholesale
Aircraft equipment and supplies—
  wholesale
Boats, except pleasure—wholesale
Combat vehicles, except trucks—whole-
  sale
Golf carts, self-propelled—wholesale
Guided missiles and space vehicles—
  wholesale

Marine propulsion machinery and
  equipment—wholesale
Marine supplies (dunnage)—wholesale
Railroad equipment and supplies—
  wholesale
Ships—wholesale
Space propulsion units and parts—
  wholesale
Tanks and tank components—whole-
  sale
Transportation equipment and supplies,
  except motor vehicles—wholesale

509   MISCELLANEOUS DURABLE GOODS

5091 Sporting and Recreational Goods and Supplies

Establishments primarily engaged in the wholesale distribution of sporting goods and accessories; billiard and pool supplies; sporting firearms and ammunition; and marine pleasure craft, equipment, and supplies. Establishments primarily engaged in the wholesale distribution of motor vehicles and trailers are classified in Industry 5012; those distributing self-propelled golf carts are classified in Industry 5088; and those distributing athletic apparel and footwear are classified in Industry Group 513.

Ammunition, sporting—wholesale
Archery equipment—wholesale
Athletic goods, except apparel and foot-
  wear—wholesale

Bait, artificial—wholesale
Bicycle tires and tubes—wholesale
Bicycles—wholesale
Billiards equipment and supplies—

Industry Group No.	Industry No.	
509		**MISCELLANEOUS DURABLE GOODS—Con.**
	5091	**Sporting and Recreational Goods and Supplies—Con.**

wholesale

Boats, pleasure: canoes, motorboats, and sailboats—wholesale
Bowling equipment—wholesale
Camping equipment—wholesale
Camping tents and equipment—wholesale
Firearms, sporting—wholesale
Gocarts—wholesale
Golf carts, except self-propelled—wholesale

Golf equipment—wholesale
Hot tubs—wholesale
Outboard motors—wholesale
Pool equipment and supplies—wholesale
Skiing equipment—wholesale
Swimming pools and equipment—wholesale
Underwater sports equipment—wholesale

5092 Toys and Hobby Goods and Supplies

Establishments primarily engaged in the wholesale distribution of games, toys, hobby goods and supplies, and related goods, such as fireworks and playing cards.

Craft kits—wholesale
Dolls—wholesale
Fireworks—wholesale
Games (including electronic), except coin-operated—wholesale
Hobby kits—wholesale

Model kits—wholesale
Playing cards—wholesale
Stamps, philatelist—wholesale
Toys (including electronic)—wholesale
Vehicles, children's—wholesale

5093 Scrap and Waste Materials

Establishments primarily engaged in assembling, breaking up, sorting, and wholesale distribution of scrap and waste materials. This industry includes auto wreckers engaged in dismantling automobiles for scrap. However, those engaged in dismantling cars for the purpose of selling secondhand parts are classified in Industry 5015.

Automotive wrecking for scrap—wholesale
Bag reclaiming—wholesale
Bottles, waste—wholesale
Boxes, waste—wholesale
Fur cuttings and scraps—wholesale
Iron and steel scrap—wholesale
Junk and scrap, general line—wholesale
Metal waste and scrap—wholesale
Nonferrous metals scrap—wholesale

Oil, waste—wholesale
Plastics scrap—wholesale
Rags—wholesale
Rubber scrap—wholesale
Scavengering—wholesale
Scrap and waste materials—wholesale
Textile waste—wholesale
Wastepaper, including paper recycling—wholesale
Wiping rags, including washing and reconditioning—wholesale

5094 Jewelry, Watches, Precious Stones, and Precious Metals

Establishments primarily engaged in the wholesale distribution of jewelry, precious stones and metals, costume jewelry, watches, clocks, silverware, and jewelers' findings. Establishments primarily engaged in the wholesale distribution of precious metal ores are classified in Industry 5052.

Bullion, precious metals—wholesale
Clocks—wholesale
Coins—wholesale
Diamonds (gems)—wholesale
Gem stones—wholesale
Jewelers' findings—wholesale
Jewelry—wholesale
Medallions—wholesale
Metals, precious—wholesale

Pearls—wholesale
Precious metal mill shapes—wholesale
Precious metals—wholesale
Precious stones (gems)—wholesale
Silverware and plated ware—wholesale
Trophies—wholesale
Watchcases—wholesale
Watches and parts—wholesale

509　　MISCELLANEOUS DURABLE GOODS—Con.

5099　Durable Goods, Not Elsewhere Classified

　　Establishments primarily engaged in the wholesale distribution of durable goods, not elsewhere classified, such as musical instruments and forest products, except lumber.

Ammunition, except sporting—wholesale
Cassettes, prerecorded: audio—wholesale
Cordwood—wholesale
Fire extinguishers—wholesale
Firearms, except sporting—wholesale
Firewood—wholesale
Game machines, coin-operated—wholesale
Gas lighting fixtures—wholesale
Logs, hewn ties, posts, and poles—wholesale

Luggage—wholesale
Machine guns—wholesale
Monuments and grave markers—wholesale
Musical instruments—wholesale
Phonograph records—wholesale
Portraits—wholesale
Pulpwood—wholesale
Roundwood—wholesale
Signs, except electric—wholesale
Tapes, audio prerecorded—wholesale
Timber products, rough—wholesale
Wood chips—wholesale

Major Group 51.—WHOLESALE TRADE—NONDURABLE GOODS

The Major Group as a Whole

This major group includes establishments primarily engaged in the wholesale distribution of nondurable goods.

Industry Group No.	Industry No.	

511   PAPER AND PAPER PRODUCTS

5111   Printing and Writing Paper

Establishments primarily engaged in the wholesale distribution of printing and writing paper, including envelope paper; fine paper; and groundwood paper.

Paper, fine or printing and writing—wholesale

Printing paper—wholesale

5112   Stationery and Office Supplies

Establishments primarily engaged in the wholesale distribution of stationery and office supplies, including computer and photocopy supplies, envelopes, typewriter paper, file cards and folders, pens, pencils, social stationery, and greeting cards.

Albums (photo) and scrapbooks—wholesale
Blankbooks—wholesale
Business forms—wholesale
Carbon paper—wholesale
Commercial stationers (not printers)—wholesale
Computer paper—wholesale
Envelopes—wholesale
File cards—wholesale
File folders—wholesale
Greeting cards—wholesale
Inked ribbons—wholesale
Looseleaf binders—wholesale
Manifold business forms—wholesale
Marking devices—wholesale
Mimeograph paper—wholesale
Office supplies—wholesale
Pencils—wholesale
Pens, writing—wholesale
Photocopying supplies—wholesale
Ribbons, inked—wholesale
Sales and receipt books—wholesale
Scrapbooks—wholesale
Stationery and stationery supplies—wholesale
Tabulation cards—wholesale
Writing ink—wholesale

5113   Industrial and Personal Service Paper

Establishments primarily engaged in the wholesale distribution of wrapping and other coarse paper, paperboard, and converted paper and related disposable plastics products, such as bags, boxes, dishes, eating utensils, napkins, and shipping supplies.

Bags, paper and disposable plastics—wholesale
Boxes, paperboard and disposable plastics—wholesale
Cardboard and products—wholesale
Closures, paper and disposable plastics—wholesale
Containers, paper and disposable plastics—wholesale
Corrugated and solid fiber boxes—wholesale
Cups, paper and disposable plastics—wholesale
Dishes, paper and disposable plastics—wholesale
Eating utensils: forks, knives, spoons-disposable plastics—wholesale
Fiber cans and drums—wholesale
Folding paperboard boxes—wholesale
Napkins, paper—wholesale
Paper and products, wrapping or coarse—wholesale
Paper, except printing or writing and office supplies—wholesale
Paperboard and products, except office supplies—wholesale
Patterns, paper—wholesale
Pressed and molded pulp goods—wholesale
Pressure sensitive tape—wholesale
Sanitary food containers: paper, paperboard, and disposable plastics—wholesale
Setup paperboard boxes—wholesale
Shipping supplies, paper and disposable plastics (e.g., cartons, gummed tapes)—wholesale
Towels, paper—wholesale

Industry Group No.	Industry No.	
512		**DRUGS, DRUG PROPRIETARIES, AND DRUGGISTS' SUNDRIES**

5122   Drugs, Drug Proprietaries, and Druggists' Sundries

Establishments primarily engaged in the wholesale distribution of prescription drugs, proprietary drugs, druggists' sundries, and toiletries. Establishments primarily engaged in the wholesale distribution of surgical, dental, and hospital equipment are classified in Industry 5047.

Antiseptics—wholesale
Bandages—wholesale
Biologicals and allied products—wholesale
Blood plasma—wholesale
Cosmetics—wholesale
Drug proprietaries—wholesale
Druggists' sundries—wholesale
Drugs—wholesale
Hair preparations—wholesale
Medical rubber goods—wholesale
Medicinals and botanicals—wholesale
Medicine cabinet sundries—wholesale

Patent medicines—wholesale
Perfumes—wholesale
Pharmaceuticals—wholesale
Proprietary (patent) medicines—wholesale
Razor blades—wholesale
Razors, nonelectric—wholesale
Toilet articles—wholesale
Toilet preparations—wholesale
Toilet soap—wholesale
Toothbrushes, except electric—wholesale
Vitamins—wholesale

513   APPAREL, PIECE GOODS, AND NOTIONS

5131   Piece Goods, Notions, and Other Dry Goods

Establishments primarily engaged in the wholesale distribution of piece goods or yard goods of natural or manmade fibers, notions (sewing and hair accessories, etc.), and other dry goods. Converters who buy fabric goods (except knit goods) in the grey, have them finished on contract, and sell at wholesale are included here. Converters of knit goods are classified in Manufacturing, Industry Group 225. This industry does not include establishments primarily engaged in the wholesale distribution of homefurnishings which are classified in Industry 5023.

Belt and buckle assembly kits—wholesale
Binding, textile—wholesale
Broadwoven fabrics—wholesale
Buttons—wholesale
Cheesecloth—wholesale
Circular knit fabrics—wholesale
Coated fabrics—wholesale
Cotton piece goods—wholesale
Drapery material—wholesale
Fiberglass fabrics—wholesale
Hair accessories—wholesale
Hat and cap material—wholesale
Jute piece goods—wholesale
Knit fabrics—wholesale
Lace fabrics—wholesale
Linen piece goods—wholesale
Millinery supplies—wholesale
Narrow fabrics—wholesale
Net goods—wholesale
Notions—wholesale

Nylon piece goods—wholesale
Piece goods—wholesale
Rayon piece goods—wholesale
Ribbon, textile—wholesale
Sewing accessories—wholesale
Sewing thread, except industrial—wholesale
Shoulder pads—wholesale
Silk piece goods—wholesale
Tape, textile—wholesale
Textile converters except knit goods—wholesale
Textiles—wholesale
Thread, except industrial—wholesale
Trimmings, apparel—wholesale
Warp knit fabrics—wholesale
Weft knit fabrics—wholesale
Woolen and worsted piece goods—wholesale
Yard goods—wholesale
Zippers—wholesale

5136   Men's and Boys' Clothing and Furnishings

Establishments primarily engaged in the wholesale distribution of men's and boys' apparel and furnishings, sportswear, hosiery, underwear, nightwear, and work clothing.

Apparel belts, men's and boys'—wholesale
Beachwear, men's and boys'—wholesale
Caps, men's and boys'—wholesale

Clothing, men's and boys'—wholesale
Coats, men's and boys'—wholesale
Furnishings, except shoes: men's and boys'—wholesale

513   **APPAREL, PIECE GOODS, AND NOTIONS—Con.**

5136   Men's and Boys' Clothing and Furnishings—Con.

Gloves (all materials), men's and boys'—wholesale

Handkerchiefs, men's and boys'—wholesale

Hats, men's and boys'—wholesale

Hosiery, men's and boys'—wholesale

Leather and sheep-lined clothing, men's and boys'—wholesale

Mittens, men's and boys'—wholesale

Mufflers, men's and boys'—wholesale

Neckwear, men's and boys'—wholesale

Nightwear, men's and boys'—wholesale

Outerwear, men's and boys'—wholesale

Overcoats, men's and boys'—wholesale

Raincoats, men's and boys'—wholesale

Robes, men's and boys'—wholesale

Scarves, men's and boys'—wholesale

Shirts, men's and boys'—wholesale

Sportswear, men's and boys'—wholesale

Suits, men's and boys'—wholesale

Ties, men's and boys'—wholesale

Trousers, men's and boys'—wholesale

Umbrellas, men's and boys'—wholesale

Underwear, men's and boys'—wholesale

Uniforms, men's and boys'—wholesale

Waterproof outergarments, men's and boys'—wholesale

Work clothing, men's and boys'—wholesale

5137   Women's, Children's, and Infants' Clothing and Accessories

Establishments primarily engaged in the wholesale distribution of women's, children's, and infants' clothing and accessories, including hosiery, lingerie, millinery, and furs.

Apparel belts: women's and children's—wholesale

Baby goods—wholesale

Blouses—wholesale

Caps and gowns: women's and children's—wholesale

Caps: women's and children's—wholesale

Clothing accessories: women's, children's, and infants'—wholesale

Clothing: women's, children's, and infants'—wholesale

Coats: women's, children's, and infants'—wholesale

Coordinate sets: women's, children's, and infants'—wholesale

Corsets—wholesale

Diapers—wholesale

Dresses—wholesale

Fur clothing—wholesale

Furnishings, clothing except shoes: women's, children's, and infants'—wholesale

Gloves, (all materials): women's, children's, and infants'—wholesale

Handbags—wholesale

Handkerchiefs: women's and children's—wholesale

Hats: women's, children's, and infants'—wholesale

Hosiery: women's, children's, and infants'—wholesale

Hospital gowns: women's and children's—wholesale

Infants' wear—wholesale

Karate uniforms: women's and children's—wholesale

Ladies' handkerchiefs—wholesale

Ladies' purses—wholesale

Leather and sheep-lined clothing: women's and children's—wholesale

Lingerie—wholesale

Millinery—wholesale

Mittens: women's, children's, and infants'—wholesale

Nightwear: women's, children's, and infants'—wholesale

Outerwear: women's, children's, and infants'—wholesale

Purses: women's and children's—wholesale

Raincoats: women's and children's—wholesale

Robes and gowns: women's and children's—wholesale

Scarves: women's, children's and infant's—wholesale

Skirts—wholesale

Sportswear: women's and children's—wholesale

Suits: women's, children's, and infants'—wholesale

Underwear: women's, children's, and infants'—wholesale

Uniforms: women's and children's—wholesale

Unisex clothing: women's and children's—wholesale

Waterproof outergarments: women's and children's—wholesale

5139   Footwear

Establishments primarily engaged in the wholesale distribution of footwear (including athletic) of leather, rubber, and other materials.

Athletic footwear—wholesale

Footwear—wholesale

Shoe accessories—wholesale

Shoes—wholesale

Industry Group No.	Industry No.	
514		**GROCERIES AND RELATED PRODUCTS**

5141 Groceries, General Line

Establishments primarily engaged in the wholesale distribution of a general line of groceries. Establishments primarily engaged in roasting coffee, blending tea, or grinding and packaging spices are classified in Manufacturing, Major Group 20.

Food brokers, general line—wholesale

Groceries, general line—wholesale

5142 Packaged Frozen Foods

Establishments primarily engaged in the wholesale distribution of packaged quickfrozen vegetables, juices, meats, fish, poultry, pastries, and other "deep freeze" products. Establishments primarily engaged in the wholesale distribution of frozen dairy products are classified in Industry 5143, and those distributing frozen poultry, fish, and meat which are not packaged are classified in Industries 5144, 5146, and 5147, respectively.

Bakery products, frozen—wholesale
Bread, frozen: packaged—wholesale
Cakes, frozen: packaged—wholesale
Dinners, frozen—wholesale
Fish, frozen: packaged—wholesale
Frozen foods, packaged—wholesale
Frozen vegetables—wholesale
Fruit juices, frozen—wholesale

Fruits, frozen—wholesale
Meat pies, frozen—wholesale
Meat, frozen: packaged—wholesale
Pies, fruit: frozen—wholesale
Poultry pies, frozen—wholesale
Poultry, frozen: packaged—wholesale
Seafoods, frozen: packaged—wholesale
Soup, frozen—wholesale

5143 Dairy Products, Except Dried or Canned

Establishments primarily engaged in the wholesale distribution of dairy products, such as butter, cheese, ice cream and ices, and fluid milk and cream. This industry does not include establishments primarily engaged in pasteurizing and bottling milk, which are classified in Manufacturing, Industry Group 202. Establishments primarily engaged in the wholesale distribution of dried or canned dairy products are classified in Industry 5149.

Butter—wholesale
Cheese—wholesale
Cream stations—wholesale
Dairy depots—wholesale
Dairy products, except dried or canned—wholesale
Frozen dairy desserts—wholesale

Ice cream and ices—wholesale
Milk and cream, fluid—wholesale
Milk cooling stations, operated by farm assemblers
Milk depots—wholesale
Yogurt—wholesale

5144 Poultry and Poultry Products

Establishments primarily engaged in the wholesale distribution of poultry and poultry products, except canned and packaged frozen products. This industry does not include establishments primarily engaged in the killing and dressing of poultry, which are classified in Manufacturing, Industry 2015. Establishments primarily engaged in the wholesale distribution of packaged frozen poultry are classified in Industry 5142, and those distributing canned poultry are classified in Industry 5149.

Eggs: cleaning, oil treating, packing, and grading—wholesale
Eggs—wholesale

Poultry products—wholesale
Poultry: live, dressed, or frozen (except packaged)—wholesale

5145 Confectionery

Establishments primarily engaged in the wholesale distribution of confectionery and related products, such as candy, chewing gum, fountain fruits,

514   **GROCERIES AND RELATED PRODUCTS—Con.**

5145 Confectionery—Con.

salted or roasted nuts, popcorn, fountain syrups, and potato, corn, and similar chips.

Candy—wholesale	Nuts, salted or roasted—wholesale
Chewing gum—wholesale	Popcorn—wholesale
Confectionery—wholesale	Potato chips—wholesale
Corn chips—wholesale	Syrups, fountain—wholesale
Fountain fruits and syrups—wholesale	Toppings, soda fountain—wholesale

5146 Fish and Seafoods

Establishments primarily engaged in the wholesale distribution (but not packaging) of fresh, cured, or frozen fish and seafoods, except canned or packaged frozen. The preparation of fresh or frozen packaged fish and other seafood, and the shucking and packing of fresh oysters in nonsealed containers, are classified in Manufacturing, Industry 2092. Establishments primarily engaged in the wholesale distribution of canned seafood are classified in Industry 5149, and those distributing packaged frozen foods are classified in Industry 5142.

Fish, cured—wholesale	Seafoods, not canned or frozen packaged—wholesale
Fish, fresh—wholesale	
Fish, frozen: except packaged—wholesale	

5147 Meats and Meat Products

Establishments primarily engaged in the wholesale distribution of fresh, cured, and processed (but not canned) meats and lard. Establishments primarily engaged in the wholesale distribution of frozen packaged meats are classified in Industry 5142, and those distributing canned meats are classified in Industry 5149.

Lard—wholesale	Meats, fresh—wholesale
Meats, cured or smoked—wholesale	

5148 Fresh Fruits and Vegetables

Establishments primarily engaged in the wholesale distribution of fresh fruits and vegetables.

Banana ripening for the trade—wholesale	Potatoes, fresh—wholesale
Fruits, fresh—wholesale	Vegetables, fresh—wholesale

5149 Groceries and Related Products, Not Elsewhere Classified

Establishments primarily engaged in the wholesale distribution of groceries and related products, not elsewhere classified. Establishments primarily engaged in the wholesale distribution of soft drinks, and in bottling and distributing natural spring and mineral waters, are classified in this industry, but establishments primarily engaged in bottling soft drinks are classified in Manufacturing, Major Group 20. This industry does not include establishments primarily engaged in the wholesale distribution of farm-product raw materials classified in Industry Group 515, nor those distributing beer, wine, and distilled alcoholic beverages of Industry Group 518.

Bagging of tea	Beverage concentrates—wholesale
Bakery products—wholesale	Bottling mineral or spring water—

Industry Group No.	Industry No.
514	

GROCERIES AND RELATED PRODUCTS—Con.

5149 Groceries and Related Products, Not Elsewhere Classified—Con.

wholesale
Breakfast cereals—wholesale
Canned goods: fruits, vegetables, fish, seafoods, meats, and milk—wholesale
Canned specialties—wholesale
Chocolate—wholesale
Cleaning of dry foods and spices—wholesale
Coffee: green, roasted, instant, freeze-dried, or extract—wholesale
Cookies—wholesale
Cooking oils—wholesale
Crackers—wholesale
Dairy products, dried or canned—wholesale
Dog and cat food—wholesale
Flavoring extract, except for fountain use—wholesale
Flour—wholesale
Fruit peel—wholesale
Fruits, dried—wholesale
Health foods—wholesale
Honey—wholesale
Hop extract—wholesale
Macaroni—wholesale
Malt extract—wholesale
Malt—wholesale

Margarine—wholesale
Milk, canned or dried—wholesale
Molasses, industrial—wholesale
Pet food—wholesale
Pickles, preserves, jellies, jams, and sauces—wholesale
Pretzels—wholesale
Rice, polished—wholesale
Salad dressing—wholesale
Salt, evaporated—wholesale
Sandwiches—wholesale
Sauces—wholesale
Sausage casings—wholesale
Shortening, vegetable—wholesale
Soft drinks—wholesale
Soups, except frozen—wholesale
Spaghetti—wholesale
Spices—wholesale
Starches—wholesale
Sugar, refined—wholesale
Syrups, except for fountain use—wholesale
Tea—wholesale
Vegetable cooking oil—wholesale
Wet corn milling products—wholesale
Yeast—wholesale

515   FARM-PRODUCT RAW MATERIALS

5153 Grain and Field Beans

Establishments primarily engaged in buying and/or marketing grain (such as corn, wheat, oats, barley, and unpolished rice); dry beans; soybeans, and other inedible beans. Country grain elevators primarily engaged in buying or receiving grain from farmers are included, as well as terminal elevators and other merchants marketing grain. Establishments primarily engaged in the wholesale distribution of field and garden seeds are classified in Industry 5191.

Barley—wholesale
Beans, dry: bulk—wholesale
Beans, inedible—wholesale
Beans, unshelled—wholesale
Corn—wholesale
Grain elevators, except storage only—wholesale

Grain—wholesale
Oats—wholesale
Rice, unpolished—wholesale
Soybeans—wholesale
Wheat—wholesale

5154 Livestock

Establishments primarily engaged in buying and/or marketing cattle, hogs, sheep, and goats. This industry also includes the operation of livestock auction markets.

Auctioning livestock—wholesale
Cattle—wholesale
Goats—wholesale
Hogs—wholesale

Livestock, except horses and mules—wholesale
Sheep—wholesale

5159 Farm-Product Raw Materials, Not Elsewhere Classified

Establishments primarily engaged in buying and/or marketing farm products, not elsewhere classified. Establishments primarily engaged in the wholesale distribution of milk are classified in Industry 5143, and those distributing live poultry are classified in Industry 5144.

515 **FARM-PRODUCT RAW MATERIALS—Con.**

5159 **Farm-Product Raw Materials, Not Elsewhere Classified—Con.**

Animal hair—wholesale
Bristles—wholesale
Broomcorn—wholesale
Buyers of raw farm products, except grain, field beans, and livestock—wholesale
Chicks—wholesale
Cotton merchants, not members of exchanges—wholesale
Cotton, raw—wholesale
Country buyers of cotton or cotton linters
Dealers in raw farm products, except grain, field beans, and livestock—wholesale
Dried beet pulp—wholesale
Feathers—wholesale
Fibers, vegetable—wholesale
Furs, raw—wholesale
Hides (may include curing)—wholesale
Hops—wholesale
Horses—wholesale
Merchants of raw farm products, except grain, field beans, and livestock—wholesale

Mohair, raw—wholesale
Moss—wholesale
Mules—wholesale
Nuts, unprocessed or shelled only—wholesale
Oil kernels—wholesale
Oil nuts—wholesale
Oilseeds—wholesale
Peanuts, bulk: unprocessed or shelled only—wholesale
Pecan—wholesale
Pelts—wholesale
Semen, bovine—wholesale
Silk, raw—wholesale
Skins, raw—wholesale
Sugar, raw—wholesale
Tobacco auctioning and warehousing—wholesale
Tobacco, leaf (including exporters)—wholesale
Wool tops and noils—wholesale
Wool, raw—wholesale

516 **CHEMICALS AND ALLIED PRODUCTS**

5162 **Plastics Materials and Basic Forms and Shapes**

Establishments primarily engaged in the wholesale distribution of plastics materials, and of unsupported plastics film, sheets, sheeting, rods, tubes, and other basic forms and shapes.

Plastics basic shapes—wholesale
Plastics film—wholesale
Plastics materials—wholesale
Plastics resins—wholesale

Plastics sheet and rods—wholesale
Resins, synthetic: except rubber—wholesale

5169 **Chemicals and Allied Products, Not Elsewhere Classified**

Establishments primarily engaged in the wholesale distribution of chemicals and allied products, not elsewhere classified, such as acids, industrial and heavy chemicals, dyestuffs, industrial salts, rosin, and turpentine. Establishments primarily engaged in the wholesale distribution of ammunition are classified in Industry Group 509; those distributing agricultural chemicals and pesticides are classified in Industry 5191; those distributing drugs are classified in Industry 5122; and those distributing pigments, paints, and varnishes are classified in Industry 5198.

Acids—wholesale
Alcohol, industrial—wholesale
Alkalies—wholesale
Ammonia, except for fertilizer—wholesale
Aromatic chemicals—wholesale
Carbon black—wholesale
Caustic soda—wholesale
Chemical bulk stations and terminals—wholesale
Chemicals, industrial and heavy—wholesale
Chlorine—wholesale
Coal tar products, primary and intermediate—wholesale
Concrete additives—wholesale

Cyclic crudes and intermediates—wholesale
Detergents—wholesale
Drilling mud—wholesale
Dry ice—wholesale
Dyestuffs—wholesale
Essential oils—wholesale
Explosives, all kinds except ammunition and fireworks—wholesale
Food additives, chemical—wholesale
Fuel additives—wholesale
Gases, compressed and liquefied: except liquefied petroleum gas—wholesale
Gelatin—wholesale
Glue—wholesale
Gum and wood chemicals—wholesale

Industry
Group   Industry
No.   No.

516   CHEMICALS AND ALLIED PRODUCTS—Con.

5169 Chemicals and Allied Products, Not Elsewhere Classified—Con.

Industrial gases—wholesale
Laundry soap, chips, and powder—wholesale
Manmade fibers—wholesale
Metal cyanides—wholesale
Metal polishes—wholesale
Metal salts—wholesale
Naval stores—wholesale
Oil additives—wholesale
Oil drilling muds—wholesale
Organic chemicals, synthetic—wholesale

Polishes: furniture, automobile, metal, shoe, etc.—wholesale
Resins, synthetic rubber—wholesale
Rosin—wholesale
Rustproofing chemicals—wholesale
Salts, industrial—wholesale
Sanitation preparations—wholesale
Sealants—wholesale
Surface active agents—wholesale
Synthetic rubber—wholesale
Turpentine—wholesale
Waxes, except petroleum—wholesale

517   PETROLEUM AND PETROLEUM PRODUCTS

5171 Petroleum Bulk Stations and Terminals

Establishments primarily engaged in the wholesale distribution of crude petroleum and petroleum products, including liquefied petroleum gas, from bulk liquid storage facilities.

Petroleum bulk stations and terminals—wholesale

5172 Petroleum and Petroleum Products Wholesalers, Except Bulk Stations and Terminals

Establishments primarily engaged in the wholesale distribution of petroleum and petroleum products, except those with bulk liquid storage facilities. Included are packaged and bottled petroleum products distributors, truck jobbers, and others marketing petroleum and its products at wholesale, but without bulk liquid storage facilities.

Butane gas, except bulk stations and terminals—wholesale
Crude oil, except bulk stations and terminals—wholesale
Fuel oil, except bulk stations and terminals—wholesale
Fueling services, aircraft—wholesale
Gases, liquefied petroleum: except bulk stations and terminals—wholesale
Gasoline, except bulk stations and terminals—wholesale

Gasoline: buying in bulk and selling to farmers—wholesale
Kerosene—wholesale
Lubricating oils and greases—wholesale
Naphtha, except bulk stations and terminals—wholesale
Petroleum and its products, except bulk stations and terminals—wholesale
Petroleum brokers—wholesale

518   BEER, WINE, AND DISTILLED ALCOHOLIC BEVERAGES

5181 Beer and Ale

Establishments primarily engaged in the wholesale distribution of beer, ale, porter, and other fermented malt beverages.

Ale—wholesale
Beer and other fermented malt liquors—wholesale

Porter—wholesale

5182 Wine and Distilled Alcoholic Beverages

Establishments primarily engaged in the wholesale distribution of distilled spirits, including neutral spirits and ethyl alcohol used in blended wines and distilled liquors.

Bottling wines and liquors—wholesale
Brandy and brandy spirits—wholesale
Cocktails, alcoholic: premixed—wholesale
Liquors, distilled—wholesale

Neutral spirits—wholesale
Spirits—wholesale
Wine coolers, alcoholic—wholesale
Wines—wholesale

Industry Group No.	Industry No.	
519		**MISCELLANEOUS NONDURABLE GOODS**

5191 Farm Supplies

Establishments primarily engaged in the wholesale distribution of animal feeds, fertilizers, agricultural chemicals, pesticides, seeds, and other farm supplies, except grains. Establishments primarily engaged in the wholesale distribution of pet food are classified in Industry 5149, and those distributing pet supplies are classified in Industry 5199.

Agricultural chemicals—wholesale	Harness made to individual order— wholesale
Agricultural limestone—wholesale	Hay—wholesale
Alfalfa—wholesale	Insecticides—wholesale
Animal feeds, except pet—wholesale	Lime, agricultural—wholesale
Beekeeping supplies—wholesale	Mineral supplements, animal—whole- sale
Farm supplies—wholesale	
Feed additives, animal—wholesale	Pesticides—wholesale
Feed, except unmixed grain—wholesale	Phosphate rock, ground—wholesale
Fertilizer and fertilizer materials— wholesale	Seeds: field, garden, and flower—whole- sale
Flower and field bulbs—wholesale	Straw—wholesale
Harness equipment—wholesale	

5192 Books, Periodicals, and Newspapers

Establishments primarily engaged in the wholesale distribution of books, periodicals, and newspapers.

Books—wholesale	Newspaper agencies—wholesale
Magazines—wholesale	Periodicals—wholesale

5193 Flowers, Nursery Stock, and Florists' Supplies

Establishments primarily engaged in the wholesale distribution of flowers, nursery stock, and florists' supplies.

Florists—wholesale	Flowers, fresh—wholesale
Flowers and florists' supplies—whole- sale	Nursery stock—wholesale
	Plants, potted—wholesale
Flowers, artificial—wholesale	

5194 Tobacco and Tobacco Products

Establishments primarily engaged in the wholesale distribution of tobacco and its products. Leaf tobacco wholesalers are classified in Industry 5159, and establishments primarily engaged in stemming and redrying tobacco are classified in Manufacturing, Industry 2141.

Chewing tobacco—wholesale	Snuff—wholesale
Cigarettes—wholesale	Tobacco products, manufactured— wholesale
Cigars—wholesale	
Smoking tobacco—wholesale	Tobacco, except leaf—wholesale

5198 Paints, Varnishes, and Supplies

Establishments primarily engaged in the wholesale distribution of paints, varnishes, wallpaper, and supplies. Establishments selling to the general public and known as retail in the trade are classified in Retail Trade, Industry 5231.

Calcimines—wholesale	Paints—wholesale
Colors and pigments—wholesale	Shellac—wholesale
Enamels—wholesale	Varnishes—wholesale
Lacquers—wholesale	Wallpaper—wholesale
Paint brushes, rollers, and sprayers— wholesale	

Industry Group No.	Industry No.	
519		**MISCELLANEOUS NONDURABLE GOODS—Con.**
	5199	**Nondurable Goods, Not Elsewhere Classified**

Establishments primarily engaged in the wholesale distribution of nondurable goods, not elsewhere classified, such as art goods, industrial yarns, textile bags, and bagging and burlap.

Advertising specialties—wholesale
Art goods—wholesale
Artists' materials—wholesale
Bags, textile—wholesale
Baskets: reed, rattan, willow, and wood—wholesale
Broom, mop, and paint handles—wholesale
Burlap—wholesale
Candles—wholesale
Canvas products—wholesale
Cats—wholesale
Chamois leather—wholesale
Charcoal—wholesale
Christmas trees, including artificial—wholesale
Clothes hangers—wholesale
Cotton yarns—wholesale
Curios—wholesale
Dogs—wholesale
Felt—wholesale
Fish, tropical—wholesale
Foam rubber—wholesale
Furs, dressed—wholesale
Gifts and novelties—wholesale
Glassware, novelty—wholesale
Greases, animal and vegetable—wholesale
Hairbrushes—wholesale
Ice, manufactured or natural—wholesale
Industrial yarn—wholesale

Jewelry boxes—wholesale
Leather and cut stock—wholesale
Leather goods, except footwear, gloves, luggage, and belting—wholesale
Lighters, cigar and cigarette—wholesale
Linseed oil—wholesale
Matches—wholesale
Novelties, paper—wholesale
Oils, except cooking: animal and vegetable—wholesale
Oilseed cake and meal—wholesale
Pet supplies, except pet food—wholesale
Pipes, smokers'—wholesale
Plant food—wholesale
Plastics foam—wholesale
Rayon yarns—wholesale
Rennet—wholesale
Rubber, crude—wholesale
Sawdust—wholesale
Sheet music—wholesale
Silk yarns—wholesale
Smokers' supplies—wholesale
Sponges—wholesale
Statuary—wholesale
Vegetable cake and meal—wholesale
Wigs—wholesale
Wood carvings—wholesale
Woolen and worsted yarns—wholesale
Worms—wholesale
Yarns—wholesale

DIVISION G

Retail Trade

The Division as a Whole

This division includes establishments engaged in selling merchandise for personal or household consumption and rendering services incidental to the sale of the goods. In general, retail establishments are classified by kind of business according to the principal lines of commodities sold (groceries, hardware, etc.), or the usual trade designation (drug store, cigar store, etc.). Some of the important characteristics of retail trade establishments are: the establishment is usually a place of business and is engaged in activities to attract the general public to buy; the establishment buys or receives merchandise as well as sells; the establishment may process its products, but such processing is incidental or subordinate to selling; the establishment is considered as retail in the trade; and the establishment sells to customers for personal or household use. Not all of these characteristics need be present and some are modified by trade practice.

For the most part, establishments engaged in retail trade sell merchandise to the general public for personal or household consumption. Exceptions to this general rule are lumber yards; paint, glass, and wallpaper stores; typewriter stores; stationery stores; and gasoline service stations which sell to both the general public for personal or household consumption and to businesses. These types of stores are classified in Retail Trade even if a higher proportion of their sales is made to other than individuals for personal or household consumption.

However, establishments that sell these products only to institutional or industrial users and to other wholesalers and establishments that sell similar merchandise for use exclusively by business establishments are classified in Wholesale Trade.

Establishments primarily engaged in selling such merchandise as plumbing equipment; electrical supplies; used automobile parts; and office furniture are classified in Wholesale Trade, even if a higher proportion of their sales is made to individuals for personal or household consumption.

Buying of goods for resale to the consumer is a characteristic of retail trade establishments that particularly distinguishes them from the agricultural and extractive industries. For example, farmers who sell only their own produce at or from the point of production are not classified as retailers.

Processing incidental or subordinate to selling often is conducted at retail stores. For example, restaurants prepare meals, and meat markets cut meat. Separate establishments selling merchandise for personal or household consumption

313

which has been manufactured by other establishments of the same company are classified in Retail Trade.

Chain store warehouses are considered auxiliary to the retail establishment served and are classified on the basis of the activity carried on by such retail stores.

Establishments primarily engaged in the retail sale of used motor vehicles, trailers, and boats are classified in Major Group 55; those selling used mobile homes are classified in Industry 5271; those selling used automobile parts are classified in Wholesale Trade, Industry 5015; and those selling all other used merchandise are classified in Industry Group 593. Establishments primarily engaged in nonstore retailing are classified in Industry Group 596.

Major Group 52.—BUILDING MATERIALS, HARDWARE, GARDEN SUPPLY, AND MOBILE HOME DEALERS

The Major Group as a Whole

This major group includes retail establishments primarily engaged in selling lumber and other building materials; paint, glass, and wallpaper; hardware; nursery stock; lawn and garden supplies; and mobile homes.

It includes lumber and other building materials dealers and paint, glass, and wallpaper stores selling to the general public, even if sales to construction contractors account for a larger proportion of total sales. These establishments are known as retail in the trade. Establishments primarily selling these products for use exclusively by businesses or to other wholesalers are classified in Wholesale Trade.

Establishments primarily selling plumbing, heating, and air-conditioning equipment and electrical supplies are classified in Wholesale Trade.

Industry Group No.	Industry No.	
521		**LUMBER AND OTHER BUILDING MATERIALS DEALERS**
	5211	**Lumber and Other Building Materials Dealers**

Establishments engaged in selling primarily lumber, or lumber and a general line of building materials, to the general public. While these establishments may sell primarily to construction contractors, they are known as retail in the trade. The lumber which they sell may include rough and dressed lumber, flooring, molding, doors, sashes, frames, and other millwork. The building materials may include roofing, siding, shingles, wallboard, paint, brick, tile, cement, sand, gravel, and other building materials and supplies. Hardware is often an important line sold by retail lumber and building materials dealers. Establishments which do not sell to the general public and those which are known in the trade as wholesale are classified in Wholesale Trade, Industry Group 503.

Brick and tile dealers—retail
Building materials dealers—retail
Buildings, prefabricated—retail
Cabinets, kitchen: to be installed—retail
Concrete and cinder block dealers—retail
Doors—retail
Fencing dealers—retail
Flooring, wood—retail
Garage doors—retail
Insulation material, building—retail
Lime and plaster dealers—retail
Lumber and building materials dealers—retail
Lumber and planing mill product dealers—retail
Millwork and lumber dealers—retail
Paneling—retail
Roofing material dealers—retail
Sand and gravel dealers—retail
Storm windows and sash, wood or metal—retail
Structural clay products—retail
Wallboard (composition) dealers—retail

523		**PAINT, GLASS, AND WALLPAPER STORES**
	5231	**Paint, Glass, and Wallpaper Stores**

Establishments engaged in selling primarily paint, glass, and wallpaper, or any combination of these lines, to the general public. While these establishments may sell primarily to construction contractors, they are known as retail in the trade. Establishments which do not sell to the general public or are known in the trade as wholesale are classified in Wholesale Trade.

523   PAINT, GLASS, AND WALLPAPER STORES—Con.

5231   Paint, Glass, and Wallpaper Stores—Con.

Glass stores—retail	Wallcovering stores—retail
Paint stores—retail	Wallpaper stores—retail

525   HARDWARE STORES

5251   Hardware Stores

Establishments primarily engaged in the retail sale of a number of basic hardware lines, such as tools, builders' hardware, paint and glass, housewares and household appliances, and cutlery.

Builders' hardware—retail	Handtools—retail
Chainsaws—retail	Hardware stores—retail
Door locks and lock sets—retail	Tools, power and hand—retail

526   RETAIL NURSERIES, LAWN AND GARDEN SUPPLY STORES

5261   Retail Nurseries, Lawn and Garden Supply Stores

Establishments primarily engaged in selling trees, shrubs, other plants, seeds, bulbs, mulches, soil conditioners, fertilizers, pesticides, garden tools, and other garden supplies to the general public. These establishments primarily sell products purchased from others, but may sell some plants which they grow themselves. Establishments primarily engaged in growing trees (except Christmas trees), shrubs, other plants, seeds, and bulbs are classified in Agriculture, Major Group 01 and those growing Christmas trees are classified in Industry 0811.

Christmas trees (natural)—retail	Power mowers—retail
Garden supplies and tools—retail	Sod—retail
Lawnmowers—retail	Soil, top—retail
Nursery stock, seeds and bulbs—retail	

527   MOBILE HOME DEALERS

5271   Mobile Home Dealers

Establishments primarily engaged in the retail sale of new and used mobile homes, parts, and equipment. Establishments primarily selling travel trailers and campers are classified in Industry 5561.

Mobile home equipment—retail	Mobile homes, new and used—retail
Mobile home parts and accessories—retail	

Major Group 53.—GENERAL MERCHANDISE STORES

The Major Group as a Whole

This major group includes retail stores which sell a number of lines of merchandise, such as dry goods, apparel and accessories, furniture and homefurnishings, small wares, hardware, and food. The stores included in this group are known by such names as department stores, variety stores, general merchandise stores, and general stores. Establishments primarily engaged in selling used general merchandise are classified in Industry Group 593, and those selling general merchandise by mail, vending machine, or direct selling are classified in Industry Group 596.

Industry
Group
No.

Industry
No.

531   **DEPARTMENT STORES**

    5311   **Department Stores**

Retail stores generally carrying a general line of apparel, such as suits, coats, dresses, and furnishings; homefurnishings, such as furniture, floor coverings, curtains, draperies, linens, and major household appliances; and housewares, such as table and kitchen appliances, dishes, and utensils. These stores must carry men's and women's apparel and either major household appliances or other homefurnishings. These and other merchandise lines are normally arranged in separate sections or departments with the accounting on a departmentalized basis. The departments and functions are integrated under a single management. The stores usually provide their own charge accounts, deliver merchandise, and maintain open stocks. These stores normally have 50 employees or more. Establishments which sell a similar range of merchandise with less than 50 employees are classified in Industry 5399. Establishments which do not carry these general lines of merchandise are classified according to their primary activity.

Department stores—retail

533   **VARIETY STORES**

    5331   **Variety Stores**

Establishments primarily engaged in the retail sale of a variety of merchandise in the low and popular price ranges. Sales usually are made on a cash-and-carry basis, with the open-selling method of display and customer selection of merchandise. These stores generally do not carry a complete line of merchandise, are not departmentalized, do not carry their own charge service, and do not deliver merchandise.

Limited price variety stores—retail

539   **MISCELLANEOUS GENERAL MERCHANDISE STORES**

    5399   **Miscellaneous General Merchandise Stores**

Establishments primarily engaged in the retail sale of a general line of apparel, dry goods, hardware, housewares or homefurnishings, groceries, and other lines in limited amounts. Stores selling commodities covered in the definition for department stores, but normally having less than 50 employees, and

539   MISCELLANEOUS GENERAL MERCHANDISE STORES—Con.

5399   Miscellaneous General Merchandise Stores—Con.

stores usually known as country general stores are included in this industry. Establishments primarily engaged in the retail sale of merchandise by television, catalog and mail-order are classified in Industry 5961.

Catalog showrooms, general merchandise: except catalog mail-order—retail

Country general stores—retail
General merchandise stores—retail
General stores—retail

Major Group 54.—FOOD STORES

The Major Group as a Whole

This major group includes retail stores primarily engaged in selling food for home preparation and consumption. Establishments primarily engaged in selling prepared foods and drinks for consumption on the premises are classified in Major Group 58, and stores primarily engaged in selling packaged beers and liquors are classified in Industry 5921.

Industry Group No.	Industry No.	

541   GROCERY STORES

5411   Grocery Stores

Stores, commonly known as supermarkets, food stores, and grocery stores, primarily engaged in the retail sale of all sorts of canned foods and dry goods, such as tea, coffee, spices, sugar, and flour; fresh fruits and vegetables; and fresh and prepared meats, fish, and poultry.

Convenience food stores—retail
Food markets—retail
Frozen food and freezer plans, except meat—retail

Grocery stores, with or without fresh meat—retail
Supermarkets, grocery—retail

542   MEAT AND FISH (SEAFOOD) MARKETS, INCLUDING FREEZER PROVISIONERS

5421   Meat and Fish (Seafood) Markets, Including Freezer Provisioners

Establishments primarily engaged in the retail sale of fresh, frozen, or cured meats, fish, shellfish, and other seafoods. This industry includes establishments primarily engaged in the retail sale, on a bulk basis, of meat for freezer storage and in providing home freezer plans. Meat markets may butcher animals on their own account, or they may buy from others. Food locker plants primarily engaged in renting locker space for the storage of food products for individual households are classified in Industry 4222. Establishments primarily engaged in the retail sale of poultry are classified in Industry 5499.

Fish markets—retail
Freezer food plans, meat—retail
Freezer provisioners, meat—retail
Frozen food and freezer plans, meat—retail

Meat markets—retail
Seafood markets—retail

543   FRUIT AND VEGETABLE MARKETS

5431   Fruit and Vegetable Markets

Establishments primarily engaged in the retail sale of fresh fruits and vegetables. They are frequently found in public or municipal markets or as roadside stands. However, establishments which grow fruits and vegetables and sell them at roadside stands are classified in Agriculture, Major Group 01.

Fruit markets and stands—retail
Produce markets and stands—retail

Vegetable markets and stands—retail

Industry Group No.	Industry No.	

544   CANDY, NUT, AND CONFECTIONERY STORES

5441 Candy, Nut, and Confectionery Stores

Establishments primarily engaged in the retail sale of candy, nuts, popcorn, and other confections.

Candy stores—retail	Confectionery stores—retail
Confectionery produced for direct sale on the premises—retail	Nut stores—retail
	Popcorn stands—retail

545   DAIRY PRODUCTS STORES

5451 Dairy Products Stores

Establishments primarily engaged in the retail sale of packaged dairy products to over-the-counter customers. Ice cream and frozen custard stands are classified in Industry 5812, and establishments selling ice cream and similar products from trucks or wagons are classified in Industry 5963. Establishments primarily engaged in processing and distributing milk and cream are classified in Manufacturing, Industry Group 202.

Butter and other dairy product stores— retail	Ice cream (packaged) stores—retail
Cheese stores—retail	Milk and other dairy products stores— retail
Dairy products stores—retail	

546   RETAIL BAKERIES

5461 Retail Bakeries

Establishments primarily engaged in the retail sale of bakery products. The products may be purchased from others or made on the premises. Establishments manufacturing bakery products for the trade are classified in Manufacturing, Industry Group 205, and those purchasing bakery products and selling house-to-house are classified in Industry 5963.

Bagel stores—retail	Doughnut shops—retail
Bakeries—retail	Pretzel stores and stands—retail
Cookie stores—retail	

549   MISCELLANEOUS FOOD STORES

5499 Miscellaneous Food Stores

Establishments primarily engaged in the retail sale of specialized foods, not elsewhere classified, such as eggs, poultry, health foods, spices, herbs, coffee, and tea. The poultry stores may sell live poultry, slaughter and clean poultry for their own account, and sell dressed fowls, or sell fowls cleaned and dressed by others.

Coffee stores—retail	Spice and herb stores—retail
Dietetic food stores—retail	Tea stores—retail
Egg dealers—retail	Vitamin food stores—retail
Health food stores—retail	Water, mineral—retail
Poultry dealers—retail	

Major Group 55.—AUTOMOTIVE DEALERS AND GASOLINE SERVICE STATIONS

The Major Group as a Whole

This major group includes retail dealers selling new and used automobiles, boats, recreational vehicles, utility trailers, and motorcycles including mopeds; those selling new automobile parts and accessories; and gasoline service stations. Automobile repair shops maintained by establishments engaged in the sale of new automobiles are also included. Establishments primarily engaged in selling used automobile parts are classified in Wholesale Trade, Industry 5015.

Industry Group No.	Industry No.	

551   MOTOR VEHICLE DEALERS (NEW AND USED)

5511   Motor Vehicle Dealers (New and Used)

Establishments primarily engaged in the retail sale of new automobiles or new and used automobiles. These establishments frequently maintain repair departments and carry stocks of replacement parts, tires, batteries, and automotive accessories. These establishments also frequently sell pickups and vans at retail.

Automobile agencies (dealers)—retail
Automobiles, new and used—retail
Cars, new and used—retail
Motor vehicle dealers, new and used cars—retail
Pickups and vans, new and used—retail

552   MOTOR VEHICLE DEALERS (USED ONLY)

5521   Motor Vehicle Dealers (Used Only)

Establishments primarily engaged in the retail sale of used cars only, with no sales of new automobiles. These establishments also frequently sell used pickups and vans at retail.

Antique autos—retail
Automobiles, used cars only—retail
Motor vehicle dealers, used cars only—retail
Pickups and vans, used only—retail

553   AUTO AND HOME SUPPLY STORES

5531   Auto and Home Supply Stores

Establishments primarily engaged in the retail sale of new automobile tires, batteries, and other automobile parts and accessories. Such establishments frequently sell a substantial amount of home appliances, radios, and television sets. Establishments dealing primarily in used parts are classified in Wholesale Trade, Industry 5015. Establishments primarily engaged in both selling and installing such automotive parts as transmissions, mufflers, brake linings, and glass are classified in Services, Industry Group 753.

Automobile accessory dealers—retail
Automobile air-conditioning equipment, sale and installation—retail
Automobile parts dealers—retail
Battery dealers, automobile—retail
Speed shops—retail
Tire dealers, automotive—retail
Tire, battery, and accessory dealers—retail

Industry
Group   Industry
No.   No.

554   GASOLINE SERVICE STATIONS

5541   Gasoline Service Stations

Gasoline service stations primarily engaged in selling gasoline and lubricating oils. These establishments frequently sell other merchandise, such as tires, batteries, and other automobile parts, or perform minor repair work. Gasoline stations combined with other activities, such as grocery stores, convenience stores, or carwashes, are classified according to the primary activity.

Automobile service stations—retail	Marine service stations—retail
Filling stations, gasoline—retail	Service stations, gasoline—retail
Gasoline and oil—retail	Truck stops—retail

555   BOAT DEALERS

5551   Boat Dealers

Establishments primarily engaged in the retail sale of new and used motorboats and other watercraft, marine supplies, and outboard motors.

Boat dealers—retail	Motorboat dealers—retail
Marine supply dealers—retail	Outboard motor dealers—retail

556   RECREATIONAL VEHICLE DEALERS

5561   Recreational Vehicle Dealers

Establishments primarily engaged in the retail sale of new and used motor homes, recreational trailers, and campers (pickup coaches). Establishments primarily engaged in the retail sale of mobile homes are classified in Industry 5271, and those selling utility trailers are classified in Industry 5599.

Campers (pickup coaches) for mounting on trucks—retail	Recreational vehicle parts and accessories—retail
Motor home dealers—retail	Travel trailers, automobile: new and used—retail
Recreational vehicle dealers—retail	

557   MOTORCYCLE DEALERS

5571   Motorcycle Dealers

Establishments primarily engaged in the retail sale of new and used motorcycles, including motor scooters and mopeds, and all-terrain vehicles.

All-terrain vehicles—retail	Motor scooters—retail
Bicycles, motorized—retail	Motorcycle dealers—retail
Mopeds—retail	Motorcycle parts—retail

559   AUTOMOTIVE DEALERS, NOT ELSEWHERE CLASSIFIED

5599   Automotive Dealers, Not Elsewhere Classified

Establishments primarily engaged in the retail sale of new and used automotive vehicles, utility trailers, and automotive equipment and supplies, not elsewhere classified, such as snowmobiles, dunebuggies, and gocarts. Also included in this industry are establishments primarily engaged in the retail sale of aircraft.

Aircraft dealers—retail	Snowmobiles—retail
Dunebuggies—retail	Trailers, utility—retail
Gocarts—retail	Utility trailers—retail

Major Group 56.—APPAREL AND ACCESSORY STORES

The Major Group as a Whole

This major group includes retail stores primarily engaged in selling new clothing, shoes, hats, underwear, and related articles for personal wear and adornment. Furriers and custom tailors carrying stocks of materials are included.

Industry Group No.	Industry No.	

561   MEN'S AND BOYS' CLOTHING AND ACCESSORY STORES

5611   Men's and Boys' Clothing and Accessory Stores

Establishments primarily engaged in the retail sale of men's and boys' ready-to-wear clothing and accessories.

Apparel accessory stores, men's and boys'—retail
Clothing stores, men's and boys'—retail
Haberdashery stores—retail

Hat stores, men's and boys'—retail
Men's wearing apparel—retail
Tie shops—retail

562   WOMEN'S CLOTHING STORES

5621   Women's Clothing Stores

Establishments primarily engaged in the retail sale of a general line of women's ready-to-wear clothing. This industry also includes establishments primarily engaged in the specialized retail sale of women's coats, suits, and dresses. Custom tailors primarily engaged in making women's clothing to individual order are classified in Industry 5699.

Bridal shops, except custom—retail
Clothing, ready-to-wear: women's—retail

Dress shops—retail
Maternity shops—retail
Ready-to-wear stores, women's—retail

563   WOMEN'S ACCESSORY AND SPECIALTY STORES

5632   Women's Accessory and Specialty Stores

Establishments primarily engaged in the retail sale of women's clothing accessories and specialties, such as millinery, blouses, foundation garments, lingerie, hosiery, costume jewelry, gloves, handbags, and furs (including custom made furs).

Apparel accessory stores, women's—retail
Blouse stores—retail
Costume jewelry stores—retail
Foundation garments—retail
Fur apparel made to custom order—retail

Fur shops—retail
Furriers—retail
Handbag stores—retail
Hosiery stores—retail
Lingerie stores—retail
Millinery stores—retail

564   CHILDREN'S AND INFANTS' WEAR STORES

5641   Children's and Infants' Wear Stores

Establishments primarily engaged in the retail sale of children's and infants' clothing, furnishings, and accessories. Such establishments may specialize in either children's or infants' wear or they may sell a combination of children's and infants' wear.

Children's wear stores—retail

Infants' wear stores—retail

Industry Group No.	Industry No.	
565		**FAMILY CLOTHING STORES**

5651 Family Clothing Stores

Establishments primarily engaged in the retail sale of clothing, furnishings, and accessories for men, women, and children, without specializing in sales for an individual sex or age group.

Family clothing stores—retail
Jeans stores—retail

Unisex clothing stores—retail

566   SHOE STORES

5661 Shoe Stores

Establishments primarily engaged in the retail sale of men's, women's, and children's footwear, including athletic footwear. These establishments frequently carry accessory lines, such as hosiery, gloves, and handbags.

Athletic shoe stores—retail
Footwear stores—retail

Shoe stores—retail

569   MISCELLANEOUS APPAREL AND ACCESSORY STORES

5699 Miscellaneous Apparel and Accessory Stores

Establishments primarily engaged in the retail sale of specialized lines of apparel and accessories, not elsewhere classified, such as uniforms, bathing suits, raincoats, riding apparel, sports apparel, umbrellas, wigs, and toupees. This industry also includes custom tailors primarily engaged in making and selling men's and women's clothing, except fur apparel. Establishments primarily engaged in making fur apparel to custom order are classified in Industry 5632.

Bathing suit stores—retail
Belts, apparel: custom—retail
Custom tailors—retail
Dresses made to order—retail
Dressmakers' shops, custom—retail
Merchant tailors—retail
Raincoat stores—retail

Riding apparel stores—retail
Shirts, custom made—retail
Sports apparel stores—retail
Tee shirts, custom printed—retail
Umbrella stores—retail
Uniforms—retail
Wig, toupee, and wiglet stores —retail

Major Group 57.—HOME FURNITURE, FURNISHINGS, AND EQUIPMENT STORES

The Major Group as a Whole

This major group includes retail stores selling goods used for furnishing the home, such as furniture, floor coverings, draperies, glass and chinaware, domestic stoves, refrigerators, and other household electrical and gas appliances. Establishments selling electrical and gas appliances are included in this group only if the major part of their sales consists of articles for home use. These stores may also repair household appliances, radios, televisions, and stereo equipment, but establishments primarily engaged in repair of these products are classified in Division I, Services. Dealers primarily engaged in selling antique and secondhand furniture are classified in Industry Group 593. Stores furnishing interior decorator service are classified according to the merchandise handled.

Industry Group No.	Industry No.	
571		**HOME FURNITURE AND FURNISHINGS STORES**

5712 Furniture Stores

Establishments primarily engaged in the retail sale of household furniture. These stores may also sell homefurnishings, major appliances, and floor coverings.

Beds and springs—retail
Cabinet work on a custom basis to individual order—retail
Cabinets, kitchen: not built in—retail
Furniture, custom made—retail
Furniture, household, with or without furnishings and appliances—retail

Juvenile furniture—retail
Mattress stores, including custom made—retail
Outdoor furniture—retail
Waterbeds—retail

5713 Floor Covering Stores

Establishments primarily engaged in the retail sale of floor coverings. Establishments included in this industry may incidentally perform installation, but contractors primarily engaged in installing floor coverings for others are classified in Construction, Industry 1752.

Carpet stores—retail
Floor covering stores—retail
Floor tile stores—retail

Linoleum stores—retail
Rug stores—retail

5714 Drapery, Curtain, and Upholstery Stores

Establishments primarily engaged in the retail sale of draperies, curtains, and upholstery materials. Establishments primarily engaged in reupholstering or repairing furniture are classified in Services, Industry 7641.

Curtain stores—retail
Drapery stores—retail

Slipcover stores—retail
Upholstery materials stores—retail

5719 Miscellaneous Homefurnishings Stores

Establishments primarily engaged in the retail sale of miscellaneous homefurnishings, such as china, glassware, and metalware for kitchen and table use; bedding and linen; brooms and brushes; lamps and shades; mirrors and pictures; venetian blinds; and window shades. Establishments primarily en-

Industry
Group   Industry
No.   No.

571   **HOME FURNITURE AND FURNISHINGS STORES—Con.**

5719   **Miscellaneous Homefurnishings Stores—Con.**

gaged in the retail sale of miscellaneous homefurnishings by house-to-house
canvass or by party-plan merchandising are classified in Industry 5963.

Aluminumware stores—retail	Glassware stores—retail
Bedding (sheets, blankets, spreads, and pillows)—retail	Housewares stores—retail
	Kitchenware stores—retail
Brooms—retail	Lamp and shade shops—retail
Brushes—retail	Linen shops—retail
China stores—retail	Metalware stores—retail
Cookware—retail	Mirrors —retail
Crockery stores—retail	Pottery stores—retail
Cutlery stores—retail	Tinware stores—retail
Enamelware stores—retail	Venetian blind shops—retail
Fireplace screens and accessories—retail	Window shade shops—retail
	Woodburning stoves—retail
Fireplace stores—retail	

572   **HOUSEHOLD APPLIANCE STORES**

5722   **Household Appliance Stores**

Establishments primarily engaged in the retail sale of electric and gas refrigerators, stoves, and other household appliances, such as electric irons, percolators, hot plates, and vacuum cleaners. Many such stores also sell radio and
television sets. Retail stores operated by public utility companies and primarily engaged in the sale of electric and gas appliances for household use are
classified in this industry.

Air-conditioning room units, self-contained—retail	Ranges, gas and electric—retail
	Refrigerators and related electric and gas appliances—retail
Electric household appliance stores—retail	
	Sewing machine stores—retail
Freezers, household—retail	Stoves and related electric and gas appliances—retail
Garbage disposers, electric—retail	
Household appliance stores, electric or gas—retail	Vacuum cleaner stores—retail
Kitchens, complete (sinks, cabinets, etc.)—retail	

573   **RADIO, TELEVISION, CONSUMER ELECTRONICS, AND MUSIC STORES**

5731   **Radio, Television, and Consumer Electronics Stores**

Establishments primarily engaged in the retail sale of radios, television sets,
record players, stereo equipment, sound reproducing equipment, and other
consumer audio and video electronics equipment (including automotive). Such
establishments may also sell additional lines, such as household appliances;
computers, computer peripheral equipment, and software; musical instruments; or records and prerecorded tapes. Establishments in this industry may
perform incidental installation and repair work on radios, television sets, and
other consumer electronic equipment. Establishments primarily engaged in
the installation and repair of these products are classified in Services, Industry 7622. Establishments primarily engaged in the retail sale of computer
equipment are classified in Industry 5734, and those selling electronic toys are
classified in Industry 5945.

Antenna stores, household—retail	Radio-phonograph stores—retail
Consumer electronic equipment stores—retail	Tape recorders and players—retail
	Television set stores—retail
High fidelity (hi-fi) equipment—retail	Video camera stores—retail
Phonograph stores—retail	Video tape recorder stores—retail
Radio stores—retail	

573   **RADIO, TELEVISION, CONSUMER ELECTRONICS, AND MUSIC STORES—Con.**

5734 Computer and Computer Software Stores

Establishments primarily engaged in the retail sale of computers, computer peripheral equipment, and software. Establishments primarily engaged in the sale of computers, computer peripheral equipment and software for business or professional use are classified in Wholesale Trade, Industry 5045.

Computer printer stores—retail   Peripheral   equipment,   computer
Computer software stores—retail   stores—retail
Computer stores—retail

5735 Record and Prerecorded Tape Stores

Establishments primarily engaged in the retail sale of phonograph records and prerecorded audio and video tapes and disks. Establishments primarily engaged in the retail sale of computer software are classified in Industry 5734, and those primarily engaged in the rental of video tapes are classified in Services, Industry 7841.

Disks, music and video—retail   Tape stores, audio and video—retail
Record stores—retail   Video tape stores—retail

5736 Musical Instrument Stores

Establishments primarily engaged in the retail sale of musical instruments, sheet music, and similar supplies.

Musical instrument stores—retail   Sheet music stores—retail
Piano stores—retail

Major Group 58.—EATING AND DRINKING PLACES

The Major Group as a Whole

This major group includes retail establishments selling prepared foods and drinks for consumption on the premises; and also lunch counters and refreshment stands selling prepared foods and drinks for immediate consumption. Restaurants, lunch counters, and drinking places operated as a subordinate service facility by other establishments are not included in this industry, unless they are operated as leased departments by outside operators. Thus, restaurants and lunch counters operated by hotels are classified in Services, Major Group 70; those operated by department stores in Major Group 53. Bars and restaurants owned by and operated for members of civic, social, and fraternal associations only are classified in Industry 8641. Mobile food and dairy wagons are classified in Industry 5963.

Industry Group No.	Industry No.	
581		**EATING AND DRINKING PLACES**
	5812	**Eating Places**

Establishments primarily engaged in the retail sale of prepared food and drinks for on-premise or immediate consumption. Caterers and industrial and institutional food service establishments are also included in this industry.

Automats (eating places)
Beaneries
Box lunch stands
Buffets (eating places)
Cafes
Cafeterias
Carry-out restaurants
Caterers
Coffee shops
Commissary restaurants
Concession stands, prepared food (e.g., in airports and sports arenas)
Contract feeding
Dairy bars
Diners (eating places)
Dining rooms
Dinner theaters
Drive-in restaurants
Fast food restaurants
Food bars
Food service, institutional
Frozen custard stands
Grills (eating places)
Hamburger stands
Hot dog (frankfurter) stands
Ice cream stands
Industrial feeding
Lunch bars
Lunch counters
Luncheonettes
Lunchrooms
Oyster bars
Pizza parlors
Pizzerias
Refreshment stands
Restaurants
Restaurants, carry-out
Restaurants, fast food
Sandwich bars or shops
Snack shops
Soda fountains
Soft drink stands
Submarine sandwich shops
Tea rooms
Theaters, dinner

5813 Drinking Places (Alcoholic Beverages)

Establishments primarily engaged in the retail sale of alcoholic drinks, such as beer, ale, wine, and liquor, for consumption on the premises. The sale of food frequently accounts for a substantial portion of the receipts of these establishments.

Bars (alcoholic beverage drinking places)
Beer gardens (drinking places)
Beer parlors (tap rooms)
Beer taverns
Beer, wine, and liquors: sale for on-premise consumption
Bottle clubs (drinking places)
Cabarets
Cocktail lounges
Discotheques, alcoholic beverage
Drinking places, alcoholic beverages
Night clubs
Saloons (drinking places)
Tap rooms (drinking places)
Taverns (drinking places)
Wine bars

Major Group 59.—MISCELLANEOUS RETAIL

The Major Group as a Whole

This major group includes retail establishments, not elsewhere classified. These establishments fall into the following categories: drug stores, liquor stores, used merchandise stores, miscellaneous shopping goods stores, nonstore retailers, fuel dealers, and miscellaneous retail stores, not elsewhere classified.

Industry Group No.	Industry No.	

591   DRUG STORES AND PROPRIETARY STORES

5912   Drug Stores and Proprietary Stores

Establishments engaged in the retail sale of prescription drugs, proprietary drugs, and nonprescription medicines, and which may also carry a number of related lines, such as cosmetics, toiletries, tobacco, and novelty merchandise. These stores are included on the basis of their usual trade designation rather than on the stricter interpretation of commodities handled. This industry includes drug stores which also operate a soda fountain or lunch counter.

Apothecaries—retail
Drug stores—retail
Pharmacies—retail

Proprietary (nonprescription medicines) stores—retail

592   LIQUOR STORES

5921   Liquor Stores

Establishments primarily engaged in the retail sale of packaged alcoholic beverages, such as ale, beer, wine, and liquor, for consumption off the premises. Stores selling prepared drinks for consumption on the premises are classified in Industry 5813.

Beer, packaged—retail
Liquor, packaged—retail

Wine, packaged—retail

593   USED MERCHANDISE STORES

5932   Used Merchandise Stores

This industry includes stores primarily engaged in the retail sale of used merchandise, antiques, and secondhand goods, such as clothing and shoes; furniture; books and rare manuscripts; musical instruments; office furniture; phonographs and phonograph records; and store fixtures and equipment. This industry also includes pawnshops. Dealers primarily engaged in selling used motor vehicles, trailers, and boats are classified in Major Group 55, and those selling used mobile homes are classified in Industry 5271. Establishments primarily selling used automobile parts and accessories are classified in Wholesale Trade, Industry 5015, and scrap and waste dealers are classified in Industry 5093. Establishments primarily engaged in automotive repair are classified in Services, Industry Group 753.

Antique stores—retail
Book stores, secondhand—retail
Building materials, used—retail
Clothing stores, secondhand—retail
Furniture stores, secondhand—retail
Furniture, antique—retail

Glassware, antique—retail
Homefurnishing stores, secondhand—retail
Homefurnishings, antique—retail
Manuscripts, rare—retail
Musical instrument stores, second-

Industry Group No.	Industry No.	
593		**USED MERCHANDISE STORES—Con.**
	5932	**Used Merchandise Stores—Con.**

hand—retail
Objects of art, antique—retail
Pawnshops

Phonograph and phonograph record stores, secondhand—retail
Shoe stores, secondhand—retail

594   MISCELLANEOUS SHOPPING GOODS STORES

5941   Sporting Goods Stores and Bicycle Shops

Establishments primarily engaged in the retail sale of sporting goods, sporting equipment, and bicycles, bicycle parts, and accessories. Retail establishments primarily engaged in selling motorized bicycles are classified in Industry 5571, and those engaged in the retail sale of athletic footwear are classified in Industry 5661. Establishments primarily engaged in repairing bicycles are classified in Services, Industry 7699, and those renting bicycles are classified in Industry 7999.

Ammunition—retail
Backpacking, hiking, and mountaineering equipment—retail
Bait and tackle shops—retail
Bicycle and bicycle parts dealers, except motorized—retail
Bowling equipment and supplies—retail
Camping equipment—retail
Exercise apparatus—retail
Firearms—retail
Fishing equipment—retail
Golf goods and equipment—retail

Golf professionals operating retail stores
Gymnasium equipment—retail
Hunters' equipment—retail
Playground equipment—retail
Pool and billiards table stores—retail
Riding goods and equipment—retail
Saddlery stores—retail
Skiing equipment—retail
Skin diving and scuba equipment—retail
Sporting goods stores—retail
Tennis goods and equipment—retail

5942   Book Stores

Establishments primarily engaged in the retail sale of new books and magazines. Establishments primarily engaged in the retail sale of used books are classified in Industry 5932.

Book stores selling new books and magazines—retail

Religious book stores—retail

5943   Stationery Stores

Establishments primarily engaged in the retail sale of stationery, such as paper and paper products (including printing and engraving), postcards, and paper novelties. These establishments may also sell additional lines of office type supplies, such as accounting and legal forms, blankbooks and forms, and office forms and supplies. Establishments primarily engaged in selling office forms and supplies are classified in Wholesale Trade, Industry 5112. Establishments primarily engaged in the retail sale of greeting cards are classified in Industry 5947.

Pen and pencil shops—retail
School supplies—retail

Stationery stores—retail
Writing supplies—retail

5944   Jewelry Stores

Establishments primarily engaged in the retail sale of any combination of the lines of jewelry, such as diamonds and other precious stones mounted in precious metals as rings, bracelets, and broaches; sterling and plated silverware; and watches and clocks. Stores primarily engaged in watch and jewelry

594   **MISCELLANEOUS SHOPPING GOODS STORES—Con.**

5944 Jewelry Stores—Con.

repair are classified in Services, Industry 7631. Establishments primarily engaged in selling costume jewelry are classified in Industry 5632.

Clocks, including custom made—retail	Silverware—retail
Jewelry, precious stones and precious metals: including custom made—retail	Watches, including custom made—retail

5945 Hobby, Toy, and Game Shops

Establishments primarily engaged in the retail sale of toys, games, and hobby and craft kits and supplies. Establishments primarily engaged in selling artists' supplies or collectors' items, such as coins, stamps, and autographs, are classified in Industry 5999.

Ceramics supplies—retail	Hobby shops—retail
Craft kits and supplies—retail	Kite (toy) stores—retail
Game shops—retail	Toy and game stores—retail

5946 Camera and Photographic Supply Stores

Establishments primarily engaged in the retail sale of cameras, film, and other photographic supplies and equipment. Establishments primarily engaged in the retail sale of video cameras are classified in Industry 5731 and those engaged in finishing films are classified in Services, Industry 7384.

Camera shops, photographic—retail	Photographic supply stores—retail

5947 Gift, Novelty, and Souvenir Shops

Establishments primarily engaged in the retail sale of combined lines of gifts and novelty merchandise, souvenirs, greeting cards, holiday decorations, and miscellaneous small art goods.

Balloon shops—retail	Greeting card shops—retail
Curio shops—retail	Novelty shops—retail
Gift shops—retail	Souvenir shops—retail

5948 Luggage and Leather Goods Stores

Establishments primarily engaged in the retail sale of luggage, trunks, and leather goods.

Leather goods, including goods made to individual order—retail	Trunks, luggage—retail
Luggage and leather goods stores—retail	

5949 Sewing, Needlework, and Piece Goods Stores

Establishments primarily engaged in the retail sale of sewing supplies, fabrics, patterns, yarn and other needlework accessories.

Fabric shops—retail	Quilting materials and supplies—retail
Knitting yarn shops—retail	Remnant stores—retail
Mill end stores—retail	Sewing supplies—retail
Needlework stores—retail	Yard goods stores—retail
Notion stores—retail	Yarn shops (knitting)—retail
Piece goods—retail	

596   **NONSTORE RETAILERS**

5961   **Catalog and Mail-Order Houses**

Establishments primarily engaged in the retail sale of products by television, catalog, and mail-order. These establishments do not ordinarily maintain stock for sale on the premises. Separate stores operated by catalog and mail-order houses for the retail sale of products on the premises are classified according to the product sold.

Book clubs, not publishing
Books, mail-order—retail
Catalog (order taking) offices of mail-order houses—retail
Cheese, mail-order—retail
Coins, mail-order—retail
Computer and peripheral equipment, mail-order—retail
Computer software, mail-order—retail
Food, mail-order—retail
Fruit, mail-order—retail
Jewelry, mail-order—retail

Magazines, mail-order—retail
Mail-order houses—retail (not including retail outlets)
Novelty merchandise, mail-order—retail
Order taking offices of mail-order houses—retail
Record clubs, mail-order—retail
Stamps, mail-order—retail
Television, mail-order (home shopping)—retail

5962   **Automatic Merchandising Machine Operators**

Establishments primarily engaged in the retail sale of products by means of automatic merchandising units, also referred to as vending machines. This industry does not include the operation of coin-operated service machines, such as music machines, amusement and game machines, and lockers and scales. Insurance policies sold through vending machines are classified in Insurance, Major Group 63 or 64. Establishments primarily engaged in operating music machines, amusement and game machines, lockers and scales, and most other coin-operated service machines, are classified in Services, Division I.

Coin-operated machines selling merchandise
Dispensing machine sale of products—retail

Merchandising, automatic (sale of products through vending machines)
Vending machine sale of products

5963   **Direct Selling Establishments**

Establishments primarily engaged in the retail sale of merchandise by telephone; by house-to-house canvass; or from trucks or wagons or other temporary locations. Included in this industry are individuals who sell products by these methods and who are not employees of the organization which they represent, and establishments which are retail sales offices from which employees operate to sell merchandise from door-to-door.

Bakery goods, purchased: house-to-house—retail
Canvassers (door-to-door), headquarters for retail sale of merchandise
Dairy products, house-to-house—retail
Direct selling organizations (headquarters of door-to-door canvassers)—retail
House delivery of purchased milk—retail
House-to-house selling of coffee, soda, beer, bottled water, or other products—retail

Hucksters—retail
Ice cream wagons—retail
Lunch wagons, mobile—retail
Magazine subscription sales, except mail-order—retail
Magazines, house-to-house selling
Milk delivery and sale of purchased milk, without processing—retail
Newspapers, home delivery: except by newspaper printers or publishers
Party-plan merchandising—retail

Industry
Group   Industry
No.   No.

598   **FUEL DEALERS**

      5983   **Fuel Oil Dealers**

Establishments primarily engaged in the retail sale of fuel oil. Establishments primarily engaged in selling fuel oil burners are classified in Wholesale Trade, Industry 5074; those primarily engaged in installing and servicing fuel oil burners are classified in Construction, Industry 1711; and those engaged in fuel oil burner repair service only are classified in Services, Industry 7699.

          Fuel oil dealers—retail

      5984   **Liquefied Petroleum Gas (Bottled Gas) Dealers**

Establishments primarily engaged in the retail sale of bottled or bulk liquefied petroleum (LP) gas.

Bottled gas—retail	Propane gas, bottled—retail
Butane gas, bottled—retail	
Liquefied petroleum (LP) gas delivered to customers' premises—retail	

      5989   **Fuel Dealers, Not Elsewhere Classified**

Establishments primarily engaged in the retail sale of coal, wood, or other fuels, not elsewhere classified.

Coal dealers—retail	Wood dealers, fuel—retail

599   **RETAIL STORES, NOT ELSEWHERE CLASSIFIED**

      5992   **Florists**

Establishments primarily engaged in the retail sale of cut flowers and growing plants. Establishments primarily engaged in the retail sale of seeds, bulbs, and nursery stock are classified in Industry 5261, and greenhouses and nurseries primarily engaged in growing seeds, bulbs, flowers, and nursery stock are classified in Agriculture, Industry 0181.

Florists—retail	Potted plants—retail
Flowers, fresh—retail	

      5993   **Tobacco Stores and Stands**

Establishments primarily engaged in the retail sale of cigarettes, cigars, tobacco, and smokers' supplies.

Cigar stores and stands—retail	Tobacconists—retail
Tobacco stores—retail	

      5994   **News Dealers and Newsstands**

Establishments primarily engaged in the retail sale of newspapers, magazines, and other periodicals. Home delivery of newspapers by other than printers or publishers is classified in Industry 5963.

Magazine stands—retail	Newsstands—retail
News dealers—retail	

      5995   **Optical Goods Stores**

Establishments primarily engaged in the retail sale of eyeglasses and contact lenses to prescription for individuals. Offices of oculists, ophthalmologists, and optometrists are classified in Services, Major Group 80, even if a majority of their revenues comes from retail sales. Establishments primarily engaged

RETAIL STORES, NOT ELSEWHERE CLASSIFIED—Con.

5995   Optical Goods Stores—Con.

in the retail sale of binoculars, telescopes, and opera glasses are classified in Industry 5999.

Optical goods—retail   Opticians—retail

5999   Miscellaneous Retail Stores, Not Elsewhere Classified

Establishments primarily engaged in the retail sale of specialized lines of merchandise, not elsewhere classified, such as artists' supplies; orthopedic and artificial limbs; rubber stamps; pets; religious goods; and monuments and tombstones. This industry also includes establishments primarily engaged in selling a general line of their own or consigned merchandise at retail on an auction basis. Establishments primarily engaged in auctioning tangible personal property of others on a contract or fee basis are classified in Services, Industry 7389.

Architectural supplies—retail
Art dealers—retail
Artificial flowers—retail
Artists' supply and material stores—retail
Auction rooms (general merchandise)—retail
Autograph and philatelist supply stores—retail
Awning shops—retail
Baby carriages—retail
Banner shops—retail
Binoculars—retail
Cake decorating supplies—retail
Candle shops—retail
Coin shops—retail, except mail-order
Cosmetics stores—retail
Electric razor shops—retail
Fireworks—retail
Flag shops—retail
Gem stones, rough—retail
Gravestones, finished—retail
Hearing aids—retail
Hot tubs—retail
Ice dealers—retail

Monuments, finished to custom order—retail
Orthopedic and artificial limb stores—retail
Pet food stores—retail
Pet shops—retail
Picture frames, ready-made—retail
Police supply stores—retail
Religious goods stores (other than books)—retail
Rock and stone specimens—retail
Rubber stamp stores—retail
Sales barns—retail
Stamps, philatelist—retail: except mail-order
Stones, crystalline: rough—retail
Swimming pools, home: not installed—retail
Telephone stores—retail
Telescopes—retail
Tent shops—retail
Tombstones—retail
Trophy shops—retail
Typewriter stores—retail
Whirlpool baths—retail

DIVISION H

Finance, Insurance, and Real Estate

The Division as a Whole

This division includes establishments operating primarily in the fields of finance, insurance, and real estate. Finance includes depository institutions, nondepository credit institutions, holding (but not predominantly operating) companies, other investment companies, brokers and dealers in securities and commodity contracts, and security and commodity exchanges. Insurance covers carriers of all types of insurance, and insurance agents and brokers. Real estate includes owners, lessors, lessees, buyers, sellers, agents, and developers of real estate. Establishments primarily engaged in the construction of buildings for sale (operative builders) are classified in Construction, Industry 1531.

Major Group 60.—DEPOSITORY INSTITUTIONS

The Major Group as a Whole

This major group includes institutions that are engaged in deposit banking or closely related functions, including fiduciary activities.

Industry Group No.	Industry No.	

601   **CENTRAL RESERVE DEPOSITORY INSTITUTIONS**

Central reserve depository institutions whose primary activity is receiving deposits from banks of deposit and providing advances to such institutions. These institutions generally do not engage in receiving deposits from or making advances to other enterprises or individuals.

6011   **Federal Reserve Banks**

The Federal Reserve banks and their branches, which serve as regional reserve and rediscount institutions for their member banks.

Federal Reserve banks   Federal Reserve branches

6019   **Central Reserve Depository Institutions, Not Elsewhere Classified**

Central reserve depository institutions, other than Federal Reserve banks, primarily engaged in providing credit to and holding deposits and reserves for their members, such as savings banks, savings and loan associations, or credit unions.

Central liquidity facility   National Credit Union Administration
Federal Home Loan Banks   (NCUA)

602   **COMMERCIAL BANKS**

Commercial banks and trust companies engaged in the business of accepting deposits from the public.

6021   **National Commercial Banks**

Commercial banks and trust companies (accepting deposits) chartered under the National Bank Act. Trust companies engaged in fiduciary business, but not regularly engaged in deposit banking, are classified in Industry 6091.

Commercial banks, National
Trust companies (accepting deposits),
    commercial: National

6022   **State Commercial Banks**

Commercial banks and trust companies (accepting deposits) chartered by one of the States or territories. Trust companies engaged in fiduciary business, but not regularly engaged in deposit banking, are classified in Industry 6091.

Commercial banks, State
Trust companies (accepting deposits),
    commercial: State

6029   **Commercial Banks, Not Elsewhere Classified**

Commercial banks (accepting deposits) which do not operate under Federal or State charter.

Commercial banks, not chartered

Industry Group No.	Industry No.	

603   SAVINGS INSTITUTIONS

     6035   **Savings Institutions, Federally Chartered**

Federally chartered savings institutions (accepting deposits) operating under Federal charter.

Federal savings and loan associations	Savings and loan associations, federally chartered
Saving banks, Federal	

     6036   **Savings Institutions, Not Federally Chartered**

State-chartered savings institutions (accepting deposits) which do not operate under Federal charter.

Savings and loan associations, not federally chartered	Savings banks, State: not federally chartered

606   CREDIT UNIONS

     6061   **Credit Unions, Federally Chartered**

Cooperative thrift and loan associations (accepting deposits) organized under Federal charter to finance credit needs of their members.

Federal credit unions

     6062   **Credit Unions, Not Federally Chartered**

Cooperative thrift and loan associations (accepting deposits) organized under other than Federal charter to finance credit needs of their members.

State credit unions, not federally chartered

608   FOREIGN BANKING AND BRANCHES AND AGENCIES OF FOREIGN BANKS

     6081   **Branches and Agencies of Foreign Banks**

Establishments operating as branches or agencies of foreign banks which specialize in commercial loans, especially trade finance. They typically fund themselves via large denomination interbank deposits, rather than through smaller denomination retail deposits. Federally licensed agencies of foreign banks may not accept deposits. Federal branches may accept deposits; however, if they choose to accept deposits in denominations of $100,000 or less, Federal deposit insurance is required. Establishments which are owned by foreign banks but primarily engaged in accepting retail deposits from the general public in the United States are classified in Industry Group 602.

Agencies of foreign banks	Branches of foreign banks

     6082   **Foreign Trade and International Banking Institutions**

Establishments of foreign trade companies operating in the United States under Federal or State charter for the purpose of aiding or financing foreign trade. Also included in this industry are Federal or State chartered banking institutions which only engage in banking outside the United States.

Agreement Corporations	Edge Act Corporations

609　　FUNCTIONS RELATED TO DEPOSITORY BANKING

6091　Nondeposit Trust Facilities

Trust companies engaged in fiduciary business, but not regularly engaged in deposit banking. Some of these establishments occasionally hold limited amounts of special types of deposits, and their uninvested trust funds are usually classified as deposits. These nondeposit trust facilities may have either National or State charters. This industry does not include establishments operating under trust company charters which limit their fiduciary business to that incidental to real estate title or mortgage loan activities, which are classified in Industry 6361.

Nondeposit trust companies

6099　Functions Related to Depository Banking, Not Elsewhere Classified

Establishments primarily engaged in performing functions related to depository banking, not elsewhere classified.

Automated clearinghouses
Check cashing agencies
Check clearinghouse associations
Clearinghouse associations: bank or check
Deposit brokers
Electronic funds transfer networks, including switching
Escrow institutions other than real estate
Fiduciary agencies other than real estate or trust

Foreign currency exchanges
Money order issuance
Regional clearinghouse associations
Representative offices of foreign banks, excluding agents and branches
Safe deposit companies
Tax certificate sale and redemption agencies
Travelers' check issuance

Major Group 61.—NONDEPOSITORY CREDIT INSTITUTIONS

The Major Group as a Whole

This major group includes establishments engaged in extending credit in the form of loans, but not engaged in deposit banking.

Industry Group No.	Industry No.	

611 FEDERAL AND FEDERALLY-SPONSORED CREDIT AGENCIES

6111 Federal and Federally-Sponsored Credit Agencies

Establishments of the Federal Government and federally-sponsored credit agencies primarily engaged in guaranteeing, insuring, or making loans. Federally-sponsored credit agencies are established under authority of Federal legislation, but are not regarded as part of the Government. They are often owned by their members or borrowers.

Banks for cooperatives
Commodity Credit Corporation
Export-Import Bank
Farmers Home Administration
Federal Home Loan Mortgage Corporation
Federal Intermediate Credit Bank
Federal Land Banks

Federal National Mortgage Association
Government National Mortgage Association
National Consumer Cooperative Bank
Rural Electrification Administration
Student Loan Marketing Association
Synthetic Fuels Corporation

614 PERSONAL CREDIT INSTITUTIONS

6141 Personal Credit Institutions

Establishments primarily engaged in providing loans to individuals. Also included in this industry are establishments primarily engaged in financing retail sales made on the installment plan and financing automobile loans for individuals.

Automobile loans (may include automobile insurance)
Consumer finance companies
Financing of automobiles, furniture, appliances, personal airplanes, etc.: not engaged in deposit banking
Industrial loan "banks", not engaged in deposit banking
Industrial loan companies, not engaged in deposit banking

Installment sales finance, other than banks
Loan companies, small: licensed
Loan societies, remedial
Morris plans not engaged in deposit banking
Mutual benefit associations
Personal finance companies, small loan: licensed

615 BUSINESS CREDIT INSTITUTIONS

Establishments primarily engaged in making loans to agricultural and other business enterprises, excluding those engaged principally in home or personal financing. Private establishments primarily engaged in extending agricultural credit are classified in Industry 6159.

6153 Short-Term Business Credit Institutions, Except Agricultural

Establishments primarily engaged in extending credit to business enterprises for relatively short periods. Private establishments primarily engaged in extending agricultural credit are classified in Industry 6159.

Business credit institutions, short-term
Credit card service, collection by central agency

Direct working capital financing
Factors of commercial paper
Financing of dealers by motor vehicle

Industry Group No.	Industry No.	
615		**BUSINESS CREDIT INSTITUTIONS—Con.**

6153 Short-Term Business Credit Institutions, Except Agricultural—Con.

manufacturers' organizations
Installment notes, buying of
Installment paper dealer
Mercantile financing

Purchasers of accounts receivable and commercial paper
Trust deeds, purchase and sale of
Working capital financing

6159 Miscellaneous Business Credit Institutions

Establishments primarily engaged in furnishing intermediate or long-term general and industrial credit, including the finance leasing of automobiles, trucks, and machinery and equipment. Included in this industry are private establishments primarily engaged in extending agricultural credit. Federal and federally-sponsored credit agencies primarily engaged in extending agricultural credit are classified in Industry 6111. Establishments primarily engaged in other types of leasing of passenger cars and trucks are classified in Industry Group 751.

Agricultural loan companies
Automobile finance leasing
Credit institutions, agricultural
Farm mortgage companies
Finance leasing of equipment and vehicles
General and industrial loan institutions
Intermediate investment "banks"
Investment companies, small business
Livestock loan companies

Loan institutions, general and industrial
Machinery and equipment finance leasing
Pari-mutuel totalizator equipment finance leasing and maintenance
Production credit association, agricultural
Truck finance leasing

616 MORTGAGE BANKERS AND BROKERS

6162 Mortgage Bankers and Loan Correspondents

Establishments primarily engaged in originating mortgage loans, selling mortgage loans to permanent investors, and servicing these loans. They may also provide real estate construction loans.

Bond and mortgage companies
Loan correspondents
Mortgage bankers

Mortgage brokers, using own money
Mortgage companies, urban

6163 Loan Brokers

Establishments primarily engaged in arranging loans for others. These establishments operate mostly on a commission or fee basis and do not ordinarily have any continuing relationship with either borrower or lender.

Agents, farm or business loan
Brokers, farm or business loan
Loan agents

Loan brokers
Mortgage brokers arranging for loans but using money of others

Major Group 62.—SECURITY AND COMMODITY BROKERS, DEALERS, EXCHANGES, AND SERVICES

The Major Group as a Whole

This major group includes establishments engaged in the underwriting, purchase, sale, or brokerage of securities and other financial contracts on their own account or for the account of others; and exchanges, exchange clearinghouses, and other services allied with the exchange of securities and commodities.

Industry Group No.	Industry No.	

621 SECURITY BROKERS, DEALERS, AND FLOTATION COMPANIES

6211 Security Brokers, Dealers, and Flotation Companies

Establishments primarily engaged in the purchase, sale, and brokerage of securities; and those, generally known as investment bankers, primarily engaged in originating, underwriting, and distributing issues of securities. Establishments primarily engaged in issuing shares of mutual and money market funds, unit investment trusts, and face amount certificates are classified in Industry Group 672. Establishments primarily engaged in providing investment advice on a contract or fee basis to establishments which deal in financial contracts are classified in Industry 6282.

Agents for mutual funds	Note brokers
Bond dealers and brokers	Oil and gas lease brokers
Distributors, security	Oil royalties, dealers in
Floor traders, security	Option dealers, stock
Investment bankers	Sale of partnership shares in real estate syndicates
Investment certificates, sale of	Security brokers
Investment firm—general brokerage	Security dealers
Mineral leases, dealers in	Security flotation companies
Mineral royalties, dealers in	Security traders
Mortgages, buying and selling (rediscounting)	Security underwriters
Mutual fund agents	Stock brokers and dealers
Mutual funds, selling by independent salesperson	Tax certificate dealers

622 COMMODITY CONTRACTS BROKERS AND DEALERS

6221 Commodity Contracts Brokers and Dealers

Establishments primarily engaged in buying and selling commodity contracts on either a spot or future basis for their own account or for the account of others. These establishments are members, or are associated with members, of recognized commodity exchanges. Establishments primarily engaged in buying and selling commodities are classified in Wholesale Trade.

Commodity brokers (contracts)	Futures dealers, commodity
Commodity dealers (contracts)	Traders, commodity contract
Futures brokers, commodity	

623 SECURITY AND COMMODITY EXCHANGES

6231 Security and Commodity Exchanges

Establishments primarily engaged in furnishing space and other facilities to members for the purpose of buying, selling, or otherwise trading in stocks, stock options, bonds, or commodity contracts.

623　SECURITY AND COMMODITY EXCHANGES—Con.

6231　Security and Commodity Exchanges—Con.

Commodity contract exchanges	Security exchanges
Futures exchanges, contract	Stock exchanges
Option exchanges, stock	

628　SERVICES ALLIED WITH THE EXCHANGE OF SECURITIES OR COMMODITIES

6282　Investment Advice

Establishments primarily engaged in furnishing investment information and advice to companies and individuals concerning securities and commodities on a contract or fee basis. Establishments that provide advice and also act as brokers or dealers are classified in Industry 6211.

Futures advisory service	Investment research
Investment advisory service	Manager of mutual funds, contract or
Investment counselors	fee basis

6289　Services Allied With the Exchange of Securities or Commodities, Not Elsewhere Classified

Establishments primarily engaged in furnishing services to security or commodity holders, brokers, or dealers, not elsewhere classified.

Bondholders protective committees	Royalty owners protective associations
Custodians of securities	Security custodians
Exchange clearinghouses, commodity	Security holders protective committees
Exchange clearinghouses, security	Stock transfer agents
Financial reporting	Transfer agents, securities
Quotation service, stock	

Major Group 63.—INSURANCE CARRIERS

The Major Group as a Whole

This major group includes carriers of insurance of all types, including reinsurance. Agents and brokers dealing in insurance and organizations rendering services to insurance carriers or to policyholders are classified in Major Group 64.

Industry Group No.	Industry No.	

631 LIFE INSURANCE

6311 Life Insurance

Establishments primarily engaged in underwriting life insurance. These establishments are operated by enterprises that may be owned by stockholders, policyholders, or other carriers.

Assessment life insurance organizations	Funeral insurance
Benevolent insurance associations	Insurance carriers, life
Burial insurance societies	Legal reserve life insurance
Cooperative life insurance organizations	Life insurance
	Life insurance funds, savings bank
Fraternal life insurance organizations	Life reinsurance
Fraternal protective associations	Reinsurance carriers, life

632 ACCIDENT AND HEALTH INSURANCE AND MEDICAL SERVICE PLANS

6321 Accident and Health Insurance

Establishments primarily engaged in underwriting accident and health insurance. This industry includes establishments which provide health insurance protection for disability income losses and medical expense coverage on an indemnity basis. These establishments are operated by enterprises that may be owned by stockholders, policyholders, or other carriers. Establishments primarily engaged in providing hospital, medical and other health services on a service basis or combination of service and indemnity bases are classified in Industry 6324.

Accident and health insurance	Insurance carriers, accident
Assessment associations, accident and health insurance	Insurance carriers, health
	Mutual accident associations
Disability health insurance	Reciprocal interinsurance exchanges, accident and health insurance
Fraternal accident and health insurance organizations	Reinsurance carriers, accident and health
Health insurance, indemnity plans: except medical service	Sick benefit associations, mutual

6324 Hospital and Medical Service Plans

Establishments primarily engaged in providing hospital, medical, and other health services to subscribers or members in accordance with prearranged agreements or service plans. Generally, these service plans provide benefits to subscribers or members in return for specified subscription charges. The plans may be through a contract under which a participating hospital or physician agrees to render the covered services without charging any additional fees. Other plans provide for partial indemnity and service benefits. Also included in this industry are separate establishments of health maintenance organizations which provide medical insurance. Establishments providing these serv-

Industry Group No.	Industry No.	

632   **ACCIDENT AND HEALTH INSURANCE AND MEDICAL SERVICE PLANS—Con.**

6324 Hospital and Medical Service Plans—Con.

ices through their own facilities or employed physicians are classified in Major Group 80.

Dental insurance (providing services by contracts with health facilities)	Hospital and medical service plans
Group hospitalization plans	Medical service plans

633   **FIRE, MARINE, AND CASUALTY INSURANCE**

6331 Fire, Marine, and Casualty Insurance

Establishments primarily engaged in underwriting fire, marine, and casualty insurance. These establishments are operated by enterprises that may be owned by stockholders, policyholders, or other carriers.

Agricultural (crop and livestock) insurance	Insurance carriers: fire, marine, and casualty
Assessment associations: fire, marine, and casualty insurance	Mutual fire, marine, and casualty insurance
Associated factory mutuals, fire and marine insurance	Plate glass insurance
Automobile insurance	Property damage insurance
Boiler insurance	Reciprocal interinsurance exchanges: fire, marine, and casualty insurance
Burglary and theft insurance	Stock fire, marine, and casualty insurance
Contact lens insurance	Workers' compensation insurance
Federal Crop Insurance Corporation	

635   **SURETY INSURANCE**

6351 Surety Insurance

Establishments primarily engaged in underwriting financial responsibility insurance.

Assessment associations, surety and fidelity insurance	Fidelity insurance
Bonding for guaranteeing job completion	Financial responsibility insurance
	Liability insurance
Bonding of employees	Mortgage guaranty insurance
Bonding, fidelity or surety	Reciprocal interinsurance exchanges, surety and fidelity insurance
Credit and other financial responsibility insurance	Surety insurance
	Warranty insurance, home

636   **TITLE INSURANCE**

6361 Title Insurance

Establishments primarily engaged in underwriting insurance to protect the owner of real estate, or lenders of money thereon, against loss sustained by reason of any defect of title.

Guaranty of titles	Title insurance
Real estate title insurance	

637   **PENSION, HEALTH, AND WELFARE FUNDS**

6371 Pension, Health, and Welfare Funds

Establishments primarily engaged in managing pension, retirement, health, and welfare funds.

Pension funds	Welfare pensions
Union trust funds	
Union welfare, benefit, and health funds	

639   **INSURANCE CARRIERS, NOT ELSEWHERE CLASSIFIED**

     6399   **Insurance Carriers, Not Elsewhere Classified**

Establishments primarily engaged in underwriting insurance, not elsewhere classified, such as insuring bank deposits and shares in savings and loan associations.

Bank deposit insurance
Deposit or share insurance
Federal Deposit Insurance Corporation
Federal Savings and Loan Insurance
  Corporation

Health insurance for pets
Warranty insurance, automobile

Major Group 64.—INSURANCE AGENTS, BROKERS, AND SERVICE

The Major Group as a Whole

This major group includes agents and brokers dealing in insurance, and also organizations offering services to insurance companies and to policyholders.

Industry Group No.	Industry No.	

641   INSURANCE AGENTS, BROKERS, AND SERVICE

6411   **Insurance Agents, Brokers, and Service**

Agents primarily representing one or more insurance carriers, or brokers not representing any particular carriers primarily engaged as independent contractors in the sale or placement of insurance contracts with carriers, but not employees of the insurance carriers they represent. This industry also includes independent organizations concerned with insurance services. Establishments engaged in searching real estate titles are classified in Industry 6541.

Fire Insurance Underwriters' Laboratories
Fire loss appraisal
Insurance adjusters
Insurance advisory services
Insurance agents
Insurance brokers
Insurance claim adjusters, not employed by insurance companies
Insurance educational services
Insurance information bureaus
Insurance inspection and investigation services
Insurance loss prevention services
Insurance patrol services
Insurance professional standards services
Insurance reporting services
Insurance research services
Insurance services
Life insurance agents
Medical insurance claims, processing of: contract or fee basis
Pension and retirement plan consultants
Policyholders' consulting service
Rate making organizations, insurance

Major Group 65.—REAL ESTATE

The Major Group as a Whole

This major group includes real estate operators, and owners and lessors of real property, as well as buyers, sellers, developers, agents, and brokers. Establishments primarily engaged in the construction of buildings for sale (operative builders) are classified in Industry 1531.

Industry Group No.	Industry No.	

651   **REAL ESTATE OPERATORS (EXCEPT DEVELOPERS) AND LESSORS**

Included in this industry group are real estate operators (except developers) and lessors. Lessees or lessors engaged in the development or improvement of unimproved real property are classified according to the principal activity performed. This group includes operators of apartment hotels and residential mobile home sites, but does not include hotels, rooming and boarding houses, camps, travel trailer parks, and other lodging places for transients which are classified in Services, Major Group 70. "Operators" in this group will be interpreted as owner-operators. Establishments primarily engaged in renting, buying, selling, managing, and appraising real estate for others are classified in Industry 6531.

6512 Operators of Nonresidential Buildings

Establishments primarily engaged in the operation of nonresidential buildings.

Bank buildings, operation of
Insurance buildings, operation of
Lessors of piers, docks, and associated buildings and facilities
Operators of commercial and industrial buildings
Operators of nonresidential buildings

Retail establishments, property operation only
Shopping centers, property operation only
Theater buildings (ownership and operation)

6513 Operators of Apartment Buildings

Establishments primarily engaged in the operation of apartment buildings. Apartment buildings are defined as containing five or more housing units. This industry does not include hotels, rooming and boarding houses, camps, and other lodging places for transients which are classified in Services, Major Group 70.

Operators of apartment buildings (five or more housing units)
Operators of apartment hotels

Operators of residential hotels
Operators of retirement hotels

6514 Operators of Dwellings Other Than Apartment Buildings

Establishments primarily engaged in the operation of dwellings other than apartment buildings. Dwellings other than apartment buildings are defined as containing four or fewer housing units. This industry does not include hotels, rooming and boarding houses, camps, and other lodging places for transients which are classified in Services, Major Group 70.

Operators of dwellings (four or fewer housing units)

Operators of residential buildings (four or fewer housing units)

Industry Group No.	Industry No.	
651		**REAL ESTATE OPERATORS (EXCEPT DEVELOPERS) AND LESSORS— Con.**

6515 Operators of Residential Mobile Home Sites

Establishments primarily engaged in the operation of residential mobile home sites. Establishments primarily engaged in the operation of sites for overnight or transient use for travel trailers are classified in Services, Industry 7033.

Operators of mobile home sites

6517 Lessors of Railroad Property

Establishments primarily engaged in leasing railroad property.

Lessors of railroad property

6519 Lessors of Real Property, Not Elsewhere Classified

Establishments primarily engaged in leasing real property, not elsewhere classified.

Airport leasing, if not operating airport	Lessors of property, except railroad,
Landholding offices	buildings, or mobile home sites

653   REAL ESTATE AGENTS AND MANAGERS

6531 Real Estate Agents and Managers

Establishments primarily engaged in renting, buying, selling, managing, and appraising real estate for others.

Agents, real estate	Housing authorities, operating
Appraisers, real estate	Listing service, real estate
Brokers of manufactured homes, on site	Managers, real estate
Brokers, real estate	Multiple listing services, real estate
Buying agents, real estate	Real estate auctions
Cemetery management service	Rental agents for real estate
Condominium managers	Selling agents for real estate
Cooperative apartment manager	Time-sharing real estate: sales, leasing,
Escrow agents, real estate	and rentals
Fiduciaries, real estate	

654   TITLE ABSTRACT OFFICES

6541 Title Abstract Offices

Establishments primarily engaged in searching real estate titles. This industry does not include title insurance companies which are classified in Industry 6361.

Title abstract companies	Title reconveyance companies
Title and trust companies	Title search companies

655   LAND SUBDIVIDERS AND DEVELOPERS

6552 Land Subdividers and Developers, Except Cemeteries

Establishments primarily engaged in subdividing real property into lots, except cemetery lots, and in developing it for resale on their own account. Establishments primarily engaged in developing lots for others are classified in Industry 1794.

Real property subdividers and developers, except of cemetery lots

LAND SUBDIVIDERS AND DEVELOPERS—Con.

6553 Cemetery Subdividers and Developers

Establishments primarily engaged in subdividing real property into cemetery lots, and in developing it for resale on their own account.

Animal cemetery operation
Cemeteries—real estate operation
Cemetery associations

Mausoleum operation
Real property subdividers and developers, cemetery lots only

Major Group 67.—HOLDING AND OTHER INVESTMENT OFFICES

The Major Group as a Whole

This major group includes investment trusts, investment companies, holding companies, and miscellaneous investment offices.

Industry Group No.	Industry No.	

671   **HOLDING OFFICES**

6712 Offices of Bank Holding Companies

Establishments primarily engaged in holding or owning the securities of banks for the sole purpose of exercising some degree of control over the activities of bank companies whose securities they hold. Companies holding securities of banks, but which are predominantly operating the banks, are classified according to the kind of bank operated.

> Bank holding companies

6719 Offices of Holding Companies, Not Elsewhere Classified

Establishments primarily engaged in holding or owning securities of companies other than banks, for the sole purpose of exercising some degree of control over the activities of the companies whose securities they hold. Companies holding securities, but which are predominantly operating companies, are classified according to the kind of business operated.

> Holding companies, except bank
> Investment holding companies, except bank
> Personal holding companies, except bank
> Public utility holding companies

672   **INVESTMENT OFFICES**

6722 Management Investment Offices, Open-End

Establishments primarily engaged in issuing shares, other than unit investment trusts and face-amount certificate companies, whose shares contain a provision requiring redemption by the company upon request of the security holder.

> Management investment funds, open-end
> Money market mutual funds
> Mutual fund sales on own account

6726 Unit Investment Trusts, Face-Amount Certificate Offices, and Closed-End Management Investment Offices

Establishments primarily engaged in issuing unit investment trusts or face-amount certificates; and establishments primarily engaged in issuing shares, other than unit investment trusts and face-amount certificate companies, whose shares contain no provision requiring redemption by the company upon request of the security holder. Unit investment trust companies (1) are organized under a trust indenture, contract of custodianship or agency, or similar instrument; (2) do not have a board of directors; and (3) issue only securities redeemable at the request of the security holder, each of which represents an undivided interest in a unit of specified securities, but does not include voting

672   **INVESTMENT OFFICES—Con.**

6726 **Unit Investment Trusts, Face-Amount Certificate Offices, and Closed-End Management Investment Offices—Con.**

trusts. Face-amount certificates, sometimes referred to as guaranteed face-amount certificates, are essentially obligations of the issuing company to pay a fixed sum at a specified maturity date and usually require periodic payments by the purchaser.

Face-amount certificate issuing
Government National Mortgage Association (GNMA) pools
Investment funds, closed-end: management of
Investors' syndicates

Issuing of face-amount installment certificates
Management investment funds, closed-end
Unit investment trusts

673   **TRUSTS**

Establishments primarily engaged in the management of the funds of individual trusts and foundations. Trusts and funds which are predominantly operating establishments are classified according to the kind of business operated.

6732 **Educational, Religious, and Charitable Trusts**

Establishments primarily engaged in the management of the funds of trusts and foundations organized for religious, educational, charitable, or nonprofit research purposes.

Charitable trusts, management of
Educational trusts, management of

Religious trusts, management of

6733 **Trusts, Except Educational, Religious, and Charitable**

Establishments primarily engaged in the management of the funds of trusts and foundations organized for purposes other than religious, educational, charitable, or nonprofit research.

Administrators of private estates (non-operating)
Personal investment trusts, management of
Trustees: except for educational, religious, or charitable trusts

Trusts except educational, religious, and charitable: management of
Vacation funds for employees

679   **MISCELLANEOUS INVESTING**

6792 **Oil Royalty Traders**

Establishments primarily engaged in investing in oil and gas royalties or leases, or fractional interest therein.

Oil leases, buying and selling on own account

Oil royalty companies

6794 **Patent Owners and Lessors**

Establishments primarily engaged in owning or leasing franchises, patents, and copyrights which they in turn license others to use.

Copyright buying and licensing
Franchises, selling or licensing
Music licensing to radio stations
Music royalties, sheet and record

Patent buying and licensing
Patent leasing
Performance rights, publishing and licensing of

Industry Group No.	Industry No.	

679   **MISCELLANEOUS INVESTING—Con.**

6798   **Real Estate Investment Trusts**

Establishments primarily engaged in closed-end investments in real estate or related mortgage assets operating so that they could meet the requirements of the Real Estate Investment Trust Act of 1960 as amended. This act exempts trusts from corporate income and capital gains taxation, provided they invest primarily in specified assets, pay out most of their income to shareholders, and meet certain requirements regarding the dispersion of trust ownership.

Mortgage investment trusts	Realty investment trusts
Mortgage trusts	Realty trusts
Real estate investment trusts (REIT'S)	

6799   **Investors, Not Elsewhere Classified**

Establishments primarily engaged in investing, not elsewhere classified.

Commodity contract pool operators	Security speculators for own account
Commodity contract trading companies	Tax liens: holding, buying, and selling
Investment clubs	Venture capital companies

DIVISION I

Services

The Division as a Whole

This division includes establishments primarily engaged in providing a wide variety of services for individuals, business and government establishments, and other organizations. Hotels and other lodging places; establishments providing personal, business, repair, and amusement services; health, legal, engineering, and other professional services; educational institutions; membership organizations, and other miscellaneous services, are included.

Establishments which provide specialized services closely allied to activities covered in other divisions are classified in such divisions.

354

Major Group 70.—HOTELS, ROOMING HOUSES, CAMPS, AND OTHER LODGING PLACES

The Major Group as a Whole

This major group includes commercial and noncommercial establishments engaged in furnishing lodging, or lodging and meals, and camping space and camping facilities.

Industry Group No. | Industry No.

701 HOTELS AND MOTELS

7011 Hotels and Motels

Commercial establishments, known to the public as hotels, motor hotels, motels, or tourist courts, primarily engaged in providing lodging, or lodging and meals, for the general public. Hotels which are operated by membership organizations and open to the general public are included in this industry. Hotels operated by organizations for their members only are classified in Industry 7041. Apartment hotels are classified in Real Estate, Industry 6513; rooming and boarding houses are classified in Industry 7021; and sporting and recreational camps are classified in Industry 7032.

Auto courts	Motels
Bed and breakfast inns	Recreational hotels
Cabins and cottages	Resort hotels
Casino hotels	Seasonal hotels
Hostels	Ski lodges and resorts
Hotels, except residential	Tourist cabins
Inns, furnishing food and lodging	Tourist courts

702 ROOMING AND BOARDING HOUSES

7021 Rooming and Boarding Houses

Establishments primarily engaged in renting rooms, with or without board, on a fee basis. Rental of apartments, apartment hotels, and other housing units are classified in Real Estate, Industry Group 651. Rooming and boarding houses operated by membership organizations for their members only are classified in Industry 7041. Homes for the aged, for children, and for the handicapped that also provide additional services, other than nursing care, are classified in Industry 8361, and homes that provide nursing care are classified in Industry Group 805.

Boarding houses, except organization	Rental of furnished rooms
Dormitories, commercially operated	Rooming houses, except organization
Lodging houses, except organization	

703 CAMPS AND RECREATIONAL VEHICLE PARKS

7032 Sporting and Recreational Camps

Establishments primarily engaged in operating sporting and recreational camps, such as boys' and girls' camps, and fishing and hunting camps. Establishments primarily engaged in operating sports instructional camps, such as baseball, basketball, football, or karate camps, and those operating day camps are classified in Industry 7999.

Boys' camps	Hunting camps
Camps, sporting and recreational	Nudist camps
Dude ranches	Summer camps, except day and sports
Fishing camps	instructional
Girls' camps	

703   CAMPS AND RECREATIONAL VEHICLE PARKS—Con.

7033 **Recreational Vehicle Parks and Campsites**

Establishments primarily engaged in providing overnight or short-term sites for recreational vehicles, trailers, campers, or tents. Establishments primarily engaged in operating residential trailer parks are classified in Real Estate, Industry 6515.

Campgrounds   Recreational vehicle parks
Campsites for transients   Trailer parks for transients

704   ORGANIZATION HOTELS AND LODGING HOUSES, ON MEMBERSHIP
             BASIS

7041 **Organization Hotels and Lodging Houses, on Membership Basis**

Lodging houses and hotels operated by membership organizations for the benefit of their constituents, and not open to the general public. Commercial hotels operated by such organizations are classified in Industry 7011 and commercial rooming and boarding houses are classified in Industry 7021. Residential homes for the aged and handicapped are classified in Industry 8361.

Boarding houses operated by organiza-   Residence clubs operated by organizations for members only   tions for members only
Boarding houses, fraternity and sorori-   Rooming houses operated by organiza-
ty   tions for members only
Fraternity residential houses   Rooming houses, fraternity and sorority
Hotels operated by organizations for   Sorority residential houses
members only
Lodging houses operated by organizations for members only

Major Group 72.—PERSONAL SERVICES

The Major Group as a Whole

This major group includes establishments primarily engaged in providing services generally to individuals, such as laundries, drycleaning plants, portrait photographic studios, and beauty and barber shops. Also included are establishments operating as industrial launderers and those primarily engaged in providing linen supply services to commercial and business establishments.

Industry Group No.	Industry No.	

721   LAUNDRY, CLEANING, AND GARMENT SERVICES

7211   Power Laundries, Family and Commercial

Establishments primarily engaged in operating mechanical laundries with steam or other power. Establishments primarily engaged in supplying laundered work clothing on a contract or fee basis are classified in Industry 7218.

Laundries, power: family and commercial
Laundry collecting and distributing outlets operated by power laundries

Power laundries, family and commercial

7212   Garment Pressing, and Agents for Laundries and Drycleaners

Establishments primarily engaged in providing laundry and drycleaning services but which have the laundry and drycleaning work done by others. Establishments in this industry may do their own pressing or finishing work. Establishments operating their own laundry plants are classified in Industry 7211, and those operating their own drycleaning plants are classified in Industry 7216.

Agents, retail: for laundries and drycleaners
Bobtailers, laundry and drycleaning
Cleaning and laundry pickup stations, not owned by laundries or cleaners

Press shops for garments
Truck route laundry and drycleaning, not operated by laundries or cleaners
Valet apparel service

7213   Linen Supply

Establishments primarily engaged in supplying to commercial establishments or household users, on a rental basis, such laundered items as uniforms, gowns, and coats of the type used by doctors, nurses, barbers, beauticians, and waitresses; and table linens, bed linens, towels and toweling, and similar items. Establishments included in this industry may or may not operate their own laundry facilities. Establishments primarily engaged in providing diaper service are classified in Industry 7219.

Apron supply service
Coat supply service
Continuous towel supply service
Gown supply service, uniform
Linen supply service

Shirt supply service
Table cover supply service
Towel supply service, except wiping
Uniform supply service, except industrial

7215   Coin-Operated Laundries and Drycleaning

Establishments primarily engaged in the operation of coin-operated or similar self-service laundry and drycleaning equipment for use on the premises, or in apartments, dormitories, and similar locations.

Industry Group No.	Industry No.	
721		**LAUNDRY, CLEANING, AND GARMENT SERVICES—Con.**

7215　Coin-Operated Laundries and Drycleaning—Con.

Coin-operated laundries
Drycleaning, coin-operated
Launderettes

Laundromats
Laundry machine routes, coin-operated
Self-service laundry and drycleaning

7216　Drycleaning Plants, Except Rug Cleaning

Establishments primarily engaged in drycleaning or dyeing apparel and household fabrics other than rugs. Press shops and agents for drycleaners are classified in Industry 7212; establishments primarily engaged in cleaning rugs are classified in Industry 7217; and establishments primarily engaged in dyeing fabrics for the trade are classified in Manufacturing, Major Group 22.

Cleaning and dyeing plants, except rug
　cleaning
Collecting and distributing agencies op-
　erated by cleaning plants

Drapery drycleaning plants
Drycleaning plants, except rug cleaning

7217　Carpet and Upholstery Cleaning

Establishments primarily engaged in cleaning carpets and upholstered furniture at a plant or on customers' premises. Establishments primarily engaged in rug repair are classified in Industry 7699, and those primarily engaged in reupholstering and repairing furniture are classified in Industry 7641.

Carpet cleaning and repairing plants
Carpet cleaning on customers' premises
Furniture cleaning on customers' prem-
　ises

Rug cleaning, dyeing, and repairing
　plants
Upholstery cleaning on customers'
　premises

7218　Industrial Launderers

Establishments primarily engaged in supplying laundered or drycleaned industrial work uniforms and related work clothing, such as protective apparel (flame and heat resistant) and clean room apparel; laundered mats and rugs; dust control items, such as treated mops, rugs, mats, dust tool covers, and cloths; laundered wiping towels; and other selected items to industrial, commercial, and government users. These items may belong to the industrial launderer and be supplied to users on a rental basis, or they may be the customers' own goods. Establishments included in this industry may or may not operate their own laundry or drycleaning facilities.

Clean room apparel supply service
Flame and heat resistant clothing
　supply service
Industrial launderers
Industrial uniform supply service
Laundered mat and rug supply service
Radiation protective garments supply
　service

Safety glove supply service
Towel supply service, wiping
Treated mats, rugs, mops, dust tool
　covers, and cloth supply service
Wiping towel supply service
Work clothing supply service, industri-
　al

7219　Laundry and Garment Services, Not Elsewhere Classified

Establishments primarily engaged in furnishing laundry and garment services, not elsewhere classified, such as the repair, alteration, and storage of clothes for individuals and for the operation of hand laundries. Custom tailors and dressmakers are classified in Retail Trade, Industry 5699; fur shops making fur apparel to custom order are classified in Retail Trade, Industry 5632; and press shops are classified in Industry 7212.

Diaper service

Dressmaking services on material

Industry Group No.	Industry No.	

721   **LAUNDRY, CLEANING, AND GARMENT SERVICES—Con.**

    7219   **Laundry and Garment Services, Not Elsewhere Classified—Con.**

owned by individual customers
Fur garments: cleaning, repairing, and storage
Garment alteration and repair shops
Hand laundries
Laundries, except power and coin-operated
Pillow cleaning and renovating

Repair of furs and other garments for individuals
Reweaving textiles (mending service)
Storage of furs and other garments for individuals
Tailor shops, except custom or merchant tailors

722   **PHOTOGRAPHIC STUDIOS, PORTRAIT**

    7221   **Photographic Studios, Portrait**

Establishments primarily engaged in still or video portrait photography for the general public. Establishments primarily engaged in commercial photography are classified in Industry 7335; those engaged in video tape production other than portrait are classified in Industry 7812; and those engaged in film developing or print processing for the trade or for the general public are classified in Industry 7384. Establishments primarily engaged in processing film for the motion picture production industry are classified in Industry 7819, and those engaged in computer photography are classified in Industry 7299.

Home photographers
Passport photographers
Photographers, portrait: still or video
Portrait photographers

School photographers
Transient photographers
Video photography, portrait

723   **BEAUTY SHOPS**

    7231   **Beauty Shops**

Establishments primarily engaged in furnishing beauty or hairdressing services. This industry also includes combination beauty and barber shops, as well as hairdressing shops serving both male and female clientele. Beauty and cosmetology schools are included in this industry.

Beauty and barber shops, combined
Beauty culture schools
Beauty shops or salons
Cosmetology schools
Cosmetology shops or salons

Facial salons
Hairdressers
Manicure and pedicure salons
Unisex hairdressers

724   **BARBER SHOPS**

    7241   **Barber Shops**

Establishments primarily engaged in furnishing barber and men's hair styling services. Barber colleges are included in this industry.

Barber colleges
Barber shops

Hair stylists, men's

725   **SHOE REPAIR SHOPS AND SHOESHINE PARLORS**

    7251   **Shoe Repair Shops and Shoeshine Parlors**

Establishments primarily engaged in repairing footwear or shining shoes. Also included are establishments engaged in cleaning and blocking hats.

Bootblack parlors
Hatcleaning and blocking shops
Shoe dyeing shops

Shoe repair shops
Shoeshine parlors

Industry Group No.	Industry No.	
726		**FUNERAL SERVICE AND CREMATORIES**

7261 Funeral Service and Crematories

Establishments primarily engaged in preparing the dead for burial, conducting funerals, and cremating the dead.

Crematories	Morticians
Funeral directors	Undertakers
Funeral homes or parlors	

729   **MISCELLANEOUS PERSONAL SERVICES**

7291 Tax Return Preparation Services

Establishments primarily engaged in providing tax return preparation services without also providing accounting, auditing, or bookkeeping services. Establishments engaged in providing income tax return preparation services which also provide accounting, auditing, or bookkeeping services are classified in Industry 8721.

Income tax return preparation services without accounting, auditing, or bookkeeping services	Tax return preparation services without accounting, auditing, or bookkeeping services

7299 Miscellaneous Personal Services, Not Elsewhere Classified

Establishments primarily engaged in providing personal services, not elsewhere classified. Establishments primarily engaged in operating physical fitness facilities, including health fitness spas and reducing salons, are classified in Major Group 70 if they provide lodging and in Industry 7991 if they do not, and those renting medical equipment are classified in Industry 7352.

Babysitting bureaus	Dress suit rental
Bartering services for individuals	Electrolysis (hair removal)
Birth certificate agencies	Escort service
Blood pressure testing, coin-operated	Genealogical investigation service
Buyers' clubs	Hair removal (electrolysis)
Car title and tag service	Hair weaving or replacement service
Checkroom concessions or services	Locker rental, except cold storage
Clothing rental, except industrial launderers and linen supply	Marriage bureaus
Coin-operated service machine operation: scales, shoeshine, lockers, and blood pressure	Massage parlors
	Porter service
	Quilting for individuals
College clearinghouses	Rest room operation
Comfort station operation	Scalp treatment service
Computer photography or portraits	Shopping service for individuals
Consumer buying service	Steam baths
Costume rental	Tanning salons
Dating service	Tattoo parlors
Debt counseling or adjustment service to individuals	Turkish baths
	Tuxedo rental
Depilatory salons	Valet parking
Diet workshops	Wardrobe service, except theatrical
	Wedding chapels, privately operated

Major Group 73.—BUSINESS SERVICES

The Major Group as a Whole

This major group includes establishments primarily engaged in rendering services, not elsewhere classified, to business establishments on a contract or fee basis, such as advertising, credit reporting, collection of claims, mailing, reproduction, stenographic, news syndicates, computer programming, photocopying, duplicating, data processing, services to buildings, and help supply services. Establishments primarily engaged in providing engineering, accounting, research, management, and related services are classified in Major Group 87. Establishments which provide specialized services closely allied to activities covered in other divisions are classified in such divisions.

Industry Group No.	Industry No.	
731		**ADVERTISING**

7311 Advertising Agencies

Establishments primarily engaged in preparing advertising (writing copy, artwork, graphics, and other creative work) and placing such advertising in periodicals, newspapers, radio and television, or other advertising media for clients on a contract or fee basis. Establishments which place advertising with media, but which perform no creative services (media buying service), are classified in Industry 7319; those which write advertising copy, but do not place the advertising with media, are classified in Industry 8999; and those which provide services in commercial art and graphics, or other creative advertising services, but do not place the advertising with media, are classified in Industry Group 733.

Advertising agencies	Advertising consultants (agencies)

7312 Outdoor Advertising Services

Establishments primarily engaged in the preparation of poster displays and painted and electric spectacular displays on billboards, panels, bulletins, and frames, principally outdoors. Such establishments may construct, repair, and maintain display boards and may post advertisements. Special trade contractors primarily engaged in erecting display boards are classified in Construction, Major Group 17. Establishments primarily engaged in manufacturing electrical, mechanical, or plate signs and advertising displays are classified in Manufacturing, Industry 3993.

Billboard advertising	Poster advertising service, outdoor
Outdoor advertising service	

7313 Radio, Television, and Publishers' Advertising Representatives

Establishments primarily engaged in soliciting advertising on a contract or fee basis for newspapers, magazines, and other publications, or for radio and television stations. Separate offices of newspapers, magazines, and radio and television stations engaged in soliciting advertising are classified as auxiliaries.

Newspaper advertising representatives, not auxiliary to publishing	Television and radio time, sale of: not auxiliary to television or radio broadcasting
Radio representatives, advertising: not auxiliary to radio broadcasting	

731 ADVERTISING—Con.

7319 Advertising, Not Elsewhere Classified

Establishments primarily engaged in furnishing advertising services, not elsewhere classified, such as aerial advertising, circular and handbill distribution, distribution or delivery of advertising material or samples, and transit advertising. Establishments primarily engaged in direct mail advertising are classified in Industry 7331; those which write advertising copy, but do not place the advertising with media, are classified in Industry 8999; and those which provide services in commercial art, graphics, or other creative advertising services, but do not place the advertising with media, are classified in Industry Group 733.

Aerial advertising	Poster advertising services, except outdoor
Bus card advertising	door
Circular distributing service	Samples, distribution of
Coupon distribution	Shopping news advertising and distributing service
Display advertising service, except outdoor	uting service
door	Sky writing
Handbill distribution service	Taxicab card advertising
Media buying service	Transit advertising

732 CONSUMER CREDIT REPORTING AGENCIES, MERCANTILE REPORTING AGENCIES, AND ADJUSTMENT AND COLLECTION AGENCIES

7322 Adjustment and Collection Services

Establishments primarily engaged in the collection or adjustment of claims, other than insurance. Establishments primarily engaged in providing credit card service with collection by a central agency are classified in Finance, Industry 6153; those providing insurance adjustment services are classified in Insurance, Industry 6411; and those providing debt counseling or adjustment services to individuals are classified in Industry 7299.

Adjustment bureaus, except insurance adjustment agencies	Collection agencies, accounts

7323 Credit Reporting Services

Establishments primarily engaged in providing mercantile and consumer credit reporting services.

Consumer credit reporting bureaus	Credit investigation services
Credit bureaus and agencies	Mercantile credit reporting bureaus
Credit clearinghouses	

733 MAILING, REPRODUCTION, COMMERCIAL ART AND PHOTOGRAPHY, AND STENOGRAPHIC SERVICES

7331 Direct Mail Advertising Services

Establishments primarily engaged in furnishing services for direct mail advertising, such as creating, producing, and mailing of direct mail advertising. This industry also includes establishments primarily engaged in compiling and selling mailing lists. Establishments primarily engaged in reproducing direct mail copy on order, but performing none of the other direct mail advertising services, are classified in Manufacturing, Industry Group 275 if they print the copy, and in Industry 7334 if they duplicate the copy by photocopying or similar reproduction methods.

Industry
Group
No.

Industry
No.

733 **MAILING, REPRODUCTION, COMMERCIAL ART AND PHOTOGRAPHY, AND STENOGRAPHIC SERVICES—Con.**

7331 **Direct Mail Advertising Services—Con.**

Address list compilers	Mail advertising service
Addressing service	Mailing list compilers
Direct mail advertising service	Mailing service

7334 **Photocopying and Duplicating Services**

Establishments primarily engaged in reproducing text, drawings, plans, maps, or other copy, by blueprinting, photocopying, mimeographing, or other methods of duplication other than printing or microfilming. Establishments primarily engaged in printing are classified in Manufacturing, Industry Group 275, and those engaged in providing microfilming services are classified in Industry 7389.

Blueprinting service	Multigraphing service
Duplicating services, except printing	Multilithing service
Mimeographing service	Photocopying service

7335 **Commercial Photography**

Establishments primarily engaged in providing commercial photography services for advertising agencies, publishers, and other business and industrial users. Establishments primarily engaged in still and video portrait photography are classified in Industry 7221, and those primarily engaged in mapmaking are classified in Industry 7389. Establishments primarily engaged in producing commercial video tape or films are classified in Industry 7812.

Aerial photographic service, except mapmaking	Commercial photography
	Photographic studios, commercial

7336 **Commercial Art and Graphic Design**

Establishments primarily engaged in providing commercial art or graphic design services for advertising agencies, publishers, and other business and industrial users. Establishments primarily engaged in art, except commercial and medical, are classified in Industry 8999; those engaged in medical art are classified in Industry 8099; and those providing drafting services are classified in Industry 7389.

Artists, commercial	Graphic arts and related design
Chart and graph design	Silk screen design
Commercial art and illustration	Slide film producers
Film strip and slide producers	Still film producers

7338 **Secretarial and Court Reporting Services**

Establishments primarily engaged in furnishing secretarial, typing, word processing, resume writing, and court reporting services.

Court reporting service	Secretarial service
Editing service	Stenographic service
Letter writing service	Typing service
Proofreading service	Word processing service (typing)
Resume writing service	

734 **SERVICES TO DWELLINGS AND OTHER BUILDINGS**

7342 **Disinfecting and Pest Control Services**

Establishments primarily engaged in disinfecting dwellings and other buildings, and in termite, insect, rodent, and other pest control, generally in dwell-

734   SERVICES TO DWELLINGS AND OTHER BUILDINGS—Con.

7342   Disinfecting and Pest Control Services—Con.

ings or other buildings. Establishments primarily engaged in pest control for lawns or agricultural production are classified in Division A, Agriculture.

Bird proofing	Pest control in structures
Deodorant servicing of rest rooms	Rest room cleaning service
Disinfecting service	Termite control
Exterminating service	Washroom sanitation service
Fumigating service	

7349   Building Cleaning and Maintenance Services, Not Elsewhere Classified

Establishments primarily engaged in furnishing building cleaning and maintenance services, not elsewhere classified, such as window cleaning, janitorial service, floor waxing, and office cleaning. General contractors and special trade contractors primarily engaged in building repair work are classified in Division C, Construction.

Acoustical tile cleaning service	Maid service on a contract or fee basis
Building cleaning service, interior	Maintenance, building: except repairs
Chimney cleaning service	Office cleaning service
Custodians of schools on a contract or fee basis	Service station cleaning and degreasing service
Floor waxing service	Telephone booths, cleaning and maintenance of
Housekeeping (cleaning service) on a contract or fee basis	Venetian blind cleaning, including work done on owners' premises
Janitorial services on a contract or fee basis	Window cleaning service
Lighting maintenance service (bulb replacement and cleaning)	

735   MISCELLANEOUS EQUIPMENT RENTAL AND LEASING

7352   Medical Equipment Rental and Leasing

Establishments primarily engaged in renting or leasing (except finance leasing) medical equipment. Establishments of this industry may also sell medical supplies. Establishments primarily engaged in the sale of medical equipment and supplies are classified in Wholesale or Retail Trade, and those primarily engaged in finance leasing are classified in Finance, Industry 6159.

Invalid supplies rental and leasing	Medical equipment rental and leasing

7353   Heavy Construction Equipment Rental and Leasing

Establishments primarily engaged in renting or leasing (except finance leasing) heavy construction equipment, with or without operators. Establishments primarily engaged in finance leasing are classified in Finance, Industry 6159.

Bulldozer rental and leasing	Crane rental and leasing
Construction equipment, heavy: rental and leasing	Earth moving equipment rental and leasing

7359   Equipment Rental and Leasing, Not Elsewhere Classified

Establishments primarily engaged in renting or leasing (except finance leasing) equipment, not elsewhere classified. Establishments primarily engaged in finance leasing are classified in Finance, Industry 6159. Establishments renting and leasing automobiles and trucks without drivers are classified in Industry Group 751; those renting automobiles with drivers are classified in Transportation and Public Utilities, Industry 4119; those renting trucks with drivers are classified in Transportation and Public Utilities, Industry Group 421;

Industry Group No.	Industry No.	
735		MISCELLANEOUS EQUIPMENT RENTAL AND LEASING—Con.
	7359	Equipment Rental and Leasing, Not Elsewhere Classified—Con.

those renting personal items such as lockers (other than refrigerated), clothes, and pillows are classified in Industry 7299; those renting amusement and recreation items, such as bicycles, canoes, and beach chairs and accessories are classified in Industry 7999; and those renting commercial boats are classified in Transportation and Public Utilities, Industry 4499. Establishments producing machinery and equipment (including computers and other data processing equipment) which lease or sell their products are classified in Division D, Manufacturing. Manufacturers' sales branches or offices leasing or selling the machinery and equipment of their manufacturing plant are classified in Division F, Wholesale Trade. Establishments primarily engaged in leasing computer time, including time sharing services, are classified in Industry 7374; and those renting or leasing computers or data processing equipment are classified in Industry 7377.

Airplane rental and leasing
Appliance rental and leasing
Coin-operated machine rental and leasing
Electronic equipment rental and leasing, except medical and computer equipment
Furniture rental and leasing
Industrial truck rental and leasing
Office machine rental and leasing, except computers
Oil field equipment rental and leasing
Oil well drilling equipment rental and leasing

Party supplies rental and leasing
Piano rental and leasing
Plants, live: rental and leasing
Rental and leasing of dishes, silverware, and tables
Television rental and leasing
Toilets, portable: rental and leasing
Tool rental and leasing
Vending machines, rental only
Video recorder and player rental and leasing

736 PERSONNEL SUPPLY SERVICES

7361 Employment Agencies

Establishments primarily engaged in providing employment services, except theatrical employment agencies and motion picture casting bureaus. Establishments classified here may assist either employers or those seeking employment. Establishments primarily engaged in operating theatrical employment agencies are classified in Industry 7922; those operating motion picture casting bureaus are classified in Industry 7819; and farm labor contractors are classified in Agriculture, Industry 0761.

Chauffeur registries
Employment agencies, except theatrical and motion picture
Executive placing services
Labor contractors (employment agencies), except farm labor

Maid registries
Model registries
Nurses' registries
Ship crew registries
Teachers' registries

7363 Help Supply Services

Establishments primarily engaged in supplying temporary or continuing help on a contract or fee basis. The help supplied is always on the payroll of the supplying establishments, but is under the direct or general supervision of the business to whom the help is furnished. Establishments which provide both management and staff to operate a business are classified according to the type of activity of the business. Establishments primarily engaged in furnishing personnel to perform a range of services in support of the operation of

<table>
<tr><td>Industry
Group
No.</td><td>Industry
No.</td></tr>
</table>

736 **PERSONNEL SUPPLY SERVICES—Con.**

7363 **Help Supply Services—Con.**

other establishments are classified in Industry 8744, and those supplying farm labor are classified in Agriculture, Industry 0761.

Employee leasing service	Modeling service
Fashion show model supply service	Office help supply service
Help supply service	Temporary help service
Labor pools	Usher service
Manpower pools	

737 **COMPUTER PROGRAMMING, DATA PROCESSING, AND OTHER COMPUTER RELATED SERVICES**

7371 **Computer Programming Services**

Establishments primarily engaged in providing computer programming services on a contract or fee basis. Establishments of this industry perform a variety of additional services, such as computer software design and analysis; modifications of custom software; and training in the use of custom software.

Applications software programming, custom	Computer software systems analysis and design, custom
Computer code authors	Computer software writers, free-lance
Computer programming services	Programming services, computer: custom
Computer programs or systems software development, custom	Software programming, custom

7372 **Prepackaged Software**

Establishments primarily engaged in the design, development, and production of prepackaged computer software. Important products of this industry include operating, utility, and applications programs. Establishments of this industry may also provide services such as preparation of software documentation for the user; installation of software for the user; and training the user in the use of the software. Establishments primarily engaged in providing preparation of computer software documentation and installation of software on a contract or fee basis are classified in Industry 7379, and those engaged in training users in the use of computer software are classified in Industry 8243. Establishments primarily engaged in buying and selling prepackaged computer software are classified in Trade; those providing custom computer programming services are classified in Industry 7371; and those developing custom computer integrated systems are classified in Industry 7373.

Applications software, computer: prepackaged	Operating systems software, computer: prepackaged
Computer software publishers, prepackaged	Software, computer: prepackaged
Games, computer software: prepackaged	Utility software, computer: prepackaged

7373 **Computer Integrated Systems Design**

Establishments primarily engaged in developing or modifying computer software and packaging or bundling the software with purchased computer hardware (computers and computer peripheral equipment) to create and market an integrated system for specific application. Establishments in this industry must provide each of the following services: (1) the development or modification of the computer software; (2) the marketing of purchased computer hardware; and (3) involvement in all phases of systems development from design

737 COMPUTER PROGRAMMING, DATA PROCESSING, AND OTHER
COMPUTER RELATED SERVICES—Con.

7373 Computer Integrated Systems Design—Con.

through installation. Establishments primarily engaged in selling computer hardware are classified in Wholesale Trade, Industry 5045, and Retail Trade, Industry 5734; and those manufacturing computers and computer peripheral equipment are classified in Manufacturing, Industry Group 357.

CAD/CAM systems services
Computer-aided design (CAD) systems services
Computer-aided engineering (CAE) systems services
Computer-aided manufacturing (CAM) systems services
Local area network (LAN) systems integrators

Network systems integration, computer
Office automation, computer systems integration
Systems integration, computer
Turnkey vendors, computer systems
Value-added resellers, computer systems

7374 Computer Processing and Data Preparation and Processing Services

Establishments primarily engaged in providing computer processing and data preparation services. The service may consist of complete processing and preparation of reports from data supplied by the customer or a specialized service, such as data entry or making data processing equipment available on an hourly or time-sharing basis.

Calculating service, computer
Computer time-sharing
Data entry service
Data processing services
Data verification service
Keypunch service

Leasing of computer time
Optical scanning data service
Rental of computer time
Service bureaus, computer
Tabulating service, computer

7375 Information Retrieval Services

Establishments primarily engaged in providing on-line information retrieval services on a contract or fee basis. The information generally involves a range of subjects and is taken from other primary sources. Establishments primarily engaged in performing activities, such as credit reporting, direct mail advertising, stock quotation services, etc., and who also create data bases are classified according to their primary activity. Establishments primarily engaged in collecting data bases from primary sources and reformatting or editing them for distribution through information retrieval services are classified in Industry 7379.

Data base information retrieval services
Information retrieval services, on-line
On-line data base information retrieval services

Remote data base information retrieval services

7376 Computer Facilities Management Services

Establishments primarily engaged in providing on-site management and operation of computer and data processing facilities on a contract or fee basis. Establishments primarily engaged in providing computer processing services at their own facility are classified in Industry 7374.

Computer facilities management services

737

COMPUTER PROGRAMMING, DATA PROCESSING, AND OTHER COMPUTER RELATED SERVICES—Con.

7377 Computer Rental and Leasing

Establishments primarily engaged in renting or leasing computers and related data processing equipment on the customers' site, whether or not also providing maintenance or support services. Establishments primarily engaged in both manufacturing and leasing computers and related data processing equipment are classified in Division D, Manufacturing, and separate establishments owned by the manufacturer and primarily engaged in leasing are classified in Division F, Wholesale Trade. Establishments primarily engaged in finance leasing of computers and related data processing equipment are classified in Finance, Industry 6159. Establishments primarily engaged in leasing computer time are classified in Industry 7374.

Computer hardware rental or leasing, except finance leasing or by the manufacturer	Leasing of computers, except finance leasing or by the manufacturer
Computer peripheral equipment, rental and leasing	Rental of computers, except finance leasing or by the manufacturer

7378 Computer Maintenance and Repair

Establishments primarily engaged in the maintenance and repair of computers and computer peripheral equipment.

Computer peripheral equipment repair and maintenance	Computer repair and maintenance

7379 Computer Related Services, Not Elsewhere Classified

Establishments primarily engaged in supplying computer related services, not elsewhere classified. Computer consultants operating on a contract or fee basis are classified in this industry. Establishments primarily engaged in producing prepackaged software are classified in Industry 7372; and those engaged in offering data processing courses or training in computer programming and in computer and computer peripheral equipment operation, repair, and maintenance are classified in Industry 8243.

Computer consultants	Requirements analysis, computer hardware
Data base developers	Tape recertification service
Data processing consultants	
Disk and diskette conversion services	
Disk and diskette recertification services	

738

MISCELLANEOUS BUSINESS SERVICES

7381 Detective, Guard, and Armored Car Services

Establishments primarily engaged in providing detective, guard, and armored car services. Establishments primarily engaged in monitoring and maintaining security systems devices, such as burglar and fire alarms, are classified in Industry 7382.

Armored car service	Investigators, private
Detective agencies	Lie detection service
Dogs, rental of: for protective service	Polygraph service
Fingerprint service	Protective service, guard
Guard service	Security guard service

MISCELLANEOUS BUSINESS SERVICES—Con.

7382 Security Systems Services

Establishments primarily engaged in monitoring and maintaining security systems devices, such as burglar and fire alarms. Establishments of this industry may sell or lease and install the security systems which they monitor and maintain. Establishments primarily engaged in the sales and installation, or installation only, of such devices are classified in Construction, Industry 1731.

Burglar alarm monitoring and maintenance	Security systems devices, burglar and fire alarm: monitoring and maintenance
Fire alarm monitoring and maintenance	

7383 News Syndicates

Establishments primarily engaged in furnishing news, pictures, and features and in supplying news reporting services to newspapers and periodicals. Separate establishments of newspaper and periodical publishers which are engaged in gathering news are classified as auxiliaries.

News correspondents, independent	News syndicates
News feature syndicates	News ticker services
News pictures, gathering and distributing	Press services (news syndicates)
News reporting services for newspapers and periodicals	

7384 Photofinishing Laboratories

Establishments primarily engaged in developing film and in making photographic prints and enlargements for the trade or for the general public. Establishments primarily engaged in processing motion picture and video film for the motion picture and television industries are classified in Industry 7819.

Developing and printing of film, except commercial motion picture film	Photofinishing laboratories, except for the motion picture industry
Developing and processing of home movies	Photograph developing and retouching
Film processing, except for the motion picture industry	Photographic laboratories, except for the motion picture industry

7389 Business Services, Not Elsewhere Classified

Establishments primarily engaged in furnishing business services, not elsewhere classified, such as bondspersons, drafting services, lecture bureaus, notaries public, sign painting, speakers' bureaus, water softening services, and auctioneering services, on a commission or fee basis. Auctions of used cars and agricultural commodities, such as livestock and produce, are classified in Wholesale Trade.

Agents and brokers for authors and nonperforming artists	Bartering services for businesses
Apparel pressing service for the trade	Batik work (handprinting on textiles)
Appraisers, except real estate appraisers	Bondspersons
	Bottle exchanges
Arbitration and conciliation services	Bronzing baby shoes
Artists' agents and brokers, except performing artists	Business brokers (buying and selling business enterprises)
Auctioneering service on a commission or fee basis	Charge account service (shopping plates)—collection by individual firms
Authors' agents and brokers	
Automobile recovery service	Check validation service
Automobile repossession service	Cloth: cutting to length, bolting, or winding for textile distributors
Automobile shows, flower shows, and home shows: promoters of	Contractors' disbursement control
	Convention bureaus

738   MISCELLANEOUS BUSINESS SERVICES—Con.

7389   Business Services, Not Elsewhere Classified—Con.

Convention decorators

Copyright protection service

Correct time service

Cosmetic kits, assembling and packaging

Cotton inspection service, not connected with transportation

Cotton sampler service

Coupon redemption service, except trading stamps

Credit card service (collection by individual firms)

Decoration service for special events

Demonstration service, separate from sale

Directories, telephone: distribution on a contract or fee basis

Divers, commercial

Drafting service, except temporary help

Drawback service, customs

Drive-a-way automobile service

Embroidering of advertising on shirts, etc.

Engrossing, e.g., diplomas and resolutions

Exhibits, building of: by industrial contractors

Field warehousing, not public warehousing

Filling pressure containers (aerosol) with hair spray, insecticides, etc.

Fire extinguishers, service of

Firefighting service, other than forestry or public

Flagging service (traffic control)

Floats, decoration of

Florists' telegraph service

Folding and refolding service: textiles and apparel

Fundraising on a contract or fee basis

Gas systems, contract conversion from manufactured to natural gas

Handtool designers

Handwriting analysis

Hosiery pairing on a contract or fee basis

Hotel reservation service

Identification engraving service

Inspection of commodities, not connected with transportation

Interior decorating consulting service, except painters and paperhangers

Interior designing service, except painters and paperhangers

Inventory computing service

Labeling bottles, cans, cartons, etc. for the trade: not printing

Laminating of photographs (coating photographs with plastics)

Lecture bureaus

Lettering service

Liquidators of merchandise on a contract or fee basis

Mannequin decorating service

Map drafting service

Mapmaking, including aerial

Message service, telephone answering: except beeper service

Metal slitting and shearing on a contract or fee basis

Meter readers, remote

Microfilm recording and developing service

Mounting merchandise on cards on a contract or fee basis

Music distribution systems, except coin-operated

Notaries public

Packaging and labeling service (not packing and crating)

Paralegal service

Parcel packing service (packaging)

Patent brokers

Patrol of electric transmission or gas lines

Photogrammetric mapping service (not professional engineers)

Photographic library service, still

Photography brokers

Pipeline and power line inspection services

Playwrights' brokers

Post office contract stations

Presorting mail service

Press clipping service

Printed circuitry graphic layout

Process serving service

Produce weighing service, not connected with transportation

Product sterilization service

Promoters of home shows and flower shows

Racetrack cleaning, except buildings

Radio broadcasting music checkers

Radio transcription service

Recording studios on a contract or fee basis

Redemption of trading stamps

Repossession service

Restaurant reservation service

Rug binding for the trade

Safety inspection service, except automotive

Salvaging of damaged merchandise, not engaged in sales

Sampling of commodities, not connected with transportation

Scrap steel cutting on a contract or fee basis

Shoe designers

Showcard painting

Shrinking textiles for tailors and dressmakers

Sign painting and lettering shops

Solvents recovery service on a contract or fee basis

Speakers' bureaus

Sponging textiles for tailors and dressmakers

Styling of fashions, apparel, furniture, and textiles

Styling wigs for the trade

Swimming pool cleaning and maintenance

Switchboard operation of private branch exchanges

Tape slitting for the trade (cutting plastics, leather, etc. into widths)

Tax collection agencies: collecting for a city, county, or State

Tax title dealers: agencies for city, county, or State

Telemarketing (telephone marketing) service on a contract or fee basis

Telephone answering, except beeper service

Industry
Group
No.

Industry
No.

738   MISCELLANEOUS BUSINESS SERVICES—Con.

7389   Business Services, Not Elsewhere Classified—Con.

Telephone solicitation service on a contract or fee basis
Textile designers
Textile folding and packing services
Time-share condominium exchanges
Tobacco sheeting service on a contract or fee basis
Tourist information bureaus
Trade show arrangement
Trading stamp promotion and sale to stores

Trading stamp redemption
Translation service
Water softener service
Weighing foods and other commodities, not connected with transportation
Welcoming service
Window trimming service
Yacht brokers

Major Group 75.—AUTOMOTIVE REPAIR, SERVICES, AND PARKING

The Major Group as a Whole

This major group includes establishments primarily engaged in furnishing automotive repair, rental, leasing, and parking services to the general public. Similar facilities owned and operated by concerns for their own use and not for the general public are treated as auxiliary establishments. Establishments primarily engaged in finance leasing of passenger cars and trucks are classified in Finance, Industry 6159. Automotive repair shops operated by establishments engaged in the sale of new automobiles are classified in Retail Trade, Industry 5511; and those operated by gasoline service stations are classified in Retail Trade, Industry 5541. Repair shops of railroad companies are classified in Railroad Transportation, Major Group 40; and establishments repairing ships and boats are classified in Manufacturing, Industry Group 373.

Industry
Group   Industry
No.   No.

751   **AUTOMOTIVE RENTAL AND LEASING, WITHOUT DRIVERS**

7513   Truck Rental and Leasing, Without Drivers

Establishments primarily engaged in short-term rental or extended-term leasing (with or without maintenance) of trucks, truck tractors, or semitrailers without drivers. Establishments primarily engaged in finance leasing of trucks are classified in Finance, Industry 6159; those renting trucks with drivers are classified in Transportation, Industry Group 421; and those primarily engaged in renting and leasing, except finance leasing, of industrial trucks are classified in Industry 7359.

Truck leasing, except industrial trucks and finance leasing: without drivers

Truck rental, except industrial: without drivers

7514   Passenger Car Rental

Establishments primarily engaged in short-term rental of passenger cars without drivers.

Automobile rental, without drivers
Hearse rental, without drivers

Limousine rental, without drivers
Passenger car rental, without drivers

7515   Passenger Car Leasing

Establishments primarily engaged in extended-term leasing of passenger cars without drivers. Establishments primarily engaged in finance leasing of automobiles are classified in Finance, Industry 6159.

Automobile leasing, except finance leasing: without drivers

Passenger car leasing, except finance leasing: without drivers

7519   Utility Trailer and Recreational Vehicle Rental

Establishments primarily engaged in daily or extended-term rental of utility trailers and recreational vehicles. Establishments primarily engaged in renting motorcycles, bicycles, golf carts, gocarts, or recreational boats are classified in Industry 7999; and those engaged in renting airplanes are classified in Industry 7359. Establishments primarily engaged in the rental of mobile homes on site are classified in Real Estate, Industry 6515.

751   AUTOMOTIVE RENTAL AND LEASING, WITHOUT DRIVERS—Con.

7519   Utility Trailer and Recreational Vehicle Rental—Con.

Mobile home rental, except on site	Trailer rental
Motor home rental	Utility trailer rental
Popup camper rental	

752   AUTOMOBILE PARKING

7521   Automobile Parking

Establishments primarily engaged in the temporary parking of automobiles, usually on an hourly, daily, or monthly contract or fee basis. Establishments primarily engaged in extended or dead storage of automobiles are classified in Transportation, Industry 4226.

Garages, automobile parking	Parking structures
Parking lots	Tow-in parking lots

753   AUTOMOTIVE REPAIR SHOPS

7532   Top, Body, and Upholstery Repair Shops and Paint Shops

Establishments primarily engaged in the repair of automotive tops, bodies, and interiors, or automotive painting and refinishing. Also included in this industry are establishments primarily engaged in customizing automobiles, trucks, and vans except on a factory basis. Establishments primarily engaged in customizing automobiles, trucks, and vans on a factory basis are classified in Manufacturing, Industry Group 371.

Antique and classic automobile restoration	Automotive trim shops
Automotive body shops	Bump shops (automotive repair)
Automotive interior shops	Collision shops, automotive
Automotive paint shops	Customizing automobiles, trucks or vans: except on a factory basis
Automotive tops (canvas or plastic), installation, repair, or sales and installation	Upholstery repair, automotive
	Van conversions, except on a factory basis

7533   Automotive Exhaust System Repair Shops

Establishments primarily engaged in the installation, repair, or sale and installation of automotive exhaust systems. The sale of mufflers, tailpipes, and catalytic converters is considered to be incidental to the installation of these products.

Catalytic converters, automotive: installation, repair, or sales and installation	Exhaust system services, automotive
	Mufflers, automotive: installation, repair, or sales and installation

7534   Tire Retreading and Repair Shops

Establishments primarily engaged in repairing and retreading automotive tires. Establishments classified here may either retread customers' tires or retread tires for sale or exchange to the user or the trade.

Rebuilding and retreading tires for the trade	Tire repair shops
Retreading tires	Tire studding and restudding
Tire recapping	Vulcanizing tires and tubes

Industry Group No.	Industry No.	
753		**AUTOMOTIVE REPAIR SHOPS—Con.**

7536 Automotive Glass Replacement Shops

Establishments primarily engaged in the installation, repair, or sales and installation of automotive glass. The sale of the glass is considered incidental to the replacement.

Glass replacement and repair, automotive

7537 Automotive Transmission Repair Shops

Establishments primarily engaged in the installation, repair, or sales and installation of automotive transmissions. The sale of transmissions and related parts is considered incidental to the installation or repair of these products.

Automatic transmission repair, automotive
Transmission repair, automotive

Transmissions, automotive: installation, repair, or sale and installation

7538 General Automotive Repair Shops

Establishments primarily engaged in general automotive repair. Establishments primarily engaged in industrial truck repair are classified in Industry 7699.

Automotive repair shops, general
Diesel engine repair, automotive
Engine repair, automotive
Engine repair, truck: except industrial

Garages, general automotive repair and service
Motor repair, automotive
Truck engine repair, except industrial

7539 Automotive Repair Shops, Not Elsewhere Classified

Establishments primarily engaged in specialized automotive repair, not elsewhere classified, such as fuel service (carburetor repair), brake relining, front-end and wheel alignment, and radiator repair. Establishments primarily engaged in automotive welding are classified in Industry 7692.

Air-conditioner repair, automotive
Automotive springs, rebuilding and repair
Axle straightening, automotive
Brake linings, sale and installation
Brake repairing, automotive
Carburetor repair
Electrical service, automotive (battery and ignition repair)

Frame repair shops, automotive
Front end repair, automotive
Fuel system conversion, automotive
Fuel system repair, automotive
Generator and starter repair, automotive
Radiator repair shops, automotive
Wheel alignment, automotive

Industry Group No.	Industry No.	
754		**AUTOMOTIVE SERVICES, EXCEPT REPAIR**

7542 Carwashes

Establishments primarily engaged in washing, waxing, and polishing motor vehicles, or in furnishing facilities for the self-service washing of motor vehicles.

Bus washing
Carwashes
Cleaning and polishing (detailing) new autos for dealers on a contract or fee basis
Detailing (cleaning and polishing) new autos for dealers on a contract or fee basis

Laundries, automotive
Truck washing
Washing and polishing, automotive
Waxing and polishing, automotive

Industry Group No.	Industry No.	
754		**AUTOMOTIVE SERVICES, EXCEPT REPAIR—Con.**
	7549	**Automotive Services, Except Repair and Carwashes**

Establishments primarily engaged in furnishing automotive services, except repair and carwashes. Establishments primarily providing automobile driving instructions are classified in Industry 8299.

Auto emissions testing, without repairs
Diagnostic centers, automotive
Emissions testing service, automotive: without repair
Garages, do-it-yourself
Inspection service, automotive
Lubricating service, automotive

Road service, automotive
Rustproofing service, automotive
Towing service, automotive
Undercoating service, automotive
Window tinting, automotive
Wrecker service (towing), automotive

Major Group 76.—MISCELLANEOUS REPAIR SERVICES

The Major Group as a Whole

This major group includes establishments engaged in miscellaneous repair services. It does not include some repair services of which the most important are: repair to structures, which is classified in Construction, Division C; electronic computer and computer peripheral equipment repair, which is classified in Industry 7378; automotive repair, which is classified in Industry Group 753; clothing repair, which is classified in Industry 7219; and shoe repair, which is classified in Industry 7251.

Industry Group No.	Industry No.	
762		**ELECTRICAL REPAIR SHOPS**

7622 Radio and Television Repair Shops

Establishments primarily engaged in repairing radios, televisions, phonographs, stereo equipment, and tape recorders. Also included are establishments engaged in installing and repairing television, amateur, and citizens' band antennas; or in installing and servicing radio transmitting and receiving equipment in homes, offices, boats, automobiles, or other vehicles. Establishments primarily engaged in installation, repair, or maintenance of radio and television broadcast transmitting antennas and towers are classified in Construction, Division C.

Aircraft radio equipment repair
Antennas, household: installation and service
Automotive radio repair shops
Citizens' band (CB) antennas, installation of
Intercommunications equipment repair
Phonograph repair: stereo, hi-fi, and tape recorder

Public address system repair
Radio and television receiver installation
Radio repair shops
Stereophonic equipment repair
Television repair shops
Video recorder or player repair

7623 Refrigeration and Air-Conditioning Service and Repair Shops

Establishments primarily engaged in servicing and repairing household and commercial electrical refrigerators and air-conditioning and refrigeration equipment. Establishments primarily engaged in servicing and repairing gas refrigeration equipment are classified in Industry 7699, and those repairing automotive air-conditioning equipment are classified in Industry 7539.

Air-conditioner repair, self-contained units: except automotive

Refrigeration repair service, electric
Refrigerator repair service, electric

7629 Electrical and Electronic Repair Shops, Not Elsewhere Classified

Establishments primarily engaged in the repair of electrical and electronic equipment, not elsewhere classified, such as electrical household appliances and electrical and electronic industrial equipment. Establishments primarily engaged in the repair of electronic computers and computer peripheral equipment are classified in Industry 7378.

Aircraft electrical equipment repair, except radio
Appliance repair, electrical
Business machine repair, electrical
Electric razor repair
Electric tool repair

Electrical measuring instrument repair and calibration
Electrical repair shops, except radio, television, and refrigerator repair
Electronic equipment repair, except computers and computer peripheral

762   **ELECTRICAL REPAIR SHOPS—Con.**

7629   **Electrical and Electronic Repair Shops, Not Elsewhere Classified—Con.**

equipment
Hearing aid repair
Medical equipment repair, electrical
Office machine repair, electrical: except
typewriters, computers, and comput-
er peripheral equipment

Telephone set repair
Washing machine repair

763   **WATCH, CLOCK, AND JEWELRY REPAIR**

7631   **Watch, Clock, and Jewelry Repair**

Establishments primarily engaged in the repair of watches, clocks, or jewelry. Establishments primarily engaged in assembling watches from purchased parts are classified in Manufacturing, Industry 3873.

Clock repair shops
Jewelry repair shops

Pearl restringing for the trade
Watch repair shops

764   **REUPHOLSTERY AND FURNITURE REPAIR**

7641   **Reupholstery and Furniture Repair**

Establishments primarily engaged in furniture reupholstery and repair. Establishments primarily engaged in selling upholstery materials for personal or household consumption are classified in Retail Trade, Industry 5714; and those making furniture and cabinets on a custom basis are classified in Retail Trade, Industry 5712.

Antique furniture repair and restoration
Furniture refinishing
Furniture repairing, redecorating, and
remodeling shops

Repair of furniture upholstery
Reupholstery shops

769   **MISCELLANEOUS REPAIR SHOPS AND RELATED SERVICES**

7692   **Welding Repair**

Establishments primarily engaged in general repair work by welding, including automotive welding. Establishments primarily engaged in welding at construction sites are classified in Construction, Industry 1799.

Brazing (welding)
Repair of cracked castings (welding
service)

Welding shops, including automotive

7694   **Armature Rewinding Shops**

Establishments primarily engaged in rewinding armatures and rebuilding or repairing electric motors. Establishments classified here may either repair customers' equipment, or repair or rebuild for sale or exchange to users or the trade.

Armature rewinding
Coil winding service
Electric motor repair
Hermetics repair

Rebuilding motors, other than automotive
Rewinding stators

7699   **Repair Shops and Related Services, Not Elsewhere Classified**

Establishments primarily engaged in specialized repair services, not elsewhere classified, such as bicycle repair; leather goods repair; lock and gun repair, including the making of lock parts or gun parts to individual order;

Industry
Group
No.
Industry
No.

769   MISCELLANEOUS REPAIR SHOPS AND RELATED SERVICES—Con.

7699   Repair Shops and Related Services, Not Elsewhere Classified—Con.

musical instrument repair; septic tank cleaning; farm machinery repair; furnace cleaning; motorcycle repair; tank truck cleaning; taxidermists; tractor repair; and typewriter repair.

Agricultural equipment repair
Antique repair and restoration, except furniture and automotive
Awning repair shops
Beer pump coil cleaning and repair service
Bicycle repair shops
Binoculars and other optical goods repair
Blacksmith shops
Boiler cleaning
Boiler repair shops, except manufacturing
Bowling pins, refinishing or repair
Camera repair shops
Catch basin cleaning
Cesspool cleaning
China firing and decorating to individual order
Cleaning and reglazing of baking pans
Cleaning bricks
Coppersmithing repair, except construction
Covering textile rolls
Dental instrument repair
Drafting instrument repair
Engine repair, except automotive
Farm machinery repair
Farriers (blacksmith shops)
Fire control (military) equipment repair
Furnace and chimney cleaning
Furnace cleaning service
Gas appliance repair service
Glazing and cleaning baking pans
Gun parts made to individual order
Gunsmith shops
Harness repair shops
Horseshoeing
Industrial truck repair
Key duplicating shops
Laboratory instrument repair, except electric
Lawnmower repair shops
Leather goods repair shops
Lock parts made to individual order
Locksmith shops
Luggage repair shops
Machinery cleaning
Mattress renovating and repair shops
Measuring and controlling instrument repair, mechanical

Medical equipment repair, except electric
Meteorological instrument repair
Microscope repair
Mirror repair shops
Motorcycle repair service
Musical instrument repair shops
Nautical and navigational instrument repair, except electric
Organ tuning and repair
Piano tuning and repair
Picture framing to individual order, not connected with retail art stores
Picture framing, custom
Pocketbook repair shops
Precision instrument repair
Rebabbitting
Reneedling work
Repair of optical instruments
Repair of photographic equipment
Repair of service station equipment
Repair of speedometers
Rug repair shops, not combined with cleaning
Saddlery repair shops
Scale repair service
Scientific instrument repair, except electric
Septic tank cleaning service
Sewer cleaning and rodding
Sewing machine repair shops
Sharpening and repairing knives, saws, and tools
Ship boiler and tank cleaning and repair—contractors
Ship scaling—contractors
Stove repair shops
Surgical instrument repair
Surveying instrument repair
Tank and boiler cleaning service
Tank truck cleaning service
Taxidermists
Tent repair shops
Thermostat repair
Tinsmithing repair, except construction
Tractor repair
Tuning of pianos and organs
Typewriter repair, including electric
Venetian blind repair shops
Window shade repair shops

Major Group 78.—MOTION PICTURES

The Major Group as a Whole

This major group includes establishments producing and distributing motion pictures, exhibiting motion pictures in commercially operated theaters, and furnishing services to the motion picture industry. The term motion pictures, as used in this major group, includes similar productions for television or other media using film, tape, or other means.

Industry Group No.	Industry No.	

781   MOTION PICTURE PRODUCTION AND ALLIED SERVICES

7812   Motion Picture and Video Tape Production

Establishments primarily engaged in the production of theatrical and nontheatrical motion pictures and video tapes for exhibition or sale, including educational, industrial, and religious films. Included in the industry are establishments engaged in both production and distribution. Producers of live radio and television programs are classified in Industry 7922. Establishments primarily engaged in motion picture and video tape reproduction are classified in Industry 7819 and those engaged in distribution are classified in Industry 7822.

Audiovisual motion picture program production
Cartoon motion picture production
Commercials, television: tape or film production
Educational motion picture production
Industrial motion picture production
Motion picture production and distribution

Music video production
Nontheatrical motion picture production
Religious motion picture production
Tape production, video or motion picture
Television film production
Training motion picture production
Video tape production

7819   Services Allied to Motion Picture Production

Establishments primarily engaged in performing services independent of motion picture production, but allied thereto, such as motion picture film processing, editing, and titling; casting bureaus; wardrobe and studio property rental; television tape services; motion picture and video tape reproduction; and stock footage film libraries.

Casting bureaus, motion picture
Developing and printing of commercial motion picture film
Directors, motion picture: independent
Editing of motion picture film
Film libraries, stock footage
Film processing, motion picture
Laboratories, motion picture
Motion picture consultants
Motion picture reproduction

Rental of motion picture equipment
Studio property rental for motion picture film production
Television tape services (e.g., editing and transfers)
Titling of motion picture film
Video tape or disk reproduction
Wardrobe rental for motion picture film production

782   MOTION PICTURE DISTRIBUTION AND ALLIED SERVICES

7822   Motion Picture and Video Tape Distribution

Establishments primarily engaged in the distribution (rental or sale) of theatrical and nontheatrical motion picture films or in the distribution of video tapes and disks, except to the general public. Establishments engaged in both distribution and production are classified in Industry 7812. Establishments

782   **MOTION PICTURE DISTRIBUTION AND ALLIED SERVICES—Con.**

7822   **Motion Picture and Video Tape Distribution—Con.**

primarily engaged in renting video tapes and disks to the general public are classified in Industry 7841, and those engaged in the sale of video tapes and disks to individuals for personal or household use are classified in Retail Trade, Industry 5735.

Film exchanges, motion picture	Tape distribution for television
Motion picture distribution, exclusive of production	Tapes, video, recorded—wholesale
Rental of motion picture film	Video tapes, recorded—wholesale

7829   **Services Allied to Motion Picture Distribution**

Establishments primarily engaged in performing auxiliary services to motion picture distribution, such as film delivery service, film purchasing and booking agencies, and film libraries.

Booking agencies, motion picture	Theatrical booking agencies, motion picture
Film delivery, motion picture	
Film libraries, motion picture	
Film purchasing agencies, motion picture	

783   **MOTION PICTURE THEATERS**

7832   **Motion Picture Theaters, Except Drive-In**

Commercially operated theaters primarily engaged in the indoor exhibition of motion pictures.

Motion picture exhibitors for airlines	Theaters, motion picture: except drive-in
Motion picture exhibitors, itinerant	

7833   **Drive-In Motion Picture Theaters**

Commercially operated theaters, commonly known as drive-ins, primarily engaged in the outdoor exhibition of motion pictures.

Drive-in theaters

784   **VIDEO TAPE RENTAL**

7841   **Video Tape Rental**

Establishments primarily engaged in renting recorded video tapes and disks to the general public for personal or household use. Establishments primarily engaged in renting video recorders and players are classified in Industry 7359. Establishments primarily engaged in selling recorded video tapes and disks to the general public are classified in Retail Trade, Industry 5735, and those engaged in the wholesale distribution of recorded video tapes and disks are classified in Industry 7822.

Motion picture film or tape rental to the general public	Video disk rental to the general public
	Video tape rental to the general public

380

Major Group 79.—AMUSEMENT AND RECREATION SERVICES
The Major Group as a Whole

This major group includes establishments engaged in providing amusement or entertainment services, not elsewhere classified. Establishments primarily engaged in operating motion picture theaters are classified in Industry Group 783, and those operating museums, art galleries, arboreta, and botanical and zoological gardens are classified in Major Group 84.

Industry Group No.	Industry No.	

791   **DANCE STUDIOS, SCHOOLS, AND HALLS**

     7911   **Dance Studios, Schools, and Halls**

Establishments primarily engaged in operating dance studios, schools, and public dance halls or ballrooms. Establishments primarily engaged in renting facilities used as dance halls or ballrooms are classified in Real Estate, Industry 6512.

Ballroom operation
Children's dancing schools
Dance hall operation
Dance instructors

Dance studios and schools
Discotheques, except those serving alcoholic beverages
Professional dancing schools

792   **THEATRICAL PRODUCERS (EXCEPT MOTION PICTURE), BANDS, ORCHESTRAS, AND ENTERTAINERS**

     7922   **Theatrical Producers (Except Motion Picture) and Miscellaneous Theatrical Services**

Establishments primarily engaged in providing live theatrical presentations, such as road companies and summer theaters. This industry also includes services allied with theatrical presentations, such as casting agencies; booking agencies for plays, artists, and concerts; scenery, lighting, and other equipment services; and theatrical ticket agencies. Also included in this industry are producers of live and taped radio programs and commercials and producers of live television programs. Establishments primarily engaged in the production of taped television programs and commercials are classified in Industry 7812. Theaters which are normally rented to theatrical producers and stock companies are classified in Real Estate, Industry 6512. Motion picture theaters and motion picture service industries are classified in Major Group 78. Establishments primarily engaged in operating dinner theaters are classified in Retail Trade, Industry 5812.

Agents or managers for entertainers
Agents, talent: theatrical
Ballet production
Booking agencies, theatrical: except motion picture
Burlesque companies
Casting agencies, theatrical: except motion picture
Community theater productions
Concert management service
Costume design, theatrical
Employment agencies: theatrical, radio, and television-except motion picture
Legitimate theater producers
Opera companies
Performing arts center productions
Plays (road companies and stock companies)
Radio programs, including commercials: producers of

Rental of theatrical scenery
Repertory or stock companies, theatrical
Road companies, theatrical
Scenery design, theatrical
Stock companies, theatrical
Summer theaters, except dinner theaters
Television programs (including commercials): live
Theatrical companies
Theatrical equipment rental
Theatrical lighting on a contract basis
Theatrical production, except motion picture
Theatrical ticket agencies
Vaudeville companies

Industry Group No.	Industry No.	
792		**THEATRICAL PRODUCERS (EXCEPT MOTION PICTURE), BANDS, ORCHESTRAS, AND ENTERTAINERS—Con.**
	7929	**Bands, Orchestras, Actors, and Other Entertainers and Entertainment Groups**

Establishments primarily engaged in providing entertainment other than live theatrical presentations. These establishments include bands, orchestras, and entertainers.

Actors
Actresses
Classical music groups or artists
Concert artists
Dance bands
Drum and bugle corps (drill teams)
Entertainers
Entertainment groups

Jazz music groups or artists
Magicians
Musicians
Orchestras
Performing artists
Popular music groups or artists
Symphony orchestras

793		**BOWLING CENTERS**
	7933	**Bowling Centers**

Establishments known to the public as bowling centers or lanes. Such establishments frequently sell meals and refreshments.

Bowling centers
Candle pin centers

Duck pin centers
Ten pin centers

794		**COMMERCIAL SPORTS**
	7941	**Professional Sports Clubs and Promoters**

Establishments primarily engaged in operating and promoting professional and semiprofessional athletic clubs; promoting athletic events, including amateur; and managing individual professional athletes. Stadiums and athletic fields are included only if the operator is actually engaged in the promotion of athletic events. Establishments primarily engaged in operating stadiums and athletic fields are classified in Real Estate, Industry Group 651. Amateur sports and athletic clubs are classified in Industry Group 799.

Arenas, boxing and wrestling (sports promotion): professional
Athletic field operation (sports promotion)
Baseball clubs, professional or semiprofessional
Basketball clubs, professional or semiprofessional
Football clubs, professional or semiprofessional
Ice hockey clubs, professional or semiprofessional

Managers of individual professional athletes
Professional or semiprofessional sports clubs
Promoters, sports events
Soccer clubs, professional or semiprofessional
Sports field operation (sports promotion)
Sports promotion: baseball, football, boxing, etc.
Stadiums (sports promotion)

	7948	**Racing, Including Track Operation**

Promoters and participants in racing activities, including racetrack operators, operators of racing stables, jockeys, racehorse trainers, and race car owners and operators.

Dog racing
Dragstrip operation
Horses, race: training
Horses, racing of
Jockeys, horseracing
Motorcycle racing
Race car drivers and owners

Racetrack operation: e.g., horse, dog, auto
Racing stables, operation of
Speedway operation
Stock car racing
Training racehorses

799   MISCELLANEOUS AMUSEMENT AND RECREATION SERVICES

7991   Physical Fitness Facilities

Establishments primarily engaged in operating reducing and other health clubs, spas, and similar facilities featuring exercise and other active physical fitness conditioning, whether or not on a membership basis. Also included in this industry are establishments providing aerobic dance and exercise classes. Sports and recreation clubs are classified in Industry 7997 if operated on a membership basis, and in Industries 7992 or 7999 if open to the general public. Health resorts and spas providing lodging are classified in Major Group 70. Establishments that promote physical fitness through diet control are classified in Industry 7299.

Aerobic dance and exercise classes	Reducing facilities, physical fitness,
Clubs, health	without lodging
Exercise salons	Slenderizing salons
Fitness salons	Spas, health fitness: except resort
Gymnasiums	lodges
Physical fitness centers	

7992   Public Golf Courses

Establishments primarily engaged in the operation of golf courses open to the general public on a contract or fee basis. Membership golf and country clubs are classified in Industry 7997. Miniature golf courses and golf driving ranges are classified in Industry 7999.

Golf clubs, nonmembership	Golf courses, public: operation of

7993   Coin-Operated Amusement Devices

Establishments primarily engaged in operating coin-operated amusement devices, either in their own or in other places of business. Such amusement devices include juke boxes, pinball machines, mechanical games, slot machines, and similar types of amusement equipment. Amusement (including video game) arcades and parlors are also included in this industry.

Amusement device parlors, coin-operated	Juke boxes, operation of
	Mechanical games, coin-operated: operation of
Amusement machines, coin-operated: operation of	Music distribution systems, coin-operated
Arcades, amusement	
Gambling establishments primarily operating coin-operated machines	Pinball machines, operation of
	Slot machines, operation of
Gambling machines, coin-operated: operation of	Video game arcades

7996   Amusement Parks

Establishments of the type known as amusement parks and kiddie parks which group together and operate in whole or in part a number of attractions, such as mechanical rides, amusement devices, refreshment stands, and picnic grounds. Amusement concessionaires operating within the park are generally classified in Industry 7999.

Amusement centers and parks (not fairs, circuses, or carnivals)	Kiddie parks
	Piers, amusement
Amusement parks	Theme parks, amusement

7997   Membership Sports and Recreation Clubs

Sports and recreation clubs which are restricted to use by members and their guests. Country, golf, tennis, yacht, and amateur sports and recreation

799   MISCELLANEOUS AMUSEMENT AND RECREATION SERVICES—Con.

7997   Membership Sports and Recreation Clubs—Con.

clubs are included in this industry. Physical fitness facilities are classified in Industry 7991.

Aviation clubs, membership
Baseball clubs, except professional and semiprofessional
Bathing beaches, membership
Beach clubs, membership
Boating clubs, membership
Bowling leagues or teams, except professional and semiprofessional
Bridge clubs, membership
Clubs, membership: sports and recreation, except physical fitness
Country clubs, membership
Flying fields maintained by aviation clubs
Football clubs, except professional and semiprofessional
Golf clubs, membership

Gun clubs, membership
Handball clubs, membership
Hockey clubs, except professional and semiprofessional
Hunt clubs, membership
Racquetball clubs, membership
Recreation and sports clubs, membership: except physical fitness
Riding clubs, membership
Shooting clubs, membership
Soccer clubs, except professional and semiprofessional
Sports and recreation clubs, membership: except physical fitness
Swimming clubs, membership
Tennis clubs, membership
Yacht clubs, membership

7999   Amusement and Recreation Services, Not Elsewhere Classified

Establishments primarily engaged in the operation of sports, amusement, and recreation services, not elsewhere classified, such as bathing beaches, swimming pools, riding academies and schools, carnival operation, exposition operation, horse shows, picnic grounds operation, rental of rowboats and canoes, and shooting galleries. Establishments primarily engaged in showing or handling animals at shows or exhibitions are classified in Agricultural Services, Industry Group 075.

Aerial tramways, amusement or scenic
Amusement concessions
Amusement rides
Animal shows in circuses, fairs, and carnivals
Archery ranges, operation of
Astrologers
Baseball instruction schools
Basketball instruction schools
Bath houses, independently operated
Bathing beaches, public
Betting information services
Billiard parlors
Bingo parlors
Boat rental, pleasure
Boats, party fishing: operation of
Bookies
Bookmakers, race
Bowling instruction
Bridge clubs, nonmembership
Bridge instruction
Cable lifts, amusement or scenic: operated separately from lodges
Canoe rental
Card rooms
Carnival operation
Cave operation
Circus companies
Concession operators, amusement devices and rides
Day camps
Exhibition operation
Exposition operation
Fairs, agricultural: operation of
Fireworks display service
Fishing piers and lakes, operation of

Fortune tellers
Gambling establishments not primarily operating coin-operated machines
Gambling machines, except coin-operated: operation of
Game parlors, except coin-operated
Games, teaching of
Gocart raceway operation
Gocart rentals
Golf courses, miniature: operation of
Golf driving ranges
Golf professionals not operating retail stores
Golf, pitch-n-putt
Gymnastics instruction
Handball courts, except membership clubs
Horse shows
Houseboat rentals
Hunting guides
Ice skating rink operation
Judo instruction
Karate instruction
Lifeguard service
Lotteries, operation of
Lottery clubs and ticket sales to individuals
Moped rental
Motorcycle rental
Natural wonders, tourist attraction: commercial
Observation tower operation
Off-track betting
Pack trains for amusement
Parachute training for pleasure
Phrenologists

Industry Group No.	Industry No.	
799		**MISCELLANEOUS AMUSEMENT AND RECREATION SERVICES—Con.**
	7999	**Amusement and Recreation Services, Not Elsewhere Classified—Con.**

Picnic grounds operation
Ping pong parlors
Pool parlors
Racquetball courts, except membership clubs
Rental of beach chairs and accessories
Rental of bicycles
Rental of golf carts
Rental of rowboats and canoes
Rental of saddle horses
Riding academies and schools
Riding stables
River rafting, operation of
Rodeo animal rental
Rodeos, operation of
Roller skating rink operation
Scenic railroads for amusement
Schools and camps, sports instructional
Scuba and skin diving instruction
Shooting galleries
Shooting ranges, operation of
Skating instruction, ice or roller
Skeet shooting facilities, except membership clubs
Ski instruction
Ski lifts, cable lifts, and ski tows operated separately from lodges

Ski rental concessions
Slot-car racetracks
Sporting goods rental
Sports instructors, professional: golf, skiing, swimming, etc.
Sports professionals
Swimming instruction
Swimming pools, except membership
Tennis clubs, nonmembership
Tennis courts, outdoor and indoor: operation of, nonmembership
Tennis professionals
Ticket sales offices for sporting events, contract
Tourist attractions, natural wonder: commercial
Tourist guides
Trampoline operation
Trapshooting facilities, except membership clubs
Waterslides, operation of
Wave pools, operation of
Wax figure exhibitions
Yoga instruction

Major Group 80.—HEALTH SERVICES

The Major Group as a Whole

This major group includes establishments primarily engaged in furnishing medical, surgical, and other health services to persons. Establishments of associations or groups, such as Health Maintenance Organizations (HMOs), primarily engaged in providing medical or other health services to members are included, but those which limit their services to the provision of insurance against hospitalization or medical costs are classified in Insurance, Major Group 63. Hospices are also included in this major group and are classified according to the primary service provided.

Industry groups 801 through 804 includes individual practitioners, group clinics in which a group of practitioners is associated for the purpose of carrying on their profession, and clinics which provide the same services through practitioners that are employees.

Industry Group No.	Industry No.	

801 **OFFICES AND CLINICS OF DOCTORS OF MEDICINE**

    8011 **Offices and Clinics of Doctors of Medicine**

Establishments of licensed practitioners having the degree of M.D. and engaged in the practice of general or specialized medicine and surgery. Establishments operating as clinics of physicians are included in this industry. Osteopathic physicians are classified in Industry 8031.

Ambulatory surgical centers	Pathologists (M.D.), offices of
Anesthesiologists, offices of	Pediatricians, offices of
Clinics of physicians (M.D.)	Physicians (M.D.), including specialists:
Dermatologists, offices of	offices and clinics of
Freestanding emergency medical (M.D.)	Plastic surgeons, offices of
centers	Primary care medical (M.D.) clinics
Gynecologists, offices of	Psychiatrists, offices of
Neurologists, offices of	Psychoanalysts, offices of
Obstetricians, offices of	Radiologists, offices of
Oculists, offices of	Surgeons (M.D.), offices of
Ophthalmologists, offices of	Urologists, offices of
Orthopedic physicians, offices of	

802 **OFFICES AND CLINICS OF DENTISTS**

    8021 **Offices and Clinics of Dentists**

Establishments of licensed practitioners having the degree of D.M.D. or D.D.S. (or D.D.Sc.) and engaged in the practice of general or specialized dentistry, including dental surgery. Establishments operating as clinics of dentists are included in this industry.

Clinics of dentists	Orthodontists, offices of
Dental surgeons, offices of	Pathologists, oral: offices of
Dentists, offices and clinics of	Periodontists, offices of
Endodontists, offices of	Prosthodontists, offices of
Oral pathologists, offices of	

803 **OFFICES AND CLINICS OF DOCTORS OF OSTEOPATHY**

    8031 **Offices and Clinics of Doctors of Osteopathy**

Establishments of licensed practitioners having the degree of D.O. and engaged in the practice of general or specialized osteopathic medicine and sur-

803   **OFFICES AND CLINICS OF DOCTORS OF OSTEOPATHY—Con.**

8031   **Offices and Clinics of Doctors of Osteopathy—Con.**

gery. Establishments operating as clinics of osteopathic physicians are included in this industry.

Osteopathic physicians, offices and clinics of

804   **OFFICES AND CLINICS OF OTHER HEALTH PRACTITIONERS**

8041   **Offices and Clinics of Chiropractors**

Establishments of licensed practitioners having the degree of D.C. and engaged in the practice of chiropractic medicine. Establishments operating as clinics of chiropractors are included in this industry.

Chiropractors, offices and clinics of   Clinics of chiropractors

8042   **Offices and Clinics of Optometrists**

Establishments of licensed practitioners having the degree of O.D. and engaged in the practice of optometry. Establishments operating as clinics of optometrists are included in this industry.

Optometrists, offices and clinics of

8043   **Offices and Clinics of Podiatrists**

Establishments of licensed practitioners having the degree of D.P. and engaged in the practice of podiatry. Establishments operating as clinics of podiatrists are included in this industry.

Podiatrists, offices and clinics of

8049   **Offices and Clinics of Health Practitioners, Not Elsewhere Classified**

Establishments of health practitioners engaged in the practice of health fields, not elsewhere classified. Practitioners may or may not be licensed or certified, depending on the State in which they practice. Establishments operating as clinics of health practitioners, not elsewhere classified, are included in this industry.

Acupuncturists, except M.D.: offices of
Audiologists, offices of
Christian Science practitioners, offices of
Dental hygienists, offices of
Dieticians, offices of
Hypnotists, offices of
Inhalation therapists, registered
Midwives, offices of
Naturopaths, offices of
Nurses, registered and practical: offices of, except home health care services

Nutritionists, offices of
Occupational therapists, offices of
Paramedics, offices of
Physical therapists, offices of
Physicians' assistants, offices of
Psychiatric social workers, offices of
Psychologists, clinical: offices of
Psychotherapists, except M.D.: offices of
Speech clinicians, offices of
Speech pathologists, offices of

805   **NURSING AND PERSONAL CARE FACILITIES**

This group includes establishments primarily engaged in providing inpatient nursing and health-related personal care. Establishments providing diagnostic, surgical, and extensive medical services are classified in Industry Group 806, and those providing residential care with incidental nursing or medical services are classified in Industry Group 836.

805		NURSING AND PERSONAL CARE FACILITIES—Con.

		8051	**Skilled Nursing Care Facilities**

Establishments primarily engaged in providing inpatient nursing and rehabilitative services to patients who require continuous health care, but not hospital services. Care must be ordered by and under the direction of a physician. The staff must include a licensed nurse on duty continuously with a minimum of one full-time registered nurse on duty during each day shift. Included are establishments certified to deliver skilled nursing care under the Medicare and Medicaid programs.

Convalescent homes with continuous nursing care	Mental retardation hospitals
Extended care facilities	Nursing homes, skilled

		8052	**Intermediate Care Facilities**

Establishments primarily engaged in providing inpatient nursing and rehabilitative services, but not on a continuous basis. Staffing must include 24-hour per day personnel with a licensed nurse on duty full-time during each day shift. At least once a week, consultation from a registered nurse on the delivery of care is required. Included are facilities certified to deliver intermediate care under the Medicaid program.

Intermediate care facilities	Nursing homes, intermediate care

		8059	**Nursing and Personal Care Facilities, Not Elsewhere Classified**

Establishments primarily engaged in providing some nursing and/or health-related care to patients who do not require the degree of care and treatment that a skilled or intermediate care facility is designed to provide. Patients in these facilities, because of their mental or physical condition, require some nursing care, including the administering of medications and treatments or the supervision of self-administered medications in accordance with a physician's orders. Establishments primarily engaged in providing day-to-day personal care without supervision of the delivery of health services prescribed by a physician are classified in Industry 8361.

Convalescent homes for psychiatric patients, with health care	Nursing homes except skilled and intermediate care facilities
Convalescent homes with health care	Personal care facilities with health care
Domiciliary care with health care	Personal care homes with health care
Homes for the mentally retarded with health care, except skilled and intermediate care facilities	Psychiatric patient's convalescent homes
	Rest homes with health care

806		HOSPITALS

This group includes establishments primarily engaged in providing diagnostic services, extensive medical treatment including surgical services, and other hospital services, as well as continuous nursing services. These establishments have an organized medical staff, inpatient beds, and equipment and facilities to provide complete health care. Convalescent homes with extended care facilities, sometimes referred to as convalescent hospitals, are classified in Industry 8051.

Industry Group No.	Industry No.	
806		**HOSPITALS—Con.**

8062 General Medical and Surgical Hospitals

Establishments primarily engaged in providing general medical and surgical services and other hospital services. Specialty hospitals are classified in Industries 8063 and 8069.

General medical and surgical hospitals

8063 Psychiatric Hospitals

Establishments primarily engaged in providing diagnostic medical services and inpatient treatment for the mentally ill. Establishments, known as hospitals, primarily engaged in providing health care for the mentally retarded are classified in Industry 8051.

Mental hospitals, except for the mentally retarded

Psychiatric hospitals

8069 Specialty Hospitals, Except Psychiatric

Establishments primarily engaged in providing diagnostic services, treatment, and other hospital services for specialized categories of patients, except mental. Psychiatric hospitals are classified in Industry 8063.

Alcoholism rehabilitation hospitals
Cancer hospitals
Children's hospitals
Chronic disease hospitals
Drug addiction rehabilitation hospitals
Eye, ear, nose, and throat hospitals: inpatient

Hospitals, specialty: except psychiatric
Maternity hospitals
Orthopedic hospitals
Rehabilitation hospitals: drug addiction and alcoholism
Tuberculosis and other respiratory illness hospitals

807   MEDICAL AND DENTAL LABORATORIES

8071 Medical Laboratories

Establishments primarily engaged in providing professional analytic or diagnostic services to the medical profession, or to the patient on prescription of a physician.

Bacteriological laboratories (not manufacturing)
Biological laboratories (not manufacturing)
Blood analysis laboratories
Chemists, biological: (not manufacturing) laboratories of
Dental laboratories, X-ray

Medical laboratories, clinical
Pathological laboratories
Testing laboratories, medical: analytic or diagnostic
Urinalysis laboratories
X-ray laboratories, including dental (not manufacturing)

8072 Dental Laboratories

Establishments primarily engaged in making dentures, artificial teeth, and orthodontic appliances to order for the dental profession. Establishments primarily engaged in manufacturing artificial teeth, except to order, are classified in Manufacturing, Industry 3843, and those providing dental X-ray laboratory services are classified in Industry 8071.

Crowns and bridges made in dental laboratories to order for the profession
Dental laboratories, except X-ray
Dentures made in dental laboratories to order for the profession

Orthodontic appliances made in dental laboratories to order for the profession
Teeth, artificial: made in dental laboratories to order for the profession

808   **HOME HEALTH CARE SERVICES**

     8082   **Home Health Care Services**

Establishments primarily engaged in providing skilled nursing or medical care in the home, under supervision of a physician. Establishments of registered or practical nurses engaged in the independent practice of their profession are classified in Industry 8049, and nurses' registries are classified in Industry 7361. Establishments primarily engaged in selling health care products for personal or household consumption are classified in Retail Trade and those engaged in renting or leasing products for health care are classified in Industry 7352.

Home health care services	Visiting nurse associations

809   **MISCELLANEOUS HEALTH AND ALLIED SERVICES, NOT ELSEWHERE CLASSIFIED**

     8092   **Kidney Dialysis Centers**

Establishments primarily engaged in providing kidney or renal dialysis services. Offices and clinics of doctors of medicine are classified in Industry 8011.

Kidney dialysis centers

     8093   **Specialty Outpatient Facilities, Not Elsewhere Classified**

Establishments primarily engaged in outpatient care of a specialized nature with permanent facilities and with medical staff to provide diagnosis, treatment, or both for patients who are ambulatory and do not require inpatient care. Offices and clinics of health practitioners are classified according to their primary activity in Industry Groups 801 through 804.

Alcohol treatment, outpatient clinics	Outpatient treatment clinics for alcoholism and drug addiction
Biofeedback centers	Rehabilitation centers, outpatient (medical treatment)
Birth control clinics (family planning)	Respiratory therapy clinics
Drug treatment, outpatient clinics	
Outpatient detoxification centers	
Outpatient mental health clinics	

     8099   **Health and Allied Services, Not Elsewhere Classified**

Establishments primarily engaged in providing health and allied services, not elsewhere classified. Offices and clinics of health practitioners are classified according to their primary activity in Industry Groups 801 through 804.

Artists, medical	Medical photography and art
Blood banks	Osteoperosis centers
Blood donor stations	Oxygen tent service
Childbirth preparation classes	Physical examination service, except by physicians
Health screening service	Plasmapheresis centers
Hearing testing service	Sperm banks
Insurance physical examination service, except by physicians	

Major Group 81.—LEGAL SERVICES

The Major Group as a Whole

This major group includes establishments which are headed by members of the bar and are engaged in offering legal advice or legal services.

Industry Group No.	Industry No.	

811   **LEGAL SERVICES**

8111 Legal Services

Establishments which are headed by members of the bar and are primarily engaged in offering legal advice or services.

Attorneys	Legal aid services
Counselors at law	Legal services
Law offices	Patent solicitors' offices
Lawyers	Referees in bankruptcy

Major Group 82.—EDUCATIONAL SERVICES

The Major Group as a Whole

This major group includes establishments providing academic or technical instruction. Also included are establishments providing educational services such as libraries, student exchange programs, and curriculum development. Schools for the instruction of beauticians and cosmetologists are classified in Industry 7231, and barber colleges are classified in Industry 7241. Establishments primarily engaged in providing job training for the unemployed, the underemployed, the handicapped, and to persons who have a job market disadvantage because of lack of education, job skill or experience are classified in Industry 8331.

Industry Group No.	Industry No.	

821   **ELEMENTARY AND SECONDARY SCHOOLS**

     8211   **Elementary and Secondary Schools**

Elementary and secondary schools furnishing academic courses, ordinarily for kindergarten through grade 12. Included in this industry are parochial schools and military academies furnishing academic courses for kindergarten through grade 12, and secondary schools which furnish both academic and technical courses.

Academies, elementary and secondary schools
Boarding schools
Finishing schools, secondary
High schools
Kindergartens
Military academies, elementary and secondary level
Parochial schools, elementary and secondary

Preparatory schools
Schools for the physically handicapped, elementary and secondary
Schools for the retarded
Schools, elementary and secondary
Seminaries, below university grade
Vocational high schools

822   **COLLEGES, UNIVERSITIES, PROFESSIONAL SCHOOLS, AND JUNIOR COLLEGES**

     8221   **Colleges, Universities, and Professional Schools**

Colleges, universities, and professional schools furnishing academic courses and granting academic degrees. The requirement for admission is at least a high school diploma or equivalent general academic training.

Colleges, except junior
Professional schools: e.g., dental, engineering, law, medical
Seminaries, theological

Service academies (college)
Theological seminaries
Universities

     8222   **Junior Colleges and Technical Institutes**

Junior colleges and technical institutes furnishing academic, or academic and technical, courses and granting associate academic degrees, certificates, or diplomas. The requirement for admission is at least a high school diploma or equivalent general academic training. Schools having junior college grades in conjunction with secondary grades are classified in Industry 8211.

Community colleges (junior)
Junior colleges

Technical institutes

Industry Group No.	Industry No.	
823		**LIBRARIES**

8231 Libraries

Establishments primarily engaged in providing library services, including the circulation of books and other materials for reading, study, and reference. Establishments primarily engaged in operating motion picture film libraries are classified in Industry 7829.

Centers for documentation	Libraries, printed matter
Circulating libraries	Rental of books
Lending libraries	

824   VOCATIONAL SCHOOLS

8243 Data Processing Schools

Establishments primarily engaged in offering data processing courses or training in computer programming and in computer and computer peripheral equipment operation, maintenance, and repair. Schools offering an academic degree in computer sciences are classified in Industry Group 822.

Computer operator training	Computer software training
Computer repair training	Data processing schools

8244 Business and Secretarial Schools

Establishments primarily engaged in offering courses in business machine operation, office procedures, and secretarial and stenographic skills. Schools offering academic degrees are classified in Industry Groups 821 and 822.

Business colleges and schools, not of college grade	Court reporting schools
	Secretarial schools

8249 Vocational Schools, Not Elsewhere Classified

Establishments primarily engaged in offering specialized vocational courses, not elsewhere classified. Also included in this industry are establishments primarily engaged in furnishing educational courses by mail. Offices maintained by such schools for the sale of correspondence courses are included. Beauty schools are classified in Industry 7231, and barber schools are classified in Industry 7241. Establishments primarily engaged in offering flying instruction are classified in Industry 8299. Schools offering academic degrees are classified in Industry Groups 821 and 822.

Aviation schools, excluding flying instruction	Nursing schools, practical
	Real estate schools
Banking schools (training in banking)	Restaurant operation schools
Commercial art schools	Trade schools
Construction equipment operation schools	Truck driving schools
	Vocational apprenticeship training
Correspondence schools, including branch offices and solicitors	Vocational schools: except high schools, data processing, or business

829   SCHOOLS AND EDUCATIONAL SERVICES, NOT ELSEWHERE CLASSIFIED

8299 Schools and Educational Services, Not Elsewhere Classified

Establishments primarily engaged in offering educational courses and services, not elsewhere classified. Included in this industry are music schools, drama schools, language schools, short-term examination preparatory schools, student exchange programs, curriculum development, and vocational counsel-

Industry Group No.	Industry No.	
829		**SCHOOLS AND EDUCATIONAL SERVICES, NOT ELSEWHERE CLASSIFIED—Con.**
	8299	**Schools and Educational Services, Not Elsewhere Classified—Con.**

ing, except rehabilitation counseling. Establishments primarily engaged in operating dance schools are classified in Industry 7911, and those providing rehabilitation counseling are classified in Industry 8331.

Art schools, except commercial
Automobile driving instruction
Baton instruction
Bible schools, not operated by churches
Ceramics schools
Charm schools
Civil service schools
Continuing education programs
Cooking schools
Curriculum development, educational
Diction schools
Drama schools
Finishing schools, charm and modeling
Flying instruction

Hypnosis schools
Language schools
Modeling schools, clothes
Music schools
Personal development schools
Public speaking schools
Reading schools
Speed reading courses
Student exchange programs
Survival schools
Tutoring
Vocational counseling, except rehabilitation counseling

394

Major Group 83.—SOCIAL SERVICES

The Major Group as a Whole

This major group includes establishments providing social services and rehabilitation services to those persons with social or personal problems requiring special services and to the handicapped and the disadvantaged. Also included are organizations soliciting funds to be used directly for these and related services. Establishments primarily engaged in providing health services are classified in Major Group 80; those providing legal services are classified in Industry 8111; and those providing educational services are classified in Major Group 82.

Industry Group No.

Industry No.

832

INDIVIDUAL AND FAMILY SOCIAL SERVICES

8322 Individual and Family Social Services

Establishments primarily engaged in providing one or more of a wide variety of individual and family social, counseling, welfare, or referral services, including refugee, disaster, and temporary relief services. This industry includes offices of specialists providing counseling, referral, and other social services. Government offices directly concerned with the delivery of social services to individuals and families, such as issuing of welfare aid, rent supplements, food stamps, and eligibility casework, are included here, but central office administration of these programs is classified in Public Administration, Industry 9441. Social Security offices are also classified in Public Administration, Industry 9441. Establishments primarily engaged in providing vocational rehabilitation or counseling are classified in Industry 8331; and fraternal, civic, and social associations are classified in Industry 8641.

Activity centers, elderly or handicapped
Adoption services
Adult day care centers
Aid to families with dependent children (AFDC)
Alcoholism counseling, nonresidential: except medical treatment
Centers for senior citizens
Child guidance agencies
Community centers
Counseling centers
Crisis centers
Crisis intervention centers
Day care centers, adult and handicapped
Disaster services
Emergency shelters
Family counseling services
Family location services
Family service agencies
Helping hand services
Homemaker's service, primarily non-medical
Hotlines

Marriage counseling services
Meal delivery programs
Multiservice centers, neighborhood
Neighborhood centers
Offender rehabilitation agencies
Offender self-help agencies
Old age assistance
Outreach programs
Parole offices
Probation offices
Public welfare centers, offices of
Referral services for personal and social problems
Refugee services
Relief services, temporary
Self-help organizations for alcoholics and gamblers
Senior citizens associations
Service leagues
Settlement houses
Social service centers
Telephone counseling service
Traveler's aid centers
Youth centers
Youth self-help organizations

JOB TRAINING AND VOCATIONAL REHABILITATION SERVICES

8331 Job Training and Vocational Rehabilitation Services

Establishments primarily engaged in providing manpower training and vocational rehabilitation and habilitation services for the unemployed, the underemployed, the handicapped, and to persons who have a job market disadvantage because of lack of education, job skill or experience. Included are upgrading and job-development services, skill training, world-of-work orientation, and vocational rehabilitation counseling. This industry includes offices of specialists providing rehabilitation and job counseling. Also included are establishments primarily engaged in providing work experience for rehabilitees.

Community service employment train-
  ing programs
Job counseling
Job training
Manpower training
Rehabilitation counseling and training,
  vocational

Sheltered workshops
Skill training centers
Vocational rehabilitation agencies
Vocational rehabilitation counseling
Vocational training agencies, except
  schools
Work experience centers

835 CHILD DAY CARE SERVICES

8351 Child Day Care Services

Establishments primarily engaged in the care of infants or children, or in providing prekindergarten education, where medical care or delinquency correction is not a major element. These establishments may or may not have substantial educational programs. These establishments generally care for prekindergarten or preschool children, but may care for older children when they are not in school. Establishments providing babysitting services are classified in Industry 7299. Head Start centers operating in conjunction with elementary schools are classified in Industry 8211.

Child care centers
Day care centers, child
Group day care centers, child
Head Start centers, except in conjunc-
  tion with schools

Nursery schools
Preschool centers

836 RESIDENTIAL CARE

8361 Residential Care

Establishments primarily engaged in the provision of residential social and personal care for children, the aged, and special categories of persons with some limits on ability for self-care, but where medical care is not a major element. Included are establishments providing 24-hour year-round care for children. Boarding schools providing elementary and secondary education are classified in Industry 8211. Establishments primarily engaged in providing nursing and health-related personal care are classified in Industry Group 805.

Alcoholism rehabilitation centers, resi-
  dential: with health care incidental
Boys' towns
Children's boarding homes
Children's homes
Children's villages
Drug rehabilitation centers, residential:
  with health care incidental
Group foster homes
Halfway group homes for persons with
  social or personal problems
Halfway homes for delinquents and of-
  fenders

Homes for children, with health care
  incidental
Homes for destitute men and women
Homes for the aged, with health care
  incidental
Homes for the deaf or blind, with
  health care incidental
Homes for the emotionally disturbed,
  with health care incidental
Homes for the mentally handicapped,
  with health care incidental
Homes for the physically handicapped,
  with health care incidental

Industry Group No.	Industry No.	
836		**RESIDENTIAL CARE—Con.**
	8361	**Residential Care—Con.**

Juvenile correctional homes
Old soldiers' homes
Orphanages
Rehabilitation centers, residential: with health care incidental

Rest homes, with health care incidental
Self-help group homes for persons with social or personal problems
Training schools for delinquents

839		**SOCIAL SERVICES, NOT ELSEWHERE CLASSIFIED**
	8399	**Social Services, Not Elsewhere Classified**

Establishments primarily engaged in providing social services, not elsewhere classified, including establishments primarily engaged in community improvement and social change. Organizations primarily engaged in soliciting contributions on their own account and administering appropriations and allocating funds among other agencies engaged in social welfare services are also included, but foundations and philanthropic trusts are classified in Finance, Industry 6732. Civic, social, and fraternal organizations are classified in Industry 8641; political organizations are classified in Industry 8651; and establishments which raise funds on a contract basis are classified in Industry 7389.

Advocacy groups
Antipoverty boards
Community action agencies
Community chests
Community development groups
Councils for social agencies, exceptional children, and poverty
Fundraising organizations, except on a contract or fee basis

Health and welfare councils
Health systems agencies
Regional planning organizations, for social services
Social change associations
Social service information exchanges: e.g., alcoholism, drug addiction
United fund councils

Major Group 84.—MUSEUMS, ART GALLERIES, AND BOTANICAL AND ZOOLOGICAL GARDENS

The Major Group as a Whole

This major group includes museums, art galleries, arboreta, and botanical and zoological gardens. These establishments are often of historical, educational, or cultural interest.

Industry
Group
No.

Industry
No.

841   **MUSEUMS AND ART GALLERIES**

8412   **Museums and Art Galleries**

Establishments primarily engaged in the operation of museums and art galleries. Art galleries and dealers primarily engaged in selling to the general public are classified in Retail Trade, Industries 5932 and 5999.

Art galleries, not primarily selling	Planetaria
Museums	

842   **ARBORETA AND BOTANICAL OR ZOOLOGICAL GARDENS**

8422   **Arboreta and Botanical or Zoological Gardens**

Establishments primarily engaged in the operation of arboreta and of botanical or zoological gardens and exhibits.

Animal exhibits	Botanical gardens
Aquariums	Reptile exhibits
Arboreta	Zoological gardens

Major Group 86.—MEMBERSHIP ORGANIZATIONS

The Major Group as a Whole

This major group includes organizations operating on a membership basis for the promotion of the interests of their members. Included are organizations such as trade associations; professional membership organizations; labor unions and similar labor organizations; and political and religious organizations. This major group does not include business establishments operated by membership organizations, which are classified according to their primary activity.

Industry Group No.	Industry No.	

861   **BUSINESS ASSOCIATIONS**

8611 Business Associations

Membership organizations engaged in promoting the business interests of their members. Associations owned by their members but organized to perform a specific business function, such as common marketing of crops or joint advertising, are classified according to the function performed.

Better business bureaus
Boards of trade, other than security and commodity exchanges
Business associations, other than civic and social
Chambers of Commerce
Contractor's associations
Growers' associations, not engaged in contract buying or selling
Growers' marketing advisory services
Industrial standards committees
Junior Chambers of Commerce
Manufacturers' institutes
Merchants' associations, not engaged in credit investigations
Public utility associations
Real estate boards
Shipping and steamship company associations
Trade associations

862   **PROFESSIONAL MEMBERSHIP ORGANIZATIONS**

8621 Professional Membership Organizations

Membership organizations of professional persons for the advancement of the interests of their profession.

Bar associations
Dental associations
Engineering associations
Medical associations
Professional membership organizations
Professional standards review boards
Scientific membership associations

863   **LABOR UNIONS AND SIMILAR LABOR ORGANIZATIONS**

8631 Labor Unions and Similar Labor Organizations

Membership organizations of workers for the improvement of wages and working conditions.

Collective bargaining units
Employees' associations for improvement of wages and working conditions
Labor organizations
Labor unions
Trade unions, local or national

864   **CIVIC, SOCIAL, AND FRATERNAL ASSOCIATIONS**

8641 Civic, Social, and Fraternal Associations

Membership organizations engaged in civic, social, or fraternal activities. Membership sports and recreation clubs are classified in Industry Group 799, and insurance offices maintained by fraternal organizations are classified in

864   **CIVIC, SOCIAL, AND FRATERNAL ASSOCIATIONS—Con.**

 8641   **Civic, Social, and Fraternal Associations—Con.**

Insurance, Major Group 63. Homeowner, tenant, and condominium associations primarily engaged in managing real estate are classified in Real Estate, Industry 6531.

Alumni associations and clubs	Fraternal lodges
Bars and restaurants owned and operated for members of organizations only	Fraternities and sororities, except residential
Booster clubs	Homeowner associations, except property management
Businesspersons clubs, civic and social	Parent-teacher associations
Citizens' unions	Singing societies
Civic associations	Social clubs, membership
Community membership clubs, other than amusement and recreation clubs	Taxpayers' associations
	Tenant associations, except property management
Condominium associations, except property management	University clubs
	Veterans' organizations
Fraternal associations, other than insurance offices	Youth associations, except hotel units

865   **POLITICAL ORGANIZATIONS**

 8651   **Political Organizations**

Membership organizations established to promote the interests of a national, State, or local political party or candidate. Also included are political groups organized to raise funds for a political party or individual candidates. Fundraising organizations operating on a contract or fee basis are classified in Industry 7389.

Political Action Committees (PACs)	Political organizations and clubs
Political campaign organizations	
Political fundraising, except on a contract or fee basis	

866   **RELIGIOUS ORGANIZATIONS**

 8661   **Religious Organizations**

Establishments of religious organizations operated for worship, religious training or study, government or administration of an organized religion, or for promotion of religious activities. Other establishments maintained by religious organizations, such as educational institutions, hospitals, publishing houses, reading rooms, social services, and secondhand stores, are classified according to their primary activity. Also included in this industry are religious groups which reach the public through radio or television media. Establishments of such religious groups which produce taped religious programming for television are classified in Industry 7812, and those which produce live religious programs are classified in Industry 7922. Establishments of such groups which operate radio or television stations are classified in Communications, Major Group 48.

Churches	Religious organizations
Convents	Shrines, religious
Monasteries	Temples
Religious instruction, provided by religious organizations	

Industry Group No.	Industry No.	
869		**MEMBERSHIP ORGANIZATIONS, NOT ELSEWHERE CLASSIFIED**
	8699	**Membership Organizations, Not Elsewhere Classified**

Membership organizations, not elsewhere classified.

Art councils
Athletic associations—regulatory only
Automobile owners' associations and clubs
Farm bureaus
Farm granges

Historical clubs, other than professional
Humane societies, animal
Poetry associations
Reading rooms, religious materials

Major Group 87.—ENGINEERING, ACCOUNTING, RESEARCH, MANAGEMENT, AND RELATED SERVICES

The Major Group as a Whole

This major group includes establishments primarily engaged in providing engineering, architectural, and surveying services; accounting, auditing, and bookkeeping services; research, development, and testing services; and management and public relations services.

Industry Group No.	Industry No.	

871   ENGINEERING, ARCHITECTURAL, AND SURVEYING SERVICES

8711 Engineering Services

Establishments primarily engaged in providing professional engineering services. Establishments primarily providing and supervising their own engineering staff on temporary contract to other firms are included in this industry. Establishments providing engineering personnel, but not general supervision, are classified in Industry 7363. Establishments primarily engaged in providing architectural engineering services are classified in Industry 8712, and those providing photogrammetric engineering services are classified in Industry 8713.

Designing: ship, boat, and machine	Machine tool designers
Engineering services: industrial, civil, electrical, mechanical, petroleum, marine, and design	Marine engineering services
	Petroleum engineering services

8712 Architectural Services

Establishments primarily engaged in providing professional architectural services. Establishments primarily engaged in providing landscape architectural services are classified in Agriculture, Industry 0781. Establishments primarily engaged in providing graphic arts and related design services are classified in Industry 7336, and those providing drafting services are classified in Industry 7389.

Architectural engineering services	Engineering services: architectural
Architectural services	House designers

8713 Surveying Services

Establishments primarily engaged in providing professional land, water, and aerial surveying services.

Engineering services: photogrammetric	Surveying: land, water, and aerial
Photogrammetric engineering	

872   ACCOUNTING, AUDITING, AND BOOKKEEPING SERVICES

8721 Accounting, Auditing, and Bookkeeping Services

Establishments primarily engaged in furnishing accounting, bookkeeping, and related auditing services. These establishments may use data processing and tabulating techniques as part of providing their services. However, establishments primarily engaged in providing data processing and tabulating services are classified in Industry 7374. Establishments providing income tax

ACCOUNTING, AUDITING, AND BOOKKEEPING SERVICES—Con.

8721 Accounting, Auditing, and Bookkeeping Services—Con.

return preparation service without also furnishing accounting, auditing, or bookkeeping services are classified in Industry 7291.

Accounting service
Auditing service, accounts
Bookkeeping and billing service

Certified public accountants (CPAs)
Payroll accounting service
Public accountants, certified

873 RESEARCH, DEVELOPMENT, AND TESTING SERVICES

8731 Commercial Physical and Biological Research

Establishments primarily engaged in commercial physical and biological research and development on a contract or fee basis. Noncommercial research establishments funded by endowments, grants, or contributions are classified in Industry 8733. Separate establishments of aircraft, guided missile, or spacecraft manufacturers primarily engaged in research and development on these products are classified in Manufacturing, Major Group 37.

Agricultural research, commercial
Biological research, commercial
Chemical laboratories, commercial research: except testing
Engineering laboratories, commercial research: except testing

Food research, commercial
Industrial laboratories, commercial research: except testing
Physical research, commercial
Research and development, physical and biological: commercial

8732 Commercial Economic, Sociological, and Educational Research

Establishments primarily engaged in performing commercial business, marketing, opinion, and other economic, sociological, and educational research on a contract or fee basis. Noncommercial economic, sociological, and educational research establishments funded from endowments, grants, or contributions are classified in Industry 8733.

Business economists, commercial
Business research, commercial
Economic research, commercial
Educational research, commercial
Market research, commercial

Opinion research, commercial
Research: economic, sociological, and educational—commercial
Sociological research, commercial

8733 Noncommercial Research Organizations

Establishments primarily engaged in performing noncommercial research into and dissemination of, information for public health, education, or general welfare. Establishments included here operate primarily on funds from endowments, contributions, and grants. The research is frequently contracted out and funded by these establishments. Establishments primarily engaged in commercial physical and biological research are classified in Industry 8731, and those engaged in commercial economic, sociological, and educational research are classified in Industry 8732.

Archeological expeditions
Biological research, noncommercial
Economic research, noncommercial
Educational research, noncommercial
Medical research, noncommercial

Physical research, noncommercial
Research, noncommercial
Scientific research, noncommercial
Sociological research, noncommercial

RESEARCH, DEVELOPMENT, AND TESTING SERVICES—Con.

8734 Testing Laboratories

Establishments primarily engaged in providing testing services. Establishments primarily engaged in performing clinical laboratory testing for the medical profession are classified in Industry 8071.

Assaying services	Metallurgical testing laboratories
Automobile proving and testing grounds	Pollution testing, except automotive emissions testing
Calibration and certification (testing)	Product testing services
Dosimetry, radiation	Radiation dosimetry laboratories
Film badge service (radiation detection)	Radiographing welded joints on pipes and fittings
Food testing services	Seed testing laboratories
Forensic laboratories	Testing laboratories, except clinical
Hydrostatic testing laboratories	Veterinary testing laboratories
Laboratories, product testing: not manufacturing auxiliaries	X-ray inspection service, industrial

874   MANAGEMENT AND PUBLIC RELATIONS SERVICES

8741 Management Services

Establishments primarily engaged in furnishing general or specialized management services on a day to day basis and on a contract or fee basis. Establishments in this industry do not provide operating staff. Management and operation of a business, where operating staff as well as management is provided, is classified according to the activity of the establishment managed.

Administrative management services	Construction management
Business management services	Motel management services
Circuit management services for motion picture theaters	Office management services

8742 Management Consulting Services

Establishments primarily engaged in furnishing operating counsel and assistance to managements of private, nonprofit, and public organizations. These establishments generally perform a variety of activities, such as strategic and organizational planning; financial planning and budgeting; marketing objectives and policies; information systems planning, evaluation and selection; human resource policies and practices planning; and production scheduling and control planning. These establishments are characterized by the breadth and scope of the problems they address.

Administrative management consultants	Marketing consultants
General management consultants	Operations research consultants
Human resource consultants	Personnel management consultants, except employment service
Management engineering consultants	Physical distribution consultants
Management information systems consultants	Site location consultants
Manufacturing management consultants	

8743 Public Relations Services

Establishments primarily engaged in the preparation of materials, written or spoken, which are designed to influence the general public or other groups in promoting the interests of their clients.

Lobbyists	Public relations services

874   **MANAGEMENT AND PUBLIC RELATIONS SERVICES—Con.**

8744   **Facilities Support Management Services**

Establishments primarily engaged in furnishing personnel to perform a range of services in support of the operations of other establishments or in providing a number of different continuing services, on a contract or fee basis, within another establishment. Included in the industry are establishments primarily engaged in the private operation of jails and adult correctional facilities, whether or not providing both management and supporting staff. Establishments primarily engaged in operating juvenile correctional homes are classified in Industry 8361. Establishments which provide management and staff to operate a business are classified according to the type of activity of the business. Establishments primarily providing one specialized service, such as janitorial services or guard services, are classified in the specialized industry. Janitorial services are classified in Industry 7349, and guard services are classified in Industry 7381. Establishments primarily engaged in providing management services only, except agricultural, are classified in Industry 8741. Computer facilities management services are classified in Industry 7376. Establishments primarily supplying temporary or continuing help are classified in Industry 7363. Establishments primarily engaged in providing temporary or continuing help for agricultural purposes and agricultural management services are classified in Agriculture, Industry Group 076.

Base maintenance (providing personnel
    on continuing basis)
Correctional facilities, adult: privately
    operated
Facilities management, except comput-
    er

Facilities support services, except com-
    puter
Jails, privately operated

8748   **Business Consulting Services, Not Elsewhere Classified**

Establishments primarily engaged in furnishing business consulting services, not elsewhere classified, on a contract or fee basis.

Agricultural consulting
City planners, except professional engi-
    neering
Economic consulting
Educational consulting, except manage-
    ment
Industrial development planning serv-
    ice, commercial
Radio consultants

Systems engineering consulting, except
    professional engineering or computer
    related
Test development and evaluation serv-
    ice, educational or personnel
Testing services, educational or person-
    nel
Traffic consultants

Major Group 88.—PRIVATE HOUSEHOLDS

The Major Group as a Whole

This major group includes private households which employ workers who serve on or about the premises in occupations usually considered as domestic service. Households classified in this major group may employ individuals such as cooks, laundresses, maids, sitters, butlers, personal secretaries, and managers of personal affairs; and outside workers, such as gardeners, caretakers, and other maintenance workers. The households of farming establishments are classified in Agriculture, Division A; individuals or groups providing amusement and entertainment services are classified in Major Group 79; individuals or groups providing baby sitting services are classified in Industry 7299; and other day care services are classified in Industries 8322 and 8351.

Industry Group No.	Industry No.	

881   **PRIVATE HOUSEHOLDS**

     8811   **Private Households**

Private households which employ workers who serve on or about the premises in occupations usually considered as domestic service.

Babysitting (private households employing babysitters in the home)
Domestic service (private households employing cooks, maids, etc.)
Estates, private
Farm homes, noncommercial
Households, private: employing cooks, maids, chauffeurs, gardeners, etc.
Personal affairs management
Residential farms, noncommercial

Major Group 89.—SERVICES, NOT ELSEWHERE CLASSIFIED

Industry
Group
No.

Industry
No.

899   **SERVICES, NOT ELSEWHERE CLASSIFIED**

8999   **Services, Not Elsewhere Classified**

Establishments primarily providing services, not elsewhere classified, such as authors, lecturers, radio commentators, song writers, weather forecasters, writers, and artists working on their own account. Establishments primarily providing commercial art services are classified in Industry 7336.

Actuaries, consulting
Advertising copy, writers of
Announcers, radio and television service
Art restoration
Artificial nucleation (cloud seeding)
Artists' studios, except commercial and medical
Artists, except commercial and medical
Authors
Chemists, consulting: not connected with business service laboratories
Christian Science lecturers
Cloud seeding
Consultants, nuclear: not connected with business service laboratories
Entomologists, consulting: not with business service laboratories

Geologists, consulting: not connected with business service laboratories
Ghost writing
Greeting cards, hand painting of
Inventors
Lecturers
Music arrangers
Newspaper columnists
Physicists, consulting: not connected with business service laboratories
Psychologists, industrial
Radio commentators
Sculptors' studios
Song writers
Stained glass artists
Weather forecasters
Weather modification (rain makers)
Writers

DIVISION J

Public Administration

The Division as a Whole

This division includes the executive, legislative, judicial, administrative and regulatory activities of Federal, State, local, and international governments. Government-owned and operated business establishments are classified in Major Groups 01-89 according to the activity in which they are engaged. Private establishments primarily engaged in the same activities as government establishments in Public Administration are classified in Major Groups 01-89 according to the activity in which they are engaged.

Major Group 91.—EXECUTIVE, LEGISLATIVE, AND GENERAL GOVERNMENT, EXCEPT FINANCE

The Major Group as a Whole

This major group includes offices of executives, legislative bodies, and general government offices, not elsewhere classified.

Industry Group No.	Industry No.	

911   EXECUTIVE OFFICES

9111   Executive Offices

Offices of chief executives and their advisory and interdepartmental committees and commissions.

Advisory commissions, executive	Governors' offices
City and town managers' offices	Mayors' offices
County supervisors' and executives' offices	President's office

912   LEGISLATIVE BODIES

9121   Legislative Bodies

Legislative bodies and their advisory and interdepartmental committees and commissions.

Advisory commissions, legislative	County commissioners
Boards of supervisors	Legislative assemblies
City and town councils	Study commissions, legislative
Congress	

913   EXECUTIVE AND LEGISLATIVE OFFICES COMBINED

9131   Executive and Legislative Offices Combined

Councils and boards of commissioners or supervisors and such bodies where the chief executive is a member of the legislative body itself.

Legislative and executive office combinations

919   GENERAL GOVERNMENT, NOT ELSEWHERE CLASSIFIED

9199   General Government, Not Elsewhere Classified

Government establishments primarily engaged in providing general support for government, which include personnel, auditing, procurement services, and building management services, and other general government establishments which cannot be classified in other industries. Public finance is classified in Industry 9311.

Civil rights commissions—government	Personnel agencies—government
Civil service commissions—government	Purchasing and supply agencies—government
General accounting offices—government	Supply agencies—government
General services departments—government	

Major Group 92.—JUSTICE, PUBLIC ORDER, AND SAFETY

The Major Group as a Whole

This major group includes government establishments engaged in justice, public order and safety.

Industry Group No.	Industry No.	

921   **COURTS**

    9211 Courts

Civilian courts of law are classified here. Military courts are classified in Industry 9711.

Civilian courts   Courts of law

922   **PUBLIC ORDER AND SAFETY**

    9221 Police Protection

Government establishments primarily engaged in law enforcement, traffic safety, police and other activities related to the enforcement of the law and preservation of order. The National Guard is classified in Industry 9711. Private establishments primarily engaged in law enforcement, traffic safety, police and other activities related to law enforcement are classified in Services, Industry 7381. Government establishments primarily engaged in prosecution are classified in Industry 9222. Military police are classified in Industry 9711. Government establishments primarily engaged in the collection of law enforcement statistics are classified in Industry 9229.

Bureaus of criminal investigations—government
Highway patrols
Marshals' offices, police

Police departments
Sheriffs' offices
State police

    9222 Legal Counsel and Prosecution

Government establishments primarily engaged in providing legal counsel to or prosecution for their governments and operation or administration of crime prevention programs. Government establishments primarily engaged in the collection of criminal justice statistics are classified in Industry 9229.

Attorneys general's offices
District attorneys' offices
Legal counsel offices—government

Public defenders' offices
Public prosecutors' offices
U.S. attorneys' offices

    9223 Correctional Institutions

Government establishments primarily engaged in the confinement and correction of offenders sentenced by a court. Private establishments primarily engaged in the confinement and correction of offenders sentenced by a court are classified in Services, Industry 8744. Half-way houses for ex-convicts and homes for delinquents are classified in Services, Industry 8361.

Correctional institutions—government
Detention centers—government
Honor camps—government
Houses of correction—government
Jails—government

Penitentiaries—government
Prison farms—government
Prisons—government
Reformatories—government

Industry Group No.	Industry No.	
922		**PUBLIC ORDER AND SAFETY—Con.**

9224 Fire Protection

Government establishments primarily engaged in firefighting and other related fire protection activities. Government and private establishments primarily engaged in forest firefighting and fire protection services are classified in Agriculture, Industry 0851. Private establishments primarily engaged in other firefighting services are classified in Services, Industry 7389.

Fire departments, including volunteer—government

Fire marshals' offices—government
Fire prevention offices—government

9229 Public Order and Safety, Not Elsewhere Classified

Government establishments primarily engaged in public order and safety, not elsewhere classified, including general administration of public order and safety programs. Collection of statistics on overall public safety is included here.

Criminal justice statistics centers—government
Disaster preparedness and management offices—government
Emergency management offices—government

Law enforcement statistics centers—government
Public safety bureaus—government
Public safety statistics centers—government

Major Group 93.—PUBLIC FINANCE, TAXATION, AND MONETARY POLICY

The Major Group as a Whole

This major group includes government establishments primarily engaged in public finance, taxation, and monetary policy.

Industry
Group
No.

Industry
No.

931   **PUBLIC FINANCE, TAXATION, AND MONETARY POLICY**

     9311   **Public Finance, Taxation, and Monetary Policy**

Government establishments primarily engaged in financial administration and taxation including monetary policy; tax administration; collection, custody and disbursement of funds; debt and investment administration; government employee retirement and other trust funds; and the like. Income maintenance program administration is classified in Industry 9441. Government establishments primarily engaged in regulation of insurance and banking institutions are classified in Industry 9651.

Budget agencies—government	Property tax assessors' offices
Controllers' offices—government	State tax commissions
Customs Bureaus	Taxation departments
Gambling control boards—government	Treasurers' offices—government
Lottery control boards—government	

Major Group 94.—ADMINISTRATION OF HUMAN RESOURCE PROGRAMS

The Major Group as a Whole

This major group includes government establishments primarily engaged in the administration of human resource programs.

Industry Group No. | Industry No.

941   **ADMINISTRATION OF EDUCATIONAL PROGRAMS**

    9411   **Administration of Educational Programs**

Government establishments primarily engaged in central coordination, planning, supervision and administration of funds, policies, intergovernmental activities, statistical reports and data collection, and centralized programs for educational administration. Government scholarship programs are classified here. Included are Federal and State education departments, commissions and similar educational organizations. Schools and local and State school boards operating schools are classified in Services, Major Group 82. Human resource training is classified in Services, Industry 8331, and administration of such programs in Group 944.

County supervisors of education, except school boards
Education offices, nonoperating
Education statistics centers—government

State education departments
Teacher certification bureaus

943   **ADMINISTRATION OF PUBLIC HEALTH PROGRAMS**

    9431   **Administration of Public Health Programs**

Government establishments primarily engaged in planning, administration, and coordination of public health programs and services, including environmental health activities, mental health, categorical health programs (e.g., cancer control, communicable disease control, maternity, child health), health statistics, and immunization services. Hospitals, including boards of directors, are classified in Services, Industry Group 806. Health services such as immunization, X-ray, and cancer detection clinics are classified in Services, Major Group 80.

Cancer detection program administration—government
Categorical health program administration—government
Communicable disease program administration—government
Environmental health programs—government

Health statistics centers—government
Immunization program administration—government
Maternity and child health program administration—government
Mental health agencies—government
Public health agencies—nonoperating

944   **ADMINISTRATION OF SOCIAL, HUMAN RESOURCE AND INCOME MAINTENANCE PROGRAMS**

    9441   **Administration of Social, Human Resource and Income Maintenance Programs**

Government establishments primarily engaged in planning, administration, and coordination of programs for public assistance, social work, and welfare

Industry Group No.	Industry No.	

944   **ADMINISTRATION OF SOCIAL, HUMAN RESOURCE AND INCOME MAINTENANCE PROGRAMS—Con.**

   9441   **Administration of Social, Human Resource and Income Maintenance Programs—Con.**

activities, such as old age assistance, child welfare, aid to families with dependent children, aid to the blind and disabled, medical assistance, human resource development, and related activities, but the operators of these programs are classified in Services, Major Group 83. Both the administration and operation of Social Security, disability benefits under OASDHI, Medicare, unemployment insurance, workman's compensation, and social insurance programs for the aged, survivors, or disabled persons are classified here, but offices that administer veterans' programs are classified in Industry 9451. Local employment service offices are classified in Services, Industry 7361.

Equal employment opportunity offices—government
Medical assistance program administration—government
Public welfare administration, nonoperating

Unemployment insurance offices—government
Women's bureaus
Workman's compensation offices—government

945   **ADMINISTRATION OF VETERANS' AFFAIRS, EXCEPT HEALTH AND INSURANCE**

   9451   **Administration of Veterans' Affairs, Except Health and Insurance**

Government establishments primarily engaged in administration of programs of assistance, training, counselling, and other services to veterans and their dependents, heirs or survivors. Also included are offices that maintain liaison and coordinate activities with other service organizations and governmental agencies. Veterans' hospitals are classified in Services, Industry Group 806, and veterans' insurance in Insurance, Major Group 63.

Veterans' affairs offices

Major Group 95.—ADMINISTRATION OF ENVIRONMENTAL QUALITY AND HOUSING PROGRAMS

The Major Group as a Whole

This major group includes government establishments primarily engaged in the administration of environmental quality and housing programs.

Industry
Group   Industry
No.   No.

951   **ADMINISTRATION OF ENVIRONMENTAL QUALITY PROGRAMS**

9511   **Air and Water Resource and Solid Waste Management**

Government establishments primarily engaged in regulation, planning, protection and conservation of air and water resources; solid waste management; water and air pollution control and prevention; flood control; drainage development, and consumption of water resources; coordination of these activities at intergovernmental levels; research necessary for air pollution abatement and control and conservation of water resources. Water systems are classified in Transportation and Public Utilities, Industry 4941. Sewage and refuse systems and other sanitary services are classified in Transportation and Public Utilities, Industry Group 495. Irrigation systems are classified in Transportation and Public Utilities, Industry 4971.

Environmental protection agencies—government
Environmental quality and control agencies—government
Pollution control agencies—government
Sanitary engineering agencies—government

Waste management program administration—government
Water control and quality agencies—government

9512   **Land, Mineral, Wildlife, and Forest Conservation**

Government establishments primarily engaged in regulation, supervision and control of land use, including recreational areas; conservation and preservation of natural resources; control of wind and water erosion; and the administration and protection of publicly and privately owned forest lands, including pest control. Planning, management, regulation, and conservation of game, fish, and wildlife populations, including wildlife management areas and field stations; and other matters relating to the protection of fish, game, and wildlife are also classified here. Parks are classified in Services, Industry 7999. Operators of forest property are classified in Forestry, Industry 0811. Operators of game or fish preserves are classified in Major Group 09. Private membership establishments primarily engaged in promoting conservation of wildlife and protection of animals are classified in Services, Division I.

Conservation and stabilization agencies—government
Fish and wildlife conservation—government
Game and inland fish agencies—government
Land management agencies—government

Recreational program administration—government
Soil conservation services—government
Wildlife conservation agencies—government
Wind and water erosion control agencies—government

Industry Group No.	Industry No.	
953		**ADMINISTRATION OF HOUSING AND URBAN DEVELOPMENT PROGRAMS**

9531 Administration of Housing Programs

Government establishments primarily engaged in planning, administration and research for housing programs. Insurance and finance are classified in Finance, Division H. The operation and rental of apartments and houses is classified in Finance, Insurance, and Real Estate, Industry Group 651.

Building standards agencies—government
Housing agencies, nonoperating—government

Housing authorities, nonoperating—government
Planning and development of housing programs—government

9532 Administration of Urban Planning and Community and Rural Development

Government establishments primarily engaged in planning, administration, and research for the development of urban and rural areas, including programs for slum clearance, community redevelopment, urban renewal and land clearance. Also included are zoning boards and commissions. Private establishments primarily engaged in urban planning, rural planning, and community development planning are classified in Services, Major Group 87.

Community development agencies—government
County development agencies—government
Redevelopment land agencies—government

Urban planning commissions—government
Urban renewal agencies—government
Zoning boards and commissions

Major Group 96.—ADMINISTRATION OF ECONOMIC PROGRAMS

The Major Group as a Whole

This major group includes government establishments primarily engaged in the administration of economic programs.

Industry Group No.	Industry No.

961   ADMINISTRATION OF GENERAL ECONOMIC PROGRAMS

9611   Administration of General Economic Programs

Government establishments primarily engaged in promotion and development of economic resources of all kinds, including tourism, business, and industry. Included are establishments responsible for the development of general statistical data and analyses and promotion of the general economic well-being of the Nation.

Consumer protection offices—government
Economic development agencies—government
Energy development and conservation agencies—nonoperating

General economic statistics agencies—government
Trade commissions—government

962   REGULATION AND ADMINISTRATION OF TRANSPORTATION PROGRAMS

9621   Regulation and Administration of Transportation Programs

Government establishments primarily engaged in regulation, licensing, planning, inspection and investigation of transportation services and facilities. Motor vehicle and operator licensing is classified here. Establishments of the Coast Guard that perform functions related to the regulation, administration and operation of transportation are included here. Also included in this industry are civilian government air traffic control and aircraft inspection establishments. Parking authorities are classified here, but the operators of lots and garages are classified in Services, Industry 7521. Operators of railroads, subways, depots, ports, toll roads and bridges, and other transportation facilities are classified in Transportation and Public Utilities, Division E. Highway construction and maintenance are classified in Construction, Industry 1611. Military establishments primarily engaged in air traffic control operations are classified in Industry 9711 and private establishments engaged in air traffic control operations are classified in Transportation and Public Utilities, Industry 4581.

Air traffic control operations—government
Aircraft inspection—government
Licensing and inspection of transportation facilities and services—government
Motor carrier licensing and inspection offices—government
Motor vehicle licensing and inspection offices—government

Port authorities and districts—nonoperating
Railroad and warehouse commissions—nonoperating
Transit systems and authorities—nonoperating
Transportation departments—government
Transportation regulatory agencies—government

963 REGULATION AND ADMINISTRATION OF COMMUNICATIONS, ELECTRIC, GAS, AND OTHER UTILITIES

9631 Regulation and Administration of Communications, Electric, Gas, and Other Utilities

Government establishments primarily engaged in regulation, licensing and inspection of communications, electric (including nuclear), gas, water, sewer, and other utilities. Operators of utilities are classified in Transportation and Public Utilities, Division E. All establishments of the U.S. Postal Service are classified in Transportation and Public Utilities, Industry 4311.

Communications commissions—government	Public service commissions, except transportation
Irrigation districts—nonoperating	Public utility commissions
Licensing and inspection of utilities	Regulation of utilities
Mosquito eradication districts	Sanitary districts—nonoperating
Nuclear energy inspection and regulation offices	

964 REGULATION OF AGRICULTURAL MARKETING AND COMMODITIES

9641 Regulation of Agricultural Marketing and Commodities

Government establishments primarily engaged in planning, administration, and coordination of agricultural programs for production, marketing, and utilization, including related research, educational, and promotional activities. Establishments responsible for regulating and controlling the grading, inspection, and warehousing of agricultural products; the grading and inspection of foods; and the handling of plants and animals are classified here. Government establishments primarily engaged in administration of programs for developing economic data about agriculture and trade in agricultural products are classified in Industry 9611. Government establishments primarily engaged in programs for conservation of agricultural resources are classified in Industry 9512. Government establishments primarily engaged in programs to provide food to people are classified in Industry 9441.

Agriculture extension services	Regulation and inspection of agricultural products—government
Agriculture fair boards—government	
Food inspection agencies—government	
Marketing and consumer services—government	

965 REGULATION, LICENSING, AND INSPECTION OF MISCELLANEOUS COMMERCIAL SECTORS

9651 Regulation, Licensing, and Inspection of Miscellaneous Commercial Sectors

Government establishments primarily engaged in regulation, licensing, and inspection of other commercial sectors, such as retail trade, professional occupations, manufacturing, mining, construction and services. Maintenance of physical standards, regulating hazardous conditions not elsewhere classified, and alcoholic beverage control are classified here. Private establishments primarily engaged in regulation, licensing, and establishment of standards are classified in Services, Division I.

Alcoholic beverage control boards—government	Insurance commissions—government
Banking regulatory agencies—government	Labor-management negotiations boards—government
Bureaus of standards—government	Licensing and permit for professional occupations—government
Inspection for labor standards—government	Licensing and permit for retail trade—government

Industry Group No.	Industry No.
965		**REGULATION, LICENSING, AND INSPECTION OF MISCELLANEOUS COMMERCIAL SECTORS—Con.**

9651 Regulation, Licensing, and Inspection of Miscellaneous Commercial Sectors—Con.

Minimum wage program administration—government
Price control agencies—government

Rent control agencies—government
Securities regulation commissions
Wage control agencies—government

966   SPACE RESEARCH AND TECHNOLOGY

9661 Space Research and Technology

Government establishments primarily engaged in programs for manned and unmanned space flights, space exploration, and the like. Research and development laboratories operated by the National Aeronautics and Space Administration are classified as auxiliaries to this industry. Private establishments primarily engaged in operation of space flights on their own account are classified in Transportation and Public Utilities, Industry 4789.

Space flight operations—government
Space research and development—government

Major Group 97.—NATIONAL SECURITY AND INTERNATIONAL AFFAIRS

The Major Group as a Whole

This major group includes government establishments primarily engaged in national security and international affairs.

Industry Group No.	Industry No.	

971   **NATIONAL SECURITY**

      9711   **National Security**

Establishments of the armed forces, including the National Guard, primarily engaged in national security and related activities. Establishments primarily engaged in manufacturing ordnance, ships and other military goods are classified in Manufacturing, Division D. Service academies are classified in Services, Industry 8221, but military training schools are classified here. Military hospitals are classified in Services, Industry Group 806. Establishments of the Coast Guard primarily engaged in the administration, operation, or regulation of transportation are classified in Industry 9621.

Air Force	Military training schools
Army	National Guard
Marine Corps	Navy

972   **INTERNATIONAL AFFAIRS**

      9721   **International Affairs**

Establishments of U.S. and foreign governments primarily engaged in international affairs and programs relating to other nations and peoples. Trade commissions and councils operated by private establishments are classified in Services, Division I and government operated trade commissions and councils are classified in Major Group 96.

Consulates	Foreign missions
Diplomatic services—government	Immigration services—government
Embassies	United Nations

DIVISION K
Nonclassifiable Establishments

Major Group 99.—NONCLASSIFIABLE ESTABLISHMENTS

The Major Group as a Whole

This major group includes establishments which cannot be classified in any other industry. Establishments which can be classified in a division should be classified in the most appropriate industry within that division.

Industry
Group
No.

Industry
No.

999   **NONCLASSIFIABLE ESTABLISHMENTS**

     9999   **Nonclassifiable Establishments**

Part II

Numerical List of Short Titles

Numerical List of Short Titles

The official SIC titles of the divisions and the two-digit major groups, three-digit industry groups, and four-digit industries are those shown in Part I. For various reasons, including presentation of statistical tables, it is desirable to have a standard list of short SIC titles so that all agencies may use the same short titles for the same codes as long as the titles fit the space requirements of the publication.

The standard short titles below have been limited to 36 spaces for four-digit industry codes and 38 spaces for two-digit major group and three-digit industry group codes. Where a two-digit major group or three-digit industry group contains only a single four-digit industry, the two-digit or three-digit titles are allowed 36 rather than 38 spaces. If the official SIC title falls within the short title space limitation above, it is generally used without change.

It is understood, of course, that just as a title itself is not sufficient to define an industry, so too a short title may not appear to represent the same content as the official title. Content can only be defined by reference to the official titles and descriptions for the relevant division, major group, industry group, and industry.

A. AGRICULTURE, FORESTRY, AND FISHING

Code	Short Title
01	**AGRICULTURAL PRODUCTION—CROPS**
011	**Cash Grains**
0111	Wheat
0112	Rice
0115	Corn
0116	Soybeans
0119	Cash grains, nec
013	**Field Crops, Except Cash Grains**
0131	Cotton
0132	Tobacco
0133	Sugarcane and sugar beets
0134	Irish potatoes
0139	Field crops, except cash grains, nec
016	**Vegetables and Melons**
0161	Vegetables and melons
017	**Fruits and Tree Nuts**
0171	Berry crops
0172	Grapes
0173	Tree nuts
0174	Citrus fruits
0175	Deciduous tree fruits
0179	Fruits and tree nuts, nec
018	**Horticultural Specialties**
0181	Ornamental nursery products
0182	Food crops grown under cover
019	**General Farms, Primarily Crop**
0191	General farms, primarily crop
02	**AGRICULTURAL PRODUCTION—LIVESTOCK**
021	**Livestock, Except Dairy and Poultry**
0211	Beef cattle feedlots
0212	Beef cattle, except feedlots
0213	Hogs
0214	Sheep and goats
0219	General livestock, nec
024	**Dairy Farms**
0241	Dairy farms
025	**Poultry and Eggs**
0251	Broiler, fryer, and roaster chickens
0252	Chicken eggs
0253	Turkeys and turkey eggs
0254	Poultry hatcheries
0259	Poultry and eggs, nec
027	**Animal Specialties**
0271	Fur-bearing animals and rabbits
0272	Horses and other equines
0273	Animal aquaculture
0279	Animal specialties, nec

Code	Short Title
029	**General Farms, Primarily Animal**
0291	General farms, primarily animal
07	**AGRICULTURAL SERVICES**
071	**Soil Preparation Services**
0711	Soil preparation services
072	**Crop Services**
0721	Crop planting and protecting
0722	Crop harvesting
0723	Crop preparation services for market
0724	Cotton ginning
074	**Veterinary Services**
0741	Veterinary services for livestock
0742	Veterinary services, specialties
075	**Animal Services, Except Veterinary**
0751	Livestock services, exc. veterinary
0752	Animal specialty services
076	**Farm Labor and Management Services**
0761	Farm labor contractors
0762	Farm management services
078	**Landscape and Horticultural Services**
0781	Landscape counseling and planning
0782	Lawn and garden services
0783	Ornamental shrub and tree services
08	**FORESTRY**
081	**Timber Tracts**
0811	Timber tracts
083	**Forest Products**
0831	Forest products
085	**Forestry Services**
0851	Forestry services
09	**FISHING, HUNTING, AND TRAPPING**
091	**Commercial Fishing**
0912	Finfish
0913	Shellfish
0919	Miscellaneous marine products
092	**Fish Hatcheries and Preserves**
0921	Fish hatcheries and preserves
097	**Hunting, Trapping, Game Propagation**
0971	Hunting, trapping, game propagation

B. MINING

Code	Short Title	Code	Short Title
10	**METAL MINING**	1311	Crude petroleum and natural gas
101	**Iron Ores**	**132**	**Natural Gas Liquids**
1011	Iron ores	1321	Natural gas liquids
102	**Copper Ores**	**138**	**Oil and Gas Field Services**
1021	Copper ores	1381	Drilling oil and gas wells
103	**Lead and Zinc Ores**	1382	Oil and gas exploration services
1031	Lead and zinc ores	1389	Oil and gas field services, nec
104	**Gold and Silver Ores**		
1041	Gold ores	**14**	**NONMETALLIC MINERALS, EXCEPT**
1044	Silver ores		**FUELS**
106	**Ferroalloy Ores, Except Vanadium**	**141**	**Dimension Stone**
1061	Ferroalloy ores, except vanadium	1411	Dimension stone
108	**Metal Mining Services**	**142**	**Crushed and Broken Stone**
1081	Metal mining services	1422	Crushed and broken limestone
109	**Miscellaneous Metal Ores**	1423	Crushed and broken granite
1094	Uranium-radium-vanadium ores	1429	Crushed and broken stone, nec
1099	Metal ores, nec	**144**	**Sand and Gravel**
		1442	Construction sand and gravel
12	**COAL MINING**	1446	Industrial sand
122	**Bituminous Coal and Lignite Mining**	**145**	**Clay, Ceramic, & Refractory Minerals**
1221	Bituminous coal and lignite—surface	1455	Kaolin and ball clay
1222	Bituminous coal—underground	1459	Clay and related minerals, nec
123	**Anthracite Mining**	**147**	**Chemical and Fertilizer Minerals**
1231	Anthracite mining	1474	Potash, soda, and borate minerals
124	**Coal Mining Services**	1475	Phosphate rock
1241	Coal mining services	1479	Chemical and fertilizer mining, nec
		148	**Nonmetallic Minerals Services**
13	**OIL AND GAS EXTRACTION**	1481	Nonmetallic minerals services
131	**Crude Petroleum and Natural Gas**	**149**	**Miscellaneous Nonmetallic Minerals**
		1499	Miscellaneous nonmetallic minerals

C. CONSTRUCTION

Code	Short Title	Code	Short Title
15	**GENERAL BUILDING CONTRACTORS**	1611	Highway and street construction
152	**Residential Building Construction**	**162**	**Heavy Construction, Except Highway**
1521	Single-family housing construction	1622	Bridge, tunnel, & elevated highway
1522	Residential construction, nec	1623	Water, sewer, and utility lines
153	**Operative Builders**	1629	Heavy construction, nec
1531	Operative builders		
154	**Nonresidential Building Construction**	**17**	**SPECIAL TRADE CONTRACTORS**
1541	Industrial buildings and warehouses	**171**	**Plumbing, Heating, Air-Conditioning**
1542	Nonresidential construction, nec	1711	Plumbing, heating, air-conditioning
		172	**Painting and Paper Hanging**
16	**HEAVY CONSTRUCTION, EX.**	1721	Painting and paper hanging
	BUILDING	**173**	**Electrical Work**
161	**Highway and Street Construction**	1731	Electrical work

Code	Short Title	Code	Short Title
174	**Masonry, Stonework, and Plastering**	177	**Concrete Work**
1741	Masonry and other stonework	1771	Concrete work
1742	Plastering, drywall, and insulation	178	**Water Well Drilling**
1743	Terrazzo, tile, marble, mosaic work	1781	Water well drilling
175	**Carpentry and Floor Work**	179	**Misc. Special Trade Contractors**
1751	Carpentry work	1791	Structural steel erection
1752	Floor laying and floor work, nec	1793	Glass and glazing work
176	**Roofing, Siding, and Sheet Metal Work**	1794	Excavation work
1761	Roofing, siding, and sheet metal work	1795	Wrecking and demolition work
		1796	Installing building equipment, nec
		1799	Special trade contractors, nec

D. MANUFACTURING

Code	Short Title	Code	Short Title
20	**FOOD AND KINDRED PRODUCTS**	2067	Chewing gum
201	**Meat Products**	2068	Salted and roasted nuts and seeds
2011	Meat packing plants	207	**Fats and Oils**
2013	Sausages and other prepared meats	2074	Cottonseed oil mills
2015	Poultry slaughtering and processing	2075	Soybean oil mills
202	**Dairy Products**	2076	Vegetable oil mills, nec
2021	Creamery butter	2077	Animal and marine fats and oils
2022	Cheese, natural and processed	2079	Edible fats and oils, nec
2023	Dry, condensed, evaporated products	208	**Beverages**
2024	Ice cream and frozen desserts	2082	Malt beverages
2026	Fluid milk	2083	Malt
203	**Preserved Fruits and Vegetables**	2084	Wines, brandy, and brandy spirits
2032	Canned specialties	2085	Distilled and blended liquors
2033	Canned fruits and vegetables	2086	Bottled and canned soft drinks
2034	Dehydrated fruits, vegetables, soups	2087	Flavoring extracts and syrups, nec
2035	Pickles, sauces, and salad dressings	209	**Misc. Food and Kindred Products**
2037	Frozen fruits and vegetables	2091	Canned and cured fish and seafoods
2038	Frozen specialties, nec	2092	Fresh or frozen prepared fish
204	**Grain Mill Products**	2095	Roasted coffee
2041	Flour and other grain mill products	2096	Potato chips and similar snacks
2043	Cereal breakfast foods	2097	Manufactured ice
2044	Rice milling	2098	Macaroni and spaghetti
2045	Prepared flour mixes and doughs	2099	Food preparations, nec
2046	Wet corn milling		
2047	Dog and cat food	21	**TOBACCO PRODUCTS**
2048	Prepared feeds, nec	211	**Cigarettes**
205	**Bakery Products**	2111	Cigarettes
2051	Bread, cake, and related products	212	**Cigars**
2052	Cookies and crackers	2121	Cigars
2053	Frozen bakery products, except bread	213	**Chewing and Smoking Tobacco**
206	**Sugar and Confectionery Products**	2131	Chewing and smoking tobacco
2061	Raw cane sugar	214	**Tobacco Stemming and Redrying**
2062	Cane sugar refining	2141	Tobacco stemming and redrying
2063	Beet sugar		
2064	Candy & other confectionery products	22	**TEXTILE MILL PRODUCTS**
2066	Chocolate and cocoa products	221	**Broadwoven Fabric Mills, Cotton**

Code	Short Title
2211	Broadwoven fabric mills, cotton
222	**Broadwoven Fabric Mills, Manmade**
2221	Broadwoven fabric mills, manmade
223	**Broadwoven Fabric Mills, Wool**
2231	Broadwoven fabric mills, wool
224	**Narrow Fabric Mills**
2241	Narrow fabric mills
225	**Knitting Mills**
2251	Women's hosiery, except socks
2252	Hosiery, nec
2253	Knit outerwear mills
2254	Knit underwear mills
2257	Weft knit fabric mills
2258	Lace & warp knit fabric mills
2259	Knitting mills, nec
226	**Textile Finishing, Except Wool**
2261	Finishing plants, cotton
2262	Finishing plants, manmade
2269	Finishing plants, nec
227	**Carpets and Rugs**
2273	Carpets and rugs
228	**Yarn and Thread Mills**
2281	Yarn spinning mills
2282	Throwing and winding mills
2284	Thread mills
229	**Miscellaneous Textile Goods**
2295	Coated fabrics, not rubberized
2296	Tire cord and fabrics
2297	Nonwoven fabrics
2298	Cordage and twine
2299	Textile goods, nec

23   APPAREL AND OTHER TEXTILE PRODUCTS

Code	Short Title
231	**Men's and Boys' Suits and Coats**
2311	Men's and boys' suits and coats
232	**Men's and Boys' Furnishings**
2321	Men's and boys' shirts
2322	Men's & boys' underwear & nightwear
2323	Men's and boys' neckwear
2325	Men's and boys' trousers and slacks
2326	Men's and boys' work clothing
2329	Men's and boys' clothing, nec
233	**Women's and Misses' Outerwear**
2331	Women's & misses' blouses & shirts
2335	Women's, juniors', & misses' dresses
2337	Women's and misses' suits and coats
2339	Women's and misses' outerwear, nec
234	**Women's and Children's Undergarments**
2341	Women's and children's underwear
2342	Bras, girdles, and allied garments
235	**Hats, Caps, and Millinery**
2353	Hats, caps, and millinery

Code	Short Title
236	**Girls' and Children's Outerwear**
2361	Girls' & children's dresses, blouses
2369	Girls' and children's outerwear, nec
237	**Fur Goods**
2371	Fur goods
238	**Miscellaneous Apparel and Accessories**
2381	Fabric dress and work gloves
2384	Robes and dressing gowns
2385	Waterproof outerwear
2386	Leather and sheep-lined clothing
2387	Apparel belts
2389	Apparel and accessories, nec
239	**Misc. Fabricated Textile Products**
2391	Curtains and draperies
2392	Housefurnishings, nec
2393	Textile bags
2394	Canvas and related products
2395	Pleating and stitching
2396	Automotive and apparel trimmings
2397	Schiffli machine embroideries
2399	Fabricated textile products, nec

24   LUMBER AND WOOD PRODUCTS

Code	Short Title
241	**Logging**
2411	Logging
242	**Sawmills and Planing Mills**
2421	Sawmills and planing mills, general
2426	Hardwood dimension & flooring mills
2429	Special product sawmills, nec
243	**Millwork, Plywood & Structural Members**
2431	Millwork
2434	Wood kitchen cabinets
2435	Hardwood veneer and plywood
2436	Softwood veneer and plywood
2439	Structural wood members, nec
244	**Wood Containers**
2441	Nailed wood boxes and shook
2448	Wood pallets and skids
2449	Wood containers, nec
245	**Wood Buildings and Mobile Homes**
2451	Mobile homes
2452	Prefabricated wood buildings
249	**Miscellaneous Wood Products**
2491	Wood preserving
2493	Reconstituted wood products
2499	Wood products, nec

25   FURNITURE AND FIXTURES

Code	Short Title
251	**Household Furniture**
2511	Wood household furniture
2512	Upholstered household furniture
2514	Metal household furniture

Code	Short Title
2515	Mattresses and bedsprings
2517	Wood TV and radio cabinets
2519	Household furniture, nec
252	**Office Furniture**
2521	Wood office furniture
2522	Office furniture, except wood
253	**Public Building & Related Furniture**
2531	Public building & related furniture
254	**Partitions and Fixtures**
2541	Wood partitions and fixtures
2542	Partitions and fixtures, except wood
259	**Miscellaneous Furniture and Fixtures**
2591	Drapery hardware & blinds & shades
2599	Furniture and fixtures, nec

Code	Short Title
26	**PAPER AND ALLIED PRODUCTS**
261	**Pulp Mills**
2611	Pulp mills
262	**Paper Mills**
2621	Paper mills
263	**Paperboard Mills**
2631	Paperboard mills
265	**Paperboard Containers and Boxes**
2652	Setup paperboard boxes
2653	Corrugated and solid fiber boxes
2655	Fiber cans, drums & similar products
2656	Sanitary food containers
2657	Folding paperboard boxes
267	**Misc. Converted Paper Products**
2671	Paper coated & laminated, packaging
2672	Paper coated and laminated, nec
2673	Bags: plastics, laminated, & coated
2674	Bags: uncoated paper & multiwall
2675	Die-cut paper and board
2676	Sanitary paper products
2677	Envelopes
2678	Stationery products
2679	Converted paper products, nec

Code	Short Title
27	**PRINTING AND PUBLISHING**
271	**Newspapers**
2711	Newspapers
272	**Periodicals**
2721	Periodicals
273	**Books**
2731	Book publishing
2732	Book printing
274	**Miscellaneous Publishing**
2741	Miscellaneous publishing
275	**Commercial Printing**
2752	Commercial printing, lithographic
2754	Commercial printing, gravure

Code	Short Title
2759	Commercial printing, nec
276	**Manifold Business Forms**
2761	Manifold business forms
277	**Greeting Cards**
2771	Greeting cards
278	**Blankbooks and Bookbinding**
2782	Blankbooks and looseleaf binders
2789	Bookbinding and related work
279	**Printing Trade Services**
2791	Typesetting
2796	Platemaking services

Code	Short Title
28	**CHEMICALS AND ALLIED PRODUCTS**
281	**Industrial Inorganic Chemicals**
2812	Alkalies and chlorine
2813	Industrial gases
2816	Inorganic pigments
2819	Industrial inorganic chemicals, nec
282	**Plastics Materials and Synthetics**
2821	Plastics materials and resins
2822	Synthetic rubber
2823	Cellulosic manmade fibers
2824	Organic fibers, noncellulosic
283	**Drugs**
2833	Medicinals and botanicals
2834	Pharmaceutical preparations
2835	Diagnostic substances
2836	Biological products exc. diagnostic
284	**Soap, Cleaners, and Toilet Goods**
2841	Soap and other detergents
2842	Polishes and sanitation goods
2843	Surface active agents
2844	Toilet preparations
285	**Paints and Allied Products**
2851	Paints and allied products
286	**Industrial Organic Chemicals**
2861	Gum and wood chemicals
2865	Cyclic crudes and intermediates
2869	Industrial organic chemicals, nec
287	**Agricultural Chemicals**
2873	Nitrogenous fertilizers
2874	Phosphatic fertilizers
2875	Fertilizers, mixing only
2879	Agricultural chemicals, nec
289	**Miscellaneous Chemical Products**
2891	Adhesives and sealants
2892	Explosives
2893	Printing ink
2895	Carbon black
2899	Chemical preparations, nec

Code	Short Title	Code	Short Title
29	**PETROLEUM AND COAL PRODUCTS**	**32**	**STONE, CLAY, AND GLASS PRODUCTS**
291	**Petroleum Refining**	**321**	**Flat Glass**
2911	Petroleum refining	3211	Flat glass
295	**Asphalt Paving and Roofing Materials**	**322**	**Glass and Glassware, Pressed or Blown**
2951	Asphalt paving mixtures and blocks	3221	Glass containers
2952	Asphalt felts and coatings	3229	Pressed and blown glass, nec
299	**Misc. Petroleum and Coal Products**	**323**	**Products of Purchased Glass**
2992	Lubricating oils and greases	3231	Products of purchased glass
2999	Petroleum and coal products, nec	**324**	**Cement, Hydraulic**
		3241	Cement, hydraulic
30	**RUBBER AND MISC. PLASTICS PRODUCTS**	**325**	**Structural Clay Products**
		3251	Brick and structural clay tile
301	**Tires and Inner Tubes**	3253	Ceramic wall and floor tile
3011	Tires and inner tubes	3255	Clay refractories
302	**Rubber and Plastics Footwear**	3259	Structural clay products, nec
3021	Rubber and plastics footwear	**326**	**Pottery and Related Products**
305	**Hose & Belting & Gaskets & Packing**	3261	Vitreous plumbing fixtures
3052	Rubber & plastics hose & belting	3262	Vitreous china table & kitchenware
3053	Gaskets, packing and sealing devices	3263	Semivitreous table & kitchenware
306	**Fabricated Rubber Products, NEC**	3264	Porcelain electrical supplies
3061	Mechanical rubber goods	3269	Pottery products, nec
3069	Fabricated rubber products, nec	**327**	**Concrete, Gypsum, and Plaster Products**
308	**Miscellaneous Plastics Products, NEC**	3271	Concrete block and brick
3081	Unsupported plastics film & sheet	3272	Concrete products, nec
3082	Unsupported plastics profile shapes	3273	Ready-mixed concrete
3083	Laminated plastics plate & sheet	3274	Lime
3084	Plastics pipe	3275	Gypsum products
3085	Plastics bottles	**328**	**Cut Stone and Stone Products**
3086	Plastics foam products	3281	Cut stone and stone products
3087	Custom compound purchased resins	**329**	**Misc. Nonmetallic Mineral Products**
3088	Plastics plumbing fixtures	3291	Abrasive products
3089	Plastics products, nec	3292	Asbestos products
		3295	Minerals, ground or treated
		3296	Mineral wool
31	**LEATHER AND LEATHER PRODUCTS**	3297	Nonclay refractories
		3299	Nonmetallic mineral products, nec
311	**Leather Tanning and Finishing**		
3111	Leather tanning and finishing		
313	**Footwear Cut Stock**	**33**	**PRIMARY METAL INDUSTRIES**
3131	Footwear cut stock	**331**	**Blast Furnace and Basic Steel Products**
314	**Footwear, Except Rubber**	3312	Blast furnaces and steel mills
3142	House slippers	3313	Electrometallurgical products
3143	Men's footwear, except athletic	3315	Steel wire and related products
3144	Women's footwear, except athletic	3316	Cold finishing of steel shapes
3149	Footwear, except rubber, nec	3317	Steel pipe and tubes
315	**Leather Gloves and Mittens**	**332**	**Iron and Steel Foundries**
3151	Leather gloves and mittens	3321	Gray and ductile iron foundries
316	**Luggage**	3322	Malleable iron foundries
3161	Luggage	3324	Steel investment foundries
317	**Handbags and Personal Leather Goods**	3325	Steel foundries, nec
3171	Women's handbags and purses	**333**	**Primary Nonferrous Metals**
3172	Personal leather goods, nec	3331	Primary copper
319	**Leather Goods, NEC**	3334	Primary aluminum
3199	Leather goods, nec		

Code	Short Title	Code	Short Title
3339	Primary nonferrous metals, nec	348	**Ordnance and Accessories, NEC**
334	**Secondary Nonferrous Metals**	3482	Small arms ammunition
3341	Secondary nonferrous metals	3483	Ammunition, exc. for small arms, nec
335	**Nonferrous Rolling and Drawing**	3484	Small arms
3351	Copper rolling and drawing	3489	Ordnance and accessories, nec
3353	Aluminum sheet, plate, and foil	349	**Misc. Fabricated Metal Products**
3354	Aluminum extruded products	3491	Industrial valves
3355	Aluminum rolling and drawing, nec	3492	Fluid power valves & hose fittings
3356	Nonferrous rolling and drawing, nec	3493	Steel springs, except wire
3357	Nonferrous wiredrawing & insulating	3494	Valves and pipe fittings, nec
336	**Nonferrous Foundries (Castings)**	3495	Wire springs
3363	Aluminum die-castings	3496	Misc. fabricated wire products
3364	Nonferrous die-casting exc. aluminum	3497	Metal foil and leaf
3365	Aluminum foundries	3498	Fabricated pipe and fittings
3366	Copper foundries	3499	Fabricated metal products, nec
3369	Nonferrous foundries, nec		
339	**Miscellaneous Primary Metal Products**	35	**INDUSTRIAL MACHINERY AND EQUIPMENT**
3398	Metal heat treating		
3399	Primary metal products, nec	351	**Engines and Turbines**
		3511	Turbines and turbine generator sets
34	**FABRICATED METAL PRODUCTS**	3519	Internal combustion engines, nec
341	**Metal Cans and Shipping Containers**	352	**Farm and Garden Machinery**
3411	Metal cans	3523	Farm machinery and equipment
3412	Metal barrels, drums, and pails	3524	Lawn and garden equipment
342	**Cutlery, Handtools, and Hardware**	353	**Construction and Related Machinery**
3421	Cutlery	3531	Construction machinery
3423	Hand and edge tools, nec	3532	Mining machinery
3425	Saw blades and handsaws	3533	Oil and gas field machinery
3429	Hardware, nec	3534	Elevators and moving stairways
343	**Plumbing and Heating, Except Electric**	3535	Conveyors and conveying equipment
3431	Metal sanitary ware	3536	Hoists, cranes, and monorails
3432	Plumbing fixture fittings and trim	3537	Industrial trucks and tractors
3433	Heating equipment, except electric	354	**Metalworking Machinery**
344	**Fabricated Structural Metal Products**	3541	Machine tools, metal cutting types
3441	Fabricated structural metal	3542	Machine tools, metal forming types
3442	Metal doors, sash, and trim	3543	Industrial patterns
3443	Fabricated plate work (boiler shops)	3544	Special dies, tools, jigs & fixtures
3444	Sheet metal work	3545	Machine tool accessories
3446	Architectural metal work	3546	Power-driven handtools
3448	Prefabricated metal buildings	3547	Rolling mill machinery
3449	Miscellaneous metal work	3548	Welding apparatus
345	**Screw Machine Products, Bolts, Etc.**	3549	Metalworking machinery, nec
3451	Screw machine products	355	**Special Industry Machinery**
3452	Bolts, nuts, rivets, and washers	3552	Textile machinery
346	**Metal Forgings and Stampings**	3553	Woodworking machinery
3462	Iron and steel forgings	3554	Paper industries machinery
3463	Nonferrous forgings	3555	Printing trades machinery
3465	Automotive stampings	3556	Food products machinery
3466	Crowns and closures	3559	Special industry machinery, nec
3469	Metal stampings, nec	356	**General Industrial Machinery**
347	**Metal Services, NEC**	3561	Pumps and pumping equipment
3471	Plating and polishing	3562	Ball and roller bearings
3479	Metal coating and allied services	3563	Air and gas compressors

Code	Short Title	Code	Short Title
3564	Blowers and fans	3652	Prerecorded records and tapes
3565	Packaging machinery	**366**	**Communications Equipment**
3566	Speed changers, drives, and gears	3661	Telephone and telegraph apparatus
3567	Industrial furnaces and ovens	3663	Radio & TV communications equipment
3568	Power transmission equipment, nec	3669	Communications equipment, nec
3569	General industrial machinery, nec	**367**	**Electronic Components and Accessories**
357	**Computer and Office Equipment**	3671	Electron tubes
3571	Electronic computers	3672	Printed circuit boards
3572	Computer storage devices	3674	Semiconductors and related devices
3575	Computer terminals	3675	Electronic capacitors
3577	Computer peripheral equipment, nec	3676	Electronic resistors
3578	Calculating and accounting equipment	3677	Electronic coils and transformers
3579	Office machines, nec	3678	Electronic connectors
358	**Refrigeration and Service Machinery**	3679	Electronic components, nec
3581	Automatic vending machines	**369**	**Misc. Electrical Equipment & Supplies**
3582	Commercial laundry equipment	3691	Storage batteries
3585	Refrigeration and heating equipment	3692	Primary batteries, dry and wet
3586	Measuring and dispensing pumps	3694	Engine electrical equipment
3589	Service industry machinery, nec	3695	Magnetic and optical recording media
359	**Industrial Machinery, NEC**	3699	Electrical equipment & supplies, nec
3592	Carburetors, pistons, rings, valves		
3593	Fluid power cylinders & actuators	**37**	**TRANSPORTATION EQUIPMENT**
3594	Fluid power pumps and motors	**371**	**Motor Vehicles and Equipment**
3596	Scales and balances, exc. laboratory	3711	Motor vehicles and car bodies
3599	Industrial machinery, nec	3713	Truck and bus bodies
		3714	Motor vehicle parts and accessories
36	**ELECTRONIC & OTHER ELECTRIC EQUIPMENT**	3715	Truck trailers
		3716	Motor homes
361	**Electric Distribution Equipment**	**372**	**Aircraft and Parts**
3612	Transformers, except electronic	3721	Aircraft
3613	Switchgear and switchboard apparatus	3724	Aircraft engines and engine parts
362	**Electrical Industrial Apparatus**	3728	Aircraft parts and equipment, nec
3621	Motors and generators	**373**	**Ship and Boat Building and Repairing**
3624	Carbon and graphite products	3731	Ship building and repairing
3625	Relays and industrial controls	3732	Boat building and repairing
3629	Electrical industrial apparatus, nec	**374**	**Railroad Equipment**
363	**Household Appliances**	3743	Railroad equipment
3631	Household cooking equipment	**375**	**Motorcycles, Bicycles, and Parts**
3632	Household refrigerators and freezers	3751	Motorcycles, bicycles, and parts
3633	Household laundry equipment	**376**	**Guided Missiles, Space Vehicles, Parts**
3634	Electric housewares and fans	3761	Guided missiles and space vehicles
3635	Household vacuum cleaners	3764	Space propulsion units and parts
3639	Household appliances, nec	3769	Space vehicle equipment, nec
364	**Electric Lighting and Wiring Equipment**	**379**	**Miscellaneous Transportation Equipment**
3641	Electric lamps	3792	Travel trailers and campers
3643	Current-carrying wiring devices	3795	Tanks and tank components
3644	Noncurrent-carrying wiring devices	3799	Transportation equipment, nec
3645	Residential lighting fixtures		
3646	Commercial lighting fixtures	**38**	**INSTRUMENTS AND RELATED PRODUCTS**
3647	Vehicular lighting equipment		
3648	Lighting equipment, nec	**381**	**Search and Navigation Equipment**
365	**Household Audio and Video Equipment**	3812	Search and navigation equipment
3651	Household audio and video equipment		

Code	Short Title
382	**Measuring and Controlling Devices**
3821	Laboratory apparatus and furniture
3822	Environmental controls
3823	Process control instruments
3824	Fluid meters and counting devices
3825	Instruments to measure electricity
3826	Analytical instruments
3827	Optical instruments and lenses
3829	Measuring & controlling devices, nec
384	**Medical Instruments and Supplies**
3841	Surgical and medical instruments
3842	Surgical appliances and supplies
3843	Dental equipment and supplies
3844	X-ray apparatus and tubes
3845	Electromedical equipment
385	**Ophthalmic Goods**
3851	Ophthalmic goods
386	**Photographic Equipment and Supplies**
3861	Photographic equipment and supplies
387	**Watches, Clocks, Watchcases & Parts**
3873	Watches, clocks, watchcases & parts

Code	Short Title
39	**MISCELLANEOUS MANUFACTURING INDUSTRIES**
391	**Jewelry, Silverware, and Plated Ware**
3911	Jewelry, precious metal
3914	Silverware and plated ware
3915	Jewelers' materials & lapidary work
393	**Musical Instruments**
3931	Musical instruments
394	**Toys and Sporting Goods**
3942	Dolls and stuffed toys
3944	Games, toys, and children's vehicles
3949	Sporting and athletic goods, nec
395	**Pens, Pencils, Office, & Art Supplies**
3951	Pens and mechanical pencils
3952	Lead pencils and art goods
3953	Marking devices
3955	Carbon paper and inked ribbons
396	**Costume Jewelry and Notions**
3961	Costume jewelry
3965	Fasteners, buttons, needles, & pins
399	**Miscellaneous Manufactures**
3991	Brooms and brushes
3993	Signs and advertising specialities
3995	Burial caskets
3996	Hard surface floor coverings, nec
3999	Manufacturing industries, nec

E. TRANSPORTATION AND PUBLIC UTILITIES

Code	Short Title
40	**RAILROAD TRANSPORTATION**
401	**Railroads**
4011	Railroads, line-haul operating
4013	Switching and terminal services
41	**LOCAL AND INTERURBAN PASSENGER TRANSIT**
411	**Local and Suburban Transportation**
4111	Local and suburban transit
4119	Local passenger transportation, nec
412	**Taxicabs**
4121	Taxicabs
413	**Intercity and Rural Bus Transportation**
4131	Intercity & rural bus transportation
414	**Bus Charter Service**
4141	Local bus charter service
4142	Bus charter service, except local
415	**School Buses**
4151	School buses
417	**Bus Terminal and Service Facilities**
4173	Bus terminal and service facilities

Code	Short Title
42	**TRUCKING AND WAREHOUSING**
421	**Trucking & Courier Services, Ex. Air**
4212	Local trucking, without storage
4213	Trucking, except local
4214	Local trucking with storage
4215	Courier services, except by air
422	**Public Warehousing and Storage**
4221	Farm product warehousing and storage
4222	Refrigerated warehousing and storage
4225	General warehousing and storage
4226	Special warehousing and storage, nec
423	**Trucking Terminal Facilities**
4231	Trucking terminal facilities
43	**U.S. POSTAL SERVICE**
431	**U.S. Postal Service**
4311	U.S. Postal Service
44	**WATER TRANSPORTATION**
441	**Deep Sea Foreign Trans. of Freight**
4412	Deep sea foreign trans. of freight

Code	Short Title	Code	Short Title
442	**Deep Sea Domestic Trans. of Freight**	4741	Rental of railroad cars
4424	Deep sea domestic trans. of freight	**478**	**Miscellaneous Transportation Services**
443	**Freight Trans. on the Great Lakes**	4783	Packing and crating
4432	Freight trans. on the Great Lakes	4785	Inspection & fixed facilities
444	**Water Transportation of Freight, NEC**	4789	Transportation services, nec
4449	Water transportation of freight, nec		
448	**Water Transportation of Passengers**	**48**	**COMMUNICATIONS**
4481	Deep sea passenger trans., ex. ferry	**481**	**Telephone Communications**
4482	Ferries	4812	Radiotelephone communications
4489	Water passenger transportation, nec	4813	Telephone communications, exc. radio
449	**Water Transportation Services**	**482**	**Telegraph & Other Communications**
4491	Marine cargo handling	4822	Telegraph & other communications
4492	Towing and tugboat service	**483**	**Radio and Television Broadcasting**
4493	Marinas	4832	Radio broadcasting stations
4499	Water transportation services, nec	4833	Television broadcasting stations
		484	**Cable and Other Pay TV Services**
45	**TRANSPORTATION BY AIR**	4841	Cable and other pay TV services
451	**Air Transportation, Scheduled**	**489**	**Communications Services, NEC**
4512	Air transportation, scheduled	4899	Communications services, nec
4513	Air courier services		
452	**Air Transportation, Nonscheduled**	**49**	**ELECTRIC, GAS, AND SANITARY SERVICES**
4522	Air transportation, nonscheduled	**491**	**Electric Services**
458	**Airports, Flying Fields, & Services**	4911	Electric services
4581	Airports, flying fields, & services	**492**	**Gas Production and Distribution**
		4922	Natural gas transmission
46	**PIPELINES, EXCEPT NATURAL GAS**	4923	Gas transmission and distribution
461	**Pipelines, Except Natural Gas**	4924	Natural gas distribution
4612	Crude petroleum pipelines	4925	Gas production and/or distribution
4613	Refined petroleum pipelines	**493**	**Combination Utility Services**
4619	Pipelines, nec	4931	Electric and other services combined
		4932	Gas and other services combined
47	**TRANSPORTATION SERVICES**	4939	Combination utilities, nec
472	**Passenger Transportation Arrangement**	**494**	**Water Supply**
4724	Travel agencies	4941	Water supply
4725	Tour operators	**495**	**Sanitary Services**
4729	Passenger transport arrangement, nec	4952	Sewerage systems
473	**Freight Transportation Arrangement**	4953	Refuse systems
4731	Freight transportation arrangement	4959	Sanitary services, nec
474	**Rental of Railroad Cars**	**496**	**Steam and Air-Conditioning Supply**
		4961	Steam and air-conditioning supply
		497	**Irrigation Systems**
		4971	Irrigation systems

F. WHOLESALE TRADE

Code	Short Title	Code	Short Title
50	**WHOLESALE TRADE—DURABLE GOODS**	5012	Automobiles and other motor vehicles
		5013	Motor vehicle supplies and new parts
501	**Motor Vehicles, Parts, and Supplies**	5014	Tires and tubes
		5015	Motor vehicle parts, used

Code	Short Title	Code	Short Title
502	**Furniture and Homefurnishings**	51	**WHOLESALE TRADE—NONDURABLE GOODS**
5021	Furniture		
5023	Homefurnishings	511	**Paper and Paper Products**
503	**Lumber and Construction Materials**	5111	Printing and writing paper
5031	Lumber, plywood, and millwork	5112	Stationery and office supplies
5032	Brick, stone, & related materials	5113	Industrial & personal service paper
5033	Roofing, siding, & insulation	512	**Drugs, Proprietaries, and Sundries**
5039	Construction materials, nec	5122	Drugs, proprietaries, and sundries
504	**Professional & Commercial Equipment**	513	**Apparel, Piece Goods, and Notions**
5043	Photographic equipment and supplies	5131	Piece goods & notions
5044	Office equipment	5136	Men's and boys' clothing
5045	Computers, peripherals & software	5137	Women's and children's clothing
5046	Commercial equipment, nec	5139	Footwear
5047	Medical and hospital equipment	514	**Groceries and Related Products**
5048	Ophthalmic goods	5141	Groceries, general line
5049	Professional equipment, nec	5142	Packaged frozen foods
505	**Metals and Minerals, Except Petroleum**	5143	Dairy products, exc. dried or canned
5051	Metals service centers and offices	5144	Poultry and poultry products
5052	Coal and other minerals and ores	5145	Confectionery
506	**Electrical Goods**	5146	Fish and seafoods
5063	Electrical apparatus and equipment	5147	Meats and meat products
5064	Electrical appliances, TV & radios	5148	Fresh fruits and vegetables
5065	Electronic parts and equipment	5149	Groceries and related products, nec
507	**Hardware, Plumbing & Heating Equipment**	515	**Farm-Product Raw Materials**
5072	Hardware	5153	Grain and field beans
5074	Plumbing & hydronic heating supplies	5154	Livestock
5075	Warm air heating & air-conditioning	5159	Farm-product raw materials, nec
5078	Refrigeration equipment and supplies	516	**Chemicals and Allied Products**
508	**Machinery, Equipment, and Supplies**	5162	Plastics materials & basic shapes
5082	Construction and mining machinery	5169	Chemicals & allied products, nec
5083	Farm and garden machinery	517	**Petroleum and Petroleum Products**
5084	Industrial machinery and equipment	5171	Petroleum bulk stations & terminals
5085	Industrial supplies	5172	Petroleum products, nec
5087	Service establishment equipment	518	**Beer, Wine, and Distilled Beverages**
5088	Transportation equipment & supplies	5181	Beer and ale
509	**Miscellaneous Durable Goods**	5182	Wine and distilled beverages
5091	Sporting & recreational goods	519	**Misc. Nondurable Goods**
5092	Toys and hobby goods and supplies	5191	Farm supplies
5093	Scrap and waste materials	5192	Books, periodicals, & newspapers
5094	Jewelry & precious stones	5193	Flowers & florists' supplies
5099	Durable goods, nec	5194	Tobacco and tobacco products
		5198	Paints, varnishes, and supplies
		5199	Nondurable goods, nec

G. RETAIL TRADE

Code	Short Title	Code	Short Title
52	**BUILDING MATERIALS & GARDEN SUPPLIES**	523	**Paint, Glass, and Wallpaper Stores**
		5231	Paint, glass, and wallpaper stores
521	**Lumber and Other Building Materials**	525	**Hardware Stores**
5211	Lumber and other building materials	5251	Hardware stores
		526	**Retail Nurseries and Garden Stores**

Code	Short Title	Code	Short Title
5261	Retail nurseries and garden stores	5621	Women's clothing stores
527	**Mobile Home Dealers**	563	**Women's Accessory & Specialty Stores**
5271	Mobile home dealers	5632	Women's accessory & specialty stores
		564	**Children's and Infants' Wear Stores**
53	**GENERAL MERCHANDISE STORES**	5641	Children's and infants' wear stores
531	**Department Stores**	565	**Family Clothing Stores**
5311	Department stores	5651	Family clothing stores
533	**Variety Stores**	566	**Shoe Stores**
5331	Variety stores	5661	Shoe stores
539	**Misc. General Merchandise Stores**	569	**Misc. Apparel & Accessory Stores**
5399	Misc. general merchandise stores	5699	Misc. apparel & accessory stores
54	**FOOD STORES**	**57**	**FURNITURE AND HOMEFURNISHINGS STORES**
541	**Grocery Stores**		
5411	Grocery stores	571	**Furniture and Homefurnishings Stores**
542	**Meat and Fish Markets**	5712	Furniture stores
5421	Meat and fish markets	5713	Floor covering stores
543	**Fruit and Vegetable Markets**	5714	Drapery and upholstery stores
5431	Fruit and vegetable markets	5719	Misc. homefurnishings stores
544	**Candy, Nut, and Confectionery Stores**	572	**Household Appliance Stores**
5441	Candy, nut, and confectionery stores	5722	Household appliance stores
545	**Dairy Products Stores**	573	**Radio, Television, & Computer Stores**
5451	Dairy products stores	5731	Radio, TV, & electronic stores
546	**Retail Bakeries**	5734	Computer and software stores
5461	Retail bakeries	5735	Record & prerecorded tape stores
549	**Miscellaneous Food Stores**	5736	Musical instrument stores
5499	Miscellaneous food stores		
		58	**EATING AND DRINKING PLACES**
55	**AUTOMOTIVE DEALERS & SERVICE STATIONS**	581	**Eating and Drinking Places**
		5812	Eating places
551	**New and Used Car Dealers**	5813	Drinking places
5511	New and used car dealers		
552	**Used Car Dealers**	**59**	**MISCELLANEOUS RETAIL**
5521	Used car dealers	591	**Drug Stores and Proprietary Stores**
553	**Auto and Home Supply Stores**	5912	Drug stores and proprietary stores
5531	Auto and home supply stores	592	**Liquor Stores**
554	**Gasoline Service Stations**	5921	Liquor stores
5541	Gasoline service stations	593	**Used Merchandise Stores**
555	**Boat Dealers**	5932	Used merchandise stores
5551	Boat dealers	594	**Miscellaneous Shopping Goods Stores**
556	**Recreational Vehicle Dealers**	5941	Sporting goods and bicycle shops
5561	Recreational vehicle dealers	5942	Book stores
557	**Motorcycle Dealers**	5943	Stationery stores
5571	Motorcycle dealers	5944	Jewelry stores
559	**Automotive Dealers, NEC**	5945	Hobby, toy, and game shops
5599	Automotive dealers, nec	5946	Camera & photographic supply stores
		5947	Gift, novelty, and souvenir shops
56	**APPAREL AND ACCESSORY STORES**	5948	Luggage and leather goods stores
561	**Men's & Boys' Clothing Stores**	5949	Sewing, needlework, and piece goods
5611	Men's & boys' clothing stores	596	**Nonstore Retailers**
562	**Women's Clothing Stores**	5961	Catalog and mail-order houses
		5962	Merchandising machine operators

Code	Short Title	Code	Short Title
5963	Direct selling establishments	599	**Retail Stores, NEC**
598	**Fuel Dealers**	5992	Florists
5983	Fuel oil dealers	5993	Tobacco stores and stands
5984	Liquefied petroleum gas dealers	5994	News dealers and newsstands
5989	Fuel dealers, nec	5995	Optical goods stores
		5999	Miscellaneous retail stores, nec

H. FINANCE, INSURANCE, AND REAL ESTATE

Code	Short Title	Code	Short Title
60	**DEPOSITORY INSTITUTIONS**	6231	Security and commodity exchanges
601	**Central Reserve Depositories**	628	**Security and Commodity Services**
6011	Federal reserve banks	6282	Investment advice
6019	Central reserve depository, nec	6289	Security & commodity services, nec
602	**Commercial Banks**		
6021	National commercial banks	63	**INSURANCE CARRIERS**
6022	State commercial banks	631	**Life Insurance**
6029	Commercial banks, nec	6311	Life insurance
603	**Savings Institutions**	632	**Medical Service and Health Insurance**
6035	Federal savings institutions	6321	Accident and health insurance
6036	Savings institutions, except federal	6324	Hospital and medical service plans
606	**Credit Unions**	633	**Fire, Marine, and Casualty Insurance**
6061	Federal credit unions	6331	Fire, marine, and casualty insurance
6062	State credit unions	635	**Surety Insurance**
608	**Foreign Bank & Branches & Agencies**	6351	Surety insurance
6081	Foreign bank & branches & agencies	636	**Title Insurance**
6082	Foreign trade & international banks	6361	Title insurance
609	**Functions Closely Related to Banking**	637	**Pension, Health, and Welfare Funds**
6091	Nondeposit trust facilities	6371	Pension, health, and welfare funds
6099	Functions related to deposit banking	639	**Insurance Carriers, NEC**
		6399	Insurance carriers, nec
61	**NONDEPOSITORY INSTITUTIONS**		
611	**Federal & Fed.-Sponsored Credit**	64	**INSURANCE AGENTS, BROKERS, & SERVICE**
6111	Federal & fed.-sponsored credit		
614	**Personal Credit Institutions**	641	**Insurance Agents, Brokers, & Service**
6141	Personal credit institutions	6411	Insurance agents, brokers, & service
615	**Business Credit Institutions**		
6153	Short-term business credit	65	**REAL ESTATE**
6159	Misc. business credit institutions	651	**Real Estate Operators and Lessors**
616	**Mortgage Bankers and Brokers**	6512	Nonresidential building operators
6162	Mortgage bankers and correspondents	6513	Apartment building operators
6163	Loan brokers	6514	Dwelling operators, exc. apartments
		6515	Mobile home site operators
62	**SECURITY AND COMMODITY BROKERS**	6517	Railroad property lessors
		6519	Real property lessors, nec
621	**Security Brokers and Dealers**	653	**Real Estate Agents and Managers**
6211	Security brokers and dealers	6531	Real estate agents and managers
622	**Commodity Contracts Brokers, Dealers**	654	**Title Abstract Offices**
6221	Commodity contracts brokers, dealers	6541	Title abstract offices
623	**Security and Commodity Exchanges**	655	**Subdividers and Developers**

Code	Short Title	Code	Short Title
6552	Subdividers and developers, nec	6722	Management investment, open-end
6553	Cemetery subdividers and developers	6726	Investment offices, nec
		673	**Trusts**
		6732	Educational, religious, etc. trusts
67	**HOLDING AND OTHER INVESTMENT OFFICES**	6733	Trusts, nec
		679	**Miscellaneous Investing**
671	**Holding Offices**	6792	Oil royalty traders
6712	Bank holding companies	6794	Patent owners and lessors
6719	Holding companies, nec	6798	Real estate investment trusts
672	**Investment Offices**	6799	Investors, nec

I. SERVICES

Code	Short Title	Code	Short Title
70	**HOTELS AND OTHER LODGING PLACES**	**73**	**BUSINESS SERVICES**
		731	**Advertising**
701	**Hotels and Motels**	7311	Advertising agencies
7011	Hotels and motels	7312	Outdoor advertising services
702	**Rooming and Boarding Houses**	7313	Radio, TV, publisher representatives
7021	Rooming and boarding houses	7319	Advertising, nec
703	**Camps and Recreational Vehicle Parks**	**732**	**Credit Reporting and Collection**
7032	Sporting and recreational camps	7322	Adjustment & collection services
7033	Trailer parks and campsites	7323	Credit reporting services
704	**Membership-Basis Organization Hotels**	**733**	**Mailing, Reproduction, Stenographic**
7041	Membership-basis organization hotels	7331	Direct mail advertising services
		7334	Photocopying & duplicating services
72	**PERSONAL SERVICES**	7335	Commercial photography
721	**Laundry, Cleaning, & Garment Services**	7336	Commercial art and graphic design
7211	Power laundries, family & commercial	7338	Secretarial & court reporting
7212	Garment pressing & cleaners' agents	**734**	**Services to Buildings**
7213	Linen supply	7342	Disinfecting & pest control services
7215	Coin-operated laundries and cleaning	7349	Building maintenance services, nec
7216	Drycleaning plants, except rug	**735**	**Misc. Equipment Rental & Leasing**
7217	Carpet and upholstery cleaning	7352	Medical equipment rental
7218	Industrial launderers	7353	Heavy construction equipment rental
7219	Laundry and garment services, nec	7359	Equipment rental & leasing, nec
722	**Photographic Studios, Portrait**	**736**	**Personnel Supply Services**
7221	Photographic studios, portrait	7361	Employment agencies
723	**Beauty Shops**	7363	Help supply services
7231	Beauty shops	**737**	**Computer and Data Processing Services**
724	**Barber Shops**	7371	Computer programming services
7241	Barber shops	7372	Prepackaged software
725	**Shoe Repair and Shoeshine Parlors**	7373	Computer integrated systems design
7251	Shoe repair and shoeshine parlors	7374	Data processing and preparation
726	**Funeral Service and Crematories**	7375	Information retrieval services
7261	Funeral service and crematories	7376	Computer facilities management
729	**Miscellaneous Personal Services**	7377	Computer rental & leasing
7291	Tax return preparation services	7378	Computer maintenance & repair
7299	Miscellaneous personal services, nec	7379	Computer related services, nec
		738	**Miscellaneous Business Services**
		7381	Detective & armored car services

Code	Short Title
7382	Security systems services
7383	News syndicates
7384	Photofinishing laboratories
7389	Business services, nec
75	**AUTO REPAIR, SERVICES, AND PARKING**
751	**Automotive Rentals, No Drivers**
7513	Truck rental and leasing, no drivers
7514	Passenger car rental
7515	Passenger car leasing
7519	Utility trailer rental
752	**Automobile Parking**
7521	Automobile parking
753	**Automotive Repair Shops**
7532	Top & body repair & paint shops
7533	Auto exhaust system repair shops
7534	Tire retreading and repair shops
7536	Automotive glass replacement shops
7537	Automotive transmission repair shops
7538	General automotive repair shops
7539	Automotive repair shops, nec
754	**Automotive Services, Except Repair**
7542	Carwashes
7549	Automotive services, nec
76	**MISCELLANEOUS REPAIR SERVICES**
762	**Electrical Repair Shops**
7622	Radio and television repair
7623	Refrigeration service and repair
7629	Electrical repair shops, nec
763	**Watch, Clock, and Jewelry Repair**
7631	Watch, clock, and jewelry repair
764	**Reupholstery and Furniture Repair**
7641	Reupholstery and furniture repair
769	**Miscellaneous Repair Shops**
7692	Welding repair
7694	Armature rewinding shops
7699	Repair services, nec
78	**MOTION PICTURES**
781	**Motion Picture Production & Services**
7812	Motion picture & video production
7819	Services allied to motion pictures
782	**Motion Picture Distribution & Services**
7822	Motion picture and tape distribution
7829	Motion picture distribution services
783	**Motion Picture Theaters**
7832	Motion picture theaters, ex drive-in
7833	Drive-in motion picture theaters
784	**Video Tape Rental**
7841	Video tape rental

Code	Short Title
79	**AMUSEMENT & RECREATION SERVICES**
791	**Dance Studios, Schools, and Halls**
7911	Dance studios, schools, and halls
792	**Producers, Orchestras, Entertainers**
7922	Theatrical producers and services
7929	Entertainers & entertainment groups
793	**Bowling Centers**
7933	Bowling centers
794	**Commercial Sports**
7941	Sports clubs, managers, & promoters
7948	Racing, including track operation
799	**Misc. Amusement, Recreation Services**
7991	Physical fitness facilities
7992	Public golf courses
7993	Coin-operated amusement devices
7996	Amusement parks
7997	Membership sports & recreation clubs
7999	Amusement and recreation, nec
80	**HEALTH SERVICES**
801	**Offices & Clinics of Medical Doctors**
8011	Offices & clinics of medical doctors
802	**Offices and Clinics of Dentists**
8021	Offices and clinics of dentists
803	**Offices of Osteopathic Physicians**
8031	Offices of osteopathic physicians
804	**Offices of Other Health Practitioners**
8041	Offices and clinics of chiropractors
8042	Offices and clinics of optometrists
8043	Offices and clinics of podiatrists
8049	Offices of health practitioners, nec
805	**Nursing and Personal Care Facilities**
8051	Skilled nursing care facilities
8052	Intermediate care facilities
8059	Nursing and personal care, nec
806	**Hospitals**
8062	General medical & surgical hospitals
8063	Psychiatric hospitals
8069	Specialty hospitals exc. psychiatric
807	**Medical and Dental Laboratories**
8071	Medical laboratories
8072	Dental laboratories
808	**Home Health Care Services**
8082	Home health care services
809	**Health and Allied Services, NEC**
8092	Kidney dialysis centers
8093	Specialty outpatient clinics, nec
8099	Health and allied services, nec
81	**LEGAL SERVICES**
811	**Legal Services**

Code	Short Title	Code	Short Title
8111	Legal services	8611	Business associations
		862	**Professional Organizations**
		8621	Professional organizations
82	**EDUCATIONAL SERVICES**	**863**	**Labor Organizations**
821	**Elementary and Secondary Schools**	8631	Labor organizations
8211	Elementary and secondary schools	**864**	**Civic and Social Associations**
822	**Colleges and Universities**	8641	Civic and social associations
8221	Colleges and universities	**865**	**Political Organizations**
8222	Junior colleges	8651	Political organizations
823	**Libraries**	**866**	**Religious Organizations**
8231	Libraries	8661	Religious organizations
824	**Vocational Schools**	**869**	**Membership Organizations, NEC**
8243	Data processing schools	8699	Membership organizations, nec
8244	Business and secretarial schools		
8249	Vocational schools, nec	**87**	**ENGINEERING & MANAGEMENT SERVICES**
829	**Schools & Educational Services, NEC**		
8299	Schools & educational services, nec	**871**	**Engineering & Architectural Services**
		8711	Engineering services
		8712	Architectural services
83	**SOCIAL SERVICES**	8713	Surveying services
832	**Individual and Family Services**	**872**	**Accounting, Auditing, & Bookkeeping**
8322	Individual and family services	8721	Accounting, auditing, & bookkeeping
833	**Job Training and Related Services**	**873**	**Research and Testing Services**
8331	Job training and related services	8731	Commercial physical research
835	**Child Day Care Services**	8732	Commercial nonphysical research
8351	Child day care services	8733	Noncommercial research organizations
836	**Residential Care**	8734	Testing laboratories
8361	Residential care	**874**	**Management and Public Relations**
839	**Social Services, NEC**	8741	Management services
8399	Social services, nec	8742	Management consulting services
		8743	Public relations services
		8744	Facilities support services
84	**MUSEUMS, BOTANICAL, ZOOLOGICAL GARDENS**	8748	Business consulting, nec
841	**Museums and Art Galleries**	**88**	**PRIVATE HOUSEHOLDS**
8412	Museums and art galleries	**881**	**Private Households**
842	**Botanical and Zoological Gardens**	8811	Private households
8422	Botanical and zoological gardens		
		89	**SERVICES, NEC**
86	**MEMBERSHIP ORGANIZATIONS**	**899**	**Services, NEC**
861	**Business Associations**	8999	Services, nec

J. PUBLIC ADMINISTRATION

Code	Short Title	Code	Short Title
91	**EXECUTIVE, LEGISLATIVE, AND GENERAL**	9121	Legislative bodies
		913	**Executive and Legislative Combined**
911	**Executive Offices**	9131	Executive and legislative combined
9111	Executive offices	**919**	**General Government, NEC**
912	**Legislative Bodies**	9199	General government, nec

Code	Short Title
92	**JUSTICE, PUBLIC ORDER, AND SAFETY**
921	**Courts**
9211	Courts
922	**Public Order and Safety**
9221	Police protection
9222	Legal counsel and prosecution
9223	Correctional institutions
9224	Fire protection
9229	Public order and safety, nec
93	**FINANCE, TAXATION, & MONETARY POLICY**
931	**Finance, Taxation, & Monetary Policy**
9311	Finance, taxation, & monetary policy
94	**ADMINISTRATION OF HUMAN RESOURCES**
941	**Admin. of Educational Programs**
9411	Admin. of educational programs
943	**Admin. of Public Health Programs**
9431	Admin. of public health programs
944	**Admin. of Social & Manpower Programs**
9441	Admin. of social & manpower programs
945	**Administration of Veterans' Affairs**
9451	Administration of veterans' affairs

Code	Short Title
95	**ENVIRONMENTAL QUALITY AND HOUSING**
951	**Environmental Quality**
9511	Air, water, & solid waste management
9512	Land, mineral, wildlife conservation
953	**Housing and Urban Development**
9531	Housing programs
9532	Urban and community development
96	**ADMINISTRATION OF ECONOMIC PROGRAMS**
961	**Admin. of General Economic Programs**
9611	Admin. of general economic programs
962	**Regulation, Admin. of Transportation**
9621	Regulation, admin. of transportation
963	**Regulation, Admin. of Utilities**
9631	Regulation, admin. of utilities
964	**Regulation of Agricultural Marketing**
9641	Regulation of agricultural marketing
965	**Regulation Misc. Commercial Sectors**
9651	Regulation misc. commercial sectors
966	**Space Research and Technology**
9661	Space research and technology
97	**NATIONAL SECURITY AND INTL. AFFAIRS**
971	**National Security**
9711	National security
972	**International Affairs**
9721	International affairs

K. NONCLASSIFIABLE ESTABLISHMENTS

Code	Short Title
99	**NONCLASSIFIABLE ESTABLISHMENTS**
999	**Nonclassifiable Establishments**

Code	Short Title
9999	Nonclassifiable establishments

Part III

Alphabetic Index

Alphabetic Index

A

2282 Acrylic and modacrylic filament yarn: throwing, winding, or spooling—*mfg*
2221 Acrylic broadwoven fabrics—*mfg*
2824 Acrylic fibers—*mfg*
2821 Acrylic resins—*mfg*
2822 Acrylic rubbers—*mfg*
2281 Acrylic yarn, made from purchased staple: spun—*mfg*
2869 Acrylonitrile—*mfg*
2824 Acrylonitrile fibers—*mfg*
2821 Acrylonitrile-butadiene-styrene resins—*mfg*
3829 Actinometers, meteorological—*mfg*
2819 Activated carbon and charcoal—*mfg*
8322 Activity centers, elderly or handicapped
7929 Actors
7929 Actresses
8999 Actuaries, consulting
3593 Actuators, fluid power: hydraulic and pneumatic—*mfg*
8049 Acupuncturists, except M.D.: offices of
3728 Adapter assemblies, hydromatic propeller—*mfg*
3537 Adapters for multiweapon rack loading on aircraft—*mfg*
3483 Adapters, bombcluster—*mfg*
2679 Adding machine rolls, paper—mfpm—*mfg*
3578 Adding machines—*mfg*
5044 Adding machines—wholesale
3313 Additive alloys, except copper—*mfg*
3579 Address labeling machines—*mfg*
7331 Address list compilers
3579 Addressing machines, plates and plate embossers—*mfg*
5044 Addressing machines—wholesale
7331 Addressing service
3842 Adhesive tape and plasters, medicated or nonmedicated—*mfg*
2891 Adhesives—*mfg*
2891 Adhesives, plastics—*mfg*
2869 Adipic acid—*mfg*
2869 Adipic acid esters—*mfg*
2869 Adiponitrile—*mfg*
2822 Adiprene—*mfg*
7322 Adjustment bureaus, except insurance adjustment agencies
6411 Adjustment services, insurance
1542 Administration building construction—general contractors
8742 Administrative management consultants
8741 Administrative management services
6733 Administrators of private estates (nonoperating)
**** Administrators of private estates (operating)—code to principal activity
3259 Adobe brick—*mfg*

8322 Adoption services
2833 Adrenal derivatives: bulk, uncompounded—*mfg*
2834 Adrenal pharmaceutical preparations—*mfg*
8322 Adult day care centers
2791 Advertisement typesetting—*mfg*
7311 Advertising agencies
3555 Advertising and newspaper mats—*mfg*
7311 Advertising consultants (agencies)
8999 Advertising copy, writers of
3999 Advertising curtains—*mfg*
3993 Advertising displays, except printed—*mfg*
2752 Advertising posters, lithographed—*mfg*
7312 Advertising service, outdoor
3993 Advertising specialties—mfpm—*mfg*
5199 Advertising specialties—wholesale
7319 Advertising, aerial
7312 Advertising, billboard
7331 Advertising, direct mail
9111 Advisory commissions, executive
9121 Advisory commissions, legislative
8399 Advocacy groups
3423 Adzes—*mfg*
3565 Aerating machines, for beverages—*mfg*
7319 Aerial advertising
3861 Aerial cameras—*mfg*
0721 Aerial dusting and spraying
1382 Aerial geophysical exploration, oil and gas field: on a contract basis
7335 Aerial photographic service, except mapmaking
7999 Aerial tramways, amusement or scenic
4119 Aerial tramways, except amusement and scenic
3531 Aerial work platforms, hydraulic or electric truck or carrier mounted—*mfg*
7991 Aerobic dance and exercise classes
5088 Aeronautical equipment and supplies—wholesale
3499 Aerosol valves, metal—*mfg*
3443 Aftercooler shells—*mfg*
3443 Aftercoolers, steam jet—*mfg*
2836 Agar culture media, except in vitro and in vivo—*mfg*
2833 Agar-agar (ground)—*mfg*
1499 Agate mining
6081 Agencies of foreign banks
7389 Agents and brokers for authors and non-performing artists
6211 Agents for mutual funds
7922 Agents or managers for entertainers
6163 Agents, farm or business loan
6531 Agents, real estate
7212 Agents, retail: for laundries and drycleaners

7629 Aircraft electrical equipment repair, except radio
3537 Aircraft engine cradles—*mfg*
3724 Aircraft engines and engine parts, internal combustion and jet propulsion—*mfg*
5088 Aircraft engines and engine parts—wholesale
5088 Aircraft equipment and supplies—wholesale
3812 Aircraft flight instruments—*mfg*
2273 Aircraft floor coverings, except rubber or plastics—*mfg*
3462 Aircraft forgings, ferrous: not made in rolling mills—*mfg*
3463 Aircraft forgings, nonferrous: not made in hot-rolling mills—*mfg*
5172 Aircraft fueling services—wholesale
3429 Aircraft hardware—*mfg*
9621 Aircraft inspection—government
3647 Aircraft lighting fixtures—*mfg*
3537 Aircraft loading hoists—*mfg*
**** Aircraft modification centers—classify according to principal activity
3728 Aircraft power transmission equipment—*mfg*
3728 Aircraft propeller parts—*mfg*
3728 Aircraft propellers, variable and fixed pitch—*mfg*
7622 Aircraft radio equipment repair
2531 Aircraft seats—*mfg*
4581 Aircraft servicing and repairing, except on a factory basis
4581 Aircraft storage at airports
4581 Aircraft upholstery repair
3564 Aircurtains (blower)—*mfg*
3724 Airfoils, aircraft engine—*mfg*
3728 Airframe assemblies, except for guided missiles—*mfg*
3769 Airframe assemblies, for guided missiles—*mfg*
3812 Airframe equipment instruments—*mfg*
4581 Airfreight handling at airports
4729 Airline ticket offices, not operated by transportation companies
3443 Airlocks—*mfg*
3728 Airplane brake expanders—*mfg*
2211 Airplane cloth, cotton—*mfg*
3999 Airplane models, except toy and hobby models—*mfg*
3944 Airplane models, toy and hobby—*mfg*
7359 Airplane rental and leasing
3721 Airplanes, fixed or rotary wing—*mfg*
4581 Airplanes, janitorial services on
3944 Airplanes, toy—*mfg*
4581 Airport hangar rental
6519 Airport leasing, if not operating airport

4581 Airport leasing, if operating airport
3612 Airport lighting transformers—*mfg*
4111 Airport limousine scheduled service
1611 Airport runway construction—general contractors
4581 Airport terminal services
4111 Airport transportation service, local: road or rail
4581 Airports
3721 Airships—*mfg*
3812 Airspeed instrumentation (aeronautical instruments)—*mfg*
1499 Alabaster mining
5063 Alarm signal systems—wholesale
2782 Albums—*mfg*
5112 Albums (photo) and scrapbooks—wholesale
2085 Alcohol for medicinal and beverage purposes, ethyl or grain—*mfg*
2821 Alcohol resins, polyvinyl—*mfg*
8093 Alcohol treatment, outpatient clinics
2869 Alcohol, aromatic—*mfg*
2869 Alcohol, fatty: powdered—*mfg*
5169 Alcohol, industrial—wholesale
2861 Alcohol, methyl: natural—*mfg*
2869 Alcohol, methyl: synthetic (methanol)—*mfg*
2861 Alcohol, wood: natural (methanol)—*mfg*
9651 Alcoholic beverage control boards—government
8322 Alcoholism counseling, nonresidential: except medical treatment
8361 Alcoholism rehabilitation centers, residential: with health care incidental
8069 Alcoholism rehabilitation hospitals
2869 Alcohols, industrial: denatured (nonbeverage)—*mfg*
2869 Alcohols, polyhydric—*mfg*
2082 Ale—*mfg*
5181 Ale—wholesale
0139 Alfalfa farms
2048 Alfalfa, cubed—*mfg*
2048 Alfalfa, prepared as feed for animals—*mfg*
5191 Alfalfa—wholesale
2869 Algin products—*mfg*
3829 Alidades, surveying—*mfg*
3728 Alighting assemblies (landing gear), aircraft—*mfg*
2819 Alkali metals—*mfg*
2812 Alkalies, not produced at mines—*mfg*
5169 Alkalies—wholesale
3691 Alkaline cell storage batteries—*mfg*
2833 Alkaloids and salts—*mfg*
2821 Alkyd resins—*mfg*
2865 Alkylated diphenylamines, mixed—*mfg*
2865 Alkylated phenol, mixed—*mfg*

2655 Ammunition cans or tubes, paperboard laminated with metal foil—mfpm—*mfg*
3484 Ammunition carts, machine gun—*mfg*
3483 Ammunition loading and assembling plants—*mfg*
5099 Ammunition, except sporting—wholesale
5091 Ammunition, sporting—wholesale
5941 Ammunition—retail
3825 Ampere-hour meters—*mfg*
3711 Amphibian motor vehicles, except tanks—*mfg*
3795 Amphibian tanks, military—*mfg*
3663 Amplifiers: RF power and IF—*mfg*
3651 Amplifiers: radio, public address, or musical instrument—*mfg*
3699 Amplifiers; magnetic, pulse, and maser—*mfg*
3221 Ampoules, glass—*mfg*
7996 Amusement centers and parks (not fairs, circuses, or carnivals)
7999 Amusement concessions
7993 Amusement device parlors, coin-operated
3999 Amusement machines, coin-operated: except coin-operated phonographs—*mfg*
7993 Amusement machines, coin-operated: operation of
7996 Amusement parks
7999 Amusement rides
3599 Amusement rides for carnivals—*mfg*
2869 Amyl acetate and alcohol—*mfg*
2834 Analgesics—*mfg*
3825 Analog-to-digital converters, electronic instrumentation type—*mfg*
5049 Analytical instruments: photometers, spectrographs, and chromatographic instruments—wholesale
3825 Analyzers for testing electrical characteristics—*mfg*
3823 Analyzers, industrial process type—*mfg*
3829 Anamometers—*mfg*
3462 Anchors, forged: not made in rolling mills—*mfg*
1459 Andalusite mining
3429 Andirons—*mfg*
3841 Anesthesia apparatus—*mfg*
8011 Anesthesiologists, offices of
2833 Anesthetics, in bulk form—*mfg*
2834 Anesthetics, packaged—*mfg*
2835 Angiourographic diagnostic agents—*mfg*
3429 Angle irons, hardware—*mfg*
3545 Angle rings—*mfg*
3812 Angle-of-attack instrumentation—*mfg*
3812 Angle-of-yaw instrumentation—*mfg*
2873 Anhydrous ammonia—*mfg*
2021 Anhydrous butterfat—*mfg*
2824 Anidex fibers—*mfg*

2865 Aniline—*mfg*
2865 Aniline oil—*mfg*
3496 Animal and fish traps, made from purchased wire—*mfg*
2816 Animal black—*mfg*
6553 Animal cemetery operation
3523 Animal clippers, hand and electric—*mfg*
8422 Animal exhibits
5191 Animal feeds, except pet—wholesale
2048 Animal feeds, prepared: except dog and cat—*mfg*
2282 Animal fiber yarn: twisting, winding, or spooling—*mfg*
5159 Animal hair—wholesale
0741 Animal hospitals for livestock
0742 Animal hospitals for pets and other animal specialties
8699 Animal humane societies
2077 Animal oils, except medicinal grade—*mfg*
2833 Animal oils, medicinal grade: refined and concentrated—*mfg*
2834 Animal remedies—*mfg*
0752 Animal shelters
7999 Animal shows in circuses, fairs, and carnivals
0291 Animal specialty and livestock farms, general
0971 Animal trapping, commercial
3429 Animal traps, iron and steel: except wire—*mfg*
2899 Anise oil—*mfg*
3842 Ankle supports, orthopedic—*mfg*
2252 Anklets, hosiery—*mfg*
2861 Annato extract—*mfg*
3443 Annealing boxes, pots, and covers—*mfg*
3398 Annealing of metal for the trade—*mfg*
2759 Announcements, engraved—*mfg*
8999 Announcers, radio and television service
3823 Annunciators, relay and solid-state types: industrial display—*mfg*
5051 Anode metal—wholesale
3559 Anodizing equipment (except rolling mill lines)—*mfg*
3471 Anodizing of metals and formed products, for the trade—*mfg*
5064 Answering machines, telephone—wholesale
2879 Ant poisons—*mfg*
2834 Antacids—*mfg*
1799 Antenna installation, except household type—contractors
5731 Antenna stores, household—retail
7622 Antennas, household: installation and service
3679 Antennas, receiving: automobile, home, and portable—*mfg*

2873 Aqua ammonia, made in ammonia plants—*mfg*
3499 Aquarium accessories, metal—*mfg*
3089 Aquarium accessories, plastics—*mfg*
8422 Aquariums
3231 Aquariums and reflectors, made from purchased glass—*mfg*
1623 Aqueduct construction—general contractors
7389 Arbitration and conciliation services
3542 Arbor presses—*mfg*
8422 Arboreta
0783 Arborist services
3545 Arbors (machine tool accessories)—*mfg*
3845 Arc lamp units, electrotherapeutic: except infrared and ultraviolet—*mfg*
3648 Arc lamps, except electrotherapeutic—*mfg*
3648 Arc lighting fixtures—*mfg*
3548 Arc-welding generators—*mfg*
3548 Arc-welder transformers (separate)—*mfg*
3548 Arc-welders, transformer-rectifier—*mfg*
3548 Arc-welding generators, a.c. and d.c.—*mfg*
7993 Arcades, amusement
3842 Arch supports, orthopedic—*mfg*
8733 Archeological expeditions
3949 Archery equipment—*mfg*
5091 Archery equipment—wholesale
7999 Archery ranges, operation of
2439 Arches, laminated lumber—*mfg*
5049 Architects' equipment and supplies—wholesale
3271 Architectural block, concrete: e.g., fluted, screen, split, slump, ground face—*mfg*
8712 Architectural engineering services
3446 Architectural metal work, ferrous and nonferrous—*mfg*
5039 Architectural metal work—wholesale
3299 Architectural sculptures, plaster of paris: factory production only—*mfg*
3299 Architectural sculptures: gypsum, clay or papier mache—*mfg*
8712 Architectural services
1761 Architectural sheet metal work—contractors
5999 Architectural supplies—retail
3259 Architectural terra cotta—*mfg*
3021 Arctics, rubber or rubber soled fabric—*mfg*
3648 Area and sports luminaries—*mfg*
3272 Areaways, basement window: concrete—*mfg*
7941 Arenas, boxing and wrestling (sports promotion): professional
1411 Argillite, dimension—quarrying
2813 Argon—*mfg*
2389 Arm bands, elastic—mfpm—*mfg*

3625 Armature relays—*mfg*
7694 Armature rewinding
3621 Armatures, industrial—*mfg*
3694 Armatures, motor vehicle—*mfg*
3483 Arming and fusing devices for missiles—*mfg*
3462 Armor plate, forged iron and steel: not made in rolling mills—*mfg*
3312 Armor plate, made in steel works or rolling mills—*mfg*
3357 Armored cable or conductor, nonferrous—mfpm—*mfg*
7381 Armored car service
9711 Army
2911 Aromatic chemicals, made in petroleum refineries—*mfg*
5169 Aromatic chemicals—wholesale
4729 Arrangement of carpools and vanpools
3643 Arrestors and coils, lightning—*mfg*
3949 Arrows, archery—*mfg*
2879 Arsenates: calcium, copper, and lead-formulated—*mfg*
1479 Arsenic mineral mining
2879 Arsenites, formulated—*mfg*
7335 Art and illustration, commercial
3269 Art and ornamental ware, pottery—*mfg*
8699 Art councils
5999 Art dealers—retail
8412 Art galleries, not primarily selling
3231 Art glass, made from purchased glass—*mfg*
3229 Art glassware, made in glassmaking plants—*mfg*
3299 Art goods: plaster of paris, papier-mache, and scagliola—*mfg*
5199 Art goods—wholesale
3272 Art marble, concrete—*mfg*
2395 Art needlework—mfpm—*mfg*
8999 Art restoration
8249 Art schools, commercial
8299 Art schools, except commercial
2273 Art squares, textile fiber—*mfg*
2273 Art squares: twisted paper, grass, reed, coir, sisal, jute, and rag—*mfg*
2033 Artichokes in olive oil, canned—*mfg*
3999 Artificial and preserved flowers, foliage, fruits, and vines: except glass—*mfg*
3999 Artificial flower arrangements—*mfg*
5999 Artificial flowers—retail
5193 Artificial flowers—wholesale
3812 Artificial horizon instrumentation—*mfg*
0752 Artificial insemination services: animal specialties
0751 Artificial insemination services: livestock
5999 Artificial limb stores—retail
8999 Artificial nucleation (cloud seeding)

3161 Attache cases, regardless of material—*mfg*
3546 Attachments for portable drills—*mfg*
3679 Attenuators—*mfg*
3564 Attic fans—*mfg*
8111 Attorneys
9222 Attorneys general's offices
5999 Auction rooms (general merchandise)—retail
**** Auction, specialized—code according to product sold
7389 Auctioneering service on a commission or fee basis
5154 Auctioning livestock—wholesale
2517 Audio cabinets, wood—*mfg*
3695 Audio range tapes, blank—*mfg*
3651 Audio recorders and players: automotive and household—*mfg*
3825 Audiofrequency oscillators—*mfg*
3845 Audiological equipment, electromedical—*mfg*
8049 Audiologists, offices of
3825 Audiometers, except medical—*mfg*
7812 Audiovisual motion picture program production
8721 Auditing service, accounts
1542 Auditorium construction—general contractors
4731 Auditors, freight rate
3532 Auger mining equipment—*mfg*
1241 Auger mining services: bituminous coal, anthracite, and lignite on a contract basis
3423 Augers (edge tools)—*mfg*
8999 Authors
7389 Authors' agents and brokers
7011 Auto courts
7549 Auto emissions testing, without repairs
2241 Auto wind lace—*mfg*
3843 Autoclaves, dental—*mfg*
3842 Autoclaves, hospital and surgical—*mfg*
3443 Autoclaves, industrial—*mfg*
3821 Autoclaves, laboratory—*mfg*
3721 Autogiros—*mfg*
5999 Autograph and philatelist supply stores—retail
2761 Autographic register forms, printed—*mfg*
3845 Automated blood and body fluid analyzers, except laboratory—*mfg*
6099 Automated clearinghouses
3826 Automatic chemical analyzers, laboratory type—*mfg*
3541 Automatic chucking machines—*mfg*
7215 Automatic laundry
3812 Automatic pilots—*mfg*
3541 Automatic screw machines—*mfg*
3578 Automatic teller machines (ATM)—*mfg*

7537 Automatic transmission repair, automotive
5812 Automats (eating places)
5531 Automobile accessory dealers—retail
5511 Automobile agencies (dealers)—retail
5531 Automobile air-conditioning equipment, sale and installation—retail
5012 Automobile auction—wholesale
5531 Automobile battery dealers—retail
3711 Automobile bodies, passenger car—*mfg*
4226 Automobile dead storage
8299 Automobile driving instruction
5013 Automobile engine testing equipment, electrical—wholesale
5015 Automobile engines, used—wholesale or retail
6159 Automobile finance leasing
2273 Automobile floor coverings, except rubber or plastics—*mfg*
5013 Automobile glass—wholesale
3429 Automobile hardware—*mfg*
3052 Automobile hose, plastics or rubber—*mfg*
3792 Automobile house trailer chassis—*mfg*
6331 Automobile insurance
7515 Automobile leasing, except finance leasing: without drivers
3469 Automobile license tags, stamped metal—*mfg*
3534 Automobile lifts (elevators)—*mfg*
6141 Automobile loans (may include automobile insurance)
8699 Automobile owners' associations and clubs
5531 Automobile parts dealers—retail
5015 Automobile parts, used—wholesale or retail
2842 Automobile polishes—*mfg*
8734 Automobile proving and testing grounds
7389 Automobile recovery service
4119 Automobile rental with drivers
7514 Automobile rental, without drivers
7389 Automobile repossession service
2399 Automobile seat covers—*mfg*
3499 Automobile seat frames, metal—*mfg*
2531 Automobile seats—*mfg*
5013 Automobile service station equipment—wholesale
5541 Automobile service stations—retail
7389 Automobile shows, flower shows, and home shows: promoters of
3496 Automobile skid chains, made from purchased wire—*mfg*
3493 Automobile springs—*mfg*
5531 Automobile tire dealers—retail
5014 Automobile tires and tubes—wholesale
3799 Automobile trailer chassis, except travel trailer—*mfg*

3799 Automobile trailers, except house and travel—*mfg*
2396 Automobile trimmings, fabric—*mfg*
3531 Automobile wrecker hoists—*mfg*
3713 Automobile wrecker-truck body—*mfg*
3711 Automobiles—*mfg*
3944 Automobiles and trucks, toy—*mfg*
3944 Automobiles, children's pedal driven—*mfg*
5511 Automobiles, new and used—retail
5521 Automobiles, used cars only—retail
5012 Automobiles—wholesale
5013 Automotive accessories—wholesale
5075 Automotive air-conditioners—wholesale
3825 Automotive ammeters and voltmeters—*mfg*
3357 Automotive and aircraft wire and cable, nonferrous—*mfg*
7532 Automotive body shops
7539 Automotive electrical service (battery and ignition repair)
5013 Automotive engines, new—wholesale
2211 Automotive fabrics, cotton—*mfg*
2221 Automotive fabrics, manmade fiber—*mfg*
3462 Automotive forgings, ferrous: not made in rolling mills—*mfg*
3463 Automotive forgings, nonferrous: not made in hot-rolling mills—*mfg*
7536 Automotive glass replacement and repair service
7549 Automotive inspection and diagnostic service
7532 Automotive interior shops
3647 Automotive lighting fixtures—*mfg*
3061 Automotive mechanical rubber goods: molded, extruded, and lathe-cut—*mfg*
7533 Automotive mufflers, sale and installation
7532 Automotive paint shops
5013 Automotive parts, new —wholesale
7622 Automotive radio repair shops
7538 Automotive repair shops, general
7539 Automotive springs, rebuilding and repair
3465 Automotive stampings: e.g., fenders, tops, hub caps, body parts, trim—*mfg*
5013 Automotive stampings—wholesale
7539 Automotive starter and generator repair
5013 Automotive supplies—wholesale
7532 Automotive tops (canvas or plastic), installation, repair, or sales and installation
7549 Automotive towing service
7532 Automotive trim shops
7532 Automotive upholstery and trim shops
7542 Automotive washing and polishing
3714 Automotive wiring harness sets, except ignition—*mfg*
5093 Automotive wrecking for scrap—wholesale

3931 Autophones (organs with perforated music rolls)—*mfg*
3799 Autos, midget: power driven—*mfg*
3612 Autotransformers for switchboards, except telephone switchboards—*mfg*
3661 Autotransformers for telephone switchboards—*mfg*
3612 Autotransformers, electric (power transformers)—*mfg*
3572 Auxiliary computer storage units—*mfg*
0279 Aviaries (e.g., parakeet, canary, love birds)
7997 Aviation clubs, membership
8249 Aviation schools, excluding flying instruction
0179 Avocado orchards and farms
3423 Awls—*mfg*
1799 Awning installation—contractors
7699 Awning repair shops
5999 Awning shops—retail
2211 Awning stripes, cotton—mitse—*mfg*
2394 Awnings, fabric—mfpm—*mfg*
3089 Awnings, fiberglass and plastics combination—*mfg*
3444 Awnings, sheet metal—*mfg*
2431 Awnings, wood—*mfg*
5039 Awnings—wholesale
3423 Axes—*mfg*
3714 Axle housings and shafts, motor vehicle—*mfg*
7539 Axle straightening, automotive
3714 Axles, motor vehicle—*mfg*
3462 Axles, railroad: forged—not made in rolling mills—*mfg*
3312 Axles, rolled or forged: made in steel works or rolling mills—*mfg*
2273 Axminster carpets—*mfg*
2892 Azides (explosives)—*mfg*
2865 Azine dyes—*mfg*
2865 Azo dyes—*mfg*
2865 Azobenzene—*mfg*
2865 Azoic dyes—*mfg*

B

3341 Babbitt metal smelting and refining, secondary—*mfg*
3339 Babbitt metal, primary—*mfg*
5999 Baby carriages—retail
2032 Baby foods (including meats), canned—*mfg*
2023 Baby formula: fresh, processed, and bottled—*mfg*
5137 Baby goods—wholesale
3069 Baby pants, vulcanized rubber and rubberized fabric—mitse—*mfg*
2844 Baby powder—*mfg*
3596 Baby scales—*mfg*

8811 Babysitting (private households employing babysitters in the home)
7299 Babysitting bureaus
3531 Backfillers, self-propelled—*mfg*
3432 Backflow preventors—*mfg*
3531 Backhoes—*mfg*
5941 Backpacking, hiking, and mountaineering equipment—retail
2514 Backs for metal household furniture—*mfg*
2013 Bacon, slab and sliced—mfpm—*mfg*
2011 Bacon, slab and sliced—mitse—*mfg*
2836 Bacterial vaccines—*mfg*
2836 Bacterins, except in vitro and in vivo—*mfg*
8071 Bacteriological laboratories (not manufacturing)
2836 Bacteriological media, except in vitro and in vivo—*mfg*
3999 Badges for policemen and firemen—metal—*mfg*
2399 Badges, made from fabric—*mfg*
3949 Badminton equipment—*mfg*
3443 Baffles—*mfg*
3554 Bag and envelope making machinery (paper machinery)—*mfg*
3111 Bag leather—*mfg*
3483 Bag loading plants, ammunition—*mfg*
3565 Bag opening, filling and closing machines—*mfg*
2621 Bag paper—mitse—*mfg*
5093 Bag reclaiming—wholesale
3559 Bag sewing and closing machines (industrial sewing machines)—*mfg*
3949 Bagatelle tables—*mfg*
5461 Bagel stores—retail
2051 Bagels—*mfg*
4212 Baggage transfer
5149 Bagging of tea
2299 Bagging, jute: made in jute weaving mills—*mfg*
3161 Bags (luggage), regardless of material—*mfg*
2259 Bags and bagging—mitse—*mfg*
2393 Bags and containers, textile: except sleeping bags—insulated or not—mfpm—*mfg*
2392 Bags, blanket: plastics—*mfg*
3199 Bags, feed: for horses—*mfg*
2392 Bags, garment storage: except paper or plastics film—*mfg*
3949 Bags, golf—*mfg*
2392 Bags, laundry—mfpm—*mfg*
5113 Bags, paper and disposable plastics—wholesale
2674 Bags, paper: uncoated—mfpm—*mfg*
2759 Bags, plastics: printed only, except lithographed or gravure (bags not made in printing plants)—*mfg*

3949 Bags, rosin—*mfg*
3069 Bags, rubber or rubberized fabric—*mfg*
2399 Bags, sleeping—*mfg*
3949 Bags, striking (punching)—*mfg*
2393 Bags, textile: including canvas—except laundry, garment, and sleeping—mfpm—*mfg*
5199 Bags, textile—wholesale
1389 Bailing wells on a contract basis
3443 Bails, ladle—*mfg*
5941 Bait and tackle shops—retail
5091 Bait, artificial—wholesale
3949 Bait, fishing: artificial—*mfg*
2032 Baked beans without meat: canned—*mfg*
5461 Bakeries with baking on the premises—retail
5461 Bakeries without baking on the premises—retail
5461 Bakeries—retail
2026 Bakers' cheese—*mfg*
2087 Bakers' colors, except synthetic—*mfg*
2499 Bakers' equipment, wood—*mfg*
1629 Bakers' oven construction—general contractors
2326 Bakers' service apparel, washable—*mfg*
5963 Bakery goods, purchased: house-to-house—retail
3556 Bakery machinery—*mfg*
5461 Bakery products produced primarily for sale on the premises—retail
2052 Bakery products, dry: e.g., biscuits, crackers, pretzels—*mfg*
2051 Bakery products, fresh: bread, cakes, doughnuts, and pastries—*mfg*
2053 Bakery products, frozen: except bread and bread-type rolls—*mfg*
5142 Bakery products, frozen—wholesale
2051 Bakery products, partially cooked: except frozen—*mfg*
5149 Bakery products—wholesale
2079 Baking and frying fats (shortening)—*mfg*
2066 Baking chocolate—*mfg*
2851 Baking japans—*mfg*
2099 Baking powder—*mfg*
3596 Balances, except laboratory—*mfg*
5046 Balances, except laboratory—wholesale
3821 Balances, laboratory—*mfg*
3559 Balancing equipment, automotive wheel—*mfg*
3446 Balconies, metal—*mfg*
2261 Bale dyeing of cotton broadwoven products—*mfg*
2262 Bale dyeing of manmade fiber and silk broadwoven fabrics—*mfg*
3523 Bale throwers—*mfg*
3496 Bale ties, made from purchased wire—*mfg*

1479	Barium ore mining
2816	Barium sulfate, precipitated (blanc fixe)—*mfg*
3295	Barium, ground or otherwise treated—*mfg*
2211	Bark cloth, cotton—*mfg*
0831	Barks, gathering of
0119	Barley farms
5153	Barley—wholesale
2258	Barmen laces—*mfg*
3523	Barn cleaners—*mfg*
3523	Barn stanchions and standards—*mfg*
3829	Barographs—*mfg*
3829	Barometers, mercury and aneroid types—*mfg*
3443	Barometric condensers—*mfg*
2429	Barrel heading and staves, sawed or split—*mfg*
3484	Barrels, gun: 30 mm. (or 1.18 inch) or less—*mfg*
3489	Barrels, gun: more than 30 mm. (or more than 1.18 inch)—*mfg*
5085	Barrels, new and reconditioned—wholesale
3412	Barrels, shipping: steel and other metal—*mfg*
2449	Barrels, wood: coopered—*mfg*
3499	Barricades, metal—*mfg*
5813	Bars (alcoholic beverage drinking places)
8641	Bars and restaurants owned and operated for members of organizations only
3354	Bars, aluminum: extruded—*mfg*
3355	Bars, aluminum: rolled—*mfg*
2064	Bars, candy: including chocolate covered bars—*mfg*
2066	Bars, candy: solid chocolate—*mfg*
3449	Bars, concrete reinforcing: fabricated steel—*mfg*
5051	Bars, concrete reinforcing—wholesale
3351	Bars, copper and copper alloy—*mfg*
3312	Bars, iron: made in steel works or rolling mills—*mfg*
5051	Bars, metal—wholesale
3423	Bars, prying (handtools)—*mfg*
3331	Bars, refinery: primary copper—*mfg*
3316	Bars, steel: cold-rolled—not made in hot-rolling mills—*mfg*
3312	Bars, steel: made in steel works or hot-rolling mills—*mfg*
3356	Bars: lead, magnesium, nickel, tin, titanium, zinc, and their alloys—*mfg*
7389	Bartering services for businesses
7299	Bartering services for individuals
3229	Barware, glass—*mfg*
2816	Barytes pigments—*mfg*
1429	Basalt, crushed and broken—quarrying
1411	Basalt, dimension—quarrying
8744	Base maintenance (providing personnel on continuing basis)
2353	Baseball caps, except plastics—*mfg*
7997	Baseball clubs, except professional and semiprofessional
7941	Baseball clubs, professional or semiprofessional
3949	Baseball equipment and supplies, except uniforms and footwear—*mfg*
7999	Baseball instruction schools
2329	Baseball uniforms: men's and boys'—*mfg*
2431	Baseboards, floor: wood—*mfg*
3442	Baseboards, metal—*mfg*
3949	Bases, baseball—*mfg*
2844	Bases, perfume: blending and compounding—*mfg*
2211	Basket weave fabrics, cotton—*mfg*
7941	Basketball clubs, professional or semiprofessional
7999	Basketball instruction schools
2329	Basketball uniforms: men's and boys'—*mfg*
3949	Basketballs and basketball equipment and supplies, except uniforms and footwear—*mfg*
2499	Baskets, except fruit, vegetable, fish, and bait: (e.g., rattan, reed, straw)—*mfg*
3949	Baskets, fish and bait—*mfg*
2449	Baskets, fruit and vegetable: e.g., till, berry, climax, round stave—*mfg*
3496	Baskets, made from purchased wire—*mfg*
3315	Baskets, steel: made in wiredrawing plants—*mfg*
3944	Baskets, toy—*mfg*
5199	Baskets: reed, rattan, willow, and wood—wholesale
2519	Bassinets, reed and rattan—*mfg*
3931	Bassoons—*mfg*
1099	Bastnasite ore mining
3531	Batching plants, bituminous—*mfg*
3531	Batching plants, for aggregate concrete and bulk cement—*mfg*
7999	Bath houses, independently operated
2392	Bath mitts (washcloths)—*mfg*
2844	Bath salts—*mfg*
3069	Bath sprays, rubber—*mfg*
1799	Bathtub refinishing—contractors
7997	Bathing beaches, membership
7999	Bathing beaches, public
3069	Bathing caps and suits, rubber—mitse—*mfg*
5699	Bathing suit stores—retail
2369	Bathing suits: girls', children's, and infants'—mfpm—*mfg*
2329	Bathing suits: men's and boys'—mfpm—*mfg*

3999	Beauty shop equipment—*mfg*
7231	Beauty shops or salons
7011	Bed and breakfast inns
2258	Bed sets, lace—*mfg*
2211	Bed tickings, cotton—*mfg*
3634	Bedcoverings, electric—*mfg*
5719	Bedding (sheets, blankets, spreads, and pillows)—retail
0181	Bedding plants, growing of
2341	Bedjackets: women's, misses', and juniors'—mfpm—*mfg*
5712	Beds and springs—retail
2599	Beds, hospital—*mfg*
5047	Beds, hospital—wholesale
2514	Beds, including folding and cabinet beds: household—metal—*mfg*
2511	Beds, including folding and cabinet beds: household—wood—*mfg*
2515	Beds, sleep-system ensembles: flotation and adjustable—*mfg*
2515	Beds, sofa and chair: on frames of any material—*mfg*
2211	Bedsheeting, cotton—mitse—*mfg*
2511	Bedside stands, wood—*mfg*
2392	Bedspreads and bed sets—mfpm—*mfg*
2211	Bedspreads, cotton: made in weaving mills—*mfg*
2258	Bedspreads, lace: made on lace machines—*mfg*
2221	Bedspreads, silk and manmade fiber—mitse—*mfg*
2259	Bedspreads—mitse—*mfg*
5023	Bedspreads—wholesale
2514	Bedspring frames, metal—*mfg*
2511	Bedspring frames, wood—*mfg*
2515	Bedsprings, assembled—*mfg*
5021	Bedsprings—wholesale
0279	Bee farms
0212	Beef cattle farms, except feedlots
0211	Beef cattle feedlots
2013	Beef stew—*mfg*
2013	Beef—mfpm—*mfg*
2011	Beef—mitse—*mfg*
3312	Beehive coke oven products—*mfg*
3999	Beekeeping supplies, except wood—*mfg*
2499	Beekeeping supplies, wood—*mfg*
5191	Beekeeping supplies—wholesale
4812	Beeper (radio pager) communications services
2082	Beer (alcoholic beverage)—*mfg*
5181	Beer and other fermented malt liquors—wholesale
3411	Beer cans, metal—*mfg*
3585	Beer dispensing equipment—*mfg*
5813	Beer gardens (drinking places)
5813	Beer parlors (tap rooms)
7699	Beer pump coil cleaning and repair service
5813	Beer taverns
2086	Beer, birch and root: bottled or canned—*mfg*
5921	Beer, packaged—retail
5813	Beer, wine, and liquors: sale for on-premise consumption
2842	Beeswax, processing of—*mfg*
0161	Beet farms, except sugar beet
0133	Beet farms, sugar
2063	Beet pulp, dried—*mfg*
2063	Beet sugar, made from sugar beets—*mfg*
2834	Belladonna pharmaceutical preparations—*mfg*
3429	Bellows, hand—*mfg*
3599	Bellows, industrial: metal—*mfg*
3931	Bells (musical instruments)—*mfg*
3699	Bells, electric—*mfg*
3944	Bells, toy—*mfg*
5131	Belt and buckle assembly kits—wholesale
3535	Belt conveyor systems for general industrial use—*mfg*
2842	Belt dressing—*mfg*
3199	Belt laces, leather—*mfg*
4013	Belt line railroads
2296	Belting (industrial) reinforcement, cord and fabric—*mfg*
3111	Belting butts, curried or rough—*mfg*
3111	Belting leather—*mfg*
3568	Belting, chain—*mfg*
2399	Belting, fabric—mfpm—*mfg*
5085	Belting, hose and packing: industrial—wholesale
3052	Belting, rubber: e.g., conveyor, elevator, transmission—*mfg*
2241	Beltings, woven or braided—*mfg*
3199	Belts and belting for machinery, leather—*mfg*
3949	Belts, ammunition (sporting goods: of all materials)—*mfg*
5699	Belts, apparel: custom—retail
2387	Belts, apparel: made of any material—*mfg*
3949	Belts, cartridge: sporting type—*mfg*
3496	Belts, conveyor: made from purchased wire—*mfg*
3496	Belts, drying: made from purchased wire—*mfg*
3484	Belts, machine gun, metallic: 30 mm. (or 1.18 inch) or less—*mfg*
2399	Belts, money: made of any material—*mfg*
3199	Belts, safety: leather—*mfg*
3842	Belts: sanitary, surgical, and corrective—*mfg*
2531	Benches for public buildings—*mfg*
3281	Benches, cut stone—*mfg*
3821	Benches, laboratory—*mfg*

2522	Benches, office: except wood—*mfg*
2521	Benches, office: wood—*mfg*
2599	Benches, work: industrial—*mfg*
3542	Bending and forming machines—*mfg*
3498	Bends, pipe: fabricated from purchased metal pipe—*mfg*
6311	Benevolent insurance associations
1459	Bentonite mining
2499	Bentwood (steam bent) products, except furniture—*mfg*
2865	Benzaldehyde—*mfg*
2865	Benzene hexachloride (BHC)—*mfg*
2865	Benzene, made in chemical plants—*mfg*
2911	Benzene, produced in petroleum refineries—*mfg*
2865	Benzoic acid—*mfg*
0782	Bermuda sprigging services
0722	Berries, machine harvesting of
3523	Berry and grain separators, farm—*mfg*
2449	Berry crates, wood: wirebound—*mfg*
2449	Berry cups, veneer and splint—*mfg*
0171	Berry farms
1099	Beryl mining
3264	Beryllia porcelain insulators—*mfg*
3369	Beryllium castings, except die-castings—*mfg*
3364	Beryllium die-castings—*mfg*
3339	Beryllium metal—*mfg*
1099	Beryllium ore mining
2819	Beryllium oxide—*mfg*
3844	Beta-ray irradiation equipment—*mfg*
3699	Betatrons—*mfg*
8611	Better business bureaus
7999	Betting information services
2789	Beveling of cards—*mfg*
2085	Beverage alcohol, ethyl and grain—*mfg*
2087	Beverage bases—*mfg*
5149	Beverage concentrates—wholesale
5078	Beverage coolers—wholesale
2087	Beverage syrups—*mfg*
2396	Bias bindings—mfpm—*mfg*
8299	Bible schools, not operated by churches
5963	Bibles, house-to-house selling—retail
3069	Bibs, vulcanized rubber and rubberized fabric—mitse—*mfg*
2385	Bibs, waterproof—mfpm—*mfg*
2819	Bichromates and chromates—*mfg*
5941	Bicycle and bicycle parts dealers, except motorized—retail
3647	Bicycle lamps—*mfg*
7999	Bicycle rental
7699	Bicycle repair shops
5091	Bicycle tires and tubes—wholesale
3751	Bicycles and parts—*mfg*
5571	Bicycles, motorized—retail
5091	Bicycles—wholesale

3261	Bidets, vitreous china—*mfg*
7312	Bill posting, advertising
7312	Billboard advertising
3547	Billet mills—*mfg*
3312	Billets, steel—*mfg*
3089	Billfold inserts, plastics—*mfg*
3172	Billfolds, regardless of material—*mfg*
2752	Billheads, lithographed—*mfg*
3949	Billiard and pool balls, cues, cue tips, and tables—*mfg*
3949	Billiard chalk—*mfg*
2231	Billiard cloths—mitse—*mfg*
7999	Billiard parlors
5091	Billiards equipment and supplies—wholesale
3578	Billing machines—*mfg*
2298	Binder and baler twine—*mfg*
2899	Binders (chemical foundry supplies)—*mfg*
2631	Binders' board—mitse—*mfg*
2782	Binders, looseleaf—*mfg*
3579	Binding machines, plastics and adhesive: for store or office use—*mfg*
2789	Binding only: books, pamphlets, magazines, etc.—*mfg*
5131	Binding, textile—wholesale
2396	Bindings, bias—mfpm—*mfg*
2396	Bindings, cap and hat—mfpm—*mfg*
2241	Bindings, textile—mitse—*mfg*
3944	Bingo boards (games)—*mfg*
7999	Bingo parlors
3161	Binocular cases—*mfg*
3827	Binoculars—*mfg*
7699	Binoculars and other optical goods repair
5999	Binoculars—retail
3443	Bins, prefabricated metal plate—*mfg*
3444	Bins, prefabricated: sheet metal—*mfg*
8093	Biofeedback centers
2836	Biological and allied products: antitoxins, bacterins, vaccines, viruses, except in vitro and in vivo—*mfg*
8071	Biological laboratories (not manufacturing)
8731	Biological research, commercial
8733	Biological research, noncommercial
2865	Biological stains—*mfg*
5122	Biologicals and allied products—wholesale
3841	Biopsy instruments and equipment—*mfg*
2086	Birch beer, bottled or canned—*mfg*
3496	Bird cages, made from purchased wire—*mfg*
2048	Bird food, prepared—*mfg*
7342	Bird proofing
2211	Bird's-eye diaper cloth, cotton—*mfg*
7299	Birth certificate agencies
8093	Birth control clinics (family planning)
2771	Birthday cards, except hand painted—*mfg*

3556 Biscuit cutters (machines)—*mfg*
2041 Biscuit dough, canned—mitse—*mfg*
2045 Biscuit mixes and doughs—mfpm—*mfg*
2051 Biscuits, baked: baking powder and raised—*mfg*
2052 Biscuits, baked: dry, except baking powder and raised—*mfg*
3339 Bismuth refining, primary—*mfg*
3423 Bits (edge tools for woodworking)—*mfg*
3545 Bits for use on lathes, planers, shapers, etc.—*mfg*
3532 Bits, rock: except oil and gas field tools—*mfg*
3533 Bits, rock: oil and gas field tools—*mfg*
2087 Bitters (flavoring concentrates)—*mfg*
1499 Bitumens (native) mining
3531 Bituminous batching plants—*mfg*
1221 Bituminous coal cleaning plants
1221 Bituminous coal crushing
1241 Bituminous coal mining services on a contract basis
1221 Bituminous coal screening plants
1241 Bituminous coal stripping service: on a contract basis
1222 Bituminous coal stripping: except on a contract, fee, or other basis
1221 Bituminous coal washeries
1499 Bituminous limestone quarrying
1241 Bituminous or lignite auger mining service: on a contract basis
2851 Bituminous paints—*mfg*
5082 Bituminous processing equipment—wholesale
1499 Bituminous sandstone quarrying
2816 Black pigments, except carbon black—*mfg*
5051 Black plate, iron and steel—wholesale
0171 Blackberry farms
3281 Blackboards, slate—*mfg*
2531 Blackboards, wood—*mfg*
2842 Blackings—*mfg*
3312 Blackplate—*mfg*
7699 Blacksmith shops
3199 Blacksmiths' aprons, leather—*mfg*
2061 Blackstrap molasses—*mfg*
1771 Blacktop work: private driveways and private parking areas—contractors
3531 Blades for graders, scrapers, dozers, and snowplows—*mfg*
3728 Blades, aircraft propeller: metal or wood—*mfg*
3421 Blades, knife and razor—*mfg*
3425 Blades, saw: for hand or power saws—*mfg*
2816 Blanc fixe (barium sulfate, precipitated)—*mfg*
3482 Blank cartridges, 30 mm. (or 1.18 inch) or less—*mfg*

2782 Blankbook making—*mfg*
5112 Blankbooks—wholesale
2392 Blanket bags, plastic—*mfg*
2221 Blanketings, manmade fiber—*mfg*
2211 Blankets and blanketings, cotton—mitse—*mfg*
2231 Blankets and blanketings, wool and similar animal fibers—mitse—*mfg*
3292 Blankets, asbestos—*mfg*
3634 Blankets, electric—*mfg*
2399 Blankets, horse—mfpm—*mfg*
3292 Blankets, insulating for aircraft: asbestos—*mfg*
2679 Blankets, insulating: paper—mfpm—*mfg*
3069 Blankets, printers': rubber—*mfg*
2392 Blankets—mfpm—*mfg*
5023 Blankets—wholesale
3229 Blanks for electric light bulbs, glass—*mfg*
3965 Blanks, button—*mfg*
3545 Blanks, cutting tool—*mfg*
3545 Blanks, tips and inserts: cutting tools—*mfg*
5084 Blanks, tips and inserts—wholesale
2426 Blanks, wood: for bowling pins, handles, and textile machinery accessories—*mfg*
3569 Blast cleaning equipment, dustless: except metalworking—*mfg*
3312 Blast furnace products—*mfg*
3295 Blast furnace slag—*mfg*
1446 Blast sand mining
2298 Blasting mats, rope—*mfg*
2892 Blasting powder and blasting caps—*mfg*
1629 Blasting, except building demolition—contractors
2819 Bleach (calcium hypochlorite), industrial—*mfg*
2819 Bleach (sodium hypochlorite), industrial—*mfg*
2531 Bleacher seating, portable—*mfg*
2844 Bleaches, hair—*mfg*
2842 Bleaches, household: liquid or dry—*mfg*
2819 Bleaches, industrial—*mfg*
3999 Bleaching and dyeing of sponges—*mfg*
2261 Bleaching cotton broadwoven fabrics—*mfg*
3552 Bleaching machinery, textile—*mfg*
2262 Bleaching manmade fiber and silk broadwoven fabrics—*mfg*
2819 Bleaching powder, industrial—*mfg*
2269 Bleaching raw stock, yarn, and narrow fabrics: except knit and wool—*mfg*
2231 Bleaching yarn and fabrics, wool and similar animal fibers: except knit—*mfg*
2261 Bleaching, kier: continuous machine—*mfg*
3825 Bleed control cabinets (engine testers)—*mfg*
1031 Blende (zinc) mining

3732 Boats, fiberglass: building and repairing—*mfg*
3089 Boats, nonrigid: plastics—*mfg*
7999 Boats, party fishing: operation of
5091 Boats, pleasure: canoes, motorboats, and sailboats—wholesale
3732 Boats, rigid: plastics—*mfg*
3732 Boats: motorboats, sailboats, rowboats, and canoes—building and repairing—*mfg*
2426 Bobbin blocks and blanks, wood—*mfg*
2258 Bobbinet (lace goods)—*mfg*
3552 Bobbins for textile machinery—*mfg*
2655 Bobbins, fiber—mfpm—*mfg*
3949 Bobsleds—*mfg*
7212 Bobtailers, laundry and drycleaning
3728 Bodies, aircraft: not complete aircraft—*mfg*
5012 Bodies, automotive—wholesale
3713 Bodies, dump—*mfg*
3711 Bodies, passenger automobile—*mfg*
3713 Bodies, truck (motor vehicle)—*mfg*
3465 Body parts, automotive: stamped—*mfg*
2844 Body powder—*mfg*
7532 Body repair, automotive
7532 Body shops, automotive
2253 Body stockings—mitse—*mfg*
3489 Bofors guns—*mfg*
1799 Boiler and pipe, insulation of—contractors
3443 Boiler casings: metal plate—*mfg*
7699 Boiler cleaning
2899 Boiler compounds, antiscaling—*mfg*
3823 Boiler controls: industrial, power, and marine type—*mfg*
3494 Boiler couplings and drains, metal—*mfg*
3292 Boiler covering (heat insulating material), except felt—*mfg*
2299 Boiler covering, felt—*mfg*
1711 Boiler erection and installation—contractors
3491 Boiler gauge cocks—*mfg*
6331 Boiler insurance
7699 Boiler repair shops, except manufacturing
3443 Boiler shop products: industrial boilers, smokestacks, and steel tanks—*mfg*
3599 Boiler tube cleaners—*mfg*
3317 Boiler tubes, wrought—mfpm—*mfg*
3433 Boilers, low-pressure heating: steam or hot water—*mfg*
5074 Boilers, power: industrial—wholesale
5074 Boilers, steam and hot water heating—wholesale
3443 Boilers: industrial, power, and marine—*mfg*
0161 Bok choy farms
2013 Bologna—mfpm—*mfg*

3261 Bolt caps, vitreous china and earthenware—*mfg*
3452 Bolts, metal—*mfg*
5072 Bolts, nuts, rivets, and screws—wholesale
3089 Bolts, plastics—*mfg*
2411 Bolts, wood: e.g., handle, heading, shingle, stave—*mfg*
3537 Bomb lifts—*mfg*
3483 Bomb loading and assembling plants—*mfg*
3728 Bomb racks, aircraft—*mfg*
3537 Bomb trucks—*mfg*
2211 Bombazine, cotton—*mfg*
3483 Bombcluster adapters—*mfg*
3483 Bombs and parts—*mfg*
2899 Bombs, flashlight—*mfg*
6162 Bond and mortgage companies
6211 Bond dealers and brokers
2621 Bond paper—mitse—*mfg*
2084 Bonded wine cellars, engaged in blending wines—*mfg*
2297 Bonded-fiber fabrics, except felt—*mfg*
3479 Bonderizing of metal and metal products, for the trade—*mfg*
6289 Bondholders protective committees
6351 Bonding for guaranteeing job completion
6351 Bonding of employees
6351 Bonding, fidelity or surety
7389 Bondspersons
2816 Bone black—*mfg*
3262 Bone china—*mfg*
3841 Bone drills—*mfg*
3999 Bone novelties—*mfg*
3841 Bone plates and screws—*mfg*
3841 Bone rongeurs—*mfg*
2211 Book cloth—mitse—*mfg*
2731 Book club publishing and printing, or publishing only—*mfg*
5961 Book clubs, not publishing
3499 Book ends, metal—*mfg*
2789 Book gilding, bronzing, edging, deckling, embossing, and gold stamping—*mfg*
3999 Book matches—*mfg*
2672 Book paper, coated—mfpm—*mfg*
2621 Book paper—mitse—*mfg*
5942 Book stores selling new books and magazines—retail
5932 Book stores, secondhand—retail
3251 Book tile, clay—*mfg*
3111 Bookbinders' leather—*mfg*
3555 Bookbinders' machines—*mfg*
2789 Bookbinding: edition, job, library, and trade—*mfg*
2514 Bookcases, household: metal—*mfg*
2511 Bookcases, household: wood—*mfg*
2522 Bookcases, office: except wood—*mfg*
2521 Bookcases, office: wood—*mfg*

7999 Bookies
7829 Booking agencies, motion picture
7922 Booking agencies, theatrical: except motion picture
8721 Bookkeeping and billing service
3578 Bookkeeping machines—*mfg*
7999 Bookmakers, race
5961 Books, mail-order—retail
2678 Books, memorandum: except printed—mfpm—*mfg*
2732 Books, music: printing or printing and binding, not publishing—*mfg*
2731 Books, music: publishing and printing, or publishing only—*mfg*
2732 Books: printing or printing and binding, not publishing—*mfg*
2731 Books: publishing and printing, or publishing only—*mfg*
5192 Books—wholesale
3949 Boomerangs—*mfg*
8641 Booster clubs
3483 Boosters and bursters—*mfg*
3612 Boosters, feeder voltage (electric transformers)—*mfg*
3131 Boot and shoe cut stock and findings—*mfg*
5087 Boot and shoe cut stock and findings—wholesale
2499 Boot and shoe lasts, regardless of material—*mfg*
3559 Boot making and repairing machinery—*mfg*
7251 Bootblack parlors
3444 Booths, spray: prefabricated sheet metal—*mfg*
2542 Booths, telephone: except wood—*mfg*
2541 Booths, telephone: wood—*mfg*
3143 Boots, dress and casual: men's—*mfg*
3199 Boots, horse—*mfg*
3021 Boots, plastics—*mfg*
3021 Boots, rubber or rubber soled fabric—*mfg*
3144 Boots: women's canvas and leather—except athletic—*mfg*
1474 Borate compounds mining
2819 Borax (sodium tetraborate)—*mfg*
1474 Borax mining
1474 Borax, crude: ground and pulverized
2879 Bordeaux mixture—*mfg*
3827 Borescopes—*mfg*
2819 Boric acid—*mfg*
1799 Boring for building construction—contractors
3545 Boring machine attachments (machine tool accessories)—*mfg*
3541 Boring machine tools, metalworking—*mfg*
3541 Boring mills—*mfg*

1081 Boring test holes for metal mining: on a contract basis
1481 Boring test holes for nonmetallic minerals, except fuels: on a contract basis
3541 Boring, drilling, and milling machine combinations—*mfg*
3291 Boron carbide abrasives—*mfg*
2819 Boron compounds, not produced at mines—*mfg*
1474 Boron mineral mining
2819 Borosilicate—*mfg*
3291 Bort, crushing—*mfg*
5085 Bort—wholesale
2834 Botanical extracts: powdered, pilular, solid, and fluid, except diagnostics—*mfg*
8422 Botanical gardens
2833 Botanical products, medicinal: ground, graded, and milled—*mfg*
2631 Bottle cap board—mitse—*mfg*
2675 Bottle caps and tops, die-cut from purchased paper or paperboard—*mfg*
3466 Bottle caps and tops, stamped metal—*mfg*
3089 Bottle caps, molded plastics—*mfg*
5813 Bottle clubs (drinking places)
2499 Bottle corks—*mfg*
2499 Bottle covers: willow, rattan, and reed—*mfg*
7389 Bottle exchanges
3496 Bottle openers, made from purchased wire—*mfg*
3469 Bottle openers, stamped metal—*mfg*
3634 Bottle warmers, household: electric—*mfg*
3089 Bottle warmers, plastics—*mfg*
5984 Bottled gas—retail
5085 Bottlers' supplies: caps, bottles, etc.—wholesale
3221 Bottles for packing, bottling, and canning: glass—*mfg*
5085 Bottles, glass or plastics—wholesale
2655 Bottles, paper fiber—mfpm—*mfg*
3085 Bottles, plastics—*mfg*
3069 Bottles, rubber—*mfg*
3429 Bottles, vacuum—*mfg*
5093 Bottles, waste—wholesale
3565 Bottling machinery: washing, sterilizing, filling, capping, and labeling—*mfg*
5149 Bottling mineral or spring water—wholesale
5182 Bottling wines and liquors—wholesale
3645 Boudoir lamps—*mfg*
2099 Bouillon cubes—*mfg*
1429 Boulder, crushed and broken—quarrying
2999 Boulets (fuel bricks), made with petroleum binder—*mfg*
3999 Boutiquing: for the trade (decorating gift items)—*mfg*

2323 Bow ties: men's and boys'—mfpm—*mfg*
3089 Bowl covers, plastics—*mfg*
1799 Bowling alley installation and service—contractors
3949 Bowling alleys and accessories—*mfg*
2599 Bowling center furniture—*mfg*
7933 Bowling centers
5941 Bowling equipment and supplies—retail
5091 Bowling equipment—wholesale
7999 Bowling instruction
7997 Bowling leagues or teams, except professional and semiprofessional
2426 Bowling pin blanks—*mfg*
3949 Bowling pin machines, automatic—*mfg*
3949 Bowling pins—*mfg*
7699 Bowling pins, refinishing or repair
3229 Bowls, glass—*mfg*
2499 Bowls, wood: turned and shaped—*mfg*
3949 Bows, archery—*mfg*
3131 Bows, shoe—*mfg*
2441 Box cleats, wood—*mfg*
2421 Box lumber—*mfg*
5812 Box lunch stands
2099 Box lunches for sale off premises—*mfg*
3554 Box making machines for paper boxes—*mfg*
3553 Box making machines for wooden boxes—*mfg*
2441 Box shooks—*mfg*
5085 Box shooks—wholesale
2515 Box springs, assembled—*mfg*
3131 Box toes, leather (shoe cut stock)—*mfg*
2631 Boxboard—mitse—*mfg*
2011 Boxed beef—mitse—*mfg*
5063 Boxes and fittings, electrical—wholesale
3499 Boxes for packing and shipping, metal—*mfg*
3499 Boxes, ammunition: metal—*mfg*
3443 Boxes, annealing—*mfg*
3469 Boxes, cash and stamp: stamped metal—*mfg*
2441 Boxes, cigar: wood and part wood—*mfg*
3443 Boxes, condenser: metal plate—*mfg*
2653 Boxes, corrugated and solid fiber—mfpm—*mfg*
5085 Boxes, crates, etc., other than paper—wholesale
3644 Boxes, electric wiring: junction, outlet, switch, and fuse—*mfg*
2657 Boxes, folding paperboard—mfpm—*mfg*
3069 Boxes, hard rubber—*mfg*
3161 Boxes, hat: except paper or paperboard—*mfg*
3199 Boxes, leather—*mfg*
2652 Boxes, newsboard: metal edged—mfpm—*mfg*

5113 Boxes, paperboard and disposable plastics—wholesale
3089 Boxes, plastics—*mfg*
2652 Boxes, setup paperboard—mfpm—*mfg*
3952 Boxes, sketching and paint—*mfg*
2655 Boxes, vulcanized fiber—mfpm—*mfg*
5093 Boxes, waste—wholesale
2441 Boxes, wood: plain or fabric covered, nailed or lock corner—*mfg*
2449 Boxes, wood: wirebound—*mfg*
3949 Boxing equipment—*mfg*
7032 Boys' camps
2252 Boys' hosiery—*mfg*
8361 Boys' towns
2341 Bra-slips: women's and misses'—mfpm—*mfg*
3842 Braces, elastic—*mfg*
3842 Braces, orthopedic—*mfg*
0721 Bracing of orchard trees and vines
3299 Brackets, architectural: plaster—factory production only—*mfg*
3429 Brackets, iron and steel—*mfg*
2431 Brackets, wood—*mfg*
3399 Brads, nonferrous metal (including wire)—*mfg*
3315 Brads, steel: wire or cut—*mfg*
5072 Brads—wholesale
2269 Braided goods, except wool: bleaching, dyeing, printing, and other finishing—*mfg*
3552 Braiding machines, textile—*mfg*
3999 Braids, puffs, switches, wigs, etc.-made of hair or other fiber—*mfg*
2241 Braids, textile—*mfg*
2241 Braids, tubular nylon and plastics—*mfg*
3569 Brake burnishing and washing machines—*mfg*
3714 Brake drums—*mfg*
2992 Brake fluid, hydraulic—mfpm—*mfg*
3292 Brake lining, asbestos—*mfg*
3069 Brake lining, rubber—*mfg*
7539 Brake linings, sale and installation
3292 Brake pads, asbestos—*mfg*
7539 Brake repairing, automotive
3321 Brake shoes, railroad: cast iron—*mfg*
3714 Brakes and brake parts, motor vehicle—*mfg*
3728 Brakes, aircraft—*mfg*
3751 Brakes, bicycle: friction clutch and other—*mfg*
3625 Brakes, electromagnetic—*mfg*
3542 Brakes, metal forming—*mfg*
3743 Brakes, railway: air and vacuum—*mfg*
2041 Bran and middlings, except rice—*mfg*
2044 Bran, rice—*mfg*
6081 Branches of foreign banks

2341 Briefs: women's, misses', children's, and infants'—mfpm—*mfg*
1479 Brimstone mining
2819 Brine—*mfg*
2035 Brining of fruits and vegetables—*mfg*
2999 Briquettes (fuel bricks): made with petroleum binder—*mfg*
2499 Briquettes, sawdust or bagasse: nonpetroleum binder—*mfg*
3999 Bristles, dressing of—*mfg*
5159 Bristles—wholesale
2631 Bristols, bogus—mitse—*mfg*
2621 Bristols, except bogus—mitse—*mfg*
3356 Britannia metal, rolling and drawing—*mfg*
3545 Broaches (machine tool accessories)—*mfg*
3843 Broaches, dental—*mfg*
5084 Broaches—wholesale
3541 Broaching machines—*mfg*
3663 Broadcast equipment (including studio), radio and television—*mfg*
4832 Broadcasting stations, radio
4833 Broadcasting stations, television
2211 Broadcloth, cotton—*mfg*
2211 Broadwoven fabrics, cotton—*mfg*
2221 Broadwoven fabrics, silk and manmade fiber—*mfg*
2299 Broadwoven fabrics: linen, jute, hemp, and ramie—*mfg*
5131 Broadwoven fabrics—wholesale
2211 Brocade, cotton—*mfg*
2211 Brocatelle, cotton—*mfg*
0161 Broccoli farms
0251 Broiler chickens, raising of
3634 Broilers, electric—*mfg*
6531 Brokers of manufactured homes, on site
7389 Brokers, business (buying and selling business enterprises)
6221 Brokers, commodity contract
4731 Brokers, custom house
6163 Brokers, farm or business loan
6411 Brokers, insurance
6531 Brokers, real estate
6211 Brokers, security
4731 Brokers, shipping
4731 Brokers, transportation
2819 Bromine, elemental—*mfg*
2869 Bromochloromethane—*mfg*
3845 Bronchoscopes, electromedical—*mfg*
3841 Bronchoscopes, except electromedical—*mfg*
3364 Bronze die castings—*mfg*
3366 Bronze foundries—*mfg*
2893 Bronze ink—*mfg*
3351 Bronze rolling and drawing—*mfg*

3341 Bronze smelting and refining, secondary—*mfg*
3952 Bronze, artists': mixtures, powders, paints, etc.—*mfg*
3555 Bronzing and dusting machines for the printing trade—*mfg*
7389 Bronzing baby shoes
2789 Bronzing books, cards, or paper—*mfg*
3523 Brooders—*mfg*
3559 Broom making machinery—*mfg*
5199 Broom, mop, and paint handles—wholesale
0139 Broomcorn farms
5159 Broomcorn—wholesale
3991 Brooms, hand and machine: bamboo, wire, fiber, splint, or other material—*mfg*
3711 Brooms, powered (motor vehicles)—*mfg*
5719 Brooms—retail
2032 Broth, except seafood: canned—*mfg*
2051 Brown bread, Boston and other: canned—*mfg*
1221 Brown coal mining
1011 Brown ore mining
3861 Brownprint paper and cloth, sensitized—*mfg*
3861 Brownprint reproduction machines and equipment—*mfg*
5044 Brownprinting equipment—wholesale
2833 Brucine and derivatives—*mfg*
1459 Brucite mining
3624 Brush blocks, carbon or molded graphite—*mfg*
2426 Brush blocks, wood: turned and shaped—*mfg*
1629 Brush clearing or cutting—contractors
3089 Brush handles, plastics—*mfg*
3624 Brushes and brush stock contacts: carbon and graphite—electric—*mfg*
3991 Brushes for vacuum cleaners, carpet sweepers, and other rotary machines—*mfg*
3952 Brushes, air: artists'—*mfg*
5963 Brushes, house-to-house or party plan selling—retail
3991 Brushes, household and industrial—*mfg*
3069 Brushes, rubber—*mfg*
5719 Brushes—retail
3541 Brushing machines (metalworking machinery)—*mfg*
3089 Bubble formed packaging, plastics—*mfg*
3443 Bubble towers—*mfg*
3432 Bubblers, drinking fountain—*mfg*
3531 Bucket and scarifier teeth—*mfg*
3535 Bucket type conveyor systems for general industrial use—*mfg*

3535 Buckets, elevator or conveyor for general industrial use—*mfg*
3531 Buckets, excavating: e.g., clamshell, concrete, dragline, drag scraper, shovel—*mfg*
3949 Buckets, fish and bait—*mfg*
3089 Buckets, plastics—*mfg*
2449 Buckets, wood: coopered—*mfg*
3965 Buckle blanks and molds—*mfg*
3965 Buckles and buckle parts, except shoe buckles—*mfg*
3131 Buckles, shoe—*mfg*
2295 Buckram: varnished, waxed, and impregnated—*mfg*
2211 Buckram—mitse—*mfg*
0119 Buckwheat farms
2041 Buckwheat flour—*mfg*
9311 Budget agencies—government
5812 Buffets (eating places)
2511 Buffets (furniture)—*mfg*
3541 Buffing and polishing machines (machine tools)—*mfg*
3291 Buffing and polishing wheels, abrasive and nonabrasive—*mfg*
3546 Buffing machines, hand: electric—*mfg*
3471 Buffing, for the trade—*mfg*
3111 Buffings, russet—*mfg*
3931 Bugles and parts (musical instruments)—*mfg*
3429 Builders' hardware, including locks and lock sets—*mfg*
5251 Builders' hardware—retail
5072 Builders' hardware—wholesale
1531 Builders, operative: on own account
1531 Builders, speculative
1541 Building alterations, industrial and warehouse—general contractors
1542 Building alterations, nonresidential: except industrial and warehouses—general contractors
1522 Building alterations, residential: except single-family—general contractors
1521 Building alterations, single-family—general contractors
3275 Building board, gypsum—*mfg*
7349 Building cleaning service, interior
1541 Building components manufacturing plant construction—general contractors
1541 Building construction, industrial and warehouse—general contractors
1542 Building construction, nonresidential: except industrial and warehouses—general contractors
1522 Building construction, residential: except single-family—general contractors

1521 Building construction, single-family—general contractors
1791 Building front installation, metal—contractors
3211 Building glass, flat—*mfg*
3274 Building lime—*mfg*
7349 Building maintenance, except repairs
5211 Building materials dealers—retail
3292 Building materials, asbestos: except asbestos paper—*mfg*
3272 Building materials, concrete: except block and brick—*mfg*
5039 Building materials, fiberglass—wholesale
5932 Building materials, used—retail
1389 Building oil and gas well foundations on a contract basis
2679 Building paper, laminated—mfpm—*mfg*
2621 Building paper: sheathing, insulation, saturating, and dry felts—mitse—*mfg*
1541 Building repairs, industrial—general contractors
1542 Building repairs, nonresidential—general contractors
1522 Building repairs, residential: except single-family—general contractors
1521 Building repairs, single family—general contractors
3822 Building services monitoring controls, automatic—*mfg*
9531 Building standards agencies—government
3272 Building stone, artificial: concrete—*mfg*
3281 Building stone, natural: cut—including combination with quarrying—*mfg*
5032 Building stone—wholesale
3251 Building tile, clay—*mfg*
6513 Buildings, apartment (five or more housing units): operators of
6514 Buildings, dwelling (four or fewer housing units): operators of
2451 Buildings, mobile: commercial use—*mfg*
6512 Buildings, nonresidential: operators of
2452 Buildings, prefabricated and portable: wood—*mfg*
3448 Buildings, prefabricated: metal—*mfg*
5211 Buildings, prefabricated—retail
3299 Built-up mica—*mfg*
3229 Bulbs for electric lights, without filaments or sockets—mitse—*mfg*
3069 Bulbs for medicine droppers, syringes, atomizers, and sprays: rubber—*mfg*
3641 Bulbs, electric light: complete—*mfg*
5191 Bulbs, flower and field—wholesale
0181 Bulbs, growing of
5261 Bulbs, seed and nursery stock—retail
7353 Bulldozer rental and leasing
3531 Bulldozers, construction—*mfg*

3542 Bulldozers, metalworking—*mfg*
3482 Bullet jackets and cores, 30 mm. (or 1.18 inch) or less—*mfg*
2499 Bulletin boards, wood and cork—*mfg*
3842 Bulletproof vests—*mfg*
1041 Bullion, gold: produced at mine, mill, or dredge site
5094 Bullion, precious metals—wholesale
1044 Bullion, silver: produced at mine or mill site
7532 Bump shops (automotive repair)
3714 Bumpers and bumperettes, motor vehicle—*mfg*
3462 Bumping posts, railroad: forged—not made in rolling mills—*mfg*
2499 Bungs, wood—*mfg*
2051 Buns, bread-type (e.g., hamburger, hot dog), including frozen—*mfg*
2051 Buns, sweet, except frozen—*mfg*
3821 Bunsen burners—*mfg*
2211 Bunting—mitse—*mfg*
2369 Buntings: infants'—mfpm—*mfg*
3823 Buoyancy instruments, industrial process type—*mfg*
3089 Buoys and floats, plastics—*mfg*
2499 Buoys, cork—*mfg*
3443 Buoys, metal—*mfg*
9221 Bureaus of criminal investigations—government
9651 Bureaus of standards—government
3669 Burglar alarm apparatus, electric—*mfg*
1731 Burglar alarm installation—contractors
7382 Burglar alarm monitoring and maintenance
6331 Burglary and theft insurance
3995 Burial cases, metal and wood—*mfg*
2389 Burial garments—mfpm—*mfg*
6311 Burial insurance societies
3272 Burial vaults, concrete and precast terrazzo—*mfg*
3995 Burial vaults, fiberglass—*mfg*
3281 Burial vaults, stone—*mfg*
2299 Burlap, jute—*mfg*
5199 Burlap—wholesale
7922 Burlesque companies
1459 Burley mining
2231 Burling and mending wool cloth for the trade—*mfg*
2411 Burls, wood—*mfg*
5074 Burners, fuel oil and distillate oil—wholesale
3433 Burners, gas: domestic—*mfg*
3433 Burners, oil: domestic and industrial—*mfg*
3398 Burning metal for the trade—*mfg*
3952 Burnishers and cushions, gilders'—*mfg*

3569 Burnishing and washing machines, brake—*mfg*
2842 Burnishing ink—*mfg*
3541 Burnishing machines (machine tools)—*mfg*
3199 Burnt leather goods for the trade—*mfg*
2087 Burnt sugar (food color)—*mfg*
3999 Burnt wood articles—*mfg*
0272 Burro farms
1499 Burrstone quarrying
3843 Burs, dental—*mfg*
3613 Bus bar structures—*mfg*
3643 Bus bars (electrical conductors)—*mfg*
5063 Bus bars and trolley ducts—wholesale
3713 Bus bodies, motor vehicle—*mfg*
7319 Bus card advertising
4142 Bus charter service, except local
4141 Bus charter service, local
4111 Bus line operation, local
4131 Bus lines, intercity
4173 Bus terminal operation
4729 Bus ticket offices, not operated by transportation companies
3715 Bus trailers, tractor type—*mfg*
7542 Bus washing
3462 Bus, truck and trailer forgings, ferrous: not made in rolling mills—*mfg*
3711 Buses, motor: except trackless trolley—*mfg*
4151 Buses, school: operation of
4119 Buses, sightseeing: operation of
3743 Buses, trackless trolley—*mfg*
5012 Buses—wholesale
3423 Bush hooks—*mfg*
3366 Bushings and bearings, except die-castings: brass, bronze, and copper—*mfg*
3325 Bushings, cast steel: except investment—*mfg*
3069 Bushings, rubber—*mfg*
2499 Bushings, wood—*mfg*
8611 Business associations, other than civic and social
7389 Business brokers (buying and selling business enterprises)
8244 Business colleges and schools, not of college grade
6153 Business credit institutions, short-term
8732 Business economists, commercial
2759 Business forms, except manifold, lithographed or gravure printed—*mfg*
2754 Business forms, except manifold: gravure printing—*mfg*
2752 Business forms, except manifold: lithographed—*mfg*
2761 Business forms, manifold—*mfg*
5112 Business forms—wholesale
7629 Business machine repair, electrical

C

4119 Cable cars, aerial: except amusement and scenic
4111 Cable cars, except aerial, amusement and scenic
5063 Cable conduit—wholesale
1623 Cable laying construction—contractors
7999 Cable lifts, amusement or scenic: operated separately from lodges
4813 Cable service, telephone
1799 Cable splicing service, nonelectrical—contractors
1731 Cable splicing, electrical—contractors
3663 Cable television equipment—*mfg*
1731 Cable television hookup—contractors
1623 Cable television line construction— contractors
4841 Cable television services
3829 Cable testing machines—*mfg*
3443 Cable trays, metal plate—*mfg*
3355 Cable, aluminum: made in rolling mills—*mfg*
2298 Cable, fiber—*mfg*
3357 Cable, nonferrous: bare, insulated, or armored—mfpm—*mfg*
3315 Cable, steel: insulated or armored—*mfg*
3496 Cable, uninsulated wire: made from purchased wire—*mfg*
5051 Cable, wire: not insulated—wholesale
4822 Cablegram services
3537 Cabs for industrial trucks and tractors—*mfg*
3523 Cabs, agricultural machinery—*mfg*
3531 Cabs, construction machinery—*mfg*
4789 Cabs, horse-drawn: for hire
2066 Cacao bean products: chocolate, cocoa butter, and cocoa—*mfg*
2066 Cacao beans: shelling, roasting, and grinding for making chocolate liquor—*mfg*
3799 Caddy cars—*mfg*
3949 Caddy carts—*mfg*
3339 Cadmium refining, primary—*mfg*
5812 Cafes
3589 Cafeteria food warming equipment—*mfg*
2599 Cafeteria furniture—*mfg*
5021 Cafeteria furniture—wholesale
5812 Cafeterias
2833 Caffeine and derivatives—*mfg*
2384 Caftans—mfpm—*mfg*
3532 Cages, mine shaft—*mfg*
3496 Cages, wire: made from purchased wire—*mfg*
1629 Caisson drilling—contractors
3489 Caisson limbers—*mfg*
3443 Caissons, metal plate—*mfg*
5999 Cake decorating supplies—retail

2099 Cake fillings, except fruits, vegetables and meat—*mfg*
2045 Cake flour—mfpm—*mfg*
2041 Cake flour—mitse—*mfg*
2099 Cake frosting mixes, dry—*mfg*
2045 Cake mixes—mfpm—*mfg*
2064 Cake ornaments, confectionery—*mfg*
2046 Cake, corn oil—*mfg*
2051 Cakes, bakery, except frozen—*mfg*
5142 Cakes, frozen: packaged—wholesale
2053 Cakes, frozen: pound, layer, and cheese—*mfg*
1031 Calamine mining
1041 Calaverite mining
1422 Calcareous tufa, crushed and broken—quarrying
1411 Calcareous tufa, dimension—quarrying
2851 Calcimines, dry and paste—*mfg*
5198 Calcimines—wholesale
2999 Calcined petroleum coke—mfpm—*mfg*
3567 Calcining kilns (industrial furnaces)—*mfg*
1499 Calcite mining
2861 Calcium acetate, product of hardwood distillation—*mfg*
2879 Calcium arsenate and arsenite, formulated—*mfg*
2819 Calcium carbide, chloride, and hypochlorite—*mfg*
2819 Calcium compounds, inorganic—*mfg*
2874 Calcium meta-phosphates—*mfg*
2819 Calcium metal—*mfg*
2869 Calcium oxalate—*mfg*
2843 Calcium salts of sulfonated oils, fats, or greases—*mfg*
3578 Calculating machines, operator paced—*mfg*
5044 Calculating machines—wholesale
7374 Calculating service, computer
3999 Calendars, framed—*mfg*
2754 Calendars, gravure printing: not publishing—*mfg*
2752 Calendars, lithographed: not published—*mfg*
2759 Calendars, printed: except lithographed or gravure—*mfg*
2741 Calendars: publishing and printing, or publishing only—*mfg*
2261 Calendering of cotton broadwoven fabrics—*mfg*
2262 Calendering of manmade fiber and silk broadwoven fabrics—*mfg*
2231 Calendering of wool, mohair, and similar animal fiber fabrics: except knit—*mfg*
3523 Calf savers (farm equipment)—*mfg*
2013 Calf's-foot jelly—*mfg*
8734 Calibration and certification (testing)

3545 Calipers and dividers—*mfg*
3462 Calks, horseshoe: forged—not made in rolling mills—*mfg*
3931 Calliopes (steam organs)—*mfg*
3821 Calorimeters, laboratory type—*mfg*
2211 Cambric, cotton—*mfg*
2295 Cambric: varnished, waxed, and impregnated—*mfg*
3011 Camelback for tire retreading—*mfg*
3161 Camera carrying bags, regardless of material—*mfg*
7699 Camera repair shops
5946 Camera shops, photographic—retail
5731 Camera stores, video—retail
5043 Cameras, equipment, and supplies—wholesale
3861 Cameras, microfilm—*mfg*
3861 Cameras, still and motion picture—*mfg*
3663 Cameras, television—*mfg*
2341 Camisoles: women's, misses', children's, and infants'—mfpm—*mfg*
2298 Camouflage nets, not made in weaving mills—*mfg*
2211 Camouflage nets—mitse—*mfg*
2514 Camp furniture, metal—*mfg*
2519 Camp furniture, reed and rattan—*mfg*
2511 Camp furniture, wood—*mfg*
5561 Campers (pickup coaches) for mounting on trucks—retail
5012 Campers (pickup coaches) for mounting on trucks—wholesale
7519 Campers (recreational vehicles), rental
3792 Campers, for mounting on trucks—*mfg*
7033 Campgrounds
2869 Camphor, synthetic—*mfg*
5941 Camping equipment—retail
5091 Camping equipment—wholesale
5091 Camping tents and equipment—wholesale
3792 Camping trailers and chassis—*mfg*
7032 Camps, sporting and recreational
7033 Campsites for transients
3545 Cams (machine tool accessories)—*mfg*
3714 Camshafts, motor vehicle gasoline engine—*mfg*
3496 Can keys, made from purchased wire—*mfg*
3411 Can lids and ends, metal—*mfg*
3542 Can making machines—*mfg*
3634 Can openers, electric—*mfg*
3423 Can openers, except electric—*mfg*
4449 Canal barge operations
1629 Canal construction—general contractors
4449 Canal freight transportation
4499 Canal operation
3579 Canceling machinery, post office—*mfg*
9431 Cancer detection program administration—government

8069 Cancer hospitals
2655 Candelabra tubes, fiber—mfpm—*mfg*
2064 Candied fruits and fruit peel—*mfg*
7933 Candle pin centers
3999 Candle shades, except glass and metal—*mfg*
5999 Candle shops—retail
3999 Candles—*mfg*
5199 Candles—wholesale
3229 Candlesticks, glass—*mfg*
2064 Candy bars, except solid chocolate—*mfg*
5441 Candy stores—retail
2064 Candy, except solid chocolate—*mfg*
2066 Candy, solid chocolate—*mfg*
5145 Candy—wholesale
0133 Cane farms, sugar
3423 Cane knives—*mfg*
2062 Cane sugar refineries—*mfg*
2061 Cane sugar, made from sugarcane—*mfg*
2061 Cane syrup, made from sugarcane—*mfg*
2062 Cane syrup, made in sugar refineries from purchased sugar—*mfg*
2499 Cane, chair: woven of reed or rattan—*mfg*
3999 Canes and cane trimmings, except precious metal—*mfg*
3842 Canes, orthopedic—*mfg*
3483 Canisters, ammunition—*mfg*
2091 Canned fish, crustacea, and mollusks—*mfg*
2033 Canned fruits and vegetables—*mfg*
5149 Canned goods: fruits, vegetables, fish, seafoods, meats, and milk—wholesale
2013 Canned meats, except baby foods and animal feeds—mfpm—*mfg*
2011 Canned meats, except baby foods and animal feeds—mitse—*mfg*
5149 Canned specialties—wholesale
3489 Cannons, more than 30 mm. (or more than 1.18 inch)—*mfg*
3841 Cannulae—*mfg*
7999 Canoe rental
3732 Canoes, building and repairing—*mfg*
2394 Canopies, fabric—mfpm—*mfg*
3444 Canopies, sheet metal—*mfg*
5085 Cans for fruits and vegetables—wholesale
3411 Cans, aluminum—*mfg*
3469 Cans, ash and garbage: stamped and pressed metal—*mfg*
2655 Cans, composite: foil-fiber and other combinations—mfpm—*mfg*
2655 Cans, fiber (metal-end or all-fiber)—mfpm—*mfg*
3411 Cans, metal—*mfg*
3479 Cans, retinning of; not done in rolling mills—*mfg*
3423 Cant hooks (handtools)—*mfg*
0161 Cantaloup farms

2221   Canton crepes—*mfg*
2211   Canton flannels, cotton—*mfg*
2421   Cants, resawed (lumber)—*mfg*
3952   Canvas board, artists'—*mfg*
2394   Canvas products, except bags and knap-
          sacks—mfpm—*mfg*
5199   Canvas products—wholesale
3021   Canvas shoes, rubber soled—*mfg*
3952   Canvas, artists': prepared on frames—*mfg*
2211   Canvas—mitse—*mfg*
5963   Canvassers (door-to-door), headquarters for
          retail sale of merchandise
2396   Cap fronts and visors—*mfg*
3469   Capacitor and condenser cans and cases:
          stamped metal—*mfg*
2621   Capacitor paper—mitse—*mfg*
3629   Capacitors, a.c.: for motors and fluorescent
          lamp ballasts—*mfg*
3675   Capacitors, electronic: fixed and variable—
          mfg
5065   Capacitors, electronic—wholesale
3629   Capacitors, except electronic: fixed and
          variable—*mfg*
5063   Capacitors, except electronic—wholesale
2337   Capes, except fur and vulcanized rubber:
          women's, misses', and juniors'—mfpm—
          mfg
2371   Capes, fur—*mfg*
3069   Capes, vulcanized rubber and rubberized
          fabric—mitse—*mfg*
2869   Caprolactam—*mfg*
2389   Caps and gowns, academic—mfpm—*mfg*
5137   Caps and gowns: women's and children's—
          wholesale
3643   Caps and plugs, attachment: electric—*mfg*
3466   Caps and tops, bottle: stamped metal—*mfg*
2675   Caps and tops, bottle: die cut from pur-
          chased paper or paperboard—mfpm—
          mfg
2892   Caps, blasting and detonating—*mfg*
3261   Caps, bolt: vitreous china and earthen-
          ware—*mfg*
3483   Caps, bomb—*mfg*
2353   Caps, cloth—mfpm—*mfg*
2899   Caps, for toy pistols—*mfg*
2371   Caps, fur—*mfg*
3131   Caps, heel and toe: leather or metal—*mfg*
2386   Caps, leather—*mfg*
5136   Caps, men's and boys'—wholesale
3089   Caps, plastics—*mfg*
3069   Caps, rubber—mitse—*mfg*
2353   Caps: textiles, straw, fur-felt, and wool-
          felt—mfpm—*mfg*
5137   Caps: women's and children's—wholesale
2253   Caps—mitse—*mfg*
3531   Capstans, ship—*mfg*

2899   Capsules, gelatin: empty—*mfg*
3711   Car bodies, including fiberglass—*mfg*
3532   Car dumpers, mining—*mfg*
4482   Car lighters (ferries)
4789   Car loading
3429   Car seals, metal—*mfg*
7299   Car title and tag service
3321   Car wheels, railroad: chilled cast iron—
          mfg
3312   Car wheels, rolled—*mfg*
3089   Carafes, plastics—*mfg*
2819   Carbide—*mfg*
3484   Carbines, 30 mm. (or 1.18 inch) or less—
          mfg
2821   Carbohydrate plastics—*mfg*
2892   Carbohydrates, nitrated (explosives)—*mfg*
3845   Carbon arc lamp units, electrotherapeutic:
          except infrared and ultraviolet—*mfg*
2869   Carbon bisulfide (disulfide)—*mfg*
2895   Carbon black—*mfg*
5169   Carbon black—wholesale
3297   Carbon brick—*mfg*
2813   Carbon dioxide—*mfg*
3955   Carbon paper—*mfg*
5112   Carbon paper—wholesale
2899   Carbon removing solvent—*mfg*
3624   Carbon specialties for electrical use—*mfg*
2869   Carbon tetrachloride—*mfg*
2819   Carbon, activated—*mfg*
2086   Carbonated beverages, nonalcoholic: bot-
          tled or canned—*mfg*
2812   Carbonates, potassium and sodium: not
          produced at mines—*mfg*
2299   Carbonized rags—*mfg*
3552   Carbonizing equipment (wool processing
          machinery)—*mfg*
2299   Carbonizing of wool, mohair, and similar
          fibers—*mfg*
3624   Carbons, electric—*mfg*
3624   Carbons, lighting—*mfg*
3221   Carboys, glass—*mfg*
7539   Carburetor repair
3592   Carburetors, all types—*mfg*
7319   Card advertising
3172   Card cases, except precious metal—*mfg*
3552   Card clothing for textile machines—*mfg*
2675   Card cutting—mfpm—*mfg*
3577   Card punching and sorting machines—*mfg*
7999   Card rooms
3577   Card-type conversion equipment, computer
          peripheral equipment—*mfg*
5113   Cardboard and products—wholesale
2675   Cardboard foundations and cutouts—
          mfpm—*mfg*
2675   Cardboard panels and cutouts—mfpm—
          mfg

3496 Carts, grocery: made from purchased wire—*mfg*
3484 Carts, machine gun and machine gun ammunition—*mfg*
2599 Carts, restaurant—*mfg*
2499 Carved and turned wood (except furniture)—*mfg*
3553 Carving machine, woodworking—*mfg*
3914 Carving sets, with metal handles and blades—*mfg*
3421 Carving sets: except all metal—*mfg*
2426 Carvings, furniture: wood—*mfg*
5087 Carwash equipment and supplies—wholesale
7542 Carwashes
3589 Carwashing machinery, including coin-operated—*mfg*
3111 Case leather—*mfg*
2824 Casein fibers—*mfg*
2821 Casein plastics—*mfg*
3089 Casein products, molded for the trade—*mfg*
2023 Casein, dry and wet—*mfg*
2211 Casement cloth, cotton—*mfg*
3442 Casements, aluminum—*mfg*
3873 Cases for watches—*mfg*
2522 Cases, filing: except wood—*mfg*
2521 Cases, filing: wood—*mfg*
3949 Cases, gun and rod (sporting equipment)—*mfg*
3172 Cases, jewelry: regardless of material—*mfg*
3161 Cases, luggage—*mfg*
2655 Cases, mailing: paper fiber (metal-end or all-fiber)—mfpm—*mfg*
3161 Cases, musical instrument—*mfg*
2441 Cases, packing: wood—nailed or lock corner—*mfg*
3089 Cases, plastics—*mfg*
2441 Cases, shipping: wood—nailed or lock corner—*mfg*
2449 Cases, shipping: wood—wirebound—*mfg*
3585 Cases, show and display: refrigerated—*mfg*
2517 Cases: radio, phonograph, and sewing machine—wood—*mfg*
3911 Cases: cigar, cigarette, and vanity—precious metal—*mfg*
3469 Cash and stamp boxes, stamped metal—*mfg*
0119 Cash grain farms: except wheat, rice, corn, and soybeans
3578 Cash registers, including adding machines with cash drawers—*mfg*
5044 Cash registers—wholesale
2869 Casing fluids for curing fruits, spices, and tobacco—*mfg*

3443 Casing, boiler: metal plate—*mfg*
1321 Casing-head butane and propane production
3769 Casings for missiles and missile components shipping and storage—*mfg*
3443 Casings, scroll—*mfg*
3444 Casings, sheet metal—*mfg*
7011 Casino hotels
3429 Casket hardware—*mfg*
5087 Caskets, burial—wholesale
3995 Caskets, metal and wood—*mfg*
2449 Casks, wood: coopered—*mfg*
3634 Casseroles, electric—*mfg*
5099 Cassettes, prerecorded: audio—wholesale
5065 Cassettes, recording—wholesale
3321 Cast iron pipe—*mfg*
5051 Cast iron pipe—wholesale
3325 Cast steel railroad car wheels—*mfg*
3272 Cast stone, concrete—*mfg*
3255 Castable refractories, clay—*mfg*
3297 Castable refractories, nonclay—*mfg*
3429 Casters, furniture—*mfg*
3429 Casters, industrial—*mfg*
7922 Casting agencies, theatrical: except motion picture
7819 Casting bureaus, motion picture
7922 Casting bureaus, theatrical: except motion picture
3089 Casting of plastics for the trade, except foam plastics—*mfg*
3365 Castings, aluminum: except die-castings—*mfg*
3321 Castings, compacted graphite iron—*mfg*
3369 Castings, except die-castings and castings of aluminum and copper—*mfg*
3366 Castings, except die-castings: brass, bronze, copper, and copper-base alloy—*mfg*
3321 Castings, gray iron and semisteel—*mfg*
3322 Castings, malleable iron—*mfg*
3369 Castings, precision, except die-castings: industrial and aircraft use—cobalt-chromium—*mfg*
5051 Castings, rough: iron and steel—wholesale
3069 Castings, rubber—*mfg*
3325 Castings, steel: except investment—*mfg*
2076 Castor oil and pomace—*mfg*
3143 Casual shoes, men's: except athletic and rubber footwear—*mfg*
6531 Casualty insurance and reinsurance
0279 Cat farms
2047 Cat food—*mfg*
5961 Catalog (order taking) offices of mail-order houses—retail
2621 Catalog paper—mitse—*mfg*
5399 Catalog showrooms, general merchandise: except catalog mail-order—retail

6019	Central liquidity facility
1629	Central station construction—general contractors
3273	Central-mixed concrete—*mfg*
3569	Centrifugal purifiers—*mfg*
3569	Centrifuges, industrial—*mfg*
3821	Centrifuges, laboratory—*mfg*
3269	Ceramic articles for craft shops—*mfg*
5032	Ceramic construction materials, except refractory—wholesale
3299	Ceramic fiber—*mfg*
3251	Ceramic glazed brick, clay—*mfg*
3567	Ceramic kilns and furnaces—*mfg*
3253	Ceramic tile, floor and wall—*mfg*
5032	Ceramic wall and floor tile—wholesale
8299	Ceramics schools
5945	Ceramics supplies—retail
2043	Cereal preparations and breakfast foods—*mfg*
2041	Cereals, cracked grain—mitse—*mfg*
1099	Cerium ore mining
2819	Cerium salts—*mfg*
1031	Cerrusite mining
2759	Certificates, security: engraved—*mfg*
8721	Certified public accountants (CPAs)
3842	Cervical collars—*mfg*
2819	Cesium metal—*mfg*
7699	Cesspool cleaning
1711	Cesspool construction—contractors
3728	Chaffing dispensers, aircraft—*mfg*
3634	Chafing dishes, electric—*mfg*
3429	Chain fittings—*mfg*
3446	Chain ladders, metal—*mfg*
3315	Chain link fencing, steel: made in wire-drawing plants—*mfg*
3546	Chain saws, portable—*mfg*
3425	Chain type saw blades—*mfg*
3568	Chain, power transmission—*mfg*
5085	Chain, power transmission—wholesale
3496	Chain, welded: made from purchased wire—*mfg*
3496	Chain, wire: made from purchased wire—*mfg*
3462	Chains, forged steel: not made in rolling mills—*mfg*
3829	Chains, surveyors'—*mfg*
5251	Chainsaws—retail
5084	Chainsaws—wholesale
2515	Chair and couch springs, assembled—*mfg*
2515	Chair beds, on frames of any material—*mfg*
2392	Chair covers, cloth—*mfg*
2426	Chair frames for upholstered furniture, wood—*mfg*
3499	Chair frames, metal—*mfg*
3429	Chair glides—*mfg*
2392	Chair pads, except felt—*mfg*
2426	Chair seats, hardwood—*mfg*
2426	Chair stock, hardwood: turned, shaped, or carved—*mfg*
2511	Chairs, bentwood—*mfg*
2519	Chairs, cane—*mfg*
3843	Chairs, dentists'—*mfg*
2511	Chairs, household: except upholstered—wood—*mfg*
2514	Chairs, household: metal—*mfg*
3999	Chairs, hydraulic: barber and beauty shop—*mfg*
5087	Chairs, hydraulic: beauty and barber shop—wholesale
2522	Chairs, office: except wood—*mfg*
2521	Chairs, office: wood—*mfg*
2531	Chairs, portable folding—*mfg*
2531	Chairs, tablet arm—*mfg*
2512	Chairs, upholstered on wood frames, except convertible beds—*mfg*
3842	Chairs, wheel—*mfg*
5021	Chairs: household, office, and public building—wholesale
1021	Chalcocite mining
1021	Chalcopyrite mining
1422	Chalk mining, crushed and broken—quarrying
3949	Chalk, billiard—*mfg*
1422	Chalk, ground or otherwise treated
3952	Chalk: e.g., carpenters', blackboard, marking, artists', tailors'—*mfg*
3281	Chalkboards, slate—*mfg*
2531	Chalkboards, wood—*mfg*
8611	Chambers of Commerce
2211	Chambrays—*mfg*
3541	Chamfering machines—*mfg*
3111	Chamois leather—*mfg*
5199	Chamois leather—wholesale
3646	Chandeliers, commercial—*mfg*
3645	Chandeliers, residential—*mfg*
3578	Change making machines—*mfg*
2895	Channel black—*mfg*
1629	Channel construction—general contractors
1629	Channel cutoff construction—general contractors
3446	Channels, furring—*mfg*
2819	Charcoal, activated—*mfg*
2861	Charcoal, except activated—*mfg*
5199	Charcoal—wholesale
7389	Charge account service (shopping plates)—collection by individual firms
3629	Chargers, battery: rectifying or nonrotating—*mfg*
6732	Charitable trusts, management of

2051 Charlotte Russe (bakery product), except frozen—*mfg*
8299 Charm schools
7336 Chart and graph design
2782 Chart and graph paper, ruled—*mfg*
4499 Chartering of commercial boats
3545 Chasers (machine tool accessories)—*mfg*
3555 Chases and galleys, printers'—*mfg*
3479 Chasing on metals for the trade, for purposes other than printing—*mfg*
3792 Chassis for travel and camping trailers—*mfg*
3799 Chassis, automobile trailer: except mobile home and travel trailer—*mfg*
3711 Chassis, motor vehicle—*mfg*
3469 Chassis, radio and television: stamped metal—*mfg*
7361 Chauffeur registries
2353 Chauffeurs' hats and caps, cloth—*mfg*
6099 Check cashing agencies
6099 Check clearinghouse associations
7389 Check validation service
3579 Check writing, endorsing, signing, numbering, and protecting machines—*mfg*
3172 Checkbook covers, regardless of material—*mfg*
2782 Checkbooks—*mfg*
3944 Checkers and checkerboards—*mfg*
7299 Checkroom concessions or services
2022 Cheese analogs—*mfg*
2399 Cheese bandages—mfpm—*mfg*
2096 Cheese curls and puffs—*mfg*
3556 Cheese making machinery—*mfg*
2022 Cheese products, imitation or substitutes—*mfg*
2022 Cheese spreads, pastes, and cheese-like preparations—*mfg*
5451 Cheese stores—retail
4222 Cheese warehouses
2026 Cheese, cottage—*mfg*
2022 Cheese, except cottage cheese—*mfg*
2022 Cheese, imitation or substitutes—*mfg*
5961 Cheese, mail-order—retail
2022 Cheese, natural: except cottage cheese—*mfg*
2022 Cheese, processed—*mfg*
5143 Cheese—wholesale
2211 Cheesecloth—*mfg*
5131 Cheesecloth—wholesale
5169 Chemical bulk stations and terminals—wholesale
2819 Chemical catalysts—*mfg*
1629 Chemical complex or facilities construction—general contractors
2899 Chemical cotton (processed cotton linters)—*mfg*

3542 Chemical explosives metal forming machines—*mfg*
3821 Chemical fume hoods—*mfg*
2865 Chemical indicators—*mfg*
3559 Chemical kilns—*mfg*
8731 Chemical laboratories, commercial research: except testing
3559 Chemical machinery and equipment—*mfg*
3599 Chemical milling job shops—*mfg*
3541 Chemical milling machines—*mfg*
3269 Chemical porcelain—*mfg*
3312 Chemical recovery coke oven products—*mfg*
3269 Chemical stoneware (pottery products)—*mfg*
2899 Chemical supplies for foundries—*mfg*
0711 Chemical treatment of soil for crops
2869 Chemical warfare gases—*mfg*
3483 Chemical warfare projectiles and components—*mfg*
1389 Chemically treating wells on a contract basis
5191 Chemicals, agricultural—wholesale
5169 Chemicals, industrial and heavy—wholesale
2819 Chemicals, laboratory: inorganic—*mfg*
2833 Chemicals, medicinal: organic and inorganic—bulk, uncompounded—*mfg*
3861 Chemicals, photographic: prepared—*mfg*
2341 Chemises: women's, misses', children's, and infants'—mfpm—*mfg*
8071 Chemists, biological: (not manufacturing) laboratories of
8999 Chemists, consulting: not connected with business service laboratories
2273 Chenille rugs—*mfg*
2211 Chenilles, tufted textile—mitse—*mfg*
2035 Cherries, brined—*mfg*
2033 Cherries, maraschino—*mfg*
0831 Cherry gum, gathering of
0175 Cherry orchards and farms
3944 Chessmen and chessboards—*mfg*
2861 Chestnut extract—*mfg*
0831 Chestnut gum, gathering of
2441 Chests for tools, wood—*mfg*
2511 Chests, cedar—*mfg*
3499 Chests, fire or burglary resistive: metal—*mfg*
3999 Chests, money: steel—*mfg*
3999 Chests, musical—*mfg*
3499 Chests, safe deposit: metal—*mfg*
2511 Chests, silverware: wood (floor standing)—*mfg*
2211 Cheviots, cotton—*mfg*
2064 Chewing candy, except chewing gum—*mfg*
2067 Chewing gum—*mfg*

2067 Chewing gum base—*mfg*
3556 Chewing gum machinery—*mfg*
5145 Chewing gum—wholesale
2131 Chewing tobacco—*mfg*
5194 Chewing tobacco—wholesale
3523 Chicken brooders—*mfg*
2032 Chicken broth and soup, canned—*mfg*
2449 Chicken coops (crates), wood: wirebound for shipping poultry—*mfg*
2452 Chicken coops, prefabricated: wood—*mfg*
0252 Chicken egg farms
0251 Chicken farms or ranches, raising for slaughter
3523 Chicken feeders—*mfg*
2048 Chicken feeds, prepared—*mfg*
0254 Chicken hatcheries
2015 Chickens, processed: fresh, frozen, canned, or cooked—*mfg*
2015 Chickens: slaughtering and dressing—*mfg*
5159 Chicks—wholesale
2099 Chicory root, dried—*mfg*
2511 Chiffoniers and chifforobes—*mfg*
8351 Child care centers
8322 Child guidance agencies
8099 Childbirth preparation classes
8361 Children's boarding homes
7911 Children's dancing schools
8361 Children's homes
2252 Children's hosiery—*mfg*
8069 Children's hospitals
8361 Children's villages
5641 Children's wear stores—retail
2032 Chili con carne, canned—*mfg*
2099 Chili pepper or powder—*mfg*
2033 Chili sauce, tomato—*mfg*
3931 Chimes and parts (musical instruments)—*mfg*
3699 Chimes, electric—*mfg*
3251 Chimney blocks, radial—clay—*mfg*
3272 Chimney caps, concrete—*mfg*
7349 Chimney cleaning service
1741 Chimney construction and maintenance—contractors
3259 Chimney pipe and tops, clay—*mfg*
3229 Chimneys, lamp: glass—pressed or blown—*mfg*
1455 China clay mining
2511 China closets—*mfg*
3262 China cooking ware—*mfg*
7699 China firing and decorating to individual order
3269 China firing and decorating, for the trade—*mfg*
5719 China stores—retail
3262 China tableware, commercial, and household: vitreous—*mfg*

5023 China—wholesale
0271 Chinchilla farms
2032 Chinese foods, canned—*mfg*
2099 Chinese noodles—*mfg*
2211 Chintz, cotton—*mfg*
3531 Chip spreaders, self-propelled—*mfg*
2631 Chipboard (paperboard)—mitse—*mfg*
2675 Chipboard, pasted—mfpm—*mfg*
2421 Chipper mills—*mfg*
3531 Chippers, commercial: brush, limb, and log—*mfg*
3546 Chipping hammers, electric—*mfg*
8041 Chiropractors, offices and clinics of
3423 Chisels—*mfg*
2869 Chloral—*mfg*
3069 Chlorinated rubbers, natural—*mfg*
2822 Chlorinated rubbers, synthetic—*mfg*
2869 Chlorinated solvents—*mfg*
2834 Chlorination tablets and kits (water purification)—*mfg*
2842 Chlorine bleaching compounds, household: liquid or dry—*mfg*
2812 Chlorine, compressed or liquefied—*mfg*
5169 Chlorine—wholesale
2869 Chloroacetic acid and metallic salts—*mfg*
2865 Chlorobenzene—*mfg*
2869 Chloroform—*mfg*
2865 Chloronaphthalene—*mfg*
2865 Chlorophenol—*mfg*
2869 Chloropicrin—*mfg*
2822 Chloroprene type rubbers—*mfg*
2822 Chlorosulfonated polyethylenes—*mfg*
2819 Chlorosulfonic acid—*mfg*
2865 Chlorotoluene—*mfg*
2064 Chocolate bars, from purchased cocoa or chocolate—*mfg*
2066 Chocolate bars, solid: from cacao beans—*mfg*
2064 Chocolate candy, except solid chocolate—*mfg*
2066 Chocolate coatings and syrups—*mfg*
2066 Chocolate liquor—*mfg*
2026 Chocolate milk—*mfg*
3556 Chocolate processing machinery—*mfg*
2066 Chocolate syrup—*mfg*
2066 Chocolate, instant—*mfg*
2066 Chocolate, sweetened or unsweetened—*mfg*
5149 Chocolate—wholesale
2032 Chop suey, canned—*mfg*
3556 Choppers, food: commercial types—*mfg*
0722 Chopping and silo filling
2032 Chow mein, canned—*mfg*
2091 Chowder, clam: canned—*mfg*
2091 Chowders, fish and seafood: canned—*mfg*
2092 Chowders, fish and seafood: frozen—*mfg*

8999 Christian Science lecturers
8049 Christian Science practitioners, offices of
2771 Christmas cards, except hand painted—*mfg*
0811 Christmas tree growing
3699 Christmas tree lighting sets, electric—*mfg*
3999 Christmas tree ornaments, except electrical and glass—*mfg*
3229 Christmas tree ornaments, from glass—mitse—*mfg*
3231 Christmas tree ornaments, made from purchased glass—*mfg*
5261 Christmas trees (natural)—retail
3999 Christmas trees, artificial—*mfg*
5199 Christmas trees, including artificial—wholesale
2819 Chromates and bichromates—*mfg*
3826 Chromatographic instruments, laboratory type—*mfg*
3823 Chromatographs, industrial process type—*mfg*
2816 Chrome pigments: chrome green, chrome yellow, chrome orange, and zinc yellow—*mfg*
2819 Chromic acid—*mfg*
1061 Chromite mining
2819 Chromium compounds, inorganic—*mfg*
1061 Chromium ore mining
3471 Chromium plating of metals and formed products, for the trade—*mfg*
3339 Chromium refining, primary—*mfg*
2819 Chromium salts—*mfg*
8069 Chronic disease hospitals
3873 Chronographs, spring wound—*mfg*
3829 Chronometers, electronic—*mfg*
3873 Chronometers, spring wound—*mfg*
3826 Chronoscopes—*mfg*
3541 Chucking machines, automatic—*mfg*
3545 Chucks: drill, lathe, and magnetic (machine tool accessories)—*mfg*
3272 Church furniture, concrete—*mfg*
3281 Church furniture, cut stone—*mfg*
2531 Church furniture, except stone or concrete—*mfg*
5021 Church pews—wholesale
1542 Church, synagogue, and related building construction—general contractors
8661 Churches
3443 Chutes, metal plate—*mfg*
3556 Cider presses—*mfg*
2099 Cider, nonalcoholic—*mfg*
3999 Cigar and cigarette holders—*mfg*
2441 Cigar boxes, wood and part wood—*mfg*
3172 Cigar cases, except precious metal—*mfg*
3911 Cigar cases, precious metal—*mfg*
3634 Cigar lighters, electric—*mfg*

3999 Cigar lighters, except precious metal and electric—*mfg*
3911 Cigar lighters, precious metal or based metal clad with precious metal—*mfg*
5993 Cigar stores and stands—retail
3559 Cigarette and cigar making machines—*mfg*
3172 Cigarette cases, except precious metal—*mfg*
3911 Cigarette cases, precious metal—*mfg*
3999 Cigarette filters, not made in chemical plants—*mfg*
3069 Cigarette holder mouthpieces, molded rubber—*mfg*
3999 Cigarette lighter flints—*mfg*
3634 Cigarette lighters, electric—*mfg*
3999 Cigarette lighters, except precious metal and electric—*mfg*
3911 Cigarette lighters, precious metal—*mfg*
2679 Cigarette paper, book—mfpm—*mfg*
2621 Cigarette paper—mitse—*mfg*
2823 Cigarette tow, cellulosic fiber—*mfg*
2111 Cigarettes—*mfg*
5962 Cigarettes, sale by vending machine—retail
5194 Cigarettes—wholesale
2121 Cigarillos—*mfg*
2121 Cigars—*mfg*
5194 Cigars—wholesale
2833 Cinchona and derivatives—*mfg*
3271 Cinder block, concrete—*mfg*
5032 Cinders—wholesale
3827 Cinetheodolites—*mfg*
1099 Cinnabar mining
3672 Circuit boards, television and radio: printed—*mfg*
3613 Circuit breakers, air—*mfg*
3613 Circuit breakers, power—*mfg*
5063 Circuit breakers—wholesale
8741 Circuit management services for motion picture theaters
7319 Circular distributing service
2257 Circular knit fabrics—*mfg*
5131 Circular knit fabrics—wholesale
2752 Circulars, lithographed—*mfg*
2759 Circulars, printed: except lithographed or gravure—*mfg*
2754 Circulars: gravure printing—*mfg*
8231 Circulating libraries
7999 Circus companies
7622 Citizens' band (CB) antennas, installation of
3663 Citizens' band (CB) radios—*mfg*
5065 Citizens' band radios—wholesale
8641 Citizens' unions
2869 Citral—*mfg*

2869 Citrates—*mfg*
2869 Citric acid—*mfg*
2899 Citronella oil—*mfg*
2869 Citronellal—*mfg*
0721 Citrus grove cultivation services
0762 Citrus grove management and maintenance, with or without crop services
0174 Citrus groves and farms
5084 Citrus processing machinery—wholesale
2048 Citrus seed meal—*mfg*
4111 City and suburban bus line operation
9121 City and town councils
9111 City and town managers' offices
8748 City planners, except professional engineering
8641 Civic associations
1542 Civic center construction—general contractors
9199 Civil rights commissions—government
9199 Civil service commissions—government
8299 Civil service schools
9211 Civilian courts
6411 Claim adjusters insurance: not employed by insurance companies
2091 Clam bouillon, broth, chowder, juice: bottled or canned—*mfg*
3423 Clamps, hand—*mfg*
3429 Clamps, hose—*mfg*
3545 Clamps, machine tool—*mfg*
3429 Clamps, metal—*mfg*
3841 Clamps, surgical—*mfg*
0913 Clams, digging of
3532 Clarifying machinery, mineral—*mfg*
3931 Clarinets and parts—*mfg*
3131 Clasps, shoe—*mfg*
7929 Classical music groups or artists
3532 Classifiers, metallurgical and mining—*mfg*
2631 Clay coated board—mitse—*mfg*
5032 Clay construction materials, except refractory—wholesale
3295 Clay for petroleum refining, chemically processed—*mfg*
3255 Clay refractories—*mfg*
3295 Clay, ground or otherwise treated—*mfg*
3952 Clay, modeling—*mfg*
1459 Clays (common) quarrying—not in conjunction with manufacturing
3559 Clayworking and tempering machines—*mfg*
7218 Clean room apparel supply service
1541 Clean room construction—general contractors
3714 Cleaners, air: motor vehicle—*mfg*
3599 Cleaners, boiler tube—*mfg*
2844 Cleaners, denture—*mfg*
3589 Cleaners, electric vacuum: industrial—*mfg*

3635 Cleaners, electric: vacuum—household—*mfg*
7212 Cleaners, not operating own drycleaning plants
2851 Cleaners, paintbrush—*mfg*
3999 Cleaners, pipe and cigarette holder—*mfg*
3471 Cleaning and descaling metal products, for the trade—*mfg*
7216 Cleaning and dyeing plants, except rug cleaning
7212 Cleaning and laundry pickup stations, not owned by laundries or cleaners
7542 Cleaning and polishing (detailing) new autos for dealers on a contract or fee basis
2044 Cleaning and polishing of rice—*mfg*
2842 Cleaning and polishing preparations—*mfg*
7699 Cleaning and reglazing of baking pans
7217 Cleaning and repairing plants, rug and carpet
7699 Cleaning bricks
1799 Cleaning building exteriors—contractors
3699 Cleaning equipment, ultrasonic: except medical and dental—*mfg*
1389 Cleaning lease tanks, oil and gas field: on a contract basis
3547 Cleaning lines, electrolytic (rolling mill equipment)—*mfg*
3532 Cleaning machinery, mineral—*mfg*
3523 Cleaning machines for fruits, grains, and vegetables: farm—*mfg*
1799 Cleaning new buildings after construction—contractors
5149 Cleaning of dry foods and spices—wholesale
4741 Cleaning of railroad cars
1221 Cleaning plants, bituminous coal
0751 Cleaning poultry coops
4789 Cleaning railroad ballasts
1389 Cleaning wells on a contract basis
2621 Cleansing tissue stock—mitse—*mfg*
2676 Cleansing tissues—mfpm—*mfg*
3647 Clearance lamps and reflectors, motor vehicle—*mfg*
1629 Clearing of land—general contractors
6099 Clearinghouse associations: bank or check
6289 Clearinghouses, commodity exchange
6289 Clearinghouses, security exchange
3264 Cleats, porcelain—*mfg*
3421 Cleavers—*mfg*
2389 Clergy's vestments—*mfg*
2449 Climax baskets—*mfg*
2835 Clinical chemistry reagents (including toxicology)—*mfg*
2835 Clinical chemistry standards and controls (including toxicology)—*mfg*

3829 Clinical thermometers, including digital—*mfg*

8041 Clinics of chiropractors

8021 Clinics of dentists

8042 Clinics of optometrists

8031 Clinics of osteopathic physicians

8011 Clinics of physicians (M.D.)

8043 Clinics of podiatrists

8093 Clinics, alcohol and drug treatment: outpatient

8093 Clinics, mental health: outpatient

3229 Clip cups, glass—*mfg*

2499 Clipboards, wood—*mfg*

3421 Clippers, fingernail and toenail—*mfg*

3999 Clippers, hair: for human use—hand and electric—*mfg*

3523 Clippers, hair: for animal use—hand and electric—*mfg*

3496 Clips and fasteners, made from purchased wire—*mfg*

3484 Clips, gun: 30 mm. (or 1.18 inch) or less—*mfg*

3069 Cloaks, vulcanized rubber and rubberized fabric—mitse—*mfg*

3873 Clock materials and parts, except crystals and jewels—*mfg*

3651 Clock radio and telephone combinations—*mfg*

3651 Clock radios—*mfg*

7631 Clock repair shops

3495 Clock springs, precision: made from purchased wire—*mfg*

3873 Clocks, assembling of—*mfg*

3873 Clocks, except timeclocks—*mfg*

5944 Clocks, including custom made—retail

5094 Clocks—wholesale

3663 Closed circuit television equipment—*mfg*

4841 Closed circuit television services

3261 Closet bowls, vitreous china—*mfg*

5113 Closures, paper and disposable plastics—wholesale

3089 Closures, plastics—*mfg*

3466 Closures, stamped metal—*mfg*

2269 Cloth mending, except wool: for the trade—*mfg*

3552 Cloth spreading machines—*mfg*

3552 Cloth stripping machines—*mfg*

2499 Cloth winding reels, wood—*mfg*

3291 Cloth, abrasive—*mfg*

3292 Cloth, asbestos—*mfg*

2257 Cloth, circular knit—*mfg*

3861 Cloth, photographic: sensitized—*mfg*

3952 Cloth, tracing (drafting material)—*mfg*

2295 Cloth, varnished glass—*mfg*

2258 Cloth, warp knit—mitse—*mfg*

2231 Cloth, wool: mending for the trade—*mfg*

3496 Cloth, woven wire: made from purchased wire—*mfg*

2672 Cloth-lined paper—mfpm—*mfg*

7389 Cloth: cutting to length, bolting, or winding for textile distributors

3291 Cloth: garnet, emery, aluminum oxide, and silicon carbide coated—*mfg*

3822 Clothes dryer controls, including dryness controls—*mfg*

2499 Clothes dryers (clothes horses), wood—*mfg*

5064 Clothes dryers, household: electric and gas—wholesale

2499 Clothes drying frames, wood—*mfg*

3089 Clothes hangers, plastics—*mfg*

5199 Clothes hangers—wholesale

2499 Clothes horses, wood—*mfg*

2499 Clothes poles, wood—*mfg*

3089 Clothespins, plastics—*mfg*

2499 Clothespins, wood—*mfg*

5137 Clothing accessories: women's, children's, and infants'—wholesale

7219 Clothing alteration and repair shops

7299 Clothing rental, except industrial launderers and linen supply

5651 Clothing stores, family—retail

5611 Clothing stores, men's and boys'—retail

5932 Clothing stores, secondhand—retail

3942 Clothing, doll—*mfg*

3699 Clothing, electrically heated—*mfg*

3842 Clothing, fire resistant and protective—*mfg*

2371 Clothing, fur—*mfg*

2386 Clothing, leather or sheep-lined—*mfg*

5136 Clothing, men's and boys'—wholesale

5621 Clothing, ready-to-wear: women's—retail

3069 Clothing, vulcanized rubber and rubberized fabric—mitse—*mfg*

2385 Clothing, waterproof—mfpm—*mfg*

5137 Clothing: women's, children's, and infants'—wholesale

2394 Cloths, drop: fabric—mfpm—*mfg*

2842 Cloths, dusting and polishing: chemically treated—*mfg*

2392 Cloths, lunch—mfpm—*mfg*

2399 Cloths, saddle—*mfg*

8999 Cloud seeding

0139 Clover farms

2514 Clubroom furniture, metal—*mfg*

2511 Clubroom furniture, wood—*mfg*

7991 Clubs, health

7997 Clubs, membership: sports and recreation, except physical fitness

2499 Clubs, police: wood—*mfg*

3949 Clubs: golf, Indian, etc. (sporting goods)—*mfg*

3292 Clutch facings, asbestos—*mfg*

3568   Clutches, except motor vehicle—*mfg*

****   Clutches, vehicle—classify by type of vehicle

2835   Coagulation diagnostic reagents—*mfg*

2836   Coagulation products—*mfg*

3532   Coal breakers, cutters, and pulverizers—*mfg*

3444   Coal chutes, prefabricated sheet metal—*mfg*

5989   Coal dealers—retail

3312   Coal gas, derived from chemical recovery coke ovens—*mfg*

1311   Coal gasification at the mine site

1311   Coal liquefaction at the mine site

1231   Coal mining, anthracite

1221   Coal mining, bituminous: surface

1222   Coal mining, bituminous—underground

1221   Coal mining—brown

4619   Coal pipeline operation

1221   Coal preparation plants, bituminous or lignite

1311   Coal pyrolysis at the mine site

3312   Coal tar crudes, derived from chemical recovery coke ovens—*mfg*

2865   Coal tar crudes, derived from coal tar distillation—*mfg*

2865   Coal tar distillates—*mfg*

2865   Coal tar intermediates—*mfg*

2951   Coal tar paving materials, not made in petroleum refineries—*mfg*

5169   Coal tar products, primary and intermediate—wholesale

2821   Coal tar resins—*mfg*

5052   Coal—wholesale

3751   Coaster brakes, bicycle—*mfg*

4424   Coastwise transportation of freight

2369   Coat and legging sets: girls' and children's—mfpm—*mfg*

3496   Coat hangers, made from purchased wire—*mfg*

2396   Coat linings, fronts, and pads: for men's coats—*mfg*

2371   Coat linings, fur—*mfg*

7213   Coat supply service

2396   Coat trimmings fabric—mfpm—*mfg*

5131   Coated fabrics—wholesale

2671   Coated paper for packaging—mfpm—*mfg*

3479   Coating (hot dipping) of metals and formed products, for the trade—*mfg*

3554   Coating and finishing machinery, paper—*mfg*

2295   Coating and impregnating of fabrics, except rubberizing—*mfg*

3479   Coating and wrapping steel pipe—*mfg*

2952   Coating compounds, tar—mfpm—*mfg*

1799   Coating of concrete structures with plastics—contractors

3479   Coating of metals with plastics and resins, for the trade—*mfg*

3479   Coating of metals with silicon, for the trade—*mfg*

2851   Coating, air curing—*mfg*

3479   Coating, rust preventive—*mfg*

2066   Coatings, chocolate—*mfg*

2337   Coats, except fur and raincoats: women's, misses', and juniors'—mfpm—*mfg*

2329   Coats, except tailored or work: men's and boys'—mfpm—*mfg*

2371   Coats, fur—*mfg*

2386   Coats, leather or sheep-lined—*mfg*

5136   Coats, men's and boys'—wholesale

2329   Coats, oiled fabric and blanket-lined: men's and boys'—mfpm—*mfg*

2339   Coats, service apparel (e.g., medical and lab)—*mfg*

2311   Coats, tailored: men's and boys'—mfpm—*mfg*

2369   Coats: girls', children's, and infants'—mfpm—*mfg*

5137   Coats: women's, children's, and infants'—wholesale

3357   Coaxial cable, nonferrous—*mfg*

5063   Coaxial cable—wholesale

2819   Cobalt 60 (radioactive)—*mfg*

2819   Cobalt chloride—*mfg*

1061   Cobalt ore mining

3339   Cobalt refining, primary—*mfg*

2819   Cobalt sulfate—*mfg*

2833   Cocaine and derivatives—*mfg*

3432   Cocks, drain (including basin)—*mfg*

5813   Cocktail lounges

2087   Cocktail mixes, nonalcoholic—*mfg*

2085   Cocktails, alcoholic—*mfg*

5182   Cocktails, alcoholic: premixed—wholesale

2066   Cocoa butter—*mfg*

2066   Cocoa mix, instant—*mfg*

2066   Cocoa, powdered: mixed with other substances—*mfg*

2076   Coconut oil—*mfg*

2099   Coconut, desiccated and shredded—*mfg*

2843   Cod oil, sulfonated—*mfg*

0912   Cod, catching of

3827   Coddington magnifying instruments—*mfg*

2833   Codeine and derivatives—*mfg*

2091   Codfish: smoked, salted, dried, and pickled—*mfg*

2095   Coffee concentrates (instant coffee)—*mfg*

2095   Coffee extracts—*mfg*

0179   Coffee farms

2087   Coffee flavorings and syrups—*mfg*

3634   Coffee makers, household: electric—*mfg*

3556 Coffee roasting and grinding machines—*mfg*

2095 Coffee roasting, except by wholesale grocers—*mfg*

5812 Coffee shops

5499 Coffee stores—retail

2043 Coffee substitutes made from grain—*mfg*

2511 Coffee tables, wood—*mfg*

5046 Coffee urns, commercial—wholesale

3589 Coffee urns, restaurant type—*mfg*

2095 Coffee, ground: mixed with grain or chicory—*mfg*

2095 Coffee, instant and freeze-dried—*mfg*

5963 Coffee-cart food service—retail

5149 Coffee: green, roasted, instant, freeze-dried, or extract—wholesale

1629 Cofferdam construction—general contractors

4119 Cog railways, except amusement and scenic

3549 Coil winding machines for springs—*mfg*

7694 Coil winding service

3677 Coil windings, electronic—*mfg*

3493 Coiled flat springs—*mfg*

3549 Coilers (metalworking machines)—*mfg*

3621 Coils for motors and generators—*mfg*

3677 Coils, chokes and other inductors, electronic—*mfg*

5065 Coils, electronic—wholesale

3694 Coils, ignition: internal combustion engines—*mfg*

3498 Coils, pipe: fabricated from purchased metal pipe—*mfg*

3354 Coils, rod: aluminum—extruded—*mfg*

3353 Coils, sheet: aluminum—*mfg*

3355 Coils, wire: aluminum—made in rolling mills—*mfg*

3578 Coin counters—*mfg*

3172 Coin purses, regardless of material—*mfg*

5999 Coin shops—retail, except mail-order

3579 Coin wrapping machines—*mfg*

3999 Coin-operated amusement machine, except phonographs—*mfg*

7215 Coin-operated drycleaning

5099 Coin-operated game machines

7215 Coin-operated laundries

7215 Coin-operated laundry and drycleaning routes

7359 Coin-operated machine rental and leasing

5962 Coin-operated machines selling merchandise

3581 Coin-operated merchandise vending machines—*mfg*

3651 Coin-operated phonographs—*mfg*

7299 Coin-operated service machine operation: scales, shoeshine, lockers, and blood pressure

5961 Coins, mail-order—retail

5094 Coins—wholesale

2299 Coir yarns and roving—*mfg*

1629 Coke oven construction—general contractors

4925 Coke oven gas, production and distribution

4925 Coke ovens, byproduct: operated for manufacture or distribution of gas

2999 Coke, petroleum: not produced in petroleum refineries—*mfg*

2911 Coke, petroleum: produced in petroleum refineries—*mfg*

3312 Coke, produced in beehive ovens—*mfg*

3312 Coke, produced in chemical recovery coke ovens—*mfg*

5052 Coke—wholesale

3585 Cold drink dispensing equipment, except coin-operated—*mfg*

3547 Cold forming type mills (rolling mill machinery)—*mfg*

2835 Cold kits for labeling with technetium—*mfg*

2834 Cold remedies—*mfg*

4222 Cold storage locker rental

5078 Cold storage machinery—wholesale

1541 Cold storage plant construction—general contractors

4222 Cold storage warehousing

3316 Cold-finished steel bars: not made in hot-rolling mills—*mfg*

3316 Cold-rolled steel strip, sheet, and bars: not made in hot-rolling mills—*mfg*

2099 Cole slaw in bulk—*mfg*

1474 Colemanite mining

3499 Collapsible tubes for viscous products, metal—*mfg*

2339 Collar and cuff sets: women's, misses' and juniors'— mfpm—*mfg*

2253 Collar and cuff sets—mitse—*mfg*

3965 Collar buttons, except precious metal and precious or semiprecious stones—*mfg*

3911 Collar buttons, precious metal and precious or semiprecious stones—*mfg*

3111 Collar leather—*mfg*

2396 Collar linings, for men's coats—*mfg*

3545 Collars (machine tool accessories)—*mfg*

3199 Collars and collar pads (harness)—*mfg*

3199 Collars, dog—*mfg*

2321 Collars, men's and boys'—mfpm—*mfg*

3568 Collars, shaft (power transmission equipment)—*mfg*

3555 Collating machines for printing and bookbinding trade use—*mfg*

3579 Collating machines for store or office use—*mfg*

7216 Collecting and distributing agencies operated by cleaning plants

7211 Collecting and distributing agencies, laundry: operated by power laundries

7212 Collecting and distributing agents, laundry and drycleaning

7322 Collection agencies, accounts

8631 Collective bargaining units

3621 Collector rings for motors and generators—*mfg*

7299 College clearinghouses

8221 Colleges, except junior

3545 Collets (machine tool accessories)—*mfg*

7532 Collision shops, automotive

2844 Colognes—*mfg*

3845 Colonscopes, electromedical—*mfg*

2752 Color cards, paint: offset printing—*mfg*

2865 Color lakes and toners—*mfg*

2752 Color lithography—*mfg*

2816 Color pigments, inorganic—*mfg*

2865 Color pigments, organic: except animal black and bone black—*mfg*

2759 Color printing: except lithographed or gravure—*mfg*

2754 Color printing: gravure—*mfg*

2796 Color separations for printing—*mfg*

3826 Colorimeters, laboratory type—*mfg*

3471 Coloring and finishing of aluminum and formed products, for the trade—*mfg*

3111 Coloring of leather—*mfg*

2087 Colorings, food: except synthetic—*mfg*

5198 Colors and pigments—wholesale

2087 Colors for bakers' and confectioners' use, except synthetic—*mfg*

2851 Colors in oil, except artists'—*mfg*

3952 Colors, artists': water and oxide ceramic glass—*mfg*

2865 Colors, dry: lakes, toners, or full strength organic colors—*mfg*

2865 Colors, extended (color lakes)—*mfg*

2865 Colors, food: synthetic—*mfg*

3842 Colostomy appliances—*mfg*

1061 Columbite mining

3339 Columbium refining, primary—*mfg*

3272 Columns, concrete—*mfg*

3443 Columns, fractionating: metal plate—*mfg*

3299 Columns, papier-mache or plaster of paris—*mfg*

3172 Comb cases, except precious metal—*mfg*

3999 Comb mounting, except precious metal—*mfg*

3731 Combat ships, building and repairing—*mfg*

5088 Combat vehicles, except trucks—wholesale

2281 Combed yarn, cotton—*mfg*

3822 Combination limit and fan controls—*mfg*

3822 Combination oil and hydronic controls—*mfg*

3523 Combines (harvester-threshers)—*mfg*

2299 Combing and converting top—*mfg*

3552 Combing machines, textile—*mfg*

0722 Combining, agricultural

3999 Combs, except hard rubber—*mfg*

3069 Combs, hard rubber—*mfg*

3089 Combs, plastics—*mfg*

3823 Combustion control instruments, **except commercial and household furnace** type—*mfg*

7299 Comfort station operation

2392 Comforters or comfortables—mfpm—*mfg*

2221 Comforters, manmade fiber—mitse—*mfg*

2721 Comic books: publishing and printing, or publishing only—*mfg*

3262 Commercial and household tableware and kitchenware: vitreous china—*mfg*

6512 Commercial and industrial buildings, operators of

7336 Commercial art and illustration

8249 Commercial art schools

6021 Commercial banks, National

6022 Commercial banks, State

6029 Commercial banks, not chartered

1542 Commercial building construction—general contractors

3263 Commercial earthenware, semivitreous—*mfg*

3646 Commercial lighting fixtures—*mfg*

6153 Commercial paper and accounts receivable, purchasers of

7335 Commercial photography

2711 Commercial printing and newspaper publishing combined—*mfg*

2754 Commercial printing, gravure—*mfg*

2752 Commercial printing, lithographic—*mfg*

2752 Commercial printing, offset—*mfg*

2759 Commercial printing: except lithographed or gravure—*mfg*

5112 Commercial stationers (not printers)—wholesale

3263 Commercial tableware and kitchenware, fine earthenware—*mfg*

3469 Commercial utensils, stamped and pressed metal: except cast aluminum—*mfg*

1541 Commercial warehouse construction—general contractors

7812 Commercials, television: tape or film production

5812 Commissary restaurants

**** Commission merchants, commodity: wholesale—code according to commodity

6111 Commodity Credit Corporation
6221 Commodity brokers (contracts)
6231 Commodity contract exchanges
6799 Commodity contract pool operators
6799 Commodity contract trading companies
6221 Commodity dealers (contracts)
**** Commodity or merchandise brokers and dealers—code according to commodity
1442 Common sand mining
9431 Communicable disease program administration—government
3661 Communications equipment and parts, telephone and telegraph—*mfg*
3661 Communications headgear, telephone—*mfg*
3357 Communications wire and cable, nonferrous—*mfg*
9631 Communications commissions—government
1731 Communications equipment installation—contractors
5065 Communications equipment, except household—wholesale
3663 Communications equipment, mobile and microwave—*mfg*
2531 Communion tables, wood—*mfg*
2052 Communion wafers—*mfg*
8399 Community action agencies
8322 Community centers
8399 Community chests
8222 Community colleges (junior)
9532 Community development agencies—government
8399 Community development groups
8641 Community membership clubs, other than amusement and recreation clubs
8331 Community service employment training programs
7922 Community theater productions
3621 Commutators, electric motor—*mfg*
3679 Commutators, electronic—*mfg*
4111 Commuter bus operation
4111 Commuter rail passenger operation
3652 Compact disc, prerecorded: except video—*mfg*
3531 Compactors, soil: vibratory—*mfg*
3961 Compacts, except precious metal and solid leather—*mfg*
3911 Compacts, precious metal—*mfg*
3172 Compacts, solid leather—*mfg*
3545 Comparators (machinists' precision tools)—*mfg*
3827 Comparators, optical—*mfg*
3812 Compasses, gyroscopic and magnetic except portable—*mfg*
3829 Compasses, magnetic: portable type—*mfg*

5031 Composite board products, wood-based—wholesale
2951 Composition blocks for paving—*mfg*
3089 Composition stone, plastics—*mfg*
2791 Composition, hand: for the printing trade—*mfg*
2791 Composition, machine: e.g., linotype, monotype—for the printing trade—*mfg*
2875 Compost—*mfg*
3843 Compounds, dental—*mfg*
3491 Compressed gas cylinder valves—*mfg*
3585 Compressors for refrigeration and air-conditioning—*mfg*
3563 Compressors, air and gas: for general industrial use—*mfg*
5075 Compressors, air-conditioning—wholesale
5084 Compressors, except air-conditioning and refrigeration—wholesale
5961 Computer and peripheral equipment, mail-order—retail
7371 Computer code authors
7379 Computer consultants
7376 Computer facilities management services
2761 Computer forms, manifold or continuous (excludes paper simply lined)—*mfg*
7377 Computer hardware rental or leasing, except finance leasing or by the manufacturer
7374 Computer input-output service
3823 Computer interface equipment for industrial process control—*mfg*
3674 Computer logic modules—*mfg*
8243 Computer operator training
3577 Computer output to microfilm units, computer peripheral equipment—*mfg*
3577 Computer paper tape punchers and devices, computer peripheral equipment—*mfg*
5112 Computer paper—wholesale
7378 Computer peripheral equipment repair and maintenance
7377 Computer peripheral equipment, rental and leasing
7299 Computer photography or portraits
5734 Computer printer stores—retail
7371 Computer programming services
7371 Computer programs or systems software development, custom
7378 Computer repair and maintenance
8243 Computer repair training
7372 Computer software publishers, prepackaged
5734 Computer software stores—retail
7371 Computer software systems analysis and design, custom

3695 Computer software tape and disks, blank: rigid and floppy—*mfg*
8243 Computer software training
7371 Computer software writers, free-lance
5961 Computer software, mail-order—retail
3572 Computer storage units—*mfg*
5734 Computer stores—retail
3575 Computer terminals—*mfg*
5045 Computer terminals—wholesale
7374 Computer time brokerage
7374 Computer time-sharing
7373 Computer-aided design (CAD) systems services
7373 Computer-aided engineering (CAE) systems services
7373 Computer-aided manufacturing (CAM) systems services
3845 Computerized axial tomography (CT/CAT scanner) apparatus—*mfg*
3571 Computers: digital, analog, and hybrid—*mfg*
5045 Computers—wholesale
2087 Concentrates, drink: except frozen fruit—*mfg*
2087 Concentrates, flavoring—*mfg*
2037 Concentrates, frozen fruit juice—*mfg*
5052 Concentrates, metallic—wholesale
2844 Concentrates, perfume—*mfg*
3532 Concentration machinery (metallurgical and mining)—*mfg*
7929 Concert artists
7922 Concert management service
3931 Concertinas and parts—*mfg*
7999 Concession operators, amusement devices and rides
5812 Concession stands, prepared food (e.g., in airports and sports arenas)
5169 Concrete additives—wholesale
5211 Concrete and cinder block dealers—retail
5032 Concrete and cinder block—wholesale
3546 Concrete and masonry drilling tools, power: portable—*mfg*
3272 Concrete articulated mattresses for river revetment—*mfg*
1741 Concrete block laying—contractors
1795 Concrete breaking for streets and highways—contractors
3531 Concrete buggies, powered—*mfg*
5032 Concrete building products—wholesale
5087 Concrete burial vaults and boxes—wholesale
1611 Concrete construction: roads, highways, public sidewalks, and streets—contractors
2899 Concrete curing compounds (blends of pigments, waxes, and resins)—*mfg*

1771 Concrete finishers—contractors
3444 Concrete forms, sheet metal—*mfg*
3531 Concrete grouting equipment—*mfg*
3531 Concrete gunning equipment—*mfg*
2899 Concrete hardening compounds—*mfg*
3531 Concrete mixers and finishing machinery—*mfg*
5032 Concrete mixtures—wholesale
3531 Concrete plants—*mfg*
5082 Concrete processing equipment—wholesale
3559 Concrete products machinery—*mfg*
3272 Concrete products, precast: except block and brick—*mfg*
1791 Concrete products, structural precast or prestressed: placing of—contractors
1791 Concrete reinforcement, placing of—contractors
5051 Concrete reinforcing bars—wholesale
3496 Concrete reinforcing mesh, made from purchased wire—*mfg*
3449 Concrete reinforcing steel bars, fabricated—*mfg*
1771 Concrete work, except paving—contractors
1771 Concrete work: private driveways, sidewalks, and parking areas—contractors
2951 Concrete, asphaltic: not made in petroleum refineries—*mfg*
2951 Concrete, bituminous—*mfg*
3272 Concrete, dry mixture—*mfg*
1321 Condensate production, cycle (natural gas)
2821 Condensation plastics—*mfg*
2023 Condensed and evaporated milk—*mfg*
3556 Condensed and evaporated milk machinery—*mfg*
3443 Condenser boxes, metal plate—*mfg*
2672 Condenser paper—mfpm—*mfg*
2621 Condenser paper—mitse—*mfg*
3585 Condensers and condensing units: refrigeration and air-conditioning—*mfg*
3629 Condensers for motors and generators—*mfg*
3443 Condensers, barometric—*mfg*
3675 Condensers, electronic—*mfg*
5065 Condensers, electronic—wholesale
3629 Condensers, except electronic: fixed and variable—*mfg*
3443 Condensers, steam—*mfg*
3621 Condensers, synchronous: electric—*mfg*
5075 Condensing units, air-conditioning—wholesale
5078 Condensing units, refrigeration—wholesale
8641 Condominium associations, except property management
1531 Condominium developers on own account
6531 Condominium managers

2835   Contrast media diagnostic products (e.g., iodine and barium)—*mfg*

3625   Control circuit devices: magnet and solid-state—*mfg*

3625   Control circuit relays, industrial—*mfg*

3621   Control equipment for buses and trucks—*mfg*

3625   Control equipment, electric—*mfg*

3714   Control equipment, motor vehicle: acceleration mechanisms and governors—*mfg*

3613   Control panels, electric power distribution—*mfg*

3559   Control rod drive mechanisms for use on nuclear reactors—*mfg*

3612   Control transformers—*mfg*

3492   Control valves, fluid power: metal—*mfg*

3674   Controlled rectifiers, solid-state—*mfg*

3823   Controllers for process variables: electric, electronic, and pneumatic—*mfg*

9311   Controllers' offices—government

5084   Controlling instruments and accessories, industrial—wholesale

3625   Controls and control accessories, industrial—*mfg*

3625   Controls for adjustable speed drives—*mfg*

3824   Controls, revolution and timing instruments—*mfg*

8059   Convalescent homes for psychiatric patients, with health care

8051   Convalescent homes with continuous nursing care

8059   Convalescent homes with health care

3631   Convection ovens, household: including portable—*mfg*

5074   Convectors—wholesale

5411   Convenience food stores—retail

3643   Convenience outlets, electric—*mfg*

7389   Convention bureaus

7389   Convention decorators

8661   Convents

3621   Converters, phase and rotary: electrical equipment—*mfg*

2515   Convertible sofas—*mfg*

3111   Convertors, leather—*mfg*

3496   Conveyor belts, made from purchased wire—*mfg*

1796   Conveyor system installation—contractors

3535   Conveyor systems for general industrial use—*mfg*

5084   Conveyor systems—wholesale

3523   Conveyors, farm (agricultural machinery)—*mfg*

3469   Cookers, pressure: stamped or drawn—*mfg*

3589   Cookers, steam: restaurant type—*mfg*

5461   Cookie stores—retail

2052   Cookies—*mfg*

5149   Cookies—wholesale

3634   Cooking appliances, household: electric, except convection and microwave ovens—*mfg*

3589   Cooking equipment, commercial—*mfg*

5046   Cooking equipment, commercial—wholesale

2079   Cooking oils, vegetable: except corn oil—refined—*mfg*

5149   Cooking oils—wholesale

8299   Cooking schools

3365   Cooking utensils, cast aluminum: except die-castings—*mfg*

3321   Cooking utensils, cast iron—*mfg*

3229   Cooking utensils, glass and glass ceramic—*mfg*

3262   Cooking ware, china—*mfg*

3263   Cooking ware, fine earthenware—*mfg*

3469   Cooking ware, porcelain enameled—*mfg*

3269   Cooking ware: stoneware, coarse earthenware, and pottery—*mfg*

5719   Cookware—retail

4961   Cooled air suppliers

5078   Coolers, beverage and drinking water: mechanical—wholesale

3585   Coolers, milk and water: electric—*mfg*

3086   Coolers, portable: foamed plastics—*mfg*

4741   Cooling of railroad cars

3724   Cooling systems, aircraft engine—*mfg*

3443   Cooling towers, metal plate—*mfg*

3444   Cooling towers, sheet metal—*mfg*

2499   Cooling towers, wood or wood and sheet metal combination—*mfg*

2449   Cooperage—*mfg*

2429   Cooperage stock mills—*mfg*

2429   Cooperage stock: staves, heading, and hoops—sawed or split—*mfg*

5085   Cooperage stock—wholesale

1531   Cooperative apartment developers on own account

6531   Cooperative apartment manager

6311   Cooperative life insurance organizations

2449   Coopered tubs—*mfg*

5137   Coordinate sets: women's, children's, and infants'—wholesale

3259   Coping, wall: clay—*mfg*

3272   Copings, concrete—*mfg*

2822   Copolymers: butadiene-styrene, butadiene-acrylonitrile, over 50 percent butadiene—*mfg*

3366   Copper and copper-base alloy castings, except die-castings—*mfg*

3366   Copper and copper-base alloy foundries—*mfg*

2879   Copper arsenate, formulated—*mfg*

8249 Correspondence schools, including branch offices and solicitors

2678 Correspondence-type tablets—mfpm—*mfg*

2899 Corrosion preventive lubricant, synthetic base: for jet engines—*mfg*

5113 Corrugated and solid fiber boxes—wholesale

3089 Corrugated panels, plastics—*mfg*

3316 Corrugating iron and steel, cold-rolled: not made in hot-rolling mills—*mfg*

3554 Corrugating machines for paper—*mfg*

2342 Corselets—mfpm—*mfg*

2342 Corset accessories: e.g., clasps and stays—mfpm—*mfg*

2241 Corset laces—*mfg*

7219 Corset repair shops

2342 Corsets and allied garments, except surgical: women's and misses'—mfpm—*mfg*

3842 Corsets, surgical—*mfg*

5137 Corsets—wholesale

3291 Corundum abrasives—*mfg*

1499 Corundum mining

3172 Cosmetic bags, regardless of material—*mfg*

2844 Cosmetic creams—*mfg*

2865 Cosmetic dyes, synthetic—*mfg*

3221 Cosmetic jars, glass—*mfg*

7389 Cosmetic kits, assembling and packaging

2844 Cosmetic lotions and oils—*mfg*

3842 Cosmetic restorations—*mfg*

2844 Cosmetics—*mfg*

5999 Cosmetics stores—retail

5963 Cosmetics, house-to-house or party plan selling—retail

5122 Cosmetics—wholesale

7231 Cosmetology schools

7231 Cosmetology shops or salons

5632 Costume accessories: handbags, costume jewelry, gloves, etc.—retail

7922 Costume design, theatrical

5632 Costume jewelry stores—retail

3961 Costume jewelry, except precious metal and precious or semiprecious stones—*mfg*

7299 Costume rental

2389 Costumes: e.g., lodge, masquerade, theatrical—mfpm—*mfg*

2515 Cot springs, assembled—*mfg*

3069 Cots, finger: rubber—*mfg*

2514 Cots, household: metal—*mfg*

2511 Cots, household: wood—*mfg*

2026 Cottage cheese, including pot, bakers', and farmers' cheese—*mfg*

2391 Cottage sets (curtains)—mfpm—*mfg*

3452 Cotter pins, metal—*mfg*

3089 Cotter pins, plastics—*mfg*

3523 Cotton balers and presses—*mfg*

2261 Cotton broadwoven fabric finishing—*mfg*

2211 Cotton broadwoven goods—*mfg*

4221 Cotton compresses and warehouses

0131 Cotton farms

2621 Cotton fiber paper—mitse—*mfg*

0724 Cotton ginning

3559 Cotton ginning machinery—*mfg*

7389 Cotton inspection service, not connected with transportation

5159 Cotton merchants, not members of exchanges—wholesale

2241 Cotton narrow fabrics—*mfg*

3523 Cotton picker and stripper harvesting machinery—*mfg*

0724 Cotton pickery

5131 Cotton piece goods—wholesale

7389 Cotton sampler service

0723 Cotton seed delinting

2284 Cotton thread—*mfg*

2281 Cotton yarn, spinning—*mfg*

5199 Cotton yarns—wholesale

3842 Cotton, absorbent: sterilized—*mfg*

3842 Cotton, including cotton balls—*mfg*

0722 Cotton, machine harvesting of

5159 Cotton, raw—wholesale

2211 Cottonades—*mfg*

2079 Cottonseed cooking and salad oil—*mfg*

0131 Cottonseed farms

2074 Cottonseed oil, cake, and meal: made in cottonseed oil mills—*mfg*

2074 Cottonseed oil, deodorized—*mfg*

2515 Couch springs, assembled—*mfg*

2515 Couches, studio: on frames of any material—*mfg*

2512 Couches, upholstered on wood frames, except convertible beds—*mfg*

2064 Cough drops, except pharmaceutical preparations—*mfg*

2834 Cough medicines—*mfg*

3823 Coulometric analyzers, industrial process type—*mfg*

3826 Coulometric analyzers, laboratory type—*mfg*

2869 Coumarin—*mfg*

2821 Coumarone-indene resins—*mfg*

8399 Councils for social agencies, exceptional children, and poverty

8322 Counseling centers

8111 Counselors at law

3829 Count rate meters, nuclear radiation—*mfg*

3089 Counter coverings, plastics—*mfg*

1799 Counter top installation—contractors

3824 Counter type registers—*mfg*

3423 Counterbores and countersinking bits, woodworking—*mfg*

4783 Crating goods for shipping
0913 Crayfish, catching of
3952 Crayons: chalk, gypsum, charcoal, fusains, pastel, and wax—*mfg*
2869 Cream of tartar—*mfg*
5084 Cream separators, except farm—wholesale
3523 Cream separators, farm—*mfg*
5083 Cream separators, farm—wholesale
3556 Cream separators, industrial—*mfg*
5143 Cream stations—wholesale
2023 Cream substitutes—*mfg*
2026 Cream, aerated—*mfg*
2026 Cream, bottled—*mfg*
2026 Cream, sour—*mfg*
2023 Cream: dried, powdered, and canned—*mfg*
2021 Creamery butter—*mfg*
2844 Creams, cosmetic—*mfg*
2844 Creams, shaving—*mfg*
6351 Credit and other financial responsibility insurance
7323 Credit bureaus and agencies
7389 Credit card service (collection by individual firms)
6153 Credit card service, collection by central agency
7323 Credit clearinghouses
6159 Credit institutions, agricultural
7323 Credit investigation services
6061 Credit unions, Federal
6062 Credit unions, State: not federally chartered
3949 Creels, fish—*mfg*
3552 Creels, textile machinery—*mfg*
3569 Cremating ovens—*mfg*
7261 Crematories
2865 Creosote oil, made in chemical plants—*mfg*
2861 Creosote, wood—*mfg*
2491 Creosoting of wood—*mfg*
2679 Crepe paper—mfpm—*mfg*
2221 Crepe satins—*mfg*
2211 Crepes, cotton—*mfg*
**** Cresines—code according to material from which made
2821 Cresol resins—*mfg*
2821 Cresol-furfural resins—*mfg*
2865 Cresols, made in chemical plants—*mfg*
2865 Cresylic acid, made in chemical plants—*mfg*
2211 Cretonne, cotton—*mfg*
3731 Crew boats, building and repairing—*mfg*
0761 Crew leaders, farm labor: contract
2252 Crew socks—*mfg*
3272 Cribbing, concrete—*mfg*
2514 Cribs, metal—*mfg*
2511 Cribs, wood—*mfg*

3949 Cricket equipment—*mfg*
9229 Criminal justice statistics centers—government
2211 Crinoline—*mfg*
8322 Crisis centers
8322 Crisis intervention centers
2284 Crochet thread: cotton, silk, manmade fibers, and wool—*mfg*
2395 Crochet ware, machine-made—*mfg*
2281 Crochet yarn: cotton, silk, wool, and manmade staple—*mfg*
3634 Crock pots, electric—*mfg*
3269 Crockery—*mfg*
5719 Crockery stores—retail
5023 Crockery—wholesale
2051 Croissants, except frozen—*mfg*
2053 Croissants, frozen—*mfg*
3523 Crop driers, farm—*mfg*
0721 Crop dusting, with/without fertilizing
0191 Crop farms, general
0721 Crop spraying, with/without fertilizing
3199 Crops, riding—*mfg*
3949 Croquet sets—*mfg*
3272 Crossing slabs, concrete—*mfg*
2491 Crossties, treated—*mfg*
8072 Crowns and bridges made in dental laboratories to order for the profession
5085 Crowns and closures, metal—wholesale
3466 Crowns, jar: stamped metal—*mfg*
3255 Crucibles, fire clay—*mfg*
3297 Crucibles: graphite, magnesite, chrome, silica, or other nonclay materials—*mfg*
1311 Crude oil production
5172 Crude oil, except bulk stations and terminals—wholesale
4612 Crude petroleum pipelines
1311 Crude petroleum production
0851 Cruising timber
2051 Crullers, except frozen—*mfg*
3523 Crushers, feed (agricultural machinery)—*mfg*
3569 Crushers, ice: except household—*mfg*
3531 Crushers, mineral: portable—*mfg*
3532 Crushers, mineral: stationary—*mfg*
3821 Crushing and grinding apparatus, laboratory—*mfg*
5084 Crushing machinery and equipment, industrial—wholesale
1221 Crushing plants, bituminous coal
5082 Crushing, pulverizing and screening machinery for construction and mining—wholesale
0273 Crustacean farms
3842 Crutches and walkers—*mfg*
3679 Cryogenic cooling devices (e.g., cryostats) for infrared detectors and masers—*mfg*

1541 Custom builders, industrial and warehouse—general contractors
1542 Custom builders, nonresidential: except industrial and warehouses—general contractors
1522 Custom builders, residential: except single-family—general contractors
1521 Custom builders, single-family houses—general contractors
3087 Custom compounding of purchased resins—*mfg*
3069 Custom compounding of rubber materials—*mfg*
3449 Custom roll formed products, metal—*mfg*
2421 Custom sawmills—*mfg*
5699 Custom tailors—retail
4731 Customhouse brokers
7532 Customizing automobiles, trucks or vans: except on a factory basis
9311 Customs Bureaus
4731 Customs clearance of freight
3231 Cut and engraved glassware, made from purchased glass—*mfg*
5992 Cut flowers—retail
5193 Cut flowers—wholesale
3131 Cut stock for boots and shoes—*mfg*
2421 Cut stock, softwood—*mfg*
3281 Cut stone products—*mfg*
5719 Cutlery stores—retail
3421 Cutlery, except table cutlery with handles of metal—*mfg*
3914 Cutlery, with metal handles and blades—*mfg*
5072 Cutlery—wholesale
3541 Cutoff machines (metalworking machinery)—*mfg*
3993 Cutouts and displays, window and lobby—*mfg*
3613 Cutouts, distribution—*mfg*
2675 Cutouts, paper and paperboard: die-cut from purchased material—*mfg*
3643 Cutouts, switch and fuse—*mfg*
3556 Cutters, biscuit (machines)—*mfg*
3532 Cutters, coal—*mfg*
3523 Cutters, ensilage—*mfg*
3423 Cutters, glass—*mfg*
3545 Cutters, milling—*mfg*
3554 Cutting and folding machines, paper—*mfg*
3544 Cutting dies, for cutting metal—*mfg*
3423 Cutting dies, paper industry—*mfg*
3423 Cutting dies: except metal cutting—*mfg*
3843 Cutting instruments, dental—*mfg*
3541 Cutting machines, pipe (machine tools)—*mfg*
2675 Cutting of cards—mfpm—*mfg*
3111 Cutting of leather—*mfg*

2992 Cutting oils, blending and compounding from purchased material—*mfg*
1629 Cutting right-of-way—general contractors
3545 Cutting tools and bits for use on lathes, planers, shapers, etc.—*mfg*
3549 Cutting up lines—*mfg*
3231 Cutware, made from purchased glass—*mfg*
2819 Cyanides—*mfg*
1459 Cyanite mining
1321 Cycle condensate production (natural gas)
3944 Cycles, sidewalk: children's—*mfg*
5169 Cyclic crudes and intermediates—wholesale
2865 Cyclic crudes, coal tar: product of coal tar distillation—*mfg*
2865 Cyclic intermediates, made in chemical plants—*mfg*
3069 Cyclo rubbers, natural—*mfg*
2822 Cyclo rubbers, synthetic—*mfg*
2865 Cyclohexane—*mfg*
3443 Cyclones, industrial: metal plate—*mfg*
2869 Cyclopropane—*mfg*
2834 Cyclopropane for anesthetic use (U.S.P. par N.F.), packaged—*mfg*
3699 Cyclotrons—*mfg*
3714 Cylinder heads, motor vehicle: gasoline engines—*mfg*
3272 Cylinder pipe, prestressed concrete—*mfg*
3272 Cylinder pipe, pretensioned concrete—*mfg*
3541 Cylinder reboring machines—*mfg*
3496 Cylinder wire cloth, made from purchased wire—*mfg*
3484 Cylinders and clips, gun: 30 mm. (or 1.18 inch) or less—*mfg*
3593 Cylinders, fluid power: hydraulic and pneumatic—*mfg*
3443 Cylinders, pressure: metal plate—*mfg*
3561 Cylinders, pump—*mfg*
3931 Cymbals and parts—*mfg*
3845 Cystoscopes, electromedical—*mfg*
3841 Cystoscopes, except electromedical—*mfg*
2835 Cytology and histology diagnostic products—*mfg*

D

2879 DDT (insecticide), formulated—*mfg*
2869 DDT, technical—*mfg*
5812 Dairy bars
5143 Dairy depots—wholesale
3523 Dairy equipment, farm—*mfg*
5083 Dairy farm machinery and equipment—wholesale
0241 Dairy farms
0241 Dairy heifer replacement farms
0751 Dairy herd improvement associations

3585 Dehumidifiers, except portable: electric—*mfg*

2034 Dehydrated fruits, vegetables, and soups—*mfg*

3556 Dehydrating equipment, food processing—*mfg*

3728 Deicing equipment, aircraft—*mfg*

2899 Deicing fluid—*mfg*

2611 Deinking of newsprint—*mfg*

3679 Delay lines—*mfg*

7319 Delivering advertising, private

3496 Delivery cases, made from purchased wire—*mfg*

3825 Demand meters, electric—*mfg*

2499 Demijohn covers: willow, rattan and reed—*mfg*

1795 Demolition of buildings or other structures, except marine—contractors

7389 Demonstration service, separate from sale

3715 Demountable cargo containers—*mfg*

2869 Denatured alcohol, industrial (nonbeverage)—*mfg*

2211 Denims—*mfg*

3861 Densitometers—*mfg*

3826 Densitometers, analytical—*mfg*

3823 Density and specific gravity instruments, industrial process type—*mfg*

3843 Dental alloys for amalgams—*mfg*

8621 Dental associations

3843 Dental chairs—*mfg*

3843 Dental engines—*mfg*

3843 Dental equipment and supplies—*mfg*

5047 Dental equipment—wholesale

3843 Dental hand instruments, including forceps—*mfg*

8049 Dental hygienists, offices of

7699 Dental instrument repair

6324 Dental insurance (providing services by contracts with health facilities)

8071 Dental laboratories, X-ray

8072 Dental laboratories, except X-ray

3843 Dental laboratory equipment—*mfg*

5047 Dental laboratory equipment—wholesale

3843 Dental metal—*mfg*

8021 Dental surgeons, offices of

2844 Dentifrices—*mfg*

5047 Dentists' professional supplies—wholesale

8021 Dentists, offices and clinics of

2844 Denture cleaners—*mfg*

3843 Denture materials—*mfg*

8072 Dentures made in dental laboratories to order for the profession

7342 Deodorant servicing of rest rooms

2842 Deodorants, nonpersonal—*mfg*

2844 Deodorants, personal—*mfg*

5311 Department stores—retail

2844 Depilatories, cosmetic—*mfg*

7299 Depilatory salons

3471 Depolishing metal, for the trade—*mfg*

6099 Deposit brokers

6399 Deposit or share insurance

3842 Depressors, tongue—*mfg*

3489 Depth charge release pistols and projectors—*mfg*

3483 Depth charges and parts (ordnance)—*mfg*

2834 Dermatological preparations—*mfg*

8011 Dermatologists, offices of

1389 Derrick building, repairing, and dismantling: oil and gas—on a contract basis

3531 Derricks, except oil and gas field—*mfg*

3533 Derricks, oil and gas field—*mfg*

5084 Derricks—wholesale

3559 Desalination equipment—*mfg*

2899 Desalter kits, sea water—*mfg*

3295 Desiccants, activated: clay—*mfg*

2819 Desiccants, activated: silica gel—*mfg*

1521 Designing and erecting combined: single-family houses—general contractors

1542 Designing and erecting, combined: commercial—general contractors

1541 Designing and erecting, combined: industrial—general contractors

1522 Designing and erecting, combined: residential, except single-family—general contractors

8711 Designing: ship, boat, and machine

3634 Desk fans, electric—*mfg*

3646 Desk lamps, commercial—*mfg*

3645 Desk lamps, residential—*mfg*

3999 Desk pads, except paper—*mfg*

2678 Desk pads, paper—mfpm—*mfg*

3281 Desk set bases, onyx—*mfg*

3199 Desk sets, leather—*mfg*

2511 Desks, household: wood—*mfg*

5021 Desks, including school—wholesale

2522 Desks, office: except wood—*mfg*

2521 Desks, office: wood—*mfg*

2024 Dessert pops, frozen: flavored ice, fruit, pudding, and gelatin—*mfg*

2024 Desserts, frozen: except bakery—*mfg*

2099 Desserts, ready-to-mix—*mfg*

3731 Destroyer tenders, building and repairing—*mfg*

7542 Detailing (cleaning and polishing) new autos for dealers on a contract or fee basis

0721 Detasseling of corn

7381 Detective agencies

3829 Detectors, scintillation—*mfg*

9223 Detention centers—government

2841 Detergents, synthetic organic and inorganic alkaline—*mfg*

5169 Detergents—wholesale
3341 Detinning of cans—*mfg*
3341 Detinning of scrap—*mfg*
2892 Detonating caps for safety fuses—*mfg*
2892 Detonators (explosive compounds)—*mfg*
3483 Detonators for ammunition more than 30 mm. (or more than 1.18 inch)—*mfg*
3483 Detonators: mine, bomb, depth charge, and chemical warfare projectile—*mfg*
8093 Detoxification centers, outpatient
3861 Developers, prepared photographic: not made in chemical plants—*mfg*
7819 Developing and printing of commercial motion picture film
7384 Developing and printing of film, except commercial motion picture film
7384 Developing and processing of home movies
5043 Developing apparatus, photographic—wholesale
3861 Developing machines and equipment, still or motion picture—*mfg*
1799 Dewatering—contractors
0171 Dewberry farms
2046 Dextrine—*mfg*
2899 Dextrine sizes—*mfg*
2046 Dextrose—*mfg*
2834 Dextrose and sodium chloride injection, mixed—*mfg*
2834 Dextrose injection—*mfg*
1429 Diabase, crushed and broken—quarrying
1411 Diabase, dimension—quarrying
2835 Diagnostic agents, biological—*mfg*
3841 Diagnostic apparatus, physicians'—*mfg*
7549 Diagnostic centers, automotive
5047 Diagnostic equipment, medical—wholesale
3643 Dial light sockets, radio—*mfg*
3845 Dialyzers, electromedical—*mfg*
2874 Diammonium phosphates—*mfg*
3496 Diamond cloth, made from purchased wire—*mfg*
3915 Diamond cutting and polishing—*mfg*
3545 Diamond cutting tools for turning, boring, burnishing, etc.—*mfg*
3544 Diamond dies, metalworking—*mfg*
3545 Diamond dressing and wheel crushing attachments—*mfg*
3291 Diamond dressing wheels—*mfg*
1799 Diamond drilling for building construction—contractors
1499 Diamond mining, industrial
3915 Diamond points for phonograph needles—*mfg*
3291 Diamond powder—*mfg*
5094 Diamonds (gems)—wholesale
5085 Diamonds, industrial: natural and crude—wholesale

2385 Diaper covers, waterproof: except vulcanized rubber—*mfg*
2211 Diaper fabrics—*mfg*
7219 Diaper service
2676 Diapers, disposable—mfpm—*mfg*
2399 Diapers, except disposable—mfpm—*mfg*
5137 Diapers—wholesale
3069 Diaphragms, rubber: separate and in kits—*mfg*
2782 Diaries—*mfg*
1459 Diaspore mining
3845 Diathermy apparatus, electromedical—*mfg*
3845 Diathermy unit—*mfg*
1499 Diatomaceous earth mining
3295 Diatomaceous earth, ground or otherwise treated—*mfg*
1499 Diatomite mining
3861 Diazo (whiteprint) paper and cloth, sensitized—*mfg*
3861 Diazotype (whiteprint) reproduction machines and equipment—*mfg*
3944 Dice and dice cups—*mfg*
2869 Dichlorodifluoromethane—*mfg*
2819 Dichromates—*mfg*
2339 Dickeys: women's, misses' and juniors'—mfpm—*mfg*
3579 Dictating machines, office types—*mfg*
8299 Diction schools
2821 Dicyandiamine resins—*mfg*
3559 Die and hub cutting equipment (jewelry manufacturing)—*mfg*
3537 Die and strip handlers—*mfg*
3542 Die-casting machines—*mfg*
3364 Die-casting nonferrous metals, except aluminum—*mfg*
3363 Die-castings, aluminum—*mfg*
2675 Die-cut paper and paperboard—mfpm—*mfg*
3554 Die-cutting and stamping machinery (paper converting machinery)—*mfg*
3111 Die-cutting of leather—*mfg*
3567 Dielectric heating equipment—*mfg*
3544 Dies and die holders for metal die-casting and metal cutting and forming, except threading—*mfg*
3556 Dies, biscuit cutting—*mfg*
3423 Dies, cutting: except metal cutting—*mfg*
3544 Dies, diamond: metalworking—*mfg*
3953 Dies, hand seal—*mfg*
3544 Dies, metalworking, except threading—*mfg*
5084 Dies, metalworking—wholesale
3544 Dies, plastics forming—*mfg*
3544 Dies, steel rule—*mfg*
3545 Dies, thread cutting—*mfg*

3519 Diesel and semidiesel engines: for stationary, marine, traction, etc.—*mfg*

3519 Diesel engine parts—*mfg*

7538 Diesel engine repair, automotive

5084 Diesel engines and engine parts, industrial—wholesale

3544 Diesets for metal stamping (presses)—*mfg*

3541 Diesinking machines—*mfg*

7299 Diet workshops

2023 Dietary supplements, dairy and nondairy base—*mfg*

5499 Dietetic food stores—retail

2869 Diethylcyclohexane (mixed isomers)—*mfg*

2869 Diethylene glycol ether—*mfg*

8049 Dieticians, offices of

3823 Differential pressure instruments, industrial process type—*mfg*

3826 Differential thermal analysis instruments—*mfg*

3714 Differentials and parts, motor vehicle—*mfg*

3443 Digesters, process: metal plate—*mfg*

3823 Digital displays of process variables—*mfg*

3663 Digital encoders—*mfg*

3825 Digital panel meters, electricity measuring—*mfg*

3825 Digital test equipment, electronic and electrical circuits and equipment—*mfg*

3825 Digital-to-analog converters, electronic instrumentation type—*mfg*

2834 Digitalis pharmaceutical preparations—*mfg*

2833 Digitoxin—*mfg*

2821 Diisocyanate resins—*mfg*

1629 Dike construction—general contractors

3281 Dimension stone for buildings—*mfg*

2426 Dimension, hardwood—*mfg*

2869 Dimethyl divinyl acetylene (di-isopropenyl acetylene)—*mfg*

2869 Dimethylhydrazine, unsymmetrical—*mfg*

2211 Dimities—*mfg*

5812 Diners (eating places)

2514 Dinette sets, metal—*mfg*

3732 Dinghies, building and repairing—*mfg*

4789 Dining car operations, not performed by line-haul railroad companies

3743 Dining cars and car equipment—*mfg*

2511 Dining room furniture, wood—*mfg*

5812 Dining rooms

5812 Dinner theaters

2038 Dinners, frozen: packaged—*mfg*

5142 Dinners, frozen—wholesale

3089 Dinnerware, plastics: except foam—*mfg*

3825 Diode and transistor testers—*mfg*

3674 Diodes, solid-state (germanium, silicon, etc.)—*mfg*

5065 Diodes—wholesale

1423 Diorite, crushed and broken—quarrying

1411 Diorite, dimension—quarrying

2865 Diphenylamine—*mfg*

2836 Diphtheria toxin—*mfg*

9721 Diplomatic services—government

3469 Dippers, ice cream—*mfg*

3479 Dipping metal in plastics solution as a preservative, for the trade—*mfg*

2879 Dips, cattle and sheep—*mfg*

2022 Dips, cheese-based—*mfg*

2099 Dips, except cheese and sour cream based—*mfg*

2026 Dips, sour cream based—*mfg*

4841 Direct broadcast satellite (DBS) services

7331 Direct mail advertising service

5963 Direct selling organizations (headquarters of door-to-door canvassers)—retail

6153 Direct working capital financing

1381 Directional drilling of oil and gas wells on a contract basis

3714 Directional signals, motor vehicle—*mfg*

2759 Directories, printed: except lithographed or gravure (not publishing)—*mfg*

7389 Directories, telephone: distribution on a contract or fee basis

2754 Directories: gravure printing (not publishing)—*mfg*

2741 Directories: publishing and printing, or publishing only—*mfg*

7819 Directors, motion picture: independent

3721 Dirigibles—*mfg*

1794 Dirt moving—contractors

3589 Dirt sweeping units, industrial—*mfg*

6321 Disability health insurance

9229 Disaster preparedness and management offices—government

8322 Disaster services

3651 Disc players, compact—*mfg*

1629 Discharging station construction, mine—general contractors

5813 Discotheques, alcoholic beverage

7911 Discotheques, except those serving alcoholic beverages

3652 Discs, laser: audio prerecorded—*mfg*

0721 Disease control for crops, with or without fertilizing

2599 Dish carts, restaurant—*mfg*

2392 Dishcloths, nonwoven textile—*mfg*

2211 Dishcloths, woven: made in weaving mills—*mfg*

2259 Dishcloths—mitse—*mfg*

3843 Dishes, abrasive: dental—*mfg*

3263 Dishes, commercial and household: fine earthenware (whiteware)—*mfg*

5113 Dishes, paper and disposable plastics—wholesale

2656 Dishes, paper: except those made from pressed or molded pulp—mfpm—*mfg*

3089 Dishes, plastics: except foam—*mfg*

2679 Dishes, pressed and molded pulp—mfpm—*mfg*

3944 Dishes, toy—*mfg*

2499 Dishes, wood—*mfg*

3262 Dishes: commercial and household—vitreous china—*mfg*

5064 Dishwashers, household: electric—wholesale

2841 Dishwashing compounds—*mfg*

3589 Dishwashing machines, commercial—*mfg*

3639 Dishwashing machines, household—*mfg*

2879 Disinfectants, agricultural—*mfg*

2842 Disinfectants, household and industrial plant—*mfg*

7342 Disinfecting service

7379 Disk and diskette conversion services

7379 Disk and diskette recertification services

3572 Disk drives, computer—*mfg*

5045 Disk drives—wholesale

3577 Disk pack inspectors, computer peripheral equipment—*mfg*

5065 Diskettes—wholesale

5735 Disks, music and video—retail

1796 Dismantling of machinery and other industrial equipment—contractors

1389 Dismantling of oil well rigs (oil field service) on a contract basis

4499 Dismantling ships

1795 Dismantling steel oil tanks, except oil field work—contractors

3999 Dispensers, soap—*mfg*

3089 Dispensers, tissue: plastics—*mfg*

3586 Dispensing and measuring pumps, gasoline and oil—*mfg*

5962 Dispensing machine sale of products—retail

2851 Dispersions, thermoplastics and colloidal: paint—*mfg*

7319 Display advertising service, except outdoor

2542 Display cases and fixtures, not refrigerated: except wood—*mfg*

2541 Display cases and fixtures, not refrigerated: wood—*mfg*

5078 Display cases, refrigerated—wholesale

2499 Display forms for boots and shoes, regardless of material—*mfg*

3999 Display forms, except shoe display forms—*mfg*

2653 Display items, corrugated and solid fiberboard—mfpm—*mfg*

2789 Display mounting—*mfg*

3993 Displays advertising: except printed—*mfg*

3993 Displays, paint process—*mfg*

3812 Distance measuring equipment (DME), aeronautical—*mfg*

2865 Distillates, coal tar—*mfg*

3312 Distillates, derived from chemical recovery coke ovens—*mfg*

2861 Distillates, wood—*mfg*

0831 Distillation of gums if carried on at the gum farm

0831 Distillation of turpentine and rosin if carried on at the gum farm

3567 Distillation ovens, charcoal and coke—*mfg*

3821 Distillation racks, laboratory—*mfg*

2899 Distilled water—*mfg*

2085 Distillers' dried grains and solubles—*mfg*

3556 Distillery machinery—*mfg*

3821 Distilling apparatus, laboratory type—*mfg*

3825 Distortion meters and analyzers—*mfg*

3613 Distribution boards, electric—*mfg*

3613 Distribution cutouts—*mfg*

5063 Distribution equipment, electrical—wholesale

1623 Distribution lines construction, oil and gas field—general contractors

7319 Distribution of advertising circulars and handbills

4961 Distribution of cooled air

4911 Distribution of electric power

4925 Distribution of manufactured gas

4924 Distribution of natural gas

3612 Distribution transformers, electric—*mfg*

3531 Distributors (construction machinery)—*mfg*

3694 Distributors, motor vehicle engine—*mfg*

6211 Distributors, security

9222 District attorneys' offices

3531 Ditchers, ladder: vertical boom or wheel—*mfg*

2834 Diuretics—*mfg*

3728 Dive brakes, aircraft—*mfg*

7389 Divers, commercial

1629 Dock construction—general contractors

4492 Docking of ocean vessels

3448 Docks, building, prefabricated: metal—*mfg*

4491 Docks, including buildings and facilities: operation and maintenance

3537 Docks, loading: portable, adjustable, and hydraulic—*mfg*

3577 Document entry conversion devices, computer peripheral equipment—*mfg*

5149 Dog and cat food—wholesale

0279 Dog farms

2047 Dog food—*mfg*

3199 Dog furnishings, leather: e.g., collars, leashes, harnesses, muzzles—*mfg*

0752 Dog grooming
0752 Dog pounds
7948 Dog racing
7381 Dogs, rental of: for protective service
5199 Dogs—wholesale
2679 Doilies, paper—mfpm—*mfg*
3944 Doll carriages and carts—*mfg*
3999 Doll wigs—*mfg*
3537 Dollies (hand or power trucks), industrial: except mining—*mfg*
3942 Dolls, doll parts, and doll clothing: except wigs—*mfg*
3942 Dolls, miniature: collectors'—*mfg*
5092 Dolls—wholesale
3297 Dolomite and dolomite-magnesite brick and shapes—*mfg*
1422 Dolomite, crushed and broken—quarrying
3274 Dolomite, dead-burned—*mfg*
1411 Dolomite, dimension—quarrying
3274 Dolomitic lime—*mfg*
1429 Dolomitic marble, crushed and broken—quarrying
1411 Dolomitic marble, dimension—quarrying
1542 Dome construction—general contractors
3647 Dome lights, motor vehicle—*mfg*
4731 Domestic forwarding
4424 Domestic freight transportation, deep sea
8811 Domestic service (private households employing cooks, maids, etc.)
3561 Domestic water pumps—*mfg*
8059 Domiciliary care with health care
3944 Dominoes—*mfg*
0272 Donkey farms
3442 Door and jamb assemblies, prefabricated: metal—*mfg*
1751 Door and window (prefabricated) installation—contractors
3429 Door bolts and checks—*mfg*
3442 Door frames and sash, metal—*mfg*
2431 Door frames and sash, wood and covered wood—*mfg*
5031 Door frames, all materials—wholesale
3272 Door frames, concrete—*mfg*
3444 Door hoods, aluminum—*mfg*
2431 Door jambs, wood—*mfg*
3429 Door locks and lock sets—*mfg*
5251 Door locks and lock sets—retail
3496 Door mats, made from purchased wire—*mfg*
3069 Door mats, rubber—*mfg*
2273 Door mats: twisted paper, grass, reed, coir, sisal, jute, and rag—*mfg*
3699 Door opening and closing devices, electrical—*mfg*
3429 Door opening and closing devices, except electrical—*mfg*

2431 Door screens, wood—*mfg*
2431 Door shutters, wood—*mfg*
2431 Door trim, wood—*mfg*
2431 Door units, prehung: wood and covered wood—*mfg*
3612 Doorbell transformers, electric—*mfg*
2431 Doors, combination screen-storm: wood—*mfg*
1751 Doors, folding: installation—contractors
3089 Doors, folding: plastics or plastics coated fabric—*mfg*
1751 Doors, garage: installation or erection—contractors
3442 Doors, louver: all metal or metal frame—*mfg*
3231 Doors, made from purchased glass—*mfg*
3442 Doors, metal—*mfg*
3499 Doors, safe and vault: metal—*mfg*
2431 Doors, wood and covered wood—*mfg*
5211 Doors—retail
2851 Dopes, paint—*mfg*
3732 Dories, building and repairing—*mfg*
7021 Dormitories, commercially operated
1522 Dormitory construction—general contractors
8734 Dosimetry, radiation
3552 Doubling and twisting frames (textile machinery)—*mfg*
3556 Dough mixing machinery—*mfg*
2045 Dough, biscuit—mfpm—*mfg*
2041 Dough, biscuit—mitse—*mfg*
2045 Doughnut mixes—mfpm—*mfg*
5461 Doughnut shops—retail
2051 Doughnuts, except frozen—*mfg*
2053 Doughnuts, frozen—*mfg*
2045 Doughs, refrigerated or frozen—mfpm—*mfg*
2041 Doughs, refrigerated or frozen—mitse—*mfg*
3553 Dovetailing machines (woodworking machinery)—*mfg*
3452 Dowel pins, metal—*mfg*
2499 Dowels, wood—*mfg*
3999 Down (feathers)—*mfg*
2329 Down-filled clothing: men's and boys'—mfpm—*mfg*
2339 Down-filled coats, jackets, and vests: women's, misses', and juniors'—mfpm—*mfg*
1761 Downspout installation, metal—contractors
3089 Downspouts, plastics—*mfg*
3444 Downspouts, sheet metal—*mfg*
3531 Dozers, tractor mounted: material moving—*mfg*
3823 Draft gauges, industrial process type—*mfg*

2851 Driers, paint—*mfg*
3861 Driers, photographic—*mfg*
3523 Driers: grain, hay, and seed (agricultural implements)—*mfg*
3634 Driers: hand, face, and hair—electric—*mfg*
3812 Driftmeters, aeronautical—*mfg*
3545 Drill bits, metalworking—*mfg*
3423 Drill bits, woodworking—*mfg*
3545 Drill bushings (drilling jig)—*mfg*
3541 Drill presses (machine tools)—*mfg*
3533 Drill rigs, all types—*mfg*
3499 Drill stands, metal—*mfg*
3731 Drilling and production platforms, floating, oil and gas—*mfg*
5084 Drilling bits—wholesale
1241 Drilling for bituminous coal, anthracite, and lignite on a contract basis
1081 Drilling for metal mining: on a contract basis
1481 Drilling for nonmetallic minerals, except fuels: on a contract basis
3545 Drilling machine attachments and accessories (machine tool accessories)—*mfg*
3541 Drilling machine tools (metal cutting)—*mfg*
2899 Drilling mud—*mfg*
5169 Drilling mud—wholesale
1381 Drilling of oil and gas wells: on a contract basis
3915 Drilling of pearls—*mfg*
3533 Drilling tools for gas, oil, or water wells—*mfg*
3546 Drilling tools, masonry and concrete: power (portable)—*mfg*
1381 Drilling water intake wells: on a contract basis
1781 Drilling water wells—contractors
1381 Drilling, service well: on a contract basis
3546 Drills (except rock drilling and coring), portable: electric and pneumatic—*mfg*
3545 Drills (machine tool accessories)—*mfg*
3532 Drills and drilling equipment, mining: except oil and gas field—*mfg*
3532 Drills, core—*mfg*
2211 Drills, cotton—*mfg*
3843 Drills, dental—*mfg*
3546 Drills, hand: electric—*mfg*
3423 Drills, hand: except power—*mfg*
3532 Drills, rock: portable—*mfg*
2087 Drink powders and concentrates—*mfg*
2656 Drinking cups, paper: except those made from pressed or molded pulp—mfpm—*mfg*
3431 Drinking fountains, except mechanically refrigerated: metal—*mfg*

3088 Drinking fountains, except mechanically refrigerated: plastics—*mfg*
3585 Drinking fountains, mechanically refrigerated—*mfg*
3261 Drinking fountains, vitreous china—*mfg*
5813 Drinking places, alcoholic beverages
2656 Drinking straws, except glass or plastics—mfpm—*mfg*
3229 Drinking straws, glass—*mfg*
5078 Drinking water coolers, mechanical—wholesale
2086 Drinks, fruit: bottled, canned, or fresh—*mfg*
3568 Drive chains, bicycle and motorcycle—*mfg*
3714 Drive shafts, motor vehicle—*mfg*
7389 Drive-a-way automobile service
5812 Drive-in restaurants
7833 Drive-in theaters
3545 Drivers, drill and cutters (machine tool accessories)—*mfg*
3572 Drives, computer: disk and drum—*mfg*
3566 Drives, high-speed industrial: except hydrostatic—*mfg*
3594 Drives, hydrostatic transmissions—*mfg*
1629 Driving piling—general contractors
2411 Driving timber—*mfg*
2394 Drop cloths, fabric—mfpm—*mfg*
3462 Drop forgings, iron and steel: not made in rolling mills—*mfg*
3542 Drop hammers, for forging and shaping metal—*mfg*
8069 Drug addiction rehabilitation hospitals
2865 Drug dyes, synthetic—*mfg*
2833 Drug grading, grinding, and milling—*mfg*
5122 Drug proprietaries—wholesale
8361 Drug rehabilitation centers, residential: with health care incidental
5912 Drug stores—retail
8093 Drug treatment, outpatient clinics
3069 Druggists' sundries, rubber—*mfg*
5122 Druggists' sundries—wholesale
5122 Drugs—wholesale
7929 Drum and bugle corps (drill teams)
3537 Drum cradles—*mfg*
3572 Drum drives, computer—*mfg*
3931 Drummers' traps—*mfg*
2655 Drums, fiber (metal-end or all-fiber)—mfpm—*mfg*
5085 Drums, new and reconditioned—wholesale
3931 Drums, parts, and accessories (musical instruments)—*mfg*
3089 Drums, plastics (containers)—*mfg*
2449 Drums, plywood—*mfg*
3412 Drums, shipping: metal—*mfg*
2449 Drums, shipping: wood—wirebound—*mfg*
3944 Drums, toy—*mfg*

2253 Dyeing and finishing knit outerwear, except hosiery, gloves, and nightwear—*mfg*
2254 Dyeing and finishing knit underwear—*mfg*
2258 Dyeing and finishing lace goods—*mfg*
2273 Dyeing and finishing of rugs and carpets—*mfg*
2231 Dyeing and finishing of wool and similar animal fibers: except knit—*mfg*
2258 Dyeing and finishing warp knit fabrics—*mfg*
2257 Dyeing and finishing weft knit fabrics—*mfg*
2251 Dyeing and finishing women's full-length and knee-length hosiery, except socks—*mfg*
2261 Dyeing cotton broadwoven fabrics—*mfg*
3999 Dyeing feathers, for the trade—*mfg*
3999 Dyeing furs—*mfg*
2381 Dyeing gloves, woven or knit: for the trade—*mfg*
3552 Dyeing machinery, textile—*mfg*
2262 Dyeing manmade fiber and silk broadwoven fabrics—*mfg*
2269 Dyeing raw stock, yarn, and narrow fabrics: except knit and wool—*mfg*
3999 Dyeing sponges—*mfg*
3999 Dyers' nets—*mfg*
2865 Dyes, food: synthetic—*mfg*
2844 Dyes, hair—*mfg*
2899 Dyes, household—*mfg*
2865 Dyes, synthetic organic—*mfg*
2861 Dyestuffs, natural—*mfg*
5169 Dyestuffs—wholesale
2892 Dynamite—*mfg*
3829 Dynamometer instruments—*mfg*
3621 Dynamos, electric: except automotive—*mfg*
3621 Dynamotors—*mfg*
3699 Dynamotrons—*mfg*
3728 Dynetric balancing stands, aircraft—*mfg*
3429 Dzus fasteners—*mfg*

E

2822 EPDM polymers—*mfg*
3842 Ear stoppers—*mfg*
7353 Earth moving equipment rental and leasing
1629 Earth moving, not connected with building construction—general contractors
1794 Earth moving—contractors
3269 Earthenware table and kitchen articles, coarse—*mfg*

3263 Earthenware: commercial and household—semivitreous—*mfg*
2048 Earthworm food and bedding—*mfg*
0279 Earthworm hatcheries
3952 Easels, artists'—*mfg*
2771 Easter cards, except hand painted—*mfg*
5113 Eating utensils: forks, knives, spoons-disposable plastics—wholesale
3444 Eaves, sheet metal—*mfg*
3281 Ecclesiastical statuary, marble—*mfg*
3299 Ecclesiastical statuary: gypsum, clay, or papier-mache—factory production only—*mfg*
3914 Ecclesiastical ware: silver, nickel silver, pewter, and plated—*mfg*
8748 Economic consulting
9611 Economic development agencies—government
8732 Economic research, commercial
8733 Economic research, noncommercial
3443 Economizers (boilers)—*mfg*
6082 Edge Act Corporations
3423 Edge tools for woodworking: augers, bits, gimlets, countersinks, etc.—*mfg*
2789 Edging books, cards, or paper—*mfg*
2258 Edgings, lace—*mfg*
3861 Editing equipment, motion picture: rewinds, viewers, titlers, and splicers—*mfg*
7819 Editing of motion picture film
7338 Editing service
9411 Education offices, nonoperating
9411 Education statistics centers—government
8748 Educational consulting, except management
7812 Educational motion picture production
8732 Educational research, commercial
8733 Educational research, noncommercial
6732 Educational trusts, management of
0912 Eels, catching of
2834 Effervescent salts—*mfg*
2015 Egg albumen—*mfg*
2675 Egg cartons, die-cut paper and paperboard—mfpm—*mfg*
2679 Egg cartons, molded pulp—mfpm—*mfg*
2679 Egg case filler flats, molded pulp—mfpm—*mfg*
2675 Egg case fillers and flats, die-cut from purchased paper or paperboard—*mfg*
2441 Egg cases, wood—*mfg*
3634 Egg cookers, electric—*mfg*
5499 Egg dealers—retail
0252 Egg farms, chicken
0259 Egg farms, poultry: except chicken and turkey
0253 Egg farms, turkey

3823 Electrodes used in industrial process measurement—*mfg*
3641 Electrodes, cold cathode fluorescent lamp—*mfg*
3548 Electrodes, electric welding—*mfg*
3845 Electroencephalographs—*mfg*
3542 Electroforming machines—*mfg*
3829 Electrogamma ray loggers—*mfg*
3845 Electrogastrograph—*mfg*
3492 Electrohydraulic servo valves, fluid power: metal—*mfg*
3471 Electrolizing steel, for the trade—*mfg*
7299 Electrolysis (hair removal)
2835 Electrolyte diagnostic reagents—*mfg*
3823 Electrolytic conductivity instruments, industrial process type—*mfg*
3826 Electrolytic conductivity instruments, laboratory type—*mfg*
3541 Electrolytic metal cutting machine tools—*mfg*
3625 Electromagnetic brakes and clutches—*mfg*
3824 Electromechanical counters—*mfg*
3845 Electromedical apparatus—*mfg*
5047 Electromedical equipment—wholesale
3845 Electromyographs—*mfg*
3671 Electron beam (beta ray) generator tubes—*mfg*
3699 Electron beam metal cutting, forming, and welding machines—*mfg*
3699 Electron linear accelerators—*mfg*
3826 Electron microprobes—*mfg*
3826 Electron microscopes—*mfg*
3826 Electron paramagnetic spin type apparatus—*mfg*
3559 Electron tube making machinery—*mfg*
3671 Electron tube parts, except glass blanks: bases, getters, and guns—*mfg*
3825 Electron tube test equipment—*mfg*
3671 Electron tubes—*mfg*
3541 Electron-discharge metal cutting machine tools—*mfg*
5065 Electronic coils and transformers—wholesale
3577 Electronic computer subassembly for film reader and phototheodolite—*mfg*
5065 Electronic connectors—wholesale
1731 Electronic control system installation—contractors
3469 Electronic enclosures: stamped or pressed—*mfg*
7359 Electronic equipment rental and leasing, except medical and computer equipment
7629 Electronic equipment repair, except computers and computer peripheral equipment

6099 Electronic funds transfer networks, including switching
3944 Electronic game machines, except coin-operated—*mfg*
3651 Electronic kits for home assembly: radio and television receiving sets, and phonograph equipment—*mfg*
4822 Electronic mail services
3931 Electronic musical instruments—*mfg*
5065 Electronic parts—wholesale
3825 Electronic test equipment for testing electrical characteristics—*mfg*
3824 Electronic totalizing counters—*mfg*
3944 Electronic toys—*mfg*
5065 Electronic tubes: receiving, transmitting, and industrial—wholesale
3826 Electrophoresis instruments—*mfg*
3559 Electroplating machinery and equipment, except rolling mill lines—*mfg*
3471 Electroplating of metals and formed products, for the trade—*mfg*
1721 Electrostatic painting on site (including of lockers and fixtures)—contractors
3699 Electrostatic particle accelerators—*mfg*
3564 Electrostatic precipitators—*mfg*
3641 Electrotherapeutic lamp units for ultraviolet and infrared radiation—*mfg*
3845 Electrotherapy unit—*mfg*
2796 Electrotype plates—*mfg*
2796 Electrotyping for the trade—*mfg*
3555 Electrotyping machines—*mfg*
3826 Elemental analyzers (CHNOS)—*mfg*
8211 Elementary schools
2879 Elements, minor or trace (agricultural chemicals)—*mfg*
1622 Elevated highway construction—general contractors
4111 Elevated railway operation
1791 Elevator front installation, metal—contractors
3534 Elevator fronts—*mfg*
3446 Elevator guide rails, metal—*mfg*
1796 Elevator installation, conversion, and repair—contractors
3534 Elevators and elevator equipment, passenger and freight—*mfg*
3728 Elevators, aircraft—*mfg*
3523 Elevators, farm—*mfg*
4221 Elevators, grain: storage only
3534 Elevators, powered: nonfarm—*mfg*
5084 Elevators—wholesale
9721 Embassies
2395 Emblems, embroidered—*mfg*
2399 Emblems, made from fabrics—*mfg*
3199 Embossed leather goods for the trade—*mfg*

3764 Engines and engine parts, guided missile—*mfg*
3519 Engines and engine parts, internal combustion— military tank—*mfg*
5084 Engines and parts, diesel—wholesale
3714 Engines and parts, except diesel: motor vehicle—*mfg*
3519 Engines, internal combustion: except aircraft and nondiesel automotive—*mfg*
3944 Engines, miniature—*mfg*
3743 Engines, steam (locomotives)—*mfg*
3511 Engines, steam: except locomotives—*mfg*
3519 Engines: diesel and semidiesel and dual fuel—except aircraft—*mfg*
0161 English pea farms
3231 Engraved glassware—*mfg*
3423 Engravers' tools, hand—*mfg*
3479 Engraving jewelry, silverware, and metal for the trade: except printing—*mfg*
3555 Engraving machinery and equipment (printing trades machinery)—*mfg*
2759 Engraving of cards, except greeting cards—*mfg*
3089 Engraving of plastics—*mfg*
2796 Engraving on copper, steel, wood, or rubber plates for printing purposes—*mfg*
2796 Engraving on textile printing plates and cylinders—*mfg*
2796 Engraving, steel line: for printing purposes—*mfg*
7389 Engrossing, e.g., diplomas and resolutions
3861 Enlargers, photographic—*mfg*
2335 Ensemble dresses: women's, misses', and juniors'—mfpm—*mfg*
3523 Ensilage blowers and cutters—*mfg*
7929 Entertainers
7929 Entertainment groups
0721 Entomological service, agricultural
8999 Entomologists, consulting: not with business service laboratories
3555 Envelope printing presses—*mfg*
3579 Envelope stuffing, sealing, and addressing machines—*mfg*
2677 Envelopes, printed or unprinted: paper, glassine, cellophane, and pliofilm—mfpm—*mfg*
2759 Envelopes, printed: except lithographed or gravure—*mfg*
2754 Envelopes: gravure printing—*mfg*
5112 Envelopes—wholesale
9431 Environmental health programs—government
9511 Environmental protection agencies—government

9511 Environmental quality and control agencies—government
2835 Enzyme and isoenzyme diagnostic reagents—*mfg*
2869 Enzymes, except diagnostic substances—*mfg*
2865 Eosine toners—*mfg*
2833 Ephedrine and derivatives—*mfg*
2821 Epichlorohydrin bisphenol—*mfg*
2821 Epichlorohydrin diphenol—*mfg*
2822 Epichlorohydrin elastomers—*mfg*
2891 Epoxy adhesives—*mfg*
1799 Epoxy application—contractors
2851 Epoxy coatings, made from purchased resin—*mfg*
2821 Epoxy resins—*mfg*
9441 Equal employment opportunity offices—government
3952 Eraser guides and shields—*mfg*
3069 Erasers: rubber, or rubber and abrasive combined—*mfg*
1389 Erecting lease tanks, oil and gas field: on a contract basis
1799 Erection and dismantling of forms for poured concrete—contractors
3944 Erector sets, toy—*mfg*
2833 Ergot alkaloids—*mfg*
3534 Escalators, passenger and freight—*mfg*
7299 Escort service
6531 Escrow agents, real estate
6099 Escrow institutions other than real estate
2899 Essential oils—*mfg*
5169 Essential oils—wholesale
2822 Estane—*mfg*
8811 Estates, private
2821 Ester gum—*mfg*
2869 Esters of phosphoric, adipic, lauric, oleic, sebacic, and stearic acids—*mfg*
2869 Esters of phthalic anhydride—*mfg*
2869 Esters of polyhydric alcohols—*mfg*
0851 Estimating timber
3555 Etching machines (printing trades machinery)—*mfg*
2796 Etching on copper, steel, wood, or rubber plates for printing purposes—*mfg*
3479 Etching on metals for purposes other than printing—*mfg*
3479 Etching: photochemical, for the trade—*mfg*
1321 Ethane (natural) production
2869 Ethanol, industrial—*mfg*
2869 Ether—*mfg*
2861 Ethyl acetate, natural—*mfg*
2869 Ethyl acetate, synthetic—*mfg*
2085 Ethyl alcohol for medicinal and beverage purposes—*mfg*

3356   Extruded shapes, nonferrous metals and alloys, except copper and aluminum—*mfg*

3542   Extruding machines (machine tools), metal—*mfg*

3544   Extrusion dies—*mfg*

3355   Extrusion ingot, aluminum: made in rolling mills—*mfg*

3334   Extrusion ingot, aluminum: primary—*mfg*

3841   Eye examining instruments and apparatus—*mfg*

8069   Eye, ear, nose, and throat hospitals: in-patient

3172   Eyeglass cases, regardless of material—*mfg*

3851   Eyeglasses, lenses, and frames—*mfg*

2395   Eyelet making, for the trade—*mfg*

3965   Eyelets, metal: for clothing, fabrics, boots and shoes, and paper—*mfg*

3851   Eyes, glass and plastics—*mfg*

F

3651   FM and AM tuners—*mfg*

2231   Fabric finishing of wool, mohair, and similar animal fibers: except knit—*mfg*

2261   Fabric finishing, cotton broadwoven fabrics—*mfg*

2262   Fabric finishing, manmade fiber and silk broadwoven—*mfg*

2258   Fabric finishing, warp knit—*mfg*

5949   Fabric shops—retail

2842   Fabric softeners—*mfg*

3498   Fabricated pipe and fittings: threading, bending, etc.—of purchased pipe—*mfg*

3441   Fabricated structural steel—*mfg*

2296   Fabrics for reinforcing rubber tires, industrial belting, and fuel cells—*mfg*

2231   Fabrics, animal fiber: broadwoven wool, mohair, and similar animal fibers—*mfg*

2241   Fabrics, animal fiber: narrow woven—*mfg*

2297   Fabrics, bonded fiber: except felt—*mfg*

2211   Fabrics, broadwoven: cotton—*mfg*

2221   Fabrics, broadwoven: manmade fiber and silk—*mfg*

2231   Fabrics, broadwoven: wool, mohair, and similar animal fibers—*mfg*

2257   Fabrics, circular knit—*mfg*

2295   Fabrics, coated and impregnated: except rubberized—*mfg*

2297   Fabrics, nonwoven: except felts—*mfg*

2952   Fabrics, roofing: asphalt or tar saturated—mfpm—*mfg*

3069   Fabrics, rubberized—*mfg*

2258   Fabrics, warp knit—mitse—*mfg*

2257   Fabrics, weft knit—*mfg*

3496   Fabrics, woven wire: made from purchased wire—*mfg*

2299   Fabrics: linen, jute, hemp, ramie—*mfg*

2844   Face creams and lotions—*mfg*

3644   Face plates (wiring devices)—*mfg*

2844   Face powders—*mfg*

6726   Face-amount certificate issuing

7231   Facial salons

2621   Facial tissue stock—mitse—*mfg*

2676   Facial tissues—mfpm—*mfg*

7376   Facilities management services, computer

8744   Facilities management, except computer

8744   Facilities support services, except computer

3541   Facing machines—*mfg*

3251   Facing tile, clay—*mfg*

2899   Facings (chemical foundry supplies)—*mfg*

3661   Facsimile equipment—*mfg*

2754   Facsimile letters: gravure printing—*mfg*

4822   Facsimile transmission services

6153   Factors of commercial paper

1541   Factory construction—general contractors

2599   Factory furniture: stools, work benches, tool stands, and cabinets—*mfg*

3253   Faience tile—*mfg*

2221   Failles—*mfg*

7999   Fairs, agricultural: operation of

2679   False faces, papier-mache—mfpm—*mfg*

5651   Family clothing stores—retail

8322   Family counseling services

8322   Family location services

8322   Family service agencies

3822   Fan control, temperature responsive—*mfg*

3599   Fan forges—*mfg*

3111   Fancy leathers—*mfg*

2672   Fancy paper, coated and glazed: except for packaging—mfpm—*mfg*

2761   Fanfold forms—*mfg*

3564   Fans, except household—*mfg*

3634   Fans, household: kitchen—except attic—*mfg*

3634   Fans, household: electric, except attic fans—*mfg*

5084   Fans, industrial—wholesale

3829   Fare registers: e.g., for streetcars and buses—*mfg*

2043   Farina, cereal breakfast food—*mfg*

2041   Farina, except breakfast food—mitse—*mfg*

1542   Farm building construction, except residential—general contractors

2452   Farm buildings, prefabricated or portable: wood—*mfg*

3448   Farm buildings, prefabricated: metal—*mfg*

8699   Farm bureaus

3523   Farm elevators—*mfg*

8699   Farm granges

8811   Farm homes, noncommercial
0761   Farm labor contractors
3523   Farm machinery and equipment—*mfg*
5083   Farm machinery and equipment—wholesale
7699   Farm machinery repair
0762   Farm management services
6159   Farm mortgage companies
4221   Farm product warehousing and storage, other than cold storage
3443   Farm storage tanks, metal plate—*mfg*
5191   Farm supplies—wholesale
4212   Farm to market hauling
3523   Farm tractors—*mfg*
3523   Farm wagons—*mfg*
6111   Farmers Home Administration
8811   Farms, residential: noncommercial
****   Farms—see type of farm
7699   Farriers (blacksmith shops)
3089   Fascia, plastics (siding)—*mfg*
2752   Fashion plates, lithographed—*mfg*
2759   Fashion plates, printed: except lithographed or gravure—*mfg*
2754   Fashion plates: gravure printing—*mfg*
7363   Fashion show model supply service
5812   Fast food restaurants
5812   Fast food stores (prepared food)
5072   Fasteners, hardware—wholesale
3965   Fasteners: glove, slide, snap, and hook-and-eye—*mfg*
3812   Fathometers—*mfg*
3829   Fatigue testing machines, industrial: mechanical—*mfg*
2843   Fats, sulfonated—*mfg*
2869   Fatty acid esters and amines—*mfg*
2899   Fatty acids: margaric, oleic, and stearic—*mfg*
3261   Faucet handles, vitreous china and earthenware—*mfg*
3432   Faucets, metal and plastics—*mfg*
2499   Faucets, wood—*mfg*
3582   Feather cleaning and sterilizing machinery—*mfg*
2077   Feather meal—*mfg*
2329   Feather-filled clothing: men's and boys'—mfpm—*mfg*
2339   Feather-filled coats, jackets, and vests: women's, misses', and juniors'—mfpm—*mfg*
3999   Feathers: curling, dyeing, and renovating—for the trade—*mfg*
5159   Feathers—wholesale
6331   Federal Crop Insurance Corporation
6399   Federal Deposit Insurance Corporation
6019   Federal Home Loan Banks
6111   Federal Home Loan Mortgage Corporation

6111   Federal Intermediate Credit Bank
6111   Federal Land Banks
6111   Federal National Mortgage Association
6011   Federal Reserve banks
6011   Federal Reserve branches
6399   Federal Savings and Loan Insurance Corporation
6061   Federal credit unions
6035   Federal savings and loan associations
6035   Federal savings banks
5191   Feed additives, animal—wholesale
3199   Feed bags for horses—*mfg*
2048   Feed concentrates—*mfg*
3523   Feed grinders, crushers, and mixers (agricultural machinery)—*mfg*
3523   Feed grinders—mixers—*mfg*
3556   Feed mixers, except agricultural machinery—*mfg*
2048   Feed premixes—*mfg*
2048   Feed supplements—*mfg*
5191   Feed, except unmixed grain—wholesale
2046   Feed, gluten—*mfg*
3612   Feeder voltage regulators and boosters (electric transformers)—*mfg*
3523   Feeders, chicken—*mfg*
3532   Feeders, ore and aggregate—*mfg*
0211   Feedlots, cattle
0213   Feedlots, hog
0214   Feedlots, lamb
2048   Feeds, prepared (including mineral): for animals and fowls—except dogs and cats—*mfg*
2048   Feeds, specialty: mice, guinea pigs, minks, etc.—*mfg*
2048   Feeds, stock: dry—*mfg*
1459   Feldspar mining
3295   Feldspar, ground or otherwise treated—*mfg*
2499   Fellies, wood—*mfg*
2299   Felt goods, except woven felts and hats: wool, hair, jute, or other fiber—*mfg*
3292   Felt roll roofing, asbestos—*mfg*
3951   Felt tip markers—*mfg*
3292   Felt, woven amosite: asbestos—*mfg*
5199   Felt—wholesale
2621   Felts, building—mitse—*mfg*
2299   Felts, pressed or needle loom—*mfg*
2952   Felts, roofing: asphalt saturated and tar saturated-roll or shingle—*mfg*
5033   Felts, tarred—wholesale
2231   Felts: wool, mohair, and similar animal fibers: woven—*mfg*
3699   Fence chargers, electric—*mfg*
1799   Fence construction—contractors
3496   Fence gates, made from purchased wire—*mfg*

3315	Fence gates, posts, and fittings: steel—made in wiredrawing plants—*mfg*
3312	Fence posts, iron and steel: made in steel works or rolling mills—*mfg*
3423	Fence stretchers (handtools)—*mfg*
3446	Fences and posts, ornamental iron and steel—*mfg*
5039	Fencing and accessories, wire—wholesale
5211	Fencing dealers—retail
3949	Fencing equipment (sporting goods)—*mfg*
3496	Fencing, made from purchased wire—*mfg*
2499	Fencing, wood: except rough pickets, poles, and rails—*mfg*
5031	Fencing, wood—wholesale
3465	Fenders, stamped and pressed—*mfg*
1061	Ferberite mining
3443	Fermenters (process vessels), metal plate—*mfg*
2869	Ferric ammonium oxalate—*mfg*
2819	Ferric chloride—*mfg*
2816	Ferric oxide pigments—*mfg*
2819	Ferric oxides, except pigments—*mfg*
4482	Ferries, operation of
3599	Ferris wheels—*mfg*
3264	Ferrite—*mfg*
3313	Ferroalloys (including high percentage)—*mfg*
5051	Ferroalloys—wholesale
3313	Ferrochromium—*mfg*
2819	Ferrocyanides—*mfg*
3313	Ferromanganese—*mfg*
3313	Ferromolybdenum—*mfg*
3313	Ferrophosphorus—*mfg*
3313	Ferrosilicon—*mfg*
3313	Ferrotitanium—*mfg*
3313	Ferrotungsten—*mfg*
3547	Ferrous and nonferrous mill equipment, auxiliary—*mfg*
3313	Ferrovanadium—*mfg*
3499	Ferrules, metal—*mfg*
3731	Ferryboats, building and repairing—*mfg*
5191	Fertilizer and fertilizer materials—wholesale
0711	Fertilizer application for crops
2819	Fertilizer materials: muriate and sulfate of potash, not produced at mines—*mfg*
2875	Fertilizers, mixed: made in plants not manufacturing fertilizer materials—*mfg*
2873	Fertilizers, mixed: made in plants producing nitrogenous fertilizer materials—*mfg*
2874	Fertilizers, mixed: made in plants producing phosphatic fertilizer materials—*mfg*
2873	Fertilizers: natural (organic), except compost—*mfg*
3523	Fertilizing machinery, farm—*mfg*

2834	Fever remedies—*mfg*
5113	Fiber cans and drums—wholesale
2519	Fiber furniture, household—*mfg*
3357	Fiber optic cable—*mfg*
3229	Fiber optics strands—*mfg*
2611	Fiber pulp: made from wood, rags, wastepaper, linters, straw, and bagasse—*mfg*
2221	Fiberglass fabrics—*mfg*
5131	Fiberglass fabrics—wholesale
3296	Fiberglass insulation—*mfg*
5033	Fiberglass insulation materials—wholesale
3624	Fibers, carbon and graphite—*mfg*
2823	Fibers, cellulose manmade—*mfg*
3229	Fibers, glass, textile—*mfg*
2824	Fibers, manmade: except cellulosic—*mfg*
2823	Fibers, rayon—*mfg*
2299	Fibers, textile: recovery from textile mill waste and rags—*mfg*
5159	Fibers, vegetable—wholesale
2823	Fibers, viscose—*mfg*
6351	Fidelity insurance
6531	Fiduciaries, real estate
6099	Fiduciary agencies other than real estate or trust
3489	Field artillery—*mfg*
2329	Field jackets, military—mfpm—*mfg*
0181	Field nurseries: growing of flowers and shrubbery, except forest shrubbery
3825	Field strength and intensity measuring equipment, electrical—*mfg*
3523	Field type rotary tillers (agricultural machinery)—*mfg*
7389	Field warehousing, not public warehousing
3714	Fifth wheels—*mfg*
0179	Fig orchards and farms
3953	Figures (marking devices), metal—*mfg*
3269	Figures, pottery: china, earthenware, and stoneware—*mfg*
3999	Figures, wax: mannikins—*mfg*
3641	Filaments for electric lamps—*mfg*
0173	Filbert groves and farms
0723	Filbert hulling and shelling
5112	File cards—wholesale
2522	File drawer frames: except wood—*mfg*
5112	File folders—wholesale
3423	Files, including recutting and resharpening—*mfg*
3545	Files, machine tool—*mfg*
2522	Filing boxes, cabinets, and cases: except wood—*mfg*
2521	Filing boxes, cabinets, and cases: wood—*mfg*
2652	Filing boxes, paperboard—mfpm—*mfg*
2675	Filing folders—mfpm—*mfg*
3541	Filing machines, metal (machine tools)—*mfg*

9224 Fire departments, including volunteer—government
3669 Fire detection systems, electric—*mfg*
3829 Fire detector systems, nonelectric—*mfg*
3442 Fire doors, metal—*mfg*
1799 Fire escape installation—contractors
3446 Fire escapes, metal—*mfg*
2899 Fire extinguisher charges—*mfg*
3999 Fire extinguishers, portable—*mfg*
7389 Fire extinguishers, service of
5099 Fire extinguishers—wholesale
3491 Fire hydrant valves—*mfg*
6411 Fire loss appraisal
9224 Fire marshals' offices—government
9224 Fire prevention offices—government
0851 Fire prevention, forest
2261 Fire resistance finishing of cotton broadwoven fabrics—*mfg*
2262 Fire resistance finishing of manmade fiber and silk broadwoven fabrics—*mfg*
2899 Fire retardant chemical preparations—*mfg*
1542 Fire station construction—general contractors
3484 Firearms, 30 mm. (or 1.18 inch) or less—*mfg*
5099 Firearms, except sporting—wholesale
5091 Firearms, sporting—wholesale
5941 Firearms—retail
3731 Fireboats, building and repairing—*mfg*
3255 Firebrick, clay—*mfg*
2311 Firefighters' dress uniforms, men's—*mfg*
3569 Firefighting apparatus, except automotive and chemical—*mfg*
5087 Firefighting equipment—wholesale
7389 Firefighting service, other than forestry or public
0851 Firefighting, forest
3569 Firehose, except rubber—*mfg*
3052 Firehose, rubber—*mfg*
3429 Fireplace equipment (hardware)—*mfg*
3433 Fireplace inserts—*mfg*
2999 Fireplace logs, made from coal—*mfg*
5719 Fireplace screens and accessories—retail
5719 Fireplace stores—retail
3272 Fireplaces, concrete—*mfg*
5074 Fireplaces, prefabricated—wholesale
1752 Fireproof flooring construction—contractors
1799 Fireproofing buildings—contractors
3251 Fireproofing tile, clay—*mfg*
2499 Firewood and fuel wood containing fuel binder—*mfg*
5099 Firewood—wholesale
2899 Fireworks—*mfg*
7999 Fireworks display service

5999 Fireworks—retail
5092 Fireworks—wholesale
7699 Firing china to individual order
3269 Firing china, for the trade—*mfg*
2449 Firkins and kits, wood: coopered—*mfg*
3842 First aid, snake bite, and burn kits—*mfg*
2092 Fish and seafood cakes, frozen—*mfg*
2091 Fish and seafood cakes: canned—*mfg*
3556 Fish and shellfish processing machinery—*mfg*
9512 Fish and wildlife conservation—government
2091 Fish egg bait, canned—*mfg*
0273 Fish farms, except hatcheries
2092 Fish fillets—*mfg*
2048 Fish food—*mfg*
0921 Fish hatcheries
2077 Fish liver oils, crude—*mfg*
2833 Fish liver oils, refined and concentrated for medicinal use—*mfg*
5421 Fish markets—retail
2077 Fish meal—*mfg*
2298 Fish nets and seines, made in cordage or twine mills—*mfg*
2077 Fish oil and fish oil meal—*mfg*
2092 Fish sticks—*mfg*
3644 Fish wire (electrical wiring tool)—*mfg*
2091 Fish, canned and cured—*mfg*
5146 Fish, cured—wholesale
5146 Fish, fresh—wholesale
5146 Fish, frozen: except packaged—wholesale
5142 Fish, frozen: packaged—wholesale
5199 Fish, tropical—wholesale
2091 Fish: cured, dried, pickled, salted, and smoked—*mfg*
2092 Fish: fresh and frozen, prepared—*mfg*
0912 Fisheries, finfish
0913 Fisheries, shellfish
7999 Fishing boats, party: operation of
3732 Fishing boats, small—*mfg*
7032 Fishing camps
5941 Fishing equipment—retail
1389 Fishing for tools, oil and gas field: on a contract basis
3421 Fishing knives—*mfg*
2298 Fishing lines, nets, seines: made in cordage or twine mills—*mfg*
2399 Fishing nets—mfpm—*mfg*
7999 Fishing piers and lakes, operation of
0921 Fishing preserves
3949 Fishing tackle (except lines, nets, and seines)—*mfg*
3731 Fishing vessels, large: seiners and trawlers—building and repairing—*mfg*
2819 Fissionable material production—*mfg*
7991 Fitness salons

3999 Flocking metal products for the trade—*mfg*

2261 Flocking of cotton broadwoven fabrics—*mfg*

2262 Flocking of manmade fiber and silk broadwoven fabrics—*mfg*

1629 Flood control project construction—general contractors

3648 Floodlights—*mfg*

3251 Floor arch tile, clay—*mfg*

2431 Floor baseboards, wood—*mfg*

3299 Floor composition, magnesite—*mfg*

2951 Floor composition, mastic: hot and cold—*mfg*

5713 Floor covering stores—retail

3996 Floor coverings, asphalted-felt-base (linoleum)—*mfg*

3089 Floor coverings, plastics—*mfg*

2273 Floor coverings, textile fiber—*mfg*

2273 Floor coverings, tufted—*mfg*

2273 Floor coverings: twisted paper, grass, reed, coir, sisal, jute, and rag—*mfg*

5023 Floor coverings—wholesale

3634 Floor fans, electric—*mfg*

3272 Floor filler tiles, concrete—*mfg*

3441 Floor jacks, metal—*mfg*

3645 Floor lamps—*mfg*

1752 Floor laying, scraping, finishing, and refinishing—contractors

2392 Floor mops—*mfg*

3441 Floor posts, adjustable: metal—*mfg*

3589 Floor sanding, washing, and polishing machines: commercial type—*mfg*

3272 Floor slabs, precast concrete—*mfg*

5713 Floor tile stores—retail

3292 Floor tile, asphalt—*mfg*

3253 Floor tile, ceramic—*mfg*

3272 Floor tile, precast terrazzo—*mfg*

3469 Floor tile, stamped metal—*mfg*

6221 Floor traders, commodity contract

6211 Floor traders, security

2842 Floor wax emulsion—*mfg*

3639 Floor waxers and polishers, household: electric—*mfg*

2842 Floor waxes—*mfg*

7349 Floor waxing service

2421 Flooring (dressed lumber), softwood—*mfg*

3251 Flooring brick, clay—*mfg*

3444 Flooring, cellular steel—*mfg*

2426 Flooring, hardwood—*mfg*

3446 Flooring, open steel (grating)—*mfg*

3069 Flooring, rubber: tile or sheet—*mfg*

2491 Flooring, wood block: treated—*mfg*

1752 Flooring, wood—contractors

5211 Flooring, wood—retail

2452 Floors, prefabricated: wood—*mfg*

3269 Florists' articles, red earthenware—*mfg*

3496 Florists' designs, made from purchased wire—*mfg*

0181 Florists' greens, cultivated: growing of

7389 Florists' telegraph service

5992 Florists—retail

5193 Florists—wholesale

6211 Flotation companies, security

3532 Flotation machinery (mining machinery)—*mfg*

2258 Flouncings, lace—*mfg*

2673 Flour bags, except fabric—mfpm—*mfg*

2393 Flour bags, fabric—mfpm—*mfg*

3556 Flour mill machinery—*mfg*

2041 Flour mills, cereals: except rice—*mfg*

2041 Flour mixes—mitse—*mfg*

2044 Flour, rice—*mfg*

2499 Flour, wood—*mfg*

2045 Flour: blended or self-rising—mfpm—*mfg*

2041 Flour: blended, prepared, or self-rising—mitse—*mfg*

2041 Flour: buckwheat, corn, graham, rye, and wheat—*mfg*

5149 Flour—wholesale

3625 Flow actuated electrical switches—*mfg*

3823 Flow instruments, industrial process type—*mfg*

5191 Flower and field bulbs—wholesale

3299 Flower boxes, plaster of paris: factory production only—*mfg*

5261 Flower bulbs—retail

3089 Flower pots, plastics—*mfg*

3269 Flower pots, red earthenware—*mfg*

5193 Flowers and florists' supplies—wholesale

3999 Flowers, artificial, except glass—*mfg*

5999 Flowers, artificial—retail

5193 Flowers, artificial—wholesale

3231 Flowers, foliage, fruits and vines: artificial glass—made from purchased glass—*mfg*

5992 Flowers, fresh—retail

5193 Flowers, fresh—wholesale

0181 Flowers, growing of

3231 Flowers, made from purchased glass—*mfg*

3999 Flowers, preserved—*mfg*

3259 Flue lining, clay—*mfg*

3444 Flues, stove and furnace: sheet metal—*mfg*

3412 Fluid milk shipping containers, metal—*mfg*

3593 Fluid power actuators, hydraulic and pneumatic—*mfg*

3593 Fluid power cylinders, hydraulic and pneumatic—*mfg*

3593 Fluid power motors—*mfg*

3594 Fluid power pumps and motors—*mfg*

3492 Fluid power valves and fittings—*mfg*

3589 Food warming equipment, commercial—*mfg*

5046 Food warming equipment, commercial—wholesale

3639 Food waste disposal units, household—*mfg*

5961 Food, mail-order—retail

3842 Foot appliances, orthopedic—*mfg*

7997 Football clubs, except professional and semiprofessional

7941 Football clubs, professional or semiprofessional

3949 Footballs and football equipment and supplies, except uniforms and footwear—*mfg*

3021 Footholds, rubber—*mfg*

2389 Footlets—mfpm—*mfg*

5661 Footwear stores—retail

3149 Footwear, children's: house slippers and vulcanized rubber footwear—*mfg*

3149 Footwear, children's: leather or vinyl with molded or vulcanized shoes—*mfg*

3143 Footwear, men's: except house slippers, athletic, and vulcanized rubber footwear—*mfg*

3143 Footwear, men's: leather or vinyl with molded or vulcanized soles—*mfg*

3021 Footwear, rubber or rubber soled fabric—*mfg*

3144 Footwear, women's: except house slippers, athletic, and vulcanized rubber footwear—*mfg*

3144 Footwear, women's: leather or vinyl with molded or vulcanized soles—*mfg*

5139 Footwear—wholesale

3523 Forage blowers—*mfg*

3523 Forage harvesters—*mfg*

**** Force account construction—code according to the use for which constructed

3843 Forceps, dental—*mfg*

3841 Forceps, surgical—*mfg*

6099 Foreign currency exchanges

4731 Foreign forwarding

9721 Foreign missions

4226 Foreign trade zone warehousing, and storage

8734 Forensic laboratories

0851 Forest management plans, preparation of

0831 Forest nurseries

6519 Forest properties, lessors of

5082 Forestry equipment—wholesale

0851 Forestry services

3599 Forges, fan—*mfg*

3542 Forging machinery and hammers—*mfg*

5051 Forgings, ferrous—wholesale

3312 Forgings, iron and steel: made in steel works or rolling mills—*mfg*

3462 Forgings, iron and steel: not made in rolling mills—*mfg*

3463 Forgings, nonferrous metal: not made in hot rolling mills—*mfg*

3483 Forgings, projectile: machined—for ammunition more than 30 mm. (or more than 1.18 inch)—*mfg*

3537 Forklift trucks—*mfg*

3914 Forks, table: all metal—*mfg*

3421 Forks, table: except all metal—*mfg*

3423 Forks: garden, hay and manure, stone and ballast—*mfg*

3315 Form ties, made in wiredrawing plants—*mfg*

2311 Formal jackets, men's and boys'—*mfg*

2869 Formaldehyde (formalin)—*mfg*

2869 Formalin—*mfg*

2869 Formic acid and metallic salts—*mfg*

3444 Forming machine work for the trade, except stampings: sheet metal—*mfg*

3542 Forming machines—*mfg*

2782 Forms and fillers, looseleaf: pen ruled or printed only—*mfg*

3444 Forms for concrete, sheet metal—*mfg*

3269 Forms for dipped rubber products, pottery—*mfg*

1799 Forms for poured concrete, erection and dismantling—contractors

3579 Forms handling equipment for store and office use—*mfg*

2761 Forms, business: manifold or continuous—*mfg*

3443 Forms, collapsible: for tunnels—*mfg*

5051 Forms, concrete construction: steel—wholesale

2499 Forms, display: for boots and shoes—regardless of material—*mfg*

3544 Forms, metal (molds): for foundry and plastics working machinery—*mfg*

3999 Forms: display, dress, and show—except shoe display forms—*mfg*

7999 Fortune tellers

4731 Forwarding, domestic

4731 Forwarding, foreign

8361 Foster homes, group

1794 Foundation digging (excavation)—contractors

2342 Foundation garments, women's—mfpm—*mfg*

5632 Foundation garments—retail

2515 Foundations, bed: spring, foam, and platform—*mfg*

1741 Foundations, building of: block, stone, or brick—contractors

1771 Foundations, building of: poured concrete—contractors

2675 Foundations, cardboard—mfpm—*mfg*
3999 Foundations, honeycomb (bookkeepers' supplies)—*mfg*
3365 Foundries, aluminum: except die-castings—*mfg*
3321 Foundries, gray iron and semisteel—*mfg*
3322 Foundries, malleable iron—*mfg*
3325 Foundries, steel: except investment—*mfg*
3366 Foundries: brass, bronze, copper, and copper-base alloy—except die-castings—*mfg*
3543 Foundry cores—*mfg*
3295 Foundry facings, ground or otherwise treated—*mfg*
3559 Foundry machinery and equipment—*mfg*
3543 Foundry patternmaking—*mfg*
5051 Foundry products—wholesale
3255 Foundry refractories, clay—*mfg*
1446 Foundry sand mining
2899 Foundry supplies, chemical preparations—*mfg*
3555 Foundry type for printing—*mfg*
5145 Fountain fruits and syrups—wholesale
3648 Fountain lighting fixtures—*mfg*
3951 Fountain pens and fountain pen desk sets—*mfg*
3069 Fountain syringes, rubber—*mfg*
3585 Fountain syrup dispensing equipment—*mfg*
3272 Fountains, concrete—*mfg*
3431 Fountains, drinking: except mechanically refrigerated—*mfg*
3585 Fountains, drinking: mechanically refrigerated—*mfg*
3499 Fountains, metal (except drinking)—*mfg*
3299 Fountains, plaster of paris: factory production only—*mfg*
3272 Fountains, wash: precast terrazzo—*mfg*
3554 Fourdrinier machines (paper manufacturing machinery)—*mfg*
3496 Fourdrinier wire cloth, made from purchased wire—*mfg*
0271 Fox farms
3443 Fractionating columns, metal plate—*mfg*
1321 Fractionating natural gas liquids
3443 Fractionating towers, metal plate—*mfg*
2911 Fractionation products of crude petroleum, produced in petroleum refineries—*mfg*
3842 Fracture appliances, surgical—*mfg*
7539 Frame repair shops, automotive
3559 Frame straighteners, automotive (garage equipment)—*mfg*
3999 Frames and handles, handbag and luggage: except precious metal—*mfg*
3851 Frames and parts, eyeglass and spectacle—*mfg*

3952 Frames for artists' canvases—*mfg*
2514 Frames for box springs or bedsprings, metal—*mfg*
2511 Frames for box springs, bedsprings, or water beds: wood—*mfg*
2426 Frames for upholstered furniture, wood—*mfg*
3499 Frames, chair: metal—*mfg*
2499 Frames, clothes drying: wood—*mfg*
3442 Frames, door and window: metal—*mfg*
2431 Frames, door and window: wood—*mfg*
3552 Frames, doubling and twisting (textile machinery)—*mfg*
3999 Frames, lamp shade—*mfg*
3714 Frames, motor vehicle—*mfg*
3751 Frames, motorcycle and bicycle—*mfg*
5048 Frames, ophthalmic—wholesale
3931 Frames, piano-back—*mfg*
3999 Frames, umbrella and parasol—*mfg*
2499 Frames: medallion, mirror, photograph, and picture—wood or metal—*mfg*
1751 Framing—contractors
6794 Franchises, selling or licensing
5812 Frankfurter (hot dog) stands
2013 Frankfurters, except poultry—mfpm—*mfg*
2011 Frankfurters, except poultry—mitse—*mfg*
2015 Frankfurters, poultry—*mfg*
6321 Fraternal accident and health insurance organizations
8641 Fraternal associations, other than insurance offices
6311 Fraternal life insurance organizations
8641 Fraternal lodges
6311 Fraternal protective associations
8641 Fraternities and sororities, except residential
7041 Fraternity residential houses
8011 Freestanding emergency medical (M.D.) centers
2095 Freeze-dried coffee—*mfg*
5421 Freezer food plans, meat—retail
5421 Freezer provisioners, meat—retail
3632 Freezers, home and farm—*mfg*
5722 Freezers, household—retail
5064 Freezers, household—wholesale
3556 Freezers, ice cream: commercial—*mfg*
3499 Freezers, ice cream: household—metal—*mfg*
3821 Freezers, laboratory—*mfg*
4731 Freight agencies, railroad: not operated by railroad companies
4789 Freight car loading and unloading, not trucking
3743 Freight cars and car equipment—*mfg*
4731 Freight consolidation
4731 Freight forwarding

4783 Freight packing and crating
4731 Freight rate auditors
4731 Freight rate information service
4231 Freight trucking terminals, with or without maintenance facilities
2221 French crepes—*mfg*
2035 French dressing—*mfg*
2038 French toast, frozen—*mfg*
3621 Frequency converters (electric generators)—*mfg*
3825 Frequency meters: electrical, mechanical, and electronic—*mfg*
3825 Frequency synthesizers—*mfg*
1743 Fresco work—contractors
3931 Fretted instruments and parts—*mfg*
3499 Friction material, made from powdered metal—*mfg*
3292 Friction materials, asbestos: woven—*mfg*
3069 Friction tape, rubber—*mfg*
2241 Fringes, weaving—*mfg*
3952 Frisket paper (artists' material)—*mfg*
2899 Frit—*mfg*
0279 Frog farms
0919 Frogs, catching of
3312 Frogs, iron and steel: made in steel works or rolling mills—*mfg*
3462 Frogs, railroad: forgings not made in rolling mills—*mfg*
7539 Front end repair, automotive
5082 Front-end loaders—wholesale
3851 Fronts and temples, ophthalmic—*mfg*
2541 Fronts, store: prefabricated—wood—*mfg*
2099 Frosting, prepared—*mfg*
2051 Frozen bread and bread-type rolls—*mfg*
2024 Frozen custard—*mfg*
5812 Frozen custard stands
5143 Frozen dairy desserts—wholesale
2024 Frozen desserts, except bakery—*mfg*
2038 Frozen dinners, packaged—*mfg*
2045 Frozen doughs—mfpm—*mfg*
2041 Frozen doughs—mitse—*mfg*
2092 Frozen fish, packaged—*mfg*
5411 Frozen food and freezer plans, except meat—retail
5421 Frozen food and freezer plans, meat—retail
2673 Frozen food bags—mfpm—*mfg*
2657 Frozen food containers, folding paperboard—mfpm—*mfg*
2656 Frozen food containers, nonfolding paperboard—mfpm—*mfg*
4222 Frozen food locker rental
5142 Frozen foods, packaged—wholesale
2037 Frozen fruits, fruit juices, and vegetables—*mfg*
2092 Frozen prepared fish—*mfg*

2038 Frozen soups, except seafood—*mfg*
5142 Frozen vegetables—wholesale
2046 Fructose—*mfg*
2086 Fruit (fresh) drinks, bottled or canned—*mfg*
2449 Fruit baskets, veneer and splint—*mfg*
2033 Fruit butters—*mfg*
2449 Fruit crates, wood: wirebound—*mfg*
0723 Fruit drying
2034 Fruit flour, meal, and powders—*mfg*
3523 Fruit grading, cleaning, and sorting machines—*mfg*
3221 Fruit jars, glass—*mfg*
2037 Fruit juice concentrates, frozen—*mfg*
2087 Fruit juices, concentrated: for fountain use—*mfg*
2037 Fruit juices, frozen—*mfg*
5142 Fruit juices, frozen—wholesale
2033 Fruit juices: canned—*mfg*
5431 Fruit markets and stands—retail
2064 Fruit peel products: candied, glazed, glace, and crystallized—*mfg*
5149 Fruit peel—wholesale
2033 Fruit pie mixes—*mfg*
2024 Fruit pops, frozen—*mfg*
4741 Fruit precooling, in connection with railroad transportation
0723 Fruit precooling, not in connection with transportation
2033 Fruit purees—*mfg*
0723 Fruit sorting, grading, and packing
0181 Fruit stocks, growing of
5431 Fruit stores—retail
0723 Fruit vacuum cooling
3231 Fruit, artificial: made from purchased glass—*mfg*
5961 Fruit, mail-order—retail
3523 Fruit, vegetable, berry, and grape harvesting machines—*mfg*
0182 Fruits grown under cover
3999 Fruits, artificial and preserved: except glass—*mfg*
3999 Fruits, artificial, except glass—*mfg*
2033 Fruits, canned—*mfg*
2087 Fruits, crushed: for soda fountain use—*mfg*
2034 Fruits, dried or dehydrated—*mfg*
5149 Fruits, dried—wholesale
5145 Fruits, fountain—wholesale
5431 Fruits, fresh—retail
5148 Fruits, fresh—wholesale
5142 Fruits, frozen—wholesale
0722 Fruits, machine harvesting of
2035 Fruits, pickled and brined—*mfg*
2037 Fruits, quick frozen and coldpack (frozen)—*mfg*

2034 Fruits, sulphured—*mfg*
2064 Fruits: candied, glazed, and crystallized—*mfg*
3589 Fryers, commercial—*mfg*
3634 Fryers, household: electric—*mfg*
0251 Frying chickens, raising of
3229 Frying pans, glass and glass ceramic—*mfg*
2064 Fudge (candy)—*mfg*
5169 Fuel additives—wholesale
2999 Fuel briquettes or boulets, made with petroleum binder—*mfg*
2679 Fuel cell forms, cardboard—mfpm—*mfg*
2296 Fuel cell reinforcement, cord and fabric—*mfg*
3629 Fuel cells, electrochemical generators—*mfg*
3069 Fuel cells, rubber—*mfg*
3674 Fuel cells, solid-state—*mfg*
5984 Fuel dealers, bottled liquefied petroleum gas—retail
3829 Fuel densitometers, aircraft engine—*mfg*
3829 Fuel mixture indicators, aircraft engine—*mfg*
1711 Fuel oil burner installation and servicing—contractors
5983 Fuel oil dealers—retail
5172 Fuel oil, except bulk stations and terminals—wholesale
2819 Fuel propellants, solid: inorganic—*mfg*
2869 Fuel propellants, solid: organic—*mfg*
3714 Fuel pumps, motor vehicle—*mfg*
7539 Fuel system conversion, automotive
3829 Fuel system instruments, aircraft—*mfg*
7539 Fuel system repair, automotive
3714 Fuel systems and parts, motor vehicle—*mfg*
2899 Fuel tank and engine cleaning chemicals, automotive and aircraft—*mfg*
3728 Fuel tanks, aircraft: including self-sealing—*mfg*
3069 Fuel tanks, collapsible: rubberized fabric—*mfg*
3443 Fuel tanks, metal plate—*mfg*
3829 Fuel totalizers, aircraft engine—*mfg*
2411 Fuel wood harvesting—*mfg*
5989 Fuel wood—retail
5052 Fuel: coal and coke—wholesale
5172 Fueling services, aircraft—wholesale
2819 Fuels, high energy: inorganic—*mfg*
2869 Fuels, high energy: organic—*mfg*
2911 Fuels, jet—*mfg*
2421 Fuelwood, from mill waste—*mfg*
1459 Fuller's earth mining
3295 Fuller's earth, ground or otherwise treated—*mfg*

2892 Fulminate of mercury (explosive compounds)—*mfg*
3821 Fume hoods, chemical—*mfg*
3443 Fumigating chambers, metal plate—*mfg*
7342 Fumigating service
3825 Function generators—*mfg*
7389 Fundraising on a contract or fee basis
8399 Fundraising organizations, except on a contract or fee basis
3578 Funds transfer devices—*mfg*
7261 Funeral directors
7261 Funeral homes or parlors
6311 Funeral insurance
2879 Fungicides—*mfg*
3069 Funnels, rubber—*mfg*
5632 Fur apparel made to custom order—retail
2371 Fur apparel: capes, coats, hats, jackets, and neckpieces—*mfg*
7219 Fur cleaning
5137 Fur clothing—wholesale
5093 Fur cuttings and scraps—wholesale
0271 Fur farms
2371 Fur finishers and liners for the fur goods trade: buttonhole making—*mfg*
7219 Fur garments: cleaning, repairing, and storage
2371 Fur plates and trimmings—*mfg*
3559 Fur sewing machines—*mfg*
5632 Fur shops—retail
4226 Fur storage for the trade
3999 Fur stripping—*mfg*
2221 Fur-type fabrics, manmade fiber—*mfg*
7699 Furnace and chimney cleaning
2895 Furnace black—*mfg*
3564 Furnace blowers (blower filter units)—*mfg*
3444 Furnace casings, sheet metal—*mfg*
7699 Furnace cleaning service
1629 Furnace construction for industrial plants—general contractors
3444 Furnace flues, sheet metal—*mfg*
1711 Furnace repair—contractors
3433 Furnaces, domestic: steam or hot water—*mfg*
5074 Furnaces, except electric and warm air—wholesale
5075 Furnaces, heating: electric—wholesale
3567 Furnaces, industrial process—*mfg*
3843 Furnaces, laboratory: dental—*mfg*
3821 Furnaces, laboratory: except dental—*mfg*
5075 Furnaces, warm air—wholesale
3585 Furnaces: gravity air flow—*mfg*
7021 Furnished rooms, rental of
5137 Furnishings, clothing except shoes: women's, children's, and infants'—wholesale

5136 Furnishings, except shoes: men's and boys'—wholesale
7217 Furniture cleaning on customers' premises
3469 Furniture components, porcelain enameled—*mfg*
2211 Furniture denim—*mfg*
2426 Furniture dimension stock, hardwood—*mfg*
2421 Furniture dimension stock, softwood—*mfg*
2426 Furniture frames for upholstering, wood—*mfg*
3429 Furniture hardware, including casters—*mfg*
2499 Furniture inlays (veneers)—*mfg*
5712 Furniture made on a custom basis to individual order—retail
3553 Furniture makers' machinery (woodworking)—*mfg*
4214 Furniture moving, local: combined with storage
4212 Furniture moving, local: without storage
3499 Furniture parts, metal—*mfg*
2842 Furniture polish and wax—*mfg*
7641 Furniture refinishing
7359 Furniture rental and leasing
7641 Furniture repairing, redecorating, and remodeling shops
7641 Furniture restoration, antique
3495 Furniture springs, unassembled: made from purchased wire—*mfg*
2426 Furniture squares, hardwood—*mfg*
4226 Furniture storage, without local trucking
5712 Furniture stores, household—retail
5932 Furniture stores, secondhand—retail
3231 Furniture tops, glass: cut, beveled, and polished—*mfg*
2396 Furniture trimmings, fabric—mfpm—*mfg*
2426 Furniture turnings and carvings, wood—*mfg*
5932 Furniture, antique—retail
3999 Furniture, beauty shop and barber shop—*mfg*
2514 Furniture, clubroom: metal—*mfg*
5712 Furniture, custom made—retail
3281 Furniture, cut stone—*mfg*
2599 Furniture, factory: stools, work benches, tool stands, and cabinets—*mfg*
3272 Furniture, garden: concrete—*mfg*
5712 Furniture, household, with or without furnishings and appliances—retail
2511 Furniture, household, wood: porch, lawn, garden, and beach—*mfg*
2511 Furniture, household, wood: unassembled or knock-down—*mfg*
2511 Furniture, household, wood: unfinished—*mfg*

2519 Furniture, household: glass and plastics (including fiberglass)—*mfg*
2514 Furniture, household: metal—*mfg*
2519 Furniture, household: rattan, reed, malacca, fiber, willow, and wicker—*mfg*
2514 Furniture, household: upholstered on metal frames, except dual-purpose sleep furniture—*mfg*
2512 Furniture, household: upholstered on wood frames, except convertible beds—*mfg*
5021 Furniture, juvenile—wholesale
3821 Furniture, laboratory—*mfg*
2522 Furniture, office: except wood—*mfg*
2521 Furniture, office: wood—*mfg*
2599 Furniture, restaurant—*mfg*
5021 Furniture, unfinished—wholesale
2531 Furniture: church, library, school, theater, and other public buildings—*mfg*
2511 Furniture: household, clubroom, novelty—wood, except upholstered—*mfg*
5021 Furniture: household, office, restaurant, and public building—wholesale
5632 Furriers—retail
3446 Furring channels—*mfg*
3251 Furring tile, clay—*mfg*
3999 Furs, dressed: bleached, curried, scraped, tanned, and dyed—*mfg*
5199 Furs, dressed—wholesale
5159 Furs, raw—wholesale
3613 Fuse clips and blocks, electric—*mfg*
3643 Fuse cutouts—*mfg*
3613 Fuse devices, power: 600 volts and over—*mfg*
3613 Fuse mountings, electric power—*mfg*
2892 Fuse powder—*mfg*
3827 Fuse setters (fire control equipment)—*mfg*
2899 Fusees: highway, marine, and railroad—*mfg*
3728 Fuselage assemblies, aircraft—*mfg*
5063 Fuses and accessories—wholesale
3483 Fuses for ammunition more than 30 mm. (or more than 1.18 inch)—*mfg*
3613 Fuses, electric—*mfg*
2892 Fuses, safety—*mfg*
3483 Fuses: mine, torpedo, bomb, depth charge, and chemical warfare projectile—*mfg*
2861 Fustic wood extract—*mfg*
6282 Futures advisory service
6221 Futures brokers, commodity
6221 Futures dealers, commodity
6231 Futures exchanges, contract

G

2211 Gabardine, cotton—*mfg*
1429 Gabbro, crushed and broken—quarrying

2389 Garter belts—mfpm—*mfg*
2389 Garters—mfpm—*mfg*
1623 Gas (natural) compressing station construction—general contractors
1311 Gas (natural) production
3443 Gas absorbers—*mfg*
3826 Gas analyzers, laboratory type—*mfg*
3519 Gas and diesel engine rebuilding, on a factory basis—*mfg*
3823 Gas and liquid analysis instruments, industrial process type—*mfg*
4932 Gas and other services combined (gas less than 95 percent of total)
3671 Gas and vapor tubes—*mfg*
7699 Gas appliance repair service
3822 Gas burner automatic controls, except valves—*mfg*
3433 Gas burners, domestic—*mfg*
3842 Gas capes (cold climate individual protective covers)—*mfg*
3826 Gas chromatographic instruments, laboratory type—*mfg*
1389 Gas compressing, natural gas at the field on a contract basis
1382 Gas field exploration: on a contract basis
3823 Gas flow computers, industrial process type—*mfg*
3433 Gas heaters, room—*mfg*
3443 Gas holders, metal plate—*mfg*
5722 Gas household appliance stores—retail
3433 Gas infrared heating units—*mfg*
1799 Gas leakage detection—contractors
3648 Gas lighting fixtures—*mfg*
5099 Gas lighting fixtures—wholesale
1623 Gas main construction—general contractors
3842 Gas masks—*mfg*
3321 Gas pipe, cast iron—*mfg*
3569 Gas producers (machinery)—*mfg*
3631 Gas ranges, domestic—*mfg*
3569 Gas separators (machinery)—*mfg*
7389 Gas systems, contract conversion from manufactured to natural gas
3443 Gas tanks, metal plate—*mfg*
3714 Gas tanks, motor vehicle—*mfg*
3511 Gas turbine generator set units, complete—*mfg*
3511 Gas turbines and parts, except aircraft type—*mfg*
3511 Gas turbines, mechanical drive—*mfg*
3491 Gas valves and parts, industrial—*mfg*
3548 Gas welding equipment—*mfg*
3496 Gas welding rods, made from purchased wire—*mfg*
1381 Gas well drilling: on a contract basis
3533 Gas well machinery and equipment—*mfg*

1389 Gas well rig building, repairing, and dismantling on a contract basis
3312 Gas, coal: derived from chemical recovery coke ovens—*mfg*
5984 Gas, liquefied petroleum: bottled—retail
4925 Gas, liquefied petroleum: distribution through mains
4925 Gas, manufactured: production and distribution
4925 Gas, mixed natural and manufactured: production and distribution
4924 Gas, natural: distribution
4922 Gas, natural: transmission
4923 Gas, natural: transmission and distribution
2911 Gas, refinery or still oil: produced in petroleum refineries—*mfg*
3433 Gas-oil burners, combination—*mfg*
2869 Gases, chemical warfare—*mfg*
5169 Gases, compressed and liquefied: except liquefied petroleum gas—wholesale
2869 Gases, fluorinated hydrocarbon—*mfg*
2813 Gases, industrial: compressed, liquefied, or solid—*mfg*
5172 Gases, liquefied petroleum: except bulk stations and terminals—wholesale
2911 Gases, liquefied petroleum: produced in petroleum refineries—*mfg*
3053 Gaskets, regardless of material—*mfg*
5085 Gaskets—wholesale
1711 Gasline hookup—contractors
3824 Gasmeters: domestic, large capacity, and industrial—*mfg*
1321 Gasoline (natural) production
5541 Gasoline and oil—retail
2911 Gasoline blending plants—*mfg*
3824 Gasoline dispensing meters (except pumps)—*mfg*
5541 Gasoline filling stations—retail
3599 Gasoline filters, internal combustion engine: except motor vehicle—*mfg*
3586 Gasoline measuring and dispensing pumps—*mfg*
4613 Gasoline pipelines, common carriers
1799 Gasoline pump installation—contractors
5172 Gasoline, except bulk stations and terminals—wholesale
2911 Gasoline, except natural gasoline—*mfg*
5172 Gasoline: buying in bulk and selling to farmers—wholesale
2269 Gassing yarn—*mfg*
3845 Gastroscopes, electromedical—*mfg*
3841 Gastroscopes, except electromedical—*mfg*
3569 Gate and bridge machinery, hydraulic—*mfg*
3452 Gate hooks—*mfg*

3089 Gate hooks, plastics—*mfg*
5039 Gates and accessories, wire—wholesale
3441 Gates, dam: metal plate—*mfg*
3496 Gates, fence: made from purchased wire—*mfg*
3523 Gates, holding (farm equipment)—*mfg*
3446 Gates, ornamental metal—*mfg*
0831 Gathering of forest products: (e.g., gums, barks, seeds)
0831 Gathering, extracting, and selling of tree seeds
3545 Gauge blocks—*mfg*
3829 Gauges except electric, motor vehicle: oil pressure and water temperature—*mfg*
3824 Gauges for computing pressure-temperature corrections—*mfg*
3545 Gauges, except optical (machine tool accessories)—*mfg*
3829 Gauging instruments, thickness: ultrasonic—*mfg*
3842 Gauze, surgical: not made in weaving mills—*mfg*
2211 Gauze—mitse—*mfg*
2499 Gavels, wood—*mfg*
3541 Gear chamfering machines (machine tools)—*mfg*
3541 Gear cutting and finishing machines—*mfg*
3423 Gear pullers, handtools—*mfg*
3542 Gear rolling machines—*mfg*
3541 Gear tooth grinding machines (machine tools)—*mfg*
3566 Gearmotors (power transmission equipment)—*mfg*
3462 Gears, forged steel: not made in rolling mills—*mfg*
3714 Gears, motor vehicle—*mfg*
3751 Gears, motorcycle and bicycle—*mfg*
3728 Gears, power transmission: aircraft—*mfg*
3566 Gears, power transmission: except motor vehicle and aircraft—*mfg*
5085 Gears—wholesale
0259 Geese farms
2015 Geese, processed: fresh, frozen, canned, or cooked—*mfg*
2015 Geese: slaughtering and dressing—*mfg*
3671 Geiger Mueller tubes—*mfg*
3829 Geiger counters—*mfg*
2899 Gelatin capsules, empty—*mfg*
2099 Gelatin dessert preparations—*mfg*
3555 Gelatin rolls used in printing—*mfg*
2833 Gelatin, vegetable (agar-agar)—*mfg*
2899 Gelatin: edible, technical, photographic, and pharmaceutical—*mfg*
5169 Gelatin—wholesale
1499 Gem stone mining
5999 Gem stones, rough—retail

5094 Gem stones—wholesale
3915 Gems, real and imitation: preparation for setting—*mfg*
7299 Genealogical investigation service
9199 General accounting offices—government
6159 General and industrial loan institutions
9611 General economic statistics agencies—government
3411 General line cans, metal—*mfg*
8742 General management consultants
8062 General medical and surgical hospitals
5399 General merchandise stores—retail
9199 General services departments—government
5399 General stores—retail
4225 General warehousing and storage
3621 Generating apparatus and parts, electrical: except internal combustion engine and arc-welding—*mfg*
4911 Generation of electric power
7539 Generator and starter repair, automotive
3613 Generator control and metering panels—*mfg*
3511 Generator set units, turbine: complete—steam, gas, and hydraulic—*mfg*
3621 Generator sets: gasoline, diesel, and dual fuel—*mfg*
3612 Generator voltage regulators, electric induction and step type—*mfg*
3548 Generators (separate) for arc-welders—*mfg*
3621 Generators and sets, electric: except internal combustion engine, welding, and turbogenerators—*mfg*
3621 Generators for gas-electric and oil-electric vehicles—*mfg*
3621 Generators for storage battery chargers, except internal combustion engine and aircraft—*mfg*
3844 Generators, X-ray—*mfg*
3694 Generators, aircraft and motor vehicle—*mfg*
5063 Generators, electrical—wholesale
3569 Generators, gas—*mfg*
3489 Generators, smoke (ordnance)—*mfg*
3569 Generators: steam, liquid oxygen, and nitrogen—*mfg*
2452 Geodesic domes, prefabricated: wood—*mfg*
1382 Geological exploration, oil and gas field: on a contract basis
8999 Geologists, consulting: not connected with business service laboratories
1081 Geophysical exploration services, for metal mining: on a contract basis
1481 Geophysical exploration services, for nonmetallic minerals, except fuels: on a contract basis

1382 Geophysical exploration, oil and gas field: on a contract basis

2221 Georgettes—*mfg*

1781 Geothermal drilling—contractors

4961 Geothermal steam production

2869 Geraniol, synthetic—*mfg*

3339 Germanium refining, primary—*mfg*

3341 Germanium refining, secondary—*mfg*

8999 Ghost writing

5947 Gift shops—retail

2679 Gift wrap paper—mfpm—*mfg*

5199 Gifts and novelties—wholesale

2789 Gilding books, cards, or paper—*mfg*

1499 Gilsonite mining

3423 Gimlets (edge tools)—*mfg*

2241 Gimps—mitse—*mfg*

2085 Gin (alcoholic beverage)—*mfg*

2086 Ginger ale, bottled or canned—*mfg*

2045 Gingerbread mixes—mfpm—*mfg*

2211 Ginghams—*mfg*

0724 Ginning cotton

3559 Ginning machines, cotton—*mfg*

0723 Ginning moss

0724 Gins, cotton: operation of

0831 Ginseng, gathering of

2259 Girdle blanks, elastic—mitse—*mfg*

2259 Girdles (elastic) and other foundation garments—mitse—*mfg*

2342 Girdles, women's and misses'—mfpm—*mfg*

7032 Girls' camps

2252 Girls' hosiery—*mfg*

2064 Glace fruits and nuts—*mfg*

2833 Gland derivatives: bulk, uncompounded—*mfg*

3229 Glass and glassware made in glassmaking establishments: for industrial, scientific, and technical use—*mfg*

3229 Glass blanks for electric light bulbs—*mfg*

5085 Glass bottles—wholesale

3229 Glass brick—*mfg*

2221 Glass broadwoven fabrics—*mfg*

3851 Glass eyes—*mfg*

1793 Glass installation, except automotive—contractors

3559 Glass making machinery: blowing, molding, forming, grinding, etc.—*mfg*

2241 Glass narrow fabrics—*mfg*

7536 Glass replacement and repair, automotive

1446 Glass sand mining

5231 Glass stores—retail

2296 Glass tire cord and tire cord fabrics—*mfg*

2211 Glass toweling, cotton—*mfg*

2842 Glass window cleaning preparations—*mfg*

3296 Glass wool—*mfg*

1793 Glass work, except automotive—contractors

3211 Glass, colored: cathedral and antique—*mfg*

3211 Glass, flat—*mfg*

5039 Glass, flat: except automotive—wholesale

5122 Glass, medical—wholesale

3231 Glass, scientific apparatus: for druggists', hospitals, laboratories—made from purchased glass—*mfg*

3231 Glass, sheet: bent—made from purchased glass—*mfg*

3231 Glass: cut, ground, leaded, laminated, ornamented, and tinted—mfpm—*mfg*

3827 Glasses, field or opera—*mfg*

3851 Glasses, sun or glare—*mfg*

3255 Glasshouse refractories—*mfg*

2674 Glassine bags, uncoated paper—mfpm—*mfg*

2621 Glassine wrapping paper—mitse—*mfg*

3221 Glassware for packing, bottling and home canning—*mfg*

5719 Glassware stores—retail

5932 Glassware, antique—retail

3231 Glassware, cut and engraved—made from purchased glass—*mfg*

3231 Glassware, cutting and engraving—*mfg*

3231 Glassware, decorated: e.g., chipped, engraved, sandblasted, etched—made from purchased glass—*mfg*

3229 Glassware, except glass containers for packing, bottling, and canning—*mfg*

5023 Glassware, household—wholesale

5199 Glassware, novelty—wholesale

3229 Glassware: art, decorative, and novelty—*mfg*

2819 Glauber's salt—*mfg*

1474 Glauber's salt mining

7699 Glazing and cleaning baking pans

2371 Glazing furs—*mfg*

1799 Glazing of concrete surfaces—contractors

3089 Glazing panels, plastics—*mfg*

1793 Glazing work—contractors

3812 Glide slope instrumentation—*mfg*

3721 Gliders (aircraft)—*mfg*

2514 Gliders (furniture), metal—*mfg*

2741 Globe covers (maps): publishing and printing, or publishing only—*mfg*

3999 Globes, geographical—*mfg*

2211 Glove fabrics, cotton—mitse—*mfg*

3111 Glove leather—*mfg*

2241 Glove lining fabrics—*mfg*

2381 Glove linings, except fur—*mfg*

2371 Glove linings, fur—*mfg*

2399 Glove mending on factory basis—*mfg*

5136 Gloves (all materials), men's and boys'—wholesale

3089 Gloves and mittens, plastics—*mfg*

1389   Grading oil and gas well foundations on a contract basis

3523   Grading, cleaning, and sorting machines: fruit, grain, and vegetable—*mfg*

1794   Grading: except for highways, streets, and airport runways—contractors

3822   Gradual switches, pneumatic—*mfg*

3842   Grafts, artificial: for surgery—made of braided or mesh artificial fibers—*mfg*

2041   Graham flour—*mfg*

1499   Grahamite mining

2085   Grain alcohol for medicinal and beverage purposes—*mfg*

2869   Grain alcohol, industrial (nonbeverage)—*mfg*

2041   Grain cereals, cracked—mitse—*mfg*

0723   Grain cleaning

3523   Grain drills, including legume planters (agricultural machinery)—*mfg*

1541   Grain elevator construction—general contractors

5153   Grain elevators, except storage only—wholesale

4221   Grain elevators, storage only

0119   Grain farms: except wheat, rice, corn, and soybeans

0723   Grain fumigation

3523   Grain grading, cleaning, and sorting machines—*mfg*

0723   Grain grinding, custom

4741   Grain leveling in railroad cars

2499   Grain measures, wood: turned and shaped—*mfg*

3556   Grain mill machinery—*mfg*

3523   Grain stackers—*mfg*

5039   Grain storage bins—wholesale

4741   Grain trimming service for railroad shipment

2082   Grain, brewers'—*mfg*

0722   Grain, machine harvesting of

5153   Grain—wholesale

3291   Grains, abrasive: natural and artificial—*mfg*

5032   Granite building stone—wholesale

1423   Granite, crushed and broken—quarrying

3281   Granite, cut and shaped—*mfg*

1411   Granite, dimension—quarrying

2064   Granola bars and clusters—*mfg*

2043   Granola, except bars and clusters—*mfg*

2041   Granular wheat flour—*mfg*

2063   Granulated beet sugar—*mfg*

3821   Granulators, laboratory—*mfg*

0172   Grape farms

0174   Grapefruit groves and farms

2899   Grapefruit oil—*mfg*

2782   Graph paper, ruled—*mfg*

7336   Graphic arts and related design

3861   Graphic arts plates, sensitized—*mfg*

3577   Graphic displays, except graphic terminals: computer peripheral equipment—*mfg*

3825   Graphic recording meters—electric—*mfg*

3624   Graphite electrodes and contacts, electric—*mfg*

1499   Graphite mining

3295   Graphite, natural: ground, pulverized, refined, or blended—*mfg*

3531   Grapples: rock, wood, etc.—*mfg*

3524   Grass catchers, lawnmower—*mfg*

3423   Grass hooks—*mfg*

0139   Grass seed farms

3999   Grasses, artificial and preserved: except glass—*mfg*

3231   Grasses, artificial: made from purchased glass—*mfg*

3446   Gratings (open steel flooring)—*mfg*

3827   Gratings, diffraction—*mfg*

3446   Gratings, tread: fabricated metal—*mfg*

1799   Grave excavation—contractors

3272   Grave markers, concrete—*mfg*

3272   Grave vaults, concrete—*mfg*

3995   Grave vaults, metal—*mfg*

1442   Gravel mining

3299   Gravel painting—*mfg*

5032   Gravel—wholesale

5999   Gravestones, finished—retail

2893   Gravure ink—*mfg*

2796   Gravure plates and cylinders, preparation of—*mfg*

3555   Gravure presses—*mfg*

2754   Gravure printing—*mfg*

2099   Gravy mixes, dry—*mfg*

3321   Gray iron castings—*mfg*

3321   Gray iron foundries—*mfg*

3599   Grease cups, metal—*mfg*

3586   Grease guns (lubricators)—*mfg*

2077   Grease rendering, inedible—*mfg*

3053   Grease retainers, leather—*mfg*

3053   Grease seals, asbestos—*mfg*

3272   Grease traps, concrete—*mfg*

2299   Grease, wool—*mfg*

2621   Greaseproof wrapping paper—mitse—*mfg*

5199   Greases, animal and vegetable—wholesale

2911   Greases, lubricating: produced in petroleum refineries—*mfg*

2992   Greases, lubricating—mfpm—*mfg*

2843   Greases, sulfonated—*mfg*

4432   Great Lakes and St. Lawrence Seaway freight transportation

0161   Green lima bean farms

0161   Green pea farms

0181   Greenhouses for floral products

0182 Greenhouses for food crops
3448 Greenhouses, prefabricated: metal—*mfg*
3523 Greens mowing equipment—*mfg*
1499 Greensand mining
1411 Greenstone, dimension—quarrying
5947 Greeting card shops—retail
2771 Greeting cards, except hand painted—*mfg*
8999 Greeting cards, hand painting of
5112 Greeting cards—wholesale
3484 Grenade launchers—*mfg*
3483 Grenades and parts—*mfg*
3999 Grenades, hand (fire extinguishers)—*mfg*
3634 Griddles and grills, household: electric—*mfg*
3699 Grids, electric—*mfg*
3496 Grilles and grillework, woven wire: made from purchased wire—*mfg*
3446 Grillework, ornamental metal—*mfg*
5812 Grills (eating places)
3523 Grinders and crushers, feed (agricultural machinery)—*mfg*
3556 Grinders, food: commercial types—*mfg*
3546 Grinders, pneumatic and electric: portable (metalworking machinery)—*mfg*
3546 Grinders, snagging—*mfg*
3531 Grinders, stone: portable—*mfg*
3532 Grinders, stone: stationary—*mfg*
3291 Grinding balls, ceramic—*mfg*
3599 Grinding castings for the trade—*mfg*
3541 Grinding machines, metalworking—*mfg*
3269 Grinding media, pottery—*mfg*
2833 Grinding of drugs and herbs—*mfg*
1499 Grinding peat
3999 Grinding purchased nut shells—*mfg*
1446 Grinding sand mining
1499 Grindstone quarrying
3291 Grindstones, artificial—*mfg*
3069 Grips and handles, rubber—*mfg*
3291 Grit, steel—*mfg*
2041 Grits and flakes, corn: for brewers' use—*mfg*
1429 Grits mining (crushed stone)
5141 Groceries, general line—wholesale
2674 Grocers' bags and sacks, uncoated paper—mfpm—*mfg*
3496 Grocery carts, made from purchased wire—*mfg*
5411 Grocery stores, with or without fresh meat—retail
3069 Grommets, rubber—*mfg*
5085 Grommets—wholesale
3541 Grooving machines (machine tools)—*mfg*
2211 Grosgrain, cotton—*mfg*
3643 Ground clamps (electric wiring devices)—*mfg*

3231 Ground glass, made from purchased glass—*mfg*
3523 Grounds mowing equipment—*mfg*
2621 Groundwood paper—mitse—*mfg*
8351 Group day care centers, child
8361 Group foster homes
6324 Group hospitalization plans
2899 Grouting material (concrete mending compound)—*mfg*
1771 Grouting work—contractors
**** Groves—see type of grove
3089 Grower pots, plastics—*mfg*
8611 Growers' associations, not engaged in contract buying or selling
8611 Growers' marketing advisory services
2879 Growth regulants, agricultural—*mfg*
1479 Guano mining
6361 Guaranty of titles
7381 Guard service
1611 Guardrail construction on highways—contractors
3444 Guardrails, highway: sheet metal—*mfg*
3446 Guards, bannisters, railings, etc.: made from metal pipe—*mfg*
3496 Guards, made from purchased wire—*mfg*
3949 Guards: e.g., football, basketball, soccer, lacrosse—*mfg*
5088 Guided missiles and space vehicles—wholesale
3761 Guided missiles, complete—*mfg*
7999 Guides, hunting
7999 Guides, tourist
2741 Guides: publishing and printing, or publishing only—*mfg*
3931 Guitars and parts, electric and nonelectric—*mfg*
5169 Gum and wood chemicals—wholesale
2861 Gum naval stores, processing but not gathering or warehousing—*mfg*
2899 Gum sizes—*mfg*
2759 Gummed labels and seals, printed: except lithographed or gravure—*mfg*
2672 Gummed paper—mfpm—*mfg*
3579 Gummed tape moisteners for store and office use—*mfg*
2672 Gummed tape, cloth and paper base—mfpm—*mfg*
0831 Gums, gathering of
3484 Gun barrels, 30 mm. (or 1.18 inch) or less—*mfg*
3949 Gun cases (sporting equipment)—*mfg*
7997 Gun clubs, membership
3312 Gun forgings, iron and steel: made in steel works or rolling mills—*mfg*
3489 Gun limbers—*mfg*

3484 Gun magazines, 30 mm. (or 1.18 inch) or less—*mfg*
7699 Gun parts made to individual order
3484 Gun sights, except optical: 30 mm. (or 1.18 inch) or less—*mfg*
3827 Gun sights, optical—*mfg*
2899 Gun slushing compounds—*mfg*
3495 Gun springs, precision: made from purchased wire—*mfg*
2426 Gun stocks, wood—*mfg*
3429 Gun trigger locks—*mfg*
3489 Gun turrets and parts for artillery more than 30 mm. (or more than 1.18 inch)—*mfg*
1771 Gunite work—contractors
3674 Gunn effect devices—*mfg*
3297 Gunning mixes, nonclay—*mfg*
2892 Gunpowder—*mfg*
3484 Guns, 30 mm. (or 1.18 inch) or less—*mfg*
3489 Guns, catapult—*mfg*
3423 Guns, caulking—*mfg*
3484 Guns, dart: except toy—*mfg*
3586 Guns, grease (lubricators)—*mfg*
3489 Guns, more than 30 mm. (or more than 1.18 inch)—*mfg*
3546 Guns, pneumatic: chip removal—*mfg*
3944 Guns, toy—*mfg*
3484 Guns: BB and pellet—*mfg*
7699 Gunsmith shops
3842 Gut sutures, surgical—*mfg*
3069 Gutta percha compounds—*mfg*
1761 Gutter installation, metal—contractors
3089 Gutters, plastics: glass fiber reinforced—*mfg*
3444 Gutters, sheet metal—*mfg*
3949 Gymnasium and playground equipment—*mfg*
2329 Gymnasium clothing: men's and boys'—mfpm—*mfg*
5941 Gymnasium equipment—retail
7991 Gymnasiums
7999 Gymnastics instruction
3842 Gynecological supplies and appliances—*mfg*
8011 Gynecologists, offices of
1499 Gypsite mining
1499 Gypsum mining
3275 Gypsum products: e.g., block, board, plaster, lath, rock, tile—*mfg*
3812 Gyrocompasses—*mfg*
3812 Gyrogimbals—*mfg*
3812 Gyropilots—*mfg*
3812 Gyroscopes—*mfg*

H

5611 Haberdashery stores—retail
0912 Haddock, catching of
5131 Hair accessories—wholesale
3523 Hair clippers for animal use, hand and electric—*mfg*
3999 Hair clippers for human use, hand and electric—*mfg*
2844 Hair coloring preparations—*mfg*
3999 Hair curlers, designed for beauty parlors—*mfg*
3634 Hair curlers, electric—*mfg*
3965 Hair curlers, except equipment designed for beauty parlor use—*mfg*
3069 Hair curlers, rubber—*mfg*
3634 Hair dryers, electric: except equipment designed for beauty parlor use—*mfg*
3999 Hair dryers, designed for beauty parlors—*mfg*
3999 Hair goods: braids, nets, switches, toupees, and wigs—*mfg*
3999 Hair nets—*mfg*
3991 Hair pencils (artists' brushes)—*mfg*
2844 Hair preparations: dressings, rinses, tonics, and scalp conditioners—*mfg*
5122 Hair preparations—wholesale
7299 Hair removal (electrolysis)
7241 Hair stylists, men's
7299 Hair weaving or replacement service
5159 Hair, animal—wholesale
2299 Hair, curled: for upholstery, pillow, and quilt filling—*mfg*
3999 Hair, dressing of, for the trade—*mfg*
5199 Hairbrushes—wholesale
2231 Haircloth: wool, mohair, and similar animal fibers—*mfg*
7231 Hairdressers
2844 Hairdressings, dyes, bleaches, tonics, and removers—*mfg*
3999 Hairpin mountings—*mfg*
3965 Hairpins, except rubber—*mfg*
3069 Hairpins, rubber—*mfg*
3495 Hairsprings, made from purchased wire—*mfg*
2026 Half and half—*mfg*
2759 Halftones, engraved—*mfg*
8361 Halfway group homes for persons with social or personal problems
8361 Halfway homes for delinquents and offenders
3674 Hall effect devices—*mfg*
2679 Halloween lanterns, papier-mache—mfpm—*mfg*
3199 Halters (harness)—*mfg*
2064 Halvah (candy)—*mfg*

2015   Ham, poultry—*mfg*
5812   Hamburger stands
3523   Hammer and roughage mills (agricultural machinery)—*mfg*
3462   Hammer forgings, not made in rolling mills—*mfg*
3531   Hammer mills (rock and ore crushing machines), portable—*mfg*
3532   Hammer mills (rock and ore crushing machines), stationary—*mfg*
3423   Hammers (handtools)—*mfg*
3542   Hammers, drop: for forging and shaping metal—*mfg*
2499   Hammers, meat: wood—*mfg*
3931   Hammers, piano—*mfg*
3531   Hammers, pile driving—*mfg*
3542   Hammers, power (forging machinery)—*mfg*
3546   Hammers: portable electric and pneumatic: e.g., chipping, riveting, caulking—*mfg*
2399   Hammocks, fabric—mfpm—*mfg*
2514   Hammocks, metal or fabric and metal combination—*mfg*
2449   Hampers, fruit and vegetable: veneer and splint—*mfg*
3444   Hampers, laundry: sheet metal—*mfg*
2499   Hampers, laundry: rattan, reed, splint, veneer, and willow—*mfg*
2653   Hampers, shipping: paperboard and solid fiber—mfpm—*mfg*
2655   Hampers, shipping: vulcanized fiber—mfpm—*mfg*
2013   Hams, except poultry—mfpm—*mfg*
2011   Hams, except poultry—mitse—*mfg*
7219   Hand laundries
3843   Hand pieces and parts, dental—*mfg*
3953   Hand stamps, stencils, and brands—*mfg*
2284   Hand-knitting thread: cotton, silk, man-made fibers, and wool—*mfg*
3999   Handbag frames—*mfg*
3111   Handbag leather—*mfg*
5632   Handbag stores—retail
3172   Handbags, men's: regardless of material—*mfg*
3911   Handbags, precious metal—*mfg*
3171   Handbags, women's: of all materials, except precious metal—*mfg*
5137   Handbags—wholesale
7997   Handball clubs, membership
7999   Handball courts, except membership clubs
7319   Handbill distribution service
3429   Handcuffs—*mfg*
2211   Handkerchief fabrics, cotton—*mfg*
2389   Handkerchiefs, except paper—mfpm—*mfg*

5136   Handkerchiefs, men's and boys'—wholesale
2676   Handkerchiefs, paper—mfpm—*mfg*
5137   Handkerchiefs: women's and children's—wholesale
3751   Handle bars, motorcycle and bicycle—*mfg*
2426   Handle blanks, wood—*mfg*
2411   Handle bolts, wood: hewn—*mfg*
2426   Handle stock, sawed or planed—*mfg*
3089   Handles, brush and tool: plastics—*mfg*
3261   Handles, faucet: vitreous china and earthenware—*mfg*
3069   Handles, rubber—*mfg*
3999   Handles, umbrella and parasol: except precious metal—*mfg*
3911   Handles, umbrella and parasol: gold and silver—*mfg*
3199   Handles, whip and luggage: leather—*mfg*
2499   Handles, wood: turned and shaped—*mfg*
5072   Handsaws—wholesale
7389   Handtool designers
5072   Handtools, except automotive and machinists' precision—wholesale
3546   Handtools, power-driven: woodworking or metalworking—*mfg*
5251   Handtools—retail
2299   Handwoven fabrics—*mfg*
7389   Handwriting analysis
3721   Hang gliders—*mfg*
3442   Hangar doors, sheet metal—*mfg*
4581   Hangar operation
2499   Hangers, garment: wood—*mfg*
3496   Hangers, garment: made from purchased wire—*mfg*
3861   Hangers: photographic film, plate, and paper—*mfg*
5063   Hanging and fastening devices, electrical—wholesale
2621   Hanging paper (wallpaper stock)—mitse—*mfg*
1629   Harbor construction—general contractors
1389   Hard banding service: on a contract basis
1221   Hard coal surface mining, except Pennsylvania anthracite
1222   Hard coal underground mining, except Pennsylvania anthracite
2298   Hard fiber cordage and twine—*mfg*
3069   Hard rubber products—*mfg*
3069   Hard surface floor coverings: rubber—*mfg*
3996   Hard surfaced floor coverings, except rubber and cork—*mfg*
2493   Hardboard—*mfg*
5031   Hardboard—wholesale
2899   Hardening compounds, concrete—*mfg*
3398   Hardening of metal for the trade—*mfg*
3829   Hardness testing equipment—*mfg*

3496 Hardware cloth, woven wire: made from purchased wire—*mfg*
5251 Hardware stores—retail
5013 Hardware, automotive—wholesale
5072 Hardware, heavy—wholesale
3089 Hardware, plastics—*mfg*
3644 Hardware, pole line—*mfg*
5063 Hardware, pole line—wholesale
5072 Hardware, shelf or light—wholesale
3999 Hardware, stage—*mfg*
2426 Hardwood dimension—*mfg*
2861 Hardwood distillates—*mfg*
1752 Hardwood flooring—contractors
2435 Hardwood plywood composites—*mfg*
2435 Hardwood veneer or plywood—*mfg*
3931 Harmonicas—*mfg*
3679 Harness assemblies for electronic use: wire and cable—*mfg*
2842 Harness dressing—*mfg*
5191 Harness equipment—wholesale
3429 Harness hardware—*mfg*
3111 Harness leather—*mfg*
5191 Harness made to individual order—wholesale
7699 Harness repair shops
3694 Harness wiring sets for internal combustion engines—*mfg*
3199 Harness, dog—*mfg*
3199 Harnesses and harness parts—*mfg*
3931 Harps and parts—*mfg*
3931 Harpsichords—*mfg*
3523 Harrows: disc, spring, and tine—*mfg*
2353 Harvest hats, straw—*mfg*
5083 Harvesting machinery and equipment—wholesale
3523 Harvesting machines—*mfg*
3634 Hassock fans, electric—*mfg*
2392 Hassocks, textile—*mfg*
5131 Hat and cap material—wholesale
2241 Hat band fabrics—*mfg*
3999 Hat blocks and display forms—*mfg*
2353 Hat bodies: fur-felt, straw, and wool-felt—*mfg*
3161 Hat boxes, except paper or paperboard—*mfg*
2396 Hat findings, men's—*mfg*
2396 Hat linings and trimmings, men's—*mfg*
3559 Hat making and hat renovating machinery—*mfg*
5611 Hat stores, men's and boys'—retail
0921 Hatcheries, fish
0254 Hatcheries, poultry
3423 Hatchets—*mfg*
7251 Hatcleaning and blocking shops
3942 Hats, doll—*mfg*
2371 Hats, fur—*mfg*

2386 Hats, leather—*mfg*
5136 Hats, men's and boys'—wholesale
2679 Hats, paper—mfpm—*mfg*
2353 Hats, trimmed—*mfg*
2353 Hats: fur-felt, straw, and wool-felt—*mfg*
2353 Hats: textiles, straw, fur-felt, and wool-felt—*mfg*
5137 Hats: women's, children's, and infants'—wholesale
2253 Hats—mitse—*mfg*
2396 Hatters' fur—*mfg*
4212 Hauling live animals, local
4212 Hauling, by dump truck
4212 Hauling, farm to market
3523 Hay balers and presses, farm—*mfg*
0139 Hay farms
3423 Hay forks—*mfg*
3423 Hay knives—*mfg*
0722 Hay mowing, raking, baling, and chopping
2048 Hay, cubed—*mfg*
5191 Hay—wholesale
5083 Haying machinery—wholesale
3523 Haying machines: mowers, rakes, loaders, stackers, balers, presses, etc.—*mfg*
4953 Hazardous waste material disposal sites
8351 Head Start centers, except in conjunction with schools
2044 Head rice—*mfg*
2511 Headboards, wood—*mfg*
2013 Headcheese—mfpm—*mfg*
3542 Headers—*mfg*
2411 Heading bolts, wood: hewn—*mfg*
2429 Heading, barrel (cooperage stock): sawed or split—*mfg*
3647 Headlights (fixtures), vehicular—*mfg*
3679 Headphones, radio—*mfg*
3931 Heads, banjo and drum—*mfg*
3679 Heads, recording for speech and musical equipment—*mfg*
3812 Heads-up display (HUD) systems, aeronautical—*mfg*
3661 Headsets, telephone—*mfg*
2369 Headwear: girls', children's, and infants'—mfpm—*mfg*
2253 Headwear—mitse—*mfg*
6321 Health and accident insurance
8399 Health and welfare councils
5499 Health food stores—retail
5149 Health foods—wholesale
6411 Health insurance coverage consulting service
6399 Health insurance for pets
6321 Health insurance, indemnity plans: except medical service
3641 Health lamps, infrared and ultraviolet—radiation—*mfg*

8099 Health screening service
9431 Health statistics centers—government
8399 Health systems agencies
7629 Hearing aid repair
3842 Hearing aids—*mfg*
5999 Hearing aids—retail
5047 Hearing aids—wholesale
8099 Hearing testing service
3713 Hearse bodies—*mfg*
4119 Hearse rental with drivers
7514 Hearse rental, without drivers
3711 Hearses (motor vehicles)—*mfg*
7514 Hearses and limousines, rental without drivers
3845 Heart-lung machine—*mfg*
5084 Heat exchange equipment, industrial—wholesale
3443 Heat exchangers: industrial, scientific, and nuclear—*mfg*
2899 Heat insulating compounds—*mfg*
3292 Heat insulating materials except felt: for covering boilers, pipes, etc.—*mfg*
3585 Heat pumps, electric—*mfg*
3861 Heat sensitized paper made from purchased paper—*mfg*
3443 Heat transfer drives (finned tubing)—*mfg*
3398 Heat treating of metal for the trade—*mfg*
3567 Heat treating ovens—*mfg*
2899 Heat treating salts—*mfg*
3052 Heater hose, plastics or rubber—*mfg*
3269 Heater parts, pottery—*mfg*
3255 Heater radiants, clay—*mfg*
3634 Heaters, immersion: household—electric—*mfg*
3714 Heaters, motor vehicle—*mfg*
3634 Heaters, space: electric—*mfg*
3433 Heaters, space: except electric—*mfg*
3569 Heaters, swimming pool: electric—*mfg*
3433 Heaters, swimming pool: oil or gas—*mfg*
3634 Heaters, tape—*mfg*
3585 Heating and air conditioning combination units—*mfg*
3433 Heating apparatus, except electric or warm air—*mfg*
1711 Heating equipment installation—contractors
3567 Heating equipment, induction—*mfg*
4741 Heating of railroad cars
3634 Heating pads, electric—*mfg*
4961 Heating systems, steam (suppliers of heat)
3567 Heating units and devices, industrial: electric—*mfg*
3634 Heating units for electric appliances—*mfg*
3634 Heating units, baseboard or wall: electric (radiant heating element)—*mfg*

1711 Heating, with or without sheet metal work—contractors
2819 Heavy water—*mfg*
3552 Heddles for loom harnesses, wire—*mfg*
3421 Hedge shears and trimmers, except power—*mfg*
3524 Hedge trimmers, power—*mfg*
3131 Heel caps, leather or metal—*mfg*
3131 Heel lifts, leather—*mfg*
3131 Heels, boot and shoe: finished wood or leather—*mfg*
3089 Heels, boot and shoe: plastics—*mfg*
3069 Heels, boot and shoe: rubber, composition, and fiber—*mfg*
3493 Helical springs, hot wound: for railroad equipment and vehicles—*mfg*
4522 Helicopter carriers
3721 Helicopters—*mfg*
2813 Helium—*mfg*
3949 Helmets, athletic—*mfg*
3199 Helmets, except athletic: leather—*mfg*
2353 Helmets, jungle-cloth: wool-lined—*mfg*
3842 Helmets, space—*mfg*
3469 Helmets, steel—*mfg*
7363 Help supply service
8322 Helping hand services
1011 Hematite mining
2835 Hematology diagnostic reagents—*mfg*
2836 Hematology products, except in vitro and in vivo reagents—*mfg*
2861 Hemlock extract—*mfg*
0831 Hemlock gum, gathering of
3841 Hemodialysis apparatus—*mfg*
2299 Hemp yarn, thread, roving, and textiles—*mfg*
2395 Hemstitching, for the trade—*mfg*
2833 Herb grinding, grading, and milling—*mfg*
2879 Herbicides—*mfg*
3679 Hermetic seals for electronic equipment—*mfg*
7694 Hermetics repair
2091 Herring: smoked, salted, dried, and pickled—*mfg*
2869 Hexamethylenediamine—*mfg*
2869 Hexamethylenetetramine—*mfg*
2211 Hickory stripes, cotton—*mfg*
5159 Hides (may include curing)—wholesale
2011 Hides and skins, cured or uncured—*mfg*
3111 Hides: tanning, currying, and finishing—*mfg*
2511 High chairs, children's: wood—*mfg*
3542 High energy rate metal forming machines—*mfg*
2892 High explosives—*mfg*
5731 High fidelity (hi-fi) equipment—retail
5064 High fidelity (hi-fi) equipment—wholesale

2046 High fructose syrup—*mfg*
3313 High percentage ferroalloys—*mfg*
3313 High percentage nonferrous additive alloys, except copper—*mfg*
2819 High purity grade chemicals, inorganic: refined from technical grades—*mfg*
2869 High purity grade chemicals, organic: refined from technical grades—*mfg*
8211 High schools
3297 High temperature mortar, nonclay—*mfg*
3443 High vacuum coaters, metal plate—*mfg*
3441 Highway bridge sections, prefabricated metal—*mfg*
4785 Highway bridges, operation of
1622 Highway construction, elevated—general contractors
1611 Highway construction, except elevated—general contractors
2899 Highway fusees—*mfg*
3444 Highway guardrails, sheet metal—*mfg*
1731 Highway lighting and electrical signal construction—contractors
9221 Highway patrols
3669 Highway signals, electric—*mfg*
1611 Highway signs, installation of—contractors
3429 Hinge tubes—*mfg*
3429 Hinges—*mfg*
8699 Historical clubs, other than professional
3799 Hitches, trailer—*mfg*
5092 Hobby kits—wholesale
5945 Hobby shops—retail
3944 Hobbyhorses—*mfg*
3545 Hobs—*mfg*
5084 Hobs—wholesale
7997 Hockey clubs, except professional and semiprofessional
3949 Hockey equipment, except uniforms and footwear—*mfg*
0721 Hoeing
3423 Hoes, garden and masons'—*mfg*
0213 Hog farms
3523 Hog feeding, handling, and watering equipment—*mfg*
3496 Hog rings, made from purchased wire—*mfg*
2011 Hog slaughtering plants—*mfg*
5154 Hogs—wholesale
2449 Hogsheads, wood: coopered—*mfg*
3537 Hoists, aircraft loading—*mfg*
3536 Hoists, except aircraft loading and automobile wrecker hoists—*mfg*
3536 Hoists, hand—*mfg*
3536 Hoists, overhead—*mfg*
5084 Hoists—wholesale
3999 Holders, cigar and cigarette—*mfg*

3952 Holders, pencil—*mfg*
3089 Holders, plastics: papertowel, grocery bag, dust mop and broom—*mfg*
3841 Holders, surgical needle—*mfg*
3861 Holders: photographic film, plate, and paper—*mfg*
6719 Holding companies, except bank
3914 Hollowware, silver, nickel silver, pewter, stainless steel, and plated—*mfg*
3199 Holsters, leather—*mfg*
8082 Home health care services
1522 Home improvements, residential: except single-family—general contractors
1521 Home improvements, single-family—general contractors
2844 Home permanent kits—*mfg*
7221 Home photographers
3651 Home tape recorders: cassette, cartridge, and reel—*mfg*
3541 Home workshop machine tools, metal-working—*mfg*
5932 Homefurnishing stores, secondhand—retail
**** Homefurnishing, except antique—retail—see kind of furnishing
5932 Homefurnishings, antique—retail
5023 Homefurnishings—wholesale
8322 Homemaker's service, primarily nonmedical
8641 Homeowner associations, except property management
8361 Homes for children, with health care incidental
8361 Homes for destitute men and women
8361 Homes for the aged, with health care incidental
8361 Homes for the deaf or blind, with health care incidental
8361 Homes for the emotionally disturbed, with health care incidental
8361 Homes for the mentally handicapped, with health care incidental
8059 Homes for the mentally retarded with health care, except skilled and intermediate care facilities
8361 Homes for the physically handicapped, with health care incidental
2043 Hominy grits prepared as cereal breakfast food—*mfg*
2041 Hominy grits, except breakfast food—*mfg*
2033 Hominy, canned—*mfg*
3556 Homogenizing machinery: dairy, fruit, vegetable, and other foods—*mfg*
3291 Hones—*mfg*
0279 Honey production
0752 Honey straining on the farm

1389 Hot oil treating of oil field tanks: on a contract basis
1389 Hot shot service: on a contract basis
3547 Hot strip mill machinery—*mfg*
3255 Hot top refractories, clay—*mfg*
3297 Hot top refractories, nonclay—*mfg*
2449 Hot tubs, coopered—*mfg*
3088 Hot tubs, plastics or fiberglass—*mfg*
5999 Hot tubs—retail
5091 Hot tubs—wholesale
3639 Hot water heaters, household: including nonelectric—*mfg*
3493 Hot wound springs, except wire springs—*mfg*
3312 Hot-rolled iron and steel products—*mfg*
1522 Hotel construction—general contractors
7389 Hotel reservation service
3262 Hotel tableware and kitchen articles, vitreous china—*mfg*
7041 Hotels operated by organizations for members only
7011 Hotels, except residential
6513 Hotels, residential: operators
7011 Hotels, seasonal
8322 Hotlines
3634 Hotplates, electric—*mfg*
3821 Hotplates, laboratory—*mfg*
1521 House construction, single-family—general contractors
5963 House delivery of purchased milk—retail
8712 House designers
1799 House moving—contractors
1721 House painting—contractors
3142 House slippers—*mfg*
7519 House trailer rental
5963 House-to-house selling of coffee, soda, beer, bottled water, or other products—retail
1521 House: shell erection, single-family—general contractors
7999 Houseboat rentals
3732 Houseboats, building and repairing—*mfg*
2384 Housecoats, except children's and infants'—mfpm—*mfg*
2369 Housecoats: girls', children's, and infants'—mfpm—*mfg*
2253 Housecoats—mitse—*mfg*
2335 Housedresses: women's, misses', and juniors'—mfpm—*mfg*
2392 Housefurnishings, except curtains and draperies—*mfg*
5722 Household appliance stores, electric or gas—retail
2842 Household bleaches, dry or liquid—*mfg*
3991 Household brooms and brushes—*mfg*
3263 Household earthenware, semivitreous—*mfg*

2512 Household furniture upholstered on wood frames, except dual-purpose sleep furniture—*mfg*
2519 Household furniture, glass and plastics—*mfg*
2511 Household furniture, wood: except upholstered—*mfg*
2519 Household furniture: rattan, reed, malacca, fiber, willow, and wicker—*mfg*
5712 Household furniture—retail
5021 Household furniture—wholesale
3069 Household gloves, rubber—*mfg*
4214 Household goods moving, local: combined with storage
4226 Household goods warehousing and storage, without local trucking
2879 Household insecticides—*mfg*
3262 Household tableware and kitchen articles, vitreous china—*mfg*
2899 Household tints and dyes—*mfg*
3365 Household utensils, cast aluminum: except die-castings—*mfg*
3469 Household utensils, porcelain enameled—*mfg*
3469 Household utensils, stamped and pressed metal—*mfg*
2499 Household woodenware—*mfg*
8811 Households, private: employing cooks, maids, chauffeurs, gardeners, etc.
7349 Housekeeping (cleaning service) on a contract or fee basis
9223 Houses of correction—government
2452 Houses, portable: prefabricated wood—except mobile homes—*mfg*
3448 Houses, prefabricated: metal—*mfg*
3792 Housetrailers, except as permanent dwellings—*mfg*
5719 Housewares stores—retail
5963 Housewares: house-to-house, telephone or party plan selling—retail
9531 Housing agencies, nonoperating—government
9531 Housing authorities, nonoperating—government
6531 Housing authorities, operating
3443 Housing cabinets for radium, metal plate—*mfg*
3272 Housing components, prefabricated: concrete—*mfg*
3444 Housings for business machines, sheet metal: except stamped—*mfg*
3469 Housings for business machines, stamped metal—*mfg*
3443 Housings, pressure—*mfg*
3489 Howitzers, more than 30 mm. (or more than 1.18 inch)—*mfg*

3559 Hub and die-cutting machines (jewelers)—*mfg*
3465 Hub caps, automotive: stamped—*mfg*
3728 Hubs, aircraft propeller—*mfg*
2499 Hubs, wood—*mfg*
2211 Huck toweling—*mfg*
0831 Huckleberry greens, gathering of
5963 Hucksters—retail
1061 Huebnerite mining
0723 Hulling and shelling of tree nuts
3523 Hulling machinery, agricultural—*mfg*
8742 Human resource consultants
8699 Humane societies, animal
5075 Humidifiers and dehumidifiers, except portable—wholesale
5064 Humidifiers and dehumidifiers, portable—wholesale
3634 Humidifiers, electric: portable—*mfg*
3585 Humidifying equipment, except portable—*mfg*
3822 Humidistats: wall, duct, and skeleton—*mfg*
3822 Humidity controls, air-conditioning types—*mfg*
3829 Humidity instruments, except industrial process and air-conditioning type—*mfg*
3823 Humidity instruments, industrial process type—*mfg*
7997 Hunt clubs, membership
5941 Hunters' equipment—retail
7032 Hunting camps
0971 Hunting carried on as a business enterprise
2329 Hunting coats and vests, men's—mfpm—*mfg*
7999 Hunting guides
3421 Hunting knives—*mfg*
0971 Hunting preserves, operation of
3423 Husking hooks—*mfg*
3674 Hybrid integrated circuits—*mfg*
2819 Hydrated alumina silicate powder—*mfg*
3274 Hydrated lime—*mfg*
5085 Hydraulic and pneumatic pistons and valves—wholesale
3593 Hydraulic cylinders, fluid power—*mfg*
3714 Hydraulic fluid power pumps for automotive steering mechanisms—*mfg*
2869 Hydraulic fluids, synthetic base—*mfg*
2992 Hydraulic fluids—mfpm—*mfg*
1389 Hydraulic fracturing wells on a contract basis
3492 Hydraulic hose assemblies—*mfg*
3594 Hydraulic pumps, aircraft—*mfg*
3511 Hydraulic turbine generator set units, complete—*mfg*
3511 Hydraulic turbines—*mfg*

3492 Hydraulic valves, including aircraft: fluid power—metal—*mfg*
2819 Hydrazine—*mfg*
2911 Hydrocarbon fluid, produced in petroleum refineries—*mfg*
2869 Hydrocarbon gases, fluorinated—*mfg*
2819 Hydrochloric acid—*mfg*
2819 Hydrocyanic acid—*mfg*
1629 Hydroelectric plant construction—general contractors
2819 Hydrofluoric acid—*mfg*
2899 Hydrofluoric acid compound, for etching and polishing glass—*mfg*
3732 Hydrofoil boats—*mfg*
3731 Hydrofoil vessels—*mfg*
2813 Hydrogen—*mfg*
2819 Hydrogen peroxide—*mfg*
2819 Hydrogen sulfide—*mfg*
3561 Hydrojet marine engine units—*mfg*
2046 Hydrol—*mfg*
3829 Hydrometers, except industrial process type—*mfg*
3823 Hydrometers, industrial process type—*mfg*
3822 Hydronic circulator control, automatic—*mfg*
5074 Hydronic heating equipment and supplies—wholesale
3822 Hydronic limit control—*mfg*
3822 Hydronic pressure and temperature controls—*mfg*
3812 Hydrophones—*mfg*
3443 Hydropneumatic tanks, metal plate—*mfg*
0182 Hydroponic crops, grown under cover
2865 Hydroquinone—*mfg*
3594 Hydrostatic drives (transmissions)—*mfg*
8734 Hydrostatic testing laboratories
3594 Hydrostatic transmissions—*mfg*
2819 Hydrosulfites—*mfg*
3842 Hydrotherapy equipment—*mfg*
3829 Hygrometers, except industrial process type—*mfg*
3829 Hygrothermographs—*mfg*
2822 Hypalon—*mfg*
8299 Hypnosis schools
8049 Hypnotists, offices of
3841 Hypodermic needles and syringes—*mfg*
2819 Hypophosphites—*mfg*

I

3841 IV transfusion apparatus—*mfg*
3069 Ice bags, rubber or rubberized fabric—*mfg*
3822 Ice bank controls—*mfg*
3632 Ice boxes, household—*mfg*
3585 Ice boxes, industrial—*mfg*
3089 Ice buckets, plastics: except foam—*mfg*

3429 Ice chests or coolers, portable, except insulated foam plastics—*mfg*

3089 Ice chests or coolers, portable, plastics: except insulated or foam plastics—*mfg*

3086 Ice chests or coolers, portable: foamed plastics—*mfg*

5451 Ice cream (packaged) stores—retail

5143 Ice cream and ices—wholesale

5078 Ice cream cabinets—wholesale

3411 Ice cream cans, metal—*mfg*

2052 Ice cream cones and wafers—*mfg*

2657 Ice cream containers, folding paperboard—mfpm—*mfg*

2656 Ice cream containers, nonfolding paperboard—mfpm—*mfg*

3469 Ice cream dippers—*mfg*

3499 Ice cream freezers, household, nonelectric: metal—*mfg*

3556 Ice cream manufacturing machinery—*mfg*

2023 Ice cream mix, unfrozen: liquid or dry—*mfg*

5812 Ice cream stands

5963 Ice cream wagons—retail

2024 Ice cream: e.g., bulk, packaged, molded, on sticks—*mfg*

3634 Ice crushers, electric—*mfg*

3569 Ice crushers, except household—*mfg*

2097 Ice cubes—*mfg*

5999 Ice dealers—retail

7941 Ice hockey clubs, professional or semiprofessional

3822 Ice maker controls—*mfg*

3585 Ice making machinery—*mfg*

5078 Ice making machines—wholesale

2023 Ice milk mix, unfrozen: liquid or dry—*mfg*

2024 Ice milk: e.g., bulk, packaged, molded, on sticks—*mfg*

2097 Ice plants, operated by public utilities—*mfg*

3949 Ice skates—*mfg*

7999 Ice skating rink operation

2097 Ice, manufactured or artificial: except dry ice—*mfg*

5199 Ice, manufactured or natural—wholesale

2086 Iced tea, bottled or canned—*mfg*

1499 Iceland spar mining (optical grade calcite)

2024 Ices and sherbets—*mfg*

4741 Icing of railroad cars

7389 Identification engraving service

3999 Identification plates—*mfg*

3999 Identification tags, except paper—*mfg*

5043 Identity recorders for photographing checks and fingerprints—wholesale

2899 Igniter grains, boron potassium nitrate—*mfg*

3483 Igniters, tracer: for ammunition more than 30 mm. (or more than 1.18 inch)—*mfg*

3694 Ignition apparatus for internal combustion engines—*mfg*

3694 Ignition cable sets or wire assemblies for internal combustion engines—*mfg*

3822 Ignition controls for gas appliances and furnaces, automatic—*mfg*

7539 Ignition service, automotive

3694 Ignition systems, high frequency—*mfg*

3825 Ignition testing instruments—*mfg*

3612 Ignition transformers—*mfg*

3229 Illuminating glass: light shades, reflectors, lamp chimneys, and globes—*mfg*

2911 Illuminating oil, produced in petroleum refineries—*mfg*

1099 Ilmenite mining

3299 Images, small: gypsum, clay, or papier-mache—factory production only—*mfg*

3634 Immersion heaters, household: electric—*mfg*

9721 Immigration services—government

9431 Immunization program administration—government

3679 Impedance conversion units, high frequency—*mfg*

3825 Impedance measuring equipment—*mfg*

3824 Impeller and counter driven flow meters—*mfg*

3842 Implants, surgical—*mfg*

1389 Impounding and storing salt water in connection with petroleum production

4971 Impounding reservoirs, irrigation

2295 Impregnating and coating of fabrics, except rubberizing—*mfg*

3843 Impression material, dental—*mfg*

2759 Imprinting, except lithographed or gravure—*mfg*

2754 Imprinting: gravure—*mfg*

2835 In vitro diagnostics—*mfg*

2835 In vivo diagnostics—*mfg*

2835 In vivo radioactive reagents—*mfg*

3822 In-built thermostats, filled system and bimetal types—*mfg*

3641 Incandescent filament lamp bulbs, complete—*mfg*

3559 Incandescent lamp making machinery—*mfg*

2899 Incense—*mfg*

3822 Incinerator control systems, residential and commercial types—*mfg*

1796 Incinerator installation, small—contractors

4953 Incinerator operation

3272 Incinerators, concrete—*mfg*

3339 Ingots, primary: nonferrous metals, except copper and aluminum—*mfg*
3312 Ingots, steel—*mfg*
5051 Ingots—wholesale
8049 Inhalation therapists, registered
3841 Inhalation therapy equipment—*mfg*
3841 Inhalators, surgical and medical—*mfg*
2899 Ink and writing fluids, except printing and drawing—*mfg*
2842 Ink eradicators—*mfg*
2842 Ink, burnishing—*mfg*
3952 Ink, drawing: black and colored—*mfg*
2893 Ink, duplicating—*mfg*
2899 Ink, indelible—*mfg*
5085 Ink, printers'—wholesale
2893 Ink, printing: base or finished—*mfg*
2899 Ink, stamp pad—*mfg*
5112 Ink, writing—wholesale
5112 Inked ribbons—wholesale
3229 Inkwells, glass—*mfg*
2499 Inlays for furniture (veneers)—*mfg*
3131 Inner soles, leather—*mfg*
3011 Inner tubes: airplane, automobile, bicycle, motorcycle, and tractor—*mfg*
7011 Inns, furnishing food and lodging
2819 Inorganic acids, except nitric or phosphoric—*mfg*
2833 Inorganic medicinal chemicals: bulk, uncompounded—*mfg*
2816 Inorganic pigments—*mfg*
3577 Input/output equipment, computer: except terminals—*mfg*
0721 Insect control for crops, with or without fertilizing
2879 Insect powder, household—*mfg*
3496 Insect screening, woven wire: made from purchased wire—*mfg*
2879 Insecticides, agricultural—*mfg*
2879 Insecticides, household—*mfg*
5191 Insecticides—wholesale
3545 Inserts, cutting tool—*mfg*
3999 Insignia, military: except textile—*mfg*
2399 Insignia, military: textile—*mfg*
9651 Inspection for labor standards—government
7389 Inspection of commodities, not connected with transportation
2899 Inspection oil, fluorescent—*mfg*
7549 Inspection service, automotive
4785 Inspection services connected with transportation
1796 Installation of machinery and other industrial equipment—contractors
6153 Installment notes, buying of
6153 Installment paper dealer

6141 Installment sales finance, other than banks
2095 Instant coffee—*mfg*
2752 Instant printing, except photocopy service—*mfg*
1542 Institutional building construction, nonresidential—general contractors
3646 Institutional lighting fixtures—*mfg*
3714 Instrument board assemblies, motor vehicle—*mfg*
3812 Instrument landing system instrumentation, airborne or airport—*mfg*
3827 Instrument lenses—*mfg*
3728 Instrument panel mockups: aircraft training units—*mfg*
3825 Instrument relays, all types—*mfg*
3825 Instrument shunts—*mfg*
3495 Instrument springs, precision: made from purchased wire—*mfg*
3612 Instrument transformers, except portable—*mfg*
3829 Instrumentation for reactor controls, auxiliary—*mfg*
3695 Instrumentation type tape, blank—*mfg*
3841 Instruments and apparatus, except electromedical: medical, surgical, ophthalmic, and veterinary—*mfg*
3823 Instruments for industrial process control—*mfg*
3825 Instruments for measuring electrical quantities—*mfg*
3825 Instruments, electric: for testing electrical characteristics—*mfg*
3952 Instruments, lettering: artists'—*mfg*
3841 Instruments, microsurgical: except electromedical—*mfg*
3931 Instruments, musical—*mfg*
3861 Instruments, photographic—*mfg*
3357 Insulated wire and cable, nonferrous—*mfg*
2679 Insulating batts, fills, and blankets: paper—mfpm—*mfg*
2899 Insulating compounds—*mfg*
3255 Insulating firebrick and shapes, clay—*mfg*
3211 Insulating glass, sealed units—mitse—*mfg*
3292 Insulating materials for covering boilers and pipes—*mfg*
2499 Insulating materials, cork—*mfg*
3275 Insulating plaster, gypsum—*mfg*
2493 Insulating siding, board—mitse—*mfg*
2952 Insulating siding, impregnated—mfpm—*mfg*
2241 Insulating tapes and braids, electric, except plastics—*mfg*
3086 Insulation and cushioning: foamed plastics—*mfg*

2062 Invert sugar—*mfg*
3629 Inverters, nonrotating: electrical—*mfg*
3621 Inverters, rotating: electrical—*mfg*
7381 Investigators, private
6282 Investment advisory service
6211 Investment bankers
3324 Investment castings, steel—*mfg*
6211 Investment certificates, sale of
6799 Investment clubs
6159 Investment companies, small business
6282 Investment counselors
6211 Investment firm—general brokerage
6722 Investment funds (management) open-end
6726 Investment funds, closed-end: management of
6719 Investment holding companies, except bank
3843 Investment material, dental—*mfg*
6282 Investment research
6726 Investment trusts, unit
6726 Investors' syndicates
2759 Invitations, engraved—*mfg*
2819 Iodides—*mfg*
2835 Iodinated diagnostic agents—*mfg*
2819 Iodine, elemental—*mfg*
2819 Iodine, resublimed—*mfg*
2834 Iodine, tincture of—*mfg*
3829 Ion chambers—*mfg*
2821 Ion exchange resins—*mfg*
2821 Ionomer resins—*mfg*
2869 Ionone—*mfg*
1099 Iridium ore mining
3339 Iridium refining, primary—*mfg*
3341 Iridium smelting and refining, secondary—*mfg*
0134 Irish potato farms
1011 Iron agglomerate and pellet production
5051 Iron and steel flat products—wholesale
5093 Iron and steel scrap—wholesale
5051 Iron and steel semifinished products—wholesale
2816 Iron blue pigments—*mfg*
3321 Iron castings, ductile and nodular—*mfg*
2891 Iron cement, household—*mfg*
2816 Iron colors—*mfg*
3842 Iron lungs—*mfg*
1011 Iron ore dressing (beneficiation) plants
1011 Iron ore mining
1011 Iron ore, blocked: mining
3399 Iron ore, recovery from open hearth slag—*mfg*
5052 Iron ore—wholesale
2816 Iron oxide, black—*mfg*
2816 Iron oxide, magnetic—*mfg*
2816 Iron oxide, yellow—*mfg*
3312 Iron sinter, made in steel mills—*mfg*

2819 Iron sulphate—*mfg*
1799 Iron work, ornamental—contractors
1791 Iron work, structural—contractors
3312 Iron, pig—*mfg*
5051 Iron, pig—wholesale
3399 Iron, powdered—*mfg*
3469 Ironer parts, porcelain enameled—*mfg*
3633 Ironers and mangles, household, except portable irons—*mfg*
3582 Ironers, commercial laundry and drycleaning—*mfg*
5064 Ironers, household: electric—wholesale
2392 Ironing board pads—mfpm—*mfg*
3499 Ironing boards, metal—*mfg*
2499 Ironing boards, wood—*mfg*
3634 Irons, domestic: electric—*mfg*
3953 Irons, marking or branding—*mfg*
3423 Ironworkers' handtools—*mfg*
3844 Irradiation equipment—*mfg*
9631 Irrigation districts—nonoperating
3523 Irrigation equipment, self-propelled—*mfg*
5083 Irrigation equipment—wholesale
3272 Irrigation pipe, concrete—*mfg*
3444 Irrigation pipe, sheet metal—*mfg*
1629 Irrigation projects construction—general contractors
4971 Irrigation system operation
0721 Irrigation system operation services (not providing water)
1321 Isobutane (natural) production
2821 Isobutylene polymers—*mfg*
2822 Isobutylene-isoprene rubbers—*mfg*
2822 Isocyanate type rubber—*mfg*
2865 Isocyanates—*mfg*
3612 Isolation transformers—*mfg*
2822 Isoprene rubbers, synthetic—*mfg*
2869 Isopropyl alcohol—*mfg*
2819 Isotopes, radioactive—*mfg*
6726 Issuing of face-amount installment certificates
2032 Italian foods, canned—*mfg*

J

3569 Jack screws—*mfg*
3482 Jackets, bullet: 30 mm. (or 1.18 inch) or less—*mfg*
2371 Jackets, fur—*mfg*
3443 Jackets, industrial: metal plate—*mfg*
2386 Jackets, leather (except welders') or sheep-lined—*mfg*
2329 Jackets, nontailored except work: men's and boys'—mfpm—*mfg*
2339 Jackets, not tailored: women's, misses', and juniors'—*mfg*

2326 Jackets, overall and work: men's and boys'—mfpm—*mfg*

2339 Jackets, service apparel (e.g., medical and lab)—*mfg*

2339 Jackets, ski: women's, misses' and juniors'—mfpm—*mfg*

2384 Jackets, smoking: men's—mfpm—*mfg*

2329 Jackets, sport, nontailored: men's and boys'—mfpm—*mfg*

2311 Jackets, tailored suit-type: men's and boys'—*mfg*

2337 Jackets, tailored, except fur, sheep-lined, and leather: women's, misses', and juniors'—mfpm—*mfg*

3199 Jackets, welders': leather—*mfg*

2369 Jackets: girls', children's, and infants'—mfpm—*mfg*

2253 Jackets—mitse—*mfg*

3569 Jacks, hydraulic: for general industrial use—*mfg*

2499 Jacks, ladder: wood—*mfg*

3531 Jacks, mud—*mfg*

3423 Jacks: lifting, screw, and ratchet (handtools)—*mfg*

3552 Jacquard card cutting machines—*mfg*

2675 Jacquard cards—mfpm—*mfg*

3552 Jacquard loom parts and attachments—*mfg*

2211 Jacquard woven fabrics, cotton—*mfg*

2221 Jacquard woven fabrics, manmade fiber and silk—*mfg*

1499 Jade mining

8744 Jails, privately operated

9223 Jails—government

3442 Jalousies, all metal or metal frame—*mfg*

2431 Jalousies, glass: wood frame—*mfg*

2033 Jams, including imitation—*mfg*

4581 Janitorial service on airplanes

7349 Janitorial services on a contract or fee basis

3589 Janitors' carts—*mfg*

5087 Janitors' supplies—wholesale

3111 Japanning of leather—*mfg*

3479 Japanning of metal—*mfg*

3567 Japanning ovens—*mfg*

2851 Japans, baking and drying—*mfg*

3466 Jar crowns and tops, stamped metal—*mfg*

3069 Jar rings, rubber—*mfg*

3221 Jars for packing, bottling, and canning: glass—*mfg*

3069 Jars, battery: hard rubber—*mfg*

3089 Jars, plastics—*mfg*

7929 Jazz music groups or artists

2211 Jean fabrics, cotton—*mfg*

2325 Jean-cut casual slacks: men's and boys'—mfpm—*mfg*

2339 Jean-cut casual slacks: women's, misses', and juniors'—mfpm—*mfg*

5651 Jeans stores—retail

2369 Jeans: girls', children's, and infants'—mfpm—*mfg*

2325 Jeans: men's and boys'—mfpm—*mfg*

2339 Jeans: women's, misses', and juniors'—*mfg*

2033 Jellies, edible: including imitation—*mfg*

2099 Jelly, corncob (gelatin)—*mfg*

2257 Jersey fabrics—*mfg*

2253 Jerseys and sweaters—mitse—*mfg*

3724 Jet assisted takeoff devices (JATO)—*mfg*

2899 Jet fuel igniters—*mfg*

2911 Jet fuels—*mfg*

3724 Jet propulsion and internal combustion engines and parts, aircraft—*mfg*

3483 Jet propulsion projectiles, complete—*mfg*

1629 Jetty construction—general contractors

3915 Jewel bearings, synthetic—*mfg*

3915 Jewel cutting, drilling, polishing, recutting, or setting—*mfg*

3915 Jewel preparing: for instruments, tools, watches, and jewelry—*mfg*

3911 Jewel settings and mountings, precious metal—*mfg*

2675 Jewelers' cards—mfpm—*mfg*

3915 Jewelers' findings and materials—*mfg*

5094 Jewelers' findings—wholesale

3423 Jewelers' handtools—*mfg*

3559 Jewelers' machines—*mfg*

5199 Jewelry boxes—wholesale

3479 Jewelry enameling, for the trade—*mfg*

3915 Jewelry parts, unassembled—*mfg*

3915 Jewelry polishing for the trade—*mfg*

7631 Jewelry repair shops

3915 Jewelry soldering for the trade—*mfg*

5632 Jewelry stores, costume—retail

5944 Jewelry stores, except costume—retail

3961 Jewelry, costume: except precious metal and precious or semiprecious stone—*mfg*

3911 Jewelry, made of precious metal or precious or semiprecious stones—*mfg*

5961 Jewelry, mail-order—retail

3911 Jewelry, natural or cultured pearls—*mfg*

5944 Jewelry, precious stones and precious metals: including custom made—retail

5094 Jewelry—wholesale

3541 Jig boring machines—*mfg*

3541 Jig grinding machines—*mfg*

3544 Jigs and fixtures (metalworking machinery accessories)—*mfg*

3544 Jigs: inspection, gauging, and checking—*mfg*

5084 Jigs—wholesale

8331 Job counseling

2711 Job printing and newspaper publishing combined—*mfg*
2759 Job printing, except lithographic or gravure—*mfg*
2754 Job printing, gravure—*mfg*
2752 Job printing, lithographic—*mfg*
2752 Job printing, offset—*mfg*
8331 Job training
7948 Jockeys, horseracing
3949 Jogging machines—*mfg*
2329 Jogging suits, men's and boys'—mfpm—*mfg*
2369 Jogging suits: girls', children's, and infants'—mfpm—*mfg*
2339 Jogging suits: women's, misses', and juniors'—mfpm—*mfg*
2253 Jogging suits—mitse—*mfg*
1751 Joinery, ship—contractors
2891 Joint compounds—*mfg*
3553 Jointers (woodworking machines)—*mfg*
3568 Joints, swivel: except motor vehicle and aircraft—*mfg*
3568 Joints, universal: except motor vehicle—*mfg*
3272 Joists, concrete—*mfg*
3449 Joists, fabricated bar—*mfg*
3441 Joists, open web steel: long-span series—*mfg*
3444 Joists, sheet metal—*mfg*
7999 Judo instruction
3221 Jugs for packing, bottling, and canning: glass—*mfg*
3429 Jugs, vacuum—*mfg*
3634 Juice extractors, electric—*mfg*
3556 Juice extractors, fruit and vegetable: commercial type—*mfg*
2024 Juice pops, frozen—*mfg*
2033 Juice, fruit: concentrated-hot pack—*mfg*
2033 Juices, fresh: fruit or vegetable—*mfg*
2033 Juices, fruit and vegetable: canned or fresh—*mfg*
3651 Juke boxes—*mfg*
7993 Juke boxes, operation of
2337 Jumpsuits: women's, misses', and juniors'—mfpm—*mfg*
8611 Junior Chambers of Commerce
8222 Junior colleges
5093 Junk and scrap, general line—wholesale
2631 Jute liner board—mitse—*mfg*
5131 Jute piece goods—wholesale
8361 Juvenile correctional homes
2514 Juvenile furniture, metal—*mfg*
2519 Juvenile furniture, rattan and reed—*mfg*
2512 Juvenile furniture, upholstered on wood frames, except convertible beds—*mfg*

2511 Juvenile furniture, wood: except upholstered—*mfg*
5712 Juvenile furniture—retail

K

2851 Kalsomines, dry or paste—*mfg*
1455 Kaolin mining
3295 Kaolin, ground or otherwise treated—*mfg*
7999 Karate instruction
5137 Karate uniforms: women's and children's—wholesale
3732 Kayaks, building and repairing—*mfg*
3275 Keene's cement—*mfg*
2449 Kegs, wood: coopered—*mfg*
2048 Kelp meal and pellets—*mfg*
2833 Kelp plants—*mfg*
3825 Kelvin bridges (electrical measuring instruments)—*mfg*
0752 Kennels, boarding
0279 Kennels, breeding and raising own stock
7948 Kennels, dogracing
1474 Kernite mining
1311 Kerogen processing
2911 Kerosene—*mfg*
3433 Kerosene space heaters—*mfg*
5172 Kerosene—wholesale
2033 Ketchup—*mfg*
2869 Ketone, methyl ethyl—*mfg*
2869 Ketone, methyl isobutyl—*mfg*
3443 Kettles (process vessels), metal plate—*mfg*
3429 Key blanks—*mfg*
3172 Key cases, regardless of material—*mfg*
7699 Key duplicating shops
3496 Key rings, made from purchased wire—*mfg*
3572 Key to tape or disk devices—*mfg*
3577 Key-disk or diskette equipment, computer peripheral equipment—*mfg*
3577 Key-tape equipment: reel, cassette, or cartridge—*mfg*
3931 Keyboards, piano or organ—*mfg*
3577 Keying equipment, computer peripheral equipment—*mfg*
5045 Keying equipment—wholesale
7374 Keypunch service
3577 Keypunch/verify cards, computer peripheral equipment—*mfg*
3429 Keys—*mfg*
3496 Keys, can: made from purchased wire—*mfg*
3541 Keyseating machines (machine tools)—*mfg*
7996 Kiddie parks
8092 Kidney dialysis centers
2261 Kier bleaching, continuous machine—*mfg*
1629 Kiln construction—general contractors

7819 Laboratories, motion picture
8734 Laboratories, product testing: not manufacturing auxiliaries
8731 Laboratories, research: commercial
8071 Laboratories: biological, medical, and X-ray (picture and treatment)
8731 Laboratory (physical) research and development
0279 Laboratory animal farms (e.g., rats, mice, guinea pigs)
2819 Laboratory chemicals, inorganic—*mfg*
2869 Laboratory chemicals, organic—*mfg*
2326 Laboratory coats: men's—mfpm—*mfg*
5047 Laboratory equipment, dental and medical—wholesale
5049 Laboratory equipment, except medical or dental—wholesale
3821 Laboratory equipment: fume hoods, distillation racks, benches, and cabinets—*mfg*
3231 Laboratory glassware, made from purchased glass—*mfg*
7699 Laboratory instrument repair, except electric
3825 Laboratory standards, electric: resistance, inductance, and capacitance—*mfg*
3069 Laboratory sundries: e.g., cases, covers, funnels, cups, bottles—rubber—*mfg*
3089 Laboratoryware, plastics—*mfg*
0831 Lac production
3552 Lace and net machines—*mfg*
5131 Lace fabrics—wholesale
2258 Lace goods: curtains, bedspreads, table covers, flouncings, and insertions—*mfg*
3111 Lace leather—*mfg*
3552 Lace machine bobbins, wood or metal—*mfg*
2241 Lace, auto wind—*mfg*
2395 Lace, burnt-out—*mfg*
2258 Lace, knit—*mfg*
2675 Lace, paper: die-cut from purchased materials—*mfg*
3131 Laces, boot and shoe: leather—*mfg*
2241 Laces, corset and shoe: textile—*mfg*
2258 Laces: Barmen, bobbinet, levers, and Nottingham—*mfg*
2241 Lacings—mitse—*mfg*
2851 Lacquer bases and dopes—*mfg*
2851 Lacquer thinner—*mfg*
2851 Lacquer, clear and pigmented—*mfg*
3479 Lacquering of metal products, for the trade—*mfg*
3567 Lacquering ovens—*mfg*
2851 Lacquers, plastics—*mfg*
5198 Lacquers—wholesale
3949 Lacrosse equipment—*mfg*
2023 Lactose, edible—*mfg*

3499 Ladder assemblies, combination workstand: metal—*mfg*
3531 Ladder ditchers, vertical boom or wheel—*mfg*
3429 Ladder jacks, metal—*mfg*
2499 Ladder jacks, wood—*mfg*
2426 Ladder round—*mfg*
2426 Ladder rounds or rungs, hardwood—*mfg*
3446 Ladders, chain: metal—*mfg*
3446 Ladders, for permanent installation: metal—*mfg*
3499 Ladders, metal: portable—*mfg*
3089 Ladders, plastics—*mfg*
2499 Ladders, wood—*mfg*
5084 Ladders—wholesale
5137 Ladies' handkerchiefs—wholesale
5137 Ladies' purses—wholesale
3443 Ladle bails—*mfg*
3255 Ladle brick, clay—*mfg*
3443 Ladles, metal plate—*mfg*
4449 Lake freight transportation, except on the Great Lakes
2865 Lake red C toners—*mfg*
2865 Lakes, color—*mfg*
2013 Lamb stew, mfpm—*mfg*
2011 Lamb—mitse—*mfg*
2679 Laminated building paper—mfpm—*mfg*
2675 Laminated cardboard—mfpm—*mfg*
3211 Laminated glass, made from glass produced in the same establishment—*mfg*
3231 Laminated glass, made from purchased glass—*mfg*
3083 Laminated plastics plate, rods, and tubes and sheet, except flexible packaging—*mfg*
2891 Laminating compounds—*mfg*
2295 Laminating of fabrics—*mfg*
7389 Laminating of photographs (coating photographs with plastics)
3399 Laminating steel for the trade—*mfg*
3641 Lamp (bulb) parts, electric—*mfg*
5719 Lamp and shade shops—retail
3281 Lamp bases, onyx—*mfg*
3089 Lamp bases, plastics—*mfg*
3269 Lamp bases, pottery—*mfg*
2816 Lamp black—*mfg*
5063 Lamp bulbs —wholesale
3641 Lamp bulbs and tubes, electric: incandescent filament, fluorescent, and vapor—*mfg*
3641 Lamp bulbs and tubes, health: infrared and ultraviolet radiation—*mfg*
3648 Lamp fixtures, infrared—*mfg*
3496 Lamp frames, wire: made from purchased wire—*mfg*

3559 Lamp making machinery, incandescent—*mfg*
3229 Lamp parts, glass—*mfg*
3446 Lamp posts, metal—*mfg*
3999 Lamp shade frames—*mfg*
3229 Lamp shades, glass—*mfg*
3645 Lamp shades, metal—*mfg*
3089 Lamp shades, plastics—*mfg*
3999 Lamp shades: except metal and glass—*mfg*
3643 Lamp sockets and receptacles (electric wiring devices)—*mfg*
3645 Lamps (lighting fixtures), residential: electric—*mfg*
3844 Lamps, X-ray—*mfg*
3641 Lamps, glow—*mfg*
3699 Lamps, insect: electric—*mfg*
3647 Lamps, marker and clearance: motor vehicle—*mfg*
3641 Lamps, sealed beam—*mfg*
3841 Lamps, slit (ophthalmic goods)—*mfg*
5023 Lamps: floor, boudoir, desk—wholesale
1629 Land clearing—contractors
1629 Land drainage—contractors
1629 Land leveling (irrigation)—contractors
9512 Land management agencies—government
5083 Land preparation machinery, agricultural—wholesale
1629 Land reclamation—contractors
3523 Land rollers and levelers (agricultural machinery)—*mfg*
8713 Land surveying
4953 Landfill, sanitary: operation of
6519 Landholding offices
3728 Landing gear, aircraft—*mfg*
3449 Landing mats, aircraft: metal—*mfg*
3731 Landing ships, building and repairing—*mfg*
3728 Landing skis and tracks, aircraft—*mfg*
0781 Landscape architects
0781 Landscape counseling
0781 Landscape planning
8299 Language schools
3229 Lantern globes, glass: pressed or blown—*mfg*
3861 Lantern slide plates, sensitized—*mfg*
2679 Lanterns, halloween: papier mache—mfpm—*mfg*
3648 Lanterns: electric, gas, carbide, kerosene, and gasoline—*mfg*
5085 Lapidary equipment—wholesale
3915 Lapidary work, contract and other—*mfg*
3541 Lapping machines—*mfg*
2013 Lard—mfpm—*mfg*
2011 Lard—mitse—*mfg*
5147 Lard—wholesale
3674 Laser diodes—*mfg*

3845 Laser systems and equipment, medical—*mfg*
3699 Laser welding, drilling and cutting equipment—*mfg*
3199 Lashes (whips)—*mfg*
2411 Last blocks, wood: hewn or riven—*mfg*
2499 Last sole patterns, regardless of material—*mfg*
2499 Lasts, boot and shoe: regardless of material—*mfg*
3069 Latex, foamed—*mfg*
3449 Lath, expanded metal—*mfg*
2493 Lath, fiber—*mfg*
3275 Lath, gypsum—*mfg*
2421 Lath, made in sawmills and lathmills—*mfg*
3496 Lath, woven wire: made from purchased wire—*mfg*
3545 Lathe attachments and cutting tools (machine tool accessories)—*mfg*
3541 Lathes, metal cutting—*mfg*
3541 Lathes, metal polishing—*mfg*
3542 Lathes, spinning—*mfg*
3553 Lathes, wood turning: including accessories—*mfg*
1742 Lathing—contractors
3111 Latigo leather—*mfg*
7218 Laundered mat and rug supply service
2399 Launderers' nets—*mfg*
7218 Launderers, industrial
7215 Launderettes
7542 Laundries, automotive
7219 Laundries, except power and coin-operated
7211 Laundries, power: family and commercial
7215 Laundromats
7211 Laundry collecting and distributing outlets operated by power laundries
3537 Laundry containers on wheels—*mfg*
5087 Laundry equipment and supplies—wholesale
2211 Laundry fabrics, cotton—*mfg*
3444 Laundry hampers, sheet metal—*mfg*
7215 Laundry machine routes, coin-operated
3582 Laundry machinery and equipment, commercial, including coin-operated—*mfg*
3633 Laundry machinery, household, including coin-operated—*mfg*
2211 Laundry nets—mitse—*mfg*
5169 Laundry soap, chips, and powder—wholesale
2899 Laundry sours—*mfg*
3272 Laundry trays, concrete—*mfg*
3261 Laundry trays, vitreous china—*mfg*
3431 Laundry tubs, enameled iron and other metal—*mfg*
3088 Laundry tubs, plastics—*mfg*

2869   Lauric acid esters—*mfg*
3431   Lavatories, enameled iron and other metal—*mfg*
3088   Lavatories, plastics—*mfg*
3261   Lavatories, vitreous china—*mfg*
9229   Law enforcement statistics centers—government
8111   Law offices
0782   Lawn care
3524   Lawn edgers, power—*mfg*
0782   Lawn fertilizing services
2514   Lawn furniture, metal—*mfg*
2519   Lawn furniture: except wood, metal, stone, and concrete—*mfg*
5021   Lawn furniture—wholesale
5083   Lawn machinery and equipment—wholesale
0782   Lawn mowing services
0782   Lawn mulching services
3524   Lawn rollers, residential—*mfg*
0782   Lawn seeding services
0782   Lawn spraying services
0782   Lawn sprigging services
1711   Lawn sprinkler system installation—contractors
7699   Lawnmower repair shops
3524   Lawnmowers, hand and power: residential—*mfg*
5261   Lawnmowers—retail
2211   Lawns, cotton—*mfg*
8111   Lawyers
2834   Laxatives—*mfg*
1094   Leaching of uranium, radium or vanadium ores at mine site
3691   Lead acid batteries (storage batteries)—*mfg*
3356   Lead and lead alloy bars, pipe, plates, rods, sheets, strip, and tubing—*mfg*
2879   Lead arsenate, formulated—*mfg*
2892   Lead azide (explosives)—*mfg*
1799   Lead burning—contractors
3364   Lead die-castings—*mfg*
3497   Lead foil, not made in rolling mills—*mfg*
1031   Lead ore mining
5052   Lead ore—wholesale
2816   Lead oxide pigments—*mfg*
2819   Lead oxides, other than pigments—*mfg*
2816   Lead pigments—*mfg*
3339   Lead pigs, blocks, ingots, and refinery shapes: primary—*mfg*
3356   Lead rolling, drawing, and extruding—*mfg*
2819   Lead silicate—*mfg*
3339   Lead smelting and refining, primary—*mfg*
3341   Lead smelting and refining, secondary—*mfg*

3295   Lead, black (natural graphite): ground, refined, or blended—*mfg*
3641   Lead-in wires, electric lamp: made from purchased wire—*mfg*
2851   Lead-in-oil paints—*mfg*
1031   Lead-zinc ore mining
5051   Lead—wholesale
3231   Leaded glass, made from purchased glass—*mfg*
3555   Leads, printers'—*mfg*
3423   Leaf skimmers and swimming pool rakes—*mfg*
3493   Leaf springs: automobile, locomotive, and other vehicle—*mfg*
3497   Leaf, metal—*mfg*
3599   Leak detectors, water—*mfg*
1389   Lease tanks, oil and gas field: erecting, cleaning, and repairing—on a contract basis
7374   Leasing of computer time
7377   Leasing of computers, except finance leasing or by the manufacturer
5199   Leather and cut stock—wholesale
5136   Leather and sheep-lined clothing, men's and boys'—wholesale
5137   Leather and sheep-lined clothing: women's and children's—wholesale
3199   Leather belting for machinery: flat, solid, twisted, and built-up—*mfg*
5085   Leather belting, packing—wholesale
3111   Leather coloring, cutting, embossing, japanning, and welting—*mfg*
3111   Leather converters—*mfg*
2842   Leather dressings and finishes—*mfg*
2865   Leather dyes and stains, synthetic—*mfg*
2843   Leather finishing agents—*mfg*
3151   Leather gloves or mittens—*mfg*
7699   Leather goods repair shops
5199   Leather goods, except footwear, gloves, luggage, and belting—wholesale
5948   Leather goods, including goods made to individual order—retail
3172   Leather goods, small: personal—*mfg*
3131   Leather welting—*mfg*
3559   Leather working machinery—*mfg*
2295   Leather, artificial or imitation—*mfg*
3111   Leather: tanning, currying, and finishing—*mfg*
2631   Leatherboard—mitse—*mfg*
2099   Leavening compounds, prepared—*mfg*
2074   Lecithin, cottonseed—*mfg*
2075   Lecithin, soybean—*mfg*
7389   Lecture bureaus
8999   Lecturers
2782   Ledgers and ledger sheets—*mfg*
2252   Leg warmers—*mfg*

8111 Legal aid services
9222 Legal counsel offices—government
6311 Legal reserve life insurance
8111 Legal services
3199 Leggings, welders': leather—*mfg*
2369 Leggings: girls', children's, and infants'—mfpm—*mfg*
9131 Legislative and executive office combinations
9121 Legislative assemblies
7922 Legitimate theater producers
0174 Lemon groves and farms
2899 Lemon oil—*mfg*
2086 Lemonade: bottled, canned, or fresh—*mfg*
8231 Lending libraries
2211 Leno fabrics, cotton—*mfg*
2221 Leno fabrics, manmade fiber and silk—*mfg*
3229 Lens blanks, optical and ophthalmic—*mfg*
3827 Lens coating—*mfg*
3851 Lens coating, ophthalmic—*mfg*
3827 Lens grinding, except ophthalmic—*mfg*
3851 Lens grinding, ophthalmic, except prescription—*mfg*
3827 Lens mounts—*mfg*
3861 Lens shades, camera—*mfg*
3229 Lenses, glass: for lanterns, flashlights, headlights, and searchlights—*mfg*
3851 Lenses, ophthalmic—*mfg*
5048 Lenses, ophthalmic—wholesale
3827 Lenses, optical: photographic, magnifying, projection, and instrument—*mfg*
3089 Lenses, plastics: except ophthalmic or optical—*mfg*
0119 Lentil farms
2369 Leotards: girls', children's, and infants'—mfpm—*mfg*
2339 Leotards: women's, misses', and juniors'—mfpm—*mfg*
2253 Leotards—mitse—*mfg*
1479 Lepidolite mining
6512 Lessors of piers, docks, and associated buildings and facilities
6519 Lessors of property, except railroad, buildings, or mobile home sites
6517 Lessors of railroad property
4513 Letter delivery, private: air
4215 Letter delivery, private: except air
3579 Letter folding, stuffing, and sealing machines—*mfg*
3545 Letter pins (gauging and measuring)—*mfg*
7338 Letter writing service
3952 Lettering instruments, artists'—*mfg*
7389 Lettering service
2893 Letterpress ink—*mfg*
2796 Letterpress plates, preparation of—*mfg*

2759 Letterpress printing—*mfg*
3953 Letters (marking devices), metal—*mfg*
3993 Letters for signs, metal—*mfg*
2675 Letters, cardboard—mfpm—*mfg*
2759 Letters, circular and form: except lithographed or gravure printed—*mfg*
2754 Letters, circular and form: gravure printing—*mfg*
2752 Letters, circular and form: lithographed—*mfg*
2499 Letters, wood—*mfg*
0161 Lettuce farms
1629 Levee construction—general contractors
3823 Level and bulk measuring instruments, industrial process type—*mfg*
3829 Level gauges, radiation type—*mfg*
3229 Level vials for instruments, glass—*mfg*
3547 Levelers, roller (rolling mill equipment)—*mfg*
3829 Levels and tapes, surveying—*mfg*
3423 Levels, carpenters'—*mfg*
6351 Liability insurance
8231 Libraries, except motion picture film
8231 Libraries, printed matter
2782 Library binders, looseleaf—*mfg*
2675 Library cards, paperboard—mfpm—*mfg*
9621 Licensing and inspection of transportation facilities and services—government
9631 Licensing and inspection of utilities
9651 Licensing and permit for professional occupations—government
9651 Licensing and permit for retail trade—government
2064 Licorice candy—*mfg*
7381 Lie detection service
6311 Life insurance
6411 Life insurance agents
6311 Life insurance funds, savings bank
2499 Life preservers, cork—*mfg*
3842 Life preservers, except cork and inflatable—*mfg*
6311 Life reinsurance
3732 Lifeboats, building and repairing—*mfg*
7999 Lifeguard service
3089 Lifejackets, plastics—*mfg*
3069 Lifejackets: inflatable rubberized fabric—*mfg*
3732 Liferafts, except inflatable (rubber and plastics)—*mfg*
3089 Liferafts, nonrigid: plastics—*mfg*
3069 Liferafts, rubber—*mfg*
3537 Lift trucks, industrial: fork, platform, straddle, etc.—*mfg*
5084 Lift trucks—wholesale
3534 Lifts (elevators), passenger and freight—*mfg*

3131 Lifts, heel: leather—*mfg*
3842 Ligatures, medical—*mfg*
1629 Light and power plant construction—general contractors
3641 Light bulbs, electric: complete—*mfg*
5063 Light bulbs, electric—wholesale
3663 Light communications equipment—*mfg*
3674 Light emitting diodes—*mfg*
3861 Light meters, photographic—*mfg*
3812 Light reconnaissance and surveillance systems and equipment—*mfg*
3671 Light sensing and emitting tubes—*mfg*
3674 Light sensitive devices, solid-state—*mfg*
3229 Light shades, glass: pressed or blown—*mfg*
3645 Light shades, metal—*mfg*
3827 Light sources, standard—*mfg*
2899 Lighter fluid—*mfg*
4499 Lighterage
3999 Lighters, cigar and cigarette: except precious metal and electric—*mfg*
5199 Lighters, cigar and cigarette—wholesale
3731 Lighters, marine: building and repairing—*mfg*
3731 Lighthouse tenders, building and repairing—*mfg*
3624 Lighting carbons—*mfg*
3648 Lighting fixtures, airport: runway, approach, taxi, and ramp—*mfg*
3646 Lighting fixtures, commercial—*mfg*
3647 Lighting fixtures, motor vehicle—*mfg*
3645 Lighting fixtures, residential, electric: e.g., garden, patio, walkway, yard—*mfg*
3648 Lighting fixtures, residential, except electric—*mfg*
3645 Lighting fixtures, residential: electric—*mfg*
3647 Lighting fixtures, vehicular—*mfg*
5063 Lighting fixtures: residential, commercial, and industrial—wholesale
3229 Lighting glassware, pressed or blown—*mfg*
7349 Lighting maintenance service (bulb replacement and cleaning)
3612 Lighting transformers, fluorescent—*mfg*
3612 Lighting transformers, street and airport—*mfg*
3643 Lightning arrestors and coils—*mfg*
1799 Lightning conductor erection—contractors
3643 Lightning protection equipment—*mfg*
3645 Lights, yard: electric—*mfg*
2821 Lignin plastics—*mfg*
1221 Lignite mining
1241 Lignite mining services on a contract basis
3489 Limbers, gun and caisson—*mfg*
3842 Limbs, artificial—*mfg*
5211 Lime and plaster dealers—retail
2819 Lime bleaching compounds—*mfg*

2869 Lime citrate—*mfg*
0174 Lime groves and farms
3274 Lime plaster—*mfg*
1422 Lime rock, ground
0711 Lime spreading for crops
5191 Lime, agricultural—wholesale
5032 Lime, except agricultural—wholesale
2879 Lime-sulfur, dry and solution—*mfg*
3281 Limestone, cut and shaped—*mfg*
1411 Limestone, dimension—quarrying
1422 Limestone, except bituminous: crushed and broken—quarrying
5032 Limestone—wholesale
3822 Limit controls, residential and commercial heating types—*mfg*
5331 Limited price variety stores—retail
1011 Limonite mining
4119 Limousine rental with drivers
7514 Limousine rental, without drivers
2879 Lindane, formulated—*mfg*
3531 Line markers, self-propelled—*mfg*
3822 Line or limit control for electric heat—*mfg*
3494 Line strainers, for use in piping systems—metal—*mfg*
3612 Line voltage regulators—*mfg*
3699 Linear accelerators—*mfg*
3824 Linear counters—*mfg*
2824 Linear esters fibers—*mfg*
2796 Linecuts—*mfg*
3842 Linemen's safety belts—*mfg*
2269 Linen fabrics: dyeing, finishing, and printing—*mfg*
5131 Linen piece goods—wholesale
5719 Linen shops—retail
7213 Linen supply service
5023 Linens—wholesale
2631 Liner board, kraft and jute—mitse—*mfg*
3259 Liner brick and plates, for lining sewers, tanks, etc.: vitrified clay—*mfg*
3069 Liner strips, rubber—*mfg*
2394 Liners and covers, fabric: pond, pit, and landfill—mfpm—*mfg*
2675 Liners for freight car doors: reinforced with metal strip—mfpm—*mfg*
3443 Liners, industrial: metal plate—*mfg*
5632 Lingerie stores—retail
5137 Lingerie—wholesale
2834 Liniments—*mfg*
2221 Lining fabrics, manmade fiber and silk: except glove lining fabrics—*mfg*
3111 Lining leather—*mfg*
2621 Lining paper—mitse—*mfg*
3259 Lining, stove and flue: clay—*mfg*
3131 Linings, boot and shoe: leather—*mfg*
2299 Linings, carpet: felt except woven—*mfg*
2392 Linings, carpet: textile, except felt—*mfg*

3452 Lock washers—*mfg*
3089 Lock washers, plastics—*mfg*
7299 Locker rental, except cold storage
2542 Lockers, not refrigerated: except wood—*mfg*
2541 Lockers, not refrigerated: wood—*mfg*
5046 Lockers, not refrigerated—wholesale
3585 Lockers, refrigerated—*mfg*
3429 Locks and lock sets: except safe, vault, and coin-operated—*mfg*
5072 Locks and related materials—wholesale
3581 Locks, coin-operated—*mfg*
3499 Locks, safe and vault: metal—*mfg*
3429 Locks, trigger, for guns—*mfg*
7699 Locksmith shops
3647 Locomotive and railroad car lights—*mfg*
3531 Locomotive cranes—*mfg*
3462 Locomotive wheels, forged: not made in rolling mills—*mfg*
3743 Locomotives, locomotive frames, and parts—*mfg*
1041 Lode gold mining
7041 Lodging houses operated by organizations for members only
7021 Lodging houses, except organization
2452 Log cabins, prefabricated: wood—*mfg*
4449 Log rafting and towing
3531 Log splitters—*mfg*
4212 Log trucking
0171 Loganberry farms
2411 Logging contractors—*mfg*
3531 Logging equipment—*mfg*
5082 Logging equipment—wholesale
4013 Logging railroads
1389 Logging wells on a contract basis
3825 Logic circuit testers—*mfg*
2411 Logs—*mfg*
3699 Logs, fireplace: electric—*mfg*
3433 Logs, fireplace: gas—*mfg*
5099 Logs, hewn ties, posts, and poles—wholesale
2861 Logwood extract—*mfg*
2211 Long cloth, cotton—*mfg*
4813 Long distance telephone communications
4213 Long-distance trucking
3552 Loom bobbins, wood or metal—*mfg*
3552 Looms (textile machinery)—*mfg*
3552 Loopers (textile machinery)—*mfg*
2395 Looping, for the trade—*mfg*
5112 Looseleaf binders—wholesale
2782 Looseleaf devices and binders—*mfg*
2678 Looseleaf fillers and ream paper in filler sizes, except printed—mfpm—*mfg*
2782 Looseleaf forms and fillers, pen ruled or printed only—*mfg*
3851 Lorgnettes—*mfg*

7999 Lotteries, operation of
7999 Lottery clubs and ticket sales to individuals
9311 Lottery control boards—government
3651 Loudspeakers, electrodynamic and magnetic—*mfg*
5813 Lounges, cocktail
2384 Lounging robes and dressing gowns, men's, boys', and women's—mfpm—*mfg*
2369 Lounging robes: girls', children's, and infants'—mfpm—*mfg*
2253 Lounging robes—mitse—*mfg*
2431 Louver windows and doors, glass with wood frame—*mfg*
3442 Louver windows, all metal or metal frame—*mfg*
3444 Louvers, sheet metal—*mfg*
3914 Loving cups, silver, nickel silver, pewter, and plated—*mfg*
2064 Lozenges, candy: nonmedicated—*mfg*
2834 Lozenges, pharmaceutical—*mfg*
2992 Lubricating greases and oils—mfpm—*mfg*
5172 Lubricating oils and greases—wholesale
2992 Lubricating oils, re-refining—mfpm—*mfg*
7549 Lubricating service, automotive
3724 Lubricating systems, aircraft—*mfg*
3569 Lubricating systems, centralized—*mfg*
3569 Lubrication equipment, industrial—*mfg*
3569 Lubrication machinery, automatic—*mfg*
3714 Lubrication systems and parts, motor vehicle—*mfg*
3743 Lubrication systems, locomotive—*mfg*
5948 Luggage and leather goods stores—retail
2211 Luggage fabrics, cotton—*mfg*
3429 Luggage hardware—*mfg*
2396 Luggage linings—*mfg*
3429 Luggage racks, car top—*mfg*
7699 Luggage repair shops
3161 Luggage, regardless of material—*mfg*
5099 Luggage—wholesale
5063 Lugs and connectors, electrical—wholesale
5211 Lumber and building materials dealers—retail
5211 Lumber and planing mill product dealers—retail
2421 Lumber stacking or sticking—*mfg*
4226 Lumber terminals, storage for hire
2426 Lumber, hardwood dimension—*mfg*
2421 Lumber, kiln drying of—*mfg*
5031 Lumber: rough, dressed, and finished—wholesale
2421 Lumber: rough, sawed, or planed—*mfg*
2329 Lumberjackets: men's and boys'—mfpm—*mfg*
2819 Luminous compounds, radium—*mfg*
3646 Luminous panel ceilings—*mfg*

3369   Magnesium castings, except die-castings—*mfg*
2819   Magnesium chloride—*mfg*
2819   Magnesium compounds, inorganic—*mfg*
3364   Magnesium die-castings—*mfg*
3339   Magnesium refining, primary—*mfg*
3356   Magnesium rolling, drawing, and extruding—*mfg*
3341   Magnesium smelting and refining, secondary—*mfg*
3357   Magnet wire, insulated—*mfg*
3674   Magnetic bubble memory device—*mfg*
3824   Magnetic counters—*mfg*
3823   Magnetic flow meters, industrial process type—*mfg*
3542   Magnetic forming machines—*mfg*
3577   Magnetic ink recognition devices, computer peripheral equipment—*mfg*
2899   Magnetic inspection oil and powder—*mfg*
3695   Magnetic recording tape, blank: reels, cassettes, and disks—*mfg*
5065   Magnetic recording tape—wholesale
3845   Magnetic resonance imaging device (diagnostic), nuclear—*mfg*
3826   Magnetic resonance imaging type apparatus, except diagnostic—*mfg*
3572   Magnetic storage devices for computers—*mfg*
3652   Magnetic tape, audio: prerecorded—*mfg*
1011   Magnetite mining
3674   Magnetohydrodynamic (MHD) devices—*mfg*
3829   Magnetometers—*mfg*
3671   Magnetron tubes—*mfg*
3264   Magnets, permanent: ceramic or ferrite—*mfg*
3499   Magnets, permanent: metallic—*mfg*
3851   Magnifiers (readers and simple magnifiers)—*mfg*
3827   Magnifying instruments, optical—*mfg*
7361   Maid registries
7349   Maid service on a contract or fee basis
7331   Mail advertising service
3469   Mail boxes, except collection boxes—*mfg*
4212   Mail carriers, bulk, contract: local
3444   Mail chutes, sheet metal—*mfg*
3444   Mail collection or storage boxes, sheet metal—*mfg*
4215   Mail delivery, private: except air
2542   Mail pouch racks, except wood—*mfg*
3579   Mail tying (bundling) machines—*mfg*
5961   Mail-order houses—retail (not including retail outlets)
4822   Mailgram services
2655   Mailing cases and tubes, paper fiber (metal-end or all-fiber)—mfpm—*mfg*

7331   Mailing list compilers
3579   Mailing machines—*mfg*
5044   Mailing machines—wholesale
2542   Mailing racks, postal service: except wood—*mfg*
7331   Mailing service
3571   Mainframe computers—*mfg*
4173   Maintenance facilities for motor vehicle passenger transportation
7349   Maintenance, building: except repairs
2519   Malacca furniture—*mfg*
4959   Malaria control
2865   Maleic anhydride—*mfg*
3423   Mallets, printers'—*mfg*
3069   Mallets, rubber—*mfg*
3949   Mallets, sports: e.g., polo, croquet—*mfg*
2499   Mallets, wood—*mfg*
2869   Malononitrile, technical grade—*mfg*
2083   Malt byproducts—*mfg*
2082   Malt extract, liquors, and syrups—*mfg*
5149   Malt extract—wholesale
3556   Malt mills—*mfg*
2083   Malt: barley, rye, wheat, and corn—*mfg*
5149   Malt—wholesale
2023   Malted milk—*mfg*
2083   Malthouses—*mfg*
8742   Management engineering consultants
8742   Management information systems consultants
6726   Management investment funds, closed-end
6722   Management investment funds, open-end
0762   Management services, farm
6282   Manager of mutual funds, contract or fee basis
7941   Managers of individual professional athletes
6211   Managers or agents for mutual funds
6531   Managers, real estate
3931   Mandolins and parts—*mfg*
3545   Mandrels—*mfg*
2819   Manganese dioxide powder, synthetic—*mfg*
3313   Manganese metal—*mfg*
1061   Manganese ore mining
1011   Manganiferous ore mining, valued chiefly for iron content
1061   Manganite mining
2861   Mangrove extract—*mfg*
1623   Manhole construction—contractors
3272   Manhole covers and frames, concrete—*mfg*
3321   Manhole covers, metal—*mfg*
7231   Manicure and pedicure salons
2844   Manicure preparations—*mfg*
5112   Manifold business forms—wholesale
3714   Manifolds, motor vehicle: gasoline engine—*mfg*

3423 Masons' handtools—*mfg*
3274 Masons' lime—*mfg*
5032 Masons' materials—wholesale
3826 Mass spectrometers—*mfg*
3826 Mass spectroscopy instrumentation—*mfg*
3999 Massage machines, electric: designed for beauty and barber shops—*mfg*
3634 Massage machines, electric: except designed for beauty and barber shop—*mfg*
7299 Massage parlors
2951 Mastic floor composition, hot and cold—*mfg*
2952 Mastic roofing composition—mfpm—*mfg*
2499 Masts, wood—*mfg*
3999 Matches and match books—*mfg*
5199 Matches—wholesale
2211 Matelasse, cotton—*mfg*
5084 Materials handling equipment—wholesale
9431 Maternity and child health program administration—government
2342 Maternity bras and corsets—mfpm—*mfg*
8069 Maternity hospitals
5621 Maternity shops—retail
2631 Matrix board—mitse—*mfg*
2621 Matrix paper—mitse—*mfg*
3496 Mats and matting, made from purchased wire—*mfg*
2273 Mats and matting, textile—*mfg*
3069 Mats and matting: e.g., bath, door—rubber—*mfg*
2273 Mats and matting: twisted paper, grass, reed, coir, sisal, jute, and rag—*mfg*
3555 Mats, advertising and newspaper (matrices)—*mfg*
2299 Mats, felt: except woven—*mfg*
0181 Mats, preseeded: soil erosion—growing of
2295 Mats, varnished glass—*mfg*
3423 Mattocks (handtools)—*mfg*
2392 Mattress pads—*mfg*
2392 Mattress protectors, except rubber—*mfg*
3069 Mattress protectors, rubber—*mfg*
7699 Mattress renovating and repair shops
5712 Mattress stores, including custom made—retail
3272 Mattresses for river revetment, concrete articulated—*mfg*
3292 Mattresses, asbestos—*mfg*
2515 Mattresses, containing felt, foam rubber, urethane, etc.—*mfg*
3069 Mattresses, pneumatic: fabric coated with rubber—*mfg*
2515 Mattresses: innerspring, box spring, and noninnerspring—*mfg*
5021 Mattresses—wholesale
2052 Matzoths—*mfg*
3423 Mauls, metal (handtools)—*mfg*

2499 Mauls, wood—*mfg*
3952 Maulsticks, artists'—*mfg*
1542 Mausoleum construction—general contractors
6553 Mausoleum operation
2035 Mayonnaise—*mfg*
9111 Mayors' offices
8322 Meal delivery programs
2077 Meal, blood—*mfg*
2048 Meal, bone: prepared as feed for animals and fowls—*mfg*
2041 Meal, corn—*mfg*
2046 Meal, gluten—*mfg*
2077 Meal, meat and bone: not prepared as feed—*mfg*
2038 Meals, frozen—*mfg*
7699 Measuring and controlling instrument repair, mechanical
5084 Measuring and testing equipment, electrical, except automotive—wholesale
3825 Measuring equipment for electronic and electrical circuits and equipment—*mfg*
3825 Measuring instruments and meters, electric—*mfg*
3545 Measuring tools and machines, machinists' metalworking type—*mfg*
3824 Measuring wheels—*mfg*
2077 Meat and bone meal and tankage—*mfg*
3556 Meat and poultry processing machinery—*mfg*
2259 Meat bagging—mitse—*mfg*
2013 Meat extracts—mfpm—*mfg*
2011 Meat extracts—mitse—*mfg*
3556 Meat grinders—*mfg*
5421 Meat markets—retail
2011 Meat packing plants—*mfg*
5142 Meat pies, frozen—wholesale
2013 Meat products: cooked, cured, frozen, smoked, and spiced—mfpm—*mfg*
2099 Meat seasonings, except sauces—*mfg*
5142 Meat, frozen: packaged—wholesale
2011 Meat—mitse—*mfg*
5147 Meats, cured or smoked—wholesale
5147 Meats, fresh—wholesale
1711 Mechanical contractors
7993 Mechanical games, coin-operated: operation of
3111 Mechanical leather—*mfg*
3462 Mechanical power transmission forgings, ferrous: not made in rolling mills—*mfg*
3463 Mechanical power transmission forgings, nonferrous: not made in hot-rolling mills—*mfg*
3061 Mechanical rubber goods: molded, extruded, and lathe-cut—*mfg*

3429 Metal fasteners, spring and cold-rolled steel, not made in rolling mills—*mfg*

3559 Metal finishing equipment for plating, except rolling mill lines—*mfg*

1791 Metal furring—contractors

3567 Metal melting furnaces, industrial—*mfg*

3674 Metal oxide silicon (MOS) devices—*mfg*

3559 Metal pickling equipment, except rolling mill lines—*mfg*

5169 Metal polishes—wholesale

3541 Metal polishing lathes—*mfg*

5084 Metal refining machinery and equipment—wholesale

5169 Metal salts—wholesale

5074 Metal sanitary ware—wholesale

7389 Metal slitting and shearing on a contract or fee basis

3559 Metal smelting and refining machinery, except furnaces and ovens—*mfg*

2899 Metal treating compounds—*mfg*

5093 Metal waste and scrap—wholesale

3291 Metallic abrasives—*mfg*

5052 Metallic concentrates—wholesale

2671 Metallic covered paper for packaging—mfpm—*mfg*

2672 Metallic covered paper, except for packaging—mfpm—*mfg*

3861 Metallic emulsion sensitized paper and cloth, photographic—*mfg*

5052 Metallic ores—wholesale

2816 Metallic pigments, inorganic—*mfg*

2869 Metallic salts of acyclic organic chemicals—*mfg*

2869 Metallic stearate—*mfg*

2295 Metallizing of fabrics—*mfg*

3827 Metallographs—*mfg*

8734 Metallurgical testing laboratories

5051 Metals, except precious—wholesale

2819 Metals, liquid—*mfg*

5094 Metals, precious—wholesale

5719 Metalware stores—retail

5084 Metalworking machinery—wholesale

5084 Metalworking tools: drills, taps, dies, grinding wheels, and files—wholesale

3829 Meteorogic tracking systems—*mfg*

7699 Meteorological instrument repair

3829 Meteorological instruments—*mfg*

3272 Meter boxes, concrete—*mfg*

3951 Meter pens—*mfg*

7389 Meter readers, remote

3613 Metering panels, electric—*mfg*

3825 Meters, electric: pocket, portable, panelboard, and graphic recording—*mfg*

3825 Meters, power factor and phase angle—*mfg*

3824 Meters: gas, liquid, tallying, and mechanical measuring—except electrical—*mfg*

2861 Methanol, natural (wood alcohol)—*mfg*

2869 Methanol, synthetic (methyl alcohol)—*mfg*

2861 Methyl acetone—*mfg*

2821 Methyl acrylate resins—*mfg*

2861 Methyl alcohol, natural (wood alcohol)—*mfg*

2821 Methyl cellulose plastics—*mfg*

2869 Methyl chloride—*mfg*

2821 Methyl methacrylate resins—*mfg*

2869 Methyl perhydrofluorine—*mfg*

2869 Methyl salicylate—*mfg*

2865 Methyl violet toners—*mfg*

2869 Methylamine—*mfg*

2869 Methylene chloride—*mfg*

2032 Mexican foods, canned—*mfg*

1499 Mica mining

3299 Mica products, built-up and sheet, except radio parts—*mfg*

1429 Mica schist, crushed and broken—quarrying

1411 Mica schist, dimension—quarrying

3299 Mica splitting—*mfg*

3295 Mica, ground or otherwise treated—*mfg*

3299 Mica, laminated—*mfg*

2835 Microbiology, virology, and serology diagnostic products—*mfg*

3674 Microcircuits, integrated (semiconductor)—*mfg*

3571 Microcomputers—*mfg*

3861 Microfiche cameras—*mfg*

3861 Microfiche readers and reader printers—*mfg*

3861 Microfilm equipment: cameras, projectors, and readers—*mfg*

7389 Microfilm recording and developing service

5044 Microfilming equipment—wholesale

1099 Microlite mining

3545 Micrometers—*mfg*

3651 Microphones—*mfg*

3826 Microprobes: electron, ion, laser, X-ray—*mfg*

3674 Microprocessors—*mfg*

3827 Microprojectors—*mfg*

2741 Micropublishing—*mfg*

7699 Microscope repair

3826 Microscopes, electron and proton—*mfg*

3827 Microscopes, except electron, proton, and corneal—*mfg*

3821 Microtomes—*mfg*

3663 Microwave communications equipment—*mfg*

3679 Microwave components—*mfg*

3631 Microwave ovens, household: including portable—*mfg*

5064 Microwave ovens, household—wholesale

3825 Microwave test equipment—*mfg*

3089 Microwaveware, plastics—*mfg*

2361 Middies: girls', children's, and infants'—mfpm—*mfg*

8049 Midwives, offices of

2261 Mildew proofing cotton broadwoven fabrics—*mfg*

2262 Mildew proofing manmade fiber and silk broadwoven fabrics—*mfg*

8211 Military academies, elementary and secondary level

3999 Military insignia, except textile—*mfg*

2899 Military pyrotechnics—*mfg*

9711 Military training schools

2311 Military uniforms, tailored: men's and boys'—*mfg*

3412 Milk (fluid) shipping containers, metal—*mfg*

5143 Milk and cream, fluid—wholesale

5451 Milk and other dairy products stores—retail

3221 Milk bottles, glass—*mfg*

3411 Milk cans, metal—*mfg*

2631 Milk carton board—mitse—*mfg*

2656 Milk cartons, paperboard—mfpm—*mfg*

5143 Milk cooling stations, operated by farm assemblers

5963 Milk delivery and sale of purchased milk, without processing—retail

5143 Milk depots—wholesale

2675 Milk filter disks, die-cut from purchased paper—*mfg*

2621 Milk filter disks—mitse—*mfg*

2026 Milk processing (pasteurizing, homogenizing, vitaminizing, bottling)—*mfg*

3556 Milk processing machinery—*mfg*

0241 Milk production, dairy cattle farm

2026 Milk production, except farm—*mfg*

0214 Milk production, goat farm

5084 Milk products manufacturing machinery and equipment—wholesale

0751 Milk testing for butterfat

2026 Milk, acidophilus—*mfg*

2026 Milk, bottled—*mfg*

5149 Milk, canned or dried—wholesale

2026 Milk, flavored—*mfg*

2026 Milk, reconstituted—*mfg*

2026 Milk, ultra-high temperature—*mfg*

2023 Milk, whole: canned—*mfg*

2023 Milk: concentrated, condensed, dried, evaporated, and powdered—*mfg*

5083 Milking machinery and equipment—wholesale

3523 Milking machines—*mfg*

2023 Milkshake mix—*mfg*

5949 Mill end stores—retail

2269 Mill enders, contract: cotton, silk, and manmade fiber—*mfg*

2231 Mill menders, contract: wool, mohair, and similar animal fibers—*mfg*

3199 Mill strapping for textile mills, leather—*mfg*

5085 Mill supplies—wholesale

3547 Mill tables (rolling mill equipment)—*mfg*

3292 Millboard, asbestos—*mfg*

2353 Millinery—*mfg*

5632 Millinery stores—retail

5131 Millinery supplies—wholesale

2396 Millinery trimmings—mfpm—*mfg*

5137 Millinery—wholesale

3545 Milling machine attachments (machine tool accessories)—*mfg*

3541 Milling machines (machine tools)—*mfg*

2041 Milling of grains, dry, except rice—*mfg*

2044 Milling of rice—*mfg*

3556 Mills and presses: beet, cider, and sugarcane—*mfg*

1499 Millstone quarrying

5211 Millwork and lumber dealers—retail

2431 Millwork products—*mfg*

2491 Millwork, treated—*mfg*

5031 Millwork—wholesale

1796 Millwrights

0119 Milo farms

5044 Mimeograph equipment—wholesale

5112 Mimeograph paper—wholesale

7334 Mimeographing service

2032 Mincemeat, canned—*mfg*

3535 Mine conveyors—*mfg*

1081 Mine development for metal mining: on a contract basis

1481 Mine development for nonmetallic minerals, except fuels: on a contract basis

1629 Mine loading and discharging station construction—general contractors

2491 Mine props, treated—*mfg*

2491 Mine ties, wood: treated—*mfg*

2411 Mine timbers, hewn—*mfg*

5082 Mineral beneficiation machinery—wholesale

2816 Mineral colors and pigments—*mfg*

2048 Mineral feed supplements—*mfg*

2911 Mineral jelly, produced in petroleum refineries—*mfg*

6211 Mineral leases, dealers in

2911 Mineral oils, natural: produced in petroleum refineries—*mfg*

1479 Mineral pigment mining

6211 Mineral royalties, dealers in

5191 Mineral supplements, animal—wholesale
2086 Mineral water, carbonated: bottled or canned—*mfg*
2911 Mineral waxes, natural: produced in petroleum refineries—*mfg*
5033 Mineral wool insulation materials—wholesale
3296 Mineral wool roofing mats—*mfg*
3648 Miners' lamps—*mfg*
3483 Mines and parts (ordnance)—*mfg*
3571 Minicomputers—*mfg*
9651 Minimum wage program administration—government
1629 Mining appurtenance construction—general contractors
3532 Mining cars and trucks (dollies)—*mfg*
3532 Mining equipment, except oil and gas field: rebuilding on a factory basis—*mfg*
3743 Mining locomotives and parts—*mfg*
3532 Mining machinery and equipment, except oil and gas field—*mfg*
5082 Mining machinery and equipment, except petroleum—wholesale
2816 Minium (pigments)—*mfg*
4225 Miniwarehouse warehousing
0271 Mink farms
0273 Minnow farms
0139 Mint farms
7699 Mirror repair shops
5719 Mirrors —retail
3231 Mirrors, framed or unframed: made from purchased glass—*mfg*
3827 Mirrors, optical—*mfg*
3231 Mirrors, transportation equipment: made from purchased glass—*mfg*
1629 Missile facilities construction—general contractors
3462 Missile forgings, ferrous: not made in rolling mills—*mfg*
3463 Missile forgings, nonferrous: not made in hot-rolling mills—*mfg*
3812 Missile guidance systems and equipment—*mfg*
3443 Missile silos and components, metal plate—*mfg*
3483 Missile warheads—*mfg*
3423 Mitre boxes, metal—*mfg*
2211 Mitten flannel, cotton—*mfg*
3151 Mittens, leather—*mfg*
5136 Mittens, men's and boys'—wholesale
3069 Mittens, rubber—*mfg*
5137 Mittens: women's, children's, and infants'—wholesale
2259 Mittens—mitse—*mfg*
2819 Mixed acid—*mfg*

3556 Mixers and whippers, electric: for food manufacturing industries—*mfg*
3443 Mixers for hot metal—*mfg*
5082 Mixers, construction and mining—wholesale
3556 Mixers, feed: except agricultural machinery—*mfg*
3556 Mixers, food: commercial types—*mfg*
3531 Mixers: e.g., concrete, ore, sand, slag, plaster, mortar, bituminous—*mfg*
2045 Mixes, flour: e.g., pancake, cake, biscuit, doughnut—mfpm—*mfg*
2041 Mixes, flour: e.g., pancake, cake, biscuit, doughnut—mitse—*mfg*
2451 Mobile buildings for commercial use (e.g., offices, banks)—*mfg*
2451 Mobile classrooms—*mfg*
3663 Mobile communications equipment—*mfg*
2451 Mobile dwellings—*mfg*
5271 Mobile home equipment—retail
5271 Mobile home parts and accessories—retail
7519 Mobile home rental, except on site
1521 Mobile home repair, on site—general contractors
1799 Mobile home site setup and tie down—contractors
2451 Mobile homes, except recreational—*mfg*
5271 Mobile homes, new and used—retail
5039 Mobile homes—wholesale
3711 Mobile lounges (motor vehicle)—*mfg*
3537 Mobile straddle carriers—*mfg*
3149 Moccasins—*mfg*
2221 Modacrylic broadwoven fabrics—*mfg*
2824 Modacrylic fibers—*mfg*
2281 Modacrylic yarn, made from purchased staple: spun—*mfg*
5092 Model kits—wholesale
7361 Model registries
3952 Modeling clay—*mfg*
8299 Modeling schools, clothes
7363 Modeling service
3842 Models, anatomical—*mfg*
3999 Models, except toy and hobby—*mfg*
3944 Models, toy and hobby: e.g., airplane, boat, ship, railroad equipment—*mfg*
3661 Modems—*mfg*
5065 Modems—wholesale
2521 Modular furniture systems, office, wood—*mfg*
2522 Modular furniture systems, office: except wood—*mfg*
1521 Modular housing, single-family (assembled on site)—general contractors
3674 Modules, solid-state—*mfg*
0214 Mohair production

2282 Mohair yarn: twisting, winding, or spooling—*mfg*
5159 Mohair, raw—wholesale
3579 Moisteners, gummed tape: for store and office use—*mfg*
3826 Moisture analysers, laboratory type—*mfg*
3823 Moisture meters, industrial process type—*mfg*
2063 Molasses beet pulp—*mfg*
2062 Molasses, blackstrap: made from purchased raw cane sugar or sugar syrup—*mfg*
2061 Molasses, blackstrap: made from sugarcane—*mfg*
5149 Molasses, industrial—wholesale
2063 Molasses, made from sugar beets—*mfg*
2061 Molasses, made from sugarcane—*mfg*
2099 Molasses, mixed or blended—mfpm—*mfg*
2821 Molding compounds, plastics—*mfg*
3089 Molding of plastics for the trade, except foam—*mfg*
3089 Molding primary plastics for the trade, except foam—*mfg*
1446 Molding sand mining
5031 Molding, all materials—wholesale
3465 Moldings and trim, automotive: stamped—*mfg*
3442 Moldings and trim, metal: except automobile—*mfg*
3299 Moldings, architectural: plaster of paris—factory production only—*mfg*
2499 Moldings, picture frame: finished—*mfg*
2431 Moldings, wood and covered wood: unfinished and prefinished—*mfg*
3544 Molds, industrial—*mfg*
3674 Molecular devices, solid-state—*mfg*
2211 Moleskins—mitse—*mfg*
0273 Mollusk farms
1061 Molybdenite mining
1061 Molybdenum ore mining
3313 Molybdenum silicon—*mfg*
1061 Molybdite mining
2211 Momie crepe, cotton—*mfg*
8661 Monasteries
1099 Monazite mining
3499 Money chests, metal—*mfg*
6722 Money market mutual funds
6099 Money order issuance
2869 Monochlorodifluoromethane—*mfg*
3826 Monochrometers, laboratory type—*mfg*
3089 Monofilaments, plastics: not suited for textile use—*mfg*
3674 Monolithic integrated circuits (solid-state)—*mfg*
2869 Monomethylparaminophenol sulfate—*mfg*
3536 Monorail systems—*mfg*

4111 Monorails, regular route: except amusement and scenic
2869 Monosodium glutamate—*mfg*
3555 Monotype machines—*mfg*
5099 Monuments and grave markers—wholesale
3272 Monuments, concrete—*mfg*
3281 Monuments, cut stone: not including only finishing or lettering to order—*mfg*
5999 Monuments, finished to custom order—retail
3589 Mop wringers—*mfg*
7999 Moped rental
3751 Mopeds and parts—*mfg*
5571 Mopeds—retail
5012 Mopeds—wholesale
2392 Mops, floor and dust—*mfg*
2843 Mordants—*mfg*
2833 Morphine and derivatives—*mfg*
6141 Morris plans not engaged in deposit banking
3531 Mortar mixers—*mfg*
3483 Mortar shells, more than 30 mm. (or more than 1.18 inch)—*mfg*
3255 Mortars, clay refractory—*mfg*
3489 Mortars, more than 30 mm. (or more than 1.18 inch)—*mfg*
6162 Mortgage bankers
6163 Mortgage brokers arranging for loans but using money of others
6162 Mortgage brokers, using own money
6162 Mortgage companies, urban
6351 Mortgage guaranty insurance
6798 Mortgage investment trusts
6798 Mortgage trusts
6211 Mortgages, buying and selling (rediscounting)
7261 Morticians
5087 Morticians' goods—wholesale
3553 Mortisers (woodworking machines)—*mfg*
3253 Mosaic tile, ceramic—*mfg*
1743 Mosaic work—contractors
3999 Mosaics: ivory, shell, horn, and bone—*mfg*
4959 Mosquito eradication
9631 Mosquito eradication districts
2258 Mosquito netting, warp knit—mitse—*mfg*
2211 Mosquito netting—mitse—*mfg*
0723 Moss ginning
0831 Moss, gathering of
5159 Moss—wholesale
1522 Motel construction—general contractors
8741 Motel management services
7011 Motels
2879 Moth repellants—*mfg*
3861 Motion picture apparatus and equipment—*mfg*

5043 Motion picture cameras, equipment, and supplies—wholesale
7819 Motion picture consultants
7822 Motion picture distribution, exclusive of production
7832 Motion picture exhibitors for airlines
7832 Motion picture exhibitors, itinerant
3861 Motion picture film—*mfg*
7841 Motion picture film or tape rental to the general public
7812 Motion picture production and distribution
7819 Motion picture reproduction
5043 Motion picture studio and theater equipment—wholesale
7833 Motion picture theaters, drive-in
3711 Motor buses, except trackless trolley—*mfg*
9621 Motor carrier licensing and inspection offices—government
3625 Motor control accessories, including overload relays—*mfg*
3625 Motor control centers—*mfg*
3625 Motor controls, electric—*mfg*
5063 Motor controls, electric—wholesale
3621 Motor generator sets, except automotive and turbogenerators—*mfg*
5561 Motor home dealers—retail
7519 Motor home rental
3716 Motor homes, self-contained: made on purchased chassis—*mfg*
3711 Motor homes, self-contained—mitse—*mfg*
5012 Motor homes—wholesale
3621 Motor housings—*mfg*
7538 Motor repair, automotive
3751 Motor scooters and parts—*mfg*
5571 Motor scooters—retail
5012 Motor scooters—wholesale
3625 Motor starters, contactors, and controllers, industrial—*mfg*
3596 Motor truck scales—*mfg*
3715 Motor truck trailers—*mfg*
3711 Motor trucks, except off-highway—*mfg*
5511 Motor vehicle dealers, new and used cars—retail
5521 Motor vehicle dealers, used cars only—retail
3714 Motor vehicle gasoline engine rebuilding on a factory basis—*mfg*
3429 Motor vehicle hardware—*mfg*
9621 Motor vehicle licensing and inspection offices—government
3714 Motor vehicle parts and accessories, except motor vehicle stampings—*mfg*
5015 Motor vehicle parts, used—wholesale or retail
5064 Motor vehicle radios—wholesale
5014 Motor vehicle tires and tubes—wholesale

5012 Motor vehicles, commercial—wholesale
3711 Motor vehicles, including amphibian—*mfg*
3751 Motorbikes and parts—*mfg*
5551 Motorboat dealers—retail
3732 Motorboats, inboard and outboard: building and repairing—*mfg*
5571 Motorcycle dealers—retail
3647 Motorcycle lamps—*mfg*
5571 Motorcycle parts—retail
5013 Motorcycle parts—wholesale
7948 Motorcycle racing
7999 Motorcycle rental
7699 Motorcycle repair service
3751 Motorcycles and parts—*mfg*
5012 Motorcycles—wholesale
3594 Motors, air or hydraulic (fluid power)—*mfg*
3594 Motors, air or hydraulic fluid power—*mfg*
3621 Motors, electric: except engine starting motors and gear motors—*mfg*
5063 Motors, electric—wholesale
3566 Motors, gear—*mfg*
3594 Motors, pneumatic—*mfg*
3694 Motors, starting: motor vehicle and aircraft—*mfg*
2371 Mounting heads on fur neckpieces—*mfg*
7389 Mounting merchandise on cards on a contract or fee basis
2789 Mounting of maps and samples, for the trade—*mfg*
3999 Mountings, comb and hairpin: except precious metal—*mfg*
3851 Mountings, eyeglass and spectacle—*mfg*
3911 Mountings, gold and silver: for pens, leather goods, and umbrellas—*mfg*
3484 Mounts for guns, 30 mm. (or 1.18 inch) or less—*mfg*
3931 Mouthpieces for musical instruments—*mfg*
3069 Mouthpieces for pipes and cigarette holders, rubber—*mfg*
2844 Mouthwashes—*mfg*
3873 Movements, watch or clock—*mfg*
3523 Mowers and mower-conditioners, hay—*mfg*
5083 Mowers, power—wholesale
0782 Mowing highway center strips and edges
2891 Mucilage—*mfg*
3531 Mud jacks—*mfg*
1389 Mud service, oil field drilling: on a contract basis
7533 Mufflers, automotive: installation, repair, or sales and installation
3714 Mufflers, exhaust: motor vehicle—*mfg*
5136 Mufflers, men's and boys'—wholesale
2323 Mufflers: men's and boys'—mfpm—*mfg*

2253 Mufflers—mitse—*mfg*
3524 Mulchers, residential lawn and garden—*mfg*
0272 Mule farms
5159 Mules—wholesale
7334 Multigraphing service
7334 Multilithing service
2741 Multimedia educational kits: publishing and printing, or publishing only—*mfg*
3825 Multimeters—*mfg*
6531 Multiple listing services, real estate
3231 Multiple-glazed insulating units, made from purchased glass—*mfg*
3211 Multiple-glazed insulating units—mitse—*mfg*
3663 Multiplex equipment, radio—*mfg*
3661 Multiplex equipment, telephone and telegraph—*mfg*
4841 Multipoint distribution systems (MDS) services
8322 Multiservice centers, neighborhood
3575 Multistation CRT/teleprinters—*mfg*
2674 Multiwall bags, paper—mfpm—*mfg*
2819 Muriate of potash, not produced at mines—*mfg*
3841 Muscle exercise apparatus, ophthalmic—*mfg*
1499 Muscovite mining
1542 Museum construction—general contractors
8412 Museums
0182 Mushroom spawn, production of
0182 Mushrooms , growing of
2033 Mushrooms, canned—*mfg*
8999 Music arrangers
2732 Music books: printing or printing and binding, not publishing—*mfg*
2731 Music books: publishing and printing, or publishing only—*mfg*
3999 Music boxes—*mfg*
3651 Music distribution apparatus, except records or tape—*mfg*
7993 Music distribution systems, coin-operated
7389 Music distribution systems, except coin-operated
6794 Music licensing to radio stations
3931 Music rolls, perforated—*mfg*
6794 Music royalties, sheet and record
8299 Music schools
3931 Music stands—*mfg*
7812 Music video production
2759 Music, sheet: except lithographed or gravure (not publishing)—*mfg*
2754 Music, sheet: gravure printing (not publishing)—*mfg*

2741 Music, sheet: publishing and printing, or publishing only—*mfg*
3999 Musical chests—*mfg*
3931 Musical instrument accessories: e.g., reeds, mouthpieces, stands, traps—*mfg*
3651 Musical instrument amplifiers—*mfg*
3161 Musical instrument cases—*mfg*
7699 Musical instrument repair shops
5932 Musical instrument stores, secondhand—retail
5736 Musical instrument stores—retail
3931 Musical instruments, including electric and electronic—*mfg*
3944 Musical instruments, toy—*mfg*
5099 Musical instruments—wholesale
7929 Musicians
2211 Muslin, cotton—*mfg*
0913 Mussels, taking of
2869 Mustard gas—*mfg*
0119 Mustard seed farms
2035 Mustard, prepared (wet)—*mfg*
2011 Mutton—mitse—*mfg*
6321 Mutual accident associations
6141 Mutual benefit associations
6331 Mutual fire, marine, and casualty insurance
6211 Mutual fund agents
6722 Mutual fund sales on own account
6211 Mutual funds, selling by independent salesperson
2861 Myrobalans extract—*mfg*

N

2833 N-methylpiperazine—*mfg*
2822 N-type rubber—*mfg*
3728 Nacelles, aircraft—*mfg*
3542 Nail heading machines—*mfg*
3399 Nails, nonferrous metal (including wire)—*mfg*
3315 Nails, steel: wire or cut—*mfg*
5051 Nails—wholesale
2211 Nainsook, cotton—*mfg*
3993 Nameplates, metal: except e.g., engraved, etched, chased—*mfg*
3479 Nameplates: engraved and etched—*mfg*
2899 Napalm—*mfg*
5172 Naphtha, except bulk stations and terminals—wholesale
2911 Naphtha, produced in petroleum refineries—*mfg*
2865 Naphtha, solvent: made in chemical plants—*mfg*
2865 Naphthalene chips and flakes—*mfg*
2869 Naphthalene sulfonic acid condensates—*mfg*

2865 Naphthalene, made in chemical plants—*mfg*
2851 Naphthanate driers—*mfg*
2869 Naphthenic acid soaps—*mfg*
2911 Naphthenic acids, produced in petroleum refineries—*mfg*
2865 Naphthol, alpha and beta—*mfg*
2865 Naphtholsulfonic acids—*mfg*
2621 Napkin stock, paper—mitse—*mfg*
2392 Napkins, fabric and nonwoven textiles—mfpm—*mfg*
2676 Napkins, paper—mfpm—*mfg*
5113 Napkins, paper—wholesale
2676 Napkins, sanitary—mfpm—*mfg*
3552 Napping machines (textile machinery)—*mfg*
2261 Napping of cotton broadwoven fabrics—*mfg*
2262 Napping of manmade fiber and silk broadwoven fabrics—*mfg*
2231 Napping of wool, mohair, and similar animal fiber fabrics—*mfg*
2231 Narrow fabrics, dyeing and finishing: wool, mohair, and similar animal fibers—*mfg*
2241 Narrow fabrics, elastic: woven or braided—*mfg*
2269 Narrow fabrics, except knit and wool: bleaching, dyeing, and finishing—*mfg*
5131 Narrow fabrics—wholesale
2241 Narrow woven fabrics: cotton, rayon, wool, silk, glass, and manmade fiber—*mfg*
2299 Narrow woven fabrics: linen, jute, hemp, and ramie—*mfg*
6111 National Consumer Cooperative Bank
6019 National Credit Union Administration (NCUA)
9711 National Guard
6021 National banks, commercial
2032 Nationality specialty foods, canned—*mfg*
2032 Native foods, canned—*mfg*
2038 Native foods, frozen—*mfg*
1499 Natural abrasives mining (except sand)
1623 Natural gas compressing station construction—general contractors
4924 Natural gas distribution
1321 Natural gas liquids production
1311 Natural gas production
4922 Natural gas storage
4922 Natural gas transmission
4923 Natural gas transmission and distribution
1321 Natural gasoline production
7999 Natural wonders, tourist attraction: commercial
8049 Naturopaths, offices of

7699 Nautical and navigational instrument repair, except electric
3812 Nautical instruments—*mfg*
3489 Naval artillery—*mfg*
3731 Naval ships, building and repairing—*mfg*
2861 Naval stores, gum: processing but not gathering or warehousing—*mfg*
2861 Naval stores, wood—*mfg*
5169 Naval stores—wholesale
3812 Navigational instruments—*mfg*
9711 Navy
2082 Near beer—*mfg*
2371 Neckpieces, fur—*mfg*
2221 Necktie fabrics, manmade fiber and silk: broadwoven—*mfg*
2396 Necktie linings, cutting of—*mfg*
2323 Neckties: men's and boys'—mfpm—*mfg*
2253 Neckties—mitse—*mfg*
5136 Neckwear, men's and boys'—wholesale
2323 Neckwear: men's and boys'—mfpm—*mfg*
2339 Neckwear: women's, misses' and juniors'—mfpm—*mfg*
0175 Nectarine orchards and farms
2033 Nectars, fruit—*mfg*
3841 Needle holders, surgical—*mfg*
3965 Needles, hand and machine—*mfg*
3841 Needles, hypodermic—*mfg*
3841 Needles, suture—*mfg*
5949 Needlework stores—retail
2395 Needlework, art—mfpm—*mfg*
2341 Negligees: women's, misses', children's, and infants'—mfpm—*mfg*
2254 Negligees—mitse—*mfg*
8322 Neighborhood centers
2813 Neon—*mfg*
3993 Neon signs—*mfg*
5046 Neon signs—wholesale
2822 Neoprene—*mfg*
1459 Nepheline syenite quarrying
3826 Nephelometers, except meteorological—*mfg*
3829 Nephoscopes—*mfg*
3552 Net and lace machines—*mfg*
5131 Net goods—wholesale
2211 Nets and nettings—mitse—*mfg*
2399 Nets, fishing—mfpm—*mfg*
3999 Nets, hair—*mfg*
2399 Nets, launderers' and dyers'—*mfg*
2298 Nets, rope—*mfg*
3949 Nets: e.g., badminton, basketball, tennis—not made in weaving mills—*mfg*
2258 Netting made on a lace or net machine—*mfg*
2258 Netting, knit—mitse—*mfg*

3366 Nonferrous foundries: brass, bronze, copper, and copper base alloy—*mfg*
3369 Nonferrous foundries: except aluminum, copper, and copper alloys—*mfg*
3369 Nonferrous metal foundries, except aluminum, copper, and die-castings—*mfg*
3369 Nonferrous metal machinery castings: except aluminum, copper, and die-castings—*mfg*
3341 Nonferrous metal smelting and refining, secondary—*mfg*
5051 Nonferrous metal, except precious: e.g., sheets, bars, rods—wholesale
5093 Nonferrous metals scrap—wholesale
3339 Nonferrous refining, primary: except copper and aluminum—*mfg*
3356 Nonferrous rolling, drawing, and extruding: except copper and aluminum—*mfg*
3339 Nonferrous smelting, primary: except copper and aluminum—*mfg*
5052 Nonmetallic minerals and concentrates, crude: except petroleum—wholesale
6512 Nonresidential buildings, operators of
7812 Nontheatrical motion picture production
2297 Nonwoven fabrics, except felt—*mfg*
2099 Noodles, fried (e.g., Chinese)—*mfg*
2099 Noodles, uncooked: packaged with other ingredients—*mfg*
2098 Noodles: egg, plain, and water—*mfg*
2869 Normal hexyl decalin—*mfg*
3769 Nose cones, guided missile—*mfg*
3842 Nose plugs—*mfg*
7389 Notaries public
6211 Note brokers
2678 Notebooks, including mechanically bound by wire, plastics, etc.—mfpm—*mfg*
5949 Notion stores—retail
5131 Notions—wholesale
2258 Nottingham lace—*mfg*
3499 Novelties and specialties, metal: except advertising novelties—*mfg*
3993 Novelties, advertising—*mfg*
3961 Novelties, costume: except precious metal and gems—*mfg*
3231 Novelties, glass: e.g., fruit, foliage, flowers, animals, made from purchased glass—*mfg*
3199 Novelties, leather—*mfg*
2679 Novelties, paper—mfpm—*mfg*
5199 Novelties, paper—wholesale
2499 Novelties, wood fiber—*mfg*
3999 Novelties: bone, beaded, and shell—*mfg*
2514 Novelty furniture, metal—*mfg*
3229 Novelty glassware: made in glassmaking plants—*mfg*
5961 Novelty merchandise, mail-order—retail

5947 Novelty shops—retail
2395 Novelty stitching, for the trade—*mfg*
3429 Nozzles, fire fighting—*mfg*
3432 Nozzles, lawn hose—*mfg*
3432 Nozzles, plumbers'—*mfg*
3499 Nozzles, spray: aerosol paint, and insecticides—*mfg*
3443 Nuclear core structurals, metal plate—*mfg*
2819 Nuclear cores, inorganic—*mfg*
9631 Nuclear energy inspection and regulation offices
2819 Nuclear fuel reactor cores, inorganic—*mfg*
2819 Nuclear fuel scrap reprocessing—*mfg*
2869 Nuclear fuels, organic—*mfg*
3829 Nuclear instrument modules—*mfg*
3844 Nuclear irradiation equipment—*mfg*
3462 Nuclear power plant forgings, ferrous: not made in rolling mills—*mfg*
3829 Nuclear radiation detection and monitoring instruments—*mfg*
1629 Nuclear reactor containment structure construction—general contractors
3559 Nuclear reactor control rod drive mechanisms—*mfg*
3823 Nuclear reactor controls—*mfg*
3443 Nuclear reactors, military and industrial—*mfg*
3443 Nuclear shielding, metal plate—*mfg*
7032 Nudist camps
3579 Numbering machines, office and store: mechanical—*mfg*
3953 Numbering stamps, with rubber type: hand—*mfg*
3625 Numerical controls—*mfg*
3541 Numerically controlled metal cutting machine tools—*mfg*
5999 Numismatist shops—retail
0831 Nurseries, forest
2514 Nursery furniture, metal—*mfg*
2511 Nursery furniture, wood—*mfg*
8351 Nursery schools
0181 Nursery stock, growing of
5261 Nursery stock, seeds and bulbs—retail
5193 Nursery stock—wholesale
7361 Nurses' registries
8049 Nurses, registered and practical: offices of, except home health care services
8059 Nursing homes except skilled and intermediate care facilities
8052 Nursing homes, intermediate care
8051 Nursing homes, skilled
8249 Nursing schools, practical
0173 Nut (tree) groves and farms
3429 Nut crackers and pickers, metal—*mfg*
0723 Nut hulling and shelling
2079 Nut margarine—*mfg*

5159　Oil nuts—wholesale
2851　Oil paints—*mfg*
3829　Oil pressure gauges, motor vehicle—*mfg*
6519　Oil properties, lessors of
1629　Oil refinery construction—general contractors
5084　Oil refining machinery, equipment, and supplies—wholesale
6211　Oil royalties, dealers in
6792　Oil royalty companies
1389　Oil sampling service for oil companies on a contract basis
1311　Oil sand mining
3053　Oil seals, asbestos—*mfg*
3053　Oil seals, leather—*mfg*
3053　Oil seals, rubber—*mfg*
1311　Oil shale mining
4959　Oil spill cleanup
2851　Oil stains—*mfg*
2911　Oil still gas, produced in petroleum refineries—*mfg*
3443　Oil storage tanks, metal plate—*mfg*
2899　Oil treating compounds—*mfg*
7359　Oil well drilling equipment rental and leasing
1381　Oil well drilling: on a contract basis
1389　Oil well logging on a contract basis
5084　Oil well machinery, equipment, and supplies—wholesale
1389　Oil well rig building, repairing, and dismantling: on a contract basis
5084　Oil well supply houses—wholesale
2911　Oil, acid: produced in petroleum refineries—*mfg*
2865　Oil, aniline—*mfg*
2046　Oil, corn: crude and refined—*mfg*
2074　Oil, cottonseed—*mfg*
2865　Oil, creosote: product of coal tar distillation—*mfg*
2079　Oil, hydrogenated: edible—*mfg*
2079　Oil, olive—*mfg*
2079　Oil, partially hydrogenated: edible—*mfg*
2861　Oil, pine: produced by distillation of pine gum or pine wood—*mfg*
2899　Oil, red (oleic acid)—*mfg*
2075　Oil, soybean—*mfg*
2843　Oil, turkey red—*mfg*
2079　Oil, vegetable winter stearin—*mfg*
5093　Oil, waste—wholesale
2295　Oilcloth—*mfg*
2672　Oiled paper—mfpm—*mfg*
2077　Oils, animal—*mfg*
2844　Oils, cosmetic—*mfg*
2899　Oils, essential—*mfg*
5199　Oils, except cooking: animal and vegetable—wholesale

2077　Oils, fish and marine animal: e.g., herring, menhaden, whale (refined), sardine—*mfg*
2077　Oils, fish and marine animal: herring, menhaden, whale (refined), sardine—*mfg*
2992　Oils, lubricating: re-fining—*mfg*
2992　Oils, lubricating—mfpm—*mfg*
2911　Oils, partly refined: sold for rerunning—produced in petroleum refineries—*mfg*
2843　Oils, soluble (textile assistants)—*mfg*
2843　Oils, sulfonated—*mfg*
2079　Oils, vegetable (except corn oil) refined: cooking and salad—*mfg*
2833　Oils, vegetable and animal: medicinal grade—refined and concentrated—*mfg*
2076　Oils, vegetable: except corn, cottonseed, and soybean—*mfg*
2861　Oils, wood: product of hardwood distillation—*mfg*
2911　Oils: fuel, lubricating, and illuminating—produced in petroleum refineries—*mfg*
2865　Oils: light, medium, and heavy: made in chemical plants—*mfg*
5199　Oilseed cake and meal—wholesale
3556　Oilseed crushing and extracting machinery—*mfg*
5159　Oilseeds—wholesale
1499　Oilstone quarrying
3291　Oilstones, artificial—*mfg*
2834　Ointments—*mfg*
2076　Oiticica oil—*mfg*
8322　Old age assistance
8361　Old soldiers' homes
2851　Oleate driers—*mfg*
2824　Olefin fibers—*mfg*
2899　Oleic acid (red oil)—*mfg*
2869　Oleic acid esters—*mfg*
3728　Oleo struts, aircraft—*mfg*
2819　Oleum (fuming sulfuric acid)—*mfg*
0179　Olive groves and farms
2079　Olive oil—*mfg*
2035　Olives, brined: bulk—*mfg*
2034　Olives, dried—*mfg*
2033　Olives, including stuffed: canned—*mfg*
1459　Olivine (nongem) mining
3812　Omnibearing instrumentation—*mfg*
7375　On-line data base information retrieval services
1521　One-family house construction—general contractors
0161　Onion farms
2035　Onions, pickled—*mfg*
1429　Onyx marble, crushed and broken—quarrying
1411　Onyx marble, dimension—quarrying

0783 Ornamental tree planting, pruning, bracing, spraying, removal, and surgery
2431 Ornamental woodwork: e.g., cornices and mantels—*mfg*
3231 Ornamented glass, made from purchased glass—*mfg*
3999 Ornaments, Christmas tree: except glass and electric—*mfg*
3229 Ornaments, Christmas tree: glass—mitse—*mfg*
3231 Ornaments, Christmas tree: made from purchased glass—*mfg*
3699 Ornaments, Christmas tree: electric—*mfg*
3961 Ornaments, costume: except precious metal and gems—*mfg*
3131 Ornaments, shoe—*mfg*
8361 Orphanages
2899 Orris oil—*mfg*
2865 Orthodichlorobenzene—*mfg*
3843 Orthodontic appliances—*mfg*
8072 Orthodontic appliances made in dental laboratories to order for the profession
8021 Orthodontists, offices of
5999 Orthopedic and artificial limb stores—retail
3842 Orthopedic devices and materials—*mfg*
5047 Orthopedic equipment—wholesale
3842 Orthopedic hosiery, elastic—*mfg*
8069 Orthopedic hospitals
8011 Orthopedic physicians, offices of
3275 Orthopedic plaster, gypsum—*mfg*
3149 Orthopedic shoes, children's: except extension shoes—*mfg*
3842 Orthopedic shoes, extension—*mfg*
3143 Orthopedic shoes, men's: except extension shoes—*mfg*
3144 Orthopedic shoes, women's: except extension shoes—*mfg*
3069 Orthopedic sundries, molded rubber—*mfg*
3825 Oscillators, audiofrequency and radiofrequency (instrument types)—*mfg*
3679 Oscillators, except laboratory type—*mfg*
3825 Oscillographs and oscilloscopes—*mfg*
1099 Osmium ore mining
3826 Osmometers—*mfg*
2211 Osnaburgs—*mfg*
2899 Ossein—*mfg*
8031 Osteopathic physicians, offices and clinics of
8099 Osteoperosis centers
3999 Ostrich feathers: curling, dyeing, and renovating for the trade—*mfg*
3845 Otoscopes, electromedical—*mfg*
3841 Otoscopes, except electromedical—*mfg*
5551 Outboard motor dealers—retail
3699 Outboard motors, electric—*mfg*

3519 Outboard motors, except electric—*mfg*
5091 Outboard motors—wholesale
7312 Outdoor advertising service
5712 Outdoor furniture—retail
2253 Outerwear handknitted: for the trade—*mfg*
5136 Outerwear, men's and boys'—wholesale
5137 Outerwear: women's, children's, and infants'—wholesale
2211 Outing flannel, cotton—*mfg*
3644 Outlet boxes (electric wiring devices)—*mfg*
3643 Outlets, convenience: electric—*mfg*
8093 Outpatient detoxification centers
8093 Outpatient mental health clinics
8093 Outpatient treatment clinics for alcoholism and drug addiction
8322 Outreach programs
1629 Oven construction for industrial plants—general contractors
1629 Oven construction, bakers'—general contractors
3822 Oven temperature controls, nonindustrial—*mfg*
3556 Ovens, bakery—*mfg*
3589 Ovens, cafeteria food warming: portable—*mfg*
3631 Ovens, household: excluding portable appliances other than microwave and convection—*mfg*
3634 Ovens, household: portable: except microwave and convection ovens—*mfg*
3567 Ovens, industrial process: except bakery—*mfg*
3821 Ovens, laboratory—*mfg*
3589 Ovens, microwave (cooking equipment): commercial—*mfg*
5046 Ovens, microwave: commercial—wholesale
5064 Ovens, microwave: household—wholesale
3567 Ovens, sherardizing—*mfg*
3569 Ovens, surveillance: for aging and testing powder—*mfg*
3229 Ovenware, glass—*mfg*
3089 Ovenware, plastics—*mfg*
4213 Over-the-road trucking
2326 Overall jackets: men's and boys'—mfpm—*mfg*
2326 Overalls, work: men's and boys'—mfpm—*mfg*
1241 Overburden removal for bituminous coal, anthracite, and lignite on a contract basis
1081 Overburden removal for metal mining: on a contract basis
1481 Overburden removal for nonmetallic minerals, except fuels: on a contract basis

3567   Paint baking and drying ovens—*mfg*

5198   Paint brushes, rollers, and sprayers—wholesale

2851   Paint driers—*mfg*

3559   Paint making machinery—*mfg*

2816   Paint pigments, inorganic—*mfg*

2865   Paint pigments, organic—*mfg*

2851   Paint primers—*mfg*

2851   Paint removers—*mfg*

3991   Paint rollers—*mfg*

3944   Paint sets, children's—*mfg*

7532   Paint shops, automotive

5084   Paint spray equipment, industrial—wholesale

3563   Paint sprayers—*mfg*

2499   Paint sticks, wood—*mfg*

5231   Paint stores—retail

3952   Paint, gold or bronze—*mfg*

2851   Paintbrush cleaners—*mfg*

3991   Paintbrushes—*mfg*

3479   Painting (enameling and varnishing) of metal products, for the trade—*mfg*

3999   Painting instrument dials, for the trade—*mfg*

1721   Painting of buildings and other structures, except roofs—contractors

1721   Painting ships—contractors

1721   Painting traffic lanes—contractors

3952   Paints for burnt wood or leather work, platinum—*mfg*

3952   Paints for china painting—*mfg*

3952   Paints, artists'—*mfg*

2851   Paints, asphalt and bituminous—*mfg*

2851   Paints, plastics texture: paste and dry—*mfg*

2851   Paints, waterproof—*mfg*

2851   Paints: oil and alkyd vehicle, and water thinned—*mfg*

5198   Paints—wholesale

2211   Pajama checks, textile—*mfg*

2322   Pajamas: men's and boys'— mfpm—*mfg*

2341   Pajamas: women's, misses', children's, and infants'—mfpm—*mfg*

2254   Pajamas—mitse—*mfg*

3952   Palettes, artists'—*mfg*

1099   Palladium ore mining

3537   Pallet assemblies for landing mats—*mfg*

2448   Pallet containers, wood or wood and metal combination—*mfg*

3537   Pallet loaders and unloaders—*mfg*

2542   Pallet racks, except wood—*mfg*

2679   Pallet spacers, fiber—mfpm—*mfg*

3537   Palletizers and depalletizers—*mfg*

2653   Pallets, corrugated and solid fiberboard—mfpm—*mfg*

3537   Pallets, metal—*mfg*

2448   Pallets, wood or wood and metal combination—*mfg*

2076   Palm kernel oil—*mfg*

2789   Pamphlets, binding only—*mfg*

2732   Pamphlets: printing or printing and binding, not publishing—*mfg*

2731   Pamphlets: publishing and printing, or publishing only—*mfg*

3479   Pan glazing, for the trade—*mfg*

2353   Panama hats—*mfg*

2045   Pancake batter, refrigerated or frozen—mfpm—*mfg*

2041   Pancake batter, refrigerated or frozen—mitse—*mfg*

2045   Pancake mixes—mfpm—*mfg*

2099   Pancake syrup, blended and mixed—*mfg*

3728   Panel assemblies (hydromatic propeller test stands), aircraft—*mfg*

2521   Panel furniture systems, office, wood—*mfg*

2522   Panel furniture systems, office: except wood—*mfg*

2431   Panel work, wood—*mfg*

3823   Panelboard indicators, recorders and controllers: receiver type—*mfg*

3613   Panelboards and distribution boards, electric—*mfg*

5063   Panelboards—wholesale

5031   Paneling, wood—wholesale

5211   Paneling—retail

3272   Panels and sections, prefabricated: concrete—*mfg*

3448   Panels for prefabricated metal buildings—*mfg*

2452   Panels for prefabricated wood buildings—*mfg*

2675   Panels, cardboard: mfpm—*mfg*

3613   Panels, electric control and metering—*mfg*

2435   Panels, hardwood plywood—*mfg*

3299   Panels, papier-mache or plaster of paris—*mfg*

3275   Panels, plaster: gypsum—*mfg*

2436   Panels, softwood plywood—*mfg*

3827   Panoramic telescopes—*mfg*

2655   Pans and voids, fiber or cardboard—mfpm—*mfg*

3469   Pans, stamped and pressed metal: except tinned—*mfg*

3411   Pans, tinned—*mfg*

2341   Panties: women's, misses', children's, and infants'—mfpm—*mfg*

2254   Panties—mitse—*mfg*

2231   Pantings: wool, mohair, and similar animal fibers—*mfg*

3952   Pantographs for drafting—*mfg*

2339   Pants outfits, except pantsuits: women's, misses', and juniors'—mfpm—*mfg*

8049   Paramedics, offices of
3679   Parametric amplifiers—*mfg*
3674   Parametric diodes—*mfg*
3999   Parasols and frames: handles, parts, and trimmings—except precious metal—*mfg*
4513   Parcel delivery, private: air
4215   Parcel delivery, private: except air
7389   Parcel packing service (packaging)
3111   Parchment leather—*mfg*
2621   Parchment paper—mitse—*mfg*
8641   Parent-teacher associations
2834   Parenteral solutions—*mfg*
2024   Parfait—*mfg*
6159   Pari-mutuel totalizator equipment finance leasing and maintenance
2879   Paris green (insecticide)—*mfg*
3479   Parkerizing, for the trade—*mfg*
3647   Parking lights, automotive—*mfg*
1771   Parking lot construction—contractors
7521   Parking lots
3824   Parking meters—*mfg*
7521   Parking structures
7299   Parking, valet
1611   Parkway construction—general contractors
4789   Parlor car operations, not performed by line-haul railroad companies
8211   Parochial schools, elementary and secondary
8322   Parole offices
2426   Parquet flooring, hardwood—*mfg*
1752   Parquet flooring—contractors
3699   Particle accelerators, high voltage—*mfg*
3826   Particle size analyzers—*mfg*
3821   Particle size reduction apparatus, laboratory—*mfg*
2493   Particleboard—*mfg*
5031   Particleboard—wholesale
2899   Parting compounds (chemical foundry supplies)—*mfg*
3251   Partition tile, clay—*mfg*
3496   Partitions and grillework, made from purchased wire—*mfg*
3446   Partitions and grillework, ornamental metal—*mfg*
2653   Partitions, corrugated and solid fiberboard—mfpm—*mfg*
2522   Partitions, office: not for floor attachment—except wood—*mfg*
2521   Partitions, office: not for floor attachment—wood—*mfg*
2542   Partitions, prefabricated: except wood and free-standing—*mfg*
2541   Partitions, prefabricated: wood—for floor attachment—*mfg*
5046   Partitions—wholesale

7359   Party supplies rental and leasing
5963   Party-plan merchandising—retail
2782   Passbooks—*mfg*
2396   Passementeries—mfpm—*mfg*
1542   Passenger and freight terminal building construction—general contractors
3711   Passenger automobile bodies—*mfg*
3535   Passenger baggage belt loaders—*mfg*
7515   Passenger car leasing, except finance leasing: without drivers
7514   Passenger car rental, without drivers
4111   Passenger transportation, regular route, road or rail: between airports and terminals
4489   Passenger water transportation on rivers and canals
3731   Passenger-cargo vessels, building and repairing—*mfg*
3679   Passive repeaters—*mfg*
7221   Passport photographers
2032   Pasta, canned—*mfg*
2099   Pasta, uncooked: packaged with other ingredients—*mfg*
2891   Paste, adhesive—*mfg*
3399   Paste, metal—*mfg*
3952   Pastels, artists'—*mfg*
2099   Pastes, almond—*mfg*
2033   Pastes, fruit and vegetable—*mfg*
3556   Pasteurizing equipment, dairy and other food—*mfg*
2013   Pastrami—mfpm—*mfg*
2051   Pastries, except frozen: e.g., Danish, French—*mfg*
2499   Pastry boards, wood—*mfg*
2899   Patching plaster, household—*mfg*
7389   Patent brokers
6794   Patent buying and licensing
2631   Patent coated paperboard—mitse—*mfg*
6794   Patent leasing
3111   Patent leather—*mfg*
5122   Patent medicines—wholesale
8111   Patent solicitors' offices
8071   Pathological laboratories
8011   Pathologists (M.D.), offices of
8021   Pathologists, oral: offices of
3845   Patient monitoring equipment: intensive care/coronary care unit—*mfg*
5047   Patient monitoring equipment—wholesale
1771   Patio construction, concrete—contractors
3731   Patrol boats, building and repairing—*mfg*
7389   Patrol of electric transmission or gas lines
3711   Patrol wagons (motor vehicles)—*mfg*
3553   Pattern makers' machinery (woodworking)—*mfg*
3469   Patterns on metal—*mfg*
3543   Patterns, industrial—*mfg*

3827 Percentage correctors—*mfg*
2819 Perchloric acid—*mfg*
2869 Perchloroethylene—*mfg*
3634 Percolators, electric—*mfg*
5064 Percolators, electric—wholesale
3482 Percussion caps, for ammunition of 30 mm. (or 1.18 inch) or less—*mfg*
3931 Percussion musical instruments—*mfg*
3469 Perforated metal, stamped—*mfg*
3443 Perforating on heavy metal—*mfg*
3469 Perforating on light metal—*mfg*
1389 Perforating well casings on a contract basis
3579 Perforators (office machines)—*mfg*
6794 Performance rights, publishing and licensing of
7929 Performing artists
7922 Performing arts center productions
2844 Perfume bases, blending and compounding—*mfg*
2869 Perfume materials, synthetic—*mfg*
2844 Perfumes, natural and synthetic—*mfg*
5122 Perfumes—wholesale
2752 Periodicals, lithographed: not published—*mfg*
2759 Periodicals, printed: except lithographed or gravure (not publishing)—*mfg*
2754 Periodicals: gravure printing (not publishing)—*mfg*
2721 Periodicals: publishing and printing, or publishing only—*mfg*
5192 Periodicals—wholesale
8021 Periodontists, offices of
5734 Peripheral equipment, computer stores—retail
5045 Peripheral equipment, computer—wholesale
3827 Periscopes—*mfg*
3295 Perlite aggregate—*mfg*
1499 Perlite mining
3295 Perlite, expanded—*mfg*
2395 Permanent pleating and pressing, for the trade—*mfg*
3999 Permanent wave equipment and machines—*mfg*
2892 Permissible explosives—*mfg*
2819 Peroxides, inorganic—*mfg*
2865 Persian orange lake—*mfg*
0175 Persimmon orchards and farms
8811 Personal affairs management
8059 Personal care facilities with health care
8059 Personal care homes with health care
3571 Personal computers—*mfg*
8299 Personal development schools
6141 Personal finance companies, small loan: licensed

6719 Personal holding companies, except bank
6733 Personal investment trusts, management of
3172 Personal leather goods, small—*mfg*
3842 Personal safety appliances and equipment—*mfg*
7299 Personal shopping service
9199 Personnel agencies—government
3711 Personnel carriers, for highway use—*mfg*
3829 Personnel dosimetry devices—*mfg*
8742 Personnel management consultants, except employment service
7342 Pest control in structures
0851 Pest control, forest
2879 Pesticides, agricultural—*mfg*
2879 Pesticides, household—*mfg*
5191 Pesticides—wholesale
5999 Pet food stores—retail
2048 Pet food, except dog and cat: canned, frozen, and dry—*mfg*
5149 Pet food—wholesale
0742 Pet hospitals
5999 Pet shops—retail
5199 Pet supplies, except pet food—wholesale
1629 Petrochemical plant construction—general contractors
2911 Petrolatums, produced in petroleum refineries—*mfg*
4226 Petroleum and chemical bulk stations and terminals for hire
5172 Petroleum and its products, except bulk stations and terminals—wholesale
5172 Petroleum brokers—wholesale
5171 Petroleum bulk stations and terminals—wholesale
2911 Petroleum coke, produced in petroleum refineries—*mfg*
8711 Petroleum engineering services
4612 Petroleum pipelines, crude
4613 Petroleum pipelines, refined
2821 Petroleum polymer resins—*mfg*
1311 Petroleum production—crude
1629 Petroleum refinery construction—general contractors
3559 Petroleum refinery equipment—*mfg*
2911 Petroleum refining—*mfg*
2531 Pews, church—*mfg*
3914 Pewter ware—*mfg*
3559 Pharmaceutical machinery—*mfg*
1541 Pharmaceutical manufacturing plant construction—general contractors
2834 Pharmaceuticals—*mfg*
5122 Pharmaceuticals—wholesale
5912 Pharmacies—retail
3825 Phase angle meters—*mfg*

3827 Phototheodolites—*mfg*
3663 Phototransmission equipment—*mfg*
2791 Phototypesetting—*mfg*
3674 Photovoltaic devices, solid-state—*mfg*
7999 Phrenologists
2869 Phthalates—*mfg*
2821 Phthalic alkyd resins—*mfg*
2865 Phthalic anhydride—*mfg*
2821 Phthalic anhydride resins—*mfg*
2865 Phthalocyanine toners—*mfg*
8742 Physical distribution consultants
8099 Physical examination service, except by physicians
7991 Physical fitness centers
3829 Physical properties testing and inspection equipment—*mfg*
8731 Physical research, commercial
8733 Physical research, noncommercial
8049 Physical therapists, offices of
8011 Physicians (M.D.), including specialists: offices and clinics of
8049 Physicians' assistants, offices of
5047 Physicians' equipment—wholesale
5047 Physicians' supplies—wholesale
8031 Physicians, osteopathic: offices and clinics of
8999 Physicists, consulting: not connected with business service laboratories
3841 Physiotherapy equipment, electrical—*mfg*
2833 Physostigmine and derivatives—*mfg*
2879 Phytoactin—*mfg*
3429 Piano hardware—*mfg*
3931 Piano parts and materials, except piano hardware—*mfg*
7359 Piano rental and leasing
5736 Piano stores—retail
7699 Piano tuning and repair
3931 Pianos, all types: e.g., vertical, grand, spinet, player, coin-operated—*mfg*
3931 Piccolos and parts—*mfg*
3552 Picker machines (textile machinery)—*mfg*
2426 Picker stick blanks—*mfg*
3552 Picker sticks for looms—*mfg*
2411 Pickets and paling: round or split—*mfg*
2092 Picking of crab meat—*mfg*
3547 Picklers and pickling lines, sheet and strip (rolling mill equipment)—*mfg*
2035 Pickles and pickle salting—*mfg*
5149 Pickles, preserves, jellies, jams, and sauces—wholesale
3423 Picks (handtools)—*mfg*
7212 Pickup and delivery station laundry not operated by laundries
3792 Pickup coaches (campers), for mounting on pickup trucks—*mfg*
3792 Pickup covers, canopies or caps—*mfg*

3651 Pickup heads, phonograph—*mfg*
5511 Pickups and vans, new and used—retail
5521 Pickups and vans, used only—retail
7999 Picnic grounds operation
3089 Picnic jugs, plastics—*mfg*
2892 Picric acid (explosives)—*mfg*
3812 Pictorial situation instrumentation—*mfg*
2499 Picture frame moldings, finished—*mfg*
5999 Picture frames, ready-made—retail
2499 Picture frames, wood or metal—*mfg*
7699 Picture framing to individual order, not connected with retail art stores
7699 Picture framing, custom
3211 Picture glass—*mfg*
3999 Picture plaques, laminated—*mfg*
2759 Picture post cards: except lithographed or gravure—*mfg*
2752 Picture postcards, lithographed—*mfg*
3671 Picture tube reprocessing—*mfg*
2099 Pie fillings, except fruits, vegetables and meat—*mfg*
5949 Piece goods—retail
5131 Piece goods—wholesale
1629 Pier construction—general contractors
3272 Pier footings, prefabricated concrete—*mfg*
**** Piers and docks, operated by oil firms—code as auxiliary to tanker fleets
7996 Piers, amusement
4491 Piers, including buildings and facilities: operation and maintenance
2051 Pies, bakery, except frozen—*mfg*
2053 Pies, bakery, frozen—*mfg*
5142 Pies, fruit: frozen—wholesale
2032 Pies, meat: canned—*mfg*
3679 Piezoelectric crystals—*mfg*
3312 Pig iron—*mfg*
5051 Pig iron—wholesale
0259 Pigeon farms
3949 Pigeons, clay (targets)—*mfg*
2865 Pigment scarlet lake—*mfg*
5198 Pigments and colors—wholesale
2816 Pigments, inorganic—*mfg*
2865 Pigments, organic: except animal black and bone black—*mfg*
2013 Pigs' feet, cooked and pickled—mfpm—*mfg*
3334 Pigs, aluminum—*mfg*
3331 Pigs, copper—*mfg*
3339 Pigs, lead—*mfg*
3339 Pigs, primary: nonferrous metals, except copper and aluminum—*mfg*
0912 Pilchard, catching of
1629 Pile driving—contractors
2257 Pile fabrics, circular knit—*mfg*
2211 Pile fabrics, cotton—*mfg*
2221 Pile fabrics, manmade fiber and silk—*mfg*

1623 Pipeline wrapping—contractors
4613 Pipelines (common carriers), gasoline
4612 Pipelines, crude petroleum
4922 Pipelines, natural gas
4613 Pipelines, refined petroleum
3714 Pipes, fuel: motor vehicle—*mfg*
3931 Pipes, organ—*mfg*
3999 Pipes, pipestems, and bits: tobacco—except hard rubber—*mfg*
5199 Pipes, smokers'—wholesale
1499 Pipestone mining
3821 Pipettes, hemocytometer—*mfg*
3498 Piping systems, metal: for pulp, paper, and chemical industries—*mfg*
1711 Piping, plumbing—contractors
2211 Piques, cotton—*mfg*
0173 Pistachio groves and farms
3484 Pistols and parts, except toy—*mfg*
3489 Pistols, depth charge release—*mfg*
3944 Pistols, toy—*mfg*
3592 Pistons and piston rings—*mfg*
5085 Pistons and valves, industrial—wholesale
2861 Pit charcoal—*mfg*
2865 Pitch, product of coal tar distillation—*mfg*
2952 Pitch, roofing—mfpm—*mfg*
2861 Pitch, wood—*mfg*
1094 Pitchblende mining
3829 Pitometers—*mfg*
2833 Pituitary gland derivatives: bulk, uncompounded—*mfg*
2834 Pituitary gland pharmaceutical preparations—*mfg*
3568 Pivots, power transmission—*mfg*
2045 Pizza mixes and doughs—mfpm—*mfg*
2041 Pizza mixes and prepared dough—mitse—*mfg*
5812 Pizza parlors
2038 Pizza, frozen—*mfg*
2099 Pizza, refrigerated: not frozen—*mfg*
5812 Pizzerias
2392 Placemats, plastics and textiles—*mfg*
1041 Placer gold mining
2211 Plaids, cotton—*mfg*
3671 Planar triode tubes—*mfg*
3531 Planers, bituminous—*mfg*
3541 Planers, metal cutting—*mfg*
3553 Planers, woodworking—*mfg*
3555 Planes, printers'—*mfg*
3423 Planes, woodworking: hand—*mfg*
8412 Planetaria
3553 Planing mill machinery—*mfg*
5211 Planing mill products and lumber dealers—retail
2421 Planing mills, independent: except millwork—*mfg*
2431 Planing mills, millwork—*mfg*

9531 Planning and development of housing programs—government
2752 Planographing—*mfg*
5199 Plant food—wholesale
2873 Plant foods, mixed: made in plants producing nitrogenous fertilizer materials—*mfg*
2874 Plant foods, mixed: made in plants producing phosphatic fertilizer materials—*mfg*
2879 Plant hormones—*mfg*
0179 Plantain farms
3089 Planters, plastics—*mfg*
0721 Planting crops, with or without fertilizing
5083 Planting machinery and equipment—wholesale
3523 Planting machines, agricultural—*mfg*
3231 Plants and foliage, artificial: made from purchased glass—*mfg*
7359 Plants, live: rental and leasing
0181 Plants, ornamental: growing of
0181 Plants, potted: growing of
5992 Plants, potted—retail
5193 Plants, potted—wholesale
3999 Plaques, picture: laminated—*mfg*
3299 Plaques: clay, plaster, or papier-mache—factory production only—*mfg*
3542 Plasma jet spray metal forming machines—*mfg*
3541 Plasma process metal cutting machines, except welding machines—*mfg*
8099 Plasmapheresis centers
2836 Plasmas—*mfg*
3275 Plaster and plasterboard, gypsum—*mfg*
3531 Plaster mixers—*mfg*
3275 Plaster of paris—*mfg*
3299 Plaster work, ornamental and architectural—*mfg*
3843 Plaster, dental—*mfg*
3275 Plaster, gypsum—*mfg*
2899 Plaster, patching: household—*mfg*
5032 Plaster—wholesale
3449 Plastering accessories, metal—*mfg*
1742 Plastering, plain or ornamental—contractors
3842 Plasters, adhesive: medicated or nonmedicated—*mfg*
3479 Plastic coating of metals for the trade—*mfg*
1459 Plastic fire clay mining
8011 Plastic surgeons, offices of
2869 Plasticizers, organic: cyclic and acyclic—*mfg*
2851 Plastics base paints and varnishes—*mfg*
5162 Plastics basic shapes—wholesale
3089 Plastics casting, for the trade—*mfg*
2295 Plastics coated fabrics—*mfg*

3081 Plastics film and sheet, unsupported—*mfg*
2671 Plastics film, coated or laminated: for packaging—mfpm—*mfg*
5162 Plastics film—wholesale
3255 Plastics fire clay bricks—*mfg*
5199 Plastics foam—wholesale
2385 Plastics gowns—*mfg*
2541 Plastics laminated over particleboard (fixture tops)—*mfg*
5162 Plastics materials—wholesale
3089 Plastics molding, for the trade—*mfg*
3255 Plastics refractories, clay—*mfg*
3297 Plastics refractories, nonclay—*mfg*
3087 Plastics resins, custom compounding of—*mfg*
5162 Plastics resins—wholesale
5093 Plastics scrap—wholesale
5162 Plastics sheet and rods—wholesale
1799 Plastics wall tile installation—contractors
3559 Plastics working machinery—*mfg*
3083 Plastics, laminated: plate, rods, tubes, profiles and sheet, except flexible packaging—*mfg*
2851 Plastisol coating compound—*mfg*
3211 Plate glass blanks for optical or ophthalmic uses—*mfg*
6331 Plate glass insurance
3211 Plate glass, polished and rough—*mfg*
5039 Plate glass—wholesale
3861 Plate holders, photographic—*mfg*
2759 Plate printing—*mfg*
3547 Plate rolling mill machinery—*mfg*
3443 Plate work, fabricated: cutting, punching, bending, and shaping—*mfg*
3083 Plate, laminated plastics—*mfg*
3914 Plated ware: flatware, hollow ware, toilet ware, ecclesiastical ware, etc.—*mfg*
2759 Plateless engraving—*mfg*
3069 Platens, except printers': solid or covered rubber—*mfg*
2796 Plates and cylinders, rotogravure printing: preparation of—*mfg*
2796 Plates for printing, embossing of—*mfg*
3579 Plates, addressing—*mfg*
3353 Plates, aluminum—*mfg*
3841 Plates, bone—*mfg*
3351 Plates, copper and copper alloy—*mfg*
3089 Plates, dinnerware, plastics: except foam—*mfg*
3644 Plates, face (wiring devices)—*mfg*
3086 Plates, foamed plastics—*mfg*
2796 Plates, lithographic: preparation of—*mfg*
3312 Plates, made in steel works or rolling mills—*mfg*
3555 Plates, metal: engravers'—*mfg*
5051 Plates, metal—wholesale

2656 Plates, paper: except those made from pressed or molded pulp—mfpm—*mfg*
2796 Plates, photoengraving—*mfg*
3861 Plates, photographic: sensitized—*mfg*
2679 Plates, pressed and molded pulp—mfpm—*mfg*
3555 Plates, printers': of all materials—*mfg*
2796 Plates, printing: preparation of—*mfg*
3356 Plates: lead, magnesium, nickel, zinc, and their alloys—*mfg*
3537 Platforms, cargo: metal—*mfg*
2899 Plating compounds—*mfg*
3471 Plating of metals and formed products, for the trade—*mfg*
3356 Platinum and platinum alloy sheets and tubing—*mfg*
3497 Platinum and platinum base alloy foil—*mfg*
1099 Platinum group ore mining
3339 Platinum-group metals refining, primary—*mfg*
3356 Platinum-group metals rolling, drawing, and extruding—*mfg*
3341 Platinum-group metals smelting and refining, secondary—*mfg*
3949 Playground equipment—*mfg*
5941 Playground equipment—retail
2752 Playing cards, lithographed—*mfg*
2759 Playing cards, printed: except lithographed or gravure—*mfg*
2754 Playing cards: gravure printing—*mfg*
5092 Playing cards—wholesale
2514 Playpens, children's: metal—*mfg*
2511 Playpens, children's: wood—*mfg*
7922 Plays (road companies and stock companies)
2369 Playsuits: girls', children's, and infants'—mfpm—*mfg*
2339 Playsuits: women's, misses', and juniors'—mfpm—*mfg*
7389 Playwrights' brokers
2395 Pleating, for the trade—*mfg*
3423 Pliers (handtools)—*mfg*
3843 Pliers, dental—*mfg*
3271 Plinth blocks, precast terrazzo—*mfg*
2673 Pliofilm bags—mfpm—*mfg*
2211 Plisse crepe, cotton—*mfg*
2261 Plisse printing of cotton broadwoven fabrics—*mfg*
2262 Plisse printing of manmade fiber and silk broadwoven fabrics—*mfg*
3577 Plotter controllers, computer peripheral equipment—*mfg*
3577 Plotters, computer—*mfg*
3827 Plotting boards (sighting and fire control equipment)—*mfg*

0711 Plowing
3524 Plows (garden tractor equipment)—*mfg*
3523 Plows, agricultural: disc, moldboard, chisel, etc.—*mfg*
3532 Plows, coal—*mfg*
3531 Plows, construction: excavating and grading—*mfg*
3711 Plows, snow (motor vehicles)—*mfg*
1389 Plugging and abandoning wells on a contract basis
3499 Plugs, drain: magnetic—metal—*mfg*
3842 Plugs, ear and nose—*mfg*
3643 Plugs, electric—*mfg*
2499 Plugs, wood—*mfg*
0175 Plum orchards and farms
2032 Plum pudding—*mfg*
3295 Plumbago: ground, refined, or blended—*mfg*
3432 Plumbers' brass goods—*mfg*
5074 Plumbers' brass goods, fittings, and valves—wholesale
3423 Plumbers' handtools—*mfg*
3069 Plumbers' rubber goods—*mfg*
3494 Plumbing and heating valves, metal—*mfg*
5074 Plumbing and heating valves—wholesale
1711 Plumbing and heating—contractors
3432 Plumbing fixture fittings and trim—*mfg*
3463 Plumbing fixture forgings, nonferrous: not made in hot-rolling mills—*mfg*
5074 Plumbing fixtures, equipment, and supplies—wholesale
3088 Plumbing fixtures, plastics—*mfg*
3261 Plumbing fixtures, vitreous china—*mfg*
3431 Plumbing fixtures: enameled iron, cast iron, and pressed metal—*mfg*
1711 Plumbing repair—contractors
1711 Plumbing, with or without sheet metalwork—contractors
3999 Plumes, feather—*mfg*
2211 Plushes, cotton—*mfg*
2221 Plushes, manmade fiber and silk—*mfg*
2435 Plywood, hardwood or hardwood faced—*mfg*
2436 Plywood, softwood—*mfg*
5031 Plywood—wholesale
3011 Pneumatic casings (rubber tires)—*mfg*
3823 Pneumatic controllers, industrial process type—*mfg*
3593 Pneumatic cylinders, fluid power—*mfg*
3492 Pneumatic hose assemblies—*mfg*
3052 Pneumatic hose, rubber or rubberized fabric: e.g., air brake and air line—*mfg*
2394 Pneumatic mattresses—mfpm—*mfg*
3822 Pneumatic relays, air-conditioning type—*mfg*

3535 Pneumatic tube conveyor systems for general industrial use—*mfg*
1796 Pneumatic tube system installation—contractors
3492 Pneumatic valves, including aircraft: fluid power—metal—*mfg*
3421 Pocket knives—*mfg*
3999 Pocketbook frames—*mfg*
2396 Pocketbook linings—*mfg*
7699 Pocketbook repair shops
3172 Pocketbooks, men's: regardless of material—*mfg*
3171 Pocketbooks, women's: of all materials, except precious metal—*mfg*
2211 Pocketing twill, cotton—*mfg*
2396 Pockets for men's and boys' suits and coats—*mfg*
8043 Podiatrists, offices and clinics of
8699 Poetry associations
3578 Point-of-sale devices—*mfg*
2371 Pointing furs—*mfg*
3541 Pointing, chamfering, and burring machines—*mfg*
3843 Points, abrasive: dental—*mfg*
2879 Poison: ant, rat, roach, and rodent—household—*mfg*
3944 Poker chips—*mfg*
3826 Polariscopes—*mfg*
3826 Polarizers—*mfg*
3826 Polarographic equipment—*mfg*
2411 Pole cutting contractors—*mfg*
1623 Pole line construction—general contractors
3644 Pole line hardware—*mfg*
3462 Pole line hardware forgings, ferrous: not made in rolling mills—*mfg*
3463 Pole line hardware forgings, nonferrous: not made in hot-rolling mills—*mfg*
5063 Pole line hardware—wholesale
2491 Poles and pole crossarms, treated—*mfg*
3272 Poles, concrete—*mfg*
2591 Poles, curtain and drapery—*mfg*
2491 Poles, cutting and preserving—*mfg*
2499 Poles, wood: e.g., clothesline, tent, flag—*mfg*
2411 Poles, wood: untreated—*mfg*
9221 Police departments
2353 Police hats and caps, except protective head gear—*mfg*
2499 Police officer's clubs, wood—*mfg*
5999 Police supply stores—retail
2311 Police uniforms, men's—*mfg*
6411 Policyholders' consulting service
2842 Polishes: furniture, automobile, metal, shoe, and stove—*mfg*

5012 Popup campers—wholesale
2891 Porcelain cement, household—*mfg*
3264 Porcelain parts, molded: for electrical and electronic devices—*mfg*
3269 Porcelain, chemical—*mfg*
2431 Porch columns, wood—*mfg*
2591 Porch shades, wood slat—*mfg*
2514 Porch swings, metal—*mfg*
2511 Porch swings, wood—*mfg*
2431 Porch work, wood—*mfg*
2032 Pork and beans, canned—*mfg*
2096 Pork rinds—*mfg*
2013 Pork: pickled, cured, salted, or smoked—mfpm—*mfg*
2011 Pork—mitse—*mfg*
9621 Port authorities and districts—nonoperating
3448 Portable buildings, prefabricated metal—*mfg*
2452 Portable buildings, prefabricated wood—*mfg*
3431 Portable chemical toilets (metal)—*mfg*
3088 Portable chemical toilets, plastics—*mfg*
3825 Portable test meters—*mfg*
2082 Porter (alcoholic beverage)—*mfg*
7299 Porter service
5181 Porter—wholesale
3241 Portland cement—*mfg*
7221 Portrait photographers
5099 Portraits—wholesale
3845 Position emission tomography (PET scanner)—*mfg*
3812 Position indicators, airframe equipment: e.g., for landing gear, stabilizers—*mfg*
3824 Positive displacement meters—*mfg*
3423 Post hole diggers, hand—*mfg*
3531 Post hole diggers, powered—*mfg*
3444 Post office collection boxes—*mfg*
1542 Post office construction—general contractors
7389 Post office contract stations
3579 Postage meters—*mfg*
4311 Postal Service, U.S.
3496 Postal screen wire equipment—mfpm—*mfg*
2542 Postal service lock boxes, except wood—*mfg*
2759 Postcards, picture: except lithographed or gravure printed—*mfg*
2754 Postcards, picture: gravure printing—*mfg*
2752 Postcards, picture: lithographed—*mfg*
7312 Poster advertising service, outdoor
7319 Poster advertising services, except outdoor
2621 Poster paper—mitse—*mfg*
2759 Posters, including billboard: except lithographed or gravure—*mfg*

2752 Posters, lithographed—*mfg*
2754 Posters: gravure printing—*mfg*
1799 Posthole digging—contractors
3462 Posts, bumping: railroad—forged (not made in rolling mills)—*mfg*
3272 Posts, concrete—*mfg*
2411 Posts, wood: hewn, round, or split—*mfg*
2491 Posts, wood: treated—*mfg*
2026 Pot cheese—*mfg*
2819 Potash alum—*mfg*
1474 Potash mining
2812 Potash, caustic—*mfg*
2819 Potassium aluminum sulfate—*mfg*
2819 Potassium bichromate and chromate—*mfg*
2869 Potassium bitartrate—*mfg*
2819 Potassium bromide—*mfg*
2812 Potassium carbonate—*mfg*
2819 Potassium chlorate—*mfg*
2819 Potassium chloride—*mfg*
1474 Potassium compounds mining
2819 Potassium compounds, inorganic: except potassium hydroxide and carbonate—*mfg*
2819 Potassium cyanide—*mfg*
2812 Potassium hydroxide—*mfg*
2819 Potassium hypochlorate—*mfg*
2819 Potassium iodide—*mfg*
2819 Potassium metal—*mfg*
2819 Potassium nitrate and sulfate—*mfg*
2819 Potassium permanganate—*mfg*
4221 Potato cellars
2096 Potato chips and related corn snacks—*mfg*
5145 Potato chips—wholesale
0723 Potato curing
3523 Potato diggers, harvesters, and planters (agricultural machinery)—*mfg*
0134 Potato farms, Irish
0134 Potato farms, except sweet potato and yam
0139 Potato farms, sweet
0139 Potato farms, yam
2034 Potato flakes, granules, and other dehydrated potato products—*mfg*
3496 Potato mashers, made from purchased wire—*mfg*
2499 Potato mashers, wood—*mfg*
3556 Potato peelers, electric—*mfg*
3421 Potato peelers, hand—*mfg*
2046 Potato starch—*mfg*
2096 Potato sticks—*mfg*
2099 Potatoes, dried: packaged with other ingredients—*mfg*
5148 Potatoes, fresh—wholesale
2099 Potatoes, peeled for the trade—*mfg*
3825 Potentiometric instruments, except industrial process type—*mfg*

1522   Prefabricated building erection, residential: except single-family—general contractors
3448   Prefabricated buildings, metal—*mfg*
2452   Prefabricated buildings, wood—*mfg*
5211   Prefabricated buildings—retail
5039   Prefabricated buildings—wholesale
1521   Prefabricated single-family houses erection—general contractors
2435   Prefinished hardwood plywood—*mfg*
2835   Pregnancy test kits—*mfg*
1521   Premanufactured housing, single-family (assembled on site)—general contractors
3999   Preparation of slides and exhibits, for classroom use—*mfg*
1231   Preparation plants, anthracite
1221   Preparation plants, bituminous coal or lignite
8211   Preparatory schools
2299   Preparing textile fibers for spinning (scouring and combing)—*mfg*
3652   Prerecorded audio magnetic tape—*mfg*
8351   Preschool centers
2033   Preserves, including imitation—*mfg*
2491   Preserving of wood (creosoting)—*mfg*
2261   Preshrinking cotton broadwoven fabrics for the trade—*mfg*
2262   Preshrinking manmade fiber and silk broadwoven fabrics for the trade—*mfg*
2231   Preshrinking wool broad woven fabrics for the trade—*mfg*
9111   President's office
2841   Presoaks—*mfg*
7389   Presorting mail service
3542   Press brakes—*mfg*
7389   Press clipping service
2211   Press cloth—*mfg*
3462   Press forgings, iron and steel: not made in rolling mills—*mfg*
7383   Press services (news syndicates)
7212   Press shops for garments
2631   Pressboard—mitse—*mfg*
5113   Pressed and molded pulp goods—wholesale
2299   Pressed felts—*mfg*
2499   Pressed logs of sawdust and other wood particles, nonpetroleum binder—*mfg*
3469   Pressed metal products (stampings)—*mfg*
2679   Pressed products from wood pulp—mfpm—*mfg*
3523   Presses and balers, farm: hay, cotton, etc.—*mfg*
3542   Presses, arbor—*mfg*
3582   Presses, finishing: commercial laundry and drycleaning—*mfg*
3569   Presses, metal baling—*mfg*
3555   Presses, printing—*mfg*

3553   Presses, woodworking: particleboard, hardboard, medium density fiberboard (MDF), and plywood—*mfg*
3556   Presses: cheese, beet, cider, and sugarcane—*mfg*
3542   Presses: forming, stamping, punching, and shearing (machine tools)—*mfg*
3542   Presses: hydraulic and pneumatic, mechanical and manual—*mfg*
2499   Pressing blocks, tailors': wood—*mfg*
3582   Pressing machines, commercial laundry and drycleaning—*mfg*
3829   Pressure and vacuum indicators, aircraft engine—*mfg*
3492   Pressure control valves, fluid power: metal—*mfg*
3822   Pressure controllers, air-conditioning system type—*mfg*
3365   Pressure cookers, domestic: cast aluminum, except die-castings—*mfg*
3469   Pressure cookers, stamped or drawn—*mfg*
3589   Pressure cookers, steam: commercial—*mfg*
3823   Pressure gauges, dial and digital—*mfg*
3823   Pressure instruments, industrial process type—*mfg*
3321   Pressure pipe, cast iron—*mfg*
3272   Pressure pipe, reinforced concrete—*mfg*
2672   Pressure sensitive paper and tape, except rubber backed—mfpm—*mfg*
5113   Pressure sensitive tape—wholesale
3829   Pressure transducers—*mfg*
3491   Pressure valves, industrial: except power transfer—*mfg*
3443   Pressure vessels, industrial: metal plate—made in boiler shops—*mfg*
3443   Pressurizers and auxiliary equipment, nuclear: metal plate—*mfg*
3272   Prestressed concrete products—*mfg*
5461   Pretzel stores and stands—retail
2052   Pretzels—*mfg*
5149   Pretzels—wholesale
9651   Price control agencies—government
3692   Primary batteries, dry and wet—*mfg*
8011   Primary care medical (M.D.) clinics
3823   Primary elements for process flow measurement: orifice plates—*mfg*
3822   Primary oil burner controls, including stack controls and cadmium cells—*mfg*
3334   Primary production of aluminum—*mfg*
3339   Primary refining of nonferrous metal: except copper and aluminum—*mfg*
3331   Primary smelting and refining of copper—*mfg*
3339   Primary smelting of nonferrous metal: except copper and aluminum—*mfg*

3483 Projectiles, chemical warfare—*mfg*
3483 Projectiles, jet propulsion: complete—*mfg*
5043 Projection apparatus, motion picture and slide: photographic—wholesale
3827 Projection lenses—*mfg*
3861 Projectors, microfilm—*mfg*
3861 Projectors, still and motion picture: silent and sound—*mfg*
3489 Projectors: antisub, depth charge release, grenade, livens, and rocket—*mfg*
3253 Promenade tile, clay—*mfg*
7389 Promoters of home shows and flower shows
7941 Promoters, sports events
7338 Proofreading service
1321 Propane (natural) production
5984 Propane gas, bottled—retail
2819 Propellants for missiles, solid: inorganic—*mfg*
2869 Propellants for missiles, solid: organic—*mfg*
3728 Propeller adapter assemblies, hydromatic—*mfg*
3728 Propeller alining tables—*mfg*
3634 Propeller fans, window-type (household)—*mfg*
3549 Propeller straightening presses—*mfg*
3824 Propeller type meters with registers—*mfg*
3599 Propellers, ship and boat: machined—*mfg*
3366 Propellers, ship and screw: cast brass, bronze, copper, and copper-base—except die-castings—*mfg*
3728 Propellers, variable and fixed pitch and parts—aircraft—*mfg*
6331 Property damage insurance
9311 Property tax assessors' offices
3069 Prophylactics, rubber—*mfg*
5912 Proprietary (nonprescription medicines) stores—retail
5122 Proprietary (patent) medicines—wholesale
2834 Proprietary drug products—*mfg*
3764 Propulsion units for guided missiles and space vehicles—*mfg*
2869 Propylene glycol—*mfg*
2869 Propylene, made in chemical plants—*mfg*
2911 Propylene, produced in petroleum refineries—*mfg*
1081 Prospect drilling for metal mining: on a contract basis
1481 Prospect drilling for nonmetallic minerals except fuels: on a contract basis
3842 Prosthetic appliances and supplies—*mfg*
8021 Prosthodontists, offices of
6289 Protective committees, security holders
7381 Protective service, guard
3579 Protectors, check (machine)—*mfg*

3851 Protectors, eye—*mfg*
3949 Protectors, sports: e.g., baseball, basketball, hockey—*mfg*
3826 Protein analyzers, laboratory type—*mfg*
2824 Protein fibers—*mfg*
2821 Protein plastics—*mfg*
0175 Prune orchards and farms
2034 Prunes, dried—*mfg*
0721 Pruning of orchard trees and vines
3423 Pruning tools—*mfg*
2816 Prussian blue pigments—*mfg*
3423 Prying bars (handtools)—*mfg*
1061 Psilomelane mining
8063 Psychiatric hospitals
8059 Psychiatric patient's convalescent homes
8049 Psychiatric social workers, offices of
8011 Psychiatrists, offices of
8011 Psychoanalysts, offices of
8049 Psychologists, clinical: offices of
8999 Psychologists, industrial
8049 Psychotherapists, except M.D.: offices of
8721 Public accountants, certified
5065 Public address equipment—wholesale
7622 Public address system repair
3651 Public address systems—*mfg*
2531 Public building fixtures—*mfg*
5021 Public building furniture—wholesale
9222 Public defenders' offices
9431 Public health agencies—nonoperating
8732 Public opinion research
9222 Public prosecutors' offices
8743 Public relations services
9229 Public safety bureaus—government
9229 Public safety statistics centers—government
9631 Public service commissions, except transportation
8299 Public speaking schools
8611 Public utility associations
9631 Public utility commissions
6719 Public utility holding companies
6519 Public utility property, lessors of
9441 Public welfare administration, nonoperating
8322 Public welfare centers, offices of
2621 Publication paper—mitse—*mfg*
7313 Publishers' representatives, advertising
2741 Publishing and printing maps, guides, directories, atlases, and sheet music—*mfg*
2731 Publishing and printing, books and pamphlets—*mfg*
2711 Publishing and printing, or publishing only: newspapers—*mfg*
2721 Publishing and printing, or publishing only: periodicals—*mfg*

5137 Purses: women's and children's—wholesale
3991 Push brooms—*mfg*
3799 Pushcarts—*mfg*
3545 Pushers—*mfg*
3199 Puttees, canvas and leather—*mfg*
2851 Putty—*mfg*
3423 Putty knives—*mfg*
2879 Pyrethrin bearing preparations—*mfg*
2879 Pyrethrin concentrates—*mfg*
3829 Pyrheliometers—*mfg*
2822 Pyridine-butadiene copolymers—*mfg*
2822 Pyridine-butadiene rubbers—*mfg*
1479 Pyrites mining
3952 Pyrography materials—*mfg*
2861 Pyroligneous acid—*mfg*
1061 Pyrolusite mining
3297 Pyrolytic graphite—*mfg*
3269 Pyrometer tubes—*mfg*
3823 Pyrometers, industrial process type—*mfg*
3269 Pyrometric cones: earthenware—*mfg*
1499 Pyrophyllite mining
3295 Pyrophyllite, ground or otherwise treated—*mfg*
2899 Pyrotechnic ammunition: flares, signals, flashlight bombs, and rockets—*mfg*
3484 Pyrotechnic pistols and projectors—*mfg*
2821 Pyroxylin—*mfg*
2295 Pyroxylin coated fabrics—*mfg*
1479 Pyrrhotite mining

Q

0259 Quail farms
3253 Quarry tile, clay—*mfg*
5082 Quarrying machinery and equipment—wholesale
3131 Quarters (shoe cut stock)—*mfg*
1499 Quartz crystal mining (pure)
3679 Quartz crystals for electronic application—*mfg*
1429 Quartzite, crushed and broken—quarrying
1411 Quartzite, dimension—quarrying
2861 Quebracho extract—*mfg*
2861 Quercitron extract—*mfg*
2752 Quick printing, except photocopy service—*mfg*
3274 Quicklime—*mfg*
1099 Quicksilver (mercury) ore mining
2299 Quilt filling: curled hair (e.g., cotton waste, moss, hemp tow, kapok)—*mfg*
2395 Quilted fabrics or cloth—*mfg*
7299 Quilting for individuals
5949 Quilting materials and supplies—retail
2395 Quilting, for the trade—*mfg*

2221 Quilts, manmade fiber and silk—mitse—*mfg*
2392 Quilts—mfpm—*mfg*
0175 Quince orchards and farms
2833 Quinine and derivatives—*mfg*
2865 Quinoline dyes—*mfg*
2869 Quinuclidinol ester of benzylic acid—*mfg*
6289 Quotation service, stock

R

2892 RDX (explosives)—*mfg*
3663 RF power amplifiers, and IF amplifiers: sold separately—*mfg*
0271 Rabbit farms
2015 Rabbits, processed: fresh, frozen, canned, or cooked—*mfg*
2015 Rabbits, slaughtering and dressing—*mfg*
7948 Race car drivers and owners
2741 Race track programs: publishing and printing, or publishing only—*mfg*
3562 Races, ball and roller bearing—*mfg*
7389 Racetrack cleaning, except buildings
7948 Racetrack operation: e.g., horse, dog, auto
3644 Raceways—*mfg*
2741 Racing forms: publishing and printing, or publishing only—*mfg*
7948 Racing stables, operation of
3949 Rackets and frames, sports: e.g., tennis, badminton, squash, racketball, lacrosse—*mfg*
3496 Racks without rigid framework, made from purchased wire—*mfg*
2511 Racks, book and magazine: wood—*mfg*
2499 Racks, for drying clothes: wood—*mfg*
2542 Racks, merchandise display and storage: except wood—*mfg*
2541 Racks, merchandise display: wood—*mfg*
3443 Racks, trash: metal plate—*mfg*
2542 Racks: mail pouch, mailing, mail sorting, etc., except wood—*mfg*
7997 Racquetball clubs, membership
7999 Racquetball courts, except membership clubs
4899 Radar station operation
3812 Radar systems and equipment—*mfg*
3825 Radar testing instruments, electric—*mfg*
3731 Radar towers, floating—*mfg*
3829 Radiac equipment (radiation measuring and detecting)—*mfg*
3567 Radiant heating systems, industrial process: e.g., dryers, cookers'—*mfg*
8734 Radiation dosimetry laboratories
3829 Radiation measuring and detecting (radiac) equipment—*mfg*

7218 Radiation protective garments supply service

3842 Radiation shielding aprons, gloves, and sheeting—*mfg*

7539 Radiator repair shops, automotive

3444 Radiator shields and enclosures, sheet metal—*mfg*

5074 Radiators and parts, heating: nonelectric—wholesale

3714 Radiators and radiator shells and cores, motor vehicle—*mfg*

3634 Radiators, electric—*mfg*

3433 Radiators, except electric—*mfg*

3651 Radio and phonograph combinations—*mfg*

3469 Radio and television chassis, stamped—*mfg*

7622 Radio and television receiver installation

3663 Radio and television switching equipment—*mfg*

3441 Radio and television tower sections, prefabricated metal—*mfg*

1623 Radio and television transmitting tower construction—general contractors

3825 Radio apparatus analyzers for testing electrical characteristics—*mfg*

7389 Radio broadcasting music checkers

4899 Radio broadcasting operated by cab companies

4832 Radio broadcasting stations

2517 Radio cabinets and cases, wood—*mfg*

2519 Radio cabinets, plastics—*mfg*

8999 Radio commentators

8748 Radio consultants

3671 Radio electron tubes—*mfg*

3812 Radio magnetic instrumentation (RMI)—*mfg*

5065 Radio parts and accessories—wholesale

7922 Radio programs, including commercials: producers of

3663 Radio receiver networks—*mfg*

5065 Radio receiving and transmitting tubes—wholesale

3651 Radio receiving sets—*mfg*

7622 Radio repair shops

7313 Radio representatives, advertising: not auxiliary to radio broadcasting

3825 Radio set analyzers, electrical—*mfg*

5731 Radio stores—retail

4822 Radio telegraph services

7389 Radio transcription service

3663 Radio transmitting and communications antennas and ground equipment—*mfg*

1623 Radio transmitting tower construction—general contractors

3825 Radio tube checkers, electrical—*mfg*

5731 Radio-phonograph stores—retail

2835 Radioactive diagnostic substances—*mfg*

2819 Radioactive isotopes—*mfg*

4953 Radioactive waste materials, disposal of

3825 Radiofrequency measuring equipment—*mfg*

3825 Radiofrequency oscillators—*mfg*

3844 Radiographic X-ray apparatus and tubes: medical, industrial, and research—*mfg*

8734 Radiographing welded joints on pipes and fittings

8011 Radiologists, offices of

5064 Radios, receiving only, household and automotive—wholesale

4812 Radiotelephone communications

4812 Radiotelephone services

2819 Radium chloride—*mfg*

3844 Radium equipment—*mfg*

2819 Radium luminous compounds—*mfg*

1094 Radium ore mining

3089 Rafts, life: nonrigid—plastics—*mfg*

3069 Rafts, life: rubber—*mfg*

2273 Rag rugs—*mfg*

2299 Rags, carbonized—*mfg*

5093 Rags—wholesale

3643 Rail bonds, electric: for propulsion and signal circuits—*mfg*

3312 Rail joints and fastenings, made in steel works or rolling mills—*mfg*

3531 Rail laying and tamping equipment—*mfg*

3446 Railings, bannisters, guards, etc.: made from metal pipe—*mfg*

3446 Railings, prefabricated metal—*mfg*

2431 Railings, stair: wood—*mfg*

9621 Railroad and warehouse commissions—nonoperating

3321 Railroad brake shoes, cast iron—*mfg*

3462 Railroad bumping posts, forged: not made in rolling mills—*mfg*

4741 Railroad car cleaning, icing, ventilating, and heating

3568 Railroad car journal bearings, plain—*mfg*

3743 Railroad car rebuilding—*mfg*

4741 Railroad car rental—without care of loading

4789 Railroad car repair, on a contract or fee basis

3321 Railroad car wheels, chilled cast iron—*mfg*

3743 Railroad cars and car equipment—*mfg*

1629 Railroad construction—general contractors

2491 Railroad cross bridge and switch ties, treated—*mfg*

3312 Railroad crossings, iron and steel: made in steel works or rolling mills—*mfg*

5088 Railroad equipment and supplies—wholesale

3493   Railroad equipment springs—*mfg*
4482   Railroad ferries
4731   Railroad freight agencies, not operated by railroad companies
2899   Railroad fusees—*mfg*
3429   Railroad hardware—*mfg*
3743   Railroad locomotives and parts—*mfg*
3999   Railroad models, except toy and hobby models—*mfg*
3944   Railroad models: toy and hobby—*mfg*
6517   Railroad property, lessors of
2531   Railroad seats—*mfg*
3669   Railroad signaling devices, electric—*mfg*
4013   Railroad switching
4013   Railroad terminals
4729   Railroad ticket offices, not operated by transportation companies
2421   Railroad ties, sawed—*mfg*
2899   Railroad torpedoes—*mfg*
3596   Railroad track scales—*mfg*
3462   Railroad wheels, axles, frogs, and related equipment: forged—mfpm—*mfg*
4013   Railroads, belt line
4011   Railroads, electric: line-haul
4011   Railroads, line-haul operating
4013   Railroads, logging
5051   Rails and accessories—wholesale
3355   Rails, aluminum: rolled and drawn—*mfg*
2411   Rails, fence: round or split—*mfg*
3312   Rails, iron and steel—*mfg*
3312   Rails, rerolled or renewed—*mfg*
3351   Rails, rolled and drawn: brass, bronze, and copper—*mfg*
3441   Railway bridge sections, prefabricated metal—*mfg*
2491   Railway crossties, wood: treated—*mfg*
3743   Railway maintenance cars—*mfg*
3743   Railway motor cars—*mfg*
3621   Railway motors and control equipment, electric—*mfg*
4111   Railway operation, local
1629   Railway roadbed construction—general contractors
3531   Railway track equipment: e.g., rail layers, ballast distributors—*mfg*
4011   Railways, interurban
3829   Rain gauges—*mfg*
5699   Raincoat stores—retail
2385   Raincoats, except vulcanized rubber—mfpm—*mfg*
5136   Raincoats, men's and boys'—wholesale
5137   Raincoats: women's and children's—wholesale
2034   Raisins—*mfg*
3423   Rakes, handtools—*mfg*
3523   Rakes, hay (agricultural machinery)—*mfg*

3531   Rakes, land clearing: mechanical—*mfg*
2299   Ramie yarn, thread, roving, and textiles—*mfg*
3297   Ramming mixes, nonclay—*mfg*
3537   Ramps, aircraft—loading—*mfg*
3537   Ramps, loading: portable, adjustable, and hydraulic—*mfg*
3448   Ramps, prefabricated: metal—*mfg*
****   Ranches—see type of ranch
3674   Random access memories (RAMS)—*mfg*
3131   Rands (shoe cut stock)—*mfg*
3433   Range boilers, galvanized iron and nonferrous metal—*mfg*
3861   Range finders, photographic—*mfg*
3589   Ranges, cooking: commercial—*mfg*
3631   Ranges, cooking: household—*mfg*
5064   Ranges, electric—wholesale
5074   Ranges, except electric—wholesale
5722   Ranges, gas and electric—retail
3631   Ranges, household cooking: electric and gas—*mfg*
3743   Rapid transit cars and equipment—*mfg*
5932   Rare book stores—retail
2819   Rare earth metal salts—*mfg*
1099   Rare-earths ore mining
0171   Raspberry farms
3423   Rasps, including recutting and resharpening—*mfg*
2879   Rat poisons—*mfg*
6411   Rate making organizations, insurance
4731   Rate services, transportation
3812   Rate-of-climb instrumentation—*mfg*
2211   Ratine, cotton—*mfg*
3612   Ratio transformers—*mfg*
2499   Rattan ware, except furniture—*mfg*
0279   Rattlesnake farms
2032   Ravioli, canned—*mfg*
2231   Raw stock dyeing and finishing: wool, mohair, and similar animal fibers—*mfg*
2269   Raw stock dyeing and other finishing, except wool—*mfg*
3111   Rawhide—*mfg*
2221   Rayon broadwoven fabrics—*mfg*
5131   Rayon piece goods—wholesale
2823   Rayon primary products: fibers, straw, strips, and yarn—*mfg*
2611   Rayon pulp—*mfg*
2284   Rayon thread—*mfg*
2299   Rayon tops, combing and converting—*mfg*
2282   Rayon yarn, filament: throwing, twisting, winding—*mfg*
2281   Rayon yarn, made from purchased staple: spun—*mfg*
2823   Rayon yarn, made in chemical plants—*mfg*
5199   Rayon yarns—wholesale

3651 Recording machines, music and speech: except dictation and telephone answering machines—*mfg*
7389 Recording studios on a contract or fee basis
3652 Records, phonograph—*mfg*
3341 Recovering and refining of nonferrous metals—*mfg*
2299 Recovering textile fibers from clippings and rags—*mfg*
3399 Recovery of iron ore from open hearth slag—*mfg*
3341 Recovery of silver from used photographic film—*mfg*
7997 Recreation and sports clubs, membership: except physical fitness
7032 Recreational camps
7011 Recreational hotels
9512 Recreational program administration—government
5561 Recreational vehicle dealers—retail
7033 Recreational vehicle parks
5561 Recreational vehicle parts and accessories—retail
5012 Recreational vehicles—wholesale
3612 Rectifier transformers—*mfg*
3629 Rectifiers (electrical apparatus)—*mfg*
3679 Rectifiers, electronic: except solid-state—*mfg*
5065 Rectifiers, electronic—wholesale
3674 Rectifiers, solid-state—*mfg*
2816 Red lead pigments—*mfg*
2899 Red oil (oleic acid)—*mfg*
7389 Redemption of trading stamps
9532 Redevelopment land agencies—government
3826 Redox (oxidation-reduction potential) instruments—*mfg*
1381 Redrilling oil and gas wells on a contract basis
2141 Redrying and stemming of tobacco—*mfg*
3494 Reducer returns, pipe: metal—*mfg*
3566 Reducers, speed—*mfg*
7991 Reducing facilities, physical fitness, without lodging
3566 Reduction gears and gear units for turbines, except automotive and aircraft—*mfg*
2519 Reed furniture—*mfg*
1499 Reed peat mining
2499 Reed ware, except furniture—*mfg*
3931 Reedboards, organ—*mfg*
3931 Reeds for musical instruments—*mfg*
3552 Reeds, loom—*mfg*
3569 Reels and racks, firehose—*mfg*
3499 Reels, cable: metal—*mfg*

2499 Reels, cloth winding: wood—*mfg*
3861 Reels, film—*mfg*
3949 Reels, fishing—*mfg*
2499 Reels, for drying clothes: wood—*mfg*
2499 Reels, plywood—*mfg*
2655 Reels, textile: fiber—mfpm—*mfg*
1741 Refactory brick construction—contractors
8111 Referees in bankruptcy
8322 Referral services for personal and social problems
4613 Refined petroleum pipelines
2062 Refineries, cane sugar—*mfg*
2911 Refineries, petroleum—*mfg*
2911 Refinery gas produced in petroleum refineries—*mfg*
3339 Refining of lead, primary—*mfg*
3339 Refining of nonferrous metal, primary: except copper and aluminum—*mfg*
3341 Refining of nonferrous metals and alloys, secondary—*mfg*
3339 Refining of zinc, primary—*mfg*
2231 Refinishing and sponging cloths: wool, mohair, and similar animal fibers, for the trade—*mfg*
2261 Refinishing and sponging cotton broadwoven fabrics for the trade—*mfg*
2262 Refinishing of manmade fiber and silk broadwoven fabrics—*mfg*
3825 Reflectometers, sliding shorts—*mfg*
3231 Reflector glass beads, for highway signs and other reflectors: made from purchased glass—*mfg*
3229 Reflectors for lighting equipment, glass: pressed or blown—*mfg*
3648 Reflectors for lighting equipment: metal—*mfg*
3647 Reflectors, clearance: vehicular—*mfg*
3827 Reflectors, optical—*mfg*
3827 Reflectors, searchlight—*mfg*
0851 Reforestation
9223 Reformatories—government
3823 Refractometers, industrial process type—*mfg*
3826 Refractometers, laboratory—*mfg*
3297 Refractories, castable: nonclay—*mfg*
3255 Refractories, clay—*mfg*
3297 Refractories, graphite: carbon bond or ceramic bond—*mfg*
3297 Refractories, nonclay—*mfg*
3255 Refractory cement and mortars, clay—*mfg*
3297 Refractory cement, nonclay—*mfg*
5085 Refractory material—wholesale
5812 Refreshment stands
4222 Refrigerated warehousing
1711 Refrigeration and freezer work—contractors

3585 Refrigeration compressors—*mfg*
3822 Refrigeration controls, pressure—*mfg*
3585 Refrigeration machinery and equipment, industrial—*mfg*
7623 Refrigeration repair service, electric
3822 Refrigeration thermostats—*mfg*
3822 Refrigeration/air-conditioning defrost controls—*mfg*
3632 Refrigerator cabinets, household—*mfg*
3229 Refrigerator dishes and jars, glass—*mfg*
3469 Refrigerator parts, porcelain enameled—*mfg*
7623 Refrigerator repair service, electric
5722 Refrigerators and related electric and gas appliances—retail
5078 Refrigerators, commercial: reach-in and walk-in—wholesale
5064 Refrigerators, household: electric and gas—wholesale
3632 Refrigerators, mechanical and absorption: household—*mfg*
3728 Refueling equipment, airplane: for use in flight—*mfg*
8322 Refugee services
4953 Refuse systems
4212 Refuse, local collecting and transporting: without disposal
2389 Regalia—mfpm—*mfg*
2823 Regenerated cellulose fibers—*mfg*
6099 Regional clearinghouse associations
8399 Regional planning organizations, for social services
8049 Registered nurses, offices of: except home care services
3446 Registers, air: metal—*mfg*
3579 Registers, autographic—*mfg*
3578 Registers, credit account—*mfg*
3829 Registers, fare: for streetcars, buses, etc.—*mfg*
3824 Registers, linear tallying—*mfg*
7361 Registries, nurses'
3541 Regrinding machines, crankshaft—*mfg*
9641 Regulation and inspection of agricultural products—government
9631 Regulation of utilities
3612 Regulators, feeder voltage (electric transformers)—*mfg*
3613 Regulators, power—*mfg*
3612 Regulators, transmission and distribution voltage—*mfg*
3694 Regulators, voltage: motor vehicle—*mfg*
8093 Rehabilitation centers, outpatient (medical treatment)
8361 Rehabilitation centers, residential: with health care incidental

8331 Rehabilitation counseling and training, vocational
8069 Rehabilitation hospitals: drug addiction and alcoholism
5051 Reinforcement mesh, wire—wholesale
3496 Reinforcing mesh concrete: made from purchased wire—*mfg*
6321 Reinsurance carriers, accident and health
6311 Reinsurance carriers, life
6311 Reinsurance, life
3625 Relays—*mfg*
3825 Relays, instrument: all types—*mfg*
5063 Relays—wholesale
8322 Relief services, temporary
5942 Religious book stores—retail
5999 Religious goods stores (other than books)—retail
8661 Religious instruction, provided by religious organizations
7812 Religious motion picture production
8661 Religious organizations
6732 Religious trusts, management of
2035 Relishes, fruit and vegetable—*mfg*
2834 Remedies, human and animal—*mfg*
5949 Remnant stores—retail
1541 Remodeling buildings, industrial and warehouse—general contractors
1542 Remodeling buildings, nonresidential: except industrial and warehouses—general contractors
1522 Remodeling buildings, residential: except single-family—general contractors
1521 Remodeling buildings, single-family—general contractors
7375 Remote data base information retrieval services
1389 Removal of condensate gasoline from field gathering lines: on a contract basis
1241 Removal of overburden for anthracite: on a contract basis
1241 Removal of overburden for bituminous coal: on a contract basis
1081 Removal of overburden for metal mining: on a contract basis
1481 Removal of overburden for nonmetallic minerals except fuels: on a contract basis
2077 Rendering plants, inedible grease and tallow—*mfg*
7699 Reneedling work
5199 Rennet—wholesale
1541 Renovating buildings, industrial and warehouse—general contractors
1542 Renovating buildings, nonresidential: except industrial and warehouses—general contractors

1522 Renovating buildings, residential: except single-family—general contractors
1521 Renovating buildings, single-family—general contractors
3999 Renovating feathers, for the trade—*mfg*
9651 Rent control agencies—government
6531 Rental agents for real estate
7359 Rental and leasing of dishes, silverware, and tables
7359 Rental and servicing of electronic equipment, except computers
7514 Rental of automobiles, without drivers
7999 Rental of beach chairs and accessories
7999 Rental of bicycles
8231 Rental of books
7359 Rental of coin-operated machines
4222 Rental of cold storage lockers
7374 Rental of computer time
7377 Rental of computers, except finance leasing or by the manufacturer
7353 Rental of construction equipment
7021 Rental of furnished rooms
7359 Rental of furniture
7999 Rental of golf carts
4119 Rental of hearses and limousines, with drivers
7819 Rental of motion picture equipment
7822 Rental of motion picture film
7359 Rental of oil field equipment
4119 Rental of passenger automobiles, with drivers
4741 Rental of railroad cars
7999 Rental of rowboats and canoes
7999 Rental of saddle horses
7922 Rental of theatrical scenery
7359 Rental of tools
7519 Rental of trailers
4212 Rental of trucks with drivers
7513 Rental of trucks, without drivers
7519 Renting automobile utility trailers
7519 Renting travel, camping, or recreational trailers
2211 Rep, cotton—*mfg*
5014 Repair materials, tire and tube—wholesale
7692 Repair of cracked castings (welding service)
7641 Repair of furniture upholstery
7219 Repair of furs and other garments for individuals
7699 Repair of optical instruments
7699 Repair of photographic equipment
1761 Repair of roofs—contractors
7699 Repair of service station equipment
7699 Repair of speedometers
7538 Repair shops, automotive: general

7217 Repairing and cleaning plants, rug and carpet
2789 Repairing books (bookbinding)—*mfg*
1541 Repairing buildings, industrial and warehouse—general contractors
1542 Repairing buildings, nonresidential: except industrial and warehouses—general contractors
1522 Repairing buildings, residential: except single-family—general contractors
1521 Repairing buildings, single-family—general contractors
1389 Repairing lease tanks, oil field: on a contract basis
3661 Repeater equipment, telephone and telegraph—*mfg*
7922 Repertory or stock companies, theatrical
5065 Replacement parts, electronic—wholesale
7389 Repossession service
6099 Representative offices of foreign banks, excluding agents and branches
8422 Reptile exhibits
7379 Requirements analysis, computer hardware
2421 Resawing lumber into smaller dimensions—*mfg*
8731 Research and development of computer and related hardware
3721 Research and development on aircraft by the manufacturer—*mfg*
3724 Research and development on aircraft engines and engine parts by the manufacturer—*mfg*
3728 Research and development on aircraft parts and auxiliary equipment by the manufacturer—*mfg*
3769 Research and development on guided missile and space vehicle components, by the manufacturer—*mfg*
3764 Research and development on guided missile and space vehicle engines, by the manufacturer—*mfg*
3761 Research and development on guided missiles and space vehicles, by the manufacturer—*mfg*
8731 Research and development, physical and biological: commercial
8733 Research, noncommercial
8732 Research: economic, sociological, and educational—commercial
2833 Reserpines—*mfg*
7389 Reservation service, hotel
1629 Reservoir construction—general contractors
7041 Residence clubs operated by organizations for members only

2044 Rice, brown—*mfg*
5149 Rice, polished—wholesale
2099 Rice, uncooked: packaged with other ingredients—*mfg*
5153 Rice, unpolished—wholesale
2044 Rice, vitamin and mineral enriched—*mfg*
2241 Rickrack braid—*mfg*
3599 Riddles, sand (hand sifting or screening apparatus)—*mfg*
7999 Riding academies and schools
5699 Riding apparel stores—retail
2329 Riding clothes: men's and boys'—mfpm—*mfg*
7997 Riding clubs, membership
3199 Riding crops—*mfg*
5941 Riding goods and equipment—retail
2339 Riding habits: women's, misses', and juniors'—mfpm—*mfg*
7999 Riding stables
2899 Rifle bore cleaning compounds—*mfg*
3541 Rifle working machines (machine tools)—*mfg*
3484 Rifles and parts, 30 mm. (or 1.18 inch) or less—*mfg*
3841 Rifles for propelling hypodermics into animals—*mfg*
3484 Rifles, high compression pneumatic: 30 mm. (or 1.18 inch) or less—*mfg*
3489 Rifles, recoilless—*mfg*
3944 Rifles, toy—*mfg*
3484 Rifles: BB and pellet—*mfg*
3484 Rifles: pneumatic, spring loaded, and compressed air—except toy—*mfg*
1389 Rig building, repairing, and dismantling: on a contract basis
3469 Rigidizing metal—*mfg*
3714 Rims, wheel: motor vehicle—*mfg*
3961 Rings, finger: gold-plated wire—*mfg*
3255 Rings, glasshouse: clay—*mfg*
3592 Rings, piston—*mfg*
3911 Rings, precious metal—*mfg*
1429 Riprap quarrying, except limestone or granite
4449 River freight transportation, except on the St. Lawrence Seaway
7999 River rafting, operation of
3546 Riveting hammers—*mfg*
3542 Riveting machines—*mfg*
3452 Rivets, metal—*mfg*
3089 Rivets, plastics—*mfg*
2879 Roach poisons—*mfg*
7922 Road companies, theatrical
3531 Road construction and maintenance machinery—*mfg*
5082 Road construction and maintenance machinery—wholesale

1611 Road construction, except elevated—general contractors
2951 Road materials, bituminous: not made in petroleum refineries—*mfg*
2911 Road materials, bituminous: produced in petroleum refineries—*mfg*
3711 Road oilers (motor vehicles)—*mfg*
2911 Road oils, produced in petroleum refineries—*mfg*
7549 Road service, automotive
4785 Roads, toll: operation of
3634 Roasters, electric—*mfg*
0251 Roasting chickens, raising of
3556 Roasting machinery: coffee, peanut, etc.—*mfg*
5137 Robes and gowns: women's and children's—wholesale
2369 Robes, lounging: children's—mfpm—*mfg*
2369 Robes, lounging: girls', children's, and infants'—mfpm—*mfg*
2384 Robes, lounging: men's, boys', and women's—mfpm—*mfg*
2253 Robes, lounging—mitse—*mfg*
5136 Robes, men's and boys'—wholesale
3535 Robotic conveyors for general industrial use—*mfg*
3541 Robots for drilling and cutting—machine type, metalworking—*mfg*
3569 Robots for general industrial use—*mfg*
3541 Robots for grinding, polishing, and deburring—metalworking—*mfg*
3542 Robots for metal forming: e.g., pressing, hammering, extruding—*mfg*
3563 Robots for spraying, painting—industrial—*mfg*
3548 Robots for welding, soldering, or brazing—*mfg*
3559 Robots, plastics: for molding and forming—*mfg*
**** Robots—code according to primary function
5999 Rock and stone specimens—retail
3531 Rock crushing machinery, portable—*mfg*
3532 Rock crushing machinery, stationary—*mfg*
3532 Rock drills, portable—*mfg*
1629 Rock removal, underwater—contractors
1479 Rock salt mining
3275 Rock, gypsum—*mfg*
2512 Rockers, upholstered on wood frames—*mfg*
2511 Rockers, wood: except upholstered—*mfg*
2869 Rocket engine fuel, organic—*mfg*
3489 Rocket launchers, hand-held—*mfg*
3724 Rocket motors, aircraft—*mfg*
3764 Rocket motors, guided missile—*mfg*
3443 Rocket transportation casings—*mfg*

2046 Root starch, edible—*mfg*
3552 Rope and cordage machines—*mfg*
2621 Rope and jute wrapping paper—mitse—*mfg*
3429 Rope fittings—*mfg*
3292 Rope, asbestos—*mfg*
2298 Rope, except asbestos and wire—*mfg*
5085 Rope, except wire rope—wholesale
3496 Rope, uninsulated wire: made from purchased wire—*mfg*
5051 Rope, wire: not insulated—wholesale
3961 Rosaries and other small religious articles, except precious metal—*mfg*
3911 Rosaries and other small religious articles, precious metal—*mfg*
1094 Roscoelite (vanadium hydromica) mining
0181 Rose growers
2821 Rosin modified resins—*mfg*
2899 Rosin sizes—*mfg*
2861 Rosin, produced by distillation of pine gum or pine wood—*mfg*
5169 Rosin—wholesale
3621 Rotary converters (electrical equipment)—*mfg*
3523 Rotary hoes (agricultural machinery)—*mfg*
2754 Rotary photogravure printing—*mfg*
3549 Rotary slitters (metalworking machines)—*mfg*
3545 Rotary tables, indexing—*mfg*
3824 Rotary type meters, consumption registering—*mfg*
3351 Rotating bands, copper and copper alloy—*mfg*
2879 Rotenone bearing preparations—*mfg*
2879 Rotenone concentrates—*mfg*
3728 Roto-blades for helicopters—*mfg*
2621 Rotogravure paper—mitse—*mfg*
2754 Rotogravure printing—*mfg*
2796 Rotogravure printing plates and cylinders—*mfg*
3621 Rotor retainers and housings—*mfg*
3621 Rotors for motors—*mfg*
3524 Rototillers (garden machinery)—*mfg*
2844 Rouge, cosmetic—*mfg*
3291 Rouge, polishing—*mfg*
3523 Roughage mills (agricultural machinery)—*mfg*
2449 Round stave baskets, for fruits and vegetables—*mfg*
2426 Rounds or rungs, ladder and furniture: hardwood—*mfg*
3312 Rounds, tube—*mfg*
5099 Roundwood—wholesale
1389 Roustabout service: on a contract basis
3553 Routing machines, woodworking—*mfg*
2299 Roves, flax and jute—*mfg*

3552 Roving machines (textile machinery)—*mfg*
7999 Rowboat rental
3732 Rowboats, building and repairing—*mfg*
1521 Rowhouse (single-family) construction—general contractors
3949 Rowing machines—*mfg*
6792 Royalty companies, oil
6289 Royalty owners protective associations
2891 Rubber cement—*mfg*
1455 Rubber clay mining
3567 Rubber curing ovens—*mfg*
3061 Rubber goods, mechanical: molded, extruded, and lathe-cut—*mfg*
5085 Rubber goods, mechanical—wholesale
5122 Rubber goods, medical—wholesale
3069 Rubber heels, soles, and soling strips—*mfg*
0831 Rubber plantations
2869 Rubber processing chemicals, organic: accelerators and antioxidants—*mfg*
2899 Rubber processing preparations—*mfg*
3559 Rubber products machinery—*mfg*
5093 Rubber scrap—wholesale
2891 Rubber sealing compounds, synthetic—*mfg*
5999 Rubber stamp stores—retail
2241 Rubber thread and yarns, fabric covered—*mfg*
3559 Rubber working machinery—*mfg*
5199 Rubber, crude—wholesale
3069 Rubber, reclaimed and reworked by manufacturing processes—*mfg*
2822 Rubber, synthetic—*mfg*
3069 Rubber-covered motor mounting rings (rubber bonded)—*mfg*
3069 Rubberbands—*mfg*
3069 Rubberized fabrics—*mfg*
1499 Rubbing stone quarrying
3291 Rubbing stones, artificial—*mfg*
4953 Rubbish collection and disposal
1411 Rubble mining
2819 Rubidium metal—*mfg*
1499 Ruby mining
3728 Rudders, aircraft—*mfg*
2395 Ruffling, for the trade—*mfg*
3069 Rug backing compounds, latex—*mfg*
7389 Rug binding for the trade
3582 Rug cleaning, drying, and napping machines: commercial laundry—*mfg*
7217 Rug cleaning, dyeing, and repairing plants
7699 Rug repair shops, not combined with cleaning
5713 Rug stores—retail
2842 Rug, upholstery, and drycleaning detergents and spotters—*mfg*
2299 Rugbacking, jute or other fiber—*mfg*
2273 Rugs, except rubber or plastics—*mfg*
5023 Rugs—wholesale

7319 Samples, distribution of
7389 Sampling of commodities, not connected with transportation
5211 Sand and gravel dealers—retail
3531 Sand mixers—*mfg*
3599 Sand riddles (hand sifting or screening apparatus)—*mfg*
5032 Sand, construction—wholesale
3149 Sandals, children's: except rubber—*mfg*
3021 Sandals, rubber—*mfg*
1799 Sandblasting of building exteriors—contractors
3471 Sandblasting of metal parts, for the trade—*mfg*
3546 Sanders, hand: electric—*mfg*
3714 Sanders, motor vehicle safety—*mfg*
3553 Sanding machines, except portable floor sanders (woodworking machinery)—*mfg*
3589 Sanding machines, floor—*mfg*
3291 Sandpaper—*mfg*
3554 Sandpaper manufacturing machines—*mfg*
1499 Sandstone, bituminous—quarrying
1411 Sandstone, dimension—quarrying
1429 Sandstone, except bituminous: crushed and broken—quarrying
5812 Sandwich bars or shops
2022 Sandwich spreads, cheese—*mfg*
2013 Sandwich spreads, meat—mfpm—*mfg*
2035 Sandwich spreads, salad dressing base—*mfg*
3634 Sandwich toasters and grills, household: electric—*mfg*
2099 Sandwiches, assembled and packaged: for wholesale market—*mfg*
5149 Sandwiches—wholesale
3842 Sanitary aprons—*mfg*
9631 Sanitary districts—nonoperating
9511 Sanitary engineering agencies—government
5113 Sanitary food containers: paper, paperboard, and disposable plastics—wholesale
2676 Sanitary napkins—mfpm—*mfg*
2656 Sanitary paper food containers, liquid tight—mfpm—*mfg*
3432 Sanitary pipe fittings—*mfg*
5074 Sanitary ware, china or enameled iron—wholesale
3431 Sanitary ware: bathtubs, lavoratories, and sinks—metal—*mfg*
2842 Sanitation preparations—*mfg*
5169 Sanitation preparations—wholesale
1499 Sapphire mining
2221 Saran broadwoven fabrics—*mfg*
2824 Saran fibers—*mfg*
2077 Sardine oil—*mfg*

2091 Sardines, canned—*mfg*
3321 Sash balances, cast iron—*mfg*
3495 Sash balances, spring—*mfg*
3442 Sash, door and window: metal—*mfg*
2431 Sash, door and window: wood and covered wood—*mfg*
5211 Sash, storm: wood or metal—retail
3161 Satchels, regardless of material—*mfg*
2211 Sateens, cotton—*mfg*
4899 Satellite earth stations
3679 Satellite home antennas—*mfg*
4841 Satellite master antenna systems (SMATV) services
4899 Satellite or missile tracking stations, operated on a contract basis
3663 Satellites, communications—*mfg*
2816 Satin white pigments—*mfg*
2221 Satins—*mfg*
3612 Saturable reactors—*mfg*
2621 Saturated felts—mitse—*mfg*
2099 Sauce mixes, dry—*mfg*
3089 Saucers, plastics: except foam—*mfg*
2035 Sauces, meat (seasoning): except tomato and dry—*mfg*
2035 Sauces, seafood: except tomato and dry—*mfg*
2033 Sauces, spaghetti—*mfg*
2033 Sauces, tomato-based—*mfg*
2035 Sauces, vegetable: except tomato and dry—*mfg*
5149 Sauces—wholesale
2035 Sauerkraut, bulk—*mfg*
2033 Sauerkraut, canned—*mfg*
3634 Sauna heaters, electric—*mfg*
5074 Sauna heaters, except electric—wholesale
2452 Sauna rooms, prefabricated: wood—*mfg*
2013 Sausage casings, collagen—*mfg*
3089 Sausage casings, synthetic—*mfg*
5149 Sausage casings—wholesale
3556 Sausage stuffers—*mfg*
2013 Sausages—mfpm—*mfg*
2011 Sausages—mitse—*mfg*
6035 Saving banks, Federal
6035 Savings and loan associations, federally chartered
6036 Savings and loan associations, not federally chartered
6036 Savings banks, State: not federally chartered
3425 Saw blades, for hand or power saws—*mfg*
5072 Saw blades—wholesale
2411 Saw logs—*mfg*
7699 Saw sharpening and repair shops
2421 Sawdust and shavings—*mfg*
2499 Sawdust, reground—*mfg*
5199 Sawdust—wholesale

3541 Sawing and cutoff machines (metalworking machinery)—*mfg*

3553 Sawmill machines—*mfg*

2421 Sawmills, custom—*mfg*

2421 Sawmills, except special product mills—*mfg*

2429 Sawmills, special product: except lumber and veneer mills—*mfg*

3425 Saws, hand: metalworking or woodworking—*mfg*

3546 Saws, portable hand held: power-driven—woodworking or metalworking—*mfg*

3553 Saws, power: bench and table (woodworking machinery)—except portable—*mfg*

3541 Saws, power: metal cutting—*mfg*

3841 Saws, surgical—*mfg*

3931 Saxophones and parts—*mfg*

1799 Scaffolding construction—contractors

5082 Scaffolding—wholesale

3446 Scaffolds, metal (mobile or stationary)—*mfg*

2499 Scaffolds, wood—*mfg*

7699 Scale repair service

3579 Scalers for gummed tape: hand—*mfg*

3829 Scalers, nuclear radiation—*mfg*

7299 Scales, coin-operated: operation of

3596 Scales, except laboratory—*mfg*

5046 Scales, except laboratory—wholesale

3545 Scales, measuring (machinists' precision tools)—*mfg*

7699 Scaling, ship—contractors

2395 Scalloping, for the trade—*mfg*

7299 Scalp treatment service

2819 Scandium—*mfg*

3553 Scarfing machines (woodworking machinery)—*mfg*

2253 Scarfs—mitse—*mfg*

3531 Scarifiers, road—*mfg*

2865 Scarlet 2 R lake—*mfg*

2339 Scarves, hoods, and headbands: women's, misses', and juniors'—mfpm—*mfg*

5136 Scarves, men's and boys'—wholesale

2392 Scarves: e.g., table, dresser—mfpm—*mfg*

2323 Scarves: men's and boys'—mfpm—*mfg*

5137 Scarves: women's, children's and infant's—wholesale

2273 Scatter rugs, except rubber or plastics—*mfg*

5093 Scavengering—wholesale

7922 Scenery design, theatrical

3999 Scenery for theaters, opera houses, halls, and schools—*mfg*

7922 Scenery, rental: theatrical

7999 Scenic railroads for amusement

2759 Schedules, transportation: except lithographed or gravure—*mfg*

2754 Schedules, transportation: gravure printing—*mfg*

2752 Schedules, transportation: lithographed—*mfg*

1061 Scheelite mining

2397 Schiffli machine embroideries—*mfg*

1411 Schist, dimension—quarrying

1542 School building construction—general contractors

4151 School buses

5021 School desks—wholesale

2531 School furniture—*mfg*

2531 School furniture, except stone and concrete—*mfg*

7221 School photographers

5943 School supplies—retail

7999 Schools and camps, sports instructional

8211 Schools for the physically handicapped, elementary and secondary

8211 Schools for the retarded

8249 Schools, correspondence: including branch offices and solicitors

7911 Schools, dance: including children's, and professionals'

8211 Schools, elementary and secondary

7999 Schools, riding

8249 Schools, vocational, except high schools, data processing, or business

3674 Schottky diodes—*mfg*

3944 Science kits: microscopes, chemistry sets, and natural science sets—*mfg*

3231 Scientific apparatus glass, made from purchased glass—*mfg*

3231 Scientific glassware, made from purchased glass—*mfg*

3229 Scientific glassware, pressed or blown: made in glassmaking plants—*mfg*

7699 Scientific instrument repair, except electric

5049 Scientific instruments—wholesale

8621 Scientific membership associations

8733 Scientific research, noncommercial

3829 Scintillation detectors—*mfg*

3634 Scissors, electric—*mfg*

3421 Scissors, hand—*mfg*

3421 Scissors: barbers', manicure, pedicure, tailors' and household—*mfg*

3949 Scoops, crab and fish—*mfg*

3423 Scoops, hand: metal—*mfg*

2499 Scoops, wood—*mfg*

3944 Scooters, children's—*mfg*

3993 Scoreboards, electric—*mfg*

1499 Scoria mining

2841 Scouring compounds—*mfg*

3559 Scouring machines, tannery—*mfg*

2299 Scouring of wool, mohair, and similar fibers—*mfg*
3291 Scouring pads, soap impregnated—*mfg*
3731 Scows, building and repairing—*mfg*
5093 Scrap and waste materials—wholesale
7389 Scrap steel cutting on a contract or fee basis
5093 Scrap, rubber—wholesale
2782 Scrapbooks—*mfg*
5112 Scrapbooks—wholesale
3532 Scraper loaders, underground—*mfg*
3531 Scrapers, construction—*mfg*
3423 Scrapers, woodworking: hand—*mfg*
2013 Scrapple—mfpm—*mfg*
3531 Screeds and screeding machines—*mfg*
3442 Screen doors, metal—*mfg*
2261 Screen printing of cotton broadwoven fabrics—*mfg*
2262 Screen printing of manmade fiber and silk broadwoven fabrics—*mfg*
2759 Screen printing on glass, plastics, paper, and metal, including highway signs—*mfg*
**** Screen printing, textiles—classify on basis of fiber
2893 Screen process ink—*mfg*
3531 Screeners, portable—*mfg*
3532 Screeners, stationary—*mfg*
3569 Screening and sifting machines for general industrial use—*mfg*
5084 Screening machinery and equipment, industrial—wholesale
1499 Screening peat
1231 Screening plants, anthracite
1221 Screening plants, bituminous coal
3089 Screening, window: plastics—*mfg*
3496 Screening, woven wire: made from purchased wire—*mfg*
3442 Screens, door and window: metal frame—*mfg*
2431 Screens, door and window: wood—*mfg*
2511 Screens, privacy: wood—*mfg*
3861 Screens, projection—*mfg*
3953 Screens, textile printing—*mfg*
3541 Screw and nut slotting machines—*mfg*
3423 Screw drivers—*mfg*
3452 Screw eyes, metal—*mfg*
3089 Screw eyes, plastics—*mfg*
3452 Screw hooks—*mfg*
**** Screw machine production of one product—code the product
3451 Screw machine products: produced on a job or order basis—*mfg*
3451 Screw machine products: produced on a job or order basis—*mfg*
3541 Screw machines, automatic—*mfg*

3366 Screw propellers: cast brass, bronze, copper, and copper base—*mfg*
3549 Screwdowns and boxes—*mfg*
3549 Screwdriving machines—*mfg*
3841 Screws, bone—*mfg*
3569 Screws, jack—*mfg*
3452 Screws, metal—*mfg*
2211 Scrim, cotton—*mfg*
3443 Scroll casings—*mfg*
2211 Scrub cloths—mitse—*mfg*
3589 Scrubbing machines—*mfg*
3089 Scrubbing pads, plastics—*mfg*
7999 Scuba and skin diving instruction
3949 Scuba diving equipment, except clothing—*mfg*
8999 Sculptors' studios
3299 Sculptures, architectural: gypsum, clay, or papier-mache—factory production only—*mfg*
3423 Scythes—*mfg*
1499 Scythestone quarrying
3291 Scythestones, artificial—*mfg*
0912 Sea herring, catching of
0919 Sea urchins, catching of
5421 Seafood markets—retail
2091 Seafood products, canned and cured—*mfg*
2092 Seafoods, fresh and frozen—*mfg*
5142 Seafoods, frozen: packaged—wholesale
5146 Seafoods, not canned or frozen packaged—wholesale
3953 Seal presses, notary, hand—*mfg*
5169 Sealants—wholesale
2851 Sealers, wood—*mfg*
2891 Sealing compounds for pipe threads and joints—*mfg*
2891 Sealing compounds, synthetic rubber and plastics—*mfg*
2295 Sealing or insulating tape for pipe, fiberglass coated with tar or asphalt—*mfg*
2891 Sealing wax—*mfg*
3953 Seals, corporation—*mfg*
5085 Seals, gaskets, and packing—wholesale
3953 Seals, hand (dies)—*mfg*
3679 Seals, hermetic: for electronic equipment—*mfg*
2752 Seals, lithographed—*mfg*
2754 Seals: gravure printing—*mfg*
2759 Seals: printing except lithographic or gravure—*mfg*
3548 Seam welding apparatus, gas and electric—*mfg*
3827 Searchlight mirrors and reflectors—*mfg*
3648 Searchlights—*mfg*
7011 Seasonal hotels
2033 Seasonings (prepared sauces), tomato—*mfg*

8322 Senior citizens associations
3861 Sensitometers, photographic—*mfg*
3845 Sentinel, cardiac—*mfg*
3532 Separating machinery, mineral—*mfg*
3569 Separators for steam, gas, vapor, and air (machinery)—*mfg*
2499 Separators, battery: wood—*mfg*
3069 Separators, battery: rubber—*mfg*
3523 Separators, cream: farm—*mfg*
3556 Separators, cream: industrial—*mfg*
3523 Separators, grain and berry: farm—*mfg*
3443 Separators, industrial process: metal plate—*mfg*
7699 Septic tank cleaning service
1711 Septic tank installation—contractors
3272 Septic tanks, concrete—*mfg*
3443 Septic tanks, metal plate—*mfg*
3089 Septic tanks, plastics—*mfg*
5039 Septic tanks—wholesale
3822 Sequencing controls for electric heat—*mfg*
2231 Serges of wool, mohair, and similar animal fibers—*mfg*
2221 Serges, manmade fiber—*mfg*
3629 Series capacitors, except electronic—*mfg*
2836 Serobacterins—*mfg*
1429 Serpentine, crushed and broken—quarrying
1411 Serpentine, dimension—quarrying
2836 Serums, except in vitro and in vivo—*mfg*
8221 Service academies (college)
1799 Service and repair of broadcasting stations—contractors
2339 Service apparel, washable: e.g., nurses', maids', waitresses', laboratory uniforms: women's, misses', and juniors'—mfpm
2326 Service apparel, washable: men's—mfpm—*mfg*
7374 Service bureaus, computer
5063 Service entrance equipment, electrical—wholesale
8322 Service leagues
7299 Service machine operation-coin-operated
7349 Service station cleaning and degreasing service
1542 Service station construction—general contractors
1799 Service station equipment installation, maintenance, and repair—contractors
5013 Service station equipment, automobile—wholesale
5541 Service stations, gasoline—retail
1381 Service well drilling: on a contract basis
3589 Servicing machines, coin-operated: except drycleaning and laundry—*mfg*
1389 Servicing oil and gas wells on a contract basis

1781 Servicing water wells—contractors
2514 Serving carts, household: metal—*mfg*
3621 Servomotors—*mfg*
8322 Settlement houses
2631 Setup boxboard—mitse—*mfg*
5113 Setup paperboard boxes—wholesale
1623 Sewage collection and disposal line construction—general contractors
3589 Sewage treatment equipment—*mfg*
1629 Sewage treatment plant construction—general contractors
7699 Sewer cleaning and rodding
3589 Sewer cleaning equipment, power—*mfg*
1623 Sewer construction—general contractors
1711 Sewer hookups and connections for buildings—contractors
3259 Sewer liner brick, vitrified clay—*mfg*
3259 Sewer pipe and fittings, clay—*mfg*
3321 Sewer pipe, cast iron—*mfg*
5032 Sewer pipe, clay—wholesale
3272 Sewer pipe, concrete—*mfg*
4952 Sewerage systems
5131 Sewing accessories—wholesale
3172 Sewing cases, regardless of material—*mfg*
3999 Sewing kits, novelty: other than sewing cases and cabinets—*mfg*
2517 Sewing machine cabinets and cases, wood—*mfg*
7699 Sewing machine repair shops
5722 Sewing machine stores—retail
3639 Sewing machines and attachments, household—*mfg*
3559 Sewing machines and attachments, industrial—*mfg*
5064 Sewing machines, household: electric—wholesale
5084 Sewing machines, industrial—wholesale
5949 Sewing supplies—retail
5131 Sewing thread, except industrial—wholesale
2284 Sewing thread: cotton, silk, manmade fibers, and wool—*mfg*
3812 Sextants, except surveying—*mfg*
3829 Sextants, surveying—*mfg*
2295 Shade cloth, coated or impregnated—*mfg*
2211 Shade cloth, window: cotton—*mfg*
2591 Shade pulls, window—*mfg*
2394 Shades, canvas—*mfg*
3999 Shades, lamp and candle: except glass and metal—*mfg*
3229 Shades, lamp: glass—*mfg*
3645 Shades, lamp: metal—*mfg*
2591 Shades, porch: made of wood slats—*mfg*
2591 Shades, window: except canvas—*mfg*
1481 Shaft sinking for nonmetallic minerals, except fuels: on a contract basis

3496 Shelving without rigid framework, made from purchased wire—*mfg*

2542 Shelving, office and store: except wood—*mfg*

2541 Shelving, office and store: wood—*mfg*

5046 Shelving—wholesale

3479 Sherardizing of metals and metal products, for the trade—*mfg*

3567 Sherardizing ovens—*mfg*

2024 Sherbets and ices—*mfg*

9221 Sheriffs' offices

4492 Shifting of floating equipment within harbors

3499 Shims, metal—*mfg*

2411 Shingle bolts, wood: hewn—*mfg*

2429 Shingle mills, wood—*mfg*

3292 Shingles, asbestos cement—*mfg*

2952 Shingles, asphalt or tar saturated felt: strip and individual—*mfg*

5033 Shingles, except wood—wholesale

2429 Shingles, wood: sawed or hand split—*mfg*

5031 Shingles, wood—wholesale

7699 Ship boiler and tank cleaning and repair—contractors

3531 Ship capstans—*mfg*

4499 Ship cleaning, except hold cleaning

3531 Ship cranes and derricks—*mfg*

7361 Ship crew registries

2599 Ship furniture—*mfg*

4491 Ship hold cleaning

1751 Ship joinery—contractors

3999 Ship models, except toy and hobby models—*mfg*

1721 Ship painting—contractors

3366 Ship propellers: cast brass, bronze, copper and copper base—*mfg*

4499 Ship registers: survey and classification of ships and marine equipment

7699 Ship scaling—contractors

3441 Ship sections, prefabricated metal—*mfg*

3531 Ship winches—*mfg*

3357 Shipboard cable, nonferrous—*mfg*

3731 Shipbuilding and repairing—*mfg*

8611 Shipping and steamship company associations

2674 Shipping bags or sacks, including multiwall and heavy duty—mfpm—*mfg*

3412 Shipping barrels, kegs, and pails: metal—light and heavy types—*mfg*

2449 Shipping cases and drums, wood: wirebound—*mfg*

2441 Shipping cases, wood: nailed or lock corner—*mfg*

4731 Shipping documents preparation

2655 Shipping hampers, vulcanized fiber—mfpm—*mfg*

3086 Shipping pads, plastics foam—*mfg*

2621 Shipping sack paper—mitse—*mfg*

2674 Shipping sacks, paper—mfpm—*mfg*

5113 Shipping supplies, paper and disposable plastics (e.g., cartons, gummed tapes)—wholesale

5088 Ships—wholesale

2329 Shirt and slack suits, nontailored: men's and boys'—mfpm—*mfg*

2396 Shirt linings—*mfg*

3965 Shirt studs, except precious metal and precious or semiprecious stones—*mfg*

3911 Shirt studs, precious metal and precious or semiprecious stones—*mfg*

7213 Shirt supply service

2211 Shirting fabrics, cotton—*mfg*

2221 Shirting fabrics, manmade fiber and silk—*mfg*

5699 Shirts, custom made—retail

5136 Shirts, men's and boys'—wholesale

2361 Shirts, outerwear: girls', children's, and infants'—mfpm—*mfg*

2331 Shirts, outerwear: women's, misses', and juniors'—mfpm—*mfg*

2321 Shirts, outerwear; except work shirts: men's and boys'—mfpm—*mfg*

2253 Shirts, outerwear—mitse—*mfg*

2322 Shirts, underwear: men's and boys'—mfpm—*mfg*

2254 Shirts, underwear—mitse—*mfg*

2326 Shirts, work: men's and boys'—mfpm—*mfg*

3714 Shock absorbers, motor vehicle—*mfg*

3542 Shock wave metal forming machines—*mfg*

5139 Shoe accessories—wholesale

2392 Shoe bags—mfpm—*mfg*

2631 Shoe board—mitse—*mfg*

2842 Shoe cleaners and polishes—*mfg*

3131 Shoe cut stock—*mfg*

3131 Shoe cut stock and findings—*mfg*

7389 Shoe designers

2499 Shoe display forms—regardless of material—*mfg*

3149 Shoe dyeing for the trade—*mfg*

7251 Shoe dyeing shops

2211 Shoe fabrics—mitse—*mfg*

3131 Shoe heels, finished wood or leather—*mfg*

3089 Shoe heels, plastics—*mfg*

3069 Shoe heels: rubber, composition, and fiber—*mfg*

5087 Shoe heels—wholesale

3161 Shoe kits, regardless of material—*mfg*

2241 Shoe laces, except leather—*mfg*

3131 Shoe laces, leather—*mfg*

3131 Shoe linings, leather—*mfg*

2259 Shoe linings— mitse—*mfg*

2231 Shrinking cloth of wool, mohair, and similar animal fibers: for the trade—*mfg*
2261 Shrinking cotton broadwoven fabrics for the trade—*mfg*
2262 Shrinking manmade fiber and silk broadwoven fabrics for the trade—*mfg*
7389 Shrinking textiles for tailors and dressmakers
0181 Shrubberies, except forest shrubbery: growing of
3825 Shunts, instrument—*mfg*
3861 Shutters, camera—*mfg*
3442 Shutters, door and window: metal—*mfg*
2431 Shutters, door and window: wood and covered wood—*mfg*
3089 Shutters, plastics—*mfg*
2426 Shuttle blocks: hardwood—*mfg*
3532 Shuttle cars, underground—*mfg*
3552 Shuttles for textile weaving—*mfg*
6321 Sick benefit associations, mutual
3423 Sickles, hand—*mfg*
1011 Siderite mining
1771 Sidewalk construction, except public—contractors
1611 Sidewalk construction, public—contractors
3292 Siding, asbestos cement—*mfg*
2952 Siding, asphalt brick—*mfg*
2421 Siding, dressed lumber—*mfg*
5033 Siding, except wood—wholesale
2621 Siding, insulating: paper, impregnated or not—mitse—*mfg*
2952 Siding, insulating: impregnated—mfpm—*mfg*
3089 Siding, plastics—*mfg*
3272 Siding, precast stone—*mfg*
3444 Siding, sheet metal—*mfg*
1761 Siding—contractors
1479 Sienna mining
2816 Siennas—*mfg*
3496 Sieves, made from purchased wire—*mfg*
3569 Sifting and screening machines for general industrial use—*mfg*
3556 Sifting machines, food—*mfg*
3827 Sighting and fire control equipment, optical—*mfg*
3484 Sights, gun: except optical 30 mm. (or 1.18 inch) or less—*mfg*
3489 Sights, gun: except optical—more than 30 mm. (or more than 1.18 inch)—*mfg*
3827 Sights, telescopic—*mfg*
4522 Sightseeing airplane services
4489 Sightseeing boats
4119 Sightseeing buses
7389 Sign painting and lettering shops
3357 Signal and control cable, nonferrous—*mfg*
2899 Signal flares, marine—*mfg*

3825 Signal generators and averages—*mfg*
3669 Signaling apparatus, electric—*mfg*
5063 Signaling equipment, electrical—wholesale
3612 Signaling transformers, electric—*mfg*
3714 Signals, directional: motor vehicle—*mfg*
3669 Signals: railway, highway, and traffic—electric—*mfg*
2499 Signboards, wood—*mfg*
5046 Signs, electrical—wholesale
5099 Signs, except electric—wholesale
3993 Signs, not made in custom sign painting shops—*mfg*
2211 Silesia, cotton—*mfg*
2819 Silica gel—*mfg*
1446 Silica mining
1446 Silica sand mining
2819 Silica, amorphous—*mfg*
2819 Silicofluorides—*mfg*
3291 Silicon carbide abrasives—*mfg*
3339 Silicon refining, primary (over 99 percent pure)—*mfg*
3674 Silicon wafers, chemically doped—*mfg*
3339 Silicon, epitaxial (silicon alloy)—*mfg*
3339 Silicon, pure—*mfg*
3295 Silicon, ultra high purity: treated purchased materials—*mfg*
2821 Silicone fluid solution (fluid for sonar transducers)—*mfg*
2821 Silicone resins—*mfg*
2822 Silicone rubbers—*mfg*
2869 Silicones—*mfg*
0279 Silk (raw) production and silkworm farms
2262 Silk broadwoven fabric finishing—*mfg*
2221 Silk broadwoven fabrics—*mfg*
2241 Silk narrow fabrics—*mfg*
5131 Silk piece goods—wholesale
7336 Silk screen design
2396 Silk screening on fabric articles—*mfg*
3552 Silk screens for the textile industry—*mfg*
2284 Silk thread—*mfg*
2282 Silk throwing, twisting, winding, or spooling—*mfg*
2281 Silk yarn, spinning—*mfg*
5199 Silk yarns—wholesale
5159 Silk, raw—wholesale
1459 Sillimanite mining
3272 Sills, concrete—*mfg*
1542 Silo construction, agricultural—general contractors
3523 Silo fillers (agricultural machinery)—*mfg*
3272 Silo staves, cast stone—*mfg*
2431 Silo staves, wood—*mfg*
2421 Silo stock, wood: sawed—*mfg*
3251 Silo tile—*mfg*
3523 Silo unloaders—*mfg*
3531 Silos, cement (batch plant)—*mfg*

7319   Sky writing
3211   Skylight glass—*mfg*
1761   Skylight installation—contractors
3444   Skylights, sheet metal—*mfg*
3334   Slabs, aluminum: primary—*mfg*
3331   Slabs, copper: primary—*mfg*
3272   Slabs, crossing: concrete—*mfg*
3339   Slabs, primary: nonferrous metals, except copper and aluminum—*mfg*
3312   Slabs, steel—*mfg*
2325   Slacks (separate): men's and boys'—mfpm—*mfg*
2325   Slacks, jean-cut casual: men's and boys'—mfpm—*mfg*
2369   Slacks: girls' and children's—mfpm—*mfg*
2339   Slacks: women's, misses', and juniors'—mfpm—*mfg*
2253   Slacks—mitse—*mfg*
3531   Slag mixers—*mfg*
3295   Slag, crushed or ground—*mfg*
3552   Slashing machines (textile machinery)—*mfg*
3281   Slate and slate products—*mfg*
1429   Slate, crushed and broken—quarrying
1411   Slate, dimension—quarrying
2441   Slats, trunk: wood—*mfg*
2048   Slaughtering of animals, except for human consumption—*mfg*
2011   Slaughtering plants: except animals not for human consumption—*mfg*
0751   Slaughtering, custom: for individuals
2099   Slaw, cole: in bulk—*mfg*
3423   Sledges (handtools)—*mfg*
3944   Sleds, children's—*mfg*
3429   Sleeper mechanisms, for convertible beds—*mfg*
2399   Sleeping bags—*mfg*
4789   Sleeping car and other passenger car operations, not performed by railroads
3743   Sleeping cars, railroad—*mfg*
3069   Sleeves, pump: rubber—*mfg*
3199   Sleeves, welders': leather—*mfg*
2295   Sleeving, textile: saturated—*mfg*
7991   Slenderizing salons
3556   Slicing machines, fruit and vegetable: commercial types—*mfg*
2241   Slide fastener tapes—*mfg*
3965   Slide fasteners (zippers)—*mfg*
7336   Slide film producers
3999   Slides and exhibits for classroom use, preparation of—*mfg*
3496   Slings, lifting: made from purchased wire—*mfg*
2298   Slings, rope—*mfg*
1455   Slip clay mining
2211   Slipcover fabrics, cotton—*mfg*

2221   Slipcover fabrics, manmade fiber and silk—*mfg*
5714   Slipcover stores—retail
5023   Slipcovers, furniture—wholesale
2392   Slipcovers: made of fabrics, plastics, and other material—except paper—*mfg*
3142   Slipper socks, made from purchased socks—*mfg*
2252   Slipper socks—mitse—*mfg*
3149   Slippers, ballet—*mfg*
3142   Slippers, house—*mfg*
3621   Sliprings for motors and generators—*mfg*
2341   Slips: women's, misses', children's, and infants'—mfpm—*mfg*
2254   Slips—mitse—*mfg*
3579   Slipsheeting machines—*mfg*
3841   Slit lamps (ophthalmic goods)—*mfg*
3549   Slitters, rotary (metalworking machines)—*mfg*
3999   Slot machines—*mfg*
7993   Slot machines, operation of
7999   Slot-car racetracks
3541   Slotting machines (machine tools)—*mfg*
2299   Slubs and nubs (cutting up fibers for use in tweeds)—*mfg*
4953   Sludge disposal sites
3589   Sludge processing equipment—*mfg*
3599   Sludge tables—*mfg*
3355   Slugs, aluminum—*mfg*
3351   Slugs, copper and copper alloy—*mfg*
3555   Slugs, printers'—*mfg*
3251   Slumped brick—*mfg*
4619   Slurry pipeline operation
1389   Slush pits and cellars, excavation of: on a contract basis
2899   Slushing compounds, gun—*mfg*
3482   Small arms ammunition, 30 mm. (or 1.18 inch) or less—*mfg*
2015   Small game dressing—*mfg*
3559   Smelting and refining machinery and equipment, except ovens—*mfg*
3339   Smelting and refining of lead, primary—*mfg*
3341   Smelting and refining of nonferrous metals, secondary—*mfg*
3339   Smelting and refining of zinc, primary—*mfg*
5084   Smelting machinery and equipment—wholesale
3339   Smelting of nonferrous metal, primary: except copper and aluminum—*mfg*
3567   Smelting ovens—*mfg*
3443   Smelting pots and retorts—*mfg*
1031   Smithsonite mining
2339   Smocks: women's, misses', and juniors'—mfpm—*mfg*

3669 Smoke detectors—*mfg*
3489 Smoke generators (ordnance)—*mfg*
2013 Smoked meats—mfpm—*mfg*
2892 Smokeless powder—*mfg*
3269 Smokers' articles, pottery—*mfg*
3229 Smokers' glassware: ashtrays, tobacco jars, etc.—*mfg*
5199 Smokers' supplies—wholesale
3999 Smokers, bee (beekeepers' supplies)—*mfg*
3443 Smokestacks, boiler plate—*mfg*
2514 Smoking stands, metal—*mfg*
2511 Smoking stands, wood—*mfg*
2131 Smoking tobacco—*mfg*
5194 Smoking tobacco—wholesale
2273 Smyrna carpets and rugs, machine woven—*mfg*
5812 Snack bars
5812 Snack shops
3546 Snagging grinders—*mfg*
0161 Snap bean farms (bush and pole)
3643 Snap switches, (electric wiring devices)—*mfg*
3421 Snips, tinners'—*mfg*
2499 Snow fence—*mfg*
2421 Snow fence lath—*mfg*
3585 Snow making machinery—*mfg*
3524 Snowblowers and throwers, residential—*mfg*
3799 Snowmobiles—*mfg*
5599 Snowmobiles—retail
5012 Snowmobiles—wholesale
3531 Snowplow attachments—*mfg*
4959 Snowplowing
3711 Snowplows (motor vehicles)—*mfg*
3949 Snowshoes—*mfg*
2369 Snowsuits: girls' and children's—mfpm—*mfg*
2329 Snowsuits: men's and boys'—mfpm—*mfg*
2339 Snowsuits: women's, misses', and juniors'—mfpm—*mfg*
3644 Snubbers for CATV systems—*mfg*
2131 Snuff—*mfg*
5194 Snuff—wholesale
3261 Soap dishes, vitreous china and earthenware—*mfg*
3999 Soap dispensers—*mfg*
2844 Soap impregnated papers and paper washcloths—*mfg*
5169 Soap, chips, and powder: laundry—wholesale
2842 Soap, saddle—*mfg*
5122 Soap, toilet—wholesale
2841 Soap: granulated, liquid, cake, flaked, and chip—*mfg*
2869 Soaps, naphthenic acid—*mfg*
1499 Soapstone quarrying

7997 Soccer clubs, except professional and semiprofessional
7941 Soccer clubs, professional or semiprofessional
3949 Soccer equipment, except apparel—*mfg*
8399 Social change associations
8641 Social clubs, membership
7299 Social escort service
8322 Social service centers
8399 Social service information exchanges: e.g., alcoholism, drug addiction
8732 Sociological research, commercial
8733 Sociological research, noncommercial
3545 Sockets (machine tool accessories)—*mfg*
3643 Sockets, electric—*mfg*
3679 Sockets, electronic tube—*mfg*
2252 Socks—*mfg*
3142 Socks, slipper: made from purchased socks—*mfg*
2252 Socks, slipper—mitse—*mfg*
3842 Socks, stump—*mfg*
0181 Sod farms
0782 Sod laying
5261 Sod—retail
2819 Soda alum—*mfg*
1474 Soda ash mining
2812 Soda ash, not produced at mines—*mfg*
5046 Soda fountain fixtures, except refrigerated—wholesale
5078 Soda fountain fixtures, refrigerated—wholesale
5812 Soda fountains
3585 Soda fountains, parts, and accessories—*mfg*
2656 Soda straws, except glass or plastics—mfpm—*mfg*
2812 Soda, caustic—*mfg*
2869 Sodium acetate—*mfg*
2869 Sodium alginate—*mfg*
2819 Sodium aluminate—*mfg*
2819 Sodium aluminum sulfate—*mfg*
2819 Sodium antimoniate—*mfg*
2879 Sodium arsenite (formulated)—*mfg*
2819 Sodium arsenite, technical—*mfg*
2869 Sodium benzoate—*mfg*
2812 Sodium bicarbonate, not produced at mines—*mfg*
2819 Sodium bichromate and chromate—*mfg*
2819 Sodium borates—*mfg*
2819 Sodium borohydride—*mfg*
2819 Sodium bromide, not produced at mines—*mfg*
2812 Sodium carbonate (soda ash), not produced at mines—*mfg*
2819 Sodium chlorate—*mfg*

2834 Sodium chloride solution for injection, U.S.P.—*mfg*
2899 Sodium chloride, refined—*mfg*
1474 Sodium compounds mining, except common salt
2819 Sodium compounds, inorganic—*mfg*
2819 Sodium cyanide—*mfg*
2869 Sodium glutamate—*mfg*
2819 Sodium hydrosulfite—*mfg*
2812 Sodium hydroxide (caustic soda)—*mfg*
2842 Sodium hypochlorite (household bleach)—*mfg*
2819 Sodium molybdate—*mfg*
2869 Sodium pentachlorophenate—*mfg*
2819 Sodium perborate—*mfg*
2819 Sodium peroxide—*mfg*
2819 Sodium phosphate—*mfg*
2819 Sodium polyphosphate—*mfg*
2834 Sodium salicylate tablets—*mfg*
2843 Sodium salts of sulfonated oils, fats, or greases—*mfg*
2819 Sodium silicate—*mfg*
2819 Sodium silicofluoride—*mfg*
2819 Sodium stannate—*mfg*
2819 Sodium sulfate-bulk or tablets—*mfg*
2869 Sodium sulfoxalate formaldehyde—*mfg*
2819 Sodium tetraborate, not produced at mines—*mfg*
2819 Sodium thiosulfate—*mfg*
2819 Sodium tungstate—*mfg*
2819 Sodium uranate—*mfg*
2819 Sodium, metallic—*mfg*
2515 Sofas, convertible—*mfg*
2512 Sofas, upholstered on wood frames, except convertible beds—*mfg*
3089 Soffit, plastics (siding)—*mfg*
5812 Soft drink stands
2086 Soft drinks, bottled or canned—*mfg*
5149 Soft drinks—wholesale
2298 Soft fiber cordage and twine—*mfg*
2843 Softeners (textile assistants)—*mfg*
7371 Software programming, custom
7371 Software systems analysis and design, custom
7372 Software, computer: prepackaged
5045 Software, computer—wholesale
2861 Softwood distillates—*mfg*
2436 Softwood plywood composites—*mfg*
2436 Softwood veneer or plywood—*mfg*
1629 Soil compacting service—contractors
3531 Soil compactors: vibratory—*mfg*
2879 Soil conditioners—*mfg*
9512 Soil conservation services—government
3321 Soil pipe, cast iron—*mfg*
3523 Soil pulverizers and packers (agricultural machinery)—*mfg*

2899 Soil testing kits—*mfg*
5261 Soil, top—retail
3674 Solar cells—*mfg*
3433 Solar energy collectors, liquid or gas—*mfg*
3433 Solar heaters—*mfg*
1711 Solar heating apparatus—contractors
5074 Solar heating panels and equipment—wholesale
3511 Solar powered turbine-generator sets—*mfg*
1742 Solar reflecting insulation film—contractors
3829 Solarimeters—*mfg*
3341 Solder (base metal), pig and ingot: secondary—*mfg*
3356 Solder wire, bar: acid core and rosin core—*mfg*
3548 Soldering equipment, except soldering irons—*mfg*
2899 Soldering fluxes—*mfg*
3915 Soldering for the jewelry trade—*mfg*
3423 Soldering guns and tools, hand: electric—*mfg*
3423 Soldering iron tips and tiplets—*mfg*
3423 Soldering irons and coppers—*mfg*
3643 Solderless connectors (electric wiring devices)—*mfg*
3111 Sole leather—*mfg*
3625 Solenoid switches, industrial—*mfg*
3492 Solenoid valves, fluid power: metal—*mfg*
3679 Solenoids for electronic applications—*mfg*
3131 Soles, boot and shoe: except rubber, composition, plastics, and fiber—*mfg*
3089 Soles, boot and shoe: plastics—*mfg*
3069 Soles, boot and shoe: rubber, composition, and fiber—*mfg*
5087 Soles, shoe—wholesale
2819 Solid fuel propellants, inorganic—*mfg*
2869 Solid fuel propellants, organic—*mfg*
3674 Solid-state electronic devices—*mfg*
3089 Soling strips, boot and shoe: plastics—*mfg*
3069 Soling strips, boot and shoe: rubber, composition, and fiber—*mfg*
3295 Solite, ground or otherwise treated—*mfg*
2843 Soluble oils and greases—*mfg*
2834 Solutions, pharmaceutical—*mfg*
2865 Solvent naphtha, made in chemical plants—*mfg*
7389 Solvents recovery service on a contract or fee basis
2899 Solvents, carbon—*mfg*
2842 Solvents, degreasing—*mfg*
2842 Solvents, drain pipe—*mfg*
2869 Solvents, organic—*mfg*
2911 Solvents, produced in petroleum refineries—*mfg*
3812 Sonabuoys—*mfg*

8049 Speech pathologists, offices of
3566 Speed changers (power transmission equipment)—*mfg*
3824 Speed indicators and recorders, vehicle—*mfg*
8299 Speed reading courses
3566 Speed reducers (power transmission equipment)—*mfg*
5531 Speed shops—retail
3824 Speedometers—*mfg*
7948 Speedway operation
3339 Spelter (zinc), primary—*mfg*
8099 Sperm banks
0831 Sphagnum moss, gathering of
1031 Sphalerite mining
3443 Spheres, for liquids or gas: metal plate—*mfg*
3841 Sphygmomanometers—*mfg*
5499 Spice and herb stores—retail
2099 Spices, including grinding—*mfg*
5149 Spices—wholesale
3313 Spiegeleisen—*mfg*
3432 Spigots, metal and plastics—*mfg*
2499 Spigots, wood—*mfg*
3312 Spike rods, made in steel works or rolling mills—*mfg*
3399 Spikes, nonferrous metal (including wire)—*mfg*
3315 Spikes, steel: wire or cut—*mfg*
2241 Spindle banding—*mfg*
3552 Spindles, textile—*mfg*
3728 Spinners, aircraft propeller—*mfg*
3542 Spinning lathes—*mfg*
3542 Spinning machines, metal—*mfg*
3552 Spinning machines, textile—*mfg*
3469 Spinning metal, for the trade—*mfg*
2284 Spinning thread: cotton, silk, manmade fibers, and wool—*mfg*
2281 Spinning wool carpet and rug yarn: wool, mohair, or animal fiber—*mfg*
2281 Spinning yarn: cotton, silk, wool, and manmade staple—*mfg*
3496 Spiral cloth, made from purchased wire—*mfg*
2899 Spirit duplicating fluid—*mfg*
2085 Spirits, neutral, except fruit—for beverage purposes—*mfg*
2834 Spirits, pharmaceutical—*mfg*
5182 Spirits—wholesale
3861 Splicers, motion picture film—*mfg*
3542 Spline rolling machines—*mfg*
2449 Splint baskets, for fruits and vegetables—*mfg*
3842 Splints, pneumatic and wood—*mfg*
3111 Splits, leather—*mfg*
1479 Spodumene mining

2499 Spokes, wood—*mfg*
2051 Sponge goods, bakery, except frozen—*mfg*
3312 Sponge iron—*mfg*
3069 Sponge rubber and sponge rubber products—*mfg*
3999 Sponges, bleaching and dyeing of—*mfg*
0919 Sponges, gathering of
3089 Sponges, plastics—*mfg*
3069 Sponges, rubber—*mfg*
3291 Sponges, scouring: metallic—*mfg*
3842 Sponges, surgical—*mfg*
5199 Sponges—wholesale
2231 Sponging and refinishing cloth: wool and similar animal fiber for the trade—*mfg*
7389 Sponging textiles for tailors and dressmakers
2426 Spool blocks and blanks, wood—*mfg*
2282 Spooling yarn: wool, mohair, or similar animal fibers—*mfg*
2282 Spooling yarn: cotton, silk, and manmade fiber continuous filament—*mfg*
2499 Spools, except for textile machinery: wood—*mfg*
2655 Spools, fiber (metal-end or all-fiber)—mfpm—*mfg*
3552 Spools, textile machinery: wood—*mfg*
2656 Spoons, paper: except those made from pressed or molded pulp—mfpm—*mfg*
2679 Spoons, pressed and molded pulp—mfpm—*mfg*
3914 Spoons: silver, nickel silver, pewter, stainless steel, and plated—*mfg*
2321 Sport shirts: men's and boys'—mfpm—*mfg*
7032 Sporting camps
7999 Sporting goods rental
5941 Sporting goods stores—retail
5091 Sporting goods, including firearms, ammunition, and bicycles—wholesale
3949 Sporting goods: except clothing, footwear, small arms, and ammunition—*mfg*
2892 Sporting powder (explosive)—*mfg*
7997 Sports and recreation clubs, membership: except physical fitness
5699 Sports apparel stores—retail
2329 Sports clothing, nontailored: men's and boys'—mfpm—*mfg*
7941 Sports field operation (sports promotion)
7999 Sports instructors, professional: golf, skiing, swimming, etc.
7999 Sports professionals
7941 Sports promotion: baseball, football, boxing, etc.
2253 Sports shirts—mitse—*mfg*
5136 Sportswear, men's and boys'—wholesale
5137 Sportswear: women's and children's—wholesale

3469 Stamping metal, for the trade—*mfg*
3532 Stamping mill mining machinery—*mfg*
2396 Stamping on finished fabric articles—*mfg*
3953 Stamps, hand: time, date, postmark, cancelling, shoe, and textile marking—*mfg*
5961 Stamps, mail-order—retail
5999 Stamps, philatelist—retail: except mail-order
5092 Stamps, philatelist—wholesale
3523 Stanchions and standards, barn—*mfg*
3949 Stand boards—*mfg*
3825 Standard cells—*mfg*
3479 Standardizing of metals and metal products, for the trade—*mfg*
3825 Standards and calibration equipment for electrical measuring, except laboratory—*mfg*
3825 Standing wave ratio measuring equipment—*mfg*
3443 Standpipes—*mfg*
3861 Stands, camera and projector—*mfg*
3537 Stands, ground servicing aircraft—*mfg*
2541 Stands, merchandise display: wood—*mfg*
2542 Stands, merchandise display: except wood—*mfg*
3931 Stands, music—*mfg*
2511 Stands: telephone, bedside, and smoking—wood—*mfg*
2819 Stannic and stannous chloride—*mfg*
3579 Staple removers—*mfg*
3399 Staples, nonferrous metal (including wire)—*mfg*
3315 Staples, steel: wire or cut—*mfg*
3496 Staples, wire: made from purchased wire—*mfg*
5072 Staples—wholesale
3579 Stapling machines, office—*mfg*
4212 Star routes, local
2842 Starch preparations, laundry—*mfg*
2046 Starch, instant—*mfg*
2046 Starch, liquid—*mfg*
2046 Starches, edible and industrial—*mfg*
2842 Starches, plastics—*mfg*
5149 Starches—wholesale
0252 Started pullet farms
7539 Starter and generator repair, automotive
3694 Starter and starter parts, internal combustion engine—*mfg*
3724 Starters, aircraft: nonelectric—*mfg*
3625 Starters, electric motor—*mfg*
3643 Starters, fluorescent—*mfg*
3621 Starting equipment, for streetcars—*mfg*
3643 Starting switches, fluorescent lamp—*mfg*
6022 State banks, commercial
6062 State credit unions, not federally chartered

9411 State education departments
9221 State police
9311 State tax commissions
3679 Static power supply converters for electronic applications—*mfg*
3822 Static pressure regulators—*mfg*
3711 Station wagons (motor vehicles)—*mfg*
3229 Stationers' glassware: inkwells, clip cups, etc.—*mfg*
3069 Stationers' sundries, rubber—*mfg*
5112 Stationery and stationery supplies—wholesale
3269 Stationery articles, pottery—*mfg*
5943 Stationery stores—retail
2759 Stationery: except lithographed or gravure—*mfg*
2754 Stationery: gravure printing—*mfg*
2678 Stationery—mfpm—*mfg*
4013 Stations operated by railway terminal companies
5143 Stations, cream—wholesale
2721 Statistical reports (periodicals), publishing and printing, or publishing only—*mfg*
3621 Stators for motors—*mfg*
3281 Statuary, marble—*mfg*
3299 Statuary: gypsum, clay, papier-mache, scagliola, and metal—factory production only—*mfg*
5199 Statuary—wholesale
2411 Stave bolts, wood: hewn—*mfg*
2429 Staves, barrel: sawed or split—*mfg*
3272 Staves, silo: concrete—*mfg*
3131 Stays, shoe—*mfg*
3053 Steam and other packing—*mfg*
7299 Steam baths
1799 Steam cleaning of building exteriors—contractors
3443 Steam condensers—*mfg*
3589 Steam cookers, restaurant type—*mfg*
3511 Steam engines, except locomotives—*mfg*
1711 Steam fitting—contractors
3494 Steam fittings and specialties, except plumbers' brass goods and fittings, metal—*mfg*
5074 Steam fittings—wholesale
3511 Steam governors—*mfg*
3433 Steam heating apparatus, domestic—*mfg*
4961 Steam heating systems (suppliers of heat)
3443 Steam jet aftercoolers—*mfg*
3443 Steam jet inter condensers—*mfg*
3822 Steam pressure controls, residential and commercial type—*mfg*
3569 Steam separators (machinery)—*mfg*
4961 Steam supply systems, including geothermal
3589 Steam tables—*mfg*

3433 Stokers, mechanical: domestic and industrial—*mfg*

3423 Stone forks (handtools)—*mfg*

3532 Stone pulverizers, stationary—*mfg*

1741 Stone setting—contractors

3559 Stone tumblers—*mfg*

3559 Stone working machinery—*mfg*

5032 Stone, building—wholesale

3272 Stone, cast concrete—*mfg*

5032 Stone, crushed or broken—wholesale

3281 Stone, cut and shaped—*mfg*

3281 Stone, quarrying and processing of own stone products—*mfg*

3423 Stonecutters' handtools—*mfg*

3291 Stones, abrasive—*mfg*

5999 Stones, crystalline: rough—retail

3299 Stones, synthetic: for gem stones and industrial use—*mfg*

3915 Stones: preparation of real and imitation gems for settings—*mfg*

1459 Stoneware clay mining

3269 Stoneware, chemical (pottery products)—*mfg*

1741 Stonework erection—contractors

2599 Stools, factory—*mfg*

2514 Stools, household: metal—*mfg*

2511 Stools, household: wood—*mfg*

2599 Stools, metal: with casters—not household or office—*mfg*

2522 Stools, office: rotating—except wood—*mfg*

2521 Stools, office: wood—*mfg*

3272 Stools, precast terrazzo—*mfg*

3494 Stop cocks, except drain: metal—*mfg*

3432 Stopcocks (plumbers' supplies)—*mfg*

2499 Stoppers, cork—*mfg*

3842 Stoppers, ear—*mfg*

3255 Stoppers, glasshouse: clay—*mfg*

3069 Stoppers, rubber—*mfg*

7219 Storage and repair of fur and other garments for individuals

3691 Storage batteries—*mfg*

5063 Storage batteries, industrial—wholesale

3621 Storage battery chargers, engine generator type—*mfg*

2511 Storage chests, household: wood—*mfg*

3572 Storage devices, computer—*mfg*

2542 Storage fixtures, except wood—*mfg*

2541 Storage fixtures, wood—*mfg*

7219 Storage of furs and other garments for individuals

4226 Storage of goods at foreign trade zones

4214 Storage of household goods: combined with local trucking

4226 Storage of household goods: without local trucking

4922 Storage of natural gas

4221 Storage other than cold storage, farm product

3272 Storage tanks, concrete—*mfg*

3443 Storage tanks, metal plate—*mfg*

1791 Storage tanks, metal: erection—contractors

4222 Storage, frozen or refrigerated goods

4226 Storage, furniture: without local trucking

4225 Storage, general

4226 Storage, special: except farm products and cold storage

1542 Store construction—general contractors

1751 Store fixture installation—contractors

1791 Store front installation, metal—contractors

3469 Store fronts, porcelain enameled—*mfg*

3442 Store fronts, prefabricated: metal, except porcelain enameled—*mfg*

2541 Store fronts, prefabricated: wood—*mfg*

3442 Storm doors and windows, metal—*mfg*

5211 Storm windows and sash, wood or metal—retail

2431 Storm windows, wood—*mfg*

2082 Stout (alcoholic beverage)—*mfg*

3444 Stove boards, sheet metal—*mfg*

3259 Stove lining, clay—*mfg*

3469 Stove parts, porcelain enameled—*mfg*

3444 Stove pipe and flues, sheet metal—*mfg*

2842 Stove polish—*mfg*

7699 Stove repair shops

5722 Stoves and related electric and gas appliances—retail

3589 Stoves, commercial—*mfg*

5064 Stoves, cooking or heating, household: electric—wholesale

5074 Stoves, cooking: except electric—wholesale

3631 Stoves, disk—*mfg*

3631 Stoves, household: cooking—*mfg*

3433 Stoves, household: heating—except electric—*mfg*

3433 Stoves, wood and coal burning—*mfg*

5074 Stoves, wood burning—wholesale

3537 Straddle carriers, mobile—*mfg*

3421 Straight razors—*mfg*

3547 Straightening machinery (rolling mill equipment)—*mfg*

3674 Strain gages, solid-state—*mfg*

3494 Strainers, line: for use in piping systems—metal—*mfg*

3714 Strainers, oil: motor vehicle—*mfg*

3569 Strainers, pipeline—*mfg*

3496 Strand, uninsulated wire: made from purchased wire—*mfg*

2493 Strandboard, oriented—*mfg*

2399 Strap assemblies, tie down: aircraft—except leather—*mfg*

3111 Strap leather—*mfg*
3423 Strapping tools, steel—*mfg*
2241 Strapping webs—*mfg*
3499 Strapping, metal—*mfg*
3199 Straps, except watch straps: leather—*mfg*
2396 Straps, shoulder: for women's underwear—mfpm—*mfg*
3172 Straps, watch: except precious metal—*mfg*
3999 Straw goods—*mfg*
2823 Straw, rayon—*mfg*
5191 Straw—wholesale
0171 Strawberry farms
2631 Strawboard, except building board—mitse—*mfg*
2353 Strawhats—*mfg*
3229 Straws, glass—*mfg*
2656 Straws, soda: except glass or plastics—*mfg*
3711 Street flushers (motor vehicles)—*mfg*
3648 Street lighting fixtures, except traffic signals—*mfg*
3612 Street lighting transformers—*mfg*
1611 Street maintenance or repair—contractors
1611 Street paving—contractors
4953 Street refuse systems
3711 Street sprinklers and sweepers (motor vehicles)—*mfg*
3991 Street sweeping brooms, hand and machine—*mfg*
4111 Streetcar operation
3743 Streetcars and car equipment—*mfg*
3829 Stress, strain, and flaw detecting and measuring equipment—*mfg*
2211 Stretch fabrics, cotton—*mfg*
3842 Stretchers—*mfg*
2499 Stretchers, curtain: wood—*mfg*
3542 Stretching machines—*mfg*
3949 Striking (punching) bags—*mfg*
3931 Stringed musical instruments and parts—*mfg*
3999 Stringing beads for the trade—*mfg*
3931 Strings, musical instrument—*mfg*
3931 Strings, piano—*mfg*
3949 Strings, tennis racket—*mfg*
2761 Strip forms (manifold business forms)—*mfg*
1481 Strip mining for nonmetallic minerals, except fuels: on a contract basis
1231 Strip mining, anthracite: except on a contract basis
1221 Strip mining, bituminous coal: except on a contract basis
1221 Strip mining, lignite: except on a contract basis
1081 Strip mining, metal: on a contract basis
3316 Strip steel, cold-rolled: not made in hot-rolling mills—*mfg*

3351 Strip, copper and copper alloy—*mfg*
5051 Strip, metal—wholesale
3356 Strip: lead, magnesium, nickel, tin, titanium, zinc, and their alloys—*mfg*
1241 Stripping services: bituminous coal, anthracite, and lignite on a contract basis
3312 Strips, galvanized iron and steel: made in steel works or rolling mills—*mfg*
3312 Strips, iron and steel: made in steel works or hot-rolling mills—*mfg*
3069 Strips, liner: rubber—*mfg*
2823 Strips, rayon—*mfg*
2823 Strips, viscose—*mfg*
3825 Stroboscopes—*mfg*
3641 Strobotrons—*mfg*
3944 Strollers, baby (vehicles)—*mfg*
1479 Strontianite mining
2819 Strontium carbonate, precipitated, and oxide—*mfg*
1479 Strontium mineral mining
2819 Strontium nitrate—*mfg*
3199 Strops, razor—*mfg*
5039 Structural assemblies, prefabricated: non-wood—wholesale
5031 Structural assemblies, prefabricated: wood—wholesale
5211 Structural clay products—retail
3211 Structural glass, flat—*mfg*
2491 Structural lumber and timber, treated—*mfg*
2439 Structural members, laminated wood: arches, trusses, timbers, and parallel chord ceilings—*mfg*
3547 Structural mills (rolling mill machinery)—*mfg*
3312 Structural shapes, iron and steel—*mfg*
5051 Structural shapes, iron and steel—wholesale
3355 Structural shapes, rolled aluminum—*mfg*
1791 Structural steel erection—contractors
3441 Structural steel, fabricated—*mfg*
3251 Structural tile, clay—*mfg*
3944 Structural toy sets—*mfg*
2833 Strychnine and derivatives—*mfg*
3299 Stucco—*mfg*
1771 Stucco construction—contractors
5032 Stucco—wholesale
3674 Stud bases or mounts for semiconductor devices—*mfg*
2421 Stud mills—*mfg*
6111 Student Loan Marketing Association
8299 Student exchange programs
3663 Studio equipment, radio and television broadcasting—*mfg*
7819 Studio property rental for motion picture film production

7911 Studios, dance
7221 Studios, portrait photography
3444 Studs, sheet metal—*mfg*
3965 Studs, shirt: except precious metal and precious or semiprecious stones—*mfg*
9121 Study commissions, legislative
3942 Stuffed toys (including animals)—*mfg*
3556 Stuffers, sausage—*mfg*
2411 Stumping for turpentine or powder manufacturing—*mfg*
2411 Stumps—*mfg*
3679 Styli, phonograph record cutting—*mfg*
7389 Styling of fashions, apparel, furniture, and textiles
7389 Styling wigs for the trade
3951 Stylographic pens—*mfg*
2892 Styphnic acid—*mfg*
2865 Styrene—*mfg*
2865 Styrene monomer—*mfg*
2821 Styrene resins—*mfg*
2821 Styrene-acrylonitrile resins—*mfg*
2822 Styrene-butadiene rubbers (50 percent or less styrene content)—*mfg*
2822 Styrene-chloroprene rubbers—*mfg*
2822 Styrene-isoprene rubbers—*mfg*
1221 Subbituminous coal surface mining
1222 Subbituminous coal underground mining
3531 Subgraders, construction equipment—*mfg*
2819 Sublimate, corrosive—*mfg*
3484 Submachine guns and parts—*mfg*
1629 Submarine rock removal—general contractors
5812 Submarine sandwich shops
3731 Submarine tenders, building and repairing—*mfg*
3544 Subpresses, metalworking—*mfg*
4841 Subscription television services
3531 Subsoiler attachments, tractor-mounted—*mfg*
4111 Suburban and urban railway operation
1629 Subway construction—general contractors
4111 Subway operation
3841 Suction therapy apparatus—*mfg*
2261 Sueding cotton broadwoven goods—*mfg*
2262 Sueding manmade fiber and silk broadwoven fabrics—*mfg*
0133 Sugar beet farms
0722 Sugar beets, machine harvesting of
2099 Sugar grinding—*mfg*
2023 Sugar of milk—*mfg*
3556 Sugar plant machinery—*mfg*
2087 Sugar, burnt (food color)—*mfg*
2046 Sugar, corn—*mfg*
2062 Sugar, granulated: made from purchased raw cane sugar or sugar syrup—*mfg*

2063 Sugar, granulated: made from sugar beets—*mfg*
2061 Sugar, granulated: made from sugarcane—*mfg*
2099 Sugar, industrial maple: made in plants producing maple syrup—*mfg*
2062 Sugar, invert: made from purchased raw cane sugar or sugar syrup—*mfg*
2063 Sugar, invert: made from sugar beets—*mfg*
2061 Sugar, invert: made from sugarcane—*mfg*
2063 Sugar, liquid: made from sugar beets—*mfg*
2062 Sugar, powdered: made from purchased raw cane sugar or sugar syrup—*mfg*
2063 Sugar, powdered: made from sugar beets—*mfg*
2061 Sugar, powdered: made from sugarcane—*mfg*
2099 Sugar, powdered—mfpm—*mfg*
2061 Sugar, raw: made from sugarcane—*mfg*
5159 Sugar, raw—wholesale
2062 Sugar, refined: made from purchased raw cane sugar or sugar syrup—*mfg*
5149 Sugar, refined—wholesale
2061 Sugar: clarified, granulated, and raw—made from sugarcane—*mfg*
0133 Sugarcane farms
0722 Sugarcane, machine harvesting of
2396 Suit and coat findings: coat fronts and linings—*mfg*
2396 Suit trimmings, fabric—mfpm—*mfg*
3429 Suitcase hardware, including locks—*mfg*
3089 Suitcase shells, plastics—*mfg*
3161 Suitcases, regardless of material—*mfg*
2211 Suiting fabrics, cotton—*mfg*
2221 Suiting fabrics, manmade fiber and silk—*mfg*
2231 Suitings: wool, mohair, and similar animal fibers—*mfg*
2369 Suits and rompers: children's and infants'—mfpm—*mfg*
2337 Suits, except playsuits and athletic: women's, misses', and juniors'—mfpm—*mfg*
3842 Suits, firefighting: asbestos—*mfg*
2329 Suits, men's and boys': warmup, jogging, snow, and ski—mfpm—*mfg*
5136 Suits, men's and boys'—wholesale
2311 Suits, tailored: men's and boys'—mfpm—*mfg*
2339 Suits, women's, misses', and juniors': ski, swim, snow, play, warmup, and jogging—mfpm—*mfg*
2326 Suits, work: men's—mfpm—*mfg*
2369 Suits: girls' and children's—mfpm—*mfg*

3825 Sweep generators—*mfg*
3825 Sweep oscillators—*mfg*
3589 Sweepers, carpet: except household electric vacuum sweepers—*mfg*
3635 Sweepers, electric: vacuum—household—*mfg*
3589 Sweepers, electric: vacuum—industrial—*mfg*
3711 Sweepers, street (motor vehicles)—*mfg*
2842 Sweeping compounds, oil and water absorbent, clay or sawdust—*mfg*
4959 Sweeping service: road, airport, parking lot, etc.
0161 Sweet corn farms
0161 Sweet pepper farms
0723 Sweet potato curing
0139 Sweet potato farms
2051 Sweet yeast goods, except frozen—*mfg*
2053 Sweet yeast goods, frozen—*mfg*
2869 Sweetners, synthetic—*mfg*
7997 Swimming clubs, membership
7999 Swimming instruction
7389 Swimming pool cleaning and maintenance
1799 Swimming pool construction—contractors
2394 Swimming pool covers and blankets, fabric—mfpm—*mfg*
3089 Swimming pool covers and blankets: plastics—*mfg*
3589 Swimming pool filter systems (home pools)—*mfg*
3648 Swimming pool lighting fixtures—*mfg*
5091 Swimming pools and equipment—wholesale
7999 Swimming pools, except membership
5999 Swimming pools, home: not installed—retail
3949 Swimming pools, plastics—*mfg*
2329 Swimsuits: men's and boys'—mfpm—*mfg*
2339 Swimsuits: women's, misses', and juniors'—mfpm—*mfg*
2253 Swimsuits—mitse—*mfg*
2329 Swimwear, men's and boys'—mfpm—*mfg*
2514 Swings, porch: metal—*mfg*
2511 Swings, porch: wood—*mfg*
2395 Swiss loom embroideries—*mfg*
3644 Switch boxes, electric—*mfg*
3643 Switch cutouts—*mfg*
7389 Switchboard operation of private branch exchanges
3281 Switchboard panels, slate—*mfg*
3613 Switchboards and parts, power—*mfg*
5063 Switchboards, electrical distribution—wholesale
3661 Switchboards, telephone and telegraph—*mfg*
3999 Switches (hair)—*mfg*

3643 Switches for electric wiring: e.g., snap, tumbler, pressure, pushbutton—*mfg*
3613 Switches, electric power: except snap, push button, tumbler, and solenoid—*mfg*
3679 Switches, electronic—*mfg*
5063 Switches, except electronic—wholesale
3625 Switches, flow activated electrical—*mfg*
3822 Switches, pneumatic positioning remote—*mfg*
3462 Switches, railroad: forged—not made in rolling mills—*mfg*
3674 Switches, silicon control—*mfg*
3679 Switches, stepping—*mfg*
3822 Switches, thermostatic—*mfg*
3613 Switchgear and switchgear accessories—*mfg*
5063 Switchgear—wholesale
3613 Switching equipment power—*mfg*
3661 Switching equipment, telephone—*mfg*
3743 Switching locomotives and parts, electric and nonelectric—*mfg*
3949 Swivels (fishing equipment)—*mfg*
3421 Swords—*mfg*
1411 Syenite (except nepheline), dimension—quarrying
1423 Syenite, except nepheline: crushed and broken—quarrying
1459 Syenite, nepheline—quarrying
1041 Sylvanite mining
7929 Symphony orchestras
3829 Synchronizers, aircraft engine—*mfg*
3621 Synchronous condensers and timing motors, electric—*mfg*
3621 Synchros—*mfg*
3825 Synchroscopes—*mfg*
3931 Synthesizers, music—*mfg*
6111 Synthetic Fuels Corporation
3559 Synthetic filament extruding machines—*mfg*
4925 Synthetic natural gas from naphtha, production and distribution
5169 Synthetic rubber—wholesale
3299 Synthetic stones, for gem stones and industrial use—*mfg*
3069 Syringes, fountain: rubber—*mfg*
3841 Syringes, hypodermic—*mfg*
2061 Syrup, cane: made from sugarcane—*mfg*
2046 Syrup, corn: unmixed—*mfg*
2062 Syrup, made from purchased raw cane sugar or sugar syrup—*mfg*
2063 Syrup, made from sugar beets—*mfg*
2087 Syrups, beverage—*mfg*
2066 Syrups, chocolate—*mfg*
5149 Syrups, except for fountain use—wholesale
2087 Syrups, flavoring—*mfg*
5145 Syrups, fountain—wholesale

2082 Syrups, malt—*mfg*

2834 Syrups, pharmaceutical—*mfg*

2062 Syrups, refiners'—*mfg*

2099 Syrups, sweetening: honey, maple syrup, sorghum—*mfg*

7371 Systems analysis and design, computer software

8748 Systems engineering consulting, except professional engineering or computer related

7373 Systems integration, computer

T

2361 T-shirts, outerwear: girls', children's, and infants'—mfpm—*mfg*

2321 T-shirts, outerwear: men's and boys'—mfpm—*mfg*

2331 T-shirts, outerwear: women's, misses', and juniors'—mfpm—*mfg*

2253 T-shirts, outerwear—mitse—*mfg*

2322 T-shirts, underwear: men's and boys'—mfpm—*mfg*

2341 T-shirts, underwear: women's, misses', children's, and infants'—mfpm—*mfg*

2254 T-shirts, underwear—mitse—*mfg*

2253 T-shirts—mitse—*mfg*

3829 T-squares (drafting)—*mfg*

2892 TNT (trinitrotoluene)—*mfg*

3914 Table and kitchen cutlery, all metal—*mfg*

3269 Table articles, coarse earthenware—*mfg*

3263 Table articles, fine earthenware (whiteware)—*mfg*

3262 Table articles, vitreous china—*mfg*

2211 Table cover fabrics, cotton—*mfg*

7213 Table cover supply service

2258 Table covers, lace—*mfg*

3914 Table cutlery, all metal—*mfg*

3421 Table cutlery, except table cutlery with handles of metal—*mfg*

2211 Table damask, cotton—*mfg*

3645 Table lamps—*mfg*

5023 Table linens—wholesale

2392 Table mats, plastics and textiles—*mfg*

2079 Table oils—*mfg*

2541 Table or counter tops, plastics laminated—*mfg*

3292 Table pads and padding, asbestos—*mfg*

2299 Table pads and padding, felt: except woven—*mfg*

2392 Table scarves—mfpm—*mfg*

2426 Table slides, for extension tables: wood—*mfg*

3231 Table tops, made from purchased glass—*mfg*

3281 Table tops, marble—*mfg*

3469 Table tops, porcelain enameled—*mfg*

2392 Tablecloths, plastics—*mfg*

2392 Tablecloths—mfpm—*mfg*

2514 Tables, household: metal—*mfg*

2511 Tables, household: wood—*mfg*

3537 Tables, lift: hydraulic—*mfg*

2522 Tables, office: except wood—*mfg*

2521 Tables, office: wood—*mfg*

3841 Tables, operating—*mfg*

3545 Tables, rotary: indexing—*mfg*

3599 Tables, sludge—*mfg*

3949 Tables: billiard, pool, bagatelle, and ping pong—*mfg*

2678 Tablets and pads, book and writing—mfpm—*mfg*

3499 Tablets, metal—*mfg*

2834 Tablets, pharmaceutical—*mfg*

3262 Tableware, commercial: vitreous china—*mfg*

3229 Tableware, glass and glass ceramic—*mfg*

3089 Tableware, plastics: except foam—*mfg*

3263 Tableware: commercial and household—semivitreous—*mfg*

2761 Tabulating card set forms (business forms)—*mfg*

2675 Tabulating cards, printed or unprinted: die-cut from purchased paperboard—*mfg*

7374 Tabulating service, computer

5112 Tabulation cards—wholesale

3825 Tachometer generators—*mfg*

3824 Tachometer, centrifugal—*mfg*

2869 Tackifiers, organic—*mfg*

3429 Tackle blocks, metal—*mfg*

2499 Tackle blocks, wood—*mfg*

3949 Tackle, fishing: except nets, seines, and line—*mfg*

3399 Tacks, nonferrous metal (including wire)—*mfg*

3315 Tacks, steel: wire or cut—*mfg*

5072 Tacks—wholesale

1011 Taconite mining

2221 Taffetas—*mfg*

3812 Taffrail logs—*mfg*

2621 Tagboard, made in paper mills—mitse—*mfg*

2631 Tagboard—mitse—*mfg*

2752 Tags, lithographed—*mfg*

2679 Tags, paper: unprinted—mfpm—*mfg*

2759 Tags, printed: except lithographed or gravure—*mfg*

3647 Tail lights, motor vehicle—*mfg*

7219 Tailor shops, except custom or merchant tailors

2311 Tailored dress and sport coats: men's and boys'—*mfg*

3952 Tailors' chalk—*mfg*
2499 Tailors' pressing blocks, wood—*mfg*
3421 Tailors' scissors—*mfg*
3421 Tailors' shears, hand—*mfg*
5087 Tailors' supplies—wholesale
5699 Tailors, custom—retail
1499 Talc mining
3295 Talc, ground or otherwise treated—*mfg*
2844 Talcum powders—*mfg*
2861 Tall oil, except skimmings—*mfg*
2851 Tallate driers—*mfg*
2077 Tallow rendering, inedible—*mfg*
2076 Tallow, vegetable—*mfg*
3824 Tally counters—*mfg*
3824 Tallying meters: except electrical instruments, watches, and clocks—*mfg*
2032 Tamales, canned—*mfg*
3531 Tampers, powered—*mfg*
3531 Tamping equipment, rail—*mfg*
3489 Tampions for guns more than 30 mm. (or more than 1.18 inch)—*mfg*
2676 Tampons—mfpm—*mfg*
0174 Tangerine groves and farms
7699 Tank and boiler cleaning service
3489 Tank artillery—*mfg*
3255 Tank blocks, glasshouse: clay—*mfg*
7699 Tank cleaning, ship
3795 Tank components, specialized: military—*mfg*
3519 Tank engines and engine parts, internal combustion: military—*mfg*
3743 Tank freight cars and car equipment—*mfg*
3259 Tank liner brick, vitrified clay—*mfg*
3795 Tank recovery vehicles—*mfg*
2331 Tank tops, outerwear: women's, misses', and juniors—mfpm—*mfg*
2361 Tank tops: girls', children's, and infants'—mfpm—*mfg*
2321 Tank tops: men's and boys'—mfpm—*mfg*
2253 Tank tops—mitse—*mfg*
3443 Tank towers, metal plate—*mfg*
7699 Tank truck cleaning service
3824 Tank truck meters—*mfg*
3511 Tank turbines—*mfg*
**** Tanker fleets of oil companies, if separate—code in transportation
3731 Tankers (ships), building and repairing—*mfg*
5088 Tanks and tank components—wholesale
3443 Tanks for tank trucks, metal plate—*mfg*
3272 Tanks, concrete—*mfg*
3261 Tanks, flush: vitreous china—*mfg*
3728 Tanks, fuel: aircraft—*mfg*
3714 Tanks, gas: motor vehicle—*mfg*
3443 Tanks, metal plate: lined—*mfg*

3795 Tanks, military: including factory rebuilding—*mfg*
3585 Tanks, soda water—*mfg*
3443 Tanks, standard and custom fabricated: metal plate—made in boiler shops—*mfg*
2449 Tanks, wood: coopered—*mfg*
3861 Tanks: photographic developing, fixing, and washing—*mfg*
3111 Tanneries, leather—*mfg*
3559 Tannery machines—*mfg*
2869 Tannic acid—*mfg*
2819 Tanning agents, synthetic inorganic—*mfg*
2869 Tanning agents, synthetic organic—*mfg*
3999 Tanning and currying furs—*mfg*
2861 Tanning extracts and materials, natural—*mfg*
7299 Tanning salons
1061 Tantalite mining
1061 Tantalum ore mining
3339 Tantalum refining—*mfg*
5813 Tap rooms (drinking places)
3577 Tape cleaners, magnetic: computer peripheral equipment—*mfg*
7822 Tape distribution for television
3999 Tape measures—*mfg*
5064 Tape players and recorders, household—wholesale
3651 Tape players, household—*mfg*
3577 Tape print units, computer peripheral equipment—*mfg*
7812 Tape production, video or motion picture
7379 Tape recertification service
7622 Tape recorder repair
5731 Tape recorders and players—retail
3572 Tape recorders for data computers—*mfg*
3651 Tape recorders, household—*mfg*
7389 Tape slitting for the trade (cutting plastics, leather, etc. into widths)
3572 Tape storage units, computer—*mfg*
5735 Tape stores, audio and video—retail
3572 Tape transports, magnetic—*mfg*
3842 Tape, adhesive: medicated or nonmedicated—*mfg*
3292 Tape, asbestos—*mfg*
3652 Tape, audio magnetic: prerecorded—*mfg*
2672 Tape, cellophane adhesive—mfpm—*mfg*
3069 Tape, friction: rubber—*mfg*
2672 Tape, gummed: cloth and paper base—mfpm—*mfg*
3965 Tape, hook-and-eye and snap fastener—*mfg*
3695 Tape, magnetic recording: blank—*mfg*
2672 Tape, masking—mfpm—*mfg*
3069 Tape, pressure sensitive (including friction), rubber—*mfg*

2672 Tape, pressure sensitive: except rubber backed—mfpm—*mfg*

2679 Tape, telegraph: paper—mfpm—*mfg*

5131 Tape, textile—wholesale

2295 Tape, varnished: plastics and other coated: except magnetic—mfpm—*mfg*

5065 Tapes, audio and video recording—wholesale

5099 Tapes, audio prerecorded—wholesale

2241 Tapes, fabric—*mfg*

3829 Tapes, surveyors'—*mfg*

7822 Tapes, video, recorded—wholesale

2211 Tapestry fabrics, cotton—*mfg*

2221 Tapestry fabrics, manmade fiber and silk—*mfg*

1742 Taping and finishing drywall—contractors

2046 Tapioca—*mfg*

5084 Tapping attachments—wholesale

3541 Tapping machines—*mfg*

3643 Taps, current: attachment plug and screw shell types—*mfg*

3545 Taps, machine tool—*mfg*

3131 Taps, shoe: regardless of material—*mfg*

2821 Tar acid resins—*mfg*

2951 Tar and asphalt mixtures for paving, not made in petroleum refineries—*mfg*

2861 Tar and tar oils, products of wood distillation—*mfg*

2911 Tar or residuum, produced in petroleum refineries—*mfg*

2621 Tar paper, building and roofing—mitse—*mfg*

2952 Tar paper, roofing—mfpm—*mfg*

2672 Tar paper: except building or roofing and packaging—mfpm—*mfg*

1311 Tar sands mining

3312 Tar, derived from chemical recovery coke ovens—*mfg*

2865 Tar, product of coal tar distillation—*mfg*

3499 Target drones for use by ships, metal—*mfg*

3728 Target drones, aircraft—*mfg*

3949 Target shooting equipment, except small arms and ammunition—*mfg*

3949 Targets, archery and rifle shooting—*mfg*

3949 Targets, clay—*mfg*

3728 Targets, trailer type: aircraft—*mfg*

4731 Tariff consultant

4731 Tariff rate information service

2211 Tarlatan, cotton—*mfg*

2394 Tarpaulins, fabric—mfpm—*mfg*

2869 Tartaric acid and metallic salts—*mfg*

2869 Tartrates—*mfg*

2284 Tatting thread: cotton, silk, manmade fibers, and wool—*mfg*

7299 Tattoo parlors

5813 Taverns (drinking places)

6211 Tax certificate dealers

6099 Tax certificate sale and redemption agencies

7389 Tax collection agencies: collecting for a city, county, or State

6799 Tax liens: holding, buying, and selling

7291 Tax return preparation services without accounting, auditing, or bookkeeping services

7389 Tax title dealers: agencies for city, county, or State

9311 Taxation departments

7319 Taxicab card advertising

4121 Taxicab operation

3711 Taxicabs—*mfg*

5012 Taxicabs—wholesale

7699 Taxidermists

3824 Taximeters—*mfg*

8641 Taxpayers' associations

2393 Tea bags, fabric—mfpm—*mfg*

2099 Tea blending—*mfg*

3634 Tea kettles, electric—*mfg*

3229 Tea kettles, glass and glass ceramic—*mfg*

5812 Tea rooms

5499 Tea stores—retail

2514 Tea wagons, metal—*mfg*

2511 Tea wagons, wood—*mfg*

2086 Tea, iced: bottled or canned—*mfg*

5149 Tea—wholesale

0831 Teaberries, gathering of

9411 Teacher certification bureaus

7361 Teachers' registries

3699 Teaching machines and aids, electronic—*mfg*

3469 Teakettles, except electric: stamped metal—*mfg*

2869 Tear gas—*mfg*

3999 Tear gas devices and equipment—*mfg*

2261 Teaseling cotton broadwoven goods—*mfg*

2262 Teaseling manmade fiber and silk broadwoven fabrics—*mfg*

2835 Technetium products—*mfg*

3229 Technical glassware and glass products, pressed or blown—*mfg*

3231 Technical glassware, made from purchased glass—*mfg*

8222 Technical institutes

2741 Technical manuals and papers: publishing and printing, or publishing only—*mfg*

2341 Teddies: women's, misses', children's, and infants'—mfpm—*mfg*

5699 Tee shirts, custom printed—retail

8072 Teeth, artificial: made in dental laboratories to order for the profession

3843 Teeth, artificial: not made in dental laboratories—*mfg*
3531 Teeth, bucket and scarifier—*mfg*
3069 Teething rings, rubber—*mfg*
1731 Telecommunications equipment installation—contractors
4822 Telegram services
3661 Telegraph and telephone carrier and repeater equipment—*mfg*
4822 Telegraph cable services
5065 Telegraph equipment—wholesale
1623 Telegraph line construction—general contractors
3661 Telegraph office switching equipment—*mfg*
7389 Telegraph service, florists'
4822 Telegraph services
3661 Telegraph station equipment and parts, wire—*mfg*
2679 Telegraph tape, paper—mfpm—*mfg*
7389 Telemarketing (telephone marketing) service on a contract or fee basis
3663 Telemetering equipment, electronic—*mfg*
3823 Telemetering instruments, industrial process type—*mfg*
1731 Telephone and telephone equipment installation—contractors
3661 Telephone answering machines—*mfg*
7389 Telephone answering, except beeper service
7349 Telephone booths, cleaning and maintenance of
2542 Telephone booths, except wood—*mfg*
2541 Telephone booths, wood—*mfg*
3661 Telephone central office equipment, dial and manual—*mfg*
8322 Telephone counseling service
3661 Telephone dialing devices, automatic—*mfg*
2759 Telephone directories, except lithographed or gravure (not publishing)—*mfg*
2754 Telephone directories, gravure printing: not publishing—*mfg*
2741 Telephone directories: publishing and printing, or publishing only—*mfg*
5065 Telephone equipment—wholesale
1623 Telephone line construction—general contractors
7629 Telephone set repair
3661 Telephone sets, except cellular radio telephone—*mfg*
7389 Telephone solicitation service on a contract or fee basis
2511 Telephone stands, wood—*mfg*
3661 Telephone station equipment and parts, wire—*mfg*
5999 Telephone stores—retail

3663 Telephones, cellular radio—*mfg*
3661 Telephones, sound powered (no battery)—*mfg*
3661 Telephones, underwater—*mfg*
3575 Teleprinters (computer terminals)—*mfg*
3827 Telescopes—*mfg*
5999 Telescopes—retail
3827 Telescopic sights—*mfg*
2679 Teletypewriter paper, rolls with carbon—mfpm—*mfg*
4822 Teletypewriter services
3469 Television and radio chassis: stamped metal—*mfg*
1799 Television and radio stations, service and repair of—contractors
7313 Television and radio time, sale of: not auxiliary to television or radio broadcasting
4833 Television broadcasting stations
2519 Television cabinets, plastics—*mfg*
2517 Television cabinets, wood—*mfg*
3663 Television closed-circuit equipment—*mfg*
7922 Television employment agencies
7812 Television film production
3663 Television monitors—*mfg*
7922 Television programs (including commercials): live
5065 Television receiving and transmitting tubes—wholesale
3651 Television receiving sets—*mfg*
7359 Television rental and leasing
7622 Television repair shops
2721 Television schedules: publishing and printing, or publishing only—*mfg*
5731 Television set stores—retail
5064 Television sets—wholesale
7819 Television tape services (e.g., editing and transfers)
3441 Television tower sections, prefabricated metal—*mfg*
3663 Television transmitting antennas and ground equipment—*mfg*
1623 Television transmitting tower construction—general contractors
3229 Television tube blanks, glass—*mfg*
3671 Television tubes—*mfg*
5961 Television, mail-order (home shopping)—retail
4841 Television, subscription or closed circuit
4822 Telex services
1041 Telluride (gold) mining
3339 Tellurium refining, primary—*mfg*
3822 Temperature controls, automatic: residential and commercial types—*mfg*
3823 Temperature instruments: industrial process type, except glass and bimetal—*mfg*

3822 Temperature sensors for motor windings—*mfg*

3569 Temperature testing chambers—*mfg*

3231 Tempered glass, made from purchased glass—*mfg*

3211 Tempered glass—mitse—*mfg*

3398 Tempering of metal for the trade—*mfg*

3829 Templates, drafting—*mfg*

8661 Temples

3851 Temples and fronts, ophthalmic—*mfg*

7363 Temporary help service

7933 Ten pin centers

8641 Tenant associations, except property management

3731 Tenders (ships), building and repairing—*mfg*

3944 Tenders, baby (vehicles)—*mfg*

3743 Tenders, locomotive—*mfg*

7997 Tennis clubs, membership

7999 Tennis clubs, nonmembership

1629 Tennis court construction, outdoor—general contractors

7999 Tennis courts, outdoor and indoor: operation of, nonmembership

5941 Tennis goods and equipment—retail

3949 Tennis goods: e.g., balls, frames, rackets—*mfg*

7999 Tennis professionals

2253 Tennis shirts— mitse—*mfg*

3553 Tenoners (woodworking machines)—*mfg*

3829 Tensile strength testing equipment—*mfg*

2499 Tent poles, wood—*mfg*

7699 Tent repair shops

5999 Tent shops—retail

3792 Tent-type camping trailers—*mfg*

2211 Tentage—mitse—*mfg*

2394 Tents—mfpm—*mfg*

4013 Terminal and switching companies, railroad

4491 Terminal operation, waterfront

4581 Terminal services, coordinated: at airports

3643 Terminals and connectors for electrical devices—*mfg*

3575 Terminals, computer—*mfg*

4231 Terminals, freight trucking: with or without maintenance facilities

7342 Termite control

3312 Terneplate—*mfg*

5051 Terneplate—wholesale

3312 Ternes, iron and steel: long or short—*mfg*

2869 Terpineol—*mfg*

3259 Terra cotta, architectural: clay—*mfg*

5032 Terra cotta—wholesale

0919 Terrapins, catching of

3272 Terrazzo products, precast—*mfg*

1743 Terrazzo work—contractors

2211 Terry woven fabrics, cotton—*mfg*

2869 Tert-butylated bis (p-phenoxyphenyl) ether fluid—*mfg*

1799 Test boring for construction—contractors

8748 Test development and evaluation service, educational or personnel

1081 Test drilling for metal mining: on a contract basis

1481 Test drilling for nonmetallic minerals except fuel: on a contract basis

3825 Test equipment for electronic and electrical circuits and equipment—*mfg*

3423 Test plugs: plumbers' handtools—*mfg*

3825 Test sets, ignition harness—*mfg*

3231 Test tubes, made from purchased glass—*mfg*

3829 Testers for checking hydraulic controls on aircraft—*mfg*

5084 Testing and measuring equipment, electrical: except automotive—wholesale

3569 Testing chambers for altitude, temperature, ordnance, and power—*mfg*

5013 Testing equipment, electrical: automotive—wholesale

3829 Testing equipment: abrasion, shearing strength, tensile strength, and torsion—*mfg*

8734 Testing laboratories, except clinical

8071 Testing laboratories, medical: analytic or diagnostic

8748 Testing services, educational or personnel

2869 Tetrachloroethylene—*mfg*

2869 Tetraethyl lead—*mfg*

2892 Tetryl (explosives)—*mfg*

2621 Text paper—mitse—*mfg*

2732 Textbooks: printing or printing and binding, not publishing—*mfg*

2731 Textbooks: publishing and printing, or publishing only—*mfg*

5131 Textile converters except knit goods—wholesale

7389 Textile cutting service

7389 Textile designers

2843 Textile finishing agents—*mfg*

3552 Textile finishing machinery: bleaching, dyeing, mercerizing, and printing—*mfg*

7389 Textile folding and packing services

3229 Textile glass fibers—*mfg*

3269 Textile guides, porcelain—*mfg*

3199 Textile leathers: apron picker leather, and mill strapping—*mfg*

5084 Textile machinery and equipment—wholesale

3552 Textile machinery parts—*mfg*

3552 Textile machinery, except sewing machines—*mfg*

3953   Textile marking stamps, hand—*mfg*
2211   Textile mills, broadwoven cotton—*mfg*
2221   Textile mills, broadwoven: silk, and manmade fiber including glass—*mfg*
2241   Textile mills, narrow woven fabric: cotton, wool, silk, and manmade fibers—including glass—*mfg*
2299   Textile mills: linen, jute, hemp, and ramie yarn, thread, and fabrics—*mfg*
5085   Textile printers' supplies—wholesale
3552   Textile printing machines—*mfg*
2843   Textile processing assistants—*mfg*
2655   Textile reels, fiber—mfpm—*mfg*
7699   Textile roll covering service
2843   Textile scouring compounds and wetting agents—*mfg*
2841   Textile soap—*mfg*
2655   Textile spinning bobbins, fiber (metal-end or all-fiber)—mfpm—*mfg*
3552   Textile turnings and shapes, wood—*mfg*
4226   Textile warehousing
2221   Textile warping, on a contract basis—*mfg*
5093   Textile waste—wholesale
3292   Textiles, asbestos: except packing—*mfg*
2297   Textiles, bonded fiber: except felt—*mfg*
7389   Textiles, sponging or shrinking: for tailors and dressmakers
5131   Textiles—wholesale
2824   Textured fibers and yarns, noncellulosic: made in chemical plants—*mfg*
2823   Textured yarns and fibers, cellulosic: made in chemical plants—*mfg*
2282   Textured yarns—mfpm—*mfg*
6512   Theater buildings (ownership and operation)
5021   Theater seats—wholesale
5812   Theaters, dinner
7833   Theaters, motion picture: drive-in
7832   Theaters, motion picture: except drive-in
7922   Theatrical booking agencies, except motion picture
7829   Theatrical booking agencies, motion picture
7922   Theatrical companies
2389   Theatrical costumes—*mfg*
7922   Theatrical employment agencies
7922   Theatrical equipment rental
2531   Theatrical furniture—*mfg*
7922   Theatrical lighting on a contract basis
7922   Theatrical production, except motion picture
3999   Theatrical scenery—*mfg*
7922   Theatrical ticket agencies
7996   Theme parks, amusement
2833   Theobromine—*mfg*
3829   Theodolites, surveying—*mfg*

8221   Theological seminaries
3844   Therapeutic X-ray apparatus and tubes: medical, industrial, and research—*mfg*
5047   Therapy equipment—wholesale
3826   Thermal analysis instruments, laboratory type—*mfg*
3826   Thermal conductivity instruments and sensors—*mfg*
3823   Thermal conductivity instruments, industrial process type—*mfg*
3674   Thermionic devices, solid-state—*mfg*
3676   Thermistors, except temperature sensors—*mfg*
3823   Thermistors, industrial process type—*mfg*
3829   Thermocouples, except industrial process, aircraft type, and glass vacuum—*mfg*
3823   Thermocouples, industrial process type—*mfg*
3822   Thermocouples, vacuum: glass—*mfg*
3674   Thermoelectric devices, solid-state—*mfg*
3629   Thermoelectric generators—*mfg*
2759   Thermography, except lithographed or gravure—*mfg*
3826   Thermogravimetric analyzers—*mfg*
3829   Thermohydrometers—*mfg*
3069   Thermometer cases, rubber—*mfg*
3823   Thermometers, filled system: industrial process type—*mfg*
3829   Thermometers, liquid-in-glass and bimetal types—*mfg*
2671   Thermoplastics coated paper for packaging—mfpm—*mfg*
2672   Thermoplastics coated paper, except for packaging—mfpm—*mfg*
3083   Thermoplastics laminates: rods, tubes, plates, and sheet, except flexible packaging—*mfg*
3083   Thermosetting laminates: rods, tubes, plates, and sheet, except flexible packaging—*mfg*
7699   Thermostat repair
3491   Thermostatic traps, heating: metal—*mfg*
3714   Thermostats, motor vehicle—*mfg*
3822   Thermostats: air-conditioning, refrigeration, comfort heating, appliance—*mfg*
3829   Thickness gauging instruments, ultrasonic—*mfg*
3259   Thimbles, chimney: clay—*mfg*
3429   Thimbles, wire rope—*mfg*
3674   Thin film circuits—*mfg*
2621   Thin paper—mitse—*mfg*
2843   Thin water (admixture)—*mfg*
2851   Thinner, lacquer—*mfg*
2851   Thinners, paint: prepared—*mfg*
0721   Thinning of crops, mechanical and chemical

3823 Time cycle and program controllers, industrial process type—*mfg*
3821 Time interval measuring equipment, electric (laboratory type)—*mfg*
3429 Time locks—*mfg*
3822 Time program controls, air-conditioning systems—*mfg*
2675 Time recording cards, die-cut from purchased paperboard—*mfg*
7374 Time sharing, computer
3613 Time switches, electrical switchgear apparatus—*mfg*
5063 Time switches—wholesale
7389 Time-share condominium exchanges
6531 Time-sharing real estate: sales, leasing, and rentals
3579 Time-stamps containing clock mechanisms—*mfg*
3579 Time-stamps: containing clock mechanisms—*mfg*
3579 Timeclocks and time recording devices—*mfg*
3873 Timers for industrial use, clockwork mechanism only—*mfg*
3625 Timing devices, mechanical and solid-state, except clockwork—*mfg*
3621 Timing motors, synchronous: electric—*mfg*
0139 Timothy farms
3356 Tin and tin alloy bars, pipe, rods, sheets, strip, and tubing—*mfg*
5051 Tin and tin base metals, shapes, forms, etc.—wholesale
3339 Tin base alloys, primary—*mfg*
3411 Tin cans—*mfg*
2819 Tin chloride—*mfg*
2819 Tin compounds, inorganic—*mfg*
3497 Tin foil, not made in rolling mills—*mfg*
1099 Tin ore mining
2819 Tin oxide—*mfg*
5051 Tin plate bars—wholesale
5051 Tin plate—wholesale
3339 Tin refining, primary—*mfg*
3356 Tin rolling and drawing—*mfg*
2819 Tin salts—*mfg*
3341 Tin smelting and refining, secondary—*mfg*
3312 Tin-free steel—*mfg*
2834 Tinctures, pharmaceutical—*mfg*
3423 Tinners' handtools, except snips—*mfg*
3421 Tinners' snips—*mfg*
3312 Tinplate—*mfg*
3999 Tinsel—*mfg*
7699 Tinsmithing repair, except construction
1761 Tinsmithing, in connection with construction work—contractors
1799 Tinting glass—contractors
2899 Tints and dyes, household—*mfg*

5719 Tinware stores—retail
2396 Tip printing and stamping on fabric articles—*mfg*
1629 Tipple construction—general contractors
3545 Tips, cutting tool—*mfg*
3131 Tips, shoe: regardless of material—*mfg*
5531 Tire (automobile) dealers—retail
5014 Tire and tube repair materials—wholesale
3496 Tire chains, made from purchased wire—*mfg*
2296 Tire cord—*mfg*
2399 Tire covers—mfpm—*mfg*
5531 Tire dealers, automotive—retail
2296 Tire fabric—*mfg*
3559 Tire grooving machines—*mfg*
3563 Tire inflators, hand or compressor operated—*mfg*
7534 Tire recapping
7534 Tire repair shops
3559 Tire retreading machinery and equipment—*mfg*
3559 Tire shredding machinery—*mfg*
7534 Tire studding and restudding
3011 Tire sundries and tire repair materials, rubber—*mfg*
3714 Tire valve cores—*mfg*
5531 Tire, battery, and accessory dealers—retail
5014 Tires and tubes, new—wholesale
3011 Tires, cushion or solid rubber—*mfg*
3089 Tires, plastics—*mfg*
5014 Tires, used—wholesale
3011 Tiring, continuous lengths: rubber, with or without metal core—*mfg*
3089 Tissue dispensers, plastics—*mfg*
2621 Tissue paper—mitse—*mfg*
2676 Tissues, cleansing: mfpm—*mfg*
3264 Titania porcelain insulators—*mfg*
1099 Titaniferous-magnetite mining, valued chiefly for titanium content
3356 Titanium and titanium alloy bars, rods, billets, sheets, strip, and tubing—*mfg*
3369 Titanium castings, except die-castings—*mfg*
3364 Titanium die-castings—*mfg*
3463 Titanium forgings, not made in hot-rolling mills—*mfg*
3356 Titanium from sponge—*mfg*
3339 Titanium metal sponge and granules—*mfg*
1099 Titanium ore mining
2816 Titanium pigments—*mfg*
6541 Title abstract companies
6541 Title and trust companies
6361 Title insurance
6541 Title reconveyance companies
6541 Title search companies
3861 Titlers, motion picture film—*mfg*

3546 Tools, hand: power-driven—woodworking or metalworking—*mfg*
3423 Tools, hand: except power-driven tools and saws—*mfg*
3541 Tools, machine: metal cutting types—*mfg*
5084 Tools, machinists' precision—wholesale
5251 Tools, power and hand—retail
3533 Tools: drilling, etc.—for artesian, gas, and oil wells—*mfg*
3634 Toothbrushes, electric—*mfg*
5064 Toothbrushes, electric—wholesale
3991 Toothbrushes, except electric—*mfg*
5122 Toothbrushes, except electric—wholesale
2844 Toothpastes and powders—*mfg*
2499 Toothpicks, wood—*mfg*
3069 Top lift sheets, rubber—*mfg*
3131 Top lifts, boot and shoe—*mfg*
7532 Top repair, automotive
3069 Top roll covering, for textile mill machinery: rubber—*mfg*
1459 Topaz (nongem) mining
2311 Topcoats: men's and boys'—*mfg*
5145 Toppings, soda fountain—wholesale
3465 Tops, automobile: stamped metal—*mfg*
2675 Tops, bottle; die-cut from purchased paper or paperboard—*mfg*
3259 Tops, chimney: clay—*mfg*
2299 Tops, combing and converting—*mfg*
3466 Tops, jar: stamped metal—*mfg*
2299 Tops, manmade fiber—*mfg*
3714 Tops, motor vehicle: except stamped metal—*mfg*
3089 Tops, plastics (e.g., dispenser, shaker)—*mfg*
3713 Tops, truck—*mfg*
5159 Tops, wool—wholesale
2899 Torches (fireworks)—*mfg*
3489 Torpedo tubes (ordnance)—*mfg*
3483 Torpedoes and parts (ordnance)—*mfg*
2899 Torpedoes, railroad—*mfg*
2892 Torpedoes, well shooting (explosives)—*mfg*
3566 Torque converters, except motor vehicle—*mfg*
3621 Torque motors, electric—*mfg*
3493 Torsion bar springs—*mfg*
3829 Torsion testing equipment—*mfg*
2032 Tortillas, canned—*mfg*
2099 Tortillas, fresh or refrigerated—*mfg*
3824 Totalizing meters, consumption registering, except aircraft—*mfg*
3999 Toupees—*mfg*
4725 Tour operation (travel)
4724 Tourist agencies for the arrangement of transportation, lodging, and car rental
7999 Tourist attractions, natural wonder: commercial

7011 Tourist cabins
7011 Tourist camps
7011 Tourist courts
7999 Tourist guides
7389 Tourist information bureaus
4725 Tours, except sightseeing buses, boats, and airplanes
3728 Tow targets, aircraft—*mfg*
2299 Tow to top mills—*mfg*
7521 Tow-in parking lots
3731 Towboats, building and repairing—*mfg*
3261 Towel bar holders, vitreous china and earthenware—*mfg*
7213 Towel supply service, except wiping
7218 Towel supply service, wiping
2844 Towelettes, premoistened—*mfg*
2621 Toweling paper—mitse—*mfg*
2211 Towels and toweling, cotton: made in weaving mills—*mfg*
2299 Towels and towelings, linen and linen-and-cotton mixtures—mitse—*mfg*
2392 Towels, fabric and nonwoven textiles—mfpm—*mfg*
2676 Towels, paper—mfpm—*mfg*
5113 Towels, paper—wholesale
2259 Towels—mitse—*mfg*
3441 Tower sections, transmission: prefabricated metal—*mfg*
2499 Towers, cooling: wood or wood and sheet metal combination—*mfg*
3443 Towers, tank: metal plate—*mfg*
3443 Towers: bubble, cooling, fractionating—metal plate—*mfg*
3799 Towing bars and systems—*mfg*
7549 Towing service, automotive
4492 Towing services, marine
1521 Townhouse construction—general contractors
2836 Toxins—*mfg*
2836 Toxoids, except in vitro and in vivo—*mfg*
5945 Toy and game stores—retail
3612 Toy transformers—*mfg*
5092 Toys (including electronic)—wholesale
3942 Toys, doll—*mfg*
3069 Toys, rubber: except dolls—*mfg*
3942 Toys, stuffed—*mfg*
3944 Toys: except dolls, bicycles, rubber toys, and stuffed toys—*mfg*
2879 Trace elements (agricultural chemicals)—*mfg*
3483 Tracer igniters for ammunition more than 30 mm. (or more than 1.18 inch)—*mfg*
3952 Tracing cloth (drafting material)—*mfg*
2211 Tracing cloth, cotton—*mfg*
3949 Track and field athletic equipment, except apparel and footwear—*mfg*

5051 Track spikes—wholesale
4899 Tracking missiles by telemetry and photography on a contract basis
5082 Tracklaying equipment—wholesale
3743 Trackless trolley buses—*mfg*
3842 Traction apparatus—*mfg*
7699 Tractor repair
5082 Tractor-mounting equipment—wholesale
5083 Tractors, agricultural—wholesale
3531 Tractors, construction—*mfg*
5082 Tractors, construction—wholesale
3531 Tractors, crawler—*mfg*
3537 Tractors, industrial: for use in plants, depots, docks, and terminals—*mfg*
5084 Tractors, industrial—wholesale
3524 Tractors, lawn and garden—*mfg*
3531 Tractors, tracklaying—*mfg*
3711 Tractors, truck: for highway use—*mfg*
5012 Tractors, truck—wholesale
3523 Tractors, wheel: farm type—*mfg*
8611 Trade associations
2789 Trade binding services—*mfg*
9611 Trade commissions—government
2721 Trade journals, publishing and printing, or publishing only—*mfg*
8249 Trade schools
7389 Trade show arrangement
8631 Trade unions, local or national
6221 Traders, commodity contract
6211 Traders, security
6799 Trading companies, commodity contract
7389 Trading stamp promotion and sale to stores
7389 Trading stamp redemption
2752 Trading stamps, lithographed—*mfg*
2759 Trading stamps, printed: except lithographed or gravure—*mfg*
2754 Trading stamps: gravure printing—*mfg*
8748 Traffic consultants
1721 Traffic lane painting—contractors
3669 Traffic signals, electric—*mfg*
1629 Trail building—general contractors
1629 Trailer camp construction—general contractors
3799 Trailer hitches—*mfg*
7033 Trailer parks for transients
7519 Trailer rental
3523 Trailers and wagons, farm—*mfg*
3799 Trailers for automobiles, except travel and mobile home—*mfg*
5012 Trailers for passenger automobiles—wholesale
3799 Trailers for transporting horses, except fifth-wheel type—*mfg*
5012 Trailers for trucks, new and used—wholesale

3799 Trailers, boat—*mfg*
3792 Trailers, camping—*mfg*
3715 Trailers, fifth-wheel type: for transporting horses—*mfg*
3792 Trailers, house: except as permanent dwellings—*mfg*
5084 Trailers, industrial—wholesale
3715 Trailers, motor truck—*mfg*
3537 Trailers, truck: for use in plants, depots, docks, and terminals—*mfg*
5599 Trailers, utility—retail
3743 Train cars and equipment, freight or passenger—*mfg*
3728 Training aids, aircraft: except electronic—*mfg*
0752 Training horses, except racing
7812 Training motion picture production
0752 Training of pets and other animal specialties
2341 Training pants (underwear) except rubber or rubberized fabric: children's and infants'—mfpm—*mfg*
7948 Training racehorses
8361 Training schools for delinquents
3944 Trains and equipment, toy: electric and mechanical—*mfg*
7999 Trampoline operation
4119 Tramways, aerial: except amusement and scenic
2834 Tranquilizers and mental drug preparations—*mfg*
3663 Transceivers—*mfg*
3845 Transcutaneous electrical nerve stimulators (TENS)—*mfg*
3679 Transducers for use in measuring and testing instruments and equipments—*mfg*
3829 Transducers, pressure—*mfg*
6289 Transfer agents, securities
2672 Transfer paper, gold and silver—mfpm—*mfg*
2752 Transferring designs (lithographing)—*mfg*
2752 Transfers, decalcomania and dry: lithographed—*mfg*
3999 Transformations, hair—*mfg*
3548 Transformers (separate) for arc-welders—*mfg*
3612 Transformers, electric power—*mfg*
5063 Transformers, electric: except electronic—wholesale
3677 Transformers, electronic types—*mfg*
5065 Transformers, electronic—wholesale
3612 Transformers, for electronic meters—*mfg*
3612 Transformers, ignition: for use on domestic fuel burners—*mfg*
3612 Transformers, instrument: except portable—*mfg*

3825   Transformers, instrument: portable—*mfg*
3612   Transformers, reactor—*mfg*
3677   Transformers: power supply electronic type—*mfg*
7221   Transient photographers
3674   Transistors—*mfg*
5065   Transistors—wholesale
7319   Transit advertising
9621   Transit systems and authorities—nonoperating
3829   Transits, surveying—*mfg*
7389   Translation service
4923   Transmission and distribution of natural gas
3612   Transmission and distribution voltage regulators—*mfg*
3199   Transmission belting, leather—*mfg*
5063   Transmission equipment, electrical—wholesale
2992   Transmission fluid—mfpm—*mfg*
3714   Transmission housings and parts, motor vehicle—*mfg*
1623   Transmission line construction—general contractors
4911   Transmission of electric power
4922   Transmission of natural gas
7537   Transmission repair, automotive
3441   Transmission towers—*mfg*
3728   Transmissions, aircraft—*mfg*
7537   Transmissions, automotive: installation, repair, or sale and installation
3594   Transmissions, hydrostatic drives—*mfg*
3714   Transmissions, motor vehicle—*mfg*
3663   Transmitter-receivers, radio—*mfg*
3823   Transmitters of process variables, standard signal conversion—*mfg*
5065   Transmitters—wholesale
3663   Transmitting apparatus, radio and television—*mfg*
3671   Transmitting electron tubes—*mfg*
3523   Transplanters—*mfg*
4731   Transport clearinghouse
3731   Transport vessels, passenger and troop: building and repairing—*mfg*
4731   Transportation brokerage
9621   Transportation departments—government
5088   Transportation equipment and supplies, except motor vehicles—wholesale
4449   Transportation of freight on bays and sounds of the oceans
4731   Transportation rate services
9621   Transportation regulatory agencies—government
2754   Transportation schedules, gravure printing—*mfg*

2752   Transportation schedules, lithographed—*mfg*
2759   Transportation schedules, printing: except lithographed or gravure—*mfg*
4011   Transportation, railroad: line-haul
3949   Trap racks (clay targets)—*mfg*
1429   Trap rock, crushed and broken—quarrying
1411   Trap rock, dimension—quarrying
0971   Trapping carried on as a business enterprise
3496   Traps, animal and fish: made from purchased wire—*mfg*
3931   Traps, drummers'—*mfg*
3432   Traps, water—*mfg*
7999   Trapshooting facilities, except membership clubs
2673   Trash bags, plastics film, foil, and coated paper—mfpm—*mfg*
3639   Trash compactors, household—*mfg*
3089   Trash containers, plastics—*mfg*
3443   Trash racks, metal plate—*mfg*
4724   Travel agencies
4724   Travel bureaus
3792   Travel trailer chassis—*mfg*
5561   Travel trailers, automobile: new and used—retail
8322   Traveler's aid centers
6099   Travelers' check issuance
3161   Traveling bags, regardless of material—*mfg*
3671   Traveling wave tubes—*mfg*
1422   Travertine, crushed and broken—quarrying
1411   Travertine, dimension—quarrying
2298   Trawl twine—*mfg*
3731   Trawlers, building and repairing—*mfg*
2599   Tray trucks, restaurant—*mfg*
2441   Trays, carrier: wood—*mfg*
3229   Trays, glass—*mfg*
3272   Trays, laundry: concrete—*mfg*
3496   Trays, made from purchased wire—*mfg*
3861   Trays, photographic printing and processing—*mfg*
3089   Trays, plastics: except foam—*mfg*
3069   Trays, rubber—*mfg*
3634   Trays, warming: electric—*mfg*
3914   Trays: silver, nickel silver, pewter, stainless steel, and plated—*mfg*
2499   Trays: wood, wicker, and bagasse—*mfg*
3011   Tread rubber (camelback)—*mfg*
3949   Treadmills—*mfg*
3069   Treads, stair: rubber—*mfg*
3446   Treads, stair: fabricated metal—*mfg*
9311   Treasurers' offices—government
7218   Treated mats, rugs, mops, dust tool covers, and cloth supply service

7513 Truck rental, except industrial: without drivers
7212 Truck route laundry and drycleaning, not operated by laundries or cleaners
5541 Truck stops—retail
5014 Truck tires and tubes—wholesale
3713 Truck tops—*mfg*
3711 Truck tractors for highway use—*mfg*
5012 Truck tractors—wholesale
3715 Truck trailers—*mfg*
3537 Truck trailers for use in plants, depots, docks, and terminals—*mfg*
5012 Truck trailers—wholesale
4731 Truck transportation brokers
7542 Truck washing
3273 Truck-mixed concrete—*mfg*
4212 Trucking logs
4213 Trucking rental with drivers, except for local use
4231 Trucking terminals, freight: with or without maintenance facilities
4212 Trucking timber
4213 Trucking, except local
4212 Trucking, local: without storage
4214 Trucking, local: combined with storage
3537 Trucks, industrial (except mining): for freight, baggage, etc.—*mfg*
5084 Trucks, industrial—wholesale
3711 Trucks, motor: except off-highway—*mfg*
3531 Trucks, off-highway—*mfg*
5012 Trucks—wholesale
0182 Truffles grown under cover
3931 Trumpets and parts—*mfg*
3429 Trunk hardware, including locks—*mfg*
2441 Trunk slats, wood—*mfg*
5948 Trunks, luggage—retail
3161 Trunks, regardless of material—*mfg*
3443 Truss plates, metal—*mfg*
2439 Trusses, laminated lumber—*mfg*
2439 Trusses, wood—*mfg*
3842 Trusses: orthopedic and surgical—*mfg*
6022 Trust companies (accepting deposits), commercial: State
6021 Trust companies with deposits, commercial: national
6091 Trust companies, nondeposit
6153 Trust deeds, purchase and sale of
6733 Trustees: except for educational, religious, or charitable trusts
6733 Trusts except educational, religious, and charitable: management of
6732 Trusts, charitable: management of
6732 Trusts, educational: management of
6733 Trusts, personal investment: management of
6732 Trusts, religious: management of

3492 Tube and hose fittings and assemblies, fluid power: metal—*mfg*
3354 Tube blooms, aluminum: extruded—*mfg*
3498 Tube fabricating (contract bending and shaping); metal—*mfg*
3469 Tube fins, stamped metal—*mfg*
3492 Tube fittings and assemblies, fluid power: metal—*mfg*
3547 Tube mill machinery—*mfg*
3679 Tube retainers, electronic—*mfg*
3312 Tube rounds—*mfg*
3679 Tube spacers, mica—*mfg*
3825 Tube testers—*mfg*
3679 Tube transformer assemblies used in firing electronic tubes—*mfg*
3354 Tube, aluminum: extruded or drawn—*mfg*
2836 Tuberculins—*mfg*
8069 Tuberculosis and other respiratory illness hospitals
3671 Tubes for operating above the X-ray spectrum (with shorter wavelength)—*mfg*
3844 Tubes, X-ray—*mfg*
3671 Tubes, cathode ray—*mfg*
3499 Tubes, collapsible: for viscous products—tin, lead, and aluminum—*mfg*
3671 Tubes, electron—*mfg*
5065 Tubes, electronic: receiving and transmitting, and industrial—wholesale
2655 Tubes, fiber or paper (with or without metal ends)—mfpm—*mfg*
2655 Tubes, for chemical and electrical uses: impregnated paper or fiber—mfpm—*mfg*
3069 Tubes, hard rubber—*mfg*
3011 Tubes, inner: airplane, automobile, bicycle, motorcycle, and tractor—*mfg*
3312 Tubes, iron and steel: made in steel works or rolling mills—*mfg*
3671 Tubes, klystron—*mfg*
3083 Tubes, laminated plastics—*mfg*
3264 Tubes, porcelain—*mfg*
3317 Tubes, seamless steel—mfpm—*mfg*
3671 Tubes, television receiving type: cathode ray—*mfg*
3082 Tubes, unsupported plastics—*mfg*
3353 Tubes, welded: aluminum—*mfg*
3317 Tubes, wrought: welded, lock joint, and heavy riveted—mfpm—*mfg*
3299 Tubing for electrical purposes, quartz—*mfg*
3292 Tubing, asbestos—*mfg*
3351 Tubing, copper and copper alloy—*mfg*
3599 Tubing, flexible metallic—*mfg*
3229 Tubing, glass—*mfg*
3317 Tubing, mechanical and hypodermic sizes: cold-drawn stainless steel—mfpm—*mfg*

3555   Typesetting machines: intertypes, linotypes, monotypes, etc.—*mfg*

2791   Typesetting, computer controlled—*mfg*

7699   Typewriter repair, including electric

2211   Typewriter ribbon cloth, cotton—*mfg*

2221   Typewriter ribbon cloth, manmade fiber—*mfg*

3955   Typewriter ribbons, cloth or paper—*mfg*

5999   Typewriter stores—retail

3579   Typewriters—*mfg*

5044   Typewriters—wholesale

7338   Typing service

2791   Typographic composition—*mfg*

3555   Typographic numbering machines—*mfg*

1094   Tyuyamunite mining

U

9222   U.S. attorneys' offices

3931   Ukuleles and parts—*mfg*

1474   Ulexite mining

2816   Ultramarine pigments—*mfg*

3541   Ultrasonic assisted grinding machines (metalworking)—*mfg*

3699   Ultrasonic cleaning equipment, except medical and dental—*mfg*

3843   Ultrasonic dental equipment—*mfg*

3699   Ultrasonic generators sold separately for inclusion in tools and equipment—*mfg*

3841   Ultrasonic medical cleaning equipment—*mfg*

3845   Ultrasonic medical equipment, except cleaning—*mfg*

3541   Ultrasonic metal cutting machine tools—*mfg*

3845   Ultrasonic scanning devices, medical—*mfg*

3829   Ultrasonic testing equipment—*mfg*

3699   Ultrasonic welding machines and equipment—*mfg*

3542   Ultrasonically assisted metal forming machines—*mfg*

3648   Ultraviolet lamp fixtures—*mfg*

3641   Ultraviolet lamps—*mfg*

3674   Ultraviolet sensors, solid-state—*mfg*

3826   Ultraviolet-type analytical instruments—*mfg*

1479   Umber mining

2816   Umbers—*mfg*

2211   Umbrella cloth, cotton—*mfg*

3911   Umbrella handles and trimmings, precious metal—*mfg*

5699   Umbrella stores—retail

3999   Umbrellas and parts, except precious metal—*mfg*

5136   Umbrellas, men's and boys'—wholesale

3999   Umbrellas: beach, garden, and wagon—*mfg*

7549   Undercoating service, automotive

2851   Undercoatings, paint—*mfg*

1622   Underpass construction—general contractors

1799   Underpinning work—contractors

7261   Undertakers

5087   Undertakers' equipment and supplies—wholesale

3648   Underwater lighting fixtures—*mfg*

5091   Underwater sports equipment—wholesale

2221   Underwear fabrics, except knit: manmade fiber and silk—*mfg*

2211   Underwear fabrics, woven: cotton—*mfg*

5136   Underwear, men's and boys'—wholesale

2322   Underwear: men's and boys'—mfpm—*mfg*

5137   Underwear: women's, children's, and infants'—wholesale

2341   Underwear: women's, misses', children's, and infants'—mfpm—*mfg*

2254   Underwear—mitse—*mfg*

6211   Underwriters, security

4492   Undocking of ocean vessels

9441   Unemployment insurance offices—government

2353   Uniform hats and caps, except protective head gear—*mfg*

2321   Uniform shirts, except athletic or work: men's and boys'—mfpm—*mfg*

7213   Uniform supply service, except industrial

2329   Uniforms, athletic and gymnasium: men's and boys'—mfpm—*mfg*

2339   Uniforms, athletic: women's, misses', and juniors'—mfpm—*mfg*

2389   Uniforms, band—mfpm—*mfg*

2337   Uniforms, except athletic and service apparel: women's, misses', and juniors'—mfpm—*mfg*

5136   Uniforms, men's and boys'—wholesale

2326   Uniforms, nontailored work type: men's—mfpm—*mfg*

2311   Uniforms, tailored: men's and boys'—*mfg*

2339   Uniforms, washable service apparel (nurses', maid, waitresses', laboratory): women's, misses', and juniors'—mfpm—*mfg*

2326   Uniforms, work: men's—mfpm—*mfg*

5137   Uniforms: women's and children's—wholesale

5699   Uniforms—retail

2254   Union suits—mitse—*mfg*

6371   Union trust funds

6371   Union welfare, benefit, and health funds

3494   Unions, pipe: metal—*mfg*

3089   Unions, plastics—*mfg*

5651 Unisex clothing stores—retail
5137 Unisex clothing: women's and children's—wholesale
7231 Unisex hairdressers
3433 Unit heaters, domestic: except electric—*mfg*
3634 Unit heaters, household: electric—*mfg*
6726 Unit investment trusts
2761 Unit sets (manifold business forms)—*mfg*
5063 Unit substations—wholesale
9721 United Nations
4311 United States Postal Service
8399 United fund councils
3711 Universal carriers, military—*mfg*
3568 Universal joints, except motor vehicle—*mfg*
3714 Universal joints, motor vehicle—*mfg*
8221 Universities
8641 University clubs
4491 Unloading vessels
2512 Upholstered furniture, household: on wood frames, except dual-purpose sleep furniture—*mfg*
5087 Upholsterers' equipment and supplies, except fabrics—wholesale
7217 Upholstery cleaning on customers' premises
2211 Upholstery fabrics, cotton—*mfg*
2221 Upholstery fabrics, manmade fiber and silk—*mfg*
2231 Upholstery fabrics, wool—*mfg*
5087 Upholstery filling and padding—wholesale
2299 Upholstery filling, textile—*mfg*
3111 Upholstery leather—*mfg*
5714 Upholstery materials stores—retail
7532 Upholstery repair, automotive
3495 Upholstery springs, unassembled: made from purchased wire—*mfg*
3111 Upper leather—*mfg*
3131 Uppers (shoe cut stock)—*mfg*
3462 Upset forgings, iron and steel: not made in rolling mills—*mfg*
3542 Upsetters (forging machines)—*mfg*
1094 Uraninite (pitchblende) mining
1094 Uranium ore mining
2819 Uranium slug, radioactive—*mfg*
4111 Urban and suburban railway operation
6162 Urban mortgage companies
9532 Urban planning commissions—government
9532 Urban renewal agencies—government
2873 Urea—*mfg*
2821 Urea resins—*mfg*
2822 Urethane rubbers—*mfg*
3088 Urinals, plastics—*mfg*
3069 Urinals, rubber—*mfg*

3261 Urinals, vitreous china—*mfg*
3431 Urinals: enameled iron, cast iron, and pressed metal—*mfg*
8071 Urinalysis laboratories
3281 Urns, cut stone—*mfg*
3634 Urns, electric: household—*mfg*
3299 Urns, gypsum or papier-mache: factory production only—*mfg*
8011 Urologists, offices of
7363 Usher service
3365 Utensils, cast aluminum—*mfg*
3469 Utensils, metal, except cast: household, commercial, and hospital—*mfg*
2656 Utensils, paper: except those made from pressed or molded pulp—mfpm—*mfg*
3469 Utensils, porcelain enameled: household, commercial, and hospital—*mfg*
2679 Utensils, pressed and molded pulp—mfpm—*mfg*
3479 Utensils, retinning of: not done in rolling mills—*mfg*
4939 Utilities, combination of
3448 Utility buildings, prefabricated: metal—*mfg*
3429 Utility carriers, car top—*mfg*
3089 Utility containers, plastics—*mfg*
0783 Utility line tree trimming services
7372 Utility software, computer: prepackaged
7519 Utility trailer rental
5599 Utility trailers—retail

V

3052 V-belts, rubber or plastics—*mfg*
6733 Vacation funds for employees
0751 Vaccinating livestock, except by veterinarians
0752 Vaccinating pets and other animal specialties, except by veterinarians
2836 Vaccines—*mfg*
3429 Vacuum bottles and jugs—*mfg*
3714 Vacuum brakes, motor vehicle—*mfg*
3743 Vacuum brakes, railway—*mfg*
3052 Vacuum cleaner hose, plastics or rubber—*mfg*
5722 Vacuum cleaner stores—retail
3635 Vacuum cleaners and sweepers, electric: household—*mfg*
3635 Vacuum cleaners and sweepers, electric: household—*mfg*
3589 Vacuum cleaners and sweepers, electric: industrial and commercial—*mfg*
5064 Vacuum cleaners, household—wholesale
1796 Vacuum cleaning systems, built-in—contractors
5087 Vacuum cleaning systems—wholesale

3567 Vacuum furnaces and ovens—*mfg*
3563 Vacuum pumps, except laboratory—*mfg*
3821 Vacuum pumps, laboratory—*mfg*
3625 Vacuum relays—*mfg*
3443 Vacuum tanks, metal plate—*mfg*
3825 Vacuum tube bridges (electrical measuring instruments)—*mfg*
3671 Vacuum tubes—*mfg*
3443 Vacuum tunnels, metal plate—*mfg*
4959 Vacuuming of airport runways
3524 Vacuums, residential lawn—*mfg*
2771 Valentine cards, except hand painted—*mfg*
7212 Valet apparel service
7299 Valet parking
3161 Valises, regardless of material—*mfg*
2861 Valonia extract—*mfg*
7373 Value-added resellers, computer systems
3714 Valve cores, tire—*mfg*
3541 Valve grinding machines—*mfg*
5085 Valves and fittings, except plumbers'—wholesale
3714 Valves, PCV—*mfg*
3491 Valves, air ventilating—*mfg*
3492 Valves, automatic control: fluid power—metal—*mfg*
3491 Valves, automatic control: industrial, except fluid power—*mfg*
3592 Valves, engine: intake and exhaust—*mfg*
3069 Valves, hard rubber—*mfg*
3492 Valves, hydraulic and pneumatic control: fluid power—metal—*mfg*
3491 Valves, industrial: gate, globe, check, pop safety, and relief—*mfg*
3491 Valves, nuclear—*mfg*
3494 Valves, plumbing and heating: metal—*mfg*
5074 Valves, plumbing and heating—wholesale
3491 Valves, power transfer: except fluid power—*mfg*
3491 Valves, relief: over 15 lbs. w.s.p.—*mfg*
3491 Valves, solenoid: except fluid power—*mfg*
3131 Vamps, leather—*mfg*
7532 Van conversions, except on a factory basis
3713 Van-type bodies, all purpose—*mfg*
1094 Vanadium ore mining
3599 Vanes, weather—*mfg*
2869 Vanillin, synthetic—*mfg*
2434 Vanities, bathroom, wood: to be installed—*mfg*
2514 Vanities, household: metal—*mfg*
3961 Vanity cases, except precious metal and leather—*mfg*
3172 Vanity cases, leather—*mfg*
3911 Vanity cases, precious metal—*mfg*
2511 Vanity dressers—*mfg*
4119 Vanpool operation

3716 Vans, self-propelled: conversion on a factory basis for recreational use—*mfg*
5012 Vans—wholesale
3822 Vapor heating controls—*mfg*
3641 Vapor lamps, electric—*mfg*
3569 Vapor separators (machinery)—*mfg*
3634 Vaporizers, electric: household—*mfg*
3674 Variable capacitance diodes—*mfg*
2674 Variety bags, uncoated paper—mfpm—*mfg*
2011 Variety meats edible organs—mitse—*mfg*
5331 Variety stores, limited price—retail
3676 Varistors—*mfg*
3991 Varnish brushes—*mfg*
2851 Varnish removers—*mfg*
2851 Varnish stains—*mfg*
2851 Varnishes—*mfg*
5198 Varnishes—wholesale
3479 Varnishing of metal products, for the trade—*mfg*
2295 Varnishing of textiles—*mfg*
3281 Vases, cut stone—*mfg*
3229 Vases, glass—*mfg*
3299 Vases, gypsum or papier-mache: factory production only—*mfg*
3269 Vases, pottery (china, earthenware, and stoneware)—*mfg*
2262 Vat dyeing of manmade fiber and silk broadwoven fabrics—*mfg*
2865 Vat dyes, synthetic—*mfg*
3443 Vats, metal plate—*mfg*
3444 Vats, sheet metal—*mfg*
2449 Vats, wood: coopered—*mfg*
2499 Vats, wood: except coopered—*mfg*
7922 Vaudeville companies
3499 Vault doors and linings, metal—*mfg*
5044 Vaults and safes—wholesale
3499 Vaults, except burial vaults: metal—*mfg*
3272 Vaults, grave: concrete and precast terrazzo—*mfg*
3995 Vaults, grave: metal—*mfg*
2011 Veal—mitse—*mfg*
5431 Vegetable and fruit stands—retail
2449 Vegetable baskets, veneer and splint—*mfg*
0181 Vegetable bedding plants, growing of
5199 Vegetable cake and meal—wholesale
2079 Vegetable cooking and salad oils, except corn oil: refined—*mfg*
5149 Vegetable cooking oil—wholesale
2449 Vegetable crates, wood: wirebound—*mfg*
0723 Vegetable drying
0161 Vegetable farms
2034 Vegetable flour, meal, and powders—*mfg*
2833 Vegetable gelatin (agar-agar)—*mfg*
3523 Vegetable grading, cleaning and sorting machines: farm—*mfg*

2033 Vegetable juices: canned, bottled and bulk—*mfg*

5431 Vegetable markets and stands—retail

3556 Vegetable oil processing machinery—*mfg*

2833 Vegetable oils, medicinal grade: refined and concentrated—*mfg*

2899 Vegetable oils, vulcanized or sulfurized—*mfg*

2033 Vegetable pie mixes—*mfg*

0723 Vegetable precooling, not in connection with transportation

2033 Vegetable purees—*mfg*

2035 Vegetable sauces, except tomato—*mfg*

0723 Vegetable sorting, grading, and packing

2076 Vegetable tallow—*mfg*

0723 Vegetable vacuum cooling

0182 Vegetables grown under cover

2099 Vegetables peeled for the trade—*mfg*

2033 Vegetables, canned—*mfg*

2034 Vegetables, dried or dehydrated—*mfg*

5148 Vegetables, fresh—wholesale

0722 Vegetables, machine harvesting of

2035 Vegetables, pickled and brined—*mfg*

2037 Vegetables, quick frozen and coldpack (frozen)—*mfg*

2034 Vegetables, sulphured—*mfg*

3429 Vehicle hardware: aircraft, automobile, railroad, etc.—*mfg*

2491 Vehicle lumber, treated—*mfg*

2426 Vehicle stock, hardwood—*mfg*

3824 Vehicle tank meters—*mfg*

3944 Vehicles except bicycles, children's—*mfg*

5092 Vehicles, children's—wholesale

3711 Vehicles, motor: including amphibian—*mfg*

2396 Veils and veiling, hat—*mfg*

3999 Veils made of hair—*mfg*

3111 Vellum leather—*mfg*

2211 Velours—*mfg*

2211 Velveteens—*mfg*

2221 Velvets, manmade fiber and silk—*mfg*

5962 Vending machine sale of products

3581 Vending machines for merchandise: coin-operated—*mfg*

7359 Vending machines, rental only

5046 Vending machines—wholesale

2449 Veneer baskets, for fruits and vegetables—*mfg*

2411 Veneer logs—*mfg*

3553 Veneer mill machines—*mfg*

2435 Veneer mills, hardwood—*mfg*

2436 Veneer mills, softwood—*mfg*

2499 Veneer work, inlaid—*mfg*

5031 Veneer—wholesale

7349 Venetian blind cleaning, including work done on owners' premises

3553 Venetian blind machines (woodworking machinery)—*mfg*

7699 Venetian blind repair shops

5719 Venetian blind shops—retail

2431 Venetian blind slats, wood—*mfg*

2241 Venetian blind tapes—*mfg*

2591 Venetian blinds—*mfg*

2836 Venoms—*mfg*

5075 Ventilating equipment and supplies—wholesale

3634 Ventilating fans, electric: household—kitchen—*mfg*

1711 Ventilating work, with or without sheet metalwork—contractors

3564 Ventilating, blowing, and exhaust fans: except household and kitchen—*mfg*

4741 Ventilation of railroad cars

3444 Ventilators, sheet metal—*mfg*

6799 Venture capital companies

1429 Verde' antique, crushed and broken—quarrying

1411 Verde' antique, dimension—quarrying

3577 Verifiers—*mfg*

2098 Vermicelli—*mfg*

1499 Vermiculite mining

3295 Vermiculite, exfoliated—*mfg*

2834 Vermifuges—*mfg*

2816 Vermilion pigments—*mfg*

3545 Verniers (machinists' precision tools)—*mfg*

3541 Vertical turning and boring machines (metalworking)—*mfg*

3443 Vessels, pressure: industrial—metal plate (made in boiler shops)—*mfg*

3443 Vessels, process and storage: metal plate (made in boiler shops)—*mfg*

2389 Vestments, academic and clerical—mfpm—*mfg*

2337 Vests, except tailored: women's, misses', and juniors'—mfpm—*mfg*

2386 Vests, leather or sheep-lined—*mfg*

2329 Vests, nontailored including sweater—men's and boys'—mfpm—*mfg*

2339 Vests, not tailored: women's, misses' and juniors—mfpm—*mfg*

2311 Vests, tailored: men's and boys'—*mfg*

9451 Veterans' affairs offices

8641 Veterans' organizations

0741 Veterinarians for livestock

0742 Veterinarians for pets and other animal specialties

3841 Veterinarians' instruments and apparatus—*mfg*

2834 Veterinary pharmaceutical preparations—*mfg*

0741 Veterinary services for livestock

0742 Veterinary services for pets and other animal specialties

8734 Veterinary testing laboratories

1622 Viaduct construction—general contractors

3221 Vials, glass: made in glassmaking establishments—*mfg*

3231 Vials, made from purchased glass—*mfg*

3089 Vials, plastics—*mfg*

3931 Vibraphones—*mfg*

3829 Vibration meters, analyzers, and calibrators—*mfg*

3531 Vibrators for concrete construction—*mfg*

3999 Vibrators, electric: designed for beauty and barber shops—*mfg*

3612 Vibrators, interrupter—*mfg*

5731 Video camera stores—retail

3651 Video camera-audio recorders, household—*mfg*

3651 Video cassette recorders/players—*mfg*

5064 Video disc players—wholesale

7841 Video disk rental to the general public

7993 Video game arcades

3944 Video game machines, except coin-operated—*mfg*

7221 Video photography, portrait

7539 Video recorder and player rental and leasing

7622 Video recorder or player repair

3695 Video recording tape, blank—*mfg*

7819 Video tape or disk reproduction

7812 Video tape production

5731 Video tape recorder stores—retail

7841 Video tape rental to the general public

5735 Video tape stores—retail

7822 Video tapes, recorded—wholesale

3651 Video triggers (remote control television devices)—*mfg*

3679 Video triggers, except remote control television devices—*mfg*

2013 Vienna sausage—mfpm—*mfg*

2221 Vinal broadwoven fabrics—*mfg*

3523 Vine pullers—*mfg*

2099 Vinegar—*mfg*

2035 Vinegar pickles and relishes—*mfg*

0721 Vineyard cultivation services

0762 Vineyard management and maintenance, with or without crop services

0172 Vineyards

2869 Vinyl acetate—*mfg*

3081 Vinyl and vinyl copolymer film and sheet, unsupported—*mfg*

3292 Vinyl asbestos tile—*mfg*

2295 Vinyl coated fabrics—*mfg*

2851 Vinyl coatings, strippable—*mfg*

2824 Vinyl fibers—*mfg*

1752 Vinyl floor tile and sheet installation—contractors

2851 Vinyl plastisol—*mfg*

2821 Vinyl resins—*mfg*

2824 Vinylidene chloride fibers—*mfg*

2221 Vinyon broadwoven fabrics—*mfg*

3931 Violas and parts—*mfg*

3931 Violins and parts—*mfg*

2835 Viral test diagnostic reagents—*mfg*

2836 Viruses—*mfg*

2823 Viscose fibers, bands, strips, and yarn—*mfg*

3829 Viscosimeters, except industrial process type—*mfg*

3823 Viscosimeters, industrial process type—*mfg*

3423 Vises, carpenters'—*mfg*

3423 Vises, except machine—*mfg*

3545 Vises, machine (machine tool accessories)—*mfg*

2752 Visiting cards, lithographed—*mfg*

2759 Visiting cards, printed: except lithographed or gravure—*mfg*

2754 Visiting cards: gravure printing—*mfg*

8082 Visiting nurse associations

2396 Visors, cap—*mfg*

2044 Vitamin and mineral enriched rice—*mfg*

5499 Vitamin food stores—retail

2834 Vitamin preparations—*mfg*

2833 Vitamins, natural and synthetic: bulk, uncompounded—*mfg*

5122 Vitamins—wholesale

8249 Vocational apprenticeship training

8299 Vocational counseling, except rehabilitation counseling

8211 Vocational high schools

8331 Vocational rehabilitation agencies

8331 Vocational rehabilitation counseling

8249 Vocational schools: except high schools, data processing, or business

8331 Vocational training agencies, except schools

2085 Vodka—*mfg*

3679 Voice controls—*mfg*

4813 Voice telephone communications, except radio telephone

2655 Voids and pans, fiber and cardboard—mfpm—*mfg*

2211 Voiles, cotton—*mfg*

2221 Voiles, manmade fiber and silk—*mfg*

1499 Volcanic ash mining

1429 Volcanic rock, crushed and broken—quarrying

1411 Volcanic rock, dimension—quarrying

3825 Volt-ohm milliammeters—*mfg*

3612 Voltage regulating transformers, electric power—*mfg*
3694 Voltage regulators, motor vehicle—*mfg*
3612 Voltage regulators, transmission and distribution—*mfg*
3825 Voltmeters—*mfg*
3523 Volume guns (irrigation equipment)—*mfg*
3579 Voting machines—*mfg*
5087 Voting machines—wholesale
2655 Vulcanized fiber boxes—mfpm—*mfg*
3089 Vulcanized fiber plate, sheet, rods and tubes—*mfg*
2822 Vulcanized oils—*mfg*
7534 Vulcanizing tires and tubes

W

3949 Wading pools, plastics coated fabric—*mfg*
2299 Wads and wadding, textile—*mfg*
3482 Wads, ammunition: 30 mm. (or 1.18 inch) or less—*mfg*
2493 Waferboard—*mfg*
3674 Wafers (semiconductor devices)—*mfg*
2052 Wafers, sugar—*mfg*
2211 Waffle cloth, cotton—*mfg*
3634 Waffle irons, electric—*mfg*
5064 Waffle irons, electric—wholesale
2038 Waffles, frozen—*mfg*
9651 Wage control agencies—government
3523 Wagons and trailers, farm—*mfg*
3524 Wagons for residential lawn and garden use—*mfg*
3944 Wagons, children's: coaster, express, and play—*mfg*
5963 Wagons, ice cream—retail
3069 Wainscoting, rubber—*mfg*
2431 Wainscots, wood—*mfg*
2396 Waistbands, trouser—*mfg*
3842 Walkers—*mfg*
3944 Walkers, baby (vehicles)—*mfg*
3534 Walkways, moving—*mfg*
3272 Wall base, precast terrazzo—*mfg*
2522 Wall cases, office: except wood—*mfg*
3259 Wall coping, clay—*mfg*
3089 Wall coverings, plastics—*mfg*
3433 Wall heaters, except electric—*mfg*
3634 Wall heaters, household: electric—*mfg*
3645 Wall lamps—*mfg*
3272 Wall squares, concrete—*mfg*
3253 Wall tile, ceramic—*mfg*
2493 Wall tile, fiberboard—*mfg*
5211 Wallboard (composition) dealers—retail
3275 Wallboard, gypsum—*mfg*
2493 Wallboard, wood fiber: cellular fiber or hard pressed—mitse—*mfg*
5031 Wallboard—wholesale

5231 Wallcovering stores—retail
3069 Wallcoverings, rubber—*mfg*
2679 Wallcoverings: paper—mfpm—*mfg*
3172 Wallets, regardless of material—*mfg*
2842 Wallpaper cleaners—*mfg*
1799 Wallpaper removal—contractors
2621 Wallpaper stock (hanging paper)—mitse—*mfg*
5231 Wallpaper stores—retail
2679 Wallpaper, embossed plastics: made on textile backing—mfpm—*mfg*
2679 Wallpaper—mfpm—*mfg*
5198 Wallpaper—wholesale
1741 Walls, retaining: block, stone, or brick—contractors
0173 Walnut groves and farms
0723 Walnut hulling and shelling
2076 Walnut oil—*mfg*
3952 Walnut oil, artists'—*mfg*
3999 Walnut shell flour—*mfg*
2673 Wardrobe bags (closet accessories), plastics film or coated paper—mfpm—*mfg*
3161 Wardrobe bags (luggage)—*mfg*
2392 Wardrobe bags—mfpm—*mfg*
7819 Wardrobe rental for motion picture film production
7299 Wardrobe service, except theatrical
2511 Wardrobes, household: wood—*mfg*
1541 Warehouse construction—general contractors
4221 Warehousing and storage, farm product: other than refrigerated
4226 Warehousing of goods at foreign trade zones
4226 Warehousing of household goods, without local trucking
4222 Warehousing, cold storage or refrigerated
4225 Warehousing, general
4225 Warehousing, self-storage
4226 Warehousing, special: except farm products and cold storage
3812 Warfare countermeasures equipment—*mfg*
5075 Warm air heating and cooling equipment—wholesale
3089 Warmers, bottle: plastics, except foam—*mfg*
2253 Warmup and jogging suits—mitse—*mfg*
2369 Warmup suits: girls', children's, and infants'—mfpm—*mfg*
2329 Warmup suits: men's and boys'—mfpm—*mfg*
2339 Warmup suits: women's, misses', and juniors'—mfpm—*mfg*
2258 Warp (flat) knit fabrics—*mfg*

3552 Warp and knot tying machines (textile machinery)—*mfg*

5131 Warp knit fabrics—wholesale

3552 Warping machines (textile machinery)—*mfg*

6399 Warranty insurance, automobile

6351 Warranty insurance, home

3272 Wash foundations, precast terrazzo—*mfg*

2326 Washable service apparel, men's: hospital, professional, barbers', etc.—*mfg*

2499 Washboards, wood and part wood—*mfg*

2211 Washcloths, woven: made in weaving mills—*mfg*

2392 Washcloths—mfpm—*mfg*

2259 Washcloths—mitse—*mfg*

1629 Washeries construction, mining—general contractors

1231 Washeries, anthracite

1221 Washeries, bituminous coal or lignite

3532 Washers, aggregate and sand: stationary type—*mfg*

3565 Washers, bottle: for food products—*mfg*

5072 Washers, hardware—wholesale

3053 Washers, leather—*mfg*

3452 Washers, metal—*mfg*

3861 Washers, photographic print and film—*mfg*

3089 Washers, plastics—*mfg*

2844 Washes, cosmetic—*mfg*

7542 Washing and polishing, automotive

2841 Washing compounds—*mfg*

3469 Washing machine parts, porcelain enameled—*mfg*

7629 Washing machine repair

5064 Washing machines, household: electric—wholesale

3633 Washing machines, household: including coin-operated—*mfg*

3582 Washing machines, laundry: commercial, including coin-operated—*mfg*

2812 Washing soda (sal soda)—*mfg*

7342 Washroom sanitation service

2673 Waste bags, plastics film and laminated—mfpm—*mfg*

5093 Waste bottles and boxes—wholesale

1629 Waste disposal plant construction—general contractors

9511 Waste management program administration—government

4953 Waste materials disposal at sea

5093 Waste rags—wholesale

5093 Waste, rubber—wholesale

2299 Waste, textile mill: processing of—*mfg*

5093 Waste, textile—wholesale

2655 Wastebaskets, fiber (metal-end or all-fiber)—mfpm—*mfg*

3469 Wastebaskets, stamped metal—*mfg*

5093 Wastepaper, including paper recycling—wholesale

3231 Watch crystals, made from purchased glass—*mfg*

3915 Watch jewels—*mfg*

7631 Watch repair shops

3172 Watch straps, except metal—*mfg*

3961 Watchbands, base metal—*mfg*

3911 Watchbands, precious metal—*mfg*

3873 Watchcases—*mfg*

5094 Watchcases—wholesale

3873 Watches and parts: except crystals and jewels—*mfg*

5094 Watches and parts—wholesale

5944 Watches, including custom made—retail

3221 Water bottles, glass—*mfg*

3069 Water bottles, rubber—*mfg*

3088 Water closets, plastics—*mfg*

3431 Water closets: enameled iron, cast iron, and pressed metal—*mfg*

3952 Water colors, artists'—*mfg*

3589 Water conditioners, for swimming pools—*mfg*

5074 Water conditioning equipment—wholesale

9511 Water control and quality agencies—government

3585 Water coolers, electric—*mfg*

2834 Water decontamination or purification tablets—*mfg*

4971 Water distribution or supply systems for irrigation

3589 Water filters and softeners, household type—*mfg*

2819 Water glass—*mfg*

3822 Water heater controls—*mfg*

5064 Water heaters, electric—wholesale

5074 Water heaters, except electric—wholesale

3639 Water heaters, household: including nonelectric—*mfg*

1381 Water intake well drilling: on a contract basis

3599 Water leak detectors—*mfg*

1623 Water main line construction—general contractors

2851 Water paints—*mfg*

3321 Water pipe, cast iron—*mfg*

9511 Water pollution control agencies

1629 Water power project construction—general contractors

3634 Water pulsating devices, electric—*mfg*

1711 Water pump installation and servicing—contractors

5084 Water pumps, industrial—wholesale

3589 Water purification equipment, household type—*mfg*

7299 Wedding chapels, privately operated
2335 Wedding dresses: women's, misses', and juniors'—mfpm—*mfg*
0721 Weed control, crop: after planting
0711 Weed control, crop: before planting
3523 Weeding machines, farm—*mfg*
2257 Weft knit fabrics—*mfg*
5131 Weft knit fabrics—wholesale
7389 Weighing foods and other commodities, not connected with transportation
3596 Weighing machines and apparatus, except laboratory—*mfg*
4785 Weighing services connected with transportation
7389 Welcoming service
3315 Welded steel wire fabric, made in wire-drawing plants—*mfg*
3199 Welders' aprons, leather—*mfg*
3151 Welders' gloves—*mfg*
3842 Welders' hoods—*mfg*
3199 Welders' jackets, leggings, and sleeves: leather—*mfg*
3548 Welding accessories, electric and gas—*mfg*
3548 Welding and cutting apparatus, gas or electric—*mfg*
1799 Welding contractors, operating at site of construction
2899 Welding fluxes—*mfg*
5084 Welding machinery and equipment—wholesale
3544 Welding positioners (jigs)—*mfg*
3356 Welding rods—*mfg*
7692 Welding shops, including automotive
3548 Welding wire, bare and coated—*mfg*
3443 Weldments—*mfg*
6371 Welfare pensions
3494 Well adapters, tipless: metal—*mfg*
3317 Well casing, wrought: welded, lock joint, and heavy riveted—mfpm—*mfg*
3312 Well casings, iron and steel: made in steel works or rolling mills—*mfg*
3272 Well curbing, concrete—*mfg*
1781 Well drilling, water: except oil or gas field water intake—contractors
1381 Well drilling: gas, oil, and water intake—on a contract basis
1389 Well foundation grading, oil and gas wells: on a contract basis
3533 Well logging equipment—*mfg*
1389 Well logging: on a contract basis
1389 Well plugging and abandoning, oil and gas wells: on a contract basis
5082 Well points (drilling equipment)—wholesale
1389 Well pumping, oil and gas: on a contract basis

1389 Well servicing, oil and gas wells: on a contract basis
2892 Well shooting torpedoes (explosives)—*mfg*
3533 Well surveying machinery—*mfg*
3531 Wellpoint systems—*mfg*
3444 Wells, light: sheet metal—*mfg*
3111 Welting leather—*mfg*
3131 Welting, leather (cut stock and findings)—*mfg*
2399 Welts—mfpm—*mfg*
3111 Wet blues—*mfg*
5149 Wet corn milling products—wholesale
2631 Wet machine board—mitse—*mfg*
3069 Wet suits, rubber—*mfg*
2843 Wetting agents—*mfg*
2077 Whale oil, refined—*mfg*
1629 Wharf construction—general contractors
2511 Whatnot shelves, wood—*mfg*
0111 Wheat farms
2043 Wheat flakes—*mfg*
2041 Wheat flour—*mfg*
2041 Wheat germ—*mfg*
2046 Wheat gluten—*mfg*
2041 Wheat mill feed—*mfg*
2046 Wheat starch—*mfg*
5153 Wheat—wholesale
3825 Wheatstone bridges (electrical measuring instruments)—*mfg*
7539 Wheel alignment, automotive
3559 Wheel balancing equipment, automotive—*mfg*
3842 Wheel chairs—*mfg*
3559 Wheel mounting and balancing equipment, automotive—*mfg*
3812 Wheel position indicators and transmitters, aircraft—*mfg*
3423 Wheel pullers, handtools—*mfg*
3545 Wheel turning equipment, diamond point and other (machine tool accessories)—*mfg*
3799 Wheelbarrows—*mfg*
3843 Wheels, abrasive: dental—*mfg*
3291 Wheels, abrasive: except dental—*mfg*
3728 Wheels, aircraft—*mfg*
3462 Wheels, car and locomotive: forged—not made in rolling mills—*mfg*
3312 Wheels, car and locomotive: iron and steel—mitse—*mfg*
3291 Wheels, diamond abrasive—*mfg*
3291 Wheels, grinding: artificial—*mfg*
3714 Wheels, motor vehicle—*mfg*
5013 Wheels, motor vehicle: new—wholesale
3499 Wheels, stamped metal, disc type: wheelbarrow, stroller, lawnmower—*mfg*
1499 Whetstone quarrying
3291 Whetstones, artificial—*mfg*

2021 Whey butter—*mfg*
2022 Whey, raw: liquid—*mfg*
2023 Whey: concentrated, condensed, dried, evaporated, and powdered—*mfg*
2353 Whimseys and miniatures (millinery)—*mfg*
2026 Whipped cream—*mfg*
2023 Whipped topping, dry mix—*mfg*
2026 Whipped topping, except frozen or dry mix—*mfg*
2038 Whipped topping, frozen—*mfg*
3634 Whippers, household: electric—*mfg*
3199 Whips, horse—*mfg*
3199 Whipstocks—*mfg*
3842 Whirlpool baths, hydrotherapy equipment—*mfg*
5999 Whirlpool baths—retail
3991 Whisk brooms—*mfg*
4226 Whiskey warehousing
2085 Whiskey: bourbon, rye, scotch type, and corn—*mfg*
2816 White lead pigments—*mfg*
3369 White metal castings, except die-castings: lead, antimony, and tin—*mfg*
3861 Whiteprint (diazo) paper and cloth, sensitized—*mfg*
3861 Whiteprint (diazotype) reproduction machines and equipment—*mfg*
5044 Whiteprinting equipment—wholesale
3263 Whiteware, fine type semivitreous tableware and kitchenware—*mfg*
1721 Whitewashing—contractors
2816 Whiting—*mfg*
1422 Whiting mining, crushed and broken—quarrying
0912 Whiting, catching of
3829 Whole body counters, nuclear—*mfg*
4725 Wholesale tour operator
3292 Wick, asbestos—*mfg*
2519 Wicker furniture—*mfg*
2241 Wicking—*mfg*
5699 Wig, toupee, and wiglet stores —retail
2211 Wignan, cotton—*mfg*
3999 Wigs, including doll wigs, toupees, or wiglets, except custom made—*mfg*
5199 Wigs—wholesale
9512 Wildlife conservation agencies—government
0971 Wildlife management
1031 Willemite mining
2519 Willow furniture—*mfg*
2499 Willow ware, except furniture—*mfg*
2273 Wilton carpets—*mfg*
3531 Winches, all types—*mfg*
5084 Winches—wholesale

9512 Wind and water erosion control agencies—government
3999 Wind chimes—*mfg*
3827 Wind correctors, military—*mfg*
3829 Wind direction indicators—*mfg*
5083 Wind machines (frost protection equipment)—wholesale
3511 Wind powered turbine-generator sets—*mfg*
3443 Wind tunnels—*mfg*
2329 Windbreakers: men's and boys'—mfpm—*mfg*
2339 Windbreakers: women's, misses', and juniors'—mfpm—*mfg*
3552 Winders (textile machinery)—*mfg*
2282 Winding yarn: wool, mohair, or similar animal fibers—*mfg*
2282 Winding yarn: cotton, silk, wool, and man-made fiber continuous filament—*mfg*
3523 Windmill heads and towers—*mfg*
3511 Windmills for generating power—*mfg*
3523 Windmills for pumping water (agricultural machinery)—*mfg*
1751 Window and door (prefabricated) installation—contractors
2541 Window backs, store and lunchroom: prefabricated—wood—*mfg*
2842 Window cleaning preparations—*mfg*
7349 Window cleaning service
3993 Window cutouts and displays—*mfg*
3442 Window frames and sash, metal—*mfg*
3089 Window frames and sash, plastics—*mfg*
2431 Window frames and sash, wood and covered wood—*mfg*
5031 Window frames, all materials—wholesale
3089 Window frames, plastics—*mfg*
3211 Window glass, clear and colored—*mfg*
5039 Window glass—wholesale
3089 Window screening, plastics—*mfg*
3442 Window screens, metal frame—*mfg*
2431 Window screens, wood—*mfg*
2211 Window shade cloth, cotton—*mfg*
2295 Window shade cloth, impregnated or coated—*mfg*
1799 Window shade installation—contractors
7699 Window shade repair shops
2591 Window shade rollers and fittings—*mfg*
5719 Window shade shops—retail
2591 Window shades, except canvas—*mfg*
3272 Window sills, cast stone—*mfg*
7549 Window tinting, automotive
2431 Window trim, wood and covered wood—*mfg*
7389 Window trimming service
2431 Window units, wood and covered wood—*mfg*
5031 Windows and doors—wholesale

3442 Windows, louver: all metal or metal frame—*mfg*

2431 Windows, louver: wood—*mfg*

3089 Windows, louver: plastics—*mfg*

3231 Windows, stained glass: made from purchased glass—*mfg*

5211 Windows, storm: wood or metal—retail

3089 Windows, storm: plastics—*mfg*

3523 Windrowers (agricultural machinery)—*mfg*

3714 Windshield frames, motor vehicle—*mfg*

3714 Windshield wiper systems, all types—*mfg*

3231 Windshields, made from purchased glass—*mfg*

3089 Windshields, plastics—*mfg*

3949 Windsurfing boards and equipment—*mfg*

5813 Wine bars

2084 Wine cellars, bonded: engaged in blending wines—*mfg*

2084 Wine coolers (beverages)—*mfg*

5182 Wine coolers, alcoholic—wholesale

5921 Wine, packaged—retail

2084 Wines—*mfg*

5182 Wines—wholesale

3728 Wing assemblies and parts, aircraft—*mfg*

3714 Winterfronts, motor vehicle—*mfg*

2899 Wintergreen oil—*mfg*

3714 Wipers, windshield: motor vehicle—*mfg*

5093 Wiping rags, including washing and reconditioning—wholesale

7218 Wiping towel supply service

5063 Wire and cables, interior—wholesale

3496 Wire and wire products mfpm: except insulated wire, and nails and spikes—*mfg*

3315 Wire carts: household, grocery, and industrial—made in wiredrawing plants—*mfg*

3357 Wire cloth, nonferrous: made in wiredrawing plants—*mfg*

3315 Wire cloth, steel: made in wiredrawing plants—*mfg*

5039 Wire fence, gates, and accessories—wholesale

3315 Wire garment hangers, steel: made in wiredrawing plants—*mfg*

4822 Wire or cable telegraph

3315 Wire products, ferrous: made in wiredrawing plants—*mfg*

3312 Wire products, iron and steel: made in steel works or rolling mills—*mfg*

5051 Wire rods—wholesale

2298 Wire rope centers—*mfg*

5063 Wire rope or cable, insulated—wholesale

5051 Wire rope or cable, not insulated—wholesale

3357 Wire screening, nonferrous: made in wiredrawing plants—*mfg*

5051 Wire screening—wholesale

4813 Wire telephone

3496 Wire winding of purchased wire—*mfg*

3355 Wire, aluminum: made in rolling mills—*mfg*

3496 Wire, concrete reinforcing: made from purchased wire—*mfg*

3351 Wire, copper and copper alloy: made in brass mills—*mfg*

3315 Wire, ferrous: made in wiredrawing plants—*mfg*

3316 Wire, flat: cold-rolled strip—not made in hot-rolling mills—*mfg*

5063 Wire, insulated—wholesale

3356 Wire, nonferrous except copper and aluminum: made in rolling mills—*mfg*

3357 Wire, nonferrous: bare, insulated, or armored—mfpm—*mfg*

5051 Wire, not insulated—wholesale

3315 Wire, steel: insulated or armored—*mfg*

3549 Wiredrawing and fabricating machinery and equipment, except dies—*mfg*

3544 Wiredrawing and straightening dies—*mfg*

3672 Wiring boards—*mfg*

5063 Wiring devices—wholesale

3714 Wiring harness sets motor vehicles: except ignition—*mfg*

5063 Wiring materials, interior—wholesale

5063 Wiring supplies—wholesale

1061 Wolframite mining

9441 Women's bureaus

2861 Wood alcohol, natural—*mfg*

5199 Wood carvings—wholesale

2421 Wood chips produced at mill—*mfg*

2411 Wood chips, produced in the field—*mfg*

5099 Wood chips—wholesale

2861 Wood creosote—*mfg*

5989 Wood dealers, fuel—retail

2861 Wood distillates—*mfg*

3559 Wood drying kilns—*mfg*

2491 Wood fence: pickets, poling, rails—treated—*mfg*

2851 Wood fillers and sealers—*mfg*

1752 Wood flooring—contractors

2499 Wood flour—*mfg*

3131 Wood heel blocks, for sale as such—*mfg*

3131 Wood heels, finished (shoe findings)—*mfg*

2861 Wood oils, product of hardwood distillation—*mfg*

2491 Wood products, creosoted—*mfg*

2611 Wood pulp—*mfg*

3452 Wood screws, metal—*mfg*

5031 Wood siding—wholesale

2851 Wood stains—*mfg*

2429 Wood wool (excelsior)—*mfg*

2499 Wood, except furniture: turned and carved—*mfg*
2899 Wood, plastic—*mfg*
5719 Woodburning stoves—retail
2499 Woodenware, kitchen and household—*mfg*
3931 Woodwind and brass wind musical instrument—*mfg*
2431 Woodwork, interior and ornamental: e.g., windows, doors, sash, and mantels—*mfg*
5084 Woodworking machinery—wholesale
3553 Woodworking machines—*mfg*
4221 Wool and mohair warehousing
3552 Wool and worsted finishing machines—*mfg*
2231 Wool broad woven fabrics—*mfg*
2299 Wool felts, pressed or needle loom—*mfg*
2231 Wool felts, woven—*mfg*
2299 Wool grease, mohair, and similar fibers—*mfg*
2241 Wool narrow woven goods—*mfg*
0214 Wool production
3999 Wool pulling—*mfg*
2299 Wool scouring and carbonizing—*mfg*
2299 Wool shoddy—*mfg*
5159 Wool tops and noils—wholesale
2299 Wool tops, combing and converting—*mfg*
2299 Wool waste processing—*mfg*
2282 Wool yarn: twisting, winding, or spooling—*mfg*
3296 Wool, mineral: made of rock, slag, and silica minerals—*mfg*
5159 Wool, raw—wholesale
3291 Wool, steel—*mfg*
5131 Woolen and worsted piece goods—wholesale
5199 Woolen and worsted yarns—wholesale
2035 Worcestershire sauce—*mfg*
3579 Word processing equipment—*mfg*
7338 Word processing service (typing)
2599 Work benches, factory—*mfg*
2599 Work benches, industrial—*mfg*
7218 Work clothing supply service, industrial
5136 Work clothing, men's and boys'—wholesale
8331 Work experience centers
2326 Work garments, waterproof, men's and boys'; except raincoats—mfpm—*mfg*
3069 Work gloves and mittens: rubber—*mfg*
2259 Work gloves and mittens—mitse—*mfg*
3151 Work gloves, leather—*mfg*
3089 Work gloves, plastics—*mfg*
2326 Work jackets—*mfg*
2326 Work pants, except jeans and dungarees: men's and boys'—*mfg*
3531 Work platforms, elevated—*mfg*
2326 Work shirts: men's and boys'—*mfg*

3143 Work shoes, men's—*mfg*
6331 Workers' compensation insurance
6153 Working capital financing
9441 Workman's compensation offices—government
2326 Workpants, except jeans and dungarees: men's and boys'—mfpm—*mfg*
3821 Worktables, laboratory—*mfg*
0279 Worm farms
5199 Worms—wholesale
5131 Worsted and woolen piece goods, woven—wholesale
2299 Worsted combing—*mfg*
2231 Worsted fabrics, broadwoven—*mfg*
3496 Woven wire products, made from purchased wire—*mfg*
2429 Wrappers, excelsior—*mfg*
2752 Wrappers, lithographed—*mfg*
2759 Wrappers, printed: except lithographed or gravure—*mfg*
2754 Wrappers: gravure printing—*mfg*
3565 Wrapping machines—*mfg*
5113 Wrapping paper and products—wholesale
2671 Wrapping paper, coated or laminated—mfpm—*mfg*
2621 Wrapping paper—mitse—*mfg*
3999 Wreaths, artificial—*mfg*
7549 Wrecker service (towing), automotive
1795 Wrecking of buildings or other structures, except marine—contractors
3423 Wrenches (handtools)—*mfg*
3633 Wringers, domestic laundry—*mfg*
3589 Wringers, mop—*mfg*
2253 Wristlets—mitse—*mfg*
8999 Writers
2899 Writing ink and fluids—*mfg*
5112 Writing ink—wholesale
2678 Writing paper and envelopes, boxed sets—mfpm—*mfg*
2621 Writing paper—mitse—*mfg*
5943 Writing supplies—retail
2678 Writing tablets, mfpm—*mfg*
3317 Wrought pipe and tubes: welded, lock joint, and heavy riveted—mfpm—*mfg*
3312 Wrought pipe and tubing, made in steel works or rolling mills—*mfg*
1061 Wulfenite mining
1499 Wurtzilite mining

X

3825 X-Y recorders (plotters), except computer peripheral equipment—*mfg*
3844 X-ray apparatus and tubes: medical, industrial, research, and control—*mfg*
3861 X-ray film—*mfg*

3844 X-ray generators—*mfg*
8734 X-ray inspection service, industrial
8071 X-ray laboratories, including dental (not manufacturing)
5047 X-ray machines and parts, medical—wholesale
3861 X-ray plates, sensitized—*mfg*
2879 Xanthone (formulated)—*mfg*
2865 Xylene, made in chemical plants—*mfg*
3931 Xylophones and parts—*mfg*

Y

3494 Y bends and branches, pipe: metal—*mfg*
4493 Yacht basins, operation of
7389 Yacht brokers
7997 Yacht clubs, membership
0139 Yam farms
5949 Yard goods stores—retail
5131 Yard goods—wholesale
3423 Yardsticks, metal—*mfg*
2499 Yardsticks, wood—*mfg*
2231 Yarn bleaching, dyeing, and finishing: wool, mohair, and similar animal fibers—*mfg*
2269 Yarn bleaching, dyeing, and other finishing: except wool—*mfg*
5949 Yarn shops (knitting)—retail
2281 Yarn spinning: cotton, silk, and manmade staple—*mfg*
3552 Yarn texturizing machines—*mfg*
2282 Yarn, animal fiber: twisting, winding, and spooling—*mfg*
3292 Yarn, asbestos—*mfg*
2281 Yarn, carpet and rug: animal fiber—spinning, twisting and spooling—*mfg*
2823 Yarn, cellulosic: made in chemical plants—*mfg*
2241 Yarn, elastic: fabric covered—*mfg*
3229 Yarn, fiberglass: made in glass plants—*mfg*
2299 Yarn, specialty and novelty—*mfg*
2281 Yarn, spun: cotton, silk, manmade fiber, wool, and animal fiber—*mfg*
2823 Yarn, viscose—*mfg*
2211 Yarn-dyed fabrics, cotton—*mfg*
2281 Yarn: cotton, silk, wool, and manmade staple—*mfg*
2299 Yarn: flax, jute, hemp, and ramie—*mfg*
2299 Yarn: metallic, ceramic, or paper fibers—*mfg*
2241 Yarns, fabric covered rubber—*mfg*
2295 Yarns, plastics coated: made from purchased yarns—*mfg*

5199 Yarns—wholesale
2741 Yearbooks: publishing and printing, or publishing only—*mfg*
2099 Yeast—*mfg*
5149 Yeast—wholesale
7999 Yoga instruction
2023 Yogurt mix—*mfg*
2026 Yogurt, except frozen—*mfg*
2024 Yogurt, frozen—*mfg*
5143 Yogurt—wholesale
8641 Youth associations, except hotel units
8322 Youth centers
8322 Youth self-help organizations

Z

2824 Zein fibers—*mfg*
3674 Zener diodes—*mfg*
3356 Zinc and zinc alloy bars, plates, pipe, rods, sheets, tubing, and wire—*mfg*
3369 Zinc castings, except die-castings—*mfg*
2819 Zinc chloride—*mfg*
3364 Zinc die-castings—*mfg*
3339 Zinc dust, primary—*mfg*
3341 Zinc dust, reclaimed—*mfg*
3497 Zinc foil, not made in rolling mills—*mfg*
2834 Zinc ointment—*mfg*
1031 Zinc ore mining
5052 Zinc ore—wholesale
2851 Zinc oxide in oil, paint—*mfg*
2816 Zinc oxide pigments—*mfg*
2816 Zinc pigments: zinc yellow and zinc sulfide—*mfg*
3356 Zinc rolling, drawing, and extruding—*mfg*
3339 Zinc slabs, ingots, and refinery shapes: primary—*mfg*
3341 Zinc smelting and refining, secondary—*mfg*
1031 Zinc-blende (sphalerite) mining
5051 Zinc—wholesale
1031 Zincite mining
3559 Zipper making machinery—*mfg*
2241 Zipper tape—*mfg*
3965 Zippers (slide fasteners)—*mfg*
5131 Zippers—wholesale
3356 Zirconium and zirconium alloy bars, rods, billets, sheets, strip, and tubing—*mfg*
3339 Zirconium metal sponge and granules—*mfg*
1099 Zirconium ore mining
3931 Zithers and parts—*mfg*
9532 Zoning boards and commissions
8422 Zoological gardens
2052 Zwieback—*mfg*

Appendixes

Relation of 1972 to 1977 SIC Industries Showing Only Changes <u>To 1977</u>

(For all industries other than those listed below, 1977 SIC industries are the same as in 1972 or the changes in the industries will affect the classification of few, if any, establishments)

1972 industry		1977 industry	
Code	Short title	Code	Short title
	D. MANUFACTURING		
3792	Travel trailers and campers		
	Motor homes	3716	**Motor homes**
	Travel trailers and campers	3792	**Travel trailers and campers**
	E. TRANSPORTATION AND PUBLIC UTILITIES		
4041	Railway Express Service	1	
	H. FINANCE, INSURANCE, AND REAL ESTATE		
		6798	**Real estate investment trusts**
6799	Investors, not elsewhere classified		
		6799	**Investors, not elsewhere classified**

See footnotes at end of appendix.

Appendix A—Section II

Relation of 1977 to 1972 SIC Industries Showing Only Changes <u>From 1972</u>

(For all industries other than those listed below, 1977 SIC industries are the same as in 1972 or the changes in the industries will affect the classification of few, if any, establishments)

1977 industry		1972 industry	
Code	Short title	Code	Short title
	D. MANUFACTURING		
3716	**Motor homes**		
3792	**Travel trailers & campers**	3792	Travel trailers & campers
	(excludes motor homes)		
	H. FINANCE, INSURANCE, & REAL ESTATE		
6798	**Real estate investment trusts**		
6799	**Investors, nec**	Part 6799	Investors, nec

See footnotes at end of appendix.

Appendix A—Section III

Relation of 1977 to 1987 SIC Industries Showing Only Changes <u>To</u> 1987

(For all industries other than those listed below, 1987 SIC industries are the same as in 1977 or the changes in the industries will affect the classification of few, if any, establishments)

\multicolumn{2}{c}{1977 industry}		\multicolumn{2}{c}{1987 industry}	
Code	Short title	Code	Short title
	A. AGRICULTURE, FORESTRY, AND FISHING		
0181	Ornamental nursery products........................	Part 0181	**Ornamental nursery products**
0182	Food crops grown under cover	Part 0182	**Food crops grown under cover**
0189	Horticultural specialties, nec		
	Ornamental nursery products....................	Part 0181	**Ornamental nursery products**
	Food crops grown under cover	Part 0182	**Food crops grown under cover**
0279	Animal specialties, nec		
	Animal aquaculture	0273	**Animal aquaculture**
	Other animal specialties, nec	0279	**Animal specialties, nec**
0721	Crop planting and protection	Part 0721	**Crop planting and protecting**
0722	Crop harvesting...	Part 0722	**Crop harvesting**
0723	Crop preparation services for market...........	Part 0723	**Crop preparation services for market**
0724	Cotton ginning...	Part 0724	**Cotton ginning**
0729	General crop services		
	Crop planting and protection	Part 0721	**Crop planting and protecting**
	Crop harvesting...	Part 0722	**Crop harvesting**
	Crop preparation services for market.......	Part 0723	**Crop preparation services for market**
	Cotton ginning...	Part 0724	**Cotton ginning**
0821	Forest nurseries and seed gathering............	}	
0843	Extraction of pine gum.................................	} 0831	**Forest products**
0849	Gathering of forest products, nec	}	
	B. MINING		
1051	Bauxite and other aluminum ores	}	
1092	Mercury ores	} 1099	**Metal ores, nec**
1099	Metal ores, nec...	}	
1111 [2]	Anthracite...	1231	**Anthracite mining**

See footnotes at end of appendix.

661

(For all industries other than those listed below, 1987 SIC industries are the same as in 1977 or the changes in the industries will affect the classification of few, if any, establishments)—Con.

1977 industry		1987 industry	
Code	Short title	Code	Short title

B. MINING—Con.

1112	Anthracite mining services............................	1241	Coal mining services
1213	Bituminous & lignite mining services		
		1221	Bituminous coal and lignite—surface
1211	Bituminous coal and lignite		
		1222	Bituminous coal—underground
1452	Bentonite..		
1453	Fire clay		
		1459	Clay and related minerals, nec
1454	Fuller's earth...		
1459	Clay and related minerals, nec....................		
1472	Barite		
1473	Fluorspar...		
1476	Rock salt..	1479	Chemical and fertilizer mining, nec
1477	Sulfur		
1479	Chemical and fertilizer mining, nec		
1492	Gypsum...		
1496	Talc, soapstone, and pyrophyllite..................	1499	Miscellaneous nonmetallic minerals
1499	Nonmetallic minerals, nec...............................		

C. CONSTRUCTION

1611	Highway and street construction		
	Recreational facilities; trailer camps........	Part 1629	Heavy construction, nec
	Culverts and curbs.............................	Part 1771	Concrete work
	Highway and street construction	1611	Highway and street construction
1629	Heavy construction, nec.................................	Part 1629	Heavy construction, nec
1771	Concrete work	Part 1771	Concrete work

D. MANUFACTURING

2016	Poultry dressing plants	2015	Poultry slaughtering and processing
2017	Poultry and egg processing............................		
2032	Canned specialties		
	Fish cakes...	Part 2091	Canned and cured fish and seafoods
	Canned specialties, except fish cakes........	2032	Canned specialties
2034	Dehydrated fruits, vegetables, soups		
	Nuts...	Part 2068	Salted and roasted nuts and seeds
	Dehydrated fruits, vegetables, soups.........	2034	Dehydrated fruits, vegetables, soups
2038	Frozen specialties		
	Bakery products.....................................	2053	Frozen bakery products, except bread

See footnotes at end of appendix.

(For all industries other than those listed below, 1987 SIC industries are the same as in 1977 or the changes in the industries will affect the classification of few, if any, establishments)—Con.

1977 industry		1987 industry	
Code	Short title	Code	Short title
	D. MANUFACTURING—Con.		
2038	Frozen specialities—Con.		
	Other frozen specialties............................	2038	Frozen specialties, nec
2047	Dog, cat, and other pet food		
	Dog and cat food	2047	Dog and cat food
	Other pet food and meat not fit for human consumption.	Part 2048	Prepared feeds, nec
2048	Prepared feeds, nec	Part 2048	Prepared feeds, nec
2065	Confectionery products		
	Salted and roasted nuts.............................	Part 2068	Salted and roasted nuts and seeds
	Other confectionery products......................	2064	Candy and other confectionery products
2066	Chocolate and cocoa products.........................	Part 2066	Chocolate and cocoa products
2091	Canned and cured seafoods............................	Part 2091	Canned and cured fish and seafoods
2099	Food preparations, nec		
	Chocolate	Part 2066	Chocolate and cocoa products
	Potato chips and similar products.............	2096	Potato chips and similar snacks
	Salted and roasted seeds	Part 2068	Salted and roasted nuts and seeds
	Food preparations, nec................................	2099	Food preparations, nec
2258	Warp knit fabric mills................................	Part 2258	Lace & warp knit fabric mills
2271	Woven carpets and rugs................................		
2272	Tufted carpets and rugs	2273	Carpets and rugs
2279	Carpets and rugs, nec		
2281	Yarn mills, except wool...............................	Part 2281	Yarn spinning mills
2282	Throwing and winding mills	Part 2282	Throwing and winding mills
2283	Wool yarn mills		
	Thread..	Part 2284	Thread mills
	Yarn, made in spinning mills...................	Part 2281	Yarn spinning mills
	Yarn, made in throwing and winding mills.	Part 2282	Throwing and winding mills
2284	Thread mills	Part 2284	Thread mills
2291	Felt goods, exc. woven felts & hats..............	Part 2299	Textile goods, nec
2292	Lace goods..	Part 2258	Lace & warp knit fabric mills
2293	Paddings and upholstery filling....................		
2294	Processed textile waste................................	Part 2299	Textile goods, nec
2299	Textile goods, nec		
2321	Men's and boys' shirts and nightwear		
	Shirts..	2321	Men's and boys' shirts
	Nightwear	Part 2322	Men's and boys' underwear & nightwear
2322	Men's and boys' underwear..........................	Part 2322	Men's and boys' underwear & nightwear
2327	Men's and boys' separate trousers...............	Part 2325	Men's and boys' trousers and slacks
2328	Men's and boys' work clothing		
	Jeans and jean-cut casual slacks..............	Part 2325	Men's and boys' trousers and slacks
	Other men's and boys' work clothing.......	2326	Men's and boys' work clothing

See footnotes at end of appendix.

(For all industries other than those listed below, 1987 SIC industries are the same as in 1977 or the changes in the industries will affect the classification of few, if any, establishments)—Con.

1977 industry		1987 industry	
Code	Short title	Code	Short title

D. MANUFACTURING—Con.

1977 industry		1987 industry	
2351	Millinery..	2353	Hats, caps, and millinery
2352	Hats and caps, except millinery		
2363	Children's coats and suits		
2369	Children's outerwear, nec	2369	Girls' and children's outerwear, nec
2411	Logging camps & logging contractors........... (excludes primarily logging but combined with sawmills)	Part 2411	Logging
2421	Sawmills and planing mills, general		
	Logging (combined with sawmills).............	Part 2411	Logging
	Other sawmills and planing mills	2421	Sawmills and planing mills, general
2431	Millwork...	Part 2431	Millwork
2492	Particleboard	Part 2493	Reconstituted wood products
2499	Wood products, nec		
	Reconstituted wood products (e.g., medium density fiberboard, waferboard, oriented strandboard, hardboard).	Part 2493	Reconstituted wood products
	Other wood products, nec............................	2499	Wood products, nec
2522	Metal office furniture	Part 2522	Office furniture, except wood
2542	Metal partitions and fixtures........................	Part 2542	Partitions and fixtures, except wood
2599	Furniture and fixtures, nec		
	Office furniture..	Part 2522	Office furniture, except wood
	Partitions and fixtures	Part 2542	Partitions and fixtures, except wood
	Other furniture and fixtures, nec..............	2599	Furniture and fixtures, nec
2611	Pulp mills..	Part 2611	Pulp mills
2621	Paper mills, except building paper		
	Pulp and paper mills, primarily pulp.......	Part 2611	Pulp mills
	Other paper mills	Part 2621	Paper mills
2631	Paperboard mills		
	Pulp and paperboard mills, primarily pulp.	Part 2611	Pulp mills
	Other paperboard mills	2631	Paperboard mills
		2671	Paper coated & laminated, packaging
2641	Paper coating and glazing...............................		
		2672	Paper coated and laminated, nec
2642 [2]	Envelopes	2677	Envelopes
		2674	Bags: uncoated paper & multiwall
2643	Bags, except textile bags		
		2673	Bags: plastics, laminated, & coated

See footnotes at end of appendix.

(For all industries other than those listed below, 1987 SIC industries are the same as in 1977 or the changes in the industries will affect the classification of few, if any, establishments)—Con.

1977 industry		1987 industry	
Code	Short title	Code	Short title

D. MANUFACTURING—Con.

Code	Short title	Code	Short title
2645 [2]	Die-cut paper and board	2675	Die-cut paper and board
2646	Pressed and molded pulp goods	Part 2679	Converted paper products, nec
2647 [2]	Sanitary paper products	2676	Sanitary paper products
2648 [2]	Stationery products	2678	Stationery products
2649	Converted paper products, nec	Part 2679	Converted paper products, nec
2651	Folding paperboard boxes	Part 2657	Folding paperboard boxes
2654	Sanitary food containers		
	Folding	Part 2657	Folding paperboard boxes
	Other sanitary food containers	2656	Sanitary food containers
2661	Building paper and board mills		
	Insulation board	Part 2493	Reconstituted wood products
	Paper	Part 2621	Paper mills
2751	Commercial printing, letterpress	Part 2759	Commercial printing, nec
2753	Engraving and plate printing		
	Platemaking	Part 2796	Platemaking services
	Printing	Part 2759	Commercial printing, nec
2754	Commercial printing, gravure		
	Platemaking	Part 2796	Platemaking services
	Printing	2754	Commercial printing, gravure
2793	Photoengraving		
2794	Electrotyping and stereotyping	Part 2796	Platemaking services
2795	Lithographic platemaking services		
2819	Industrial inorganic chemicals, nec	Part 2819	Industrial inorganic chemicals, nec
		2835	Diagnostic substances
2831	Biological products		
		2836	Biological products, exc. diagnostic
2869	Industrial organic chemicals, nec		
	Hydrazine	Part 2819	Industrial inorganic chemicals, nec
	Other	2869	Industrial organic chemicals, nec
3031	Reclaimed rubber	Part 3069	Fabricated rubber products, nec
3041 [2]	Rubber and plastics hose and belting	3052	Rubber & plastics hose & belting
3069	Fabricated rubber products, nec	3061	Mechanical rubber goods
		Part 3069	Fabricated rubber products, nec
		3081	Unsupported plastics film & sheet
		3083	Laminated plastics plate & sheet
		3084	Plastics pipe
		3085	Plastics bottles
		3082	Unsupported plastics profile shapes
3079	Miscellaneous plastics products	3086	Plastics foam products
		3087	Custom compounded purchased resins
		3088	Plastics plumbing fixtures
		3089	Plastics products, nec
		Part 3432	Plumbing fixture fittings and trim

See footnotes at end of appendix.

(For all industries other than those listed below, 1987 SIC industries are the same as in 1977 or the changes in the industries will affect the classification of few, if any, establishments)—Con.

1977 industry		1987 industry	
Code	Short title	Code	Short title

D. MANUFACTURING—Con.

Code	Short title	Code	Short title
3264	Porcelain electrical supplies...............	Part 3264	Porcelain electrical supplies
3293 [2]	Gaskets, packing, and sealing devices	3053	Gaskets, packing, and sealing devices
3332	Primary lead....................		
3333	Primary zinc.....................	3339	Primary nonferrous metals, nec
3339	Primary nonferrous metals, nec.................		
		3363	Aluminum die-castings
3361	Aluminum foundries.......................		
		3365	Aluminum foundries
		Part 3364	Nonferrous die-castings, exc. aluminum
3362	Brass, bronze, and copper foundries		
		3366	Copper foundries
		Part 3364	Nonferrous die-castings, exc. aluminum
3369	Nonferrous foundries, nec..................		
		3369	Nonferrous foundries, nec
3423	Hand and edge tools, nec	Part 3423	Hand and edge tools, nec
3432	Plumbing fittings and brass goods	Part 3432	Plumbing fixture fittings and trim
3433	Heating equipment, except electric		
	Incinerators, metal: domestic and commercial.	Part 3567	Industrial furnaces and ovens
	Other heating equipment, except electric	3433	Heating equipment, except electric
3442	Metal doors, sash, and trim		
	Doors, windows, etc. of wood covered with metal.	Part 2431	Millwork
	Other metal doors, sash, and trim.............	3442	Metal doors, sash, and trim
3444	Sheet metal work		
	Curtain wall......................	Part 3449	Miscellaneous metal work
	Other sheet metal work................	3444	Sheet metal work
3449	Miscellaneous metal work................	Part 3449	Miscellaneous metal work
3469	Metal stampings, nec		
	Curtain wall......................	Part 3449	Miscellaneous metal work
	Other metal stampings, nec................	3469	Metal stampings, nec
		Part 3492	Fluid power valves & hose fittings
3494	Valves and pipe fittings	3491	Industrial valves
		3494	Valves and pipe fittings, nec
3531	Construction machinery................	Part 3531	Construction machinery
3536	Hoists, cranes, and monorails		
	Aerial work platforms; automobile wrecker hoists.	Part 3531	Construction machinery
	Automatic stacking machines	Part 3537	Industrial trucks and tractors
	Other hoists, cranes, and monorails..........	3536	Hoists, cranes, and monorails
3537	Industrial trucks and tractors................	Part 3537	Industrial trucks and tractors

See footnotes at end of appendix.

(For all industries other than those listed below, 1987 SIC industries are the same as in 1977 or the changes in the industries will affect the classification of few, if any, establishments)—Con.

1977 industry		1987 industry	
Code	Short title	Code	Short title

D. MANUFACTURING—Con.

3549	Metalworking machinery, nec		
	Welding and soldering machines, nonelectric.	Part 3548	Welding apparatus
	Automotive maintenance equipment........	Part 3559	Special industry machinery, nec
	Other metalworking machinery, nec........	3549	Metalworking machinery, nec
3551	Food products machinery		
	Food packaging machinery.........................	Part 3565	Packaging machinery
	Other food products machinery	3556	Food products machinery
3555	Printing trades machinery		
	Printers' rolls, blankets, and roller covers.	Part 3069	Fabricated rubber products, nec
	Printers mallets...	Part 3423	Hand and edge tools, nec
	Other printing trades machinery	3555	Printing trades machinery
3559	Special industry machinery, nec	Part 3559	Special industry machinery, nec
3561	Pumps and pumping equipment		
	Fluid power equipment...............................	Part 3594	Fluid power pumps and motors
	Other pumps and pumping equipment.....	3561	Pumps and pumping equipment
3565 [2]	Industrial patterns	3543	Industrial patterns
3566	Speed changers, drives, and gears		
	Hydrostatic drives (transmissions)	Part 3594	Fluid power pumps and motors
	Other speed changers, drives, and gears..	3566	Speed changers, drives, and gears
3567	Industrial furnaces and ovens.......................	Part 3567	Industrial furnaces and ovens
3569	General industrial machinery, nec		
	Fluid power pumps and motors	Part 3594	Fluid power pumps and motors
	Packaging machinery, except food	Part 3565	Packaging machinery
	Other general industrial machinery, nec.	3569	General industrial machinery, nec
3572	Typewriters...	Part 3579	Office machines, nec
		3571	Electronic computers
		3572	Computer storage devices
3573	Electronic computing equipment...................	Part 3575	Computer terminals
		3577	Computer peripheral equipment, nec
		Part 3695	Magnetic and optical recording media
3574 [2]	Calculating and accounting machines..........	3578	Calculating and accounting equipment
3576 [2]	Scales and balances, exc. laboratory............	3596	Scales and balances, exc. laboratory
3579	Office machines, nec	Part 3579	Office machines, nec
3585	Refrigeration and heating equipment	Part 3585	Refrigeration and heating equipment
3599	Machinery, except electrical, nec		
	Fluid power cylinders and actuators	Part 3593	Fluid power cylinders & actuators
	Other machinery, except electrical, nec...	3599	Industrial machinery, nec
3613	Switchgear and switchboard apparatus		
	Relays...	Part 3625	Relays and industrial controls

See footnotes at end of appendix.

(For all industries other than those listed below, 1987 SIC industries are the same as in 1977 or the changes in the industries will affect the classification of few, if any, establishments)—Con.

1977 industry		1987 industry	
Code	Short title	Code	Short title
	D. MANUFACTURING—Con.		
3613	Switchgear and switchboard apparatus—Con.		
	Other switchgear and switchboard apparatus.	3613	**Switchgear and switchboard apparatus**
3622	Industrial controls.............................	Part 3625	**Relays and industrial controls**
3623	Welding apparatus, electric.............................	Part 3548	**Welding apparatus**
3636	Sewing machines		
	Household..............................	Part 3639	**Household appliances, nec**
	Commercial and industrial	Part 3559	**Special industry machinery, nec**
3639	Household appliances, nec..............................	Part 3639	**Household appliances, nec**
3641	Electric lamps..............................	Part 3641	**Electric lamps**
3661	Telephone and telegraph apparatus		
	Teletypewriters	Part 3575	**Computer terminals**
	Other telephone and telegraph apparatus.	Part 3661	**Telephone and telegraph apparatus**
3662	Radio and TV communications equipment		
	Modems and other interface equipment ..	Part 3661	**Telephone and telegraph apparatus**
	Radio and TV communications systems and equipment, and broadcast and studio equipment.	3663	**Radio and TV communications equipment**
	Search, detection, navigation, and guidance systems and equipment.	Part 3812	**Search and navigation equipment**
	Other communications equipment	3669	**Communications equipment, nec**
	Hydrological, hydrographic, meteorological, and geophysical equipment.	Part 3829	**Measuring and controlling devices, nec**
	Other radio and television communications equipment.	Part 3699	**Electrical equipment & supplies, nec**
3671	Electron tubes, receiving type......................	} Part 3671	**Electron tubes**
3672	Cathode ray television picture tubes		
3673	Electron tubes, transmitting		
3679	Electronic components, nec		
	Ferrite electronic parts and porcelain electronic supplies.	Part 3264	**Porcelain electrical supplies**
	Relays..............................	Part 3625	**Relays and industrial controls**
	Electron tube parts....................................	Part 3671	**Electron tubes**
	Printed circuit boards...............................	3672	**Printed circuit boards**
	Recording media	Part 3695	**Magnetic and optical recording media**
	Other electronic components, nec	3679	**Electronic components, nec**
		3844	**X-ray apparatus and tubes**
3693	X-ray apparatus and tubes .... {		
		3845	**Electromedical equipment**
3699	Electrical equipment & supplies, nec		
	Electric lamp bulb parts..............................	Part 3641	**Electric lamps**
	Electric comfort heating equipment	Part 3585	**Refrigeration and heating equipment**

See footnotes at end of appendix.

(For all industries other than those listed below, 1987 SIC industries are the same as in 1977 or the changes in the industries will affect the classification of few, if any, establishments)—Con.

1977 industry		1987 industry	
Code	Short title	Code	Short title

D. MANUFACTURING—Con.

3699	Electrical equipment & supplies—Con:		
	Other electrical equipment & supplies, nec.	Part 3699	Electrical equipment & supplies, nec
3728	Aircraft equipment, nec		
	Hydraulic and pneumatic valves	Part 3492	Fluid power valves & hose fittings
	Fluid power pumps and motors	Part 3594	Fluid power pumps and motors
	Fluid power cylinders and actuators	Part 3593	Fluid power cylinders & actuators
	Other aircraft equipment, nec	3728	Aircraft parts and equipment, nec
3811	Engineering & scientific instruments		
	Search, detection, navigation, and guidance instruments.	Part 3812	Search and navigation equipment
	Laboratory apparatus and furniture	3821	Laboratory apparatus and furniture
	Analytical instruments	Part 3826	Analytical instruments
	Surveying and drafting apparatus	Part 3829	Measuring & controlling devices, nec
3829	Measuring & controlling devices, nec	Part 3829	Measuring & controlling devices, nec
3832	Optical instruments and lenses		
	Analytical instruments	Part 3826	Analytical instruments
	Meteorological, hydrographic, hydrological, and geophysical instruments.	Part 3829	Measuring & controlling devices, nec
	Optical instruments	3827	Optical instruments and lenses
3962	Artificial flowers	Part 3999	Manufacturing industries, nec
3963	Buttons		
		3965	Fasteners, buttons, needles, & pins
3964	Needles, pins, and fasteners		
3999	Manufacturing industries, nec	Part 3999	Manufacturing industries, nec

E. TRANSPORTATION AND PUBLIC UTILITIES

4171	Bus terminal facilities		
		4173	Bus terminal and service facilities
4172	Bus service facilities		
4212	Local trucking, without storage		
	Trucking	4212	Local trucking, without storage
	Courier services	Part 4215	Courier services, except by air
4213	Trucking, except local		
	Trucking	4213	Trucking, except local
	Courier services	Part 4215	Courier services, except by air
4224	Household goods warehousing		
		4226	Special warehousing and storage, nec
4226	Special warehousing and storage, nec		

See footnotes at end of appendix.

(For all industries other than those listed below, 1987 SIC industries are the same as in 1977 or the changes in the industries will affect the classification of few, if any, establishments)—Con.

1977 industry		1987 industry	
Code	Short title	Code	Short title

E. TRANSPORTATION AND PUBLIC UTILITIES—Con.

Code	Short title	Code	Short title
4411	Deep sea foreign transportation		
	Deep sea foreign transportation, freight..	4412	Deep sea foreign transportation of freight
	Deep sea foreign transportation, passenger.	Part 4481	Deep sea passenger transportation, except by ferry
4421	Noncontiguous area transportation		
	Noncontiguous territories transportation, freight.	Part 4424	Deep sea domestic transportation of freight
	Noncontiguous territories transportation, passenger.	Part 4481	Deep sea passenger transportation, except by ferry
4422	Coastwise transportation		
	Coastwise transportation, freight..............	Part 4424	Deep sea domestic transportation of freight
	Coastwise transportation, passenger.........	Part 4481	Deep sea passenger transportation, except by ferry
4423	Intercoastal transportation		
	Intercoastal transportation, freight..........	Part 4424	Deep sea domestic transportation of freight
	Intercoastal transportation, passenger.....	Part 4481	Deep sea passenger transportation, except by ferry
4431	Great Lakes transportation		
	Great Lakes-St Lawrence Seaway, freight.	Part 4432	**Freight transportation on the Great Lakes**
	Great Lakes-St Lawrence Seaway, passengers.	Part 4481	Deep sea passenger transportation, except by ferry
	Great Lakes-St Lawrence Seaway, ferries.	Part 4482	Ferries
4441	Transportation on rivers and canals		
	Transportation on rivers and canals, freight.	4449	**Water transportation of freight, nec**
	Transportation on rivers and canals, passenger.	Part 4489	Water passenger transportation, nec
4452	Ferries...	Part 4482	Ferries
4453	Lighterage..	Part 4499	Water transportation of freight, nec
4454 [2]	Towing and tugboat service..........................	4492	**Towing and tugboat service**
4459	Local water transportation, nec		
	Local water transportation of passengers, nec.	Part 4489	Water passenger transportation, nec
	Local water transportation of freight, nec.	Part 4449	Water transportation of freight, nec
4463 [2]	Marine cargo handling.................................	4491	**Marine cargo handling**
4464	Canal operation....................................	Part 4499	Water transportation services, nec
4469	Water transportation services, nec		
	Marinas...	4493	**Marinas**
	Oil spill cleanup...................................	Part 4959	**Sanitary services, nec**

See footnotes at end of appendix.

(For all industries other than those listed below, 1987 SIC industries are the same as in 1977 or the changes in the industries will affect the classification of few, if any, establishments)—Con.

1977 industry		1987 industry	
Code	Short title	Code	Short title

E. TRANSPORTATION AND PUBLIC UTILITIES—Con.

4469	Water transportation services, nec—Con.		
	Other water transportation services, nec.	Part 4499	Water transportation services, nec
4511	Certificated air transportation		
	Air transportation-scheduled......................	Part 4512	Air transportation, scheduled
	Air courier services	Part 4513	Air courier services
4521	Noncertificated air transportation		
	Air transportation-scheduled, except sightseeing and airport services.	Part 4512	Air transportation, scheduled
	Air courier services	Part 4513	Air courier services
	Other noncertificated air transportation.	4522	Air transportation, nonscheduled
4582	Airports and flying fields...............................		
		4581	Airports, flying fields, & services
4583	Airport terminal services...............................		
4712	Freight forwarding		
		4731	Freight transportation arrangement
4723	Freight transportation arrangement............		
		4724	Travel agencies
4722	Passenger transportation arrangement	4725	Tour operators
		4729	Passenger transport arrangement, nec
4742	Railroad car rental with service....................		
		4741	Rental of railroad cars
4743	Railroad car rental without service..............		
4782	Inspection and weighing services..................		
		4785	Inspection & fixed facilities
4784	Fixed facilities for vehicles, nec....................		
		4812	Radiotelephone communications
4811	Telephone communications		
		4813	Telephone communications, exc. radio
4821	Telegraph communication	Part 4822	Telegraph & other communications
4833	Television broadcasting		
	Subscription television...............................	Part 4841	Cable and other pay TV services
	Other television broadcasting.....................	4833	Television broadcasting stations
4899	Communications services, nec		
	Cable television	Part 4841	Cable and other pay TV services
	Message communications............................	Part 4822	Telegraph & other communications
	Other communication services, nec...........	4899	Communication services, nec
4959	Sanitary services, nec	Part 4959	Sanitary services, nec

F. WHOLESALE TRADE

5013	Automotive parts and supplies		
	New automotive parts and automotive equipment.	5013	Motor vehicle supplies and new parts

See footnotes at end of appendix.

(For all industries other than those listed below, 1987 SIC industries are the same as in 1977 or the changes in the industries will affect the classification of few, if any, establishments)—Con.

1977 industry		1987 industry	
Code	Short title	Code	Short title

F. WHOLESALE TRADE—Con.

1977 industry		1987 industry	
5013	Automotive parts and supplies—Con.		
	Used automotive parts..............................	Part 5015	Motor vehicle parts, used
		5032	Brick, stone, & related materials
5039	Construction materials, nec............................	5033	Roofing, siding, & insulation
		5039	Construction materials, nec
5041 [2]	Sporting and recreational goods....................	5091	Sporting & recreational goods
5042 [2]	Toys and hobby goods and supplies..............	5092	Toys and hobby goods and supplies
5063	Electrical apparatus and equipment		
	Communications equipment......................	Part 5065	Electronic parts and equipment
	Measuring and testing equipment.............	Part 5084	Industrial machinery and equipment
	Other electrical apparatus and equipment.	5063	Electrical apparatus and equipment
5065	Electronic parts and equipment	Part 5065	Electronic parts and equipment
		5044	Office equipment
5081	Commercial machines and equipment	5045	Computers, peripherals & software
		5046	Commercial equipment, nec
5084	Industrial machinery and equipment...........	Part 5084	Industrial machinery and equipment
		5047	Medical and hospital equipment
5086	Professional equipment and supplies...........	5048	Ophthalmic goods
		5049	Professional equipment, nec
5133	Piece goods...		
		5131	Piece goods & notions
5134	Notions and other dry goods		
5152	Cotton..		
		5159	Farm-product raw materials, nec
5159	Farm-product raw materials, nec..................		
		5162	Plastics materials & basic shapes
5161	Chemicals and allied products		
		5169	Chemicals & allied products, nec
		5192	Books, periodicals, & newspapers
5199	Nondurable goods, nec.................................	5193	Flowers & florists' supplies
		5199	Nondurable goods, nec

G. RETAIL TRADE

1977 industry		1987 industry	
5311	Department stores		
	Having fewer than 50 employees..............	Part 5399	Misc. general merchandise stores
	Other department stores	5311	Department stores
5399	Misc. general merchandise stores.................	Part 5399	Misc. general merchandise stores
5422	Freezer and locker meat provisioners		
		5421	Meat and fish markets
5423	Meat and fish (seafood) markets...................		

See footnotes at end of appendix.

(For all industries other than those listed below, 1987 SIC industries are the same as in 1977 or the changes in the industries will affect the classification of few, if any, establishments)—Con.

1977 industry		1987 industry	
Code	Short title	Code	Short title

G. RETAIL TRADE—Con.

1977 industry		1987 industry	
5462	Retail bakeries—baking and selling	5461	**Retail bakeries**
5463	Retail bakeries—selling only.........................		
5561	Recreation and utility trailer dealers		
	Utility trailers.....................................	Part 5599	**Automotive dealers, nec**
	Other recreation and utility trailer dealers.	5561	**Recreational vehicle dealers**
5599	Automotive dealers, nec..............................	Part 5599	**Automotive dealers, nec**
5631	Women's accessory and specialty stores	5632	**Women's accessory & specialty stores**
5681	Furriers and fur shops................................		
		5734	**Computer and software stores**
5732	Radio and television stores..........................	5731	**Radio, TV, & electronic stores**
		5735	**Record & prerecorded tape stores**
5733	Music stores..	5736	**Musical instrument stores**
5931	Used merchandise stores		
	Automotive parts, used...............................	Part 5015	**Motor vehicle parts, used**
	Other used merchandise stores..................	5932	**Used merchandise stores**
5982	Fuel and ice dealers, nec		
	Ice	Part 5999	**Miscellaneous retail stores, nec**
	Other fuel and ice dealer, nec....................	5989	**Fuel dealers, nec**
5999	Miscellaneous retail stores, nec		
	Opticians stores..	5995	**Optical goods stores**
	Other miscellaneous retail stores, nec......	Part 5999	**Miscellaneous retail stores, nec**

H. FINANCE, INSURANCE, AND REAL ESTATE

1977 industry		1987 industry	
6022	State banks, Federal Reserve		
	Stock savings banks	Part 6036	**Savings institutions, except federal**
	Commercial banks	Part 6022	**State commercial banks**
6023	State banks, not Federal Reserve, FDIC		
	Stock savings banks	Part 6036	**Savings institutions, except federal**
	Commercial banks	Part 6022	**State commercial banks**
6024	State banks, not Federal Reserve, not FDIC		
	Stock savings banks	Part 6036	**Savings institutions, except federal**
	Commercial banks	Part 6022	**State commercial banks**
6025	National banks, Federal Reserve	6021	**National commercial banks**
6026	National banks, not Federal Reserve, FDIC		
6027	National banks, not FDIC............................		
6028 [2]	Private banks, not incorp., not FDIC...........	6029	**Commercial banks, nec**
6032	Mutual savings banks, Federal Reserve.......	Part 6036	**Savings institutions, except federal**
[3]	Federal savings banks..................................	Part 6035	**Federal savings institutions**

See footnotes at end of appendix.

(For all industries other than those listed below, 1987 SIC industries are the same as in 1977 or the changes in the industries will affect the classification of few, if any, establishments)—Con.

1977 industry		1987 industry	
Code	Short title	Code	Short title

H. FINANCE, INSURANCE, AND REAL ESTATE—Con.

Code	Short title	Code	Short title
6033	Mutual savings banks, nec..............................	Part 6036	Savings institutions, except federal
6034	Mutual savings banks, not FDIC...................		
6042	Nondeposit trust, Federal Reserve...............	6091	Nondeposit trust facilities
6044	Nondeposit trust, not FDIC...........................		
6052	Foreign exchange establishments		
	Branches and agencies of foreign banks ..	6081	Foreign bank & branches & agencies
	Other foreign exchange establishments...	Part 6099	Functions related to deposit banking
6054	Safe deposit companies.................................	Part 6099	Functions related to deposit banking
6055	Clearinghouse associations		
6056	Corporations for banking abroad		
	Foreign trade and international banking institutions.	6082	Foreign trade & international banks
	Other corporations for banking abroad....	Part 6099	Functions related to deposit banking
6059	Functions related to banking, nec.................	Part 6099	Functions related to deposit banking
6112	Rediscounting, not for agricultural		
	Federal and federally sponsored credit agencies.	Part 6111	Federal and federally-sponsored credit
	Central reserve depository institutions....	6019	Central reserve depository, nec
6113	Rediscounting for agricultural......................	Part 6111	Federal and federally-sponsored credit
6122	Federal savings and loan associations..........	Part 6035	Federal savings institutions
6123	State associations, insured............................		
6124	State associations, noninsured, FHLB.........	Part 6036	Savings institutions, except federal
6125	State associations, noninsured, nec..............		
6131	Agricultural credit institutions		
	Federal and federally sponsored...............	Part 6111	Federal and federally-sponsored credit
	Other agricultural credit institutions (i.e., private).	Part 6159	Misc. business credit institutions
6142 [2]	Federal credit unions....................................	6061	Federal credit unions
6143 [2]	State credit unions	6062	State credit unions
6144	Nondeposit industrial loan companies		
6145	Licensed small loan lenders	Part 6141	Personal credit institutions
6146	Installment sales finance companies............		
6149	Miscellaneous personal credit institutions ..		

See footnotes at end of appendix.

(For all industries other than those listed below, 1987 SIC industries are the same as in 1977 or the changes in the industries will affect the classification of few, if any, establishments)—Con.

1977 industry		1987 industry	
Code	Short title	Code	Short title

H. FINANCE, INSURANCE, AND REAL ESTATE—Con.

6159	Miscellaneous business credit institutions		
	Federal and federally sponsored...............	Part 6111	Federal and federally-sponsored credit
	Other miscellaneous business credit institutions.	Part 6159	Misc. business credit institutions
6281	Security and commodity services	6282	Investment advice
		6289	Security & commodity services, nec
6411	Insurance agents, brokers, and service	Part 6411	Insurance agents, brokers, & service
6531	Real estate agents and managers.................	Part 6531	Real estate agents and managers
6611	Combined real estate, insurance, etc.		
	Loans, personal..	Part 6141	Personal credit institutions
	Loans, business...	Part 6159	Misc. business credit institutions
	Insurance...	Part 6411	Insurance agents, brokers, & service
	Real estate...	Part 6531	Real estate agents and managers
	Law offices ,...	Part 8111	Legal services
6711	Holding offices..	6712	Bank holding companies
		6719	Holding companies, nec
6723	Management investment, closed-end............		
6724	Unit investment trusts.................................	6726	Investment offices, nec
6725	Face-amount certificate offices		
6793	Commodity traders...		
		6799	Investors, nec
6799	Investors, nec...		

I. SERVICES

7214	Diaper service...		
		Part 7219	Laundry and garment services, nec
7219	Laundry & garment services, nec..................		
7299	Miscellaneous personal services		
	Tax return preparation services...............	7291	Tax return preparation services
	Medical equipment rental...........................	7352	Medical equipment rental
	Health clubs and spas.................................	Part 7991	Physical fitness facilities
	Seamstress and dressmaking services, except custom.	Part 7219	Laundry and garment services, nec
	Other miscellaneous personal services.....	7299	Miscellaneous personal services, nec
		7322	Adjustment & collection services
7321	Credit reporting and collection.....................	7323	Credit reporting services

See footnotes at end of appendix.

(For all industries other than those listed below, 1987 SIC industries are the same as in 1977 or the changes in the industries will affect the classification of few, if any, establishments)—Con.

1977 industry		1987 industry	
Code	Short title	Code	Short title

I. SERVICES—Con.

1977 industry		1987 industry	
7332	Blueprinting and photocopying....................	Part 7334	Photocopying and duplicating services
7333	Commercial photography and art	7335	Commercial photography
		7336	Commercial art and graphic design
7339	Stenographic and reproduction, nec		
	Stenographic and court reporting services.	7338	Secretarial & court reporting
	Duplicating services	Part 7334	Photocopying & duplicating services
7341	Window cleaning	7349	Building maintenance services, nec
7349	Building maintenance services, nec		
7351 [2]	News syndicates...	7383	News syndicates
7362	Temporary help supply services	Part 7363	Help supply services
7369	Personnel supply services, nec		
	Facilities support management services ..	8744	Facilities support services
	Other personnel supply services, nec........	Part 7363	Help supply services
7372	Computer programming and software..........	7371	Custom computer programming services
		7372	Prepackaged software
		7373	Computer integrated systems design
7374	Data processing services.............................	7374	Data processing and preparation
		7375	Information retrieval services
		7376	Computer facilities management
7379	Computer related services, nec	7377	Computer rental & leasing
		7378	Computer maintenance & repair
		7379	Computer related services, nec
7391 [2]	Research and development laboratories	8731	Commercial physical research
		8732	Commercial nonphysical research
7392	Management and public relations...............	8741	Management services
		8742	Management consulting services
		8743	Public relations services
		8748	Business consulting, nec
7393	Detective and protective services	7381	Detective & armored car services
		7382	Security systems services
7394	Equipment rental and leasing.......................	7353	Heavy construction equipment
		7359	Equipment rental and leasing, nec
		7841	Video tape rental
7395 [2]	Photofinishing laboratories	7384	Photofinishing laboratories
7396	Trading stamp services.................................	Part 7389	Business services, nec
7397 [2]	Commercial testing laboratories...................	8734	Testing laboratories

See footnotes at end of appendix.

(For all industries other than those listed below, 1987 SIC industries are the same as in 1977 or the changes in the industries will affect the classification of few, if any, establishments)—Con.

1977 industry		1987 industry	
Code	Short title	Code	Short title

I. SERVICES—Con.

Code	Short title	Code	Short title
7399	Business services, nec	Part 7389	Business services, nec
		7514	Passenger car rental
7512	Passenger car rental and leasing		
		7515	Passenger car leasing
7523	Parking lots		
		7521	Automobile parking
7525	Parking structures		
7531	Top and body repair shops.............................		
		7532	Top & body repair & paint shops
7535	Paint shops		
		7533	Auto exhaust system repair shops
		7536	Automotive glass replacement shops
7539	Automotive repair shops, nec.........................	7537	Automotive transmission repair shops
		7539	Automotive repair shops, nec
7813	Motion picture production, except TV		
		7812	Motion picture & video production
7814	Motion picture production for TV		
7823	Motion picture film exchanges		
		7822	Motion picture and tape distribution
7824	Film or tape distribution for TV		
7932	Billiard and pool establishments..................	Part 7999	Amusement and recreation, nec
7997	Membership sports and recreation clubs		
	Physical fitness facilities...........................	Part 7991	Physical fitness facilities
	Other membership sports and recreation clubs.	7997	Membership sports & recreation clubs
7999	Amusement and recreation, nec		
	Nonmembership physical fitness facilities.	Part 7991	Physical fitness facilities
	Other amusement and recreation services, nec.	Part 7999	Amusement and recreation, nec
	Museums (commercial)	Part 8412	Museums and art galleries
	Botanical and zoological gardens (commercial).	Part 8422	Botanical and zoological gardens
8011	Offices of physicians.......................................	Part 8011	Offices & clinics of medical doctors
8021	Offices of dentists	Part 8021	Offices and clinics of dentists
		8043	Offices and clinics of podiatrists
8049	Offices of health practitioners, nec..............	8049	Offices of health practitioners, nec
		8052	Intermediate care facilities
8059	Nursing and personal care facilities, nec.....	8059	Nursing and personal care, nec

See footnotes at end of appendix.

(For all industries other than those listed below, 1987 SIC industries are the same as in 1977 or the changes in the industries will affect the classification of few, if any, establishments)—Con.

1977 industry		1987 industry	
Code	Short title	Code	Short title

I. SERVICES—Con.

1977 industry		1987 industry	
8081	Outpatient care facilities		
	Clinics of physicians.....................................	Part 8011	**Offices & clinics of medical doctors**
	Clinics of dentists...	Part 8021	**Offices and clinics of dentists**
	Kidney dialysis centers...............................	8092	**Kidney dialysis centers**
	Specialty outpatient clinics.......................	8093	**Specialty outpatient clinics, nec**
		8082	**Home health care services**
8091	Health and allied services, nec		
		8099	**Health and allied services, nec**
8111	Legal services	Part 8111	**Legal services**
8241	Correspondence schools		
		8249	**Vocational schools, nec**
8249	Vocational schools, nec.................................		
8321	Individual and family services......................	Part 8322	**Individual and family services**
8399	Social services, nec		
	Services to individuals and families (e.g., self-help; agencies for retarded, blind, etc.).	Part 8322	**Individual and family services**
	Other social services, nec	8399	**Social services, nec**
8411	Museums and art galleries	Part 8412	**Museums and art galleries**
8421	Botanical and zoological gardens..................	Part 8422	**Botanical and zoological gardens**
		8711	**Engineering services**
8911	Engineering and architectural services........	8712	**Architectural services**
		8713	**Surveying services**
8922 [2]	Noncommercial research organizations	8733	**Noncommercial research organizations**
8931 [2]	Accounting, auditing, and bookkeeping	8721	**Accounting, auditing, & bookkeeping**

See footnotes at end of appendix.

Relation of 1987 to 1977 SIC Industries Showing Only Changes <u>From 1977</u>

(For all industries other than those listed below, 1987 SIC industries are the same as in 1977 or the changes in the industries will affect the classification of few, if any, establishments)

1987 industry		1977 industry	
Code	Short title	Code	Short title
	A. AGRICULTURE, FORESTRY, AND FISHING		
0181	**Ornamental nursery products**		
	Ornamental nursery products, 50 percent or more.	0181	Ornamental nursery products
	Other ornamental nursery products........	Part 0189	Horticultural specialties, nec
0182	**Food crops grown under cover**		
	Food crops grown under cover, 50 percent or more.	0182	Food crops grown under cover
	Other food crops grown under cover	Part 0189	Horticultural specialties, nec
0273	**Animal aquaculture**...		
		0279	Animal specialties, nec
0279	**Animal specialties, nec**		
0721	**Crop planting and protecting**		
	Crop planting and protection, 50 percent or more.	0721	Crop planting and protecting
	Other crop planting and protection.........	Part 0729	General crop services
0722	**Crop harvesting**		
	Crop harvesting, 50 percent or more.......	0722	Crop harvesting
	Other crop harvesting	Part 0729	General crop services
0723	**Crop preparation services for market**		
	Crop preparation services for market, 50 percent or more.	0723	Crop preparation services for market
	Other crop preparation services for market.	Part 0729	General crop services
0724	**Cotton ginning**		
	Cotton ginning, 50 percent or more........	0724	Cotton ginning
	Other cotton ginning................................	Part 0729	General crop services
		0821	Forest nursery and seed gathering
0831	**Forest products**...	0843	Extraction of pine gum
		0849	Gathering of forest products, nec

See footnotes at end of appendix.

(For all industries other than those listed below, 1987 SIC industries are the same as in 1977 or the changes in the industries will affect the classification of few, if any, establishments)—Con.

1987 industry		1977 industry	
Code	Short title	Code	Short title

B. MINING

1987 industry		1977 industry	
		1051	Bauxite and other aluminum ores
1099	Metal ores, nec	1092	Mercury ores
		1099	Metal ores, nec
1221	Bituminous coal and lignite—surface		
		1211	Bituminous coal and lignite
1222	Bituminous coal—underground		
1231 [2]	Anthracite mining	1111	Anthracite
		1112	Anthracite mining services
1241	Coal mining services		
		1213	Bituminous and lignite mining services
		1452	Betonite
		1453	Fire clay
1459	Clay and related minerals, nec		
		1454	Fuller's earth
		1459	Clay and related minerals, nec
		1472	Barite
		1473	Fluorspar
1479	Chemical and fertilizer mining, nec	1476	Rock salt
		1477	Sulfur
		1479	Chemical and fertilizer mining, nec
		1492	Gypsum
1499	Miscellaneous nonmetallic minerals	1496	Talc, soapstone, and pyrophyllite
		1499	Nonmetallic minerals, nec

C. CONSTRUCTION

1987 industry		1977 industry	
1611	Highway and street construction	Part 1611	Highway and street construction
1629	Heavy construction, nec		
	Heavy construction, nec	1629	Heavy construction, nec
	Recreational facilities, trailer camps	Part 1611	Highway and street construction
1771	Concrete work		
	Concrete work	1771	Concrete work
	Culverts and curbs	Part 1611	Highway and street construction

D. MANUFACTURING

1987 industry		1977 industry	
		2016	Poultry dressing plants
2015	Poultry slaughtering and processing		
		2017	Poultry and egg processing
2032	Canned specialties	Part 2032	Canned specialties
	(excludes fish cakes)		
2034	Dehydrated fruits, vegetables, soups	Part 2034	Dehydrated fruits, vegetables, soups
	(excludes dried or dehydrated nuts)		

See footnotes at end of appendix.

(For all industries other than those listed below, 1987 SIC industries are the same as in 1977 or the changes in the industries will affect the classification of few, if any, establishments)—Con.

1987 industry		1977 industry	
Code	Short title	Code	Short title

D. MANUFACTURING—Con.

1987 industry		1977 industry	
2038	Frozen specialties, nec..................................... (excludes frozen bakery products)	Part 2038	Frozen specialties
2047	Dog and cat food... (excludes other pet food)	Part 2047	Dog, cat, and other pet food
2048	Prepared feeds, nec		
	Prepared feeds, nec......................................	2048	Prepared feeds, nec
	Pet foods, except dog and cat food	Part 2047	Dog, cat, and other pet food
2053	Frozen bakery products, except bread........	Part 2038	Frozen specialties
2064	Candy and other confectionery products ...	Part 2065	Confectionery products
2066	Chocolate and cocoa products		
	Chocolate and cocoa products, mitse	2066	Chocolate and cocoa products
	Chocolate and cocoa products, mfpm	Part 2099	Food preparations, nec
2068	Salted and roasted nuts and seeds		
	Dried or dehydrated nuts............................	Part 2034	Dehydrated fruits, vegetables, soups
	Salted and roasted nuts.............................	Part 2065	Confectionery products
	Salted and roasted seeds............................	Part 2099	Food preparations, nec
2091	Canned and cured fish and seafoods		
	Canned and cured seafoods, nec...............	2091	Canned and cured seafoods
	Fish cakes	Part 2032	Canned specialties
2096	Potato chips and similar snacks		
2099	Food preparations, nec (excludes chocolate, mfpm; salted and roasted seeds; potato chips and similar snacks)	Part 2099	Food preparation, nec
		2258	Warp knit fabric mills
2258	Lace and warp knit fabric mills...................		
		2292	Lace goods
		2271	Woven carpets and rugs
2273	Carpets and rugs...	2272	Tufted carpets and rugs
		2279	Carpets and rugs, nec
2281	Yarn spinning mills		
	Yarn mills, except wool..............................	2281	Yarn mills, except wool
	Yarn mills, wool...	Part 2283	Wool yarn mills
2282	Throwing and winding mills		
	Throwing and winding mills, except wool.	2282	Throwing and winding mills
	Throwing and winding mills, wool...........	Part 2283	Wool yarn mills
2284	Thread mills		
	Thread mills, except wool	2284	Thread mills
	Thread mills, wool	Part 2283	Wool yarn mills
		2291	Felt goods, except woven felts and hats
2299	Textile goods, nec...	2293	Paddings and upholstery filling
		2294	Processed textile waste
		2299	Textile goods, nec

See footnotes at end of appendix.

(For all industries other than those listed below, 1987 SIC industries are the same as in 1977 or the changes in the industries will affect the classification of few, if any, establishments)—Con.

1987 industry		1977 industry	
Code	Short title	Code	Short title
	D. MANUFACTURING—Con.		
2321	**Men's and boys' shirts** .... (excludes nightwear)	Part 2321	Men's and boys' shirts and nightwear
2322	**Men's and boys' underwear and nightwear**		
	Nightwear...	Part 2321	Men's and boys' shirts and nightwear
	Underwear	2322	Men's and boys' underwear
2325	**Men's and boys' trousers and slacks**		
	Separate trousers and slacks....................	2327	Men's and boys' separate trousers
	Jean and jean-cut casual slacks	Part 2328	Men's and boys' work clothing
2326	**Men's and boys' work clothing**	Part 2328	Men's and boys' work clothing
		2351	Millinery
2353	**Hats, caps, and millinery**		
		2352	Hats and caps, except millinery
		2363	Children's coats and suits
2369	**Girls' and children's outerwear, nec**...........		
		2369	Children's outerwear, nec
2411	**Logging**		
	Logging...	2411	Logging camps and logging contractors
	Logging combined with sawmills and planing mills, primarily logging.	Part 2421	Sawmills and planing mills, general
2421	**Sawmills and planing mills**	Part 2421	Sawmills and planing mills, general
	(excludes logging combined with saw-mills)		
2431	**Millwork**		
	Millwork, nec	2431	Millwork
	Doors, windows, etc. of wood covered with metal.	Part 3442	Metal doors, sash, and trim
2493	**Reconstituted wood products**		
	Particleboard...	2492	Particleboard
	Reconstituted wood products, nec (medium density, fiberboard, wafer board, etc.).	Part 2499	Wood products, nec
	Insulation board...	Part 2661	Building paper and board mills
2499	**Wood products, nec**	Part 2499	Wood products, nec
	(excludes reconstituted wood prod-ucts)		
2522	**Office furniture, except wood**		
	Office furniture, metal...............................	2522	Metal office furniture
	Office furniture, nec...................................	Part 2599	Furniture and fixtures, nec
2542	**Partitions and fixtures, except wood**		
	Partitions and fixtures, metal..................	2542	Metal partitions and fixtures
	Partitions and fixtures, nec......................	Part 2599	Furniture and fixtures, nec

See footnotes at end of appendix.

(For all industries other than those listed below, 1987 SIC industries are the same as in 1977 or the changes in the industries will affect the classification of few, if any, establishments)—Con.

1987 industry		1977 industry	
Code	Short title	Code	Short title

D. MANUFACTURING—Con.

Code	Short title	Code	Short title
2599	Furniture and fixtures, nec	Part 2599	Furniture and fixtures, nec
2611	Pulp mills		
	Pulp mills..	2611	Pulp mills
	Pulp and paper mills, primarily pulp......	Part 2621	Paper mills, except building paper
	Pulp and paperboard mills, primarily paperboard.	Part 2631	Paperboard mills
2621	Paper mills		
	Paper mills not combined with pulp mills.	Part 2621	Paper mills, except building paper
	Building paper mills.................................	Part 2661	Building paper and board mills
2631	Paperboard mills......................................	Part 2631	Paperboard mills
	(excludes paperboard mills combined with pulp mills)		
2656	Sanitary food containers.............................	Part 2654	Sanitary food containers
2657	Folding paperboard boxes		
	Folding paperboard boxes, nec	2651	Folding paperboard boxes
	Folding sanitary food boxes......................	Part 2654	Sanitary food containers
2671	Paper coated and laminated, packaging.....		
		2641	Paper coating and glazing
2672	Paper coated and laminated, nec		
2673	Bags: plastics, laminated, and coated.........		
		2643	Bags, except textile bags
2674	Bags: uncoated paper and multiwall		
2675 [2]	Die-cut paper and board................................	2645	Die-cut paper and board
2676 [2]	Sanitary paper products................................	2647	Sanitary paper products
2677 [2]	Envelopes..	2642	Envelopes
2678 [2]	Stationery products	2648	Stationery products
		2646	Pressed and molded pulp goods
2679	Converted paper products, nec		
		2649	Converted paper products, nec
2754	Commercial printing, gravure.......................	Part 2754	Commercial printing, gravure
	(excludes platemaking)		
2759	Commercial printing, nec		
	Commercial printing, letterpress and screen.	2751	Commercial printing, letterpress
	Plate printing..	Part 2753	Engraving and plate printing
2796	Platemaking services		
	Engraving plates	Part 2753	Engraving and plate printing
	Gravure plates...	Part 2754	Commercial printing, gravure
	Photoengraving	2793	Photoengraving
	Electrotyping and stereotyping.................	2794	Electrotyping and stereotyping
	Lithographic platemaking services..........	2795	Lithographic platemaking services
2819	Industrial inorganic chemicals, nec		
	Industrial inorganic chemicals, nec.........	2819	Industrial inorganic chemicals, nec

See footnotes at end of appendix.

(For all industries other than those listed below, 1987 SIC industries are the same as in 1977 or the changes in the industries will affect the classification of few, if any, establishments)—Con.

1987 industry		1977 industry	
Code	Short title	Code	Short title

D. MANUFACTURING—Con.

Code	Short title	Code	Short title
2819	Industrial organic chemicals, nec—Con.		
	Hydrazine..	Part 2869	Industrial organic chemicals, nec
2835	Diagnostic substances.............................	} 2831	Biological products
2836	Biological products, except diagnostic.......		
2869	Industrial organic chemicals, nec...............	Part 2869	Industrial organic chemicals, nec
	(excludes hydrazine)		
3052 [2]	Rubber and plastics hose and belting	3041	Rubber and plastics hose and belting
3053 [2]	Gaskets, packing and sealing devices..........	3293	Gaskets, packing, and sealing devices
3061	Mechanical rubber goods.............................	Part 3069	Fabricated rubber products, nec
3069	Fabricated rubber products, nec		
	Reclaimed rubber.....................................	3031	Reclaimed rubber
	Fabricated rubber products, nec...............	Part 3069	Fabricated rubber products, nec
	Printers' rolls, blankets, and roller covers.	Part 3555	Printing trades machinery
3081	Unsupported plastics film and sheet		
3082	Unsupported plastics profile shapes...........		
3083	Laminated plastics plate and sheet.............		
3084	Plastics pipe		
3085	Plastics bottles..	} Part 3079	Miscellaneous plastics products
3086	Plastics foam products		
3087	Custom compound purchased resins...........		
3088	Plastics plumbing fixtures..........................		
3089	Plastics products, nec		
3264	Porcelain electrical supplies		
	Porcelain electrical supplies.....................	3264	Porcelain electrical supplies
	Electronic parts and porcelain electronic supplies.	Part 3679	Electronic components, nec
3339	Primary nonferrous metals, nec..................	{ 3332	Primary lead
		3333	Primary zinc
		3339	Primary nonferrous metals, nec
3363	Aluminum die-castings	Part 3361	Aluminum foundries
3364	Nonferrous die-castings, except aluminum		
	Die-castings, copper.................................	Part 3362	Brass, bronze, and copper foundries
	Other die-castings, except aluminum	Part 3369	Nonferrous foundries, nec
3365	Aluminum foundries...................................	Part 3361	Aluminum foundries
3366	Copper foundries..	Part 3362	Brass, bronze, and copper foundries
3369	Nonferrous foundries, nec	Part 3369	Nonferrous foundries, nec
	(excludes aluminum and copper)		
3423	Hand and edge tools, nec		
	Hand and edge tools, nec	3423	Hand and edge tools, nec
	Printers' mallets.....................................	Part 3555	Printing trades machinery

See footnotes at end of appendix.

(For all industries other than those listed below, 1987 SIC industries are the same as in 1977 or the changes in the industries will affect the classification of few, if any, establishments)—Con.

1987 industry		1977 industry	
Code	Short title	Code	Short title

D. MANUFACTURING—Con.

Code	Short title	Code	Short title
3432	**Plumbing fixture fittings and trim**		
	Plumbing fittings and trim, metal............	3432	Plumbing fittings and brass goods
	Plumbing fixture fittings: plastics............	Part 3079	Miscellaneous plastics products
3433	**Heating equipment, except electric**..............	Part 3433	Heating equipment, except electric
	(excludes incinerators)		
3442	**Metal doors, sash, and trim**...........................	Part 3442	Metal doors, sash, and trim
	(excludes wood covered with metal)		
3444	**Sheet metal work**.....................................	Part 3444	Sheet metal work
	(excludes curtain wall)		
3449	**Miscellaneous metal work**		
	Curtain walls, sheet metal...........................	Part 3444	Sheet metal work
	Miscellaneous metal work.........................	3449	Miscellaneous metal work
	Curtain walls for buildings, steel	Part 3469	Metal stampings, nec
3469	**Metal stampings, nec**................................	Part 3469	Metal stampings, nec
	(excludes curtain wall)		
3491	**Industrial valves**.............................	Part 3494	Valves and pipe fittings
3492	**Fluid power valves and hose fittings**		
	Hydraulic and pneumatic valves and hose fittings and assemblies.	Part 3494	Valves and pipe fittings
	Hydraulic and pneumatic valves, air-craft.	Part 3728	Aircraft equipment, nec
3494	**Valves and pipe fittings, nec**	Part 3494	Valves and pipe fittings, nec
	(excludes fluid power and industrial valves and hose fittings)		
3531	**Construction machinery**		
	Construction machinery............................	3531	Construction machinery
	Aerial work platforms; automobile wrecker hoists.	Part 3536	Hoists, cranes, and monorails
3536	**Hoists, cranes, and monorails**......................	Part 3536	Hoists, cranes, and monorails
	(excludes aerial work platforms; auto wrecker hoists; and automatic stacking machines)		
3537	**Industrial trucks and tractors**		
	Automatic stacking machines...................	Part 3536	Hoists, cranes, and monorails
	Industrial trucks and tractors..................	3537	Industrial trucks and tractors
3543 [2]	**Industrial patterns**.................................	3565	Industrial patterns
3548	**Welding apparatus**		
	Welding and soldering machines, none-lectric.	Part 3549	Metalworking machinery, nec
	Welding apparatus, electric	3623	Welding apparatus, electric
3549	**Metalworking machinery, nec**......................	Part 3549	Metalworking machinery, nec
	(excludes welding, soldering and automotive maintenance)		
3555	**Printing trades machinery**...........................	Part 3555	Printing trades machinery
	(excludes rolls and covers, blankets and mallets)		

See footnotes at end of appendix.

(For all industries other than those listed below, 1987 SIC industries are the same as in 1977 or the changes in the industries will affect the classification of few, if any, establishments)—Con.

1987 industry		1977 industry	
Code	Short title	Code	Short title

D. MANUFACTURING—Con.

1987 industry		1977 industry	
3556	Food products machinery	Part 3551	Food products machinery
3559	Special industry machinery, nec		
	Automotive maintenance equipment	Part 3549	Metalworking machinery, nec
	Special industry machinery, nec	3559	Special industry machinery, nec
	Sewing machines, commercial and industrial.	Part 3636	Sewing machines
3561	Pumps and pumping equipment	Part 3561	Pumps and pumping equipment
	(excludes fluid power pumps)		
3565	Packaging machinery		
	Foods products packaging machinery.....	Part 3551	Food products machinery
	General industrial packaging machinery.	Part 3569	General industrial machinery, nec
3566	Speed changers, drives, and gears	Part 3566	Speed changers, drives, and gears
	(excludes hydrostatic drives)		
3567	Industrial furnaces and ovens		
	Incinerators, metal: domestic and commercial.	Part 3433	Heating equipment, except electric
	Industrial furnaces and ovens	3567	Industrial furnaces and ovens
3569	General industrial machinery, nec	Part 3569	General industrial machinery, nec
	(excludes packaging, and fluid power pumps)		
3571	Electronic computers	Part 3573	Electronic computing equipment
3572	Computer storage devices		
3575	Computer terminals		
	Terminals.......................................	Part 3573	Electronic computing equipment
	Teletypewriters	Part 3661	Telephone and telegraph apparatus
3577	Computer peripheral equipment, nec..........	Part 3573	Electronic computing equipment
3578 [2]	Calculating and accounting equipment	3574	Calculating and accounting machines
		3579	Office machines, nec
3579	Office machines, nec................................	3572	Typewriters
3585	Refrigeration and heating equipment		
	Refrigeration and heating equipment	3585	Refrigeration and heating equipment
	Electric comfort heating equipment........	Part 3699	Electrical equipment and supplies, nec
3593	Fluid power cylinders and actuators		
	Fluid power cylinders and actuators, nec.	Part 3599	Machinery, except electrical, nec
	Fluid power cylinders and actuators, aircraft.	Part 3728	Aircraft equipment, nec

See footnotes at end of appendix.

(For all industries other than those listed below, 1987 SIC industries are the same as in 1977 or the changes in the industries will affect the classification of few, if any, establishments)—Con.

1987 industry		1977 industry	
Code	Short title	Code	Short title

D. MANUFACTURING—Con.

Code	Short title	Code	Short title
3594	Fluid power pumps and motors		
	Fluid power equipment..............................	Part 3561	Pumps and pumping equipment
	Hydrostatic drives......................................	Part 3566	Speed changer, drives, and gears
	General industrial fluid power pumps and motors.	Part 3569	General industrial machinery, nec
	Aircraft fluid power pumps and motors.	Part 3728	Aircraft equipment, nec
3596 [2]	Scales and balances, except laboratory	3576	Scales and balances, except laboratory
3599	Industrial machinery, nec.............................	Part 3599	Machinery, except electrical, nec
	(excludes fluid power cylinders and actuators)		
3613	Switchgear and switchboard apparatus......	Part 3613	Switchgear and switchboard apparatus
	(excludes relays)		
3625	Relays and industrial controls		
	Switchgear and switchboard relays	Part 3613	Switchgear and switchboard apparatus
	Industrial controls.......................................	3622	Industrial controls
	Relays, electronic...	Part 3679	Electronic components, nec
3639	Household appliances, nec		
	Household sewing machines.......................	Part 3636	Sewing machines
	Household appliances, nec...........................	3639	Household appliances, nec
3641	Electric lamps		
	Electric lamps...	3641	Electric lamps
	Electric lamp bulb parts.............................	Part 3699	Electrical equipment and supplies, nec
3661	Telephone and telegraph apparatus		
	Modems and other interface equipment.	Part 3662	Radio and TV communications equipment
	Other telephone and telegraph apparatus.	Part 3661	Telephone and telegraph apparatus
3663	Radio and TV communications equipment	Part 3662	Radio and TV communications equipment
3669	Communications equipment, nec		
3671	Electron tubes		
	Electron tubes, receiving type....................	3671	Electron tubes, receiving type
	Cathode ray television picture tubes	3672	Cathode ray television picture tubes
	Electron tubes, transmitting......................	3673	Electron tubes, transmitting
	Electron tube parts......................................	Part 3679	Electronic components, nec
3672	Printed circuit boards.................................	Part 3679	Electronic components, nec
3679	Electronic components, nec.........................		

See footnotes at end of appendix.

(For all industries other than those listed below, 1987 SIC industries are the same as in 1977 or the changes in the industries will affect the classification of few, if any, establishments)—Con.

1987 industry		1977 industry	
Code	Short title	Code	Short title

D. MANUFACTURING—Con.

Code	Short title	Code	Short title
3679	Electronic components, nec—Con.		
	(excludes printed circuit boards, electron tube parts, relays, ceramic supplies and recording media)		
3695	Magnetic and optical recording media		
	Recording media, nec..................................	Part 3679	Electronic components, nec
	Magnetic disks..............................	Part 3573	Electronic computing equipment
3699	Electrical equipment and supplies, nec		
	(excludes lamp bulb parts and comfort heating)		
	Other communication equipment.............	Part 3662	Radio and TV communications equipment
	Other electrical equipment and supplies, nec.	Part 3699	Electrical equipment and supplies, nec
3728	Aircraft parts and equipment, nec...............	Part 3728	Aircraft equipment, nec
	(excludes fluid power pumps, motors, cylinders, actuators, and valves)		
3812	Search and navigation equipment		
	Search, detection, and navigation systems.	Part 3662	Radio and TV communications equipment
	Search, detection, and navigation instruments.	Part 3811	Engineering and scientific instruments
3821	Laboratory apparatus and furniture..........	Part 3811	Engineering and scientific instruments
3826	Analytical instruments		
	Analytical engineering and scientific instruments.	Part 3811	Engineering and scientific instruments
	Analytical instruments, optical.................	Part 3832	Optical instruments and lenses
3827	Optical instruments and lenses	Part 3832	Optical instruments and lenses
3829	Measuring and controlling devices, nec		
	Surveying and drafting apparatus	Part 3811	Engineering and scientific instruments
	Measuring and controlling devices, nec..	3829	Measuring and controlling devices, nec
	Hydrological, hydrographic, meteorological, and geophysical systems.	Part 3662	Radio and TV communications equipment
	Meteorological, hydrographic, hydrological, and geophysical instruments.	Part 3832	Optical instruments and lenses
3844	X-ray apparatus and tubes	3693	X-ray apparatus and tubes
3845	Electromedical equipment		
3965	Fasteners, buttons, needles, and pins..........	3963	Buttons
		3964	Needles, pins, and fasteners

See footnotes at end of appendix.

(For all industries other than those listed below, 1987 SIC industries are the same as in 1977 or the changes in the industries will affect the classification of few, if any, establishments)—Con.

1987 industry		1977 industry	
Code	Short title	Code	Short title
	D. MANUFACTURING—Con.		
		3962	Artificial flowers
3999	**Manufacturing industries, nec**......................		
		3999	Manufacturing industries, nec
	E. TRANSPORTATION AND PUBLIC UTILITIES		
		4171	Bus terminal facilities
4173	**Bus terminal and service facilities**...............		
		4172	Bus service facilities
4212	**Local trucking, without storage** .... (excludes courier services)	Part 4212	Local trucking, without storage
4213	**Trucking, except local**................................. (excludes courier services)	Part 4213	Trucking, except local
4215	**Courier services, except by air**		
	Courier services, local without storage...	Part 4212	Local trucking without storage
	Courier services, except local....................	Part 4213	Trucking, except local
		4224	Household goods warehousing
4226	**Special warehousing and storage, nec**		
		4226	Special warehousing and storage, nec
4412	**Deep sea foreign transportation of freight**	Part 4411	Deep sea foreign transportation
4424	**Deep sea domestic transportation of freight**		
	Noncontiguous area transportation, freight.	Part 4421	Noncontiguous area transportation
	Coastwise transportation, freight............	Part 4422	Coastwise transportation
	Intercoastal transportation, freight.........	Part 4423	Intercoastal transportation
4432	**Freight transportation on the Great Lakes.**	Part 4431	Great Lakes transportation
		Part 4441	Transportation on rivers and canals
4449	**Water transportation of freight, nec**		
		Part 4459	Local water transportation, nec
4481	**Deep sea passenger transportation, except by ferry.**		
	Deep sea foreign transportation, passenger.	Part 4411	Deep sea foreign transportation
	Domestic and noncontiguous territories transportation, passenger.	Part 4421	Noncontiguous area transportation
	Coastwise transportation, passenger	Part 4422	Coastwise transportation
	Intercoastal transportation, passenger ...	Part 4423	Intercoastal transportation
	Great Lakes transportation, passenger, except ferry.	Part 4431	Great Lakes transportation
4482	Ferries		
	Great Lakes-St. Lawrence Seaway...........	Part 4431	Great Lakes transportation
	Other...	4452	Ferries

See footnotes at end of appendix.

(For all industries other than those listed below, 1987 SIC industries are the same as in 1977 or the changes in the industries will affect the classification of few, if any, establishments)—Con.

1987 industry		1977 industry	
Code	Short title	Code	Short title

E. TRANSPORTATION AND PUBLIC UTILITIES—Con.

Code	Short title	Code	Short title
4489	Water passenger transportation, nec		
	Transportation on rivers and canals, passenger.	Part 4441	Transportation on rivers and canals
	Local water transportation of passengers, nec.	Part 4459	Local water transportation, nec
4491 [2]	Marine cargo handling	4463	Marine cargo handling
4492 [2]	Towing and tugboat service	4454	Towing and tugboat service
4493	Marinas	Part 4469	Water transportation services, nec
4499	Water transportation services, nec		
	Lighterage	4453	Lighterage
	Water transportation services, nec	Part 4469	Water transportation services, nec
	Canal operations	4464	Canal operations
4512	Air transportation, scheduled		
	Certificated air transportation	Part 4511	Certificated air transportation
	Noncertificated air transportation scheduled, except sightseeing and airport services.	Part 4521	Noncertificated air transportation
4513	Air courier services		
	Air courier services, certificated	Part 4511	Certificated air transportation
	Air courier services, noncertificated	Part 4521	Noncertificated air transportation
4522	Air transportation, nonscheduled	Part 4521	Noncertificated air transportation
4581	Airports, flying fields, and services	4582	Airports and flying fields
		4583	Airport terminal services
4724	Travel agencies		
4725	Tour operators	4722	Passenger transportation arrangement
4729	Passenger transport arrangement, nec		
4731	Freight transportation arrangement	4712	Freight forwarding
		4723	Freight transportation arrangement
		4742	Railroad car rental with service
4741	Rental of railroad cars	4743	Railroad car rental without service
		4782	Inspection and weighing services
4785	Inspection and fixed facilities	4784	Fixed facilities for vehicles, nec
4812	Radiotelephone communications	4811	Telephone communications
4813	Telephone communications, except radio		
4822	Telegraph and other communications		
	Telegraph communications	4821	Telegraph communications
	Message communications	Part 4899	Communications services, nec

See footnotes at end of appendix.

(For all industries other than those listed below, 1987 SIC industries are the same as in 1977 or the changes in the industries will affect the classification of few, if any, establishments)—Con.

1987 industry		1977 industry	
Code	Short title	Code	Short title
	E. TRANSPORTATION AND PUBLIC UTILITIES—Con.		
4833	**Television broadcasting stations** .... **(excludes subscription)**	Part 4833	Television broadcasting
4841	**Cable and other pay TV services**		
	Subscription television................................	Part 4833	Television broadcasting
	Cable television...	Part 4899	Communications services, nec
4899	**Communications services, nec**.................... **(excludes message communications and cable TV)**	Part 4899	Communications services, nec
4959	**Sanitary services, nec**		
	Sanitary services, nec.................................	4959	Sanitary services, nec
	Oil spill cleanup	Part 4469	Water transportation services, nec
	F. WHOLESALE TRADE		
5013	**Motor vehicle supplies and new parts**......... **(excludes used automotive parts)**	Part 5013	Automotive parts and supplies
5015	**Motor vehicle parts, used**		
	Used parts, wholesale.................................	Part 5013	Automotive parts and supplies
	Used parts, retail..	Part 5931	Used merchandise stores
5032	**Brick, stone, and related materials**..............	}	
5033	**Roofing, siding, and insulation**....................	5039	Construction materials, nec
5039	**Construction materials, nec**		
5044	**Office equipment**...	}	
5045	**Computers, peripherals, & software**............	5081	Commercial machines and equipment
5046	**Commercial equipment, nec**		
5047	**Medical and hospital equipment**	}	
5048	**Ophthalmic goods**..	5086	Professional equipment and supplies
5049	**Professional equipment, nec**		
5063	**Electrical apparatus and equipment**........... **(excludes communications equipment and measuring and testing equipment)**	Part 5063	Electrical apparatus and equipment
5065	**Electronic parts and equipment**		
	Communications equipment......................	Part 5063	Electrical apparatus and equipment
	Electronic parts and equipment	5065	Electronic parts and equipment
5084	**Industrial machinery and equipment**		
	Measuring and testing equipment............	Part 5063	Electrical apparatus and equipment
	Industrial machinery and equipment......	5084	Industrial machinery and equipment
5091 [2]	**Sporting & recreational goods**......................	5041	Sporting and recreational goods
5092 [2]	**Toys and hobby goods and supplies**	5042	Toys and hobby goods and supplies

See footnotes at end of appendix.

(For all industries other than those listed below, 1987 SIC industries are the same as in 1977 or the changes in the industries will affect the classification of few, if any, establishments)—Con.

1987 industry		1977 industry	
Code	Short title	Code	Short title
	F. WHOLESALE TRADE—Con.		
5131	**Piece goods and notions**............................	5133	Piece goods
		5134	Notions and other dry goods
		5152	Cotton
5159	**Farm-product raw materials, nec**...............		
		5159	Farm-product raw materials, nec
5162	**Plastics materials and basic shapes**...........		
		5161	Chemicals and allied products
5169	**Chemicals and allied products, nec**...........		
5192	**Books, periodicals, & newspapers**.............		
5193	**Flowers & florists' supplies**..........................	5199	Nondurable goods, nec
5199	**Nondurable goods, nec**...............................		
	G. RETAIL TRADE		
5311	**Department stores**...	Part 5311	Department stores
	(excludes department stores with fewer than 50 employees)		
5399	**Miscellaneous general merchandise stores**		
	Stores with fewer than 50 employees	Part 5311	Department stores
	Miscellaneous general merchandise stores.	5399	Miscellaneous general merchandise stores
		5422	Freezer and locker meat provisioners
5421	**Meat and fish markets**..................................		
		5423	Meat and fish (seafood) markets
		5462	Retail bakeries—baking and selling
5461	**Retail bakeries**..		
		5463	Retail bakeries—selling only
5561	**Recreational vehicle dealers**.........................	Part 5561	Recreation and utility trailer dealers
	(excludes utility trailer dealers)		
5599	**Automotive dealers, nec**		
	Utility trailers	Part 5561	Recreation and utility trailer dealers
	Automotive dealers, nec	5599	Automotive dealers, nec
		5631	Women's accessory and specialty stores
5632	**Women's accessory and specialty stores**		
		5681	Furriers and fur shops
5731	**Radio, television, and electronic stores**		
		5732	Radio and television stores
5734	**Computer and software stores**.....................		
5735	**Record and prerecorded tape stores**...........		
		5733	Music stores
5736	**Musical instrument stores**		
5932	**Used merchandise stores**...............................	Part 5931	Used merchandise stores

See footnotes at end of appendix.

(For all industries other than those listed below, 1987 SIC industries are the same as in 1977 or the changes in the industries will affect the classification of few, if any, establishments)—Con.

1987 industry		1977 industry	
Code	Short title	Code	Short title
	G. RETAIL TRADE—Con.		
5989	**Fuel dealers, nec**	Part 5982	Fuel and ice dealers, nec
5995	**Optical goods stores**	Part 5999	Miscellaneous retail stores, nec
5999	**Miscellaneous retail stores, nec (excludes optical goods stores)**		
	Ice	Part 5982	Fuel and ice dealers, nec
	Miscellaneous retail stores, nec	Part 5999	Miscellaneous retail stores, nec
	H. FINANCE, INSURANCE, AND REAL ESTATE		
6019	**Central reserve depository, nec**	Part 6112	Rediscounting, not for agriculture
		6025	National banks, Federal Reserve
6021	**National commercial banks**	6026	National banks, not Federal Reserve, FDIC
		6027	National banks, not FDIC
6022	**State commercial banks**		
	Commercial banks, Federal Reserve	Part 6022	State banks, Federal Reserve
	Commercial banks, not Federal Reserve, FDIC.	Part 6023	State banks, not Federal Reserve, FDIC
	Commercial banks, not Federal Reserve, not FDIC.	Part 6024	State banks, not Federal Reserve, not FDIC
6029 [2]	**Commercial banks, nec**	6028	Private banks, not incorporated, not FDIC
6035	**Federal savings institutions**		
	Federal savings banks	[3]	Federal savings banks
	Federal savings and loans	6122	Federal savings and loan associations
6036	**Savings institutions, except federal**		
	Stock savings banks, Federal Reserve	Part 6022	State banks, Federal Reserve
	Stock savings banks, not Federal Reserve, FDIC.	Part 6023	State banks, not Federal Reserve, FDIC
	Stock savings banks, not Federal Reserve, not FDIC.	Part 6024	State banks, not Federal Reserve, not FDIC
	State mutual savings banks, Federal Reserve.	6032	Mutual savings banks, Federal Reserve
	State mutual savings banks, not Federal Reserve, FDIC.	6033	Mutual savings banks, nec
	State mutual savings banks, not FDIC ...	6034	State mutual savings banks, not FDIC
	State savings and loan associations, insured.	6123	State associations, insured
	State savings and loan associations, noninsured, FHLB.	6124	State associations, noninsured, FHLB
	State savings and loan associations, noninsured, nec.	6125	State agencies, noninsured, nec

See footnotes at end of appendix.

(For all industries other than those listed below, 1987 SIC industries are the same as in 1977 or the changes in the industries will affect the classification of few, if any, establishments)—Con.

1987 industry		1977 industry	
Code	Short title	Code	Short title
	H. FINANCE, INSURANCE, AND REAL ESTATE—Con.		
6061 [2]	**Federal credit unions**...............................	6142	Federal credit unions
6062 [2]	**State credit unions**..............................	6143	State credit unions
6081	**Foreign bank and branches and agencies..**	Part 6052	Foreign exchange establishments
6082	**Foreign trade and international banks**.......	Part 6056	Corporations for banking abroad
6091	**Nondeposit trust facilities**...........................	6042	Nondeposit trust, Federal Reserve
		6044	Nondeposit trust, not FDIC
6099	**Functions related to deposit banking**	Part 6052	Foreign exchange establishments
		6054	Safe deposit companies
		6055	Clearinghouse associations
		Part 6056	Corporations for banking abroad
		6059	Functions related to banking, nec
6111	**Federal and federally-sponsored credit**		
	Federal and federally sponsored credit agencies.	Part 6112	Rediscounting, not for agricultural
	Rediscounting for agricultural	6113	Rediscounting, for agricultural
	Agricultural credit institutions, federal and federally sponsored.	Part 6131	Agricultural credit institutions
	Miscellaneous business credit institutions, federal and federally sponsored.	Part 6159	Miscellaneous business credit institutions
6141	**Personal credit institutions**..........................	6144	Nondeposit industrial loan companies
		6145	Licensed small loan lenders
		6146	Installment sales finance companies
		6149	Miscellaneous personal credit institutions
		Part 6611	Combined real estate, insurance, etc.
6159	**Miscellaneous business credit institutions**		
	Other agricultural credit institutions......	Part 6131	Agricultural credit institutions
	Other miscellaneous business credit institutions.	Part 6159	Miscellaneous business credit institutions
	Combination services, primarily credit...	Part 6611	Combined real estate, insurance, etc.
6282	**Investment advice**	6281	Securities and commodity services
6289	**Security and commodity services, nec**		
6411	**Insurance agents, brokers, and service**		
	Insurance agents, brokers, and service...	6411	Insurance agents, brokers, and service
	Combination services, primarily insurance.	Part 6611	Combined real estate, insurance, etc.
	Real estate agents and managers	6531	Real estate agents and managers
	Combination services, primarily real estate.	Part 6611	Combined real estate, insurance, etc.

See footnotes at end of appendix.

(For all industries other than those listed below, 1987 SIC industries are the same as in 1977 or the changes in the industries will affect the classification of few, if any, establishments)—Con.

1987 industry		1977 industry	
Code	Short title	Code	Short title
	H. FINANCE, INSURANCE, AND REAL ESTATE—Con.		
6712	**Bank holding companies**..............................		
6719	**Holding companies, nec**................................	6711	Holding offices
		6723	Management investment, closed-end
6726	**Investment offices, nec**...............................	6724	Unit investment trusts
		6725	Face-amount certificate offices
		6793	Commodity traders
6799	**Investors, nec**..		
		6799	Investors, nec
	I. SERVICES		
7219	**Laundry and garment services, nec**		
	Diaper services..	7214	Diaper service
	Laundry and garment services, nec.........	7219	Laundry and garment services, nec
	Seamstress and dressmaking services, on customer material.	Part 7299	Miscellaneous personal services
7291	**Tax return preparation services**....................	Part 7299	Miscellaneous personal services
7299	**Miscellaneous personal services, nec**	Part 7299	Miscellaneous personal services
	(excludes tax return preparation; health clubs and spas; seamstress and dressmaking services and medical equipment rental)		
7322	**Adjustment & collection services**................		
		7321	Credit reporting and collection
7323	**Credit reporting services**..............................		
7334	**Photocopying & duplicating services**		
	Blueprinting and photocopying service.	7332	Blueprinting and photocopying
	Duplicating services	Part 7339	Stenographic and reproduction, nec
7335	**Commercial photography**...............................		
		7333	Commercial photography and art
7336	**Commercial art and graphic design**.............		
7338	**Secretarial & court reporting**.......................	Part 7339	Stenographic and reproduction, nec
		7341	Window cleaning
7349	**Building maintenance services, nec**.............		
		7349	Building maintenance services, nec
7352	**Medical equipment rental**	Part 7299	Miscellaneous personal services
7353	**Heavy construction equipment rental**.........		
		Part 7394	Equipment rental and leasing
7359	**Equipment rental and leasing, nec**		

See footnotes at end of appendix.

(For all industries other than those listed below, 1987 SIC industries are the same as in 1977 or the changes in the industries will affect the classification of few, if any, establishments)—Con.

1987 industry		1977 industry	
Code	Short title	Code	Short title

I. SERVICES—Con.

1987 industry		1977 industry	
7363	Help supply services		
	Temporary help supply services	7362	Temporary help supply services
	Other personnel supply services, nec	Part 7369	Personnel supply services, nec
7371	Custom computer programming services ...		
7372	Prepackaged software.....................................	7372	Computer programming and software
7373	Computer integrated systems design...........		
7374	Data processing and preparation.................		
7375	Information retrieval services	7374	Data processing services
7376	Computer facilities management..................		
7377	Computer rental & leasing		
7378	Computer maintenance & repair.................	7379	Computer related services, nec
7379	Computer related services, nec...................		
7381	Detective and armored car services............		
		7393	Detective and protective services
7382	Security systems services		
7383 [2]	News syndicates..	7351	News syndicates
7384 [2]	Photofinishing laboratories.........................	7395	Photofinishing laboratories
		7396	Trading stamp services
7389	Business services, nec		
		7399	Business services, nec
7514	Passenger car rental......................................		
		7512	Passenger car rental and leasing
7515	Passenger car leasing....................................		
		7523	Parking lots
7521	Automobile parking..		
		7525	Parking structures
		7531	Top and body repair shops
7532	Top & body repair & paint shops.................		
		7535	Paint shops
7533	Auto exhaust system repair shops		
7536	Automotive glass replacement shops...........		
		7539	Automotive repair shops, nec
7537	Automotive transmission repair shops		
7539	Automotive repair shops, nec......................		
		7813	Motion picture production, except TV
7812	Motion picture & video production		
		7814	Motion picture production for TV
		7823	Motion picture film exchanges
7822	Motion picture and tape distribution..........		
		7824	Film or tape distribution for TV
7841	Video tape rental...	Part 7394	Equipment rental and leasing

See footnotes at end of appendix.

(For all industries other than those listed below, 1987 SIC industries are the same as in 1977 or the changes in the industries will affect the classification of few, if any, establishments)—Con.

1987 industry		1977 industry	
Code	Short title	Code	Short title

I. SERVICES—Con.

Code	Short title	Code	Short title
7991	**Physical fitness facilities**		
	Physical fitness facilities............................	Part 7997	Membership sports and recreation clubs
	Health clubs and spas	Part 7299	Miscellaneous personal services
	Nonmembership physical fitness facilities.	Part 7999	Amusement and recreation, nec
7997	**Membership sports and recreation clubs....** (excludes physical fitness facilities)	Part 7997	Membership sports and recreation clubs
		Part 7999	Amusement and recreation, nec
7999	**Amusement and recreation, nec ....** (excludes museums, botanical and zoological gardens and physical fitness facilities)		
		7932	Billiard and pool establishments
8011	**Offices and clinics of medical doctors**		
	Offices of physicians.................................	8011	Offices of physicians
	Clinics of physicians	Part 8081	Outpatient care facilities
8021	**Offices and clinics of dentists**		
	Offices of dentists	8021	Offices of dentists
	Clinics of dentists......................................	Part 8081	Outpatient care facilities
8043	**Offices and clinics of podiatrists.................**		
		8049	Offices of health practitioners, nec
8049	**Offices of health practitioners, nec ....**		
8052	**Intermediate care facilities...........................**		
		8059	Nursing and personal care, nec
8059	**Nursing and personal care, nec ....**		
8082	**Home health care services ....**	Part 8091	Health and allied services, nec
8092	**Kidney dialysis centers.................................**		
8093	**Specialty outpatient clinics, nec...................**	Part 8081	Outpatient care facilities
8099	**Health and allied services, nec ....**	Part 8091	Health and allied services, nec
8111	**Legal services**		
	Legal services..	8111	Legal services
	Combination services, primarily legal.....	Part 6611	Combined real estate, insurance, etc.
		8241	Correspondence schools
8249	**Vocational schools, nec ....**		
		8249	Vocational schools, nec
8322	**Individual and family services**		
	Individual and family social services......	8321	Individual and family services
	Services to individuals and families	Part 8399	Social services, nec
8399	**Social services, nec ....** (excludes services to individuals and families)	Part 8399	Social services, nec

See footnotes at end of appendix.

(For all industries other than those listed below, 1987 SIC industries are the same as in 1977 or the changes in the industries will affect the classification of few, if any, establishments)—Con.

1987 industry		1977 industry	
Code	Short title	Code	Short title
	I. SERVICES—Con.		
8412	**Museums and art galleries**		
	Commercial museums and art galleries..	Part 7999	Amusement and recreation, nec
	Noncommercial museums and art galleries.	8411	Museums and art galleries
8422	**Botanical and zoological gardens**		
	Noncommercial botanical and zoological gardens.	8421	Botanical and zoological gardens
	Commercial botanical and zoological gardens.	Part 7999	Amusement and recreation, nec
8711	**Engineering services**	⎫	
8712	**Architectural services**	8911	Engineering and architectural services
8713	**Surveying services**	⎭	
8721 ²	**Accounting, auditing, & bookkeeping**.........	8931	Accounting, auditing, and bookkeeping
8731 ²	**Commercial physical research**......................	7391	Research and development laboratories
8732	**Commercial nonphysical research**..............	Part 7392	Management and public relations
8733 ²	**Noncommercial research organizations**	8922	Noncommercial research organizations
8734 ²	**Testing laboratories**..	7397	Commercial testing laboratories
8741	**Management services**	⎫	
8742	**Management consulting services**..................	Part 7392	Management and public relations
8743	**Public relations services**................................	⎭	
8744	**Facilities support services**.............................	Part 7369	Personnel supply services, nec
8748	**Business consulting, nec**	Part 7392	Management and public relations

¹ There is no longer any activity in this industry.

² No change in content.

³ Federal Savings banks did not exist prior to 1982.

Appendix B

Principles and Procedures for the Review of the SIC

A. Introduction

The Standard Industrial Classification (SIC) is a system for classifying establishments by type of economic activity. Its purposes are: (1) to facilitate the collection, tabulation, presentation, and analysis of data relating to establishments, and (2) to promote uniformity and comparability in the presentation of statistical data describing the economy. The SIC is used by agencies of the United States Government that collect or publish data by industry. It is also widely used by State agencies, trade associations, private businesses, and other organizations.

The SIC system is designed for statistical purposes. Although the classification is also used for various administrative purposes, the requirements of government agencies that use it for nonstatistical purposes play no role in development and revision of the SIC.

B. Principles of Classification

Following are the basic principles underlying the SIC classification (described more fully in the SIC Manual):

(1) The classification is organized to reflect the structure of the U.S. economy. It does not follow any single principle, such as end use, nature of raw materials, product, or market structure.

(2) The unit classified is the establishment. An establishment is an economic unit that produces goods or services—for example, a farm, mine, factory, or store. In most instances, the establishment is at a single physical location and is engaged in one, or predominantly one, type of economic activity. An establishment is not necessarily identical with a company or enterprise.

(3) Each establishment is classified according to its primary activity. Primary activity is determined by identifying the predominant product or group of products produced or handled, or service rendered.

(4) An industry (four-digit SIC) consists of a group of establishments primarily engaged in the same activity. To be recognized as an industry, such a group of establishments must meet certain criteria of economic significance, as described in Section D.

C. Purpose and Scope of Review

The SIC is reviewed and revised periodically to reflect the changing structure of the U.S. economy. Revisions take into account the technological change and economic growth and decline of individual industries. They may include changes in industry detail or coverage, improvements to industry definitions, or the clarification of the classification of individual activities.

Review and revision of the SIC are the responsibility of the Office of Management and Budget, which has developed these principles and procedures with the assistance of the Technical Committee on Industrial Classification. Committee members include the following agencies: Office of Management and Budget (Chair), Board of Governors of the Federal Reserve System, Bureau of Economic Analysis, Bureau of Labor Statistics, Bureau of Mines, Bureau of the Census, Department of Transportation, Economic Research Service (USDA), Federal Emergency Management Agency, Federal Trade Commission, Internal Revenue Service, International Trade Administration, Interstate Commerce Commission, National Center for Health Statistics, National Science Foundation, Small Business Administration, Social Security Administration, and U.S. International Trade Commission.

Proposals for revision are accepted from Federal agencies and the public and are reviewed by the Technical Committee on Industrial Classification. Final decisions on revisions will be made by the Office of Management and Budget based on the recommendations of the Technical Committee.

Persons considering submitting proposals should note that it is not always necessary to revise the SIC to obtain more detailed statistical information. If statistical information is needed for specific products rather than establishments, it may be more appropriate to seek changes in the level of detail of data collected and published by individual Government agencies than to change the SIC.

D. Guidelines for Reviewing Proposed Changes in the Classification

Proposals for revisions to the SIC will be reviewed based on the following considerations:

(1) *Structure of the Classification.*—The overall structure is a general-purpose framework which can have its four-digit detail rearranged for various analytical purposes. Proposed changes should be designed to fit within this structure with minimum disruption to the existing configuration.

For example, a change which consists of breaking one four-digit industry into two or more within the same three-digit industry group is easier and less expensive than a change which affects three-digit groups, particularly if this in turn affects the two-digit or divisional groupings. Changes to the basic two- or three-digit structure require exceptionally strong justification showing that they reflect changes in the economy and not simply a different view of what the basic structure should be.

(2) *Historical Continuity.*—Maintaining the continuity of major Federal statistical series will be an important consideration in evaluating proposed changes in the SIC. Changes that result in weakening principal economic indicators or that neces-

sitate costly backward revision of time series will require very strong justification on other grounds to be acceptable.

(3) *Economic Significance.*—To be recognized as an industry, a group of establishments must have economic significance measured in terms of numbers of establishments, employment, payroll, value added, and volume of business (value of shipments or receipts). The following scoring system is used to evaluate economic significance for SIC purposes:

Values for the "average" industry are calculated by division (manufacturing, construction, retail trade, etc.) for each of the five factors. These values are used in evaluating the economic significance of a proposed SIC industry by comparing the division averages to the values for the proposed industry, as illustrated below. For each factor, a proposed industry is assigned points. The number of points is equal to the value of the factors for a proposed industry as a percentage of the value for the division average.

The number of employees and value added are considered more significant and reliable measures of industry importance and are therefore given double weight when calculating the final score. The table below presents calculations (based on 1977 data) for a proposed potato chip and similar snack industry in Division D (manufacturing). The final score for this industry is 59 (column E total divided by column D total).

Data Items	Proposed industry	Average industry	Number of points (A as percent of B)	Weights	Weighted points (C × D)
	(A)	(B)	(C)	(D)	(E)
Number of establishments	230	796	29	1	29
Number of employees (thousands)	26.7	43.0	62	2	124
Payroll (million dollars)	301.3	584.0	52	1	52
Value added (million dollars)	934.5	1,295.0	72	2	144
Shipments (million dollars)	1,929.0	3,006.0	64	1	64

In general, a score of at least 20 is needed to warrant recognition as a new SIC industry. However, an existing SIC industry will be retained if it has a score of at least 10.

The 1987 review will be based on the most recent data available. In cases where data are not available for all five factors, scores will be weighted averages of those factors for which data are available.

(4) *Specialization and Coverage.*—For an industry to properly reflect the activity being measured, the output of the industry should: (1) Consist mainly of the goods or services defining the industry, and (2) account for the bulk of the specified goods and services provided by all establishments. For manufacturing industries, these factors are measured by the primary product specialization ratio and the coverage ratio.

The primary product specialization ratio indicates how much the establishments in a given industry concentrate on the activities that define the industry. This ratio is calculated by dividing the value of the primary product shipments of the establishments classified in the industry by the value of all shipments (both primary and secondary) for the same establishments.

The coverage ratio indicates the volume of shipments of products which define the industry that are accounted for by establishments classified in the industry. The coverage ratio is the proportion of products defining the industry shipped by establishments classified in the industry to total shipments of these products by all manufacturing establishments.

For example, establishments classified in 1977 as primarily producing transformers (SIC 3612) had shipments of $2,051.1 million for transformers, total shipments for all products of $2,160.6 million, and a resulting specialization ratio of 95. Total shipments of transformers by all industries were $2,117.8 million, yielding a coverage ratio of 97.

A four-digit SIC industry should have a minimum primary product specialization ratio of 80. The minimum for the coverage ratio is generally 70 for establishments producing for commercial sale. This may be reduced somewhat for industries having significant interplant transfers or production for use within the same establishment (e.g., Gray Iron Foundries, Iron and Steel Forgings) or for industries producing the same final product as another industry but made from materials that are at a more advanced stage of manufacture (e.g., Blended and Prepared Flour). Where existing industries have relatively few large plants producing a wide range of products, the coverage ratio criterion often precludes the establishment of further industry detail.

(5) *Other Statistical Considerations.*—In general, proposed new industries should meet each of the criteria of economic significance, specialization, and coverage. However, industries that substantially exceed one or two of the criteria and fall slightly short on the others also may be accepted in some cases.

For example, industries which are not yet large enough, but are growing rapidly, may be accepted based on current size and evidence of growth by a specified time. Proposed industries which meet the criteria only marginally should also show substantial current growth and likelihood of future growth.

Special consideration will be given to new industries and industry changes that increase comparability of the SIC with the United Nation's International Standard Industrial Classification and that increase the capability for assessing the impact of international trade on domestic industries such as increasing possibilities for comparability with the Customs Cooperation Council's Harmonized System.

Proposed new industries will be evaluated to make sure they provide for relatively stable classification of individual establishments. In some fields of activity, it is normal for the primary activity, if defined restrictively, to fluctuate from year to year. For example, shipbuilding establishments may work on defense contracts one year and on civilian contracts the next; or establishments may perform primarily new work one year and rebuilding another. Separate industries will not be created where the distinction would result in industry shifts for establishments that are still engaged in similar industrial activity.

In some cases, a proposed industry may meet all previously stated criteria but be rejected because the remaining part of the existing industry is too small for separate industry status and cannot logically be merged into other industries.

(6) *Administrative Considerations.*—Cost to the Government, as well as cost and burden to businesses that furnish data to the Government, will be major considerations in evaluating proposed changes in the SIC. Revisions that involve major changes in record-keeping by business or in government agencies' procedures, records, and data series will require very strong justification to be considered.

The ability of government agencies to classify, collect, and publish data on the proposed basis will also be taken into account. Proposed changes must be such that they can be applied by agencies within their normal processing operations.

Proposed industries must also include a sufficient number of companies so that industry data can be published without disclosing information about the operations of individual firms.

☆ GPO : 1987 O - 185-718 : QL 3

Appendix C

Glossary of Abbreviations

admin................................ administration
&.. and
etc...................................... et cetera (and so forth)
exc. or ex.......................... except
Intl.................................... International
inst.................................... institutions
mach.................................. machinery
misc................................... miscellaneous
mfg.................................... manufacturing
mfpm .... made from purchased materials or materials
                                              transferred from another establishment
mitse .... made in the same establishment as the basic
                                              materials
nec..................................... not elsewhere classified
trans .... transportation

Other Titles Available from

JIST publishes a variety of books on careers and job search topics. Please consider ordering one or more from your dealer, local bookstore, or directly from JIST.

Orders from Individuals: Please use the form below (or provide the same information) to order additional copies of this or other books listed on this page. You are also welcome to send us your order (please enclose money order, check, or credit card information), or simply call our toll free number at 1-800-648-JIST or 1-317-264-3720. Our FAX number is 1-317-264-3709 or *toll free* 1-800-JIST-FAX. Qualified schools and organizations may request our catalog and obtain information on quantity discounts (we have over 400 career-related books, videos, and other items). Our offices are open weekdays 8 a.m. to 5 p.m. local time and our address is:

JIST Works, Inc. • 720 North Park Avenue • Indianapolis, IN 46202-3431

QTY	BOOK TITLE	TOTAL ($)
	Getting the Job You Really Want, J. Michael Farr • ISBN 0-942784-15-4 • **$9.95**	
	The Very Quick Job Search: Get a Good Job in Less Time, J. Michael Farr •ISBN 0-942784-72-3 • **$9.95**	
	America's 50 Fastest Growing Jobs: An Authoritative Information Source • ISBN 0-942784-61-8 • **$10.95**	
	America's Top 300 Jobs: A Complete Career Handbook (trade version of the *Occupational Outlook Handbook*) • ISBN 0-942784-45-6 • **$17.95**	
	America's Federal Jobs: A Complete Directory of Federal Career Opportunities • ISBN 0-942784-81-2 • **$14.95**	
	America's Top Medical Jobs: Good Jobs in Health Related Occupations • ISBN 1-56370-046-8 • **$9.95**	
	America's Top Technical and Trade Jobs: Good Jobs that Don't Require Four Years of College • ISBN 1-56370-041-7 • **$9.95**	
	America's Top Office, Management and Sales Jobs: Good Jobs that Offer Advancement and Excellent Pay • ISBN 1-56370-041-7 • **$9.95**	
	The Resume Solution: How to Write and Use a Resume That Gets Results, David Swanson • ISBN 0-942784-44-8 • **$8.95**	
	The Job Doctor: Good Advice on Getting a Good Job, Phillip Norris, Ed.D. • ISBN 0-942784-43-X • **$5.95**	
	The Right Job for You: An Interactive Career Planning Guide, J. Michael Farr • ISBN 0-942784-73-1 • **$9.95**	
	Exploring Careers: A Young Person's Guide to over 300 Jobs • ISBN 0-942784-27-8 • **$19.95**	
	Work in the New Economy: Careers and Job Seeking into the 21st Century, Robert Wegmann 0-942784-19-78 • **$14.95**	
	The Occupational Outlook Handbook • ISBN 0-942784-38-3 • **$16.95**	
	The Enhanced Guide for Occupational Exploration: Descriptions for the 2,500 Most Important Jobs • ISBN 0-942784-76-6 • **$29.95**	
	U.S. Industrial Outlook '92: Business Forecasts for 350 Industries • ISBN 1-56370-062-X • **$29.95**	
	The Career Connection: Guide to College Majors and Their Related Careers, Dr. Fred Rowe • ISBN 0-942784-82-0 • **$15.95**	
	The Career Connection II: Guide to Technical Majors and Their Related Careers, Dr. Fred Rowe • ISBN 0-942784-83-9 • **$13.95**	

Subtotal _____

Sales Tax _____

Shipping: ($3 for first book, $1 for each additional book.) _____

(*U.S. Currency only*) **TOTAL ENCLOSED WITH ORDER** _____

(Prices subject to change without notice)

❑ Check ❑ Money order Credit Card: ❑ MasterCard ❑ VISA ❑ AMEX

Card # (if applies)_____Exp. Date _____

Name (please print)_____

Name of Organization (if applies) _____

Address _____

City/State/Zip_____

Daytime Telephone ( ) _____—_____

Thank-you for your order!

Agriculture, Forestry, and Fishing

Mining

Construction

Manufacturing

Transportation and Public Utilities

Wholesale Trade

Retail Trade

Finance, Insurance, and Real Estate

Services

Public Administration

Nonclassifiable Establishments

Numerical List

Alphabetic Index

Conversion Tables

Principles and Procedures

Abbreviations

HOW TO USE THE MARGIN INDEX

To locate desired section bend pages and follow margin index to page with corresponding black edge marker.